MOON HANDBOOKS

CUBA

CHRISTOPHER P. BAKER

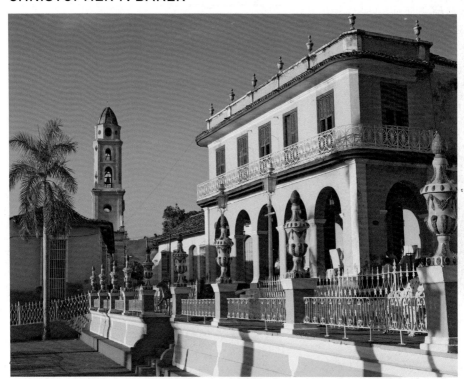

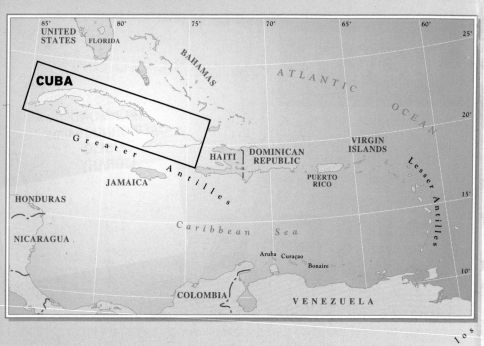

© AVALON TRAVEL

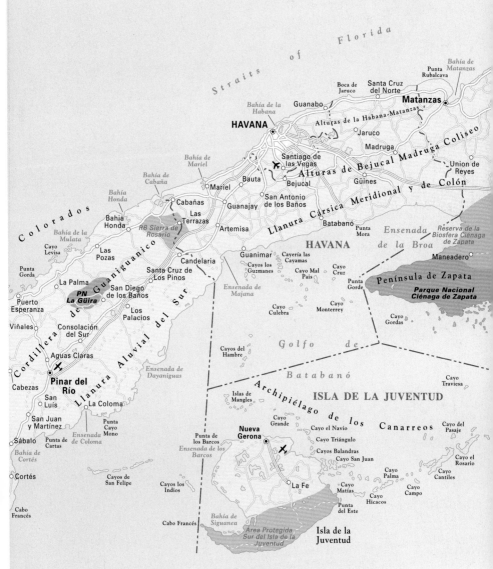

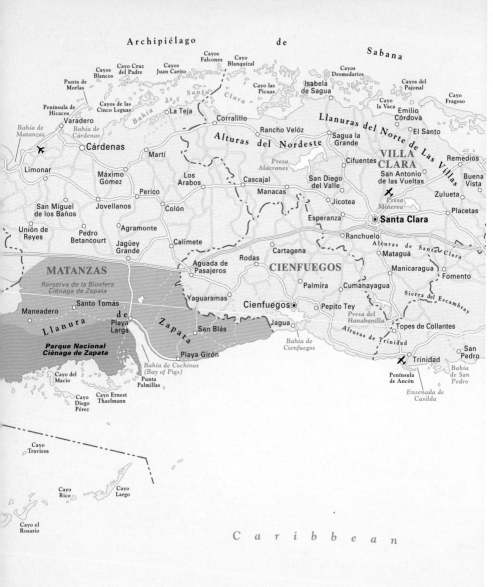

Archipiélago   de   Sabana

Cayos Blancos
Punta de Morlas
Cayo Cruz del Padre
Cayos Falcones
Cayo Blanquizal
Cayos Juan Carito
Cayos Dromedarios
Cayos del Pajonal
Cayo Fragoso

Península de Hicacos
Cayos de las Cinco Leguas
Bahía de Santa Clara
Cayo las Picuas
Isabela de Sagua
Cayo la Vaca
Emilio Córdova
El Santo

Varadero
La Teja
Bahía de Matanzas
Bahía de Cárdenas
Corralillo
Rancho Velóz
Sagua la Grande
Llanuras del Norte de las Villas

Cárdenas
Martí
Alturas del Nordeste
San Diego del Valle
Cifuentes
VILLA CLARA
Remedios
Buena Vista

Limonar
Máximo Gómez
Los Arabos
Cascajal
Presa Alacranes
San Diego del Valle
San Antonio de las Vueltas
Zulueta

Perico
Jovellanos
Colón
Manacas
Jicotea
Placetas
Presa Minerva

San Miguel de los Baños
Agramonte
Esperanza
Ranchuelo
Santa Clara

Unión de Reyes
Pedro Betancourt
Jagüey Grande
Calimete
Rodas
Cartagena
CIENFUEGOS
Matagua
Alturas de Santa Clara
Manicaragua
Fomento

MATANZAS
Reserva de la Biosfera Ciénaga de Zapata
Aguada de Pasajeros
Palmira
Cumanayagua
Sierra del Escambray

Maneadero
Santo Tomás
Yaguaramas
Cienfuegos
Pepito Tey
Presa del Hanabanilla
Topes de Collantes

Llanura
Playa Larga
Zapata
San Blás
Jagua
Alturas de Trinidad
San Pedro

Parque Nacional Ciénaga de Zapata
Playa Girón
Bahía de Cienfuegos
Trinidad
Bahía de San Pedro

Cayo del Macio
Bahía de Cochinos (Bay of Pigs)
Punta Palmillas
Península de Ancón
Ensenada de Casilda

Cayo Diego Pérez
Cayo Ernest Thaelmann

Cayo Traviesa

Cayo Rico
Cayo Largo

Cayo el Rosario

Caribbean

0   25 mi

0   25 km

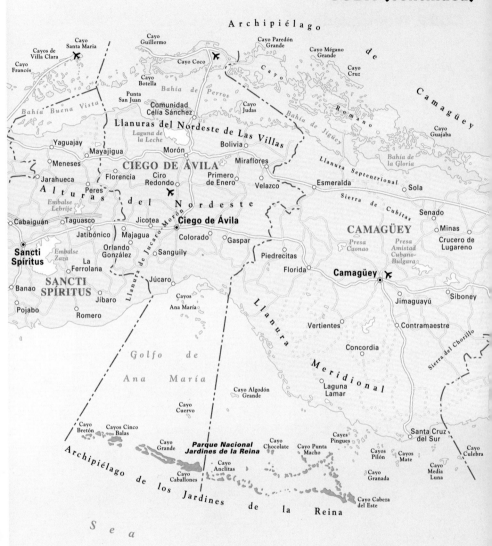

CUBA (continued)

Archipiélago de Camagüey

Cayos de Villa Clara
Cayo Santa María
Cayo Frances
Cayo Guillermo
Cayo Coco
Cayo Paredón Grande
Cayo Mégano Grande
Cayo Cruz
Cayo Guajaba

Cayo Botella
Cayo
Bahía de Perros
Cayo Judas
Bahía de Jiguey
Romano
Bahía de la Gloria

Bahía Buena Vista
Punta San Juan
Comunidad Celia Sánchez
Llanuras del Nordeste de Las Villas
Laguna de la Leche
Morón
Bolivia
Miraflores

Yaguajay
Mayajigua
CIEGO DE ÁVILA
Llanura Septentrional
Esmeralda
Sola
Senado

Meneses
Jarahueca
Peres
Florencia
Ciro Redondo
Primero de Enero
Velazco
Sierra de Cubitas

Cabaiguán
Taguasco
Alturas del Nordeste
Jicotea
Ciego de Ávila
CAMAGÜEY
Minas
Crucero de Lugareno

Sancti Spíritus
Embalse Lebrije
Jatibónico
Majagua
Colorado
Gaspar
Presa Caonao
Presa Amistad Cubano-Bulgara

Embalse Zaza
Orlando González
Sanguily
Piedrecitas
Florida
Camagüey
Siboney

Banao
La Ferrolana
SANCTI SPÍRITUS
Júcaro
Llanura
Jimaguayú

Pojabo
Jíbaro
Romero
Cayos Ana María
Vertientes
Contramaestre
Sierra del Chorillo

Golfo de Ana María
Meridional
Concordia
Laguna Lamar

Cayo Algodón Grande
Cayo Cuervo
Santa Cruz del Sur
Cayo Culebra

Cayo Bretón
Cayos Cinco Balas
Cayo Grande
Parque Nacional Jardines de la Reina
Cayo Chocolate
Cayo Punta Macho
Cayes Pingues
Cayos Pilón
Cayos Mate
Cayo Media Luna

Archipiélago de los Jardines de la Reina
Cayo Caballones
Cayo Anclitas
Cayo Granada
Cayo Cabeza del Este

Sea

© AVALON TRAVEL

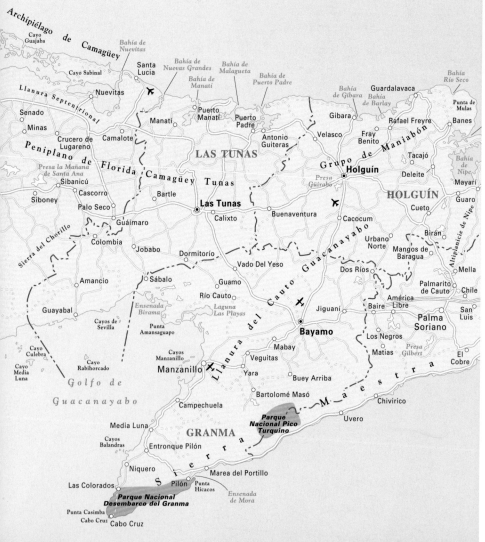

© AVALON TRAVEL

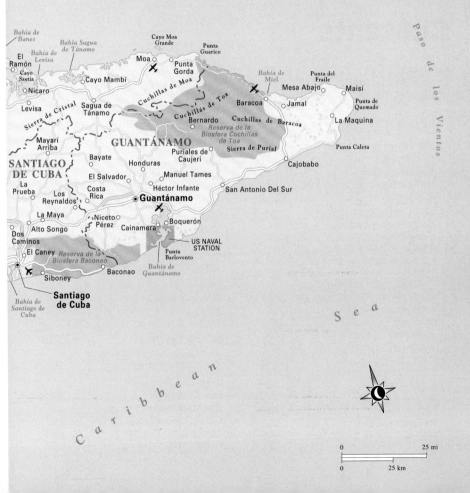

O C E A N

Bahía de
Banes

Bahía Sagua
de Tánamo

El
Ramón

Bahía de
Levisa

Cayo
Saetia

Cayo Moa
Grande

Moa

Punta
Guarico

Punta
Gorda

Bahía de
Miel

Punta del
Fraile

Mesa Abajo

Maisí

paso de los Vientos

Nicaro

Cayo Mambí

Cuchillas de Moa

Punta de
Quemado

Levisa

Sagua de
Tánamo

Sierra de Cristal

Baracoa

Jamal

Cuchillas de Toa

Bernardo

Cuchillas de Baracoa

La Maquina

Mayarí
Arriba

GUANTÁNAMO

Reserva de la
Biosfera Cuchillas
de Toa

Punta Caleta

Bayate

Puriales de
Caujeri

Sierra de Purial

SANTIAGO
DE CUBA

Honduras

La
Prueba

El Salvador

Manuel Tames

Cajobabo

Los
Reynaldos

Costa
Rica

Héctor Infante

San Antonio Del Sur

La Maya

Guantánamo

Niceto
Pérez

Boquerón

Alto Songo

Cainamera

Dos
Caminos

US NAVAL
STATION

El Caney

Reserva de la
Biosfera Baconao

Punta
Barlovento

Siboney

Baconao

Bahía de
Guantánamo

Santiago
de Cuba

Bahía de
Santiago de
Cuba

C a r i b b e a n

S e a

| 0 | 25 mi |
| 0 | 25 km |

Contents

Discover Cuba

In October 1959, Fidel Castro spoke to the American Society of Travel Agents (ASTA) convention, held in Havana. "We have sea," said Castro. "We have bays, we have beautiful beaches, we have medicinal waters in our hotels, we have mountains, we have game and we have fish in the sea and the rivers, and we have sun. Our people are noble, hospitable, and most important, they hate no one. They love visitors, so much in fact that our visitors feel completely at home."

Nothing has changed but the politics. Five decades after Castro closed the doors to outsiders, Cuba is enjoying cult status again. Every year, more than two million visitors arrive.

With all the hoopla about politics, it's easy to overlook the sheer beauty of the place: the diamond-dust beaches and bathtub-warm seas the color of peacock feathers; the bottle-green mountains and jade valleys full of dramatic formations; the ancient cities, with their cobbled colonial plazas and castles evocative of the once mighty power of Spain; and, above all, the sultriness and spontaneity of a people and place called the most emotionally involving in the Western hemisphere.

Divers are delirious over Cuba's deep-sea treasures. Birding is the best in the Caribbean. There are crocodiles, too, lurking leery-eyed in well-preserved everglades. Horseback-riding options abound. Cuba is a

prime destination for fishing and bicycle touring, and hikers can head for the Sierra Maestra to tread revolutionary trails trod by Fidel Castro and Che Guevara. There is *santería* and salsa, sunny days on talcum beaches, *mojitos* and Cuba libres to enjoy, and the world's finest cigars to smoke fresh from the factory. Deluxe all-inclusive resorts are well-established, as are urbane boutique hotels.

Cuba's most enigmatic appeal, however, is the sense that you are living inside a romantic thriller. Cuba is still intoxicating, still laced with the sharp edges and sinister shadows that made Federico García Lorca, the Spanish poet, write to his parents, "If I get lost, look for me in Cuba," and that made Ernest Hemingway want "to stay here forever." No other Western nation offers such sensual and surreal sensations, made more poignant by Cuba's romantic caught-in-a-time-warp setting. You don't want to sleep for fear of missing a vital experience. Before the Revolution, Cuba had a reputation as a place of intrigue and tawdry romance. The whiff of conspiracy, the intimation of liaison, is still in the air. For foreign visitors, it is heady stuff.

Planning Your Trip

▶ WHERE TO GO

Havana

Habana Vieja (Old Havana) is the colonial core, full of plazas, cathedrals, museums, and bars. Parque Histórico Militar Morro-Cabaña preserves the largest castle in the Americas. The Vedado district teems with Beaux-Arts, art nouveau, and art deco mansions; a magnificent cemetery; and the one-of-a-kind Plaza de la Revolución. There are even gorgeous beaches nearby.

Pinar del Río

These valleys are where the world's finest tobacco is grown. Viñales has magnificent scenery, plus preeminent climbing and caving. Scuba divers rave about Cayo Levisa and María la Gorda. Península de Guanahacabibes has birding and hiking trails, as does Las Terrazas, Cuba's most developed eco-resort. Head to Finca El Pinar San Luis for Tobacco 101.

IF YOU HAVE...

- **ONE WEEK:** Explore Habana Vieja and the Vedado district in Havana, plus two days in Viñales.
- **TWO WEEKS:** Add Trinidad via Zapata, Cienfuegos, and Playa Girón (Bay of Pigs).
- **THREE WEEKS:** Add Santa Clara, Remedios, and the Cayos de Villa Clara.
- **FOUR WEEKS:** Head east for Santiago de Cuba and Baracoa.

Isla de la Juventud Special Municipality

Slung beneath Cuba, this archipelago draws few visitors. The exception is Cayo Largo, a coral jewel with stupendous beaches. Isla de la Juventud boasts Presidio Modelo

traditional costumes, Habana Vieja, Havana

© AVALON TRAVEL

(the prison where Fidel was held); Refugio Ecológico Los Indios, great for birding; and Cuba's finest diving off Punta Francés. Two days is all that's required to explore Isla de la Juventud, plus two days more for Cayo Largo.

Matanzas

Cuba's premier beach resort, Varadero has the lion's share of hotels, plus Cuba's only 18-hole golf course and exceptional diving. Colonial-era Matanzas is a center for Afro-Cuban music and dance. The Caribbean's largest swamp—the Ciénaga de Zapata—offers fantastic birding and fishing. Nearby, Playa Girón, site of the 1961 Bay of Pigs invasion, has an engaging museum.

Playa Mayor, Varadero

Cienfuegos and Villa Clara

Bird-watchers and hikers are enamored of the Sierra Escambray, where forest trails lead to waterfalls. Santa Clara draws visitors to the mausoleum and museum of Che Guevara. Sleepy Remedios explodes with fireworks during the year-end *parranda* and is gateway to the beaches of Cayos de Villa Clara. Cienfuegos offers colonial architecture and a world-class botanical garden, the Jardín Botánico Soledad.

Sancti Spíritus

Sancti Spíritus is a charming hill town that is a crown jewel of colonial architecture. It's a

Antiguo Convento de San Francisco de Asís, Trinidad

great base for hiking at Topes de Collantes, lazing at Playa Ancón, or a steam-train ride into the Valle de los Ingenios. The provincial capital, Sancti Spíritus, also has a colonial core worth exploring, and anglers are lured to Embalse Zaza to hook world-prize bass.

Ciego de Ávila and Camagüey

Tiny Ciego de Ávila Province is the setting for Cayo Coco, the most developed isle of the Jardines del Rey archipelago. Come here for magnificent beaches and to view flamingos. Playa Santa Lucía has some of Cuba's best diving. The less developed Jardines de la Reina is a new frontier for anglers and divers. Camagüey city has quaint cobbled plazas and colonial architecture.

Las Tunas and Holguín

For travelers, Las Tunas Province is a place to pass through en route to history-packed Holguín, with its intriguing plazas and lively artistic culture. Nearby are the beaches

of Guardalavaca, an archaeological site at Museo Aborigen Chorro de Maíta, the alpine setting of Pinares de Mayarí, and Fidel Castro's birthplace at the Museo Conjunto Histórico Birán.

Granma

Off-the-beaten-path Granma Province is dominated by the Sierra Maestra, the mountainous base for Fidel Castro's guerrilla war. You can hike to his headquarters, La Comandancia de la Plata, and to the summit of Pico Turquino, Cuba's highest peak. Independence was launched in Bayamo, touting a vibrant colonial plaza. For scenery, the lonesome coast road east of the ho-hum beach resort of Marea del Portillo can't be beat.

Santiago de Cuba

The city of Santiago de Cuba, founded in 1514, predates Havana and has strong Haitian and Jamaican influences. Much of Cuba's musical heritage was birthed here. The

Moncada barracks, museums, and mausoleums recall the city's revolutionary fervor. At sunset, visitors flock to Castillo de San Pedro del Morro for a cannon-firing ceremony; in July it hosts Cuba's preeminent Carnaval. Explore the eclectic attractions of nearby Reserva de la Biosfera Baconao and the basilica at El Cobre.

Guantánamo

This mountainous province is synonymous with the U.S. naval base, which can be viewed from the Cuban military outpost at Caimanera. The otherwise dreary town of Guantánamo is alive with traditional music. Nearby the Zoológico de Piedra—literally a stone zoo!—fascinates. The La Farola mountain road leads to Baracoa, Cuba's oldest city, full of vernacular charm. Some of the nation's best birding and hiking can be enjoyed at El Yunque and Parque Nacional Alejandro de Humboldt.

► WHEN TO GO

Cuba has fairly distinct seasons: a relatively dry and mild winter (November–April) and a hot and wet summer (May–October). Early spring is the ideal time to travel, especially in the Oriente (the eastern provinces), which can be insufferably hot in summer. Christmas and New Year's are the busiest periods, and many accommodations and car rental agencies sell out then, while finding a domestic flight is nearly impossible. Hotel prices are usually lower in summer—the low season (*temporada baja*)—when hurricanes are a slim possibility. Tropical storms can lash the island even in winter, however.

You might want to time your visit to coincide with a major festival, such as Carnaval in Santiago de Cuba or the International Festival of New Latin American Cinema in Havana.

A cocker spaniel surveys the street in Trinidad.

▶ BEFORE YOU GO

Passports and Visas

Visitors to Cuba need a pass-port valid for at least six months beyond their intended length of stay; a ticket for onward travel; plus a tourist visa, typically issued when you check in for your plane to Cuba. Stays of up to 30 days are permitted (90 days for Canadians), extendable one time.

What to Take

Dress for a tropical climate. Pack a warm sweater and a wind-breaker for winter visits. In summer, the weather is hot and humid; you'll want light, loose-fitting shirts and shorts. Ideally, everything should be drip-dry, wash-and-wear. Cubans dress informally, though neatly, for all occasions.

1958 Edsel Corsair, near Trinidad

A comfortable, well-fitting pair of sneak-ers will work for most occasions. Pack a pair of dress shoes for your evening ensemble.

Take all the toiletries you think you'll need, including toilet paper and face cloth. Medicines are rarely available except in Havana and other key tourist venues; come prepared with aspirin and other essentials.

International (except U.S.) credit cards are accepted throughout Cuba, although the system is dysfunctional and unreliable. U.S. citizens will need to operate on a cash-only basis.

Transportation

Most international visitors fly into either Havana's José Martí International Airport or Varadero's Juan Gualberto Gómez International Airport. Cuba is a large island (more than 1,000 kilometers east–west). In Havana, getting around is simple thanks to an efficient taxi system. Traveling between cities by public transportation, however, can be a challenge. Víazul tourist buses connect major cities and resorts. Domestic flights are best avoided. Renting a car is recommended for serendipitous travelers, but cars are in short supply and roads are full of hazards.

U.S. Citizens

U.S. citizens may ask "Can I travel to Cuba legally?" U.S. law currently restricts legal travel to individuals who meet specific criteria for licensed travel (such as journalists). To visit Cuba legally, you must either spend no money there or qualify for a license. However, restrictions loosen and tighten with shifts in the political breeze. Thousands of U.S. citizens simply hop a plane to Cuba via Canada, Mexico, or other countries.

Explore Cuba

▶ THE BEST OF CUBA

Cuba is a large island, and exploring the isle fully would take at least a month, but the following fast-paced itinerary combines a sampling of the top scenery, beaches, and cities for those intent on seeing the best of all the island. Rent a car and plan to spend at least four days sampling Havana before heading out to the provinces (don't underestimate how much there is to see in the capital city).

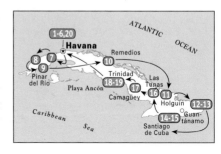

Day 1

Arrive at José Martí International Airport in Havana; transfer to a hotel or *casa particular* in the Habana Vieja or Vedado district.

Day 2

Take a self-guided walking tour of Habana Vieja, including the Plaza de Armas, Plaza de la Catedral, and the museums,

galleries, and shops along the surrounding streets. Return at night to savor the plazas lit by traditional gas lanterns. Don't fail to sip a *mojito* at La Bodeguita del Medio.

Day 3

Continue exploring Habana Vieja, including the Plaza de San Francisco, Plaza

Fuente de los Leones, Havana

BEST BEACHES

Cuba boasts glorious beaches. Most are scattered along the north shore, with concentrations immediately east of Havana; in Varadero; Cayo Largo; the Jardines del Rey (Ciego de Ávila and Camagüey Provinces); and Holguín. The south coast has relatively few noteworthy beaches. Swimming requires caution, as many beaches are known for riptides. Arrive with plenty of mosquito repellent, and avoid most beaches at dusk, when minuscule but ferocious no-see-ums are active.

Playas del Este: A series of lovely beaches within a 30-minute drive of Havana; they get lively with *habaneros* on weekends. The best sections are Tarará and Playa Mégano.

Playa El Francés: Tucked at the very southwestern extreme of Isla de la Juventud, there's a reason this white-sand beach draws big cruise ships. It's a beauty, with turquoise waters for snorkeling. You'll need an obligatory EcoTur guide in Nueva Gerona to get here.

Playa Sirena: Reached by a sandy unpaved road, this stunning beach is the best that Cayo Largo (and Cuba) can offer. The turquoise waters must be seen to be believed – but the waters shelve deeply and are not safe for children.

Playa Mayor: Varadero's main beach has silvery sands that run unbroken for five miles or more. Although it's lined with hotels and thatched restaurants the whole way, you can still find quiet spots all to your lonesome.

Playa Ancón: If you tire of wandering the cobbled streets of Trinidad, explore this beach just a few minutes away. The scuba diving here is superb, and there's a dive shop at the Hotel Playa Ancón; you can use the recreational services for a fee.

Playa Flamingo: The miles-long, palm-shaded, white-sand beach at Cayo Coco is lined with all-inclusive resorts, all with water sports.

Playa Pilar: The high point of Cayo Guillermo, this beach is backed by sand dunes and has a rustic seafood restaurant.

Playa Los Pinos: Sugar-white sand dissolves into turquoise shallows that stretch as far as the eye can see. Magical! It's just you and whatever day-trippers call in on excursions from Playa Santa Lucía. Bring your snorkeling gear to explore the coral reefs farther out.

Playa Flamingo at Cayo Coco, Ciego de Ávila

daiquiri in El Floridita, Havana

Vieja, and the surrounding area; be sure not to miss the Museo de Ron. In the late afternoon, head to the Parque Histórico Militar Morro-Cabaña, lingering to enjoy the sunset *cañonazo* ceremony.

Day 4

This morning, concentrate your time around Parque Central and Paseo de Martí. You'll want to visit the Capitolio Nacional, Fábrica de Tabaco Partagás, the Museo Nacional de Bellas Artes, and the Museo de la Revolución. A daiquiri at El Floridita is a must! At dusk, walk the Malecón.

Hemingway museum in Hotel Ambos Mundos, Havana

Day 5

Spend the morning exploring the streets of Vedado, being sure to call in at the Hotel Nacional, the Hotel Habana Libre Tryp, and University of Havana. After cooling off with an ice cream at Coppelia (with pesos in hand, stand in line with the Cubans), walk along Calle 17, calling in at the Museo de Artes Decorativas. Then hail a taxi to take you to Cementerio Colón and Plaza de la Revolución.

Day 6

Rent a car and set out on a tour of suburban Havana, calling in at Iglesia de Santa María del Rosario and Museo Ernest Hemingway. Continue to the village of Cojímar for lunch at La Terraza, then head to Playas del Este for time on the beach. I recommend the Playa Mégano section at Tarará.

Day 7

Head west along the Circuito Norte highway to Las Terrazas, an eco-resort and rural community in the heart of the Sierra del Rosario. Hike the trails and visit the artists' studios. Overnight at Hotel La Moka.

beach at María la Gorda, Pinar del Río

Mausoleo de Martí, Cementerio de Santa Ifigenia

Day 8

Continue west to Valle de Viñales. Spend the afternoon exploring Viñales village, the Cuevas del Indio, and tobacco fields. Overnight either in a *casa particular* or at the Horizontes La Ermita.

Day 9

This morning, head to the town of Pinar del Río and take the Autopista east to Havana and onward to Santa Clara. Visit the mausoleum and museum of Che Guevara and spend the night in town.

Day 10

Continue east to the historic town of Remedios. During Christmas week, you'll want to overnight in Remedios to enjoy the local fireworks battles called *parrandas.* Once done, follow the coast road east via Morón to Cayo Coco, arriving midafternoon in time to enjoy the beach and water sports.

Day 11

Follow the Circuito Norte east to Las Tunas, then continue along the Carretera Central to Holguín. I recommend staying at a *casa particular.*

Day 12

After walking the main plazas, set out for Museo Conjunto Histórico Birán, birthplace of Fidel Castro, before following the coast road east via Moa to Baracoa, arriving in this isolated and charming town in early evening. Overnight at Hotel El Castillo or a *casa particular.*

Day 13

Stroll the streets of Baracoa, savoring its unique laid-back flavor. In the afternoon, head to El Yunque, where you can hike to the summit of this fantastic mountain formation.

Day 14

Continue over La Farola, a switchback mountain road, dropping to the city of Guantánamo. En route, be sure to visit the Zoológico de Piedra. Continue to Santiago de Cuba, arriving in the early evening. Check into the Hotel Casagranda or a *casa particular.*

Day 15

After visiting the Cuartel Moncada and Museo de la Revolución, spend the balance of the day exploring the historic quarter of Santiago de Cuba, being sure to include the Cementerio de Santa Ifigenia. Before dusk, head out to Castillo de San Pedro del Morro to watch the *cañonazo* ceremony, when soldiers in period costume put a light to an ancient cannon. In the evening, call in at the Casa de la Trova to hear traditional Cuban music at its best.

Day 16

This morning depart Santiago and follow the Carretera Central northwest to the town of Bayamo. En route, call in at El Cobre to visit the shrine of the Virgen de la Caridad. After sightseeing around the main plaza of Bayamo, continue northwest via Yasa to Las Tunas. Overnight at a *casa particular*.

Basílica Metropolitana Santa Ifigenia at night, Santiago de Cuba

Day 17

Continue west along the Carretera Central to Camagüey, arriving midday with time to explore the three major colonial plazas. For digs, I recommend the charmingly restored 18th-century Hotel Colón, which also has one of the best restaurants in town.

Day 18

Get an early start today for the drive west via the provincial capitals of Ciego de Ávila and Sancti Spíritus, then through the Valle de los Ingenios, where you should have a late lunch at Hacienda Iznaga. Arriving in Trinidad, spend the rest of the afternoon perambulating the ancient plazas.

Day 19

After further walking the cobbled colonial heart of Trinidad, drive out to Playa Ancón for beach time and perhaps even some scuba diving. Tonight, check out an Afro-Cuban performance before heading to the Disco Ayala, set in a cave.

Day 20

Get up early again to follow the long and winding road over the Sierra Escambray to Topes de Collantes. Continue north to Santa Clara, then head back to Havana via the Autopista. This evening, visit the Tropicana cabaret, being sure to have made reservations. Fly home the next day.

▶ *¡VIVA LA REVOLUCIÓN!*

Many a traveler departs Cuba wearing a T-shirt emblazoned with the world-renowned image of Che Guevara. That doesn't necessarily indicate a fondness for Communism, or even Che. Still, thousands of visitors *do* arrive every year to pay homage to, or at least learn about, the *revolución*. Whatever

your politics, a pilgrimage along the revolutionary trail following the footsteps of Fidel Castro & Co. makes for a fascinating historical journey.

Day 1

Arrive at José Martí International Airport in

Complejo Escultórico Memorial Comandante Ernesto Che Guevara, Santa Clara

Havana; transfer to a hotel or *casa particular* in the Habana Vieja or Vedado district.

Day 2

Start the day with a visit to the Museo de la Revolución, housed in the former presidential palace of corrupt dictator Fulgencio Batista, whom the Revolution overthrew. Of course, you'll want to spend some time viewing the other fascinating sites nearby. In the afternoon, your tour of Habana Vieja should include the Museo Casa Natal de José Martí, birthplace of the national hero whom Fidel Castro named the "intellectual author" of the Revolution; and Museo de la Comandancia de Che, in Fortaleza de San Carlos de la Cabaña.

Day 3

Today, concentrate your sightseeing around Vedado. Must-see sights include the Casa Museo Abel Santamaría, a former apartment that was the secret headquarters for Castro's 26th of July Movement; the Universidad de la Habana, where the Escalinata (staircase) was a venue for clashes with Batista's police; Galería 23 y 12, where Castro first announced that Cuba was socialist; and Plaza de la Revolución, the seat of Communist government.

Day 4

Head west from Havana to Pinar del Río Province to visit Cuevas de los Portales, used as Che Guevara's command center during the Cuban Missile Crisis. Continue to Viñales to visit the tobacco fields and overnight.

Day 5

Depart Pinar del Río along the Autopista for the town of Santa Clara, setting for the seminal battle that toppled the Batista regime. Arriving midafternoon, your tour of the town should include the Tren Blindado (a troop train destroyed by Che Guevara's troops) and the Complejo Escultórico Memorial Comandante Ernesto Che Guevara, with an excellent museum devoted to the Argentinian revolutionary, whose remains are interred here.

Day 6

A long day's drive today along the Carretera Central to reach Holguín, with time for exploring the colonial heart of the city. Check out the Plaza de la Revolución.

Day 7

Leaving the city, take Avenida Simón Bolívar, lined with monuments to nationalist and revolutionary heroes, including a pop-art rendition of Che. Your destination is Museo Conjunto Histórico Birán, Fidel Castro's birthplace and home into adolescence. Afterwards, continue via Palma Soriano, arriving in Santiago de Cuba in the afternoon.

Day 8

The first stop today is Cuartel Moncada, site of the 1953 attack that launched the Revolution; today the former barracks holds the Museo de la Revolución. Nearby is the Museo Abel Santamaría, named for a prominent revolutionary tortured to death following the failed attack. This afternoon, tour the historic town center, including Parque

Che Guevara paraphernalia for sale

Céspedes (where Fidel Castro gave his victory speech after Batista was toppled); the Colegio Jesuita Dolores, where Fidel attended school; and the Museo Lucha Clandestina, recalling the clandestine war in the cities.

Day 9

Head out to Siboney to visit the farmhouse from where Castro and his revolutionaries set out to attack the Moncada barracks. The route is lined with monuments to those who died in the attack. Afterwards, head into the mountains to Mayarí Arriba and the Museo Comandancia del Segundo Frente (Museum of the Second Front) and the nearby mausoleum, recalling the "Second Front" led by Raúl Castro. Return to Santiago for the evening.

Day 10

Head west along the coast via Chivírico—a stupendous drive! Beyond Ocujal, visit Museo Comandancia de la Plata, with exhibits detailing the revolutionary war in the mountains. Continue to the Parque Nacional Desembarco del Granma, site of the landing of Fidel's army in 1956. Overnight in Niquero.

Day 11

Call in at Media Luna to view the Casa Museo Celia Sanchez, birthplace of the revolutionary heroine who ran the secret supply line to Fidel's army in the Sierra Maestra. In Manzanillo, visit the Monumento Celía Sánchez then continue via Bartolomé Masó to Santo Domingo, where a small museum features a 3-D map of the war in the Sierra Maestra. Overnight in Santo Domingo.

Day 12

This morning hike to La Comandancia de la Plata, Fidel's headquarters deep in the Sierra Maestra. In the afternoon, continue via Bayamo, arriving in Las Tunas in early evening.

Day 13

Prepare for the long drive back to Havana today via the Carretera Central and Autopista. In the morning, transfer to the airport for your departure flight.

BEST SCENIC DRIVES

Cuba is a visual delight, and anyone who enjoys driving (and can handle the sometimes daunting obstacles that pave the way) will thrill to these eight scenic drives.

- **Mariel to Valle de Viñales via Circuito Norte:** This winding ridge-top drive between mountain and sea begins one hour west of Havana and offers lovely views of the *mogotes* of the Sierra del Rosario.

- **Chambas to Caibarién via Circuito Norte:** This route offers quintessentially Cuban rural scenery: tobacco fields tended by ox-drawn plows and shaded by royal palms, with rustic *bohíos* in the lee of mountains.

- **Trinidad to Sancti Spíritus via Circuito Sur:** A roller-coaster ride through swathes of lime-green sugarcane in the Valle de los Ingenios. Farther east, you'll pass the rugged Alturas de Banao.

- **Trinidad to Santa Clara via Manicaragua:** This mountain drive with steep climbs and hairpin turns winds through forests and rolling tobacco country. Drive cautiously on the switchback ascent to Topes de Collantes.

- **Bartolomé Masó to Marea del Portillo:** A four-wheel drive challenge via the Sierra Maestra, with a steep, looping road in awful condition – but the staggering mountain vistas are topped by views over the coast and sea.

- **Marea del Portillo to Santiago de Cuba:** This lonesome drive features awesome coastal scenery – copper-colored cliffs loom massively out of the sea, with Cuba's highest peaks within fingertip distance beyond the stark low-desert plains.

- **Cajobabo to Baracoa via La Farola:** A steep ascent through the pine-clad Sierra Cristal, with snaking bends and occasional pullouts for savoring the vistas.

Valle de Viñales at dusk, Pinar del Río

▶ CARS, CIGARS, AND CABARETS

Cuba is a mother lode for anyone who loves classic American autos, fine cigars, quality rums, and Las Vegas–style cabaret revues. Before 1959, Havana was the hottest spot in the Caribbean, notorious for its glittering cabarets, smooth rum, and chrome-laden Cadillacs. The good news is that the tail fins of '57 Eldorados still glint beneath the floodlit mango trees of nightclubs such as the Tropicana, the open-air extravaganza now in its seventh decade of stiletto-heeled paganism. OK, big spender, let the fun begin.

Day 1

Arrive at José Martí International Airport in Havana; transfer to a hotel or *casa particular* in Habana Vieja or Vedado.

Day 2

This morning, concentrate your time around Parque Central, where the highlight will be a guided tour of the Fábrica de Tabaco Partagás. After buying some premium smokes, head to either the earthy art deco bar in the Edificio Bacardí or the sophisticated bar in the Hotel NH Parque Central to enjoy your stogie with a Cuba libre. Then rent a classic 1950s auto from Gran Car and set out for a tour of the city. In the evening, enjoy dinner at the Comedor de Aguiar restaurant in the Hotel Nacional, then thrill to the sexy spectacle of the hotel's Cabaret Parisien.

Day 3

Today, follow Hemingway's ghost. Drive out to the village of San Miguel del Padrón and the Museo Ernest Hemingway, in the author's former home. Afterwards, head to Cojímar for a seafood lunch at La Terraza restaurant, once popular with Papa and his former skipper, the late local resident

worker rolling a cigar at Finca El Pinar San Luis, Pinar del Río

Gregorio Fuentes. Return to Havana for a *mojito* and stogie at La Bodeguita del Medio. Explore Plaza de la Catedral and Plaza de Armas, being sure to stop in at the Hotel Ambos Mundos (Room 511, where Hemingway was a long-time guest, is a museum) and the Museo de Ron, a splendid museum giving insight into production of Cuba's fine rums. This evening, sample the daiquiris at El Floridita.

Day 4

Rent a car (pick it up the day before if possible), or hire a taxi for a day trip to Pinar del Río. Set out early to visit the tobacco fields of Valle de Viñales, and the Finca El Pinar San Luis, *finca* of the late Alejandro Robaina, a legend after whom the Cuban state named a brand of cigar. Return to Havana in the evening for dinner at El Aljibe. Share fine cigars and *añejo* rums with connoisseur cigar lovers at the Casa del Habano in Miramar.

1953 Chevrolet Bel Air in Havana

dancer at Tropicana nightclub

1952 Oldsmobile Super in Santa Clara

Day 5

Head out to Marina Hemingway for a full day of sportfishing for blue marlin in Hemingway's "great blue river." This evening, enjoy dinner at one of Havana's chicest restaurants. If you still have energy after a day battling game fish, sample the retro nightlife at the Café Concierto Gato Tuerto nightclub.

Days 6-7

This morning, head to Club Habana, a private and very chic members club (open to nonmembers for a fee) where you can relax on the fine beach, partake of water sports, and sample cocktails and fine cigars. After dinner at Cocina de Lilliam *paladar,* head to the Tropicana nightclub for the sauciest cabaret in Cuba. In the morning, transfer to the airport for your departure flight.

▶ BIRDING AT ITS BEST

With more than 350 bird species, Cuba is an ornithologist's paradise. Birders flock to spy the isle's 21 endemic species found nowhere else, among them the world's smallest bird—the thimble-sized *zunzuncito* hummingbird. The following 10-day tour covers sufficiently diverse terrain to check off a vast list of avian fauna. You'll want an experienced guide, prearranged through Cuba's EcoTur tour agency.

Day 1

Arrive at José Martí International Airport in Havana; transfer to a hotel in Habana Vieja or Vedado.

Day 2

Meet your guide and head west to Las Terrazas, an eco-resort in Reserva Sierra del Rosario, Cuba's first biosphere reserve. The trill of Cuban green woodpeckers and the haunting song of the endemic Cuban solitaire accompany you on the trails. Overnight at Hotel La Moka.

Day 3

After a morning hike at Las Terrazas, continue west to Parque Nacional Viñales, and your base at Hotel Horizontes Rancho San Vicente. Exploring the Sierra de los Órganos grants a chance to spot the Cuban parrot, the yellow-headed warbler, and the minuscule bee hummingbird.

Day 4

Head east to the wetlands of the Península de Zapata to search for the Zapata wren, the Zapata rail, and other endemic species. Arrive

DIVE INTO CUBA

diving off Cayo Levisa

Cuba has some of the Caribbean's most spectacular diving, much of it almost entirely virgin. The coral formations rival those of anywhere else in the region, and the wreck diving is varied and fascinating: take your pick from Spanish galleons to 20th-century Soviet warships. These are the major venues worth planning a trip around:

- **The "Blue Circuit":** You don't have to leave Havana to dive. Wrecks litter the Atlantic seabed, with dive sites extending for 10 kilometers east, beginning at Bacuranao.

- **Playa María la Gorda:** This site near the western tip of Cuba is the place to dive with whale sharks. El Valle de Coral Negro (Black Coral Valley) is another highlight, and there are Spanish wrecks in the bay.

- **Cayo Levisa:** This tiny, coral-fringed cay off the north coast of Pinar del Río Province is a dedicated dive resort.

- **Punta Francés:** Spanish galleons and coral formations await divers a short distance off the south shore of Isla de la Juventud.

- **Ciénaga de Zapata:** The Club Octopus International Dive Center, at Playa Larga, will take you diving in *cenotes,* water-filled limestone sinkholes. You can even dive wrecks of landing craft that grounded during the Bay of Pigs invasion.

- **Playa Santa Lucía:** Although the hotels here aren't much to speak of, the diving is sensational. A big draw is shark-feeding, performed by the divemaster.

- **Jardines de la Reina:** Never mind shark feeding. How about *riding* a shark? The "Garden of the Queens," south of Camagüey, are virgin territory, with stupendous coral reefs, colorful fishes, marine turtles, moray eels, and other desirable stars of the show.

roseate spoonbill

in time for an afternoon hike in the deciduous forests near Bermejas, where endangered Fernandina's flickers are often seen. An afternoon swim in the *cenote* at Cueva de los Peces precedes an overnight at Playa Larga.

Day 5

Drive to the tidal flats at La Salina, world-famous for its waders and water fowl, including flamingos. Look en route for such endemics as the Cuban martin and Gundlach's hawk. Then depart Zapata via the Museo Playa Girón, recalling the Bay of Pigs invasion of 1961. After a late-afternoon lunch in Cienfuegos, continue to the Sierra Escambray for a night at Topes de Collantes.

Day 6

Plan an early morning departure by Russian truck or jeep to Parque El Nicho, with time to swim at the base of the cascades. After hiking Sendero El Reino de las Aguas, enjoy a rustic lunch before continuing to Trinidad

to savor this colonial city. Tonight, enjoy dinner at Restaurante El Jigüe and traditional music and dance at the Casa de la Trova.

Day 7

Passing through Sancti Spíritus, take the Carretera Central east to Camagüey, then south to the Finca La Belén, where denizens of the semideciduous woodland and tropical montane forest include Cuban parrots, the endangered giant kingbird, and *tocororos,* or Cuban trogons.

Day 8

Spend the morning hiking the trails of the Belén reserve before departing for Cayo Coco, with its fabulous beaches and bird-filled lagoons. Time your arrival to coincide with the flamingo flyover at dusk.

Day 9

Roseate spoonbills, egrets, piping plovers, and Oriente warblers are among the birds to look for as you explore Parque Nacional El Bagá and nearby Cayo Guillermo. You'll want to relax this afternoon with a sunset catamaran cruise.

Days 10-12

Return to Havana via the Circuito Norte or Autopista.

It would be sacrilege to visit Cuba without exploring Havana, so spend the next day on an all-day, hop-on/hop-off HabanaBusTour. Tonight, celebrate your birding skills with a cocktail at the Hotel Nacional followed, perhaps, by a night at the Cabaret Parisien. In the morning, transfer to the airport for your departure flight.

HAVANA

Havana (pop. 2.2 million), political, cultural, and industrial heart of the nation, lies 150 kilometers (93 miles) due south of Florida on Cuba's northwest coast. It is built on the west side of a sweeping bay—Bahía de la Habana—and extends west 12 kilometers to the Río Jaimanitas and south for an equal distance.

Countless writers have commented on the exhilarating sensation that engulfs visitors to this most beautiful and beguiling of Caribbean cities. The city's ethereal mood, little changed through the centuries, is so pronounced that it finds its way into novels. "I wake up feeling different, like something inside me is changing, something chemical and irreversible. There's a magic here working its way through my veins," says Pilar, a Cuban-American character from New York who returns to Havana in Cristina García's novel *Dreaming in Cuban.* Set foot one time in Havana and you can only succumb to its enigmatic allure. It is impossible to resist the city's mysteries and contradictions.

Havana has a flavor all its own, a strange amalgam of colonialism, capitalism, and Communism merged into one. One of the great historical cities of the New World, Havana is a far cry from the Caribbean backwaters that call themselves capitals elsewhere in the Antilles. Havana is a city, notes architect Jorge Rigau, "upholstered in columns, cushioned by colonnaded arcades." The buildings come in a spectacular amalgam of styles—from the academic classicism of aristocratic homes, rococo residential exteriors, Moorish interiors, and art deco and art nouveau to stunning exemplars of 1950s moderne.

© CHRISTOPHER P. BAKER

HIGHLIGHTS

((Museo Nacional de Bellas Artes: Divided into national and international sections, this art gallery competes with the world's finest (pages 42 and 46).

((Capitolio Nacional: Cuba's former congressional building is an architectural glory reminiscent of Washington's own Capitol (page 42).

((Plaza de la Catedral: This small, atmospheric plaza is hemmed in by colonial mansions and a baroque cathedral (page 48).

((Plaza de Armas: The restored cobbled plaza at the heart of Old Havana features a castle, museums, and tons of charm (page 55).

((Plaza Vieja: Still undergoing restoration, this antique plaza offers offbeat museums, Havana's only brewpub, flashy boutiques, and heaps of ambience (page 64).

((Hotel Nacional: A splendid landmark with magnificent architecture and oodles of history, this hotel is a great place to relax with a *mojito* and cigar while soaking in the heady atmosphere of the past (page 82).

((Necrópolis Cristóbal Colón: This is one of the New World's great cemeteries, with dramatic tombstones that comprise a who's who of Cuban history (page 89).

((Parque Histórico Militar Morro-Cabaña: An imposing castle complex contains the Castillo de los Tres Reyes del Morro and massive Fortaleza de San Carlos de la Cabaña, with cannons in situ and soldiers in period costume (page 106).

((Tropicana: Havana at its most sensual, the Tropicana hosts a spectacular cabaret with more than 200 performers and dancers (page 116).

((Museo Ernest Hemingway: "Papa's" former home is preserved as it was on the day he died. His sportfishing boat, the *Pilar*, stands on the grounds (page 177).

LOOK FOR ((TO FIND RECOMMENDED SIGHTS, ACTIVITIES, DINING, AND LODGING.

At the heart of the city is enchanting Habana Vieja (Old Havana), a living museum inhabited by 60,000 people and containing perhaps the finest collection of Spanish-colonial buildings in all the Americas. Baroque churches, convents, and castles that could have been transposed from Madrid or Cádiz still reign majestically over squares embraced by the former palaces of Cuba's ruling gentry and cobbled streets still haunted by Ernest Hemingway's ghost. Hemingway's house, Finca Vigía, is one of dozens of museums dedicated to the memory of great men and women. And although most of the older monuments—those of politically incorrect heroes—were pulled down, at least they were replaced by dozens of grandiose monuments to those on the correct side of history.

Balmy city streets with walls in faded tropical pastels still smolder gold in the waxing sun. Sunlight still filters through stained-glass *mediopuntos* to dance on the cool marble floors. And time cannot erase the sound of the "jalousies above the colonnades creaking in the small wind from the sea," in the words of Graham Greene.

The heart of Habana Vieja has been in the process of restoration, and most of the important structures have been given facelifts, or better. Some have even metamorphosed into boutique hotels. Nor is there a shortage of 1950s-era modernist hotels steeped in Mafia associations. And hundreds of *casas particulares* provide an opportunity to live life alongside the *habaneros* themselves. There's something for every budget. As for food, Havana is the only place in Cuba where you can dine well every night of the week.

Then there's the arts scene, perhaps unrivaled in Latin America. The city offers some first-rate museums and galleries. Not only formal galleries, but informal ones where contemporary artists produce unique works of amazing profundity and appeal. There are tremendous crafts markets and boutique stores. Afro-Caribbean music is everywhere, quite literally on the streets. Lovers of sizzling salsa have dozens of venues from which to choose. Havana even has a hot jazz scene. Classical

© CHRISTOPHER P. BAKER

the Capitolio Nacional, from the roof of the Hotel Saratoga

music and ballet is world class, with numerous venues to choose from. And neither Las Vegas, Paris, nor Rio de Janeiro can compare with Havana for sensational and sexy cabarets, with top billing now, as back in the day, being the Tropicana.

PLANNING YOUR TIME

Havana is so large and the sights to be seen so many, that one week is the bare minimum needed. Metropolitan Havana sprawls over 740 square kilometers (286 square miles) and incorporates 15 *municipios* (municipalities). Havana is a collection of neighborhoods, each with its own distinct character that owes much to the century that each developed. Since the city is so spread out, it is best to explore Havana in sections, concentrating your time on the three main districts of touristic interest—Habana Vieja, Vedado, and Miramar—in that order.

If you have only one or two days in Havana, book a get-your-bearings trip by HabanaBusTour or hop on an organized city tour offered by Havanatur or a similar agency.

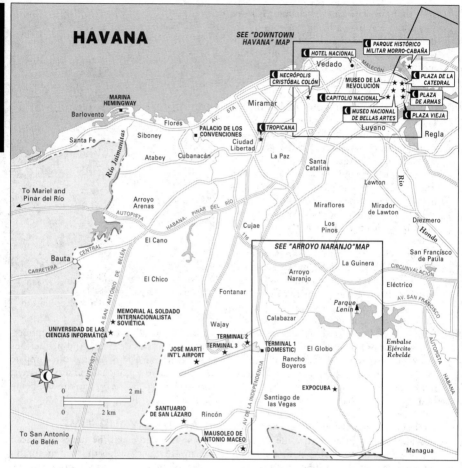

HAVANA

SEE "DOWNTOWN HAVANA" MAP

PARQUE HISTÓRICO MILITAR MORRO-CABAÑA

HOTEL NACIONAL

Vedado

NECRÓPOLIS CRISTÓBAL COLÓN

MUSEO DE LA REVOLUCIÓN

PLAZA DE LA CATEDRAL

CAPITOLIO NACIONAL

PLAZA DE ARMAS

MARINA HEMINGWAY

Barlovento

Florés

Miramar

MUSEO NACIONAL DE BELLAS ARTES

PLAZA VIEJA

AV. 5TA

Santa Fe

Siboney

PALACIO DE LOS CONVENCIONES

TROPICANA

Luyano

Regla

Río Jaimanitas

Atabey

Cubanacán

Ciudad Libertad

La Paz

Santa Catalina

Lawton

Río

To Mariel and Pinar del Río

Arroyo Arenas

AUTOPISTA

HABANA PINAR DEL RÍO

Cujae

Miraflores

Mirador de Lawton

Diezmero

Hondo

El Cano

SEE "ARROYO NARANJO" MAP

Los Pinos

San Francisco de Paúla

CENTRAL

Bauta

CARRETERA

El Chico

Fontanar

Arroyo Naranjo

La Guinera

CIRCUNVALACIÓN

Eléctrico

AV. SAN FRANCISCO

A SAN ANTONIO DE BELÉN

Parque Lenin

MEMORIAL AL SOLDADO INTERNACIONALISTA SOVIÉTICA

Calabazar

Embalse Ejército Rebelde

UNIVERSIDAD DE LAS CIENCIAS INFORMÁTICA

Wajay

TERMINAL 2

TERMINAL 3

TERMINAL 1 (DOMESTIC)

El Globo

AUTOPISTA HABANA

AUTOPISTA

JOSÉ MARTÍ INT'L AIRPORT

Rancho Boyeros

EXPOCUBA

AV. DE LA INDEPENDENCIA

Santiago de las Vegas

0   2 mi

0   2 km

SANTUARIO DE SAN LÁZARO

Rincón

To San Antonio de Belén

MAUSOLEO DE ANTONIO MACEO

Managua

This will provide an overview of the major sites. Concentrate the balance of your time around Parque Central, **Plaza de la Catedral,** and **Plaza de Armas.** Your checklist of must-sees should include the **Capitolio Nacional,** Gran Teatro, Fábrica de Tabaco Partagás, **Museo de la Revolución, Museo Nacional de Bellas Artes,** the Catedral de la Habana, and the Museo de la Ciudad de la Habana (in the Palacio de los Capitanes Generales).

Habana Vieja (Old Havana), the original colonial city within the 17th-century city walls (now demolished), will require at least three

days to fully explore. You can base yourself in one of the charming historic hotel conversions close to the main sights of interest. Be sure to journey across the harbor to visit **Parque Histórico Militar Morro-Cabaña,** featuring two restored castles attended by soldiers in period costume.

Centro Habana has many *casas particulares* but few sites of interest, and its rubble-strewn, dimly lit streets aren't the safest. Skip Centro for Vedado, the modern heart of the city that evolved in the early 20th century, with many ornate mansions in Beaux-Arts and art nouveau

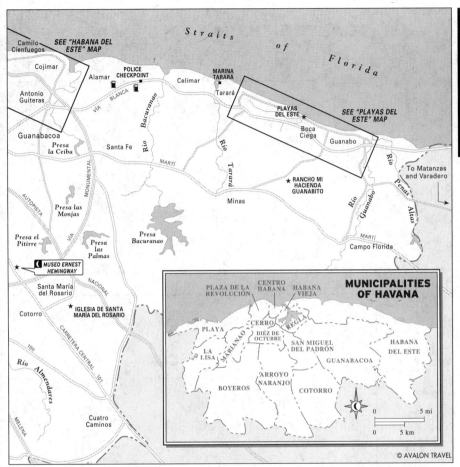

© AVALON TRAVEL

style. Its leafy streets make for great walking. Many of the city's best *casas particulares* are here, as are most businesses, *paladares,* and nightclubs. The **Hotel Nacional,** Universidad de la Habana, Cementerio Colón, and Plaza de la Revolución are among the prime sights not to miss.

If you're interested in Beaux-Arts, art deco, or even 1950s moderne architecture, then once-glamorous Miramar, Cubanacán, and Siboney regions, west of Vedado, are worth exploring. Miramar also has excellent restaurants, deluxe hotels, and some of my favorite nightspots.

Most other sections of Havana are run-down residential districts of little interest to tourists. A few exceptions lie on the east side of Havana harbor. Regla and neighboring Guanabacoa are together a center of *santería* and Afro-Cuban music. The 18th-century fishing village of Cojímar has Hemingway associations, and the nearby community of San Miguel de Padrón is where the great author lived for 20 years. A visit to his home, Finca Vigía, today the **Museo Ernest Hemingway,** is de rigueur. Combine it with a visit to the exquisite colonial **Iglesia de Santa María del Rosario.** About

HAVANA

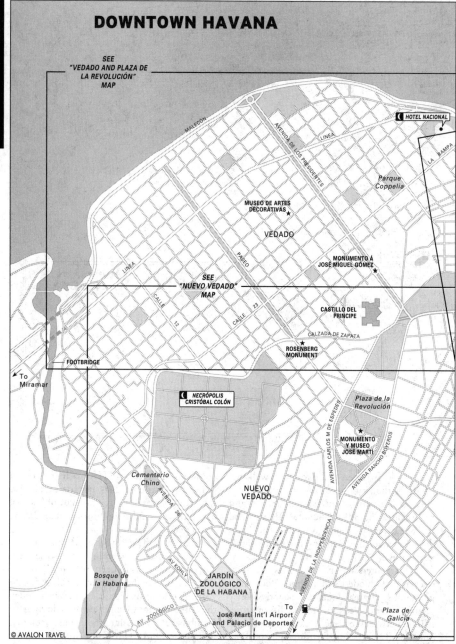

DOWNTOWN HAVANA

SEE
"VEDADO AND PLAZA DE
LA REVOLUCIÓN"
MAP

MALECÓN

AVENIDA DE LOS PRESIDENTES

LINEA

🍸 HOTEL NACIONAL

LA RAMPA

Parque
Coppelia

MUSEO DE ARTES
DECORATIVAS ★

VEDADO

PASEO

LINEA

CALLE 12

CALLE 23

SEE
"NUEVO VEDADO"
MAP

MONUMENTO A
JOSÉ MIGUEL GÓMEZ ★

CASTILLO DEL
PRINCIPE

CALZADA DE ZAPATA

ROSENBERG
MONUMENT ★

FOOTBRIDGE

↖ To
Miramar

🌙 NECRÓPOLIS
CRISTÓBAL COLÓN

AVENIDA CARLOS M DE ESPEDES

Plaza de la
Revolución

★
MONUMENTO
Y MUSEO
JOSÉ MARTÍ

AVENIDA RANCHO BOYEROS

Cementerio
Chino

AVENIDA 26

NUEVO
VEDADO

AVENIDA DE LA INDEPENDENCIA

AV KOHLY

Bosque de
la Habana

JARDÍN
ZOOLÓGICO
DE LA HABANA

AV. ZOOLÓGICO

To
José Martí Int'l Airport
and Palacio de Deportes

Plaza de
Galicia

© AVALON TRAVEL

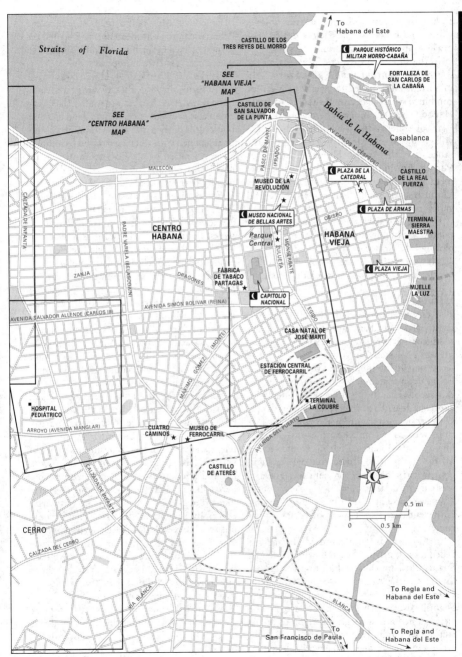

Straits of Florida

To Habana del Este

CASTILLO DE LOS TRES REYES DEL MORRO

PARQUE HISTÓRICO MILITAR MORRO-CABAÑA

FORTALEZA DE SAN CARLOS DE LA CABAÑA

SEE "HABANA VIEJA" MAP

CASTILLO DE SAN SALVADOR DE LA PUNTA

Bahía de la Habana

Casablanca

SEE "CENTRO HABANA" MAP

AV CARLOS M CÉSPEDES

MALECÓN

PASEO DE MARTÍ (PRADO)

MUSEO DE LA REVOLUCIÓN

PLAZA DE LA CATEDRAL

CASTILLO DE LA REAL FUERZA

MUSEO NACIONAL DE BELLAS ARTES

OBISPO

PLAZA DE ARMAS

CALZADA DE INFANTA

CENTRO HABANA

PADRE VARELA (BELASCOAÍN)

Parque Central

MONSERRATE

ZULUETA

HABANA VIEJA

TERMINAL SIERRA MAESTRA

ZANJA

DRAGONES

FÁBRICA DE TABACO PARTAGAS

PLAZA VIEJA

CAPITOLIO NACIONAL

EGIDO

MUELLE LA LUZ

AVENIDA SIMÓN BOLÍVAR (REINA)

MÁXIMO GÓMEZ (MONTE)

CASA NATAL DE JOSÉ MARTÍ

ESTACIÓN CENTRAL DE FERROCARRIL

HOSPITAL PEDIÁTRICO

ARROYO (AVENIDA MANGLAR)

AVENIDA SALVADOR ALLENDE (CARLOS III)

TERMINAL LA COUBRE

CUATRO CAMINOS

MUSEO DE FERROCARRIL

AVENIDA DEL PUERTO

CALZADA DE INFANTA

CASTILLO DE ATERÉS

0   0.5 mi
0   0.5 km

CERRO

CALZADA DEL CERRO

VÍA BLANCA

VÍA BLANCA

To Regla and Habana del Este

To San Francisco de Paula

To Regla and Habana del Este

15 kilometers east of the city, a series of long, white-sand beaches—the **Playas del Este**—prove tempting on hot summer days.

In the suburban district of Boyeros, to the south, the **Santuario de San Lázaro** is an important pilgrimage site. A visit here can be combined with the nearby **Mausoleo Antonio Maceo,** where the mulatto-hero general of the Wars of Independence is buried outside the village of Santiago de las Vegas. A short distance east, the Arroyo Naranjo district has **Parque Lenin,** a vast park with an amusement park, horseback rides, boating, and more. Enthusiasts of botany can visit the botanical garden, **Jardín Botánico Nacional.**

Despite Havana's great size, most sights of interest are highly concentrated, and most exploring is best done on foot.

All touristed areas are patrolled by police, but don't let your guard down for a second.

HISTORY

The city was founded in July 1515 as San Cristóbal de la Habana, and was located on the south coast, where Batabanó stands today. The site was a disaster. On November 25, 1519, the settlers moved to the shore of the flask-shaped Bahía de la Habana. Its location was so advantageous that in July 1553 the city replaced Santiago de Cuba as the capital of the island.

Every spring and summer, Spanish treasure ships returning from the Americas crowded into Havana's sheltered harbor before setting off for Spain in an armed convoy—*la flota.* By the turn of the 18th century, Havana was the third-largest city in the New World after Mexico City and Lima. The 17th and 18th centuries saw a surge of ecclesiastical construction.

In 1762, the English captured Havana but ceded it back to Spain the following year. The Spanish lost no time in building the largest fortress in the Americas—San Carlos de la Cabaña. Under the supervision of the new Spanish governor, the Marqués de la Torre, the city attained a new focus and rigorous architectural harmony. The first public gas lighting arrived in 1768, along with a workable system

of aqueducts. Most of the streets were cobbled. Along them, wealthy merchants and plantation owners erected beautiful mansions fitted inside with every luxury in European style.

By the mid-19th century, Havana was bursting its seams. In 1863, the city walls came tumbling down, less than a century after they were completed. New districts went up, and graceful boulevards pushed into the surrounding countryside, lined with a parade of *quintas* (summer homes) fronted by classical columns. By the mid-1800s, Havana had achieved a level of modernity that surpassed that of Madrid.

Following the Spanish-Cuban-American War, Havana entered a new era of prosperity. The city spread out, its perimeter enlarged by parks, boulevards, and dwellings in eclectic, neoclassical, and revivalist styles, while older residential areas settled into an era of decay.

By the 1950s Havana was a wealthy and thoroughly modern city with a large and prospering middle class, and had acquired skyscrapers such as the Focsa building and the Hilton (now the Habana Libre). Ministries were being moved to a new center of construction, the Plaza de la República (today the Plaza de la Revolución), inland from Vedado. Gambling found a new lease on life, and casinos flourished.

Following the Revolution, a mass exodus of the wealthy and the middle class began, inexorably changing the face of Havana. Tourists also got the message, dooming Havana's hotels, restaurants, and other businesses to bankruptcy. Festering slums and shanty towns marred the suburbs. The government ordered them razed. Concrete high-rise apartment blocks were erected on the outskirts, especially in Habana del Este. That accomplished, the Revolution turned its back on the city. Havana's aged housing and infrastructure, much of it already decayed, have ever since suffered benign neglect. Even the mayor of Havana has admitted that "the Revolution has been hard on the city."

Meanwhile, tens of thousands of poor peasant migrants poured into Havana from Oriente, shipped in by the Castro government to bolster Fidel's natural base of support. The

THE MOB IN HAVANA

For three decades, the Mafia had dealings in Cuba, and prerevolutionary Havana will forever be remembered for its presence.

During U.S. Prohibition (1920-1933), mobsters such as Al Capone had contracted with Cuban refineries to supply molasses for their illicit rum factories. When Prohibition ended, the Mob turned to gambling. The Mafia's interests were represented by Meyer Lansky, the Jewish mobster from Miami who arrived in 1939 and struck a deal with Fulgencio Batista, Cuba's strongman president – "the best thing that ever happened to us," Lansky told national crime syndicate boss Salvatore "Lucky" Luciano. Lansky, acting as lieutenant for Luciano, took over the Oriental Park racetrack and the casino at Havana's Casino Nacional, where he ran a straight game that attracted high rollers.

World War II effectively put an end to the Mob's business, which was relatively small scale at the time. Lansky returned to Florida; Batista followed him in 1944 when he lost to Ramón Grau in the national election. Lansky's above board operation soon withered in the Mob's absence, replaced by rigged casinos, and Havana's gambling scene developed a bad reputation.

Following the war, the United States deported Luciano to Italy. In 1946, he moved to Cuba, where he intended to establish a gambling and narcotics operation and regain his status as head of the U.S. Mob. He called a summit in Havana's Hotel Nacional. The meeting was immortalized in *The Godfather*, and the official cover, records Alan Ryan, "was that it was meant to honor a nice Italian boy from Hoboken called Frank Sinatra," who went down to Havana to say thanks. The United States, however, pressured Grau to deport Luciano back to Italy. Before leaving, Luciano named Lansky head of operations in Cuba.

The Mob's Cuba presence was given a boost when Florida's casinos were closed down, followed by a federal campaign to suppress the Mob. Mobsters decided Cuba was the place to be. A new summit was called at Batista's house in Daytona Beach, attended by Cuban politicians and military brass. A deal was struck: Batista would return to Cuba, regain power, and open the doors to large-scale gambling. In return, he and his crooked pals would receive a piece of the take. A gift of US$250,000 personally delivered by Lansky helped convince President Grau to step aside, and on March 10, 1952, Batista again occupied the presidential palace. New laws were quickly enacted to attract investment in hotels and casinos, and banks were set up as fronts to channel money into the hands of Cuban politicos.

The "family," headed by Cuban-Italian Amleto Batistti, controlled the heroin and cocaine routes to the United States and an emporium of illegal gambling from Batistti's base at the Hotel Sevilla. Tampa's Mafia boss, Santo Trafficante Jr., operated the Sans Souci casino-nightclub, plus the casinos in the Capri, Comodoro, Deauville, and Sevilla-Biltmore Hotels. Watching over everyone was Lansky, who ran the Montmartre Club and the Internacional Club of the Hotel Nacional. Anything was permissible: gambling, pornography, drugs. Nonetheless, no frivolities were allowed. Games were regulated, and cardsharps and cheats were sent packing, although cocaine and prostitutes were supplied to high rollers. (In 1957, Mob boss Santo Trafficante claims to have set John F. Kennedy up with a private party, supplying three prostitutes in a special suite in the Hotel Comodoro.)

The tourists flocked. Lansky's last act was to build the ritziest hotel and casino in Cuba – the US$14 million Hotel Riviera and Gold Leaf Casino, which opened on December 10, 1958. Once Castro took power, the casinos were closed down, and in June 1959, Lansky, Trafficante, and other "undesirable aliens" were kicked out of Cuba. Said Lansky: "I crapped out."

settlers changed the city's demographic profile: Most of the immigrants were black (as many as 400,000 *"palestinos,"* immigrants from Santiago and the eastern provinces, live in Havana, their presence resented by a large segment of *habaneros*).

Finally, in the 1980s, the revolutionary government established a preservation program for Habana Vieja, and the Centro Nacional de Conservación, Restauración, y Museología was created to inventory Havana's historic sites and implement a restoration program that would return much of the ancient city to pristine splendor. Much of the original city core now gleams afresh with confections in stone, while the rest of the city is left to crumble.

Sights - Habana Vieja

Habana Vieja (4.5 square km) is defined by the limits of the early colonial settlement that lay within fortified walls. The legal boundary of Habana Vieja includes the Paseo de Martí (colloquially called the Prado) and everything east of it.

Habana Vieja is roughly shaped like a diamond, with the Castillo de la Punta its northerly point. The Prado runs south at a gradual gradient from the Castillo de la Punta to Parque Central and, beyond, Parque de la Fraternidad, from where Avenida de la Bélgica runs southeast, tracing the old city wall to the harborfront at the west end of Desamparados. East of Castillo de la Punta, Avenida Carlos Manuel de Céspedes (Avenida del Puerto) runs along the harbor channel and curls south to Desamparados.

The original settlement extended roughly north–south from Castillo de la Real Fuerza to Plaza Vieja. Here are the major sites of interest, centered on the Plaza de Armas and the smaller but more imposing Plaza de la Catedral. Each square has its own flavor. The plazas and surrounding streets shine after a complete restoration. The restoration now extends to the area east of Avenida de Bélgica and southwest of Plaza Vieja, between Calles Brasil and Merced. This was the great ecclesiastical center of colonial Havana and is replete with churches and convents.

In the 20th century, many grandiose structures went up around Parque Central. Today, the park is the social hub of Habana Vieja and forms a nexus for sightseeing.

Habana Vieja is a living museum—as many as 60,000 people live within the confines of the old city wall—and suffers from inevitable ruination brought on by the tropical climate, hastened since the Revolution by years of neglect. The grime of centuries has been soldered by tropical heat into the chipped cement and faded pastels. Beyond the restored areas, Habana Vieja is a quarter of sagging, mildewed walls and half-collapsed balconies. The much-deteriorated (mostly residential) southern half of Habana Vieja requires caution.

PASEO DE MARTÍ (PRADO)

Paseo de Martí, colloquially known as the Prado, is a kilometer-long tree-lined boulevard that slopes southward, uphill, from the harbor mouth to Parque Central. The beautiful boulevard was initiated by the Marquis de la Torre in 1772 and completed in 1852, when it had the name Alameda de Isabella II. It lay *extramura* (outside the old walled city) and was Havana's most notable thoroughfare. Mansions of aristocratic families rose on each side and it was a sign of distinction to live here. The *paseo*—the daily carriage ride—along the boulevard was an important social ritual, with bands positioned at regular intervals to play to the parade of *volantas* (carriages).

French landscape artist Jean-Claude Nicolas Forestier remodeled the Prado to its present form in 1929. It sits guarded by eight bronze lions, with an elevated central walkway bordered by an ornate wall with alcoves containing marble benches carved with scroll motifs.

At night it is lit by brass gas lamps with globes atop wrought-iron lampposts in the shape of griffins. Schoolchildren sit beneath shade trees, listening attentively to lessons presented alfresco. An art fair is held on Sundays.

Castillo de San Salvador de la Punta

The small, recently restored Castillo de San Salvador de la Punta (Av. Carlos M. de Céspedes, esq. Prado y Malecón, tel. 07/860-3196, Tues.–Sat. 9:30 A.M.–5 P.M., Sun. 9 A.M.–12:30 P.M., free) guards the entrance to Havana's harbor channel at the base of the Prado. The fortress was initiated in 1589 directly across from the Morro castle so that the two fortresses could catch invaders in a crossfire. A great chain was slung between them each night to secure Havana harbor. There are still a few cannons.

Gazing over the plaza on the west side of the castle is a life-size statue of Venezuelan general Francisco de Miranda Rodríguez (1750–1816), while 100 meters east of the castle is a statue of Pierre D'Iberville (1661–1706), a Canadian explorer who died in Havana.

Parque de Mártires and Parque de los Enamorados

The park immediately south of the castle, on the south side of Avenida Carlos Manuel de Céspedes, at the base (and east) of the Prado, is divided in two by Avenida de los Estudiantes.

Parque de los Enamorados (Park of the Lovers), on the north side of Avenida de los Estudiantes, features a statue of an Indian couple, plus the **Monumento de Estudiantes de Medicina,** a small Grecian-style temple shading the remains of a wall used by Spanish-colonial firing squads. Here on November 27, 1871, eight medical students met their deaths after being falsely accused of desecrating the tomb of a prominent loyalist, Gonzalo Castañón. A trial found them innocent, but enraged loyalist troops—the Spanish Volunteers—held their own trial and shot the students. The students are commemorated with a national holiday each November 27.

Parque de Mártires (Martyrs' Park), on the south side of Avenida de los Estudiantes, occupies the ground of the former Tacón prison, built in 1838. Nationalist hero José Martí was imprisoned here 1869–1870. The prison was demolished in 1939. Preserved are two of the punishment cells and the chapel used by condemned prisoners before being marched to the firing wall.

PARQUE CENTRAL

Spacious Parque Central is the social epicenter of Habana Vieja. The park—bounded by the Prado, Neptuno, Zulueta, and San Martín—is presided over by stately royal palms shading a marble **statue of José Martí.** Erected on the 10th anniversary of the national hero's death, it was sculpted by José Vilalta de Saavedra and inaugurated in 1905. Baseball fanatics gather at a point called *esquina caliente* ("hot corner") to discuss and argue the intricacies of *pelota* (baseball).

The park is surrounded by historic hotels, including the triangular **Hotel Plaza** (Zulueta #267), built in 1909, on the northeast face of the square. In 1920, Babe Ruth stayed in room 216, preserved as a museum with his signed bat and ball in a case.

Hotel Inglaterra

Much of the social action happens in front of the Hotel Inglaterra (Paseo de Martí #416), opened in 1856 and today the oldest Cuban hotel still extant. The sidewalk Café Louvre, known in colonial days as the Acera del Louvre, was a focal point for rebellion against Spanish rule. A plaque outside the hotel entrance honors the "lads of the Louvre sidewalk" who died for Cuban independence.

Inside, the hotel boasts elaborate wrought-ironwork and exquisite Mudejar-style detailing, including arabesque archways and *azulejos* (patterned tile). A highlight is the sensuous life-size bronze statue of a Spanish dancer—*La Sevillana*—in the main bar.

Gran Teatro

Immediately south of the Inglaterra, the Gran Teatro (Paseo de Martí #452, e/ San Rafael y

HABANA VIEJA

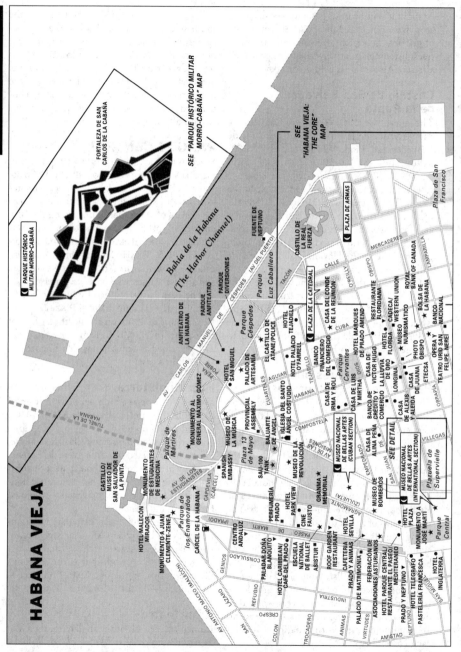

PARQUE HISTÓRICO
MILITAR MORRO-CABAÑA

FORTALEZA DE SAN
CARLOS DE LA CABAÑA

SEE "PARQUE HISTÓRICO MILITAR
MORRO-CABAÑA" MAP

SEE
"HABANA VIEJA:
THE CORE"
MAP

Bahía de la Habana
(The Harbor Channel)

Plaza de San
Francisco

PLAZA DE ARMAS

CASTILLO DE
LA REAL
FUERZA

FUENTE DE
NEPTUNO

MERCADERES

Parque
Luz Caballero

TACÓN

CALLE

CÉSPEDES   (AV DEL PUERTO)

O'REILLY

OBISPO

CUBA

ROYAL
BANK OF CANADA

LAMPARILLA

PARQUE
DIVERSIONES

PLAZA DE LA CATEDRAL

CASA DEL CONDE
DE LA REUNIÓN

RESTAURANTE
FLORIDIANA

HOTEL
SAN MIGUEL

HOTEL
PALACIO TEJADILLO
O'FARRILL

BANCO
FINANCIERO
DEL COMERCIO

HOTEL MARQUES
DE PRADO AMEND

CADECA!

BOLSA DE
LA HABANA

BANCO
NACIONAL

EL CASTILLO DE
ATANE/POLICE

Parque
Cervantes

CASA DE
VICTOR HUGO

LA LLUVIA
DE ORO

MUSEO WESTERN UNION

NUMISMÁTICO

PHOTO
OBISPO

ANFITEATRO DE
LA HABANA

PARQUE
ANFITEATRO

Parque
Céspedes

PALACIO DE
ARTESANÍA

MUSEO DE
LA MÚSICA

CASA DE
IRMA Y ROLI

CASA DE LUIS
Y MIRTHA

BANCO DE
CRÉDITO Y
COMERCIO

CASA DE PRADO
FLORIDA

LONGINA!

ETECSA

OPERA Y
TEATRO URID SAN
FELIPE NERE!

OBRAPÍA

PROVINCIAL
ASSEMBLY

BALUARTE
DE ÁNGEL

IGLESIA DEL SANTO
ÁNGEL COSTUDIO

CASA DE
ALINA PEÑA

CASA
DE ALEXIS
Y ALEIDA

CASA DE JUANA

MONUMENTO AL
GENERAL MÁXIMO GÓMEZ

SPANISH
EMBASSY

SAU-100
TANK

MUSEO DE LA
REVOLUCIÓN

MUSEO NACIONAL
DE BELLAS ARTES
(CUBAN SECTION)

VILLEGAS

Plazuela de
Supervielle

Plaza 13
de Mayo

GRANMA
MEMORIAL

MUSEO NACIONAL
DE BELLAS ARTES
(INTERNATIONAL SECTION)

MUSEO DE
BOMBEROS

SEE DETAIL

Parque de
los Enamorados

CASTILLO/
MUSEO DE
SAN SALVADOR DE
LA PUNTA

MONUMENTO A
LAS ESTUDIANTES
DE MEDICINA

Parque de
Mártires

PERFUMERÍA
PRADO

HOTEL
PARK VIEW

HOTEL
PLAZA

MONUMENTO A
JOSÉ MARTÍ

Parque
Central

CARCEL DE LA HABANA

CINE
FAUSTO

HOTEL MALECÓN
MIRADOR

MONUMENTO A JUAN
CLEMENTE-ZENEA

CENTRO
ANDALUZ

ESCUELA
NATIONAL
DE BALLET

ROOF GARDEN
RESTAURANT

HOTEL
SEVILLA

PRADO Y ANIMAS

FEDERACIÓN DE
ASOCIACIONES ASTURIANOS

HOTEL
CARIBBEAN/
CAFÉ DEL PRADO

CAFETERÍA

HOTEL TELEGRAFO

HOTEL
INGLATERRA

PALADAR DOÑA
BLANQUIT▼

PRADO Y NEPTUNO

PALACIO DE MATRIMONIA

PASTELERÍA FRANCESCA

HOTEL PARQUE CENTRAL/
RESTAURANTE PASEO/
RESTAURANTE MEDITERANEO

ASBISTUR

TÚNEL DE LA
HABANA

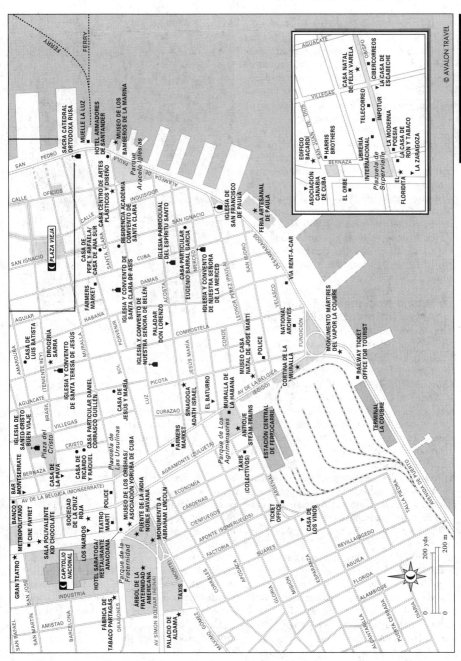

© AVALON TRAVEL

Neptuno, tel. 07/861-3077, daily 9 A.M.–5 P.M., CUC2 with guided tour) originated in 1837 as the Teatro Tacón, drawing operatic luminaries such as Enrico Caruso and Sarah Bernhardt. The current neo-baroque structure dates from 1915, when a social club—the Centro Gallego—was built around the old Teatro Tacón for the Galician community.

Its exorbitantly baroque facade drips with caryatids and has four towers, each tipped by a white marble angel reaching gracefully for heaven. The entire edifice is crumbling dangerously, however, though it still functions as a theater for the Ballet Nacional and Opera Nacional de Cuba. The main auditorium—the exquisitely decorated 2,000-seat Teatro García Lorca—features a painted dome and huge chandelier. Smaller performances are hosted in the 500-seat Sala Alejo Carpentier and the 120-seat Sala Artaud.

◖ Museo Nacional de Bellas Artes (International Section)

The international section of the Museo Nacional de Bellas Artes (National Fine Arts Museum, San Rafael, e/ Zulueta y Monserrate, tel. 07/863-9484 or 862-0140, www.museonacional.cult.cu, Tues.–Sat. 10 A.M.–6 P.M., Sun. 10 A.M.–2 P.M., entrance CUC5, or CUC8 for both sections, guided tour CUC2) occupies the Centro Asturiano, on the southeast side of the square. The building, lavishly decorated with neoclassical motifs, was erected in 1885 but rebuilt in Renaissance style in 1927 following a fire and until recently housed the postrevolutionary People's Supreme Court. A highlight is the stained-glass window above the main staircase showing Columbus's three caravels.

The art collection is displayed on five floors covering 4,800 square meters. The works are separated by nationality and span the United States, Latin America, Asia, and Europe—including masters such as Gainsborough, Goya, Murillo, Rubens, Velásquez, and various Impressionists. The museum also boasts Latin America's richest trove of Roman, Greek, and Egyptian antiquities.

A 248-seat theater hosts cultural activities.

the baroque facade of the Gran Teatro

© CHRISTOPHER P. BAKER

◖ Capitolio Nacional

The statuesque Capitolio (Capitol, Paseo de Martí, e/ San Martín y Dragones, tel. 07/861-5519, daily 9 A.M.–7 P.M., entrance CUC3, guided tours CUC1, cameras CUC2), one block south of Parque Central, dominates Havana's skyline. It was built between 1926 and 1929 as Cuba's Chamber of Representatives and Senate and designed after Washington's own Congress building. The 692-foot-long edifice is supported by flanking colonnades of Doric columns, with semicircular pavilions at each end of the building. The lofty stone cupola rises 61.75 meters, topped by a replica of 16th-century Florentine sculptor Giambologna's famous bronze *Mercury* in the Palazzo de Bargello.

A massive stairway—flanked by neoclassical figures in bronze by Italian sculptor Angelo Zanelli that represent Labor and Virtue—leads up to an entrance portico with three tall bronze doors sculpted with 30 bas-reliefs that depict important events of Cuban history. Inside, facing the door is the *Estatua de la República* (Statue of the Republic), a

A WALK DOWN THE PRADO

Begin your walk of the Prado at Parque Central and Neptuno. Heading downhill, the first building of interest, the **Palacio de Matrimonio** (Prado #306, esq. Ánimas, tel. 07/862-5781, Tues.–Fri. 8 A.M.–4 P.M.), on the west side, at the corner of Ánimas, is where many of Havana's wedding ceremonies are performed. The palace boasts a magnificent neo-baroque facade and an ornate stuccoed interior in desperate disrepair.

Up and down the Prado you'll see tiled mosaics reflecting the Moorish style that influenced Havana's colonial architecture. The most stunning example is the lobby of the **Hotel Sevilla** (Trocadero #55), which is like entering a Moroccan medina. It was inspired by the Patio of the Lions at the Alhambra in Granada, Spain. The hotel opened in 1908 and became a place of repose for fashionable society. The gallery walls are festooned with black-and-white photos of famous figures who have stayed here, from singer Josephine Baker and boxer Joe Louis to Al Capone, who took the entire sixth floor (Capone occupied room 615). The top-story restaurant is a magnificent exemplar of neoclassical decor – perfect for sampling

a Mary Pickford (rum, pineapple juice, and grenadine), invented here. The Sevilla was the setting for the comical intrigues of Wormold in Graham Greene's *Our Man in Havana*.

At Trocadero, budding dancers train for potential ballet careers in the **Escuela Nacional de Ballet** (National School of Ballet, Prado #207, e/ Colón y Trocadero, tel. 07/862-7053; call 07/803-0817 for permission to visit). Across the street, on the west side, the **Casa de los Científicos** (Prado #212, esq. Trocadero, tel. 07/862-1607), the former home of President José Miguel Gómez, first president of the republic, is now a hotel; pop in to admire the fabulous stained-glass work and chapel where locals come to make offerings.

At Prado and Colón, note the **Cine Fausto,** a modernist building with an ornamental band on its upper facade harking back to art deco; two blocks north, examine the mosaic mural of a Nubian beauty on the upper wall of the **Centro Cultural de Árabe** (between Refugio and Trocadero).

The bronze **statue of Juan Clemente-Zenea** (1832–1871), at the base of the Prado, honors a nationalist poet shot for treason in 1871.

massive bronze sculpture (also by Zanelli) of Cuba's voluptuous Indian maiden. At 17.54 meters (56 feet) tall, she is the world's third-largest indoor statue (the other two are the gold Buddha in Nava, Japan, and the Lincoln Memorial in Washington, D.C.). In the center of the floor is a 24-carat diamond replica that marks Kilometer 0, the point from which all distances on the island are calculated (rumor has it that the original is kept in Fidel's office). Above, the gilt-covered dome has a barrel-vaulted ceiling carved in refulgent relief.

The 394-foot-long **Salón de los Pasos Perdidos** (Great Hall of the Lost Steps), so named because of its acoustics, is inlaid with patterned marble motifs and features bronze bas-reliefs, green marble pilasters, and massive lamps on carved pedestals of glittering copper. Renaissance-style candelabras dangle from

the frescoed ceiling. The semicircular Senate chamber and Chamber of Representatives are at each end; former congressional offices line the hallway, and there's a mahogany-paneled former congressional library.

The Capitolio is the headquarters of the **Academia de Ciencias** (Academy of Sciences); the library—the **Biblioteca Nacional de Ciencias y Naturales**—is on the Capitolio's south side (Mon.–Sat. 8 A.M.–5 P.M.).

PARQUE DE LA FRATERNIDAD AND VICINITY

Paseo de Martí (Prado) runs south from Parque Central three blocks, where it ends at the junction with Avenida Máximo Gómez (Monte). Here rises the **Fuente de la India Noble Habana** in the middle of the Prado. Erected in 1837, the fountain is surmounted by a Carrara-marble statue of the legendary Indian queen after whom the province is named. In one hand she bears a cornucopia, in the other a shield with the arms of Havana. Four fish at her feet occasionally spout water.

The **Asociación Cultural Yoruba de Cuba** (Prado #615, e/ Dragones y Monte, tel. 07/863-5953, daily 9 A.M.–5 P.M.) has an upstairs **Museo de los Orishas** (CUC10, students CUC3) dedicated to the *orishas* of *santería*.

The constitution for the republic was signed in 1901 in the **Teatro Martí** (Dragones, esq. Zulueta), one block west of the Prado. It was being restored at time of publication. Around the corner, the **Sociedad de la Cruz Roja** (Red Cross Society, Zulueta, e/ Muralla y Brasil) is housed in an exquisite classical building.

Parque de la Fraternidad

The Parque de la Fraternidad (Friendship Park) was laid out in 1892 on an old military drill square, the Campo de Marte, to commemorate the fourth centennial of Columbus's discovery of America. By the mid-1850s, it was the site of the city's train station, terminating the railway that ran along today's Zanja and Dragones. The current layout by Jean-Claude Nicolas Forestier dates from 1928, with a redesign to celebrate the sixth Pan-American Conference, held in Havana that year. The **Árbol de la Fraternidad Americana** (the Friendship Tree) was planted at its center on February 24, 1928, to cement goodwill between the nations of the Americas. Busts and statues of outstanding American leaders such as Simón Bolívar and Abraham Lincoln watch over.

Palacio de Aldama

The Palacio de Aldama, on the park's far southwest corner, is a grandiose mansion built in neoclassical style in 1844 for a wealthy Basque, Don Domingo Aldama y Arrechaga. Its facade is lined by Ionic columns and the interior features murals of scenes from Pompeii; the garden courtyard features ornamental fountains. When the owner's nationalist feelings became known, it was ransacked and the interior defaced in 1868 by the

Spanish Volunteers militia. Today it houses the **Instituto de la Historia del Movimiento Comunista y de la Revolución Socialista de Cuba** (Institute of the History of the Communist Movement and the Socialist Revolution of Cuba, Amistad #510, e/ Reina y Estrella, tel. 07/862-2076) but is not open to the public.

Fábrica de Tabaco Partagás

A highlight of any stay in Havana is a visit to the Fábrica de Tabaco Partagás (Partagás Cigar Factory, Industria #520, e/ Dragones y Barcelona, tel. 07/863-5766, Mon.–Fri. 9–11 A.M. and noon–3 P.M., guided tour CUC10), on the west side of the Capitolio. The classical Spanish-style facade of this four-story structure is capped by a roofline of baroque curves topped by lions. Here you can see Cuba's premium cigars being hand-rolled for export. The factory specializes in full-bodied cigars such as the Montecristo and, of course, the Partagás, one of the oldest of the Havana brands, started in 1843 by Catalan immigrant Don Jaime Partagás Ravelo. Partagás was murdered in 1868—some say by a rival who discovered that Partagás was having an affair with his wife—and his ghost is said to haunt the factory.

Guided tours (45 minutes) are offered every 15 minutes. Buy tickets in advance at either Hotel Saratoga (Paseo del Pradode Martí #603, esq. Dragones, tel. 07/868-1000) or Hotel Habana Libre Tryp (Calle L, e/ 23 y 25, tel. 07/834-6100).

ZULUETA (CALLE AGRAMONTE)

Calle Agramonte, more commonly referred to by its colonial name of Zulueta, parallels the Prado and slopes gently upward from Avenida de los Estudiantes to the northeast side of Parque Central. Traffic runs one-way uphill.

On the north side of Avenida de los Estudiantes (Cárcel) is the **Monumento al General Máximo Gómez.** This massive monument of white marble by sculptor Aldo Gamba was erected in 1935 to honor the Dominican-

VISITING HAVANA'S CIGAR FACTORIES

You'll forever remember the pungent aroma of a cigar factory, a visit to which is de rigueur. The factories, housed in fine old colonial buildings, remain much as they were in the mid-19th century. Though now officially known by ideologically sound names, they're still commonly referred to by their prerevolutionary names, which are displayed on old signs outside. Each specializes in a number of cigar brands of a particular flavor – the government assigns to certain factories the job of producing particular brands.

The six major factories welcome visitors. Unfortunately, the tours are not well organized and often crowded with tour groups. Explanations of tobacco processes and manufacturing procedures are also sparse. Tours usually bypass the tobacco preparations and instead begin in the *galeras* (rolling rooms), then pass to the quality-control methods. Visitors therefore miss out on seeing the stripping, selecting, and dozens of other steps that contribute to producing a handmade cigar. Duties vary by floor, with leaf handling on the ground floor and stemming, sorting, rolling, box decorating, and ringing on the upper two floors. No cameras are permitted.

FACTORIES WITH ORGANIZED TOURS

Fábrica de Tabaco Partagás (Calle Industria #502, e/ Dragones y Barcelona, Habana Vieja, tel. 07/862-0086 or 878-4368, Mon.-Fri. 9-11 A.M. and noon-3 P.M.) offers 45-minute guided group tours (CUC10).

Fábrica Corona (20 de Mayo #520, e/ Marta Abreu y Línea, Cerro, tel. 07/873-0131, Mon.-Fri. 9-11 A.M. and 1-3 P.M., CUC10 with guide) has guided group tours.

Tickets must be purchased from the Hotel Saratoga or Hotel Habana Libre Tryp.

FACTORIES REQUIRING PERMISSION TO VISIT

Requests to visit the following factories should be made through **Tabacuba** (Virtudes #609, e/ Escobar y Gervasio, Centro Habana, tel. 07/877-6861), which is in charge of the industry.

Fábrica H. Upmann (Calle 23, e/ 14 y 16, tel. 07/835-1371) makes the famous H. Upmann brand of cigars, plus cigarettes. Note that this is *not* the original H. Upmann factory (Amistad #407, e/ Barcelona y Dragones), which no longer manufactures cigars.

Fábrica El Laguito (Av. 146 #2302, e/ 21 y 21A, Cubanacán, tel. 07/208-2486) makes Cohibas. Since Cohibas are made from only the finest leaves, El Laguito is given first choice from the harvest – "the best selection of the best selection," says factory head Emilia Tamayo. El Laguito also makes the best cigar in the world – the Trinidad, a 7.5-inch-long cigar made exclusively for Castro to present to diplomats and dignitaries.

Fábrica Héroes del Moncada (Av. 57 #13403, e/ 134 y 136, Marianao, tel. 07/260-6723) makes most major brands of export cigars, including Cohibas.

Fábrica de Tabaco Romeo y Julieta (Padre Varela, e/ Desague y Peñal Verno, Centro Habana, tel. 07/878-1059 or 879-3927), although it formerly permitted visits, is now a cigar-rollers' school.

---

born hero of the Cuban Wars of Independence who led the Liberation Army as commander-in-chief. Generalissimo Gómez (1836–1905) is cast in bronze, reining in his horse. Its base features bas-reliefs.

Museo de la Revolución

The ornate building facing north over Plaza 13 de Mayo was initiated in 1913 to house the provincial government. Before it could be finished (in 1920), it was earmarked as the Palacio Presidencial (Presidential Palace), and Tiffany's of New York was entrusted with its interior decoration. It was designed by Belgian Paul Belau and Cuban Carlos Maruri in an eclectic style, with a lofty dome. Following the Revolution, the three-story palace (now much deteriorated) was converted into the dour Museo de la Revolución (Museum of the Revolution, Refugio #1, e/ Zulueta y Monserrate, tel. 07/862-4091, daily 10 A.M.–5 P.M., CUC5, cameras CUC2, guide CUC2).

The marble staircase leads upstairs to the Salón de los Espejos (the Mirror Room), a replica of that in Versailles (replete with paintings by Armando Menocal and other notable Cuban painters); and Salón Dorado (the Gold Room), decorated with yellow marble and gold leaf and highlighted by its magnificently decorated dome.

Rooms are divided chronologically, from the colonial period to the modern day. Maps describe the progress of the revolutionary war. Guns and rifles are displayed alongside grisly photos of dead and tortured heroes. One section is dedicated to the revolutionaries who died in an assault on the palace on March 13, 1957, when Batista escaped through a secret door. The Rincón de los Cretinos ("Corner of Cretins") pokes fun at Batista, Ronald Reagan, and George Bush.

A room to the right of the entrance celebrates the ill-fated efforts of Che to inspire a revolution in Bolivia.

At the rear, in the former palace gardens, is the **Granma Memorial,** preserving the vessel that brought Castro and his revolutionaries from Mexico to Cuba in 1956. The *Granma* is encased in a massive glass structure. It's surrounded by vehicles used in the revolutionary war: armored vehicles, the bullet-riddled "Fast Delivery" truck used in the student commandos' assault on the Presidential Palace in 1957, and Castro's Toyota jeep from the Sierra Maestra. There's also a turbine from the U-2 spy plane downed during the missile crisis in 1962, plus a naval Sea Fury and a T-34 tank.

◖ Museo Nacional de Bellas Artes (Cuban Section)

The Cuban section of the Museo Nacional de Bellas Artes (National Fine Arts Museum, Trocadero, e/ Zulueta y Monserrate, tel. 07/863-9484 or 862-0140, www.museonacional.cult.cu, Tues.–Sat. 10 A.M.–6 P.M., Sun. 10 A.M.–2 P.M., entrance CUC5, or CUC8 for

both sections, guided tour CUC2) is housed in the soberly classical Palacio de Bellas Artes. The museum features an atrium garden from which ramps lead up to two floors exhibiting more than 1,200 works of art—a complete spectrum of Cuban paintings, engravings, sketches, and sculptures laid out according to eight themes in 24 *salas*. Works representing the vision of early 16th- and 17th-century travelers merge into colonial-era pieces, early 20th-century Cuban interpretations of Impressionism, Surrealism, and works spawned by the Revolution.

MONSERRATE (AVENIDA DE LOS MISIONES)

Avenida de los Misiones, or Monserrate as everyone knows it, parallels Zulueta one block to the east (traffic is one-way, downhill) and follows the space left by the ancient city walls after they were demolished last century.

Iglesia del Santo Ángel Custodio

The Gothic Iglesia del Santo Ángel Custodio (Monserrate y Cuarteles, tel. 07/861-8873), immediately east of the Palacio Presidencial, sits atop a rock known as Angel Hill. The church was founded in 1687 by builder-bishop Diego de Compostela. The tower dates from 1846, when a hurricane toppled the original, while the facade was reworked in neo-Gothic style in the mid-19th century. It's immaculate yet simple within. Cuba's national hero, José Martí, was baptized here on February 12, 1853.

The church was the setting for both the opening scene and the tragic marriage scene that ends in the violent denouement on the steps of the church in the 19th-century novel *Cecilia Valdés* by Cirilo Villaverde. A bust of the author stands in the *plazuela* outside the main entrance, to the rear of the church, on the corner of Calles Compostela and Cuarteles.

Edificio Bacardí

The Edificio Bacardí (Bacardí Building, Monserrate #261, esq. San Juan de Dios), former headquarters of the Bacardí rum empire, is a stunning exemplar of art deco design. Designed by Cuban architect Esteban

A WALK DOWN ZULUETA AND MONSERRATE

A stroll down Zulueta from Parque Central, returning via Monserrate, reveals several sites of interest, in addition to the "must-sees."

One block north of Parque Central, at the corner of Zulueta and Ánimas, a mosaic on the paving announces your arrival at **Sloppy Joe's,** commemorated as Freddy's Bar in Hemingway's *To Have and Have Not.* At last visit, the near-derelict building remained shuttered, its interior a dusty shambles, awaiting the restoration now sweeping Habana Vieja. Across the way is the old Cuartel de Bomberos fire station, housing the tiny **Museo de Bomberos** (Museum of Firemen, Zulueta #257, e/ Neptuno y Ánimas).

As you cross Refugio, on your right is a **SAU-100 Stalin tank** fronting the Museo de la Revolución; it was used in the Bay of Pigs. Immediately beyond is **Plaza 13 de Mayo,** a grassy park named to commemorate the ill-fated attack of the presidential palace by student martyrs on March 13, 1957. It was laid out by French landscaper Jean-Claude Nicolas Forestier. At the base of Zulueta, at the junction with Cárcel, note the flamboyant art nouveau building housing the **Spanish Embassy.**

Turn right and cross Plaza 13 de Mayo to reach Monserrate.

At the base of Monserrate, at its junction with Calle Tacón, is the **Museo y Archivo de la Música** (Capdevila #1, tel. 07/861-9846 and 863-0052; closed for restoration at last visit), housed in the sober Casa de Pérez de la Riva, built in Italian Renaissance style in 1905. The museum traces the evolution of Cuban music since early colonial days; its collection of antique instruments includes venerable pianos and drums. In a separate room, you can listen to old scores drawn from the record library.

Following Monserrate uphill, southward, you'll pass the **Iglesia del Santo Ángel Custodio** (Monserrate y Cuarteles, tel. 07/861-8873). Opposite, a semi-derelict watchtower – **Baluarte de Ángel** – erected in 1680 stands in front of Museo de la Revolución. Monserrate continues south three blocks to Edificio Bacardí and **Plazuela de Supervielle,** commemorating Dr. Manuel Fernández Supervielle, mayor of Havana during the 1940s.

One block south brings you to **Plazuela de Albear,** with a bust of Francisco de Albear, who last century engineered the Malecón and Havana's first water-drainage system. On its south side, adjoining El Floridita, is the **Casa del Ron,** where free rum samples are given.

Rodríguez and finished in December 1929, it is clad in Swedish granite and local limestone. Terra-cotta of varying hues accents the building, with motifs showing Grecian nymphs and floral patterns. It's crowned by a Lego-like pyramidal bell tower topped with a brass-winged bat—the famous Bacardí motif.

The building now houses various offices. Access is restricted to the Café Barrita bar (daily 9 A.M.–6 P.M.)—a true gem of art deco design—to the right of the lobby, up the stairs.

El Floridita

The famous El Floridita (corner of Monserrate and Calle Obispo, tel. 07/867-9299, 11:30 A.M.–midnight) restaurant and bar has been serving food since 1819, when it was called Pina de Plata. It is haunted by Ernest Hemingway's ghost. You expect a spotlight to come on and Desi Arnaz to appear conducting a dance band, and Hemingway to stroll in as he would every morning when he lived in Havana and drank with Honest Lil, the Worst Politician, and other real-life characters from his novels.

Hemingway's bronze bust watches over from its pedestal above the dark mahogany bar where Constante Ribailagua once served frozen daiquiris to the great writer (Hemingway immortalized both the drink and the venue in his novel *Islands in the Stream*) and such illustrious guests as Gary Cooper, Tennessee Williams, Marlene Dietrich, and Jean-Paul Sartre. There's even a life-size bronze statue of Hemingway, by sculptor José Villa, leaning with an elbow upon the bar.

El Floridita has been spruced up for tourist consumption with a 1930s art deco polish. They've overpriced the place for the package-tourist crowd, but sipping a (watery) daiquiri at El Floridita is still a must.

THE HARBOR CHANNEL

Throughout most of the colonial era, sea waves washed up on a beach that lined the southern shore of the harbor channel and bordered what is today Calle Cuba and, eastward, Calle Tacón, which runs along the site of the old city walls forming the original waterfront. In the early 19th century, the area was extended with landfill, and a broad boulevard—**Avenida Carlos Manuel de Céspedes** (Avenida del Puerto)—was laid out along the new harborfront. **Parque Luz Caballero,** between the Avenida and Calle Tacón, is pinned by a statue of José de la Luz Caballero (1800–1862), a philosopher and nationalist.

Overlooking the harborfront at the foot of Empedrado is the **Fuente de Neptuno** (Neptune Fountain), erected in 1838.

Calles Cuba and Tacón

Calle Cuba extends east from the foot of Monserrate. At the foot of Calle Cuarteles is the Palacio de Mateo Pedroso y Florencia, known today as the **Palacio de Artesanía** (Artisans Palace, Cuba #64, e/ Tacón y Peña Pobre, Mon.–Sat. 8 A.M.–8 P.M., Sat. 9 A.M.–2 P.M., free). This magnificent mansion was built in Moorish style for nobleman Don Mateo Pedroso (a slave trader and former mayor) around 1780. Pedroso's home displays the typical architectural layout of period houses, with stores on the ground floor, slave quarters on the mezzanine, and the owner's dwellings above. Today it houses craft shops and boutiques, and has folkloric music in the patio.

Immediately east is **Plazuela de la Maestranza,** where a remnant of the old city wall is preserved. On its east side, in the triangle formed by the junction of Cuba, Tacón, and Chacón, is a medieval-style fortress,

El Castillo de Atane, a police headquarters built in 1941 as a pseudo-colonial confection.

The **Seminario de San Carlos y San Ambrosio** (e/ Chacón y Empedrado, tel. 07/862-8790, Mon.–Sat. 9 A.M.–5 P.M., free), a massive seminary running the length of Tacón east of El Castillo de Atane, was established by the Jesuits in 1721 and is still a center for ecclesiastics in training. The downstairs cloister is open to the public as the **Museo Arquidioscesana;** in the rear right corner, note the fabulous antique chest engraved with figures from *Don Quixote.*

The entrance to the seminary overlooks an excavated site showing the foundations of the original seafront section of the city walls—here called the **Cortina de Valdés.** (An artisans' market that took up the length of Tacón is now at the southern end of the Alameda de Paula.)

Tacón opens to a tiny *plazuela* at the junction with Empedrado, where horse-drawn cabs called *calezas* offer guided tours to tourists. From here, Tacón leads to Plaza de Armas. The **Museo de Arqueología** (Tacón #12, e/ O'Reilly y Empedrado, tel. 07/861-4469, Tues.–Sat. 9 A.M.–5 P.M., Sun. 9 A.M.–1 P.M., CUC1) displays pre-Columbian artifacts, plus a miscellany of ceramics and other household items from the early colonial years. The museum occupies Casa de Juana Carvajal, a beautiful mansion first mentioned in documents in 1644. Its most remarkable feature is a series of eccentric floor-to-ceiling murals depicting life as it was lived in the 1700s.

◖ PLAZA DE LA CATEDRAL

The exquisite cobbled Plaza de la Catedral (Cathedral Square) was the last square to be laid out in Habana Vieja. It occupied a lowly quarter where rainwater and refuse collected (it was originally known as the Plazuela de la Ciénaga—Little Square of the Swamp). A cistern was built in 1587, and only in the following century was the area drained. Its present texture dates from the 18th century.

The square is Habana Vieja at its most quintessential, the atmosphere enhanced by mulattas in traditional costume who will pose for your camera for a small fee. One Saturday a month, the plaza is a venue for the **Noche en las Plazas** *espectáculo.*

Catedral San Cristóbal de la Habana

This intimate cathedral, on the north side of the plaza, is known colloquially as Catedral Colón (Columbus Cathedral) but is officially called the Catedral San Cristóbal de la Habana (Saint Christopher's Cathedral, tel. 07/861-7771, Mon.–Sat. 10:30 A.M.–2 P.M., Sun. 9 A.M.–noon, free guided tour, tower tour CUC1). The cathedral was initiated by the Jesuits in 1748. The order was kicked out of Cuba by Carlos III in 1767, but the building was eventually completed in 1777 and altered again in the early 19th century. Thus the original baroque interior (including the altar) is gone, replaced in 1814 by a new classical interior.

The baroque facade is adorned with clinging columns and ripples like a great swelling sea; Cuban novelist Alejo Carpentier thought it "music turned to stone." A royal decree of December 1793 elevated the church to a cathedral. On either side of the facade are mismatched towers (one fatter and taller than the other) containing bells supposedly cast with a dash of gold and silver, said to account for their musical tone.

Columns divide the rectangular church into three naves. The neoclassical main altar is simple and made of wood; the murals above are by Italian painter Guiseppe Perovani. The chapel immediately to the left has several altars, including one of Carrara marble inlaid with gold, silver, onyx, and carved hardwoods. Note, too, the wooden image of Saint Christopher, patron saint of Havana, dating to 1633.

The Spanish believed that a casket brought to Havana from Santo Domingo in 1796 and that resided in the cathedral for more than a century held the ashes of Christopher Columbus. It was returned to Spain in 1899. All but the partisan *habaneros* now believe that the ashes were those of Columbus's son Diego.

Catedral San Cristóbal de la Habana and statue of Antonio Gades, Plaza de la Catedral

HABANA VIEJA: PLAZA DE LA CATEDRAL AND VICINITY

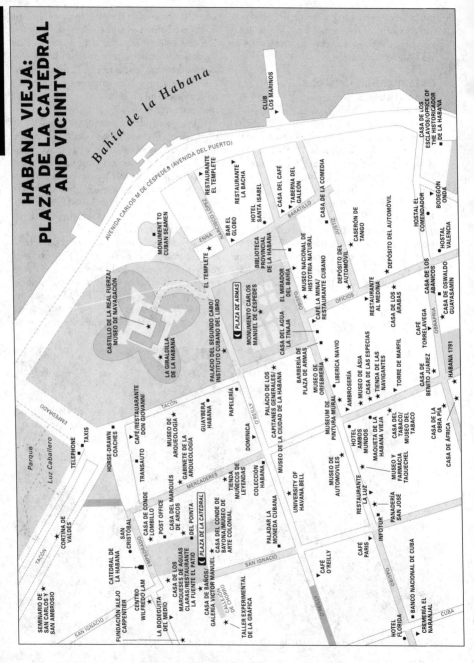

Bahía de la Habana

CLUB LOS MARINOS

CASA DE LOS ESCLAVOS/OFFICE OF THE HISTORIADOR DE LA HABANA

AVENIDA CARLOS M DE CÉSPEDES (AVENIDA DEL PUERTO)

RESTAURANTE EL TEMPLETE
RESTAURANTE LA BACHA
CASA DEL CAFÉ
TABERNA DEL GALEÓN
CASA DE LA COMEDIA
HOSTAL EL COMENDADOR
BODEGÓN ONDA
HOSTAL VALENCIA

BAR EL GLOBO
HOTEL SANTA ISABEL
BARATILLO
CASERÓN DE TANGO

MONUMENT TO CUBAN SEAMEN

ENNA
NARCISO LÓPEZ

EL TEMPLETE

BIBLIOTECA PROVINCIAL DE LA HABANA
MUSEO NACIONAL DE HISTORIA NATURAL
DEPÓSITO DEL AUTOMÓVIL
JUSTIZ
DEPÓSITO DEL AUTOMÓVIL

CASTILLO DE LA REAL FUERZA/ MUSEO DE NAVAGACIÓN

PLAZA DE ARMAS
MONUMENTO CARLOS MANUEL DE CÉSPEDES
EL MIRADOR DEL BAHÍA
MUSEO NACIONAL DE HISTORIA NATURAL
CAFÉ LA MINA/ RESTAURANTE CUBANO
OFICIOS
RESTAURANTE AL MEDINA

CASA DEL AGUA LA TINAJA

LA GIRALDILLA DE LA HABANA

PALACIO DEL SEGUNDO CABO/ INSTITUTO CUBANO DEL LIBRO

OBISPO

CASA DE LOS ÁRABAS
CASA DE OSWALDO GUAYASAMÍN
CASA DE LOS ABANICOS
CAFÉ TORRELAVEGA
OBRAPRÍA
CASA DE BENITO JUÁREZ
HABANA 1791

BARBERÍA DE PLAZA DE ARMAS
MUSEO DE ORFEBRERÍA
LIBRERÍA NAVIO
AMBROSERÍA
MUSEO DE ÁSIA
CASA DE LAS ESPECIAS
TIENDA DE LAS NAVIGANTES
TORRE DE MARFIL
CASA DE LA OBRA PÍA
CASA DE ÁFRICA

PALACIO DE LOS CAPITANES GENERALES/ MUSEO DE LA CIUDAD DE LA HABANA

TACÓN
CAFÉ/RESTAURANTE DON GIOVANNI
MUSEO DE ARQUEOLOGÍA
GABINETE DE LA ARQUEOLOGÍA
GUAYABERA HABANA
PAPELERÍA
O'REILLY
DOMINICA

HORSE-DRAWN COACHES
TRANSAUTO
CASA DE CONDE LOMBILLO
CASA DEL MARQUÉS DE ARCOS
DEL POINTA
MERCADERES
TIENDA MUÑECOS DE LEYENDAS
COLECCIÓN HABANA

PARQUE
Luz Caballero
TELEPHONE
TAXIS

EMPEDRADO
CORTINA DE VALDÉS
SAN CRISTÓBAL
POST OFFICE

TACÓN
SEMINARIO DE SAN CARLOS Y SAN AMBROSIO
CENTRO WILFREDO LAM
FUNDACIÓN ALEJO CARPENTIER
LA BODEGUITA DEL MEDIO
CATEDRAL DE LA HABANA
CASA DE LOS MARQUESES DE AGUAS CLARAS/RESTAURANTE LA FUENTE EL PATIO
PLAZA DE LA CATEDRAL
CASA DEL CONDE DE BAYONA/MUSEO DE ARTE COLONIAL
CASA DE BAÑOS/ GALERÍA VICTOR MANUEL
CALLEJÓN DE CHORRO
TALLER EXPERIMENTAL DE LA GRÁFICA

SAN IGNACIO

MUSEO DE PINTURA MURAL
HOTEL AMBOS MUNDOS
MAQUETA DE LA HABANA VIEJA
CASA DEL TABACO/ MUSEO DEL TABACO
MUSEO Y FARMACIA TAQUECHEL

MUSEO DE AUTOMÓVILES
UNIVERSITY OF HAVANA BELL
RESTAURANTE LA LUZ
PALADAR LA MONEDA CUBANA
PANADERÍA SAN JOSÉ
INFOTUR
CAFÉ PARIS

SAN IGNACIO
CAFÉ O'REILLY
HOTEL FLORIDA
CREMERÍA EL NARANJAL

OBISPO
BANCO NACIONAL DE CUBA
CUBA

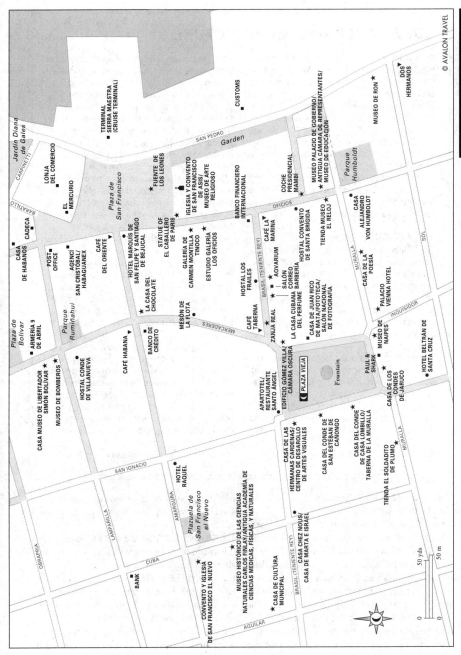

© AVALON TRAVEL

Jardín Diana de Gales

CARPINETTI

BARATILLO

Plaza de San Francisco

SAN PEDRO   Garden

Plaza de Bolívar

Parque Rumiñahui

MERCADERES

BRASIL (TENIENTE REY)

OFICIOS

MURALLA

SOL

INQUISIDOR

Parque Humboldt

DOS HERMANOS ★

MUSEO DE RON ★

CUSTOMS ■

TERMINAL SIERRA MAESTRA (CRUISE TERMINAL) ■

LONJA DEL COMERCIO ■

EL MERCURIO ■

CASA DE HABANOS ★

CADECA ■

POST OFFICE ■

AGENCI SAN CRISTÓBAL HABAGUANEX ■

CAFÉ DEL ORIENTE ▼

FUENTE DE LOS LEONES ★

IGLESIA Y CONVENTO DE SAN FRANCISCO DE ASÍS/ MUSEO DE ARTE RELIGIOSO ■

MUSEO PALACIO DE GOBIERNO/ ANTIGUA CÁMARA DE REPRESENTANTES/ MUSEO DE EDUCACIÓN ■

COCHE PRESIDENCIAL MAMBÍ

BANCO FINANCIERO INTERNACIONAL ■

CASA ALEJANDRO VON HUMBOLDT ★

CAFÉ LA MARINA ▼

HOSTAL CONVENTO DE SANTA BRIGIDA ●

TIENDA MUSEO EL RELOJ ★

CASA DE LA POESÍA ★

PALACIO VIENNA HOTEL ●

HOTEL MARQUIS DE SAN FELIPE Y SANTIAGO DE BEJUCAL ★

STATUE OF EL CABALLERO DE PARIS ★

GALERÍA DE CARMEN MONTILLA TINOCO ★

ESTUDIO GALERÍA LOS OFICIOS ★

AQUARIUM ■

SALÓN CORREO BARBERÍA

CASA DE JUAN RICO DE MATA/FOTOTECA/ SALÓN NACIONAL DE FOTOGRAFÍA ★

CASA CUBANA DEL PERFUME ★

HOSTAL LOS FRAILES ●

CAFÉ TABERNA ▼

ZANJA REAL

MESÓN DE LA FLOTA ▼

LA CASA DEL CHOCOLATE ★

BANCO DE CRÉDITO ■

CAFÉ HABANA ▼

ARMERÍA 9 DE ABRIL ■

CASA MUSEO DE LIBERTADOR SIMÓN BOLÍVAR ★

MUSEO DE BOMBEROS ●

HOSTAL CONDE DE VILLANUEVA ●

APARTOTEL/ RESTAURANTE SANTO ÁNGEL ●

EDIFICIO GÓMEZ VILLA/ CÁMARA OSCURA ✦

PLAZA VIEJA

Fountain

PAUL & SHARK ★

CASA DE LOS CONDES DE JARUCO ★

MUSEO DE NAIPES ★

HOTEL BELTRÁN DE SANTA CRUZ ●

CASA DE LAS HERMANAS CÁRDENAS/ CENTRO DE DESARROLLO DE ARTES VISUALES ★

CASA DEL CONDE DE SAN ESTÉBAN DE CAÑONGO ★

CASA DEL CONDE DE CASA LOMBILLO/ TABERNA DE LA MURALLA ★

MURALLA

TIENDA EL SOLDADITO DE PLUMO ●

HOTEL RAQUEL ●

SAN IGNACIO

AMARGURA

LAMPARILLA

Plazuela de San Francisco el Nuevo

MUSEO HISTÓRICO DE LAS CIENCIAS NATURALES CARLOS FINLAY/ANTIGUA ACADEMIA DE CIENCIAS MÉDICAS, FÍSICAS, Y NATURALES ★

CASA CHEZ NOUS/ CASA DE MARTA E ISRAEL ●

BRASIL (TENIENTE REY)

OBRAPIA

CUBA

BANK ■

CONVENTO Y IGLESIA DE SAN FRANCISCO EL NUEVO ★

CASA DE CULTURA MUNICIPAL ★

AGUILAR

50 yds

50 m

0

0

CUBAN COLONIAL ARCHITECTURE

Cuba boasts the New World's finest assemblage of colonial buildings. Spanning four centuries, these palaces, mansions, churches, castles, and more simple structures catalog an astonishing progression of styles. The academic classicism of aristocratic 18th-century Spanish homes blends with 19th-century French rococo, while art deco and art nouveau exteriors from the 1920s fuse into the cool, columned arcades of ancient palaces in Mudejar style. They were laid out along ruler-straight roads arranged in a grid pattern as decreed by the Laws of the Indies and usually intentionally narrow, conducive to shade.

THE COLONIAL HOME

The 17th-century home was made of limestone and modeled on the typical Spanish house, with a simple portal and balconies with lathe-turned *rejas,* and tall, generously proportioned rooms and shallow-stepped staircases. By the 18th century, those houses that faced onto squares had adopted a portico and loggia (supported by arched columns) to provide shelter from sun and rain.

Colonial homes grew larger with ensuing decades and typically featured two small courtyards, with a dining area between the two, with a central hallway, or *zaguán,* big enough for carriages and opening directly from the street. Arrayed around the ground floor courtyard were warehouses, offices, and other rooms devoted to the family business, with stables and servants' quarters to the rear, while the private family quarters were sequestered above around the galleried second story reached by a stately inner stairway. The design was unique to Havana houses. Commercial activity on the ground floor was relegated to those rooms (*dependencias*) facing the street (these were usually rented out to merchants). Laundry and other household functions were relegated to the inner, second patio, or *traspatio,* hidden behind massive wooden doors often flanked by pillars that in time developed ornate arches. The formal layout of rooms on the ground floor was usually repeated on the main, upper story. Another design borrowed from Spain was the *entresuelo,* a mezzanine of half-story proportions tucked between the two stories and used to house servants.

By the 19th century, the wealthy were building summer homes in Havana's hilly suburbs. These *quintas* were typically in neoclassical style, with extensive front porticos and gardens to the rear. Many, however, were influenced by the Palladian style, fashionable in Europe.

Throughout the colonial period, windows evolved as one of the most decorative elements. Ground floor windows were full height from ground level and featured shutter-doors to permit a free flow of air. Later windows acquired ornate grilled wooden balusters, which often protruded where streets were sufficiently wide. In the 19th century, glass was introduced, though usually only for decoration in multicolored stained-glass panes inserted

Casa de los Marqueses de Aguas Claras

This splendid old mansion, on the northwest side of the plaza, was built during the 16th century by Governor General Gonzalo Pérez de Angulo and has since been added to by subsequent owners. Today a café occupies the *portico,* while the inner courtyard, with its fountain amid lush palms and clinging vines, houses the Restaurante La Fuente del Patio. The restaurant extends upstairs, where the middle classes once dwelled in apartments. Sunlight pouring in through stained-glass *mediopuntos* saturates the floors with shifting fans of red and blue.

Casa del Conde de Bayona

This simple two-story structure, on the south side of the square, is a perfect example of the traditional Havana merchant's house of the period, with side stairs and an *entresuelo* (mezzanine of half-story proportions). It was built in the 1720s for Governor General Don Luis Chacón and later passed to Pancho Marty, a former smuggler-turned-entrepreneur. In

between or above the louvered wooden panels. Meanwhile, ornate metal grills called *guardavecinos* were adopted for upper stories to divide balconies of contiguous properties and so prevent intrusion.

Certain styles evolved unique to individual cities, as with the *arco mixtilíneo* (doorway lintel) and projecting turned-wood roof brackets unique to Camagüey; the mail-order gingerbread wooden homes (imported from Key West) common in Varadero; and the trompe l'oeil interior murals found in homes of Sancti Spíritus.

Cuban structures were heavily influenced by traditional Spanish and Mudejar (Moorish) styles that included:

- **alfarje:** a pitched wooden roof combining parallel and angled beams, providing a conceptual shift in emphasis to enhance a room's sense of space; normally found in churches and smaller homes, they adopted a star pattern

- **antepecho:** an ornamented window guard flush with the building facade

- **barrote:** lathe-turned vertical window rods that served to keep out burglars

- **cenefa:** band of colored plasterwork used as decorative ornamentation on interior walls

- **entresuelo:** shallow mezzanine level between ground and upper stories housing slaves

- **luceta:** long rectangular window along the edges of a doorway or window, usually containing stained or marbled glass

- **mamparas:** double-swing half doors that serve as room dividers or as partial outer doors to protect privacy; typically contained colored or frosted glass

- **mediopunto:** half-moon stained-glass window (*vitral*) above windows or doorways

- **patio:** an open space in the center of Spanish buildings – a Spanish adaptation of the classic Moorish inner court – that permits air to circulate through the house; the patios of more grandiose buildings are surrounded by columned galleries

- **persiana:** slatted shutter in tall, glassless windows, designed to let in the breezes while keeping out the harsh light and rain

- **portal:** the main doorway; early *portales* were fairly simple but evolved to monumental proportions and featured elaborate stone molding on the lintel and bas-relief pilasters to each side

- **reja:** metal window screen, replaced *barrotes*

- **vitral:** window of stained glass in geometric designs that diffuse the sunlight, saturating a room with shifting color

the 1930s, it housed the Havana Club Bar, which was used by Graham Greene as the setting for Wormold's meeting with Captain Segura (based on Batista's real-life police chief, Ventura) in *Our Man in Havana*. Today it houses the **Museo de Arte Colonial** (Colonial Art Museum, San Ignacio #61, tel. 07/862-6440, daily 9:30 A.M.–5 P.M., entrance CUC2, cameras CUC2, guides CUC1), which re-creates the lavish interior of an aristocratic colonial home. One room is devoted to colorful stained-glass *vitrales*.

Callejón de Chorro

At the southwest corner of the plaza, this short cul-de-sac is where an original cistern was built to supply water to ships in the harbor. The *aljibe* (cistern) marked the terminus of the Zanja Real (the "royal ditch," or *chorro*), a covered aqueduct that brought water from the Río Almendares some 10 kilometers away. A small sink and spigot remain.

The **Casa de Baños,** which faces onto the square, looks quite ancient but was built in the 20th century in colonial style on the site of a bathhouse erected over the *aljibe*. Today the building contains the **Galería Victor Manuel** (San Ignacio #56, tel. 07/861-2955, daily 10 A.M.–9 P.M.), selling quality arts.

At the far end of Callejón de Chorro is the **Taller Experimental de la Gráfica** (Experimental Graphics Workshop, tel. 07/864-7622, tgrafica@cubarte.cult.cu, Mon.–Fri. 9 A.M.–4 P.M.), where you can watch artists make prints for sale.

Casa de Conde de Lombillo

On the plaza's east side is the Casa de Conde de Lombillo (tel. 07/860-4311, Mon.–Fri. 9 A.M.–5 P.M., Sat. 9 A.M.–1 P.M., free). Built in 1741, this former home of a slave trader houses a small post office (Cuba's first), as it has since 1821. The building now holds historical lithographs. The mansion adjoins the **Casa del Marqués de Arcos** (closed to visitors), built in the 1740s for the royal treasurer. What you see is the rear of the mansion; the entrance is on Calle Mercaderes, where the building facing the entrance is graced by the *Mural Artístico-Histórico,* by Cuban artist Andrés Carrillo.

The two houses are fronted by a wide *portico* supported by thick columns. Note the mailbox set into the outside wall, a grotesque face (that of a tragic Greek mask) carved in stone, with a scowling mouth as its slit. A life-size bronze statue of the late Spanish flamenco dancer Antonio Gades (1936–2004) leans against one of the columns.

Centro Wilfredo Lam

The Centro Wilfredo Lam (San Ignacio #22, esq. Empredado, tel. 07/861-2096 and 861-3419, wlam@artsoft.cult.cu, Mon.–Fri. 8 A.M.–5 P.M.), on cobbled Empedrado, on the northwest corner of the plaza, occupies the former mansion of the Counts of Peñalver. This art center displays works by the eponymous Cuban artist as well as artists from developing nations (primarily Latin America). The institution studies and promotes contemporary art from around the world.

La Bodeguita del Medio

No visit to Havana is complete without popping into Ernest Hemingway's favorite watering hole, La Bodeguita del Medio (Empedrado #207, tel. 07/862-6121, daily 10:30 A.M.–midnight), half a block west of the cathedral. This neighborhood hangout was originally the coach house of the mansion next door. Later it was a *bodega,* a mom-and-pop grocery store where Spanish immigrant Ángel Martínez served food and drinks.

The bar is to the front, with the restaurant behind. Troubadours move among the thirsty *turistas.* Between tides, you can still savor the proletarian fusion of dialectics and rum. The house drink is the *mojito,* the rum mint julep that Hemingway brought out of obscurity and turned into the national drink.

Adorning the walls are posters, paintings, and faded photos of Papa Hemingway, Carmen Miranda, and other famous visitors. The walls were once decorated with the signatures and scrawls of visitors dating back decades. Alas, a renovation wiped away much of the original charm; the artwork was erased and replaced in ersatz style, with visitors being handed blue pens (famous visitors now sign a chalkboard). In 2010 it was undergoing yet another makeover. The most famous graffiti is credited to Hemingway: *"Mi Mojito en La Bodeguita, Mi Daiquirí en El Floridita,"* he supposedly scrawled on the sky-blue walls. According to Tom Miller in *Trading with the Enemy,* Martínez concocted the phrase as a marketing gimmick after the writer's death. Errol Flynn thought it "A Great Place to Get Drunk." They are there, these ribald fellows, smiling at the camera through a haze of cigar smoke and rum.

Casa del Conde de la Reunión

Built in the 1820s, at the peak of the baroque era, this home has a trefoil-arched doorway opening onto a *zaguán* (courtyard). Exquisite *azulejos* (painted tiles) decorate the walls. Famed novelist Alejo Carpentier used the house as the main setting for his novel *El siglo de las luces* (The Enlightenment). A portion of the home, which houses the Centro de Promoción Cultural, is dedicated to his memory as the **Fundación Alejo Carpentier** (Empedrado #215, tel. 07/861-5500, Mon.–Fri. 8:30 A.M.–4:30 P.M., free). Displayed are his early works, with his raincoat thrown stylishly over his old desk chair.

One block west, tiny **Plazuela de San Juan de Dios** (Empedrado, e/ Habana y Aguiar) is pinned by a white marble life-size facsimile of Miguel de Cervantes, author of *Don Quixote,* sitting in a chair, book and pen in hand, lending the plaza its colloquial name: Parque Cervantes.

Edificio Santo Domingo

Calle San Ignacio leads 50 meters south from Plaza de la Catedral to Calle Obispo. On the southeast corner of the junction, the Edificio Santo Domingo—a looming contemporary building faced in glass—occupies the site of the early Convento de Santo Domingo, which between 1727 and 1902 housed the original University of Havana. The building was remodeled in eye-pleasing fashion, with a replica of the original baroque doorway and a bell tower containing the original bell that once tolled students to class.

The building today houses offices of the current university. On the ground floor, the **Museo de la Universidad** (no tel., Tues.–Sat. 9:30 A.M.–5 P.M., Sun. 9:30 A.M.–1 P.M.) displays a model of the original structure plus miscellany related to the early university.

◖ PLAZA DE ARMAS

The most important plaza in Habana Vieja, and the oldest, handsome Plaza de Armas square was laid out in 1519 and named Plaza de Iglesia for the church that was demolished in 1741 after an English warship, the ill-named HMS *Invincible,* was struck by lightning and exploded, sending its main mast sailing down on the church. Later, Plaza de Armas evolved to become the settlement's administrative center.

The plaza seems still to ring with the cacophony of the past, when military parades and musical concerts were held under the watchful eye of the governor and the gentry would take their formal evening promenade. The plaza is ringed by stalls selling tatterdemalion antiquarian books (Wed.–Sat.).

At its heart, verdant **Parque Céspedes** is shaded by palms and tall kapok (ceiba) trees that surround a white marble **statue of Manuel de Céspedes,** hero of the Ten Years War.

Palacio de los Capitanes Generales

The somber yet stately Palacio de los Capitanes Generales (Palace of the Captains-Generals) was completed in 1791 and became home to 65 governors of Cuba between 1791 and 1898. After that, it was the U.S. governor's residence during Uncle Sam's occupation and, 1902–1920, the early seat of the Cuban government. Between 1920 and 1967, it served as Havana's city hall.

The palace is fronted by a loggia supported by Ionic columns and by "cobblewood," laid instead of stone to soften the noise of carriages and thereby lessen the disturbance of the governor's sleep. The three-story structure surrounds a courtyard that contains a statue of Christopher Columbus by Italian sculptor Cucchiari. Arched colonnades rise on all sides. In the southeast corner, a hole containing the coffin of an unknown nobleman is one of several graves from the old Cementerio de Espada.

Today, the palace houses the **Museo de la Ciudad de la Habana** (City of Havana Museum, Tacón #1, e/ Obispo y O'Reilly, tel. 07/861-5001, Tues.–Sun. 9:30 A.M.–5:30 P.M., last entry at 4:30 P.M., entrance CUC3, cameras CUC2, videos CUC10, guide CUC1). The great flight of marble stairs leads to palatially furnished rooms. The Salón del Trono (Throne Room), made for the king of Spain but never used, is of breathtaking splendor and brims with treasures. The museum also features the Salón de las Banderas (Hall of Flags), with magnificent artwork that includes *The Death of Antonio Maceo* by Menocal, plus exquisite collections illustrating the story of the city's (and Cuba's) development and the 19th-century struggles for independence. One top-floor

A WALK ALONG CALLE OBISPO

Pedestrians-only Calle Obispo links Plaza de Armas with Parque Central and is Habana Vieja's busiest street. The name means "Bishop's Street," supposedly because it was the path favored by ecclesiastics of the 18th century. It became Havana's premier shopping street early on and was given a boost when the city walls went up in the mid-1700s, linking the major colonial plaza with the Monserrate Gate, the main entranceway into the city.

Begin at Plaza Albear and walk east. Fifty meters on your left you'll pass the Infotur office; one block farther, also on your left, is the **Casa Natal de Félix Varela** (Obispo, e/ Aguacate y Villegas), the birthplace of the Cuban nationalist philosophy-priest.

The next few blocks are lined with boutiques, small art galleries, and simple cafés and bars.

Crossing Calle Havana, five blocks east of Plaza Albear, you arrive at Havana's erstwhile "Wall Street," centered on Calles Obispo, Cuba, and Aguiar, where the main banks were concentrated prior to the Revolution. The former neoclassical Banco Mendoza today houses the **Museo Numismático** (Coin Museum, Obispo, e/ Habana y Aguiar, tel. 07/861-5811, Tues.-Sat. 9 A.M.-4:45 P.M., Sun. 9:30 A.M.-5 P.M., CUC1). The broad-ranging collection of coins and banknotes spans the Greco, Roman, and Phoenician epochs, as well as Spanish *reales* and *escudos*, plus Cuban money dating back to the republican era.

At Calle Aguiar, divert south one block to the **Opera y Teatro Lírico San Felipe Neri** (Aguiar, esq. Obrapía, tel. 07/862-3243), a converted church – Iglesia San Felipe Neri – now hosting performances by the Coro Nacional de Cuba (National Chorus of Cuba).

At the corner of Calle Cuba you reach the **Hotel Florida** (Obispo #252, esq. Cuba, tel.

07/862-4127), a beautifully restored colonial mansion with a fine bar and restaurant. Catercorner to the hotel, the former **Banco Nacional de Cuba** (Obispo #211, esq. Cuba), in a splendid neoclassical building fronted by fluted Corinthian columns, is occupied by the Ministerio de Finanzas y Precios (Ministry of Finance and Prices).

Havana is replete with dusty old apothecaries, but the **Museo y Farmacia Taquechel** (Obispo #155, esq. Aguiar, tel. 07/862-9286, daily 9 A.M.-6 P.M., free) is surely the most interesting, with its mixing vases, mortars and pestles, and colorful ceramic jars full of herbs and potions. Dating from 1898, it's named for Dr. Francisco Taquechel y Mirabal.

Across the street, on the north side of Obispo, is the original site of the University of Havana, founded in January 1728. An antique bell that once tolled to call the students to class has been placed in a campanile on the north side of the new university building.

Fifty meters beyond Museo y Farmacia Taquechel you'll arrive at the rose-pink **Hotel Ambos Mundos** (Obispo #153, esq. Mercaderes, tel. 07/860-9530), dating from 1925. Off and on throughout the 1930s, Hemingway laid his head in room 511, where he wrote *The Green Hills of Africa* and *Death in the Afternoon*. The room is today a museum (daily 10 A.M.-5 P.M., CUC2). Hemingway's quarters – "a gloomy room, 16 square meters, with a double bed made of ordinary wood, two night tables, and a writing table with a chair," recalled author Gabriel García Márquez – has been preserved, with furnishings from his home, Finca Vigía. The themed exhibitions change every year. Esperanza, the multilingual *custodio*, gives a great spiel.

One block farther brings you to Plaza de Armas.

room contains the shattered wings of the eagle that once crested the Monumento del Maine in Vedado, along with other curios suggestive of U.S. voracity. Old horse-drawn carriages and artillery are among the other exhibits.

To the south side of the palace, along a 50-meter-long cobbled pedestrian section of Calle Obispo, is a row of ancient mansions each hosting a unique site of interest. For example, the **Casa del Agua la Tinaja** (Obispo #111) sells mineral water (CUC0.25 a glass), and the **Museo de la Orfebrería** (Museum of Silverwork, Obispo #113, tel. 07/863-9861, Tues.–Sat. 9:30 A.M.–5 P.M., Sun. 9:30 A.M.–12:30 P.M., free) is crammed with silver and gold ornaments from the colonial era. Upstairs you'll find candelabras, a beautiful replica in silver of Columbus's *Santa María,* walking sticks, and a splendid collection of swords and firearms. Next door, the **Librería Navío** (Obispo #117–119, daily 10 A.M.–7 P.M.) antiquarian bookstore is housed in the oldest house in Havana, dating from around 1570. It adjoins the **Museo de Pintura Mural** (Painted Mural Museum, Obispo #119, tel. 07/864-2354, Tues.–Sat. 9:30 A.M.–5 P.M., Sun. 9:30 A.M.–1 P.M.), displaying colonial murals, plus a *quitrín* (traditional low-slung, horse-drawn cart of the colonial nobility) in the foyer.

Palacio del Segundo Cabo

The austere, quasi-Moorish, pseudo-baroque, part neoclassical Palacio del Segundo Cabo (Palace of the Second Lieutenant, O'Reilly #14, tel. 07/862-8091, Mon.–Fri. 6 A.M.–midnight) dates from 1770, when it was designed as the city post office. Later it became the home of the vice-governor general and, after independence, the seat of the Senate. Today, it houses the **Instituto Cubano del Libro** (Cuban Book Institute), which hosts cultural events. Upstairs, the mezzanine is occupied by the **Galería Raúl Martínez** (Mon.–Fri. 10 A.M.–5 P.M., Sat. 10 A.M.–3 P.M.) art gallery.

Immediately east of the loggia is a marble **statue of Fernando VII,** holding a scroll of parchment that from the side appears jauntily cocked and is the butt of ribald jokes among locals.

Castillo de la Real Fuerza

The pocket-size Castillo de la Real Fuerza (Royal Power Castle, O'Reilly #2, tel. 07/864-4488, Tues.–Sun. 9:30 A.M.–5 P.M., entrance CUC1, cameras CUC1), on the northeast corner of the plaza, was begun in 1558 and completed in 1577. It's the oldest of the four forts that guarded the New World's most precious harbor. Built in medieval fashion, with walls 6

meters wide and 10 meters tall, the castle forms a square with enormous triangular bulwarks at the corners, their sharp angles slicing the dark waters of the moat. It was almost useless from a strategic point of view, being landlocked far from the mouth of the harbor channel and hemmed in by surrounding buildings that would have formed a great impediment to its cannons in any attack. The governors of Cuba lived here until 1762.

Visitors enter the fortress via a courtyard full of cannons and mortars. Note the royal coat of arms representing Seville, Spain, carved in stone above the massive gateway as you cross the moat by a drawbridge.

The castle also houses the **Museo de Navegación** (Naval Museum), displaying treasures from the golden age when the riches of the Americas flowed to Spain. The air-conditioned Sala de Tesoro gleams with gold bars, chains, coins, toothpicks, and brooches, plus precious jewels, bronze astrolabes, pewter dishes, rosary beads, clay pipes, and silver *reales* ("pieces of eight"). Labels are in Spanish only. Another *sala* has naval uniforms, swords, pistols, and model ships spanning three centuries.

You can climb to the top of a cylindrical tower rising from the northwest corner and containing a patinated brass bell. The tower is topped by a bronze weathervane called **La Giraldilla de la Habana** showing a voluptuous figure with hair braided in thick ropes; in her right hand she holds a palm tree and in her left a cross. This figure is the official symbol of Havana. The vane is a copy; the original, which now resides in the foyer, was cast in 1631 in honor of Isabel de Bobadilla, the wife of Governor Hernando de Soto, the tireless explorer who fruitlessly searched for the Fountain of Youth in Florida. De Soto named his wife governor in his absence, and she became the only female governor ever to serve in Cuba. Every afternoon for four years she scanned the horizon in vain for his return.

Immediately east of the castle, at the junction of Avenida del Puerto and O'Reilly, is an obelisk to the 77 Cuban seamen killed during World War II by German submarines.

El Templete

A charming copy of a Doric temple, El Templete (The Pavilion, daily 9:30 A.M.–5 P.M., CUC1 including guide) stands on the square's northeast corner. It was inaugurated on March 19, 1828, on the site where the first mass and town council meeting were held in 1519, beside a massive ceiba tree. The original ceiba was felled by a hurricane in 1828 and replaced by a column fronted by a small bust of Christopher Columbus. A ceiba has since been replanted and today shades the tiny temple, whose interior features a wall-to-ceiling triptych depicting the first mass, the first town council meeting, and El Templete's inauguration. In the center of the room sits a bust of the artist, Jean-Baptiste Vermay (1786–1833).

Hotel Santa Isabel

Immediately south of El Templete is the former Palacio del Conde de Santovenia (Baratillo, e/ Narciso López y Baratillo y Obispo), now the Hotel Santa Isabel. Its quintessentially Cuban-colonial facade is graced by a becolumned portico and, above, wrought-iron railings on balconies whose windows boast stained-glass *mediopuntos*. The *conde* (count) in question was famous for hosting elaborate parties, most notoriously a three-day bash in 1833 to celebrate the accession to the throne of Isabel II that climaxed with the ascent of a gaily decorated gas-filled balloon. Later that century it served as a hotel, as it is today. President Carter stayed here during his visit to Havana in 2002.

Half a block east of the hotel, on Calle Baratillo, the **Casa del Café** (tel. 07/866-8061, Mon.–Sat. 9 A.M.–7 P.M., Sun. 9 A.M.–2 P.M.) serves all kinds of Cuban coffees; next door stands the **Taberna del Galeón** (tel. 07/866-8476, Mon.–Sat. 9 A.M.–7 P.M., Sun. 9 A.M.–2 P.M.), the "House of Rum" (a rum and cigar store).

Museo Nacional de Historia Natural

On the south side of the plaza, the Museo Nacional de Historia Natural (Natural History Museum, Obispo #61, e/ Oficios y Baratillo, tel. 07/863-9361, museo@mnhnc. inf.cu, Tues.–Sun. 9:30 A.M.–7:30 P.M., CUC3) shows off the rather paltry collection of the Academía de Ciencias and encompasses the Museo de Ciencias Naturales (Museum of Natural Sciences) and the Museo de Ciencias y Técnicas (Museum of Science and Technology), which covers evolution in a well-conceived display. The museum houses collections of Cuban flora and fauna—many in clever reproductions of their natural environments—plus stuffed tigers, apes, and other beasts from around the world. Children will appreciate the interactive displays.

Immediately east, the **Biblioteca Provincial de la Habana** (Havana Provincial Library, tel. 07/862-9035, Mon.–Fri. 8:15 A.M.–7 P.M., Sat. 8:15 A.M.–4:30 P.M., Sun. 8:15 A.M.–1 P.M.) once served as the U.S. Embassy.

Casa de los Árabes

The Casa de los Árabes (Arabs' House, Oficios #12, tel. 07/861-5868, Tues.–Sat. 9 A.M.–4:30 P.M., Sun. 9 A.M.–1 P.M., free), 50 meters south of Plaza de Armas and comprising two 17th-century mansions, was formerly the Colegio de San Ambriosio, and is a fine example of Moorish-inspired architecture. It is the only place in Havana where Muslims can practice the Islamic faith (the prayer hall is decorated with hardwoods inlaid with mother-of-pearl). It houses a small museum dedicated to the many Levantine immigrants who settled Cuba throughout the centuries.

Depósito del Automóvil

Opposite Casa de los Árabe, the Depósito del Automóvil (Depository of Automobiles, Oficios #13, tel. 07/863-9942, Tues.–Sat. 9 A.M.–5 P.M., Sun. 9 A.M.–1 P.M., entrance CUC2, cameras CUC2, videos CUC10) includes an eclectic range of 30 antique automobiles—from a 1905 Cadillac (under restoration in 2010) to Che Guevara's 1959 mint green Chevrolet Bel Air. Classic Harley-Davidson motorcycles are also exhibited.

HAVANA

© CHRISTOPHER P. BAKER

Depósito del Automovil, Habana Vieja

PLAZA DE SAN FRANCISCO

Cobbled Plaza de San Francisco, two blocks south of Plaza de Armas, at Oficios and the foot of Amargura, faces onto Avenida del Puerto. During the 16th century the area was the waterfront of the early colonial city. Iberian emigrants disembarked, slaves were unloaded, and galleons were replenished for the passage to Spain. A market developed on the plaza, which became the focus of the annual Fiesta de San Francisco each October 3, when a gambling fair was established. At its heart is the **Fuente de los Leones** (Fountain of the Lions) by Giuseppe Gaggini, erected in 1836 and, though moved to different locations at various times, finally ensconced where it began.

The five-story neoclassical building on the north side is the **Lonja del Comercio** (Goods Exchange, Amargura #2, esq. Oficios, tel. 07/866-9588, Mon.–Sat. 9 A.M.–6 P.M.), dating from 1907, when it was built as a center for commodities trading. Restored, it houses offices of international corporations, news bureaus, and tour companies. The dome is crowned by a bronze figure of the god Mercury.

Behind the Lonja and entered by a wrought-iron archway topped by a most-uncommunist fairytale crown, is the **Jardín Diana de Gales** (Diana of Wales Garden, Baratillo, esq. Carpinetti, daily 9 A.M.–6 P.M.), a park unveiled in 2000 in memory of Diana, Princess of Wales. The 3-meter-tall column is by acclaimed Cuban artist Alfredo Sosabravo. There's also an engraved Welsh slate and stone plaque from Althorp, Diana's childhood home, donated by the British Embassy.

The garden backs onto the **Casa de los Esclavos** (Obrapía, esq. Av. del Puerto), a slave-merchant's home that now serves as the principal office of the city historian.

Iglesia y Convento de San Francisco de Asís

Dominating the plaza on the south side, the Iglesia y Convento de San Francisco de Asís (Oficios, e/ Amargura y Brasil, tel. 07/862-9683, daily 9 A.M.–5:30 P.M., entrance CUC2, guide CUC1, cameras CUC2, videos CUC10) was launched in 1719. The great church was reconstructed in 1730 in baroque style with a 40-meter bell tower crowned by St. Helen holding a sacred Cross of Jerusalem. The church was eventually proclaimed a Minorite basilica, and it was from its chapel that the processions of the Vía Crucis (Procession of the Cross) departed every Lenten Friday, ending at the Iglesia del Santo Cristo del Buen Vieja. The devout passed down Calle Amargura (Street of Bitterness), where Stations of the Cross were set up at street corners.

The Protestant English worshiped in the church during their tenure in Havana in 1762; Catholics refused thereafter to use it.

The church and adjoining convent reopened in October 1994 after a complete restoration. The main nave, with its towering roof supported by 12 columns, each topped by an apostle, features a trompe l'oeil that extends the perspective of the nave. The sumptuously adorned altars are gone, replaced by a huge crucifix suspended above a grand piano. (The cathedral also serves as a concert hall, with classical music performances hosted 6 P.M. Sat. and 11 A.M. Sun. Sept.–June). Members of the most aristocratic families of the times were buried in the crypt; some bodies are open to view. You can climb the campanile (CUC1) for a panoramic view over Habana Vieja.

RESTORING OLD HAVANA

Old Havana has been called the "finest urban ensemble in the Americas." The fortress colonial town that burst its walls when Washington, D.C., was still a swamp is a 140-hectare repository of antique buildings in an astounding amalgam of styles. More than 900 of Habana Vieja's 3,157 structures are of historical importance. Of these, only 101 were built in the 20th century. Almost 500 are from the 19th; 200 are from the 18th; and 144 are from the 16th and 17th. Alas, many buildings are crumbling into ruins around the people who occupy them.

In 1977, the Cuban government named Habana Vieja a National Monument. In 1982, UNESCO's Inter-Governmental Committee for World Cultural and Natural Protection named Habana Vieja a World Heritage Site worthy of international protection. Cuba formalized a plan to rescue much of the old city from decades of neglect under the guidance of Eusebio Leal Spengler, the official city historian, who runs the **Oficina del Historiador de la Ciudad de La Habana** (Av. del Puerto, esq. Obrapí, Habana Vieja, tel. 07/861-5001, www. ohch.cu). Leal, who grew up in Habana Vieja, is a member of Cuba's National Assembly, the Central Committee of the Communist Party, and the all-important Council of State.

The ambitious plan stretches into the future and has concentrated on four squares: Plaza de Armas, Plaza de la Catedral, Plaza Vieja, and Plaza de San Francisco. The most important buildings have received major renovations; others have been given facelifts. Priority is given to edifices with income-generating tourist value. Structures are ranked into one of four levels according to historical and physical value. The top level is reserved for museums; the second level for hotels, restaurants, offices, and schools; and the bottom levels for housing. Restoration is being run as a self-financing business. **Habaguanex** (Calle 24 #4313, e/ 43 y 45, Rpto. Almenderes, Playa, and Calle Oficios #110, Plaza de San Francisco, Havana, tel. 07/204-9201, www.habaguanexhotels.com) has responsibility for opening and operating commercial entities such as hotels, restaurants, cafés, and shops. The profits help finance further infrastructural improvements; 33 percent of revenues are supposedly devoted to social projects. Not every palace ends up converted for tourist use, however; some become schools, while one restored mansion is now a pediatric rehabilitation center.

Still, there is little evidence of actual homes being restored. In southern Habana Vieja, where there are relatively few structures of touristic interest, talk of restoration raises hollow laughs from the inhabitants. Because of overcrowding, some 30,000 longtime residents will be moved out for good. Many occupants have already been moved to new apartments in Alamar, the monstrous housing project east of the city; those who've been moved complain about having been transferred from ancient slum quarters to what many consider a modern and soulless slum.

The nave opens to the cloisters of a convent that today contains the **Museo de Arte Religioso,** featuring religious silver icons plus the lectern and armchairs used by Fidel and the pope during the latter's visit in 1998. A music school occupies part of the building.

A life-size bronze statue (by José Villa Soberón) of an erstwhile and once-renowned tramp known as *El Caballero de París* graces the sidewalk in front of the cathedral entrance. Many Cubans believe that touching his beard will bring good luck.

Calle Oficios

The west side of cobbled Calle Oficios facing the cathedral is lined with 17th-century colonial buildings that possess a marked Mudejar style, exemplified by their wooden balconies. The entire block has been magnificently restored and many of the buildings converted into art galleries. One of the gems is the **Galería de Carmen Montilla Tinoco** (Oficios #162, tel. 07/866-8768, Mon.–Sat. 9 A.M.–5 P.M., free). Only the front of the house remains, but the architects have made creative use of the empty shell. Next door, **Estudio Galería Los Oficios** (Oficios #166, tel. 07/863-0497, Mon.–Sat. 9:30 A.M.–5 P.M., Sun. 9 A.M.–1 P.M., free) displays works by renowned artist Nelson Domínguez.

Midway down the block, cobbled Calle Brasil extends west about 80 meters to Plaza Vieja. Portions of the original colonial-era aqueduct (the Zanja Real) are exposed. Detour to visit the **Aqvarium** (Brasil #9, tel. 07/863-9493, Tues.–Sat. 9 A.M.–5 P.M., Sun. 9 A.M.–1 P.M., CUC1, children free), displaying tropical fish. Children's events are hosted the second Wednesday of each month; video screenings every third Wednesday; and lectures every fourth Wednesday. Next door, **La Casa Cubana del Perfume** (Brasil #13, tel. 07/866-3759, Mon.–Sat. 10 A.M.–6 P.M.) displays colonial-era distilleries, has aromatherapy demos, and sells handmade perfumes made on-site.

On Oficios, the former Casa de Don Lorenzo Montalvo today houses a convent and the **Hostal Convento de Santa Brígida.**

Museo Palacio de Gobierno, Habana Vieja

© CHRISTOPHER P. BAKER

Opposite the hotel, the **Coche Presidencial Mambí** (Mon.–Fri. 8:30 AM.–4:45 P.M., CUC1) railway carriage stands on rails at Oficios and Churruca. It served as the official presidential carriage of five presidents, beginning in 1902 with Tomás Estrada Palma. Its polished hardwood interior gleams with brass fittings.

Immediately east is the **Museo Palacio de Gobierno** (Government Palace Museum, Oficios #211, esq. Muralla, tel. 07/863-4358, Tues.–Sat. 9:30 AM.–5 P.M., Sun. 9:30 A.M.–1 P.M.). This 19th-century neoclassical building housed the Cámara de Representantes (Chamber of Representatives) during the early Republic. Later it served as the Ministerio de Educación (1929–1960) and, following the Revolution, housed the Ministry of Education and the Poder Popular Municipal (Havana's local government office). Today it has uniforms, documents, and other items relating to its past use, and the office of the President of the Senate is maintained with period furniture. The interior lobby is striking for its magnificent stained-glass skylight.

The **Tienda Museo el Reloj** (Watch Museum, Oficios, esq. Muralla, tel. 07/864-9515, Mon.–Sat. 9 A.M.–6 P.M., Sun. 10 A.M.–1 P.M.) doubles as a watch and clock museum and a deluxe store selling watches and pens made by Cuervo y Sobrinos, a Swiss-Italian company that began life in Cuba in 1882.

Cater-corner to the Palacio, on the southeast side of Oficios and Muralla, is **Casa Alejandro Von Humboldt** (Oficios #254, tel. 07/863-1144, Tues.–Sat. 9 A.M.–5 P.M., Sun. 9 A.M.–noon, CUC1), a museum dedicated to the German explorer (1769–1854) who lived here while investigating Cuba in 1800–1801.

Museo de Ron

The Fundación Destilería Havana Club, or Museo de Ron (Museum of Rum, Av. San Pedro #262, e/ Muralla y Sol, tel. 07/861-8051, www.havana-club.com, Mon.–Thurs. 9 A.M.–5 P.M., Fri.–Sun. 9 A.M.–4 P.M., CUC7 including guide and drink), two blocks south of Plaza de San Francisco, occupies the former harborfront colonial mansion of the Conde de la Mortera. It's a must-see and provides an introduction to the mystery and manufacture of Cuban rum. Your tour begins with an audiovisual presentation. Exhibits include a mini-cooperage, *pailes* (sugar boiling pots), original wooden *trapiches* (sugarcane presses), and *salas* dedicated to an exposition on sugarcane, and to the colonial sugar mills and factories where the cane was pressed and the liquid processed. An operating mini-production unit replete with bubbling vats and copper stills demonstrates the process that results in some of the world's finest rums.

The highlight is a model of an early 20th-century sugar plantation at 1:22.5 scale, complete with working steam locomotives. Your tour ends in the Bar Havana Club.

Hemingway once favored **Dos Hermanos** (Av. San Pedro #304, esq. Sol, tel. 07/861-3514), a simple bar immediately south of the museum. It was closed for restoration at time of publication.

CALLE MERCADERES

Cobbled Calle Mercaderes between Obispo and Plaza Vieja, four blocks south, is full of attractions. Not least is the **Maqueta de la Habana**

Tienda Museo el Reloj, Habana Vieja

© CHRISTOPHER P. BAKER

A WALK DOWN CALLE MERCADERES

Setting out toward Plaza Vieja from the Hotel Ambos Mundos, after 20 meters you'll pass the charming **Museo de Ásia** (Asia Museum, Mercaderes #111, tel. 07/863-9740, Tues.-Sat. 9 A.M.-5 P.M., Sun. 9 A.M.-1 P.M., entrance CUC1, cameras CUC2, videos CUC10) on your left. Next door, the **Casa de las Especias** (Mon.-Sat. 9 A.M.-5 P.M., Sun. 9 A.M.-4 P.M.) sells natural herbs, such as oregano, in cloth bags. The scent upon entering is worth the visit. Nearby, call in to the **Pabellón de la Maqueta de la Habana** (Model of Havana, Calle 28 #113, e/ 1ra y 3ra, tel. 07/206-1268, maqueta@gdic.cu, Tues.-Sat. 9:30 A.M.-5 P.M., adults CUC3, students, seniors, and children CUC1, guided tour CUC1, cameras CUC2). On the west side, 20 meters farther south, are the **Casa de Puerto Rico** and **Casa del Tabaco,** both at Mercaderes #120. Besides a fine stock of cigars, the latter houses the **Museo del Tabaco** (tel. 07/861-5795, Tues.-Sat. 10 A.M.-5 P.M., Sun. 9 A.M.-1 P.M., free), a cigar museum upstairs.

At the end of the block, at the corner of Obrapía, the pink building with the Mexican flag fluttering above the doorway is the **Casa de Benito Juárez** (across called Casa de México, Mercaderes #116, tel. 07/861-8186, Tues.-Sat. 9:30 A.M.-4:45 P.M., Sun. 9:30 A.M.-1 P.M., entrance by donation), displaying artwork and costumes from Mexico, including a collection of priceless Aztec jewelry.

Turn west onto Obrapía to visit the Casa de la Obra Pía (House of Charitable Works, Obrapía #158, tel. 07/861-3097, Tues.-Sat. 9:30 A.M.-5 P.M., Sun. 9:30 A.M.-noon, free) and Casa de África (Africa House, Obrapía #157, e/ Mercaderes y San Ignacio, tel. 07/861-5798, Tues.-Sat. 9:30 A.M.-5 P.M., Sun. 9:30 A.M.-noon, CUC2). One block east, between Mercaderes and Oficios, is the **Casa de Oswaldo Guayasamín** (Obrapía #112, tel. 07/861-3843, Tues.-Sat. 9 A.M.-5:30 P.M., Sun. 9 A.M.-1:30 P.M., free), housing a museum of art and photographs from Latin America. Guayasamín, a famous Ecuadorian painter, lived and worked here for many years; you can see his works –

many are portraits of Fidel – on the upper story, where his living quarters are displayed as he left them upon his death in 1999.

Next door is the **Casa de los Abanicos** (Obrapía #107, tel. 07/863-4452, abanicos @oeetp.ohc.cu, Mon.-Sat. 10 A.M.-7 P.M., Sun. 10 A.M.-1 P.M., free), where traditional Spanish fans (abanicos) are hand-made and painted.

Return to Mercaderes and pop into **Habana 1791** (Mercaderes #176, tel. 07/861-3525, daily 10 A.M.-6 P.M.), on the southwest corner of Obrapía, where traditional fragrances are made and sold. Continue south half a block to **Casa-Museo del Libertador Simón Bolívar** (Mercaderes #160, tel. 07/861-3988, Tues.-Sat. 9 A.M.-5 P.M., Sun. 9 A.M.-1 P.M., CUC1), displaying cultural works and art from Venezuela. The collection includes portraits of the "Great Liberator," ceremonial swords, coins minted in his honor, and paintings by contemporary artists. Bolívar stayed here in March 1799 and is commemorated in the small **Plaza de Bolívar** at the corner of Mercaderes and Obrapía.

Across the street is the **Armería 9 de Abril** (Mercaderes #157, tel. 07/861-8080, Mon.-Sat. 9 A.M.-5 P.M., CUC1), a museum that commemorates four members of Castro's 26th July Movement killed in an assault on the armory on April 9, 1958.

Crossing Lamparilla, peek in at the **Hostal Conde de Villanueva,** one of Havana's finest boutique hotels. One block south, the corner of Mercaderes and Amargura is known as the Cruz Verde – Green Cross – as it was the first stop on the annual Vía Crucis pilgrimage. Today it houses the **Casa del Chocolate** (tel. 07/866-4431, daily 10 A.M.-8:30 P.M.), selling chocolate rolls and beverages and featuring a museum collection of porcelains and wall pieces relating the history of chocolate.

Midway down this curling block you'll pass **Mesón de la Flota,** a Spanish bodega with live flamenco. About 75 meters beyond, you'll arrive at Plaza Vieja.

Vieja (Model of Old Havana, Mercaderes #114, tel. 07/866-4425, daily 9:30 A.M.–6:30 P.M., entrance CUC1, guide CUC1, cameras CUC2, videos CUC5). This 1:500 scale model of Habana Vieja measures eight by four meters, with every building delineated and color coded by use. Guides give a spiel.

Museo de Ásia

The charming Museo de Ásia (Asia Museum, Mercaderes #111, tel. 07/863-9740, Tues.–Sat. 9 A.M.–5 P.M., Sun. 9 A.M.–1 P.M., entrance CUC1, cameras CUC2, videos CUC10) displays a collection of Asiatica comprising gifts to Fidel from Asian nations. The best rooms are upstairs, containing an array of carved ivory, silverware, mother-of-pearl furniture, kimonos, and Oriental armaments. The museum also includes a small bonsai garden. One of the rooms downstairs doubles as a school classroom.

Casa de la Obra Pía

The Casa de la Obra Pía (House of Charitable Works, Obrapía #158, tel. 07/861-3097, Tues.–Sat. 9:30 A.M.–5 P.M., Sun. 9:30 A.M.–noon, free), 20 meters west of Mercaderes, comprises two adjacent houses that were later combined. This splendid mansion was built in 1665 by Capitán Martín Calvo de la Puerta y Arrieta, the Cuban solicitor general. (The house and street are named for his *obra pía,* or pious act, of devoting a portion of his wealth to sponsoring five orphan girls every year.) The Calvo de Puertas family built additions in baroque style. Their coat of arms, surrounded by exuberant baroque stonework, is emblazoned above the massive *portal,* brought from Cádiz in 1686. The mansion exemplifies the Spanish adaptation of a Moorish inner courtyard, illuminated by daylight filtering through *mediopuntos* fanning out like a peacock's tail. It features art galleries, plus an exhibition of works by Alejo Carpentier in the foyer (including, rather incongruously, his blue Volkswagen brought back from Paris after his tenure as Cuban ambassador to UNESCO).

Casa de África

Dedicated to a celebration of African culture, Casa de África (Africa House, Obrapía #157, e/ Mercaderes y San Ignacio, tel. 07/861-5798, Tues.–Sat. 9:30 A.M.–5 P.M., Sun. 9:30 A.M.–noon, CUC2), opposite Casa de la Obra Pía, is full of African artwork and artifacts. On the third floor is a collection of paraphernalia used in *santería,* including statues of the leading deities in the Yoruban pantheon.

◖ PLAZA VIEJA

The last of the four main squares to be laid out in Habana Vieja, Plaza Vieja (Old Square, bounded by Calles Mercaderes, San Ignacio, Brasil, and Muralla) originally hosted a covered market. It is surrounded by mansions and apartment blocks where, in colonial times, residents looked down on processions, executions, and bullfights.

Last century many of the square's beautiful buildings sank into disrepair. Today it is in the final stages of restoration. Even the white Carrara marble fountain—an exact replica of the original by Italian sculptor Giorgio Massari—has reappeared. Until recently, the upper stories of most buildings housed tenement apartments; tenants have moved out as the buildings have metamorphosed into boutiques, restaurants, museums, and luxury apartments for foreign residents.

The tallest building is the **Edificio Gómez Villa,** on the northeast corner. Take the elevator to the top for views over the plaza and to visit the **Cámara Oscura** (daily 9:30 A.M.–7 P.M., CUC2). The optical reflection camera revolves 360 degrees, projecting a real-time picture of Havana at 30 times the magnification onto a two-meter-wide parabola housed in a completely darkened room.

Casa de los Condes de Jaruco

The restored 18th-century Casa de los Condes de Jaruco (House of the Counts of Jaruco, Muralla #107), or "La Casona," on the southeast corner, was built between 1733 and 1737 by the father of the future Count of Jaruco and is highlighted by mammoth

A WALK AROUND PLAZA VIEJA

After visiting the **Cámara Oscura** on the northeast corner of the plaza (daily 9:30 A.M.-7 P.M., CUC2), begin your clockwise tour by following the shaded arcade along the plaza's east side. Midway, you'll pass the **Casa de Juan Rico de Mata,** today the headquarters of **Fototeca** (Mercaderes #307, tel. 07/862-2530, fototeca @cubarte.cult.cu, Tues.-Sat. 10 A.M.-5 P.M.), the state-run agency that promotes the work of Cuban photographers. It offers international photo exhibitions in the Salón Nacional de Fotografía. Note the ceramic wall mural designed by Amelia Peláez.

Next door, the **Planetario Habana** (Mercaderes #309) opened in February 2010 as a cultural center for science and technology, with a 66-seat planetarium displaying 6,500 stars, interactive exhibitions about the universe, and a computerized library. The four-level museum tops out with a state-of-the-art Goto telescope.

The old **Palacio Vienna Hotel** (also called the Palacio Cueto), on the southeast corner of Plaza Vieja, is a phenomenal piece of Gaudíesque art nouveau architecture dating from 1906. At last visit it was being restored as a deluxe hotel.

Moving to the south side, the Casa de Marqués de Prado Amero today houses the **Museo de Naipes** (Museum of Playing Cards, Muralla #101, tel. 07/860-1534, Tues.-Sat. 8:30 A.M.-5 P.M., Sun. 9 A.M.-2 P.M., entrance by donation), displaying playing cards through the ages. On the plaza's southwest corner, call in at the **Casa de los Condes de Jaruco** (House of the Counts of Jaruco, Muralla #107,

Tues.-Sat. 9 A.M.-5 P.M.) to view the various art galleries, then cross San Ignacio and follow Muralla half a block to the **Tienda El Soldadito de Plumo** (Muralla #164, Mon.-Fri. 9 A.M.-5 P.M., Sat. 9 A.M.-1:30 P.M.), selling miniature soldiers made of lead! A large glass window lets you watch artists painting the pieces.

Return to the plaza, turn left to follow San Ignacio north, and cool off with a chilled beer brewed on-site in the **Taberna de la Muralla** (San Ignacio #364, tel. 07/866-4453, daily 11 A.M.-1 A.M.), in the former **Casa del Conde de Casa Lombillo.** The copper stills are displayed in the main bar, where a 1913 Ford delivery truck now sits and artworks by such famous Cuban artists as Kcho and Nelson Domínguez are displayed.

Fifty meters to the north, the **Casa del Conde de San Estéban de Cañongo** (San Ignacio #356, tel. 07/868-3561, Mon.-Fri. 9:30 A.M.-5:30 P.M., Sat. 9:30 A.M.-1 P.M.) opened in 2009 following restoration as a cultural center. Adjoining, on the northwest corner of the plaza, is the **Casa de las Hermanas Cárdenas,** recently restored and today housing the **Centro de Desarollo de Artes Visuales** (San Ignacio #352, tel. 07/862-2611, Tues.-Sat. 10 A.M.-6 P.M.). The inner courtyard is dominated by an intriguing sculpture by Alfredo Sosabravo. Art education classes are given on the second floor, reached via a wide wooden staircase. The top story has an art gallery.

Well worth the side trip is **Hotel Raquel** (San Ignacio, esq. Amargura, tel. 07/860-8280), one block north of the plaza. This restored hotel is an art deco and neoclassical jewel.

doors opening into a cavernous courtyard surrounded by lofty archways festooned with hanging vines. Whimsical murals are painted on the walls, touched in splashy color by the undulating play of light through *mediopuntos*. It hosts offices of the **Fondo Cubano de Bienes Culturales** (Cultural Property Fund, tel. 07/860-8577). Art galleries occupy the downstairs rooms (Tues.–Sat. 9 A.M.–5 P.M.).

Museo Histórico de las Ciencias Naturales Carlos Finlay

Physicians and scientists inclined to a busman's holiday might walk one block west and one north of the plaza and check out the Museo Histórico de las Ciencias Naturales Carlos Finlay (Museum of Natural History, Cuba #460, e/ Amargura y Brasil, tel. 07/863-4824, Mon.–Fri. 9 A.M.–5 P.M., Sat. 9 A.M.–3 P.M., CUC2). Dating from 1868 and once the headquarters of the Academy of Medical, Physical, and Natural Sciences, today it contains a pharmaceutical collection and tells the tales of Cuban scientists' discoveries and innovations. The Cuban scientist Dr. Finlay is honored, of course; it was he who on August 14, 1881, discovered that yellow fever is transmitted by the *Aedes aegipti* mosquito. The museum also contains a medical library and, on the third floor, a reconstructed period pharmacy.

Adjoining the museum to the north, the **Convento y Iglesia de San Francisco el Nuevo** (Cuba, esq. Amargura, tel. 07/861-8490, Mon.–Thurs. 9 A.M.–6 P.M., Sun. 8 A.M.–1 P.M., free) was completed in 1633 for the Augustine friars. It was consecrated anew in 1842, when it was given to the Franciscans, who then rebuilt it in renaissance style in 1847. The church has a marvelous domed altar and nave.

SOUTHERN HABANA VIEJA

The mostly residential southern half of Habana Vieja, south of Calle Brasil, was the ecclesiastical center of Havana during the colonial era and is studded with churches and convents. Most have been restored or are in the process. Before the Revolution, this was also Havana's Jewish quarter.

Southern Habana Vieja is enclosed by Avenida del Puerto, which swings along the harborfront and becomes Avenida San Pedro, then Avenida Leonor Pérez, then Avenida Desamparados as it curves around to Avenida de Bélgica (colloquially called Egido). The waterfront boulevard is overshadowed by warehouses. Here were the old P&O docks where the ships from Miami and Key West used to dock and where Pan American World Airways had its terminal when it was still flying the old clipper flying-boats. Before World War II, when the U.S. Navy took over the docks, Calle San Isidro, which runs inland perpendicular to Desamparados, had been lined with brothels.

Calle Egido

Egido follows the hollow once occupied by Habana Vieja's ancient walls. It is a continuation of Monserrate and flows downhill to the

HAVANA'S CITY WALLS

Construction of Havana's fortified city walls began on February 3, 1674. They ran along the western edge of the bay and, on the landward side, stood between today's Calle Egido, Monserrate, and Zulueta. Under the direction of engineer Juan de Siscaras, African slaves labored for 23 years to build the 1.4-meter-thick, 10-meter-tall city wall that was intended to ring the entire city, using rocks hauled in from the coast. The 4,892-meter-long wall was completed in 1697, with a perimeter of five kilometers. The damage inflicted by the British artillery in 1762 was repaired in 1797, when the thick wall attained its final shape. It formed an irregular polygon with nine defensive bastions with sections of wall in between, and moats and steep drops to delay assault by enemy troops. In its first stage it had just two entrances (nine more were added later), opened each morning upon the sound of a single cannon and closed at night the same way.

As time went on, the *intramuros* (the city within the walls) burst its confines. In 1841, Havana authorities petitioned the Spanish Crown for permission to demolish the walls. Just 123 years after the walls went up, they came down again. The demolition began in 1863, when African slave-convicts were put to work to destroy what their forefathers had built. The demolition wasn't completed until well into the 20th century. Only fragments remain.

harbor. The **Puerta de la Tenaza** (Egido, esq. Fundición) is the only ancient city gate still standing; a plaque inset in the wall shows a map of the city walls as they once were. About 100 meters south, on Avenida de Puerto, the **Monumento Mártires del Vapor La Coubre** is made of twisted metal fragments of *La Coubre,* the French cargo ship that exploded in Havana harbor on March 4, 1960 (the vessel was carrying armaments for the Castro government). The monument honors the seamen who died in the explosion.

Egido is lined with once-beautiful mid-19th-century buildings, now dilapidated. Egido's masterpiece is the **Estación Central de Ferrocarril** (esq. Arsenal), or Terminal de Trenes, Havana's Venetian-style railway station. Designed in 1910, it blends Spanish Revival and Italian Renaissance styles and features twin towers displaying the shields of Havana and Cuba. It is built atop the former Arsenal, or Spanish naval shipyard.

On the station's north side, the small, shady **Parque de los Agrimensores** (Park of the Surveyors) features a remnant of the **Cortina de la Habana,** the old city wall. The park is now populated by Baldwin steam trains retired from hauling sugar cane (the oldest dates from 1878). *Colectivo* taxis—old *yanqui* jalopies—park here, awaiting custom.

Museo Casa Natal de José Martí

The birthplace of the nation's preeminent national hero, Museo Casa Natal de José Martí (Leonor Pérez #314, esq. Av. de Bélgica, tel. 07/861-3778, Tues.–Sat. 9 A.M.–5 P.M., entrance CUC1, guide CUC1, cameras CUC2, videos CUC10) sits one block south of the railway station at the end of a street named after Martí's mother. This simple house with terra-cotta tile floors is a shrine for Cubans. The national hero and leader of the independence movement was born on January 28, 1853, and spent the first four years of his life here. The house displays many of his personal effects, including a beautiful lacquered *escritorio* (writing desk), original texts, poems, sketches, and even a lock of Martí's hair from when he was a child.

Plaza del Cristo

Plaza del Cristo lies at the west end of Amargura, between Lamparilla and Brasil, one block east of Avenida de Bélgica (Monserrate). It was here that Wormold, the vacuum-cleaner salesman turned secret agent, was "swallowed up among the pimps and lottery sellers of the Havana noon" in Graham Greene's *Our Man*

a 1951 Chevrolet Bel Air on Plaza del Cristo

© CHRISTOPHER P. BAKER

in Havana. Wormold and his wayward daughter Millie lived at the fictional 37 Lamparilla.

The plaza is dominated by the tiny **Iglesia de Santo Cristo Buen Vieja** (Villegas, e/ Amargura y Lamparilla, tel. 07/863-1767, daily 9 A.M.–noon), dating from 1732, but with a Franciscan hermitage—called Humilladero chapel—dating from 1640. Buen Viaje was the final point of the Vía Crucis (the Procession of the Cross) held each Lenten Friday and beginning at the Iglesia de San Francisco de Asís. The church, which was named for its popularity among sailors and travelers, who used to pray here for safe voyages, has an impressive cross-beamed wooden ceiling and exquisite altars, including one to the Virgen de la Caridad showing three boatmen being saved from the tempest.

Iglesia y Convento de Santa Teresa de Jesús

The handsome Iglesia y Convento de Santa Teresa de Jesús (Brasil, esq. Compostela, tel. 07/861-1445), two blocks east of Plaza del

JEWS IN CUBA

Today, Havana's Jewish community (La Comunidad Hebrea, www.chcuba.org) is thought to number only about 1,300, about 5 percent of its prerevolutionary size, when it supported five synagogues and a college.

The first Jew in Cuba, Luis de Torres, arrived with Columbus in 1492 as the explorer's translator. He was followed in the 16th century by Jews escaping persecution at the hands of the Spanish Inquisition. Later, Ashkenazic Jews from Florida founded the United Hebrew Congregation in 1906, and Turkish Jews flocking to avoid World War I concentrated in southern Habana Vieja, many starting out in Cuba selling ties and cloth. Other Jews emigrating from Eastern Europe passed through Cuba en route to the United States in significant numbers until the United States slammed its doors in 1924, after which they settled in Cuba. They were relatively poor compared to the earlier Jewish immigrants and were disparagingly called *polacos*. Sephardic Jews came later and were profoundly religious. They formed social clubs, opened their own schools, and married their own. By contrast, many Ashkenazic men married Cuban (Catholic) women and eventually were assimilated into Cuban society, says author Robert M. Levine. The Ashkenazim were fired with socialist ideals and were prominent in the founding of both the labor and Cuban Communist movements.

Cuba seems to have been relatively free of anti-Semitism. (Batista was a friend to Jews fleeing Nazi Europe). Levine, however, records how during the late 1930s the U.S. government bowed to isolationist, labor, and anti-Semitic pressures at home and convinced the Cuban government to turn back European Jews. This sordid chapter in U.S. history is reflected in the tragic story of the SS *St. Louis* and its 937 passengers trying to escape Nazi Germany in 1939. The ship languished in Havana harbor for a week while U.S. and Cuban officials deliberated on letting passengers disembark; tragically, entry was refused, and the passengers were sent back to Europe and their fate.

By the 1950s, about 20,000 Jews lived in Havana, concentrated around Calle Belén and Calle Acosta, which bustled with kosher bakeries, cafés, and clothes stores. Jews knew the lessons of Nazi Germany and the totalitarian regimes of Eastern Europe and so, following the Revolution, became part of the Cuban diaspora. About 95 percent of them fled, although a few joined the Castro government; two became early cabinet members. Some 500 Cuban Jews were secretly allowed to emigrate to Israel beginning in 1994.

Although the Castro government discouraged Jews from practicing their faith, Jewish religious schools were the only parochial schools allowed to remain open after the Revolution. The government has always made matzo available and even authorized a kosher butcher shop on Calle Acosta to supply meat for observant Jews. The Jewish community also has its own cemetery, in Guanabacoa, dating from 1910. However, the community has no rabbi, and marriages and circumcisions must often wait for foreign religious officials passing through Havana.

Still, a renaissance in the Jewish faith is occurring. In 1994, the first bar mitzvah in over 12 years took place and the first formal bris in over five years. A Hebrew Sunday School even teaches Hebrew and Yiddish.

JEWISH HERITAGE SITES
The Cuban government proposes to reconstruct Habana Vieja's Jewish quarter, having made a start by rehabilitating the **Sinagoga Adath Israel** (Picota #52, esq. Acosta, tel.

Cristo, was built by the Carmelites in 1705. The church is still in use, although the convent ceased to operate as such in 1929, when the nuns were moved out and the building was converted into a series of homes.

Across the road is the **Drogería Sarrá** (Brasil, e/ Compostela y Habana, tel. 07/866-7554, daily 9 A.M.–5 P.M., free), a fascinating apothecary—also known as Farmacia La Reunión—with paneled cabinets still stocked with herbs and pharmaceuticals in colorful old bottles and ceramic jars.

United Hebrew Congregation Cemetery, Guanabacoa

© CHRISTOPHER P. BAKER

07/861-3495, daily 8 A.M.-noon and 5-8 P.M.), which sports a new wooden altar carved with scenes from Jerusalem and historic Havana. Services are Monday-Friday 8 A.M. and 6 P.M., Saturday at 9 A.M. and 6 P.M., and Sunday at 9 A.M. **Chevet Achim** (Inquisidor, e/ Luz y Santa Clara, tel. 07/832-6623) was built in 1914 and is the oldest synagogue in Cuba. The building is owned and maintained by the Centro Sefardí but is not used for ritual or community purposes. It can be viewed by appointment.

In Vedado, the **Casa de la Comunidad Hebrea de Cuba** (Calle I #241, e/ 13 y 15, tel. 07/832-8953, Mon.-Sat. 9:30 A.M.-5 P.M.), or Patronato, works to preserve Cuba's Hebrew traditions and contains an active community center and a large library on Judaica. Services at the adjacent **Bet Shalon Sinagogo** are Fri-

day at 7:30 P.M. (May-Sept.) or 6 P.M. (Oct.-Apr.) and Saturday at 10 A.M. (year-round). Nearby, the run-down **Centro Sefardí** (Calle 17 #462, esq. E, tel. 07/832-6623) is a Conservative Jewish synagogue completed in 1960.

Guanabacoa, on the east side of Havana harbor, has two Jewish cemeteries. The **Cementerio de la Comunidad Religiosa Ebrea Adath Israel** (Av. de la Independencia Este, e/ Obelisco y Puente, tel. 07/97-6644, Mon.-Fri. 8-11 A.M. and 2-5 P.M.), also known as the United Hebrew Congregation Cemetery, is for Ashkenazim. It dates from 1912 and is entered by an ocher-colored Spanish-colonial frontispiece with a Star of David. A **Holocaust memorial** immediately to the left of the gate stands in memory of the millions who lost their lives to the Nazis: "Buried in this place are several cakes of soap made from Hebrew human fat, a fraction of the six million victims of Nazi savagery in the 20th century. May their remains rest in peace."

Behind the Ashkenazic cemetery is the **Cementerio de la Unión Hebrea Chevet Ahim** (Calle G, e/ 5ta y Final, tel. 07/97-5866, daily 7 A.M.-5 P.M.), for Sephardic Jews. It too has a memorial to the Holocaust victims; turn north off Avenida de la Independencia Este at Avenida de los Mártires (4ta) to reach it.

JEWISH AID ORGANIZATIONS
The following organizations send humanitarian aid to Cuba and/or offer organized trips: the **Cuban Jewish Relief Project** (1831 Murray Ave. #208, Pittsburgh, PA 15217, tel. 412/521-2390, www.cubanjewishrelief.org), the **Cuba-America Jewish Mission** (1442A Walnut St. #224, Berkeley, CA 94709, www.thecajm.org), and **Jewish Solidarity** (100 Beacom Blvd., Miami, FL 33135, tel. 305/642-1600, http://jewishcuba.org/solidarity).

Iglesia y Convento de Nuestra Señora de Belén
The Iglesia y Convento de Nuestra Señora de Belén (Church and Convent of Our Lady of Bethlehem, Compostela y Luz, tel. 07/860-3150, Mon.–Sat. 9 A.M.–5 P.M., Sun.

9 A.M.–1 P.M., free), the city's largest religious complex, occupies an entire block. The convent, completed in 1718, was built to house the first nuns to arrive in Havana and later served as a refuge for convalescents. In 1842, Spanish authorities ejected the religious order

GRAHAM GREENE: OUR MAN IN HAVANA

No contemporary novel quite captures the tawdry intrigue and disreputable aura of Batista's Havana than does Graham Greene's *Our Man in Havana*, published in 1958 and set amid the torrid events of Havana in 1957.

The comic tale tells of Wormold, an English vacuum-cleaner salesman based in Havana and short of money. His daughter has reached an expensive age, so he accepts an offer of £300 a month and becomes Agent 59200/5, MI6's man in Havana. To keep his job, he files bogus reports and dreams up military apparatuses from vacuum-cleaner parts. Unfortunately, Wormold becomes trapped by his own deceit and the workings of a hopelessly corrupt city and society.

Graham Greene (1904-1991) was already a respected author when he was recruited to work for the Foreign Office, serving the years 1941-1943 in Sierra Leone, Africa. In the last years of the war, he worked for the British Secret Service dealing with counterespionage on the Iberian Peninsula, where he learned how the Nazi Abwehr (the German Secret Service) sent home false reports – perfect material for his novel. He traveled widely and based many of his works, including *Our Man in Havana*, on his experiences. He visited Havana several times in the 1950s and was disturbed by the mutilations and torture practiced by Batista's police officers and by social ills such as racial discrimination: "Every smart bar and restaurant was called a club so that a Negro could be legally excluded." But he confessed to enjoying the "louche atmosphere" of Havana and seems to have savored the fleshpots completely. "I came there...for the brothel life, the roulette in every hotel," he later wrote.

Castro condoned *Our Man in Havana* but complained that it didn't do justice to the ruthlessness of the Batista regime. Greene agreed: "Alas, the book did me little good with the new rulers in Havana. In poking fun at the British Secret Service, I had minimized the terror of Batista's rule. I had not wanted too black a background for a light-hearted comedy, but those who had suffered during the years of dictatorship could hardly be expected to appreciate that my real subject was the absurdity of the British agent and not the justice of a revolution." Nonetheless, Castro permitted the screen version, starring Alec Guinness as Wormold, to be filmed in Havana in 1959.

Greene returned to Cuba in the years 1963-1966. Although initially impressed by Castro's war on illiteracy (he called it "a great crusade"), he later soured after witnessing the persecution of homosexuals, intellectuals, and Catholics. Perhaps for this reason, the author isn't commemorated in Cuba in any way.

and turned the church into a government office before making it over to the Jesuits. They in turn established a college for the sons of the aristocracy. The Jesuits were the nation's official weather forecasters and in 1858 erected the Observatorio Real (Royal Observatory) atop the tower. It was in use until 1925. At last visit, the convent was still being renovated.

The church and convent are linked to contiguous buildings across the street by an arched walkway—the Arco de Belén (Arch of Bethlehem)—spanning Acosta.

Iglesia y Convento de Santa Clara de Asís

The Iglesia y Convento de Santa Clara de Asís (Convent of Saint Clair of Assisi, Cuba #610, e/ Luz y Sol, tel. 07/866-9327, Mon.–Fri. 9 A.M.–5 P.M., CUC2), two blocks east of Belén, is a massive former nunnery completed in 1644. The nuns moved out in 1922. It is a remarkable building, with a lobby full of beautiful period pieces. The cloistered courtyard is surrounded by columns. Note the 17th-century fountain of a Samaritan woman, and the beautiful cloister roof carved with geometric designs—a classic *alfarje*—in the Salón Plenario, a marble-floored hall of imposing stature. Wooden carvings abound. The second cloister contains the so-called Sailor's House, built by a wealthy ship owner for his daughter, whom he failed to dissuade from a life of asceticism.

Iglesia Parroquial del Espíritu Santo

The Iglesia Parroquial del Espíritu Santo (Parish Church of the Holy Ghost, Acosta #161, esq. Cuba, tel. 07/862-3410, Mon.–Fri. 8:30 A.M.–4 P.M.), two blocks south of Santa Clara de Asís, is Havana's oldest church, dating from 1638 (the circa-1674 central nave and facade, and circa-1720 Gothic vault are later additions) when it was a hermitage for the devotions of free *negros*. Later, King Charles III granted the right of asylum here to anyone hunted by the authorities, a privilege no longer bestowed.

The church's many surprises include a gilded, carved wooden pelican in a niche in the baptistry. The sacristy, where parish archives dating back through the 17th century are preserved, boasts an enormous cupboard full of baroque silver staffs and incense holders. Catacombs to each side of the nave are held up by subterranean tree trunks. You can explore the eerie vault that runs under the chapel, with the niches still containing the odd bone as well as the body of Bishop Gerónimo Valdés, who remained in a kind of limbo, his whereabouts unknown, until he turned up buried under the floor during a restoration in 1936. The tower holds four bells; steps lead up to the gallery.

Iglesia y Convento de Nuestra Señora de la Merced

Two blocks south of Espíritu Santo is Iglesia y Convento de Nuestra Señora de la Merced (Our Lady of Mercy, Cuba #806, esq. Merced, tel. 07/863-8873, daily 8 A.M.–noon and 3–6 P.M.), a small handsome church and convent with an ornate interior containing romantic dome paintings and the Capilla de Lourdes (Lourdes Chapel), also with early-20th-century

religious frescoes. The church, begun in 1755, has strong Afro-Cuban connections (the Virgin of Mercy is also Obatalá, goddess of earth and purity), and it is not unusual to see devotees of *santería* kneeling in prayer. Each September 24, scores of worshippers cram in for the Virgen de la Merced's feast day. More modest celebrations are held on the 24th of every other month.

Alameda de Paula

The 100-meter-long Alameda de Paula promenade runs alongside the waterfront boulevard between Luz and Leonor Pérez. It is lined with marble and iron street lamps. Midway along the Alameda stands a carved column with a fountain at its base, erected in 1847 in homage to the Spanish navy. It bears an unlikely Irish name: **Columna O'Donnell**, for the Capitán-General of Cuba, Leopoldo O'Donnell, who dedicated the monument. It is covered in relief work on a military theme and crowned by a lion with the arms of Spain in its claws.

At the southern end of the Alameda, **Iglesia de San Francisco de Paula** (San Ignacio y Leonor Pérez, tel. 07/860-4210, daily 9 A.M.–5 P.M.) studs circular Plazuela de Paula. The quaint, restored church features marvelous artworks including stained-glass pieces. It is used for baroque and chamber concerts.

Sacra Catedral Ortodoxa Rusa

Opened in October 2008, the beautiful, gleaming white, waterfront Sacra Catedral Ortodoxa Rusa (Russian Orthodox church, Av. del Puerto and Calle San Pedro, daily 9 A.M.–5:45 P.M.), officially the Iglesia Virgen de María de Kazan, whisks you allegorically to Moscow with its bulbous, golden minarets. No photos are allowed inside, where a gold altar and chandeliers hang above gray marble floors. Exquisite!

Sights - Centro Habana and Cerro

Centro Habana (Central Havana, pop. 175,000) lies west of the Paseo de Martí and south of the Malecón. The 19th-century region evolved following demolition of the city walls in 1863. Prior, it had served as a glacis. The buildings are deep and tall, of four or five stories, built mostly as apartment units. Hence, the population and street life are dense. Laid out in a near-perfect grid, Centro is mostly residential, with few sights of note, except for the remnants of Chinatown—Barrio Chino—delineated by Calles Zanja, Dragones, Salud, Rayo, San Nicolás, and Manrique.

The major west–east thoroughfares are the Malecón to the north and Zanja and Avenida Salvador Allende through the center, plus Calles Neptuno and San Rafael between the Malecón and Zanja. Three major thoroughfares run perpendicular, north–south: Calzada de Infanta, forming the western boundary; Padre Varela, down the center; and Avenida de Italia (Galiano), farther east.

In prerevolutionary days, Centro Habana hosted Havana's red-light district, and prostitutes roamed such streets as the ill-named Calle Virtudes (Virtues). Neptuno and San Rafael formed the retail heart of the city. In recent years, they have regained some of their life and the famous department stores of prerevolutionary days have reopened; many still bear neon signs promoting U.S. brand names from yesteryear. Many houses, however, are in a tumbledown state—about one in three houses has collapsed—conjuring up images of what Dresden, Germany, must have looked like after it was bombed in World War II.

South of Centro, the land rises gently to Cerro, which developed during the 19th century as the place to retire for the torrid midsummer months; many wealthy families maintained two homes in Havana—one in town, another on the cooler *cerro* (hill). The area is replete with once-stately *quintas* (summer homes) in neoclassical, Beaux-Arts, and art nouveau styles. Alas, the region is terribly deteriorated, and the majority of buildings transcend sordid.

Caution is required, as muggings are common in these districts.

THE MALECÓN (CENTRO)

Officially known as Avenida Antonio Maceo, and more properly the Muro de Malecón (literally "embankment," or "seawall"), Havana's seafront boulevard winds dramatically along the Atlantic shoreline between the Castillo de San Salvador de la Punta and the Río Almendares. The six-lane seafront boulevard was designed as a jetty wall in 1857 by Cuban engineer Francisco de Albear but not laid out until 1902, by U.S. governor General Woods. It took 50 years to reach the Río Almendares, almost five miles to the west.

The Malecón is lined with once-glorious high-rise houses, each exuberantly distinct from the next. Unprotected by seaworthy paint since the Revolution, they have proven incapable of withstanding the salt spray that crashes over the seawall in great airy clouds and then floats off in rainbows. Many buildings have already collapsed, and those that were painted in haste for the pope's visit in 1998 have faded again. An ongoing restoration seems to make little headway against the elements, although wrought-iron street lamps in classical style have gone up.

All along the shore are the worn remains of square baths—known as the "Elysian Fields"—hewn from the rocks below the seawall, originally with separate areas for men, women, and *negros*. These **Baños del Mar** preceded construction of the Malecón. Each is about four meters square and two meters deep, with rock steps for access and a couple of portholes through which the waves wash in and out.

The Malecón offers a microcosm of Havana life: the elderly walking their dogs; the shiftless selling cigars and cheap sex to tourists; the young passing rum among friends; fishermen tending their lines and casting off on giant inner tubes (*neumáticos*); and always, scores of couples courting and necking. The Malecón is known as "Havana's sofa" and acts, wrote Claudia Lightfoot, as "the city's drawing room, office, study, and often bedroom." All through the night, lovers' murmurings mingle with the crash of the waves.

The Malecón—the setting for spontaneous riots in the early 1990s—is also a barometer of the political state of Havana. During times of tension, the police presence is abnormally strong and the Malecón becomes eerily empty.

Every October 26, schoolchildren are bused here to throw flowers over the seawall in memory of revolutionary leader Camilo Cienfuegos, killed in a mysterious air crash on that day in 1959.

Parque Maceo

Dominating the Malecón to the west, at the foot of Avenida Padre Varela, is the massive bronze **Monumento Antonio Maceo,** atop a marble base in a plaza with a fountain. The classical monument was erected in 1916 in honor of the mulatto general and hero of the Wars of Independence who was known as the "Bronze Titan." The motley tower that stands at the west end of the plaza is the 17th-century **Torreón de San Lázaro,** with loopholes for snipers aiming along the Malecón. Although it looks fairly modern, it was built in 1665 to guard the former cove of San Lázaro.

To the south, the **Hospital Hermanos Almeijeiras** looms over the park. The **Convento y Capilla de la Inmaculada Concepción** (San Lázaro #805, e/ Oquendo y Lucena, tel. 07/878-8404, Mon.–Sun. 9 A.M.–5 P.M.) is immediately west of the hospital. This beautiful church and convent was built in Gothic style in 1874 and features notable stained-glass windows and a painted altar.

BARRIO CAYO HUESO

Immediately west of the Plaza Antonio Maceo, a triangular area bordered by the Malecón, San Lázaro, and Calzada de Infanta forms the northwest corner of Centro Habana. Known as Barrio Cayo Hueso, the region dates from the early 20th century when tenement homes

were erected atop what had been the Espada cemetery (hence the name, Cay of Bones). Its several art deco inspirations include the **Edificio Solimar** (Soledad #205, e/ San Lázaro y Ánimas) apartment complex, built in 1944.

The pseudo-castle at the corner of Calle 25 and the Malecón was—before the Revolution—the **Casa Marina,** Havana's most palatial brothel. Carousing English travel writer Graham Greene was among its celebrity habitués.

Museo Fragua Martiana

Hallowed ground to Cubans, the small Museo Fragua Martiana (Museum of Martí's Forging, Principe #108, esq. Hospital, tel. 07/870-7338, Mon.–Fri. 9 A.M.–4:30 P.M., Sat. 9 A.M.–1 P.M., free) occupies the site of the former San Lázaro quarry, where national hero José Martí and fellow prisoners were forced to break rocks. The museum displays manuscripts and even shackles. To its rear, the quarry has been turned into a garden, with a life-size bronze statue of Martí.

"Salvador's Alley"

Almost every dance enthusiast in the know gravitates to **Callejón de Hamel** (e/ Aramburu y Hospital), an alley where local artist Salvador González Escalona has adorned the walls with evocative murals in sun-drenched yellow, burnt orange, and blazing reds, inspired by *santería.* The alley features a *santería* shrine and fantastical totemic sculptures. González, a bearded artist with an eye for self-promotion, has an eclectic gallery, **Estudio-Galería Fambá** (Callejón de Hamel #1054, tel. 07/878-1661, eliasasef@yahoo.es, daily 9:30 A.M.–6 P.M.). On Sunday, he hosts Afro-Cuban rumbas.

Nearby, **Parque de los Mártires Universitarios** (Infanta, e/ Calles Jovellar y San Lázaro), one block west of Callejón de Hamel, honors students who lost their lives during the fights against the Machado and Batista regimes.

Convento y Iglesia del Carmen

Soaring over Calle Infanta, about 100 meters

south of San Lázaro, Convento y Iglesia del Carmen (Infanta, e/ Neptuno y Concordia, tel. 07/878-5168, Mon.–Sat. 8–10 A.M. and 4–7 P.M., Sun. 7:30 A.M.–12:30 P.M. and 4:30–7:30 P.M.) is one of Havana's largest and most impressive churches. Built in baroque fashion, the church is capped by a 60.5-meter-tall tower atop which soars a 7.5-meter-tall sculpture of Our Lady of Carmen.

GALIANO

This broad boulevard, lined with arcaded porticos, runs south from the Malecón to Avenida Salvador Allende and is Centro's main north–south artery.

The **Hotel Lincoln** (Galiano, e/ Ánimas y Virtudes) was where Argentina's world-champion racecar driver Fangio was kidnapped by Castro's revolutionaries in 1958 during the Cuban Grand Prix. Room #810 is today the **Museo de Juan Manuel Fangio,** with photos and magazines from the period presenting a predictably one-sided version of the affair. Also on an Argentinian theme, fans of tango might check out the **Caserón del Tango** (Neptuno #303, e/ Águila y Italia, tel. 07/863-0097, daily 10 A.M.–8 P.M.), a tiny cultural center-cum-museum run by tango lover Edmundo Daubal in honor of the Argentinian dance.

Cine América (Galiano #253, esq. Concordia, tel. 07/862-5416) dates from 1941 and is one of the world's great art deco theaters, albeit severely deteriorated. The foyer features a terrazzo floor inlaid with zodiac motifs and a map of the world, with Cuba at the center in polished brass. Cater-corner, the rarely open **Iglesia de Nuestra Señora de Monserrate** dates from 1843 and is where Padre Fernando de la Vega runs Proyecto SIDA de Cuba (the Cuba AIDS Project) for HIV/AIDS patients.

Museo Lezama Lima

Literature buffs might detour to this museum (Trocadero #162, e/ Crespo y Industria, tel. 07/863-4161, Tues.–Sat. 9 A.M.–5 P.M., Sun. 9 A.M.–1 P.M., entrance CUC2, guide CUC1), four blocks east of Galiano, in the former home of writer José Lezama Lima. The novelist is

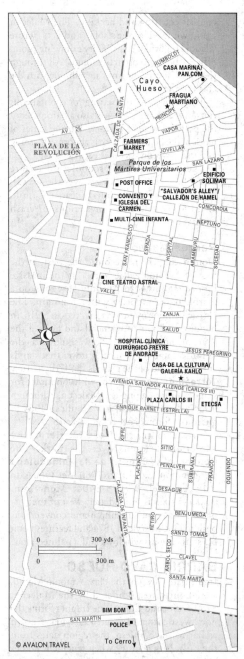

© AVALON TRAVEL

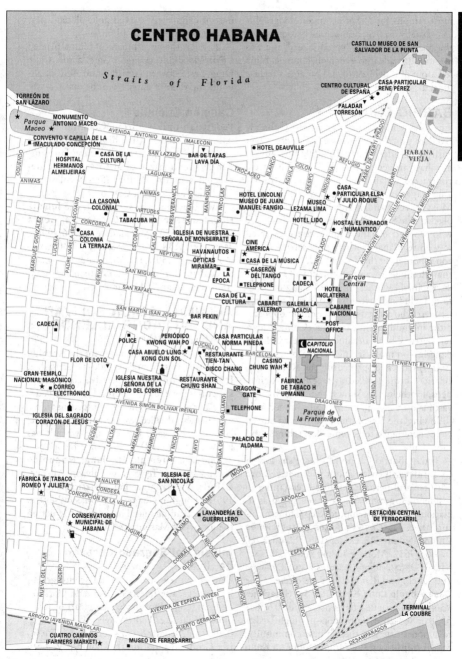

CENTRO HABANA

Straits of Florida

CASTILLO MUSEO DE SAN SALVADOR DE LA PUNTA

TORREÓN DE SAN LÁZARO

Parque Maceo

MONUMENTO ANTONIO MACEO

CENTRO CULTURAL DE ESPAÑA

CASA PARTICULAR RENE PÉREZ

PALADAR TORRESÓN

AVENIDA ANTONIO MACEO (MALECÓN)

CONVENTO Y CAPILLA DE LA IMACULADO CONCEPCIÓN

HOSPITAL HERMANOS ALMEIJEIRAS

CASA DE LA CULTURA

SAN LÁZARO

BAR DE TAPAS LAVA DÍA

HOTEL DEAUVILLE

HABANA VIEJA

ANIMAS

LAGUNAS

TROCADERO

BLANCO

AGUILA

COLÓN

CRESPO

INDUSTRIA

REFUGIO

PASEO DE MARTÍ (PRADO)

MORRO

ANIMAS

LA CASONA COLONIAL

VIRTUDES

TABACUBA HQ

CONCORDIA

HOTEL LINCOLN/ MUSEO DE JUAN MANUEL FANGIO

MUSEO LEZAMA LIMA

CASA PARTICULAR ELSA Y JULIO ROQUE

ZULUETA

AVENIDA DE LAS MISIONES

CASA COLONIA LA TERRAZA

NEPTUNO

IGLESIA DE NUESTRA SEÑORA DE MONSERRATE

HOTEL LIDO

HOSTAL EL PARADOR NUMANTICO

AGRAMONTE

MARQUÉS GONZÁLEZ

LUCENA

PADRE VARELA (BELASCOAÍN)

ESCOBAR

LEALTAD

CAMPANARIO

MANRIQUE

SAN NICOLÁS

PRESEVERANCIA

CINE AMÉRICA

CONSULADO

AGUACATE

GERVASIO

SAN MIGUEL

HAVANAUTOS

ÓPTICAS MIRAMAR

CASA DE LA MÚSICA

CASERÓN DEL TANGO

Parque Central

SAN RAFAEL

LA ÉPOCA

TELEPHONE

CADECA

SAN MARTÍN (SAN JOSÉ)

CASA DE LA CULTURA

CABARET PALERMO

GALERÍA LA ACACIA

HOTEL INGLATERRA

CABARET NACIONAL

BERNAZA

VILLEGAS

CADECA

BAR PEKIN

AMISTAD

POST OFFICE

AVENIDA DE BÉLGICA (MONSERRATE)

POLICE

PERIÓDICO KWONG WAH PO

CUCHILLO

CASA PARTICULAR NORMA PINEDA

CAPITOLIO NACIONAL

(TENIENTE REY)

FLOR DE LOTO

CASA ABUELO LUNG KONG CUN SOL

RESTAURANTE TJIEN-TAN

BARCELONA

CASINO CHUNG WAH

BRASIL

DISCO CHANG

GRAN TEMPLO NACIONAL MASÓNICO

CORREO ELECTRÓNICO

IGLESIA NUESTRA SEÑORA DE LA CARIDAD DEL COBRE

RESTAURANTE CHUNG SHAN

DRAGON GATE

FÁBRICA DE TABACO H UPMANN

AVENIDA SIMÓN BOLÍVAR (REINA)

TELEPHONE

DRAGONES

Parque de la Fraternidad

IGLESIA DEL SAGRADO CORAZÓN DE JESÚS

ESCOBAR

LEALTAD

CAMPANARIO

MANRIQUE

SAN NICOLÁS

RAYO

AVENIDA DE ITALIA (GALIANO)

PALACIO DE ALDAMA

SITIO

IGLESIA DE SAN NICOLÁS

(MONTE)

APONTE SOMERUELOS

CIENFUEGOS

CÁRDENAS

ECONOMÍA

FÁBRICA DE TABACO ROMEO Y JULIETA

PENALVER

CONDESA

CONCEPCIÓN DE LA VALLA

LAVANDERÍA EL GUERRILLERO

ESTACIÓN CENTRAL DE FERROCARRIL

EGIDO

CONSERVATORIO MUNICIPAL DE HABANA

FIGURAS

MÁXIMO

SAN NICOLÁS

GOMEZ

MISIÓN

ESPERANZA

FACTORIA

SUÁREZ

REVILLAGIGEDO

NUEVA DEL PILAR

LINDERO

CORRALES

GLORIA

ALZAMBIQUE

FLORIDA

AGUILA

ARROYO (AVENIDA MANGLAR)

AVENIDA DE ESPAÑA (VIVES)

PUERTO GERRADA

TERMINAL LA COUBRE

CUATRO CAMINOS (FARMERS MARKET)

MUSEO DE FERROCARRIL

DESAMPARADOS

most famous for *Paradiso*, an autobiographical, sexually explicit, homoerotic baroque novel that viewed Cuba as a "paradise lost" and was eventually made into a renowned movie. Lima fell afoul of Fidel Castro and became a recluse until his death in 1975.

BARRIO CHINO

The first Chinese immigrants to Cuba arrived in 1847 as indentured laborers. Over ensuing decades, as many as 150,000 Chinese may have arrived to work the fields. They were contracted to labor for eight years for miserable wages insufficient to buy their return. Most stayed, and many intermarried with blacks. The Sino-Cuban descendants of those who worked off their indenture gravitated to Centro Habana, where they settled in the zones bordering the Zanza Real, the aqueduct that channeled water to the city. They were later joined by other Chinese fleeing persecution, including a wealthy group of California Chinese who arrived with investment opportunities in mind. In time Havana's Chinese quarter, Barrio Chino, became the largest in Latin America—a mini-Beijing in the tropics.

In the decades preceding the Revolution, Barrio Chino evolved as a center of opium dens, brothels, peep shows, and sex clubs. The vast majority of Chinese left Cuba immediately following the Revolution; those who stayed were encouraged to become "less Chinese and more Cuban."

Today, Barrio Chino is a mere shadow of its former self, with about 400 native-born Chinese and perhaps 2,000 descendants still resident. Approximately a dozen social associations (*casinos*) attempt to keep Chinese culture alive. The **Casa de Artes y Tradiciones Chinas** (Salud #313, e/ Gervasio y Escobar, tel. 07/863-9632, Mon.–Fri. 8:30 A.M.–5:30 P.M., Sat. 8:30 A.M.–noon) features a small gallery, and tai chi and dance classes are offered. The **Casa Abuelo Lung Kong Cun Sol** (Dragones #364, e/ Manrique y San Nicolás, tel. 07/862-5388 or 863-2061, daily noon–midnight) exists to support elders in the Chinese community; on the third floor, the **Templo San Fan Kong**

has an exquisitely carved gold-plated altar. Visitors are welcome at all *casinos.*

In 1995, the government of China funded a **Pórtico Chino** (Dragon Gate) across Calle Dragones, between Amistad and Aguila, announcing visitors' entry from the east.

Callejón Cuchillo

Pedestrian-only Callejón Cuchillo (Knife Alley) is lined with Chinese restaurants and glows at night with Chinese lanterns. Ernest Hemingway used to eat at the defunct Restaurante Pacífico (San Nicolás, esq. Cuchillo), as did Fidel Castro.

Two blocks to the southwest, the **Iglesia Nuestra Señora de la Caridad del Cobre** (Manrique #570, esq. Salud, tel. 07/861-0945, Tues.–Fri. 7:30 A.M.–6 P.M., Sat. 7:30 A.M.–noon, Sun. 7:30 A.M.–noon and 4–6 P.M.), erected in 1802, features exquisite statuary, stained glass, and gilt altar.

AVENIDAS SIMÓN BOLÍVAR AND SALVADOR ALLENDE (CARLOS III)

Avenida Simón Bolívar (formerly Avenida Reina) runs west from Parque de la Fraternidad. It is lined with once-impressive colonial-era structures gone to ruin. Beyond Avenida Padre Varela (Belascoain), the street broadens into a wide boulevard called Avenida Salvador Allende, laid out in the early 19th century (when it was known as Carlos III) by Governor Tacón.

The **Gran Templo Nacional Masónico** (Grand Masonic Temple, Av. Salvador Allende, e/ Padre Varela y Lucena) was established in 1951. Though no longer a Freemasons' lodge, it retains a fading mural in the lobby depicting the history of Masonry in Cuba.

Iglesia del Sagrado Corazón de Jesús

One of the few structures not seemingly on its last legs, the Iglesia del Sagrado Corazón de Jesús (Church of the Sacred Heart of Jesus, Simón Bolívar, e/ Padre Varela y Gervasio, tel. 07/862-4979, daily 8 A.M.–noon and 4–7 P.M.) is a Gothic inspiration that could have been transported from medieval England. It was built in 1922 with a beamed ceiling held aloft by great marbled columns. Gargoyles and Christian allegories adorn the exterior, featuring a 77-meter-tall spire topped by a bronze cross.

CUATROS CAMINOS AND CERRO

South of Avenidas Simón Bolívar and Salvador Allende, the down-at-the-heels neighborhoods of southern Centro Habana extend into the *municipalidad* of Cerro. Caution is required when walking these streets.

Several key arterial roads meet at Cuatros Caminos, an all-important junction where the **Mercado Agropecuario Cuatros Caminos** (Four Roads Farmers Market, tel. 07/870-5934, Tues.–Sat. 7 A.M.–6:30 P.M., Sun. 7 A.M.–2 P.M.) takes up an entire block between Máximo Gómez and Cristina (also called Avenida de la México), and Manglar Arroyo and Matadero. This much-dilapidated 19th-century market hall has functioned as such for two centuries and is worth a visit for its bustling ambience and to photograph the live goats, geese, and pig's heads sold here.

Museo de Ferrocarril

On the east side of Cristina, facing the market, is the Museo de Ferrocarril (Railway Museum, tel. 07/879-3546, Mon.–Sat. 9 A.M.–4:30 P.M., Sun. 9 A.M.–12:30 P.M., entrance CUC2, camera CUC5), housed in the former Estación Cristina. You'd have to be a serious rail buff to get a thrill from the exhibits (from model trains to bells, signals, and even telegraph equipment) that tell the history of rail in Cuba. Sitting on rails in its lobby is an 1843 steam locomotive (Cuba's first) called *La Junta*. Three other antique steam trains are displayed, along with various diesel locomotives, albeit without any information whatsoever.

Fábrica de Tabaco Romeo y Julieta

Cigar connoisseurs the world over know the name Romeo y Julieta, a fine cigar brand made at Fábrica de Tabaco Romeo y Julieta (Romeo and Juliet Tobacco Factory, Padre Varela #852, e/ Desagüe y Peñal Verno, tel. 07/878-1058 or 879-3927, closed to the public), five blocks northwest of Cuatro Caminos. The factory was founded in 1875 by Inocencia Álvarez and is today a cigar-rolling school.

One block south is the **Conservatorio Municipal de Habana** (Padre Varela, esq. Carmen), a music conservatory boasting a well-preserved classical facade.

Avenida Máximo Gómez and Calzada de Cerro

Avenida Máximo Gómez (popularly called Monte; the name changes to Calzada de Cerro west of Infanta) snakes southwest from Parque de la Fraternidad and connects Habana Vieja with Cerro. During the 19th century, scores of summer homes in classical style were erected here, each more extravagantly Italianate than the next. It has been described by writer Paul Goldberger as "one of the most remarkable streets in the world: three unbroken kilometers of 19th-century neoclassical villas, with colonnaded arcades making an urban vista of heartbreaking beauty." Heartbreaking is correct. The avenue ascends southward, marching backward into the past like a classical ruin, with once-stunning arcades and houses collapsing behind decaying facades.

One of the most splendid mansions still extant is the **Quinta del Conde de Santovenia** (Calzada de Cerro #1424, e/ Patria y Auditor), erected in 1845 in subdued neoclassical style, with a 1929 neo-Gothic chapel addition. It has served as a home for the elderly (*hogar de ancianos*) for more than a century. Farther west, one block south of Calzada de Cerro, is the tiny **Plaza de Galicia** (Peñon, esq. Santo Tomás). Shaded by venerable ceiba trees and bougainvillea bowers, the square features the diminutive **Iglesia de Peñon,** with a Corinthian frontage and round spire. **Iglesia de San Nicolás,** on San Nicolás one block west of Monte, is another tiny church with a circular bell tower.

Fábrica de Ron Bocoy

The most intriguing site in Cerro is Fábrica de

Ron Bocoy (Máximo Gómez #1417, e/ Patria y Auditor, tel. 07/870-5642, bocoy@tuhv.cha.cyt. cu, Mon.–Fri. 7 A.M.–5 P.M., Sat. 9 A.M.–3 P.M.), a distillery that makes Legendario rums and liquors. Bocoy once manufactured the choicest rum in Cuba, intended solely for Fidel Castro to gift to notable personalities. An example of the special libation (packaged in a bulbous, earthenware bottle and set inside a miniature pirate's treasure chest labeled La Isla del Tesoro, or Treasure Island) is on display in the small upstairs museum, which also boasts an original 19th-century copper distillery. The vaults contain great oak casks stacked in dark recesses. Free tours are offered.

The distillery occupies the former home of the counts of Villanueva. The two-tone pink facade is decorated with four dozen cast-iron swans marching wing to wing, "each standing tall and slim, its long neck bent straight down in mortal combat with an evil serpent climbing up its legs to sink its fangs," wrote James Michener, who chose this building as a setting in his novel *Caribbean*. Hence the building's colloquial nickname, Casa de Culebras (House of Snakes). The swans were a symbol of wealth that the snakes were meant to guard.

Quinta las Delicias

The art nouveau Quinta las Delicias (Av. Santa Catalina, esq. Palatino, tel. 07/867-0205 or 841-1526, Mon.–Fri. 8 A.M.–5 P.M., by appointment only), on Calzada Palatino, a westerly extension of Calzada de Cerro, was built in 1905 by Charles Brun for Rosalia Abreu, a socialite who populated the extensive grounds

Fábrica de Ron Bocoy

© CHRISTOPHER P. BAKER

with almost 200 monkeys—hence the popular name, Finca de los Monos (Villa of Monkeys). The vestibule is graced with a mural by Cuban artist Arturo Mendocal, and by glorious stained glass. It functions today as a youth center.

If you've come this far, you may as well peek at the **Pabellón de los Depósitos del Acueducto de Albear** (Fomento, e/ Chaple y Recreo), two blocks east of Calzada Palatino. This neoclassical reservoir with giant frogs in each corner was designed in 1856 by Francisco de Albear to supply gravity-fed water to the ever-expanding city. It still functions as the modern, albeit much dilapidated, waterworks and supplies one-fifth of Havana's water. Visitors are not allowed inside.

Sights - Vedado and Plaza de la Revolución

The *municipio* of Plaza de la Revolución (pop. 165,000), west of Centro Habana, comprises the leafy residential streets of Vedado and, to the southwest, the modern enclave of Nuevo Vedado and Plaza de la Revolución.

Vedado—the commercial heart of "modern" Havana—has been described as "Havana at its middle-class best." The University of Havana

is here. So are many of the city's prime hotels and restaurants, virtually all its main commercial buildings, and block after block of handsome mansions and apartment houses in art deco, eclectic, Beaux-Arts, and neoclassical styles—luxurious and humble alike lining streets shaded by stately jagüeys dropping their aerial roots to the ground.

MODERN ARCHITECTURAL TREASURES

The turn of the 20th century spawned a desire for modernity. Cuba, a nation seeking to free itself of a parochial past, adopted North American and European influences with remarkable fervor. The arrival of U.S. architects spearheaded an American influence, while Cuba developed its own world-class Cuban School of Architecture, whose graduates showed occasional displays of genuine brilliance. The period 1925–1965 was uniquely inventive. Although no uniquely Cuban architecture evolved, a subtle "Cubanization" transformed styles introduced to the island. Modernist designs with a tropical twist, from streamlined art deco apartment blocks to modernist villas, complemented Havana's astonishing trove of colonial structures.

Art nouveau arrived from Europe around 1905, with Franco-Belgian, Viennese, and Catalan versions in overlapping succession, such as the highly decorative, even whimsical, Palacio Cueto (on the southeast corner of Plaza Vieja), built in 1906 in a style influenced by Barcelona's Gaudí-inspired *modernismo*. The 1920s Beaux-Arts style, influenced by the École de Beaux-Arts in Paris, fused baroque, classical, Renaissance, and neoclassical elements. Corinthian columns, Pompeian frescoes, with a lavish use of symbolic statues (such as those adorning the staircase to the Capitolio Nacional), conveyed a message of Havana's power and grandeur. Purely neo-Renaissance edifices – such as the legendary Hotel Nacional (1930) – also went up in quintessentially Cuban versions of Italian, French, and Spanish styles. Other structures, such as the Palacio Presidencial, completed in 1919, adopted the so-called Eclectic style, which melded revivalist trends to elements of neoclassicism, Renaissance, and Beaux-Arts forms.

Art deco followed and coincided with the heyday of Hollywood movies. Public edifices were adorned with lavish ornamentation inside and out, as with Esteban Rodríguez's masterful Edificio Bacardí (1930), on Monserrate, and the Cine América (1940), on Galiano. This was the great age of transport, and Cuban architects were inspired to infuse their art deco buildings with slick streamlined forms. Decorative panels and geometric motifs were relegated to the interiors of buildings, while exteriors were graced by gradually rounded curves and horizontally banded parapets and verandas representing bodies streaking through air. Centro Habana, in particular, boasts many apartment buildings in this streamlined style, such as the Edificio Solimar (Soledad #205, e/ San Lázaro y Ánimas).

MODERNISMO

Wed to a contemporary avant-garde style led by architects Eugenio Batista, Mario Romañach, and Max Borges Recio, "modernism" came into its glory in the 1950s and continued into the early years of the Revolution. Thousands of magnificent homes in experimental contemporary fashion blossomed in Miramar, Cubanacán, and other western suburbs. Back came stained glass, tile detailing, jalousies, and the inner patio, fused with asymmetrical cubist elements, cantilevered stairs, parabolic structures, and cast shell roofs popularized by Borges. His masterpiece is the Tropicana nightclub, combining complexity with a tropical sensuality defined by graceful curves.

Modernismo reached for the sky. Cuba's pioneering architects changed the Vedado skyline with towering hotels and apartment buildings funded, often, by Mafia money, as with the Hotel Capri (1957), Hotel Riviera (1957), and Habana Libre (1958). Meanwhile, the influence of monumentalist edifices associated with European fascist regimes was assimilated into new public structures, such as the Palace of Justice (now the Palace of the Revolution).

Following the Revolution, leading architects fled the country, and the closure of the School of Architecture in 1965 spelled the end of a glorious era.

The http://havanaarchitecture.org website is a good resource.

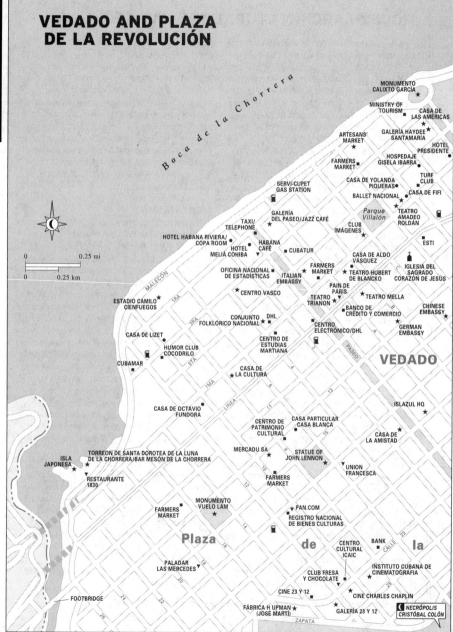

VEDADO AND PLAZA DE LA REVOLUCIÓN

Boca de la Chorrera

MONUMENTO CALIXTO GARCÍA

MINISTRY OF TOURISM

CASA DE LAS AMÉRICAS

ARTESANS' MARKET

GALERÍA HAYDEE SANTAMARÍA

HOTEL PRESIDENTE

HOSPEDAJE GISELA IBARRA

FARMERS MARKET

CASA DE YOLANDA PIQUERAS

TURF CLUB

SERVI-CUPET GAS STATION

BALLET NACIONAL

CASA DE FIFI

Parque Villalón

TEATRO AMADEO ROLDÁN

GALERÍA DEL PASEO/JAZZ CAFÉ

TAXI/ TELEPHONE

CLUB IMÁGENES

HOTEL HABANA RIVIERA/ COPA ROOM

ESTI

HABANA CAFÉ

CUBATUR

HOTEL MELIÁ COHIBA

CASA DE ALDO VÁSQUEZ

IGLESIA DEL SAGRADO CORAZÓN DE JESÚS

OFICINA NACIONAL DE ESTADÍSTICAS

FARMERS MARKET

TEATRO HUBERT DE BLANCKO

ITALIAN EMBASSY

PAIN DE PARIS

TEATRO MELLA

CENTRO VASCO

ESTADIO CAMILO CIENFUEGOS

TEATRO TRIANON

BANCO DE CRÉDITO Y COMERCIO

CHINESE EMBASSY

CONJUNTO FOLKLÓRICO NACIONAL

DHL

GERMAN EMBASSY

CASA DE LIZET

CENTRO ELECTRÓNICO/DHL

HUMOR CLUB COCODRILO

CENTRO DE ESTUDIAS MARTIANA

VEDADO

CUBAMAR

CASA DE LA CULTURA

CASA DE OCTAVIO FUNDORA

ISLAZUL HQ

CENTRO DE PATRIMONIO CULTURAL

CASA PARTICULAR CASA BLANCA

CASA DE LA AMISTAD

ISLA JAPONESA

TORREON DE SANTA DOROTEA DE LA LUNA DE LA CHORRERA/BAR MESÓN DE LA CHORRERA

MERCADU SA

STATUE OF JOHN LENNON

UNION FRANCESCA

RESTAURANTE 1830

FARMERS MARKET

FARMERS MARKET

MONUMENTO VUELO LAM

PAN.COM

REGISTRO NACIONAL DE BIENES CULTURAS

Plaza

de

CENTRO CULTURAL ICAIC

BANK

CALLE

23

la

PALADAR LAS MERCEDES

INSTITUTO CUBANA DE CINEMATOGRAFIA

CLUB FRESA Y CHOCOLATE

FOOTBRIDGE

CINE 23 Y 12

CINE CHARLES CHAPLIN

FÁBRICA H UPMAN (JOSE MARTÍ)

GALERÍA 23 Y 12

NECRÓPOLIS CRISTÓBAL COLÓN

ZAPATA

MALECÓN

1RA

3RA

5TA

7MA

LINEA

11

13

15

17

19

10

12

14

16

18

20

22

24

26

PASEO

A

25

0   0.25 mi

0   0.25 km

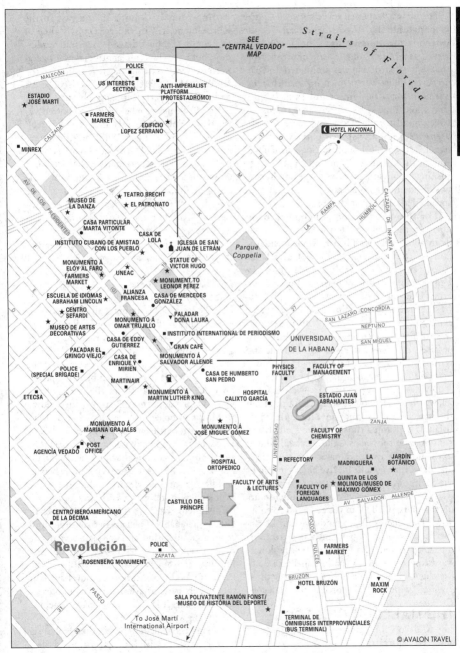

Straits of Florida

SEE "CENTRAL VEDADO" MAP

POLICE

US INTERESTS SECTION

ANTI-IMPERIALIST PLATFORM (PROTESTADRÓMO)

MALECÓN

ESTADIO JOSÉ MARTÍ

FARMERS MARKET

EDIFICIO LOPEZ SERRANO

HOTEL NACIONAL

MINREX

CALZADA

AV. DE LOS PRESIDENTES

MUSEO DE LA DANZA

TEATRO BRECHT

EL PATRONATO

CASA PARTICULAR MARTA VITONTE

CASA DE LOLA

INSTITUTO CUBANO DE AMISTAD CON LOS PUEBLO

IGLESIA DE SAN JUAN DE LETRÁN

Parque Coppelia

STATUE OF VICTOR HUGO

MONUMENTO Á ELOY AL FARO

UNEAC

MONUMENT TO LEONOR PEREZ

FARMERS MARKET

ESCUELA DE IDIOMAS ABRAHAM LINCOLN

ALIANZA FRANCESA

CASA DE MERCEDES GONZÁLEZ

CENTRO SEFARDI

MUSEO DE ARTES DECORATIVAS

MONUMENTO Á OMAR TRUJILLO

PALADAR DOÑA LAURA

INSTITUTO INTERNATIONAL DE PERIODISMO

UNIVERSIDAD DE LA HABANA

PALADAR EL GRINGO VIEJO

CASA DE EDDY GUTIERREZ

CASA DE ENRIQUE Y MIRIEN

GRAN CAFÉ

MONUMENTO Á SALVADOR ALLENDE

PHYSICS FACULTY

FACULTY OF MANAGEMENT

POLICE (SPECIAL BRIGADE)

MARTINAIR

CASA DE HUMBERTO SAN PEDRO

ESTADIO JUAN ABRAHANTES

ETECSA

MONUMENTO Á MARTIN LUTHER KING

HOSPITAL CALIXTO GARCÍA

ZANJA

MONUMENTO Á MARIANA GRAJALES

MONUMENTO Á JOSÉ MIGUEL GÓMEZ

FACULTY OF CHEMISTRY

AGENCIA VEDADO

POST OFFICE

HOSPITAL ORTOPEDICO

REFECTORY

LA MADRIGUERA

JARDÍN BOTÁNICO

QUINTA DE LOS MOLINOS/MUSEO DE MÁXIMO GÓMEX

CENTRO IBEROAMERICANO DE LA DÉCIMA

FACULTY OF ARTS & LECTURES

FACULTY OF FOREIGN LANGUAGES

CASTILLO DEL PRÍNCIPE

AV. SALVADOR ALLENDE

Revolución

POLICE

ZAPATA

ROSENBERG MONUMENT

FARMERS MARKET

BRUZÓN

HOTEL BRUZÓN

MAXIM ROCK

PASEO

SALA POLIVATENTE RAMÓN FONST/ MUSEO DE HISTÓRIA DEL DEPORTE

TERMINAL DE ÓMNIBUSES INTERPROVINCIALES (BUS TERMINAL)

To José Martí International Airport

SAN LAZARO   CONCORDIA

NEPTUNO

SAN MIGUEL

LA RAMPA

HUMBOLT

CALZADA DE INFANTA

© AVALON TRAVEL

Formerly a vast open space between Centro Habana and the Río Almendares, Vedado (which means "forest reserve" or "forbidden") served as a buffer zone in case of attack from the west; construction was prohibited. In 1859, however, plans were drawn up for urban expansion. Strict building regulations defined that there should be 15 feet of gardens between building and street, and more in wider *avenidas*. Regularly spaced parks were mandated. The conclusion of the Spanish-Cuban-American War in 1898 brought U.S. money rushing in. Civic structures, large hotels, casinos, department stores, and lavish restaurants sprouted alongside nightclubs.

The sprawling region is hemmed to the north by the Malecón, to the east by Calzada de Infanta, to the west by the Río Almendares, and to the southeast by the Calzada de Ayestaran and Avenida de la Independencia. Vedado follows a grid pattern laid out in quadrants. Odd-numbered streets (*calles*) run east–west, parallel to the shore. Even-numbered *calles* run perpendicular. (To confuse things, west of Paseo, *calles* are even-numbered; east of Paseo, *calles* run from A to P.) The basic grid is overlaid by a larger grid of broad boulevards (*avenidas*) an average of six blocks apart.

Dividing the quadrants east–west is Calle 23, which rises (colloquially) as La Rampa from the Malecón at its junction with Calzada de Infanta. La Rampa runs uphill to Calle L and continues on the flat as Calle 23. Paralleling it to the north is a second major east–west thoroughfare, Línea (Calle 9), five blocks inland of the Malecón, which it meets to the northeast.

Four major roadways divide the quadrants north–south: Calle L to the east, and Avenida de los Presidentes, Paseo, and Avenida 12 farther west. Vedado slopes gently upward from the shore to Calle 23 and then gently downward toward Nuevo Vedado and Plaza de la Revolución, connected to Vedado by the three *avenidas,* which extend north to the Malecón.

THE MALECÓN (VEDADO)

The Malecón runs along the bulging, wave-battered shorefront of northern Vedado, curling from La Rampa in the east to the Río Almendares in the west, a distance of three miles. The sidewalk is pitted underfoot, but a stroll its full length makes for good exercise while taking in such sights as the **Monumento Calixto García** (Malecón y Av. de los Presidentes), featuring a bronze figure of the 19th-century rebel general on horseback; the **Hotel Habana Riviera** (Malecón y Paseo), opened by the Mafia in 1958 and recently remodeled to show off its spectacular modernist lobby; and the **Torreón de Santa Dorotea de la Luna de la Chorrera** (Malecón y Calle 20), a small fortress built in 1762 to guard the mouth of the Río Almendares. Immediately beyond "La Chorrera," the Restaurante 1830 features a Gaudí-esque garden that includes a dramatic cupola and a tiny island—**Isla Japonesa**—in Japanese style.

🄲 Hotel Nacional

The landmark Hotel Nacional (Calles O y 21, tel. 07/836-3564) is dramatically perched atop a small cliff at the junction of La Rampa and the Malecón. Now a national monument, this grande dame hotel was designed by the same architects who designed The Breakers in Palm Beach, which it closely resembles. It opened on December 30, 1930, in the midst of the Great Depression. In 1933, army officers loyal to Machado holed up here following Batista's coup; a gun battle ensued. More famously, in December 1946 Lucky Luciano called a mobster summit (ostensibly they were here to honor Frank Sinatra) to discuss carving up Havana.

The elaborately detailed, Spanish-style neoclassical hotel was greatly in need of refurbishment when, in 1955, mobster Meyer Lansky persuaded General Batista to let him build a grand casino and convert some of the rooms to luxurious suites for wealthy gamblers. Luminaries from Winston Churchill and the Prince of Wales to Marlon Brando have laid their heads here, as attested by the photos in the lobby bar. It is still the preferred hotel for visiting bigwigs.

Beyond the Palladian porch, the vestibule is lavishly adorned with Mudejar patterned tiles.

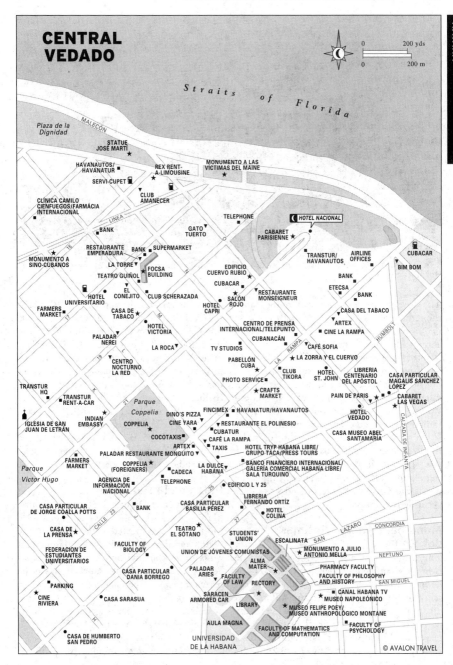

CENTRAL VEDADO

0   200 yds
0   200 m

Straits of Florida

Plaza de la Dignidad

MALECÓN

STATUE JOSÉ MARTÍ ★

HAVANAUTOS/ HAVANATUR ■   REX RENT- A-LIMOUSINE

MONUMENTO A LAS VÍCTIMAS DEL MAINE ★

SERVI-CUPET 🏛

CLUB AMANECER

CLÍNICA CAMILO CIENFUEGOS/FARMÁCIA INTERNACIONAL ■

LINEA

TELEPHONE

HOTEL NACIONAL

BANK ■

GATO TUERTO ▼

CABARET PARISIENNE ★

MONUMENTO A SINO-CUBANOS ★

RESTAURANTE EMPERADURA ★   BANK ■   SUPERMARKET

LA TORRE ▼

TEATRO GUIÑOL ★   FOCSA BUILDING

EDIFICIO CUERVO RUBIO ■

TRANSTUR/ HAVANAUTOS ▼   AIRLINE OFFICES

CUBACAR ■

BIM BOM ■

BANK ■

CUBACAR ■

RESTAURANTE MONSEIGNEUR ▼

ETECSA ■

BANK ■

EL CONEJITO ■   CLUB SCHERAZADA ■

HOTEL UNIVERSITARIO ■

SALÓN ROJO ■

HOTEL CAPRI ■

CASA DEL TABACO ■

FARMERS MARKET ■

CASA DE TABACO ★

CENTRO DE PRENSA INTERNACIONAL/TELEPUNTO ■

ARTEX ■

CINE LA RAMPA ■

HOTEL VICTORIA ■

PALADAR NEREI ■

CUBANACÁN ■

RAMPA

LA ROCA ▼

TV STUDIOS ■

CAFÉ SOFIA ▼

HUMBOLT

CENTRO NOCTURNO LA RED ■

PABELLÓN CUBA ■

LA ZORRA Y EL CUERVO ▼

PHOTO SERVICE ■

CLUB TIKORA ■

HOTEL ST. JOHN ■

LIBRERIA CENTENARIO DEL APÓSTOL ■

CASA PARTICULAR MAGALIS SÁNCHEZ LÓPEZ ■

TRANSTUR HQ ■

TRANSTUR RENT-A-CAR ■

CRAFTS MARKET ★

PAIN DE PARIS ▼ ★

CABARET LAS VEGAS ★

IGLESIA DE SAN JUAN DE LETRÁN ✝

INDIAN EMBASSY ★

Parque Coppelia

FINCIMEX ■   HAVANATUR/HAVANAUTOS ■

HOTEL VEDADO ■

CALZADA DE INFANTA

DINO'S PIZZA ▼

COPPELIA ★

CINE YARA ■

RESTAURANTE EL POLINESIO ▼

CASA MUSEO ABEL SANTAMARÍA ■

COCOTAXIS ■

CUBATUR ▼

ARTEX ■

CAFÉ LA RAMPA ▼

PALADAR RESTAURANTE MONGUITO ▼

TAXIS ■

HOTEL TRYP HABANA LIBRE/ GRUPO TACA/PRESS TOURS ■

Parque Victor Hugo

FARMERS MARKET ■

COPPELIA (FOREIGNERS) ★

CADECA ■

LA DULCE HABANA ▼

BANCO FINANCIERO INTERNACIONAL/ GALERÍA COMERCIAL HABANA LIBRE/ SALA TURQUINO ■

AGENCIA DE INFORMACIÓN NACIONAL ■

TELEPHONE ■

EDIFICIO L Y 25 ●

CASA PARTICULAR DE JORGE COALLA POTTS ■

CALLE 23

BANK ■

CASA PARTICULAR BASILIA PÉREZ ■

LIBRERIA FERNANDO ORTÍZ ■

HOTEL COLINA ■

CASA DE LA PRENSA ★

TEATRO EL SÓTANO ★

STUDENTS' UNION ■

LAZARO

CONCORDIA

FEDERACIÓN DE ESTUDIANTES UNIVERSITARIOS ■

FACULTY OF BIOLOGY ■

UNIÓN DE JÓVENES COMUNISTAS ■

ESCALINATA   SAN

MONUMENTO A JULIO ANTONIO MELLA ★

NEPTUNO

ALMA MATER ★

PHARMACY FACULTY ■

CASA PARTICULAR DANIA BORREGO ●

PALADAR ARIES ▼

FACULTY OF LAW ■

RECTORY ★

FACULTY OF PHILOSOPHY AND HISTORY ■

SAN MIGUEL

PARKING ■

SARACEN ARMORED CAR ★

LIBRARY ■

CANAL HABANA TV ■

MUSEO NAPOLEÓNICO ■

CINE RIVIERA ★

CASA SARASUA ●

MUSEO FELIPE POEY/ MUSEO ANTHROPOLÓGICO MONTANE ★

AULA MAGNA ■

FACULTY OF MATHEMATICS AND COMPUTATION ■

FACULTY OF PSYCHOLOGY ■

CASA DE HUMBERTO SAN PEDRO ●

UNIVERSIDAD DE LA HABANA

© AVALON TRAVEL

© CHRISTOPHER P. BAKER

Hotel Nacional

The sweeping palm-shaded lawns to the rear—the terrace bar is a de rigueur spot to enjoy a *mojito* and cigar—slope toward the Malecón, above which sits a battery of cannons from the Wars of Independence. The cliff is riddled with defensive tunnels built since the 1970s.

The **Edificio Cuervo Rubio** (Calles 21 y O), cater-corner to the hotel entrance, is an art deco stunner. Nip inside the lobby, which has an Italian marble statue, and look up through the "tube" of the spiral staircase augering up seven flights. The modernist **Hotel Capri** (Calles 21 y N) was built in 1958 by the American gangster Santo Trafficante and was a setting in the movie *The Godfather*. At last visit it was a shell awaiting restoration.

Monumento a las Víctimas del Maine

The Monumento a las Víctimas del Maine (Maine Monument, Malecón y Calle 17) was dedicated by the republican Cuban government to the memory of the 260 sailors who died when the USS *Maine* exploded in Havana harbor in 1898, creating a prelude for U.S. intervention in the Wars of Independence. Two rusting cannons tethered by chains from the ship's anchor are laid out beneath 12-meter-tall Corinthian columns dedicated in 1925 and originally topped by an eagle with wings spread wide. Immediately after the failed Bay of Pigs invasion in 1960, a mob toppled the eagle from its roost and broke its wings—its body is now in the Museum of the City of Havana, while the head hangs on the wall of the cafeteria in the U.S. Interests Section. The Castro government later dedicated a plaque that reads, "To the victims of the *Maine*, who were sacrificed by imperialist voracity in its eagerness to seize the island of Cuba."

Plaza de la Dignidad

The Plaza de la Dignidad (Plaza of Dignity, Malecón y Calzada), west of the Maine Monument, was created at the height of the Elián González fiasco in 1999–2000 from what was a grassy knoll in front of the U.S. Interests Section. A **statue of José Martí** stands at the plaza's eastern end, bearing in one arm a bronze likeness of young Elián while with the other he points an accusatory finger at the Interests Section—*habaneros* joke that Martí is trying to tell them, "Your visas are that way!"

The Cuban government also pumped

A WALK ALONG VEDADO'S CALLE 17

Allow one hour for this walk along one of the most astonishing streets in the city.

From the Monumento del Maine, follow Calle 17 west toward the landmark 35-story **Focsa** (Calle 17 e/ M y N), a V-shaped apartment building built 1954-1956 as one of the largest reinforced concrete structures in the world. Following the Revolution it was used to house East European and Soviet personnel.

Continue west two blocks to Calle J. Turn left and after one block turn right onto Calle 19 to view the Gothic **Iglesia San Juan de Letrán,** which dates from the 1880s and has fine stained-glass windows. One block west of the church is **Parque Victor Hugo** (Calle 19, e/ I y H). Circle the park counterclockwise, passing a monument to the 19th-century French novelist (author of Les Miserables) on the northeast corner. At the corner of Calles 19 and H is a memorial to Leonor Pérez Cabrera, mother of José Martí, with a letter to his dearly beloved mamá inscribed in metal. The southeast corner (Calle 21 y I) bears a monument to Bobby Sands and nine other IRA terrorists ("martyrs" says the plaque) who died on hunger strike in Crumlin Road jail, Northern Ireland, in 1981.

Return to Calle 17 and continue westward, passing the **Instituto Cubano de Amistad con los Pueblos** (Cuban Institute for People's Friendship, Calle 17 #301, e/ H y I), occupying a palatial Beaux-Arts villa. One block west, call in at the equally magnificent mansion on the southwest corner of Calle H: The Casa de Juan Gelats, a spectacular exemplar of the Beaux-Arts style, was built in 1920 and today houses the **Unión Nacional de Escritores y Artistas de Cuba** (National Union of Cuban Writers and Artists, UNEAC, Calle 17 #351, esq. H, tel. 07/832-4551, www.uneac.co.cu), which hosts cultural events and is open to the public.

Cross Avenida de los Presidentes and detour 20 meters uphill to the **Escuela de Idiomas Abraham Lincoln** (Presidentes, e/ 17 y 19) to admire a magnificent bronze statue of the former U.S. president in the front garden.

Venerable jagüey trees provide shade as you continue west along Calle 17 two blocks

to the **Museo de Artes Decorativas** (Museum of Decorative Arts, Calle 17 #502, e/ D y E, tel. 07/830-9848, Tues.-Sat. 11 A.M.-7 P.M., entrance CUC3 with guide, cameras CUC5, videos CUC10), housed in the former mansion of a Cuban countess. It brims with a lavish collection of furniture, paintings, textiles, and chinoiserie from the 18th and 19th centuries. Upstairs, a boudoir is decorated in Asian style, its furniture inlaid with mother-of-pearl.

At Calle C, turn right and head downhill one block to Calle 15. Turn left and visit the **Galería Marianao** (Calle 15 #607, e/ B y C, tel. 07/838-2702, Tues.-Sat. 10 A.M.-5 P.M.), containing the 6,000-piece Art Collection of New America.

Return to Calle 17 and continue west four blocks to Paseo. Cross this wide boulevard. On the west side, on the left, is the **Casa de la Amistad** (Paseo #406, e/ 17 y 19, tel. 07/830-3114), an Italian Renaissance mansion – Casa de Juan Pedro Baró – built in 1926 with a surfeit of Carrara marble. It's no longer open to the public.

Continue two blocks west along Calle 17 to Calle 6 and **Parque Lennon.** Following John Lennon's death in 1980, a gathering of Havana bohemia took place at this small quiet park. In 2000, on the 20th anniversary of his death, a life-size bronze statue was unveiled in the presence of Fidel (who had previously banned Beatles music). Lennon, who is dressed in open-neck shirt, sits on a bench, his head slightly tilted, right leg resting on his left knee, with his arm draped casually over the back of the dark-green cast-iron bench, and plenty of room for anyone who wants to join him. The sculpture is by Cuban artist José Villa, who inscribed the words "People say I'm a dreamer, but I'm not the only one," at Lennon's feet. By night, a spotlight denies him sleep. A custodio is there 24/7; he takes care of Lennon's spectacles.

One block east, turn north one block to **Parque de Lam** (Calles 14 y 15), studded by a huge bronze statue by Alberto Lescay Merencio representing a human as a bird in flight – a universal element in the works of Cuban painter Wilfredo Lam.

US$2 million into constructing the **Tribuna Abierta Anti-Imperialista** (José Martí Anti-Imperialist Platform)—called jokingly by locals the *"protestadromo"*—at the west end of the plaza to accommodate the masses bused in to taunt Uncle Sam. The concrete supports bear plaques inscribed with the names of Communist and revolutionary heroes, plus those of prominent North Americans—from Benjamin Spock to Malcolm X—at the fore of the fight for social reforms.

At the western end of the plaza is the **U.S. Interests Section** (formerly the U.S. Embassy), where U.S. diplomats and CIA agents serve Uncle Sam's whims behind a veil of mirrored-glass windows. A forest of 73 huge flagstaffs was erected in front of the building in 2007 to block the ticker-tape anti-Castroite propaganda that the Bush administration churlishly initiated (each black flag represents one of the Cubans killed in a bombing of a Cubana airliner in 1976 by Cuban-American terrorists; the main perpetrator, Louís Posada Carriles, currently lives as a free man in the United States). President Obama sensibly ended the ticker.

One block south of the plaza, the H-shaped **Edificio López Serrano** (Calle L e/ 11 y 13) *rascacielo* (skyscraper) is one of the city's most astonishing art deco apartment buildings. Built in 1932, it resembles a truncated Empire State Building. Pop inside to admire the deteriorated lobby of Moroccan red marble and the nickel-silver relief panel of *Time*.

LA RAMPA (CALLE 23)

Calle 23 rises from the Malecón to Calle L and climbs steadily past the major airline offices, nightclubs, cinemas, travel agencies, TV studios, and art deco apartment buildings mingling with high-rise office buildings. La Rampa (The Ramp) was the setting of *Three Trapped Tigers*, Guillermo Cabrera Infante's famous novel about swinging 1950s Havana, for it was here that the ritziest hotels, casinos, and nightclubs were concentrated in the days before the Revolution. Multicolored granite tiles created by Wilfredo Lam, René Portocarrero,

and other leading artists are laid at intervals in the sidewalks.

Parque Coppelia

At the top of La Rampa is the Parque Coppelia (Calle 23 y L, Tues.–Sun. 10 A.M.–9:30 P.M.), the name of a park in Havana, of the flying saucer–like structure at its heart, and of the brand of excellent ice cream served here. In 1966, the government built this lush park with a parlor in the middle as the biggest ice creamery in the world, serving up to an estimated 30,000 customers a day. Cuba's rich diversity can be observed standing in line at Coppelia on a sultry Havana afternoon.

The strange concrete structure, suspended on spidery legs and looming over the park, shelters a marble-topped bar where Cubans sit atop bar stools slurping ice cream from stainless steel bowls. A series of circular rooms lie overhead like a four-leaf clover, offering views over open-air sections where *helados* (ice cream) is enjoyed beneath the dappled shade of lush jagüey trees. Each section has its own *cola* (line), proportional in length to the strength of the sun. Even on temperate days, the *colas* snake out of the park like lethargic serpents and onto nearby streets. Waitresses serve customers at communal tables made of local marble.

Coppelia was featured in Tomás Gutiérrez Alea's trenchant classic movie, *Fresa y Chocolate,* based on Senel Paz's short story, "The Woods, the Wolf, and the New Man." The movie is named for the scene at Coppelia where Diego, a gay man, orders strawberry ice cream, much to the consternation of David, a loyal *fidelista*: "Although there was chocolate that day, he had ordered strawberry. Perverse." After the movie's success, Cuban males, concerned with their macho image, avoided ordering strawberry.

Hotel Habana Libre

The 416-foot-tall Hotel Habana Libre (Free Havana Hotel, Calle L, e/ 23 y 25) was once *the* place to be after opening as the Havana Hilton in April 1958. Castro even had his headquarters here briefly in 1959. For years the hotel teemed with shady foreigners—many of them, reported

National Geographic, "not strictly tourists" and all "watched by secret police agents from the 'ministry,' meaning MININT, the Ministry of the Interior." The hotel is fronted by a spectacular contemporary mural—*Carro de la Revolución* (the Revolutionary Car)—by ceramist Amelia Peláez, made of 525 pieces in the style of Picasso. The modernist lobby contains many fine contemporary art pieces, including a mosaic mural by René Portocarrero.

Casa Museo Abel Santamaría

Of interest primarily to students of Cuba's revolutionary history, this museum (Calle 25 #164, e/ Infanta y O, tel. 07/835-0891, Mon.–Fri. 9 A.M.–5 P.M., Sat. 10 A.M.–1 P.M., free) occupies a simple two-room, sixth-floor apartment (#603) where Fidel Castro's revolutionary movement, the M-26-7, had its secret headquarters in the former home of the eponymous martyr. Abel Santamaría was brutally tortured and murdered following the attack on the Moncada barracks in 1953. Original furnishings include Fidel's work desk.

UNIVERSIDAD DE LA HABANA AND VICINITY

The Universidad de la Habana (University of Havana, Calle L y San Lázaro, tel. 07/878-3231, www.uh.cu, Mon.–Fri. 8 A.M.–6 P.M.) was founded by Dominican friars in 1728 and was originally situated on Calle Obispo in Habana Vieja. During the 20th century, the Federación de Estudiantes Universitarios (University Students' Federation) was an extremely influential group amid the jungle of Cuban politics, and the university was an autonomous "sacred hill" that neither the police nor the army could enter—although gangsters and renegade politicians roamed the campus. (The student federation is in a beautiful Beaux-Arts mansion at the corner of Calles 27 and K.) Visitors are allowed to stroll the grounds, although, ostensibly, you need authorization to take photos (tel. 07/832-9844). The campus is off-limits on weekends, and the campus and museums are closed July–August.

From Calle L, the university is entered via an immense, 50-meter-wide stone staircase: the 88-step **Escalinata** (staircase). A patinated bronze **statue of the Alma Mater** cast by Czech sculptor Mario Korbel in 1919 sits atop the staircase. The twice-life-size statue of a woman is seated in a bronze chair with six classical bas-reliefs representing various disciplines taught at the university. She is dressed in a long-sleeve tunic and extends her bare arms, beckoning all those who desire knowledge.

The staircase is topped by a columned portico beyond which lies the peaceful **Plaza Ignacio Agramonte** surrounded by classical buildings. (The campus was loosely modeled after New York's Columbia University.) A **Saracen armored car** in the quadrant was captured in 1958 by students in the fight against Batista. The **Aula Magna** (Great Hall; special events only) features a marble urn containing the ashes of Félix Varela, plus a magnificent mural by Armando Menocal.

The **Monumento a Julio Antonio Mella,** across Calle L at the base of the Escalinata, contains the ashes of Mella, founder of the University Students' Federation and, later, of the Cuban Communist Party.

Museo de Ciencias Naturales Felipe Poey

The Escuela de Ciencias (School of Sciences), on the south side of the quadrant, contains the Museo de Ciencias Naturales Felipe Poey (Felipe Poey Museum of Natural Sciences, tel. 07/877-4221, Mon.–Fri. 9 A.M.–noon and 1–3 P.M., free, no photos allowed), displaying endemic species from alligators to sharks, stuffed or pickled for posterity. The museum dates from 1842 and is named for its French-Cuban founder. Poey (1799–1891) was versed in every field of the sciences and founded the Academy of Medical Sciences, the Anthropological Society of Cuba, and a half dozen other societies.

The **Museo Antropológico Montane** (Montane Anthropology Museum, tel. 07/879-3488, Mon.–Fri. 9 A.M.–noon and 1–3 P.M.), on the second floor of the Escuela de Ciencias (Sciences School), displays pre-Columbian artifacts.

A WALK ALONG AVENIDA DE LOS PRESIDENTES

Avenida de los Presidentes (Calle G), with wide, grassy, tree-lined pedestrian medians, runs perpendicular to Calle 23 and climbs from the Malecón toward Plaza de la Revolución. The avenue is named for the statues of Cuban and Latin American presidents that grace its length. (The busts of Tomás Estrada Palma and José Miguel Gómez, the first and second presidents of the Cuban republic, were toppled following the Revolution, as they were accused of being "puppets" of the U.S. government.)

First, admire the bas-reliefs that adorn the **Monumento Calixto García** at the Malecón. One block south, on your right, is the **Casa de las Américas** (Presidentes, esq. 3ra, tel. 07/832-2706, fax 07/834-4554, www.casa.cult.cu, Mon.-Fri. 8 A.M.-4:45 P.M.), a cultural center formed in 1959 to study and promote the cultures of Latin America and the Caribbean. Housed in an astonishing, cathedral-like art deco building, the center contains the **Galería Latinamericano** art gallery (Mon.-Thurs. 10 A.M.-5 P.M. and Fri. 10 A.M.-4 P.M.) and hosts concerts and cultural programs. Fifty meters south along Presidentes you'll pass the Casa's **Galería Haydee Santamaría** (e/ 5ta and G; closed for repair in 2009).

At 5ta you'll pass the **Hotel Presidente,** an art deco high-rise dating from 1927. Across Presidentes, on the east side, is the headquarters of **MINREX** (Ministerio de Relaciones Exteriores), the Foreign Relations Ministry, taking up two blocks including a beautiful neo-baroque building on the north side of Calzada (Calle 7ma).

At Calzada, detour west along 5ta for four blocks to **Parque Villalón** (5ta y D). On its southeast side is the Romanesque **Teatro Amadeo Roldán** (tel. 07/832-1168), restored to grandeur as a concert hall. Next door is the headquarters of the **Ballet Nacional de Cuba** (Calzada #510 e/ D y E, Vedado, tel. 07/835-2952, www.balletcuba.cu). The facility is closed to visitors, but sometimes you can spot the dancers practicing.

Turn north onto Calle D and walk one block to Línea. On the far side, peek into the 19th-century **Iglesia del Sagrado Corazón de Jesús** (Línea, e/ C y D, tel. 07/832-6807), Vedado's parish church, colloquially called Parroquia del Vedado. Exiting, head east one block along Línea to Presidentes. On the south side of Línea note the bronze **statue of Alejandro Rodríguez y Velasco** (Presidentes y Línea), a brigadier general in the Cuban Wars of Independence, atop a granite pedestal guarded by a bronze figure of Perseus.

Cross Presidentes to view the **Museo de la Danza** (Calle Línea #365, esq. Presidentes, tel. 07/831-2198, musdanza@cubarte.cult. cu, Tues.-Sat. 11 A.M.-6:30 P.M., CUC2, guide

Museo Napoleónico

Who would imagine that so much of Napoleon Bonaparte's personal memorabilia would end up in Cuba? But it has, housed in the Museo Napoleónico (Napoleonic Museum, San Miguel #1159, e/ Ronda y Masón, tel. 07/879-1460, musnap@cubarte.cult.cu, Tues.–Sat. 9 A.M.–4:30 P.M., Sun. A.M.–noon, entrance CUC3, guide CUC2) in a Florentine Renaissance mansion on the south side of the university. The collection (7,000 pieces) was the private work of Orestes Ferrara, one-time Cuban ambassador to France. Ferrara brought back from Europe such precious items as the French emperor's death mask, his toothbrush, and the pistols Napoleon used at the Battle of Borodino. Other items were seized from Julio Lobo, the former National Bank president, when he left Cuba for exile. The museum—housed in Ferrara's former three-story home (Ferrara was also forced out by the Revolution)—is replete with portraits of the military genius. The museum was closed for restoration at last visit.

CUC1), in a restored mansion on the southeast corner of the junction. The museum has four salons dedicated to Russian ballet, modern dance, the National Ballet of Cuba, and other themes. Exhibits include wardrobes, recordings, manuscripts, and photographs relating to the history of dance.

From here, walk south along the central median. Ascending the avenue, you'll pass statues to Ecuadorian president Eloy Alfaro (e/ 15 y 17), Mexican president Benito Juárez (e/ 17 y 19), Venezuelan Simón Bolívar (e/ 19 y 21), Panamanian strongman president Omar Torrijos (e/ 19 y 21), and Chilean president Salvador Allende (e/ 21 y 23).

Cross Calle 23 and walk west one block to Calle F, where on the southwest corner of the junction the **Monumento a Martin Luther King** is a marble and bronze tableaux of the Afro-American civil rights leader.

Return to Presidentes and continue south (the park on the southeast corner of Calle 23 is colloquially named **Parque de los Roqueros** for the goths and *roqueros* – "rockers" – who gather at night in black leather, black eyeliner, and pink-tinted hair). The tree-shaded boulevard climbs two blocks to the **Monumento a José Miguel Gómez** (Calle 29), designed by Italian sculptor Giovanni Nicolini and erected in 1936 in classical style to honor the former Republican president (1909-1913). Beyond, the road drops through a canyon lined with giant jagüey trees, which form a glade over the road. Hidden from sight on the bluff to the west is the **Castillo del Príncipe,** built between 1767 and 1779 following the English invasion. The castle is off-limits as it is now a military zone and houses a prison.

Arriving at the junction with Avenida Salvador Allende, Zapata, and Avenida Rancho Boyeros, turn left onto Salvador Allende. After 100 meters, on the north side of the road, you'll arrive at the once-graceful **Quinta de los Molinos** (e/ Infanta y Luaces), reached via a decrepit cobbled, gladed drive. The mansion, built between 1837 and 1840, originated as a summer palace for the captains-general and in 1899 was granted as the private residence of General Máximo Gómez, the Dominican-born commander-in-chief of the liberation army. It now houses the motley **Museo de Máximo Gómez** (tel. 07/879-8850; closed for restoration at last visit).

The *quinta* grounds now form the **Jardín Botánico** (Botanical Gardens, Tues.–Sun. 7 A.M.-7 P.M.). Following the Revolution, the once exquisite pleasure gardens of the governor's summer palace were transferred to the University of Havana and are now an overgrown mess littered with tumbledown statues, fountains, and grottoes with giant jagüeys and other trees twining around them, many with voodoo dolls and other *santería* offerings stuffed in their interstices.

◖ NECRÓPOLIS CRISTÓBAL COLÓN

Described as "an exercise in pious excesses," the Necrópolis Cristóbal Colón (Columbus Cemetery, Zapata, esq. 12, tel. 07/830-4517, daily 8 A.M.–5 P.M., entrance CUC5 includes guide and right to photograph) covers 56 hectares and contains more than 500 major mausoleums, chapels, vaults, tombs, and galleries (in addition to countless gravestones) embellished with angels, griffins, cherubs, and other flamboyant ornamentation. You'll even find Greco-Roman temples in miniature, an Egyptian pyramid, medieval castles, plus baroque, Romantic, Renaissance, art deco, and art nouveau art by a pantheon of Cuba's leading sculptors and artists. The triple-arched entrance gate, inspired by the Triumphal Arch in Rome, has marble reliefs depicting the crucifixion and Lazarus rising from the grave and is topped by a marble coronation stone representing the theological virtues: Faith, Hope, and Charity.

Today a national monument, the cemetery

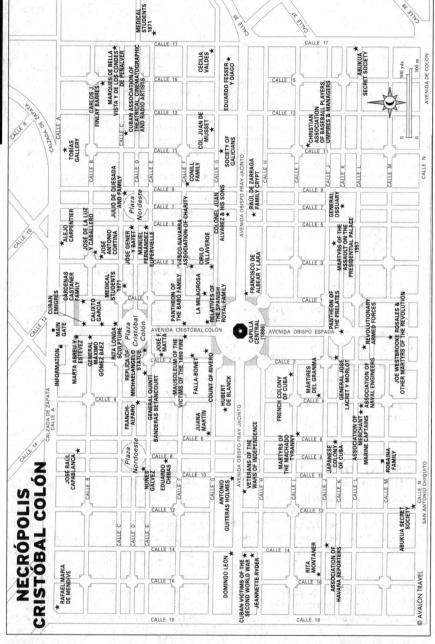

NECRÓPOLIS CRISTÓBAL COLÓN

RAFAEL MARIA DE MENDIVE

JOSÉ RAÚL CAPABLANCA

NÚÑEZ GÁLVEZ

EDUARDO CHIBÁS

ANTONIO GUITERAS HOLMES

DOMINGO LEÓN

CUBAN VICTIMS OF THE SECOND WORLD WAR

JEANNETTE RYDER

RITA MONTANER

ASSOCIATION OF HAVANA REPORTERS

ABUKUA SECRET SOCIETY

CALLE 8 y ZAPATA
CALZADA DE ZAPATA
CALLE 10
CALLE 12
CALLE 14
INFORMATION
MAIN GATE
CUBAN EMIGRÉS
CÁRDENAS CASTAÑER FAMILY
CALIXTO GARCÍA
MEDICAL STUDENTS 1871
MARTA ABREU Y ESTÉVEZ
GENERAL MÁXIMO GÓMEZ BÁEZ
RITA LONGA SCULPTURE
REPLICA OF MICHELANGELO STATUE
JOSÉ F. MATTA
FRANCHI-ALFARO
GENERAL QUINT BANDERAS BETANCOURT
JUANA MARTÍN
FALLA-BONET
COUNT OF RIVERO
MAUSOLEUM OF THE VICTIMS OF THE 1890 FIRE
HUBERT DE BLANCK
VETERANS OF THE WARS OF INDEPENDENCE
MARTYRS OF THE MACHADO TYRANNY
JAPANESE COLONY OF CUBA
ASSOCIATION OF MERCHANT MARINE CAPTAINS
FRENCH COLONY OF CUBA
ROBAINA FAMILY

Plaza Nordeste
Plaza Cristóbal Colón
Plaza Nordeste

AVENIDA CRISTÓBAL COLÓN
AVENIDA OBISPO ESPADA
AVENIDA OBISPO FRAY JACINTO
AVENIDA OBISPO FRAY JACINTO

ALEJO CARPENTIER
JOSÉ Y CABALLERO
JOSÉ ANTONIO CORTINA
JOSÉ GENER Y BATET
MANUEL FERNÁNDEZ SUPERVIELLE
PANTHEON OF THE BARÓ FAMILY
LA MILAGROSA
RELATIVES OF THE SPANISH ROYAL FAMILY
VASCO-NAVARRA ASSOCIATION OF CHARITY
CIRILO VILLAVERDE
FRANCISCO DE ALBEAR Y LARA

CAPILLA CENTRAL (1886)

TOBIAS GALLERY
CARLOS J. FINLAY BARRES
MARQUÉS DE BELLA VISTA Y DE LOS CONDES DE PEÑALVER
CUBAN ASSOCIATION OF THEATRICAL, CINEMATOGRAPHIC AND RADIO ARTISTS
MEDICAL STUDENTS 1871
CECILIA VALDÉS
EDUARDO FESSER Y DIAGO
COL. JUAN DE MUSSET
CONILL FAMILY
SOCIETY OF GALICIANS
JULIO DE QUESADA AND FAMILY
COLONEL JUAN ÁLVAREZ & HIS SONS
RAÚL DE ZÁRRAGA FAMILY CRYPT
MARTYRS OF THE ASSAULT ON THE PRESIDENTIAL PALACE 1957
PANTHEON OF THE PRELATES
REVOLUTIONARY ARMED FORCES
MÁRTIRES DEL GRANMA
GENERAL JOSÉ LACRET Y MORLOT
ASSOCIATION OF NAVAL ENGINEERS
JOE WESTBROOKE ROSALES & OTHER MARTYRS OF THE REVOLUTION
GENERAL OSSUARY
CHRISTIAN ASSOCIATION OF BASEBALL PLAYERS, UMPIRES & MANAGERS
ABUKUA SECRET SOCIETY

AVENIDA DE COLÓN
CALLE 17
CALLE 15
CALLE 13
CALLE 11
CALLE 9
CALLE 7
CALLE 5
CALLE 3
CALLE 1
CALLE 2
CALLE 4
CALLE 6
CALLE 8
CALLE 10
CALLE 12
CALLE 14
CALLE 16
CALLE 18

CALLE A
CALLE B
CALLE C
CALLE D
CALLE E
CALLE F
CALLE G
CALLE H
CALLE I
CALLE J
CALLE K
CALLE L
CALLE M
CALLE N

CALLE 39
CALLE 37
CALLE 35
CALLE N
SAN ANTONIO CHIQUITO

300 yds
300 m

© AVALON TRAVEL

© CHRISTOPHER P. BAKER

The Necrópolis Cristóbal Colón is one of the world's greatest collections of flamboyant funerary architecture.

was laid out between 1871 and 1886 in 16 rectangular blocks, like a Roman military camp. The designer, a Spaniard named Calixto de Loira, divided the cemetery by social status, with separate areas for non-Catholics and for victims of epidemics. It was originally open only to nobles, who competed to build the most elaborate tombs, with social standing dictating the size and location of plots. The cemetery is a petrified version of society of the times, combining, says the *Guía Turística* (available at the entrance gate), a "grandeur and meanness, good taste and triviality...and even an unusual black humor, as in the gravestone carved as a double-three, devoted to an emotional elderly lady who died with that domino in her hand, thus losing both game and life at a time." The *doble tres* was that of Juana Martín, a domino fanatic who indeed died as described (Calles 6 y G).

Famous *criollo* patricians, colonial aristocrats, and war heroes such as Máximo Gómez are buried here alongside noted intellectuals and politicians. The list goes on and on: José Raúl Capablanca, the world chess champion 1921–1927 (his tomb is guarded by a marble queen chess piece); Alejo Carpentier, Cuba's most revered contemporary novelist; Hubert de Blanck, the noted composer; Celia Sánchez, Haydee Santamaría, and a plethora of other revolutionaries killed for the cause, and even some of the Revolution's enemies. Many monuments belong to such communities as the Abakuá secret society, the Asturians, and the Galicians, and to groups such as film and radio stars. The **Galería Tobias** is one of several underground galleries; this one is 100 meters long and contains 256 niches containing human remains.

The major tombs line Avenida Cristóbal Colón, the main avenue, which leads south from the gate to an ocher-colored, octagonal neo-Byzantine church, the **Capilla Central,** containing a fresco of the Last Judgment.

La Milagrosa

The most visited grave is the flower-bedecked tomb of Amelia Goyri de Hoz (Calles 3 y F), revered as La Milagrosa (The Miraculous One) and to whom miraculous healings are ascribed. According to legend, she died during childbirth in 1901 and was buried with her stillborn child at her feet. When her sarcophagus was later opened, the baby was supposedly cradled in her arms. Ever since, superstitious Cubans have paid homage by knocking three times on the tombstone with one of its brass rings, before touching the tomb and requesting a favor (one must not turn one's back on the tomb when departing). Many childless women pray here in hopes of a pregnancy.

Cementerio Chino

The Chinese built their own cemetery immediately southwest of Cementerio Colón, on the west side of Avenida 26 (e/ 28 y 33, tel. 07/831-1645, daily 8 A.M.–4 P.M., free). Beyond the circular gateway, traditional lions stand guard over hundreds of graves beneath highly pitched burial chapels with upward-curving roofs of red and green tile in the traditional *xuan-shan* (hanging mountain) gabled style.

Galería 23 y 12

The northwest corner of Calles 23 and 12, one block north of Cementerio Colón, marks the spot where on April 16, 1961, Castro announced (on the eve of the Bay of Pigs invasion) that Cuba was henceforth socialist. The anniversary of the declaration of socialism is marked each April 16, when Castro speaks here. The facade bears a bronze bas-relief showing Fidel surrounded by the heroes who were killed in the U.S.-sponsored strike on the airfield at Marianao that was a prelude to the invasion.

PLAZA DE LA REVOLUCIÓN

Havana's largest plaza, Plaza de la Revolución (Revolution Plaza), which occupies the Loma de los Catalanes (Hill of the Catalans), is an ugly tarred square accurately described by P. J. O'Rourke as "a vast open space resembling the Mall in D.C., but dropped into the middle of a massive empty parking lot in a tropical Newark." The trapezoidal complex spanning 11 acres was laid out during the Batista era, when it was known as the Plaza Cívica. It forms the administrative center for Cuba. All the major edifices date back to the 1950s. Huge rallies are held here on May 1. The plaza is under close surveillance and loitering is discouraged.

Camilo Cienfuegos mural at night

© CHRISTOPHER P. BAKER

Among the important buildings are the **Biblioteca Nacional** (National Library, tel. 07/855-5442, Mon.–Sat. 8:30 A.M.–5:30 P.M.), Cuba's largest library, built 1955–1957 on the east side of the plaza in a similar monumental style as the Palace of Justice; the 21-story **Ministerio de Defensa,** originally built as the municipal seat of government on the plaza's southeast side; and the **Teatro Nacional** (National Theater, Paseo y Av. Carlos M. de Céspedes, tel. 07/879-6011), one block to the northwest of the plaza, built 1954–1960 with a convex glazed facade. Paseo climbs northwest from the plaza to Zapata, where in the middle of the road rises the **Memorial a Ethel y Julius Rosenberg,** bearing cement doves and an inset sculpture of the U.S. couple executed in Sing Sing Prison, New York, in 1953 for passing nuclear secrets to the Soviet Union. An inscription reads, "Assassinated June 19, 1953." The Cuban government holds a memorial service here each June 19.

To the rear of the library is the **Monumento El Legado Cultural Hispánico,** a larger-than-life bronze statue by American sculptor Anna

Hyatt Huntington of two naked men (one on horseback) passing a baton.

One block northeast of the plaza is the **Museo de Historia del Deporte** (Sports History Museum, Av. Rancho Boyeros, e/ 19 de Mayo and Bruzón, tel. 07/881-4696, Tues.–Sun. 10 A.M.–5 P.M., CUC1), in the **Sala Polivatente Ramón Fonst** stadium.

To get from Vedado to the plaza, you can take bus #84 from the bottom of La Rampa, at Calle O and Humboldt.

Monumento y Museo José Martí

The massive Monumento José Martí on the south side of the square sits atop a 30-meter-tall base that is shaped as a five-pointed star. It is made entirely of gray granite and marble and was designed by architect Enrique Luis Varela. Completed in 1958, it predates the Revolution. To each side, arching stairways lead to an 18-meter-tall (59-foot) gray-white marble statue of national hero José Martí sitting in a contemplative pose, like Rodin's *The Thinker*.

Behind looms a 109-meter-tall marble edifice stepped like a soaring ziggurat from a sci-fi movie. It's the highest point in Havana. The edifice houses the **Museo José Martí** (tel. 07/859-2351, Mon.–Sat. 9 A.M.–5 P.M., entrance CUC3, cameras CUC5, videos CUC10). Among the exhibits are first-edition works, engravings, drawings, maps, and artifacts relating to Martí's life. New Age music plays in the background, drawing you to a multiscreen broadcast on the Wars of Independence and the Revolution. An art gallery features portraits of Martí. For an additional CUC2 an elevator whisks you to the top of the tower for a 360-degree view over Havana.

Palacio de la Revolución

The center of government is the Palacio de la Revolución (Palace of the Revolution, tel. 07/879-6551), immediately south of the José Martí monument. This monumental structure was inspired by the architecture then popular in Fascist Europe and was built 1954–1957 as the Palace of Justice. Today, it is where the Castro brothers and Council of Ministers work out their policies of state. The labyrinthine, ocher-colored palace adjoins the buildings of the Central Committee of the Communist Party. Before the Revolution, the buildings served as the Cuban Supreme Court and national police headquarters. No visitors are allowed.

Ministerio del Interior

Commanding the northwest side of the plaza is the seven-story Ministerio del Interior (Ministry of the Interior, MININT, in charge of national security), built in 1953 to be the Office of the Comptroller. On its east side is a windowless horizontal block that bears a soaring "mural" of **Che Guevara**—the image is from Alberto "Korda" Gutiérrez's world-renowned photo—and the words *Hasta la Victoria Siempre* ("Always Toward Victory"), erected in 1995 from steel railings donated by the French government. See it by day, *and* by night, when it is illuminated.

Ministerio de Comunicaciones

In October 2009, a visage of Comandante Camilo Cienfuegos (identical in style to that of Che) was erected on the facade of the Ministry of Communications, on the plaza's northeast corner. The 100-ton steel mural was raised for the 50th anniversary of Cienfuegos's death and is accompanied by the words *Vas bien, Fidel* ("You're doing fine, Fidel"). Cienfuegos's famous response was in reply to Fidel's question "Am I doing all right, Camilo?" at a rally on January 8, 1959. The ground floor **Museo Postal Cubano** (Cuban Post Museum, Av. Rancho Boyeros, esq. 19 de Mayo, tel. 07/882-8255, Mon.–Thurs. 8 A.M.–5:30 P.M., Fri. 8 A.M.–5:30 P.M., entrance CUC1) has a well-catalogued philatelic collection, including a complete range of Cuban postage stamps dating from 1855, plus stamps from almost 100 other countries. A *filatelica* sells stamps.

NUEVO VEDADO

Nuevo Vedado, which stretches southwest of Plaza de la Revolución, is a sprawling complex of mid-20th-century housing, including high-rise,

JOSÉ MARTÍ

A knowledge of José Martí is an absolute prerequisite to understanding contemporary Cuba. He is the most revered figure in Cuban history: the canonical avatar of Cuba's independence spirit and the "ideological architect" of the Cuban Revolution, claims Castro. His works have been seized upon by Cubans on both sides of the Straits of Florida, being "full of the lament of exile and the passion for the lost homeland," thought Claudia Lightfoot. "Cubans take José Martí into their consciousness with their first breath and their mother's milk." There is hardly a quadrant in Havana that does not have a street, square, or major building named in his honor. Every year on January 28 the entire country honors Martí's birth.

José Julian Martí de Pérez was born in 1853 in a small house on Calle Paula (today known as Leonor Pérez, to honor his mother) in Habana Vieja. His father was from Valencia, Spain, and became a policeman in Cuba; his mother came from the Canary Islands. He spent much of his youth in Spain before his parents returned to Cuba. When the War of Independence erupted in 1868, Martí was 15 years old. Already he sympathized with the nationalist cause. At the age of 16, he published his first newspaper, *La Patria Libre* (Free Fatherland). He also wrote a letter denouncing a school friend for attending a pro-Spanish rally. The letter was judged to be treasonous, and Martí was sentenced to six years' imprisonment, including six months' hard labor. Martí suffered a hernia and gained permanent scars from his shackles. In 1871, his sentence was commuted to exile on the Isla de Pinos, and briefly thereafter he was exiled to Spain, where he earned a degree in law and philosophy and gravitated to the revolutionary circles then active in Madrid.

Later, he settled in Mexico, where he became a journalist, and Guatemala, where he taught, but was expelled for incendiary activities. In 1878, as part of a general amnesty, he was allowed to return to Cuba but was then deported again. He traveled through France and Venezuela and, in 1881, to the United States, where he settled in New York for the next 14 years, with his wife and son. He worked as a reporter and acted as a consul for Argentina, Paraguay, and Uruguay.

THE PEN AND THE SWORD

Dressed in his trademark black frock coat and bow tie, with his thick moustache waxed into pointy tips, Martí devoted more and more of his time to winning independence for Cuba. He wrote poetry heralding the liberation of his homeland, wedding the rhetoric of nationalism to calls for social justice and fashioning a vision of a free Cuba that broke through class

postrevolutionary apartment blocks. There are also some magnificent modern edifices, notably private homes built in modernist style in the 1950s, plus the **Palacio de Deportes** (Sports Palace, colloquially called "El Coliseo"), on the southeast side of the traffic circle at Avenida 26, Avenida de la Independencia (Rancho Boyeros), and Vía Blanca.

Note: Those with children in tow might be tempted to visit the poorly managed Jardín Zoológico de la Habana (Havana Zoological Garden, Av. 26 y Zoológico, tel. 07/881-9926 or 881-8915, zoohabana@ch.gov.cu, Wed.–Sun. 9:30 A.M.–5:30 P.M., CUC2), but this depressing zoo is best avoided.

Bosque de la Habana and Parque Metropolitano de la Habana

Follow Avenida Zoológica west to the bridge over the Río Almendares to enter the Bosque de la Habana (Havana Forest). This ribbon of wild, vine-draped woodland stretches alongside the river. There is no path—you must walk along Calle 49C, which parallels the river—and going alone is not advised, as robberies have occurred.

North of Bosque de la Habana, and accessed from Avenida 47, the motley riverside Parque Metropolitano de la Habana has pony rides, rowboats (don't fall in; the river stinks of sewage), mini-golf, and an excellent

and racial barriers. He was one of the most prolific and accomplished Latin American writers of his day, unsurpassed in the inspiration he ignited. Martí's writing helped define the school of modern Latin American poetry.

He admired the liberty of America but became an arch-anticolonialist, and his voluminous writings are littered with astute critiques of U.S. culture and politics. He despised the expansionist nature of the United States, arguing that U.S. ambitions toward Cuba were as dangerous as the rule of Spain. "It is my duty... to prevent, through the independence of Cuba, the USA from spreading over the West Indies and falling with added weight upon other lands of Our America. All I have done up to now and shall do hereafter is to that end."

Prophetically, Martí's writings are full of invocations to death. It was he who coined the phrase *"La Victoria o el Sepulcro"* (Victory or the Tomb), which Fidel Castro has turned into a call for *"Patria o Muerte"* (Patriotism or Death) and more recently *"Socialismo o Muerte."*

THEORY INTO ACTION
In 1892, Martí presented his "Fundamentals and Secret Guidelines of the Cuban Revolutionary Party," outlining the goals of the nationalists: independence for Cuba, equality of all Cubans, and establishment of democratic

processes. That year, Martí began publishing *Patria*. Having established himself as the acknowledged political leader of the independence cause, he melded the various exile factions together and integrated the cause of Cuban exiled workers into the crusade – they contributed 10 percent of their earnings to his cause. He also founded a revolutionary center, Cuba Libre (Free Cuba), and La Liga de Instrucción, which trained revolutionary fighters.

In 1895, Martí was named major general of the Armies of Liberation; General Máximo Gómez was named supreme commander. On April 11, 1895, Martí, Gómez, and four followers landed at Cajobabo, in a remote part of eastern Cuba. Moving secretly through the mountains, they gathered supporters and finally linked up with Antonio Maceo and his army of 6,000. The first skirmish with the Spanish occurred at Dos Ríos on May 19, 1895. Martí was the first casualty. He had determined on martyrdom and committed sacrificial suicide by riding headlong into the enemy line. Thus, Martí – the "Apostle of the Nation" – brought the republic to birth, says Guillermo Cabrera Infante, "carrying a cadaver around its neck."

The **Centro de Estudios Martiana** (Calzada. e/ Calles 2 y 4, Vedado, Havana, tel. 07/833-2203, cem@josemarti.co.cu, Mon.-Fri. 9 A.M.-4 P.M.) studies his life and works.

children's playground (donated by the British Embassy).

To the south, the woods extend to **Los Jardines de la Tropical** (Calle Rizo, tel. 07/881-8767, Tues.–Sun. 9 A.M.–6 P.M.), a landscaped park built 1904–1910 on the grounds of a former brewery for promotional purposes. The park found its inspiration in Antoni Gaudí's Parque Güell in Barcelona. Today it is near-derelict and looks like an abandoned set from *Lord of the Rings*. The Polar brewing company competed by opening the smaller **Jardines de la Polar,** on the north side of Calzada de Puentes Grandes.

The **Aula Ecológica** (Ciclovía, tel. 07/881-

9979, Mon.–Fri. 9 A.M.–5 P.M.) features a meager visitor center with a 1:2,000 scale model of the project.

Museo Camilo Cienfuegos

Southeast of Nuevo Vedado, the residential district of Víbora extends to Lawton and the house Camilo Cienfuegos (a future *comandante* in Fidel's revolutionary army) was born in. Now a museum (Calle Pocito #228, esq. Calle Lawton, no tel., Tues.–Sat. 9 A.M.–5 P.M., Sun. 9 A.M.–noon, CUC1), it displays suitably revolutionary miscellany recalling the life of this popular leader, who died mysteriously in an air crash in 1959.

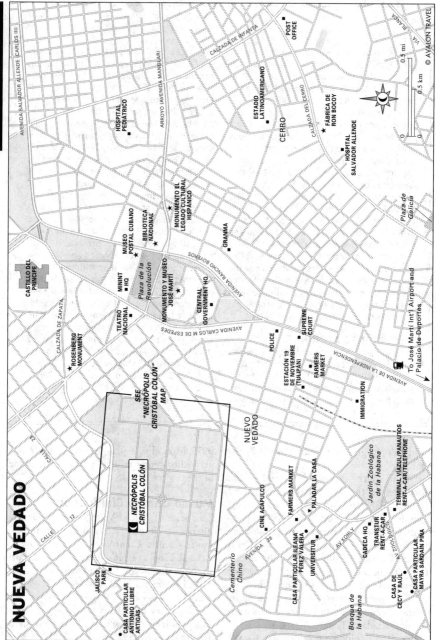

NUEVA VEDADO

AVENIDA SALVADOR ALLENDE (CARLOS III)

CALZADA DE INFANTA

POST OFFICE

HOSPITAL PEDIATRICO

ESTADIO LATINOAMERICANO

CERRO

CALZADA DEL CERRO

FÁBRICA DE RON BOCOY ★

HOSPITAL SALVADOR ALLENDE ■

ARROYO (AVENIDA MANGLAR)

Plaza de Galicia

VÍA BLANCA

© AVALON TRAVEL

0.5 mi
0.5 km

MUSEO POSTAL CUBANO

BIBLIOTECA NACIONAL

MONUMENTO EL LEGADO CULTURAL HISPÁNICO

GRANMA

CASTILLO DEL PRÍNCIPE

MININT HQ

MONUMENTO Y MUSEO JOSÉ MARTÍ ★

Plaza de la Revolución

CENTRAL GOVERNMENT HQ

AVENIDA RANCHO BOYEROS

CALZADA DE ZAPATA

★ ROSENBERG MONUMENT

TEATRO NACIONAL

AVENIDA CARLOS M DE ESPEDES

SUPREME COURT

POLICE

CALLE 23

CALLE 12

ESTACION 19 DE NOVIEMBRE (TULIPAN)

FARMERS MARKET

IMMIGRATION

AVENIDA DE LA INDEPENDENCIA

To José Martí Int'l Airport and Palacio de Deportes

SEE "NECRÓPOLIS CRISTÓBAL COLÓN" MAP

NUEVO VEDADO

NECRÓPOLIS CRISTÓBAL COLÓN

JALISCO PARK

CASA PARTICULAR ANTONIO LLIBRE ARTIGAS

Cementerio Chino

AVENIDA 26

CINE ACAPULCO

FARMERS MARKET

PALADAR LA CASA

CASA PARTICULAR ILEANA PÉREZ VALERA

UNIVERSTUR

Jardín Zoológico de la Habana

AV ZOOLÓGICO

AV KOHLY

CADECA HQ

TRANSTUR RENT-A-CAR

CASA DE CECY Y RAÚL

CASA PARTICULAR MAYRA SARDAIN PIÑA

TERMINAL VÍAZUL/PANAUTOS RENT-A-CAR/TELEPHONE

Bosque de la Habana

Sights - Playa (Miramar and Beyond)

West of Vedado and the Río Almendares, the *municipio* of Playa extends to the western boundary of Havana as far as the Río Quibu. Most areas were renamed following the Revolution. Gone are Country Club and Biltmore, replaced with politically acceptable names such as Atabey, Cubanacán, and Siboney, in honor of Cuba's indigenous past.

MIRAMAR

Miramar is Havana's upscale residential district, laid out in an expansive grid of tree-shaded streets lined by fine mansions. Most of their original owners fled Cuba following the Revolution, and many of the mansions have fallen into ruin. Nonetheless, Miramar is at the forefront of Cuba's quasi-capitalist remake. The best-stocked stores are here, as are the foreign embassies.

Primera Avenida (First Avenue, 1ra Av.) runs along the shore. Time-worn *balnearios* (bathing areas) are found along Miramar's waterfront, cut into the shore. Of limited appeal to tourists, they draw Cubans on hot summer days.

Inland, running parallel at intervals of about 200 meters, are 3ra Avenida, 5ta Avenida (the main thoroughfare), and 7ma Avenida.

Tunnels under the Río Almendares connect Miramar to Vedado. The Malecón connects with 5ta Avenida; Línea (Calle 9) connects with 7ma Avenida and Avenida 31, which leads to the Marianao district; Calle 11 also connects with 7ma Avenida; Calle 23 becomes Avenida 47, linking Vedado with the Kohly district and Marianao.

Buses #132 and 232 run to Miramar from Dragones y Industria, on the northwest side of Parque de la Fraternidad. Bus #264 runs to Miramar from Desamparados (e/ Compostela y Picota), near the railway station in Habana Vieja. In Vedado, the P1 runs along Calle 23 to Miramar (you can board at Coppelia, esq.

© CHRISTOPHER P. BAKER

Bathers cool off in the summer heat at *balnearios* (bathing areas) lining 1ra Avenida, Miramar.

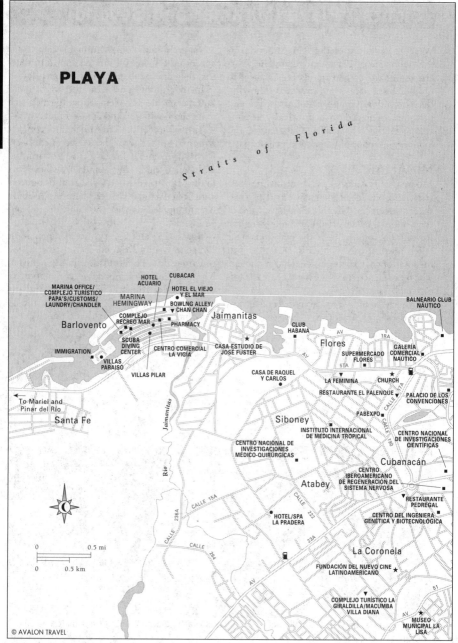

PLAYA

Straits of Florida

MARINA OFFICE/
COMPLEJO TURÍSTICO
PAPA'S/CUSTOMS/
LAUNDRY/CHANDLER

HOTEL
ACUARIO

CUBACAR

HOTEL EL VIEJO
Y EL MAR

MARINA
HEMINGWAY

BOWLNG ALLEY/
CHAN CHAN

COMPLEJO
RECREO MAR

PHARMACY

Jaimanitas

BALNEARIO CLUB
NÁUTICO

Barlovento

SCUBA
DIVING
CENTER

CENTRO COMERCIAL
LA VIGÍA

CASA-ESTUDIO DE
JOSÉ FUSTER

CLUB
HABANA

Flores

AV

1RA

SUPERMERCADO
FLORES

5TA

GALERÍA
COMERCIAL
NÁUTICO

IMMIGRATION

VILLAS
PARAISO

VILLAS PILAR

CASA DE RAQUEL
Y CARLOS

AV

LA FEMININA

CHURCH

RESTAURANTE EL PALENQUE

PALACIO DE LOS
CONVENCIONES

To Mariel and
Pinar del Río

Santa Fe

Jaimanitas

Siboney

PABEXPO

INSTITUTO INTERNACIONAL
DE MEDICINA TROPICAL

CENTRO NACIONAL
DE INVESTIGACIONES
CIENTÍFICAS

Río

CENTRO NACIONAL DE
INVESTIGACIONES
MÉDICO-QUIRURGICAS

Cubanacán

Atabey

CENTRO
IBEROAMERICANO
DE REGENERACIÓN DEL
SISTEMA NERVOSA

RESTAURANTE
PEDREGAL

CALLE 15A

CALLE 222

HOTEL/SPA
LA PRADERA

CALLE 238A

CENTRO DEL INGENIERA
GENÉTICA Y BIOTECNOLÓGICA

0   0.5 mi

0   0.5 km

CALLE 234

CALLE 28A

La Coronela

FUNDACIÓN DEL NUEVO CINE
LATINOAMERICANO

AV

COMPLEJO TURÍSTICO LA
GIRALDILLA/MACUMBA
VILLA DIANA

AV

51

MUSEO
MUNICIPAL LA
LISA

© AVALON TRAVEL

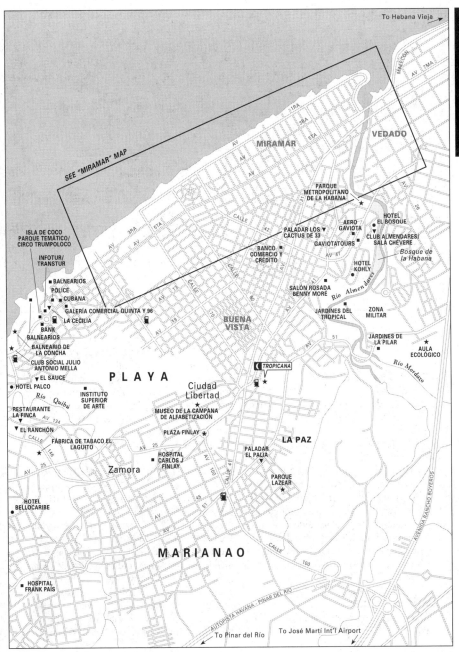

To Habana Vieja

VEDADO

MIRAMAR

SEE "MIRAMAR" MAP

PARQUE METROPOLITANO DE LA HABANA

ISLA DE COCO PARQUE TEMATICO/ CIRCO TRUMPOLOCO

INFOTUR/ TRANSTUR

PALADAR LOS CACTUS DE 33
AERO GAVIOTA
GAVIOTATOURS
HOTEL EL BOSQUE
CLUB ALMENDARES/ SALA CHÈVERE

BANCO COMERCIO Y CREDITO

Bosque de la Habana

HOTEL KOHLY

BALNEARIOS
POLICE
CUBANA
GALERÍA COMERCIAL QUINTA Y 96
LA CECILIA
BANK
BALNEARIOS
BALNEARIO DE LA CONCHA
CLUB SOCIAL JULIO ANTONIO MELLA
EL SAUCE
HOTEL PALCO

SALÓN ROSADA BENNY MORÉ
Río Almendares
JARDINES DEL TROPICAL
ZONA MILITAR
JARDINES DE LA PILAR
AULA ECOLÓGICO
Río Mordazo

BUENA VISTA

TROPICANA

PLAYA
Ciudad Libertad

INSTITUTO SUPERIOR DE ARTE

Río Quibú

RESTAURANTE LA FINCA
EL RANCHÓN
FÁBRICA DE TABACO EL LAGUITO

MUSEO DE LA CAMPANA DE ALFABETIZACIÓN

PLAZA FINLAY

LA PAZ

PALADAR EL PALIA

Zamora

HOSPITAL CARLOS J FINLAY

PARQUE LAZEAR

HOTEL BELLOCARIBE

MARIANAO

HOSPITAL FRANK PAÍS

AUTOPISTA HAVANA - PINAR DEL RÍO

To Pinar del Río

To José Martí Int'l Airport

AVENIDA RANCHO BOYEROS

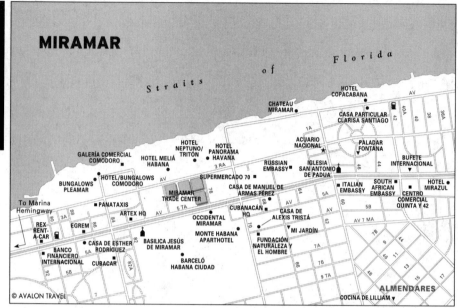

MIRAMAR

© AVALON TRAVEL

L), where it runs along 4ra Avenida, and the P4 runs along Línea.

Pabellón de la Maqueta de la Habana

The Pabellón de la Maqueta de la Habana (Model of Havana, Calle 28 #113, e/ 1ra y 3ra, tel. 07/206-1268, maqueta@gdic.cu, Tues.–Sat. 9:30 A.M.–5 P.M., adults CUC3, students, seniors, and children CUC1, guided tour CUC1, cameras CUC2) is a 1:1,000 scale model of the city housed in a hangar-sized building. The 144-square-meter *maqueta* (model) represents 144 square kilometers of Havana and its environs. The model took more than 10 years to complete and shows Havana in the most intimate detail, color-coded by age. A visit here puts the entire city in accessible 3-D perspective.

Acuario Nacional

The Acuario Nacional (National Aquarium, 3ra Av., esq. 62, tel. 07/203-6401 or 202-

5872, www.acuarionacional.cu, Tues.–Sun. 10 A.M.–6 P.M., adults CUC7, children CUC5) exhibits 450 species of sealife, including corals, exotic tropical fish, sharks, hawksbill turtles, sea lions, and dolphins. The tanks and displays are disappointing by international standards. A sea lion show is held daily at noon, 2:15 P.M., and 4 P.M.; dolphin shows are daily at 11 A.M., 3 P.M., and 5 P.M.

Museo del Ministerio del Interior

The Museo del Ministerio del Interior (Museum of the Ministry of the Interior, 5ta Av., esq. 14, tel. 07/203-4432, Tues.–Fri. 9 A.M.–5 P.M., Sat. 9 A.M.–3 P.M., entrance CUC2, guide CUC1) is dedicated to the CIA's inept efforts to dethrone Fidel. The seal of the CIA looms over a room full of photos and gadgets straight from a spy movie. It also features exhibits honoring MININT's good work in solving homicides—there's even a stuffed German shepherd that was used by police in their sleuthing. To make things easier for the

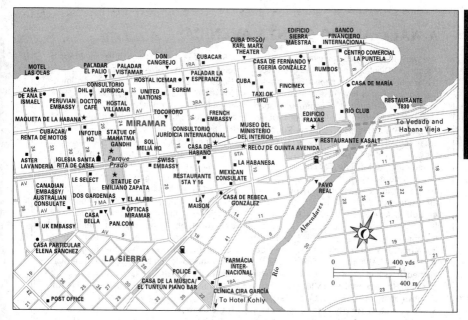

CIA should it ever take another stab at Fidel, the museum shows a video giving details of Castro's security plans, including tunnels from his residence in Jaimanitas to the Ciudad Libertad military airstrip. Surreal!

Fundación Naturaleza y El Hombre

The Fundación Naturaleza y El Hombre (Foundation of Man and Nature, Av. 5B #6611, e/ 66 y 70, tel. 07/209-2885, halcma@ fanj.cult.cu, Mon.–Fri. 8:30 A.M.–4:30 P.M., CUC2) honors Cuban naturalist and explorer Antonio Nuñez Jiménez and features his personal collection. Much of the eclectic exhibit is dedicated to the 10,889-mile journey by a team of Cubans (led by Nuñez) that paddled from the source of the Amazon to the Bahamas in dugout canoes in 1996. A replica of the canoe is there, along with indigenous artifacts such as weapons, headdresses, and ceramics showing figures copulating and masturbating.

NÁUTICO, FLORES, AND JAIMANITAS

Beyond Miramar, 5ta Avenida curls around the half-moon Playa Marianao and passes through the Náutico and Flores districts, the setting for Havana's elite prerevolutionary social clubs and *balnearios*. Following the Revolution they were reopened to the hoi polloi and rechristened. The beaches—collectively known as Playas del Oeste—are popular with Cubans on weekends, when they get crowded. There was even an eponymous mini-version of New York's famous Coney Island theme park, re-created in 2008 as **Isla de Coco Parque Temático,** Havana's only amusement park.

Commanding the scene are the palatial Mudejar-style former **Balneario de la Concha** (5ta e/ 112 and 146) and, immediately west, the **Balneario Club Náutico** with its sweeping modernist entrance. Beyond the Río Quibu, 5ta Avenida passes into the Flores district. The Havana-Biltmore Yacht and Country Club was here, dating from

A WALK ALONG QUINTA AVENIDA

The wide, fig-tree-lined boulevard called Fifth Avenue, or "Quinta," runs ruler-straight through the heart of Miramar. It is flanked by mansions, many of which have been restored and are now occupied by various Cuban commercial agencies or leased to foreign corporations. Quinta Avenida (5ta Av.) is also "Embassy Row." The broad central median is tailor-made for walking the boulevard's eight-kilometer length.

Begin at the **Edificio Fraxas,** a restored Beaux-Arts mansion on the north side of Quinta at Calle 2. Walking west you'll arrive, after four blocks, at Calle 10, pinned by **Reloj de Quinta Avenida,** a large clock erected in 1924 in the central median. At Calle 12, cross to the north side of the street to visit the **Museo del Ministerio del Interior;** then, one block west, cross to the south side to admire the stained glass and large cigar collection in the **Casa del Habano** (5ta, e/ 14 y 16).

Continue west four blocks to Calle 24, where **Parque de los Ahorcados** (Park of the Hanged), spanning Quinta between Calles 24 and 26, is shaded by massive jagüey trees, seemingly supported by their aerial roots dangling like cascades of water. On the south side of the road is **Plaza Emiliano Zapata,** with a life-size stone statue of Zapata, Mexico's revolutionary hero; on the north side is **Parque Prado,** with a Romanesque temple and a bronze bust to Mahatma Gandhi.

Rising over the west side of Parque Prado is **Iglesia de Santa Rita de Casia** (5ta, esq. Calle 26, tel. 07/204-2001). This exemplar of modernist church architecture dates from 1942 and mixes neocolonial and modern features. Its main feature is a modernist statue of Santa Rita by Rita Longa.

The next 10 blocks are lined with gracious mansions, many of them foreign embassies.

Crossing Calle 60, call in at the modernist-style Romanesque **Iglesia San Antonio de Padua** (Calle 60 #316, esq. 5ta, tel. 07/203-5045), which dates from 1951 and boasts a magnificent, albeit nonfunctional, organ. One block west, on the north side of Quinta, you pass a monstrous Cubist tower that can be seen virtually the length of the avenue. Formerly the Soviet Embassy, it is now the **Russian Embassy** (5ta, e/ 62 y 66).

At Calle 70, on your left, is the **Occidental Miramar** hotel and, on your right, the **Miramar Trade Center.**

One block farther, on the south side of Quinta, rises the massive Roman-Byzantine-style **Basilica Jesús de Miramar** (5ta #8003, e/ 80 y 82, tel. 07/203-5301, daily 9 A.M.-noon and 4-6 P.M.), built in 1953 with a magnificent organ with 5,000 pipes. The restored church features 14 splendid oversize paintings of the Stations of the Cross by Spanish artist César Hombrados Oñativa.

1928 and fronting Havana's most beautiful expanse of white sand. After the Revolution, the beach was opened to all Cubans and the former casino and hotel became a workers' social club. The "Yacht" was founded in 1886 and became the snootiest place in Havana (it was here that mulatto President Fulgencio Batista was famously refused entry for being too "black") until the Revolution, when it became the Club Social Julio Antonio Mella, for workers. Today, as the **Club Habana** (5ta Av., e/ 188 y 192, Playa, tel. 07/204-5700), it has reverted to its former role as a private club for the (mostly foreign) elite. Nonmembers are welcome (Mon.–Fri.

9 A.M.–7 P.M., entrance CUC20 includes CUC10 *consumo mínimo*).

Havana's huge yachting marina, **Marina Hemingway** (5ta Av. y Calle 248, tel. 07/204-1150, fax 07/204-1149, comercial@comermh.cha.cyt.cu) is in the Jaimanitas district, 15 kilometers west of downtown.

Buses #9 and #420 run to Marina Hemingway from 5ta Avenida and Calle 0.

Casa-Estudio de José Fuster

Artist José R. Fuster, a world-renowned painter and ceramist nicknamed the "Picasso of the Caribbean," has an open-air workshop-gallery at his home (Calle 226, esq. Av. 3A, tel. 07/271-2932 or cell 05/264-6051, www. josefuster.com, daily 9 A.M.–5 P.M.). You step through a giant doorway—La Puerta de Fuster—to discover a surreal world made of ceramics. Many of the naive, childlike works are inspired by farmyard scenes, such as *El Torre del Gallo* (Rooster's Tower), a 12-foot-tall statement on male chauvinism that also doubles as an oven. Other allegorical creations—puppet-like forms, buses bulging with people—pay tribute to Compay Segundo (of Buena Vista Social Club fame) and other provincial figures. Call ahead to arrange a visit.

Fuster's creativity now graces the entryways, benches, roofs, and facades of houses throughout his local community.

(Fidel Castro's main domicile is nearby, but you can't see it. The home is set in an expansive compound surrounded by pine trees and electrified fences and heavy security. All streets surrounding it are marked as one-way, heading away from the house.)

CUBANACÁN AND VICINITY

Cubanacán is—or was—Havana's Beverly Hills, a reclusive area on either side of the Río Quibu. It was developed in the 1920s with winding tree-lined streets on which the most grandiose of Havana's mansions arose. An 18-hole golf course at the Havana Country Club served Havana's wealthy classes, lending the name Country Club Park to what is now called Cubanacán, still the swankiest address in town.

Following the Revolution, most of the area's homeowners fled Cuba. Their mansions were dispensed to Communist Party officials, many of whom live in a lap of luxury that the vast majority of Cubans can only dream of and, of course, never see. The Castros maintain several homes here, and the area is replete with

---

THE CIA'S ATTEMPTS TO KILL CASTRO

The bitter taste left by the CIA's botched Bay of Pigs invasion led to an all-out secret war against Castro, an effort code-named Operation Mongoose and headed by Bobby Kennedy. Mongoose eventually involved 500 caseworkers handling 3,000 anti-Castro Cubans at an expense of more than US$100 million a year. The CIA's attempts (now defunct) to oust Castro were set in motion by President Eisenhower as early as March 1959. In *Inside the Company: CIA Diary*, ex-CIA agent Philip Agee described how the dirty-tricks campaign included bombings of public venues meant to discredit Cuba (the CIA claims that Agee later worked for Cuban intelligence; he settled in Havana, where he died in 2008). The agency also invented protest demonstrations, sowed discord in Cuban intelligence by fingering top officials as CIA agents, and even recruited Cuban Embassy staff by "dangling stunning beauties...exceptionally active in amorous adventures."

The CIA's plans read like a James Bond novel. Or a comedy of errors! Some plots were straightforward, like the attempt to kill Castro with a bazooka. The CIA's Technical Services Division (TSD) was more imaginative. It impregnated a box of cigars with botulism (they were tested on monkeys and "did the job expected of them") and hoped – in vain – to dupe Castro into smoking one. No one knows whether they reached Castro or whether some innocent victim smoked them. The spooks also tried to damage Castro's image by sprinkling his shoes with thallium salts (a strong depilatory), hoping that his beard would fall out.

Eventually the CIA turned to the Mob. It hired assassins hand-picked by Johnny Rosselli, who had run the syndicate's Sans Souci casino in Havana. The killers were on both the FBI's 10 Most Wanted and Bobby Kennedy's target list of organized crime figures. The marksmen disguised as Marxmen didn't fool Castro – he correctly assumed the CIA would hire assassins, whom he considered inefficient. Several assassins were caught and executed.

A BIOTECH SUCCESS STORY

Cuba is a biotech minipower. Under Fidel Castro's personal patronage, Cuba has evolved one of the world's most advanced genetic engineering and biotechnology industries, with large-scale investment coming from public sources such as the Pan American Health Organization and the World Food Program.

Cuba has developed some 200 products, both innovative and derivative. It invented and manufactures vaccines for cerebral meningitis, cholera, hepatitis B, interferon for the treatment of AIDS and cancer, and a skin growth factor to speed the healing of burns. For years, Cuba has touted a cure for the skin disease vitiligo. Recently it developed PPG, a "wonder drug" that reputedly washes cholesterol out of blood (and, incidentally, is Cuba's equivalent of Viagra). Other advances have been made in agriculture and industrial bioengineering. Unfortunately, U.S. law prevents these lifesaving wonders from being sold in the United States.

fax 07/208-4329, www.cpalco.com), was built in 1979 for the Non-Aligned Conference. The main hall (one of 15), seating 2,200 delegates, hosts twice-yearly meetings of the Cuban National Assembly. To its rear, **Pabexpo** (Av. 17 y 180, tel. 07/271-6775) has four exhibition halls for trade shows.

Cuba's biotechnology industry is also centered here and extends westward into the districts of Atabey and Siboney, earning the area the moniker "Scientific City." The **Centro de Ingeniería Genética y Biotecnología** (Center for Genetic Engineering and Biotechnology, Av. 31, e/ 158 y 190, Havana, tel. 07/271-6022, http://gndp.cigb.edu.cu), Cuba's main research facility, is perhaps the most sophisticated research facility in any developing nation.

The convoluted roads of Siboney and Cubanacán follow no logical order. Bus #32 operates between La Rampa in Vedado and Cubanacán (five pesos).

Instituto Superior de Arte

Following the Revolution, Fidel Castro and Che Guevara famously played a few rounds of golf at the exclusive Havana Country Club before tearing it up and converting the grounds to house Cuba's leading art academy, the Instituto Superior de Arte (Higher Art Institute, Calle 120 #1110, esq. 9na, tel. 07/208-0017 or 208-0288, isa@cubarte.cult.cu, by appointment only), featuring the Escuela de Música (School of Music), Escuela de Ballet (Ballet School), Escuela de Baile Moderno (School of Modern Dance), and Escuela de Bellas Artes (School of Fine Arts). The school was designed by three young "rebel" architects: Italians Roberto Gottardi and Vittorio Garatti, and Cuban Ricardo Porro. Porro's art school was a deliberate evocation of the female form complete with fountain shaped as a *mamey*, or papaya—an overt reference to the female vulva. As the five main buildings emerged, they were thought too sensual, too avant-garde for grim Communist tastes. The project was halted, though the school did open. The ghostly complex fell into ruin, with long tentacles of

military camps and security personnel. Other homes serve either as "protocol" houses— villas where foreign dignitaries and VIPs are housed during visits—or as foreign embassies and ambassadors' homes, among them the U.S. Residency (even the U.S. Marines have a house).

One of the swankiest mansions was built in 1910 for the Marqués de Pinar del Río; it was later adorned with 1930s art deco glass and chrome, a spiral staircase, and abstract floral designs. Today it is the **Fábrica El Laguito** (Av. 146 #2302, e/ 21 y 21A, tel. 07/208-4654, by appointment only), the nation's premier cigar factory, making Montecristos and the majority of Cohibas—*the* premium Havana cigar.

Havana's impressive convention center, the **Palacio de las Convenciones** (Convention Palace, Calle 146, e/ 11 y 13, tel. 07/202-6011,

branches and roots creeping into the buildings. Amazingly, in 2001 the Cuban government approached the three architects and asked them to complete the project. Restoration was completed in 2009.

For the best views, drive along Calles 15 and 134. In summer the facility is closed.

MARIANAO AND LA CORONELA

This dilapidated *municipio,* on the heights south of Miramar, evolved in the mid-19th century, when wealthy Cubans built fine summer homes along newly laid streets. During the 1920s, Marianao boasted the Marianao Country Club, the Oriental Park racetrack, and Grand Nacional Casino, and was given a further boost on New Year's Eve 1939 when the Tropicana opened as the ritziest nightclub Havana had ever seen. After the Revolution, the casinos, racetrack, and even Tropicana (briefly) were shut down.

Following the U.S. occupation of Cuba in 1898, the U.S. military governor, General Fitzhugh Lee, established his headquarters in Marianao and called it Camp Columbia: Campamento Columbia later became headquarters for Batista's army; it was from here that the sergeant effected his *golpes* in 1933 and 1952. Camp Columbia was bombed on April 15, 1960, during the prelude to the CIA-run Bay of Pigs invasion. Five of Castro's planes were destroyed, but the bombers also struck houses in the neighborhood, killing 7 people and wounding 52, giving Castro a grand political victory in his calls for solidarity against U.S. aggression. The following day he announced for the first time that Cuba was "socialist."

A tower in the center of the traffic circle— **Plaza Finlay**—outside the main entrance, at Avenida 31 and Avenida 100, was erected in 1944 as a beacon for the military airfield. In 1948 a needle was added so that today it is shaped like a syringe in honor of Carlos Finlay, the Cuban who in 1881 discovered the cause of yellow fever.

Bus #34 departs Dragones y Industria, on the northwest side of Parque de la Fraternidad, Habana Vieja, for Marianao.

Museo de la Campaña de Alfabetización

Following the Revolution, Castro turned the barracks of Camp Columbia into a school complex—Ciudad Escolar Libertad—which in 1961 became the headquarters for Castro's national literacy campaign. The Museo de la Campaña de Alfabetización (Museum of the Literacy Campaign, Av. 29E, esq. 76, tel. 07/260-8054, Mon.–Fri. 8 A.M.–5 P.M., free) is dedicated to the amazing campaign initiated on January 1, 1960, when 120,632 uniformed *brigadistas,* mostly students, spread out across the country to teach illiterate peasantry to read and write.

Tropicana

The Tropicana (Calle 72 e/ 41 y 45, tel. 07/207-0110, fax 07/207-0109) is an astonishing exemplar of modernist architecture. Most of the structures date from 1951, when the nightclub was restored with a new showroom—the **Salon Arcos de Cristal** (Crystal Bows)—designed by Max Borges Recio with a roof of five arcing concrete vaults and curving bands of glass to fill the intervening space. Built in decreasing order of height, they produce a telescopic effect that channels the perspective toward the orchestra platform. Borges also added the famous geometric sculpture that still forms the backdrop to the main stage, in the outdoor **Salón Bajo las Estrellas.**

Visitors can only view the exterior features by day, when the dancers practice. To admire the Salon Arcos de Cristal, you must visit at night, when the statuesque showgirls perform beneath the stars.

A ballet dancer (shown pirouetting on the tips of her toes) by the renowned Cuban sculptor Rita Longa dances amid the lush foliage in front of the entrance. The statue—Tropicana's motif—is surrounded by Greek maenads, with the bacchantes performing a wild ritual dance to honor Dionysius.

Sights - Across the Harbor

The harbor channel and Bahía de la Habana (Havana Bay) separate Habana Vieja from the communities of Casablanca, Regla, and Guanabacoa. The latter districts draw tourists interested in *santería* and Afro-Cuban music and dance, while Casablanca is an access point to the Parque Histórico Militar Morro-Cabaña.

Little ferries bob their way across the harbor, connecting Casablanca and Regla with each other and with Habana Vieja.

◖ PARQUE HISTÓRICO MILITAR MORRO-CABAÑA

Looming over Habana Vieja, on the north side of the harbor channel, the rugged cliff face of the Cabaña is dominated by two great fortresses that constitute Parque Histórico Militar Morro-Cabaña (Morro-La Cabaña Historical Military Park, Carretera de la Cabaña, Habana del Este). Together, the castles comprise the largest and most powerful defensive complex built by the Spanish in the Americas.

Visitors arriving by car reach the complex via the harbor tunnel (no pedestrians or motorcycles without sidecars are allowed) that descends beneath the Máximo Gómez Monument off Avenida de Céspedes. Buses from Parque de la Fraternidad pass through the tunnel and stop by the fortress access road.

Castillo de Los Tres Reyes del Morro

The Castillo de Los Tres Reyes del Morro (Castle of the Three Kings of the Headland, tel. 07/863-7941, daily 8 A.M.–8 P.M., entrance CUC5, children under 12 free, guide CUC1, cameras CUC2, videos CUC5) is built into the rocky palisades of Punta Barlovento at the entrance to Havana's narrow harbor channel. Canted in its articulation, the fort—designed by Italian engineer Bautista Antonelli and initiated in 1589—forms an irregular polygon that follows the contours of the rocky headland, with a sharp-angled bastion at the apex,

stone walls 10 feet thick, and a series of batteries stepping down to the shore. Slaves toiled under the lash of whip and sun to cut the stone in situ, extracted from the void that forms the moats. El Morro took 40 years to complete and served its job well, repelling countless pirate attacks and withstanding for 44 days a siege by British cannons in 1762.

Originally the castle connected with the outside world by sea, to which it was linked via the **Plataforma de la Estrella,** the wharf at the southern foot of the cliff. Today you enter via a drawbridge across the deep moat that leads through the **Túnel Aspillerado** (Tunnel of Loopholes) to vast wooden gates that open to the **Camino de Rondas,** a small parade ground (Plaza de Armas) containing a two-story building atop water cisterns that supplied the garrison of 1,000 men.

To the right of the plaza, a narrow entrance

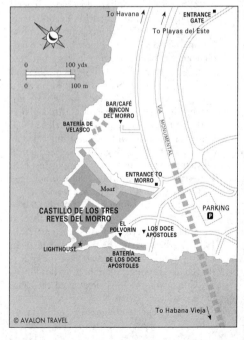

© AVALON TRAVEL

leads to the **Baluarte de Austria** (Austrian Bastion), with cannon embrasures for firing down on the moat. A cobbled ramp leads up to other *baluartes*. Various plaques commemorate heroic figures of the siege—even the Royal Navy is honored.

To the left of the Plaza de Armas, the **Sala de Historia del Faro y Castillo** profiles the various lighthouses and castles in Cuba. Beyond is the **Surtida de los Tinajones**, where giant earthenware vases are inset in stone. They once contained rapeseed oil as lantern fuel for the 25-meter-tall **Faro del Morro** (8 A.M.–7 P.M., CUC2 extra), a lighthouse constructed in 1844. Today an electric lantern still flashes twice every 15 seconds. You can climb to the top for a bird's-eye view of the castle—the climb is tight and not for claustrophobics.

All maritime traffic in and out of Havana harbor is controlled from the **Estación Semafórica,** the semaphore station atop the castle, accessed via the Baluarte de Tejeda. The harbormaster will invite you up, but you'll be expected to tip.

Below the castle, facing the city on the landward side and reached by a cobbled ramp, is the **Batería de los Doce Apóstoles** (Battery of the Twelve Apostles). It boasts massive cannons and a little bar—El Polvorín (The Powderhouse).

Fortaleza de San Carlos de la Cabaña

The massive Fortaleza de San Carlos de la Cabaña (Saint Charles of the Flock Fortress, Carretera de la Cabaña, tel. 07/862-4095, daily 10 A.M.–10 P.M., entrance CUC5 adults, children under 12 free, CUC8 for the *cañonazo* ceremony, guide CUC1), half a kilometer east of the Morro, enjoys a fantastic strategic position overlooking the city and harbor. It is the largest fort in the Americas, covering 10 hectares and stretching 700 meters in length. It was built 1763–1774 following the English invasion, and cost the staggering sum of

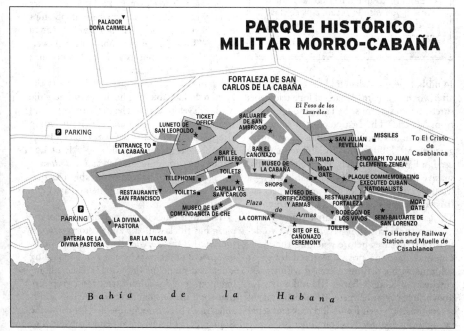

PARQUE HISTÓRICO MILITAR MORRO-CABAÑA

THE *CAÑONAZO*

The *ceremonía del cañonazo* (cannon-firing ceremony, CUC6) is held nightly at 8:30 P.M. at the Fortaleza de San Carlos de la Cabaña, where troops dressed in 18th-century military garb and led by fife and drum light the fuse of a cannon to announce the closing of the city gates, maintaining a tradition going back centuries. You are greeted at the castle gates by soldiers in traditional uniform, and the place is lit by flaming lanterns. About 8:50 P.M. a cry rings out, announcing the procession of soldiers marching across the plaza bearing muskets, while a torchbearer lights flaming barrels. The soldiers ascend to the cannon, which they prepare with ramrod and live charge. When the soldier puts the torch to the cannon, you have about three seconds before the thunderous boom. Your heart skips a beat. But it's all over in a millisecond, and the troops march away.

Be sure to get there no later than 8 P.M. if you wish to secure a place close to the cannon. Hotel tour desks offer excursions.

14 million pesos—when told the cost, the king after whom it is named reached for a telescope; surely, he said, it must be large enough to see from Madrid. The castle counted some 120 bronze cannons and mortars, plus a permanent garrison of 1,300 men. While never actually used in battle, it has been claimed that its dissuasive presence won all potential battles—a tribute to the French designer and engineer entrusted with its conception and construction. The castle has been splendidly restored.

From the north, you pass through two defensive structures before reaching the monumental baroque portal flanked by great columns with a pediment etched with the escutcheon of Kings Charles III, and a massive drawbridge over a 12-meter-deep moat, one of several moats carved from solid rock and separating individual fortress components.

Beyond the entrance gate a paved alley leads to the **Plaza de Armas,** centered on a grassy, tree-shaded park fronted by a 400-meter-long curtain wall. The wall—**La Cortina**—runs the length of the castle on its south side and formed the main gun position overlooking Havana. It is lined with cannons engraved with lyrical names such as La Hermosa (The Beautiful). The *cañonazo* (cannon-lighting) ceremony is held here nightly.

Opening to the plaza is a small **chapel** with a baroque facade and charming vaulted interior. Facing it is the **Museo de la Comandancia de Che,** where, following the Triunfo del Revolución, Che Guevara set up his tribunals for "crimes against the security of the state." The small museum salutes the Argentinian doctor-turned-revolutionary who played such a key part in the Cuban Revolution. His M-1 rifle, submachine gun, radio, and rucksack are among the exhibits.

A cobbled street leads west from the entrance gate to a large cannon-filled courtyard, from where steps lead down to La Divina Pastora restaurant, beside the wharf where supply ships once berthed. The adjoining **Bar La Tasca** (tel. 07/860-8341, daily noon–11 P.M.) overhangs the harbor and is a great place to relax with a *mojito* and cigar.

Facing the plaza on its north side is the **Museo de la Cabaña.** The museum traces the castle's development and features uniforms and weaponry from the colonial epoch, including a representation of the *cañonazo* ceremony. A portal here leads into a garden—**Patio de Los Jagüeyes**—that once served as a *cortadura*, a defensive element packed with explosives that could be ignited to foil the enemy's attempts to gain entry.

The stone block on the northeast side of the plaza has thick-walled, vaulted storage rooms (*bovedas*). One *boveda* displays 3-D models (*maquetas*) of each of Cuba's castles, including a detailed model of the Cabaña. The adjoining room contains suits of armor and weaponry that span the ancient Arab and Asian worlds and stretch back through medieval times to the Roman era. The *bovedas* open to the north to cobbled **Calle de la Marina,** where converted barracks, armaments stores, and prisoners' cells now contain restaurants and the **Casa del Tabaco y Ron,** displaying the world's longest cigar (11 meters long).

Midway down Marina, a gate leads down to **El Foso de los Laureles,** a massive moat containing the execution wall where nationalist sympathizers were shot during the Wars of Independence. A cenotaph is dedicated to Juan Clemente Zenea, executed in 1871. Following the Revolution, scores of Batista supporters and "counterrevolutionaries" met a similar fate here.

On the north side of the moat, a separate fortress unit called **San Julián Revellín** contains examples of Soviet missiles installed during the Cuban Missile Crisis (called the October 1962 Crisis or the Caribbean Crisis by Cubans). The rest of the fortress grounds is still used as a military base and is off-limits. It includes the domed **Observatorio Nacional** (National Observatory).

A ferry (10 centavos) runs to Casablanca every 20 minutes or so from the Muelle Luz (Av. del Puerto y Calle Santa Clara) in Habana Vieja. You can walk uphill from Casablanca to an easterly entrance gate to the Foso de los Laureles. This gate closes at dusk, so don't take this route if you plan on seeing the *cañonazo*.

Estatua Cristo de la Habana

The Estatua Cristo de la Habana (Havana Christ Statue, Carretera del Asilo, daily 9 A.M.–8 P.M., entrance CUC1, children under 12 free) looms over Casablanca, dominating the cliff face immediately east of the Fortaleza. The 15-meter-tall statue, unveiled on December 25, 1958, was hewn from Italian Carrara marble by Cuban sculptor Jilma Madera. From the *mirador* surrounding the statue, you have a bird's-eye view of the harbor. The views are especially good at dawn and dusk, and it is possible, with the sun gilding the waters, to imagine great galleons slipping in and out of the harbor laden with treasure en route to Spain.

The adjoining **Casa del Che** (daily 9 A.M.–8 P.M., entrance CUC4, guide CUC1,

camera CUC2) café/restaurant has a small museum, with personal effects, dedicated to the revolutionary.

The statue is a 10-minute uphill walk from the Casablanca dock.

REGLA

Regla, a working-class *barrio* on the eastern shore of Havana harbor, evolved in the 16th century as a fishing village and eventually became Havana's foremost warehousing and slaving center. It developed into a smugglers' port in colonial days, a reputation it maintained until recent days, when pirates (who made their living stealing off American yachts anchored in the harbor) were known as *terribles reglanos*. Havana's main electricity-generating plant is here, along with petrochemical works, both of which pour bilious plumes over town.

The slaves who settled here infused Regla with a profound African heritage. Regla is a center of *santería;* walking its streets, note the tiny shrines outside many houses. Calle Calixto García has many fine examples. Many *babalawos* (*santería* priests) live here and will happily dispense advice for a fee; try **Eberardo Marero** (Ñico López #60, e/ Coyola y Camilo Cienfuegos).

The **Museo Municipal de Regla** (Martí #158, e/ Facciolo y La Piedra, tel. 07/797-6989, Tues.–Sat. 9 A.M.–6 P.M., Sun. 9 A.M.–1 P.M., entrance CUC2, guide CUC1), two blocks east of the harborfront, tells the tale of the town's *santería* associations. Other displays include colonial-era swords, slave shackles, and the like.

Ferries (10 centavos) run between Regla and the Muelle Luz (Av. San Pedro y Santa Clara) in Habana Vieja.

Bus #6 departs for Regla from Zulueta and Genios in Habana Vieja; bus #106 departs from Zulueta and Refugio.

Iglesia de Nuestra Señora de Regla

The Iglesia de Nuestra Señora de Regla (Church of Our Lady of Regla, Sanctuario #11, e/ Máximo Gómez y Litoral, tel. 07/797-6228, daily 7:30 A.M.–5:30 P.M.), built in 1810 on the harborfront, is one of Havana's loveliest churches. The church's inner beauty is highlighted by a gilt altar, lit with votive candles. Figurines of miscellaneous saints dwell in wall alcoves, including a statue of St. Anthony leading a wooden suckling pig wearing a dog collar and a large blue ribbon. *Habaneros* flock to pay homage to the black Virgen de Regla, patron saint of sailors and Catholic counterpart to Yemayá, the African goddess of the sea in the Yoruba religion. Time your visit for the seventh of each month, when large masses are held, or for a pilgrimage each September 7, when the Virgin is paraded through town.

Outside, 20 meters to the east and presiding over her own private chapel, is a statue of the Virgen de la Caridad del Cobre, Cuba's patron saint. Syncretized as the *orisha* Ochún, she also draws adherents of *santería*.

Colina Lenin

Calle Martí, the main street, leads southeast to the city cemetery; from there, turn east onto Avenida Rosario for two blocks, where steps ascend to Colina Lenin (Lenin Hill, Calle Vieja, e/ Enlase y Rosaria). A three-meter-tall bronze face of the Communist leader is carved into the cliff face. A dozen life-size figures (in cement) cheer him from below. A pitiful museum (tel. 07/797-6899, Tues.–Sat. 9 A.M.–5 P.M., free) atop the hill is dedicated to Lenin and various martyrs of the Cuban revolution.

The Colina is more directly reached from Parque Guaycanamar (Calle Martí, six blocks east of the harborfront) via Calle Albuquerque and 24 de Febrero; you'll reach a metal staircase that leads to the park. Bus #29 will take you there from the Regla dock.

GUANABACOA

Guanabacoa, three kilometers east of Regla, was founded in 1607 and developed as the major trading center for slaves. An Afro-Cuban culture evolved here, expressed in a strong musical heritage. The **Casa de la Trova** (Martí #111, e/ San Antonio y Versalles, tel. 07/797-7687, Tues.–Sun. 9 A.M.–11 P.M., entrance one peso) hosts performances of Afro-Cuban

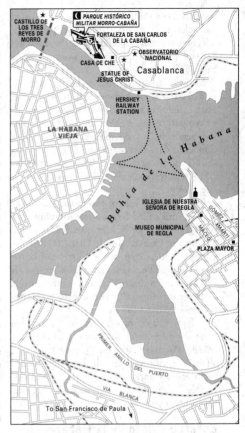

music and dance, as does **Restaurante Las Orishas** (Calle Martí, e/ Lamas y Cruz Verde, tel. 07/794-7878, daily noon–midnight). Guanabacoa is also Cuba's most important center of *santería*. So strong is the association that all over Cuba, folks facing extreme adversity will say "I'm going to have to go to Guanabacoa," implying that only the power of a *babalawo* can fix the problem.

Guanabacoa also boasts several religious sites (most are tumbledown and await restoration), including two Jewish cemeteries on the east side of town. Combined with a visit to Regla, it makes an intriguing excursion from downtown Havana.

To get there, bus #29 runs to Guanabacoa

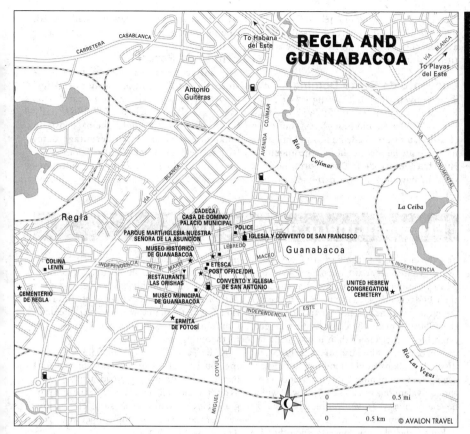

REGLA AND GUANABACOA

from the Regla dock. Bus #3 departs for Guanabacoa from Máximo Gómez and Aponte, on the south side of Parque de la Fraternidad, in Habana Vieja; and bus #95 from the corner of Corrales and Zulueta. From Vedado, you can take bus #195; from the Plaza de la Revolución, take bus #5.

Parque Martí

The sprawling town is centered on the small tree-shaded Parque Martí (Calles Martí, División Pepe Antonio, y Adolfo del Castillo Cadenas), dominated by the recently restored **Iglesia Nuestra Señora de la Asunción** (División #331, e/ Martí y Cadenas, tel. 07/797-7368, Mon.–Fri. 8 A.M.–noon and 2–5 P.M., Sun. 8–11 A.M.), commonly called the Parroquial Mayor. Completed in 1748, it features a lofty Mudejar-inspired wooden roof and baroque gilt altar dripping with gold, plus 14 Stations of the Cross. If the doors are locked, try the side entrance on Calle Enrique Güiral.

The **Museo Histórico de Guanabacoa** (Historical Museum of Guanabacoa, Martí #108, e/ Valenzuela y Quintín Bandera, tel. 07/797-9117, Tues.–Sat. 10 A.M.–6 P.M., Sun. 9 A.M.–1 P.M., entrance CUC2), one block west of the plaza, tells of Guanabacoa's development and the evolution of Afro-Cuban culture.

One block southwest of the park, the **Convento y Iglesia de San Antonio** (Máximo

Gómez, esq. San Antonio, tel. 07/797-7241), begun in 1720 and completed in 1806, is now a school. The *custodio* may let you in to admire the exquisite *alfarje* ceiling.

Convento de Santo Domingo

This convent (Santo Domingo #407, esq. Rafael de Cadena, tel. 07/797-7376, Tues.– Fri. 9–11:30 A.M. and 3:30–5 P.M. but often closed) dates from 1728 and has an impressive neo-baroque facade. Its church, the **Iglesia de Nuestra Señora de la Candelaria,** boasts a magnificent blue-and-gilt baroque altar plus

an intricate *alfarje.* The door is usually closed; ring the doorbell to the left of the entrance.

Ermita de Potosí

The only ecclesiastical edifice thus far restored is the tiny hilltop Ermita de Potosí (Potosí Hermitage, Calzada Vieja Guanabacoa, esq. Calle Potosí, tel. 07/797-9867, daily 8 A.M.–5 P.M.), the highlight of a visit to Guanabacoa. The simple hermitage dates back to 1644 and is the oldest religious structure still standing in Cuba. It has an intriguing cemetery.

Entertainment and Events

Yes, the city has lost the Barbary Coast spirit of prerevolutionary days, but *habaneros* love to paint the town red (so to speak) as much as their budgets allow. Many venues are seedier (albeit without the strippers) than they were in the 1950s; in many the decor hasn't changed! Nightlife is a lot tamer than it was just a decade ago, not least because pricey entrance fees dissuade Cubans from attending. Cubans are even priced out of most bars (one beer can cost the equivalent of a week's salary), few of which have any energy. *Habaneros* mostly socialize impromptu, on the street.

For theater, classical concerts, and other live performances it's difficult to make a reservation by telephone. Instead, go to the venue and buy a ticket in advance or just before the performance. Call ahead to double-check dates, times, and venue.

Havana lacks a reliable, widely circulated forum for announcements of upcoming events. Word of mouth is the best resource. A good Internet source is **Egrem** (in Spanish only, tel. 07/204-4685, http:// promociones.egrem.co.cu), which maintains a weekly update of live concerts nationwide on its website. *Cartelera* (www.lajiribilla.cu/ cartelera_cultural.html) also has weekly updates on its website; its weekly publication with information on exhibitions, galleries,

performances, and more in both Spanish and English is available in many hotel lobbies, as is the monthly *Guía Cultural de la Habana,* which provides up-to-date information on what's on in town. *Granma,* the daily Communist Party newspaper, also lists the forthcoming week's events.

Radio Taíno (1290 AM and 93.3 FM), serving tourists, offers information on cultural happenings with nightly broadcasts 5–7 P.M., as does Radio Habana (94.9 FM); the TV program Hurón Azul (Cubavision) gives a preview of the next week's top happenings every Thursday at 10:25 P.M.

NIGHTLIFE
Bars
HABANA VIEJA

Every tourist in town wants to sip a *mojito* at **La Bodeguita del Medio** (Empredado #207, e/ Cuba y Tacón, tel. 07/862-6121, daily noon– midnight), as Ernest Hemingway did almost daily. However, the *mojitos* are weak and far too small for the CUC4 tab. Go for the ambience, aided by troubadours.

Another Hemingway favorite offering far better and cheaper (CUC3) *mojitos* is the **Dos Hermanos** (Av. San Pedro #304, esq. Sol, tel. 07/861-3514, 24 hours), a down-to-earth wharf-front saloon where Hemingway bent

CINEMAS

Most of Havana's cinemas are mid-20th-century gems that have been allowed to deteriorate to the point of near-dilapidation. Movie houses on La Rampa, in Vedado, tend to be less rundown than those in Habana Vieja and Centro Habana. *Granma* and *Cartelera* list what's currently showing.

The **Sala Glauber Rocha** (Av. 212, esq. 31, La Coronela, tel. 07/271-8967), in the Fundación del Nuevo Cine Latinoamericano, shows mostly Latin American movies.

The most important cinemas are:

· **Cine Acapulco** (Av. 26, e/ 35 y 37, Vedado, tel. 07/833-9573).

· **Cine Charles Chaplin** (Calle 23 #1155, e/ 10 y 12, Vedado, tel. 07/831-1101).

· **Cine La Rampa** (Calle 23 #111, e/ O y P, Vedado, tel. 07/878-6146); it mostly shows Cuban and Latin American films, plus the occasional obscure foreign movie.

· **Cine Payret** (Prado #503, esq. San José, Habana Vieja, tel. 07/863-3163) is Havana's largest cinema and has as many as six showings daily.

· **Cine Riviera** (Calles 23, e/ H y G, Vedado, tel. 07/832-9564).

· **Cine-Teatro Astral** (Calzada de Infanta #501, esq. San Martín, Centro Habana, tel. 07/878-1001) is the comfiest *cine* in Havana. It functions mostly as a theater for political features.

· **Cine Yara** (Calle 23 y Calle L, Vedado, tel. 07/832-9430) is Havana's "main" theater.

· **Multi-Cine Infanta** (Infanta, e/ Neptuno y San Miguel, tel. 07/878-9323) has four up-to-date auditoriums.

---

elbows with sailors and prostitutes at the long wooden bar. There's often live music.

Hemingway enjoyed his daily daiquiri at **El Floridita** (Obispo, esq. Monserrate, tel. 07/867-9299, bar open daily 11:30 A.M.–1 A.M.). It may not quite live up to its 1950s aura, when *Esquire* magazine named it one of the great bars of the world, but to visit Havana without sipping a (weak) daiquiri here would be like visiting France without tasting the wine.

The wood-paneled **Bar Monserrate** (Monserrate, esq. Obrapía, tel. 07/860-9751, daily noon–midnight), just south of El Floridita, is popular with Cubans and is noted for its Coctel Monserrate: one teaspoon of sugar, two ounces of grapefruit juice, five drops of grenadine, two ounces of white rum, ice, and a sprig of mint (CUC2.50). It's a good spot to while away the afternoon listening to live music. It draws *jineteros* and *jineteras*. Count your change!

I love the **Café Barrita** (Monserrate #261, esq. San Juan de Dios, tel. 07/862-9310, ext. 131, daily 9 A.M.–6 P.M.), in Edificio Bacardí.

Formerly the private bar of the Bacardí family, it casts you back to the 1930s. It's popular with a cigar-smoking foreign crowd, and the *mojitos* are strong.

Lluvia de Oro (Obispo #316, esq. Habana, tel. 07/862-9870, daily 9 A.M.–midnight) is a lively, down-to-earth bar popular with foreigners come to sample the live music and meet wayward *cubanas* and *cubanos*. It serves cheap but strong *mojitos* (CUC2.50) and features live *son* music. Nearby, the similar, once-rocking **Café París** (San Ignacio #202, esq. Obispo, tel. 07/862-0466, daily 9 A.M.–midnight) has yet to reignite its former spark.

Hotel bars receive few clients (except a sprinkling of tourists) and are often boring. The lobby piano-bar in the **Hotel Ambos Mundos** (Obispo, esq. Mercaderes, tel. 07/860-9530, 24 hours) is a delightful place to tipple, as is the **Bar La Marina** (Av. San Pedro, esq. Luz, tel. 07/862-8000) in the Hotel Armadores de Santander. The latter has an upscale mood and nautical motif (including staff in mariners' uniforms). The chicest bars are the one in the **Hotel Saratoga** (Paseo de Martí #603, esq. Dragones, tel. 07/868-1000, noon–midnight) and the art deco **Bar Lejaim** (San Ignacio, esq. Amargura, tel. 07/860-8280) in the Hotel Raquel, which has an open bar each Wednesday evening. Lejaim has Cuban cocktails and *bocas* (snacks).

Beer lovers should head to Plaza Vieja, where the **Taberna de la Muralla** (San Ignacio #364, tel. 07/866-4453, daily 11 A.M.–1 A.M.), a Viennese-style brewpub, produces delicious Pilsen (light) and Munich (dark) beer. You can order half-liters (CUC2), liters, or a whopping three-liter dispenser, called a *dispensa*. This tall glass cylinder is fitted with a tap and filled with beer kept chilled by a thin center tube filled with ice.

VEDADO AND PLAZA DE LA REVOLUCIÓN

The Hotel Nacional's **Bar Vista del Golfo** (Calle O, esq. 21, tel. 07/874-3564) has a jukebox and walls festooned with photos of famous visitors such as Errol Flynn and assorted mobsters. It rarely has patrons, however; they prefer the hotel's airy **Bar La Terraza,** where one can sit in a sofa chair with a cigar and cocktail while musicians entertain with live music.

The small **El Relicario Bar** (Paseo, e/ 1ra y 3ra, tel. 07/204-3636, 1 P.M.–1 A.M.), in the mezzanine of the Hotel Meliá Cohiba, is popular with a monied, cigar-loving crowd and offers an elegant Edwardian ambience and relative serenity. It also has a pool table. I like the small lobby bar in the **Hotel Habana Riviera** (Malecón y Paseo, tel. 07/836-4051) and the sedate lobby bar of the **Hotel Habana Libre Tryp** (Calle L, e/ 23 y 25, tel. 07/834-6100, daily 7 A.M.–11 P.M.).

For superb views of the city, try the **Salón Turquino** (25th floor inside Habana Libre Tryp, Calle L, e/ 23 y 25, tel. 07/834-6100) or **La Torre** (Calle 17 #55, e/ M y N, tel. 07/832-2451), atop the Focsa building.

Penny-pinchers wanting to sup with Cubans should head to **Gran Café** (Calle 23, esq. Av. de los Presidentes, tel. 07/830-9375,

daily 10 A.M.–2 A.M.), serving CUC1 *mojitos* and CUC0.50 rum shots. The surroundings are simple. Also popular with Cubans is **Mesón de la Chorrera** (Malecón y Calle 20, tel. 07/838-3896, daily noon–midnight), upstairs in the old fortress at the mouth of the Río Almendares; this atmospheric place even has cannons pointing through the windows.

PLAYA (MIRAMAR AND BEYOND)

This district has very few bars. The classy **Paleta Bar** (tel. 07/204-7311, daily 11:30 A.M.–midnight), in the Miramar Trade Center, draws expats-in-the-know. The hip, minimalist place occasionally has live music.

The class act in town on Saturday night is the bar at the Occidental Miramar (5ta Av., e/ 72 y 76, tel. 07/204-3584), with live music and a trend-setting young crowd.

Two piano bars to consider are **Dos Gardenias** (7ma Av. y 26, tel. 07/204-2353, daily noon–midnight) and **Piano Bar Piel Canela** (Calle 16 #701, esq. 7ma, tel. 07/204-1543, daily 3–8 P.M. and 10 P.M.–3 A.M., entrance CUC1), at La Maison.

Traditional Cuban Music and Dance

HABANA VIEJA

Agencia de Viajes San Cristóbal (Oficios #110, e/ Lamparilla y Amargura, tel. 07/861-9171, www.viajessancristobal.cu) hosts **Noche en las Plazas** (Night in the Plazas) one Saturday a month at 9 P.M. in the Plaza de la Catedral or Plaza de San Francisco, with folkloric *espectáculos* (CUC22 with dinner). Reservations can be made at hotel tour desks.

The last Saturday of each month, the **Peña de Heydi Igualada** features the eponymous *trova* singer in the Palacio de Segundo Caballo (O'Reilly #14, tel. 07/862-8091), at 3 P.M. on Plaza de Armas.

The **Asociación Cultural Yoruba de Cuba** (Prado #615, e/ Dragones y Monte, tel. 07/863-5953) hosts the Peña Oyú Obbá, with traditional Afro-Cuban music and dance, Thursday 6–8 P.M. and Friday 9 A.M.–8 P.M. (CUC5).

CENTRO HABANA AND CERRO

The place to be on Sunday is "Salvador's Alley" for **Rumba del "Salvador's Alley"** (Callejón de Hamel, e/ Aramburo y Hospital, tel. 07/878-1661, eliasasef@yahoo.es), where Salvador González Escalona hosts a rumba with Afro-Cuban music and dance (Sun. noon–3 P.M.) and traditional music (9 P.M. last Friday of each month).

The **Casa de la Trova** (San Lázaro #661, e/ Padre Varela y Gervasio, tel. 07/879-3373l, Mon.–Fri. 8:30 A.M.–4:30 P.M., CUC5) has live music—everything from *filin* to *son* and *nueva trova*. Friday evening is best. Adherents of *filin* music flock to **La Peña de Joya** (San Lázaro #667, Apto. 9, e/ Padre Varela y Gervasio), two doors down, Friday 10 P.M.–1 A.M.

VEDADO AND PLAZA DE LA REVOLUCIÓN

My favorite hangout in Havana is **Café Concierto Gato Tuerto** (Calle O #14, e/ 17 y 19, tel. 07/833-2224, CUC5 cover), a cramped and moody 1950s-style nightclub that hosts *música filin, trova,* and *bolero* nightly until 3 A.M. It gets packed, mostly with middle-aged Cubans (and a smattering of expats with their trophy Cuban girlfriends) jammed cheek-to-jowl against the postage stamp–size stage tucked into a corner. It's the kind of place Sinatra and his Rat Pack might have hung out. The show normally doesn't begin until 11 P.M. Don't miss the Voces Negras, a quintet that sings everything from Aretha Franklin and Frank Sinatra to salsa.

Nearby, the **Sala 1830** (in the Hotel Nacional, Calle O y 21, tel. 07/873-3564) hosts Grupo Compay Segundo each Saturday at 9:45 P.M. (CUC25 cover, CUC50 with dinner).

Club Imágenes (Calzada #602, esq. C, tel. 07/833-3606, daily 11 P.M.–3 A.M., CUC5 cover), a stylish piano bar, hosts *boleros* and other traditional music for the late-night (and more mature) crowd. It also has karaoke and comedy (Fri.–Sun. 3:30–8 P.M., CUC2).

El Hurón Azul (UNEAC, Calle 17 #351, esq. H, tel. 07/832-4551, daily 5 P.M.–2 A.M.) hosts a *peña* with Afro-Cuban music and dance on Wednesday at 5 P.M. (CUC5), *trovas* on Thursday at 5 P.M. (CUC1), plus *boleros* on Saturday at 9 P.M. (CUC1). This is ground zero for bohemian intellectual life in Havana, and many of Cuba's top writers and artists hang out here.

The acclaimed **Conjunto Folklórico Nacional** (National Folklore Dance Group, Calle 4 #103, e/ Calzada y 5ta, tel. 07/830-3060, CUC5) performs *Sábado de rumba* alfresco each Saturday at 3 P.M. This is Afro-Cuban music and dance at its best.

Casa de las Américas (3ra Calle, esq. Av. de los Presidentes, tel. 07/832-2706, www.casa.cult.cu) hosts an eclectic range of concerts (Mon.–Fri. 8 A.M.–4:30 P.M.).

On the third Sunday of each month, head to the Centro Iberoamericano de la Décima (Calle A, e/ 25 y 27, tel. 07/837-5383, decimal@cubarte.cult.cu) for **El Jardín de la Gorda** (5 P.M.), when Sara Gonzaléz—the *gorda* (fat lady)—belts out *nueva trova*. And at 6 P.M. on the last Saturday of every month, Frank Delgado performs *nueva trova* live at the **Cine Riviera** (Calle 23, e/ F y G, tel. 07/830-9564).

PLAYA (MIRAMAR AND BEYOND)

For *boleros,* head to **Rincón de Boleros** (7ma Av., esq. 26, tel. 07/204-2353, daily 10:30 P.M.–3 A.M., CUC10), in the Dos Gardenias complex.

Cabarets Espectáculos
HABANA VIEJA

The **Hotel Telégrafo** (Paseo de Martí #408, esq. Neptuno, tel. 07/861-1010, CUC5) has a small *cabaret espectáculo* on Friday at 5 P.M. and Saturday at 9 P.M.

CENTRO HABANA AND CERRO

Cabaret Nacional (San Rafael, esq. Prado, tel. 07/863-2361, CUC5), in the dingy basement of the Gran Teatro, has a modest *espectáculo* nightly at 10 P.M. The campy show normally doesn't begin until later, and is followed by a disco. A dress code applies. It packs in Cubans on weekends for steamy dancing; ostensibly only couples are admitted.

You can safely skip the *cabaret espectáculo* in the basement of the Hotel Deauville without fear of missing a stunning experience.

VEDADO AND PLAZA DE LA REVOLUCIÓN

The most lavish show is the **Cabaret Parisien** (Calle O, esq. 21, tel. 07/836-3863, CUC29, or CUC58 with dinner), in the Hotel Nacional. The *Cubano cubano* show is offered nightly at 10 P.M. The dinner special (CUC50–70) is best avoided. The place is cramped and fills with smoke, and while the show is nowhere near the scale of the Tropicana, it has plenty of color and titillation. It's handily right in the heart of Vedado and thus beats the long trek out to Marianao for the Tropicana.

The **Cabaret Copa Room** (Paseo y Malecón, tel. 07/836-4051, CUC20, or CUC45 with dinner and cocktail), in the Hotel Habana Riviera, hosts a cabaret (Thurs.–Sun. at 10 P.M.). The venue specializes in the Latin beat and often features the top names in live Cuban music, such as Los Van Van. It's one of Havana's top spots for serious salsa fans.

Catering mostly to a tourist crowd, the contrived **Habana Café** (Paseo, e/ 1ra y 3ra, tel. 07/833-3636, ext. 147, nightly 8 P.M.–3 A.M.), adjoining the Hotel Meliá Cohiba, offers cabaret. A classic Harley-Davidson, an old Pontiac, and a 1957 open-top, canary-yellow Chevy add a dramatic effect, as does an airplane suspended from the ceiling. (Suddenly the car horns beep, the headlamps flash, and you'll hear the roar of an airplane taking off. Then the curtains open and—voilà—the show begins.) Entrance is usually free, but a CUC5 *consumo mínimo* applies (entrance costs CUC20 when top bands such as Los Van Van and Charanga Habanera play). It also has a disco on Friday nights. You can make a night of it by dining on overpriced but reasonable-quality burgers (from CUC5) and even a banana split (CUC5). The venue relies heavily on the tourist trade, and there's no shortage of *jineteras*—check your bill carefully, as scams are frequent.

Similar third-tier venues catering mostly to Cubans are **Karachi Club** (Calles 17 y K, tel. 07/832-3485, nightly 10 P.M.–4 A.M., CUC5); **Centro Nocturno La Red** (Calle 19 #151, esq. L, tel. 07/832-5415, 10 P.M.–4 A.M., CUC1–2), with karaoke on Monday, Latin music on Wednesday, comedy Thursday–Saturday, followed by disco; and the dingy **Club Amanecer** (Calle 15, e/ O y N, 10 P.M.–3 A.M., CUC5), with a small *cabaret espectáculo* Monday–Tuesday, karaoke Wednesday–Thursday, and live music Friday–Saturday.

PLAYA (MIRAMAR AND BEYOND)

The **Tropicana** is Havana's top cabaret.

The small open-air cabaret at **La Cecilia** (5ta Av. #11010, e/ 1110 y 112, tel. 07/204-1562, Fri.–Sat. 9:30 P.M., Fri. CUC5, Sat. CUC10) has improved and draws monied foreign residents and Cuba's youthful hipsters for the disco that follows. Top bands often perform (CUC20–25).

Macumba Habana (Calle 222, e/ 37 y 51, tel. 07/273-0568, Sat. 5 P.M.–midnight, Sun. 5–11 P.M., CUC5–15), in the La Giraldilla complex in the La Coronela district, offers a small *espectáculo* at 9:30 P.M. with a different theme nightly. Other second-tier venues include the **Hotel Comodoro** (1ra Av. y Calle 84, tel. 07/204-5551) and **Hotel Kohly** (Av. 49 y 36A, Rpto. Kohly, Playa, tel. 07/204-0240, free), on Monday and Wednesday at 9 P.M.

Cuba's catwalk divas strut at **La Maison** (Calle 16 #701, esq. 7ma, Miramar, tel. 07/204-1543, CUC5), renowned for its *desfiles de modas* (fashion shows) and *cabaret espectáculo* (Thurs.–Sun. 10 P.M.) in the terrace garden of an elegant old mansion. Reservations are recommended. Matinees show at 4 P.M. Wednesday–Thursday and Saturday–Sunday.

◀ TROPICANA

Cuba's premier Las Vegas–style nightclub is the Tropicana (Calle 72 #4504 y Línea del Ferrocarril, Marianao, tel. 07/267-1717, www.cabaret-tropicana.com, entrance CUC70–90, cameras CUC5, videos CUC15, dinner CUC10), boasting more than 200 performers,

PARADISE UNDER THE STARS

Tropicana, the prerevolutionary extravaganza, has been in continuous operation since New Year's Eve 1939, when it opened (in the gardens of a mansion – Villa Mina – that once housed the U.S. ambassador) as the most flamboyant nightclub in the world. The club soon eclipsed all other clubs in the grandeur and imagination of its productions. The Congo Pantera revue, which simulated a panther's nocturnal hunt in lush jungle, established the Tropicana's trademark, with dancers in the thick vegetation illuminated by colored spotlights – the name Tropicana melds the wold *trópico* (tropics) with *palma cana* (fan palm).

In its heyday, international celebrities such as Nat "King" Cole, Josephine Baker, and Carmen Miranda headlined the show, which was so popular that a 50-passenger "Tropicana Special" flew nightly from Miami for an evening of entertainment that ended in the nightclub's casino, where a daily US$10,000-bingo jackpot was offered and a new automobile was raffled every Sunday.

Talent scouts scoured Cuba for the most beautiful models and dancers. The more than 200 performers are still handpicked from the crème de la crème of Cuba's singers and dancers, though the latter no longer dance topless. Patrons watch mesmerized as rainbow-hued searchlights sweep over the hordes of long-legged showgirls, gaudily feathered with sensational headdresses more ostentatious than peacocks, parading 20 feet up among the floodlit palm trees, quivering beseechingly like tropical birds.

In 2005, the Ministry of Tourism, headed by a new, austere military figure, took control of Tropicana. Immediately, it was announced that the infamously erotic show would be tamed down and replaced with "Drums in Concert," a theatrical show with more emphasis on stage sets and high-tech lighting. Even the dancers bemoan the change, which meant goodbye to much of the gratuitous skin marked by the opening act, when a troupe of near-naked showgirls paraded down the aisles wearing see-through body stockings and glowing chandeliers atop their heads.

figurante with chandelier at Tropicana nightclub, Havana

© CHRISTOPHER P. BAKER

a fabulous orchestra, and astonishing acrobatic feats. Famous international entertainers occasionally perform. The cabaret takes place in the open-air Salón Bajo Las Estrellas (Tues.–Sun. 10 P.M.). A superb violin octet—the Violines de Tropicana—entertains early arrivers. The entrance fee is outrageous but includes a quarter bottle of rum with cola, a glass of cheap champagne, and a cheap cigar. Purchase tickets at the reservation booth (10 A.M.–6 P.M.) or directly at the entrance from 8:30 P.M. (call ahead to check availability); however, it's best to book in advance through your hotel tour desk, as the show often sells out. It's also a 20-minute taxi ride downtown. Whole or partial refunds are offered if the show is rained out. Cocktails cost CUC5. (Beware rip-offs by the waiters, who typically wait until the end of the show to bill you for any incidentals, then disappear without giving you your change as you get caught in the rush to depart.) The Tropicana also has two eateries: the elegant sky-lit **Los Jardines,** serving tasty continental fare (6 P.M.–1 A.M.), and the 1950s diner–style **Rodney Café** (noon–2 A.M.).

Discos and Nightclubs
HABANA VIEJA
Disco Karaoke, atop the Hotel Plaza (Zulueta #267, esq. Neptuno, tel. 07/860-8583, nightly 11 P.M.–5 A.M., CUC5), packs Cubans in thick as sardines.

CENTRO HABANA AND CERRO
One of the city's most popular venues is **Casa de la Música** (Galiano #253, e/ Concordia y Neptuno, tel. 07/862-4165, daily 4–7 P.M. and 10 P.M.–2 A.M., CUC10–20). A modern theater known as "Dos" (for Casa de la Música 2, or *dos*), it fills with a mostly Cuban crowd for concerts and dancing. The venue is run by Egrem, the state recording company.

A bit more raw and rough around the edges, **Cabaret Palermo** (San Miguel, esq. Amistad, tel. 07/861-9745, Thurs.–Sun. 10 P.M.–4 A.M., CUC2–5) is one of Havana's major rap scenes. Shows are sometimes preceded by a *cabaret espectáculo.*

VEDADO AND PLAZA DE LA REVOLUCIÓN
Salón Turquino (Calle L, e/ 23 y 25, tel. 07/834-4011, nightly 10:30 P.M.–3 A.M., CUC10 cover), atop the Hotel Habana Libre, offers a medley of entertainment that varies nightly, followed by salsa dancing. Top bands often perform and the place will close for VIP parties. The popular venue draws tourists and Cubans with dollars to spend. No single Cubans are allowed (foreigners are propositioned at the door by women seeking admission). Salsa lessons are offered in the mezzanine bar each Saturday at 4 P.M.

The **Salón Rojo** (Calle 21, e/ N y O, tel. 07/833-3747 or 832-0511, nightly 10 P.M.–2 A.M., CUC10–25), beside the Hotel Capri, ditched its cabaret in favor of a nightclub venue hosting Havana's hottest acts, such

HAVANA'S GAY SCENE

Gay life in Havana has expanded noticeably in recent years, although homosexual venues remain subject to police crackdowns. There are no established gay bars or clubs, which are banned, and the gay "scene" revolves around "hangout" street locales. Most venues attract male prostitutes, called *pingueros* (from the Spanish word *pinga*, or prick). Several recent murders of foreigners in Havana have been linked to transvestites and the homosexual underground.

Most nights there's one or more gay parties known as *fiestas de diez pesos* at private venues (entrance typically costs 10 pesos, or sometimes CUC1-2). Havana society is non-exclusionary, however; everyone is welcome, and the mix usually includes a sprinkling of straight, lesbian, and even *transvestis*. Private parties often feature drag shows. The "floating party" venues change nightly as they try to stay one step ahead of the police.

To find out where the night's gay party is, head to the **Cine Yara** (La Rampa y L, Vedado). However, in 2009 this area had cooled and Havana's main nighttime cruising spot is now the **Malecón,** opposite Fiat Café near the foot of La Rampa.

BARS, CAFÉS, AND CLUBS
A *transvesti* show is hosted at the **Sociedad Cultural Rosalía de Castro** (Av. de Bélgica #504 altos, e/ Máximo Gómez y Dragones, tel. 07/862-3193).

In Vedado, **Café Fresa y Chocolate** (Calle 13 y 12, Vedado) and **La Arcada** (Calle M y 23, open 24 hours) are effectively the only gay bars in town. The cramped, humid **Club Tropical** (Línea, esq. F, tel. 07/832-7361, daily 10 P.M.-3 A.M.) occasionally acts as a gay venue, as does the steamy cellar bar, **Club Saturno** (Línea, e/ 10 y 12, tel. 07/833-7942, daily 11 P.M.-2:30 A.M.).

Bar de las Estrellas (Calle A #507, e/ 15 y 16), in the Lawton district, south of Cerro, is a *paladar* (private restaurant) with a transvestite cabaret at 10 P.M.

as Los Van Van and Bandolero. It's now the hottest spot in town for sexy dancing and searing sounds.

Penny-pinchers might head to the **Cabaret Pico Blanco** (Calle O #206, e/ 23 y 25, tel. 07/833-3740, nightly 9 P.M.–3 A.M., CUC5–10) in the glass-enclosed top floor of the Hotel St. John. It hosts salsa, *boleros,* and *trova,* though the mood runs hot and cold. Occasionally a top name is featured; other times you may have to suffer through karaoke. A disco follows. Around the corner, Calle 23 between Calles O y N has several dingy clubs drawing a young Cuban crowd for merengue and salsa.

Cubans flock to one of the city's hottest venues, **Café Cantante** (Paseo, esq. 39, tel. 07/879-7011, Tues.–Sat. 9 P.M.–5 A.M., CUC3, or CUC10–20 when top groups perform) in the basement of the Teatro Nacional. No hats, T-shirts, or shorts are permitted for men, and no photos are allowed. Friday afternoons have live salsa (4–6 P.M.); only Cubans go and with luck you'll be charged in pesos. The plusher **Delirio Habanero** (tel. 07/873-5713), a lounge on the third floor of the Teatro Nacional (Av. Carlos M. de Céspedes, esq. Paseo), also has afternoon *peñas* (3–7 P.M.) and live music (Tues.–Sun. 10 A.M.–2 A.M., CUC5–CUC15), when the place can rock everything from *boleros* to *timba.* Also in the Teatro Nacional, **Mi Habana** has music and dance the same hours.

Popular with a gay crowd, **Café Fresa y Chocolate** (Calle 23 y 12, tel. 07/836-2096, Mon.–Wed. 10 A.M.–10 P.M., Thurs.–Sat. noon.–midnight) has music videos on weekdays, plus comedy and variety shows on weekends.

PLAYA (MIRAMAR AND BEYOND)

Run by Egrem, the state recording company, the **Casa de la Música** (Av. 25, esq. 20, tel. 07/204-0447, Wed.–Sun. 5–9 P.M. and 11 P.M.–3:30 A.M., CUC10–20) sometimes has sizzling-hot afternoon salsa sessions as well as nightly (Tues.–Sun.) performances by such legends as Bamboleo and Chucho Valdés. The place is preferred by Cubans with some money to burn, and the fact that the audience usually includes some of Cuba's hottest performers says

it all. The headliner normally doesn't come on until 1 A.M. Also here is the **Disco Tun Tún** (nightly 11 P.M.–6 A.M., CUC10), which keeps in the groove until dawn.

Unfathomably popular at last visit, **Don Cangrejo** (1ra Av., e/ 16 y 18, tel. 07/204-3837, daily noon–midnight, entrance CUC5) is a most unlikely venue. The restaurant's open-air oceanfront pool complex hosts live music, attracts a chic in-crowd (mostly well-heeled foreign men, monied white Cubans with high-positioned parents, and beautiful *habaneras,* many of whom are drawn by the former). There's no room to dance.

Cubans of lesser means head to **Club Río** (Calle A #314, e/ 3ra y 5ta, tel. 07/209-3389, Tues.–Sun. 10 P.M.–3 A.M., CUC5), colloquially called Johnny's. DJs spin up-to-date tunes. It also has a cabaret on the sunken dance floor. Couples only are permitted. It has a reputation for pickpockets, violence, and scams.

Salón Chévere (Club Almendares, Calle 49C y 28A, Rpto. Kohly, tel. 07/204-4990, daily noon–4 A.M.) has live music and dancing alfresco, with the real action beginning after 10 P.M. The CUC15 entrance includes an open bar.

Cubans also find their fun at **Teatro Karl Marx** (1ra Av., e/ 8 y 10, tel. 07/203-0801, Fri.–Sun. 9 P.M.–2 A.M., CUC10–20). Los Van Van, Isaac Delgado, and other big names play here. The vast theater also plays host to many of the city's big-ticket events (such as the closing galas of the Latin American Film Festival).

Farther out, **Salón Rosado Benny Moré** (Av. 41, esq. 48, tel. 07/209-1281, Fri.–Mon. 7 P.M.–2 A.M. for live groups, Tues.–Wed. for cabaret, CUC5–10), an open-air concert arena known as El Tropical, is immensely popular on weekends when top-billed Cuban salsa bands perform. Probably the wildest place in town on a Saturday night, it features kick-ass music and dancing—the dancing is salacious, and rum-induced fights often break out. For better or worse, foreigners are sometimes kept apart from *habaneros.*

Another popular venue for Cubans is **El Sauce** (9ta #12015, e/ 120 y 130, tel. 07/204-

6248), hosting live bands from rock (such as the Cuban group Dimensión Vertical, Sun. 4 P.M.) to salsa.

Jazz
HABANA VIEJA
Jazz trios perform upstairs nightly in **Café del Oriente** (Oficios #112, esq. Amargura, tel. 07/860-6686) and five nights a week in the lobby of the **Hotel NH Parque Central** (Neptuno, e/ Prado y Zulueta, tel. 07/866-6627).

However, the key jazz venue is the **Bar Chico O'Farrill** (Cuba #102, esq. Chacón, tel. 07/860-5080), in the Hotel Palacio O'Farrill. It hosts Cuba's top performers Friday–Sunday evenings.

VEDADO AND PLAZA DE LA REVOLUCIÓN
The **Jazz Café** (1ra at the base of Paseo, tel. 07/838-3556, daily noon–2 A.M., CUC10 *consumo mínimo*), on the third floor of the Galería del Paseo, is a classy supper-club with some of the best live jazz in town, including resident maestro Chucho Valdés. The music doesn't get going until about 11:30 P.M., though the seats usually fill up well before.

La Zorra y el Cuervo (Calle 23, e/ N y O, tel. 07/833-2402, zorra@cbcan.cyt.cu, 10 P.M.–2 A.M., CUC10) is a jazz club in a dreary basement setting. Occasional foreign bands perform here, as do the Cuban greats such as Chucho Valdés. It has "blues" on Thursdays. The first set normally kicks off at 10:30 P.M.

UNEAC's **El Hurón Azul** (Calle 17 #351, e/ G y H, Vedado, tel. 07/832-4551, www.uneac. com) has *tardes del jazz* (jazz afternoons) every second Thursday of the month at 5 P.M. The **Peña de Rembert Duharte** is hosted in the garden adjoining the Teatro Mella (Línea e/ A y B, tel. 07/830-4987) the last Friday of each month at 5 P.M.

PLAYA (MIRAMAR AND BEYOND)
A jazz group performs at the **Tocororo** (Calle 18 y 3ra Av., tel. 07/202-2209) restaurant. The

piano bar at the **Hotel Panorama Havana** (Calle 70, esq. 3ra, tel. 07/204-0100, 9 P.M.–2 A.M.) hosts jazz nightly.

Rap and Rock
VEDADO AND PLAZA DE LA REVOLUCIÓN
If ever you doubted that Cuba has a rock scene, head to **Maxim Rock** (Bruzón, e/ Almendares y Ayasterán, tel. 07/877-5925) for live concerts Wednesday–Saturday 8 P.M.–midnight.

Roqueros also gravitate to **Patio de María** (Calle 37 #262, e/ Paseo y 2, Vedado, tel. 07/881-0722, daily 7:30 A.M.–11 P.M., five pesos), one block west of Teatro Nacional, where rock concerts and varied *peñas* are hosted. Meanwhile, the theater hosts the **Peña de Los Kents** in the Café Cantante (Sun. 4 P.M.), when the eponymous and aging rock band plays oldster classics.

Rap, reggaeton, and other innovative avante-garde music concerts are hosted at **La Madriguera** (Av. Salvador Allende, e/ Infanta y Luaces, tel. 07/879-8175, 5–10 pesos, Mon.–Wed. and Fri.–Sat. 9 A.M.–7 P.M. and Thurs. 9 A.M.–midnight). A disco is hosted Thursday nights. La Madriguera, home to the Asociación Hermanos Saíz (youth group of UNEAC), is entered off Infanta in an unlikely spot in the overgrown botanical gardens.

Comedy
HABANA VIEJA
The **Casa de la Comedia** (Calle Justíz #18, esq. Baratillo, tel. 07/863-9282, CUC2), one block southeast of Plaza de Armas, hosts comic theater on weekends at 7 P.M.

Cine-Teatro Fausto (Prado #201, esq. Colón, Habana Vieja, tel. 07/862-5416) has comedy Friday–Saturday at 8:30 P.M. and Sunday at 5 P.M.

CENTRO HABANA AND CERRO
Comedy is a staple at **Teatro América** (Av. de Italia #253, e/ Concordia y Neptuno, tel. 07/862-5416) every Saturday at 8:30 P.M. and Sunday at 5 P.M.

VEDADO AND PLAZA
DE LA REVOLUCIÓN

The hot spot at last visit was **La Roca** (Calle 21, esq. M, tel. 07/834-4501, Tues.–Wed., Fri., and Sun. 10 P.M.–2 A.M., CUC5), which packs in Cubans for slapstick comedy; dine here first to secure a good seat. Bring a sweater.

Comedy is also performed at the **Humor Club Cocodrilo** (Av. 3ra y 10, Vedado, tel. 07/837-0305, nightly 10 P.M.–3 A.M., CUC5). Magicians perform as well. The **Teatro Bertolt Brecht** (Calle 13, esq. I, tel. 07/832-9359) specializes in comedy, offered Tuesday at 8:30 P.M.

THE ARTS
Tango and Flamenco
HABANA VIEJA

Flamenco is hosted at **Centro Andaluz en Cuba** (Prado #104, e/ Genios y Refugio, tel. 07/863-6745, free) each Wednesday, Friday, and Saturday at 9 P.M. Lessons are offered Tuesday–Thursday 9–11 A.M. (CUC15 per hour).

The touristy **El Mesón de la Flota** (Mercaderes #257, e/ Amargura y Brasil, tel. 07/863-3838, free) hosts flamenco shows daily 1:30–3 P.M. and 9–11 P.M.; you can even watch through the bars from the street.

The **Caserón de Tango** (Calle Justíz #21, e/ Baratillo y Oficios, tel. 07/861-0822) has tango *peñas* on Wednesday and Friday at 5 P.M., shows on Saturday at 10 P.M. and Sunday at 9:30 P.M., and tango lessons (CUC5) Thursday 4–6 P.M. and Saturday 2–4 P.M. (other days by arrangement).

CENTRO HABANA AND CERRO

Caserón del Tango (Neptuno #303, e/ Águila y Italia, tel. 07/863-0097) hosts tango *peñas* on Monday 7–8 P.M.

Theater, Classical Music, and Ballet
HABANA VIEJA

The most important theater in Havana is the **Gran Teatro de la Habana** (Paseo de Martí #458, e/ San Rafael y San Martín, Habana

---

CLOWNS

Clowns (*payasos*) are everywhere in Cuba. They roam the streets entertaining the populace. And they're a favorite at kids' birthday parties. Havana even has a Barnum & Bailey's equivalent.

Named for a famous but deceased Cuban clown, Havana's **Circo Trompoloco** (Calle 112, esq. 5ta Av., Miramar, tel. 07/206-5609 or 206-5641, Thurs.–Sun. 7 P.M. and Sat.–Sun. 4 P.M., CUC10) opened in 2007 to much fanfare as the headquarters of the National Circus of Cuba, which performs beneath a red-and-white-striped "big top" on Thursday and Friday at 4 P.M. and Saturday and Sunday at 4 P.M. and 7 P.M.

Adjoining the circus is **Isla del Coco Parque Temático** (tel. 07/208-0330, Wed.–Fri. 4-10 P.M., Sat.–Sun. 10 A.M.–10 P.M.). This theme park can't quite match Disney World, but it's still an admirable venue for kids to thrill to go-karts, a big-dipper, carousels, etc.

Vieja, tel. 07/861-3077, CUC20 for best orchestra seats), on the west side of Parque Central. It's the main stage for the acclaimed Ballet Nacional de Cuba, Ballet Español de la Habana, and the national opera company. The ballet is usually performed to taped music. The building has three theaters—the Teatro García Lorca, where ballet and concerts are held, and the smaller Sala Alejo Carpentier and Sala Antonin Artaud, for less commercial, experimental performances. Performances are Thursday–Saturday at 8:30 P.M. and Sunday at 5 P.M. A dress code applies.

On Friday, a symphony band strikes up at 4 P.M. in **Plaza de Armas.**

The **Basílica de San Francisco de Asís** (Calle Oficios, e/ Amargura y Brasil, tel. 07/862-9683) hosts weekly but irregular, classical concerts at 6 P.M. (CUC2–10).

For choral music, head to **Hostal Frailes** (Brasil, e/ Oficios y Mercaderes, tel. 07/862-9383, daily 10 A.M.–5 P.M.), hosting sacred music in the lobby. Classical and ecclesiastical concerts are also featured in the **Iglesia de San Francisco de Paula** (Av. del Puerto, esq. Leonor Pérez, tel. 07/860-4210, free or CUC5) on Fridays and Saturdays at 7 P.M., and in the **Oratorio San Felipe Neri** (Calle Aguiar, esq. Obrapía) daily at 7 P.M.

VEDADO AND PLAZA DE LA REVOLUCIÓN

Performances of the Orquesta Sinfónica Nacional de Cuba (National Symphony) and Danza Contemporánea de Cuba are hosted at the **Teatro Nacional** (Av. Carlos M. de Céspedes, esq. Paseo, Vedado, tel. 07/879-6011, tnc@cubarte.cult.cu) every Friday–Saturday at 8:30 P.M. and Sunday at 5 P.M. (CUC1.80–8.90). The ticket office is open Tuesday–Thursday (10 A.M.–6 P.M.) and Friday–Sunday (3–9 P.M.).

The **Teatro Mella** (Línea #657, e/ A y B, Vedado, tel. 07/833-5651) is noted for contemporary dance, theater, and ballet (CUC5–10), and hosts the Conjunto Folklórico Nacional.

For something more intimate, head to the monthly **Peña de Manuel Argudín** (Agencia Cubana de Derecho de Autor Musical, Calle 6 #313, e/ 13 y 15, Vedado, tel. 07/830-0724, www.acdam.cu), the last Saturday of each month at 6 P.M. The eponymous guitarist is often accompanied by such renowned performers as pianist Frank Fernández.

The last Thursday of each month, UNEAC (Calle 17 #351, e/ G y H, Vedado, tel. 07/832-4551, www.uneac.com) hosts an open *peña* for chamber musicians at 6 P.M.

Teatro Cine Trianón (Línea #706, e/ Paseo y A, tel. 07/832-9648, five pesos) often features foreign classics, such as the works of Tennessee Williams, performed by the Teatro el Público Company.

The **Teatro Amadeo Roldán** (Calzada y D, Vedado, tel. 07/832-1168, CUC5–10) has two *salas* and features classical concerts year-round. The Orquesta Sinfónica Nacional is based here, with concerts in season (Thurs.–Sun. 5 P.M.); many lesser classical groups also perform.

Nearby is the **Teatro Hubert de Blanck** (Calzada #657, e/ A y B, tel. 07/830-1011, CUC5), known for both modern and classical plays. Shows (in Spanish) are usually Friday–Saturday at 8:30 P.M. and Sunday at 5 P.M.

The 150-seat **Teatro Buendía** (Calle Loma y 38, Nuevo Vedado, tel. 07/881-6689, five pesos), in a converted Greek Orthodox church, hosts performances by the eponymous theater company, considered to be Cuba's most innovative and accomplished. It performs here Friday–Sunday at 8:30 P.M.

The **Teatro Guiñol** (Calle M, e/ 17 y 19, tel. 07/832-6262, CUC2), on the west side of the Focsa building, is Cuba's leading children's theater, with comedy and puppet shows Friday at 3 P.M., Saturday at 5 P.M., and Sunday at 10:30 A.M. and 5 P.M.

Aguas Espectáculo

VEDADO AND PLAZA DE LA REVOLUCIÓN

Choreographed water ballets are offered at the **Hotel Meliá Cohiba** (Paseo, e/ 1ra y 3ra, tel. 07/833-3636, Mon.–Sat. 8 A.M.–10 P.M., nightly 9:30 P.M., CUC10) and at the **Hotel Nacional** (Calle O y 21, tel. 07/873-3564, fax 07/873-5054, Sun. 9 P.M., CUC10).

Literary Events

CENTRO HABANA AND CERRO

The **La Moderna Poesía** (Calle Obispo #525, esq. Bernaza, Habana Vieja, tel. 07/861-5600) bookshop hosts literary events, as does UNEAC's **Casa de la Poesía** (Calle Muralla #63, e/ Oficios y Inquisidor, Habana Vieja, tel. 07/861-8251) and the **Fundación Alejo Carpentier** (Empedrado #215, Habana Vieja, tel. 07/861-3667).

VEDADO AND PLAZA DE LA REVOLUCIÓN

The **Unión Nacional de Escritores y Artistas de Cuba** (UNEAC, Calle 17, esq. H, Vedado, tel. 07/832-4551) and the **Casa de las Américas** (3ra Calle, esq. Av. de los Presidentes, tel. 07/832-2706, www.casa.cult.cu) host literary and other cultural events.

Centro Cultural Fresa y Chocolate
(Vedado and Plaza de la Revolución, Calle 23 y
12, tel. 07/833-9278, Fri.–Sun. 6 P.M.–2 A.M.),
attached to the INEAC film institute, hosts
films, live music, and poetry. It typically has
trova on Fridays, jazz on Saturdays, and comedy on Sundays.

FESTIVALS AND EVENTS

For a list of forthcoming festivals, conferences, and events visit www.cubaabsolutely.
com/events.html or contact **Paradiso** (Calle
19 #560, esq. C, Vedado, Havana, tel. 07/836-
2124, www.paradiso.cu) or the **Buró de
Convenciones** (Hotel Neptuno, 3ra Av., e/ 70
y 74, 3er piso, Miramar, tel. 07/204-8273, fax
07/204-8162, www.cubameeting.travel).

January

The **Cabildos** festival is held on January 6,
when Habana Vieja resounds with festivities
recalling the days when Afro-Cuban *cabildos*
danced through the streets. Contact Agencia
de Viajes San Cristóbal (Oficios #110, e/
Lamparilla y Amargura, tel. 07/861-9171,
www.viajessancristobal.cu).

February

The star-studded **Festival Internacional de
Jazz** (International Havana Jazz Festival, Calle
15, esq. F, Vedado, tel. 07/862-4938, romeu@
cubarte.cult.cu), now held in February, is highlighted by the greats of Cuban jazz, such as
Chucho Valdés and Irakere, and Juan Formell
and Los Van Van. Concerts are held at various venues.

The **Habanos Festival** (tel. 07/204-0510,
www.habanos.com) celebrates Cuban cigars.
It opens at the Tropicana (Calle 72 #4504 y
Línea del Ferrocarril, Marianao, tel. 07/267-
1717, www.cabaret-tropicana.com), with an
elegant dinner and auction for big spenders.
Tickets are hard to come by.

The **Feria Internacional del Libro de la
Habana** (Havana Book Fair) is organized by
the Instituto Cubano del Libro (Cuban Book
Institute, Calle O'Reilly #14, Habana Vieja,

tel. 07/862-4789, www.cubaliteraria.cult.cu)
and held in Plaza de Armas.

April

The **Festival Internacional de Percusión**
(International Percussion Festival, tel. 07/203-
8808, percuba@mail.com) is held at various
venues.

The prestigious **Bienal de la Habana**
(Havana Biennial, tel. 07/209-6569, www.bienaldelahabana.cu) features artists from more
than 50 countries. It is hosted in even-numbered years by the Centro Wilfredo Lam (Calle
San Ignacio #22, tel. 07/861-2096, www.cnap.
cult.cu).

May

On May 1, head to the Plaza de la Revolución
for the **Primero de Mayo** (May Day Parade) to
honor workers. Intended to appear as a spontaneous demonstration of revolutionary loyalty, in reality it is carefully choreographed.
While loyalists display genuine enthusiasm,
the majority of attendees are bused in and attend for fear of being black-marked by CDRs
and party officials at work. Stooges use loudspeakers to work up the crowd with chants
of *"¡Viva Fidel!"* and *"¡Viva Raúl!"* Each year's
theme reflects the anti–United States flavor of
the day. You'll be surrounded by as many as
500,000 people waving colorful banners and
placards and wearing T-shirts painted with
revolutionary slogans.

The **Festival Internacional de Guitarra**
(International Guitar Festival and Contest) is
held at the Teatro Roldán in even-numbered
years.

The **Festival de Danzón** (tel. 07/838-3113,
promeven@uneac.co.cu) celebrates the traditional dance form.

June

The **Festival Internacional Boleros de Oro**
(International Boleros Festival, UNEAC, Calle
17 #351, e/ G y H, Vedado, tel. 07/832-4551,
www.uneac.co.cu) features traditional Latin
American folk music.

July

The **Coloquio Internacional Hemingway** (International Hemingway Colloquium) takes place in early July every odd-numbered year.

August

The amateurish **Carnaval de la Habana** (Carnival in Havana, tel. 07/832-3742, atic@ cubarte.cult.cu) is now held the first or second week of August on the Malecón.

September

The 10-day biennial **Festival Internacional de Teatro** (International Theater Festival of Havana), sponsored by the Consejo Nacional de Artes Escénicas (National Council of Scenic Arts, Calle 4 #257, Miramar, tel. 07/832-4126), is held in odd-numbered years and features international theater companies covering drama, street theater, musicals, and dance.

October

The **Festival Internacional de Ballet** (International Ballet Festival) features ballet corps from around the world, plus the acclaimed Ballet Nacional de Cuba (BNC, Calzada #510, e/ D y E, Vedado, Ciudad Habana, tel. 07/832-4625, www.balletcuba. cult.cu).

The annual **Festival de la Habana de Música Contemporánea** (Havana Festival of Contemporary Music, c/o UNEAC, Calle 17 #351, e/ G y H, Vedado, tel. 07/832-0194, www.uneac.com.cu) spans a week in early October, with performances ranging from choral to electro-acoustic.

November

Expo Canina (tel. 07/641-9006, balance@ minag.cu) is Havana's answer to the Crufts and Westminster dog shows. It also has a show in April.

December

The **Festival del Nuevo Cine Latinoamericano** (Festival of New Latin American Cinema, c/o the Instituto de Cinematografía Calle 23 #1155, Vedado, tel. 07/838-2354, www.habana-filmfestival.com or www.cubacine.cu) is one of Cuba's most glittering events. Cuban actors and directors schmooze with Hollywood counterparts at parties in the Hotel Nacional and Hotel Habana Libre. Movies from throughout the Americas and Europe are shown across the city and the festival culminates with Cuba's own version of the Oscar, the Coral prizes. Buy your tickets for particular cinemas well before the programming is announced; you can buy a pass (CUC25) good for the duration of the festival.

Every odd year sees the **Festival Internacional de Música Popular Benny Moré,** featuring a panorama of popular Cuban music.

© CHRISTOPHER P. BAKER

Expo Canina dog show, Havana

Shopping

Havana offers superb shopping for arts and crafts, as well as hand-crafted scents, Spanish fans, and rum and cigars.

ANTIQUES
Habana Vieja
The Cuban government bans the sale and export of antiques. Hence, there are no stores selling antiques to tourists. **Colección Habana** (Mercaderes, esq. O'Reilly, Habana Vieja, tel. 07/861-3388, daily 9 A.M.–6 P.M.) sells antique reproductions and decorative items.

ARTS AND CRAFTS
For information on formal galleries, contact the **Fondo Cubano de Bienes Culturales** (Av. 47 #4702, esq. 38, Rpto. Kohly, tel. 07/204-8005, fcbc@cubarte.cult.cu).

Marisel González Milian (tel. 07/832-9032) is a knowledgeable source for meeting local artists and purchasing their works.

Habana Vieja
The largest market is the **Centro Cultural Almacenes de San José** (Avenida Desamparados at San Ignacio, tel. 07/864-7793, daily 10 A.M.–6 P.M.), a.k.a. as Feria de la Artesanía, selling everything from little ceramic figurines, miniature bongo drums, and papiermâché 1950s autos to banana-leaf hats, crocheted bikinis, straw hats, and paintings. In late 2009 it moved from Calle Tacón to a restored waterfront warehouse in southern Habana Vieja. It has an **Agencia San Cristóbal** (tel. 07/864-7784) travel agency, Etecsa office with Internet, plus cafés and restaurants. On the waterfront side of the Alameda, just south of the church, is the **Feria de la Artesanía,** the city's main artisans' market, formerly located in Calle Tacón.

Habana Vieja contains dozens of galleries, many selling naive works by the artists themselves; these galleries, called *expo-ventas* (commercial galleries representing freelance artists), concentrate along Calle Obispo. The **Asociación Cubana de Artesana Artistas** (Obispo #411,

tel. 07/860-8577, Mon.–Sat. 10 A.M.–8 P.M., Sun. 10 A.M.–6 P.M.) represents various artists.

The **Fondo Cubano de Bienes Culturales** (Muralla #107, Habana Vieja, tel. 07/862-2633, galeriahab@cubarte.cult.cu, Mon.–Fri. 10 A.M.–5 P.M., Sat. 10 A.M.–2 P.M.), in Plaza Vieja, sells quality work in its **Génesis Galerías.** The best works are upstairs. Nearby, experimental art is for sale at the **Centro de Desarrollo de las Artes Visuales** (Casa de las Hermanas Cárdenas, Plaza Vieja, tel. 07/862-2611, Tues.–Sat. 10 A.M.–6 P.M.).

One of the best galleries is **Galería La Acacia** (San José #114, e/ Industria y Consulado, tel. 07/863-9364, Mon.–Sat. 9 A.M.–5 P.M.), selling artwork of international standard by many of Cuba's leading artists. Similar pieces can be found at **Galería Victor Manuel** (San Ignacio #46, e/ Callejón del Chorro y Empedrado, tel. 07/861-2955, daily 10 A.M.–9 P.M.), on the west side of Plaza de la Catedral. Around the corner is the **Taller Experimental de la Gráfica** (Callejón del Chorro, tel. 07/867-7622, tgrafica@cubarte.cult.cu, Mon.–Fri. 9 A.M.–4 P.M.), which has exclusive lithographic prints for sale.

You can buy handmade Spanish fans (*abanicos*) for CUC2–150 at the **Casa del Abanicos** (Obrapía #107, e/ Mercaderes y Oficios, tel. 07/863-4452, Mon.–Sat. 10 A.M.–7 P.M. and Sun. 10 A.M.–1 P.M.).

The **Tienda El Soldadito de Plano** (Muralla #164, tel. 07/866-0232, Mon.–Fri. 9 A.M.–5 P.M., Sat. 9 A.M.–1:30 P.M.) sells miniature lead (!) soldiers, including a 22-piece Wars of Independence collection, for CUC5.45 apiece.

The **Tienda Muñecos de Leyendas** (Mercaderes, e/ O'Reilly y Empedrado, Tues.–Sat. 10 A.M.–5:30 P.M., Sun. 10 A.M.–1 P.M.) sells dolls of *duendes* (goblins).

Vedado and Plaza de la Revolución
Vedado has an artisans' market on La Rampa (e/ M y N, 8 A.M.–6 P.M.).

The **Casa de las Américas** (Av. de los Presidentes, esq. 3ra, tel. 07/55-2706, www.casa.cult.cu, Mon.–Fri. 8 A.M.–4:45 P.M.) hosts exhibitions with works for sale. The small gallery in the lobby of the **Hotel Nacional** (Calle O y 21) and the Hotel Meliá Cohiba's **Galería Cohiba** (Paseo, e/ 1ra y 3ra) also sell quality artwork.

BOOKS AND OFFICE SUPPLIES

Havana is desperately in need of a Barnes & Noble, and newspapers or magazines are sold only in a few tourist hotels.

Habana Vieja

The **Instituto Cubano del Libro** (Cuban Book Institute, O'Reilly #4, esq. Tacón, tel. 07/863-2244, Mon.–Sat. 10 A.M.–5:30 P.M.), on Plaza de Armas in the Palacio del Segundo Cabo, has three small bookshops; most books are in Spanish. The plaza is also the setting for the **Mercado de Libros** (Wed.–Sat. 9 A.M.–7 P.M.), a secondhand book fair where you can rummage through a dreary collection of tattered tomes.

Librería La Internacional (Obispo #528, Habana Vieja, tel. 07/861-3238, daily 10 A.M.–5:30 P.M.) stocks a limited selection of texts in English, plus a small selection of English-language novels. **La Moderna Poesía** (Obispo #527, esq. Bernaza, tel. 07/861-6983, Mon.–Sat. 10 A.M.–8 P.M.) is Cuba's largest bookstore, although virtually the entire stock is in Spanish.

La Papelería (O'Reilly #102, esq. Tacón, Habana Vieja, tel. 07/863-4263, Mon.–Sat. 9 A.M.–6:30 P.M.), cater-corner to the Plaza de Armas, sells pens and other office supplies.

Vedado and Plaza de la Revolución

Librería Fernando Ortíz (Calle L, esq. 27, tel. 07/832-9653, Mon.–Sat. 10 A.M.–5:30 P.M.) is your best bet for English-language books. Its meager collection spans a wide range.

Librería Centenario del Apóstol (Calle 25 #164, e/ Infanta y O, tel. 07/870-7220, daily 9 A.M.–9 P.M.) has used texts.

Playa (Miramar and Beyond)

Ofimática (tel. 07/204-0632), in Edificio

Feria de la Artesanía, Habana Vieja

© CHRISTOPHER P. BAKER

Habana in the Miramar Trade Center (3ra Av., e/ 76 y 80, Miramar, Mon.–Fri. 8 A.M.–6 P.M.), sells computer and office accessories.

CIGARS AND RUM

Havana has about two dozen Casas del Habano (official cigar stores). Buy here; if you buy off the street, you're almost certainly going to be sold fakes, even if they look real. Most Casas del Habano are open daily 9 A.M.–5 P.M.

The airport departure lounge has the best-stocked rum and liquor shop in town, as well as a fine cigar selection and a full range of Cuban and import scents and colognes, though don't expect better prices.

Habana Vieja

The best cigar store is the Casa del Habano (Industria #520, e/ Barcelona y Dragones, tel. 07/862-0086, Mon.–Fri. 9 A.M.–7 P.M., Sat. 9 A.M.–5 P.M., Sun. 10 A.M.–4 P.M.) in **Fábrica de Tabaco Partagás.** It has a massive walk-in humidor, plus a hidden lounge with a narrow humidified walk-in cigar showcase for serious smokers.

My other favorites are the Casa del Habano (Mercaderes #202, esq. Lamparilla, tel. 07/862-9682, daily 10:30 A.M.–7 P.M.) in **Hostal Conde de Villanueva** and **Salón Cuba** (Neptuno, e/ Prado y Zulueta, tel. 07/866-6627, daily 8:30 A.M.–9:15 P.M.), in the Hotel NH Parque Central. Each has a sumptuous smoker's lounge.

The **Casa del Habano** (Mercaderes #120, esq. Obrapía, tel. 07/861-5795, daily 9 A.M.–5 P.M.) has a limited selection. And the **Casa del Ron y Tabaco** (Obispo, e/ Monserrate y Bernaza, tel. 07/866-0911, daily 10 A.M.–6 P.M.), above El Floridita, has knowledgeable staff. This store also lets you sample the rums before buying, as does the **Fundación Havana Club** (Av. del Puerto #262, e/ Churruca y Sol, tel. 07/861-8051, daily 9 A.M.–9 P.M.), adjoining the Museo de Ron.

Taberna del Galeón (Baratillo, esq. Obispo, tel. 07/33-8476, Mon.–Fri. 9 A.M.–7 P.M.), off the southeast corner of Plaza de Armas, is well-stocked with rums.

Centro Habana and Cerro

Fábrica de Ron Bocoy (Máximo Gómez #1417, e/ Patria y Auditor, Cerro, tel. 07/877-5781, Mon.–Fri. 7 A.M.–5 P.M., Sat. 9 A.M.–3 P.M.) has a well-stocked store, plus a bar for tasting as a prelude to buying.

Vedado and Plaza de la Revolución

The **Casas del Habano** in the Hotel Nacional (Calle O y 21, tel. 07/873-3564), Hotel Habana Libre Tryp (Calle L, e/ 23 y 25, tel. 07/834-6100), Hotel Meliá Cohiba (Paseo, e/ 1ra y 3ra, tel. 07/833-3636), and Hotel Habana Riviera (Malecón y Paseo, tel. 07/836-4051) are well-stocked.

Playa (Miramar and Beyond)

Miramar has some of the best cigar stores in town. The **Casa del Habano** (5ta Av., esq. 16, tel. 07/204-7975, Mon.–Sat. 10 A.M.–6 P.M.) boasts a vast humidor, executive rooms, bar and lounge, and good service.

Club Habana's **Casa del Habano** (5ta Av. e/ 188 y 192, tel. 07/204-5700, daily 9 A.M.–5 P.M.) is run by Enrique Mons, who for most of the 1970s and '80s was in charge of quality control for the Cuban cigar industry.

Other sources include **Tabaco El Aljibe** (7ma Av., e/ 24 y 26, tel. 07/204-1012), **Tabaco La Giraldilla** (Calle 222 y Av. 37, La Coronela, tel. 07/33-1155), and the tobacco stores in the Hotel Comodoro (1ra Av. y Calle 84, tel. 07/204-5551), Hotel Meliá Habana (3ra Av., e/ 76 y 80, tel. 07/206-9406), and Hotel Occidental Miramar (5ta Av., e/ 72 y 76, tel. 07/204-3584).

CLOTHING AND SHOES
Habana Vieja

Men seeking a classic *guayabera* shirt should head to **El Quitrín** (Obispo #163, e/ San Ignacio y Mercaderes, tel. 07/862-0810, daily 9 A.M.–5 P.M.) or **Guayabera Habana** (Calle Tacó #20, e/ O'Reilly y Empedrado, Mon.–Sat. 9 A.M.–6 P.M.). El Quitrín also sells embroideries and lace for ladies, plus chic blouses and skirts. Most items are Cuban-made and of merely average quality.

Nearby, **Sombreros Jipi Japa** (Obispo, esq. Compostela, Mon.–Fri. 9 A.M.–5 P.M.) is the place to go for hats of every shade. **La Habana** (Obispo, e/ Habana y Compostela, tel. 07/861-5292; and Obispo, esq. Aguacate; Mon.–Fri. 9 A.M.–5 P.M.) offers a reasonable stock of shoes and leather goods.

For hip Italian items head to **Paul & Shark** (Muralla #105, e/ San Ignacio y Mercaderes, tel. 07/866-4326, www.paulshark.it, Mon.–Sat. 10 A.M.–7 P.M., Sun. 10 A.M.–1 P.M.), on Plaza Vieja. This upscale boutique sells quality silk blouses, skirts, and other designer wear, including jackets and pants for men.

Vedado and Plaza de la Revolución

Galerías Amazonas (Calle 12, e/ 23 y 25, tel. 07/66-2438, Mon.–Sat. 10 A.M.–7 P.M., Sun. 10 A.M.–2 P.M.) is a mall with several shops devoted to fashion, including designer labels. For quality imported shoes, try the gallery's Peletería Claudia.

Adidas and Nike have their own well-stocked branches selling sportswear in the **Galería Habana Libre** (Calle 25, e/ L y M, daily 8 A.M.–7 P.M.).

Playa (Miramar and Beyond)

The **Complejo Comercial Comodoro** (3ra Av., esq. 84, tel. 07/204-5551, daily 8 A.M.–7 P.M.), adjoining the Hotel Comodoro, has outlets for United Colors of Benetton, Givenchy, Versace, and other name-brand designers.

The boutiques at **La Maison** (Calle 16 #701, esq. 7ma, tel. 07/204-1543, Mon.–Sat. 10 A.M.–6:45 P.M.) sell upscale imported clothing, shoes, and duty-free items. Likewise, **Le Select** (5ta Av., esq. 30, tel. 07/204-7410, Mon.–Sat. 10 A.M.–8 P.M., Sun. 10 A.M.–2 P.M.), with its ritzy chandeliers and marble statues, is as close as you'll come to Bond Street or Rodeo Drive. This little Harrods in the tropics even has a ground-floor delicatessen, plus an array of boutiques selling high fashion, cosmetics, and the like. **Casa Verano** (Calle 18 #4706, e/ 41 y 43, tel. 07/204-1982, Mon.–Fri. 10:30 A.M.–6:30 P.M.,

Sat. 9:30 A.M.–1 P.M.) sells Cuban-designed clothes, including beautiful one-of-a-kind Verano dresses and straw hats; upstairs men's fashions are for sale, including shoes.

Adidas (3ra Av., e/ 70 y 82, Mon.–Sat. 9:30 A.M.–7 P.M., Sun. 9:30 A.M.–1:30 P.M.), in the Miramar Trade Center, sells sportswear. The Miramar Trade Center also has a dozen or so upscale boutiques selling imported designer clothing.

MUSIC AND FILM
Habana Vieja

Longina Música (Obispo #360, tel. 07/862-8371, Mon.–Sat. 10 A.M.–7 P.M., Sun. 10 A.M.–1 P.M.) sells musical instruments and has a large CD collection.

Centro Habana and Cerro

You can buy instruments at their source at **Industria de Instrumentos Musicales Fernando Ortíz** (Pedroso #12, esq. Nueva, Cerro, tel. 07/879-3161), where guitars, drums, and claves are made.

Vedado and Plaza de la Revolución

The **Centro Cultural Cinematográfico** (Calle 23 #1155, e/ 10 y 12, tel. 07/833-6430, Mon.–Sat. 9 A.M.–5 P.M.) sells posters and videos of Cuban films; it's on the fourth floor of the Cuban Film Institute (ICAIC).

Playa (Miramar and Beyond)

For the widest CD selection in town, head to the **Casa de la Música Egrem** (Calle 10 #309, tel. 07/202-6900, www.egrem.com.cu), the sales room of Egrem, the state recording agency. The **Casa de la Música** (Calle 20 #3309, e/ 33 y 35, tel. 07/204-0447, daily 10 A.M.–12:30 P.M.) also has a large selection.

PERFUMES, TOILETRIES, AND JEWELRY
Habana Vieja

Havana 1791 (Mercaderes #156, esq. Obrapía, tel. 07/861-3525, daily 10 A.M.–6 P.M.) sells locally made scents (CUC6–18) in exquisitely engraved bottles with not entirely trustworthy cork tops, in an embossed linen bag. The 12 fragrances—*aromas coloniales*—include Tabaco, which smells surprisingly unlike cigars. It also sells brand-name French perfumes at duty-free prices. Yanelda, the official "Alchemist of Old Havana," will make up a fragrance to order. In a similar vein is **La Casa Cubana del Perfume** (Brasil #13, tel. 07/866-3759, Mon.–Sat. 10 A.M.–6 A.M.), on the south side of Plaza Vieja.

Farmacia Taquechel (Obispo #155, e/ Mercaderes y San Ignacio, tel. 07/862-9286, daily 9 A.M.–5 P.M.) sells face creams, lotions, and other natural products made in Cuba.

Perfumería Prado (Prado, e/ Refugio y Colón, Habana Vieja, 10 A.M.–6 P.M.) has a large selection of imported perfumes, as do boutique stores in most of the city's upscale hotels.

Tienda Museo el Reloj (Oficios, esq. Muralla, tel. 07/864-9515, Mon.–Sat. 9 A.M.–6 P.M. and Sun. 10 A.M.–1 P.M.) will cause a double-take. At this deluxe store, gold-plated fountain pens (each in an elegant cedar humidor with five cigars) sell for CUC1,000 and the cheapest watch costs US$2,000. These are limited editions made by Cuevos y Sobrionos.

Playa (Miramar and Beyond)

Most upscale hotels have quality jewelry stores, as do **La Maison** (Calle 16 #701, esq. 7ma, Miramar, tel. 07/204-1543, daily 9 A.M.–5 P.M.) and **Le Select** (5ta Av., esq. 30, Miramar, tel. 07/204-7410, daily 9 A.M.–5 P.M.). Also try **Joyería La Habanera** (Calle 12 #505, e/ 5ta y 7ma, tel. 07/204-2546, Mon.–Sat. 10 A.M.–6 P.M.) and the Club Habana's **Joyería Bella Cantando** (5ta Av. y 188, tel. 07/204-5700, daily 9 A.M.–5 P.M.).

DEPARTMENT STORES AND SHOPPING CENTERS
Habana Vieja

Harris Brothers (Monserrate #305, e/ O'Reilly y Progreso, Habana Vieja, tel. 07/861-1644, daily 9 A.M.–6 P.M.) has four stories of separate stores that sell everything from fashion and children's items to toiletries.

Centro Habana and Cerro

The **Plaza Carlos III** (Av. Salvador Allende, e/ Árbol Seco y Retiro, Centro Habana, tel. 07/873-6370, Mon.–Sat. 9:30 A.M.–6:30 P.M.) is intended for Cubans, not tourists. Its many stores range from electronics and clothing to a take on the original Woolworth's dime store (with separate stores where everything costs CUC1, CUC5, or CUC10, respectively).

East of Av. de Italia (Galiano) is Calle San Rafael—a pedestrian-only shopping zone, known colloquially as "El Bulevar." Havana's main shopping street retains many department stores from prerevolutionary days. **La Época** (Av. de Italia, esq. Neptuno, Centro Habana, tel. 07/66-9414, Mon.–Sat. 9:30 A.M.–7 P.M., Sun. 9:30 A.M.–2 P.M.) is a good place for clothing, including kiddie items and designer fashions. The former Woolworth's, today called **Variedades Galiano** (Av. de Italia, esq. San Rafael, tel. 07/862-7717, Mon.–Sat. 9 A.M.–5 P.M.), still has its original lunch counter.

Vedado and Plaza de la Revolución

Galerías de Paseo (1ra Calle, e/ Paseo y A, tel. 07/833-9888, Mon.–Sat. 9 A.M.–6 P.M., Sun. 9 A.M.–1 P.M.), at the foot of Paseo, has more than two dozen stores of varying kinds.

Playa (Miramar and Beyond)

La Puntilla Centro Comercial (1ra Av., esq. 0, tel. 07/204-7309, daily 8 A.M.–8 P.M.) has four floors of stores covering electronics, furniture, clothing, and more. Similarly, there's **Quinta y 42** (5ta Av. y 42, Miramar, tel. 07/204-7070, Mon.–Sat. 10 A.M.–6 P.M., Sun. 9 A.M.–1 P.M.) and **Complejo Comercial Comodoro** (3ra Av., esq. 84, Miramar, tel. 07/204-5551, daily 8 A.M.–7 P.M.).

The largest supermarket is **Supermercado 70** (3ra Av., e/ 62 y 70, Mon.–Sat. 9 A.M.–6 P.M. and Sun. 9 A.M.–1 P.M.), with all manner of imported foodstuffs.

Sports and Recreation

Havana has many *centros deportivos* (sports centers). The largest are the **Complejo Panamericano** (Vía Monumental, Km 1.5, Ciudad Panamericano, Habana del Este, tel. 07/795-4140), with an Olympic athletic stadium, tennis courts, swimming pool, and even a velodrome for cycling; and **Ciudad Deportiva** (Vía Blanca, esq. Av. Rancho Boyeros, tel. 07/854-5022), or Sports City, colloquially called "El Coliseo," in Nuevo Vedado.

BOWLING
You can practice your 10-pin bowling in the **Hotel Kohly** (Av. 49, esq. 36A, Rpto. Kohly, Vedado, tel. 07/204-0240, 3 P.M.–3 A.M., CUC5 per game).

GOLF
The **Club Habana** (5ta Av., e/ 188 y 192, Rpto. Flores, tel. 07/204-5700) has a practice range. Nonmembers are welcome (entrance CUC20 Mon.–Fri.).

Club de Golf Habana (Carretera de Vento, Km 8, Boyeros, tel. 07/649-8918, 8:30 A.M.–sunset) is in the industrial-residential area called Capdevilla, about 20 kilometers south of Havana. "Golfito" (as the locals know it) opened as the Rover's Athletic Club in 1948 by the British community and was maintained by the British Embassy until given to the Cuban government in 1980. The nine-hole course has 18 tees positioned for play on both sides of the fairway. There is a minimally stocked pro shop, five tennis courts, a swimming pool, and two restaurants. Johan Vega is the club pro. Membership costs CUC70 plus CUC45 monthly. A round costs nonmembers CUC20 for nine holes (CUC30 for 18). Clubs can be rented for CUC15; caddies cost CUC6.

GYMS AND SPAS
Upscale hotels have tiny gyms and/or spas, though most are a letdown by international standards. Recommended hotel gyms include: **Hotel Raquel** (San Ignacio, esq. Amargura,

tel. 07/860-8280, gym CUC5, sauna CUC5, or CUC20 per month), **Hotel NH Parque Central** (Neptuno, e/ Prado y Zulueta, tel. 07/866-6627), **Hotel Nacional** (Calle O y 21, tel. 07/873-3564, nonguests CUC15), **Hotel Meliá Cohiba** (Paseo, esq. 1ra, tel. 07/833-3636), and **Hotel Meliá Habana** (3ra Av., e/ 76 y 80, tel. 07/206-9406).

One of the best facilities is at **Club Habana** (5ta Av., e/ 188 y 192, Rpto. Flores, tel. 07/204-5700, Mon.–Fri. 7:30 A.M.–7 P.M., nonmembers CUC20).

RUNNING
The Malecón is a good place to jog, but beware the uneven surface and massive potholes. One alternative is the central median of 5ta Avenida, in Miramar. For wide-open spaces, head to Parque Lenin; the road circuit provides a perfect running track. Runners in search of a track might head to the **Estadio José Martí** (Calle I, e/ 5ta y Malecón, Vedado); **Estadio Juan Abrahantes** (Zapata), south of the university; or **Ciudad Deportiva** (Vía Blanca, esq. Av. Rancho Boyeros, Nuevo Vedado, tel. 07/854-5022).

Annual road races include the 5K International Terry Fox Race (February), the 98K Ultra Marabana (April), the 5K Día de la Madre (Mother's Day Race; May), the 10K Clásico Internacional Hemingway (May), and the Habana Marabana (Havana Marathon; November; CUC40 entry fee). Contact the **Comisión Marabana** at the Ciudad Deportiva (Vía Blanca, esq. Av. Rancho Boyeros) for information.

SAILING
Club Habana (5ta Av., e/ 188 y 192, Playa, tel. 07/204-5700, dircom@clubhaba.clubhabana.get.cu) has Hobie Cats for rent. Full-size yachts and motor vessels can be rented at **Marina Hemingway** (5ta Av., esq. 248, Santa Fe, tel. 07/204-1150, comercial@comermh.cha.cyt.cu).

SCUBA DIVING

There's excellent diving offshore of Havana. The Gulf Stream and Atlantic Ocean currents meet west of the city, where many ships have been sunk through the centuries. The so-called "Blue Circuit," a series of dive sites, extends east from Bacuranao, about 10 kilometers east of Havana, to the Playas del Este, where there's a decompression chamber at Hospital Luis Díaz Soto (Vía Monumental y Carretera, Habana del Este, tel. 07/95-4251).

Centro de Buceo La Aguja (Marina Hemingway, 5ta Av. y 248, Santa Fe, tel. 07/204-5088 or 07/271-5277, fax 07/204-6848, 8:30 A.M.–4:30 P.M.) rents equipment and charges CUC30 for one dive, CUC50 for two dives, CUC60 for a "resort course," and CUC360 for an open-water certification.

The **Centro Internacional Buceo Residencial Club Habana** (5ta Av., e/ 188 y 192, Rpto. Flores, tel. 07/204-5700, Mon.–Fri. 7:30 A.M.–7 P.M., nonmembers entrance CUC20) also has scuba.

SPORTFISHING

Marlin, S.A. (Canal B, Marina Hemingway, tel. 07/204-1150, ext. 735) charges from CUC275 for four hours and from CUC375 for eight hours, including skipper and tackle.

SWIMMING

Most large tourist hotels have pools that permit use by nonguests. Many are popular with Cubans in summer and can be noisy and crowded on weekends.

Habana Vieja

Head to the small rooftop pool of the Hotel NH Parque Central (Neptuno, e/ Prado y Zulueta, tel. 07/866-6627) or that of the Hotel Saratoga (Paseo de Martí #603, esq. Dragones, tel. 07/868-1000). Also try **Piscina Hotel Mercure Sevilla** (Prado, esq. Ánimas, tel. 07/860-8560, daily 10 A.M.–6 P.M., entrance CUC20, including CUC16 *consumo mínimo,* free for hotel guests).

© CHRISTOPHER P. BAKER

guests sunning at the Hotel Nacional swimming pool

Vedado and Plaza de la Revolución

The **Hotel Nacional** (Calle O y 21, tel. 07/873-3564, CUC18 *consumo mínimo* for nonguests) and **Hotel Habana Libre Tryp** (Calle L, e/ 23 y 25, tel. 07/834-6100, CUC15 *consumo mínimo*) have excellent pools. The **Hotel Victoria** (Calle 19 #101, tel. 07/833-3510, esq. M) charges CUC3 to use its small pool.

Playa (Miramar and Beyond)

The **Occidental Miramar** (5ta Av., e/ 72 y 76, tel. 07/204-3584) and **Hotel Meliá Habana** (3ra Av., e/ 76 y 80, tel. 07/206-9406) have excellent pools. **Club Habana** (5ta Av., e/ 188 y 192, Playa, tel. 07/204-5700, dircom@club-haba.clubhana.get.cu, Mon.–Fri. 9 A.M.–7 P.M., entrance CUC20, including CUC10 *consumo mínimo*) has a large swimming pool, plus a splendid beach that shelves gently into calm waters. The pool at **Club Almendares** (Av. 49C, esq. 28A, Rpto. Kohly, tel. 07/204-4990, daily 11 A.M.–6 P.M., CUC10 adults including CUC8 *consumo mínimo*, CUC5 children) gets mobbed by Cubans on weekends.

Farther west, the **Complejo Turístico La Giraldilla** (Calle 222, e/ 37 y 51, tel. 07/273-0568, daily 10 A.M.–6 P.M., CUC5 entry with CUC3 *consumo mínimo*), in La Coronela, has a nice and relatively peaceful pool. The pool at Papa's in **Marina Hemingway** (5ta Av., esq. 248, Santa Fe, tel. 07/204-1150) can get crowded.

ROLLER SKATING

The **Complejo de Pelota Vasca y Patinodromo,** at Ciudad Deportiva (Vía Blanca, esq. Av. Rancho Boyeros, tel. 07/854-5022), has a roller skating track.

SQUASH AND TENNIS

The national *equipo* (team) trains at **Complejo Panamericano** (Vía Monumental, Km 4, Ciudad Panamericano, tel. 07/797-4140), where six tennis courts (*canchas de tenis*) can be rented. **Club Habana** (5ta Av., e/ 188 y 192, Playa, tel. 07/204-5700, dircom@clubhaba.clubhana.get. cu, Mon.–Fri. 9 A.M.–7 P.M., entrance CUC20)

has squash and tennis courts, as do the **Hotel Copacabana** (1ra Av., e/ 34 y 36, tel. 07/204-1037); **Hotel Meliá Habana** (tennis only, Paseo, e/ 1ra y 3ra, tel. 07/206-9406); **Hotel Nacional** (tennis only, Calle O y 21, tel. 07/873-3564); and **Hotel Occidental Miramar** (5ta Av., e/ 72 y 76, tel. 07/204-3584).

For information, contact the **Federación Cubana de Ténis** (tel. 07/97-2121).

VOLLEYBALL

Voleibol is a major sport in Cuba; the national women's team—Las Morenas del Caribe (the Caribbean Brown Sugars)—is the best in the world. Volleyball games are hosted at the **Sala Polivalente Kid Chocolate** (Prado, e/ San Martín y Brasil, Habana Vieja, tel. 07/862-8634) and **Sala Polivalente Ramón Fonst** (Av. de la Independencia, esq. Bruzón, Plaza de la Revolución, tel. 07/882-0000). Major tournament games are held at the **Coliseo de Deportes** (Vía Blanca, esq. Av. Rancho Boyeros, Nuevo Vedado), which hosts the Liga Mundial de Voleibol (World Volleyball League) each spring. For further information, contact the **Federación Cubana de Voleibol** (tel. 07/841-3557).

SPECTATOR SPORTS
Baseball

Havana has two teams: the Industriales (colloquially called "Los Azules," or "The Blues"), considered the best team in the National League, and the Metropolitanos (known as "Los Metros"). Both teams play at the 60,000-seat **Estadio Latinoamericano** (Consejero Aranjo y Pedro Pérez, Cerro, tel. 07/870-6526), the main baseball stadium. Games are played November–May, Tuesday–Thursday and Saturday at 8 P.M., and Sunday at 2 P.M. (CUC3). Tickets are sold on a first-come, first-served basis, although a few seats are reserved for foreigners.

For further information, contact the **Federación Cubana de Béisbol** (tel. 07/879-7980).

Basketball

The Liga Superior de Baloncesto (National

Basketball League) comprises four teams—Havana's team is the Capitalinos—and runs September–November. Games are played at the **Coliseo de Deportes** (Vía Blanca, esq. Av. Rancho Boyeros, Nuevo Vedado, tel. 07/40-5933, Mon.–Fri. 8 A.M.–5 P.M.), at Ciudad Deportiva; and at the **Sala Polivalente Ramón Fonst** (Av. de la Independencia, esq. Bruzón, Plaza de la Revolución, tel. 07/882-0000, Mon.–Sat. 8:30 P.M., Sun. 3 P.M.).

For further information, contact the **Federación Cubana de Baloncesto** (tel. 07/857-7156).

Boxing

Championship matches are hosted at the **Coliseo de Deportes** (Vía Blanca, esq. Av. Rancho Boyeros, tel. 07/854-5022), base for the **Federación Cubana de Boxeo** (tel. 07/857-7047, www.cendecomb.cu).

The main training center is the **Centro de Entrenmiento de Boxeo** (Carretera Torrens, Wajay, tel. 07/202-0538), in the Boyeros district, south of Havana. You can also watch boxing and martial arts at the **Gimnasio de Boxeo Rafael Trejo** (Calle Cuba #815, Habana Vieja, tel. 07/862-0266, Mon.–Fri. 8 A.M.–5 P.M.) and at **Sala Polivalente Kid Chocolate** (Prado, e/ San Martín y Brasil, Habana Vieja, tel. 07/862-8634).

Soccer

Fútbol has been adopted as the sport of choice when baseball season ends. Cuba's soccer league is not well developed, although there *is* a national league. Havana's team is Ciudad Havana (nicknamed "Los Rojos"—"The Reds"). Games are played at the **Estadio Pedro Marrero** (Av. 41 #4409, e/ 44 y 50, Rpto. Kohly, tel. 07/203-4698).

Accommodations

Havana is blessed with accommodations of every stripe. All are run by one of the Cuban government's five hotel groups, which assigns at least one star too many to its hotel ratings (thus a "four-star" hotel would be considered a three- or even two-star hotel in Europe or North America). After a few years of being overpriced, most hotels are now fairly priced.

The hotels listed have air-conditioned rooms with satellite TVs, telephones, and safes. *Casas particulares* (privite room rentals) have air-conditioning and private bathrooms, unless noted.

Which District?

Location is important in choosing your hotel.

Habana Vieja puts you in the heart of the old city, within walking distance of Havana's main tourist sights. A dozen or so colonial-era mansions administered by Habaguanex (www.habaguanexhotels.com) have opened after splendid makeovers, and there are some good, upscale, business-oriented hotels behind colonial facades.

Centro Habana, although offering few sites of interest, has three budget-oriented hotels close to the Prado and Habana Vieja; Cuba's state tour agencies push the Hotel Deauville, used by many budget package-tour companies, but this gloomy cement tower is terrible and everyone who stays there has a complaint. This predominantly run-down residential district also has many *casas particulares,* but safety on the dark, rubble-strewn streets is a concern.

Vedado and Plaza de la Revolución offer mid-20th-century accommodations well situated for sightseeing, including several first-class modernist hotels with modest decor. Vedado also has the best *casas particulares.*

Playa (Miramar and Beyond) has a number of moderate hotels popular with tour groups, as well as modern deluxe hotels aimed at business travelers. All are far away from the main tourist sights and you'll need wheels or taxis to get around. One hotel to avoid is the Hotel Neptuno/Triton, dreary siblings that face consistent plumbing and other infrastructural problems.

HABANA VIEJA
Casas Particulares

Casa de Daniel Carrasco Guillén (Cristo #16, 2ndo piso, e/ Brasil y Muralla, tel. 07/866-2106, carrascohousing@yahoo.com, CUC25) is recommended. The owner and his friendly family rent two lofty-ceilinged rooms with modest furnishings. Take a pick from rooms in the colonial home. Modern rooms atop the roof can get hot during midday but are cross-ventilated. Only one has a private bathroom. Farther north, **Casa de Raquel y Ricardo** (Calle Cristo #12, e/ Brasil y Muralla, tel. 07/867-5026, casaraquel@ cubacaribemail.com, CUC25–30) is a gracious upstairs home; the spacious, airy lounge has rockers and *mediopuntos*. There are two rooms with lofty ceilings; one is air-conditioned and has its own bathroom.

Casa de Eugenio Barral García (San Ignacio #656, e/ Jesús María y Merced, tel. 07/862-9877, CUC30), in southern Habana Vieja, is one of the best private room rentals with two bedrooms with fans, refrigerators, and modern hot-water bathrooms. The old home is graciously and eclectically appointed with antiques and precious ornaments. **Casa de Paula y Norma** (San Ignacio #654, e/ Merced y Jesús María, tel. 07/863-1279, CUC25–30), next door, is an identical home but much more simply furnished.

For historic ambience, I like **Casa de Luis Batista** (Amargura #255, e/ Habana y Compostela, tel. 07/863-0622, CUC30). Beyond its nail-studded door, this 1717 colonial gem has *vitrales* and a stunning *alfarje* ceiling. Four rooms with fans open to a long narrow patio where you can relax on rockers, shaded by an arbor of vines.

I also recommend **Casa Chez Nous** (Brasil #115, e/ Cuba y San Ignacio, tel. 07/862-6287, cheznous@ceiai.inf.cu, CUC30), one block from Plaza Vieja. This delightful upstairs colonial home has two large rooms with *vitral* windows, fridges, simple antique furnishings, and balconies. They share a spacious bathroom

with hot water. There's an airy TV lounge, plus a shaded patio with songbirds. Adjoining, in the same building, **Casa de Marta e Israel** (tel. 07/862-0948, martha@secomar.telemar. cu, CUC30) is similar, though rooms are smaller, darker, and more simply furnished.

Casa de Pepe y Rafaela (San Ignacio #454, e/ Sol y Santa Clara, tel. 07/867-5551, CUC30), on the second floor of a colonial home, has a spacious lounge full of antiques and songbirds. The owners rent two rooms with tall ceilings, fridges, fans, antique beds and furniture, glass chandeliers, and heaps of light pouring in from the balcony windows. Modern bathrooms have large showers.

I enjoyed my stay at **Casa de Irma y Roly** (Compostela #117, e/ Tejadillo y Empedrado, tel. 07/861-1004). The hosts are a delight and make filling breakfasts (CUC4–5). The two upstairs rooms are small and lack windows. A stone's throw away, **Casa de Luis y Mirtha** (Compostela #119, esq. Empedrado, tel. 07/860-0650, CUC30) has one room up and one room down; each has double-pane windows, air-conditioning, modern private bathrooms with hot water, and firm mattresses.

Around the corner, and perhaps the best bet in Habana Vieja, is ■ **Casa de Alina Peña** (Calle San Juan de Dios #154, Apto. 9, e/ Villegas y Aguacate, tel. 07/862-1533, adrpa1955@yahoo.com, CUC25 low season, CUC30 high season). Located on the seventh floor, this lovely, spacious, well-lit and beautifully furnished home has fabulous views over Habana Vieja. The single rented room features a high ceiling with fan and the same views. A small but modern bathroom is across the lounge. There's even a computer with Internet.

Run by a pleasant couple, the nearby **Casa de Alexis y Aleida** (Compostela #310B, e/ Obispo y Obrapía, tel. 07/861-0637, CUC30) has one room with a private bathroom and a small window opening onto a private patio. I like the clinically clean **Casa de Juana** (Lamparilla #254, e/ Habana y Compostela, tel. 07/862-6797, CUC25), festooned with colorful tiles, marble, and limestone. The two upstairs rooms have air-conditioning and external bathrooms.

Hotels

UNDER CUC50

Residencia Académica Convento de Santa Clara (Cuba #610, e/ Luz y Sol, tel. 07/861-3335, fax 07/866-5696, reaca@cencrem.cult. cu, CUC25 per person, CUC35 suite, including breakfast), in a former 17th-century convent, is a bargain. It has nine charming, modestly furnished but well-kept dorm rooms plus some private rooms. However, the rooms lack air-conditioning and can be stifling in summer. A café serves refreshments.

Seeking silent repose in a *real* convent? Try **Hotel Convento de Santa Brígida** (Oficios #204, e/ Teniente Rey y Muralla, tel. 07/866-4064, fax 07/866-4066, brigidahabana@enet. cu, CUC35 pp including breakfast), attached to the still-functioning nunnery.

Hotel Caribbean (Prado #164, e/ Colón y Refugio, tel. 07/860-8241, reservas@lidocaribbean.hor.tur.cu, CUC33 s, CUC48 d low season, CUC36 s, CUC54 d high season, including breakfast) serves budget travelers. The 38 small rooms are meagerly yet adequately furnished in lively colors, with tiny yet pleasant bathrooms. There's a simple bar and café.

CUC50-100

Hostal Valencia (Oficios #53, e/ Obrapía y Lamparilla, tel. 07/857-1037, fax 07/860-5628, www.habaguanexhotels.com, from CUC70 s, CUC110 d low season, from CUC80 s, CUC130 d high season) might induce a flashback to the romantic *posadas* of Spain. The 18th-century mansion-turned-hotel originated as the home of Governor Count Sotolongo. It exudes charm, with its lobby of hefty oak beams, Spanish tiles, and wrought-iron chandeliers. The 12 spacious rooms (some air-conditioned) and junior suites have cool marble floors and are simply furnished (hot water is said to be unreliable). The La Paella restaurant is a mega-bonus. Attached to Hostal Valencia, the **Hotel El Comendador** (Oficios #53, e/ Obrapía y Lamparilla, tel. 07/857-1037, fax

07/860-5628, www.habaguanexhotels.com, from CUC70 s, CUC110 d low season, from CUC80 s, CUC130 d high season) is another endearingly restored colonial home. Its 14 exquisite rooms feature marble floors, iron-frame beds, antique reproduction furnishings, local TVs, old-style phones, and mini-fridges. Modern bathrooms have claw-foot bathtubs, hair dryers, and toiletries. Rooms on the mezzanine are cramped; take an upper-story room with lofty ceilings.

El Mesón de la Flota (Mercaderes #257, e/ Amargura y Brasil, tel. 07/863-3838, www. habaguanexhotels.com, CUC55 s, CUC86 d low season, CUC64 s, CUC105 d high season) is a classic Spanish *bodega* bar-restaurant with five intimate rooms. Each features antique reproductions; one has a magnificent *vitral*. It's overpriced, despite its charm.

Hotel Park View (Colón, esq. Morro, tel. 07/861-3293, fax 07/863-6036, www.habaguanexhotels.com, CUC57 s, CUC86 d low season, CUC57 s, CUC90 d high season, including breakfast), in a sober green-and-ocher color scheme, has 55 lofty-ceilinged rooms, nicely furnished with green marble highlights. Some bathrooms have stand-up showers; others have tubs. Third-floor rooms have balconies. It has minimal facilities, but the Hotel Sevilla is around the corner.

CUC100-150

Hotel Plaza (Zulueta #267, esq. Neptuno, tel. 07/860-8583, fax 07/860-8869, www. gran-caribe.com, from CUC84 s, CUC120 d year-round), built in 1909, occupies the northeast corner of Parque Central. The lobby is supported by Corinthian columns. A marble stairway leads upstairs to 188 lofty-ceilinged rooms and suites, refurbished in 2009 for its 100th anniversary and featuring antique reproductions. Some rooms are gloomy, and those facing the street can be noisy. A pianist hits the ivories in the gracious lobby bar lit by stained-glass skylights and gilt chandeliers. It has a chic restaurant, a gift store, and solarium.

The overpriced **Hotel Inglaterra** (Prado #416, esq. San Rafael, tel. 07/860-8594, fax

07/860-8254, www.gran-caribe.com, CUC84 s, CUC120 d year-round), on the west side of Parque Central, has an extravagant lobby bar and restaurant that whisk you off to Morocco with their arabesque details. It has 83 rooms with hair dryers and minibars. Noise from the square can be a problem, and many rooms are dark.

Overpriced **Hotel Ambos Mundos** (Obispo #153, e/ San Ignacio y Mercaderes, tel. 07/860-9530, fax 07/860-9532, www.habaguanexhotels.com, from CUC80 s, CUC130 d low season, from CUC100 s, CUC160 d high season), one block west of Plaza de Armas, lets you rest your head where Ernest Hemingway found inspiration in the 1930s. The hotel offers 59 rooms and three junior suites arranged atrium style. Most rooms are small, dark, and have undistinguished furnishings. Those facing the interior courtyard are quieter. It has a pleasant lobby bar, plus rooftop restaurant and solarium. Avoid the fifth floor—a thoroughfare for sightseeing gawkers.

I like the **Hotel del Tejadillo** (Tejadillo, esq. San Ignacio, tel. 07/863-7283, fax 07/863-8830, www.habaguanexhotels.com, from CUC70 s, CUC110 d low season, from CUC80 s, CUC130 d high season), another converted colonial mansion. Beyond the huge doors is an airy marble-clad lobby with a quaint dining area. It offers 32 rooms around two courtyards with fountains. The cool, high-ceilinged rooms are graced by *mediopuntos* and modern furniture.

On the harborfront, **Hotel Armadores de Santander** (Luz #4, esq. San Pedro, tel. 07/862-8000, fax 07/862-8080, www.habaguanexhotels.com, from CUC85 s, CUC130 d low season, from CUC100 s, CUC160 d high season, CUC300 s/d suite year-round) has 39 spacious rooms, including three duplexes, a junior suite, and a fabulous contemporary suite with a whirlpool tub in the center of the mezzanine bedroom with a four-poster bed. All rooms feature colonial tile floors, handsome furnishings, and state-of-the-art bathrooms. One room is for travelers with disabilities. It has a 24-hour bar, billiards room, and a fine restaurant.

Playing on a monastic theme, the **Hostal Los Frailes** (Brasil, e/ Oficios y Mercaderes, tel. 07/862-9383, fax 07/862-9710, www.habaguanexhotels.com, from CUC70 s, CUC110 d low season, from CUC80 s, CUC130 d high season), another restored historic property, has staff dressed in monks' habits, plus lots of medieval-style heavy timbers, stained glass, and wrought-iron. It has 22 rooms around a patio with an *aljibe* and fountain. The rooms have patterned terra-cotta tile floors, sponge-washed walls, religious prints, period telephones, and spacious bathrooms. It has Internet and a bar, but no restaurant.

Hotel Beltrán de Santa Cruz (San Ignacio #411, e/ Muralla y Sol, tel. 07/860-8330, fax 07/860-8363, www.habaguanexhotels.com, from CUC70 s, CUC110 d low season, from CUC80 s, CUC135 d high season) is a handsome conversion of an elegant, three-story 18th-century mansion with exquisite *mediopuntos* and other architectural features (the atrium still features the original *aljibe*). Its 11 rooms and one junior suite exude historic ambience courtesy of gracious antique reproductions; all have modern bathrooms.

Another fine colonial conversion, the romantic **Hotel Palacio O'Farrill** (Cuba #102, esq. Chacón, tel. 07/860-5080, fax 07/860-5083, www.habaguanexhotels.com, from CUC85 s, CUC130 d low season, from CUC100 s, CUC160 d high season) is centered on a three-story atrium courtyard lit by a skylight and adorned with antique marble plus bronze statues. It has 38 graciously furnished rooms on three floors, with decor reflecting the 18th (mezzanine), 19th (3rd floor), and 20th (fourth floor) centuries. All have modern bathrooms. Facilities include a cybercafé, an elegant restaurant, and a jazz café.

C **Hotel Raquel** (San Ignacio, esq. Amargura, tel. 07/860-8280, fax 07/860-8275, www.habaguanexhotels.com, from CUC85 s, CUC130 d low season, from CUC100 s, CUC160 d high season, including breakfast), dating to 1905, is a dramatic exemplar of art nouveau styling. The lobby gleams with marble columns and period detailing, including

Tiffany lamps and a mahogany bar. The theme carries into the charming rooms featuring tile floors, wrought-iron beds, and hair dryers. It has an elegant restaurant, and there's a rooftop solarium plus gym. On the edge of the old Jewish quarter, the Hotel Raquel caters to Jewish travelers. Richly illustrated passages from the Old Testament cover the walls, rooms on the second floor are named for Biblical patriarchs, the restaurant serves kosher food, and the chandeliers in the lobby are inspired by the Star of David.

Another historic Habaguanex hotel to consider is the pleasant 10-room **Hotel San Miguel** (Calle Cuba #52, esq. Peña Pobre, tel. 07/862-7656, from CUC85 s, CUC130 d low season, from CUC100 s, CUC160 d high season). The **Hotel Palacio del Marqués de San Felipe y Santiago de Bejucal** (Calle Oficios 152, esq Mercaderes, tel. 7/204-9201, www.habaguanexhotels.com, CUC93–124) is slated to open on Plaza de San Francisco in 2010. The converted 1771 mansion of Don Sebastián de Peñalver is the latest addition to the Habaguanex roster, blending a 21st-century interior with a baroque exterior. Meanwhile, work is advancing on rebuilding the old **Hotel Packard** (Paseo de Martí, esq. Carcel), due to open in 2011. An entirely new interior will arise behind a preserved historic facade.

CUC150-250

Entered via giant brass-studded carriage doors, ◖ **Hotel Conde de Villanueva** (Mercaderes #202, esq. Lamparilla, tel. 07/862-9293, fax 07/862-9682, www.habaguanexhotels.com, from CUC95 s, CUC140 d low season, from CUC110 s, CUC175 d high season) is an exquisite conversion of the mansion of the Conde de Villanueva. The spacious lobby-lounge, with its bottle-green sofas and blood-red cushions, terra-cotta floor, and beamed ceiling with chandeliers, opens to an intimate courtyard with caged birds and tropical foliage. It has nine large, airy, simply appointed rooms and one suite (with whirlpool tub) with 1920s reproduction furnishings. There's a small restaurant and bar, plus Internet. The hotel aims at

cigar smokers with a Casa del Habano outlet and smokers' lounge.

◖ **Hotel Florida** (Obispo #252, esq. Cuba, tel. 07/862-4127, fax 07/862-4117, www.habaguanexhotels.com, from CUC85 s, CUC130 d low season, from CUC100 s, CUC160 d high season) is a compact colonial charmer built around an atrium courtyard with rattan lounge chairs, stained-glass skylight, and black-and-white checkered marble floors. Sumptuously furnished, its 25 rooms feature tasteful colonial decor including marble floors and wrought-iron beds. The restaurant is elegant and has above-average cuisine, while the upstairs piano bar is a marvelous place for evening cocktails. Immediately behind the Hotel Florida, and part of the same building, is the upscale **Hotel Marqués de Prado Ameno** (Obispo #252, esq. Cuba, tel. 07/862-4127, fax 07/862-4117, www.habaguanexhotels.com, from CUC85 s, CUC130 d low season, from CUC100 s, CUC160 d high season). The restored 18th-century mansion has 16 stylishly furnished rooms, all with modern bathrooms. A *bodega* (colonial-style bar/restaurant) will whisk you back 200 years. Lovely!

On Parque Central, **Hotel Telégrafo** (Paseo de Martí #408, esq. Neptuno, tel. 07/861-1010, fax 07/861-4744, www.habaguanexhotels.com, from CUC80 s, CUC130 d low season, from CUC95 s, CUC160 d high season) melds its classical elements into an exciting contemporary vogue. It has 63 rooms with beautiful furnishings and trendy color schemes, including sponge-washed walls and bare stone, plus marble floors and classy bathrooms. The hip lobby bar is skylit within an atrium framed by colonial ruins.

The **Hotel Mercure Sevilla** (Trocadero #55, e/ Prado y Zulueta, tel. 07/860-8560, fax 07/860-8875, www.accorhotels.com, CUC99 s, CUC149 d low season, CUC154 s, CUC201 d high season), built in 1924, is famous as the setting for Graham Greene's *Our Man in Havana* (Wormold stayed in room 501). The lobby is straight out of *1,001 Arabian Nights*. Its 178 rooms are done up in ocher and red color schemes, with antique reproductions, but are rather modest and overpriced. The sumptuous top-floor restaurant serves continental fare. There's a tour and car rental desk, swimming pool, four bars, assorted shops, plus an Internet café and WiFi in the lobby.

Hotel Santa Isabel (Baratillo #9, e/ Obispo y Narciso López, tel. 07/860-8201, fax 07/860-8391, www.habaguanexhotels.com, from CUC190 s, CUC240 d year-round), a small and intimate hostelry in the former 18th-century palace of the Count of Santovenia, enjoys a fabulous setting overlooking Plaza de Armas (some rooms face the harbor). The hotel has 27 lofty-ceilinged rooms furnished with marble or stone floors, plus four-poster beds, reproduction antique furniture, plus leather recliners on wide balconies. Suites have whirlpool tubs. There's an elegant restaurant and two bars. A recent guest list read like a *Who's Who*—former President Jimmy Carter, Jack Nicholson, Robert Redford, and Sting. Still, plumbing has been an issue, many rooms have mold, and readers report that staff are indifferent, which makes the rates all the more outrageous.

OVER CUC250

(Hotel NH Parque Central (Neptuno, e/ Prado y Zulueta, tel. 07/866-6627, fax 07/866-6630, www.hotelnhparquecentral.com, from CUC205 s, CUC270 d year-round) occupies the north side of Parque Central and fuses colonial and contemporary styles. This Dutch-managed hotel is one of the most sophisticated in town and is popular with businessfolk. Its 281 rooms are tastefully appointed with antique reproduction furnishings, king-size beds, and heaps of moden amenities, including Internet modems and marble-clad bathrooms. For views, ask for an exterior room. There are two choice restaurants, a cigar lounge-bar, a business center, boutiques, a rooftop swimming pool, and a fitness room. A 150-room annex, the **NH Parque Central Torre** (www.hotelnhparquecentral.com) opens in 2010 as the hippest hotel in the country, with its 21st-century modernist design.

The finest rooms in Havana are at the **(Hotel Saratoga** (Paseo de Martí #603, esq. Dragones, tel. 07/868-1000, fax 07/868-1001,

Hotel Santa Isabel, Plaza de Armas

www.habaguanexhotels.com, from CUC170 s, CUC235 d low season, from CUC200 s, CUC275 d high season, CUC424–715 suite year-round). European architects and designers have turned this colonial edifice into a visual stunner inside. Imbued throughout with a hip aesthetic, the hotel effuses sophistication on a par with New York or London. Guestroom decor varies from colonially inspired to thoroughly contemporary. Most rooms have king-size four-poster beds; all have rich color schemes, gorgeous halogen-lit bathrooms, and 21st-century amenities. A rooftop pool, spa, and gym offer fabulous views over the city. And the bar and restaurant are New York–chic (although the food is disappointing).

CENTRO HABANA
Casas Particulares

In a high-rise overlooking the Malecón, **Casa de Rene Pérez** (Malecón #51, e/ Tenios y Carcel, tel. 07/861-8108, rmichelpd@yahoo.com, CUC40) is an unusually lavish option with two spacious and windowless yet romantic rooms decorated with antiques. They share a mediocre hot-water bathroom. The vast lounge is sumptuously appointed and has a TV/VCR plus views along the Malecón. Entry is to the rear, via the parking lot (CUC1).

I also recommend **Casa de Elsa y Julio Roque** (Consulado #162, Apto. 2, e/ Colón y Trocadero, tel. 07/861-8027, julioroq@yahoo.com, CUC20, CUC25 with fridge and TV), with a pleasant lounge with leather sofas. Run by erudite and delightful owners, it has two rooms with fans, wicker furniture, and modern bathrooms, and each has an independent entrance.

Hostal el Parador Numantino (Consulado #223, e/ Ánimas y Trocadero, tel. 07/863-8733, CUC30) is a contemporary conversion with a spacious lounge with gleaming ceramic floor and comfy leather sofas. The two bedrooms upstairs are small and feature fans, TV, and mini-fridge.

La Casa Colonial (Gervasio #216, e/ Concordia y Virtudes, tel. 07/862-7109, CUC25) is a gracious place with two spacious and pleasantly furnished bedrooms with fans, and filled with antiques. It has a nice courtyard. Other room rentals nearby include **Casa Colonial La Terraza** (Calle Belascoain #207, e/ Concordia y Neptuno, tel. 07/864-1275, www.casaterraza.com, CUC20–25).

Hotels
UNDER CUC50

Hotel Lincoln (Av. de Italia #164, esq. Virtudes, tel. 07/862-8061, www.islazul.cu, CUC30 s, CUC40 d low season, CUC39 s, CUC46 d high season) dates from 1926 and features graceful public arenas, including a lobby boasting chandeliers and Louis XVI–style furnishings. The 135 rooms are no great shakes. Facilities include two eateries, a rooftop bar, and entertainment.

The budget **Hotel Islazul Lido** (Consulado, esq. Ánimas, tel./fax 07/867-1102, CUC26 s, CUC36 d low season, CUC36 s, CUC46 d high season) has 63 rooms with lackluster utility furniture and tiny balconies. Safes can be rented (the Lido has a reputation for theft), and the dreary, overly air-conditioned lobby has a snack bar and Internet service. The rooftop restaurant is open 24 hours.

The **Hotel Hotetur Deauville** (Calle Galiano y Malecón, tel. 07/866-8812, www.hotetur.com, CUC25 s, CUC30 d), billed ridiculously as three-star, was in the midst of yet another refurbishment at last visit. It remains a totally lackluster hotel to be avoided.

VEDADO AND PLAZA DE LA REVOLUCIÓN
Casas Particulares

C **Casa de Jorge Coalla Potts** (Calle I #456, Apto. 11, e/ 21 y 23, Vedado, tel. 07/832-9032 or cell 5283-1237, www.havanaroomrental.com, CUC30–35) is my favorite *casa particular* in Havana; it's where I stay, if possible, when in town. This delightful home is run by Jorge and his wife, Marisel, who offer a large, well-lit and well-furnished bedroom to the rear of their spotless ground-floor apartment, only two blocks from the Hotel Habana Libre Tryp. The room has a telephone, refrigerator,

lounge at Casa de Jorge Coalla Potts, Vedado

a double bed with a firm orthopedic mattress, a lofty ceiling with fan, and a spacious tiled bathroom with plentiful hot water. There's a TV lounge with rockers. There's also secure parking nearby. The couple and their daughter Jessica (fluent in English) go out of their way to make you feel at home.

The remarkable art deco Edificio Cuervo Rubio, at the corner of Calles 21 and O, has 14 *casas particulares*. They're more or less identical in layout; consider **Casa de Alejandria García** (#42, tel. 07/832-0689, CUC35), on the fourth floor. Take an east-facing apartment for ocean views.

Also on Calle 21, and highly recommended by a reader, is **Casa Mercedes González** (Calle 21 #360, Apto. 2-A, e/ G y H, tel. 07/832-5846, CUC30). This graciously furnished abode has a mix of antique and utility furnishings, a modern bathroom, and its own balcony. And I like it, too!

Casa de Magalis Sánchez López (Calle 25 #156, e/ Infanta y O, tel. 07/870-7613, magalissanlop@correosdecuba.cu, CUC30 low season, CUC35 high season) has two rooms to the rear of a patio. Both have a TV, fridge, and radio-cassette player. Guests get use of the centenary home with lofty ceilings, a kitchen, and TV lounge. There's secure parking.

Casa de Basilia Pérez (Calle 25 #361, Apto. 7, e/ K y L, tel. 07/832-3953, basiliapcu@yahoo.es, CUC25–30) has two rooms in a pleasant home secluded behind an apartment block. Each has an independent entrance, fridge, fan, TV, and telephone. Nearby, **Casa de Dania Borrego** (Calle J #564B, e/ 25 y 27, tel. 07/832-9956, CUC20–25) has two upstairs rooms in the home of this pleasant family. Each room has fans and modern furnishings. Guests have use of a well-lit lounge, plus secure parking.

I also like **Casa de Enrique y Mirien** (Calle F #509, e/ 21 y 23, tel. 07/832-4201, mirien@enet.cu, CUC30), a beautiful option with an independent entrance, security box, a nice modern bathroom, a delightful bedroom with TV, and a patio with rockers and a shade tree. Another independent apartment nearby is **Casa de Humberto San Pedro** (Calle 25 #567 e/ G y H, tel. 07/833-9670, sanpalbearcuba@yahoo.es, CUC30), tucked behind a massive vine. It has a small kitchen and tiny lounge downstairs; the bedroom and small modern bathroom are upstairs. The only drawback is the low ceiling, and it can get hot. I've stayed here twice with no regrets.

The breakfasts—including crêpes with honey—are reason enough to choose **Casa de Eddy Gutiérrez** (Calle 21 #408, e/ F y G, tel. 07/832-5207, carmeddy2@yahoo.es, CUC35). Two independent apartments are to the rear of the owner's colonial mansion; both have fans and refrigerators. One apartment has its own small kitchen; the other is larger. There is secure parking.

Casa de Marta Vitorte (Av. de los Presidentes #301, e/ 17 y 19, tel. 07/832-6475, martavitorte@hotmail.com, CUC40) is a splendid two-room, two-bath apartment that takes up the entire 14th floor and boasts wraparound glass windows on a balcony offering fabulous views. The beautifully maintained rooms feature antique beds. Martha is an engaging conversationalist who speaks fluent English. The only drawback is the rickety elevator.

Hospedaje Gisela Ibarra (Calle F #104 altos, e/ 5ta y Calzada, tel. 07/832-3891, lat inhouse@enet.cu, CUC30) is a beautiful colonial-era home decorated with antiques and modern art. The delightful owners, Gisela and her daughter Marta, have two rooms with antiques (including antique double beds), safety deposit boxes, and refrigerators. There's a roof terrace, plus parking, and a TV lounge gets the breezes. Meals are served in a gracious dining room.

Nearby, I like **Casa de Fifi** (Calzada #508, e/ D y E, tel. 07/832-3133, fifiacosta@yahoo.com, CUC30), an 1892 house in colonial style entered via a dramatic carriage door and opening to an arched terrace with planters. The two rooms, simply furnished with aged pieces, are spacious and have lofty ceilings and large modern bathrooms. The hostess is a delight.

Run by a savvy, politically well-placed owner, **Casa de Aldo Vásquez** (Calle B #154, e/ Línea y Calzada, tel. 07/832-3223, CUC30) is another well-kept colonial home with a wide front porch with rockers, plus a TV lounge full of antiques. The two spacious bedrooms each have TV, fan, and modern clean private bathroom. There's secure parking.

One of the best options in town, **Casa Blanca** (Calle 13 #917, e/ 6 y 8, tel. 07/833-5697, CUC25), in the heart of western Vedado, is a gracious colonial home with a front garden riotous with bougainvillea. The home is replete with antiques. It has one room with two double beds, stereo, safe deposit box, and a clean, modern bathroom. It has email service for guests.

In Nuevo Vedado, **Casa Mayra Sardaín Piña** (Av. Zoológico #160, e/ 38 y 40, tel. 07/881-3792, CUC40 low season, CUC50 high season), close to the Víazul bus station, is a graciously decorated house with a sun-kissed lounge with wicker furnishings and modern art. Two pleasingly furnished rooms, reached by a spiral staircase, have TVs and fridges. There's a small swimming pool in the rear courtyard. Nearby, **Casa de Cecy y Raul** (Av. Zoológico #112, e/ 36 y 28, tel. 07/881-3727, ceciraul@enet.cu, CUC40) is a pleasant 1950s home with an independent apartment complete with lounge and kitchen. **Casa Jorge Araoz Agero** (Calle San Juan Bautista #62, e/ 35 y 37, tel. 07/883-7378 or 05/270-3364, CUC35–45) is another lovely property with two rooms.

Hotels
UNDER CUC50
Handy for the nearby bus station, **Hotel Bruzón** (Calle Bruzón, e/ Av. Rancho Boyeros y Pozos Dulces, tel. 07/877-5682, CUC16 s, CUC24 d low season, CUC18 s, CUC28 d high season), just north of Plaza de la Revolución, offers the cheapest digs in town. Its 48 rooms are barebones, with utility furniture.

CUC50-100
Hotel St. John's (Calle O #206, e/ 23 y 25, tel. 07/833-3740, fax 07/833-3561, www.gran-caribe.com, CUC38 s, CUC60 d low season, CUC56 s, CUC80 d high season) is a popular bargain. Beyond the chill lounge, this 14-story property has 87 rooms. A cabaret is offered in the rooftop nightclub, plus there's a rooftop swimming pool, a tourism bureau, and

the Steak House Toro. Nearby, **Hotel Vedado** (Calle O #244, e/ 23 y 25, tel. 07/836-4072, fax 07/834-4186, www.gran-caribe.com, CUC45 s, CUC60 d low season, CUC63 s, CUC80 d high season) is of similar standard. Its 203 pastel-hued rooms are small, with tile floors and small bathrooms; remodeled in 2008, they now have firm mattresses and are eye-pleasing. There's a restaurant, piano bar, disco and cabaret, a tiny, uninspired lounge, and a swimming pool.

Hotel Victoria (Calle 19 #101, esq. M, tel. 07/833-3510, fax 07/833-3109, www.gran-caribe.com, CUC65 s, CUC80 d low season, CUC80 s, CUC100 d high season, CUC130 suites year-round) is a charming Victorian-style, neoclassical hotel that focuses on a business clientele. It has 31 elegant, albeit small, rooms with antique reproduction furnishings, plus Internet modems. There's a small swimming pool, intimate lobby bar, and elegant restaurant. In 2009, the hotel awaited a restoration by England's Esencia hotel group.

For unfussy budget-minded travelers, my last resort would be the lackluster **Hotel Colina** (Calle L, esq. 27, tel. 07/836-4071, reservas@colina.gca.tur.cu, CUC40 s, CUC50 d), near the Hotel Habana Libre Tryp.

CUC100-150
The art deco high-rise **Hotel Presidente** (Calzada #110, esq. Av. de los Presidentes, tel. 07/855-1801, fax 07/833-3753, reserva@hpdte.gca.tur.cu, CUC90 s, CUC140 d standard, CUC200 s/d suites year-round) was inaugurated in 1927 and retains its maroon and pink interior, with sumptuous Louis XIV–style furnishings and Grecian urns and busts that rise from a beige marble floor. It has 160 spacious rooms with tasteful contemporary furnishings, including marble bathrooms. One suite is appointed in Louis XIV style. It has an elegant restaurant, an outdoor swimming pool, plus gym and sauna.

Mobster Meyer Lansky's 23-story **Hotel Habana Riviera** (Malecón y Paseo, tel. 07/836-4051, fax 07/833-3739, www.gran-caribe.com, from CUC50 s, CU80 d low season, from

CUC71 s, CUC130d high season, CUC300 suite year-round) underwent refurbishing to recapture its 1950s luxe, but the hotel is still badly deteriorated. The fabulous modernist lobby, with acres of marble and glass and original furnishings, is the high point and has a pleasant cocktail lounge. The 352 spacious rooms have jaded and conservative furniture; cleanliness and bad plumbing are of concern, and some rooms have mildew. There are two mediocre restaurants, a 24-hour snack bar, an average swimming pool (packed with noisy Cubans and clamorous with piped-in music), a gym (sauna and massage service), a cigar store, and the swank Copa Room nightclub.

CUC150-250
◖ **Hotel Nacional** (Calle O y 21, tel. 07/873-3564, fax 07/873-5054, www.hotelnacionaldecuba.com, from CUC120 s, CUC170 d year-round) is Havana's flagship hotel, to which celebrities flock. A restoration revived much of the majesty of this 1930s eclectic-style gem, perched overlooking the Malecón. Furnishings in the 475 large rooms are dowdy. The Executive Floor has 63 specially appointed rooms and suites. The Comedor de Aguiar (one of four restaurants) is one of the city's most elegant eateries, and the Cabaret Parisien, the top-floor cocktail lounge, and the open-air terrace bar are all high points. There are two swimming pools, upscale boutiques, a beauty salon, spa, tennis courts, bank, and business center. Theft from guest rooms is a problem.

Hotel Habana Libre Tryp (Calle L, e/ 23 y 25, tel. 07/834-6100, fax 07/834-6365, www.solmeliacuba.com, from CUC140 s, CUC150 d low season, from CUC190 s, CUC200 d high season, CUC440 s/d suite year-round), managed by Spain's Sol Meliá, is Havana's landmark high-rise hotel. It was built in the 1950s by the Hilton chain and became a favorite of mobsters. The modernist atrium lobby with glass dome exudes a '50s retro feel. Although the 533 rooms feature desired amenities, furnishings are dowdy, plumbing is finicky, and guests complain about poor housekeeping. The hotel is loaded with facilities, including a 24-

---

HOTELS FOR STUDENTS

Various state agencies operate accommodations for visiting students and educators; all charge CUC15-25 s, CUC20-38 d.

In Vedado, **Villa Residencial Estudiantíl** (Calle 2, e/ 15 y 17, tel. 07/830-5250), run by the Ministry of Public Health (MINSAP), is in a converted mansion with simple rooms. It has a small restaurant and a broad, breeze-swept veranda with rockers.

Hotel Universitario (Calle L y 17, tel. 07/838-2373, hoteluni@enet.cu), run by the Ministerio de Educación (MINED), is a basic, wood-paneled affair with a gloomy student union-style bar and a pleasant restaurant downstairs behind the glum lobby. Its 21 rooms offer the bare essentials.

At last visit, these were being used exclusively for Venezuelan medical staff: In Miramar, **Hostal Icemar** (Calle 16, e/ 1 y 3, tel. 07/203-7735 or 203-6130), a 1950s Miami-style hotel operated by MINED with 54 rooms and six minimally furnished apartments; MINED's **Hotel Universitaria Ispaje** (1ra, esq. 22, tel. 07/203-5370), with eight rooms; **Villa Universitaria Miramar** (Calle 62 #508, e/ 5ta-A y 5ta-B Av., tel. 07/832-1034), with 25 rooms; **Hostal Costa Sol** (3ra y Calle 60, tel. 07/209-0828), with 11 rooms; and **Hotel Mirazúl** (5ta #3603, e/ 36 y 40, tel. 07/204-0088, fax 07/204-0045, hotelmi@enet.cu), with eight spacious rooms.

---

hour café, four restaurants (the Polinesio and El Baracón are dismal; the rooftop Las Antillas is recommended), an excellent open-air swimming pool, business center, underground parking, and one of Havana's best nightclubs.

Also managed by Spain's Sol Meliá, the deluxe postmodern, 22-story ◖ **Hotel Meliá Cohiba** (Paseo, esq. 1ra, tel. 07/833-3636, fax 07/834-4555, www.solmeliacuba.com, from CUC175 s/d low season, from CUC225 s/d high season) is perhaps the city's finest all-round hotel. Its 462 spacious and elegant rooms feature brass lamps, marble floors, and Romanesque chairs with contemporary fabrics. The bathrooms dazzle with halogen lights and huge mirrors. South-facing rooms can get hot. It has first-rate executive services, plus a magnificent swimming pool, gym, squash court, solarium, boutiques, five top-ranked restaurants, four bars, and the Habana Café nightclub.

PLAYA (MIRAMAR AND BEYOND)
Casas Particulares

Casa de Fernando y Egeria González (1ra #205, e/ 2 y 4, Miramar, tel. 07/203-3866, egeria@finagri.co.cu, CUC35) is a superb property. This gracious family home offers two

spacious and airy rooms with huge and exquisite tiled bathrooms. Secure parking is available and there's a patio to the rear.

Casa de Clarisa Santiago (1ra #4407, e/ 44 y 46, tel. 07/209-1739, CUC30) is another excellent option, with an independent apartment in the rear patio. It's modern throughout and has a nicely decorated bedroom with TV and fan, plus a bathroom with a small hot-water shower. A separate, well-stocked kitchen (by Cuban standards) has a tall refrigerator. There's secure parking.

Inland, ◖ **Casa de Elena Sánchez** (Calle 34 #714, e/ 7ma y 17, tel. 07/202-8969, gerardo@enet.cu, CUC100) is one of the nicest 1950s-style rentals in town. You rent the entire two-story modernist home. It has two rooms, each with TV, fridge, private hot-water bathroom, and a mix of antiques, 1950s modernist pieces, and contemporary furniture. A large TV lounge opens to a shaded garden patio with rockers. There's secure parking.

Casa de María (3ra #37, esq. B, Miramar, tel. 07/209-5297, fffmiramar@yahoo.com, CUC200 to CUC300) is a four-bedroom modernist home circa 1950s that's rented out in its entirety. Downstairs it has a large TV lounge and separate dining room with period pieces.

The two upstairs bedrooms, reached by a spiral staircase, each have a large marble-clad bathroom from the era, plus huge walk-in closet with wall safe. The rear garden even has its own swimming pool overlooking the mouth of the Río Almendares. It has secure parking.

If you want to know how Communist bigwigs live, check out **Casa de Raquel y Carlos** (7ma #21602, e/ 216 y 218, Siboney, tel. 07/271-4319, fax 07/469-5404, figueredos@hotmail.com, CUC300 daily, CUC5,000 monthly). This fantastic modernist home, built in 1958 and confiscated when its original owner fled Cuba following the Revolution, is graciously furnished with rattan furnishings, original Tiffany lamps, plus paintings and eclectic items such as antique pistols. The vast kitchen features contemporary appliances and would do Betty Crocker proud. It has two huge bedrooms, each with fabulous rattan king-size bed, large satellite TVs, and fans, plus humongous bathrooms with his and hers sinks. The vast garden has a swimming pool with heated whirlpool tub. How is all this permitted? Well, the owner is a former head of MININT, the Ministry of the Interior.

Others to consider include: **Casa de Manuel de Armas Pérez** (5ta #6607, e/ 66 y 68, tel. 07/203-7429, CUC50), a beautiful old home with a huge, pleasantly furnished, independent apartment with a patio and parking; **Casa de Esther Rodríguez** (5ta #8609, e/ 86 y 88, tel. 07/203-8480, CUC30), a 1950s home with one room simply furnished with period pieces, plus secure parking; **Casa de Ana e Ismael** (Calle 32 #101, esq. 1ra, tel. 07/202-9486, CUC120), a two-story 1950s home full of antique furnishings and enclosed in spacious, well-kept grounds with secure parking; and **Casa de Alexis Tristá** (5taB Av. #6612, e/ 66 y 70, tel. 07/203-2388 or 05/283-3392, angelad@infomed.sld.cu, CUC100 up to four people), a lovely home that rents an entire floor with kitchen and patio garden.

Hotels
CUC50-100
Hotel Kohly (Av. 49 y 36A, Rpto. Kohly, Playa, tel. 07/204-0240, fax 07/204-1733, comercial@ kohly.gav.tur.cu, www.gaviota-grupo.com, CUC50 s, CUC65 d) is a 1970s-style property popular with budget tour groups despite its out-of-the-way location. The 136 rooms have tasteful albeit simple furniture. Most have a balcony. Facilities include two modest restaurants, a tour desk, car rental, bar, and 10-pin bowling alley, plus a twice-weekly cabaret. Nearby, and run jointly with the Hotel Kohly, the **Hotel el Bosque** (Calle 28A, esq. Av. 47, tel. 07/204-9232, fax 07/204-5637, www.gaviota-grupo.com, CUC45 s, CUC60 d) has 62 modestly furnished rooms with French windows opening to balconies (some rooms only). It has car rental, a laundry, and a tour desk. There's no restaurant; guests must walk downhill to Club Almendares.

Used principally by package-tour groups, the bargain-priced **Hotel Copacabana** (1ra Av., e/ 34 y 36, tel. 07/204-1037, fax 07/204-2846, www.hotelescubanacan.com, CUC58 s, CU70 d year-round) is an oceanfront hotel with a Brazilian flavor: an Itapoa steak house, Caipirinha bar and grill, and more. The hotel, including all 168 rooms, was undergoing a total refurbishing at last visit. Facilities include a swimming pool (popular with locals on weekends) and discotheque.

Refurbished in 2008, the beachfront **Hotel Comodoro** (1ra Av. y Calle 84, tel. 07/204-5551, fax 07/204-2089, www.hotelescubanacan.com, from CUC61 s, CUC76 d standard year-round) has 134 spacious rooms, including 15 suites, with modern furnishings. Some rooms have a balcony. The contemporary lobby lounge opens to four restaurants, several bars, and a meager bathing area. It adjoins a major shopping complex. A shuttle runs to Habana Vieja five times daily. The Comodoro's **Bungalows Pleamar** (CUC61–150 s, CUC76–150 d year-round) are the closest thing to a beach resort in the city. The 320 aesthetically striking, two-story villas (one-, two-, and three-bedroom) are built around two sinuous swimming pools.

Way out west, **Hotel y Villas Marina Hemingway** (5ta Av. y Calle 248, Santa Fe, tel. 07/204-7628, fax 07/204-4379, comercial@comermh.cha.cyt.cu), in the Marina

Hemingway complex, offers modestly attractive waterfront suites and villas with terrace, TV and video, safe, and kitchen.

CUC100-150

The lonesome **Hotel Chateau Miramar** (1ra Av., e/ 60 y 62, tel. 07/204-1951, fax 07/204-0224, www.hotelescubanacan.com, CUC95 s, CUC120 d standard, CUC150 s/d junior suite, CUC170 s/d suite), on the shorefront, aims at business clientele. The handsome five-story hotel has 50 nicely furnished rooms (suites have whirlpool tubs), a pool, elegant restaurant, and business center.

Aiming at convention traffic, the **Hotel Palco** (Av. 146, e/ 11 y 13, tel. 07/204-7235, fax 07/204-7236, info@hpalco.gov.cu, from CUC74 s, CUC94 d low season, from CUC91 s, CUC111 d high season) adjoins the Palacio de Convenciones. The 144 rooms and 36 junior suites are spacious and have modern decor in lively colors. Facilities include a business center, elegant restaurant, split-level pool, and small sauna and gym. It sometimes has low-season specials that include car rental.

The Spanish-run **Barceló Habana Ciudad** (5ta Av. e/ 78 y 80, tel. 809/200-227-2356, www.barcelo.com, CUC114–233) opened in 2010 with 186 rooms and a colorful contemporary decor.

CUC150-250

Directly across from the Miramar Trade Center, **Hotel Meliá Habana** (3ra Av., e/ 76 y 80, tel. 07/206-9406, fax 07/204-8505, www.solmeliacuba.com, CUC225 s/d standard, CUC500 suites), with its huge atrium lobby, is a luxury hotel that aims at a business clientele. The 405 marble-clad rooms and four suites are up to international standards. The executive floor offers more personalized service plus data ports.

Facilities include five restaurants, five bars, a cigar lounge, a beautiful swimming pool, plus tennis courts, gym, and business center.

The Spanish-managed **C Occidental Miramar** (5ta Av., e/ 72 y 76, tel. 07/204-3584, fax 07/204-9227, www.occidental-hoteles.com, from CUC100 s, CUC130 d year-round) lives up to its deluxe billing. This beautiful modern property features a mix of neoclassical wrought-iron furniture and hip contemporary pieces in the vast marble-clad lobby. Its 427 cavernous rooms, including eight junior suites, eight suites, and five handicap-accessible rooms, are done up in regal dark blue and gold. Cabarets are held beside a huge swimming pool. It has a beauty salon, squash court, health center, tennis courts, business center, and three restaurants.

Tucked behind the Occidental, the garish **Montehabana Aparthotel** (tel. 07/206-9595, www.gaviota-grupo.com, CUC80–175 s/d) has pleasantly furnished rooms, studios, and one-to three-bedroom apartments, notwithstanding its tasteless architecture and lack of facilities. At least the atrium lobby is flooded with light, and you have the Occidental Miramar at hand for restaurants and services.

With an exterior of blue-tinted glass, the mammoth and contemporary **Hotel Oasis Panorama** (Calle 70, esq. 3ra, tel. 07/204-0100, fax 07/204-4969, comercial@panorama.co.cu, from CUC90 s, CUC120 d) might be too gauche for some tastes. Still, I like the decor in its 317 rooms, all with Internet modems. The executive rooms and suites get their own top floor restaurant. Other facilities include a piano bar, squash court, Internet room, Italian- and German-themed restaurants, swimming pool and deck, plus top-floor piano bar with live jazz.

HAVANA

Food

Havana reflects all the horror stories about Cuban dining. Fortunately, it *does* have some fine restaurants, many in the top-class hotels. The number of private restaurants (*paladares*) had fallen from 600 to fewer than 40 at last visit.(The four state-run vegetarian restaurants, launched in 2004, also ceased functioning as such.) Some establishments mentioned in this book may close by the time of your visit.

HABANA VIEJA
Breakfast

Most hotel restaurants are open to nonguests for breakfast. I recommend the buffet at the **Mediterráneo** (tel. 07/860-6627, daily 7–10 A.M., CUC15) in the Hotel NH Parque Central.

If all you want is a croissant and coffee, head to **Pastelería Francesca** (Prado #410, e/ Neptuno y San Rafael, tel. 07/862-0739, daily 8 A.M.–11 P.M.), on the west side of Parque Central (note that this is a pickup spot for *jineteras* and foreign males). The 【 **Café El Escorial** (Mercaderes #317, tel. 07/868-3545, daily 9 A.M.–9 P.M.), on Plaza Vieja, is the closest in Havana you'll come to a European-style coffee shop. This atmospheric venue with a Tuscan mood sells croissants, truffle cream cakes, ice cream, and gourmet coffees and coffee liqueurs. It's a lovely spot to relax.

Paladares

The pocket-size **La Moneda Cubana** (San Ignacio #77, e/ O'Reilly y Plaza de la Catedral, tel. 07/867-3852, daily noon–11 P.M.) is a tiny, well-run place with speedy service and huge portions. The menu offers Cuban staples such as grilled chicken or fried fish (CUC9) and even pork chops (CUC10) served with rice and beans, mixed salad, and bread.

Paladar Don Lorenzo (Acosta #260A, e/ Habana y Compostela, tel. 07/861-6733, daily noon–midnight) is a rooftop restaurant with musicians and a thatched bar. The large and creative menu includes stuffed tomatoes

(CUC2.50) and octopus vinaigrette (CUC5) appetizers, and main dishes such as squid in ink (CUC14), crocodile in mustard sauce (CUC18), and roast chicken in cider (CUC15).

Criollo

【 **La Bodeguita del Medio** (Empedrado #207, e/ San Ignacio y Cuba, tel. 07/862-1374, comercial@bdelm.gca.tur.cu, restaurant daily noon–midnight, bar 10:30 A.M.–midnight, CUC10–20), one block west of Plaza de la Catedral, specializes in traditional Cuban dishes—most famously its roast pork, steeped black beans, fried bananas, garlicky yucca, and sweet guava pudding "overflowing," thought Nicolás Guillén (Cuba's national poet), "with surges of aged rum." Though Ernest Hemingway liked to drink *mojitos* here, today they are the worst in Havana. You may have to wait for an hour or more to be seated, but a tip or friendly banter with Tito or Caesar, the "house captains," should get you a good table. The service is relaxed to a fault, and the atmosphere bohemian and lively. Troubadours entertain. Reservations are advised.

Restaurante El Patio (tel. 07/867-1035, café daily 8 A.M.–midnight, restaurant noon–midnight), on Plaza de la Catedral, has heaps of ambience, as you dine at tables spilling into the plaza, with live music. It serves sandwiches (CUC3.50), hamburgers (CUC3), and gazpacho (CUC4.50), plus hot dishes such as roasted pork leg (CUC9). The main restaurant has three dining rooms and an upstairs grill where the overpriced dishes (CUC16–28) include shrimp *al ajillo* (in garlic) and T-bone steak.

Similar, but facing onto Plaza de Armas, is the touristy and always packed **Café/ Restaurante La Mina** (Obispo #109, esq. Oficios, tel. 07/862-0216, daily noon–midnight), offering shaded patio dining and a menu of snacks and salads (CUC3–5) and Cuban dishes (CUC4–12). The waiters are efficient, the setting is wonderful, and there's

© CHRISTOPHER P. BAKER

Restaurante El Patio, Habana Vieja

always live music. The courtyard to the rear has free-roaming peacocks.

Penny-pinchers once knew to head to the former Restaurante Hanoi. Now the **Casa de la Pava** (Brasil, esq. Bernaza, tel. 07/867-1029, daily 11:45 A.M.–midnight), it is promoted as Vietnamese cuisine but is, in reality, limited to a typical Cuban menu that offers "combination specials" for below CUC5. *Mojitos* cost a mere CUC2.

To dine with Cubans, you can't beat 🌙 **Los Nardos** (Paseo de Martí #563, e/ Teniente Rey y Dragones, tel. 07/863-2985, daily 11:30 A.M.–11:30 P.M.), upstairs in a run-down building opposite the Capitolio. The long lines at night hint at how good this place is. It has restaurants on three levels; be sure to dine in the atmospheric Los Nardos, not the more ascetic El Trofeo or El Asturianito, on the upper levels. Los Nardos has a soaring ceiling, fabulous wooden furnishings, and a wall lined with soccer trophies, plus a wine cellar. The huge meals include garlic shrimp, lobster in Catalan sauce, paella, and Cuban staples such as pork dishes. For drinks, opt for the house sangria, served in a pitcher. Service is on the ball. The place

is run by Cuba's Spanish Asturian association. Best yet, it's bargain priced, and a pianist sometimes performs. No credit cards accepted.

Similar, but less atmospheric, is the hidden restaurant in the **Asociación Canaria de Cuba** (Monserrate #258, e/ Neptuno y Ánimas, tel. 07/862-5284, Wed.–Sun. noon–8:30 P.M.). Tucked into the rear at the top of the stairs, it serves fruit cocktails (CUC0.50), shredded beef stew (CUC2), and shrimp enchiladas (CUC5) amid garish surroundings. Completing the Spanish social club triptych, the **Centro Andaluz** (Prado #104, e/ Genios y Refugio, tel. 07/863-6745, www.centro-andaluz.galeon.com, Tues.–Sat. 10 A.M.–10 P.M., CUC5–10) is another bargain-priced, albeit no-frills *criollo* restaurant. I recommend the paella (CUC8) followed by a *locura flamenco* cocktail (CUC1.75). On Thursday and Saturday, stick around for the flamenco show at 9 P.M.

Café Taberna (Mercaderes #531, esq. Brasil, tel. 07/861-1637, daily 10 A.M.–midnight), on the northeast side of Plaza Vieja, is a lively place serving creative *criollo* fare (CUC5–15), and the long bar is a handsome place to bend an elbow. A nine-piece band performs. Inspect

HAVANA

your bill; I've been scammed by the waiters *every* visit!

Taberna de la Muralla (San Ignacio #364, tel. 07/866-4453, daily 11 A.M.–1 A.M.) serves a good cheese and onion soup (CUC1.50), shrimp skewers (CUC9), and grilled sausage (CUC4), plus burgers. The shaded patio overlooking Plaza Vieja is a great place to sit.

Nouvelle Cuban

The Moorish-themed **Restaurante Anacaona** (Paseo de Martí #603, esq. Dragones, tel. 07/868-1000, daily noon–11 P.M.), in the Hotel Saratoga, exudes chic. The menu promises mixed sushi (CUC7), oysters Rockefeller (CUC13.50), chicken supreme Marsala (CUC13.50), and fondues (CUC23). You'd expect this deluxe hotel to perform kitchenwise, but both of my meals here were total duds! Perhaps Canadian chef Michel Cascione wasn't in the house those nights.

Far better is ◖ **Restaurante Santo Ángel** (Brasil, esq. San Ignacio, tel. 07/861-1626, café daily 9 A.M.–11 P.M., restaurant noon–midnight), on the northwest corner of Plaza Vieja and one of my favorite restaurants. The menu features gazpacho (CUC2), garlic mushrooms (CUC3.75), curried shrimp (CUC15), and pork chops in mustard (CUC10). Fresh-baked breads come with a superb *comport de champiñones* (mushroom paté) in olive oil; the bread is charged extra on your bill, which includes a 10 percent service charge. A large wine list includes California labels (CUC14–25). It has live music.

The ballroom **Roof Garden Restaurant** (Trocadero #55, e/ Prado y Zulueta, tel. 07/860-8560, daily 6:30–10 P.M.), atop the Hotel Mercure Sevilla, offers a Renaissance paneled ceiling and marble floors, and tall French doors open to balconies—a great spot to catch the breeze. One reader raves about the food, a fusion of Cuban and French (CUC5–30), but my experience was mediocre, as was the service.

The elegant **Restaurante El Paseo** (Neptuno, e/ Prado y Zulueta, tel. 07/866-6627, daily 6–11 P.M.), in the Hotel NH Parque Central, has a creative menu that includes

salmon carpaccio (CUC12.50) as a starter and lobster casserole (CUC24) for a main course. An alternative is the hotel's **Restaurante Mediterráneo** (daily 7–10 A.M., noon–4 P.M., and 6–11 P.M.), which in 2009 had turned to offering *tapas fusión* cuisine. The cuisine is well executed, if overpriced, but service can be indifferent.

The elegant **Restaurante Floridiana** (Obispo #252, esq. Cuba, tel. 07/862-4127, daily 7–10 P.M.), in the Hotel Florida, also offers well-prepared dishes, such as roast pork (CUC8) and an overpriced lobster with orange (CUC27).

Arabic

Restaurante al Medina (Oficios, e/ Obispo y Obrapía, tel. 07/861-1041, daily noon–11 P.M.), in the Casa de los Árabes, one block south of Plaza de Armas, offers predominantly *criollo* items such as fish and rice (CUC3), salsa chicken (CUC2.50), and vegetarian specialties. But you'll also find couscous and lamb dishes (CUC6), as well as kebabs (CUC5.50), kibbe (minced meatballs, CUC5), and hummus (CUC3). It has value-priced set meals for CUC9–12.

Italian

The best Italian restaurant in Habana Vieja is **Dominica** (O'Reilly #108, esq. Mercaderes, tel. 07/860-2918, daily 9 A.M.–6 P.M., CUC7–24), serving pasta, pizza, spaghetti, and more in elegant air-conditioned surroundings. Live musicians perform. The place is foreign-managed and the food and service are above average. The modern **Restaurante Prado y Neptuno** (Prado, esq. Neptuno, tel. 07/860-9636, daily 11 A.M.–5 P.M. and 6:30–11:30 P.M.) is popular with expats in Havana for its reasonable Italian fare and pizzas. The contemporary decor is jazzy, and there's a bar with high stools.

Spanish

I love the rustic ambience at **El Mesón de la Flota** (Mercaderes #257, e/ Amargura y Brasil, tel. 07/863-3638, daily noon–11 P.M., bar 24 hours), a classic Spanish *bodega* with

Iberian decor and *tapas,* tortillas, *criollo* entrées (CUC4–18), and Spanish wines (CUC1.50 a glass). It hosts flamenco shows.

Similarly, the *bodega*-style 🍸 **La Paella** (Oficios #53, esq. Obrapía, tel. 07/867-1037, daily noon–11 P.M.), in the Hostal Valencia, serves paella for two people only (although one person could ostensibly eat a double serving) for CUC7–15. The *caldo* (soup) and bread is a meal in itself (CUC3). You can also choose steak, grilled fish, and chicken dishes (CUC2–10), washing them down with Spanish wines (CUC6–12). Try the excellent house vegetable soup. The kitchen also serves the **Bodegón Ouda** (Obrapía, esq. Baratillo, tel. 07/867-1037, Mon.–Sat. noon–7 P.M.), a quaint tapas bar around the corner in the Hotel El Comendador. It serves empanadas, tortillas (CUC1–2), *piquillos* (fried green peppers, CUC1.50), and pizza washed down with sangria.

La Zaragoza (Monserrate #352, e/ Obispo y Obrapía, tel. 07/867-1040, daily noon–midnight), a moody Spanish-style *bodega,* serves mostly *criollo* fare but offers seafood such as squid rings (CUC6), garlic shrimp (CUC12), and *ceviche peruano* (CUC2.50), plus lamb stew (CUC9), tortillas (CUC3), and pizza (from CUC2).

The **Restaurant Jardín del Edén** (San Ignacio, esq. Amargura, tel. 07/860-8280, daily noon–midnight), in the Hotel Raquel, offers old-world elegance and an eclectic menu that includes Hungarian goulash (CUC10.50), curried fish (CUC12), and mushroom sirloin (CUC15), plus Jewish dishes such as potato latkes, red-beet borscht, and matzo-ball soup.

Asian

Torre de Márfil (Mercaderes #121, e/ Oficios y Obrapía, tel. 07/867-1038, daily noon–midnight) has all the trappings: the Chinese lanterns, screens, and even a banquet table beneath a pagoda. It's staffed by Chinese waiters, but the service can be excruciatingly slow. The menu includes authentic spring rolls and reasonable chop suey, chow mein, fried wontons (CUC1.50), and shrimp and lobster dishes (CUC14). It has set dinners from CUC6.

Surf and Turf

El Floridita (Obispo #557, esq. Monserrate, Habana Vieja, tel. 07/ 07/867-1300, daily noon–11 P.M.) has a fantastic fin de siècle ambience—the sole reason to dine here, due to the excessive air-conditioning, ridiculous prices, and surly service. A shrimp cocktail costs CUC15; oyster cocktails cost CUC5. The house special is *langosta mariposa* (lobster grilled with almonds, pineapple, and butter; CUC42). Many of the dishes are disappointing; stick with simple dishes such as prawns flambéed in rum. The wine list is impressive.

The simple **La Casa del Escabeche** (Obispo, esq. Villegas, tel. 07/863-2660, daily noon–11 P.M.), open to the street, serves delicious *escabeche* (cube chunks of fish marinated with lime and salsa) for pennies. You can opt for a modern air-conditioned area.

The ritzy 🍸 **Café del Oriente** (Oficios, esq. Amargura, tel. 07/860-6686, daily noon–midnight), on Plaza de San Francisco, serves some of the best food in town. It has a marble-top bar, tux-clad waiters (service here is top-notch), and a jazz pianist downstairs in the Bar Café—heck, you could be in New York or San Francisco. Upstairs is even more elegant, with sparkling marble and antiques, French drapes, and a magnificent stained-glass ceiling. It offers mostly steaks and seafood dishes (CUC12–30), including calf's brains with mustard and brandy cream sauce and a divine filet mignon.

🍸 **Restaurante El Templete** (Av. del Puerto, esq. Narciso López, tel. 07/866-8807, daily noon–midnight) is recommended for its harborfront position, where it receives the breezes. Housed in a restored colonial mansion, this seafood restaurant with rustic decor has heaps of ambience, plus a diverse menu ranging from oyster cocktails (CUC5) to overpriced lobster (CUC28) and a delicious chocolate brownie dessert, all prepared by Gallego chef Arkaitz Etxarte. The adjoining sibling **Restaurante La Barca** (tel. 07/866-8807, daily noon–midnight) serves pastas and continental dishes.

HAVANA

CENTRO HABANA
Breakfast
The best of your meager choices is **Pan.Com** (Malecón y Calle 25, tel. 07/878-1853, daily 11 A.M.–11 P.M.), serving sandwiches and pastries.

Paladares
Private restaurants are few and far between in residential Centro. After succeeding for more than a decade in the face of constant threat of fines from inspectors, the world-renowned La Guarida restaurant sadly ceased operation in December 2009.

The popular **Paladar Doña Blanquita** (Prado #158, e/ Colón y Refugio, tel. 07/867-4958, daily noon–midnight) offers a choice of dining in the elegant *sala* or on a balcony overlooking the Prado. The *criollo* menu delivers large portions for CUC5–10. The place overflows with whimsical Woolworth's art such as cheap *muñequitas* (dolls), plastic flowers, animals, and cuckoo clocks.

Continental
Restaurant Colonial (Galiano #164, esq. Virtudes, tel. 07/861-0702, daily 11 A.M.–midnight), in the Hotel Lincoln, is one of the better

---

SELF-CATERING

Farmers markets (*agromercados* or *mercados agropecuarios*) exist throughout the city. State-run hard-currency groceries charge exorbitantly for packaged goods, but you have no other option.

HABANA VIEJA
The *agromercado* is on Avenida de la Bélgica (Egido) (e/ Apodaca y Corrales).

Imported meats are sold at **La Monserrate** (Monserrate, e/ Brasil y Muralles), an air-conditioned butcher shop, and at **Harris Brothers** (Monserrate #305, e/ O'Reilly y Progreso, Habana Vieja, tel. 07/861-1644, daily 9 A.M.–6 P.M.), a department store with various foodstuff sections.

Supermercado Isla de Cuba (Máximo Gómez #213, esq. Factoria, tel. 07/33-8793, Mon.-Sat. 10 A.M.–6 P.M., Sun. 9 A.M.–1 P.M.), on the south side of Parque de la Fraternidad, is reasonably well stocked.

CENTRO HABANA
Havana's largest *agromercado* is **Cuatro Caminos** (Máximo Gómez, esq. Manglar, tel. 07/870-5934, Tues.-Sat. 7 A.M.–6:30 P.M., Sun. 7 A.M.–2 P.M.).

Almacenes Ultra (Av. Simón Bolívar #109, esq. Rayo, Mon.-Sat. 9 A.M.–6 P.M., Sun. 9 A.M.–1 P.M.) is a reasonably well-stocked grocery. Similarly, try the basement su-

permarket in **La Época** (Galiano, esq. Neptuno, Mon.-Sat. 9:30 A.M.–9:30 P.M., Sun. 9 A.M.–1 P.M.).

VEDADO
There are *agromercados* at Calle 15 (esq. 10), Calle 17 (e/ K y L), Calle 19 (e/ F y Av. de los Presidentes), Calle 21 (esq. J), (Calle 16 e/ 11 y 13), and Pozos Dulces (e/ Av. Salvador Allende and Bruzón).

There's a grocery stocking Western goods, plus a bakery, on Calle 17 (e/ M y N, Mon.-Sat. 9 A.M.–6 P.M., Sun. 9 A.M.–1 P.M.). Also try **Supermercado Meridiano** (1ra, esq. Paseo, in the Galería del Paseo, Mon.-Sat. 10 A.M.–5 P.M., Sun. 10 A.M.–2 P.M.).

PLAYA (MIRAMAR AND BEYOND)
Supermercado 70 (3ra Av., e/ 62 y 70, Miramar, tel. 07/204-2890, Mon.-Sat. 9 A.M.–6 P.M., Sun. 9 A.M.–1 P.M.) is Cuba's largest supermarket selling imported foodstuffs. The next best-stocked grocery is **Diplo Mercado Miramar** (Mon.-Sat. 10 A.M.–6 P.M., Sun. 9 A.M.–1 P.M.), in the Havana Trade Center.

You can buy delicious pastries and breads at **Doña Neli Panadería Dulcería** (5ta Av., esq. 42, Mon.-Sat. 7 A.M.–6 P.M., Sun. 7 A.M.–1 P.M.), in the Quinta y 42 shopping complex, and at **La Francesa del Pan** (Calle 42, esq. 19, tel. 07/204-2211).

restaurants in Centro and serves soups, fish, shrimp, and chicken dishes for less than CUC4. The service is swift and conscientious.

Remarkable for its sensational modernist architecture (the facade features trifold Gothic-inspired curving peaks, like those of an Indonesian temple), the glass-fronted **Bar de Tapas Lava Día** (Malecón #407, e/ Manrique y Campanario, tel. 07/864-4432, daily noon–midnight) is a bit yuppyish, but I like its ambience. No surprise, it serves tapas and sangria.

Asian

Barrio Chino boasts a score of Chinese restaurants, many with waitstaff in traditional costumes. Most are concentrated along Calle Cuchillo and offer both indoor and patio dining. However, this isn't Hong Kong or San Francisco, so temper your expectations.

 Restaurante Tien-Tan (Cuchillo #17, tel. 07/861-5478, taoqi@net.cu, daily 11 A.M.– midnight) is the best of a dozen options on Cuchillo. Chef Tao Qi hails from Shanghai. The extensive menu includes such tantalizing offerings as sweet-and-sour fried fish balls with vinegar and soy, and pot-stewed liver with seasoning. The budget-minded will find many dishes for around CUC2, but dishes run to CUC18 (medium and large portions are offered). Wash everything down with a chilled Xing Tao. A 20 percent service fee is charged.

One of the best bargains in town is **Flor de Loto** (Salud #313, e/ Gervasio y Escobar, tel. 07/860-8501, daily noon–midnight). Though the staff dress in Chinese robes, about the only Asian item on the menu is *maripositas* (fried wontons). However, the *criollo* fare, such as spicy shrimp (CUC6.50) and grilled lobster (CUC7.50), is tasty and filling.

Casa Abuelo Lung Kong Cun Sol (Dragones #364, e/ Manrique y San Nicolás, tel. 07/862-5388, daily noon–midnight) has a restaurant upstairs serving classics such as *mariposas chinas* (fried wontons) and chop suey (CUC0.40–2.70). This is the real McCoy: Chinese staff, Chinese ambience, and Chinese patrons. Likewise, **Sociedad Chang Weng Chung Tong** (San Nicolás #517,

e/ Zanja y Dragones, tel. 07/862-1490, Mon.– Fri. 6 P.M.–midnight, Sat.–Sun. 12:30–5 P.M. and 6:30 P.M.–midnight) has an all-you-can-eat buffet (CUC12).

VEDADO AND PLAZA DE LA REVOLUCIÓN
Breakfast

Late-risers (and budget hounds shunning other tourists) might head to the **Café TV** (Calle 17, e/ M y N, tel. 07/832-4499, daily 10 A.M.–9 P.M.), tucked into the depths of the Edificio Focsa skyscraper. Entered via a tunnel, this classic (and chilly) café space has TV-related decor and serves a North America breakfast for CUC2. It also has burgers, salads, pastas, garlic shrimp (CUC6), and grilled fish (CUC7) dishes. It rocks at night with karaoke and comedy.

 Café La Rampa (Calle 23, esq. L, tel. 07/838-4011 ext. 125, 24 hours), outside the Hotel Habana Libre Tryp, serves American-style breakfasts, including a breakfast special of toast, eggs, bacon, coffee, and juice for CUC7. The burgers here are surprisingly good (CUC5), as are the tuna and fried egg sandwiches and hot chocolate brownie (CUC3.50). The hotel also offers a varied breakfast buffet (CUC9) in its mezzanine restaurant.

Pain de Paris (Línea, e/ Paseo y A, and at Calle 25 #164, esq. O, tel. 07/833-3347, 24 hours) sells excellent croissants and pastries.

Most hotels have buffet breakfasts open to nonguests.

Paladares

Two of my favorite *paladares,* the Hurón Azul (Humboldt #153, esq. P) and Le Chansonnier (Calle J #259, e/ 15 y Línea) were closed by authorities at last visit, leaving only a handful of options.

Restaurante Gringo Viejo (Calle 21 #454, e/ E y F, Vedado, tel. 07/831-1946, daily noon–11 P.M.) is favored by Cuban celebrities and is granted extensive leeway by the authorities. It has a consistently great *ropa vieja* (CUC11), and the *flan de la casa* is delicious. Check your bill carefully.

I'm recommending **Paladar Nerei** (Calle 19, esq. L, tel. 07/832-7860, Mon.–Fri. noon–midnight, Sat.–Sun. 6 P.M.–midnight) for its terrace dining and filling fish fillet in garlic (CUC12), but this is another place where the owners sometimes scam patrons. The once-wide-ranging menu was limited at last visit to standard Cuban fare. You'll do better at **Paladar Los Amigos** (Calle M #253, e/ 19 y 21, tel. 07/830-0880, daily noon–midnight). This cramped and popular little spot is adorned with posters and photographs of famous Cuban musicians who've dined here. It serves huge plates of traditional Cuban dishes for about CUC10.

The tiny and cramped **Paladar Restaurante Monguito** (Calle L, e/ 23 y 25, Fri.–Wed. 11 A.M.–10 P.M.), directly opposite the Hotel Habana Libre Tryp, is a bargain and for that reason almost always full. "China," your hostess, serves simple but filling Cuban dishes such as *pollo asado,* grilled fish, and pork dishes (CUC3–6).

Paladar Las Mercedes (Calle 18 #204, e/ 15 y 17, tel. 07/831-5706, daily noon–midnight) is a charming option in the style of a thatched rural *bohío.* Excellent quality *criollo* dishes with an imaginative twist are served, along with tapas and pastas. I recommend the *pescado a la Mercedes* (two types of fish with cheese sauce), plus calamari. The *brocheta* (kebab) is also good. All dishes cost CUC17, including a set menu. It has a student special for CUC5 before 7 P.M.

A last resort is **Paladar Aries** (Av. Universidad #456, e/ J y K, tel. 07/832-4118, daily noon–midnight). Not personally reviewed, but recommended by a reader is **Casa Sarasua** (Calle 25 #510, e/ H y I, tel. 07/832-2114, Mon.–Sat. noon–11 P.M.), serving traditional Cuban fare. The place is adorned with antique weaponry.

In Nuevo Vedado, (**La Casa** (Calle 30 #865, e/ 26 y 41, tel. 07/881-7000, daily noon–midnight) is worth the drive. This 1950s modernist house still has its original modish decor and is lush with tropical plantings. An indoor-outdoor patio features waterfalls and pools full

ICE-CREAM PARLORS

Street stalls sell ice-cream cones for about 2.50 pesos. However, the milk may not be pasteurized, and hygiene is always a question.

Habana Vieja: The **Cremería el Naranjal** (Obispo, esq. Cuba) sells ice-cream sundaes, including a banana split (CUC1.50-3), as does **Heladería La Mina** (Oficios, esq. Obispo). A better bet is **Cremería Obispo** (Obispo, esq. Villegas), selling various flavors for pesos.

Vedado: An institution in its own right, **Coppelia** (Calle 23, esq. Calle L, tel. 07/832-6119, Tues.-Sun. 10 A.M.-9:30 P.M.) serves ice cream of excellent quality. Tourists are normally steered toward a special section that, though offering immediate service, charges CUC2.60 for an *ensalada* (three scoops), while the half a dozen communal peso sections for Cubans (choose from indoor or outdoor dining) offer larger *ensaladas* (five scoops) for only five pesos, a *jimagua* (two scoops) for two pesos, and a *marquesita* (two scoops plus a sponge cake) for 2.50 pesos. Be prepared for a *long* wait in summer. Some lines are for inferior (lower fat) Veradero ice cream. **Bim Bom** (Calle 23, esq. Infanta, tel. 07/879-2892, 11 A.M.-11 P.M.), at the bottom of La Rampa, is run along the lines of Baskin-Robbins and charges accordingly, as does **Dulce Habana** (Calle 25, daily 10 A.M.-9 P.M.), on the south side of the Hotel Habana Libre Tryp.

Playa (Miramar and Beyond): Try **Bosque de la Habana** (3ra Av., e/ 78 y 80, tel. 07/204-8500, open 24 hours), in the Hotel Meliá Habana, or **La Casa de Helado** (Calle 84, 3ra Av., noon-7 P.M.), in the Galería Comercial Comodoro.

of drowsy terrapins. La Casa serves such delicious dishes as octopus and onions (CUC9), ceviche (CUC5), and caramel flan (CUC1.20). Matt Dillon and the Kennedys are among the famous clientele.

Criollo

El Conejito (Calle M #206, esq. Av. 17, tel. 07/832-4671, daily 10 A.M.–11 P.M.) is a good option, not least for its Teutonic ambience. A pianist plays while guests dine on *conejo* (rabbit), served any of a dozen ways. Also served are beef, chicken, and pasta dishes, plus a decent grilled fish. Entrées average CUC8. It has "student night" on Wednesdays and weekends.

Nearby, **La Roca** (Calle 21, esq. M, tel. 07/836-3219, daily noon–midnight) has set meals for CUC3.25–4.50, including beer. It's perhaps the best bargain in town. And the retro-1950s decor is a plus. A comedy show is hosted at 10:30 P.M. Bring a sweater.

Continental

There's no shortage of little in-house *cafeterías* around the university serving *cajitas* (boxed lunches) for CUC1 or so, or the equivalent in pesos. Try **Cajitas** (Calle L, esq. 25; go down the stairs into the home). Nearby, **Doña Laura's** (Calle H, e/ 21 y 23, daily 11 A.M.–4 P.M.) is a porch-based cafeteria serving sandwiches for five pesos, *cajitas* (25 pesos), and splendid *batidos* (shakes).

Penny-pinching pizza hounds should head to **Pizza Celina** (Infanta y San Rafael), alias "Pie-in-the-Sky." Reports student Bridget Murphy: "Celina the capitalist genius hasn't let the fact that she lives on the third floor stop her from running a successful pizza business. Scream up your order from across the street, and then in a few minutes pick up your pizzas from, and drop your pesos into, the plastic basket (complete with red bows) that comes crashing down." It's pretty good pizza, too.

The **Comedor de Aguiar** (Calle O, esq. 21, tel. 07/873-5054, daily 7 A.M.–midnight), in the Hotel Nacional, fairly glitters with chandeliers and silverware and appeals to those with money to burn. The waiters are liveried to the T and trained to provide top-notch service. The well-executed menu features creative international cuisine and is highlighted by shrimp with rum flambé and smoked salmon with capers and onion for starters. Main courses are priced CUC13–40.

La Torre (Calle 17 #155, e/ M y N, tel. 07/832-2451, daily noon–11:30 P.M., bar 11:30 A.M.–12:30 A.M.), atop the Focsa building, offers splendid all-around views of the city. Its French-inspired nouvelle cuisine is of higher than usual standard: I recommend the prawns and mushrooms in olive oil and garlic starter (CUC9). I also enjoyed a fish fillet poached in white wine, butter, and cream, and roasted with cheese, served with mashed potatoes and crisp vegetables (CUC14). Order the mountainous and delicious profiteroles (CUC5) for dessert! Only one wine is served by the glass (CUC3.50); it's tiny and not very good.

Competing for the loftiest views in town, the **Sierra Maestra** (Calle 23 y L, tel. 07/834-6100, noon–midnight), atop the Hotel Habana Libre Tryp, is virtually unknown to tourists (other than the hotel guests). I haven't dined here, but both the service and continental dishes are said to rank highly.

When I'm in town, you might find me dining upstairs at **Café Concierto Gato Tuerto** (Calle O #14, e/ 17 y 19, tel. 07/833-2224, daily 6 P.M.–midnight). Chef Ricardo Curbelo Ferrer has spiced up the menu with creative dishes such as sautéed shrimp with curry and coconut sauce (CUC10), and roasted leg of lamb with rosemary sauce (CUC8). Modern art festoons the walls.

If you want to experience Havana's gauche 1950s-redux decor, dine at either **Restaurante Monseigneur** (Calle O, esq. 21, tel. 07/832-9884, daily 11:30 A.M.–1 A.M.), with its black marble bar and kitsch, or at the **El Emperador** (Calle 17 e/ M y N, tel. 07/832-4998, daily noon–2 A.M.), with its blood-red curtains and Louis XIV–style furnishings. Both serve such dishes as carpaccio (CUC5), grilled shrimp (CUC10), and rabbit in creole sauce (CUC8), but you really come for the ambience.

The Meliá Cohiba's **El Abanico Restaurante Gourmet** (Paseo, esq. 1ra, tel. 07/833-3636, daily 7–11 P.M.) is one of the most elegant in town. Its nouvelle dishes might seem a bit ambitious, but execution is accomplished. I recommend the medallions of caramelized trout with tarragon starter (CUC7), followed by walnut sole with risotto (CUC17). Also in the mezzanine of the Meliá Cohiba, the best place for Italian fare is the baseball-themed **La Piazza Ristorante** (tel. 07/833-3636, daily 1 P.M.–midnight). It offers 17 types of pizza (CUC7–20) but also has minestrone (CUC7.50), gnocchi (CUC10), seafood (from CUC11), and an excellent risotto with mushrooms (tinned). It even has pizza to go! Smoking is tolerated and fouls the place.

The Basque cultural center's **Centro Vasco** (Calle 4, esq. 3ta, tel. 07/833-9354, daily noon–midnight) serves grilled shrimp (CUC7), paella (CUC7.50), and lamb stew (CUC7).

PLAYA (MIRAMAR AND BEYOND)
Breakfast
All the tourist hotels have buffet breakfasts. Those of the Hotel Meliá Habana (Paseo, e/ 1ra y 3ra, tel. 07/206-9406) and Occidental Miramar (5ta Av., e/ 72 y 76, tel. 07/204-3584) are recommended.

For fresh-baked croissants and good coffee, I like **Pain de Paris** (Calle 26 e/ 5ta y 7ma, daily 8 A.M.–10 P.M.).

Paladares
⊂ **La Esperanza** (Calle 16 #105, e/ 1ra y 3ra, tel. 07/202-4361, Fri.–Wed. 7–11:30 P.M.) is an exceptional *paladar* inside a 1930s middle-class home with a *sala* full of art nouveau furnishings, antiques, books, and intriguing miscellany. Jazz or classical music normally plays. The waiter will read off the day's French inspirations, served with lively sauces. At last visit, I enjoyed a superb eggplant *de ochún* (in honey) stuffed with chicken. The service is friendly and professional, and prices are fair (budget CUC25 for a meal), although a 10 percent service charge is automatically added. Reservations are essential.

Reservations are also vital at ⊂ **Cocina de Lilliam** (Calle 48 #1311, e/ 13 y 15, Miramar, tel. 07/209-6514, Sun.–Fri. noon–3 P.M. and 7–10 P.M.), in the lush grounds of a 1939s-era mansion romantically lit at night. The brick-lined patio is shaded by trees and set with colonial lanterns and wrought-iron tables and chairs. Lilliam Domínguez conjures up tasty nouvelle Cuban. Her appetizers include tartlets of tuna and onion, and a savory dish of garbanzo beans and ham with onion and red and green peppers. Entrées include such Cuban classics as simmered lamb with onions and peppers; chicken breast with pineapple; plus fresh fish dishes and oven-roasted meats served with creamy mashed potatoes. Budget CUC15–25 apiece. The place has been jam-packed ever since President Jimmy Carter dined here in May 2002. The house often runs out of more popular dishes by 9 P.M. and closes for two weeks in summer and the month of December.

By the shore, **Paladar Vistamar** (1ra Av. #2206, e/ 22 y 24, tel. 07/203-8328, daily noon–midnight), in a modern house on the seafront, is popular for its high-quality cuisine and has the advantage of ocean views. It serves continental fare as well as Cuban staples. Starters include fish cocktail (CUC3) and mushroom soup (CUC3.50), while main dishes include *pescado milanesa* (CUC12) and grilled fish with garlic (CUC11.50). **Paladar Ristorante El Palio** (1ra Av. #2402, esq. 24, tel. 07/202-9869, daily noon–midnight) serves Italian-*criollo* cuisine and is popular with elite Cubans. You dine on a shaded patio, with suitably Italian decor.

La Fontana (3ra Av. #305, esq. 46, tel. 07/202-8337, daily noon–midnight, CUC2–15) specializes in barbecued meats from an outdoor grill serving T-bone steak. Starters include salads, *escabeche* (ceviche), and onion soup; main dishes include a greasy fillet grilled with garlic. Rice and extras cost additional. Review your bill closely. Choose cellar or garden seating in a traditional country *bohío* setting. It has caged birds and animals. Service is hit or miss.

Mi Jardín (Calle 66 #517, esq. 5ta Av. B, tel. 07/203-4627, daily noon–midnight), in a beautiful 1950s home full of antiques, is run by an affable and conscientious Mexican and his Italian wife. They serve genuine Mexican fare—well, as much as the government prohibition on beef allows. The chicken *molé mexicano* and house special fish Veracruz are recommended. You'll also find enchiladas and *totopos* (nachos), plus Italian and *criollo* dishes. You can dine inside or on a patio beneath an arbor. Budget CUC10 per person.

Named for the huge cactus in the front garden, **Paladar Los Cactus de 33** (Av. 33 #3405, e/ 34 y 36, Rpto. Kohly, tel. 07/203-5139, daily noon–midnight) justifies its prices with splendid fare (they do have off nights, however) enjoyed in a Gothic-style home with a garden garlanded by fairy lights. Try the grilled snapper with creole sauce or the house chicken breast with olives, mushrooms, and cheese, plus baked custard. Budget CUC25 per head.

Out in Marianao, **Paladar El Palia** (Av. 51A #8827, esq. 88B, tel. 07/267-0282, daily noon–3 P.M. and 6–11 P.M.), handily close to the Tropicana nightclub, has tables in a lantern-lit garden. Imagine starters of octopus and mango salad, or tomato bruschetta, and grilled wahoo filets with shrimp! You can dine with a drink for less than CUC15.

Criollo

I find myself returning time and again to **(El Aljibe** (7ma Av., e/ 24 y 26, tel. 07/204-1583, daily noon–midnight), my favorite state-run restaurant in Havana. It serves the best Cuban fare in town and is popular with tour groups, the Havana elite, and foreign expats showing off their trophy Cuban girlfriends. You dine beneath a soaring thatch roof. The superb house dish, the *pollo asado el aljibe*, is glazed with a sweet orange sauce, then baked and served with fried plantain chips, rice, French fries, and black beans served until you can eat no more. It's a tremendous bargain at CUC12; desserts and beverages cost extra. Other *criollo* dishes are served (CUC10–20), but you really should order the house chicken. The bread and side salad delivered to your table will be charged to your bill even if you didn't order it, and a 10 percent service charge is automatically billed. The wine cellar has almost 27,000 bottles! Service is prompt and efficient.

Restaurant 5ta y 16 (5ta Av., esq. 16, tel. 07/206-9509, daily noon–1 A.M.) is acclaimed as one of Havana's best restaurants for traditional Cuban cooking, notably grilled fish and meats (the grilled pork chops are particularly good) from a *churrasquería*. More creative dishes include a delicious appetizer of stuffed red peppers with tuna, plus a daily special, from roast beef to lamb chops. The food is well prepared and the portions are huge. Choose from a downstairs buffet or à la carte upstairs. Budget CUC10–25.

The Communist elite can often be found dining at **El Rancho Palco** (Av. 19, esq. 140, tel. 07/208-9346, daily noon–11 P.M.), set in jungly surroundings in the heart of Cubanacán. It's a handsome, open-sided *bohío* with terracotta floor, Tiffany-style lamps, decor featuring saddles, and wooden toucans and parrots on swings. You can opt to dine on a patio or beneath thatch, or in an air-conditioned dining room. It serves meat dishes (CUC10–30), seafood (CUC12–26), and the usual *criollo* fare. Quality is hit or miss, depending on your timing; on a good night it serves the best filet mignon (CUC11) in Cuba. It has floor shows at night. Scan your bill carefully as scams are frequent.

Pretending to be a *paladar*, **(Doctor Café** (Calle 28 #111, e/ 1ra y 3ra, tel. 07/203-4718, daily noon–midnight) has some of the most creative gourmet dishes in town, courtesy of Chef Juan Carlos. Every dish I've eaten here was sublime. Try the crab ceviche and smoked salmon appetizers, and the filet mignon, venison, lobster, and rabbit entrées. Choose patio dining or the atmospheric air-conditioned interior. Reservations required.

Seafood

Don Cangrejo (1ra Av., e/ 16 y 18, tel. 07/204-3837, daily noon–midnight) offers some of the finest seafood in town, served in a converted colonial mansion offering views out to sea. It's popular with the monied Cuban elite. The menu features crab cocktail (CUC6), crab-filled wontons (CUC3), house specialties such as crab claws (CUC15) and garlic shrimp

(CUC13), plus paella, lobster, and fish dishes. The wine list runs to more than 150 labels. An open bar is offered on Monday (CUC10). You can use the swimming pool 10 A.M.–6 P.M. (CUC10 with CUC7 *consumo mínimo*).

Continental

A favorite of the Cuban elite, the overpriced **Tocororo** (Calle 18 #302, esq. 3ra, tel. 07/204-2209, daily noon–midnight), housed in a neoclassical mansion, has an antique-filled lobby extending into a garden patio with rattan furniture, Tiffany lamps, potted plants, and wooden parrots hanging from gilt perches, plus real parrots in cages. A pianist (by day) and jazz ensemble (by night) entertain. The food is typical Cuban fare with an exotic international twist; crocodile and ostrich occasionally feature. Expect to pay CUC25 and up (I ask you, CUC40 for a lobster?). Even the bread will be charged, and a 10 percent service charge is automatic. Although El Aljibe and other upscale restaurants have stolen Tocororo's thunder, it attempted a comeback in 2009 with a new tapas bar (noon–2 A.M.).

The bigwigs in town also dine at the rather gauche **La Ferminia** (5ta Av. #18207, e/ 182 y 184, tel. 07/273-6786, daily noon–midnight), which serves creative fare crafted by student chefs of the Escuela de Gastronomía across the street.

Paleta Bar y Amelia Restaurante (3ra Av., e/ 70 y 82, tel. 07/204-7311, daily 11:30 A.M.–midnight), on the ground floor of the Miramar Trade Center, is an elegant contemporary restaurant decorated with modern art. The hip marble-topped bar is a fine place to relax. The fairly simple menu includes sandwiches, burgers (CUC3), steaks, and shrimp enchiladas (CUC7).

For jungly ambience try **La Cecilia** (5ta Av. #11010, e/ 110 y 112, tel. 07/204-1562, daily noon–midnight), another elegant option in the middle of a large garden surrounded by bamboo, although it has an air-conditioned section. It serves typical Cuban dishes such as *ajiaco* (a stew, and the national dish), *tasajo* (jerked beef), *churrasco* (broiled steak), and *pollo con*

mojo (chicken with onion and garlic), as well as grilled lobster. Entrées cost CUC12–25. It hosts a *cabaret espectáculo* Friday and Saturday nights; there's live music other nights.

The **Complejo Turístico La Giraldilla** (Calle 222, e/ 37 y 51, tel. 07/27-0568, 10 A.M.–5 A.M.), in La Coronela, has gone downhill since the disco here was canceled, but is worth the visit if you're this far west. Choose from a selection of dining rooms in the Patio Los Naranjos. A few years ago, I enjoyed a superb creamed vegetable soup (CUC4), sautéed prawns in garlic (CUC17), and sautéed salmon (CUC19). On Saturdays it hosts a "La Noche del Búfalo" special for groups only (CUC18). La Bodega del Vino basement tapas bar serves everything from tacos to chicken mole, washed down with sangria. It has an extensive wine list.

Asian

For sushi and traditional Japanese fare, head to **Sakura** (Calle 18, esq. 3ra, tel. 07/204-2209, daily noon–midnight), in the Tocororo. The sushi menu is restricted, but quality is surprisingly good. Miso soup (CUC3), tempura (CUC12), and sashimi (CUC12) are served, as are sake and Japanese beers. Likewise, the **Fusion El Abanico,** in the Hotel Meliá Cohiba (Paseo, esq. 1ra, tel. 07/833-3636, daily 7–11 P.M.), offers Japanese fare including sushi.

Fast Food and Snacks

Pan.Com (Calle 26, esq. 7ma, Mon.–Fri. 8 A.M.–2 A.M., Sat.–Sun. 10 A.M.–2 A.M.), pronounced "pahn POOHN-to com," makes every kind of sandwich. It also has omelets, burgers, and tortillas, all for less than CUC5, plus yogurts, fruit juices, *batidos,* and cappuccinos.

ACROSS THE HARBOR

You'll be hard-pressed to find any place worthy of dining in Regla and Guanabacoa (one wonders how the locals get by). However, Parque Histórico Militar Morro-Cabaña has a few good touristy restaurants: **La Divina Pastora** (below the Fortaleza de San Carlos de la Cabaña, daily 9 A.M.–8 P.M.) and **Casa**

del Che (daily 9 A.M.–8 P.M.) immediately east of the castle. Both offer creole fare in a setting that plays on traditional colonial ambience, although the latter features an everything-Che motif. Surprisingly, there's even a private restaurant here: **Paladar Doña Carmela** (Calle B #10, tel. 07/863-6048, daily 7–11 P.M.), serving *criolla* fare in an outdoor setting.

Information and Services

MONEY
Banks and Exchange Agencies
The **Banco Financiero Internacional** (Mon.–Fri. 8 A.M.–3 P.M., 8 A.M.–noon only on the last working day of each month) is the main bank, with eight branches throughout Havana, including one in Edificio Jerusalem in the Miramar Trade Center (3ra Av., e/ 70 y 82, Miramar). Its main outlet, in the Hotel Habana Libre Tryp (Calle L, e/ 23 y 25), has a special desk handling travelers checks and credit card advances for foreigners. The Banco de Crédito y Comercio (Bandec), Banco Internacional de Comercio, Banco Popular, and Banco Metropolitano also serve foreigners.

The foreign exchange agency **Cadeca** (Obispo, e/ Cuba y Aguiar, Habana Vieja, tel. 07/866-4152, daily 8 A.M.–10 P.M.) represents Western Union (Mon.–Sat. 8 A.M.–5 P.M., Sun. 8:30 A.M.–noon). Cadeca has outlets through the city, including a branch by the swimming pool of the Hotel Nacional (Calle O y 21, Mon.–Sat. 10 A.M.–7 P.M., Sun. until 6:30 P.M.), good on Sunday when banks are closed.

ATMs
ATMs allowing cash advances of Cuban convertible pesos from Visa cards (but not MasterCard or U.S.-issued Visa cards) are located at Cadeca (Obispo, e/ Cuba y Aguiar, Habana Vieja, tel. 07/866-4152, daily 8 A.M.–10 P.M.); in Etecsa (Obispo, esq. Habana, tel. 07/866-0089, daily 8:30 A.M.–9 P.M.); and at the Hotel NH Parque Central, Hotel Cohiba, Hotel Nacional, and Miramar Trade Center; plus the Banco Internacional de Comercio (3ra Av., esq. 78, Miramar) and Banco Metropolitano (5ta Av., esq. 113, Miramar). All dispense up to CUC300.

COMMUNICATIONS
Post Offices
Most major tourist hotels have small post offices and will accept your mail for delivery. In Habana Vieja, there are post offices on the east side of Plaza de la Catedral; at Obispo #102, on the west side of Plaza de San Francisco; at Obispo #518; next to the Gran Teatro on Parque Central; and on the north side of the railway station on Avenida de Bélgica.

In Vedado, there's a 24-hour post office in the lobby of the Hotel Habana Libre Tryp (Calle L, e/ 23 y 25). Havana's main post office is **Correos de Cuba** (tel. 07/879-6824, 24 hours) on Avenida Rancho Boyeros, one block north of the Plaza de la Revolución.

Servi-Postal (Havana Trade Center, 3ra Av., e/ 76 y 80, Miramar, tel. 07/204-5122, Mon.–Sat. 10 A.M.–6 P.M.) has a copy center and Western Union agency.

Express Mail Services
DHL Worldwide Express (1ra Av. y Calle 26, Miramar, tel. 07/204-1578, fax 07/204-0999, commercial@dhl.cutisa.cu, Mon.–Fri. 8 A.M.–8 P.M., Sat. 8:30 A.M.–4 P.M.) has offices in Vedado (Calzada #818, e/ 2 y 4, tel. 07/832-2112) and at Edificio Habana in the Miramar Trade Center (3ra Av., e/ 76 y 80, Miramar).

Telephone and Fax Service
The **Empresa de Telecomunicaciones de Cuba** (Etecsa) is headquartered at the Miramar Trade Center (3ra Av., e/ 76 y 80, Miramar). The main international telephone exchange (tel.

07/834-6106, 24 hours) is in the lobby of the Hotel Habana Libre Tryp (Calle L, e/ 23 y 25).

Key *centros telefónicos* (telephone kiosks) are on the ground floor of the Lonja del Comercio (Mon.–Fri. 8:30 A.M.–5:30 P.M.) on Plaza de San Francisco and at Obispo and the corner Habana in Habana Vieja, and in Vedado at the foot of Paseo.

CELLULAR PHONES

You can rent or buy (CUC49–331) cellular phones from **Cubacel** (Calle 28 #510, e/ 5 y 7, Miramar, tel. 05/264-2266 or 07/880-2222, www.cubacel.com, Mon.–Fri. 8:30 A.M.–7:30 P.M., Sat. 8 A.M.–noon); they can also activate your own cell phone for CUC40. The main Havana office is in Edificio Santa Clara in the Miramar Trade Center (3ra Av., e/ 70 y 82), but you may be sent to the office at Desamparados, at the corner of Habana (Mon.–Thurs. 8:30 A.M.–5 P.M. and Fri. 8:30 A.M.–4 P.M.).

Internet Access

As of 2009, all Internet access was relegated to Etecsa *telepuntos* and hotel outlets using Etecsa servers. Users must buy a prepaid card (CUC6 for one hour, CUC10 in upscale hotels).

HABANA VIEJA

The best outlets are **Etecsa** (Obispo, esq. Habana, tel. 07/866-0089, daily 8:30 A.M.–9 P.M.) and the business center at the **Hotel NH Parque Central** (Neptuno, e/ Prado y Zulueta, tel. 07/866-6627, Mon.–Fri. 8 A.M.–8 P.M., Sat.–Sun. 8 A.M.–4 P.M., CUC12 per hour). Most other hotels have Internet service in the lobby at cheaper rates; those at the Hotel Plaza (Zulueta #267, esq. Neptuno, tel. 07/860-8583) and Hotel Inglaterra (Prado #416, esq. San Rafael, tel. 07/860-8594) cost CUC6 per hour.

CENTRO HABANA

The *telecorreos* on Salvador Allende (esq. Padre Varela, tel. 07/879-5795, 24 hours) and Zanja (e/ Infanta y San Francisco, daily 8:30 A.M.–7 P.M.) offer Internet access.

VEDADO

The business centers in the **Hotel Nacional** (Calle O y 21, tel. 07/836-3564, daily 8 A.M.–8 P.M.) and **Hotel Meliá Cohiba** (Paseo, e/ 1ra y 3ra, tel. 07/833-3636, Mon.–Sat. 8 A.M.–10 P.M.) charge CUC12 per hour; the **Hotel Habana Libre Tryp** (Calle L, e/ 23 y 25, tel. 07/834-6100, daily 7 A.M.–11 P.M.) charges CUC10.

Students at the University of Havana have free Internet service in the Biblioteca Central (San Lázaro, esq. Ronda, tel. 07/878-5573), at the faculty of Artes y Letras (you need to sign up the day before), and at the faculty of Filosofía y Historia, with long lines for use.

GOVERNMENT OFFICES
Immigration and Customs

Requests for visa extensions (*prórrogas*) and other immigration issues relating to foreigners are handled by **Inmigración** (Desamparados #110 e/ Habana y Compostela, c/o tel. 07/861-3462, Mon.–Wed. and Fri. 8:30 A.M.–4 P.M., Thurs. and Sat. 8:30–11 A.M.), in the Centro de Negocios Alameda de Paula. Journalists and others requiring special treatment are handled by the **Ministerio de Relaciones Exteriores** (Ministry of Foreign Relations, Calzada #360, e/ G y H, Vedado, tel. 07/830-9775, www.cubaminrex.cu).

The main customs office is on Avenida del Puerto, opposite Plaza de San Francisco.

Consulates and Embassies

The following nations have embassies/consulates in Havana. Those of other countries can be found in the local telephone directory under Embajadas, and at the Ministerio de Relaciones Exteriores website (www.cubaminrex.cu/DirectorioDiplomatico/Articulos/Cuba/A.html).

- **Australia:** c/o Canadian Embassy

- **Canada:** Calle 30 #518, esq. 7ma, Miramar, tel. 07/204-2516, fax 07/204-2044

- **United Kingdom:** Calle 34 #702, e/ 7ma y 17-A, Miramar, tel. 07/204-1771, fax 204-8104

- **United States:** Interests Section, Calzada, e/ L y M, Vedado, Havana, tel. 07/833-3551 to 07/833-3559, emergency/after hours tel. 07/833-3026, http://havana.usinterestsection.gov

MAPS AND TOURIST INFORMATION
Information Bureaus

Infotur (tel. 07/204-0624, www.infotur.cu), the government tourist information bureau, has nine information bureaus in Havana, including in the arrivals lounges at José Martí International Airport (Terminal Three, tel. 07/641-6101, infoaereo@enet.cu, 24 hours) and at the Terminal de Cruceros (Cruise Terminal), plus the following outlets in Havana (daily 8:30 A.M.–8:30 P.M.):

- Calle Obispo, e/ Bernazas y Villegas, Habana Vieja, tel. 07/866-3333, obispodir@enet.cu

- Calle Obispo, esq. San Ignacio, Habana Vieja, tel. 07/863-6884

- 5ta Avenida, esq. Calle 112, Miramar, tel. 07/204-3977, miramar@enet.cu

Travel Agencies

There are no independent travel agencies. Hotel tour bureaus can make reservations for excursions, car rental, and flights, as can **San Cristóbal Agencia de Viajes** (Oficios #110, e/ Lamparilla y Amargura, tel. 07/861-9171, fax 07/860-9586, ventas@viajessancristobal.cu, Mon.–Sat. 9 A.M.–6 P.M., Sun. 9:30 A.M.–1 P.M.), specializing in excursions in Havana.

Maps

Tienda de los Navegantes (Mercaderes #115, e/ Obispo y Obrapía, Habana Vieja, tel. 07/861-3625, Mon.–Fri. 8:30 A.M.–5 P.M., Sat. 8:30 A.M.–noon) has a wide range of tourist maps of Havana and the provinces.

MEDICAL SERVICES

Most large tourist hotels have nurses on duty. Other hotels will be able to request a doctor for in-house diagnosis.

Hospitals

Tourists needing medical assistance are usually steered to the **Clínica Internacional Cira García** (Calle 20 #4101, esq. Av. 41, Miramar, tel. 07/204-4300 or 204-2811, fax 07/204-2660, ciragcu@infomed.sld.cu, 24 hours), a full-service hospital dedicated to serving foreigners.

The **Centro Internacional Oftalmológica Camilo Cienfuegos** (Calle L, e/ Línea y 13, Vedado, tel. 07/832-5554, fax 07/833-3536, www.retinosis.sld.cu) specializes in eye disorders but also offers a range of medical services.

Pharmacies

Local pharmacies serving Cubans are meagerly stocked. For homeopathic remedies try **Farmacia Ciren** (Calle 216, esq. 11B, Playa, tel. 07/271-5044) and **Farmacia las Praderas** (Calle 230, e/ 15A y 17, Siboney, tel. 07/273-7473).

Your best bets are the foreigners-only *farmacias internacionales,* stocked with imported medicines. They're located at the **Hotel Mercure Sevilla** (Trocadero #55, e/ Prado y Zulueta, tel. 07/861-5703), **Hospital Camilo Cienfuegos** (Calle L, e/ Línea y 13, Vedado, tel. 07/832-5554, fax 07/33-3536, cirpcc@infomed.sid.cu, 8 A.M.–8 P.M.), the **Galería Comercial Habana Libre** (Calle 25 y L, Vedado, Mon.–Sat. 10 A.M.–7:30 P.M.), the **Clínica Internacional Cira García** (Calle 20 #4101, esq. Av. 41, Miramar, tel. 07/204-2880, 24 hours), the **Farmacia Internacional** (Av. 41, esq. 20, Miramar, tel. 07/204-4350, daily 8:30 A.M.–8:30 P.M.), and in the Edificio Habana at the **Miramar Trade Center** (3ra Av., e/ 76 y 80, Miramar, Mon.–Fri. 8 A.M.–6 P.M.).

Opticians

Ópticas Miramar (Neptuno #411, e/ San Nicolás y Manrique, Centro Habana, tel. 07/863-2161, and 7ma Av., e/ Calle 24 y 26, Miramar, tel. 07/204-2990) provides full-service optician and optometrist services.

SAFETY

Muggings and petty crime have been drastically reduced since January 1999, when thousands of policeman took to the streets 24/7. Still, Havana is not entirely safe despite this policing. Most crime is opportunistic, and thieves seek easy targets. Bad apples hang out at major tourist haunts.

Avoid dark back streets at night, especially southern Habana Vieja and Centro Habana, and anywhere in the Cerro district and other slum districts or wherever police are not present (these areas can be unsafe by day). I was mugged on a main street in Centro in broad daylight.

Beyond Habana Vieja, most parks should be avoided at night. Public masturbation is a problem along Avenida de los Presidentes, especially south of Monumento Gúmez.

Be cautious and circumspect of all *jineteros*.

PRACTICALITIES
Haircuts

I recommend the **Barbería de Plaza de Armas** (Obispo, e/ Oficios y Mercaderes, Habana Vieja, tel. 07/863-0943, Mon.–Sat. 8 A.M.–noon and 2–5 P.M.) or **Salón Correo Barbería** (Brasil, e/ Oficios y Mercaderes, Habana Vieja, Mon.–Sat. 8 A.M.–6 P.M.), two old-style barber shops.

For private stylists you can't beat **Lázaro and Ariel** (Calle D #504, e/ 21 y 23, Vedado, tel. 07/832-5855).

Laundry

In Habana Vieja, **Lavandería El Guerrillero** (Máximo Gómez #521, e/ San Nicolás y Indio, tel. 07/863-7585, daily 6 A.M.–6 P.M.) offers a wash and dry service for three pesos. Another small launderette is at the corner of Villegas and Lamparilla. You drop off your clothes and, hey presto, they're usually ready a few hours later, crisp and folded, for CUC3 a load.

In Miramar, **Aster Lavandería** (Calle 34 #314, e/ 3ra y 5ta, Miramar, tel. 07/204-1622, Mon.–Fri. 8 A.M.–5 P.M., Sat. 8 A.M.–noon) has a wash-and-dry service (CUC3 per load) and dry cleaning (CUC2 for pants, CUC1.50 for shirts, for three-day service; more for same-day service). There's also a laundry in the **Complejo Comercial Comodoro** (3ra Av., esq. 84, tel. 07/204-5551).

Most upscale hotels offer dry-cleaning and laundry service. Many locals will wash your clothes for a few dollars, but be prepared to have them stretched, beaten, and faded.

Legal Services

Consultoría Jurídica Internacional (CJI, International Judicial Consultative Bureau, Calle 16 #314, e/ 3ra y 5ta, Miramar, tel. 07/204-2490, fax 07/204-2303, www.cji.co.cu) provides legal advice and services, as does the **Bufete Internacional** (5ta Av. #16202, esq. 162, Miramar, tel. 07/204-6749, bufete@ bufeteinternacional.cu).

Libraries

The **Biblioteca Nacional** (National Library, Av. de la Independencia, esq. 20 de Mayo, tel. 07/881-5442, fax 07/881-6224, aponce@ jm.lib.cult.cu, Mon.–Fri. 8:15 A.M.–6 P.M., Sat. 8:15 A.M.–4 P.M.), on the east side of Plaza de la Revolución, has about 500,000 texts. Getting access, however, is another matter. Five categories of individuals are permitted to use the library, including students and professionals, but not lay citizens. Foreigners can obtain a library card valid for one year (CUC3) if they have a letter from a sponsoring Cuban government agency and/or ID establishing academic credentials, plus two photographs and a passport, which you need to hand over whenever you wish to consult books. The antiquated, dilapidated file system makes research a Kafkaesque experience. There is no open access to books. Instead, individuals must request a specific work, which is then brought to you; your passport or (for Cubans) personal ID is recorded along with the purpose of your request.

The University of Havana, in Vedado, has several libraries, including the **Biblioteca Central** (San Lázaro, esq. Ronda, tel. 07/878-5573 or 878-3951, ranero@dict. uh.cu).

The **Biblioteca Provincial de la Habana** (Obispo, Plaza de Armas, tel. 07/862-9035, Mon.–Fri. 8:15 A.M.–7 P.M., Sat. 8:15 A.M.– 4:30 P.M.) is a meagerly stocked affair. It's closed the first Monday of each month.

Photography

The best resource is **Photo Obispo** (Obispo #307, esq. Habana, Mon.–Sat. 9 A.M.–9 P.M., Sun. 9 A.M.–1 P.M.), which develops film, sells digital cameras, and makes CDs.

Also try **Agfa Photo Center,** in the Miramar Trade Center (3ra Av., e/ 76 y 80, Miramar).

Toilets

The only modern public toilet to Western standards is on the ground floor of the Lonja del Comercio, Plaza de Armas.

Most hotels and restaurants will let you use their facilities. An attendant usually sits outside the door dispensing a few sheets of toilet paper for pocket change (also note the bowl with a few coins meant to invite a tip).

Getting There

BY AIR
José Martí International Airport

José Martí International Airport (switchboard tel. 07/266-4644, www.airportcuba.com) is 25 kilometers southwest of downtown Havana, in the Wajay district. It has five terminals spaced well apart and accessed by different roads (nor are they linked by a connecting bus service).

Terminal One: This terminal (tel. 07/275-1200) serves domestic flights.

Terminal Two: Charter flights from the U.S. arrive at Terminal Two carrying passengers with OFAC licenses. Occasionally other flights pull in here, although outbound flights will invariably depart Terminal Three.

Terminal Three: All international flights except United States–Havana charters arrive at Terminal Three (tel. 07/642-6225 or 266-4133 for arrivals and departures) on the north side of the airport. Immigration proceedings are slow. All carry-on baggage is X-rayed. Beware porters who grab your bags outside; they'll expect a tip for hauling your bag the few meters to a taxi. A 24-hour Infotur (tel. 07/266-4094) tourist information office is outside the customs lounge. Check in here if you have prepaid vouchers for accommodations or transfers into town. A foreign exchange counter is also outside the customs lounge.

Terminal Four: This terminal serves the military.

Terminal Five: Aero Caribbean flights arrive here.

Getting into Town
BUS

There's no public bus service from either of the international terminals. A public bus marked Aeropuerto departs from Terminal One (domestic flights) for Vedado and Parque Central (one peso). The bus is intended for Cubans, and foreigners may be refused. It runs about once every two hours.

Alternatively, you can catch **Metrobus P12** (originating in Santiago de las Vegas) or Ómnibus #480 from the east side of Avenida de la Independencia, about a 20-minute walk east of the terminal—no fun with baggage. The bus goes to Parque de la Fraternidad on the edge of Habana Vieja (20 pesos). The journey takes about one hour, but the wait can be just as long; the bus gets incredibly crowded and is renowned for pickpockets.

TAXI

Cubataxi taxis wait outside the arrivals lounges. Official rates are CUC15–20 to downtown hotels, but most drivers will not

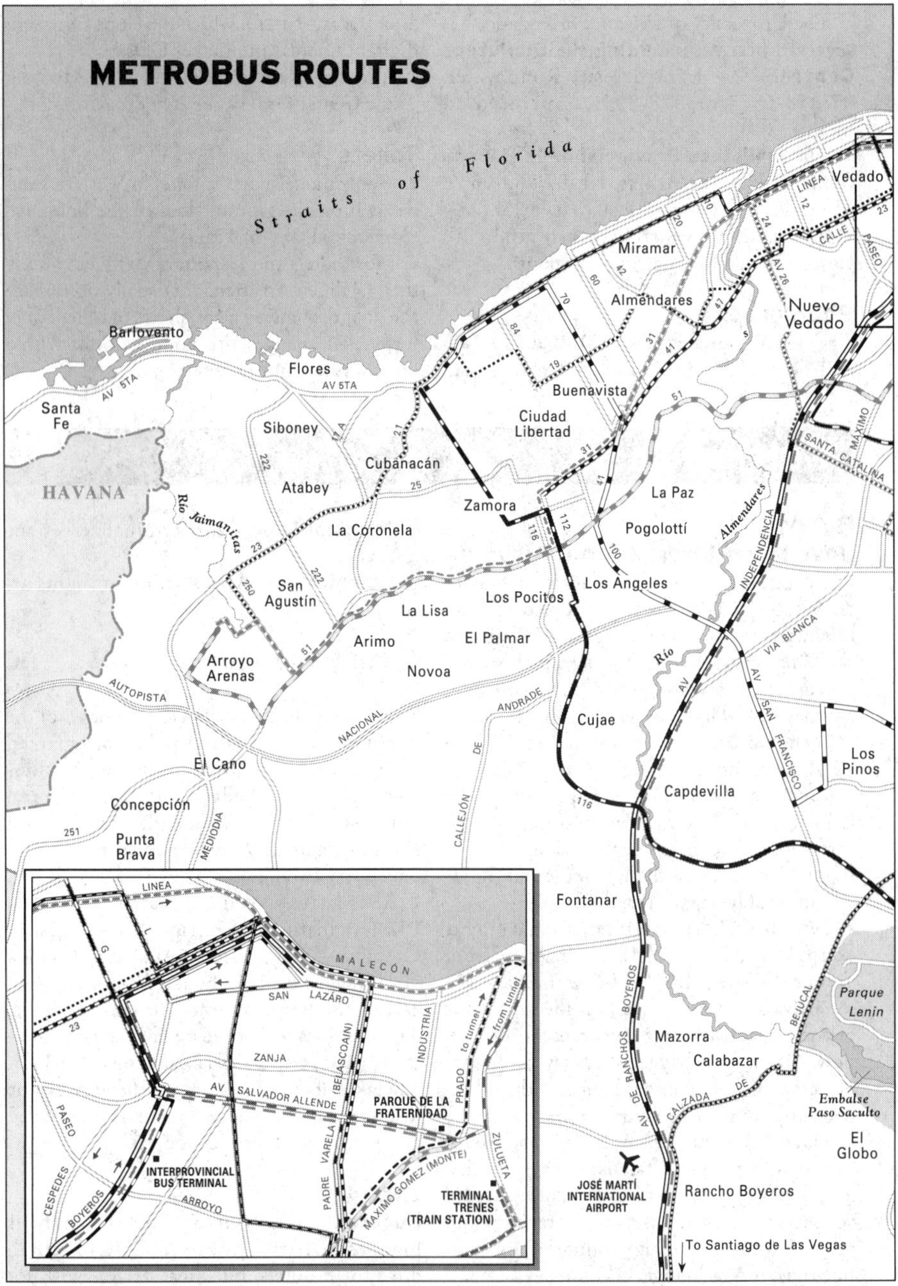
METROBUS ROUTES
Straits of Florida
Vedado
LINEA
CALLE
PASEO
AV 26
Miramar
Almendares
Nuevo Vedado
Barlovento
Flores
AV 5TA
Santa Fe
Buenavista
Ciudad Libertad
Siboney
Cubanacán
MÁXIMO
SANTA CATALINA
HAVANA
Río Jaimanitas
Atabey
Zamora
La Paz
La Coronela
Pogolottí
Almendares
INDEPENDENCIA
San Agustín
Los Pocitos
Los Angeles
La Lisa
Arimo
El Palmar
VIA BLANCA
Río
Arroyo Arenas
Novoa
AUTOPISTA
NACIONAL
ANDRADE
AV
SAN FRANCISCO
Cujae
Los Pinos
El Cano
CALLEJÓN DE
Capdevilla
Concepción
MEDIODIA
Punta Brava
Fontanar
LINEA
MALECÓN
SAN LAZARO
ZANJA
INDUSTRIA
PRADO
to tunnel
from tunnel
(BELASCOAIN)
AV SALVADOR ALLENDE
PARQUE DE LA FRATERNIDAD
PASEO
CESPEDES
BOYEROS
INTERPROVINCIAL BUS TERMINAL
ARROYO
PADRE VARELA
MAXIMO GOMEZ (MONTE)
ZULUETA
TERMINAL TRENES (TRAIN STATION)
Parque Lenin
BEJUCAL
AV DE RANCHOS BOYEROS
Mazorra
Calabazar
CALZADA DE
Embalse Paso Saculto
El Globo
JOSÉ MARTÍ INTERNATIONAL AIRPORT
Rancho Boyeros
To Santiago de Las Vegas

HAVANA

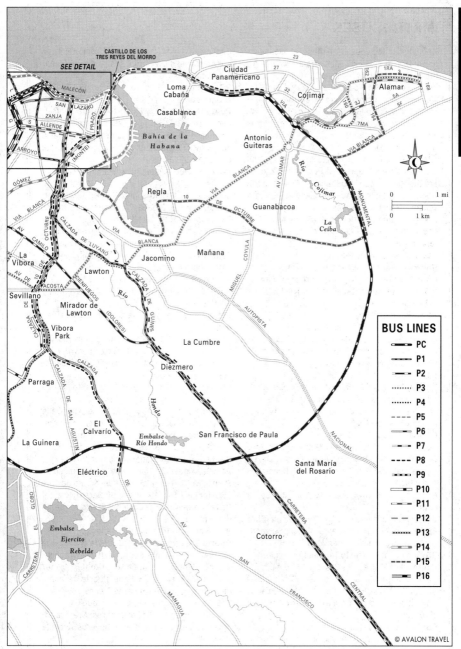

© AVALON TRAVEL

METROBUSES

About half of the one million trips that *habaneros* make daily are aboard "Metrobuses," which formerly carried the "M" designation (for Metrobus) but since 2008 have been designated with "P." Most services originate from Parque de la Fraternidad. Formerly operated by *camellos* (uncomfortable and crowded homemade articulated bodies hauled by trucks), the Metrobus service now uses modern and comfortable Chinese-made articulated buses. Seventeen routes span Havana and the most distant suburbs. Two key routes to know are the P11 (Vedado to Habana del Este) and P12 (Parque de la Fraternidad to Santiago de las Vegas via the international airport).

Most begin operation at 4 A.M., with the last departure at 10 or 11 P.M. A standard 20 centavo fare applies.

PC: Hospital Naval to Playa
Route: Ciudad Panamericano-Circunvalación-Rpto. San Pedro-Rpto. Eléctrico-Cujae-51 y 114-Hospital Militar-Escuela Nacional de Artes-Playa

P1: La Rosita to Playa
Route: Carretera Central-(Cotorro)-(San Francisco de Paula)-Calzada de Güines-Vía Blanca-Cuatro Caminos-Arroyo-Infanta-La Rampa-Calle L-Línea-3ra Avenida-Playa

P2: Alberro (Cotorro) to Vedado
Route: Carretera Central-(Cotorro)-(San Francisco de Paula)-Avenida Camilo Cienfuegos-Ciudad Deportivo-Avenida Independencia-Avenida Rancho Boyeros-Avenida G-Línea

P3: Alamar to Vedado
Route: Alamar-Rpto. Antonio Guiteras-Semaforo Guanabacoa-Vía Blanca-Avenida de Acosta-La Víbora-Avenida Santa Catalina-Ciudad Deportiva-Avenida 26-Tunel Línea

P4: San Agustín (Lisa) to Parque de la Fraternidad
Route: Náutico-Playa-19 y 70-41 y 42-Kohly-Calle 23-La Rampa-Avenida Infanta-Avenida Salvador Allende-Parque de la Fraternidad

P5: San Agustín (Lisa) to Terminal de Trenes
Route: Calle 270 (e/ 25 y 27)-51 y 250-La Lisa-51 y 114-Hospital Militar-La Ceguera-31 y 66-31 y 56-31 y 30-Línea-La Rampa-Hospital Hermanos Ameijenas-Malecón-Avenida del Puerto-Terminal de Trenes

P6: Rpto. Eléctrico to Playa
Route: 13 de Mayo-Lacret y 10 de Octubre-Cuatro Caminos-Avenida Padre Varela-Hospital Hermanos Ameijanes-Malecón-La Rampa-Calle L-Línea-3ra Avenida-Playa

P7: Alberro (Cotorro) to Parque de la Fraternidad
Route: Avenida 99 (y Final)-Carretera Central-Avenida 101-Calzada de Güines-Lindero-Calzada de Luyanó-10 de Octubre-Cuatro Caminos-Máximo Gómez (Monte)-Industria-Dragones-Parque de la Fraternidad

P8: Rpto. Eléctrico to Ciudad Panamericano
Route: 13 de Mayo-Lacret y 10 de Octubre-Cuatro Caminos-Máximo Gómez-Parque de la Fraternidad-Tunel-La Cabaña-Ciudad Panamericano

P9: Víbora to Hospital Militar
Route: Lacret y 10 de Octubre-Cuatro Caminos-Padre Varela-Hospital Hermanos Ameijanes-La Rampa-Calle 23-Kohly-41 y 42-Hospital Militar

P10: Víbora to Náutico
Route: Ciro Frias-Poey-100 y Aldabas-Autopista Pinar del Río-100 y 51-19 y 70-3ra Avenida y 70-Náutico

P11: Alamar to Avenida de los Presidentes (Hospitals)
Route: Micro X-Calle 168-Rpto. Guiteras-Vía Monumental-La Cabana-Tunel-Zulueta-Parque de la Fraternidad-Simón Bolívar (Reina)-Salvador Allende-Avenida G

P12: Santiago de las Vegas (Boyeros) to Parque de la Fraternidad
Route: Avenida 349 (y Final)-Calle 17-Calle 2-Avenida Boyeros-Salvador Allende-Simón Bolívar (Reina)-Parque de la Fraternidad

P13: Santiago de las Vegas (Boyeros) to Víbora
Route: Parque Santiago-Calabazar-Víbora

P14: San Agustín to Parque de la Fraternidad
Route: Rpto. Barbosa-Novia del Mediodia-51 y 250-La Lisa-51 y 114-100 y 51-Cerro-Hospital Covadonga-Cuatro Caminos-Parque de la Fraternidad

P15: Alamar to Terminal del Trenes
Route: 3ra Avenida-Calle 160-Vía Blanca-Vía Monumental-Puente Santa Fé-10 de Octubre-Independencia (Guanabacoa)-(Regla)-Primer Anillo del Puerto-Avenida del Puerto-Terminal de Coubre-Egido-Terminal de Trenes

P16: Santiago de las Vegas to Vedado
Route: Parque Santiago-Boyeros-Avenida Independencia-Avenida Rancho Boyeros-Avenida G-Línea

want to use their meter and may ask you how much you're prepared to pay; quote below the fares given here and expect to bargain. Avoid private (illegal) taxis, as several foreigners have been robbed.

CAR RENTAL
These companies have booths at Terminal Three: **Cubacar** (tel. 07/649-9800), **Havanautos** (tel. 07/649-5197), and **Rex** (tel. 07/266-6074). These have booths at Terminal Two: **Cubacar** (tel. 07/649-5546), **Havanautos** (tel. 07/649-5215), and **Rex** (tel. 07/649-0306).

BY SEA
By Cruise Ship
Havana's **Terminal Sierra Maestra** (Av. del Puerto, tel. 07/862-1925) is a natty conversion of the old customs building. Passengers step through the doorways directly onto Plaza de San Francisco, in the heart of Havana.

By Private Vessel
Private yachts berth at **Marina Hemingway** (Av. 5ta y Calle 248, Santa Fe, tel. 07/204-5088, fax 07/204-5280, www.nauticamarlin.

com), 15 kilometers west of downtown. The harbor coordinates are 23° 5'N and 82° 29'W. You should announce your arrival on VHF Channel 16, HF Channel 68, and SSB 2790.

Visas are not required for stays of less than 72 hours. For longer stays you'll need a tourist card (CUC20), issued at the harbormaster's office (tel. 07/204-1150, ext. 2884) at the end of channel B. Docking fees (CUC0.35 per foot per day) include water, electricity, and custodial services. Gasoline and diesel are available 8 A.M.–7 P.M. (tel. 07/204-1150, ext. 450).

The 24-hour medical post (ext. 737) is in Complejo Turístico Papa's, as are a 24-hour launderette (ext. 451), bathrooms with showers, soda bar, and TV lounge, storage room (security boxes can be rented), ship chandler (ext. 2344), plus a beach volleyball court and tennis courts. The post office (ext. 448) is at the entrance of Intercanal C, where you'll also find the Hemingway International Nautical Club (ext. 701), which offers fax and telephone facilities. The shopping mall is at the east end of Intercanal B (ext. 739).

Rental cars are also available (ext. 87), as are microbuses and taxis (ext. 85).

Getting Around

ON FOOT
Havana is a walker's city, easily and best explored on foot. Only when traveling between districts will you need transport. Except in the restored section of Habana Vieja, sidewalks are in atrocious repair. Beware potholes, broken curbs, and dog excrement. And be wary of walking beneath corroded porticos. If *habaneros* are walking in the street to avoid certain arcades, so should you.

BY BUS
Tourist Bus
Havana has a double-decker tourist bus service, the **HabanaBusTour** (tel. 07/835-000, www.transtur.cu, daily 9 A.M.–9 P.M.), which

is perfect for first-time visitors who want to get their bearings and catch the main sights of Havana. For just CUC5 a day, you can hop on and off as many times as you wish at any of the 44 stops served by a fleet of 12 buses (three are open-top double-deckers) covering 95 miles of route. Although there are three routes, the red-and-blue, Chinese-made double-deckers only serve one route. The other two routes are by minibus, which takes away the fun.

The T1 route (double-decker) begins on the west side of Parque Central and does a figure eight around the perimeter of Habana Vieja, and then heads through Vedado as far as Plaza de la Revolución via the Hotel Habana Libre. At Plaza de la Revolución you can hop

HAVANA

aboard the T2 minibus for a sightseeing tour of Nuevo Vedado and Miramar and as far afield as Marina Hemingway, on the western fringe of the city. The T3 minibus is a great way to get out to the Playas del Este beaches.

Public Bus

Hurrah! Havana's formerly crowded and uncomfortable public buses, or *guaguas* (pronounced WAH-wahs), have been replaced with modern imported buses. No buses operate within Habana Vieja except along the major peripheral thoroughfares. Buses are often packed to the gills, especially during rush hours—7–10 A.M. and 3–6 P.M. Public transportation comes to a halt on May 1 and other days of major political celebrations, as buses are redirected to transporting the masses to demonstrations.

Bus service is the responsibility of three agencies: Asociación de Transportes de Servicios de Ómnibus (Astro), Transmetro, and Ómnibus Metropolitano.

Coco-taxis await customers

© CHRISTOPHER P. BAKER

SCHEDULES AND FARES

Most buses run 24 hours, at least hourly during the day but on reduced schedules 11 P.M.–5 A.M. The standard fare for any journey throughout the city is 20 centavos, or 40 centavos on smaller buses called *ómnibuses ruteros,* which have the benefit of being uncrowded. *Taxibuses*—buses that ply a fixed, non-stop route to the airport and bus and train stations—charge one peso.

ROUTES AND ROUTE MAPS

Many buses follow a loop route, traveling to and from destinations along different streets. Few routes are in a circle. (If you find yourself going in the wrong direction, don't assume that you'll eventually come around to where you want to be.) Most buses display the bus number and destination above the front window. Many buses arrive and depart from Parque Central and Parque de la Fraternidad in Habana Vieja and La Rampa (Calle 23) in Vedado, especially at Calle L and at Calzada de Infanta.

BY TAXI

Modern taxis—including top-of-the-line Mercedes—serve the tourist trade while locals make do with wheezing jalopies. Most taxis lack seatbelts or are otherwise in a poor state of repair.

Dollar Taxis

Since 2008, the various competing state-run taxi companies have been amalgamated. Now, Transtur operates all *turistaxis* as **Cubataxi** (tel. 07/855-5555), which can be hailed outside hotels or by calling for radio dispatch. Taxis range from modern Mercedes to beat-up Ladas, the Russian-made Fiat described by Martha Gellhorn as "tough as a Land Rover, with iron-hard upholstery and, judging by sensation, no springs." Only the most modern vehicles have functioning seatbelts.

Some taxis are metered (CUC1 at flag drop, then CUC0.45 a kilometer), but not all. Few drivers will use the meter, but will instead ask how much you want to pay. You will rarely pay more than CUC10 or so for any journey within town. Expect to pay about CUC5 between Habana Vieja and the Hotel Habana Libre Tryp. A light above the cab signifies if the taxi is *libre* (free).

Classic Cars

Fancy tooling around in a 1950 Studebaker or a 1959 Buick Invicta convertible? **Gran Car** (Calle Marino, esq. Santa María, Nuevo Vedado, tel. 07/855-5567, grancardp@transnet.cu) rents classic-car taxis for CUC30 per hour (20-km limit the first hour, with shorter limits per extra hour). Daily rates decline from CUC110 for one day to CUC90 per day for five days (120-km daily limit). Set prices apply for provincial touring. They can be found outside major hotels.

You can also rent a taxi and driver (CUC13 per person two hours, CUC25 four hours, CUC50 eight hours, CUC85 14 hours).

Peso Taxis

Privately owned 1950s-era *colectivos* or *máquinas* run along fixed routes, much like buses, and charge 10 or 50 pesos for a ride anywhere along the route. Parque de las Agrimensores, on the north side of the railway station, is the official starting point for set routes throughout the city. They are officially barred from accepting foreigners but occasionally will do so.

Bici-taxis

Hundreds of homespun tricycle taxis with shade canopies ply the streets of Habana Vieja and Centro. The minimum fare is usually CUC1 (or five pesos for Cubans on peso-only *bici-taxis*). You can go the full length of the Malecón, from Habana Vieja to Vedado, for CUC3–5. Always agree to a fare before setting off.

These jalopies are barred from certain streets and areas, so you might end up taking a zigzag route to your destination.

Coco-taxis

These cutesy three-wheeled eggshells on wheels whiz around the touristed areas of Havana and charge CUC0.50 per kilometer. However, they are inherently unsafe.

Coches

Horse-drawn coaches offer a popular way of exploring the Malecón and Old Havana, although the buggies are barred from entering the pedestrian-only quarter. They're operated by **San Cristóbal Agencia de Viajes** (Oficios #110, e/ Lamparilla y Amargura, Habana Vieja, tel. 07/861-9171). Their official starting point is the junction of Empedrado and Tacón, but you can hail them wherever you see them. Others can be hailed outside the Hotel Inglaterra, on Parque Central, and at Plaza de la Revolución. They charge CUC10 per person for one hour.

BY CAR

The narrow one-way streets in Habana Vieja are purgatory for motor vehicles. The main plazas and the streets between them are barred to traffic.

A treacherously potholed, four-lane freeway—the **Autopista Circular** (route Calle 100 or *circunvalación*)—encircles southern and eastern Havana, linking the arterial highways and separating the core from suburban Havana. The intersections are dangerous.

Parking

A capital city without parking meters? Imagine. Parking meters were detested during the Batista era, mostly because they were a source of *botellas* (skimming) for corrupt officials. After the triumph of the Revolution, *habaneros* smashed the meters. However, the state is increasingly applying fees to park roadside, with *custodios* (in red vests) on hand to collect fees.

No Parking zones are well marked. Avoid these like the plague, especially if it's an officials-only zone. Havana has an efficient towing system.

Never leave your car parked unguarded. In central Vedado, the Hotel Habana Libre Tryp has an underground car park (CUC0.60 for one hour, CUC6 max. for 24 hours).

Car Rental

All hotels have car rental booths, and there are scores of outlets citywide.

Transtur (Calle L #456, e/ 25 y 27, Vedado, tel. 07/835-0000, www.transtur.cu) operates the two main car rental agencies: **Cubacar** (Calle 21, e/ N y O, Vedado, Havana, tel. 07/836-4038) and **Havanautos** (tel. 07/285-0703, http://havanautos.com). They have a selection of small and mid-range cars; Cubacar even rents BMW 5-series cars (CUC185 daily, or CUC180 per day for week-long rentals).

Rex (tel. 07/273-9166 or 683-0303, www.rex-rentacar.com) competes with Audis and has offices at the airport; in Vedado (Malecón y Línea, tel. 07/835-6830); in Miramar at Hotel Copacabana (tel. 07/202-7684) and 5ta Av. y 92 (tel. 07/209-2207); in Siboney (Av. 194, e/ 15 y 17, tel. 07/273-9166); at the cruise terminal (tel. 07/862-6343); and near the airport (Avenida Rancho Boyeros y Calzada de Bejucal, Plaza de la Revolución, tel. 07/683-0303).

Car Repair

Your car rental company will arrange repairs. However, if you need emergency treatment, **Oro Negro** has three *servicentros* (5ta Av., esq. 120, Miramar, tel. 07/208-6149; Calle 2, esq. 7ma, Miramar, tel. 07/204-5760; and Av. 13, esq. 84, Playa, tel. 07/204-1938), all with the same hours (Mon.–Sat. 8 A.M.–7 P.M.). Cubalse, which oversees sales of cars in Cuba, has an automotive repair shop at **Agency Multimarcas** (Av. 222, esq. La Lisa, tel. 07/204-8743).

You can arrange a tow through **Agencia Peugeot** (tel. 07/766-1463 or 879-3854), which charges CUC1 per kilometer outbound and CUC1 per kilometer for the tow.

BY MOTORCYCLE AND SCOOTER

Renta de Motos (3ra Av., esq. Miramar, tel. 07/204-5491, daily 9 A.M.–9 P.M.) rents scooters for CUC12 for two hours, CUC15 three hours, or CUC23 per day (CUC21 per day for rentals of 3–10 days). It does not offer insurance.

If you're staying in Cuba any length of time, consider buying a Chinese-made Dayang scooter (CUC1,845) or Suzuki GN125 (CUC2,332) from **Agencia Vedado** (Calle

23 #753, e/ B y C, Vedado, tel. 07/833-3994, ventas23@23c.automotriz.cubalse.cu).

BY BICYCLE

Bicycling offers a chance to explore the city alongside the Cubans themselves, although the roads are dodgy (an average of two cyclists are killed in traffic accidents in Havana every three days).

Specially converted buses—the *ciclobuses*—ferry cyclists and their *bicis* through the tunnel beneath Havana harbor (10 centavos). Buses depart from Parque de la Fraternidad and Avenida de los Estudiantes.

Alas, bike rentals are no longer available, but you can buy bikes from **El Orbe** (Monserrate #304, e/ O'Reilly y San Juan de Dios, Habana Vieja, tel. 07/860-2617, Mon.–Fri. 9 A.M.–6 P.M., Sat. 9 A.M.–5 P.M.).

BY FERRY

Tiny ferries (standing room only—no seats) bob across the harbor between the Havana waterfront and Regla (on the east side of the bay) and Casablanca (on the north side of the bay). The ferries leave on a constant yet irregular basis 24 hours from Muelle Luz wharf on Avenida San Pedro at the foot of Calle Santa Clara in Habana Vieja (tel. 07/797-7473 in Regla); it costs 10 centavos and takes five minutes.

ORGANIZED EXCURSIONS
City Tours

Havanatur (Calle 23, esq. M, Vedado, tel. 07/830-3107 or 201-9800, daily 8 A.M.–8 P.M.) offers a city tour, including walking tour, plus excursions to key sights in the suburbs and, of course, farther afield.

Agencia de Viajes San Cristóbal (Oficios #110, e/ Lamparilla y Amargura, tel. 07/861-9171, www.viajessancristobal.cu, daily 8:30 A.M.–5 P.M.) offers a wide range of excursions throughout the city—from a walking tour of Habana Vieja (daily 10 A.M.) to an "Eclecticismo y Modernismo" tour of modern Havana for architecture buffs.

You can book through hotel tour bureaus.

Private Guides

Agencia de Viajes San Cristóbal (Oficios #110, e/ Lamparilla y Amargura, tel. 07/861-9171, www.viajessancristobal.cu, daily 8:30 A.M.–5 P.M.) can arrange guides.

Jineteros (street hustlers) will offer to be your guide. Perhaps they can show you the offbeat scene that most tourists miss, but they're usually useless as sightseeing guides and most will pull a scam.

Getting Away

DEPARTING CUBA
By Air

Airlines serving Havana have flights that usually depart Havana on the same days they arrive.

Cubana (Calle 23 #64, e/ P y Infanta, Vedado, tel. 07/838-1039 or 834-4446, www.cubana.cu, Mon.–Fri. 8:30 A.M.–4 P.M., Sat. 8 A.M.–1 P.M.) has a fully computerized reservation system. Cubana also has a sales office in Miramar (Calle 110, esq. 5ta, tel. 07/202-9367, Mon.–Fri. 8:30 A.M.–4 P.M.).

JOSÉ MARTÍ INTERNATIONAL AIRPORT

The airport (switchboard tel. 07/266-4644, www.airportcuba.com), at Wajay, 25 kilometers southwest of downtown Havana, is accessed by Avenida de la Independencia (Avenida Rancho Boyeros). Make sure you arrive at the correct terminal for your departure.

U.S.-bound charter flights depart **Terminal Two** (Terminal Nacional, tel. 07/275-1200), on the north side of the runway.

Terminal Three (tel. 07/642-6225, or tel. 07/266-4133 for arrivals and departures), about one kilometer west of Terminal Two, handles all international flights. The departure tax (CUC25) must be paid at a separate counter after you've checked in with the airline. The foreign exchange bank refuses to accept Cuban pesos. There's an Internet café in the departure lounge.

Terminal Five (also called Terminal Caribbean), about three kilometers west of the international terminal, at the northwest corner of the airport, handles small-plane flights (mostly domestic) offered by Aero Caribbean.

GETTING TO THE AIRPORT

No buses serve the international terminals. A tourist **taxi** to the airport will cost about CUC15–20 from Havana. You may be able to negotiate less with the driver.

A **bus** marked Aeropuerto operates to Terminal One—the domestic terminal—from the east side of Parque Central in Habana Vieja. It's intended for Cubans only. The *cola* (line) begins near the José Martí statue. There are two lines: one for people wishing to be seated (*sentados*) and one for those willing to stand (*de pie*). The journey costs one peso, takes about one hour, and is very unreliable (departures are about every two hours). You can also catch Ómnibus #480 or Metrobus P12 from the west side of Parque de la Fraternidad (you can also get on the P12 near the University of Havana on Avenida Salvador Allende). Both go to Santiago de las Vegas via the domestic terminal (Terminal One) but will let you off about 400 meters east of Terminal Two. Do *not* use this bus for the international terminal.

EXPLORING BEYOND HAVANA

Make your reservations as far ahead as possible.

By Air

Cubana (Calle 23 #64, e/ P y Infanta, Vedado, tel. 07/838-1039 or 834-4446, www.cubana.cu, Mon.–Fri. 8:30 A.M.–4 P.M., Sat. 8 A.M.–1 P.M.) offers service to all major Cuban cities.

Most domestic flights leave from José Martí International Airport's **Terminal One** (Av. Van Troi, off Av. Rancho Boyeros, tel. 07/266-4644 or 275-1200).

INTERNATIONAL AIRLINE OFFICES IN HAVANA

The following airlines have offices in the Hotel Habana Libre Tryp (Calle L, e/ 23 y 25, Vedado):

- **Air Europa** (tel. 07/839-6917, ofic.cuba@air-europa.com)

- **Taca** (tel. 07/833-3114, fax 07/833-3728, www.grupotaca.com)

The following have offices at Calle 23 #64 (e/P y Infanta, Vedado):

- **Aerocaribbean** (tel. 07/879-7525, fax 07/836-5016)

- **Air Canada** (tel. 07/836-3226, www.air-canada.com)

- **Air France** (tel. 07/833-2642, www.air-france.com/cu)

- **Air Jamaica** (tel. 07/833-2447, www.air-jamaica.com)

- **Blue Panorama** (tel. 07/833-2248, www.blue-panorama.com)

- **Cubana** (tel. 07/834-4446, 07/834-4447, 07/834-4448, 07/834-4449, www.cubana.cu)

- **Havanatur** (tel. 07/201-9800, for U.S. flights only)

- **LanChile** (tel. 07/831-6186, www.lanchile.com)

- **LTU** (tel. 07/833-3525, www.ltu.com)

- **Mexicana** (tel. 07/833-3532, www.mexicana.com)

The following have offices at the Miramar Trade Center (5ta Av. y 76, Miramar):

- **Aero Caribe** (tel. 07/873-3621, fax 07/873-3871)

- **Aeroflot** (tel. 07/204-5593, www.aeroflot.com)

- **Air Europa** (Edificio Santiago, tel. 07/204-6904, fax 07/204-6905, ofic.cuba@air-europa.com)

- **COPA** (Edificio Barcelona, tel. 07/204-1111, www.copa.com)

- **Iberia** (Edificio Santiago, tel. 07/204-3444, www.iberia.com)

- **Virgin Atlantic** (Edificio Santa Clara, tel. 07/204-0747, fax 07/204-4094, www.virgin-atlantic.com)

The following also have offices in Havana:

- **Martinair** (Calle 23, esq. E, Vedado, tel. 07/833-3729, fax 07/833-3732, www.martinair.com)

AeroGaviota (Av. 47 #2814, e/ 28 y 34, Rpto. Kohly, tel. 07/204-2621 or 203-0668) flights depart from Aeropuerto Baracoa, on the Autopista Habana–Mariel, about three kilometers west of Marina Hemingway.

By Bus
TOURIST BUSES
Modern **Víazul** buses (Av. 26, esq. Zoológico, Nuevo Vedado, tel. 07/881-1413, fax 07/66-6092, www.viazul.cu, daily 7 A.M.–9 P.M.) serve provincial capitals and major tourist destinations throughout the country. They depart Terminal Víazul, which has a café and free luggage storage. City bus #27 connects the Víazul

terminal to Vedado and Centro Habana. Víazul buses make a 10-minute stop at the **Terminal de Ómnibuses Nacionales** (Av. Independencia #101, esq. 19 de Mayo, Víazul tel. 07/870-3397, daily 6:30 A.M.–9:30 P.M.), two blocks north of Plaza de la Revolución. You can also make reservations and board the buses here. The terminal is served by local bus #47 from the Prado (at Ánimas) in Habana Vieja; by bus #265 from the east side of Parque Central; and by buses #67 and 84 from La Rampa in Vedado. Facilities include a bank, snack bars, and an information booth (tel. 07/870-9401).

Cuban tour agencies such as Havanatur and Veracuba offer transfer seats on tour buses serving key tourist destinations. Check with tour desks in hotel lobbies.

PUBLIC BUSES
Astro buses to destinations throughout the country leave from the Terminal de Ómnibuses Nacionales. However, in 2009 Astro ceased accepting foreigners, except for students with appropriate ID who can travel like Cubans for pesos. Make your reservation as early as possible, either at the bus terminal or at the **Agencia Reservaciones de Pasaje** (Factor y Tulipán, Nuevo Vedado, tel. 07/881-5931 or 07/55-5537). Your name will be added to the scores of names ahead of you. If you don't have a reservation or miss your departure, you can try getting on the standby list (*lista de espera,* tel. 07/862-4341) at **Terminal La Coubre** (Av. del Puerto y Egido, tel. 07/872-3726), in southwest Habana Vieja.

Buses to towns throughout Havana Province depart from Calle Apodaca, between Zulueta and Avenida de Bélgica.

By Train
Estación Central de Ferrocarril: The main station is the Central Railway Station (Egido, esq. Arsenal, Habana Vieja, tel. 07/861-2959 or 862-1920), or Terminal de Trenes. Trains depart here for major cities. Unfortunately, Cuba's Kafaesque Communist system comes into play when you try to buy a ticket, which must be done from the hideously dysfunctional **Terminal La Coubre** (Av. del Puerto, tel. 07/862-1012), 400 meters south of the main railway station at *taquilla* (booth) #3. Tickets

can be purchased up to one hour prior to departure, but you must purchase your ticket before 8 P.M. for a nighttime departure.

Estación 19 de Noviembre: Local commuter trains (*ferro-ómnibuses*) operate from this station (Calle Tulipán and Hidalgo, tel. 07/881-4431), also called Estación Tulipán, south of Plaza de la Revolución. Trains depart to San Antonio de los Baños at 10:05 A.M. and 4:25 and 8:30 P.M. (CUC1.50); to Artemisa at 8:30 A.M. and 5:45 P.M. (CUC2.20); and to Batabanó at 5 P.M. (CUC1.80).

Estación Casablanca: The Hershey Train operates to Matanzas five times daily from Casablanca's harborfront station (tel. 07/862-4888) on the north side of Havana harbor.

By Taxi
Cubataxi (tel. 07/855-5555) and the three car rental companies offer chauffeured excursions by car or minivan within a 150-mile radius of Havana. Typical round-trip prices are: to Varadero CUC180, Bay of Pigs CUC320, and Viñales CUC250. Hourly rates for a chauffeured taxi are on a sliding scale, from about CUC15 for the first hour (20-km limit) to CUC80 for eight hours (125-km limit), typically with CUC0.80 per kilometer for extra distance.

Organized Tours and Excursions
You can book excursions in tourist hotels.

Belgian-owned **Transnico** (Lonja del Comercio #6D, Habana Vieja, tel. 07/866-9954) specializes in special-interest tours, including bicycle tours, music and dance programs, and train trips.

Havana Suburbs

SANTIAGO DE LAS VEGAS

This colonial-era rural town lies in the midst of the country, 20 kilometers south of Havana. It is accessed via Avenida de la Independencia, a fast-paced highway running south through the industrial area of Rancho Boyeros to the José Martí International Airport, beyond which it becomes Avenida de los Mártires before entering Santiago de las Vegas.

Mausoleo de General Antonio Maceo Grajales

Avenida de los Mártires rises south of Santiago de las Vegas, passes through pine forests, and deposits you at El Cacahual. Here, Antonio Maceo Grajales (1845–1896), the black general and hero of the Wars of Independence, slumbers in a mausoleum engraved in the style of Mexican artist Diego Rivera. The mausoleum also contains the tomb of Capitán Ayudante (Captain-Adjutant) Francisco Gómez Toro (1876–1896), General Máximo Gómez's son, who gave his life alongside Maceo at the Battle of San Pedro on December 7, 1896. The park forms a giant traffic circle; on the east side stands a monument in bronze to Coronel (Colonel) Juan Delgado, chief of the Santiago de las Vegas regiment, who recovered Maceo's body.

The tiny main square in Santiago de las Vegas is pinned by the marble **Monumento a Juan Delgado Gonzáles.**

SANTUARIO DE SAN LÁZARO

Cuba's most important pilgrimage site is the Sanctuary of San Lázaro (Carretera de San Antonio de los Baños, tel. 047/683-2396, daily 7 A.M.–6 P.M., free), on the west side of Rincón, a rustic hamlet about four kilometers southwest of Santiago de las Vegas. The church, **Iglesia de San Lázaro,** is busy with mendicants come to have their children baptized, while others fill bottles with holy water from a fountain behind the church, where the Los Cocos sanatorium houses leprosy and AIDS patients.

San Lázaro is the patron saint of the sick, and is an immensely popular figure throughout Cuba (in *santería,* his avatar is Babalú Ayé). His symbol is the crutch. His stooped figure is usually covered in sores, and in effigy he goes about attended by his two dogs. Limbless beggars and other unfortunates crowd at the gates and plead for a charitable donation.

A procession to the sanctuary takes place the 17th of each month. The annual **Procesión de los Milagros** (Procession of the Miracles) takes place December 17, drawing thousands of pilgrims to beseech or give thanks to the saint for miracles they imagine he has the power to grant. The villagers of Rincón do a thriving business selling votive candles and flowers. Penitents crawl on their backs and knees as others sweep the road ahead with palm fronds.

Getting There and Away

Buses P12 (from Parque de la Fraternidad) and P16 (from outside Hospital Hermanos Ameijeiras, in Centro Habana) link Havana to Santiago de las Vegas. Ómnibus #480 also serves Santiago de las Vegas from Havana's main bus terminal (Av. Independencia #101, Plaza de la Revolución, tel. 07/870-9401). The **Terminal de Ómnibus** (Calle al Rincón #43, tel. 07/683-3159) is on the southwest side of town, on the road to Rincón.

A three-car train departs Havana's Estación 19 de Noviembre (Tulipán) at 10:05 A.M. and 4:25 and 8:30 P.M., stopping at Rincón (CUC1). Trains run continuously on December 17.

If driving, follow Carretera al Rincón, which begins at the bus station on the southwest edge of Santiago de las Vegas; bus #476 also runs from here.

ARROYO NARANJO

This *municipio* lies east of Boyeros and due south of Havana.

Parque Zoológico Nacional

Cuba's national zoo, on Avenida Zoo–Lenin (Av. 8, esq. Av. Soto, tel. 07/644-8063,

© CHRISTOPHER P. BAKER

figures of San Lázaro, Santuario de San Lázaro

Wed.–Sun. 9:30 A.M.–3:15 P.M. winter, until 4:15 summer, adults CUC3, children CUC2), southeast of the village of Arroyo Naranjo, about 16 kilometers south of central Havana, covers 340 hectares and contains about 1,000 animals and more than 100 species. You can drive your own car through the park. A walk-through section houses a leopard, tiger, chimps, monkeys, and birds, but the cages are small and bare, many of the animals look woefully neglected, and the conditions are deplorable. The zoo also breeds endangered species. A children's area provides pony rides.

Tour buses (CUC2) depart the parking lot about every 30 minutes and run through the African wildlife park (*pradera africana*), taking you through an area resembling the African savanna. Elephants come to the bus and stick their trunks in through the window to glean tidbits. The tour also loops through the *foso de leones* (lion pit)—a quarry with a viewing platform.

To get to the main entrance, take Avenida de la Independencia to Avenida San Francisco (the *parque* is signed at the junction), which merges with the *circunvalación*. Take the first exit to the right and follow Calzada de Bejucal south. Turn right onto Avenida Zoo–Lenin (signed).

Buses 473 and 177 operate between La Víbora and Arroyo Naranjo, as does P13 (the P9 bus from Calle 23 and L links downtown Havana to La Víbora). A taxi will cost about CUC15 each way.

Parque Lenin

Lenin Park (Calle 100 y Carretera de la Presa, tel. 07/647-1100 or 647-1165, Tues.–Sun. 9 A.M.–5 P.M.), east of the zoo, was created from a former hacienda and landscaped mostly by volunteer labor from the city. The vast complex features wide rolling pastures and small lakes surrounded by forests. What Lenin Park lacks in grandeur and stateliness, it makes up for in scale.

The park, which is administered by Flora y Fauna, is bounded by the *circunvalación* to the north and Calzada de Bejucal to the west; there is an entrance off Calzada de Bejucal. A second road—Calle Cortina de la Presa—enters from the *circunvalación,* runs down the center of the park, and is linked to Calzada de Bejucal by a loop road.

The **Galería del Arte Amelia Peláez,** at the south end of Cortina, displays works by the eponymous Cuban ceramist. Behind the

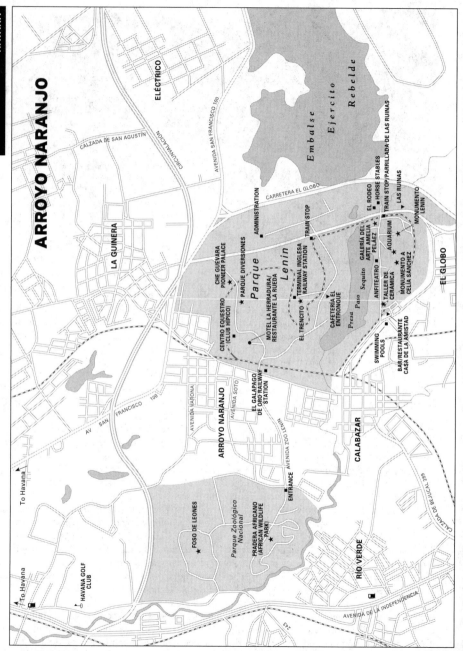

ARROYO NARANJO

ELÉCTRICO

LA GUINERA

CALZADA DE SAN AGUSTÍN

CIRCUNVALACIÓN

AVENIDA SAN FRANCISCO 100

Embalse Ejercito Rebelde

CARRETERA EL GLOBO

ADMINISTRATION

TRAIN STOP

EL RODEO
HORSE STABLES
TRAIN STOP/PARRILLADA DE LAS RUINAS
LAS RUINAS
MONUMENTO LENIN

CHE GUEVARA PIONEER PALACE

PARQUE DIVERSIONES

Parque

Lenin

CENTRO EQUESTRO (CLUB HIPICO)

MOTEL LA HERRADURA/
RESTAURANTE LA RUEDA

EL TRENCITO

TERMINAL INGLESA
RAILWAY STATION

CAFETERÍA EL ENTRONQUE

GALERIA DE ARTE AMELIA PELÁEZ
AQUARIUM

ANFITEATRO
TALLER DE CERÁMICA
MONUMENTO A CELIA SÁNCHEZ

Presa Paso Sequito

EL GLOBO

SWIMMING POOLS

BAR/RESTAURANTE CASA DE LA AMISTAD

AVENIDA VARONA

AVENIDA SOTO

EL GALAPAGO DE ORO RAILWAY STATION

ARROYO NARANJO

AVENIDA ZOO LENIN

AV. SAN FRANCISCO 100

CALABAZAR

CALZADA DE BEJUCAL 289

To Havana

ENTRANCE

FOSO DE LEONES

Parque Zoológico Nacional

PRADERA AFRICANO (AFRICAN WILDLIFE PARK)

RIO VERDE

To Havana

HAVANA GOLF CLUB

AVENIDA DE LA INDEPENDENCIA

243

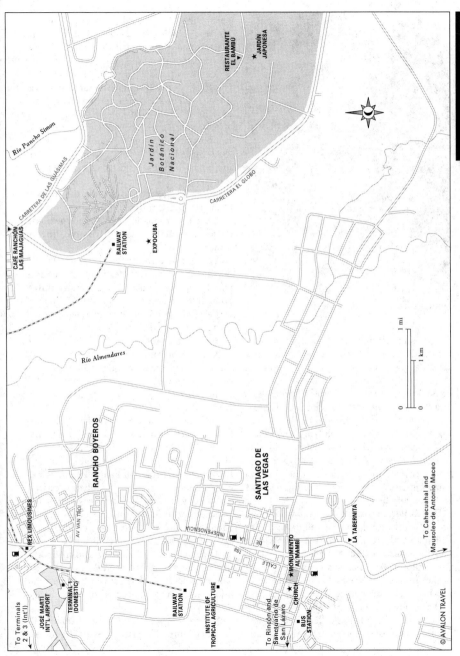

RESTAURANTE EL BAMBÚ

★ JARDÍN JAPONESA

Jardín Botánico Nacional

Río Pancho Simon

CARRETERA DE LAS QUASIMAS

CARRETERA EL GLOBO

CAFÉ RANCHÓN LAS MAJAGUAS

■ RAILWAY STATION

★ EXPOCUBA

Río Almendares

RANCHO BOYEROS

SANTIAGO DE LAS VEGAS

AV VAN TRÓI

LA INDEPENDENCIA

CALLE 188

AV DE

★ MONUMENTO AL MAMBÍ

▲ LA TABERNITA

To Cahacuahal and
Mausoleo de Antonio Maceo

REX LIMOUSINES

To Terminals
2 & 3 (Int'l)

JOSÉ MARTÍ
INT'L AIRPORT

TERMINAL 1
(DOMESTIC)

■ RAILWAY
STATION

INSTITUTE OF
TROPICAL AGRICULTURE

To Rincón and
Santuario de
San Lázaro

★ CHURCH

BUS
STATION

0   1 mi

0   1 km

© AVALON TRAVEL

© CHRISTOPHER P. BAKER

Monumento Lenin, Parque Lenin

gallery is a series of bronze busts inset in rock. A short distance to the west is the **Monumento Lenin,** a huge granite visage of the Communist leader and thinker in Soviet-realist style, carved by Soviet sculpture I. E. Kerbel. Farther west, you'll pass an **aquarium** (entrance CUC1) displaying freshwater fish and turtles, including the antediluvian garfish (*manjuari*) and a couple of Cuban crocodiles. About 400 meters farther west is the **Monumento a Celia Sánchez.** Here, a trail follows a wide apse to a small museum fronting a bronze figure of the revolutionary heroine.

The **Taller Cerámica** (ceramic workshop), on the southwest corner of the park, is also worth a visit. On the north side, the **Palacio de Pioneros Che Guevara** displays stainless-steel sculptures of Che, plus a full-scale replica of the *Granma* (the vessel that brought Castro and his revolutionaries from Mexico).

An equestrian center, **Centro Ecuestre** (daily 9 A.M.–5 P.M.), also called Club Hípico, immediately east of the entrance off Calzada de Bejucal, offers one-hour trips (CUC15)

plus riding lessons, and you can rent horses. Horseback riding is also offered on weekends at **El Rodeo,** the national rodeo arena, in the southeast corner of the park. El Rodeo offers rodeo every Sunday, with *rodeo pionero* (for youth) at noon and competitive adult rodeo at 3 P.M. The Feria de Rodeo (the national championships) is held each August 25.

A narrow-gauge railway circles the park, stopping at four stages. The old steam train (Sat.–Sun. 10 A.M.–4 P.M., four pesos), dating from 1870, departs Estación Galapagos de Oro and takes 25 minutes to circle the park. Another old steam train is preserved in front of the disused Terminal Inglesa.

You can rent aquatic **bicycles** and **rowboats** on the lake at El Rodeo (five pesos for 30 minutes).

A *parque de diversiones* (theme park) in the northwest quarter includes carousels, a Ferris wheel, and pony rides. There are **swimming pools** in the Palacio de Pioneros Che Guevara and east of the community of Calabazar, on the south side of the park (five pesos).

Bus P13 operates between La Víbora and the park. Buses 88 and 113 leave from the north side of Havana's main railway station and continue to ExpoCuba.

ExpoCuba

ExpoCuba, on the Carretera del Globo (official address Carretera del Rocío, Km 3.5, Arroyo Naranjo, tel. 07/697-4269, Wed.–Sun. 10 A.M.–5 P.M., closed Sept.–Dec., CUC1), three kilometers south of Parque Lenin, houses a permanent exhibition of Cuban industry, technology, sports, and culture touting the achievements of socialism. The facility covers 588,000 square meters and is a museum, trade expo, world's fair, and entertainment hall rolled into one. It has 34 pavilions, including booths that display the crafts, products, music, and dance of each of Cuba's provinces. There's an information office, plus a currency exchange and bank.

A train linking ExpoCuba to Estación 19 de Noviembre (Tulipán, Nuevo Vedado, tel. 07/881-4431) was not operating at last visit.

Jardín Botánico Nacional

This 600-hectare botanical garden (tel. 07/697-9364, daily 8 A.M.–4 P.M., CUC1, or CUC4 including guide), directly opposite ExpoCuba, doesn't have the fine-trimmed herbaceous borders of Kew or Butchart, but nonetheless is worth the drive for enthusiasts. Thirty-five kilometers of roads lead through the park, which was laid out between 1969 and 1984. You can drive your own vehicle, with a guide.

The garden consists mostly of wide pastures planted with copses divided by Cuban ecosystems and by regions of the tropical world (from coastal thicket to Oriental humid forest). The geographic center contains palm trees from around the world. There is even an "archaic forest" containing species such as *Microcyca calocom,* Cuba's cork palm. The highlight is the **Jardín Japonés** (Japanese garden), landscaped with tiered cascades, fountains, and a jade-green lake full of koi. The **Invernáculo Rincón Eckman** is a massive greenhouse named after Erik Leonard Eckman (1883–1931), who documented Cuban flora between 1914 and 1924. It is laid out as a triptych with greenhouses for cactus, epiphytes, ferns, insectivorous plants, and tropical mountain plants.

Food

Cubans travel from Havana to dine at ◖ **Las Ruinas** (Calle 100 y Cortina, tel. 07/643-8527, Tues.–Sun. noon–5 P.M.), in Parque Lenin. Looking like something Frank Lloyd Wright might have conceived, the restaurant was designed in concrete and encases the ruins of an old sugar mill. It serves continental and *criollo* cuisine (lobster Bellevue is a specialty, CUC20); I enjoyed a tasty shrimp enchilada (CUC12).

Parque Lenin has several basic restaurants, including air-conditioned **Restaurante La Rueda** (no tel., daily 11 A.M.–5 P.M.) and open-air **Parillada de las Ruinas** (no tel., Tues.–Sun. noon–5 P.M.), each serving simple *criollo* dishes in pesos.

The ◖ **Restaurante El Bambú** (tel. 07/697-9364, Wed.–Sun. 1–5 P.M.), overlooking the Japanese garden in the Jardín Botánico

Nacional, bills itself as an *eco-restorán* and serves vegetables—beetroot, cassava, pumpkin, spinach, taro, and more—grown right there in the garden. I recommend the *fufo* (mashed boiled banana with garlic) and eggplant cooked in cheese sauce. Free refills permitted. Locals and foreign students with ID are charged 40 pesos for a meal; other foreigners pay CUC12 for an all-you-can-eat buffet. The restaurant is often booked solid; make reservations.

SAN MIGUEL DEL PADRÓN

The *municipio* of San Miguel del Padrón, southeast of Habana Vieja, is mostly residential, with factory areas by the harbor and timeworn colonial housing on the hills south of town. The region is accessed from the Vía Blanca or (parallel to it) Calzada de Luyano via the Carretera Central (Calzada de Güines), which ascends to the quintessential colonial village of San Francisco de Paula on the city's outskirts, 12.5 kilometers south of Habana Vieja.

En route, you'll pass through the suburb of Luyano, where Cubans come to throw coins into the **Fuente de la Virgen del Camino** (Virgin of the Way), a fountain by acclaimed sculptor Rita Longa at the junction of Calzada de Luyano and Carretera Central (the money goes to pay for the indigent). Two blocks east is the **Monumento a Doña Leonor Pérez** (Balear, esq. Leonor Pérez), dedicated to José Martí's mother. The patinated bronze figure sits in a dignified pose atop a marble pedestal. Bas-reliefs depict key moments in Martí's life.

◖ Museo Ernest Hemingway

In 1939, Hemingway's third wife, Martha Gellhorn, saw and was struck by Finca Vigía (Vigía y Steinhart, tel. 07/691-0809, mushem@cubart.cult.cu, Mon.–Sat. 10 A.M.–5 P.M., Sun. 10 A.M.–1 P.M., entrance CUC3, guided tours CUC1, cameras CUC5), a one-story Spanish-colonial house built in 1887 and boasting a wonderful view of Havana. They rented Lookout Farm for US$100 a month. When Hemingway's first royalty check from *For Whom the Bell Tolls* arrived in 1940, he bought the house for US$18,500. In August 1961, his

ERNEST HEMINGWAY AND CUBA

Ernest Hemingway first set out from Key West to wrestle marlin in the wide streaming currents off the Cuban coast in April 1932. The blue waters of the Gulf Stream, chock-full of billfish, brought him closer and closer until eventually, "succumbing to the other charms of Cuba, different from and more difficult to explain than the big fish in September," he settled on this island of sensual charm. Hemingway loved Cuba and lived there for 20 years. Once, when Hemingway was away from Cuba, he was asked what he worried about in his sleep. "My house in Cuba," he replied, referring to Finca Vigía, in the suburb of San Francisco de Paula, 12.5 kilometers southeast of Havana.

Walking Havana's streets you can still feel Hemingway's presence. It is easy to imagine the sun-bronzed writer driving in his brand-new Chrysler New Yorker convertible, white mane and beard haloed in tropical light, hoary chest showing beneath khaki shirt, en route for his daily double daiquiri with his friends.

THE CULT OF HEMINGWAY

Havana's marina is named for the prize-winning novelist. Hemingway's room in the Hotel Ambos Mundos and his former home, Finca Vigía, are preserved as museums. And his likeness adorns T-shirts and billboards. "We admire Hemingway because he understood the Cuban people," a friend told me. "His friends were fishermen, jai alai players, bullfighters. He never related to high society," adds Evelio González, a guide at Finca Vigía.

Yet the cult of Hemingway is very real. The novelist's works are required reading in Cuban schools. His books are bestsellers. The Cuban understanding of Hemingway's "Cuban novels" is that they support a core tenet of Communist ideology – that humans are only fulfilled acting in a "socialist" context for a moral purpose, not individualistically. (Many of Hemingway's novels appear to condemn economic and political injustices.) "All the works of Hemingway are a defense of human rights," claims Castro, who once claimed that *For Whom the Bell Tolls*, Hemingway's fictional account of the Spanish

Civil War, inspired his guerrilla tactics. Castro has said the reason he admires Hemingway so much is that he envies the adventures he had. The two headstrong fellows met only once, during the 10th Annual Ernest Hemingway Billfish Tournament in May 1960. As sponsor and judge of the competition, Hemingway invited Cuba's youthful new leader as his guest of honor. Castro was to present the winner's trophy; instead, he hooked the biggest marlin and won the prize for himself. Hemingway surrendered the trophy to a beaming Fidel. They never met again.

With the Cold War and the United States' break with Cuba, Hemingway had to choose. Not being able to return to Cuba contributed to Hemingway's depression, says his son Patrick: "He really loved Cuba, and I think it was a great shock to him at his age to have to choose between his country, which was the United States, and his home, which was Cuba."

PAPA AND THE REVOLUTION

There has been a great deal of speculation about Hemingway's attitude toward the Cuban Revolution. Cuba, of course, attempts to portray him as sympathetic, not least because Hemingway's Cuban novels are full of images of prerevolutionary terror and destitution. "There is an absolutely murderous tyranny that extends over every little village in the country," he wrote in *Islands in the Stream*.

Hemingway's widow, Mary Welsh, told the journalist Luis Báez that "Hemingway was always in favor of the Revolution." Another writer, Lisandro Otero, records Hemingway as saying, "Had I been a few years younger, I would have climbed the Sierra Maestra with Fidel Castro." Papa was away from Cuba all of 1959, but he returned in 1960, recorded *New York Times* correspondent Herbert Matthews, "to show his sympathy and support for the Castro Revolution." Papa even used his legendary 38-foot sportfishing boat, the *Pilar*, to run arms for the Rebel Army, claimed Gregorio Fuentes, the skipper of the *Pilar* for 23 years. Welsh claims, however, to have been

© CHRISTOPHER P. BAKER

Ernest Hemingway's office, Museo Ernest Hemingway

on board when Hemingway dumped his sporting guns and ammunition into the sea so that neither side would get them.

Hemingway's enigmatic farewell comment as he departed the island in 1960 is illuminating: "*Vamos a ganar. Nosotros los cubanos vamos a ganar.* [We are going to win. We Cubans are going to win.] I'm not a Yankee, you know." Before leaving Cuba, however, Hemingway expressed hope that the Revolution would not become Communist, claims writer Claudia Lightfoot. Prophetically, in *Islands in the Stream*, a character says: "The Cubans... double cross each other. They sell each other out. They got what they deserve. The hell with their revolutions."

FINCA VIGÍA'S FATE

After Hemingway's death, Finca Vigía was seized by the Castro government, though the writer had willed the property to his fourth wife, Mary Welsh. The Cuban government allowed her to remove 200 pounds of papers, but insisted that most of their home's contents remain untouched, including 3,000 letters and documents, 3,000 photographs, and 9,000 books – all kept secreted in the humid basement, where they deteriorated to the point of near ruin. Only in 2002 was this invaluable resource opened to scholars, when a joint Cuba-U.S. effort to save them was launched (www.hemingwaypreservationfoundation.org).

In his will, the author left his sportfishing vessel, the *Pilar*, to Gregorio Fuentes (the former skipper couldn't afford its upkeep and it, too, became the property of the government). Meanwhile, Hemingway's sleek black 1955 Chrysler New Yorker escaped and apparently passed into the hands of Augustín Nuñez Gutiérrez, a Cuban policeman, according to writer Joann Biondi. Later, Nuñez hid the car and hopped on a raft for Miami. Popular legend says the car's whereabouts are still a mystery and that the Chrysler still awaits discovery.

widow, Mary Welsh, was forced to sign papers handing over the home to the Castro government, along with its contents. On July 21, 1994, on the 95th anniversary of Papa's birthday, Finca Vigía reopened its doors as a museum. The house is preserved in suspended animation, just the way the great writer left it. (In ensuing decades, it fell into decay, but a five-year, US$1 million restoration completed in 2009 has salvaged the home from termites and clime.)

Bougainvilleas frame the gateway to the 20-acre hilltop estate. Mango trees and jacarandas line the driveway leading up to the gleaming white house. No one is allowed inside—reasonably so, since every room can be viewed through the wide-open windows, and the temptation to pilfer priceless trinkets is thus reduced. Through the large windows, you can see trophies, firearms, bottles of spirits, old issues of *The Field, Spectator,* and *Sports Afield* strewn about, and more than 9,000 books and magazines, arranged the way he supposedly liked them, with no concern for authors or subjects.

It is eerie being followed by countless eyes—those of the guides (one to each room) and those of the beasts that found themselves in the crosshairs of Hemingway's hunting scope. "Don't know how a writer could write surrounded by so many dead animals," Graham Greene commented when he visited. There are bulls, too, including paintings by Joan Miró and Paul Klee; photographs and posters of bullfighting scenes; and a chalk plate of a bull's head, a gift from Picasso.

Here Hemingway wrote *Islands in the Stream, Across the River and into the Trees, A Moveable Feast,* and *The Old Man and the Sea.* The four-story tower next to the house was built at his fourth wife's prompting so that he could write undisturbed. Hemingway disliked the tower and continued writing amid the comings and goings of the house, surrounded by papers, shirtless, in Bermuda shorts. Today, the tower contains exhibitions with floors dedicated to Hemingway's sportfishing and films.

Hemingway's legendary cabin cruiser, the *Pilar,* is poised beneath a wooden pavilion on

ALAMAR

Immediately east of Cojímar, you'll pass a dormitory city long prized by Fidel Castro as an example of the achievements of socialism. In April 1959, Alamar (pop. 100,000) emerged on the drawing board as the first revolutionary housing scheme in postrevolutionary Cuba, featuring 4- to 11-story prefabricated concrete apartment blocks. The sea of concrete high-rise complexes (extending east to the adjacent town of Celimar) was built with shoddy materials by microbrigades of untrained "volunteer" workers borrowed from their normal jobs.

Despite its overwhelming deficiencies (the plumbing came from the Soviet Union, the wiring from China, the stoves from North Korea), Alamar was vastly expanded beginning in 1976 and today covers 10 square kilometers. Today it is a virtual slum. Refuse litters the potholed roads, and the roadside parks are untended. There are no jobs here, either, and few stores, no proper transportation, and no logic to the maze of streets or to the addresses of buildings, so that finding your way around is a study in maddening frustration.

the former tennis court, shaded by bamboo and royal palms. Nearby are the swimming pool where Ava Gardner swam naked and the graves of four of the novelist's favorite dogs.

The P7 metro-bus departs from Industria, between Dragones and Avenida Simón Bolívar, Parque de la Fraternidad, in Habana Vieja. P1 runs from La Rampa; the P2 runs from Paseo, in Vedado. **Paradiso** (Calle 19 #560, esq. C, Vedado, Havana, tel. 07/832-6928, paradis@paradiso.artex.com.cu) offers excursions.

SANTA MARÍA DEL ROSARIO

The charming colonial village of Santa María del Rosario, 20 kilometers south of Parque Central, is in the *municipio* of Cotorro, about five kilometers southeast of San Francisco de Paula. The village was founded in 1732 by

José Bayona y Chacón, the Conde (Count) de Casa Bayona, and was an important spa in colonial days. Venerable 18th- and 19th-century buildings surround **Plaza Mayor,** the main square. Here **Casa del Conde Bayona** (Calle 33 #2404, esq. 24, tel. 07/682-3510, daily noon–10 P.M.), the count's former home, comprises three adjacent structures complete with coach house.

The **Casa de la Cultura** (Calle 33 #202, esq. 24, tel. 07/682-4259) hosts a *peña* with local musicians each Sunday at 8:30 P.M. Note the patio mural by the world-renowned Cuban artist Manuel Mendive.

From Havana, take the P1 from La Rampa; P2 from Paseo in Vedado; or the P7 from Parque de la Fraternidad to Cotorro, then catch the #97.

Iglesia de Santa María del Rosario

The main reason to visit the village is to view the baroque Iglesia de Santa María del Rosario (Calle 24, e/ 31 y 33, tel. 07/682-2183, Tues.–Sat. 8 A.M.–noon, Sun. 3:30–6 P.M.), dominating the plaza. One of the nation's finest churches, this national monument is colloquially called the Catedral del Campo de Cuba (Cathedral of the Fields of Cuba). The highlights are the spectacular baroque altar of cedar dripping with gold leaf, the resplendent carved ceiling of indigo, plus four priceless art pieces by José Nicolás de Escalera.

CIUDAD PANAMERICANO AND COJÍMAR

Beyond the tunnel under Havana harbor, you pass through a heavily policed toll booth (no toll is charged), beyond which the six-lane Vía Monumental freeway leads east to modern Ciudad Panamericano and, immediately beyond, the time-worn fishing village of Cojímar.

Ciudad Panamericano, three kilometers east of Havana, dates from the 1991 Pan-American Games, when a high-rise village was built in hurried, jerry-rigged style. Sports stadiums rise to each side of the Vía Monumental, most significantly the 55,000-seat **Estadio**

Panamericano (Vía Monumental, Km 4, Ciudad Panamericano).

Cuban tour agencies promote stays at the Hotel Panamericano, but anyone who overnights here will find themselves cut off from Havana in a desultory place rapidly becoming a slum. Fortunately, you can walk to **Cojímar,** a forlorn fishing village with a waterfront lined with weather-beaten cottages. Whitecaps are often whipped up in the bay, making the Cuban flag flutter above **Fuerte de Cojímar** (locally called El Torreón), a pocket-size fortress guarding the cove. It was here in 1762 that the English put ashore and marched on Havana to capture Cuba for King George III. The fortress, built in the 1760s, is still in military hands, and you will be shooed away if you get too close.

Ernest Hemingway berthed his sportfishing boat, the *Pilar,* in Cojímar. When he died, every angler in the village donated a brass fitting from his boat. The collection was melted down to create a bust—**Monumento Ernest Hemingway**—that stares out to sea

© CHRISTOPHER P. BAKER

a man fishing at Fuerte de Cojímar

from within a columned rotunda at the base of El Torreón. A plaque reads: "Parque Ernest Hemingway. In grateful memory from the population of Cojímar to the immortal author of *Old Man and the Sea,* inaugurated July 21, 1962, on the 63rd anniversary of his birth."

Cojímar was most famous as the residence of Gregorio Fuentes, Hemingway's former skipper and friend, and the model for "Antonio" in *Islands in the Stream,* and—albeit less contentiously—for Santiago, the angler cursed by bad luck in *The Old Man and the Sea.* Fuentes died in 2002 at the grand old age of 104. The old man (who lived at Calle 98 #209, esq. 3D) could often be found regaling travelers in La Terraza, where you can toast to his memory with a turquoise cocktail—Coctel Fuentes.

Accommodations

Islazul's **Hotel Panamericano** (Calle A y Av. Central, tel. 07/766-1000, fax 07/766-3913, market@epr.islazul.tur.cu, CUC26 s, CUC40 d low season, CUC28 s, CUC44 d high season) is popular with budget-tour operators. Despite a refurbishing, modern bathrooms, and a swimming pool, it offers nothing but regret for tourists. **Aparthotel Islazul Costazul** (from CUC27 low season, CUC35 high season) is part of the hotel complex and offers 475 meagerly furnished two- and three-bedroom apartments.

In Cojímar, the shorefront **Casa Hostal Marlins** (Calle Real #128A, e/ Santo Domingo y Chacón, tel. 07/766-6154, CUC30–35) has a nice, independent, air-conditioned apartment upstairs with kitchenette, TV, an enclosed dining patio, and modern bathroom, plus parking. Owner Juan Carlos y Blanco can point you to alternatives.

Food

After exploring, appease your hunger with soup and paella at Hemingway's favorite restaurant, **La Terraza** (Calle 152 #161, esq. Candelaria, tel. 07/766-5151, daily 10:30 A.M.–10:30 P.M.), with a gleaming mahogany bar at the front. You sense that Papa could stroll in at any moment. His favorite corner table is still there. He

is there, too, patinated in bronze atop a pedestal, and adorning the walls in black and white, sharing a laugh with Fidel. The wide-ranging menu includes paella (CUC6–12), pickled shrimp (CUC5.50), oyster cocktail (CUC2), and sautéed calamari (CUC6).

Services

Services along Avenida 78 in Ciudad Panamericano include a bank (esq. Calle 5), Cadeca exchange bureau (esq. 5D), post office (e/ 5 y 3), *telecorreo* (esq. 5C), medical center (esq. 5D), and a **Farmacia Internacional** in the Hotel Villa Panamericana.

Getting There and Around

Heading east from Havana on the Vía Monumental, take the first exit marked Cojímar and cross over the freeway to reach Ciudad Panamericano. For Cojímar, take the *second* exit.

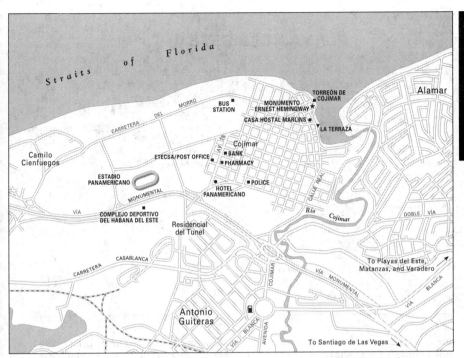

Metrobus P11 departs Paseo de Martí, opposite the Capitolio Nacional, in Habana Vieja, and runs along the Vía Monumental to Ciudad Panamericano. You can also catch it at the corner of Avenida de los Presidentes y 27 in Vedado. Buses #195 and 265 also run to Ciudad Panamericano.

Bus #58 departs Avenida Rancho Boyeros and Bruzón, Plaza de la Revolución, for Cojímar; you can also catch it at the bottom of Paseo de Martí, at the junction with Avenida de los Estudiantes (10 centavos). The return bus departs Cojímar from Calle 99 y 3A.

Cubacar (tel. 07/795-1093), at the Hotel Panamericano, rents cars and scooters.

PLAYAS DEL ESTE

On hot summer weekends all of Havana seems to come down to Playas del Este to tan their bodies and flirt. The beaches stretch unbroken for six kilometers east–west, divided by name.

A nearly constant breeze is usually strong enough to conjure surf from the warm turquoise seas—a perfect scenario for lazing, with occasional breaks for grilled fish from thatch-roofed *ranchitas,* where you can eat practically with your feet in the water.

Playas del Este is pushed as a hot destination for foreign tourists and, in the mid-1990s, enjoyed some success, bringing tourists and Cubans together for rendezvous under *palapas* and palms. Then a police crackdown (to temper the foreigner-Cuban coupling) initiated in early 1999 knocked the wind clear out of Playas del Este's sails. The place has ever since deteriorated year by year. By international standards, it's a nonstarter other than for a day visit.

Take care when swimming: Riptides are common. In winter, the seas are full of jellyfish (*agua mala*). The beaches also get terribly littered.

When driving from Havana via the Vía Monumental, it's easy to miss the turnoff,

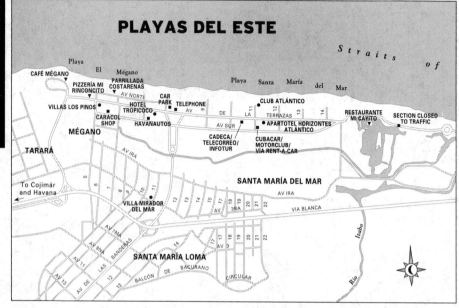

one kilometer east of the second (easternmost) turnoff for Cojímar, where the Vía Monumental splits awkwardly. Take the narrow Vía Blanca exit to the left to reach Playas del Este; the main Vía Monumental swings south (you'll end up circling Havana on the *circunvalación*).

Playa Bacuranao

This small horseshoe cove with a white-sand beach lies immediately east of Alamar and is popular on weekends with residents of Alamar. The wreck of an 18th-century galleon lies just off the tiny beach. Coral grows abundantly, so if you have snorkeling gear, bring it. Food and beverages are available at **Villa Islazul Bacuranao** (tel. 07/765-7645, daily 7 A.M.–8 P.M.), which has simple cabins.

Tarará

Beyond Bacuranao, you'll cross the Río Tarará and pass Tarará, a villa resort (reception tel. 07/798-2937) at the far western end of Playas del Este, at Vía Blanca, Km 19. Before 1990 it was the Campamento de Pioneros José Martí, used by Cuban schoolchildren, who combined study with beachside pleasures. Here, too, victims of the 1988 Chernobyl nuclear disaster in the Ukraine were treated free of charge. (It was here also that Castro operated his secret government after Batista was ousted; Che Guevara was convalescing here after his debilitating years of guerrilla warfare in the Sierra Maestra, and the location away from Havana proved perfect for secret meetings.) At last visit in 2009, it was a Spanish-language school for Chinese students.

It is also a tourist complex. To the west is a delightful pocket-size beach that forms a spit at the rivermouth; it has a volleyball court and shady *palapas*, plus a restaurant and marina with water sports. (The rivermouth channel is renowned for its coral, great for snorkeling and scuba diving.) The main beach, **Playa El Mégano**, to the east, has a sand volleyball court and is served by the **Casa Club Cubanacán**

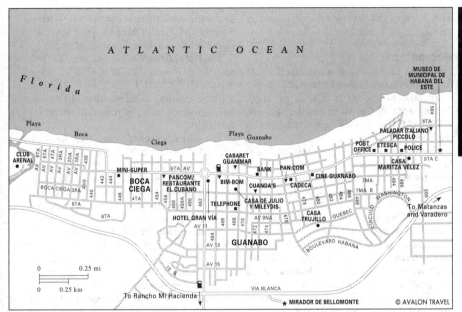

complex (Tarará, tel. 07/797-1330, entrance CUC10 including CUC7 *consumo mínimo*), with a swimming pool with grill and restaurant.

Entry is free, but you must show ID—bring your passport in case the occasionally mule-minded *custodios* get a case of *burro-cracía*.

Santa María del Mar

Playa El Mégano extends east from Tarará and merges into Playa Santa María del Mar, the broadest and most beautiful swathe, with golden sand shelving into turquoise waters. The beaches are palm-shaded and studded with shade umbrellas. Most of Playas del Este's tourist facilities are here, including bars and water sports, plus a fistful of tourist hotels.

Playa Santa María runs east for about three kilometers to the mouth of the Río Itabo—a popular bathing spot for Cuban families. A large mangrove swamp centered on **Laguna Itabo** extends inland from the mouth of the river, where waterfowl can be admired. A coral reef runs offshore.

Boca Ciega and Guanabo

Playa Boca Ciega begins east of the Río Itabo estuary and is popular with Cuban families, many of whom choose to rent simple *cabinas* in the residential and rental complex called Boca Ciega. Playa Boca Ciega merges eastward into Playa Guanabo, the least-attractive beach, running for several kilometers along the shorefront of Guanabo, a Cuban village with plantation-style wooden homes.

For grand views up and down the beaches, head inland of Guanabo to **Mirador de Bellomonte** (Vía Blanca, Km 24.5, tel. 07/96-3431, daily noon–10 P.M.), a restaurant above the Circuito Norte; it's signed, just off the highway.

Entertainment

Casa Club Cubanacán (Av. de Terrazas, daily 9 A.M.–6 P.M.) has a pool hall and dance club.

The liveliest spot in town is **Cabaret Guanimar** (3ra Av. y Calle 468, tel. 07/796-2747, Wed.–Sun. 9 P.M.–2 A.M., CUC3–5), with a simple *cabaret espectáculo* followed by a disco.

Recreation

Outlets on the beach rent watercraft (CUC15 for 15 minutes), Hobie Cats (CUC20 per hour), and beach chairs (CUC2 per day). **Restaurante Mi Cayito** (Av. las Terrazas, tel. 07/797-1339) rents kayaks and water bikes on the lagoon.

Horses can be rented in front of Hotel Horizontes Tropicoco, and are a specialty of **Rancho Mi Hacienda Guanabito** (Calzada de Jústiz, Km 4, Guanabo, tel. 07/796-4712, daily 9 A.M.–8 P.M.), four kilometers inland of Guanabo. This dude ranch raises animals and features bloodless cockfights.

Scuba diving is available at **Caribbean Diving Center** (Casa 4, Tarará, tel. 07/796-0242, www.caribscuba.com) in **Marina Tarará** (tel. 07/796-0242, channel VHF 77 or 108, marina@mit.tur.cu), at the Tarará rivermouth. You can rent yachts and pedal boats, and sport-fishing charters are offered. Boat excursions include six-hour "seafaris" at 9:30 A.M. (CUC55 based on a minimum of four passengers).

Accommodations

One of the best *casas particulares* options is **C** **Casa de Julio y Mileydis** (Calle 468 #512, e/ 5ta y 7ma, Guanabo, tel. 07/796-0100, CUC30–35). Set in a beautiful garden, the apartment is equipped for people with disabilities and has a security box, large lounge with a kitchen, simply furnished bedroom, and a small pool for children. A bungalow for guests was added in 2009. The owners are a pleasure.

Casa Maritza Vélez (Calle 5D #49610, e/ 496 y 498, Guanabo, tel. 07/796-4389, CUC30–35) is a handsome 1950s house with a beautiful interior and a well-maintained garden. It has two rooms with modern furnishings, old metal-frame beds, soothing pastel colors, and modern tiled bathrooms (but no toilet seats). Of similar standard is **Casa Trujillo** (Av. Quebec #55, e/ 478 y 482, Guanabo, tel. 07/796-3325, CUC30–35), a two-story family unit with one spacious bedroom, a TV lounge, and a modern

kitchen to which guests have access. Miriam Trujillo and Alberto Mendes, your hosts, are fluent in Spanish, French, and English.

The **Hotel Gran Vía** (Av. 5ta, e/ 502 y 504, tel. 07/796-4300, CUC18 s, CUC21 d low season, CUC22 s, CUC26 d high season) is a simple training hotel catering to Cubans, but with three basically furnished rooms for foreigners.

The **Villa Bacuranao** (Vía Blanca, Km 15.5, tel. 07/765-7645, fax 07/765-6332, www.islazul.cu, from CUC23 s, CUC25 d low season, CUC26 s, CUC30 d high season) has 52 rooms in modestly furnished one- and two-bedroom cabanas. Facilities include a restaurant and swimming pool.

Villas Marina Tarará (Calle 9na, esq. 14, Villa Tarará, tel. 07/797-1462, comercial@tarara.m.it.tur.cu, from CUC75 low season, CUC100 high season), run by Cubanacán, offers 94 two- to five-bedroom villas—*casas confort*—many with swimming pools. All have a kitchen and private parking. No Cuban guests are allowed, and no guests may stay overnight without authority of the management. A grocery, laundry, restaurants, and pharmacy are on-site.

The **Club Amigo Mégano** (Av. de las Terrazas), at the far west end of Playas del Este, was operating as a hotel for Cuba's military elite at last visit.

For great views, check into Islazul's **Villa Mirador del Mar** (Calle 11, e/ 1ra y 3ra, tel. 07/797-1262, from CUC26 low season, CUC40 high season) in Santa María. It primarily serves Cubans and has two-, three-, and four-bedroom hilltop villas.

Cubanacán's five-story **Hotel Horizontes Tropicoco** (Av. de las Terrazas, e/ 5 y 7, tel. 07/797-1371, fax 07/797-1389, rrpp@htropicoco.hor.tur.cu, CUC58 s, CUC87 d low season, CUC66 s, CUC95 d high season) has 188 air-conditioned rooms with bamboo furniture plus modern bathrooms. Services include a pleasing restaurant, bar, tour desk, shops, and car rental.

Gran Caribe's **Villas los Pinos** (Av. 4ta, tel. 07/797-1361, fax 07/797-1524, www.

villalospinos.com, CUC120–220 low season, CUC160–250 high season) offers the most elegant option, with 27 two-, three-, and four-bedroom villas; some have private pools. Visitors are prohibited.

The nicest place, and the only beachfront option, is **Club Atlántico Gran Caribe** (tel. 07/797-1085, reservas@club-atlantico.com, CUC87 d), now opened to all tourists after previously serving only Italian tour groups. The refurbished rooms are pleasant enough, with modern bathrooms, and it has water sports.

Formerly a desultory all-inclusive Cubanacán property, the Club Arenal (Lago de Boca Ciega), in the midst of the lagoon between Playas Santa María del Mar and Boca Ciega, was undergoing a much-needed restoration at last visit.

Food

Mi Casita de Coral (Av. de las Terrazas, e/ 7 y 9, 24 hours daily), 100 meters east of the Hotel Horizontes Tropicoco, serves *criollo* fare and seafood, including grilled fillet of fish (CUC5) plus spicy lobster enchiladas (CUC8). Likewise, the airy **Casa Club** (tel. 07/797-1344, ext. 178, 24 hours) offers spaghetti, plus a chicken lunch special (CUC2). Air-conditioned **Parrillada Costarenas** (Av. Norte, esq. Av. de las Terrazas, tel. 07/797-1361, daily noon–6 P.M.) serves inexpensive grilled fare (CUC5) at its beachside diner, as does the no-frills thatched **Café Mégano** (tel. 07/797-1404, daily 10 A.M.–7 P.M.) atop the sands. Nearby, **Pizzería Mi Rinconcito** (daily 10 A.M.–6 P.M.) serves ho-hum pizza.

Restaurante Mi Cayito (Av. las Terrazas, tel. 07/797-1339, daily 10 A.M.–6 P.M.), overhanging the mangroves of Laguna Itabo, has the usual fare: grilled fish, shrimp, and lobster.

In Guanabo, the best place is ◖ **Paladar Italiano Piccolo** (5ta Av., e/ 502 y 504, tel. 07/796-4300, noon–midnight daily), a spacious private restaurant with riverstone walls adorned with Greek murals. Run by Greek owners, it offers surprisingly tasty Mediterranean fare, including wood-fired pizzas, served with hearty salads at low prices (CUC5–10).

Need breakfast? **Pan.Com** (5ta Av., esq. 454, tel. 07/794-4061, daily noon–11 P.M.) is a modern eatery with a choice of airy patio or air-conditioned interior serving *criollo* dishes, sandwiches, omelets, burgers, and tortillas.

Air-conditioned **Bim-Bom** (5ta Av., esq. 464, tel. 07/796-6205) serves 32 flavors of ice cream along the lines of Baskin-Robbins.

Services

Infotur (Av. Las Terrazas, e/ 10 y 11, tel. 07/796-1261, Mon.–Fri. 8:15 A.M.–4:45 P.M., Sat. 8:15 A.M.–12:15 P.M.) has an information bureau.

There are two **post offices** (Edificio Los Corales at Av. de las Terrazas, e/ 10 y 11, and, in Guanabo, at 5ta-C Av. y 492).

The **bank** (tel. 07/796-3320) is at 5ta Avenida (e/ 468 y 470).

Getting There and Around

Tarará, at Vía Blanca, Km 17, 27 kilometers east of Havana, is signed off the Vía Blanca, as is Playas del Este, with three exits farther east. A taxi will cost about CUC20. Beware the *punto de control* (police control) near Bacuranao; keep to the posted speed limit!

The T3 **HabanaBusTour** (tel. 07/835-000, www.transtur.cu, daily 9 A.M.–9 P.M.) charges CUC3 from Parque Central to Playas del Este. Public buses #62, 162, and 262 also serve Playas del Este from Parque Central; bus #219 departs from the main bus terminal.

The marina is *not* an international entry port.

Cubacar has car rental outlets at Tarará (tel. 07/796-1997) and in the parking lot of Hotel Horizontes Tropicoco (tel. 07/797-1535). There's also **Vía Rent-a-Car** (5ta Av., esq. 11, tel. 07/797-1494). A scooter is the perfect vehicle: rent one from **MotoClub** in the parking lot of Hotel Horizontes Tropicoco (CUC22 daily).

Cubataxi (tel. 07/796-6666) has taxis at the Hotel Horizontes Tropicoco.

Havana Province

Encircling Havana is a freeway, the *circunvalación*. Beyond this, the suburban residential districts gradually merge into the countryside of the eponymous province, which extends 65 kilometers east and west and 40 kilometers south of the city limits.

Sprinkled throughout the province are colonial towns that seem trapped in a centenary time-warp. Much of the province is hilly and quite dramatic, such as the Escaleras de Jaruco, southeast of the city. The low-lying southern plain is the breadbasket of the city and the wealthiest region in Cuba. In counterpoint, the southern shore is a soggy no-man's-land of swamps and mangroves, where lowly fishing villages are among the most deprived and down at the heels in Cuba.

The main sights can be broken into two one-day excursions. Though buses run to most towns, few of the stand-alone sites are served by public transport. You'll need wheels, but be warned: The roads that fan out south from Havana are crisscrossed by minor roads that together form an unfathomable labyrinth.

HAVANA TO MARIEL

Westward, beyond Marina Hemingway, leave Havana behind as 5ta Avenida becomes the coast road (Route 2-1-3) to Pinar del Río Province. The shore is unremarkable, except for **Playa Baracoa,** 16 kilometers west of Havana and popular with Cubans on hot weekends. Some five kilometers farther west, the rather dull **Playa Salado** is the setting for a go-kart racetrack.

About 45 kilometers beyond the marina, you arrive at **Mariel.** Set deep inside a flask-shaped bay, this sleepy yet important port city, founded in 1792, is best known as the site of the famous April 1980 "boatlift" when 120,000 Cubans departed the island for Florida. Mariel is ringed by docks and factories, including a cement factory that casts a pall of dust over town. In 2009, Cuba inked a deal with Brazil for the latter to rebuild Mariel as a mega-container port to replace Havana's harbor as Cuba's main port.

The Moorish-inspired hilltop castle north of town is a military zone and off-limits.

Beyond Mariel, Route 2-1-3 continues west to **Cabañas,** beyond which you pass into Pinar del Río Province. It's a stunning drive.

Buses depart and drop off at Calle 71.

THE CARRETERA CENTRAL

The old Carretera Central (Route 2-N1) was the main thoroughfare to Pinar del Río before the Autopista was built. To get there, take Avenida 51 from Marianao to La Lisa and follow the signs. Atmospheric colonial towns line the route.

This day trip will take you through Bauta, Caimito, and Guanajay. **Caimito** has an attractive ocher-colored colonial-era church, which is fronted by an intriguing mural displaying a fierce bald eagle painted in the Stars and Stripes voraciously attacking a noble Cuban Indian and peasant. **Guanajay** has the baroque Teatro Vicente Mora on the town square. South of Guanajay, midway to Artemisa, is a restored remnant of the **Trocha Mariel-Majana,** a 19th-century fortification built by the Spanish to forestall the Army of Liberation during the Wars of Independence.

El Cano, a small village two kilometers east of the Carretera Central on Havana's southwestern outskirts, was founded in 1723 and has retained its historic charm. Immigrants from the Canary Islands and Majorca brought a tradition of pottery making. Their descendants are still known as skilled potters (*alfareros*), who use local red clays shaped on foot-operated wheels and fired in traditional wood-fired kilns.

ARTEMISA AND VICINITY

Artemisa (pop. 35,000), 60 kilometers southwest of Havana, dates from the early 19th century and has a wide main street lined by neoclassical houses fronted with verandas supported by Doric and Ionic columns. The cubist

Mausoleo a las Mártires (Av. 28 de Enero, Tues.–Sat. 8 A.M.–5 P.M., Sun. 8 A.M.–noon, CUC1) honors 28 Artemisa rebels who participated in the attack on the Moncada barracks in Santiago in 1953; 14 rebels were either killed in the assault or later tortured to death. They lie buried beneath the cube, which features brass bas-reliefs.

Rancho Azucarero, a 2,200-hectare ranch 2.5 km west of Artemisa, serves as Cuba's main equestrian center. The *rancho* breeds English purebred horses for international competition and has a horseracing track. Although plans to create a polo club and African-style lodge have not been fulfilled, it planned to open to the public in 2010 for horse exhibitions and races.

Antiguo Cafetal Angerona

Antiguo Cafetal Angerona lies two kilometers westward of Rancho Azucarero and midway to Cayajabos. The site was founded as a coffee (and, later, sugar) plantation in 1813 by Cornelio Sauchay, who kept almost 500 slaves. It is now a national monument, albeit in ruins. Novelist James Michener used the site as the setting for the sugar plantation in his novel *The Caribbean*. The watchtower and huge cisterns are still intact. There's no entrance fee or official hours of operation, but you should tip any guide.

Rancho Charco Azul

Horses are the theme at this breeding center (c/o EcoTur, tel. 07/204-5188, www.ecoturcuba.co.cu), at Cayajabos 14 kilometers west of Artemisa. An old farm that once belonged to cattle breeder Rosando Palacios, today Empresa Flora y Fauna breeds English thoroughbred horses and Gertrudis cattle. The stars of the show, however, are Pecheron and Belgian draft horses. (No, the horses aren't sold or used; apparently Raúl Castro thinks it's a good idea in case of war with Uncle Sam. Shades of World War I!) Horseback rides are offered (CUC10); so too, are pony rides for kids as well as guided birding.

Rancho Charco Azul is immediately north of the Autopista exit for Cayajabos. Take the first left as you enter Cayajabos.

Accommodations

Flora y Fauna has created a tremendous boutique hotel from a stone mansion at **Rancho Charco Azul** (c/o EcoTur, tel. 07/204-5188, www.ecoturcuba.co.cu) in Cayajabos, 14 kilometers west of Artemisa. Restored and furnished with antiques, it has four rooms with modern bathrooms. You can also choose from six modern cabins with state-of-the-art fittings and amenities, plus showers with a wall of glass. A lovely swimming pool, an outside bar and grill, and an elegant restaurant round out the picture.

Getting There

Bus #215 operates from Havana's main bus terminal and runs to Artemisa's **Terminal de Ómnibus** (Carretera Central, Km 58, tel. 047/36-3527). Trains depart Estación Tulipán in Havana at 5:45 P.M. and 8:30 P.M. for Artemisa (Av. Héroes del Moncada, five blocks west of the main plaza, CUC2.20).

SAN ANTONIO DE LOS BAÑOS

This small ramshackle town, founded in 1775 on the banks of the Río Ariguanabo (30 kilometers southwest of Havana), is lent charm by its tiny triangular plaza, ocher church (Calles 66 y 41), and streets lined with colonnaded arcades.

The town boasts the **Museo del Humor** (Calle 60 #4116, esq. 45, tel. 047/38-2817, Tues.–Sat. 10 A.M.–6 P.M., Sun. 9 A.M.–1 P.M., CUC2), which displays cartoons and hosts the **Humor Bienal Internacional** (International Humor Festival), drawing some of the best cartoonists from around the world, each odd year. It was closed for reparation at last visit.

A freeway—the Autopista a San Antonio—links San Antonio with Havana. Midway between the two cities, you'll pass the **Universidad de las Ciencias Informáticas** (Carretera de San Antonio de los Baños, Km 2½, Torrens, tel. 07/837-2548, www.uci.cu), Cuba's university dedicated to making the country a world power in software technology. Immediately north is the gray marble **Memorial**

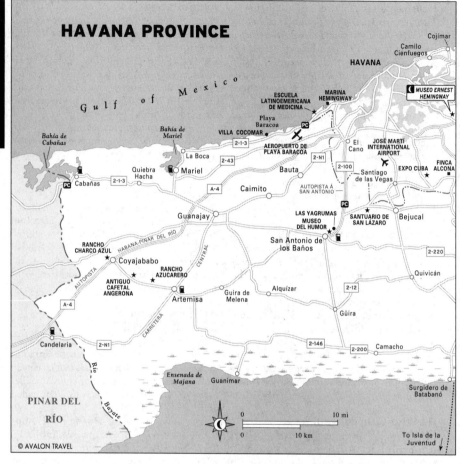

HAVANA PROVINCE

© AVALON TRAVEL

---

al Soldado Internacionalista Soviético, with an eternal flame dedicated to Soviet military personnel who died in combat.

Escuela Internacional de Cine y Televisión

The prestigious Escuela Internacional de Cine y Televisión (International Cinema and Television School, Carretera Villa Nueva, Km 4.5, tel. 047/38-3152), presided over by the great Colombian writer Gabriel García Márquez, trains cinema artists from developing nations.

Accommodations

Islazul's **Hotel Las Yagrumas** (Calle 40 y Final Autopista, tel. 047/38-4460, fax 047/38-5392, reservas@yagrumas.co.cu, CUC19 s, CUC26 d) overlooks the banks of the Río Ariguanabo one kilometer northeast of town on the Havana road. This colonial-style, red-tiled, two-story property has 120 pleasantly decorated rooms, plus a pool, tennis and racquetball courts, bicycle and boat rentals, plus boat excursions.

Getting There

Buses serve San Antonio de los Baños from

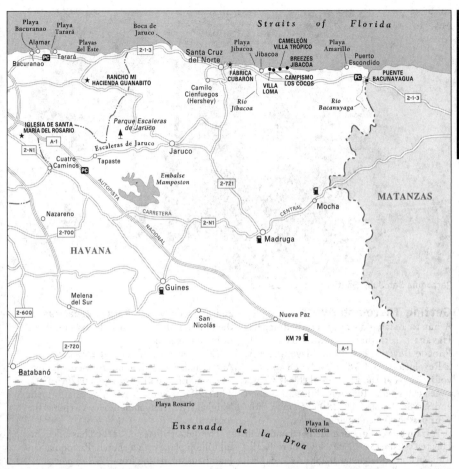

Calle Apodaca between Agramonte and Avenida de Bélgica, Habana Vieja, and arrive or depart San Antonio at the Terminal de Ómnibus (Av. 55, tel. 047/38-2737). Trains serve San Antonio de los Baños from the Estación Tulipán, in Nuevo Vedado, Havana, at 10:05 A.M. and 4:25 and 8:30 P.M. (CUC1.50), returning from San Antonio at 5:35 A.M. and 1:55 and 6:15 P.M.

BATABANÓ

This funky town, 51 kilometers due south of Havana, was site of the original city, founded in 1515 by Pánfilo de Narváez and named San Cristóbal de la Habana. The settlers lasted only four years before uprooting and establishing a new city on the north coast—today's Havana. Today Batabanó is an agricultural town surrounded by ugly dormitories for field hands.

About three kilometers south is **Surgidero de Batabanó,** a rundown hamlet of ramshackle wooden houses and of significance only as the port town from which ferries depart for Isla de la Juventud. There are no accommodations, so plan your arrival and departure accordingly.

© CHRISTOPHER P. BAKER

Parroquia San Juan Bautista church, Jaruco

Getting There and Away

A bus to Batabanó's ferry terminal departs Havana's Terminal de Ómnibus (Av. de Rancho Boyeros, esq. 19 de Mayo, Plaza de la Revolución, tel. 07/870-9401) at 8 A.M. Buy your tickets at the kiosk marked NCC, between gates 9 and 10 (Mon.–Fri. 8 A.M.–noon and Sat. 8–11 A.M., CUC2.10). You must show your passport when buying a ticket.

A train serves Surgidero de Batabanó from Havana's Estación 19 de Noviembre (Calle Tulipán and Hidalgo, tel. 07/881-4431 or 881-3642) at 5 P.M. (CUC1.80). The return train to Havana departs Surgidero at 5:25 A.M. from the rail station at the end of Calle 68.

There's a Cupet gas station in Batabanó (Calle 64, esq. Av. 73).

ESCALERAS DE JARUCO AND VICINITY

The rolling Escaleras de Jaruco (Jaruco Staircase) rising east of the Autopista are popular among *habaneros* escaping the heat for walks and horseback rides. The hills are composed of limestone terraces denuded in places into rugged karst formations laced with caves

and protected within **Parque Escaleras de Jaruco** (tel. 047/87-3266). It has horseback riding on weekends.

Take the turnoff for **Tapaste** from the Autopista, about 15 kilometers east of Havana. The road rises to **El Arabe** (tel. 047/87-3292, Thurs.–Sun. noon–5 P.M.), a restaurant in Mughal style with fabulous views as far as the Atlantic.

The quaint village of **Jaruco** has a delightful hilltop plaza with a church, Parroquia San Juan Bautista, dating from 1778.

To the south of the Escaleras, the Carretera Central (Route 2-N1) runs southeast through the Havana suburbs of San Francisco de Paula and Cotorro and, beyond, eastward through the rolling hills of the Alturas de Habana–Matanzas via the provincial town of Madruga. It's a scenic route to the city of Matanzas.

SANTA CRUZ DEL NORTE

East of the Playas del Este, the Atlantic shore is hemmed by low hills. Following the coast road (Route 2-1-3), you'll pass small oil derricks bobbing languidly atop the cliffs. **Santa Cruz**, some 30 kilometers east of Havana, is a ramshackle industrial and oil-processing town steeping in a miasma of photo-chemical fumes and fronted by badly polluted waters. Cuba's largest rum factory, **Fábrica Cubarón,** also known as Ronera Santa Cruz, is here, producing the famous Havana Club rums. No visits are permitted.

About four kilometers south of Santa Cruz and worth the detour is the community of **Camilo Cienfuegos,** formerly called Hershey and built as a model town by the Hershey chocolate company, which owned the now-derelict Central Camilo Cienfuegos sugar mill. Hershey's town had a baseball field, movie theater, an amusement park, the Hershey Hotel, and wooden homes for workers. The facilities still stand, forming a kind of lived-in museum. The mill closed in 2002. The **Hershey Train** stops here between Havana and Matanzas.

PLAYA JIBACOA AND VICINITY

This beautiful beach, also known as **Playa Amarillo,** about four kilometers east of Santa Cruz, extends east of the Río Jibacoa for several kilometers. A smaller beach—**Playa Arroyo Bermejo**—is tucked between cliffs at the mouth of the Río Jibacoa. The beaches are popular with Cubans, who are served by basic *campismos* (holiday camps).

In 2008, the British leisure group Havana Holdings announced it was partnering with the Cuban government to build the **Carbonera Country Club** (www.esenciahotelsandresorts. com). If this happens, it will be the first residential resort complex to be funded by villa and condo sales to foreigners. Famed architect Sir Terence Conran has been hired to design the site, while Esencia Hotels and Resorts will spend about US$400 million to build the flagship 170-hectare resort. Plans include a hotel, beach and water sports club, tennis club, and an 18-hole golf course, plus 720 private one-, two- and three-bedroom apartments and villas. Membership (US$1,000) in the club is a prerequisite for private villa ownership.

About eight kilometers east of the Río Jibacoa, a road leads north to the small coastal

THE MAKING OF RUM

Christopher Columbus introduced sugarcane to Cuba in 1493. Trapiches (rudimentary ox-powered mills) squeezed guarapo from the cane, which was fermented and mixed with miel de caña (molasses), the dark-brown residue left after crystallized sugar has been processed from cane, to produce a crude type of "molasses wine."

The introduction of steam power (and of distilleries in the manufacturing process) in the early 1800s increased sugar production and permitted production of more-refined rum. Production involves fermentation, distillation, aging, and blending. Molasses is first fermented with yeast (which occurs naturally in sugarcane) to transform the sugar into ethanol. The fermented liquid is then heated with compressed vapor and then diluted with distilled water. It is distilled in copper vats to eliminate unpleasant flavors and then aged in oak barrels for 1-15 years. Distilled rums are clear. Darker rums gain their distinct color and flavor from caramels added during the aging process, or naturally from the tannins of the oak barrels. The resulting overproof rum is then diluted and bottled.

About one dozen distilleries make about 60 brands of ron today.

village of **Puerto Escondido,** a "wonderfully cool inlet a few miles down the Cuban coast," wrote Ernest Hemingway, who arrived aboard the *Pilar* to escape the hot summer nights. Alas, the spectacular setting—within a wide bend of a deep ravine—is today off-limits to tourists.

Puente Bacunayagua

Camera at the ready? Then take a deep breath for your stop at this bridge, 106 kilometers from Havana and 10 kilometers east of Puerto Escondido (about 2 km after crossing the Havana–Matanzas provincial boundary; it's 14 km from here to Matanzas). The 313-

Campismo Los Cocos, Jibacoa

meter-long bridge spans the Río Bacunayagua, which slices through the narrow coastal mountain chain. The Yumurí Valley rolls away to the south, fanning out spectacularly as if contrived for a travel magazine's double-page spread.

The bridge is a favorite stop for tour buses and has a restaurant and *mirador* (lookout).

Accommodations

Budget-focused foreigners can stay at **Campismo Los Cocos** (Playa Jibacoa, tel. 047/29-5231, www.cubamarviajes.cu, CUC8 low season, CUC19 high season), which has simply furnished concrete *cabinas* amid well-kept lawns; they have kitchenettes and modern bathrooms. There's a swimming pool, game room, and basic restaurant. You'll be among Cubans here, as you will at Islazul's **Villa Loma** (Playa Jibacoa, tel. 047/29-5316, CUC20–60 per unit low season, CUC30–80 high season). The third-rate, clifftop, holiday camp–style hotel has simply appointed and deteriorated two- to five-bedroom villas.

At the east end of the beach, Gran Caribe's **Cameleón Hotel Villa Trópico** (Vía Blanca km 60, tel. 47/29-5205, fax 047/29-5208, reserve@ clubtropico.co.cu, CUC29 s, CUC46 d low season, CUC70 s, CUC100 d high season) offers nicely furnished bungalows with modern bathrooms, plus water sports and other activities. Most guests are Canadian snowbirds.

A more upscale option, the all-inclusive **Breezes Jibacoa** (Vía Blanca, Km 60, tel. 020/8339-4150 in the U.K., www.superclub-scuba.com, from CUC80 per person), run by the Jamaican chain SuperClubs, is a splendid four-star resort. Its 250 spacious and tastefully decorated rooms and 10 suites center around a vast swimming pool. It has heaps of facilities. Reservations are required.

Getting There

Bus #669 departs Terminal La Coubre, on Desamparados in Habana Vieja, and travels to San Cruz del Norte, where you can catch a taxi or bus #126. Alternatively, take a Havana–Matanzas bus and ask the driver to let you off. The Hershey Train departs Casablanca and stops at Jibacoa Pueblo, five kilometers from Jibacoa, and at the Arcos de Canasí station, three kilometers from El Abra, but it's a lonesome walk.

PINAR DEL RÍO

Pinar del Río is Cuba's westernmost province and its most scenic. Ox-drawn plows transport you back in time amid quintessentially Cuban landscapes that attain their most dramatic beauty in Viñales Valley, known for its incredible limestone formations called *mogotes*. Here, and in the neighboring region of Vuelta Abajo, the world's finest tobacco is grown.

Pinar del Río is dominated by a low mountain chain—the Cordillera de Guaniguanico—which forms an east–west spine through the province. The chain is divided by the Río San Diego into two mountain ranges—the Sierra del Rosario in the east and the Sierra de los Órganos in the west. The pine-forested mountains reach 692 meters atop Pan de Guajaibón. Opportunities for ecotourism are being developed, notably at Soroa, known for its orchid garden, and at Las Terrazas, a model community with a first-rate hotel (billed, euphemistically as an eco-resort) plus artists studios, nature trails, cascades, thermal pools, and the remains of 18th-century *cafetales* (coffee plantations) and thermal baths. Although undeveloped for tourism, Parque Nacional La Güira is great for bird-watching and for history buffs investigating the history of Che Guevara.

A slender pencil of uninhabited land—the Península de Guanahacabibes—forms the western tip of Cuba, jutting west 50 kilometers into the Gulf of Mexico. Smothered in dense brush and cactus, the peninsula is a nature reserve. Playa María la Gorda, in Bahía de Corrientes, is a center for scuba diving. This area was inhabited at least 4,000 years ago by the Guanahatabey, the island's initial

© CHRISTOPHER P. BAKER

HIGHLIGHTS

◖ Cayo Levisa: Scintillating white-sand beaches and turquoise shallows surround Cayo Levisa, offering fantastic diving (page 198).

◖ Orquideario Soroa: Hundreds of orchid species, as well as other botanicals, fill this exquisite hillside garden (page 201).

◖ Las Terrazas: This unique mountain community is home to artist studios, hiking trails, thermal baths, and Cuba's only zipline (page 202).

◖ Cuevas de los Portales: Che Guevara used this huge cave, adorned with dripstone formations, as his headquarters during the Cuban Missile Crisis (page 206).

◖ Parque Nacional de Viñales: Among Cuba's most famous and fascinating landscapes, skyscraper-scale *mogotes* provide a magnificent backdrop for tobacco fields; there's also great climbing and caving (page 213).

◖ Caverna de Santo Tomás: Cuba's largest cave system is a fascinating underworld of dripstone formations that can be explored on guided excursions (page 220).

◖ Finca El Pinar San Luis: At the tobacco farm of world-renowned farmer Alejandro Robaina, visitors gain a complete knowledge of tobacco production (page 220).

◖ Diving at María la Gorda: Whale sharks, manta rays, and fantastic coral formations are among the highlights (page 224).

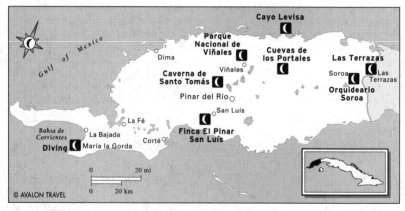

LOOK FOR ◖ TO FIND RECOMMENDED SIGHTS, ACTIVITIES, DINING, AND LODGING.

aboriginal settlers; later the region became a last refuge for the Ciboney Indians, who retreated before the advance of the Taíno. Aboriginal sites are being unearthed.

The region is regularly mauled by hurricanes.

PLANNING YOUR TIME

Most visitors to this province justifiably set their sights on **Viñales,** a rustic time-warp village fully deserving of two days or more. There's plenty to see and do in the national park that bears its name, and you may wish to budget longer to savor Viñales's fabulous scenery, slow pace, and yesteryear way of life.

To get there, most tourists follow the six-lane Autopista, the concrete highway linking Havana with the provincial capital of Pinar del Río, which can be skipped without regret. There's relatively little traffic, and the route is pleasingly scenic, notably in the east, where the lowlands are smothered in oceans of green sugarcane. There are two refreshment stops along the highway, one about a kilometer east of the turnoff for the eco-resort of **Las Terrazas,** about four kilometers west of Coyajabos, and a second at Las Barrigonas, 27 kilometers east of Pinar del Río. The only gas station is at the turnoff for **Soroa,** with its lovely orchid garden.

A more interesting route is the Carretera Central through sleepy provincial towns such as Candelaria, Santa Cruz de los Pinos, and Consolación del Sur—towns memorable for their old churches, faded pastel houses, and covered walkways with neoclassical pillars. The two-lane highway parallels the Autopista along the southern edge of the mountains and grants easy access to Soroa and Parque Nacional La Güira, which should be visited for the enormous cavern that once formed a military headquarters for Che Guevara.

For scenery, I prefer the Circuito Norte along the picturesque north coast. Offshore, a necklace of cays—the Archipiélago de los Colorados—are protected by a coral reef. There are beaches, though few of great appeal. (West of Puerto Esperanza, the road is very badly deteriorated.) The star attractions are **Cayo Levisa,** offering fabulous diving, and Cayo Jutía, with a super beach. Scuba enthusiasts should also head west to **María la Gorda,** where the diving is first-rate; and nature enthusiasts might enjoy a day or two exploring **Reserva de la Biosfera Península de Guanahacabibes.**

The northwest coast and southern plains can be skipped, although anglers might be tempted by lagoons stocked with bass. And historical attractions are few, although modernity overlays a way of life that has changed little since the end of the 19th century. This is especially so in the tobacco fields that are the province's main claim to fame, and never more so than on the outskirts of the sleepy town of San Juan y Martínez at **Finca El Pinar San Luis,** the *finca* of Alejandro Robaina, renowned worldwide to cigar aficionados. A visit here is de rigueur.

PINAR DEL RÍO

The North Coast

BAHIA HONDA TO CAYO LEVISA

The coast road west from Havana between Mariel and San Vicente is one of the most scenic in Cuba: a gentle roller-coaster ride. (West of San Vicente, there is little to hold your attention.) The road runs a few miles inland of the coast. There are few beaches.

Beyond the town of Bahía Honda, 20 kilometers west of Mariel, the road twists and loops and grows ever more scenic. Soon you are edging along beneath *mogotes,* with lower slopes covered with coffee bushes. The sensuously rounded **Pan de Guajaibón** (692 meters, 2,294 feet) looms ahead like the Sugarloaf of Rio de Janeiro. The dramatic peak lies within the 18,160-hectare **Área Protegida Mil Cumbres,** part of the Sierra del Rosario Biosphere Reserve. One kilometer east of Las

Pozas, you can turn south to follow a road into the Sierra del Rosario; it fizzles out at the hamlet of **Rancho Canelo,** from where a rough track probes to the base of Pan de Guajaibón.

West of Las Pozas you'll see the first cays of the Archipiélago de los Colorados beckoning offshore. Scuba diving is sensational. Ernest Hemingway had a fondness for beach-fringed **Cayo Paraíso,** linked to the mainland by a seven-kilometer causeway. The coral is superb, and there's a sunken vessel to explore eight meters down. Hemingway's presence is venerated by a small monument beside the small wooden dock, which reads:

From the beginning of the 1940s, this place was the refuge of the great North American author Ernest Hemingway, who visited it assiduously, sometimes remaining on the cay

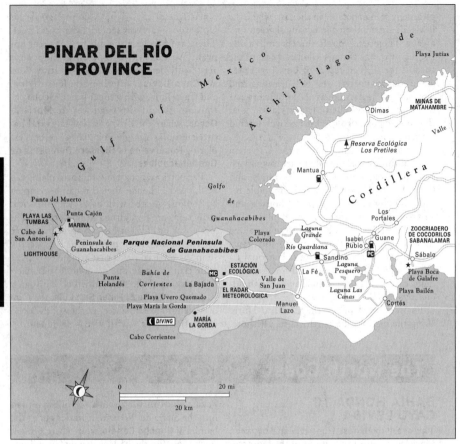

for up to 20 days at a time. Here he wrote, rested, roamed the beach, swam, and loved it so much he used it as a base for antisubmarine operations from his yacht the Pilar *during the Second World War.*

◖ Cayo Levisa

About 10 kilometers west of Cayo Paraíso (the turnoff from the Circuito Norte is 15 kilometers west of Las Pozas, just west of the village of Las Cadenas) is Cayo Levisa, two kilometers offshore and ringed by beaches. Only a section on the north side is accessible for walking, due to mangroves.

Cayo Levisa is popular with divers (the resort has a dive shop; dives cost CUC45). Snorkel gear can be rented for the day in early morning. In the past few years, hurricanes have trashed the hotel twice, but it keeps rising like a phoenix. A boat leaves for Cayo Levisa at 10 A.M. and 6 P.M. (CUC15 hotel guests; CUC20 day excursion, including sandwich and cocktail; CUC30 per person private hire after 10 A.M.) from adjacent to the coast guard station at Palma Rubia. The return boats depart the cay at 9 A.M. and 5 P.M. Excursions to Cayo Levisa are offered from tour agencies in Pinar del Río and Viñales.

No Cubans are permitted to visit.

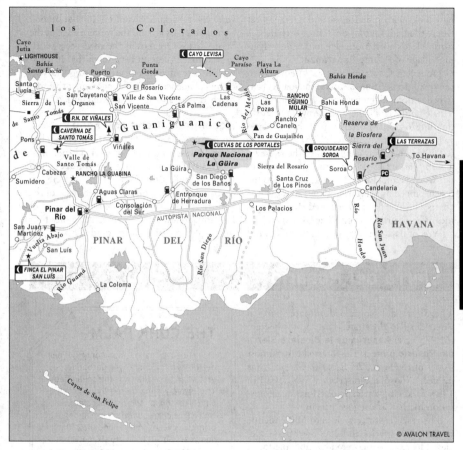

© AVALON TRAVEL

Accommodations

Missed the ferry to Cayo Levisa? No sweat. Set amid banana fields, **Casa Mario y Antonia** (tel. 048/5230-1983, CUC20), 500 meters before the dock, offers one cross-ventilated room with double and single beds and a cold-water bathroom. The charming owners make meals.

Cubanacán Cayo Levisa (tel. 048/75-6501, www.hotelescubanacan.com, CUC109 s, CUC136 d year-round, including breakfast and dinner) is all-new following back-to-back hurricanes in 2008. It now has 33 handsome thatched, air-conditioned log cabins furnished with satellite TVs, safes, fridges, plus pine pieces, including four-poster beds with mosquito nets. All have modern bathrooms. The restaurant-bar is poorly stocked and food is bland.

WEST OF CAYO LEVISA

La Palma is the only town of consequence in the area, with a tiny museum and shops. A road leads south from here over the mountains to Parque Nacional La Güira and San Diego de los Baños. The scenery continues to inspire.

Ten kilometers west of La Palma is the junction for Viñales and the town of Pinar del Río. Continue straight, though, and you reach **San Cayetano,** beyond which the land takes on a new look, with pine forests and, farther west where the land flattens out, citrus orchards. A turnoff leads north from here to the sleepy fishing village of **Puerto Esperanza.**

From San Cayetano it is 22 kilometers to the small port of **Santa Lucía** (the road is brutally deteriorated; far better is to head inland via Viñales and Matahambre). Nearby **Cayo Jutía** (tel. 048/64-8317) offers superb beaches and swimming, plus diving (CUC25) and kayaks (CUC5). The cay is connected to the shore by a *pedraplén,* accessed by a turnoff, four kilometers west of Santa Lucía; it's 13 kilometers to the beach, pinned by a metal lighthouse. A toll booth charges CUC5; passport required. Tour companies offer excursions from Viñales (CUC22).

West of Baja, there's not a soul for miles until you arrive at the pretty hamlet of **Dimas.** Beyond Dimas you pass around the western edge of the Sierra de los Órganos as the road veers south to Mantua, a pleasant little town that in 1896 was the site of a major battle during the War of Independence. This is a lonesome drive; the parched land is scrub-covered and boring.

Accommodations and Food

Accommodations are few and far between, but several locals rent rooms in Puerto Esperanza.

The field station at **Mil Cumbres** (c/o EcoTur, tel. 048/79-6120 or 75-3844, ecoturpr@enet.cu), on the southern base of the Pan de Guajaibón and 22 kilometers east of La Palma, on the road to Nieto Pérez, has four rooms plus camping. It has guided hikes.

Sierra del Rosario

The Sierra del Rosario dominates eastern Pinar del Río Province. The 25,000-hectare (61,775-acre) **Reserva de la Biosfera Sierra del Rosario** protects the forested easternmost slopes of the Sierra del Rosario. The area was named a biosphere reserve by UNESCO in 1985, following a decade of efforts at reforestation by the Cuban government.

The reserve protects close to 600 endemic higher plant species and 250 lower plant species. The reserve is covered by montane forest of pine and spruce. In springtime the slopes blaze with bright red blossoms of *flamboyanes,* and *poma rosa* grows wild by the roadside, which is also lined in season with white *yagruma* and the fiery blossoms of *popili.* At any time, the air smells piney fresh.

The 98 bird species (including 11 of Cuba's 24 endemic species) include the national bird, the *tocororo.* Terrestrial turtles and frogs are common, including the smallest frog in the world (*Sminthilus limbatus*). There's an outlandish-looking water lizard, found only here, along with bats, deer, and large guinea pig–like rodents called *jutías.*

It can get cool at night—bring a sweater.

THE CORK PALM

This endemic "palm," found only in Pinar del Río, is a souvenir of the Carboniferous era, when this valley was the ocean floor. The gravely endangered living fossil – *palma corcho,* or *Microcycas calocoma* – isn't a true palm, but rather a member of a primitive cycad family abundant 270 million years ago. It grows to six meters and sheds leaves every other year, leaving a ring around its fuzzy trunk that marks its age. It differs by sex: the masculine and feminine reproductive cells are emitted at different times, thus limiting the plant's propagation. Although some living species are 300 years old, there are no young ones known, suggesting that whichever insect acted as a fertilizing agent may have been wiped out.

SOROA

Soroa is an "eco-retreat" set in a valley at about 250 meters elevation. It is called the "the Rainbow of Cuba" for its natural beauty,

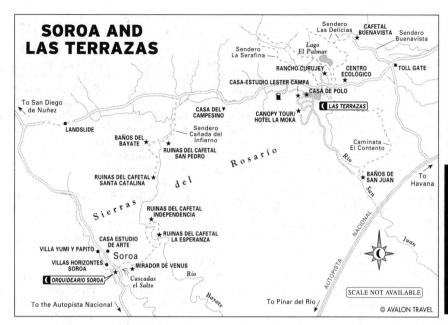

although you need to get above the valley to fully appreciate the setting. The resort is named for Jean-Paul Soroa, a Frenchman who owned a coffee estate here two centuries ago. In the 1930s, it became fashionable as a spa. Since the Revolution, it has gained a new lease on life.

Attractions include **Cascadas El Salto** (CUC3), a small waterfall reached by deteriorated stairs that descend 400 meters through fragrant woodlands to the bottom of the falls, which tumble 35 meters into pools good for bathing. The waters have medicinal properties. A bar and restaurant overlooks the river at the top of the falls.

A rugged dirt track leads uphill from the entrance to the El Salto parking lot to **Mirador de Venus,** a hilltop lookout. It's a stiff one-kilometer climb (or you can ride a horse, CUC3) that deposits you far above the valley with stupendous views. Another rugged trail from the parking lot leads to the ruins of **Cafetal Independencia,** a French coffee plantation (six hours round-trip). After hiking, enjoy a massage in the **Baños Romanos** (CUC5 per hour, open 9 A.M.–4 P.M.), at the entrance to El Salto.

Orquideario Soroa

Soroa's prize attraction is this orchid garden (Carretera Soroa, Km 8, tel. 048/52-3871, daily 8:30 A.M.–4:30 P.M., CUC3 with obligatory guide, cameras CUC1, videos CUC2), which covers three hectares. It was created in 1943 by Spaniard Tomás Felipe Camacho. The craggy hillside garden offers views down the palm-tufted valley. The garden, nourished by the humid climate and maintained by the University of Pinar del Río, contains more than 20,000 plants representing over 700 species—250 of them indigenous to Cuba. Begonias flourish along with other ornamentals beneath the shade of tall palms and towering epiphyte-clad trees.

Recreation

The **Hotel and Villa Horizontes Soroa** (Carretera de Soroa, Km 8, Candelaria, tel. 048/52-3534) offers hiking, horseback riding

PINAR DEL RÍO

(CUC5 per hour), and guided bird-watching (CUC15–25).

Accommodations and Food

About a dozen families who live along the road linking Soroa with the Autopista rent rooms; others line the Carretera Central around Candelaria. My favorite is **[Casa Estudio de Arte** (tel. 048/59-8116, infosoroa@hvs. co.cu, CUC20), one kilometer north of the Orquideario Soroa. Delightful hosts Alyshka and Jesús run this large home in its own garden ablaze with frangipani and bougainvillea. They have a cross-ventilated TV lounge. The large, simply appointed bedroom has its own bathroom and two double beds. Jesús's art adorns the walls, and Alyshka offers basic Spanish classes with room packages.

For a more rustic retreat, try **Villa Yumi y Papito** (200 meters north, tel. 048/59-8487, CUC25), with one simply furnished room in a tiny home with its own organic garden. You'll dine under thatch, with lovely views.

Cubanacán's **Hotel and Villa Horizontes Soroa** (Carretera de Soroa, Km 8, Candelaria, tel. 048/52-3534, reserva@hvs.co.cu, CUC 48 s, CUC60 d low season, CUC66 s, CUC82 d

high season cabins, from CUC43–72 s/d low season, CUC46–77 s/d high season *casas*) is a delightful resort complex. Stone pathways lead through landscaped grounds to an Olympic-size swimming pool surrounded by 49 small and pleasantly furnished *cabinas* with cable TV and modern bathrooms, on slopes backed by forest. The resort also has 20 three- and four-bedroom houses—Casitas de Soroa—with kitchenettes and private pools. The hotel's attractive **Restaurant Centro** (daily 7–9:45 A.M. and 7–9:45 P.M.) serves continental and *criollo* dishes.

The thatched **Bar y Restaurante El Salto** (daily 9 A.M.–4 P.M.), by the entrance to the cascade, serves *criollo* fare (CUC4–7) and has a Friday-night *cabaret espectáculo*.

Getting There

Soroa is seven kilometers north of the Autopista. The turnoff is about 80 kilometers west of Havana. Trains from Havana and Pinar del Río (one per day each direction) stop at Candelaria, from where you can take a taxi or hitch to Soroa, nine kilometers north. The Havana–Pinar Víazul bus will drop you at the Cupet gas station at the Candelaria junction on the Autopista.

[LAS TERRAZAS

This one-of-a-kind model village, 20 kilometers northeast of Soroa and 4 kilometers northwest of the Autopista, is touted as one of Cuba's prime ecotourism sites. **Complejo Turístico Las Terrazas** (tel. 048/57-8700, www.last-errazas.cu, 8 A.M.–5 P.M. and CUC1 for day visits) was founded in 1971 and is situated in a narrow valley above the shores of Lago San Juan with mountains to every side. It lies at the heart of a comprehensive rural development project. It gets cool here; bring a sweater.

French settlers who fled Haiti in 1792 planted coffee in these hills. After the plantations failed, the local campesinos continued to fell the trees for export and eke out a living as charcoal burners. Hillside by hillside, much of the region was deforested. In 1967 the government initiated a 5,000-hectare

swimming pool at Villa Horizontes Soroa

Las Terrazas

reforestation project, employing the impoverished campesinos and providing them with housing in a prize model village. Las Terrazas is named for the terraces of trees (teak, cedar, mahogany, pine) that were planted. The houses of whitewashed concrete are aligned in terraces that cascade down the hillside to the lake, where **Casa de Polo** (daily 9 A.M.–4:30 P.M.) is a museum in the former home of the late singer Polo Montañez. The village **community center,** facing a tiny *plazuela* with a fountain, houses a small **museum** that tells the tale of Las Terrazas' development.

Rancho Curujey (tel. 048/57-8555), the administrative center about 400 meters east of the village, offers a thatched restaurant and bar over its own lake with an inflatable trampoline. The **Centro Ecológico** (tel. 048/57-8726, Mon.–Fri. 7 A.M.–5 P.M.), a basic ecological center, welcomes visitors.

Bookings for Las Terrazas are also handled by the Oficina Comercial (Calle 8 #306, e/ 3ra y 5ta, Miramar, Havana, tel. 07/204-3739, reservas@conmoka.get.tur.cu).

If driving between Soroa and Las Terrazas, note that a massive landslide took out the road.

You can squeeze by along a makeshift road along the rim. Nervous types might opt to take the Autopista.

Cafetal Buenavista

The "Beautiful View Coffee Estate," about two kilometers east of La Moka, preserves the ruins of a French coffee plantation constructed in 1801. The buildings have been lovingly restored. The main building is now a handsome restaurant. Behind the restaurant are stone terraces where coffee beans were laid out to dry, the remains of the old slave quarters, and, on the uppermost terrace, an ox-powered coffee grinder where coffee beans were ground to remove the husks. It offers spectacular views over the expansive plains.

Ruinas del Cafetal San Pedro y Cafetal Santa Catalina

Eight kilometers west of Las Terrazas, the **Sendero Cañada del Infierno** follows the Río Bayate south two kilometers to the overgrown ruins of San Pedro French coffee plantation and the sulfur baths of Santa Catalina (CUC2 Mon.–Thurs., free Fri.–Sun.). It's easy to miss the turnoff; look for the bridge over the Río Bayate.

Baños de San Juan

A paved road leads south from Las Terrazas three kilometers to the Río San Juan (9 A.M.–7 P.M., CUC4 entrance Mon.–Thurs., free Fri.–Sun.). From the parking lot a paved path leads along the river's edge past deep pools (good for swimming) and sunning platforms above cascades. A thatched bar and grill serves snacks, and the Restaurante El Bambú sits above the falls.

Entertainment and Events

The two community bars in the Las Terrazas complex, **El Almácigo** and **Casa de Bota**, down by the lake, usually have someone playing guitar, and **Casa de Polo** hosts live music every second Tuesday (9 P.M.–2 A.M., free). The **Dos Hermanos** bar in La Moka is plusher but lacks life.

Discotemba kicks it up a notch every Wednesday and Saturday nights.

Cine Las Yagrumas shows movies on Tuesdays at 8 P.M.

Recreation

Cuba's only zipline **canopy tour** (CUC25) is here. Costa Ricans—the world's top experts—were brought in to build this two-cable run spanning the lake. Book at Hotel La Moka (tel. 048/57-8600), where the run begins.

Several poorly marked trails lead into the mountains. **Sendero Las Delicias** climbs Lomas Las Delicias, from where you have a fine view down the valley; the trip ends at the Buena Vista coffee plantation, also reached via the **Sendero Buenavista** (2 km). **Sendero La Serafina** (4 km) is good for birding; the Cuban trogon, the Cuban solitaire, woodpeckers, and the Cuban tody are common. Guided hikes and birding trips (CUC5–26), plus bicycle tours (CUC22), can be booked at Hotel La Moka (tel. 048/57-8600) and Rancho Curujey (tel. 048/57-8555); the Centro Ecológico (tel. 048/57-8726) also has guides (CUC4 per person).

Hotel La Moka (tel. 048/57-8600) also rents horses (CUC5 per hour) and mountain bikes (CUC2). Rowboats and kayaks can be rented on the lake at **Casa de los Botes** (tel. 082/75-8519, CUC2 per hour).

EcoTur (tel. 07/204-5188, www.ecoturcuba. co.cu) offers jeep tours.

Accommodations

The government has furnished five lakefront cabins (CUC40 s, CUC50 d low season, CUC60 s, CUC85 d high season) in similar fashion as the Hotel La Moka (tel. 048/57-8600), which handles bookings. Three rooms are with families; two are independent apartments.

You can rent rustic thatched cabins on stilts (CUC15 s, CUC25 d) or pitch a tent (CUC5 per person own tent, CUC12 tent rental) at **Camping Baños de San Juan** through Complejo Turístico Las Terrazas (tel. 048/57-8700, www.lasterrazas.cu).

(Hotel La Moka (tel. 048/57-8600, fax 048/57-8603, alojamiento@hotel.terraz.co.cu, CUC50 s, CUC64 d low season, CUC80 s, CUC110 d high season) is a contemporary interpretation of Spanish-colonial architecture and features an atrium lobby surrounding a lime tree disappearing through the skylight, while the two-story accommodations block has magnificent red-barked trees growing up through the balconies and ceiling. The 26 rooms are designed to international standards. Each has a floor-to-ceiling glass window and French door leading onto a spacious balcony with tables, reclining chairs, and views through the trees to the lake. Take an upper-story room with high sloping wooden ceilings and antique ceiling fans. Facilities include a tennis court, swimming pool, and lido café and bar.

Food

At **(La Fondita de Mercedes** (c/o Hotel Moka, Unit 9, tel. 048/57-8600, Sat.–Thurs. 9 A.M.–4 P.M. and 7–9 P.M.), Mercedes Dache cooks fabulous meals enjoyed on a terrace. My beef in a tangy sauce with rice and beans, plantain, and pimento was excellent (CUC12, including beer and dessert).

The menu (CUC5–10) at the upscale **La Moka** restaurant (Hotel Moka, daily 7:30–10 A.M., noon–4 P.M., and 7–10 P.M.) includes beef stew, roast chicken, and butterfly lobster.

At **Cafetal Buenavista** (Hotel Moka, daily 11:30 A.M.–3 P.M.) you can have lunch on a tree-shaded terrace. A set lunch costs CUC13, including coffee, dessert, and a fabulous main dish of baked garlic chicken.

The most atmospheric place is **C Casa del Campesino** (radio tel. 082/77-8555, daily 9 A.M.–9 P.M.), two kilometers west of Las Terrazas, a typical peasant's farm on the ruins of the old Hacienda Unión coffee plantation. Here Gustavo Golnega and his family raise fowl and serve traditional meals prepared in the open kitchen with wood-fired oven. Most dishes are overpriced but you can enjoy a hearty meal for around CUC15, including coffee. Reservations are required for meals after 5 P.M. The place is often packed with tour groups and the kitchen often runs out.

Vegetarians should head to the **Eco-Restaurante El Romero** (tel. 08/77-8555, daily 9 A.M.–10 P.M.), which gets rave reviews for its creative organic dishes.

Café de María (no tel., daily 9 A.M.–11 P.M.) is a quaint, open-air coffee shop and a great place to sip a cappuccino while enjoying the view over the village.

Shopping

Whether you intend to invest or not, call at **Casa-Estudio Lester Campa** (tel. 082/77-8590, lester@terraz.co.cu, 8 A.M.–4 P.M. daily), on the lakeshore. Lester Campa's fabulous works display staggering detail; prices begin at around CUC300 (Campa's larger paintings fetch thousands of dollars on the international market).

This tiny hamlet also has a pottery workshop and **Taller de Serigrafo** (daily 8 A.M.–5 P.M.), a serigraphy workshop.

You can buy souvenirs at **Callejón de la Moka** (daily 9 A.M.–11 P.M.), a small gallery of three shops below Café de María.

Getting There

Las Terrazas, 75 kilometers west of Havana, is four kilometers north of the Autopista, at Km 51 (there's a sign), where a road runs into the mountains. You can also reach Las Terrazas north from Soroa (the road is signed as closed due to a massive landslide, but it was passable by car at last visit), and from the Circuito Norte via an unmarked turnoff.

Tour agencies in Havana offer excursions.

The Cupet gas station (daily 8 A.M.–5 P.M.) is hidden off the main road, 400 meters west of the turnoff into Las Terrazas.

SAN DIEGO DE LOS BAÑOS

The small but once important spa town of San Diego de los Baños is on the banks of the Río San Diego, 120 kilometers west of Havana, 60 kilometers east of Pinar del Río, and 10 kilometers north of the Autopista. It's centered on a tree-shaded plaza with a Greek Orthodox-style church. The spa waters of the Templado springs were discovered in the 17th century and launched to fame when a leprous slave was supposedly miraculously cured after bathing here. German scholar and explorer Baron Alexander von Humboldt hyped the San Diego waters. Subsequently, the resort was promoted in the United States as the Saratoga of the Tropics (the deteriorated Hotel Saratoga, one block west of the park, recalls the era).

The mineral waters (a near-constant 37–40°C) are a salve for rheumatism, skin disorders, and other ailments. A modern facility with subterranean whirlpool baths was built after the Revolution; the deteriorated **Balneario San Diego** (tel. 048/54-8880) was closed for restoration at last visit but a **Farmacia Internacional** (Mon.–Fri. 8 A.M.–4:30 P.M. and Sat. 8 A.M.–12:30 P.M.) was open.

Accommodations and Food

Casa de Caridad y Julio Gutiérrez (Calle 29 #4009, e/ 40 y 42, tel. 048/54-8037, CUC20), 50 meters west of Hotel Saratoga, has two simple air-conditioned rooms with private hot-water bathrooms. Meals are served on a shady terrace fronting the pleasant garden with parking.

Catching the breezes, the bargain-priced hillside **Hotel Mirador** (Calle 23 final, tel.

© CHRISTOPHER P. BAKER

dusk in San Diego de los Baños

048/77-8338, www.islazul.cu, CUC19 s, CUC23 d low season, CUC30 s, CUC37 high season including breakfast) is set above landscaped grounds with a swimming pool. Contemporary flourishes highlight the 30 attractive air-conditioned rooms with simple furnishings, satellite TVs, direct-dial telephones, and modern bathrooms. The classy restaurant is lit by Tiffany lamps, although the menu is limited to *criollo* staples. It offers guided birding (CUC5 per person) and hiking.

Transtur (tel. 048/54-8869) rents cars.

PARQUE NACIONAL LA GÜIRA

Parque Nacional La Güira protects 54,000 acres of wilderness that rise to pine forests on the higher slopes of the Sierra de los Órganos. Much of the park occupies the former estate of Manuel Cortina, a wealthy landowner who traded in precious woods. Following the Revolution, the land was expropriated and made a preserve, although it sees few visitors.

You enter the park through a mock fortress gate with turrets (4 km west of San Diego de los Baños), beyond which the road rises to Cortina's former mansion—now in ruins—and a series of modest and deteriorated gardens including a Japanese garden, a Cuban garden, and a formal English garden with statuary and topiary.

⟨ Cuevas de los Portales

This dramatic cave (daily 8 A.M.–7 P.M., entrance CUC1, guide CUC1, cameras CUC1), on the northwestern edge of the park, has a stunning setting beside the Río Caiguanabo flowing beneath a fantastically sculpted natural arch that the river has carved through a great *mogote*. The cave, reaching 30 meters high, lies inside one wall of the arch. The curved walls and vaulted ceilings are stippled with giant dripstones.

The caves' remoteness and superb natural position made them a perfect spot for Che Guevara to establish his staff headquarters during the 1962 Cuban Missile Crisis, when he commanded the Western Army. The cave opens out to the rear, where stands Che's breeze-block office and dormitory, still containing the original table and chairs. Inside, a portal leads to another tiny cave with a floor of rough-hewn boards still supporting Che's narrow, iron bed.

A jeep is essential to negotiate the horribly denuded road that leads north through the park to the caves. Far better is to take the scenic road that connects La Palma (on the north coast) with Entronque de Herradura (on the Autopista), 20 kilometers west of San Diego de los Baóos. The caves are one kilometer east of this road. (Nine kilometers south of La Palma, you can turn left via San Andrés to Viñales.)

Accommodations and Food

Campismo Cuevas Portales has spartan concrete *cabinas* but was not accepting foreigners at last visit.

Pinar del Río and Vicinity

PINAR DEL RÍO

Pinar del Río (pop. 125,000), 178 kilometers west of Havana, is named for the native pine trees that once flourished along the banks of the Río Guamá. It was founded in 1669. Tobacco farmers established themselves nearby, in Viñales and Vuelta Abajo, and the city prospered on the tobacco trade—the first tobacco factory was founded nearby in 1761. The town is known for its neoclassical buildings with decorative art nouveau frontages. Tourist sites are few, but it makes a good base for exploring the province.

Orientation

The town is laid out in a grid, although many streets are aligned or curve at odd angles. The Autopista slides into town from the east. It becomes Calle Martí, a wide boulevard dividing the town north and south. Martí is the main street, and most places of interest are here, or along adjacent Calle Máximo Gómez (one block south). The main cross street is Isabel Rubio, which leads north and south, respectively, to the regions of Viñales and Vuelto Abajo. The city rises westward: At the "top" of Calle Martí is Plaza de la Independencia.

© CHRISTOPHER P. BAKER

1958 Oldsmobile, Pinar del Río

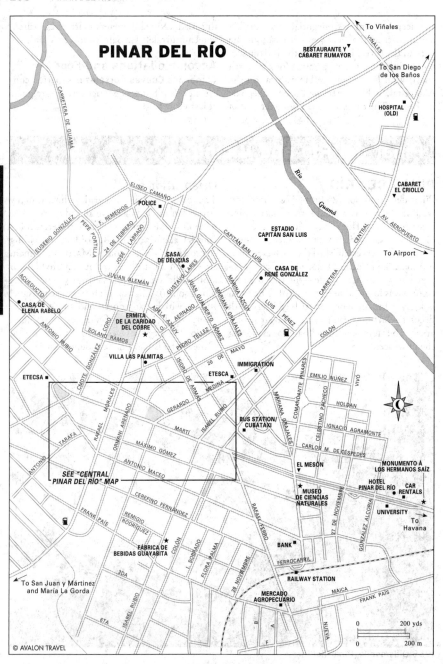

PINAR DEL RÍO

To Viñales

RESTAURANTE Y
CABARET RUMAYOR

To San Diego
de los Baños

VIÑALES

HOSPITAL
(OLD)

Río

CABARET
EL CRIOLLO

Guamá

AV. AEROPUERTO

CARRETERA DE GUAMA

ELISEO CAMAÑO

POLICE

ESTADIO
CAPITÁN SAN LUIS

CENTRAL

To Airport

EUSEBIO GONZÁLEZ

PEPE PORTILLA

F. REMEDIOS

24 DE FEBRERO

JOSÉ LABRADO

CAPITÁN SAN LUIS

CASA
DE DELICIAS

CASA DE
RENÉ GONZÁLEZ

JULIÁN ALEMÁN

GUSTAVO LARES

JUAN GUALBERTO GÓMEZ

MARIANA GRAJALES

MARINA AZCUY

LUIS PÉREZ

CARRETERA

ACUEDUCTO

CASA DE
ELENA RABELO

ANTONIO RUBIO

CORO

SOLANO RAMOS

ERMITA
DE LA CARIDAD
DEL COBRE

ADELA AZKUY

ISABRADO

PEDRO TELLEZ

COLON

CMDTE. IGONZÁLEZ

RAFAEL MORALES

VILLA LAS PALMITAS

ISIDRO DE ARMAS

20 DE MAYO

IMMIGRATION

ETECSA

ETECSA

MEDINA

EMILIO NUÑEZ

VIVO

TARAFA

ORMANI ARENADO

GERARDO

ISABEL RUBIO

BUS STATION/
CUBATAXI

COMANDANTE PINARES

CELESTINO PACHECO

HOLDAN

IGNACIO AGRAMONTE

ANTONIO

MÁXIMO GÓMEZ

MARTÍ

MARIANA GRAJALES

CARLOS M. DE CÉSPEDES

ANTONIO MACEO

SEE "CENTRAL
PINAR DEL RÍO" MAP

EL MESÓN

MONUMENTO A
LOS HERMANOS SAÍZ

CEREFINO FERNÁNDEZ

HOTEL
PINAR DEL RÍO

CAR
RENTALS

FRANK PAÍS

REMIGIO
RODRÍGUEZ

MUSEO
DE CIENCIAS
NATURALES

27 DE NOVIEMBRE

GONZÁLEZ ALCORTA

UNIVERSITY

To
Havana

COLÓN

FÁBRICA DE
BEBIDAS GUAYABITA

I. SOBRIAO

FLORA PALMA

RAFAEL FERRO

BANK

To San Juan y Mártinez
and María La Gorda

2DA

26 NOVIEMBRE

FERROCARRIL

RAILWAY STATION

ISABEL RUBIO

6TA

MERCADO
AGROPECUARIO

B A

F

MAICA

FRANK PAÍS

NUEVA

0   200 yds

0   200 m

© AVALON TRAVEL

Street numbers begin at Calle Martí (which runs east–west) and Calle Gerardo Medina (which runs north–south). Thus addresses suffixed by "Este" lie east of Gerardo Medina, and addresses suffixed by "Oeste" are west of Gerardo Medina. Similarly, any streets suffixed by "Norte" lie north of Calle Martí and those suffixed by "Sur" lie south of Calle Martí.

Museo de Ciencias Naturales

The small and mediocre Museum of Natural Sciences (Calle Martí Este #202, esq. Av. Comandante Pinares, tel. 048/77-9483, Mon.–Sat. 9 A.M.–5 P.M., Sun. 9 A.M.–1 P.M., CUC1) displays the natural history of the province and includes stuffed mammals, birds, fish, and a collection of seashells. Concrete dinosaurs stand transfixed in the courtyard, including a T-Rex and a *Megalocnus rodens* (an extinct oversized rodent once found in Cuba). The museum is housed in an ornately stuccoed building, the Palacio Gausch, built in 1914 by a Spanish doctor to reflect elements from his world travels. Thus, the columned entrance is supported by Athenian columns bearing Egyptian motifs, while Gothic griffins and gargoyles adorn the facade.

WALKING TOUR OF PINAR DEL RÍO

Begin at the **Museo de Ciencias Naturales** (Calle Martí Este #202, esq. Av. Comandante Pinares, tel. 048/77-9483, Mon.-Sat. 9 A.M.-5 P.M., Sun. 9 A.M.-1 P.M., CUC1), at the foot of Martí. After perusing the museum, follow Martí west two blocks to the **Teatro José Jacinto Milanés** (Martí, esq. Calle Colón, tel. 048/75-3871, Mon.-Fri. 9 A.M.-5 P.M., CUC1) to admire its ornate interior, restored to fin-de-siècle splendor. It dates to 1898. Immediately west, the **Museo Provincial de Historia** (Martí Este #58, e/ Isabel Rubio y Colón, tel. 048/75-4300, Mon. noon-4 P.M., Tues.-Sat. 8 A.M.-10 P.M., Sun. 9 A.M.-1 P.M., CUC1) traces local history. Aboriginal artifacts (including a mock cave dwelling) are displayed, along with antique furniture and weaponry.

Turn left onto Isabel Rubio and walk four blocks to the **Fábrica de Bebidas Guayabita** (Isabel Rubio Sur #189, e/ Cerefino Fernández y Frank País, tel. 048/75-2966, Mon.-Fri. 9 A.M.-5 P.M., Sat. 9 A.M.-1 P.M.), which since 1892 has made *guayabita*, a spicy, brandy-like alcoholic drink made from rum and the fruit of a wild bush – *Psidium guayabita* – that grows only in Pinar del Río. There are two kinds: a sweet *licor de guayabita* and a dry *guayabita seca* brandy. Tours are offered (CUC1).

Retrace your steps two blocks to Antonio Maceo. Turn left and walk west to the **Catedral de San Rosendo** (Maceo Este #2, esq. Gerardo Medina), which dates from 1833 and has a barrel vaulted wooden ceiling and fine gilt altar.

Continuing west, uphill, call in at the **Galería Korda** (Maceo #21, esq. Ormani Arenado, tel. 048/75-2758, Mon.-Fri. 8 A.M.-5 P.M.). Art is also displayed in the **Casa Natal de Antonio Guiteras Holmes** (Maceo Este #52, e/ San Juan y Ormani Avenado), in the former house of a local pharmacist and revolutionary hero brutally murdered in 1935 by the Machado regime.

One block farther west you come to the **Fábrica de Tabacos Francisco Donatién** (Antonio Maceo Oeste #157, esq. Ajete, tel. 048/77-3069, Mon.-Fri. 9 A.M.-noon and 1-4 P.M., Sat. 9 A.M.-noon, guided tour CUC5), a quaint cigar factory housed in the former jail. You can peer through windows to watch the 30 or so *tabaqueros* producing cigars. No photos are permitted.

Continue uphill one block west to **Plaza Independencia.** Those with a religious bent might turn east down Martí and follow Rafael Morales west three blocks to the little **Ermita de la Caridad del Cobre** (Rafael Morales, e/ Ramos y Isidro de Armas, daily 8 A.M.-noon and 3-5:30 P.M.), a small church with a splendid classical aesthetic. Otherwise, turn right onto Martí and descend three blocks to the **Museo de Arte MAPRI** (tel. 048/77-4671, Mon.-Fri. 9 A.M.-5 P.M., alternate Saturdays 10 A.M.-4 P.M., free), a small gallery displaying impressive contemporary art.

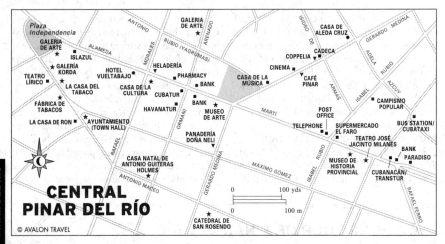

CENTRAL PINAR DEL RÍO

© AVALON TRAVEL

Entertainment

Pinar hosts a four-day **Carnaval** in early July, when *carrozas* (floats) and *comparsas* (costumed troupes) followed by conga lines of revel-making locals wind through the streets.

Cabaret Rumayor (Carretera Viñales, tel. 048/76-3007, Thurs.–Sun. at 10 P.M., CUC3 including one drink), one kilometer north of town, offers a modest two-hour-long *cabaret espectáculo*. The show begins at 10 P.M. and is followed by a disco. You need ID to enter. Fans of flesh and feathers might get a kick, too, at **Cabaret El Criollo** (tel. 048/76-3050, Wed., Fri., and Sat., CUC5) on the Carretera Central northeast of town. It's the happening spot Monday–Wednesday.

Café Pinar (Gerardo Medina Norte #34, tel. 048/77-8199, daily 7 P.M.–2 A.M., CUC3 including one drink) draws the young crowd for live music from *bolero* to rap; bring ID. **Disco Azul** (Tues.–Sun. at 10 P.M., CUC3 including drink), in the Hotel Pinar del Río, is preceded by karaoke.

For traditional music, try the **Casa de Cultura** (Máximo Gómez #108, tel. 048/75-2324, free), with live music nightly at 9 P.M., and the **Casa de la Música** (Gerardo Medina Norte #21 y Antonio Rubio, tel. 048/75-3605, CUC1). And **Museo Provincial de Historia** (Calle Martí Este #58, e/ Isabel

Rubio y Colón, tel. 082/75-4300) has music programs.

The Vegueros, the local **baseball team,** host visiting teams at the Estadio Capitán San Luis (Calle Capitán San Luis), three blocks west of the Carretera Central for Viñales (Oct.–Mar.).

Accommodations
CASAS PARTICULARES

There are dozens to choose from. I enjoyed my stay with Bertha and Agustín at **Villas Las Palmitas** (Calle Pedro Téllez #53, esq. Ormani Arenado, tel. 048/75-4247, CUC20). The two simply appointed rooms with private bathrooms are upstairs. One has a kitchen. Its heart-of-town locale is reason enough to stay here.

Secure parking (CUC1) and a fathoms-deep spa-tub in the tree-shaded stone patio are pluses at **Casa de Elena Rabelo** (Antonio Rubio #284, e/ Méndez Capote y Coronel Pozo, tel. 048/75-4295, ghernandez@fcm.pri.sld.cu, CUC20). It has two pleasantly furnished air-conditioned rooms with private bathrooms.

Casa de Aleda Cruz (Gerardo Medina 67, tel. 048/75-3173, CUC20 with fans, CUC25 with air-conditioning) is a venerable colonial home with a choice of two basically furnished rooms with private hot-water bathrooms. A patio has an exquisite garden, Jacuzzi, bar, and secure parking.

© CHRISTOPHER P. BAKER

Museo de Ciencias Naturales, Pinar del Río

Casa de René González (Calle Unión #13, e/ Capitán San Luis y Carmen, Rpto. Villamil, tel. 048/75-7515, CUC20) has two clean air-conditioned rooms upstairs, each with independent entrance, spacious balcony, separate lounge. There's secure parking.

HOTELS

Charm exudes from the restored **Hotel Vueltabajo** (Martí #103, esq. Rafael Morales, tel./fax 048/75-9381, www.islazul.cu, CUC34 s, CUC55 d year-round), a historic hotel featuring beautiful antiques and stained glass and whose marble staircase leads to 39 lofty-ceilinged rooms with simple antique-repro furnishings. It has the best restaurant in town, plus Internet and an Infotur desk.

Bargain rates are a draw at **Hotel Pinar del Río** (Martí y Final Autopista, tel. 048/75-5070, fax 048/77-1699, www.islazul.cu, CUC17 s, CUC24 d low season, CUC29 s, CUC38 d high season), on the eastern fringe of town. This post-Stalinist structure has 136 air-conditioned rooms and 13 junior suites with satellite TVs, telephones, and safes. It has car rental, a nightclub, a restaurant, and a swimming pool that draws locals on weekends.

Villa Aguas Claras (Carretera de Viñales, Km 7.5, tel. 048/77-8426, CUC22 s, CUC36 d including breakfast), eight kilometers north of town on the road to Viñales (bus #7 from town passes by), bills itself as an eco-resort. It has 50 thatched and modestly furnished air-conditioned *cabinas* amid landscaped grounds. Folkloric shows are performed beside the swimming pool, and it has guided hikes and horse rental. Loud music is a problem when Cuban groups are in, and mosquitoes thrive.

Food

The town's sole *paladar,* **El Mesón** (Calle Martí Este #205, tel. 082/75-2867, Mon.–Sat. noon–10 P.M.), opposite the Museo de Ciencias Naturales, serves the usual *criollo* fare for CUC4–6. The tablecloths were dirty at last visit, the food mediocre, and flies were abundant.

Far better to opt for the air-conditioned **Restaurant Vueltabajo** (daily 7:15–9:30 A.M., noon–2:45 P.M., and 7–9:45 P.M.), in the Hotel Vueltabajo. It serves *criollo* staples for below CUC5 but is clean.

For ambience, try the **Restaurante y Cabaret Rumayor** (tel. 048/76-3007, daily noon–midnight), one kilometer north of town on Carretera Viñales. The thatch-and-log dining room is decorated with African drums, shields, and religious icons. Service is keen, but the food is mediocre at best. *Criollo* dishes include the famous house special, *pollo ahumado* (smoked chicken, CUC5) and *chirna frita* (fish sautéed with garlic, CUC7).

Coppelia (Gerardo Medina Norte #33, Tues.–Sun. noon–midnight), one block east of Martí, has ice cream for 60 centavos per scoop.

For baked goods, head to **Panadería Doña Neli** (Gerado Medina Sur y Máximo Gómez, daily 7 A.M.–10 P.M.). You can buy produce at the *mercado agropecuario* (Rafael Ferro y Ferrocarril), four blocks south of Martí.

Information and Services

Infotur (tel. 048/72-8616, Mon.–Fri. 9 A.M.–5:30 P.M.) has a tour desk in the Hotel Vueltabajo.

There's a **post office** in the Hotel Pinar del Río. The main post office and DHL station is at Calle Martí Este #49 (esq. Isabel Rubio, tel. 048/75-5916). **Etecsa**'s *telepunto* (Gerardo Medina, esq. Juan Gualberto Gómez, daily 8:30 A.M.–7:30 P.M.) has international phone plus Internet service.

The many banks include **Banco Financiero Internacional** (Gerardo Medina Norte #44, esq. Isidro de Armas). You can change foreign currency at **Cadeca** (Gerardo Medina Norte #35, esq. Isidro de Armas, and Martí, e/ Medina y Isabel Rubio).

Hotel Pinar del Río hosts a **Farmacia Internacional** (tel. 048/75-0117, daily 8 A.M.–8:40 P.M.). **Hospital Abel Santamaria** (tel. 048/76-7379) is on the Carretera Central, one kilometer northeast of town.

Campismo Popular (Isabel Rubio Norte #20, tel. 048/75-5316, Mon.–Fri. 8 A.M.–5 P.M., Sat. 8 A.M.–noon) can let you know which *campismos* accept foreigners.

Getting There and Away
BY BUS
Víazul (tel. 048/75-2571) buses depart Havana at 9 A.M. and continue to Viñales at 12:05 A.M., and go to Havana from Pinar at 8:50 A.M. (CUC12). Buses arrive and depart the **Terminal de Ómnibus** (Adela Azcuy, e/ Colón y Comandante Pinares, tel. 048/75-2571). The Víazul office (8 A.M.–7 P.M.) is upstairs.

Colectivo taxis and *camiones* also leave from the bus station.

BY TRAIN
The railway station (Comandante Pinares y Ferrocarril, tel. 048/75-2272) is three blocks south of Calle Martí. Train #35 departs Havana's main railway station daily at 5 P.M. (six hours, CUC6.50), plus train #21 departs Havana every second day at 10:35 P.M. Train #40 departs Pinar del Río for Havana at 5:10 A.M., and train #25 departs every second day at 8:45 A.M.

TOUR AGENCIES
Tour agencies include **Cubatur** (Martí #115, esq. Ormani Arenado, tel. 048/77-8405), **Cubanacán** (Martí #109, esq. Colón, tel. 048/75-0178), and **Havanatur** (Calle Ormani Orenado e/ Martí y Máximo Gómez, tel. 082/77-8494). **Paradiso** (Martí #125, e/ Recreo y Colín, tel. 048/77-8045, www.paradiso.cu) offers cultural tours, and **EcoTur** (Carretera a Luis Lazo, Km 21.5, tel. 048/79-6120, ecoturpr@enet.cu) offers ecotourism excursions.

Getting Around
Pinar is small enough to walk most places. You can flag down *bici-taxis* virtually anywhere. Horse-drawn *coches* gather on Máximo Gómez e/ Rafael Ferro and Ciprian Valdes. **Cubataxi** (tel. 048/75-8080) is at the bus station.

Car rental agencies include **Cubacar** (tel. 048/77-8278), **Havanautos** (tel. 048/77-8015), and **Vía** (tel. 048/75-7663), all at Hotel Pinar del Río (Martí y Final Autopista).

There's a gas station at the bottom of Rafael Morales on the south side of town, and two more stations northeast of town, on the Carretera Central.

RANCHO LA GUABINA

Equestrians will delight at a visit to this horse-breeding and recreational center (Carretera de Luís Lazo, Km 9.5, tel. 048/75-7616, ranchoguabina@enet.cu) in the rolling, lake-studded hills near Mestanza, northwest of Pinar del Río. The sublime setting is icing on the cake of a relaxing day or two. The former private finca is now run by Flora y Fauna. The main focus is the breeding of Cuban horses like Pinto Cubano and Appaloosa, which are trotted out for display.

Explore the farm on a horse-drawn coach (CUC10), then opt for a horseback ride (CUC7 per hour) or rent rowboats (CUC5) or a motor-launch (CUC10).

Accommodations and Food

Surprise! ◖ **Rancho La Guabina** (CUC39 per person, including breakfast and lunch) has some of the nicest rural digs in all Cuba. The two-story private mansion of the former owner has metamorphosed into lovely air-conditioned accommodations, with five cross-ventilated rooms with huge windows, ceiling fans, and two double beds. Two rooms share a bathroom. It also has three cabins.

© CHRISTOPHER P. BAKER

PINAR DEL RÍO

coche at Rancho La Guabina, Pinar del Río

The elegant restaurant at Rancho La Guabina has lake views and a lovely patio with arbor. Tasty *criollo* meals are served. A rustic thatched lakeside restaurant has a barbecue grill.

Sierra de los Órganos

Northwest Pinar del Río Province is dominated by the Sierra de los Órganos range of mountains, boasting the most spectacular scenery in Cuba. The dramatic karst scenery is most fantastic within the Valle de Viñales. The valley (about 11 kilometers long and 5 kilometers wide) is scattered with precipitous *mogotes* that tower over *hoyos,* small depressions filled with deep deposits of rich red soil. Thanks to a very special microclimate of moist nights and cool mornings, tobacco grows well here, dominating the valley economy. One of the special memories you'll take home is the image of farmers in straw hats, machetes at their sides, plowing their fields with ox-drawn plows. Farmers will be delighted to take you out into their *vegas* and curing sheds to demonstrate the skill of raising tobacco, much of which lies under acres of cheesecloth stretched over the plants to protect against insects and an excess of sun.

◖ PARQUE NACIONAL DE VIÑALES

The Valle de Viñales is enshrined within Viñales National Park. Dominating the valley are the dramatic *mogotes* in whose shadows *guajiros* lovingly tend their plots of tobacco and maize. The setting resembles a Vietnamese or Chinese painting, particularly in the early morning, when mists settle above the valley.

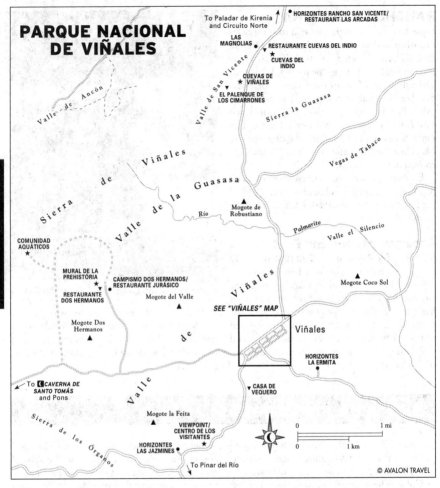

Viñales

In the heart of the valley is the eponymous village (pop. 10,000), whose sleepy yesteryear charm is a draw unto itself. Viñales is 26 kilometers north of Pinar del Río and 212 kilometers west of Havana, and was founded in 1875. Calle Salvador Cisneros, Viñales's wide main street, is lined with late-19th-century, red tile–roofed cottages shaded by rows of stately pine trees. The handsome main square is shaded by palms and has a bust of José Martí at its center. To one side is a pretty 19th-century church.

On the north side, a beautiful arcaded colonial building houses the **Casa de Cultura** (tel. 048/77-8128), which hosts cultural events and adjoins the tiny **Galería de Arte** (Wed.–Mon. 9 A.M.–noon and 1–11 P.M.).

Museo Municipal Adela Azcuy (Salvador Cisneros #115, tel. 048/79-3395, Tues.–Sat. 8 A.M.–10 P.M., Sun. 9 A.M.–4 P.M., CUC1) has motley displays telling the history of the region. Outside stands a bronze bust of Adela Azcuy Labrador (1861–1914), a local captain in the War of Independence.

The other local treasure is the restored **Casa de Don Tomás** (Salvador Cisneros #140), dating to 1822 and now an atmospheric restaurant.

María Lezcano offers guided tours of **Jardín Botánico de Viñales** (Salvador Cisneros #5, 8 A.M.–7 P.M., entry by contribution), a 0.8-hectare garden full of fruit trees, medicinal plants, and orchids totaling 189 species. The garden is festooned with plastic teddy bears, decapitated dolls' heads, and desiccated fruits, giving it airs of shamanic intrigue.

Cuevas del Indio

The Caves of the Indian (tel. 048/79-6280, daily 9 A.M.–5 P.M., CUC5), five kilometers north of Viñales, is named for the Indian remains found inside. The large grotto is entered via a slit at the foot of a *mogote*. You can explore the cave with or without a guide. The cave is four kilometers long, although you only explore the first kilometer by foot. A flight of steps leads to a well-lit path (slippery in parts) through the catacomb, which soars 135 meters. Eventually you reach an underground pier

© CHRISTOPHER P. BAKER

A tour boat emerges from Cuevas del Indio, Viñales.

where a motor-boat departs every 15 minutes for a trip up the subterranean river that runs deep beneath the mountain and is a habitat for opaque fish and blind crustaceans. It is like a crossing of the Styx, setting your imagination racing in the Stygian gloom. Try to avoid it when tour groups are in.

Cueva de Viñales (CUC1 with a guide), one kilometer south of Cuevas del Indio, is mostly a curiosity. The cave entrance has been converted into a bar-restaurant and, by night, a discotheque replete with laser lights. At the rear, a natural tunnel snakes for 100 meters and emerges into another cave entrance with another restaurant—El Palenque—that plays up the slave theme.

Mural de la Prehistoria

The much-touted Prehistoric Mural (tel. 08/79-6260, daily 8 A.M.–7 P.M., CUC1), five kilometers west of Viñales, is painted onto the exposed cliff face of Mogote Dos Hermanos. The mural illustrates evolution in the Sierra de los Órganos, from mollusk and dinosaur to club-wielding Guanajay Indian, the first human inhabitants of the region. The mural, which measures 200 feet high and 300 feet long, was commissioned by Castro and painted by 25 campesinos in 1961 while the artist, Leovigilda González, directed from below with a megaphone. The cliff face has been repainted in gaudy colors—a red brontosaurus, a yellow tyrannosaurus, and a blood-red *homo sapiens!* What was formerly a modestly appealing curiosity is now a testament to bad taste splotched on the wall of what is otherwise a splendidly beautiful valley. Horseback (CUC5 per hour) and ox-cart (CUC1) rides are offered.

A small **Museo de la Prehistoria** (daily 9 A.M.–6 P.M., CUC1) in the Campismo Dos Hermanos (opposite the entrance to the mural) displays pre-Columbian artifacts and nature specimens.

Comunidad Los Acuáticos

The Comunidad Los Acuáticos comprises 12 families who live midway up the east-facing slope of Sierra de Viñales and rarely descend

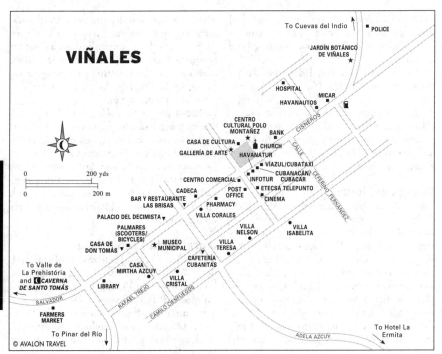

VIÑALES

To Cuevas del Indio
POLICE
JARDÍN BOTÁNICO
DE VIÑALES
HOSPITAL
MICAR
HAVANAUTOS
CISNEROS
CENTRO
CULTURAL POLO
MONTAÑEZ   BANK
CASA DE CULTURA
CHURCH
GALLERÍA DE ARTE   HAVANATUR
CALLE
VÍAZUL/CUBATAXI
CUBANACÁN/
CENTRO COMERCIAL   CUBACAR
INFOTUR   CUBACAR
CEFERINO FERNÁNDEZ
CADECA   POST   ETECSA TELEPUNTO
BAR Y RESTAURANTE   OFFICE
LAS BRISAS   PHARMACY   CINEMA
PALACIO DEL DECIMISTA   VILLA CORALES
PALMARES   VILLA   VILLA
(SCOOTERS/   NELSON   ISABELITA
BICYCLES)
CASA DE   MUSEO   VILLA
DON TOMÁS   MUNICIPAL   TERESA
CAFETERÍA
CASA   CUBANITAS
To Valle de   MIRTHA AZCUY
La Prehistória   VILLA
and CAVERNA   LIBRARY   CRISTAL
DE SANTO TOMÁS
SALVADOR
RAFAEL TREJO
FARMERS   CAMILO CIENFUEGOS
MARKET
To Pinar del Río
© AVALON TRAVEL   ADELA AZCUY   To Hotel La
Ermita

0   200 yds
0   200 m

into the valley. The community, which believes in the healing power of water, was founded in 1943 by Antoñica Izquierdo, who Cuban authorities later judged insane (she was institutionalized and died in an asylum in 2002). Her followers continued their ritual practice, which included three daily baths and drying off in the wind. The tradition is virtually dead.

The trailhead to the community is about three kilometers along a dirt road that begins at Campismo Dos Hermanos, opposite the entrance to the mural. A more direct trail begins on the Viñales–Pons road, about 500 meters west of the turn for Mogote Dos Hermanos; the actual trailhead begins about one kilometer from the main road. You can make a complete loop.

You can hire freelance guides in Viñales.

Entertainment
In Viñales, ARTex's **Palacio del Decimista**

(Salvador Cisneros #102, tel. 048/79-6014, CUC1) has live music nightly at 9:30 P.M. The happening scene, however, is the **Centro Cultural Polo Montañez** (tel. 048/77-6164), on the patio of the Casa de la Cultura on the main plaza. It has live music, including *noches campesinas* ("peasant nights," Thursday) and a nightly (Mon.–Sat.) *cabaret espectáculo.*

Cueva de Viñales (tel. 048/79-6290) hosts a *cabaret espectáculo*—Cabaret El Palenque—and disco each Saturday at 10 P.M. (CUC4 including a cocktail), four kilometers north of Viñales.

There's a **cinema** at Calle Ceferino Fernández (esq. Rafael Temos).

Recreation
The area is evolving as a mecca for caving and climbing. Scores of climbing routes have been mapped up the *mogotes.* The unofficial base camp is the Viñales home of **Oscar Jaime**

MOGOTES

Dramatic mountain formations called *mogotes* ("haystacks") stud the landscape of Cuba. The isolated, sheer-sloped, round-topped mounds are the remnants of a great limestone plateau that rose from the sea during the Jurassic era, about 160 million years ago. Over the ensuing eons, rain and rivers dissolved and eroded the porous limestone mass, leaving hummocks as high as 1,000 feet. The terrain is also found in Jamaica, Puerto Rico, China's Guangxi Province, and the eponymous Karst region of the Dalmatian coast.

Rainwater interacts with limestone to produce a mild carbonic acid, which assists the erosive action of underground streams, carving a system of underground caverns that become so huge that eventually their roofs collapse, forming sheer-sided valleys. Many caverns can be reached by traipsing through natural tunnels to follow rivers that suddenly disappear down holes in their own valley floors.

Many species of flora and fauna are found only atop the mesas. Fauna is so highly endemic that certain species of snails are found only on one or a few *mogotes*. Although the surface soil is thin, and water scarce (it percolates rapidly into the rock), the formations are luxuriantly festooned with epiphytes, ferns, and the rare and ancient cork palm (*Mycrocycas calocoma*), a botanical relic that grows only here.

Rodgríguez (Adela Azcuy #43, tel. 048/69-5516, oscar.jaime59@gmail.com), who is also a good source of information. Oscar can put you in touch with local climbers. *Cuba Climbing,* by Anibal Fernández and Armando Menocal, is an indispensable guide that includes photos and diagrams of scores of routes (www.quickdrawpublications.com). For further information, visit www.cubaclimbing.com.

Local tour agencies offer five specialist hiking excursions (CUC8–10), plus biking tours (CUC20 including lunch). You can book at

hotels and at **Museo Municipal Adela Azcuy** (Salvador Cisneros #115, tel. 048/79-3395).

You can buy a day pass to use the pool and facilities at Villa Horizontes (CUC7, including CUC6 food and drink).

Accommodations
CASAS PARTICULARES

There are more than 300 private house rentals to choose from. All charge CUC15 low-season and CUC20 high-season, are air-conditioned, and offer meals (CUC3 breakfast, CUC5–10 dinner).

I enjoyed a stay at **Villa Corales** (Salvador Cisneros #89, tel. 048/69-6654), where I dined alfresco in the rear patio. The two rooms are small but clean and have fans and hot water bathrooms.

You get secure parking at **Casa Mirtha Azcuy** (Calle Rafael Trejo #106, tel. 048/79-3278, anubis@pricesa.pri.sld.cu), with two rooms with fans and private bathrooms; one is an independent apartment.

Villa Isabelita (Camilo Cienfuegos #1B, tel. 048/79-3267) is nicely kept and has one bedroom with two double beds plus fan and a private bathroom with hot water. The delightful hosts prepare filling breakfasts. One block west, **Villa Nelson** (Camilo Cienfuegos #4, tel. 048/79-3268) is recommended for its simply furnished independent apartment with hot water. Meals are served in the rear patio, and taxi service is offered.

A reader highly recommends **Villa Cristal** (Rafael Trejo #99, tel. 5270-1284, villacristal@yahoo.es, http://villacristal.netfirms.com); I agree! Owner Francisco Martínez is an English-speaking tour guide.

HOTELS

The **Campismo Dos Hermanos** (tel. 048/79-2223, CUC15 s/d), a pleasing camp resort opposite the entrance to the Mural de la Prehistoria, has 54 basic cabins. It was not open to foreigners in early 2010, but has been in past years.

Las Magnolias (tel. 048/79-6280, CUC20 s/d rooms, CUC5 per person tents), opposite

Valle de Viñales, seen from Horizontes Las Jazmines, Viñales

© CHRISTOPHER P. BAKER

Cuevas del Indio, is a converted home with three air-conditioned rooms for rent. Each is clean and adequate, with radio, two single beds, utility furniture, and private bathroom with cold water only. You can camp in tree-shaded nylon tents.

Cubanacán's **Hotel Horizontes Rancho San Vicente** (tel. 048/79-6201, fax 048/79-6265, reserva@vinales.hor.tur.cu, from CUC40 s, CUC50 d low season, CUC56 s, CUC70 d high season, including breakfast), 200 meters north of Cuevas del Indio, has a delightful woodsy ambience. There are 53 basic, modestly furnished *cabinas* spread among forested lawns surrounding a pool. Twenty newer cabins are more spacious and appealing. Therapeutic thermal water and hot mud treatments are offered, and there's Internet service and a delightful restaurant.

Cubanacán's **Horizontes La Ermita** (Carretera de la Ermita, Km 2, Viñales, tel. 048/79-6071, fax 048/79-6069, reservas@vinales.hor.tur.cu, CUC47 s, CUC60 d low season, CUC50 s, CUC64 d high season), one kilometer south of town, is magnificently nestled atop the valley, with great views. The gracious property wraps around a sundeck and swimming pool with poolside bar. The 62 air-conditioned rooms are nicely decorated and have balconies (not all have views, however).

Unrivaled in setting, Cubanacán's ridgecrest **Horizontes Las Jazmines** (Carretera de Viñales, Km 25, tel. 048/79-6205, fax 048/79-6215, reserva@vinales.hor.tur.cu, from CUC40 s, CUC50 d low season, CUC57 s, CUC71 d high season) is an older but restored hotel, with fancy wrought-iron grillwork and fabulous vistas. The 16 air-conditioned *cabinas* stairstep the hillside, while 62 rooms are split between those in the original hotel and newer rooms in a separate block. An Olympic-size swimming pool hovers over the valley, and the colonial-style second-floor restaurant-bar offers classical elegance.

Viñales is set to get a luxury "eco-spa" hotel, the 70-room **Casa Viñales,** run by Britain's Esencia Hotels and Resort (www.esenciahotelsandresorts.com).

Food

Most owners of *casas particulares* will prepare filling breakfasts and dinners, as will **Paladar de Kirenia** (tel. 048/76-8680, 24 hours,

CUC10 for set meals), at the junction for Valle de Ancón. In town, **Restaurant Las Brisas** (Salvador Cisnero, esq. Adela Azcuy, tel. 048/79-3353, daily 11:30 A.M.--10 P.M.) offers a modicum of elegance plus *criollo* staples.

For traditional ambience, try **Casa de Don Tomás** (Salvador Cisneros #141, tel. 048/79-6300, daily 10 A.M.–9:30 P.M.), a historic wooden structure festooned with climbing plants. This is a favorite of tour groups, although the meals are meager and mediocre. The menu includes *delicias de Don Tomás* (a rice dish with pork, sausage, and lobster, US$10), and *criollo* staples such as pork steak (CUC5.50) and lobster enchiladas (CUC12.50). Troubadours serenade while you eat on the airy rear patio.

For variety, the restaurants at both Horizontes La Ermita and Las Jazmines are good bets (CUC5–12). Even better is the **Restaurant Las Arcadas** (tel. 048/79-6201, daily 7:15–10 A.M., noon–3 P.M., and 7–10 P.M.), at Horizontes Rancho San Vicente, serving spaghetti, seafood, and *criollo* staples. Try its *ajiaco* (meat and vegetable stew) or charcoal-grilled chicken. The glass-enclosed **Restaurante Cuevas del Indio** (tel. 048/79-6280, 11:30 A.M.–4 P.M.), outside the entrance to Cuevas del Indio, specializes in freshwater prawns. It also has *criollo* staples, plus inclusive meals for CUC8.

The thatched **Casa del Vequero** (tel. 048/79-6080, daily 9 A.M.–5 P.M.), on a tobacco farm 600 meters southwest of the village, also has heaps of ambience. It offers complete lunches for CUC10. Before or after your meal, you can visit the thatched *secadero* (curing shed) for a course in Tobacco 101.

Despite doing a reasonable job of a *criollo* menu, **El Palenque de los Cimarrones** (tel. 048/79-6290, daily noon–4 P.M.), accessible via a tunnel through the Cueva de Viñales, is a bit of a cheesy joke, as the waitstaff are dressed as *cimarrones* (runaway slaves).

For snacks, head to **Cafetería Cubanitas** (Azcuy, esq. Rafael Temos, no tel., daily 9:30 A.M.–10 P.M.), an open-air eatery serving pizzas, hot dogs, *bocaditos,* beers, and sodas.

Services

The hospital is two blocks east of the plaza. There's a 24-hour **pharmacy** (tel. 048/79-3169) one block west of the plaza. **Etecsa** (Calle Ceferino Fernández, Mon.–Sat. 8:30 A.M.–4 P.M.), one block south of the plaza, has telephone and Internet service. The post office is across the street from Etecsa. The police station is 100 meters north of the gas station. **Bandec** (Cisneros #57, Mon.–Fri. 8 A.M.–noon and 1:30–3 P.M.) is immediately east of the plaza.

Getting There and Around

The **Víazul** buses depart Havana for Viñales daily at 8 A.M. and 2 P.M., and Viñales for Havana at 8 A.M. and 2 P.M. (CUC12). Buses depart Viñales from outside the ticket office (Cisneros #63A, tel. 048/79-3195, 7 A.M.–6 P.M.) opposite the plaza.

Taxis are available on the plaza in Viñales. You can rent cars from **Havanautos** (tel. 048/79-6330), opposite the Cupet gas station, and **Cubacar** (tel. 048/79-6060), opposite the plaza.

Tour agencies offer excursions to Viñales from Havana. In Viñales, **Cubanacán** (tel. 048/79-6393) offers excursions to Cayo Levisa (CUC29), María la Gorda (CUC32), etc., including a "Ruta de Che."

Cubataxi (tel. 048/79-3195) offers service from the plaza. A three-hour tour of the valley costs CUC20. **Palmares** (tel. 048/79-6300), outside Casa Don Tomás, rents scooters (CUC12 two hours, CUC23 per day) and bicycles (CUC1 per hour, CUC10 per day).

WEST OF VIÑALES

West of Viñales the Sierra de los Órganos provides for a fulfilling day's excursion. It's a very beautiful drive for the first few miles, with serrated *mogotes* to the north. Farther west, tobacco gives way to coffee as you rise to El Moncada and the saddle separating the Valle de Viñales and Valle de Santo Tomás, a scrub-covered, uncultivated valley. At Pons, about 20 kilometers west of Viñales, the road to the right leads via **Matahabre** to **Santa Lucía,** on the north coast. Santa Lucía was once known for its copper mines; the mines are now derelict, but the industry is honored in a tiny and basic museum (Tues.–Thurs. 8 A.M.–5 P.M., Fri.–Sat. 8 A.M.–10 P.M.) on the west side of the town plaza, with its pretty hilltop church.

If you turn south at Pons, the deteriorated road leads through the Valle de Quemado and beyond Cabezas to **Valle San Carlos,** hidden off the tourist beaten path yet offering scenery to rival Viñales. Traveling southwest via sleepy **Sumidero,** you'll arrive on the southwest plains at the town of **Guane.**

You can turn southeast from Cabezas to reach Pinar del Río.

Caverna de Santo Tomás

At El Moncada, 15 kilometers west of Viñales, a turnoff leads through coffee fields to the orderly community of **Santo Tomás,** in the cusp of *mogotes.* This is the setting for Cuba's largest cave system, the Caverna de Santo Tomás (daily 9 A.M.–3:30 P.M.), which has more than 45 kilometers of galleries on eight levels, making it one of the largest underground systems in the New World. Guided 90-minute tours (CUC10) involve some tricky scrambling up and down ladders. Helmets with lamps are provided.

It has a small visitor center. The Centro Nacional de Espeleología (National Center of Speleology, tel. 048/68-11273) is here.

South and Southwestern Pinar del Río

The south-central province is flatland given to agriculture, but much of the shore is swampy, and mangrove and marsh lagoons extend inland for miles. West of the town of Pinar del Río, the climate becomes increasingly dry and the vegetation correspondingly stunted. María la Gorda, in the Bay of Corrientes, offers great diving, and the Península de Guanahacabibes, Cuba's slender westernmost point, is being developed for ecotourism.

VUELTA ABAJO

The Vuelto Abajo area, centered on the town of San Juan y Martínez, about 15 kilometers southwest of Pinar del Río city, has none of the dramatic beauty of Viñales, but due to a unique combination of climate and soil, the tobacco grown here is considered the finest in the world, better even than that of the Valle de Viñales. The choicest leaves of all are grown in about 6,500 hectares around San Juan y Martínez and San Luis, where the premier *vegas* are given over exclusively to production of wrapper leaves for the world's preeminent cigars.

San Juan y Martínez, 23 kilometers west of Pinar del Río, has a pretty main avenue lined with colorful columned streets.

Finca El Pinar San Luis

If you want an immersion in Tobacco 101 from the master, visit the 16-hectare private farm of the late Alejandro Robaina (tel. 048/79-7470, Mon.–Sat. 9 A.M.–5 P.M.), the unofficial "official" ambassador for Cuba's cigar industry. For six generations, the Robaina family has been renowned for the excellence of their tobacco (the family has farmed their *vegas* since 1845). So renowned was Alejandro Robaina that the Cuban government even granted him his own cigar label. There's even a postage stamp with his visage. Alejandro passed away in 2010; his son Hernán carries on the tradition.

Forty-minute tours (CUC2) are given. December and January are the best times to visit, as is August 5, when local *guajiros* (peasant farmers) make a pilgrimage to a shrine of Nuestra Señora de los Nieves (patron saint of tobacco), beneath a ceiba tree in Robaina's garden. Guests are received in a reception room full of photos of Robaina with various heads of state, fashion models, and other celebs on his various world tours. (Robaina cigars come in five different strengths; they're not sold on the *finca.* Locals will sell you fakes as "genuine" Robaina cigars.)

In 2008, a thatched restaurant was opened

TOBACCO

It is generally acknowledged that the world's best tobacco comes from Cuba (the plant is indigenous to the island), and in particular from the 41,000-hectare Vuelta Abajo area of Pinar del Río Province, where the climate and rich reddish-brown sandy loam are ideal. Rainfall is about 165 centimeters per year, but, significantly, only 20 centimeters or so fall during the main growing months of November–February, when temperatures average a perfect 27°C and the area receives around eight hours of sunshine daily.

Most tobacco is grown on small holdings – many privately owned but selling tobacco to the government at a fixed rate. *Vegueros* (tobacco growers) can own up to 60 hectares, although most cultivate less than 4 hectares.

RAISING TOBACCO

Tobacco growing is labor intensive. The seeds are planted around the end of October in well-irrigated and fertilized channels in flat fields – maize is often grown on the same land outside the tobacco season. It is planted in patches at different stages to allow for progressive harvesting when every tobacco plant is at its peak. Straw is laid down for shade, then removed as the seeds germinate. After one month the seeds are transplanted to the *vegas*. About 120 days after planting, they are ready for harvesting in March and April.

There is a range of leaf choices, from *libra de pie*, at the base, to the *corona*, at the top. The art of making a good cigar is to blend these in such proportions as to give the eventual cigar a mild, medium, or full flavor and to ensure that it burns well. The binder leaf that holds the cigar together is taken from the coarse, sun-grown leaves on the upper part of the plant, chosen for their tensile strength. Dark and oily, they have a very strong flavor

and have to be matured for up to three years before use. The finest leaves from the lower part of the plant are used as wrappers; these must be soft and pliable and free of protruding veins. Plants designated to produce wrappers are grown under fine muslin sheets (*tapados*) to prevent the leaves from becoming too oily in a protective response to sunlight. The darker the color, the sweeter the taste.

At harvest, leaves are bundled in a *plancha*, or hand, of five leaves and taken to a barn where they are hung like kippers and cured for about 40 days on poles or *cujes*. Modern barns are temperature and humidity controlled. Traditional thatched barns face west so that the sun heats one end in the morning and the other in the late afternoon, and temperature and humidity are controlled by opening and closing the doors. Gradually the green chlorophyll in the leaves turns to brown carotene. After 45-60 days, they are taken down and stacked into bundles, then taken in wooden cases to the *escogida* – sorting house – where they are shaken to separate them, then dampened and aired before being flattened and tied in bunches of 50. These are then fermented in large piles like compost heaps for anywhere up to three months. Ammonia and impurities are released. When the temperature reaches 44°C, the pile is "turned" so that fermentation takes place evenly.

The leaves are then graded for different use according to color, size, and quality. They are stripped of their mid-ribs and flattened, then sprayed with water to add moisture. Finally they are covered with burlap, fermented again, reclassified, and sent to the factories in *tercios* – square bales wrapped in palm bark to help keep the tobacco at a constant humidity. After maturing for up to two years, they are ready to be rolled into cigars.

for groups. Call-in visitors can dine if groups are dining (12:30–2 P.M., CUC30, including tour). And a single thatched room for guests was being built in 2010.

Turn south 12 kilometers west of Pinar del Río; San Luis is 3.3 kilometers south of the

highway—turn left onto a dirt road. There are several turns along the unsigned country lanes. *Jineteros* will wave you down on the main road. Many claim to be guides or workers at the finca. Some take you to alternative farms that claim to be Robaina's.

ISABEL RUBIO AND VICINITY

The landscape grows increasingly spartan as you exit the Vuelta Abajo region heading west, with the road arcing close to the coast.

About 15 kilometers southwest of San Juan y Martínez, a turnoff leads south three kilometers to **Playa Boca de Galafre,** a somewhat muddy beach. Five kilometers farther west, near Sábalo, another turnoff leads south eight kilometers to **Playa Bailén.** Both beaches are popular on weekends with Cubans, but they're unappealing. Midway between the highway and Playa Bailén you pass **Zoocriadero de Cocodrilos Sabanalamar** (daily 8 A.M.–5 P.M., CUC2 entrance, CUC3 cameras, CUC5 video), a crocodile farm within the Reserva Florística Manejado San Subaldo Sabanahlamar. Some 1,000 American crocs of varying ages can be viewed.

Twelve kilometers west of Sábalo you pass through **Isabel Rubio,** a small yet relatively prosperous agricultural town that thrives on the harvest of citrus groves. Beyond is the small town of **Sandino.** The area is studded with lagoons stocked with tilapia and bass, including **Laguna Grande,** 18 kilometers northwest of Sandino and reached via a turnoff from the main highway about five kilometers east of town.

North of Isabel Rubio lies **Guane,** at the base of the Cordillera de Guaniguanico, popular with Cubans for hiking and exploring caves.

Two trains run daily between Pinar del Río and Guane via Sábalo and Isabel Rubio. *Camiones* connect Sandino and other towns. If continuing to María la Gorda, tank up on gas at Isabel Rubio or Sandino; there are no gas stations farther west.

Accommodations

Motel Alexis Aragón (Zona L #33, tel. 048/84-3282, CUC20), off the main road in Sandino, is a *casa particular* with two air-conditioned rooms.

Anglers who don't mind basic conditions might check into Islazul's **Villa Laguna Grande** (tel. 048/84-3453, CUC15 per person, including meals). It has 12 simple thatched cabins. You need to bring your own fishing gear.

PENÍNSULA DE GUANAHACABIBES

This willowy peninsula (90 kilometers long and 30 kilometers wide) juts out into the Strait of Yucatán and narrows down to the tip at Cabo San Antonio. The geologically young peninsula is composed of limestone topped by scrubby woodland. The entire peninsula (nowhere higher than 25 meters above sea level) is encompassed within the 121,572-hectare Guanahacabibes Peninsula Biosphere Reserve, created by UNESCO in 1987 to protect the semideciduous woodland, mangroves, and wildlife that live here. The reserve is split into the El Veral and Cabo de Corrientes nature reserves. At least 14 of the more than 600 woody species are found only on the peninsula. More than 170 bird species have been identified here; endemic birds include the tiny *torcaza* and *zunzuncito* hummingbirds. *Jutías* are abundant, as are wild pigs, deer, iguanas, and various species of lizards, and land crabs that cross the road en masse in springtime.

Several archaeological sites have been uncovered. The region became the final refuge for Cuba's aboriginal population as they were driven west by the more advanced and aggressive Taíno (a Museo de Guanahacabibes, dedicated to pre-Columbian culture, was to be inaugurated in 2010). The few people who live here today eke out a meager living from fishing and farming.

The peninsula shelters the Bahía de Corrientes, with waters famed for diving.

The access road reaches the shore at **La Bajada,** where you may need to present your passport at a military barrier to reach Cabo San Antonio (to the right), the western tip of Cuba. The road to the left swings around the bay and leads 14 kilometers to María la Gorda.

The road to Cabo San Antonio is stunningly scenic and constantly changes. After 40 kilometers or so, beyond Punta Holandés, the road opens onto a cactus-studded coral platform (the sharp limestone formations are called *diente de perro*—dog's tooth). After 61 kilometers you reach Cabo San Antonio, dominated by a military post and **Faro Roncali** lighthouse, built in 1859. Nearby is **Cueva La Sorda,** a labyrinthine cave system that can be explored. The cape hooks around to **Playa Las Tumbas** (a mediocre beach with an "eco-hotel") and dead-ends three kilometers beyond at a small pier (billed as a "marina") at Punta Cajón, where the tarpon fishing is said to be good right off the dock. Scuba divers can explore a wreck off the cape. Offshore, the **Cayos de la Leúa** are a breeding ground for fishing eagles and other seabirds.

María la Gorda, which also has a narrow, white-sand beach, is named, according to legend, for a buxom barmaid, María la Gorda (Fat Mary), who turned to leasing her body to passing sailors. She prospered and her venue became known as Casa de las Tetas de María la Gorda (House of Fat Mary's Tits). The *tetas* in question may actually refer to the two protuberances jutting from the cliffs of nearby Punta Caíman.

Stay clear of the beaches at dusk; tiny no-see-ums (*jejenes*) emerge to feast on unsuspecting humans.

A **Museo de Miel** (Museum of Honey) was planned. Apparently honey from this region is acclaimed.

In 2001, explorers using a miniature submarine discovered strange stone formations on the seabed that resembled a "lost city." The formations (640 meters down) resemble pyramids, buildings, and roadways, causing some imaginative folks to speculate that they'd found a real-life Atlantis.

Hiking and Bird-Watching

Estación Ecológico (tel. 048/75-0366, www.ecovida.pinar.cu, daily 8 A.M.–sunset), at La Bajada, has hiking and birding trips (CUC5–10), and a "Seafari" to Cabo San Antonio (CUC10) that in summer includes viewing turtle nestings (July–Aug. is best). The station has a 3-D map, plus information on local ecology.

The 1.5-kilometer-long **Sendero Bosque al Mar** (CUC6 including guide) leads from the ecological station to the ocean, where a cave with a *cenote* is good for swimming; much of the "trail" is along the blazing white road. The **Sendero Cuevas Las Perlas** (three hours

the turquoise waters of Bahía de Corrientes, María la Gorda

round-trip, CUC8) leads 1.5 kilometers to the namesake cave system, where about 400 meters is accessible. The **Sendero El Tesoro de María** (four hours round-trip, CUC10) leads from María la Gorda.

◖ Diving

Divers rave about the waters, with sites (ranging from vertical walls to coral canyons, tunnels, and caves) just 200 meters from Playa María la Gorda. There are even hulks of Spanish galleons. El Valle de Coral Negro (Black Coral Valley) has 100-meter-long coral walls. Huge whale sharks are commonly seen, as are packs of dolphin and tuna.

Centro Internacional de Buceo María la Gorda (tel. 048/77-1306) has dives at 8:30 and 10:30 A.M. and 3:30 P.M. (CUC35, CUC40 at night) plus a four-day certification course (CUC365). Use of equipment costs CUC7.50 extra. Snorkeling costs CUC12.

Diving and fishing are also offered at **Marina Cabo de San Antonio** (tel. 033/75-0118, diradjunto@marinasgaviota.co.cu). Check ahead, as the boat is often "under repair."

Accommodations and Food

If the two Gaviota-run hotels are full, there's at least one *casa particular* in Manuel Lazo, the nearest town (33 kilometers east of La Bajada). Check ahead and reserve in advance, as you're a long way from the nearest alternative accommodation if the resort is full.

The better option is **Hotel María la Gorda** (tel. 048/778131, fax 048/77-8077, from CUC34 s, CUC48 d low season, CUC39 s, CUC58 d high season), which doubles as a dive resort. The 55 air-conditioned rooms come in three types: older and simple cabins with basic bathrooms; newer and pleasing rooms in two-story units; and 20 spacious wooden cabins set

back from the beach. It has a small bar, and the Restaurante El Carajuel serves mediocre à la carte buffet lunches and dinners (CUC15). Credit cards are not accepted.

In 2008, Gaviota opened the **Villa Cabo San Antonio** (tel. 048/77-8131 ext. 204, www.gaviota-grupo.com, CUC51 s, CUC66 d low season, CUC56 s, CUC76 d high season) at Playa Las Tumbas, at the tip of the peninsula. Billed as an "eco-resort," it has 16 huge and nicely equipped duplex cabins on stilts. Each has a telephone, satellite TV (the only place I've viewed a hardcore adult movie in Cuba), fridge, and safe; some have king beds. French doors open to balconies, but none has sea views as the cabins are in the woods. It has a dive center and arranges sportfishing. The lackluster restaurant was hardpressed to come up with anything beyond fried chicken and stale bread during my stay. Despite the rooms, a motley place!

The marina at Punta Cajón has an elegant restaurant (7:30–10 A.M., 1–3 P.M., and 7:30–10 P.M.), but you will likely be the only diner.

Getting There and Away

A taxi from Pinar del Río costs about CUC70 one-way. **Transgaviota** has transfers to/from Pinar del Río (CUC60 one-way, CUC100 round-trip one person, CUC50/80 per person two people), departing María la Gorda at 2 P.M. It also has a shuttle between María la Gorda and Cabo San Antonio (CUC19). A jeep-taxi from María la Gorda to Cabo San Antonio costs CUC50 (up to four people).

Gaviota's **Vía** rents scooters and cars at Hotel María la Gorda.

Yachters can moor at **Marina Cabo de San Antonio** (tel. 033/75-0118, diradjunto@marinasgaviota.co.cu) and **Marina María la Gorda** (tel. 082/77-8131, commercial@miagorda.co.cu).

ISLA DE LA JUVENTUD SPECIAL MUNICIPALITY

Slung below the underbelly of Havana Province in the shallow Gulfo de Batabanó is Isla de la Juventud, the largest of Cuba's many offshore islands and one with an intriguing history and individuality. Scattered across the ocean to the east are 350 or so isles and cays that make up the Archipiélago de los Canarreos. Together they make up the special municipality of Isla de la Juventud.

Isla de la Juventud (Isle of Youth, so named for the erstwhile socialist experiment of International Youth Brigades), about 100 kilometers south of the mainland, receives relatively few visitors and is sparsely populated. The island was once smothered with native pine and previously called the Isle of Pines. The island's appeal lies in some of the finest diving in the Caribbean, several historical sites of importance, and untapped nature reserves. The entire southern half of Isla de la Juventud comprises brush and marsh that harbor wild boar, deer, *jutías,* and *Crocodilus rhombifer,* the endemic Cuban crocodile that is aggressive from the moment it emerges from its egg.

Most of the islands of the 160-kilometer-long Archipiélago de los Canarreos necklace are girt by beaches of purest white and haloed by barrier reefs guarding bathtub-warm waters. For now, tourism development is limited to Cayo Largo, the easternmost island and the only one accessible from the mainland.

Besides their spectacular beaches, the cays are a scuba diver's delight. In addition to astounding coral formations, some 200 shipwrecks have been reported in the Canarreos. The Nueva España treasure fleet, for example,

HIGHLIGHTS

◖ Presidio Modelo: Fidel Castro and other revolutionaries who survived the attack on the Moncada barracks were imprisoned in this prison-turned-museum (page 235).

◖ Refugio Ecológico Los Indios: This swampy and scrubby wilderness area offers fabulous bird-watching and is home to the Cuban sandbill crane (page 236).

◖ Criadero de Cocodrilos: Get up close and personal with Cuba's endemic crocodile at this breeding farm (page 237).

◖ Scuba Diving off Punta Francés: Just off the coast scuba divers will find fantastic coral formations, sponges, and both Spanish galleons and Soviet military vessels to explore (page 238).

◖ Cayo Largo: Secluded from the mainland, the gorgeous beaches and turquoise waters of Cayo Largo provide the perfect spot to get that all-over tan (page 238).

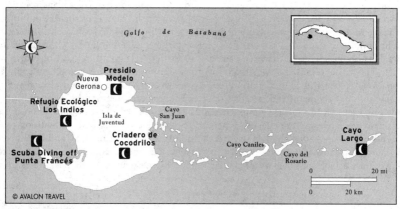

LOOK FOR ◖ TO FIND RECOMMENDED SIGHTS, ACTIVITIES, DINING, AND LODGING.

foundered in 1563 on the reefs between Cayo Rosarío and Cayo Largo. One of the best sites is Cabeza Sambo, 70 kilometers west of Cayo Largo. Over 800 species of fish gambol among the exquisite coral.

The cays shelter tens of thousands of seabirds, including crab-eating sparrow hawks; fishing orioles, cormorants, and pelicans that prey on the schools of fish; and egrets, majestic white and black herons, and other stilt-legged waders. Marine turtles are always in the water, particularly during the nesting seasons, when females lay their eggs above the high-water mark.

PLANNING YOUR TIME

Unless you're keen on bird-watching or diving, or are an aficionado of revolutionary history, you can safely skip Isla de la Juventud. Nonetheless, it is popular with backpackers and budget travelers keen to sample an offbeat part of Cuba. Two days is sufficient, although scuba divers will want to pack in a few more days for exploring the waters off **Punta Francés,** where the diving rivals anywhere in the Caribbean.

Nueva Gerona, the capital city, can be explored in mere hours, its colonnaded main street and ceramic workshops being the only sights of any appeal. Outside town, however, be sure to visit the **Presidio Modelo,** formerly Cuba's main prison, where Fidel Castro and other participants of the attack on the Moncada barracks were held; and El Abra, a historic farmstead where national hero José Martí once labored under sentence for sedition.

An entire day is needed for a visit to the Área Protegida Sur de la Isla de la Juventud, a swampy wilderness area offering fabulous bird-watching and wildlife-viewing. Guided excursions (easily arranged locally) are compulsory, including to the glorious white-sand beach of Playa Punta del Este, where the Cueva del Punta del Este is adorned with pre-Columbian paintings; to the **Criadero de Cocodrilos,** where you can learn the ecology of the Cuban crocodile; and to the **Refugio Ecológico Los Indios,** where Cuba's endemic crane and parrots can be seen.

Cayo Largo is reserved exclusively for foreigners, many of whom arrive from abroad on package tours. Its beaches shelving into warm turquoise waters are superb. It can be visited on day-long and overnight excursions from Havana.

Traveling between Isla de la Juventud and Cayo Largo is impossible. You need to backtrack to Havana.

Isla de la Juventud

Isla de la Juventud (pop. 70,000), or "La Isla," as it is known throughout Cuba, is shaped like a giant comma. At 3,050 square kilometers, it is about the size of Greater London. Most of the island is flat, with a hilly central core that reaches 310 meters in elevation. Marmoreal hills—the **Sierra de Caballo** and **Sierra del Casas**—flank the city of Nueva Gerona and are the source of most of the gray marble found in buildings throughout Cuba.

The north is predominantly flat or rolling lowland, perfect for raising cattle in the east and citrus (especially grapefruit) in the west, where the fertile flatlands are irrigated by streams dammed to create reservoirs. The sweet smell of jasmine floats over the island January–March, when the citrus trees bloom. To the south, the marshy **Ciénaga Lanier** swamp extends the width of the island and is a habitat for crocodiles, wild pigs, and waterfowl. Beautiful white-sand beaches rim the south shore. The entire southern half of the island is a protected area and ecotourism to the region is nascent. It is accessed by a single dirt road; an official guide is compulsory for visitors.

The people are called *pineros* and *pineras*. Many make their living as ceramists (the world-famous artist Kcho hails from La Isla). The local drink—a mix of grapefruit juice, white rum, and ice—is named a *pinerito*. Local lore says it's an aphrodisiac.

History

The island was inhabited in pre-Columbian days by the Ciboney, whose legacy can be seen in cave paintings at Punta del Este on the south coast. The early Indians knew the island as Siguanea. Columbus named it La Evangelista. Pirates, who used the isle as a base, named it the Isle of Parrots for the many endemic *cotorras.* The southwestern shore is known as the Pirate Coast. And the island claims, unconvincingly, to be the setting for Robert Louis Stevenson's *Treasure Island.* The English pirate Henry Morgan even gave his name to one of the island's small towns.

Although the Spanish established a fort to protect the passing treasure fleets, it remained a neglected backwater and the first colony wasn't established until 1826, on the banks of the Río Las Casas. Throughout the century, the Spanish used the island they had renamed Isla de los Pinos (Isle of Pines) as a prison, while the Spanish military sent soldiers with tropical diseases to the mineral springs in Santa Fe. After the Santa Rita hotel was built in 1860, tourists from North America began to arrive. Settlers of English and Scottish descent from the Cayman Islands also arrived in the 19th century and founded a turtle-hunting community called Jacksonville (now called Cocodrilo) on the south coast.

The War of Independence left the island in legal limbo. Although the Platt Amendment in 1902 recognized Cuba's claim on the island, only in 1925 did the island officially became part of the national territory. In consequence, Yankee real estate speculators bought much of the land and sold it for huge profits to gullible Midwestern farmers, who arrived expecting to find an agricultural paradise. The 300 or so immigrants established small communities and planted the first citrus groves, from which they eked out a meager living. Many U.S. citizens stayed; their legacy can still be seen in the cemetery and the ruined settlement at Columbia, near the Presidio Modelo, the prison that President Gerardo Machado built in 1931 and in which Fidel Castro and 25 followers were later imprisoned following their abortive attack on the Moncada barracks.

The U.S. Navy established a base here during World War II and turned the Presidio Modelo into a prisoner-of-war camp for Axis captives. In the post-war years, the island became a vacation spot, and gambling and prostitution were staples.

Following the Revolution, the Castro government launched a settlement campaign and planted citrus, which today extends over 25,000 hectares. Thousands of young Cubans went to work as "voluntary laborers" in the citrus groves. In 1971, the first of over 60 schools was established for foreign students—primarily from Africa, Nicaragua, Yemen, and North Korea—who formed what were called International Work Brigades and came to learn the Cuban method of work-study. The Cuban government paid the bill, and, in exchange, the foreign students joined Cuban students in the citrus plantations. To honor them, in 1978 the Isle of Pines was formally renamed the Isle of Youth. At the height of Cuba's internationalist phase, more than 150,000 foreign students were studying on the island.

The Special Period dealt the international

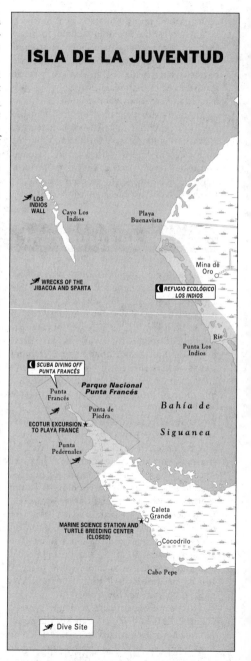

ISLA DE LA JUVENTUD

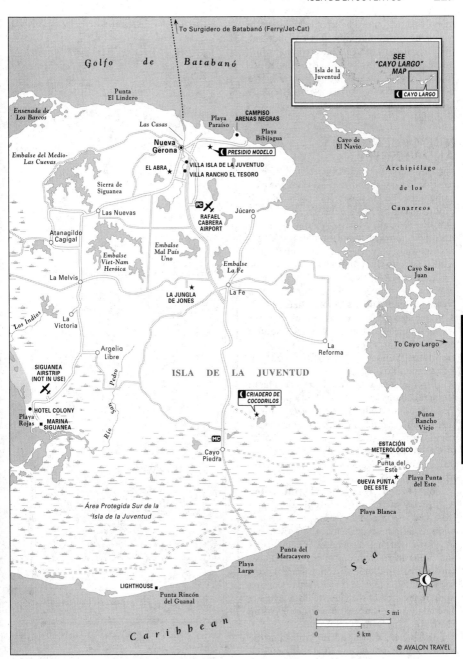

To Surgidero de Batabanó (Ferry/Jet-Cat)

Golfo   de   Batabanó

SEE
"CAYO LARGO"
MAP

Isla de la
Juventud

CAYO LARGO

Punta
El Lindero

Ensenada de
Los Barcos

Las Casas

Playa
Paraíso

CAMPISO
ARENAS NEGRAS

Playa
Bibijagua

Cayo de
El Navío

Nueva
Gerona

Embalse del Medio-
Las Cuevas

PRESIDIO MODELO

Archipiélago

EL ABRA

VILLA ISLA DE LA JUVENTUD

VILLA RANCHO EL TESORO

de   los

Sierra de
Siguanea

Canarreos

Las Nuevas

PC

Júcaro

RAFAEL
CABRERA
AIRPORT

Atanagildo
Cagigal

Embalse
Mal País
Uno

Embalse
Viet-Nam
Heróica

Embalse
La Fe

Cayo San
Juan

La Melvis

LA JUNGLA
DE JONES

La Fe

Los Indios

La
Victoria

To Cayo Largo

Argelia
Libre

La
Reforma

SIGUANEA
AIRSTRIP
(NOT IN USE)

ISLA   DE   LA   JUVENTUD

CRIADERO DE
COCODRILOS

HOTEL COLONY

Punta
Rancho
Viejo

Playa
Rojas

MARINA
SIGUANEA

ESTACIÓN
METEROLÓGICO

MC

Cayo
Piedra

Punta del
Este

CUEVA PUNTA
DEL ESTE

Playa Punta
del Este

Área Protegida Sur de la
Isla de la Juventud

Playa Blanca

Punta del
Maracayero

S e a

LIGHTHOUSE

Playa
Larga

Punta Rincón
del Guanal

C a r i b b e a n

0   5 mi

0   5 km

© AVALON TRAVEL

schools a death blow. The schools (and many of the citrus groves) have since been abandoned; in 2005, the government converted many into hospitals-cum-hotels for Latin American medical patients. Meanwhile, the isle was trashed in 2008 by hurricanes. At last visit in late 2009 Nueva Gerona was still struggling to get back on its feet.

NUEVA GERONA AND VICINITY

Nueva Gerona (pop. 36,000) lies a few kilometers inland from the north coast along the west bank of the Río Las Casas. It's a port town and exports primarily marble and citrus.

Calle 39 (Calle Martí), the main street, is lined with restored colonial buildings; it's pedestrian-only between Calles 20 and 30. The node is **Parque Guerrillero Heróico** (between Calles 28 and 30), a wide-open plaza facing a pretty, ocher-colored colonial church, **Iglesia Nuestra Señora de los Dolores** (tel. 046/32-3791), erected in 1929 in Mexican colonial style with a simple marble altar. Note the side altar dedicated to the Virgen de la Caridad. Masses are offered Sunday at 9 A.M., Wednesday at 7 P.M., and Friday at 9 A.M.

Also of interest is the **Galería de Arte Marta Machado** (daily 9 A.M.–10 P.M.), in a pretty colonial house on Calle 39. A *plazuela* a stone's throw south features a ceramic mural and intriguing ceramic seats. At last visit, the **Taller de Cerámica Artística** (Calles 37, esq. 26, tel. 061/32-2634), a ceramics studios, awaited repair due to hurricane damage.

The **Museo de Ciencias Naturales** (Calle 41 y 46, tel. 046/32-3143, Tues.–Sat. 9:30 A.M.–noon and 1–5 P.M., Sun. 8 A.M.–noon, CUC1 museum), about 0.8 kilometer south of town, has displays of endemic flora and fauna in re-creations of native habitats, plus stuffed (and somewhat moth-eaten) exotics, including a tiger and apes. There's even a small re-creation of the Cueva Punta del Este. The adjoining planetarium was destroyed by Hurricane Gustav in 2008.

For a précis on local history, call in at the **Museo Municipal** (Calle 30, e/ 37 y 39, tel.

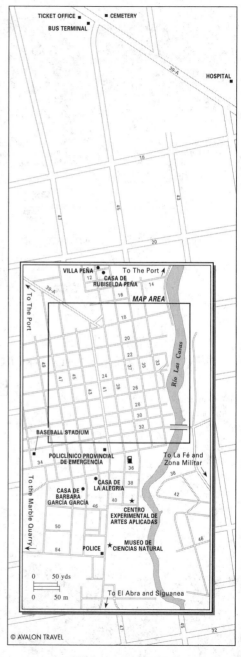

© AVALON TRAVEL

ISLA DE LA JUVENTUD

061/32-3791, Tues.–Sat. 9 A.M.–10 P.M., Sun. 9 A.M.–1 P.M., CUC1), in the Casa de Gobierno (the former town hall), built in 1853.

Once the town's major draw, *El Pinero* (Calle 33, e/ 26 y 28), the large ferry that carried Fidel to freedom following his release from prison on the Isle of Pines, is now merely a hulk and only the hull remains.

Museo Finca El Abra

This farm-cum-museum (Carretera Siguanea, Km 2, tel. 5219-3054, Tues.–Sat. 9 A.M.–4 P.M., Sun. 9 A.M.–1 P.M., CUC1), one kilometer south of Nueva Gerona, was where José Martí lived under house arrest in 1870 after being sentenced to six years' imprisonment for sedition. After a brief spell in prison on the mainland, Martí was released into the custody of José Sardá (a family friend and respected Catalonian landowner) at El Abra. Martí remained for only three months before departing for exile in Spain.

The museum is reached off the main highway by a long driveway shaded by Cuban oak trees. At the end is the farmhouse, still a family home, with a large bronze bust of Martí outside.

The exhibits include personal belongings, documents, and other artifacts of Martí's life.

Entertainment and Events

The **Festival de la Toronja** (Grapefruit Festival), held in February or March, depending on the harvest, features a carnival.

Watch for performances by Mongo Rivas and his relatives, who form **La Tumbita Criolla,** masters of the compelling dance rhythm *sucusuco,* born here early in the 19th century. The word comes from the onomatopoeic sound of feet moving to its infectious rhythm. They and other exponents of traditional music perform at the **Casa de la Cultura** (Calle 24, esq. 37, tel. 046/32-3591), which has a rumba on Saturday at 3 P.M.

The nicest nightclub in town is **Cabaret La Cubana** (Calle 39 e/ 16 y 18, tel. 046/32-3740), at Hotel La Cubana. It screens music videos and has a sexy *cabaret espectáculo* (Thurs., Fri., and Sun. at 10 P.M., 20 pesos). **Cabaret El Patio** (Calle 24, e/ Martí y 37, tel. 046/32-2346) was closed for restoration at last visit.

For a quiet tipple, try **Casa del Vino** (Calle 20, esq. 41, no tel., Fri.–Wed. 1–10 P.M.), a

Cine Caribe, Nueva Gerona

rustic wooden home festooned with fishing net. It sells flavored wines for pesos.

Cine Caribe (Calle 37, tel. 046/32-2416), on the main square, charges two pesos.

Baseball games are played October–April at **Estadio Cristóbal Labra** (Calle 32, e/ 49 y 51, tel. 046/32-1044).

Recreation

The Sierra del Casas, immediately southwest of town, is good for hiking. By following Calle 22 westward you can ascend via a dirt track to the summit of **Loma de Cañada** (310 meters), which offers good views over the island. At the base are three caves worth a peek for their dripstones and petroglyphs.

By following Calle 54 west you'll loop around to where gray *mármol* (marble) is quarried—the island has Cuba's largest reserves of marble.

Accommodations

All the state-run hotels are outside town; in early 2010, all remained closed due to low tourism numbers. Owners of *casas particulares* in town meet arriving ferries.

CASAS PARTICULARES

One of the best private rentals is **Casa de la Alegría** (Calle 43 #3602, e/ 36 y 38, tel. 046/32-3664, CUC15–20), which offers two modestly furnished, air-conditioned rooms. One has an independent entrance. The home has parking plus a patio where meals are served.

Villa Peña (Calle 10 #3710, e/ 37 y 39, tel. 046/32-2345, CUC10–15 year-round) is a pleasant home with a two-room air-conditioned unit with telephone, double and single bed, plus private hot-water bath. Meals (including vegetarian) are offered. It has secure parking. In the same family, **Casa de Rubiselda Peña** (Calle 10 #3707, e/ 37 y 39, tel. 046/32-2345, CUC10) is run by a gracious hostess who rents two well-lit air-conditioned rooms upstairs with fans and a small shared hot-water bathroom. There's a TV lounge with rockers, private bathrooms, and a rooftop terrace.

Barbarita, a delightful owner, plays host at **Casa de Barbara García García** (Calle 45 #3606, e/ 36 y 38, tel. 046/32-2038, gracia93@correodecuba.com). A highlight is the lovely brick-paved patio with arbor and grill.

HOTELS

Gran Caribe's **Complejo Hotelero Rancho Villa** combines two hotels. The **Villa Isla de la Juventud** (Carretera La Fe, Km 1.5, tel. 046/32-3290, ranchoij@enet.cu), known locally as Villa Gaviota, is a mediocre property that was in the midst of a much-needed renovation at last visit. A better bet is the nearby **Hotel Rancho El Tesoro** (Carretera La Fe, Km 2.5, tel. 046/32-3035, fax 046/32-3657, ranchoik@enet.cu).

The Hotel La Cubana is for Cubans only.

Food

The owners of *casas particulares* serve better meals than the mediocre state restaurants.

Restaurante Dragón (Calle 39, esq. 26, tel. 046/32-4479), one block north of the church, has a strong Chinese flavor and a menu featuring a chop suey special and other quasi-Chinese dishes. It serves workers until 3 P.M., then offers set meals on the hour until 10 P.M. **Restaurante El Cochinito** (Calle 39, esq. 24, tel. 046/32-2809, daily noon–10 P.M.) specializes in pork dishes, especially roast suckling pig. Shorts and tank tops are not permitted, and meals are served at set hours.

Basic pizza costs five pesos per slice at **Pizzería La Góndola** (Calle 30, esq. 35, tel. 046/32-4857). Take-out slices are sold in the back courtyard.

Coppelia (Calle 32, esq. 37, tel. 046/32-2225, Thurs.–Tues. 11 A.M.–9:45 P.M.) sells ice cream for pesos.

You can buy fresh produce from the *mercado agropecuario* at Calles 24 and 35, and on Calle 41 at the south end of town; Western groceries at the meagerly stocked **Cubalse** supermarket (Calle 30, e/ 35 y 37, Mon.–Sat. 9:30 A.M.–6 P.M.); and bread at the **Cadena de Pan** (Martí, e/ 22 y 24, daily 8 A.M.–noon and 1–4 P.M.).

Information and Services

Nueva Gerona has a **Bandec** (Calle 39, esq.

18, tel. 046/32-4805) and **Banco Popular** (Calle Martí, esq. 26, tel. 046/32-2742). You can obtain pesos at **Cadeca** (Calle 39 y 20, tel. 046/32-3462, Mon.–Sat. 8:30 A.M.–12:30 P.M. and 1–3 P.M.).

Services include a **post office** (Calle 39, esq. Calle 18, tel. 046/32-2600, Mon.–Sat. 8:30 A.M.–10 P.M.) and **Etecsa** (Calles 41 y 28, daily 8:30 A.M.–7:30 P.M.). At last visit there was *no* Internet service on the island.

The **Hospital Héroes de Baire** (Calles 18 y 41, tel. 046/32-3012) has a recompression chamber. Foreigners are also treated at the **Policlínico Provincial de Emergencia** (Calle 41, e/ 32 y 34, tel. 046/32-2236). The **pharmacy** (Calle 39, esq. 24, tel. 046/32-6084, Mon.–Sat. 8 A.M.–11 P.M.) is meagerly stocked.

The **police station** (Calle 41, esq. 54) is one kilometer south of town.

Getting There and Away

A passport is compulsory for travel to Isla de la Juventud.

BY AIR

The **Aeropuerto Rafael Cabrera** (tel. 046/32-2690) is 15 kilometers south of Nueva Gerona. **Cubana** (tel. 046/32-4259, Mon.–Fri. 8:30 A.M.–noon and 1:30–4:30 P.M.), in the ferry terminal, operates three flights most days from Havana but just two on Tuesday and Thursday (CUC64 round-trip). **AeroCaribbean** flies twice daily. Demand outstrips supply; book a round-trip ticket as far in advance as possible.

A bus marked Servicio Aereo connects flights with downtown Nueva Gerona (one peso). The bus to the airport departs from Calle 53 and passes by Cine Caribe (Calle 37, e/ 28 y 30). A taxi costs CUC5.

BY FERRY

Three high-speed catamarans serve Nueva Gerona from Surgidero de Batabanó, 70 kilometers south of Havana (CUC50, plus CUC5 bus from Havana, two hours). Departures from Surgidero are scheduled for Monday, Thursday, and Sunday at 12:30 P.M. (plus

Friday and Saturday at 4 P.M.), but the actual departure times depend on the number of passengers (sometimes only one cat departs). The 350-passenger cat has 20 seats reserved for foreigners; the 240-passenger cat has 10 seats for foreigners. The journey takes two hours (CUC50).

You'll need your passport when buying a ticket and when boarding. In Surgidero, buy your ticket at the wharfside **Viajero** (tel. 047/58-824, direccion@viajeroi.j.transnet.cu) ticket office. In Havana, buy your ticket 24 hours in advance from **Astro** (tel. 07/878-1841) in the main bus terminal in Havana, then check in at 7 A.M. for the bus to Surgidero (CUC5). I recommend buying return (*regreso*) tickets when you purchase your outbound (*ida*) tickets. There's a 20-kilogram baggage limit. No bicycles are permitted. On board, you're served a sandwich and drink. There's also a small snack bar wharfside in Surgidero.

In Nueva Gerona vessels berth at the **Naviera Cubana Caribeña** (Calles 31 y 24, tel. 046/32-3164, Mon.–Thurs. and Sat. 8 A.M.–3 P.M., Fri. 9 A.M.–4 P.M.) ferry terminal. Catamarans depart Nueva Gerona for Surgidero on Mon., Thurs., and Sun. at 8 A.M., and Fri. and Sat. at 8 A.M. and 1 P.M. and are timed to connect with a bus to Havana (buy your bus tickets at the ferry terminal when you buy your catamaran passage).

TAKING A VEHICLE

You can ship your car (CUC44 each way) or motorbike (CCU13) aboard a *transitaria* (flatbed barge) towed by a tug. You, however, will have to take a catamaran and meet the barge in Nueva Gerona. The barge departs Surgidero Tuesday, Thursday, and Saturday at 11 P.M. The dock is next to the ferry terminal in Surgidero (tel. 062/58-8495, ask for Jorge); you must register your vehicle at least two hours in advance. The barge arrives in Nueva Gerona at 7 A.M. the following day, docking two kilometers north of the ferry terminal. The return barge departs Nueva Gerona at noon, arriving in Batabanó at 11 P.M.; make your reservations in advance at the *transitaria* office (tel. 046/32-7224, Mon.–Fri. 8 A.M.–11 P.M.).

BY PRIVATE VESSEL
Private vessels can berth upstream of the ferry terminal.

BY BUS
Buses for around the isle depart from Calles 39A and 45 (ticket office tel. 046/32-2413, 8 A.M.–noon and 1–5 P.M.).

EXCURSIONS
EcoTur (Calle 24 e/ 31 y 33, tel./fax 046/32-7101, Mon.–Fri. 8 A.M.–5 P.M., Sat. 8 A.M.–noon) offers ecotourism excursions (CUC8–12, including guide; you'll need to provide your own transport).

Getting Around
Nueva Gerona is small enough that you can walk most places. Horse-drawn buggies congregate around the main square and by the ferry terminal when boats arrive. Taxis congregate at the corner of Calles 32 and 39.
Cubacar (Calles 39 y 32, tel. 046/32-4432, daily 7 A.M.–7 P.M.) rents cars. You have to pay cash for a full tank of gas (CUC38.50;

supposedly you get your money back for any gas left over above 10 liters).

EAST OF NUEVA GERONA
Calle 32 leads east from Nuevo Gerona to **Playa Paraíso** and **Playa Bibijagua,** two unremarkable beaches. **Campismo Arenas Negras** (tel. 046/32-5323), about 0.5 kilometer beyond Bibijagua, has basic cabins but was closed to foreigners at last visit.

◖ Presidio Modelo
The island's most interesting attraction—the Model Prison—is five kilometers east of Nueva Gerona. It was built 1926–1931 during President Machado's repressive regime and was based on the model of the penitentiary at Joliet, Illinois. The prison was designed to house 6,000 inmates in four five-story circular buildings. At the center of each rondel was a watchtower that put prisoners under constant surveillance. A fifth circular building, in the center, housed the mess hall, dubbed "The Place of 3,000 Silences" because talking was prohibited. Prisoners were woken at 5 A.M., *silencio* was at 9 P.M. The last prisoner went home in 1967. Only the shells remain.

The two oblong buildings that now house

Presidio Modelo

the **Museo Presidio Modelo** (tel. 046/32-5112, Mon.–Sat. 8 A.M.–4 P.M., Sun. 8 A.M.–noon, entrance CUC2, cameras CUC3, videos CUC25) were used during World War II to intern Japanese-Cubans and Germans captured in Cuban waters. The first wing of the museum contains black-and-white photos and memorabilia from the Machado era (it was closed for restoration in early 2010). Another wing was the hospital, which in 1953 housed Fidel Castro and 25 other revolutionaries sentenced to imprisonment here following the attack on the Moncada barracks. They lived apart from the other prisoners and were privileged. Their beds are still in place, with a black-and-white photo of each prisoner on the wall. Fidel's bed is next to last, to the left, facing the door. Castro used his time here to good effect. Batista foolishly allowed him to set up a school (Academía Ideológica Abel Santamaría), where the group studied economics, revolutionary theory, and guerrilla tactics. On May 15, 1955, the revolutionaries were released to much fanfare. Immediately to the left of the museum entrance is the room where Fidel—prisoner RN3859—was later kept in solitary confinement (ostensibly for heckling dictator Fulgencio Batista during a visit). It's surprisingly large, with a spacious bathroom with shower of gleaming white tiles. A glass case contains some of his favorite books.

A taxi will cost about CUC6 round-trip.

Getting There and Away

Buses depart Nueva Gerona for Presidio Modelo and Bibijagua at 7 A.M., 4:10 P.M., and 5:30 P.M. A taxi will cost about CUC6 round-trip.

SOUTHWEST OF NUEVA GERONA

Carretera Siguanea leads southwest from Nueva Gerona through a rolling landscape studded with reservoirs and stands of pines amid citrus groves. Side roads lead west to the Bahía de Siguanea, lined with mangroves. Supposedly, Columbus landed here on June 13, 1494. Later, the bay was a harbor for pirates.

The region is served by the motley Hotel Colony, 30 kilometers southwest of Nueva Gerona. It began life in the 1950s as a Hilton and backs a mediocre beach whose shallows have sea grasses and urchins; day passes can be purchased for CUC1 (you'll need your passport). The **Marina El Colony** (tel. 046/39-8181) offers fishing for bonefish and tarpon, and the International Scuba Diving Center is also here (it has a decompression chamber). An Italian company, **Avalon Fishing Center** (http://cubanfishingcenters.com/perola.php), offers fishing packages about the *Perola,* a classy 75-foot luxury live-aboard yacht.

◖ Refugio Ecológico Los Indios

Much of the bayshore is a 4,000-hectare reserve protecting a fragile environment that includes mangroves, savanna, and endemic pines and palms. There are at least 60 native floral species, 15 of them limited to this particular spot (14 are endangered, including a species of carnivorous plant). The 153 species of birds include the endemic Cuban sandbill crane (called *la grulla*) and the *cotorra*—the equally threatened Cuban parrot (*Amazona leucocephala*).

Rough trails lead into the reserve from Siguanea. A guide is compulsory and can be arranged through the hotel or EcoTur, in Nueva Gerona (CUC8).

Accommodations

The totally lackluster **Hotel Colony** (tel. 046/39-8181, fax 046/39-8420, reservas@colony.co.cu, CUC20 s, CUC36 d low season, CUC25 s, CUC42 d high season) is a deteriorated 1950s hotel with 24 modestly decorated, air-conditioned bungalows plus 77 rooms. It has water sports.

Getting There and Away

Buses depart Nueva Gerona for Siguanea at 5 A.M., 11 A.M., 2:30 P.M., 5:30 P.M., 7 P.M., and 10 P.M. A taxi from Nueva Gerona will cost about CUC20.

Marina El Colony (tel. 046/39-8181) has 15 berths with electricity, water, gas, and diesel.

SOUTH OF NUEVA GERONA

A four-lane freeway runs south from Nueva Gerona to **La Fe,** an agricultural town that was founded by U.S. citizens and originally called Santa Fe. Some of their plantation-style houses still stand around the main square. The ruins of the **Manantial Agua La Cotorra** mineral springs are touted as an attraction but aren't worth the drive.

Serious botanists might get a thrill at **La Jungla de Jones** (no tel.), about three kilometers west of La Fe. This 30-hectare botanical reserve was founded in 1902 by a U.S. couple, Harry and Helen Jones, who introduced exotic tree species for study in cooperation with the U.S. Department of Agriculture. It was abandoned in 1976. Today the woodsy reserve boasts about 72 species, including 10 bamboo species and 20 mangrove species, plus dozens of bird species that include parrots, woodpeckers, and owls. The highlight is the "Bamboo Cathedral," a 100-meter-long vaulted glade. It's been badly battered by hurricanes in recent years and is closed to the public except for guided excursions offered by **EcoTur,** in Nueva Gerona (CUC8).

Criadero de Cocodrilos

This crocodile breeding farm (daily 8 A.M.–5 P.M., CUC9), 30 kilometers south of Nueva Gerona, has over 500 crocodiles separated by age, as older crocs are cannibalistic. A trail leads to natural lagoons where mature beasts swim freely. The oldest and biggest male is a mean-looking sexagenarian giant who guards his harem jealously. The juveniles feast upon the remains of sardines and lobster, while the full-grown monsters are fed hacked-up cattle. Feeding time is usually between 9 and 10 A.M.

ÁREA PROTEGIDA SUR DEL ISLA DE LA JUVENTUD

The entire isle south of Cayo Piedra along its east–west parallel lies within the South of the Isle of Youth Protected Area, a wilderness of bush and swamp populated by wild pig, deer, and crocodiles. The coast is lined with beaches whose sugar-white sands slope down to calm turquoise waters protected by reefs.

There's a military checkpoint just south of Cayo Piedra. An official guide is compulsory, arranged through EcoTur in Nueva Gerona.

From Cayo Piedra, a dirt road leads east 20 kilometers through the Ciénaga de Lanier to Punta del Este. There's a beautiful beach here—**Playa Punta del Este**—but the main attraction is **Cuevas Punta del Este,** a group of caves containing 238 aboriginal pictographs that date from about A.D. 800 and are among the most important aboriginal petroglyphs in the Antilles. The petroglyphs seem to form a celestial plan thought to represent the passage of days and nights. Among them are 28 concentric circles of red and black, pierced by a red arrow of two parallel lines and thought to represent the lunar month. Each day the sun's rays enter through the portal of the most important cave. As the sun follows its astral route, it illuminates different sections of the mural. On March 22, when spring begins, the sun appears in the very center of the cave entrance, revealing a red phallus penetrating a group of concentric circles on the back wall, an obvious allusion to procreation.

Cayo Piedra to Punta Francés

The road south from Cayo Piedra leads directly to **Playa Larga,** a real stunner of a beach. Five kilometers before the beach is a turnoff to the right that leads west 28 kilometers to Punta Francés. The badly deteriorated road runs inland of the shore the whole way, and there is no view of the beautiful shoreline until you reach the tiny seaside community of **Cocodrilo,** formerly Jacksonville (named for Atkin Jackson, who founded the hamlet in 1904). The isolated villagers eke a living as anglers. Many are descendants of immigrants who arrived from the Cayman Islands over a century ago; a lilting Caribbean English is still spoken.

Parque Nacional Punta Francés

Covering 6,079 hectares, of which 4,313 are ocean terrain, this national park is at the southwesterly tip of the island, some 120 kilometers from Nueva Gerona. Its semideciduous forest distinguishes it from the Lanier swamp. Blind shrimp inhabit *cenotes* (water-filled sinkholes) that stud the shore. Offshore, gorgonias, corals, and marine turtles abound.

The main draws are the gorgeous beaches at **Playa El Francés,** where Spanish galleons and coral formations await scuba divers a short distance from shore. Amenities include a pleasant restaurant, lounge chairs, and water sports. Cruise ships (*Columbus, Europa, Les Levants,* and *Sea Cloud*) berth offshore and tender passengers ashore for day visits, so the place can be crowded.

◖ Scuba Diving off Punta Francés

The bay offers spectacular diving. There are 56 dive sites concentrated along **La Costa de los Piratas** (the Pirate Coast), whose tranquil waters are protected from the Gulf Stream currents. The sites extend along a 15-kilometer-long axis between Punta Pedernales and Punta Francés. Off Punta Francés, the basin's wall begins at 20 meters and plummets into the depths of the

Gulf of Mexico. The wall is laced with canyons, caves, and grottoes. Site 39 is renowned for the **Caribbean Cathedral,** said to be the tallest coral column in the world. Two other sites of interest are **Black Coral Wall** and **Stingray Paradise,** where you may stroke these friendly fish.

A naval battle between Thomas Baskerville's pirate ships and a Spanish fleet resulted in many ships being sunk near Siguanea. Northeast of Punta Francés are three well-preserved Spanish galleons. Several freighters were scuttled several decades ago to provide bombing and naval gunnery targets for the Cuban armed forces.

The **Centro Internacional del Buceo** (International Scuba Diving Center, tel. 046/39-8181), 1.5 kilometers south of the Hotel Colony, offers dives (CUC35). It takes well over one hour to reach the dive spots—a tedious journey in basic launches. Drop-in visitors hoping for a day's diving are often taken to the nearest sites, rather than the most interesting. Diving with a guide is compulsory.

It's a full-day drive from Nueva Gerona and back. **EcoTur,** in Nueva Gerona, offers excursions (CUC8).

Archipiélago de los Canarreos

◖ CAYO LARGO

Cayo Largo, 177 kilometers south of Havana and 120 kilometers east of Isla de la Juventud, is a 3-kilometer-wide, 25-kilometer-long, boomerang-shaped sliver of land fringed by an unbroken 20-kilometer stretch of beaches with sand as blindingly white as Cuban sugar. The beaches merge gently into waters that run from lightest green through turquoise and jade. There are water sports and a top-class hotel (plus several less impressive options). Cayo Largo is favored by Canadians and Europeans in budget package groups. Uniquely, the Cuban government tolerates nude sunbathing here, and many people on the beach are in the buff. You won't learn a thing about Cuban life, however, as everything here is a tourist contrivance, and the only Cubans are hotel staff who

live in their community—El Pueblo—north of the airport.

In recent years several hurricanes have swept over the cay, stripping away much of the sand and leaving the place looking deteriorated.

A single road links the airport, at the northwest end of Cayo Largo, with the resort (3 kilometers south) and continues east, unpaved as far as Playa Los Cocos (14 kilometers). **El Pueblo** (CUC1 payable in the adjacent Buro de Turismo) is a turtle farm where you can see turtles in pools. If lucky, you'll witness hatchlings emerging from their nests (Cayo Largo is Cuba's main turtle-nesting site). To date, some 12,000 baby green and leatherback turtles have been released to the sea (you can join in the release for CUC3). Free guided tours to witness nestings are offered.

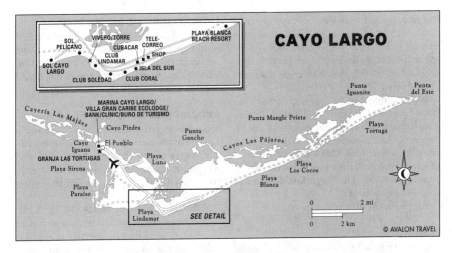

CAYO LARGO

Hidden away in the undergrowth east of Sol Pelicano, the **Vivero Torre** (no tel.) is a tiny garden where crocodiles, freshwater turtles, and tarpon lurk amid the reeds of an inky black lagoon. Agustina, the delightful gardener, will show you.

newborn leatherback turtle, Cayo Largo

© CHRISTOPHER P. BAKER

Entertainment and Events

Each September, Cayo Largo hosts the **International Marlin Tournament.**

The Cuban hotel workers have an open-air bar—**La Carpa**—in El Pueblo that gets lively with dancing. Nearby, the waterfront **El Pirata Taberna** (tel. 045/24-8213) is a good spot to imbibe.

Recreation

Catamaran excursions to Isla Iguana (CUC10–36), including a sunset "seafari," are offered from the marina (CUC49).

BEACHES AND WATER SPORTS

Cayo Largo has 27 kilometers of serene beaches, which run the entire length of the seaward side (the leeward side is composed of mangroves and salty lagoons). Swimming is forbidden when the sea gets too rough; red flags are posted.

The loveliest beach is 2.3-kilometer-long **Playa Sirena,** on the west side of Punta Sirena, the western end of the island. Facilities include a souvenir kiosk, toilets, game room, and restaurant, and sailboards and catamarans can be rented. Playa Sirena slopes steeply below the waterline—wading is not recommended for children. The beach is reached by dirt road. The *trencito* shuttle operates to **Playa**

ISLA DE LA JUVENTUD

Paraíso, immediately west of Playa Sirena, at 9, 10:30, and 11:30 A.M. (CUC2); it departs Paraíso at 1, 3, and 5 P.M. A free bus runs to the marina at 9 and 10:30 A.M. (returning at 1:15 and 3:15 P.M.). Hotels offer excursions to Playa Sirena.

Playa Lindamar, setting for the Sol Club Cayo Largo and Sol Pelícano hotels, is a scimitar-shaped beach extending east about one kilometer, where a rocky point divides it from seven-kilometer-long **Playa Blanca** (stripped of sand by hurricanes in 2005 and 2008). Immediately east are **Playa Los Cocos** and then **Playa Tortuga.**

All the hotels offer water sports.

FISHING

Bonefish (*macabí*) and tarpon (*sábalo*) abound inshore. **Villa Gran Caribe Ecolodge** (tel. 045/5282-7715), in El Pueblo, offers fly-fishing packages and day trips. Bookings are handled by **Avalon Fishing Club** (www.avalonfishing-center.com).

SNORKELING AND SCUBA DIVING

Several galleons and corsairs lie on the seabed amid the coral reefs teeming with fish. Dives are available from **Marina Marlin** (tel. 045/24-8214, buceo.marina@repgc.cls.tur.cu, CUC37 one dive, plus CUC10 equipment rental).

Accommodations and Food

Most guests arrive on an all-inclusive basis. There are no eateries outside the resort hotels, most of which serve mediocre fare. Nonguests can buy day passes to the Sol properties (CUC60) and can also dine at their restaurants.

Villa Gran Caribe Ecolodge (tel. 045/5282-7715, luisa.sacerdote@divingcuba.com, prices on request), at El Pueblo, operates as a fishing lodge and has 16 nicely furnished air-conditioned log cabins overlooking the mangrove-lined shallows. French doors open to balconies with lounge chairs. Rooms adjoin to form family units. An elegant clubhouse with Internet and pool table wards off boredom by night. No

Villa Gran Caribe Ecolodge, Cayo Largo

© CHRISTOPHER P. BAKER

ISLA DE LA JUVENTUD

walk-ins are accepted; you must buy a package with **Avalon Fishing Club** (www.avalonfishingcenter.com), which has exclusive rights.

All other hotels are operated on an all-inclusive basis by Cuba's Gran Caribe chain. All have air-conditioning, satellite TV, refrigerators, and safes in guest rooms, plus water sports and entertainment.

Hotel Club Cayo Largo (tel. 045/24-8111) comprises four adjacent and mediocre properties. Its **Club Isla del Sur,** a.k.a. Eden Village, is used exclusively by Italy's Eden Viaggi. The neighboring **Club Lindamar** is used exclusively by Italy's VeraClub. The adjacent and ludicrously overpriced **Club Coral** (CUC102 s, CUC144 d low season, CUC112 s, CUC164 d high season) has 24 rooms in two-story duplex units surrounding a half-moon pool with swim-up bar atop a coral ledge above the beach. Rooms are done up in a lively Caribbean color scheme and have king-size beds, but the club is dismal, as is the neighboring and similarly priced **Club Soledad,** with 63 thatched bungalows.

Sol Pelícano Hotel (tel. 045/24-8333, fax 045/24-8243, www.solmeliacuba.com, CUC85 s, CUC120 d standard, CUC125 s, CUC170 d junior suite low season, CUC140 s, CUC230 d standard, CUC180 s, CUC280 d junior suite high season), managed by the Meliá chain, is a mediocre and overpriced low-rise hotel built haphazardly in vaguely Spanish-colonial style around a freeform pool amid unkempt grounds. It has 324 rooms, including two suites and 110 *cabinas,* all with modest yet appealing decor.

Far better is the more upscale yet inexplicably lower-priced ◖ **Sol Cayo Largo** (tel. 045/24-8260, fax 045/24-8265, www.solmeliacuba.com, from CUC125 s, CUC175 d low season, from CUC190 s, CUC24 d high season), a deluxe all-inclusive with 301 spacious rooms in four-plex units graced by sponge-washed walls, lively ice-cream colors, and pleasingly understated furnishings. A splendid beach restaurant serves an impressive buffet luncheon; there's a 24-hour snack bar, plus specialist restaurant, game room, choice of bars, and Internet service.

The former Barceló Cayo Largo Beach Resort was ill-fated when it opened in 2005 just in time to see its beach washed away by Hurricane Wilma. In early 2010, Gran Caribe reopened it as the all-Cuban-operated **Playa Blanca Beach Resort** (tel. 045/24-8080, fax 045/24-8088, reservas.pb@cayolargo.co.cu, CUC85 s, CUC150 d low season, CUC140 s, CUC250 d high season, suites cost CUC30 additional), with 306 rooms in two-story bungalows and the three-story main building. Its contemporary design won't suit all tastes, the grounds are poorly laid out, and construction standards are questionable, but it has plenty of amenities.

In 2010, plans were announced for a Qatari company to build the 450-room, 60-villa five-star **Gran Paraíso** hotel.

Information and Services

The **Buro de Turismo** (tel. 045/24-8214, daily 7 A.M.–7 P.M.) adjoins the marina in El Pueblo. The **Clínica Internacional** (tel. 045/24-8238, 24 hours), across the street, has a dentist. The **bank** (tel. 045/24-8225, 9 A.M.–noon) is also here; you'll need to bring your passport.

The **post office** (8 A.M.–noon and 4–6:30 P.M. Mon.–Fri.) opposite the Isla del Sur Hotel has telephone, DHL, and fax service.

Inmigración (tel. 045/24-8250) and **customs** (tel. 045/24-8244) are at the airport.

A store (daily 9:30 A.M.–9:30 P.M.) opposite the Club Isla del Sur sells beachwear, etc.

Getting There and Away

International travelers (including sailors) can arrive without a visa if they don't intend to visit the mainland. You can obtain a visa upon arrival in Cayo Largo.

Charter flights operate from Canada, Europe, Mexico, and Grand Cayman to **Vilo Acuña International Airport** (tel. 045/24-8141). **Cubana** (www.cubana.cu) serves Cayo Largo from Havana and Varadero. **AeroGaviota** (tel. 045/24-8364, CUC99 plus CUC30 tax) flies from the Baracoa airstrip, 15 kilometers west of Havana.

The cheapest option is a package excursion through a Cuban tour agency (one-day package from CUC167 including tax and catamaran cruise, two-day from CUC200 including overnight).

Private yachters can berth at **Cayo Largo del Sur Marina** (tel. 045/24-8133, fax 045/24-8212, VHF channel 16). It has 90 berths with 110- and 220-volt electricity, water hookups, and gas and diesel, plus a chandler, laundry, and repair service.

Getting Around

You can rent bicycles and scooters (CUC10 hours, CUC18 per day), plus jeep rental (CUC33 three hours, CUC52 per day) at the hotels.

OTHER CAYS

West of Cayo Largo, uninhabited cays extend all the way to the shores of Isla de la Juventud. Sprinkled like diamonds across a sapphire sea, they are a yachting and diving paradise. There are no facilities.

The Archipiélago de los Canarreos deserves a reputation for some of the best wildlife-viewing in Cuba, from a small population of monkeys on **Cayo Cantiles** (the only monkeys in Cuba) to the flamingos inhabiting the lagoons of **Cayo Pasaje. Cayo Iguana,** a nature reserve immediately north of Cayo Largo, is noted for its large population of endemic iguanas.

Cruise excursions are offered from Cayo Largo to Cayo Iguana. Book at tour desks on Cayo Largo.

MATANZAS

Matanzas Province is a triptych of diverse appeal. Its north shore boasts some of the island's finest beaches. The lodestone is Varadero, Cuba's biggest beach resort. The resort, occupying the slender 20-kilometer-long Península de Hicacos, is a mini-Cancún with almost three-quarters of all hotel rooms on the island. Betwixt Havana and Varadero is the namesake city of Matanzas, a once-wealthy sugar- and slave-trading port known as the Athens of Cuba for its literary and artistic vitality. Today, it is a center for Afro-Cuban culture, although the predominant impression when passing through is of modern port industries, not least petrochemicals.

Hills separate the coastal strip from a vast plain where red soils support sugarcane fields and vast citrus orchards that extend east into Villa Clara Province, providing the bulk of Cuba's citrus.

The southern part of Matanzas Province is taken up by the low-lying Península de Zapata, the Caribbean's largest marshland system harboring fantastic bird life and a large population of Cuban crocodiles. In April 1961 the Zapata region was launched from obscurity to fame as the setting for the Bay of Pigs invasion. Today the region is enshrined within Parque Natural Ciénaga de Zapata, luring travelers keen on bird-watching, fishing, and a sampling of revolutionary history. There are pleasant beaches at Playa Larga and Playa Girón, both major landing sites for the CIA-inspired invasion by Cuban exiles. Memories of the fiasco—and Cuba's proud moment (Cubans refer to it as *la victoria*)—are kept

© CHRISTOPHER P. BAKER

HIGHLIGHTS

◖ **Castillito de San Severino:** The restored fortress houses the Museo de la Ruta del Esclavo, an intriguing museum on slavery and Afro-Cuban religions (page 251).

◖ **Cuevas de Bellamar:** Visitors will find dripstones galore in this cool underground cavern system (page 251).

◖ **Las Américas at Mansión Xanadú:** An exorbitant mansion built by industrial magnate Irénée Du Pont overhangs the crashing Atlantic in Varadero (page 260).

◖ **Scuba Diving and Snorkeling off Varadero:** The wreck diving revolves around a Russian frigate, patrol boat, and airplane (page 263).

◖ **Parque Echevarría:** This quiet colonial plaza in Cárdenas has three museums, including the superb Museo Oscar María de Roja and even one to Elián González (page 274).

◖ **Parque Nacional Ciénaga de Zapata:** The Caribbean's preeminent wetland area is chock-full of birdlife, crocodiles, and game fish (page 281).

◖ **Museo Playa Girón:** Featuring warplanes and U.S. and Soviet military hardware, this excellent museum recalls the failed CIA-sponsored Bay of Pigs invasion (page 284).

LOOK FOR ◖ TO FIND RECOMMENDED SIGHTS, ACTIVITIES, DINING, AND LODGING.

alive at a museum. The area even offers good scuba diving.

Note for Boaters: The entire coastline from the Bay of Pigs (21° 45') to Cienfuegos harbor (21° 50') is strictly off-limits.

PLANNING YOUR TIME

The Vía Blanca, or Circuito Norte, runs along the coast between Havana and Matanzas (102 kilometers), and thence to Varadero, 34 kilometers farther east. Many visitors make Varadero their main center for a vacation in Cuba. There are better beach resorts, if sun and sand are your main interests. Two or even three days relaxing on the beach here should suffice anyone. That said, the scuba diving is excellent, boat excursions are fun, and organized excursions to the timeworn historic city of Cárdenas—with its must-see Museo Oscar María de Roja on **Parque Echevarría**—and further afield provide an adequate sampling of Cuba's broader pleasures.

The city of Matanzas appeals for its heritage of Afro-Cuban music and dance; for its faded colonial architecture highlighted by the restored **Castillito de San Severino,** with an important museum recalling the era of slavery; and for the **Cuevas de Bellamar,** full of fabulous dripstone formations. One day is more than adequate to explore the city. Day trips to Matanzas are offered from Varadero.

Between Havana and Matanzas sits the Valle de Yumurí, a huge basin lushly cultivated with sugarcane. It is enfolded by a crescent of low mountains famed for their mineral springs, most notably at San Miguel de los Baños, whose once-fine mansions are now in tragic decay.

The Zapata region deserves at least a day's visit. At Boca de Guamá, Cuba's most important crocodile farm is open for visits. Bird-watchers and wildlife enthusiasts are in their element. Laguna del Tesoro and Las Salinas set a world standard for tarpon and bonefish angling (anglers might plan on two or three days casting). Scuba divers can dive a *cenote* (flooded sinkhole) while snorkelers can enjoy Caleta Buena. The **Museo Playa Girón** is worth the visit for Cuba's take on the Bay of Pigs story.

When traveling east–west or vice versa, take your pick of the super-fast Autopista, which skips all towns and runs through flat agricultural lands from Havana to Santa Clara, or the winding Carretera Central, which runs north of and parallel to the Autopista, linking the city of Matanzas with Santa Clara and passing through dusty old country towns.

Matanzas and Vicinity

MATANZAS

The city of Matanzas (pop. 142,000) lies within the deep, 11-kilometer-long, five-kilometer-wide Bahía de Matanzas. The city was founded at the end of the 17th century on the site of an Indian village, Yacayo. In 1694 a castle—Castillo de San Severino—was initiated to guard the bay. A decade later lots were distributed among settlers from the Canary Islands.

During the 18th century, Matanzas grew as a port city exporting beef, salted pork, coffee, and tobacco. During the the mid-19th century, the region accounted for more than 50 percent of national sugar production. The city was a center for the importation of slaves and established itself as Cuba's most important center of cult religions such as Regla Iyessá and Regla Arará (Matanzas remains Cuba's most potent center for *santería* and other African-derived religions, and for Afro-Cuban music and dance). Many white citizens grew immensely wealthy on the sugar and slave trades, and a fashionable café society evolved. Matanzas sponsored the arts and sciences. In 1828 the citizens began printing Cuba's first newspaper. A philharmonic society and a library were formed, followed by three theaters, and the city quickly acquired its Athens of Cuba moniker.

More than 20 Spanish galleons lie at the bottom of Matanzas Bay, sunk by Dutch admiral Piet Heyn in 1628. Later, Matanzas became a battleground during the Wars of Independence and was even bombarded by the USS *New York.* Today the bay is filled with oil tankers and freighters waiting to be loaded with sugar. Tall chimney stacks that rise above the bay belong to a geothermal, a chemical factory (pouring out insipid, sulfurous fumes), and a paper mill that uses *bagazo* (crushed cane fiber). Nonetheless, the town's setting is pleasing, in the cusp of gentle hills.

East of the city, the Vía Blanca (Matanzas–Varadero Expressway) hugs the coast. Oil derricks by the water's edge suck forth black gold from atop coral platforms.

Orientation

Matanzas lies on the western and southern bayshore and is divided by the Ríos Yumurí and San Juan into three distinct sections. To the north is **Reparto Versalles,** a late colonial addition climbing the gentle slopes. The predominantly 19th-century **Pueblo Nuevo** extends south of the Río San Juan along flatlands. The historic city center—**Reparto Matanzas**—lies between them and rises gradually to the west. The 20th-century **Reparto Playa,** to the east, fronts the bay.

The Vía Blanca from Havana descends into town from the north and skirts the Reparto Playa bayshore as Calle General Betancourt (Calle 129) en route to Varadero.

The town is laid out in a near-perfect grid. Odd-numbered streets run east–west, even-numbered streets north–south. Many streets have both a name *and* a number; most also have *two* names, one pre- and one postrevolution. For example, Calle 79 is also called Calle Contreras, though locals still refer to it as Calle Bonifacio Byrne. Contreras and Calle 83 (Milanés) run west from the Vía Blanca six blocks to the main square, Plaza de la Libertad. Calle Santa Teresita (Calle 290) runs perpendicular to the west, and Calle Ayuntamiento (Calle 288) to the east.

The first three digits of a house number refer to the nearest cross street.

For a fabulous view over town, follow Calle Contreras uphill westward from Plaza de la Libertad to **Parque René Fraga,** which contains a bronze bust of Bonifacio Byrne, National Poet (1861–1936). En route, turn right (north) onto Calle 306 and follow it to **Ermita de Monserrate** (Monserrate Hermitage), a *mirador* offering spectacular views over both Matanzas and the Valle de Yumurí.

Plaza de la Libertad

The old parade ground (once known as Plaza de Armas) is a pleasant place to sit under the shade trees and watch the world go by. At its heart is a granite edifice topped by the **Monumento a José Martí,** with life-size bronze figures of Martí and the Indian maiden breaking free of her chains. Buildings of architectural note include the much-deteriorated **Casa de la Cultura** in the former Lyceum Club, and the **Biblioteca** in the former Casino Club, both on the north side. The former city hall on Calle Ayuntamiento today houses the **Poder Popular,** on the east side.

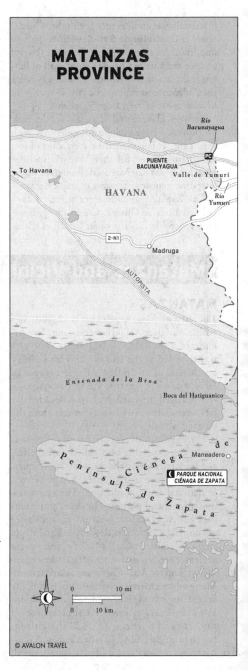

MATANZAS PROVINCE

To Havana

HAVANA

Río Bacunayagua

PUENTE BACUNAYAGUA

Valle de Yumurí

Río Yumurí

Madruga

AUTOPISTA

Ensenada de la Broa

Boca del Hatiguanico

Maneadero

Península de Zapata

Ciénega de

PARQUE NACIONAL CIÉNAGA DE ZAPATA

0   10 mi

0   10 km

© AVALON TRAVEL

SCUBA DIVING AND SNORKELING

WRECK OF RUSSIAN PATROL BOAT AND AN-24 AIRPLANE

WRECK OF BARCO HUNDIDO

Cayo Piedra

RESERVA ECOLÓGICA VARAHICACOS

BARRERA CORAL Y ÁREA PROTEGIDA LAGUNA DE MAYA

LAS AMÉRICAS

Punta Hicacos

Cayo Blanco

Cayo   Punta   Arenas

Bahía de Matanzas

JUAN GUALBERTO GÓMEZ AIRPORT

Varadero

Santa Marta

Bahía de Cárdenas

Bahía de Santa Clara

La Teja

CASTILLITO DE SAN SEVERINO

Carbonera

VIA BLANCA

CUEVA DE SATURNO

PC

Cárdenas

Matanzas

TROPICANA

CASTILLO DE MORRILLO/ PARQUE TURÍSTICO RÍO CANIMAR

PARQUE ECHEVARRÍA

LA ARBOLEDA

CUEVAS DE BELLAMAR

Limonar

Canal del Rogue

Martí

3-1-3

3-1-3

Coliseo

CARRETERA

San Miguel de los Baños

Máximo Gomez

3-N1

3-1-2

Union de Reyes

Jovellanos

CENTRAL

Perico

M A T A N Z A S

Colón

Pedro Betancourt

Los Arabos

3-N1

Agramonte

3-1-2

Buenavista

NACIONAL

Jagüey Grande

Calimete

To Santa Clara

Río Hatiguanico

Z a p a t a

PARRADA DE CARRETERA

Australia

FINCA FIESTA CAMPESINA

MUSEO MEMORIAL COMANDANCIA FAR

Aguada de Pasajeros

CIENFUEGOS

Santo Tomás

LA BOCA DE GUAMÁ

Laguna del Tesoro

Playa Larga

MC

Yaguaramas

Laguna de las Salinas

Bahía

de

Canal de Soplillar

Cienfuegos

CUEVA DE LOS PECES

Cayo Ramona

San Blás

Cochinos

Girón

MUSEO PLAYA GIRÓN

Playa Girón

CALETA BUENA

MILITARY BARRIER

Guasasas

Cayos   Blanco   del   Sur

Dive Site

MATANZAS

MATANZAS

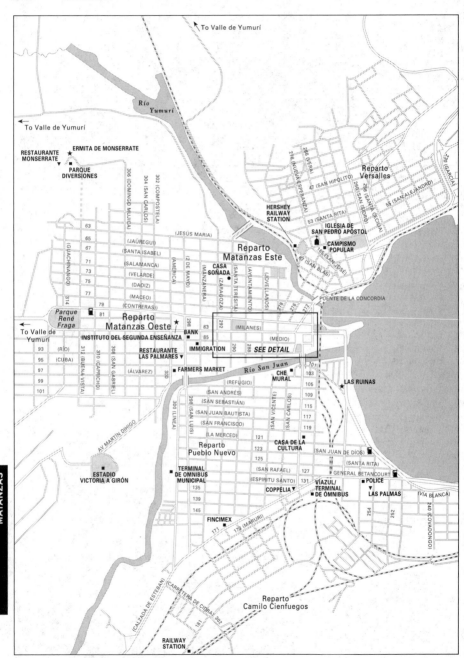

To Valle de Yumurí

Río Yumurí

To Valle de Yumurí

RESTAURANTE MONSERRATE
ERMITA DE MONSERRATE
PARQUE DIVERSIONES

306 (DOMINGO MUJICA)
304 (SAN CARLOS)
302 (COMPOSTELA)

63
65
67
71
73
75
77
79
81

(JESÚS MARIA)
(JAÚREGUI)
(SANTA ISABEL)
(SALAMANCA)
(VELARDE)
(DAOIZ)
(MACEO)
(CONTRERAS)

(GUACHINANGO)
314
(AMÉRICA)
(2 DE MAYO)
(MANZANERA)
(ZARAGOZA)
SANTA TERESITA
(AYUNTAMIENTO)
(JOVELLANOS)

286 (VERA)
218 (NUEVA ESPERANZA)
47 (SAN HIPÓLITO)
53 (SANTA RITA)
256 (SANTA CECILIA)
256 (SAN ISIDRO)
58 (SAN ALEJANDRO)
330 (GARCÍA)

Reparto Versalles

HERSHEY RAILWAY STATION

CASA SOÑADA

Reparto Matanzas Este

IGLESIA DE SAN PEDRO APÓSTOL
CAMPISMO POPULAR
155 (SAN JOSÉ)
67 (SAN BLAS)

PUENTE DE LA CONCORDIA

Parque René Fraga

To Valle de Yumurí

Reparto Matanzas Oeste

BANK

INSTITUTO DEL SEGUNDA ENSEÑANZA

IMMIGRATION

RESTAURANTE LAS PALMARES

FARMERS MARKET

83
85
298
292
290
288
(MILANES)
(MEDIO)
SEE DETAIL

312 (BUENA VISTA)
310 (CAPRICHO)
308 (SAN GABRIEL)

93 (RÍO)
95 (CUBA)
97
99
101

(ÁLVAREZ)
300

Río San Juan

CHE MURAL

LAS RUINAS

103
105
109
115
117
119

(REFUGIO)
(SAN ANDRÉS)
298 (SAN LUIS)
(SAN SEBASTIÁN)
(SAN JUAN BAUTISTA)
(SAN FRANCISCO)
(LA MERCED)

300 (LÍNEA)

(SAN VICENTE)
(SAN CARLOS)

121
123
125
127
131
135
139
145

CASA DE LA CULTURA

(SAN JUAN DE DIOS)
(SANTA RITA)
GENERAL BETANCOURT

Reparto Pueblo Nuevo

AV MARTÍN DIHIGO

ESTADIO VICTORIA A GIRÓN

TERMINAL DE OMNIBUS MUNICIPAL

(SAN RAFAEL)
(ESPÍRITU SANTO)

COPPELIA

VÍAZUL/ TERMINAL DE ÓMNIBUS

POLICE
LAS PALMAS

(VÍA BLANCA)

254
252
240 (COVADONGA)

FINCIMEX

171
179 (MÁRURI)

(CALZADA DE ESTEBAN)
(CARRETERA DE CIDRA)
302
181

Reparto Camilo Cienfuegos

RAILWAY STATION

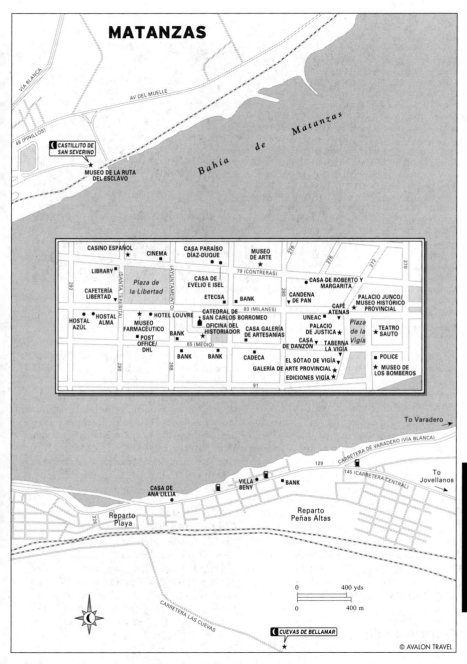

statue of Cuba's Indian maiden breaking free of her chains, Plaza de la Libertad

On the south side, the **Museo Farmacéutico** (Pharmaceutical Museum, Calle 83 #49501, tel. 045/24-3179, daily 10 A.M.–5 P.M., CUC3) is a wood-paneled pharmacy dating from 1882, when a pharmacy—La Botica Francesa—was opened by a French pharmacist, Trilet. It functioned as a family-owned pharmacy until 1964, when it metamorphosed into a museum preserving the store just as it was the day it closed, with salves, dried herbs, pharmaceutical instruments, and original porcelain jars neatly arranged on the shelves. Out back a laboratory contains copper distilleries. Note the bright red and orange *vitrales*. Originally they were red, white, and blue—the colors of France—but Spanish authorities insisted that they be replaced with Spain's national colors.

One block east, the **Museo de Arte** (Calle 9 #28007, e/ 280 y 282, tel. 045/29-0735, Tues.–Sat. 10 A.M.–5 P.M., Sun. 8 A.M.–noon, CUC1) displays a modest collection of art and antiques.

Catedral de San Carlos Borromeo

This restored cathedral (Calle 282, e/ 83 y 85, Mon.–Fri. 8 A.M.–noon and 3–5 P.M., Sun. 9 A.M.–noon), one block southeast of Plaza de la Libertad, was built in 1878. Today the opulently frescoed ceiling gleams. The curator has an office at the side of the church (Tues.–Sun.).

The tiny **Plaza de la Iglesia** fronting the church has a bronze statue of local poet José Jacinto Milanés (1814–1863), whose former home is now the **Archivo Histórico** (Calle 83 #28013, e/ 280 y 282, tel. 045/24-4212). One block east, the **Asociación de Artesanas y Artistas** (Calle 85 #26, e/ 280 y 282, tel. 045/25-3657, Mon.–Sat. 9 A.M.–5 P.M.) displays art.

Plaza de la Vigía

The city's other plaza of note is four blocks east of Plaza de la Libertad, at the junction of Milanés and Calle 270, immediately north of the **Puente Calixto García** over the Río San Juan. At its heart is a marble statue of an unnamed freedom fighter during the Wars of Independence. The **Teatro Sauto** (tel. 045/24-2721 or 2803223, Tues.–Sat. 9 A.M.–5 P.M., Sun. 2–4 P.M., CUC2 guided), considered one of Cuba's preeminent neoclassical buildings, was built in 1863 at the height of the city's prosperity. In its heyday it attracted the likes of Sarah Bernhardt, Enrico Caruso, and Anna Pavlova. The three-tiered auditorium with circular balconies supported by thin bronze columns is heartbreaking in its dereliction, yet it still hosts performances on weekend evenings.

On the plaza's north side is the Palacio de Junco, a sky-blue 1840 mansion housing the city's **Museo Histórico Provincial** (Calles 83 y 91, tel. 045/24-3195, Tues.–Sat. 9 A.M.–noon and 1–5 P.M., Sun. 9 A.M.–noon, CUC2), which traces the city's development. The antique furnishings, clocks, and weaponry are impressive.

South of the theater, the neoclassical fire station houses the **Museo de los Bomberos** (Mon.–Fri. 10 A.M.–5 P.M., Sat. 1–5 P.M.), displaying antique fire engines; the oldest, from London, dates from 1864.

Facing the fire station is the **Galería de Arte Provincial** (Calle 272, Calles 85 y 91, Mon.–Fri. 9 A.M.–5 P.M., Sat. 10 A.M.–2 P.M., Sun. 9 A.M.–1 P.M., free). Next door, the **Ediciones Vigía** (Plaza de la Vigias, e/ 85 y 91, Mon.–Fri. 9 A.M.–6 P.M., CUC1) produces handmade books in limited editions.

Castillito de San Severino

This partially restored fortress (Carretera del Puerto), completed in 1745 on the west side of the bay, is the most intriguing site in town. A cannon dating from 1775 stands by the entrance gate, and a brace of cannons still point across the harbor. Slaves were landed here and held in dungeons, awaiting sale and transfer to sugar plantations. During the 19th century, Cuban nationalists were imprisoned here; according to a plaque, 61 patriots were executed here, and you can see the bullet holes in the moat on the south side of the castle. Today, the fortress houses the excellent little **Museo de la Ruta del Esclavo** (tel. 045/28-3259, Tues.–Sat. 9 A.M.–4:30 P.M., Sun. 9 A.M.–noon, entrance CUC2, with guide CUC5, camera CUC1). One room regales visitors with local pre-Columbian and colonial history. The Sala

de Orishas is dedicated to Afro-Cuban religions and displays life-size figures of the *orishas*. A third exhibit is dedicated to the legacy of slavery.

The castle stands at the east end of Reparto Versalles, accessed from downtown via the **Puente de la Concordia,** built in 1878 over the Río Yumurí with decorative Babylonian-style columns at each end. The region was settled last century by French-Haitian refugees and is pinned by the twin-towered **Iglesia de San Pedro Apóstol** (Calles 57 and 270).

Cuevas de Bellamar

These caves (tel. 045/25-3538 or 045/25-3190, Tues.–Sun. 9:30 A.M.–5 P.M., CUC5 for one-hour guided tour, cameras and videos CUC5), in the hills about three kilometers southeast of downtown Matanzas, form one of Cuba's largest cave systems. A 159-step staircase leads to more than 3,000 meters of galleries full of stalactites and stalagmites, including the 80-meter-long, 26-meter-high Gothic Temple, plus gurgling streams and shimmering flower-like crystal formations known as dahlias. A small museum describes the geological formations. Tours (45 minutes) depart at 9:30 A.M., 10:30 A.M., 11:30 A.M., 1:15 P.M., 2:15 P.M., 3:15 P.M., and 4:15 P.M. There's a thatched restaurant. Avoid weekends.

Bus #16 departs Calle 300 (esq. 83), and will drop you at Calle 226 from where it's a 30-minute uphill hike along the road to the caves (cars will need to take Calle 254).

Valle de Yumurí

The eight-kilometer-wide Yumurí Valley is held in the cusp of 150-meter-high limestone cliffs—the Cuchillas de Habana–Matanzas—immediately west of Matanzas, from which it is separated by a high ridge. The hills form a natural amphitheater hidden from the modern world. Two rivers, the Yumurí and Bacunayagua, thread their silvered way to the sea through a landscape as archetypically Cuban as any you will find on the island.

The Hershey Train passes through the valley.

A SUGAR OF A JOURNEY

Rail journeys hold a particular magic, none more so in Cuba than the Hershey Train, which runs lazily between Casablanca and Matanzas year-round, four times a day.

Before the Revolution, the Hershey estates belonging to the Pennsylvania-based chocolate company occupied 69 square miles of lush canefields around a modern sugar-factory town (now called Camilo Cienfuegos), with a baseball field, movie theater, amusements, and a hotel.

At its peak, the estate had 19 steam locomotives. Their sparks, however, constituted a serious fire hazard, so they were replaced with seven 60-ton electric locomotives built especially for the Hershey-Cuban Railroad. Milton

Hershey also introduced a three-car passenger train service between Havana and Matanzas every hour, stopping at Hershey. Alas, the diminutive vermilion MU-train locomotive that looked like it could have fallen from the pages of a story about Thomas, the little "live" engine, was replaced in 1998 with antique Spanish cars.

The train winds in and out among palm-studded hills, speeds along the coast within sight of the Atlantic, then slips past swathes of sugarcane through the Yumurí Valley. Two hours into the journey, you'll arrive at a station still bearing the Hershey sign. You're now in the heart of the old Hershey sugar factory. After a mesmerizing four-hour journey, you finally arrive at the Matanzas station.

Entertainment and Events

In mid-October, the Teatro Sauto hosts the **Festival del Bailador Rumbero,** with performances by Cuba's finest Afro-Cuban rumba bands, including the homegrown Los Muñequitos. The **Festival del Danzón** (tel. 045/24-3512) is a biennial held in November, with workshops and competitions of *danzón* and folk dance.

The barebones **Casa de Danzón** (Calle Medio #27405, e/ 280 y 282, tel. 045/28-7061) has programs Saturday at 8 P.M. and Sunday at 2 P.M. Afro-Cuban musicians also play the **Casa de la Cultura Bonifacio Byrne** (Calle 272 #11916, e/ 119 y 121, tel. 045/29-2709), with programs most evenings.

Teatro Sauto (Plaza de la Vigía, tel. 045/24-2721, CUC5) also hosts classical and folkloric performances Friday–Sunday evenings plus Sunday at 3 P.M.

Resembling a Boston Irish bar, the **Taberna La Vigía** (Calle 85, esq. Plaza de la Vigía, tel. 045/25-3076, ext. 106, 8:30 A.M.–1 A.M.) causes a double-take. This historic venue is clean, well-run, and serves a mean pint of beer in real pint glasses (CUC1.25). This is Cuba? Below, the basement **El Sotano de Vigía** nightclub (Mon.–Fri. 9:30 P.M.–2 A.M.,

Sat.–Sun. 6:30 P.M.–2 A.M.) has a varied program, including classical music (Monday), Spanish night (Wednesday), romantic music (Thursday), and contemporary sounds Saturday and Sunday.

The hot dance spot on weekends is Artex's open-air **Las Palmas** (tel. 045/25-3252, Mon.–Wed. noon–midnight, Fri.–Sun. noon–2 A.M.), a.k.a. "El Palacio" because it's next to the Palacio de Los Matrimonios. It has live music nightly.

Las Ruinas (Vía Blanca y Calle 101, tel. 045/25-3387, 24 hours) has live music and disco Friday–Sunday at 9 P.M. and recorded music on other nights.

For sexy Las Vegas-style cabaret, head to **Tropicana Matanzas** (Autopista Varadero, Km 4.5, tel./fax 045/26-5555, reservas@trpivar.co.cu, Tues.–Sat. 10 P.M., CUC35, including a half-bottle of rum). A separate karaoke bar with dance floor is the hottest ticket in town for hip locals (10 P.M.–3 A.M., CUC.2.50); the dirty dancing here seems straight out of a X-rated hip-hop video.

Matanzas's baseball team—the Matanzas—play at **Estadio Victoria a Girón** (Av. Martín Dihigo), one kilometer west of town, October–May.

Accommodations

Amazingly, there are no hotels in town. There are more than 100 *casas particulares* to choose from, though; those listed are air-conditioned.

One block from Plaza Independencia, **Hostal Alma** (Calle 83 #29008 altos, e/ 290 y 292, tel. 045/24-2449, hostalalma@gmail.com, CUC20–25) is run by a pleasant lady. Two rooms have high ceilings, fans, radio-cassette players, fridges, and modern private bathrooms with hair dryers. The vast upstairs lounge has a balcony. Next door, and owned by the same family, is **Hostal Azul** (Calle 83 #29012, e/ 290 y 292, tel. 045/24-2449, hostalazul.cu@gmail.com, CUC20), a huge colonial home with two simply furnished rooms with small modern bathrooms.

Huge (and tasty) dinners are reason enough to stay at **Casa de Roberto y Margarita** (Calle 79 #27608, e/ 276 y 280, tel. 045/24-2577, CUC20), a colonial home with two spacious rooms with floor-to-ceiling windows opening to a courtyard. They share a hot-water bathroom.

Seeking an independent apartment? **Casa Soñada** (Santa Teresa #6701, esq. Santa Isabel, tel. 045/24-2761, mandy_rent_habitaciones@yahoo.com, CUC25) is a colonial home with a spacious, airy lounge. The apartment is to the rear with a mezzanine bedroom, a kitchenette, and clean tub-shower.

OK, it's upstairs, but 🕮 **Casa de Evelio e Isel** (Calle 79 #28201, e/ 282 y 288, tel. 045/24-3090 or 5281-4966, CUC20) gets my thumbs up. This condo home has two rooms furnished with good mattresses and modern accoutrements, including refrigerator, fan, TV, safe, and private hot-water bathrooms. You can join Evelio and Isel in their TV lounge with stereo system. This building has several other *casas particulares*. Nearby, **Casa Paraíso Díaz-Duque** (Calle 79 #28205, e/ 282 y 288, tel. 045/24-3397, CUC20) has two cross-ventilated, air-conditioned rooms that share a modern bathroom.

In the Reparto Playa district, **Casa de Ana Lilia** (Calle General Betancourt 129/#21603, e/ 216 y 218, tel. 045/26-1576, CUC25) is a bayfront 1940s home with two spacious rooms with modern bathrooms. A rear garden gets the breezes. Nearby, **Villa Beny** (Calle 129 #20813, e/ Abra y San Miguel, tel. 045/29-3800, CUC20) is a similar option.

The **Horizontes Casa del Valle** (Carretera de Chirno, Km 2, Valle del Yumurí, tel. 045/25-3584), in the Valle de Yumuri, was closed to tourists at last visit.

Food

Matanzas has no legal *paladares*. Fortunately, it has one of Cuba's best regional restaurants: 🕮 **Taberna La Vigía** (Calle 85, esq. Plaza de la Vigí, tel. 045/25-3076, ext. 106, 8:30 A.M.–1 A.M.), serving good burgers (CUC1–3), best washed down with draft beer. One block north, the air-conditioned **Café Atenas** (Calle 82, esq. 272, tel. 045/25-3493, daily 8 A.M.–11 P.M.) serves simple pizzas, sandwiches, and snacks.

The only other worthy eatery is the hilltop **Restaurante Monserrate** (no tel., daily noon–10:30 P.M.), at the end of Calle 306. This modestly elegant open-air eatery serves a limited *criollo* menu (all dishes CUC5 and under). Come for the views.

You can buy groceries at **Mercado San Luis** (Calles 298 y 291) and produce at the **Mercado La Plaza** farmers market (Calles 97 y 298), where peso stalls sell fried foods and *batidos*.

Information and Services

The **post office** (Calles 85 and 290, tel. 045/24-3231, Mon.–Sat. 7 A.M.–8 P.M.) has DHL service. **Etecsa** (Calle 83, esq. 282, daily 8:30 A.M.–7:30 P.M.) has Internet and international telephones.

Bandec (Calle 85, e/ 282 y 288, tel. 045/24-2781) and **Banco Financiero Internacional** (Calles 85 y 298, tel. 045/25-3400, Mon.–Fri. 8 A.M.–3 P.M.) have branches. And you can change foreign currency at **Cadeca** (Calle 286, e/ 83 y 85, Mon.–Sat. 8 A.M.–6 P.M., Sun. 8 A.M.–noon).

Hospital Faustino Pérez (tel. 045/25-3426) is on the Carretera Central about two kilometers southwest of town.

MATANZAS

© CHRISTOPHER P. BAKER

Taberna La Vigía, Matanzas

Getting There and Away

BY AIR

International flights arrive and depart the **Juan Gualberto Gómez International Airport** (tel. 045/61-2133), 20 kilometers east of Matanzas.

BY BUS

Buses operate to and from the **Terminal de Ómnibus Nacional** (Calles 131 and 272, tel. 045/29-1473) on the south side of town. **Víazul** buses (tel. 045/29-2943) depart Havana for Matanzas at 8 A.M., 10 A.M., noon, and 6 P.M. They depart from Varadero westbound at 8 A.M., 11:25 A.M., 3:30 P.M., and 6 P.M. Buses depart Matanzas for Havana at 9 A.M., 12:15 P.M., 4:30 P.M., and 7 P.M., and for Varadero at 10:15 A.M., 12:10 P.M., 2:10 P.M., and 8:20 P.M.

The **Terminal de Óminibus Municipal** (Calles 298 y 127, tel. 045/29-2701) serves destinations throughout Matanzas Province.

Once on the ground, a taxi will cost about CUC80 one-way between Matanzas and Havana and about CUC40 between Matanzas and Varadero.

BY TRAIN

The rail station (Calle 181, tel. 045/29-9590) is on the south side of town. All trains between Havana and Santiago de Cuba stop here, calling at provincial capitals en route: Camagüey (CUC22), Santa Clara (CUC6.50), Sancti Spíritus (CUC11), Ciego de Ávila (CUC14), Las Tunas (CUC20), and Holguín (CUC24). Eight trains serve Havana (CUC4) daily.

The slow Hershey Train (CUC2.80) from Havana departs the Estación de Casablanca (Carretera de los Cocos, tel. 07/862-4888), on the north side of Havana harbor at 4:43 and 8:35 A.M. and 12:39, 5:21, and 9:17 P.M., arriving Matanzas 3.5 hours later. Return trains depart **Terminal Hershey** (Calles 55 y 67, tel. 045/24-4805), in Reparto Versalles, three blocks northeast of the Río Yumurí bridge at 7:28 and 11:28 A.M., 3:23 and 8:16 P.M., and 12:10 A.M.

Getting Around

The **Matanzas Bus Tour** (CUC10, eight times daily, 9:30 A.M. to 5:15 P.M.) leaves from Plaza de la Libertad and makes a simple circuit along

Contreras to Parque Reve Fraga and down Calle José, then on to Varadero.

Bus #16 runs to the Terminal de Ómnibus Municipal from Calle 79, one block west of the main square. Most locals get around by *coches* (horse-drawn cabs) and *bici-taxis.*

There are gas stations on the Vía Blanca, east of downtown. You can rent cars from **Havanautos** (Calle 129, esq. 208, tel. 045/25-3294).

RÍO CANIMAR AND PLAYA CORAL

Four kilometers east of Matanzas, immediately beyond the bridge over the Río Canimar, a road to the left loops downhill into **Parque Turístico Río Canimar** (tel./fax 045/26-1516, daily 9 A.M.–5 P.M.), with a tiny beach and restaurant, and a tri-level disco boat (Mon., Wed., and Sat. 4 P.M.–close, CUC2).

A small fort, **Castillo El Morrillo** (Tues.–Sun. 10 A.M.–5 P.M., CUC1), stands over the west bank of the rivermouth. Built in 1720, it is now a museum dedicated to revolutionary leaders Antonio Guiteras Holmes (1906–1935), founder in 1934 of the radical student group Joven Cuba (Young Cuba), and Venezuela revolutionary Carlos Aponte Hernández (1901–1935), who were executed nearby by General Machado's henchmen. They are buried in the fort. Prehistoric artifacts and Indian remains are displayed upstairs. Guides give a spiel. Bus #16 departs Calle 300 (esq. 83) in Matanzas and will drop you here.

Immediately east of the rivermouth, a broad peninsula bulges into the Atlantic. A coast road loops around the peninsula, passing **Playa Coral** (daily 8 A.M.–5 P.M.), a tiny beach popular with excursion groups from Varadero. It's part of the Reserva Barrera Coralina y Laguna de Mayo, which protects an offshore barrier reef and, onshore, a lagoon. It has lounge chairs, beach volleyball, and a simple thatch restaurant. The Matanzas Bus Tour passes by here eight times daily.

Recreation

Parque Turístico Río Canimar rents Jet Skis (CUC15 15 minutes, CUC45 one hour, CUC140 six hours). A 45-minute boat trip upriver (CUC10, or CUC20 with snorkeling, plus horseback riding and lunch) includes a visit to Cueva La Eloísa (a flooded cave where you may swim) and Arboleda, a *finca* with crocodiles, buffalo, and hiking trails. You can book this excursion through **Cubamar** (tel. 045/66-8855).

You can snorkel (CUC5) at **Playa Coral,** which has a dive center (tel. 045/66-8063). The center also has trips to **Cueva de Saturno** (tel. 045/25-3272, daily 8 A.M.–6 P.M., CUC3 entrance, CUC5 extra for snorkeling), one kilometer south of the Vía Blanca on the road to Varadero airport about 10 kilometers east of Matanzas. The 17-kilometer-long cave system with a lagoon and dripstones is touted for sightseers, but they're less impressive than Cuevas de Bellamar. A small museum explains the geology.

Accommodations

The **Campismo Canimar Abajo** (tel. 045/26-1516), on the north bank of the Río Canimar, and **Campismo Faro de Maya** (tel. 045/26-3129, CUC5 per person), on the eastern side of the Bahía de Matanzas, about 16 kilometers east of town, have basic cabins. Neither was taking foreigners at last visit. Check with **Campismo Popular** (Calle 270, e/ Vera y Santa Cristina, tel. 045/24-3951) in Matanzas.

Islazul's **Hotel Canimao** (tel. 045/26-1014, fax 045/26-1037, comercial@canimao.co.cu, CUC12 s, CUC18 d low season, CUC15 s, CUC18 d high season), off the Vía Blanca about eight kilometers east of Matanzas, is a pleasant no-frills bargain. The 158 air-conditioned rooms are modestly furnished, with satellite TV, safes, and modern bathrooms. The hotel, adjacent to the Tropicana nightclub, has a swimming pool.

Varadero

"In all the beaches in Cuba the sand was made of grated silver," says a character in Robert Fernández's *Raining Backwards*, "though in Varadero it was also mixed with diamond dust." Varadero, 34 kilometers east of Matanzas and 140 kilometers east of Havana, is Cuba's tourist mecca, the artificial Cuba frequented by budget-minded Canadian and European charter groups.

There are more than 60 hotels, and the gaps are being filled in. All-inclusive resorts dominate the scene. No private restaurants or room rentals are permitted. Varadero lacks vitality. At night the onshore breeze brings rotten-egg fumes from the petrochemical works across Bahía de Cárdenas (usually to the western end of Varadero). More importantly, it bears no relation to Cuban reality. The fully stocked stores belie the shortages affecting ordinary Cubans; few tourists know that the Cuban service staff in hotels are paid less than US$1 per day in near-worthless pesos. And although the resort spans a Cuban village, visitation by Cubans from outside the area is regulated, social interactions between Cubans and foreigners are minimal, and local residents pretty much keep to themselves.

Strictly speaking, Varadero is the name of the *beach* area. It lies on the ocean-facing side of an 20-kilometer-long peninsula called Península de Hicacos, which encloses Bahía de Cárdenas and is separated from the mainland by the Laguna de Paso Malo. The peninsula is only 1.2 kilometers at its widest point. It slants to the northeast, where its tip—Punta Hicacos—is the northernmost point in Cuba. The scrub-covered eastern half is broken by a series of flat-topped mesas and low-lying raised coral platforms pitted with sinkholes and caves.

The main beach, Playa Mayor, is a virtually unbroken 11.5-kilometer-long swath that widens eastward, where most of the deluxe hotels sit over their own "private" beaches. The beaches shelve gently into waters the color of a Maxfield Parrish painting. A coral reef lies offshore, good for diving (principally wreck-diving). Water sports abound.

HISTORY

The Spanish settled the region around 1587, when charcoal and salt-pork enterprises supplied Spanish fleets. A small community of fisherfolk later sprouted on the south shore, in the village today known as Las Moralas. In the 1870s, families from Cárdenas built wooden summer homes and developed the beach with boardinghouses for summer vacationers.

© CHRISTOPHER P. BAKER

beach with Meliá Varadero in the background

Rowing regattas evolved, necessitating more lodging, and the first hotel—the Varadero Hotel—opened in 1915.

In 1926, U.S. industrialist Irénée Du Pont bought much of the peninsula and built himself a large estate, complete with golf course. Other wealthy *norteamericanos* followed, albeit in less grandiose style (Du Pont, who had paid four centavos a square meter, sold them the land for 120 pesos a square meter). Al Capone bought a house here. So did the dictator Fulgencio Batista. By the 1950s, Varadero had a casino and was a favored hangout of Hollywood stars, high-class prostitutes, and

mobsters. On the eve of the Revolution, much of the peninsula was in private hands. The Castro government likes to claim that Cubans were banned from the beach, but in reality this was only on privately owned sectors, and villagers had access to the long swath in front of the village. Ironically, during the 1990s only Cubans who lived in the village were permitted access to Varadero.

ORIENTATION

There is only one way onto the island-peninsula: the bridge over Laguna de Paso Malo, at the extreme west end of the Hicacos Peninsula

MATANZAS

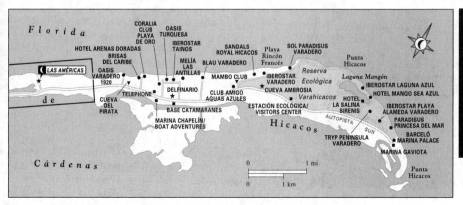

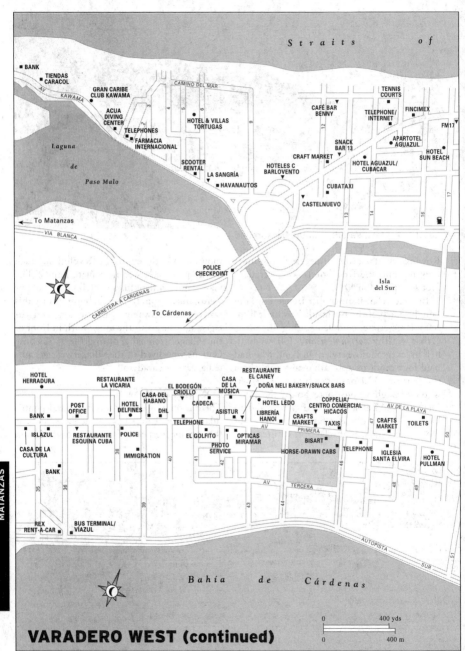

MATANZAS

VARADERO WEST (continued)

Straits of

BANK
TIENDAS CARACOL
AV KAWAMA
GRAN CARIBE CLUB KAWAMA
CAMINO DEL MAR
ACUA DIVING CENTER
TELEPHONES
FARMACIA INTERNACIONAL
HOTEL & VILLAS TORTUGAS
SCOOTER RENTAL
LA SANGRÍA
HAVANAUTOS
Laguna de Paso Malo
To Matanzas
VIA BLANCA
POLICE CHECKPOINT
CARRETERA A CÁRDENAS
To Cárdenas

CAFÉ BAR BENNY
TENNIS COURTS
TELEPHONE/ INTERNET
FINCIMEX
FM17
SNACK BAR 13
APARTOTEL AGUAZUL
HOTEL SUN BEACH
CRAFT MARKET
HOTELES C BARLOVENTO
HOTEL AGUAZUL/ CUBACAR
CUBATAXI
CASTELNUEVO
Isla del Sur

HOTEL HERRADURA
RESTAURANTE LA VICARIA
RESTAURANTE EL CANEY
DOÑA NELI BAKERY/SNACK BARS
EL BODEGÓN CRIOLLO
CASA DE LA MÚSICA
CASA DEL HABANO
COPPELIA/ CENTRO COMERCIAL HICACOS
AV DE LA PLAYA
BANK
POST OFFICE
HOTEL DELFINES
DHL
CADECA
ASISTUR
HOTEL LEDO
LIBRERÍA HANOI
CRAFTS MARKET
TAXIS
CRAFTS MARKET
TOILETS
TELEPHONE
AV PRIMERA
ISLAZUL
RESTAURANTE ESQUINA CUBA
POLICE
EL GOLFITO
PHOTO SERVICE
OPTICAS MIRAMAR
BISART
HORSE-DRAWN CABS
TELEPHONE
IGLESIA SANTA ELVIRA
HOTEL PULLMAN
CASA DE LA CULTURA
IMMIGRATION
BANK
AV TERCERA
REX RENT-A-CAR
BUS TERMINAL/ VIAZUL
AUTOPISTA SUR
Bahía de Cárdenas

0   400 yds
0   400 m

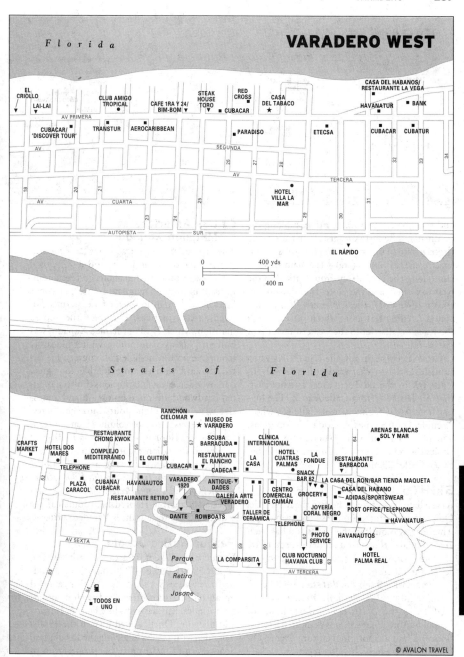

VARADERO WEST

Florida

EL CRIOLLO ▼

LAI-LAI ▼

CLUB AMIGO TROPICAL ●

CAFE 1RA Y 24/ BIM-BOM ▼

STEAK HOUSE TORO ▼

RED CROSS ■ CUBACAR

CASA DEL TABACO ★

CASA DE LOS HABANOS/ RESTAURANTE LA VEGA

HAVANATUR ■   ■ BANK

CUBACAR/ 'DISCOVER TOUR' ■

TRANSTUR   AEROCARIBBEAN

■ PARADISO

ETECSA ■

CUBACAR ■   CUBATUR ■

AV PRIMERA

SEGUNDA

AV

TERCERA

HOTEL VILLA LA MAR ●

AUTOPISTA   SUR

▼ EL RÁPIDO

0 ————— 400 yds
0 ————— 400 m

Straits   of   Florida

RANCHÓN CIELOMAR ▼

MUSEO DE VARADERO ★

RESTAURANTE CHONG KWOK

SCUBA BARRACUDA ▼

CLÍNICA INTERNACIONAL

ARENAS BLANCAS SOL Y MAR ●

CRAFTS MARKET ■

HOTEL DOS MARES ●

COMPLEJO MEDITERRÁNEO ■

EL QUITRÍN ■

RESTAURANTE EL RANCHO ■

LA CASA ■

HOTEL CUATRAS PALMAS ▼

LA FONDUE ▼

RESTAURANTE BARBACOA ■

TELEPHONE ■

CUBACAR ■

CADECA ▼

SNACK BAR 62 ●

LA CASA DEL RON/BAR TIENDA MAQUETA

PLAZA CARACOL

CUBANA/ CUBACAR

HAVANAUTOS

VARADERO 1920

ANTIGUE-DADES ▼

CENTRO COMERCIAL DE CAIMÁN

GROCERY ■

CASA DEL HABANO ●

ADIDAS/SPORTSWEAR ■

RESTAURANTE RETIRO ▼

GALERÍA ARTE VERADERO

POST OFFICE/TELEPHONE ■

DANTE   ROWBOATS

TALLER DE CERÁMICA

JOYERÍA CORAL NEGRO ■

HAVANATUR ■

TELEPHONE ■

AV SEXTA

PHOTO SERVICE ■

HAVANAUTOS ■

Parque Retiro Josone

LA COMPARSITA ▼

CLUB NOCTURNO HAVANA CLUB ▼

HOTEL PALMA REAL ●

AV TERCERA

TODOS EN UNO ■

MATANZAS

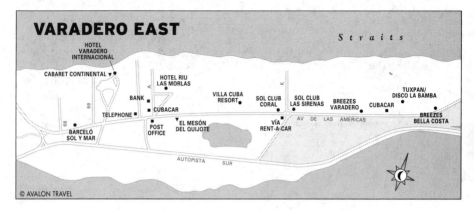

and from where two roads run east along the peninsula. The fast Autopista Sur runs along the bayfront all the way to the end of the peninsula. Avenida Primera (1ra)—the main street— runs along the oceanfront from Calle 8 in the west to Calle L and the Hotel Internacional in the east. West of Calle 8, Avenida Primera becomes Avenida Kawama, which runs through the Kawama district to the westernmost tip of the island.

Cross streets begin at Calle 1, in the Kawama suburb, and run eastward consecutively to Calle 69, in the La Torre area. Farther east, they are lettered, from Calle A to L. The luxury hotel zone begins east of Calle 69, where Avenida 1ra becomes Avenida las Américas. The old village of funky wooden houses occupies the central section of town, roughly between Calles 23 and 54.

SIGHTS

A castellated water tower next to the Mesón del Quijote restaurant, atop a rise on Avenida las Américas, was built in the 1930s and has been given a quaint touch by a modernist sculpture of Don Quixote on his trusty steed, galloping across the hillcrest.

The small **Museo de Varadero** (Calle 57 y 1ra, tel. 045/61-3189, daily 10 A.M.–6 P.M., CUC1), in the 1920s-era summer home of Leopoldo Abreu, has sections dedicated to local flora and fauna, aboriginal culture, Irénée Du Pont, and Varadero's historic regattas.

◖ Las Américas at Mansión Xanadú

The most interesting attraction is Las Américas (Carretera Las Morlas, tel. 045/66-8482, closed to sightseers other than its hotel and restaurant guests), munitions magnate Irénée Du Pont's Spanish-style mansion at the far eastern end of Avenida las Américas. The green tile–roofed mansion, which Du Pont named Xanadu, was built in 1926 as a sumptuous winter hideaway (complete with nine-hole golf course). He fitted his house with a Carrara marble floor, great dark wooden eaves and precious timbers, original hardwood antiques, an organ, and a massive wine cellar. Light pours into the library, where the vast array of volumes went unread. On the top floor is a bar (once a ballroom) decorated in Italian rococo. A tapestry in the dining room transcribes the lines of Samuel Coleridge's poem: *In Xanadu did Kubla Khan, A stately pleasure dome decree.*

The six marble-floored bedrooms can be rented and the restaurant is Varadero's finest.

Parque Retiro Josone

Varadero's well-kept landscaped park (Av. 1ra, e/ 54 y 59, tel. 045/66-7228, daily 9 A.M.–midnight, activities 9 A.M.–5 P.M., free) is centered on an old mansion furnished with colonial-era antiques. Businessman José Fermín Iturrioz and his wife, Onelia, lived here in the 1950s. After departing Cuba following the Revolution, Señor Fermín had to give his property up to

of Florida

LAS AMÉRICAS

PALACIO DE LA RUMBA

VARADERO GOLF COURSE

VARADERO GOLF CLUB

MELIÁ LAS AMÉRICAS

MELIÁ VARADERO

PALACIO DE LOS CONVENCIONES/ PLAZA DE LAS AMÉRICAS

SOL CLUB PALMERAS

AUTOPISTA SUR

CUBACAR

Bahía de

Cárdenas

0   0.25 mi

0   0.25 km

the Castro regime in exchange for safe passage from the country. Today the romantic park is favored for photo shoots for *fiestas de quinces.*

Facilities include a lake with geese, and there are ostriches, a swimming pool (CUC3 entrance, including CUC2 *consumo mínimo*), four restaurants, pedal-boats (CUC5 one hour), bicycles (CUC5 per hour), and even camel rides (CUC5 adults, CUC2.50 children).

Reserva Ecológica Varahicacos

This 450-hectare reserve (tel. 045/61-3594, varahicacos@csam.cu, daily 9 A.M.–4:30 P.M., CUC3) of scrub and woodland at the eastern tip of the peninsula is riddled with limestone caves. The most important is **Cueva Ambrosia,** accessed by trail from the park entry. It displays pre-Columbian petroglyphs. A second trail leads to **Cueva de los Musulmanes** (Cave of Muslims), once used as an aboriginal tomb (replete with a replica of a cadaver). A separate 17-hectare section of the reserve surrounds **Cueva de la Pirata** (closed by day, it hosts a cabaret by night).

Mansión Xanadú

Alas, the government drained Laguna Mangón (a prime bird sanctuary) to build three new hotels, significantly reducing the area protected.

Delfinario

Dolphins are the star performers at the Delfinario (Autopista, Km 11, tel. 045/66-8031, daily 9 A.M.–5 P.M.), in a coral-rimmed lagoon 400 meters east of Marina Chapelín. Shows are offered at 11 A.M. and 3:30 P.M. (CUC15 adults, children under five free, cameras CUC5). You can even swim with the dolphins at 9:30 A.M., 11:30 A.M., 2:30 P.M. and 4 P.M. (CUC75 adults, CUC60 children).

ENTERTAINMENT AND EVENTS

Varadero is relatively dead at night. The majority of guests stay in the all-inclusive hotels, which feature their own bars, cabarets, and entertainment.

Nightlife

Snack Bar 62 (Av. 1ra, esq. 62, 24 hours) hosts free live music nightly 9:30 P.M.–midnight, when the plaza fills shoulder to shoulder with tourists.

Todo En Uno (Autopista Sur y Calle 54, Tues.–Thurs. 6–11 P.M., Fri.–Sun. 11 A.M.–11 P.M., CUC1 per ride) also has a 24-hour *bolera* (bowling alley), plus *carros locos* (bumper cars) and a small roller coaster.

BARS

Other than hotel bars, you'll find several unremarkable open-air bars along Avenida 1ra. **Café Bar Benny** (Camino del Mar, e/ 12 y 13, 24 hours) is lent ambience by silky jazz riffs on the sound system and occasional live music. The genteel **Bar Mirador Casablanca** (Carretera Las Morlas, daily 10 A.M.–11:45 P.M.), in Mansión Xanadú, has live jazz each afternoon at 4 P.M.

To sample rums, head to **Bar Tienda Maqueta** (Av. 1ra, esq. 63, tel. 045/66-8393, daily 9 A.M.–9 P.M.), in La Casa del Ron. It serves 96 types of rum and offers sample

shots, and there's a scale model reproduction of Distilería Santa Elena rum factory (1906–1938) with a working railway. The tiny open-air **Varadero 1920** (daily 9 A.M.–9 P.M.) in Parque Retiro Josone specializes in piña coladas (CUC3).

TRADITIONAL MUSIC AND DANCE

Many of the hotels provide Afro-Cuban shows. The rundown **Casa de la Cultura** (Av. 1ra y Calle 34, tel. 045/61-2562, CUC5) has occasional folkloric music and dance shows.

CABARETS ESPECTÁCULOS

Hotel tour desks sell excursions to the Tropicana Varadero, in Matanzas. It's not worth the journey, as the **Cabaret Continental** (Carretera las Américas, tel. 045/66-7038, Tues.–Sun. at 11 P.M., CUC22, or CUC40 with lobster dinner), at Hotel Varadero International, is a sufficiently satisfying emporium of exotica, with kaleidoscopes of stiletto-heeled showgirls teasingly swirling their boas. It's followed by the New Age disco (CUC10 disco only).

At **Cueva del Pirata** (Autopista Sur, Km 11, tel. 045/66-7751, Mon.–Sat. at 11 P.M., CUC8 including all drinks), a swashbuckling cabaret—think eye-patches and cutlasses with g-strings and high heels—takes place in a natural cave. It's followed by a disco.

A free open-air mini-cabaret is hosted nightly at 9:30 P.M. at **FM-17** (Av. 1ra y Calle 17, tel. 045/61-4831).

DISCOS AND NIGHTCLUBS

Several all-inclusive hotels have their own discos. The plaza at Avenida 1ra and Calle 46 is a hot spot for dancing to live music on weekend, when Cubans pack in thick as sardines.

In 2009, the Cine Varadero converted to the **Casa de la Música** (Av. de la Playa y Calle 42, Wed.–Sun. 10:30 A.M.–2 A.M., CUC5–10), a classy venue hosting live bands. It has a dress code, and ID is needed for entry. It's *the* hot spot in town.

La Comparsita (Calle 60, esq. 3ra, tel. 045/66-7415, Wed.–Mon. 10:30 P.M.–2:30 A.M., CUC3) also packs 'em in. The open-air venue downstairs hosts a *cabaret espectáculo* and/or live music nightly at 11:30 P.M., with disco to follow. It has karaoke upstairs.

Cubans from out of town flock on weekends to the **Palacio de la Rumba** (Carretera Las Américas, Km 3.5, tel. 045/66-8210, daily 11 P.M.–5 A.M., CUC10 including all drinks), a Western-style disco with dress code; **Club Nocturno Havana Club** (Calle 62 final, tel. 045/66-7500, daily 10:30 P.M.–3 A.M., CUC10 including all drinks), in Centro Comercial Copey; **Mambo Club** (Carretera Las Morlas, Km 14, tel. 045/66-8565, Tues.–Sun. 11 P.M.–5 A.M., CUC10 including all drinks), outside the Club Amigo Varadero at the east end of the peninsula, and featuring a cabaret before the disco; and the newly reminted **Disco La Bamba** (Av. Las Américas, Km 2, tel. 045/66-7560, Wed.–Sun., 11 P.M.–5 A.M., CUC5) in the Hotel Tuxpan.

Festivals and Events
Varadero's **World Music Festival,** each June, attracts artists from throughout Latin America.

Varadero has a full-blown **Centro de Convenciones** (Autopista Sur, Km 11, tel. 045/66-8181, comercial@plamer.var.cyt.cu) at Plaza América.

SPORTS AND RECREATION
Most resort hotels have tennis courts (nonguests pay a court fee) and include water sports in their room rates. Beach outlets offer snorkeling (CUC3 per hour), sea kayaks and Aquabikes (CUC5 per hour), sailboards (CUC10), and banana-boat rides (CUC5 for 10 minutes). There's a free public tennis court at Calle 15 and Avenida 1ra.

Golf
You can practice your swing at **Varadero Golf Club** (Carretera Las Morlas, tel. 045/66-7788, fax 045/66-8481, www.varaderogolfclub.com, daily 7 A.M.–7 P.M., greens fees CUC77, club rental CUC55, golf cart CUC55). The 18-hole, par-72 course has a well-stocked pro shop (daily 8 A.M.–5 P.M.), electric carts, and caddie house, plus restaurant and snack bar. Golf classes are

offered. Bring your own golf balls: The club has a shortage and sells them for CUC5 each!

Fans of mini-golf can putt around a crude "crazy golf" course at **El Golfito** (Av. 1ra e/ 41 y 42, 9 A.M.–10 P.M., CUC0.50).

Scuba Diving and Snorkeling
There are more than 30 dive sites off Varadero, several with old wrecks. However, the diving for corals here is not as good as elsewhere in Cuba. Most sites are in **Parque Marino Cayo Piedras del Norte,** northeast of Varadero, and a one-hour boat ride. It features an AN-24 aircraft, a 102-meter frigate, and even a gunboat with missiles. Another good site is the Blue Hole—**Ojo de Mégano**—an underwater cave east of Varadero. When seas are too rough, divers are transferred to the Playa Girón (Bay of Pigs, a three-hour ride). You can also dive at Cueva de Saturno (CUC30, 9 A.M.).

Marlin S.A. (www.nauticamarlin.com) operates three dive outlets (resort course CUC70, two-tank dive CUC40, night dive CUC55, certification course CUC365). **Barracuda Scuba Cuba** (Av. 1ra, e/ 58 y 59, tel. 045/61-3481, fax 045/66-7072, daily 8 A.M.–5 P.M.) is the main outlet; it has a decompression chamber. **Scuba Diving Center Acua** (Av. Kawama y Calle 1, tel. 045/66-8063, daily 8 A.M.–5 P.M.) has Nitrox. **Diving Center Marina Chapelín** (tel. 045/66-8871, daily 9 A.M.–4 P.M.), at Marina Chapelín, is solely for certified divers.

Many all-inclusive hotels have dive facilities, which rent snorkeling gear (CUC5) and offer snorkeling trips.

Sportfishing
Sportfishing trips are offered at the three marinas: **Marina Dársena** (tel. 045/66-8060), on the Vía Blanca, one kilometer west of Varadero; **Marina Chapelín** (tel. 045/66-8727), toward the east end of the Autopista Sur; and **Marina Gaviota Varadero** (tel. 045/66-4115, dir_marina@delvar.gav.tur.cu), at the far east end of the Autopista. Typical prices are CUC350 for four people, 9 A.M.–4 P.M.

Varadero hosts the **Gregorio Fuentes White Marlin Fishing Tournament** in June.

Wind Sports

Barracuda Scuba Cuba (Av. 1ra, e/ 58 y 59, tel. 045/61-3481) rents sailboards and kitesurfers and offers *parapente* (kitesurf) instruction.

Boat Excursions

Marlin runs all water-based activities, including a 90-minute **Boat Adventure** (tel. 045/66-8440, commercial @marlinv.var.cyt.cu, CUC41) where you tour the mangroves and lagoons in convoy on a Jet Ski (9 A.M., 11 A.M., 1 P.M., and 3 P.M.) or in a speedboat (10 A.M., noon, 2 P.M., and 4 P.M.). You can hop aboard a catamaran at Marina Chapelín for a "Seafari Cayo Blanco" to Cayo Blanco (CUC75 adult, CUC38 child, including lunch) or a snorkeling cruise (CUC30 adult, CUC15 child).

ACCOMMODATIONS

There are scores of hotels to choose from, but low-price options are few. All hotels here have air-conditioning and satellite TV; most have safes and fridges or minibars. Reservations are wise in high season. Air-hotel packages from abroad offer discounts. No *casas particulares* are allowed in Varadero.

Most hotels are all-inclusive; meals, alcoholic beverages, entertainment, and water sports are included in the room rate. You're divorced from any interaction with Cubans other than hotel staff. Guests must wear colored plastic bands, not least so that security guards can keep all others out. Few live up to the standards of all-inclusives elsewhere in the Caribbean, although prices have plunged in recent years and in many cases offer good bargains. Standards are generally higher in foreign-managed hotels than in purely Cuban-managed properties.

Hotels become more upscale eastward. The easterly properties are far from the action, which concentrates between Calles 11 and 64. Constantly to-ing and fro-ing can rack up a hefty taxi bill.

Hotels are categorized according to high-season rates for twin occupancy, and arranged west to east. There are more hotels in actuality than are listed here.

Under CUC50

All hotels in this price bracket are operated by Islazul (www.islazul.cu).

Recommended as a great bargain, **⟨ Motel Punta Blanca** (tel. 045/66-2410, director@pblanca.m.tz.tur.cu, CUC15 s, CUC22.50 d low season, CUC29 s, CUC40 d high season) opened in 2009. Comprising three converted 1950s modernist villas, it has 21 spacious rooms with quasi-functional furnishings, plus a restaurant and bar. For better or worse, you're at the western tip, away from the crowds.

Hotel Ledo (Av. de la Playa, e/ 43 y 44, tel. 045/61-3206, ledo@varade2.var.cyt.cu, CUC15 s, CUC22 d low season, CUC18 s, CUC26 d high season) is a simple, older property with 20 rooms with local TV and hot water. It has a small restaurant.

Also a favorite of budget travelers, down-to-earth **Hotel Pullman** (Av. 1ra y Calle 49, tel. 045/66-2702, fax 045/66-7499, recepcion@dmares.hor.tur.cu, CUC27 s, CUC37 d low season, CUC34 s, CUC47 d high season, including a meager breakfast) occupies a colonial mansion. The 15 rooms have colonial furniture and modern bathrooms; however, not all inspire. It has a small, airy restaurant and a patio bar. One block away, and operated jointly with the Pullman, is the slightly better **Hotel Dos Mares** (Av. 1ra and Calle 53, same rates as the Hotel Pullman), with a certain bed-and-breakfast charm. It has 34 large, modestly furnished, no-frills rooms and a meager restaurant and bar.

Hotel Herradura (Av. de la Playa, e/ 35 y 36, tel. 045/61-3703, fax 045/66-7496, carpeta@herradura.co.cu, CUC21 s, CUC34 d low season, CUC25 s, CUC41 d high season, including breakfast) is a favorite of Germans. This small, intimate option has 75 rooms in apartments.

Others to consider in this price bracket are **Villa La Mar** (3ra Av., e/ 28 y 30, tel. 045/61-3910, fax 045/61-2508, vlamar@enet.cu) and **Hotel Oasis** (Vía Blanca, Km 130, Varadero, tel. 045/66-7380, fax 045/66-7489, jcarpeta@oasis.hor.tur.cu).

CUC50-100

Although popular with independent budget travelers, **Hotel Aguazul** (Av. 1ra y Calle 13, tel. 045/66-7132, fax 045/66-7245, www.islazul.cu, CUC35 s, CUC48 d low season, CUC45 s, CUC60 d high season) is an uninspired high-rise with 240 rose-pink rooms and 69 one-bedroom apartments.

Islazul targets Italians at its **Hotel Los Delfines** (Av. 1ra, e/ 38 y 39, tel. 045/66-7720, fax 045/66-7727, direccion@delfines.hor.tur.cu, CUC40 s, CUC70 d low season, CUC75 s, CUC85 d high season) but is open to all comers. The 89 rooms have a lively contemporary decor. It has four suites and nine junior suites, and is one of the better bargains.

CUC100-150

I like the contemporary motif at **Hotel & Villas Tortuga** (Calle 7, e/ Camino del Mar y Bulevar, tel. 045/61-4747, reservas@villatortuga.tur.cu, from CUC64 s, CUC88 d low season, from CUC84 s, CUC128 d high season), a modern, 280-room, two-story complex centered on a pool. The rooms have heaps of light but no TVs or telephones. You can also rent villas.

One of the few resort hotels offering a non-all-inclusive option, the **Hoteles C Arenas Doradas** (tel. 045/66-8150, fax 045/66-8158, reserva@arenas.gca.tur.cu, CUC50 s, CUC80 d low season, CUC80 s, CUC110 d high season) has 316 rooms set amid 20 acres of landscaped grounds surrounding a freeform pool with sunken pool bar and open-air whirlpool tub. Interior decor is attractive, and the prices are fair, though this is no Ritz. It has water sports and entertainment, plus an all-inclusive option.

Cubanacán's **Club Amigo Tropical** (Av. 1ra, e/ 21 y 22, tel. 045/61-3915, fax 045/66-2035, reserva@tropical.hor.tur.cu, CUC64 s, CUC80 d low season, CUC69 s, CUC112 d high season) is an all-inclusive property with 143 rooms and apartments with lively fabrics. Its pleasant lobby bar and elegant restaurant appeal. Otherwise don't expect much here, as this two-star (officially three) property is all-Cuban run.

Gran Caribe's lively, 282-room, all-inclusive **Mercure Cuatro Palmas** (Av. 1ra, e/ 61 y 62, tel. 045/66-7040, fax 045/66-7208, www.mercure.com, CUC75 s, CUC85 d low season, CUC105 s, CCU148 d high season) has a great location at the hub of local action. This popular hotel, run by the French Accor chain, is built on the grounds of Fulgencio Batista's summer house and is centered on an attractive

MATANZAS

old car and horse-drawn *coche* outside Mercure Cuatro Palmas

swimming pool. Nonguests can buy a pass (CUC25 day, CUC25 night). It has apartment units across the street.

Guests have complained of water leaks, molds, and other ongoing plagues at Cubanacán's all-inclusive, six-story postmodernist **Hotel Tuxpan** (Av. Las Américas, Km 2, tel. 045/66-7560, reservas@tuxpan.var.cyt. cu), which reopened in December 2008 after a lengthy renovation. It boasts a large swimming pool and plenty of recreational facilities, including tennis, beach volleyball, and Hobie Cats, as well as the La Bamba disco. Its 232 smallish bedrooms have pleasant travertine-clad bathrooms, but furnishings are uninspired.

Slashing its rates in 2009, Gran Caribe's all-inclusive **Gran Hotel Club Kawama** (Av. 1ra, esq. 1, Rpto. Kawama, tel. 045/66-4416, fax 045/66-7254, www.grancaribe.cu, CUC54 s, CUC99 d low season, CUC88 s, CUC112 d high season) dominates the Kawama peninsula on seven hectares and has 235 nicely albeit modestly furnished villas. The resort has several bars and restaurants, plus water sport, bike, scooter, and car rentals. Its clientele is mostly German.

The landmark Puntarena-Paraíso twin tower complex, at the western tip of the peninsula, has had more lives than a cat. In 2009 it was split (even the common swimming pool was divided in two) into two hotels and renamed. Both the **Hoteles C Playa Caleta** (Av. Kawama y Final, tel. 045/66-7120, reserva@ playacaleta.gca.tur.cu) and **Hotel Puntarena** (tel. 045/66-7125, fax 045/66-7014, reservas@ puntarena.gca.tur.cu), retaining identical interiors and furnishings, are also-rans in this price bracket.

If all else is full, try Gran Caribe' 272-room all-inclusive **Hotel Sun Beach** (Calle 17 e/ Av. 1ra y 3ra, tel. 045/66-7490, reservas@sunbeach.hor.tur.cu).

CUC150-250

Families might opt for **Breezes Bella Costa** (Carretera Las Américas 3.5, tel. 045/66-7210, fax 045/66-7713, www.superclubscuba.net, from CUC98 s, CUC155 d low season, from CUC105 s, CUC168 high season), which lay fallow for many years under another guise. The grounds remain uninspired, but it has a huge pool complex, family suites, a kids' club, and three specialist restaurants.

Managed by Spain's Raytur, **Hoteles C Barlovento** (Av. 1ra, e/ 10 y 12, tel. 045/66-7140, fax 045/66-7218, www.hotelesc.es, CUC88 s, CUC140 d low season, CUC133 s, CUC190 d high season) is a handsome, modern all-inclusive hotel done up in a contemporary interpretation of Spanish-colonial style, with 269 attractively appointed rooms and three suites. The complex surrounds a large swimming pool and offers water sports and entertainment.

The contemporary aesthetic of the all-inclusive **Hotel Palma Real** (Av. 2da y 64, tel. 045/61-4555, fax 045/61-4550, jrecep.palmreal@hotetur.com, CUC97 s, CUC154 d low season, CUC114 s, CUC186 d high season) appeals, although this hotel faces over the bay, not the sea. It has 297 rooms with lively decor, plus two restaurants and three bars, and entertainment. The twin-tiered pool is a highlight.

Often sold out to tour groups, Gran Caribe's venerable 1950s-era **Hotel Varadero Internacional** (Carretera las Américas, tel. 045/66-7038, fax 045/66-7246, reserva@ gcinter.gca.tur.cu, from CUC69 s, CUC110 d, CUC140 s/d suite low season, CUC110 s, CUC157 d, CUC165 s/d suite high season) successfully combines period decor with an elegant contemporary look. There the good points end, according to many guests.

Facilities abound at Gran Caribe's all-inclusive, 245-room **Villa Cuba Resort** (tel. 045/66-8280, fax 045/66-8282, director@vcuba.gca.cma.net, CUC75 s, CUC129 d, CUC250 s/d suite low season, CUC132 s, CUC189 d, CUC250 s/d suite high season), centered on a beautiful pool complex and offering a range of accommodations furnished in contemporary vogue, including 23 beachfront chalets with valet service (seven villas have their own pools).

For a uniquely romantic experience, check into ▐ **Mansión Xanadú** (Carretera Las Morlas, tel. 045/66-8482, fax 045/66-8481, www.varaderogolfclub.com, CUC120 s, CUC150 d low season, CUC160 s, CUC210 d high season, including breakfast and green fees) at the Varadero Golf Club. This mansion's six gracious rooms feature marble floors, wrought-iron beds, throw rugs, and all-marble bathrooms with vast walk-in showers. There's a splendid restaurant.

Further east, there's not much to choose between the following three-star all-inclusive hotels: **Oasis Turquesa** (Carretera las Américas, tel. 045/66-8471, fax 045/66-8495, www.hotelesoasis.com); **Barceló Arenas Blancas** (Calle 64, esq. 1ra, tel. 045/61-4450, fax 045/61-4491, rsv@arblcas.gca.tur.cu), the closest all-inclusive to the action; the gracious **Iberostar Taínos** (Carretera Los Taínos, tel. 045/66-8656, fax 045/68-8657, comercial@ibstain.gca.tur.cu); the 444-room **Oasis Brisas del Caribe** (Carretera Las Morlas, Km 22.5, tel. 045/66-8030, www.hotelesoasis.com); the ungainly **Club Amigo Varadero Hotel** (Carretera Las Morlas, Km 11.5, tel. 045/66-8243, gerencia@granhot.var.cyt.cu); ho-hum **Oasis Las Morlas** (Av. las Américas, tel. 045/66-7230, www.hotelesoasis.com); the **Iberostar Playa Alameda** (tel. 045/66-8822); **Hotel Oasis Playa Varadero 1920** (tel. 045/66-8288); and Gran Caribe's **Coralia Club Playa de Oro** (Carretera Las Morlas, Km 12.5, tel. 045/61-4872, comercial@poro.gca.tur.cu), run by the French Accor chain.

Over CUC250

I like Gran Caribe's all-inclusive ◖ **Barceló Solymar Beach Resort** (Carretera Las Américas y Calle 69, tel. 045/61-4499, fax 045/61-1086, www.barcelo.com, from CUC119 s, CUC270 d low season, CUC156 s, CUC330 d high season), a modern resort with a dynamic contemporary vogue. Its 525 rooms and 193 bungalows all have exquisite marble-top bathrooms. The resort enfolds a vast pool complex and offers upscale shops and even miniature golf.

Managed by Spain's Sol Meliá, the **Meliá Las Américas Suites & Golf Resort** (tel. 045/66-7600, fax 045/66-7625, www.solmeliacuba.com, from CUC155 s, CUC220 d low

season, from CUC170 s, CUC265 d high season) boasts a stunning lobby. Arched terraces support a beautiful pool and sundeck overlooking its own private beach. Its 335 rooms and 25 suites feature kitchenettes and small lounges below mezzanine bedrooms with pleasing bamboo and wicker furniture. Meliá's elegant 650-room all-inclusive **Sol Sirenas Coral Resort** (Av. las Américas y Calle K, tel. 045/66-8070, fax 045/66-8076, www.solmeliacuba.com, from CUC170 s, CUC230 d standard low season, from CUC200 s, CUC270 d high season) offers an equally satisfying alternative.

The all-inclusive **Meliá Varadero** (tel. 045/66-7013, fax 045/66-7012, reservas@solmeliacuba.com, from CUC175 s, CUC260 d low season, from CUC195 s, CUC305 d high season), adjoining Plaza Las Américas, also makes a dramatic first impression with 500 rooms and suites in six arms that fan out from a soaring circular atrium with a curtain of vines cascading down from the balconies. The effect is enhanced by the chattering of parrots. The **Sol Palmeras** (tel. 045/66-7009, fax 045/66-7209, www.solmeliacuba.com, from CUC175 s, CUC260 d low season, from CUC195 s, CUC305 d high season), immediately east, is a sprawling and gracious property also entered through a lobby with lush foliage, fountains, and caged birds. It has 375 rooms, 32 suites, and 200 *cabinas* arrayed around a huge pool with a thatched bar. Better still is the sibling ◖ **Sol Meliá Paradisus Varadero** (Carretera Las Morlas, tel. 045/66-8700, fax 045/66-8705, www.solmeliacuba.com, from CUC260 s, CUC340 d low season, from CUC290 s, CUC380 d high season), a beautiful all-inclusive with a quasi-Thai motif. Centered on a huge freeform pool, it has 420 exquisitely appointed junior suites and suites, and a garden villa (with butler service) with sponge-washed walls, canopy beds, and wrought-iron and rattan furniture. Facilities include a football court, water polo, archery, volleyball, and tennis courts.

Hotel Tryp Peninsula Varadero (tel. 045/66-8800, fax 045/66-8805, www.solmeliacuba.com, from CUC180 s, CUC250 d low season, from CUC330 s, CUC400 d high season), at the far eastern extreme of the peninsula, follows Meliá's standard format, with a beautiful freeform pool and ice-cream pastels in the 591 rooms in 20 three-story units.

One of the outstanding options, the **Blau Varadero Hotel** (Carretera Las Morlas, Km 15, tel. 045/66-7545, fax 045/66-7494, www.blauhotels.com, from CUC135 s, CUC200 d low season, from CUC248 s, CUC426 d season) is a dramatic take on a Mayan pyramid. The lobby opens to a dramatic soaring atrium with blue-tinted skylight. A contemporary vogue infuses the guest rooms, with marble-clad bathrooms and spacious balconies with brushed steel and glass rails. A hip buffet restaurant, an alfresco poolside restaurant, beach grill, a bi-level pool, large kids' club, and state-of-the-art theater and gym are among the amenities.

Iberostar Varadero (tel. 045/66-999, fax 045/66-8842, reservas@iberostar.co.cu, CUC155 s, CUC220 d low season, CUC185 s, CUC280 d high season, CUC45 more for junior suites) gets two thumbs up for its calming mood and creative design subtly infused with Mughal influences. At its heart is a vast freeform pool.

For couples only **Sandals Royal Hicacos Resort & Spa** (Carretera Las Morlas, Km 14, tel. 045/66-8844, fax 045/66-8851, www.sandalshicacos.com, per person rates from CUC140 low season, from CUC250 high season) is one of the most resplendent and impressive hotels in Varadero. The entrance plays on a Polynesian theme, with thatched walkways over landscaped water courses. Lively Caribbean colors meld with rich ocher. It has 404 junior suites with a lovely contemporary feel.

Readers report favorably on one of my faves, Gaviota's **Barceló Marina Palace Resort** (Punta Hicacos Final, tel. 045/66-9966, fax 045/66-7022, www.barcelo.com, from CUC205 s, CUC290 d low season, from CUC335 s, CUC430 d high season), at the very tip of the peninsula. Sprawling along the shore betwixt road and sand dunes, it boasts pleasing architecture and a contemporary quasi-maritime vogue to its 296 junior suites and four suites. All the required facilities are here, including a waterslide augering down to a huge pool.

Also in this price bracket, families might consider **Breezes Varadero** (Carretera Las Américas, Km 3, tel. 045/66-7030, fax 045/66-7005, www.superclubscuba.com, North America tel. 800/467-8737, U.K. tel. 01/749-677200), a 270-suite all-inclusive property managed by Jamaica's SuperClubs chain.

A deluxe newcomer that opened in 2009 on land previously part of the nature reserve, the 998-room **Hotel Sirenis La Salina** (Autopista Sur km 18.5, tel. 045/66-7599, www.sirenishotels.com) sprawls over an obscene amount of land; so much for Cuba's vaunted eco-sensitivity! And it seems to have niggling problems. However, even here you don't get face cloths or toiletries. Gaviota's adjoining and equally sprawling **Iberostar Laguna Azul** (tel. 045/66-7900, commercial@laguna.co.cu) more accurately matches expectations for a five-star resort with its 814 rooms (and complete services, although the yesteryear-style furnishings aren't to my taste). Why the designers can't arrange rooms facing the ocean is a mystery; most face a sensational pool area (one of six pools).

The Sandals chain has pulled out of two hotels. The former Beaches Varadero is now **Meliá Las Antilles** (Carretera Las Morlas, Km 15, tel. 045/66-8470, fax 045/66-8554, www.solmeliacuba.com), and the Sandals Princesa del Mar is now the 434-room **Paradisus Princesa del Mar** (tel. 045/66-7200, fax 045/66-7201, sales@princesadelmar.co.cu).

FOOD

Buffet meals in most all-inclusive hotels are mediocre, while menus in streetside restaurants vary little. Deluxe hotels managed by international hotel groups usually offer fare approaching international quality (some allow nonguests to eat for a day-pass fee). Private restaurants—*paladares*—aren't permitted.

Even in high season you may be the only diner in the street restaurants.

Criollo

Despite its modern, rather soulless ambience,

Chez Plaza (Plaza América, tel. 045/66-8181, ext. 270, daily 10 A.M.–9 P.M.) offers creative dishes such as shrimp in rum (CUC6). Shrimp in rum is also on the menu at **Restaurante La Vega** (Av. 1ra y 31, tel. 045/61-1431, daily 10 A.M.–11 P.M.), where you can dine alfresco with ocean views.

Lobster in pepper sauce (CUC6) and beef filet stuffed with bacon (CUC7) feature at **Restaurante El Criollo** (Av. 1ra y 18, tel. 045/61-4794, daily noon–midnight), a rustic colonial home-turned-restaurant whose menu also includes bean soup (CUC1.50). **Restaurante La Vicaria** (Av. 1ra y 38, tel. 045/67-4721, daily noon–10:45 P.M.) offers alfresco dining under thatch, with the usual roast chicken and fish dishes (CUC5–8). Live music, a 1914 Ford, and a 1955 Oldsmobile add ambience to the **Restaurante Esquina Cuba** (Av. 1ra 7 y 38, tel. 045/61-4019, daily noon–11 P.M.), an open-air restaurant offering *ropa vieja* (CUC8).

El Bodegón Criollo (Av. de la Playa y Calle 40, tel. 045/66-7784, daily noon–11 P.M.) attempts to replicate the famous Bodeguita de Medio in Havana with its graffiti. You can dine on a shady veranda or in a rustic setting with eaves and ships' wheels turned lamps hanging from the ceiling. Typical dishes include roast chicken (CUC6.50) and grilled pork steak (CUC7.50).

Continental

The upscale **Restaurante Antigüedades** (Av. 1ra y 59, tel. 045/66-7329, daily noon–10:45 P.M.), outside Parque Retiro Josone, exudes charm with its old clocks, lanterns, and bric-a-brac. It's like dining in an antique store, with music from a scratchy old radio, too! It offers set dinners, including filet mignon (CUC14) and lobster (CUC22–38), served on antique porcelain. Thumbs up for my dinner of beef broth, garlic shrimp with boiled potato, and gelato-style ice cream.

Restaurante La Fondue (Av. 1ra, esq. 62, tel. 045/66-7747, daily noon–10 P.M.) lists a large range of fondues using Cuban cheeses (CUC7–18). Special cheeses such as Gruyère, Sbrinz, and Gouda cost extra. It also has grilled chicken breast (CUC4.50), lobster (CUC12), and the like, plus a good selection of wines.

Fancy over-the-top old world elegance? The **Restaurante Las Américas** (Carretera Las Morlas, tel. 045/66-7388, daily noon–5 P.M. and 7–11:45 P.M.), on the ground floor of Mansión Xanadú, will oblige. It specializes in French-style seafood and meats, such as appetizers of shrimp in sherry vinaigrette (CUC10), and seared goose liver with cabbage and balsamic (CUC11). My seared ahi tuna with green sauce (CUC20) was first-rate; so, too, my artistically presented tiramisu.

For Italian fare, head to the stylish **Dante** (tel. 045/66-7738, daily 11 A.M.–11:45 P.M.), in Parque Retiro Josone, with views over the lake. It has air-conditioned and open-air options, and features pastas (from CUC6) and pizzas (from CUC4.50) plus a large wine list. **Restaurante Castel Nuevo** (Av. 1ra y 11, tel. 045/66-7786, daily 2–10 P.M.) has an appropriately Italianate motif and serves spaghetti, pastas, and pizzas (CUC2–10). The best pizza around, however, is at **Pizza Nova** (tel. 045/66-8585, daily 11 A.M.–10 P.M.), a fast-food style pizzeria upstairs in Plaza Las Américas.

Al Capone's former oceanfront home (built in 1934 on the Kawama Peninsula) is today the atmospheric **Casa de Al** (tel. 045/66-7090, 10 A.M.–10 P.M.). Paella (CUC7) and filet mignon (CUC15) feature.

In 2009, the **Restaurant Kike-Kcho** (tel. 045/66-4115, reserve@marina.gov.co.cu, daily noon–midnight) opened at Marina Gaviota.

Seafood

Several beach grills overhang the sands. I like **Ranchón Cielo Mar** (Calle 57, 24 hours). **El Rancho** (tel. 045/61-4760, daily 11 A.M.–10 P.M.), opposite the entrance to Parque Retiro Josone, also serves grilled seafood (CUC6–14) in a handsome thatched roadside setting with live musicians. In the park, the antique-filled, classically elegant **Restaurante El Retiro** (tel. 045/66-7316, daily 3–10 P.M.) specializes in lobster dishes (CUC15).

© CHRISTOPHER P. BAKER

El Mesón del Quijote restaurant, Varadero

Also specializing in lobster, albeit pricier, the hilltop 【 **El Mesón del Quijote** (Av. las Américas, tel. 045/66-7796, daily noon–11 P.M.) boasts beamed ceilings, metal lamps, brass plaques, and potted plants and climbing ivy on a solarium dining terrace (CUC10–30).

Steak House
Bull heads on the wall and rawhide seats adorn **Steak House Toro** (Av. 1ra y 25, tel. 045/66-7145, daily noon–11 P.M.), where you can dine alfresco or inside. The menu runs from veal chops (CUC14) to smoked salmon with capers (CUC6) and mussels in spiced tomato sauce (CUC4.50).

Asian
Two restaurants take a stab at Oriental fare. **Restaurant Chong Kwok** (Av. 1ra, esq. 55, tel. 045/61-3526, daily noon–10 P.M.) is a little charmer with Oriental decor plus menu featuring fried wontons, soups, chicken chop suey, and sweet-and-sour lobster (CUC11). **Lai-Lai** (Av. 1ra, e/ 18 y 19, tel. 045/66-7793,

daily 1–9:30 P.M.), also with a strong Chinese ambience, features spring rolls, fried rice with shrimp or lobster, and lobster chop suey (CUC5–15).

Fast Food and Snacks
Midnight snacks? The **Complejo Mediterráneo** (Av. 1ra, e/ 54 y 55, tel. 045/62460) has two eateries in one: **Café Aladdin** offers sandwiches 24 hours, and **D'Prisa Mediterráneo** is a 24-hour open-air grill serving *criollo* fare and pizzas.

The best sandwiches are served at **Pan. Com** (Centro Comercial Hicacos (Av. 1ra, e/ 44 y 46, tel. 045/61-4613, daily 9 A.M.–9 P.M.). Clean and modern, it would fit well in L.A. or London.

Cafés and Desserts
Coppelia (Av. 1ra, e/ 44 y 46, tel. 045/66-7147, daily noon–8 P.M.) sells ice cream at CUC0.50 per tiny scoop.

All the **Casa del Habano** tobacco shops (Av. 1ra y 27, tel. 045/66-7696; Av. 1ra y 39, tel. 045/61-4719; Calle 63, e/ 1ra y 3ra, tel. 045/66-7843; Av. Playa y 31, tel. 045/61-1431; and Plaza América, tel. 045/66-8181, ext. 251; daily 9 A.M.–9 P.M.) have pleasant espresso bars.

Self-Catering
Doña Neli (Av. 1ra y 43) is a 24-hour bakery selling croissants, pastries, and breads. You can buy Western foodstuffs at **Grocery Caracol** (Calle 15 e/ 1ra y 3ra), **Grocery La Trovatta** (Av. 1ra y A), and in **Plaza América,** which has a fully stocked supermarket (daily 8:30 A.M.–8 P.M.).

SHOPPING
Arts and Crafts
The largest crafts market is on Avenida Primera at Calle 44. For world-class ceramics head to **Taller de Cerámica Artística** (Av. 1ra y 59, tel. 045/66-7554, daily 9 A.M.–7 P.M.). Look for dining sets and individual plates by renowned artists such as Osmany Betancourt and Alfredo Sosabravo. Next door is Varadero's **Galería de Arte** (tel. 045/66-8260, daily

MATANZAS

8:30 A.M.–7 P.M.), with wooden statues, paintings, and other artwork.

Books and Music

The best outlet is **La Casa** (Av. 1ra, e/ 59 y 60, tel. 045/61-3033, daily 9 A.M.–9 P.M.), with a bookstore and music store. **Librería Hanoi** (Av. 1ra, esq. 44, tel. 045/61-2694, daily 9 A.M.–9 P.M.) is meagerly stocked with social, historical, and political works on a leftist theme.

Boutiques

Centro Comercial de Caimán (Av. 1ra, e/ 61 y 62) has boutiques and cosmetic stores; and **Adidas** has a sportswear outlet on Calle 63. **Plaza América** has designer boutiques and a duty-free jewelry store. **Joyería Coral Negro** (Calle 64 y 3ra, tel. 045/61-4870) sells duty-free name-brand watches plus perfumes and quality Cuban jewelry. And **El Quitrín** (Av. 1ra, e/ 55 y 56, tel. 045/61-2580) sells handmade *guayaberas,* lace skirts, and blouses.

Cigars, Coffee, and Rum

The five outlets of **Casa del Habano** (Av. 1ra y 27, tel. 045/66-7696; Av. 1ra y 39, tel. 045/61-4719; Calle 63, e/ 1ra y 3ra, tel. 045/66-7843; Av. Playa y 31, tel. 045/61-1431; and Plaza América, tel. 045/66-8181, ext. 251) are the best-stocked cigar shops in town. Each has a bar and smokers' lounge and also sells rare Serrano coffee, Cuba's finest export grade.

La Casa del Ron (Av. 1ra, esq. 63, tel. 045/66-8393, daily 9 A.M.–9 P.M.) stocks about 100 rum labels.

INFORMATION AND SERVICES

Infotur (Calle 13 y 1ra, tel. 045/66-2966, infovar@enet.cu, daily 8 A.M.–5 P.M.) provides tourist information.

Money

Euros are accepted as direct payment in Varadero. Banks include **Banco Financiero Internacional** (Av. Playa y 32, and in Plaza América, Mon.–Fri. 8 A.M.–12:30 P.M. and 1:30–7 P.M.); **Bandec** (Av. 1ra y 36, Mon.–Fri. 8 A.M.–3 P.M.); and **Banco Popular** (Av. 1ra y 36, Mon.–Fri. 8 A.M.–noon and 1:30–4:30 P.M.).

Fincimex (Av. 1ra y 15, tel. 045/61-4413,

© CHRISTOPHER P. BAKER

staff and cigars at Casa del Habano, Varadero

MATANZAS

Mon.–Sat. 8:30 A.M.–noon and 1–4 P.M.) represents foreign credit card companies.

Communications

Varadero has post offices at Avenida 1ra and Calle 36 (Mon.–Sat. 8 A.M.–7 P.M., Sun. 8 A.M.–5:30 P.M.), and in the gate house at Avenida las Américas and Calle A (tel. 045/61-4551, 8 A.M.–8 P.M.). **DHL** (Av. 1ra #3903, e/ 39 y 40, tel./fax 045/66-7730, dhl--var@enet.cu, Mon.–Fri. 8 A.M.–noon and 1–5 P.M., Sat. 8 A.M.–noon) offers international courier service.

Etecsa (daily 8:30 A.M.–7:30 P.M.) has international phone and Internet service in three locations (Av. 1ra, esq. 30; upstairs in Plaza Las Américas; and in Centro Comercial Hicacos, Av. 1ra e/ 44 y 46).

Medical Services

Clínica Internacional (Av. 1ra y 61, tel. 045/66-7710 or 045/66-8611, open 24 hours, CUC25 per consultation, CUC30 after 4 P.M., CUC60 after 11 P.M., CUC50 for hotel visits) has an ambulance and pharmacy. There are also international pharmacies at Plaza América (tel. 045/66-4610), Avenida Kawama (e/ 3 y 4, tel. 045/61-4470), and Centro Comercial Hicacos (Av. 1ra e/ 44 y 46, tel. 045/61-4610 ext. 145, daily 8 A.M.–7 P.M.).

Ópticas Miramar (Av. 1ra, esq. 43, tel. 045/66-7525, daily 8 A.M.–7 P.M.) has optician service.

Legal Aid and Safety

The **police** station is at Avenida 1ra (e/ 38 y 39). The **Canadian Consulate** (Calle 13 #422, e/ 1ra y Camino del Mar, tel. 045/61-2078, honconvdero@canada.com) also represents the hamlet of Australia.

Asistur (Edificio Marbella, Apto. 6, Av. 1ra, e/ 42 y 43, tel./fax 045/66-7277, www.asistur.cu, Mon.–Fri. 9 A.M.–noon and 1:30–4:30 P.M., Sat. 9 A.M.–noon) can provide assistance in an emergency.

Petty theft is common on the beaches; never leave your possessions unguarded. Red flags are flown when swimming is dangerous. Jellyfish are common in winter and spring.

GETTING THERE AND AWAY
By Air

The **Aeropuerto Juan Gualberto Gómez** (tel. 045/61-2133 or 045/61-3036) is 16 kilometers west of Varadero. A taxi will cost about CUC25. **Víazul** buses link the airport and Varadero (CUC6).

Cubana (Av. 1ra, e/ 54 y 55, tel. 045/61-1823) has an office, but its flights do not serve Varadero.

By Sea

You can berth at **Marina Marlin Dársena** (Vía Blanca, Km 31, tel. 045/66-8060, fax 045/66-7456, HF-2790 or VHF-1668) and **Marina Gaviota Varadero** (Carretera Las Morlas, Km 21, tel. 045/66-4115, fax 045/66-4107, reserve@marinagav.co.cu), which has dry-dock facilities.

By Bus

Víazul buses (tel. 045/61-4886, daily 7 A.M.–6 P.M.) arrive and depart the **Terminal de Ómnibus Interprovinciales** (Calle 36 y Autopista Sur, tel. 045/61-2626). Buses for Varadero depart Havana at 8 A.M., 10 A.M., noon, and 6 P.M. (CUC10.80); and for Santiago de Cuba (stopping at cities in between) at 8:15 P.M. (CUC56). Buses depart Varadero for Havana at 8 A.M., 11:25 A.M., 3:30 P.M., and 6 P.M.; and for Santiago de Cuba at 9:25 P.M.

Bus #236 departs hourly for Cárdenas from the **Terminal Ómnibus de Cárdenas,** next to the main bus station, and from Avenida 1ra y Calle 13 (CUC1).

You can also travel to Havana by excursion tour buses (CUC25 each way). Hotel tour desks can make reservations; the buses pick you up at your hotel.

By Car and Taxi

Most hotels have car rental outlets. Main offices include **Havanautos** (Av. 1ra y Calle 31, tel. 045/61-8196, and Av. 1ra y 64, tel. 045/66-7094), **Cubacar** (Av. 1ra y 21, tel. 045/66-0302; Av. 1ra, e/ 54 y 55, tel. 045/61-1875; and Av. las Américas y A, tel. 045/61-7336, www.transturvaradero.com), and **Vía Rent-**

a-Car (Av. 1ra, e/ 25 y 26, tel. 045/61-4391).
Rex (tel. 045/66-2112) has outlets at the Hotel Iberostar Varadero (tel. 045/66-7739) and the airport (tel. 045/66-7539).

Foreign drivers pay a CUC2 toll on the Vía Blanca, about two kilometers west of Varadero.

There are several gas stations (Autopista Sur, esq. 17; Autopista, esq. 54; and next to Marina Aqua on the Vía Blanca west of town).

A taxi from Havana costs about CUC100 one-way.

Organized Excursions

You can book excursions to Havana, Trinidad, Bay of Pigs, etc. in the major tourist hotels.

Tour agencies include **Cubanacán** (Calle 24 y Playa, tel. 045/33-7061); **Cubatur** (Av. 1ra y 33, tel. 045/66-7217); **Havanatur** (Av. 3ra, e/ 33 y 34, tel. 045/66-7027); and **Paradiso** (Calle 26, e/ 1ra y 2da, tel. 045/61-4759).

GETTING AROUND
By Bus

The **Varadero Beach Tour** (daily 9:30 A.M.–5 P.M., CUC5) double-decker bus runs up and down Avenida 1ra and the length of the peninsula hourly. It stops at all the major hotels and you can hop on or off at any stop. Your ticket can be purchased at hotels and is valid all day.

With pesos you can also hop aboard buses #47 and 48 (20 centavos), which run along Avenida 1ra between Calle 64 and the Santa Marta district, west of the access bridge; and #220, which runs the full length of the Autopista Sur.

By Taxi and *Coche*

Cubataxi taxis (tel. 045/61-4444) wait outside tourist hotels. No journey between Calle 1 and Calle 64 should cost more than CUC5. **Grancar** (tel. 045/66-2454, CUC30 per hour) rents chauffeured prerevolutionary cars.

Coco-taxis, hollow egg-shaped three-wheel vehicles known as *huevitos* ("little eggs") locally, cost CUC3 minimum and rent for CUC20 hourly.

Horse-drawn *coches* ply Avenida 1ra (CUC10 per person one hour).

By Bicycle and Scooter

Scooters can be rented at most hotels and along Avenida 1ra (CUC12 for two hours, CUC24 per day). Bicycles cost CUC2 for one hour and CUC10 per day.

Central Matanzas

From Havana the Autopista runs east–west through south-central Matanzas Province. There are no diversions to distract you until you reach Km 142 and the turnoff for Jagüey Grande, Australia, and the Zapata Peninsula. There's a Cupet gas station in Jagüey Grande. Alternatively, you can follow the Carretera Central (Route 3-N-1) through a string of dusty old towns or the Circuito Norte coast road, an unremarkable route whose only town of interest is Cárdenas.

CÁRDENAS

The Península de Hicacos forms a natural breakwater protecting Bahía de Cárdenas, whose southern shore is fringed with oil derricks amid scrub and henequen plantations. In their midst is the town of Cárdenas (pop. 82,000), a world away from the commercialism of Varadero, 10 kilometers to the northwest.

The city was founded in 1828. The town developed rapidly as a port serving the prosperous sugar-producing hinterland. Otherwise, Cárdenas has a lackluster history, punctuated by a singular event in 1850, when the Cuban flag was first flown here. That year, a Venezuelan adventurer called Narciso López came ashore with a mercenary army to free the locals from Spanish rule and annex Cuba himself. Although López's ragtag army captured the town, his

MATANZAS

meager force failed to rally local support and the invaders beat a hasty retreat. Cárdenas has forever since been called the Flag City.

Cárdenas is hyped for its architectural interest and, being close to Varadero, is favored for excursions. Most of the town is dilapidated, despite being spruced up for news photographers after hometown boy Elián González was rescued in November 1999 after his mother and 10 others drowned at sea in a bid to flee Cuba for the United States. However, Cárdenas boasts a colonial cathedral and one of the nation's most impressive museums.

Orientation

Deplorably potholed streets running northeast–southwest are called *avenidas,* and streets running northwest–southeast are *calles.* Those *avenidas* northwest of Avenida Céspedes—the main boulevard—are suffixed with *oeste* (west); those to the southeast are *este* (east). *Calles* run consecutively from the bay. From Varadero, you enter town along Calle 13 (Calzada) but exit eastward along Calle 14.

19th-century hearse in Museo Oscar María de Roja, Cárdenas

© CHRISTOPHER P. BAKER

C Parque Echevarría

This charming tree-shaded plaza, one block east of Avenida Céspedes, is the cultural heart of town. On its east side stands a life-size bronze bust of José Antonio Echevarría, the leader of the anti-Batista Directorio Revolucionario Estudantil (Students Revolutionary Directorate). Echevarría led the students' assault on Batista's palace in March 1957; from a captured radio station he announced that Batista had been killed and called for a general strike, but the plug had been pulled and his words never made the air. He was killed later that day in a shootout with police. **Museo Casa Natal de José Antonio Echevarría** (Av. 4 Este #560, esq. 12, tel. 045/52-4145, Tues.–Sat. 9 A.M.–6 P.M., Sun. 9 A.M.–1 A.M., CUC1 entrance, CUC5 camera), on the park's west side, is a two-story house built in 1873. The namesake hero was born in this house in 1932. Downstairs features memorabilia relating to the Wars of Independence and fight against Batista; upstairs is accessed

by a beautiful, hand-carved spiral staircase and honors Echevarría and locals martyred for the Revolution.

The park's highlight is the superb, not-to-be-missed **Museo Oscar María de Roja** (Av. 4 Este, e/ Echevarría y Martí, tel. 045/52-2417, Tues.–Sat. 9 A.M.–6 P.M., Sun. 9 A.M.–1 P.M., CUC5 entrance including guide, cameras CUC5, videos CUC25), on the south side. Housed in the former home of the lieutenant governor (1861–1878), then the town hall (1878–1966), it's one of Cuba's oldest (founded in 1900), finest, and most expansive museums. Fourteen rooms are arrayed by theme, ranging from pre-Columbian culture to armaments, coins, the Wars of Independence, José Martí, and so on. The pièce de résistance, however, is an ornate baroque 19th-century horse-drawn hearse that stands in the foyer.

On the park's northeast corner, the **Museo de Batalla de Ideas** (Av. 6, e/ 11 y 12, tel. 045/52-7599, www.museobatalladeideas. cult.cu, Tues.–Sat. 9 A.M.–5 P.M., Sun. 9 A.M.–1 P.M., CUC2 entrance, CUC5 camera), or Museum of the Battle, is housed in the old yellow-painted firehouse (dating from 1872). Also known as the Elián Museum, it is dedicated to Elian González's father's fight with Miami's Cuban-American extremists for custody of his son. Mementos include photographs of the boy at Disneyland wearing Mickey Mouse ears, a statue showing Elián walking on a sea of human hands, even the T-shirt worn by Donato Dalrymple, the angler who plucked the plucky Elián from the sea.

Elián lives with his father, Juan Miguel, at Avenida Céspedes #275 in a one-story house behind a chain-link fence.

Avenida Céspedes

Tiny **Parque Colón** (Céspedes, e/ 8 y 9), or Columbus Park, is dominated by the **Catedral de la Concepción Inmaculada,** a neoclassical cathedral fronted by an impressive statue of Columbus with a globe at his feet (it dates from 1858). The church, built in 1846, has notable stained-glass windows. Cater-corner, the former mayor's mansion, now the near-derelict **Hotel Dominica,** is a national monument—it was here that Narciso López first raised the Cuban flag. Avenida Céspedes continues northeast to a **flagpole** and monument commemorating the events of 1850.

At the southwest end of Céspedes, a small fortress named for Oscar María de Roja stands in the central median (Elián González's home faces the fortress on the east side of the street). There's a similar fortress at the west end of town, on Avenida 13 (Calzada).

Plaza Molokoff

Occupying an entire city block (Av. 3 Oeste, e/ 12 y 13), this two-story plaza is taken up by a farmers market. The historic market building was built of iron in 1856 in the shape of a cross, with a metal domed roof in Islamic style. Its wrought-iron balustrades are held aloft by colonnades. Molokoff refers to the "dome-like" crinoline skirts fashionable in the mid-19th century.

Entertainment and Events

Cárdenas holds a **culture week** in early March to honor the founding of the city. The **Casa de la Cultura** (Av. Céspedes #706, e/ 15 y 16, tel. 045/52-1292), in a faded but charming colonial

© CHRISTOPHER P. BAKER

Columbus statue outside Catedral de la Concepción Inmaculada, Cárdenas

MATANZAS

building, offers traditional music and dance, plus other cultural events.

Accommodations and Food

Casas particulares are illegal in Cárdenas. Nor are there any hotels.

You'll be equally hard-pressed to find anywhere exciting to eat. The best place is **Café Espriu** (Calle 12, e/ Av. 4 y 6, tel. 045/52-3273, noon–10 P.M.), on the north side of Parque Echevarría. It can usually rustle up a salad, garlic chicken, etc.

Services

There's a **post office** (Céspedes y Calle 8, Mon.–Sat. 8 A.M.–6 P.M.); an **Etecsa** *telepunto* (Céspedes y Calle 13, daily 7 A.M.–11 P.M.); **Bandec** (Céspedes #252, esq. 11); and a **Cadeca** (Av. 3 Oeste, e/ 12 y 13, daily 8 A.M.–5 P.M.), where you change dollars for pesos.

Hospital José M. Aristegui (Calle 13, tel. 045/52-4011, 24 hours daily) is one kilometer west of town.

Getting There and Away

Buses depart the **Terminal de Ómnibus Provincial** (Céspedes, e/ 21 y 22, tel. 045/52-1214). Bus #376 runs between Varadero and Cárdenas (30 minutes, CUC1), arriving and departing from Calle 14 and Avenida 8. Also serving Varadero, bus #236 arrives and departs Calle 13 and Avenida 13 Oeste.

A taxi from Varadero costs about CUC15.

Trains connect Cárdenas with Jovellanos and Colón, departing and arriving **Estación San Martín** (Av. 8 Este y Calle 5, tel. 045/52-1362).

Getting Around

Horse-drawn *coches* gather by Parque Colón and ply Avenida Céspedes. For a taxi call **Cubataxi** (tel. 045/52-3160).

There's a Cupet gas station at the west end of Calle 13, on the road to Varadero.

SAN MIGUEL DE LOS BAÑOS

San Miguel de los Baños is a little spa town hidden deep amid rolling hills. It's reached via

gingerbread house in San Miguel de los Baños

© CHRISTOPHER P. BAKER

a turnoff from the Carretera Central at Coliseo, 37 kilometers east of Matanzas, at the junction with Route 3-1-1 to Cárdenas. The town's lofty setting combined with the healing properties of its mineral waters to foster growth last century as a popular health spa. The gentry built villas here in neoclassical and French provincial style, with gingerbread woodwork. Most are in tumbledown condition.

As you enter town, you'll pass the ornate but derelict **Balneario San Miguel** on your left, topped by Islamic-style turrets. Pathways lead down the garden to disused *baños,* resembling Roman or Turkish baths.

JOVELLANOS TO COLÓN

The Carretera Central continues east past fields of sugarcane. Sixteen kilometers east of Coliseo, you reach the small agricultural town of Jovellanos, a center of Afro-Cuban music and dance. There's a Cupet gas station on the Carretera Central at the east end of town.

South of Jovellanos, Route 3-182 runs southwest to **Pedro Betancourt,** a pleasant colonial town with a beautiful church at its core. Pedro Betancourt is the gateway to mile upon mile of citrus groves extending all the way south to the Autopista.

Colón, 33 kilometers east of Jovellanos, is worth a quick browse. Its colonnaded streets are lined with tumbledown neoclassical structures centered on **Parque de Libertad,** two blocks south of the main street, Máximo Gómez. At its heart is a life-size, patinated bronze statue of the town's namesake, Christopher Columbus (Cristóbal Colón).

There's a Cupet gas station on Máximo Gómez and another on Route 3-1-2, which leads south to the Autopista.

JAGÜEY GRANDE AND VICINITY

Jagüey Grande, one kilometer north of the Autopista at Km 142, is an agricultural town encircled by citrus and sugarcane fields. Km 142 is a major hub at the junction (south) for the Zapata Peninsula and Playa Girón (Bay of Pigs). Five miles east of Jagüey Grande an ungated railway track crosses the Autopista. *Slow down!*

Finca Fiesta Campesina (tel. 045/92045, daily 9 A.M.–5 P.M., free, parking CUC1), 200 yards south of the junction at Km 142, is a contrived "peasant's farm" popular with tour groups. It has a small zoo with deer, agoutis, snakes, crocodiles, and birds. You can sample fruits, Cuban coffee, and *guarapo* (sugarcane juice) crushed in a traditional *trapiche*. A restaurant serves *criollo* cuisine. Horseback rides cost CUC1, and you can even ride a bull!

There are gas stations 100 meters west of Parador de Carretera and at the junction of Calles 13 and 70, at the south end of Jagüey Grande.

Museo Memorial Comandancia FAR

The derelict Central Australia sugar factory looms over the sugarcane fields two kilometers south of Jagüey Grande and one kilometer south of the Km 142 junction, on the road to Playa Girón. Fidel Castro set up his military headquarters here on the afternoon of April 15, 1961, during the Bay of Pigs invasion. Castro, who knew that the sugar factory had the only telephone for miles around, directed his troops from the *central* before dashing off to lead a barrage of howitzers against the invaders.

Remains of aircraft shot up in the fighting lie outside the small Revolutionary Armed Forces Command Center Memorial Museum (tel. 045/91-2504, Tues.–Sat. 9 A.M.–5 P.M., Sun. 8 A.M.–noon, entrance CUC1, guide CUC1, cameras CUC1), which has photographs, the desk and telephone used by Fidel, plus an anti-aircraft gun and uniforms. A steam train ride was to be introduced.

Accommodations and Food

Cubanacán's delightfully rustic **Villa Horizontes Batey Don Pedro** (tel. 045/91-2825, comercial@peninsual.cyt.cu, CUC19 s, CUC24 d low season, CUC24 s, CUC30 d high season), adjoining Finca Fiesta Campesina about 200 yards south of the junction at Km 142, has two modern air-conditioned cabins plus 10 roomy thatched log cottages with satellite TVs, ceiling fans, large bathrooms, and small kitchenettes. Some have loft bedrooms for four people. *Criollo* meals are served.

Pío Cua (tel. 045/91-2525, CUC24 s/d, CUC30 including breakfast), south of Jagüey Grande about two kilometers south of the Central Australia factory, has three simply furnished, air-conditioned cabins: one for two people, two each for four people. All have local TV and modern bathrooms. The two larger concrete ones are musty; the smaller is of wood but gets hot. It has an atmospheric restaurant (11:30 A.M.–4 P.M.) and bar popular with tour groups.

Parador de Carretera (tel. 045/91-3224, sistema@cienaga.var.cyt.cu), at the Km 142 junction, is a café-restaurant (daily 11:30 A.M.–10 P.M.) that doubles as a tourist information center (daily 8 A.M.–8 P.M.) that arranges guides, sells excursions, and handles bookings for the two hotels.

Península de Zapata and Vicinity

South of the hamlet of Australia, the sugarcane fields end, and the sawgrass and reed brush begins. This swampland (the Ciénega de Zapata) sweeps south to the Caribbean Sea, smothering the Zapata Peninsula, a great shoe-shaped extension jutting west into the Golfo de Batabanó. Most of the 4,230-square-kilometer limestone landmass is within Parque Nacional Ciénaga de Zapata, a wildlife reserve within the larger Reserva de la Biosfera Ciénaga de Zapata.

Zapata extends west of a deep, finger-like bay, the 20-kilometer-long Bahía de Cochinos—Bay of Pigs, named for the local *cochinos cimarrones,* wild pigs, which once formed a staple diet for local Indians. The bay is renowned as the site for the Bay of Pigs invasion, when about 1,300 heavily armed, CIA-trained Cuban exiles came ashore to topple the Castro regime.

Route 3-1-18 runs like a plumb line from Australia to Playa Larga, a small fishing village tucked into the head of the bay. Concrete monuments rise along the coast road, each one representing a Cuban soldier (161 in all) who fell during the three-day battle in April 1961.

The region was inhabited by pre-Columbian Indians. The Spanish conquistadores destroyed the Taíno population before abandoning the region. It has remained a virtual no-man's-land ever since. About 8,000 souls inhabited the area on the eve of the Revolution, when there were no roads, schools, or electricity. Charcoal-making was the major occupation of the impoverished population. The *cenagueros* were among the first beneficiaries of the Revolution. The youthful Castro government built highways into the swamps, established a small hospital and schools, and more than 200 teachers from the national literacy campaign arrived. Today *carboneros* still build their ovens, but their charcoal now goes to town on trucks.

RESERVA DE LA BIOSFERA CIÉNAGA DE ZAPATA

This 628,171-hectare UNESCO Biosphere Reserve enshrines the entire Península de Zapata and surrounding wilderness. The park entrance (no fee) is midway along Route 3-1-18. The entrance to the actual wildlife reserve is at Buena Ventura, two kilometers west of Playa Larga, 32 kilometers south of Australia; a fee applies and a guide is obligatory.

For a perspective on the reserve, call in at the

CRABS!

Mid-March through April, giant land crabs (*cangrejos*) emerge from the vegetation and swarm, legion upon legion, to meeting grounds where they gather for vast orgies and egg-laying parties. They move in such numbers that the coast road between Playa Larga and Playa Girón, and those along much of the southern and eastern coasts of Cuba, become a veritable carpet of crushed crabs, like giant M&Ms crushed underfoot. For travelers it can be a daunting challenge to avoid a puncture.

In *Mi Moto Fidel: Motorcycling Through Castro's Cuba,* I write: "The air stank of fetid crabmeat. Vultures hopped about, drawn greedily to the prodigal banquet. I passed my first live crab scurrying toward the sea. Bright orange. A newborn. Then a large black crab with terrifying red pincers ran across my path, the forerunner of a lethal invasion heading the other way. Suddenly I was surrounded by a battalion of armored, surly crustaceans that turned to snap at my tires. I slalomed between them as they rose in the road with menacing claws held high. Then I hit one square on. POOF! It sounded like bubble wrap exploding."

The surreal crabfest is usually over by May. Until then, there's no way around them. If you choose to drive, be sure to have a spare tire – it's a matter of luck as to whether you get through without a puncture.

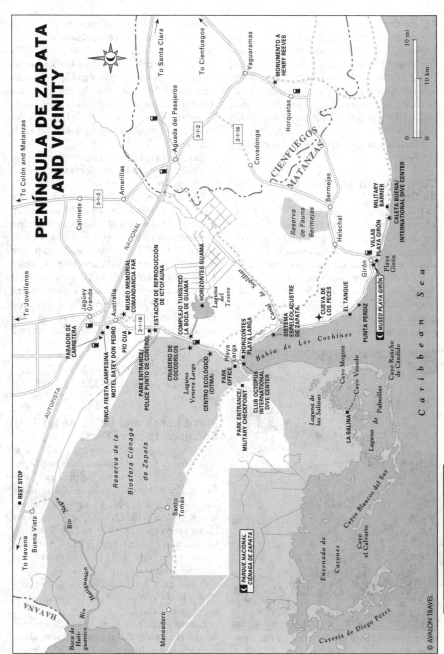

PENÍNSULA DE ZAPATA AND VICINITY

To Colón and Matanzas
To Santa Clara
To Cienfuegos

Yaguaramas
MONUMENTO A HENRY REEVES

Aguada del Pasajeros

3-1-2

3-1-16

Horquetas

Covadonga

Amarillas

CIENFUEGOS
MATANZAS

3-1-2

Bermejas

Calimete

NACIONAL

Reserva de Fauna Bermejas

Helechal

MILITARY BARRIER

VILLAS PLAYA GIRÓN

CALETA BUENA/ INTERNATIONAL DIVE CENTER

To Jovellanos

Jagüey Grande

Australia

MUSEO MEMORIAL COMANDANCIA FAR

ESTACIÓN DE REPRODUCCIÓN DE ICTOFAUNA

HORIZONTES GUAMA

Laguna del Tesoro

Girón

Playa Girón

MUSEO PLAYA GIRÓN

PARADOR DE CARRETERA

FINCA FIESTA CAMPESINA/ MOTEL BATEY DON PEDRO

PÍO CUA

3-1-18

COMPLEJO TURÍSTICO LA BOCA DE GUAMA

Canal de Sopillar

SISTEMA ESPELEOLACUSTRE DE ZAPATA

CUEVA DE LOS PECES

EL TANQUE

PUNTA PERDIZ

PARK ENTRANCE/ POLICE PUNTO DE CONTROL

CRIADERO DE COCODRILOS

Laguna Venera Largo

CENTRO ECOLÓGICO (CITMA)

HORIZONTES PLAYA LARGA

Playa Larga

Canal

Bahía de Los Cochinos

Caribbean Sea

AUTOPISTA

Reserva de la Biosfera Ciénaga de Zapata

PARK OFFICE

PARK ENTRANCE/ MILITARY CHECKPOINT

CLUB OCTOPUS INTERNATIONAL DIVE CENTER

Cayo Mogote

Cayo Venado

Cayo Rancho de Cándido

To Havana

REST STOP

Buena Vista

Río Negro

Río Hanábanico

Santo Tomás

Laguna de las Salinas

LA SALINA

Laguna de Padmillas

PARQUE NACIONAL CIÉNAGA DE ZAPATA

Ensenada de Cazones

Cayos Blancos del Sur

Cayo el Calvario

HAVANA

Boca de Haití guanico

Maneadero

Cayería de Diego Pérez

10 mi

10 km

© AVALON TRAVEL

MATANZAS

Centro Ecológico (tel. 045/91-5539, Mon.–Fri. 8 A.M.–4 P.M., CUC2 including an interpretive trail walk), a visitors ecological center five kilometers south of La Boca de Guamá. It features an exhibition on the region. A live *manjuarí* swims in a fish tank. Leaf-cutter ants go about their business farming fungi in a glass case, and a separate exhibit details the Indian heritage.

Mosquitoes are ferocious here; bring repellent!

Complejo Turístico La Boca de Guamá

La Boca Tourist Complex (tel. 045/91-5551), 19 kilometers south of Jagüey Grande, is an important roadside stop at the edge of Laguna del Tesoro. It has restaurants, a souvenir shop, and a gas station. No credit cards are accepted.

Raised wooden platforms provide vistas down over Cuban crocodiles (daily 9 A.M.–5 P.M., CUC5 adults, CUC3 children) in lagoons. The awesome beasts lie still as death, jaws agape, hoping obviously for a careless

© CHRISTOPHER P. BAKER

MATANZAS

crocodiles at Complejo Turístico La Boca de Guamá

visitor to stumble and fall into the pit. Across the road, the **Criadero de Cocodrilos** (tel. 045/91-5666, daily 9 A.M.–5:30 P.M., CUC5 adults, CUC3 children), run by Flora y Fauna, is Cuba's most important crocodile farm, with more than 3,000 crocodiles. Visitors can learn about the entire breeding cycle and ecology. When they're seven years old, some are released to the wild; others are killed for meat and leather.

You can watch potters churning out simple ceramics at the **Taller de Cerámica** (Mon.–Sat. 9 A.M.–6 P.M.).

The 16-square-kilometer **Laguna del Tesoro** (Treasure Lagoon) is stocked with bass, tarpon, and meter-long *manjuarí*. The lake, reached via a five-kilometer-long canal from La Boca, is named for the Taíno religious objects that have been raised from the water and are now exhibited at **Villa Guamá,** on an island in the middle of the lake; this hotel features a mock Indian village and 32 life-size sculptures depicting Taíno engaged in daily activities. An open-air tour boat leaves La Boca for Villa Guamá on a regular basis (CUC12).

Jet Skis (CUC35 for 90 minutes) and rowboats (CUC2) can be hired. Fishing trips are offered (tel. 045/91-3224, CUC92 for six hours).

Playa Larga and Bahía de los Cochinos (Bay of Pigs)

Playa Larga, a fishing community at the head of the Bahía de los Cochinos, was one of the two main landing sites during the Bay of Pigs fiasco. The motley village has a military dock and a small beach with a water sports outlet (c/o Rigo, tel. 015227-9637) at Villas Playa Larga (pedal boat CUC4 per hour, kayaks CUC2, and Hobie Cats CUC10). A marina is slated to be built, and catamaran excursions and even a mini-sub are to be added.

A road leads west from Playa Larga two kilometers to the entrance to the Parque Nacional Ciénaga de Zapata.

East of Playa Larga, white beaches extend around the bay. At **Caleta del Rosario,** about three kilometers from Playa Larga, is a splendid little cove with good swimming. The route is also lined with *cenotes,* limestone sinkholes filled with freshwater. **Cueva de los Peces** (Cave of Fishes, daily 9 A.M.–5 P.M.), 15 kilometers from Playa Larga, is one of the largest *cenotes:* 70 meters deep, it's a superb spot for swimming and scuba diving. The beach in front of the *cenote* also offers good snorkeling in jade-colored waters.

A little way east of Cueva de los Peces is **Bar/Restaurante Punta Perdiz** (daily 9 A.M.–4 P.M.), a small recreation area with a bird-watching trail. Nearby, the **Sistema Espeleolacustre de Zapata** investigates marine caverns. It has two one-kilometer-long trails through endemic woodlands. The first leaves to Cuevo El Brinco and a stone bridge. The second leads to Cueva Clara. You can swim in *cenotes.* Guided hikes are offered four times daily.

The **Club Octopus International Dive Center** (Playa Larga, tel. 045/98-7294) offers dives daily 8 A.M.–5 P.M. (CUC25 one dive, CUC40 cave dive and Nitrox dives, CUC365 certification) and rents snorkeling gear (CUC3). Marlin also has a dive outlet at El Tanque, about 10 kilometers south of Playa Larga. It also has guided snorkeling trips to the barrier reef (CUC10).

◖ Parque Nacional Ciénaga de Zapata

The 490,417-hectare Zapata Swamp National Park protects Cuba's most important wetland area. The ecosystems include marsh grass, mangrove thickets, and thickly wooded swamp forest. It is a biological mirror of the Everglades of Florida—there are even beautifully banded *liguus* snails, a kind of tree snail common in the Everglades. Vegetation includes the button tree, so small that it looks like a bonsai. Zapata harbors more than 900 species of flora, 171 species of birds, 31 of reptiles, and 12 of mammals, including the pygmy *jutía* native to the Zapata swamp, and manatees. The alligator gar (*manjuarí*), the most primitive of Cuban fish, is found in lagoons, as are crocodiles and caimans.

Refugio de Fauna Bermejas, accessed from north of Playa Girón, is a separate section of the park (the entrance fee is payable in the Hotel Playa Larga) with a bird-watching trail.

BIRD-WATCHING

Of Cuba's 22 endemic bird species, 18 inhabit the marshes. Zapata protects the bee hummingbird (the world's smallest bird) as well as an endemic tanager and *gallinuela de Santo Tomás,* the Zapata sparrow, Zapata rail, Zapata wren, the Cuban trogon or *tocororo,* and Cuban parrots. Zapata is also a favorite stop for tens of thousands of migratory birds. The best time is October to April, when overwhelming numbers of birds flock in, among them sandhill cranes and wood ibis.

The best spots for bird-watching are **Laguna de las Salinas,** a 36,400 hectare expanse of flats, watercourses, and islets on the southern shores of Zapata and where flamingos flock in their thousands; and also around **Santo Tomás,** about 30 kilometers west of Playa Larga (CUC10 per person by jeep, including guide).

Early morning is best for bird-watching, and springtime is the best time of year.

FISHING

Zapata has been isolated from fishing pressure since 1959, making this huge reserve as close to a virgin fishery as one can find in today's world. There are said to be places where you can catch the fish with your bare hands, the way the indigenous Indians did. There are two distinct areas for fishing—the Río Hatiguanico (for tarpon) and La Salina (for bonefish). Several well-traveled anglers consider La Salina the standard by which all other locations should be judged worldwide. Bonefishing is most productive late fall through June; tarpon fishing peaks late February/early March through June. Underpowered skiffs mean long periods getting to the best lagoons.

PERMITS AND GUIDES

Access is by permit only (CUC12 per person, including an obligatory guide), obtained from the **Oficina Parque Nacional** (tel. 045/98-7249,

BAY OF PIGS

The Bay of Pigs invasion – Cubans call it *la victoria* (the victory) – was the brainchild of Richard Bissell, deputy director of the CIA. The plan was to infiltrate anti-Castro guerrillas onto the island so that they could link up with domestic opponents. The "Program of Covert Action Against the Castro Regime" called for creation of a Cuban government in exile, covert action in Cuba, and "a paramilitary force outside of Cuba for future guerrilla action." In August 1959 President Eisenhower approved a US$13 million budget with the proviso that "no U.S. military personnel were to be used in a combat status."

Under a flexible mandate, Bissell radically expanded the original concept. By the time President Kennedy was briefed, in November 1960, the plan had grown to include 1,500 men backed by a rebel air force of B-26s.

THE UNITED STATES PREPARES TO INVADE

The CIA recruited Cuban exiles for the invasion force and used an abandoned naval base at Opa-Locka, outside Miami, to train the brigade. They were later moved to U.S. military locations in Guatemala and Puerto Rico (in violation of U.S. law). Meanwhile, a "government in exile" was chosen from within a feud-riven group of political exiles, many of them corrupt right-wing politicians nostalgic for Batista days. The group was to be transformed into a provisional government once it gained a foothold.

The plan called for the invasion force to link up with guerrillas operating out of the Sierra Escambray, more than 100 kilometers east of the Bay of Pigs, where the brigade would land at three beaches 25 kilometers apart and surrounded by swamps. In photos taken by U-2 spy planes, the CIA's photo interpreter identified what he claimed was seaweed offshore. "They are coral heads," said Dr. Juan Sordo, a brigade member: "I know them. I have seen them." Another brigade member agreed. The water would be too shallow for the landing craft, he said. But the CIA wouldn't listen.

The invasion plan relied on eliminating the Cuban air force. The CIA wanted U.S. air support; the State Department wanted it kept to a minimum so that the planes could later be claimed to have originated in Cuba. On April 15, 1961, two days before the invasion, B-26 bombers painted in Cuban air force colors struck Cuba's three military air bases. Thus Castro was fully forewarned. Worse, only five aircraft were destroyed, and Cuba still had at least three T-33 jet fighters and four British-made Sea Fury light-attack bombers.

THE INVASION

The U.S. Navy aircraft carrier *Essex* and five destroyers escorted six freighters carrying the Cuban fighters and their supplies. The landings began about 1:15 A.M. on April 17 at Playa Girón

sistema@cienaga.var.cyt.cu, Mon.–Sat. 8 A.M.–4:30 P.M.), beside the highway in Playa Larga. You can also hire a guide and arrange hikes, bird-watching, fishing (CUC170 full-day), and crocodile tours through Parador de Carretera, at Km 142. You'll need your own vehicle (4WD recommended), with a spare seat for the guide.

Accommodations

LA BOCA DE GUAMÁ

Laguna Tesoro was one of Castro's favorite fishing spots. The Cuban leader spent many weekends in a *cabina* that became known as "Fidel's Key." One day he supposedly announced, "We're going to build a Tahitian village here!" And they did. The result is a replica Taíno village, now **Horizontes Guamá** (tel. 045/91-5551, www.hotelescubanacan.com, CUC24 s, CUC30 d), with 13 tiny islands connected by hanging bridges. At last visit, the 44 thatched, air-conditioned bungalows on stilts had been rebuilt after yet another trashing by hurricanes. They have TVs (why?). There's a swimming pool. Bring bug spray!

and Playa Larga. Landing craft (LCVPs) came roaring in. About 140 meters offshore, they hit the coral reefs the CIA had dismissed as seaweed. The brigade had to wade ashore. Meanwhile, the fiberglass boats used by the Second and Fifth Battalions capsized. The Cubans had installed tall, extremely bright lights right on the beach. "It looked like Coney Island," recalls Gray Lynch, the CIA point man who ended up directing the invasion. The brigade had also been told that "no communications existed within 20 miles of the beach." In fact, there was a radio station only 100 meters inland. By the time the brigade stormed it, Castro had been alerted.

Kennedy had approved taking the Cubans to the beaches; beyond that, they were on their own. Worried about repercussions at the United Nations, Kennedy ordered cancellation of a second strike designed to give the invasion force cover. With that decision, the operation was lost.

Castro set up headquarters in the Central Australia sugar mill and from there directed the Cuban defense. As the exiles landed, Cuba's aircraft swooped down. Two supply ships containing ammunition and communications equipment were sunk. Two other ammunition vessels fled and had to be turned back by the USS *Eaton*. The brigade did, however, manage to unload WWII-era Sherman tanks. They fought the "battle of the rotunda" against Cuba's equally outdated T-34 and Stalin tanks.

Despite the CIA's predictions, the local people ("armed only with M-52 Czech rifles," writes Peter Wyden in *Bay of Pigs*) defended their homeland until the first Cuban battalion of 900 student soldiers arrived in buses (half the cadet troops were killed when the convoy was strafed by the brigade's B-26s). Reinforcements poured in and encircled the invasion forces, and the fight became a simple matter of whittling away at the exiles.

A U.S. jet-fighter squadron flew reconnaissance over the invasion but was forbidden to engage in combat. Nonetheless, six U.S. pilots flew combat missions under CIA orders without President Kennedy's knowledge. Four were shot down and killed. The Cubans recovered the body of one of the pilots – Thomas Ray – and found his dog tags (his corpse remained in a Havana morgue unclaimed by the U.S. government; Ray's daughter brought his body home for burial in 1979).

ABANDONING THE *BRIGADISTAS*
On the third day of the battle, the U.S. destroyers advanced on the shore. The destroyers picked up those *brigadistas* who had made it back to sea, then sailed away, leaving the survivors to fend for themselves. The brigade had lost 114 men (the Cubans lost 161), but a further 1,189 were captured. Eventually, 1,091 prisoners were returned to the United States in exchange for US$53 million in food and medical supplies.

PLAYA LARGA
Several homeowners in Playa Larga rent rooms. My favorite is ◖ **Villa Juana** (tel. 045/98-7308, caribesolpz@yahoo.es, CUC20–25), a pleasant home with modern amenities. The single air-conditioned room with its own refrigerator, fan, and modern bathroom opens to a charming garden patio where meals are served. The family is a delight.

Casa de Enrique Rivas (tel. 045/98-7178, CUC25 per person including breakfast and dinner), at Caletón, one kilometer west of

Playa Larga, offers one spacious, clean air-conditioned room with private hot-water bathroom.

The beachfront **Horizontes Playa Larga** (tel. 045/98-7212 ext. 106, fax 045/98-7294, www.hotelescubanacan.com, CUC37 s, CUC46 d low season, CUC38 s, CUC44 d high season, including breakfast) has 68 spacious, modestly furnished, air-conditioned *cabinas* with basic kitchenettes. The restaurant is elegant and the swimming pool lively. It has water sports.

MATANZAS

Food

At La Boca, the modestly elegant **Colibrí Restaurant** (daily 8 A.M.–8 P.M., CUC5–12) serves *criollo* fare, including crocodile (CUC10) and lobster (CUC11). The open-air **Bar y Restaurante La Rionda** (daily 9:30 A.M.–8 P.M., CUC5–12), adjacent, is nicer on cooler days.

Cueva de los Peces (daily 8 A.M.–5 P.M., CUC5–12), overhanging the *cenote,* has a thatched restaurant serving *criollo* fare.

Getting There and Around

The 8 A.M. Havana–Trinidad **Víazul** and 3 P.M. Trinidad–Havana buses travel via Playa Larga and Girón. In January 2010, Transtur introduced the hop-on/hop-off **Guamá Bus Tour** (CUC5), twice daily between Guamá (departs at 11:30 A.M. and 4 P.M.) and Caleta Buena via Playa Larga and Playa Girón (departs 9 A.M. and 2:30 P.M.).

Tour agencies in Havana and Varadero offer excursions.

PLAYA GIRÓN

Finally you arrive at the spot where socialism and capitalism slugged it out, and what do you find? Vacationers from cool climates, lathered with suntan oil, splashing in the shallows where 30-odd years before blood and bullets mingled with the sand on the surf.

Playa Girón is a small, single-road *pueblo* of a few hundred people. It was named in honor of Gilbert Girón, a French pirate captured here. The community lies inland of the tourist facility and beach, which has been off-limits to Cubans since 1998 and at last visit was being used exclusively for Venezuelans receiving medical treatment. The beautiful white-sand beach is enclosed within a concrete barrier (*rompeola*), which protects against any future wave of CIA-backed anti-Castroites foolish enough to come ashore. Nonetheless, it's a carbuncle on the coast and made worse by the military watchtower to the east end, where soldiers with high-powered binoculars have a vantage for spying on topless bathers.

The paved coastal highway (Route 3-1-16) turns inland at Playa Girón and runs 39 kilometers through scrubland to Yaguaramas (forsake the road from Covavango; it's terribly deteriorated). Here, it connects with Route 3-1-2, which runs north to the Autopista and east to Cienfuegos. About five kilometers south of Yaguaramas, the **Monumento a Henry Earl Reeves** marks the site where the eponymous U.S. mercenary, who rose to be a general in the Cuban army (he is known to Cubans as "El Inglesito"), was killed in 1876 during the first Cuban War of Independence.

◖ Museo Playa Girón

This small museum (tel. 045/98-4122, daily 8 A.M.–5 P.M., entrance CUC2, guide CUC1, cameras CUC1, videos CUC5), outside the entrance to Villas Playa Girón, gives an accurate portrayal of the drama of the Bay of Pigs invasion. Black-and-white photographs confirm the appalling poverty of the local peasantry before the Revolution. Others profile the events preceding the invasion and culminating in the act to which the museum is dedicated—the invasion of April 15, 1961, by 1,297 CIA-trained Cubans.

Maps trace the evolution of the 72-hour battle. There are photographs, including gory pictures of civilians caught in the midst of explosions, and of all the martyrs—the "Heroes de Girón"—killed in the fighting (the youngest, Nelson Fernández Estevez, was only 16 years old; the oldest, Juan Ruíz Serna, was 60). Note the photo of a young militiaman, Eduardo García Delgado, who wrote "Fidel" on a wall with his own blood before dying, face-down, with his hand on the L. And, of course, Fidel is there, leaping from a T-34 tank. Other displays include weapons and a Sea Fury fighter-aircraft, which sits on the forecourt alongside Soviet T-34 and SAU-100 tanks.

Caleta Buena

This exquisite cove (tel. 045/98-5587, daily 10 A.M.–5 P.M., CUC15), eight kilometers east of Playa Girón, contains a natural pool good for swimming. There are pocket-size beaches

© CHRISTOPHER P. BAKER

Sea Fury at Museo Playa Girón

atop the coral platform, with red-tiled *ranchitas* for shade and lounge chairs for sunning. The seabed is a multicolored garden of coral and sponges, ideal for snorkeling (CUC3 one hour, CUC5 per day) and diving (CUC25). Lunch is served 12:30–3 P.M. (the bar is open until 5 P.M.).

Caleta Buena is the end of the road; beyond is a military zone.

Accommodations

There are more than two dozen *casas particulares,* most being similar in style and price (CUC20). The standout is **(** **Villa Merci** (tel. 045/98-4304, CUC20), set in a lovely garden (with secure parking) on the road to Caletas Buena, 300 meters east of the main junction in town. Mercedes, the owner, is a delightful hostess.

Hostal Silvia Acosta Lima (tel. 045/98-4249) has two rooms that appeal for their cleanliness and decor. They're well-lit, cross-ventilated, and have fans and private bathrooms with large hot-water showers. A TV lounge boasts leather sofas. Meals are offered.

Lackluster is an understatement for Cubanacán's beachfront **Villas Playa Girón** (tel. 045/98-4110, fax 045/98-4117, www.hotelescubanacan.com, CUC37 s, CUC46 d all-inclusive), with 282 rooms in villas scattered amid lawns. Some have shared bathrooms; all have satellite TV, telephone, and fridge, but furnishings are basic. The restaurant's buffet is pathetic. Treat it as a place to overnight, *not* to vacation!

Services

There's a coin laundry, a pharmacy, and a post office opposite the museum.

Getting There and Around

The **Víazul** bus departs Girín for Havana at 6:20 P.M. and for Cienfuegos and Trinidad at 11:35 A.M.

Most tour agencies in Havana and Varadero offer excursions.

Cubacar (tel. 045/98-4144) has a rental agency opposite the museum. There's a gas station adjacent.

MATANZAS

CIENFUEGOS AND VILLA CLARA

Villa Clara and Cienfuegos Provinces lie due east of Matanzas Province, with Villa Clara north of Cienfuegos. Together they share some of the prettiest scenery in Cuba. The region is skipped by most tourists, who whiz by along the Autopista or Carretera Central bound for Oriente or the colonial city of Trinidad, in Sancti Spíritus Province. Such haste is a pity, for you are likely to miss one of my favorite regions in Cuba.

The southern and eastern portions of Villa Clara Province are dominated by beautiful rolling uplands called the Alturas de Santa Clara. The Alturas rise gradually to the steep, pine-clad Sierra Escambray. Today cool forests tantalize bird-watchers and hikers, with artificial lakes good for fishing, a famous health spa, and an invigorating climate. The mountains extend south and west into Cienfuegos Province, which surpasses even Havana in industrial output.

Industry is centered on the city of Cienfuegos, a major port town that also boasts some splendid colonial architecture and, nearby, a fine botanical garden, while the city of Santa Clara (also an important industrial and university city) should be on every traveler's itinerary for the fascinating Museo de Che (Guevara). Nearby, the historic town of Remedios is caught in a delightful time-warp.

Villa Clara is second only to Pinar del Río as a center of tobacco production, centered on the scenic Vuelta Arriba region, east of the provincial capital. Here, Remedios and neighboring villages are renowned for their *parrandas*, unique year-end carnival-style revelries that

HIGHLIGHTS

◖◗ Parque Martí: Cienfuegos's expansive central plaza is surrounded by impressive neoclassical structures and a cathedral (page 290).

◖◗ Palacio del Valle: This Mogul-inspired confection is a one-of-a-kind mansion turned restaurant; sure, the food and service win no awards, but the setting is memorable (page 293).

◖◗ Jardín Botánico Soledad: This vast botanical garden on the outskirts of Cienfuegos has separate sections for cactus, rubber trees, and other plants (page 298).

◖◗ El Nicho: The placid Sierra Escambray setting of this recreational site features beautiful waterfalls and horseback riding, hiking, and other activities (page 302).

◖◗ Complejo Escultórico Memorial Comandante Ernesto Che Guevara: A splendid museum sits beneath the imposing Che Guevara monument in Santa Clara. A reverential mausoleum contains the revolutionary hero's remains (page 304).

◖◗ Remedios: Time your visit to this beautiful colonial town for year's end to catch the *parranda* – a fireworks battle like no other (page 313).

◖◗ Cayos de Villa Clara: A 50-kilometer-long land bridge provides access to stunning white-sand beaches and jade waters on remote cays with great fishing and scuba diving and top-class resorts (page 318).

LOOK FOR ◖◗ TO FIND RECOMMENDED SIGHTS, ACTIVITIES, DINING, AND LODGING.

border on mayhem. Nearby, gorgeous beaches lie at hand in the Cayos de Villa Clara.

PLANNING YOUR TIME

All the main highways merge into (or radiate out from) the city of Santa Clara, which boasts the must-see **Complejo Escultórico Memorial Comandante Ernesto Che Guevara.** A full day is sufficient for this city, which has several good *casas particulares.*

Northwest of Santa Clara, the Circuito Norte linking Villa Clara with Matanzas Province skirts the north coast and offers little of visual appeal. You can enjoy a massage and steep in mud at Baños de Elguea. Northeast of Santa Clara, the route passes through Vuelta Arriba and is superbly scenic. I recommend overnighting in the town of **Remedios** to savor its historic charm. If possible, time your visit for Christmas week, when the entire town

explodes in revelry; accommodation is in short supply at year's end, so book well in advance. When the dust settles, head out to **Cayos de Villa Clara** for sunning, swimming, and to reel in some game fish from the placid jade waters.

The Carretera Central through central Villa Clara will take you through aged provincial towns, although there are no sites of significance. Similarly, the Autopista runs through northern Cienfuegos and southern Villa Clara Province and should be used for rapid transit through the region. (East of Santa Clara city, the scenery takes a dramatic turn as the Autopista cuts through the beautiful hills of the Alturas de Santa Clara and passes into Sancti Spíritus Province.) The main turnoff for the city of Cienfuegos is at Aguada de los Pasajeros, where there's a gas station alongside an appealing restaurant and eight-room hotel (tel. 043/56-2457, econ.aguada@cienf.palmares.cu), with an antique steam engine on display. Just east of Ranchuelo, an ungated railway track runs across the Autopista.

The city of Cienfuegos is a popular destination with an intriguing historic city core. Nearby, the ho-hum beach at Playa Rancho Luna has a Delfinario with dolphin shows, and anyone with a love of flora will find fascination in the **Jardín Botánico Soledad.** By following the scenic southern coast road, you can use Cienfuegos as a gateway for exploring the Sierra Escambray, although Trinidad, in Sancti Spíritus Province, is the best base.

You'll need at least a week to see all the highlights, with two days for Cienfuegos, a day in the Sierra Escambray, one night in Santa Clara, at least one night in Remedios, and one or two days in the Cayos de Villa Clara.

Santa Clara and Cienfuegos are served by Víazul buses, and Santa Clara is a main stop for the Havana–Santiago de Cuba train service.

Cienfuegos and Vicinity

CIENFUEGOS

Cienfuegos (pop. 105,000), 340 kilometers east of Havana and 69 kilometers southwest of Santa Clara, lies on the east side of the Bahía de Cienfuegos, a deep, 88-square-kilometer bay with an umbilical entrance. It's Cuba's third-largest port and shelters a large fishing and shrimping fleet.

Cienfuegos means "100 fires" and is sometimes written "100 fuegos." Citizens call their town La Perla del Sur (The Pearl of the South). The city's appeal lies partly in the French flavor of its colonial hub, with a wide Parisian-style boulevard and elegant colonnades (Cienfuegos even had its own Chinatown (now long since devoid of Chinese people). Nonetheless, Cienfuegos has neither the grace of Trinidad nor the flair of Havana. Still, there is an ambience that inspired Benny Moré, the celebrated Cuban *sonoro,* to sing, "Cienfuegos is the city I like best." Not least, it has a swinging nightlife and tremendous *casas particulares.*

Orientation

Approaching from the Autopista, the highway enters the city from the north and becomes a broad boulevard, the Paseo del Prado (Calle 37), the city's main thoroughfare leading to the historic core, called Pueblo Nuevo. Parque Martí, the main plaza, is four blocks west of the Prado and reached via Avenidas 54 and 56. Avenida 54 (El Bulevar), the principal shopping street, is pedestrian-only.

At Avenida 46, the Prado becomes the Malecón, a wide seafront boulevard stretching south one kilometer along a narrow peninsula ending at Punta Gorda, a once-exclusive residential district that recalls 1950s North American suburbia, with Detroit classics still parked in the driveways of mid-20th-century homes. Beyond Punta Gorda is a short, slender isthmus lined with old wooden homes.

The city is laid out in a grid: even-numbered *calles* run north–south, crossing odd-numbered *avenidas* running east–west. A six-lane highway, the *circunvalación,* bypasses the city to the north.

History

Columbus supposedly discovered the bay in 1494. Shortly after the Spanish settled Cuba and established their trade restrictions, the bay developed a thriving smuggling trade. Sir Francis Drake and Henry Morgan were among privateers who called for plunder. Construction of a fortress—Castillo de Jagua—was begun in 1738 to protect the bay and to police smuggling through the straits. It wasn't until 1817 that Louis D'Clouet, a French émigré from Louisiana, devised a settlement scheme that he presented to Don José Cienfuego, the Spanish captain-general. The Spanish government would pay for the transportation of white colonists from Europe. The Spanish Parliament approved. By April 1819, the first 137 French settlers arrived. Cienfuegos grew rapidly to wealth thanks to the deep-water harbor, and merchants and plantation owners graced the city with a surfeit of stucco.

The city continued to prosper during the early 20th century and had an unremarkable history until September 5, 1957, when young naval officers and sailors (supported by the CIA) at the Cienfuegos Naval Base rebelled against the Batista regime and took control of the city's military installations. Members of Castro's revolutionary 26th of July Movement and students joined them. Batista's troops managed to recapture the city by nightfall.

Since the Revolution, the city's hinterland has grown significantly, mostly to the west, where a port and industrial complex were initiated in the 1980s.

◖ Parque Martí

Most of Cienfuegos's buildings of note surround Parque Martí, on the ground where the founding of the first settlement was proclaimed on April 22, 1819. The city's most prominent and illustrious sons are commemorated in bronze or stone, including a statue to José Martí, guarded

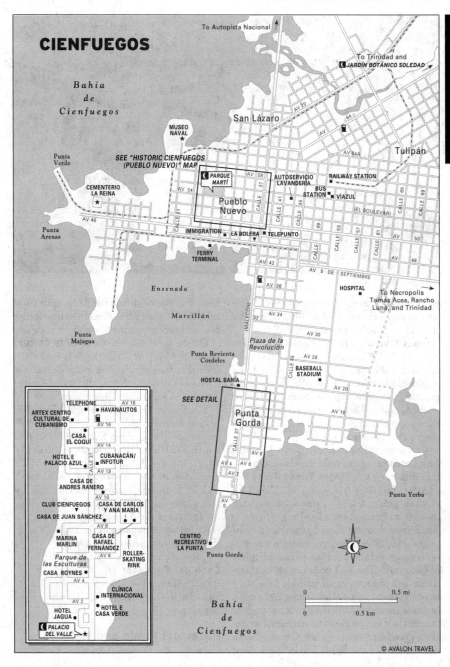

CIENFUEGOS

Bahía
de
Cienfuegos

To Autopista Nacional

To Trinidad and
JARDÍN BOTÁNICO SOLEDAD

San Lázaro

Tulipán

MUSEO
NAVAL

Punta
Verde

SEE "HISTORIC CIENFUEGOS
(PUEBLO NUEVO)" MAP

CEMENTERIO
LA REINA

PARQUE
MARTÍ

AUTOSERVICIO
LAVANDERÍA

RAILWAY STATION

BUS
STATION

VIAZUL

AV 58

AV 54

Pueblo
Nuevo

AV 48

Punta
Arenas

IMMIGRATION   LA BOLERA   TELEPUNTO

CALLE 21

CALLE 37

CALLE 41

CALLE 45

CALLE 49

CALLE 53

CALLE 57

CALLE 61

CALLE 65

CALLE 69

(EL BOULEVAR)

AV 50

AV 46

FERRY
TERMINAL

AV 42

AV 5 DE SEPTIEMBRE

Ensenada

AV 38

HOSPITAL

To Necropolis
Tomás Acea, Rancho
Luna, and Trinidad

Marcillán

AV 34

AV 30

Punta
Majagua

Plaza de la
Revolución

Punta Revienta
Cordeles

CALLE 45

AV 26

BASEBALL
STADIUM

HOSTAL BAHÍA

SEE DETAIL

Punta
Gorda

CALLE 37

AV 20

AV 16

AV 8

AV 4   AV 6

AV 2

Punta Yerba

AV 0

CENTRO
RECREATIVO
LA PUNTA

Punta Gorda

Bahía
de
Cienfuegos

Detail inset (Punta Gorda)

TELEPHONE

ARTEX CENTRO
CULTURAL DE
CUBANISMO

HAVANAUTOS

AV 18

AV 16

CASA
EL COQUÍ

HOTEL E
PALACIO AZUL

CUBANACÁN/
INFOTUR

AV 14

CALLE 37

AV 12

CASA DE
ANDRES RANERO

AV 10

CLUB CIENFUEGOS

CASA DE JUAN SÁNCHEZ

CASA DE CARLOS
Y ANA MARÍA

AV 8

MARINA
MARLIN

CASA DE
RAFAEL
FERNÁNDEZ

AV 6

ROLLER-
SKATING
RINK

Parque de
las Esculturas

CASA ROYNES

AV 4

AV 2

CLÍNICA
INTERNACIONAL

HOTEL E
CASA VERDE

HOTEL
JAGUA

PALACIO
DEL VALLE

0   0.5 mi

0   0.5 km

© AVALON TRAVEL

Colegio San Lorenzo

© CHRISTOPHER P. BAKER

by two marble lions. Note the triumphal arch on the west side, unveiled in 1902 on the day the Cuban Republic was constituted.

The **Catedral de la Purísima Concepción** (tel. 043/52-5297, daily 7 A.M.–noon), on the east side of the square, dates from 1870. It has a splendid interior, with marble floors and a pristine gilt Corinthian altar beneath a Gothic vaulted ceiling. The stained-glass windows of the 12 apostles were brought from France following the revolution of 1789.

On the north side is the deteriorated **Colegio San Lorenzo,** a handsome neoclassical building. Adjoining it is **Teatro Tomás Terry** (tel. 043/51-3361, daily 9 A.M.–6 P.M., CUC2 including guide, CUC2 camera), completed in 1895 and named for a local sugar baron, a Venezuelan who had arrived penniless in Cuba in the mid-1800s. The proscenium is sumptuously decorated and has a bas-relief centerpiece of Dionysius. The auditorium, with its three-tiered balconies, is made entirely of Cuban hardwoods and can accommodate 900 people in old-fashioned, fold-down wooden seats. The theater floor can be raised to stage level to create a grand ballroom. Enrico Caruso, Sarah Bernhardt, and the Bolshoi Ballet performed

here. The Nacional Ballet and Ópera de Cuba still perform, bringing the bats from their hiding places to swoop over the heads of the audience.

On the west side, the **Casa de la Cultura** (Calle 25 #5403, tel. 043/51-6584, 8:30 A.M.–midnight, free) occupies the much-dilapidated Palacio Ferrer, an eclectically styled former mansion of sugar baron José Ferrer Sirés.

The former Spanish Club (the initials CE, inset in the pavement, stand for Club Español), on the south side, dates from 1898 and now houses the **Museo Histórico Provincial** (Av. 54 #2702, esq. Calle 27, tel. 043/51-9722, Tues.–Sat. 10 A.M.–6 P.M., Sun. 9 A.M.–noon, CUC2). It displays a modest assortment of antiques, plus an archaeological room honoring the Indians of the Americas. Fifty meters east is the **Primer Palacio,** now the Poder Popular, the local government headquarters.

Cater-corner to the Poder Popular is the **Casa del Fundador** (Av. 54, esq. 29, tel. 043/55-2144, Mon.–Sat. 9 A.M.–5:30 P.M., Sun. 9 A.M.–12:30 P.M., CUC1), where lived city founder Don Luis D'Clouet.

Paseo del Prado and Malecón

Calle 37—the Prado—is lined with a central

median with plaques and busts honoring illustrious citizens, including a life-size bronze figure of Benny Moré (esq. Av. 54). The Prado remains a social center and bustles with gossipy life. Note the **Casa de los Leones** (e/ 58 y 60), an old mansion guarded by two life-size bronze lions.

The **Club Cienfuegos** (Calle 37, e/ Av. 8 y 12, tel. 043/52-6510), a baroque building erected in 1920, served for decades as the yacht club. The lobby exhibits antique silver trophies and other yachting memorabilia.

One block south, at the tip of the peninsula, a cultural park exhibits avant-garde sculptures.

◖ Palacio del Valle

Cienfuegos's architectural pride and joy is a palace (Calle 37, esq. Av. 2, tel. 043/51-1003 ext. 812, daily 10 A.M.–11 P.M., CUC2 including cocktail) at the tip of Punta Gorda. This architectural stunner—now a restaurant of the Hotel Jagua—originated as a modest home for a trader, Celestino Caceres. It passed out of his hands and was given as a wedding present to a member of the local Valle family, who added to it in virile Mogul style, with carved floral motifs, cupped arches, bulbous cupolas,

and delicate arabesques in alabaster. Note the mural of the Magi on the Carrara marble staircase. A spiral staircase deposits you at a rooftop *mirador* (free after 5 P.M.).

Necrópolis Tomás Acea

This cemetery (Av. 5 de Septiembre, tel. 043/52-5257, daily 9 A.M.–5 P.M., free, CUC1 guide), two kilometers east of town on the road to Rancho Luna, has impressive neoclassical structures and tombs. It is entered via a gate supported by 64 Doric columns.

Cementerio La Reina

Anyone with a morbid fascination for graveyards, or a love of baroque architecture, might find this evocative Carrara marble cemetery (Avenida 50 y Calle 7, 7 A.M.–7 P.M., free) appealing. The walls contain tombs of soldiers from the War of Independence. Many tombs are caved in, with the skeletons open to view. It was being restored at last visit. Take Avenida 48 west, then turn right.

Museo Histórico Naval

Formerly a motley affair, the Historic Naval Museum (Calle 21, e/ 60 y 62, tel. 043/51-9143, Tues.–Sat. 10 A.M.–6 P.M., Sat.–Sun.

Palacio del Valle at dusk

HISTORIC CIENFUEGOS (PUEBLO NUEVO)

To Railway Station

To Autopista

To Bus Station

To Punta Gorda

CASE DE LOS LEONES ★

CINE PRADO

CASA DE LA CULTURA

POST OFFICE

CAMPISMO POPULAR

CUBATUR

STATUE OF BENNY MORÉ ★

TELECORREO

LA CASA DE BATIDO

COPPELIA

CINE TEATRO LUISA

CADECA

(SAN CARLOS)

CADENA DE PAN/ CENTRO DRAMÁTICO

RESTAURANTE LA VERJA

DINO'S PIZZA NOVA

TRANSTUR/ TAXI/PARKING

ETECSA

CUBARTESANÍA

BANK

PHOTO SERVICE

CALLE 37
CALLE 35
CALLE 33
CALLE 31
CALLE 29
CALLE 27
CALLE 25

BANK

CATHEDRAL DE LA PURÍSIMA CONCEPCIÓN ★

CASA LA AMISTAD

COLEGIO SAN LORENZO ★

HOTEL E LA UNIÓN

CLUB BENNY MORÉ

SAL TEATRO CUESTAS

HAVANATUR

CONSULTORIA JURÍDICA INTERNACIONAL

BANK

BANK

CAFÉ TEATRO TERRY

TEATRO TOMÁS TERRY

PARQUE MARTÍ

MONUMENTO MARTÍ ★

CUBANACÁN

CASA DE EL FUNDADOR

MUSEO HISTÓRICO PROVINCIAL

PALATINO/ INFOTUR

UNEAC

CASA DE LA CULTURA

GALERÍA MAROYA ★

To Ferry Terminal and Immigration

AV 60
AV 58
AV 56
AV 54
AV 52
AV 50

0 100 yds
0 100 m

© AVALON TRAVEL

9 A.M.–1 P.M., CUC1 entrance, CUC1 camera), in the former navy headquarters, is now worth a visit for its model ships, colonial armory, and nautical miscellany up to the present day. It was here in 1957 that naval officers rebelled against the Batista regime.

Entertainment and Events

Cienfuegos hosts the week-long **Festival Naútica** in mid-July, featuring a parade, water sports, and regattas. The **Benny Moré International Festival of Popular Music** is held each alternate August.

Locals flock on weekends to the Malecón, between Calles 32 and 36, where simple open-air bars pump out free music.

The **Teatro Tomás Terry** (tel. 043/51-3361, box office 11 A.M.–3 P.M. and 90 minutes prior to performances, CUC1), on Parque Martí, hosts performances ranging from classical symphony to live salsa music.

For bowling or billiards, head to **La Bolera** (Calle 37, esq. 48, tel. 043/55-1379, 11 A.M.–2 A.M., CUC2 per hour).

BARS

The **Palatino,** on the west side of Parque Martí, is a pleasant spot to savor a drink while being serenaded. Lovers congregate at **Centro Recreativo La Punta** (no tel., daily 10 A.M.–6 P.M. and 8 P.M.–1 A.M.) at the tip of the peninsula.

For elegance, check out the **Bar Terrazas** upstairs in the Hotel Unión (live music at 10 P.M.) or the terrace bar of **Club Cienfuegos** (Calle 37, e/ Av. 8 y 12, tel. 043/52-6510, nightly 10 P.M.–2 A.M.), which has views across the bay; a dress code applies. The club also has an English pub downstairs.

TRADITIONAL MUSIC

The **Casa de la Cultura** (Calle 37 #5615, esq. Av. 58, tel. 043/51-6584, daily 8:30 A.M.–midnight, free) hosts traditional music and dance and other cultural events. **UNEAC** (Calle 25 #5425, tel. 043/51-6117, www.uneac.com), on the west side of Parque Martí, also has cultural events in an open-air patio, ranging from Afro-Cuban folkloric events to *bolero*. Nearby, the **Café Teatro Terry** hosts live entertainment Tues.–Sun. 9 A.M.–1 A.M.

Flamenco? Head to **Sal Teatro Cuestas** (Av. 54, e/ 29 y 31), a Spanish-focused performance space.

CABARET AND DISCO

The **Club Benny Moré** (Av. 54 #2907, e/ 29 y 31, tel. 043/55-1105, Thurs.–Sun. 10 P.M.–3 A.M., CUC1–2) is an elegant cabaret theater with live music, comedians, etc. followed by disco. You need ID to enter; it has a dress code.

The only *cabaret espectáculo* in town is the laser-lit **Noche en el Cabaret Costa Sur** (Av. 40, esq. Calle 35, tel. 043/52-5808, Thurs.–Sun. 9 P.M.–2 A.M., CUC5), followed by disco.

Artex's lively, open-air **Centro Cultural El Cubanismo** (Calle 35, e/ 16 y 18, tel. 043/55-1255, 9 P.M.–2 A.M.) offers a medley that draws local youth: Monday for rumba, Tuesday for Cuban music, comedy on Wednesday, folkloric music on Thursday, Caribbean beat on Friday, a *cabaret espectáculo* on Saturday, and karaoke on Sunday.

Recreation

Marina Marlin Cienfuegos (Calle 35, e/ 6 y 8, tel. 043/55-1699, operativo@nautica.cfg. tur.cu) offers scuba diving (CUC30 one dive) from Hotel Rancho Luna. Marina Marlin also offers two-hour bay excursions aboard the *Flipper* catamaran (9 A.M., 11 A.M., 2 P.M., and 5 P.M., CUC10 per person). Germany-based **Plattensail** (www.platten-sailing.de) offers long-term yacht charters at the marina, and you can rent catamarans (one-day to one-month rentals) with **Bluesail** (tel. 043/55-6119, www. bluesail-caribe.com) at **Club Cienfuegos** (Calle 37, e/ Av. 8 y 12, Sun.–Fri. 10 P.M.–2 A.M., Sat. until 2 A.M.). The club grounds also have crazy cars (*carros locos*, CUC1), go-karts, and tennis.

The **Hotel Unión** has a gym, aerobics, swimming pool, and sauna, all open to the public.

Estadio 5 de Septiembre (Av. 20, e/ 45 y 55, tel. 043/51-3644) hosts baseball games October–May.

Accommodations

You can book *campismos* with **Campismo Popular** (Calle 37, e/ 54 y 56, tel. 043/51-9423, Mon.–Fri. 8 A.M.–noon and 1–4:30 P.M.). All accommodations listed are air-conditioned.

CASAS PARTICULARES

Cienfuegos has scores of *casas particulares,* notably in Punta Gorda.

An excellent downtown option in Pueblo Nuevo, **Casa La Amistad** (Av. 56 #2927, e/ 29 y 31, tel. 043/51-6143, CUC20), one block east of Parque Martí, is upstairs in a creaky colonial home. The two simple rooms share a bathroom. The place is highly recommended by past guests and I, too, have always enjoyed the hospitality of the welcoming hosts, who are dedicated socialists. Leonora welcomes you with her "Gato Negro" and gets rave reviews for her special chicken dish.

Book early to snag a room at Omar and Diana's remarkable ◖ **Hostal Bahía** (Av. 20 #3502 altos, esq. 35, tel. 043/52-6598, hostalbahia@yahoo.es, CUC35) in Punta Gorda. Sure, it's expensive, but here you get a shaded bay-view balcony, a 40-inch plasma TV in the cross-ventilated lounge, and a huge selection of wines to accompany filling meals that can include paella (CUC8–15). Modern art adorns the walls.

Otherwise, my favorite is ◖ **Casa de Juan Sánchez** (Av. 8 #3703, e/ 37 y 39, tel. 043/51-7986, CUC25 including breakfast), a striking modernist home built in 1959, with original furnishings and heaps of stained glass. The lounge connects to a garden with shade trees. Its single, spacious room is well-lit and cross-ventilated, with a large handsome bathroom.

Worthy alternatives include the lovely **Casa de Carlos y Ana María** (Av. 8 #3901, tel. 043/51-6624, illyanet2006@yahoo.es, CUC20–25) and **Casa de Rafael "Pipe" Fernández** (Av. 8 #3903, e/ 39 y 41, tel. 043/52-5274, CUC20–25). I've enjoyed stays at both.

Casa de Andrés Ranero (Av. 10 #3707, e/ 37 y 39, tel. 043/51-7993, josera@jagua.cfg.sld.cu, CUC20–25) is a great option and has two well-lit rooms, each with handsome hot-water bathrooms. Guests have their own small lounge.

Casa de Juan Sánchez

© CHRISTOPHER P. BAKER

Meals are served on an outside patio with fish pond and parrots. There's secure parking.

HOTELS

Cienfuegos has some excellent hotels, all with satellite TV, safes, and modern bathrooms. Cubanacán's **Hostal E Palacio Azul** (Calle 37 #1201, e/ 12 y 14, tel. 043/55-5828, fax 043/55-1685, reserva@union.cfg.tur.cu, CUC60 s/d year-round, including breakfast) offers seven huge rooms with high ceilings and colonial tile floors in a restored mansion on the Malecón. It has a charming little bar and restaurant.

Cubanacán's ◖ **Hotel E La Unión** (Av. 54 y Calle 31, tel. 043/55-1020, fax 043/55-1686, reserva@union.cfg.tur.cu, from CUC64 s, CUC80 d year-round), one block east of Parque Martí, is a beautifully restored neoclassical re-creation of a 19th-century hotel. It has 49 rooms (11 are junior suites, two are suites, one is a signature suite) arrayed around a courtyard. The open-air pool has a Romanesque setting, and you get a sauna, whirlpool tub, gym, business center, and commendable restaurant.

In 2008, Cubanacán introduced another converted mansion as a hotel. With eight rooms, the ◖ **Hotel E Casa Verde** (Calle 37 e/ 0 y 2, Punta Gorda, tel. 053/55-1003, fax 053/55-1245, CUC65 s, CUC80 d) is up to European standards with its gracious furnishings, plasma TVs, and mobile phones. Two rooms have king beds. It has a pool with snack bar, and buffet lunch and dinner are served.

Britain's Esencia group (www.esenciahotelsandresorts.com) is planning on opening a posh club-style hotel, the Casa Cienfuegos.

Gran Caribe's high-rise **Hotel Jagua** (Calle 37, e/ 0 y 2, tel. 043/55-1003, fax 043/55-1245, reservas@jagua.co.cu, CUC60 s, CUC85 d low season, CUC74 s, CUC105 d high season) boasts contemporary furnishings and lively color schemes in its gracious lobby and 149 large rooms plus 13 poolside *cabinas*. You get more facilities than at the other hotels, including a swimming pool. The buffet restaurant, however, fails miserably.

For a resort feel, head east of town to **Hotel Islazul Punta La Cueva** (Carretera a Rancho Luna, Km 3.5 y Circunlavación, tel. 043/57-3952, www.islazul.cu, CUC13 s, CUC16 d low season, CUC16 s, CUC22 d high season), a 67-room low-rise hotel looking west across a bay to Cienfuegos.

Food

Legal *paladares* had all closed at last visit.

Budget hounds might try **Café Cantante Benny Moré** (Prado y Av. 54, Sun.–Fri. 9 A.M.–9 P.M., Sat. 9 A.M.–6 P.M.), serving simple *criollo* fare for pesos. No tank tops are allowed. **Dino's Pizza Nova** (Calle 31, e/ 54 y 56, tel. 043/55-2020, daily noon–4 P.M. and 6:30–10:30 P.M.) has a Mediterranean feel suitable to its menu of basic pizzas and pastas (from CUC5).

On the east side of Parque Martí, **Restaurante Polinesia** (tel. 043/51-5723, daily noon–3 P.M. and 6–10 P.M.) retains a 1950s tiki motif, and pineapple finds its way onto the *criollo* menu (CUC5 and under). For colonial atmosphere, opt for **Restaurante La Verja** (Av. 54, e/ 33 y 35, tel. 043/51-6311, daily noon–3 P.M. and 6–10 P.M.), which serves *criollo* staples (lobster CUC10) in a colonial home full of antiques.

Despite the filthy tablecloths, plan on dining at Hotel Jagua's **Palacio de Valle** (tel. 043/55-1003 ext. 812, daily 10 A.M.–10 P.M.) for the remarkable ambience. It has a large seafood menu, including overpriced lobster (CUC25), though dishes are average. Carmen Iznaga tickles the ivories of an out-of-tune piano.

You might want to go dressy to **Restaurant Marinero** (tel. 043/51-2891, daily noon–10 P.M.), a chic seafront restaurant with walls of glass. The seafood menu features paella (CUC10) and lobster (CUC15), plus chicken with wine (CUC9).

Downtown, the nicest place is **Restaurante 1869** (Av. 54 y Calle 31, tel. 043/55-1020, daily 7–9:45 A.M., noon–2:45 P.M., and 7–9:45 P.M.) in the Hotel Unión, with elegant period decor. The menu features ceviche (CUC5), cream of seafood soup (CUC3.50), garlic shrimp (CUC15), and grilled sirloin with green pepper and asparagus (CUC14).

Coppelia (Calle 37, esq. 52, 11 A.M.–11 P.M. Tues.–Sun.) is good for ice cream (pesos only). For an espresso or cappuccino head to the **Café Teatro Terry** on Parque Martí. Delicious fresh fruit *batidos* (shakes) will help you beat the heat at **La Casa del Batido** (Av. 37, e/ 52 y 54, daily 9 A.M.–10 P.M.).

Shopping

Galería Maroya (Av. 54 #2506, tel. 043/55-1208, Mon.–Sat. 9 A.M.–6 P.M., Sun. 9 A.M.–1 P.M.), on the west side of Parque Martí, has a splendid collection of arts and crafts.

For cigars or rum, head to **Casa El Embajador** (Av. 54, esq. 29, tel. 043/55-2144, Mon.–Sat. 9 A.M.–5:30 P.M., Sun. 9 A.M.–12:30 P.M.), in the Casa del Fundador.

Information and Services

Infotur (daily 8 A.M.–5 P.M.) has a tour bureau at the Palatino restaurant, on the south side of Parque Martí. These companies sell excursions, including a four-hour city tour (CUC10): **Cubanacán** (Av. 54, e/ 29 y 31, tel. 043/55-1680, Mon.–Fri. 8 A.M.–5 P.M., Sat. 8 A.M.–1 P.M.), **Cubatur** (Calle 37 e/ 54 y 56, tel. 043/55-1242, Mon.–Sat. 8:30 A.M.–5 P.M.), and **Havanatur** (Av. 54 #2906, e/ 29 y 31, tel. 043/51-1639, daily 8:30 A.M.–noon and 1–5 P.M.).

The **post office** is at Avenida 54 and Calle 35, but the ***telecorreo*** (Av. 54 #3514, tel. 043/55-6102) has DHL service.

Etecsa (Av. 54, e/ 35 y 37, daily 8:30 A.M.–6:30 P.M.) has international phone and Internet service.

Banks include **Banco Financiero Internacional** (Av. 54 y Calle 29, Mon.–Fri. 8 A.M.–3 P.M.), on the southeast corner of Parque Martí, and **Bandec** (Av. 56 y Calle 31). **Cadeca** (Av. 56, e/ 33 y 35) also converts foreign currency for pesos.

The **Clínica Internacional** (Calle 37, e/ 2 y 4, tel. 043/55-1622) is opposite the Hotel Jagua (consultations CUC25). It has a pharmacy, as does the Hotel 242.

The **Consultoría Jurídica Internacional** (Calle 54 #2904, e/ 29 y 31, tel. 043/55-1572, fax 043/55-1323) provides legal services.

Dirty laundry? Head to **Autoservicio Lavandería El Lavatin** (56 e/ 41 y 43, Mon.–Sat. 8 A.M.–7 P.M. and Sun. 8 A.M.–noon), a self-service Laundromat.

Getting There and Away

Note that the Aeropuerto Internacional Jaime Gonzalez (tel. 043/55-2047) was not functioning at last visit.

BY BUS

The bus terminal (Calle 49 e/ Av. 56 y 58) is six blocks east of the Prado. **Víazul** (tel. 043/51-5720) buses serve Cienfuegos daily en route between Havana and Trinidad, departing Havana at 8:15 A.M. and 1 P.M. (CUC21.60) and Trinidad at 7:30 A.M. and 3 P.M. (CUC6.48). Buses depart Cienfuegos for Havana at 9:10 A.M. and 4:30 P.M., for Trinidad at 1:20 P.M. and 5:10 A.M.

BY TRAIN

The train station (Calle 49, e/ Av. 58 y 60, tel. 043/52-5495) is one block north of the bus station. Trains depart Cienfuegos for Havana at 7 A.M. (and 11 P.M. by bus each second day, CUC11) and for Santa Clara at 4:10 A.M.

(CUC2.10, second-class only). You can also catch an *especial* from Havana to Santa Clara and then connect to Cienfuegos, which lies at the end of a branch line off the main Havana–Santiago railroad. Trains depart Havana for Cienfuegos at 7:30 A.M. (and 4 P.M. by bus each second day) and from Santa Clara at 5:20 P.M.

BY SEA

Arriving yachters must report for clearance at the **Guardía Frontera** post on the western shores of the entrance to Bahía de Cienfuegos. **Marina Marlin Cienfuegos** (Calle 35, e/ 6 y 8, tel. 043/55-1699) has moorings for 30 yachts.

Getting Around

Bus #9 runs the length of Calle 37 (10 centavos). Horse-drawn *coches* ply Calle 37 and the major thoroughfares (one peso).

Cubataxi (Av. 50 #3508, esq. 37, tel. 043/51-9145) charges CUC3 between the Hotel Jagua and downtown.

You can rent cars from **Cubacar** (Hotel La Unión, tel. 043/55-1700; Calle 37 y Av. 18, tel. 043/55-1211; and Hotel Jagua, tel. 043/55-2166).

There are gas stations at Calle 37 (e/ Av. 18); about 10 kilometers east of town on the road to Rancho Luna; and at the north end of Calle 37, at the entrance to town.

◖ JARDÍN BOTÁNICO SOLEDAD

This splendid garden (tel. 043/54-5115, daily 8 A.M.–4:30 P.M., CUC2.50), is about 10 kilometers east of Cienfuegos, on the main coast road to Trinidad, between the communities of San Antón and Guaos. It was begun in 1899 by a New Englander, Edward Atkins, who owned vast sugar estates in the area and brought in Harvard botanists to develop more productive sugarcane strains. Later, Harvard University assumed control under a 99-year lease, and a general collection making up one of the tropical world's finest botanical gardens was amassed. Since the Revolution, the garden has been maintained by the Cuban Academy of Science's Institute of Botany.

Pathways lead through the 97-hectare garden, reached along an avenue of royal palms. It harbors a collection of some 2,000 species, 70 percent of which are exotics. A bamboo collection has 23 species. Of rubber trees, there are 89 species; of cactus, 400. The prize collection is the 307 varieties of palms. The facility includes a laboratory and library. A basic café serves drinks.

The bus from Cienfuegos to Cumanayagua passes the garden. A taxi will cost about CUC40 round-trip. Tour agencies in Cienfuegos offer tours (CUC10).

PLAYA RANCHO LUNA AND PASACABALLO

About 15 kilometers southeast of Cienfuegos, the pleasant beach of Playa Rancho Luna hosts two small resort hotels used by package tour groups. The coast road swings west past the **Faro Luna** lighthouse and follows the rocky coast eight kilometers to Pasacaballo, facing the Castillo de Jagua across the 400-meter-wide mouth of Cienfuegos Bay, 22 kilometers from Cienfuegos.

Recreation

There are better beaches in Cuba. The main draw is the **Delfinario** (tel. 043/54-8120, Thurs.–Tues. 8:30 A.M.–4 P.M., CUC10 adults, CUC6 children), an enclosed lagoon offering dolphin shows at 10 A.M. and 2 P.M. You can kiss the dolphins for CUC10, and even swim with them (CUC50 adults, CUC33 children).

Scuba diving is offered at the **Club Amigo Rancho Luna** (Carretera de Rancho Luna, Km 18, tel. 043/54-8087, operative@nautica.cfg.tur.cu). At least eight ships lie amid the coral reefs.

You can rent catamarans and pedal-boats at the beach by **Villa Rancho Luna** (tel. 045/54-8189), a simple beachfront restaurant (8–9:45 P.M., 12:30–2:45 P.M. and 6–8 P.M.).

Accommodations
CASAS PARTICULARES
There are several private rentals to choose from near the Hotel Faro Luna, including **Casa de**

dolphins kissing tourists at the Delfinario, Playa Rancho Luna
© CHRISTOPHER P. BAKER

Julio Cortizo Hernández (tel. 043/51-5744, CUC25), with one simply appointed room with modern bathroom.

Farther west, **Finca los Colorados B&B** (Carretera de Pasacaballo, Km 18, Playa Rancho Luna, tel. 043/54-8044, fax 043/51-3265, www.casapineiro.com, CUC30) is a *casa particular* enjoying a breeze-swept position on the cliffs 100 meters east of the lighthouse. English-speaking owner José Piñeiro prepares Cuban cuisine served beneath an arbor. The home abounds in antiques and modern furnishings. Two modestly furnished, cross-ventilated rooms have metal-frame antique beds (readers report that mattresses aren't too comfy).

HOTELS
The **Club Amigo Rancho Luna** (Carretera de Rancho Luna, Km 18, tel. 043/54-8012, fax 043/54-8131, www.hotelescubanacan.com, CUC56 s, CUC70 d low season, CUC80 s, CUC110 d high season) is a staple of Canadian and European tour groups. Boasting lively tropical pastels and rattan furnishings, it's a pleasant option with 222 nicely furnished rooms,

two restaurants, water sports, game room, and a large swimming pool. In early 2010, the nearby 46-room **Club Amigo Faro Luna** was undergoing repair and was to be merged.

The Soviet-style **Hotel Pasacaballo** (Carretera de Rancho Luna, Km 22, tel. 043/59-2100, www.islazul.cu, CUC19 s, CUC30 d low season, CUC25.50 s, CUC37 d high season, including meals) is out on a limb atop cliffs on the east side of the bay. I like its modernist interior stylish, despite its ugly exterior. The new look in bedrooms appeals too, and mod-cons have been added; some rooms have king beds.

Getting There
Buses ostensibly depart Cienfuegos every two hours. A taxi will cost you about CUC10. Ferries leave for Rancho Luna on a regular basis from the terminal on Avenida 46 and Calle 25 (CUC1).

FORTALEZA DE NUESTRA SEÑORA DE JAGUA
Across the bay from Pasacaballo, a restored 17th-century Spanish fort (tel. 043/96-5402, Tues.–Sat. 9 A.M.–5 P.M., Sun. 9 A.M.–1 P.M., CUC1 entrance, CUC1 camera) guards the entrance to the Bahía de Cienfuegos. The original fortress was expanded in the 18th century to defend against the English Royal Navy. Two Ordoñez cannons guard the entrance. At midnight, a ghost—the Blue Lady—is said to haunt the small fortress that overlooks a fishing village perched above the water.

Hungry? **Paladar Juana Jiménez** (Av. del Mar #109, Castillo, tel. 043/96-5421, 24 hours) serves seafood lunches and dinners. Juana's father offers bay and fishing excursions (CUC25 up to four people).

Up on the hill behind Jagua is **Ciudad Nuclear** (Nuclear City), a modern city built in the 1980s to house workers constructing Cuba's first nuclear power station nearby at Juragua. The half-completed reactor, about two kilometers west of town, stands idle. Construction began in 1983, when Soviet aid flowed freely. Construction was mothballed in 1992.

Ordoñez cannon at Fortaleza de Nuestra Señora de Jagua

Getting There
Passenger ferries depart Cienfuegos (Av. 46 and Calle 25) at 8 A.M., 1 P.M., and 5:30 P.M. (30 minutes, CUC1). Ferries also link Jagua and Pasacaballo six times daily.

To get there by road, exit Cienfuegos on Calle 37 past the industrial complexes.

SANTA ISABEL DE LAS LAJAS AND VICINITY
Famed musician Benny Moré (1919–1963) was born in the village of Santa Isabel de las Lasas, eight kilometers north of the town of Cruces (30 kilometers northeast of Cienfuegos). The **Museo Municipal** (Calle Dr. Machín 99 e/ Martí y Calixto García, lajaz@azurina.cult.cu, Tues.–Sat. 10 A.M.–6 P.M., Sun. 9 A.M.–1 P.M.) pays homage to the crooner considered Cuba's most influential musician of his era, who is buried in the town cemetery. The **Festival Internacional de Música Benny Moré** is held here every other December. The **Café Cuba** (Paseo Dr. Machín 69 esq. Goitizolo), where he first performed, was being restored to its 1950s ambience at last visit.

Serious railroad buffs might call in at **Central Maltiempo,** five kilometers southeast of Cruces. The *central* (sugar mill) is now derelict, but an antique Baldwin steam locomotive is preserved (barely). An obelisk in Cruce's plaza commemorates the Battle of Mal Tiempo, in 1895, when Mambí generals Antonio Maceo and Máximo Gómez defeated Spanish forces.

Palmira, midway between Cienfuegos and Cruce, has deep Afro-Cuban roots and is a center for *santería,* as told in its **Museo Municipal** (Villuendas 41 e/ Cisneros y Agramontetel, tel. 043/54-4533, Tues.–Sat. 10 A.M.–6 P.M., Sun. 9 A.M.–1 P.M.,CUC1).

THE CIRCUITO SUR

The Circuito Sur coast road dips and rises east of Cienfuegos, with the Sierra Escambray to the north. Beaches lie hidden at the mouths of rivers that wash down from the hills, as at the mouth of the Río La Jutía, 42 kilometers from Cienfuegos, and eight kilometers farther east, at Playa Inglés.

Hacienda La Vega (tel. 043/55-1126, daily 9 A.M.–6 P.M.), about three kilometers west of Playa Inglés, is a cattle farm (*vaquería*) where horseback riding is offered (CUC4 per hour) and demonstrations of traditional farm life are given. A roadside restaurant serves snacks and *criollo* fare. Lather up with insect repellent!

Three kilometers east of the turnoff for Playa Ingles, you'll cross the **Río Yaguanabo** and pass into Sancti Spíritus Province. You can follow a rugged dirt track seven kilometers inland to **Finca Protegida Yaguanabo-Arriba,** also with horseback riding and guided birding in the foothills of the Escambray mountains. The highlight is the **Cueva Martín Infierno,** a stupendous cavern that boasts Latin America's largest stalagmite (67 meters tall) and gypsum flowers (*flores de yeso*).

Accommodations and Food

Wow! Who knew Cubamar had what it takes to produce such a lovely hotel? **[** **Villa Guajimico** (tel. 043/55-0941, www.cubamarviajes.com, CUC25 s, CUC40 d low season, CUC35 s,

Villa Guajimico

© CHRISTOPHER P. BAKER

CUC50 d high season) sits over the mouth of the Río La Jutía. Some of the 51 air-conditioned brick cabins line a tiny white-sand beach in the river estuary. Others stair-step a hill where a swimming pool and restaurant offer spectacular views. It has scuba diving daily at 9 A.M. and 2:30 P.M., plus Hobie Cats.

A lesser option, the **Villa Yaguanabo** (Carretera a Trinidad, Km 55, tel. 042/54-1905, fax 042/54-1921, jcarpeta@yaguanabo. cfg.tur.cu, islazul.cu, CUC14 s, CUC22 d low season, CUC28 s, CUC28 d high season) has 34 rooms at the rivermouth.

SIERRA ESCAMBRAY

The Sierra Escambray, Cuba's second-highest mountain range, lies mostly within Cienfuegos Province, descending gradually into Villa Clara Province to the north, edging into Sancti Spíritus Province to the east, and dropping steeply to the southern coast. The Escambray's peaks (which reach 1,140 meters atop Pico San Juan) and forests are protected in Parque Nacional Topes de Collantes, in the chain's southeast corner.

In the late 1950s, these mountains were the site of a revolutionary front against Fulgencio Batista, led by Che Guevara. After the revolutionaries triumphed in 1959, the Escambray hid counterrevolutionaries who opposed Castro. The CIA helped finance and arm these resistance fighters, whom the Castro regime tagged "bandits." Castro formed counterinsurgency units called Battalions of Struggle Against Bandits, and forcibly evacuated campesinos to deny the anti-Castroites local support. The *bandidos* weren't eradicated until 1966.

Access from Cienfuegos is via the Circuito Sur and the community of La Sierrita, about 30 kilometers east of Cienfuegos (the road continues to Topes de Collantes but was badly washed out at last visit and was suitable for 4WD only). It's a stupendously scenic route that rises past sheer-walled, cave-riddled limestone *mogotes*, at their most impressive near the town of **San Blas,** eight kilometers east of La Sierrita. San Blas sits in the lee of great cliffs where huge stalactites and stalagmites are exposed in an open cave high atop the mountains.

El Nicho

This recreational site (tel. 043/43-3351, daily 10 A.M.–5 P.M., CUC5), seven kilometers north of La Sierrita and 48 kilometers east of Cienfuegos, is popular with locals for its spectacular waterfalls and chilly pools good for swimming. Simple meals are served at a *ranchón*, where horseback riding is also offered (CUC2 per hour).

If driving, you'll need a four-wheel drive, as the access road is in terrible shape. You can take a *colectivo* to Cumanayagua from either Cienfuegos or Santa Clara; another *colectivo* runs from Cumanayagua at 5:30 A.M. and 5 P.M. Excursions are offered from Santa Clara.

Santa Clara and Vicinity

SANTA CLARA

Santa Clara (pop. 175,000), 300 kilometers east of Havana, is the provincial capital of Villa Clara. Straddling the Carretera Central and within five minutes of the Autopista, it is strategically located at the center of Cuba. The city was established within the confluence of the Ríos Bélico and Cubanicay in 1689, when residents of Remedios grew tired of constant pirate raids and moved inland. Later it functioned as a plum in Cuba's Wars of Independence. On December 31, 1958, Che Guevara's Rebel Army attacked the town and derailed a troop train carrying reinforcements and U.S. armaments bound for Oriente. Two days later, the Rebel Army captured the city, which became known as *el último reducto de la tiranía batistiana* (the last fortress of Batista's tyranny). Within 24 hours, the dictator fled the island.

Today Santa Clara is an important industrial town. It is also home to the Universidad Central de las Villas.

Orientation

Santa Clara is a large city laid out roughly in a rectilinear grid of one-way streets. The city is encircled by a ring road (*circunvalación*). The Carretera Central enters from the west and arcs south around the town center, accessed from the west by Rafael Tristá and from the south by Calle Cuba, which runs to Parque Vidal, the main square. Calle Marta Abreu runs west from the square and connects with the Carretera Central, which continues east to Placetas.

Independencia, one block north of Parque Vidal, runs parallel to Marta Abreu, crosses the Río Cubanicay (eastward), and (as Avenida de Liberación) leads to Remedios. (Independencia between Zayas to the west and Maceo to the east is a pedestrian precinct known as El Bulevar—The Boulevard.)

Máximo Gómez (Cuba) and Luis Estévez (Colón) run perpendicular to Abreu, on the west and east side of the park. Maceo (one

© CHRISTOPHER P. BAKER

view over Parque Vidal from Hotel Santa Clara Libre

block east of Estévez) runs north seven blocks to the railway station and becomes Avenida Sagua, which leads to Sagua la Grande and the north coast. Enrique Villanueva (one block west of Máximo Gómez) runs south to Manicaragua.

Parque Vidal

This large paved square is named for the revolutionary hero Leoncio Vidal, who—according to a monument—was killed at this exact spot. A curiosity of the square is its double-wide sidewalk. In colonial days, this was divided by an iron fence: whites perambulated on the inner half while blacks kept to the outside. The bandstand at its center hosts concerts on weekends.

Keeping her eye on things is a bronze **Monumento Marta Abreu de Estévez.** Abreu (1845–1904) was a local heroine and philanthropist who funded construction of the **Teatro la Caridad** (Marta Abreu, e/ Máximo Gómez y Lorda, tel. 042/20-5548, daily 9 A.M.–5 P.M., CUC1), built in 1885 on the north side of the square. Albeit tragically deteriorated due to water damage, the four-story, horseshoe-shaped theater boasts its original cast-iron seats plus stunning murals representing the works of Shakespeare and Spanish writers.

Fifty meters east of the theater is the **Museo de Artes Decorativos** (e/ Luis Estévez y Lorda, tel. 042/20-5368, Mon., Wed., and Thurs. 8 A.M.–6 P.M., Fri.–Sat. 1–6 P.M. and 7–10 P.M., Sun. 6–10 P.M., CUC2 entrance, CUC1 guide, CUC5 camera), featuring an eclectic array of stunning colonial antiques and furniture.

On the square's east side, the old **Palacio Provincial** houses the city library; its imposing neoclassical frontage is supported by Ionic columns.

The **Galería de Arte** (Máximo Gómez #3, tel. 042/20-7715, Tues.–Sun. 9 A.M.–10:30 P.M.), immediately northwest of the square, has revolving art exhibitions. Step one block west to shop at the **Mercado Artesanal** (Abreu, esq. Villanueva).

◖ Complejo Escultórico Memorial Comandante Ernesto Che Guevara

Looming over the hilltop Plaza de la Revolución, at the west end of Rafael Tristá, this complex is dominated by the **Monumento de Che,** a massive plinth with bas-reliefs and a 6.8-meter-tall bronze statue of Che bearing his rifle, by sculptor José Delarra. Beneath the monument, on the north side, is the **Museo de Che** (tel. 042/20-5878, Tues.–Sun. 9:30 A.M.–5 P.M., free, no photos allowed), which worships the Argentinian revolutionary and has a detailed account of the capture of Santa Clara in December 1958. Che Guevara's history is traced from childhood. Exhibits include his pistol from the Sierra Maestra, his green PVC jacket with brown corduroy elasticized sides, and his black beret with the five-pointed star.

Che's remains (discovered in Bolivia) were laid to rest in October 1997 in an adjacent mausoleum that has empty space for the 37 other guerrillas who lost their lives in Guevara's last campaign. Walls of granite are inset with the 3-D motifs of the revolutionaries, including Che's, with a small five-point star illumined top-right from a light beam inset in the ceiling.

On the north side is the "Garden of Tombs," opened in 2009. Framed by symbolic palms, it has tiered rows of 220 marble tombs, one for each of Che's *combatientes* (soldiers), arcing around an eternal flame.

Museo Provincial Abel Santamaría

Housed in the Escuela Abel Santamaría (tel. 042/20-3041, Mon.–Fri. 8:30 A.M.–5 P.M., Sat. 9 A.M.–1 P.M., CUC1), at the north end of Calle Esquerra in the Reparto Osvaldo Herrera neighborhood, this museum is full of colonial furniture but is dedicated to the province's role in the Wars of Independence and the fight against Batista. It features weaponry plus natural-history exhibits. The school was formerly a military barracks, fulfilling Castro's dictum to turn all Batista's barracks into centers of learning.

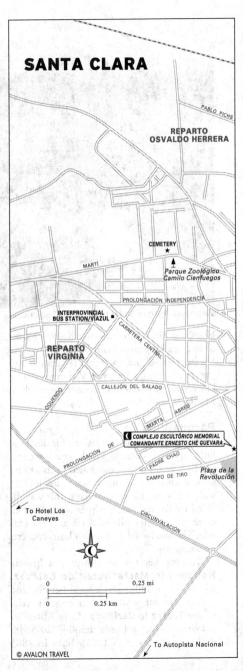

SANTA CLARA

© AVALON TRAVEL

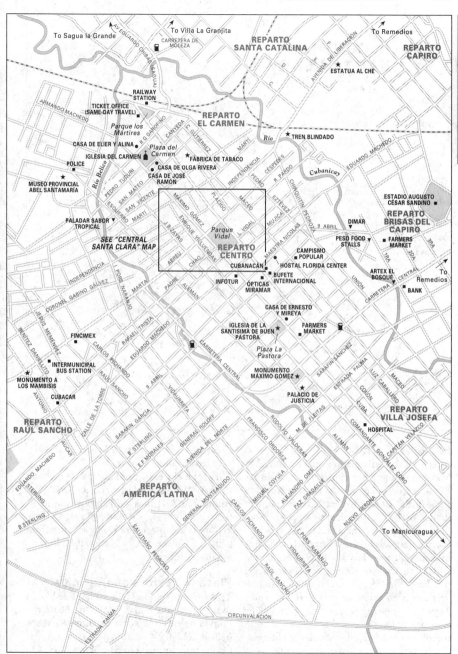

To Sagua la Grande

To Villa La Granjita

To Remedios

AV. EDUARDO CHIBÁS (SAGUA)

CARRETERA DE MOLEZA

REPARTO SANTA CATALINA

AVENIDA DE LIBERACIÓN

D

C

REPARTO CAPIRO

★ ESTATUA AL CHE

RAILWAY STATION

ARMANDO MACHEDO

TICKET OFFICE (SAME-DAY TRAVEL)

Parque los Mártires

R.G. GAROFINO

CANVEDA

A.C. GUTIÉRREZ

REPARTO EL CARMEN

Río

● TREN BLINDADO

EDUARDO MACHEDO

CASA DE ELIER Y ALINA

Plaza del Carmen

MARTÍ

Cubanicay

ESTADIO AUGUSTO CÉSAR SANDINO

IGLESIA DEL CARMEN

★ FÁBRICA DE TABACO

INDEPENDENCIA

CÉSPEDES

R. PARDO

CHINQUITÍN PEDROZA

POLICE

CASA DE OLGA RIVERA

PEDRO

REPARTO BRISAS DEL CAPIRO

Río Bélico

CASA DE JOSÉ RAMÓN

ESTÉVEZ

9 ABRIL

DIMAR ▼

■ FARMERS MARKET

MUSEO PROVINCIAL ABEL SANTAMARÍA

PEDRO TUDURI

SAN MATEO

PLÁCIDO

MACEO

MÁXIMO GÓMEZ

VIDAL

MAESTRA NICOLAS

MUJICA

PESO FOOD STALLS ▼

REPARTO CENTRO

3RA

39A

2DA

PALADAR SABOR TROPICAL ▼

SAN VICENTE

MARTÍ

ENRIQUE VILLUENDAS

J.B. ZAYAS

Parque Vidal

CAMPISMO POPULAR ●

ARTEX EL BOSQUE ■

To Remedios

SEE "CENTRAL SANTA CLARA" MAP

ESGUERRO

ABREU

CHAO

CUBANACÁN ■

HOSTAL FLORIDA CENTER

UNIÓN

CENTRAL

CARRETERA

● BANK

INDEPENDENCIA

J. PÉREZ NARANJO

MARTA

PADRE ALEMÁN

INFOTUR ■

ÓPTICAS MIRAMAR

BUFETE INTERNACIONAL

CASA DE ERNESTO Y MIREYA ■

CORONEL GABINO GALVEZ

JESÚS MENÉNDEZ

FINCIMEX ●

RAFAEL TRISTA

EDUARDO MACHEDO

IGLESIA DE LA SANTÍSIMA DE BUEN PASTORA ★

Plaza La Pastora

FARMERS MARKET ●

SERAFÍN SÁNCHEZ

ESTRADA PALMA

LUZ CABALLERO

MACEO

BENÍTEZ DANIELITO

■ INTERMUNICIPAL BUS STATION

CARLOS PICHANDO

RAÚL SANCHO

9 ABRIL

VIDAURRETA

MONUMENTO MÁXIMO GOMEZ ★

COLÓN

CUBA

COMANDANTE GONZÁLEZ CORO

CAPITÁN VELAZCO

★ MONUMENTO A LOS MAMBISIS

ANTONIO

CALLE DE LA TORRE

PALACIO DE JUSTICIA ★

REPARTO VILLA JOSEFA

■ CUBACAR

SARAFÍN GARCÍA

GENERAL ROLOFF

RODOLFO VALDERAS

M. DE FLEITAS

ALEMÁN

HOSPITAL ■

REPARTO RAÚL SANCHO

AUGAR

B STERLING

L E F MORALES

AVENIDA DEL NORTE

FRANCISCO ORDÓÑEZ

EDUARDO MACHEDO

B STERLING

REPARTO AMÉRICA LATINA

SALUTIANO PEDROSO

GENERAL MONTEAGUDO

CARLOS PICHANDO

MIGUEL COYULA

ALEJANDRO OMS

PAZ GRADAILLE

J. PORS NARANJO

VIDAURRETA

RAÚL SANCHO

NUEVO GERONA

To Manicaragua

ESTRADA PALMA

CIRCUNVALACIÓN

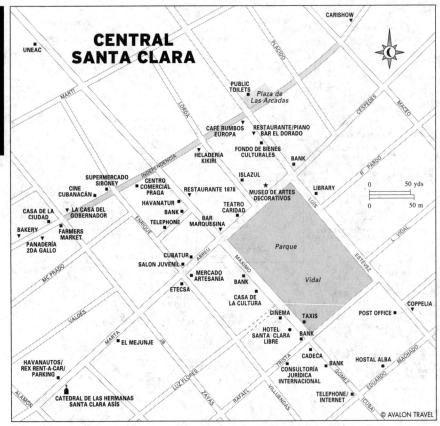

CENTRAL SANTA CLARA

Plaza del Carmen

This exquisite little plaza, at the north end of Máximo Gómez, five blocks north of Parque Vidal, is dominated by the **Iglesia Nuestra Señora del Carmen,** a national monument dating to 1748. It is fronted by a granite monument that arcs around a tamarind tree where the first mass was held to celebrate the founding of Santa Clara on July 15, 1689. The church, which was used as a women's prison during the Wars of Independence, is riddled with bullet holes fired from the police station—now named El Vaquerito—across the street during the battle of December 29, 1958. On the north side of the church is a life-size figure of revolutionary hero Roberto Rodríquez Fernández—*el*

vaquerito—of whose death Che Guevara said, "We have lost one hundred men."

Two blocks east, the **Fábrica de Tabaco** (Maceo #181, e/ Julyo Jover and Berenguer, tel. 042/20-2211) has guided tours of the tobacco factory (9–11 A.M. and 1–3 P.M., CUC4). You need to buy your ticket in advance from Cubatur, Cubanacán, or Havanatur. No photos are permitted.

Plaza la Pastora and Vicinity

This small plaza, on Calle Cuba, five blocks south of Parque Vidal, has at its heart the **Iglesia de la Santísima de Buen Pastora** (tel. 042/20-6554, daily 10 A.M.–4 P.M.). It features a beautiful stained-glass window. On its northeast corner is **Monumento a Miguel Gerónimo Gutiérrez,** honoring a local patriot.

Two blocks south, the **Monumento General Máximo Gómez** stands in front of the neoclassical **Palacio de Justicia,** the courthouse.

Tren Blindado

This site (tel. 042/20-2758, Mon.–Sat. 9 A.M.–5:30 P.M., CUC1 entrance, CUC1 camera), at the east end of Independencia beyond the railway crossing, was the setting where on December 29, 1958, rebel troops led by Che Guevara derailed one of Batista's troop trains, setting in rapid motion the train of events that toppled Batista. Four rust-colored carriages are preserved higgledy-piggledy in suspended animation as they came to rest after the train was run off the rails. There is an exhibit inside one of the carriages.

Continue east 100 meters along Carretera de Camaguany to the Communist Party headquarters; in the forecourt stands the bronze **Estatua al Che** showing Che holding a boy in his arms.

Entertainment and Events

Troubadours play most evenings and weekend afternoons at the **Casa de la Cultura** (tel. 042/20-7181), on the west side of Parque Vidal. **UNEAC** (National Union of Cuban Writers and Artists, Máximo Gómez e/ Martí/Vicente, www.uneac.com) has cultural events. The no-frills, overly air-conditioned **Piano Bar** (Luis Estevez #13, e/ Independencia y Parque Vidal, tel. 042/21-5215, daily 9 P.M.–1 A.M.) hosts *boleros,* instrumental music, and *trova.*

Casa de la Ciudad (Independencia #102, esq. Juan Bruno Zayas, tel. 042/20-5593, Mon. 8 A.M.–noon, Tues.–Fri. 8 A.M.–noon and 1–5 P.M., Sat. 1:30–10 P.M., Sun. 6–10 P.M., CUC1) hosts cultural activities.

Everything from comedy to live music is featured at **Bar Club Bulevá** (Independencia #225, e/ Unión y Maceo, tel. 042/21-6236, daily 10 P.M.–2:30 A.M., CUC2), a hip space where performances are followed by disco. Get the ball rolling with a shot of rum at

Bar Marquesina (tel. 043/22-4848, daily 10 A.M.–1 A.M.), on the northwest corner of Plaza Vidal.

El Mejunje (Marta Abreu #107, e/ Zayas y Alemán, Tues.–Fri. 10 P.M.–4 A.M., Sat. 5 P.M.–4 A.M., Sun. 10 A.M.–4 P.M.), an open-air space amid brick ruins, hosts a varying program, from rap to traditional *trova* (some of the best in Cuba), but is famous nationwide for its LGBTQ (lesbian/gay/bisexual/transgender/queer) Saturday night parties.

A small cabaret is hosted at **La Casa del Gobernador** (Independencia, esq. Zayas, tel. 042/20-2273, Fri.–Sun. 9 P.M.–2 A.M., CUC5). **Artex El Bosque** (Carretera Central, tel. 042/20-4444, Wed.–Sun. 9 P.M.–2 A.M., CUC1), overhanging the Río Cubanicay, also has an open-air cabaret at 10:30 P.M. And outside town, **Cubanacán Villa La Granjita** (Carretera Malez, Km 2.5, tel. 042/22-8190) has a nightly "Fiesta Campesina" show poolside at 9:30 P.M.

There's a **cinema** on the west side of the main square and another, **Cine Cubanacán,** on the Bulevar; pop into the **Bar Daiquiri** for a post-movie *trago* (daily noon–midnight). Classical and other performances are hosted at **Teatro la Caridad** (Tues., Wed., Sat., and Sun. at 9 P.M., 5 pesos).

Baseball is hosted October–May at **Estadio Sandino** (Avenida 9 de Abril), about one mile east of Parque Vidal.

Children may get a kick out of the lions, leopards, hyenas, etc. at **Parque Zoológico Camilo Cienfuegos** (Av. Martí, Tues.–Sun. 9 A.M.–5 P.M., one peso), but the beasts are kept in primitive conditions.

Accommodations

No *campismos* in Santa Clara Province were taking foreigners at last visit. Check with **Campismo Popular** (Maceo Sur #315, e/ San Miguel y Nazareno, tel. 0422/20-4905, Mon.–Fri. 8 A.M.–noon and 1–4:30 P.M.).

CASAS PARTICULARES

I always enjoy staying at **Casa de Elier y Alina** (Calle San Pablo #19, e/ Carolina y

CHE GUEVARA

Ernesto "Che" Guevara was born into a leftist middle-class family in Rosario, Argentina, in 1928. He received a medical degree from the University of Buenos Aires in 1953, then set out on an eight-month motorcycle odyssey through South America that had a profound influence on his radical thinking (as regaled in Brazilian director Walter Salle's 2004 movie, *The Motorcycle Diaries*, which canonizes Che and his awakening).

In 1954, he spent a brief period working as a volunteer doctor in Guatemala and was on hand when the Arbénz government was overthrown by a CIA-engineered coup (his experience left him intensely hostile to the United States). He fled Guatemala and went to Mexico where, in November 1955, he met Fidel Castro and joined the revolutionary cause.

The two had much in common. Guevara was a restless soul who, like Castro, was also daring and courted danger. They were both brilliant intellectuals (Guevara wrote poetry and philosophy and was probably the only true intellectual in Cuba's revolutionary leadership). Each had a relentless work ethic, total devotion, and an incorruptible character. Although the handsome, pipe-smoking rebel was a severe asthmatic, Che also turned out to be Castro's best field commander, eventually writing two books on guerrilla warfare. He commanded the Third Front in the Sierra Escambray and led the attack that on December 28, 1958, captured Santa Clara and finally toppled the Batista regime. It was Che Guevara who took command of Havana's main military posts on New Year's Day, 1959.

SHAPING THE REVOLUTION

The revolutionary regime declared Guevara a native Cuban citizen, rendering him legally entitled to hold office in Cuba. Che (an affectionate Argentinian appellation meaning "pal" or "buddy") became head of the National Bank of Cuba and Minister of Finance and, in 1961, Minister of Industry. He also led the tribunals that dispensed with scores of Batista supporters – Guevara never flinched from pulling the trigger

himself – and was instrumental in the repression that was meant to crush "counterrevolutionaries." To U.S. officials, says biographer Jon Lee Anderson, he was "the fearsome Rasputin of the regime." His mystical influence attracted to him a crowd of loyal disciples, *los hombres del Che.* Nonetheless, Guevara narrowly escaped an assassination attempt on February 24, 1961, outside his home on Calle 18 in Miramar.

Guevara supervised the radical economic reforms that swept through Cuba and embraced the Soviet Union with innocent fervor as a bulwark for the coming break with the United States. He negotiated the trade deals with the Soviet Union.

Though born into a bourgeois family, he developed an obsessive hatred of bourgeois democracy, the profit motive, and U.S. interests. He believed that the individualistic motivations that determine behavior in a capitalist system would become obsolete when collective social welfare became the stated goal. Che believed that liberty eroded moral values: Individualism was selfish and divisive.

Guevara's ambition was to export peasant revolution around the world. "Stealthily, Che was setting up the chessboard for his game of continental guerrilla warfare, the ultimate prize being his homeland," wrote Anderson. He worked ceaselessly to goad a conflict between the Soviet Union and United States. The forces he helped set in motion in Latin America created a dark period of revolutionary violence and vicious counter-repression throughout the continent.

FALL FROM GRACE

However, Guevara was greatly at odds with Castro on fundamental issues. Although they were intellectual equals, in many ways Che and Fidel were unmatched. Where Castro was pragmatic, Guevara was ideological. And Guevara was fair-minded toward Cubans critical of the Castro regime, unlike Castro. Guevara gradually lost his usefulness to Fidel's revolution. His frankness eventually disqualified him, forcing him into suicidal exile.

© CHRISTOPHER P. BAKER

Complejo Escultórico Memorial Comandante Ernesto Che Guevara

Guevara left Cuba in early 1965. He renounced all his positions in the Cuban government, as well as his honorary Cuban citizenship. Guevara apparently severed his ties with Cuba voluntarily, although the reasons have never been adequately explained.

DEATH AND ETERNAL GLORY

Che fought briefly in the Congo with the Kinshasa rebels before returning in secret to Cuba. He reemerged in 1966 in Bolivia, where he unsuccessfully attempted to rouse the Bolivian peasantry and "to create another Vietnam in the Americas" as a prelude to what he hoped would be a definitive world war in which socialism would be triumphant. Che was betrayed to the Bolivian Army Rangers by the peasants he had hoped to set free. He died on October 9, 1967, ambushed and executed along with several loyal members of the Cuban Communist Party.

Critics claim that he was abandoned by Castro, who may have foreseen the benefits that would derive from Che as martyr. Castro has since built an entire cult of worship around Che. He has become an icon, exploited as a "symbol of the purest revolutionary virtue." Che became the official role model of the *hombre nuevo*, the "New Man." The motto *seremos como Che* ("We will be like Che") is the official slogan of the Young Pioneers, the nation's youth organization. His image is everywhere. (The photographer Korda shot the famous image – "The Heroic Guerrilla" – showing Guevara wearing a windbreaker zippered to the neck, in his trademark black beret with five-point revolutionary star, his head tilted slightly, "his eyes burning just beyond the foreseeable future," wrote Tom Miller.) Che has been turned into a modern myth the world over. He became a hero to the New Left radicals of the 1960s. The ultimate and most absurd, tribute perhaps came from the French philosopher Jean-Paul Sartre, who honored Guevara as "the most complete man of our age."

In 1997 Che's remains were delivered to Cuba and interred in Santa Clara.

Máximo Gómez, tel. 042/22-7704 or 5337-8499, CUC25), on the north side of Plaza del Carmen. The delightful young hosts have a spacious lounge with color TV, nicely decorated in 1950s style. Two spacious air-conditioned bedrooms have private bathrooms; take the room with king bed. Filling meals can be enjoyed in a shady patio.

Casa de Olga Rivera (Yanes #20, e/ Máximo Gómez y Callejón del Carmen, tel. 042/21-1711, CUC20–25), on the south side of Plaza del Carmen, is a well-kept colonial home with two air-conditioned rooms that open to a lounge graced by plush sofas. You get TV, fridge, and private hot-water bathroom. There's parking. Meals are served in an exquisite patio with caged birds. Olga's home opens directly to an adjoining *casa particular*—**Hostal Zaida Barreto**—hence families and groups can rent four bedrooms together. Around the corner, **Casa de José Ramón** (Máximo Gómez #208 altos, e/ Berenguer y Yanes, tel. 042/20-7239, josetur2009@gmail.com, CUC15–20) has an independent upstairs apartment with full kitchen and stairs to a rooftop terrace.

English-speaking gay owner Angel Rodríguez runs a remarkable rental at [C] **Hostal Florida Center** (Maestra Nicolasa #56, e/ Colón y Maceo, tel. 042/20-8161, angel.floridacenter@ yahoo.com, CUC20 s, CUC25 d). Teeming with astounding antiques, including Baccarat chandeliers, this colonial home opens to a lush patio with aviary. One bedroom is colonial-themed and has bronze and wrought-iron beds; the other features art deco. Angel's boyfriend also has a rental with similarly impressive furnishings at **Hostal Alba** (Machado #7, e/ Cuba y Colón, tel. 042/29-4108, albahostal@yahoo. com, CUC20 s, CUC25 d).

Casa de Ernesto y Mireya (Calle Cuba #227 altos, e/ Sindico y Pastora, tel. 042/27-3501, ernesto_tama@yahoo.com, CUC15) is a bargain for its independent upstairs apartment with handsome lounge overlooking Plaza la Pastora. The spacious, simply appointed air-conditioned bedroom has an attractive bathroom. There's parking. Ernesto and Mireya also have a lovely 1950s home—you'll love the

'50s features—with two rooms around the corner. Together, the units are perfect for a family or group.

HOTELS

The only downtown option is Islazúl's lackluster high-rise **Hotel Santa Clara Libre** (tel. 042/20-7548, fax 042/20-2771, CUC17 s, CUC24 d year-round), overlooking Parque Vidal. There's a mediocre restaurant on the 10th floor. Water supply is never guaranteed, and noise from the basement disco is a problem.

A better bet is **Cubanacán Los Caneyes** (Av. de los Eucaliptos y Circunvalación de Santa Clara, tel./fax 042/21-8140, comercial@ caneyes.hor.tur.cu, CUC42 s, CUC52 d low season, CUC52 s, CUC60 d high season), two kilometers west of town and favored by tour groups. It has 96 appealing air-conditioned rooms in thatched, wooden octagonal *cabinas* spread amid landscaped grounds. Facilities include an attractive restaurant and a swimming pool. Its similarly priced sibling, **Cubanacán Villa La Granjita** (Carretera Malez, Km 2.5, Santa Clara, tel. 042/22-8190, fax 042/22-8149, reserva@granjita.vcl.tur.cu) also has 71 thatched cabins around a handsome pool and sundeck. It has a tennis court, restaurant, and shop.

Food

The only *paladar* is **Paladar Sabor Tropical** (Esquerra #157, e/ Julio Jover y Berenguer, tel. 042/22-4279, lafaraonallatina@yahoo.es, 24 hours), a small private restaurant serving *criollo* dishes and seafood.

In 2009, **Restaurante 1878** (Máximo Gómez, e/ Independencia 7 Abreu, tel. 042/20-2428, daily noon–4 P.M. and 7–11 P.M.) opened in a colonial mansion, adding a touch of much-needed elegance to the dining scene. It serves *criollo* fare.

The top-floor restaurant in the **Hotel Santa Clara Libre** (tel. 042/20-7548, daily 7:15–9:30 A.M., noon–2:30 P.M., and 7:15–9:30 P.M.) has views over the square, the sole reason to dine here.

The Bulevar has several snack bars, including **Café Europa** (tel. 042/21-6350, daily

9 A.M.–1:30 A.M.) facing Plaza de las Arcadas. It's a hangout for tourists, not least for its draft Cristal beer.

For seafood, head to the clean, air-conditioned **Dimar** (9 Abril, esq. 1ra, tel. 042/20-1375, daily 10 A.M.–10 P.M.). I recommend the garlic shrimp (CUC2.50) and lobster enchiladas (CUC6.25). A stone's throw away, *peso* food stalls around the *mercado agropecuario* (1ra, e/ Morales y General Roloff, Mon.–Sat. 8 A.M.–5 P.M., Sun. 8 A.M.–noon), which sells fresh produce.

Bakeries include **Panadería Doña Neli** (Maceo Sur, esq. Av. 9 de Abril, 6:30 A.M.–6 P.M.), selling in CUC, and the simpler **Panadería Segundo Gallo** (Independencia, esq. Zayas, daily 7 A.M.–7 P.M.), selling in pesos.

Coppelia (Calle Colón, esq. Mujica, tel. 0422/20-6426, Tues.–Sun. 10 A.M.–11:30 P.M.), one block south of the main square, sells ice cream for pesos. **Dulce Crema** (Independencia, esq. Luis Estéves, daily 10 A.M.–10 P.M.) charges in CUC.

Information and Services

An **Infotur** bureau (Máximo Gómez e/ Machado y Maestro Nicolás) was to open in 2010.

The **post office** (tel. 042/20-3862, Mon.–Fri. 9 A.M.–6 P.M., Sat. 8:30 A.M.–noon) is at Colón #10 (e/ Parque Vidal y Machado). **DHL** (Cuba 7, e/ Tristá y San Cristóbal, tel. 042/21-4069) is one block west.

Etecsa (Marta Abreu, esq. Villuendas, daily 8 A.M.–7:30 P.M.) has international telephone and Internet service.

Bandec (Marta Abreu y Luis Estéves, and Máximo Gómez y Rafael Tristá) and **Banco Financiero Internacional** (Cuba #6, e/ Triste y Machado) have branches on Parque Vidal. You can change foreign currency at **Cadeca** (Máximo Gómez, esq. Rafael Tristá). **Fincimex** (Carretera Central #103 e/ Virtudes y San Pedro, tel. 042/20-0972) can assist with problems with credit cards.

Eye issues? Go to **Opticas Miramar** (Colón e/ Maestro Nicolás y 9 Abril, Mon.–Fri. 9 A.M.–4:30 P.M. and Sat. until noon).

The **Bufete Internacional** (Luis Estévez #119, e/ San Miguel y 9 de Abril, tel. 0422/20-8458) and **Consultoría Jurídica Internacional** (Trista #5, e/ Villuendas y Cuba, tel./fax 0422/21-8114, cjivillaclara@ enet.cu) offer legal assistance.

Getting There and Away
BY AIR

Flights arrive at **Aeropuerto Internacional Abel Santamaría** (tel. 042/21-4402), 10 kilometers northeast of the city. **Havanatur** (Máximo Gómez #13, e/ Independencia y Barreras, tel. 042/20-4001) sells Cubana tickets.

BY BUS

The **Terminal de Ómnibus Nacionales** (Av. Cincuentenario, Independencia y Oquendo, tel. 042/29-2214) is on the Carretera Central, 2.5 kilometers west of the city center. **Víazul** (tel. 042/22-2523) buses between Havana and Santiago stop in Santa Clara. Buses depart Santa Clara eastbound at 12:50 A.M., 1:50 A.M., 2 P.M., and 7:30 P.M., and westbound at 3:15 A.M., 7:40 A.M., and 8:20 P.M.

BY TRAIN

Most trains traveling between Havana and Santiago de Cuba stop in Santa Clara. The **Estación de Ferrocarriles** (tel. 042/20-2895) is at the northern end of Luis Estévez, seven blocks from Parque Vidal. Same-day tickets are sold at the ticket office (tel. 042/20-0854) on the *south* side of the square. Seats on the *regular* are sold up to 24 hours in advance; seats on the *especial* can be bought only one hour in advance of departure.

The *especial* (Tren Francés) departs Santa Clara for Santiago at 10:53 A.M. (CUC41 first class, CUC33 second class). Slower eastbound trains depart for Sancti Spíritus at 2:06 A.M. (CUC3.50), Bayamo and Manzanillo at 3:42 A.M. (CUC15.50), Santiago at 8 A.M. (CUC20), and Guantánamo at noon (CUC22).

The westbound *especial* (Tren Francés) departs for Havana at 4:57 A.M. (CUC20). Slower westbound trains depart for Havana at 1:17 A.M., 12:56 P.M., 9:27 P.M., and 10:42 P.M. (CUC10), and for Cienfuegos at 5:40 P.M. (CUC2).

A train runs to Caibarién at 5:30 P.M. (CUC1.95) and to Cienfuegos at 5:40 P.M. in July–August only, and from Caibarién at 4 A.M. and Cienfuegos at 4:20 A.M. The local train ticket office is to the rear of the national train office.

BY CAR
You can rent cars from **Cubacar** (Marta Abreu #130, tel. 042/20-9118) and **Rex** (Marta Abreu #130, tel. 042/22-2244, irl@rexz.com).

BY ORGANIZED EXCURSION
Tour agencies include **Cubanacán** (Colón, e/ Candelaria y San Cristóbal, tel. 042/20-5189), **Cubatur** (Martha Abreu #10, e/ Máximo Gómez y Villuendas, tel. 042/20-8980, cubaturvc@enet.cu), and **Havanatur** (Máximo Gómez #13, e/ Independencia y Barreras, tel. 042/20-4001).

Getting Around
Local buses depart the **Terminal de Ómnibus Intermunicipal** (Marta Abreu, tel. 042/20-3470), 10 blocks west of Parque Vidal. Bus #11 runs between Parque Vidal and Hotel Los Caneyes.
   Cubataxi (tel. 0422/22-2691) taxis can be hailed from outside the Hotel Santa Clara Libre.
   There are gas stations on the Carretera Central at the corner of General Roloff and two blocks north at Carretera Central and the corner of Avenida 9 de Abril.
   Palmares (Marta Abreu #130, tel. 042/22-7595) rents scooters (CUC24 one day, CUC126 weekly).

ALTURAS DE SANTA CLARA
The Alturas de Santa Clara rise south and east of the city and merge into the Sierra Escambray. The hills and valleys are pocked with quaint timeworn villages and quilted by tobacco fields.
   The Autopista and Carretera Central pass through the region. One of the most scenic drives in Cuba is Route 4-474 south from

Santa Clara to Manicaragua and Topes de Collantes.

Embalse Hanabanilla
This huge (32-square-kilometer) artificial lake beautifies the northern foothills of the Escambray, below a backdrop of pine-studded mountains. It is stocked with trout and bass. The Hotel Hanabanilla offers fishing trips (CUC25–50 per person), guided hikes (CUC5), and boat excursions to El Nicho (CUC12), **Río Negro Restaurante,** and the **Casa del Campesino** (CUC3), a small working farm where you can get a taste for the campesino lifestyle.
   The turnoff for Hanabanilla is midway between Cumanayagua and Manicuragua, on Route 4-206, at La Macagua, just west of Ciro Redondo.

Accommodations and Food
The only hotel for miles was once a place of last resort. Yet in 2009 Islazúl's Soviet-style **Hotel Hanabanilla** (tel. 042/20-8550, fax 042/20-1100, carpeta@hanabanilla.vcl.cyt.cu, CUC14 s, CUC22 d low season including breakfast, CUC21 s, CUC36 d all-inclusive) was transformed from ugly duckling to swan. Perched on the lake's western shore, it offers great views. The 125 air-conditioned rooms are pleasantly furnished and have modern bathrooms, plus French doors opening to balconies.
   Criollo lunches such as roast pork or chicken with pineapple (the house specialty) are served at the **Río Negro Restaurante,** on the southern shores of the lake.

THE NORTH COAST
There is little to recommend along the coast northwest of Santa Clara. The Circuito Norte (Route 4-13) parallels the shore, providing an easy route for travelers heading between Santa Clara and Varadero.
   Encrucijada, 25 kilometers due north of Santa Clara, was the birthplace of revolutionary heroes Abel Santamaría and Jesús Menéndez. Their houses are now museums.

East of Encrucijada, Route 4-13 runs through **San Antonio de las Vueltas,** a sleepy town that wakes up for the year-end *parranda*. The highway then merges with Route 4-321, which runs west to Santa Clara and east to Remedios and Caibarién.

Beach-fringed cays lie scattered offshore. The cays' landward shores are fringed by mangroves—havens for herons, flamingos, roseate spoonbills, and other stilt-legged waders, as well as manatees, while marine turtles come ashore to lay eggs. The **Área Protegida Las Picuas-Cayo del Cristo** (tel. 042/69-0141) has no facilities for tourists (not even tours), although flamingos can sometimes be seen in lagoons by the office in the fishing community of Carahatas, 14 kilometers north of the Circuito Norte. It has a small *jutía* breeding facility.

Baños de Elguea

The Elguea Thermal Center, about five kilometers northwest of Corralillo and 135 kilometers northwest of Santa Clara, is supplied by hypothermal (up to 50°C) springs good for treating rheumatism, skin ailments, and respiratory problems. It has swimming pools, a marching tank, mud baths, gym, solarium, massage rooms, and more. Facilities are crude and, at last visit, deteriorated.

Accommodations

Islazúl's dead-as-a-doornail **Hotel Elguea & Spa** (tel. 042/68-6298, fax 042/68-6442, danelis@elguea.vcl.cyt.cu, CUC13 s, CUC20 d year-round) is promoted as a spa resort but receives few guests. It has 49 simply furnished air-conditioned rooms with satellite TVs and modern bathrooms. One room serves travelers with disabilities. The swimming pool was empty at last visit (as was the hotel), and the restaurant (the only eatery for miles) was closed.

Eastern Villa Clara

VUELTA ARRIBA

East of Santa Clara, the Carretera Central and Route 4-321 run through the Vuelta Arriba region, one of Cuba's premier tobacco-growing regions. The scenery is marvelous as you pass fields tilled by ox-drawn plows and stir up the dust in small agricultural towns lent a Wild West feel by horses tethered to sagging arcades that line the main streets.

The district is unique within Cuba for the year-end *parrandas,* festivals in which rockets whiz through the streets and hand-held fireworks and "mortars" explode with a military boom as the townsfolk of each community divide into two historic camps and vie to see who can produce the best parade float and the loudest din. In all, 14 local communities hold *parrandas,* most notably Placetas, Remedios, Zulueta, and San Antonio de las Vueltas, which uniquely holds its *parranda* in August.

◖ REMEDIOS

This time-warp town (pop. 18,000), 45 kilometers northeast of Santa Clara, is full of Spanish colonial charm. It is in a good state of preservation and the entire city is justifiably a national monument.

Remedios was founded in 1514 when a land grant was given to a conquistador named Vasco Porcallo de Figueroa. A city hall wasn't built, however, and supposedly for that reason the town was never acknowledged as one of the first seven cities. It was originally situated closer to the shore. In 1544, it was moved a short distance inland to escape pirates. The town continued to come under constant attack, and in 1578, the townsfolk uprooted again and founded a new settlement. In 1682, a group of citizens uprooted and founded Santa Clara, which in time grew to become the provincial capital. Apparently, in 1691 the clique returned to Remedios, determined to

and wrought-iron benches. Dominating the square is the venerable **Parroquia de San Juan Batista** (Camilo Cienfuegos #20, Mon.–Sat. 9–11 A.M.), dating from 1692. Its pious exterior belies the splendor within, not least a carved cedar altar that glimmers with 24-carat gold leaf, a statue of the Immaculate Virgin heavy with child, and a Moorish-style ceiling of carved mahogany, splendidly gabled and fluted. The church has an impressive bell tower. It was badly damaged by an earthquake in 1939 and restored over the ensuing 15 years at the behest of a local benefactor, who also donated European paintings.

Museo de la Música Alejandro García Caturla (Camilo Cienfuegos #5, tel. 042/39-6851, Tues.–Sat. 9 A.M.–noon and 1–5 P.M., Sun. 9 A.M.–1 P.M., CUC1 entrance, CUC5 camera), on the north side, honors one of Cuba's foremost avant-garde composers. The house features period furniture and Caturla's original manuscripts. The musical prodigy began writing music in 1920, when he was only 14. He was heavily influenced by the rhythms and sounds of Africa and fell under the sway of Stravinsky. The iconoclastic composer was a noted liberal and an incorruptible lawyer who rose to become judge for the city. He was assassinated in 1940.

On the park's northwest corner stands the **Iglesia Buen Viaje** (Alejandro del Río #66), a prim little church with a three-tiered bell-tower with a life-size figure of the Virgin Mary and Jesus in the "dove-hole." It is fronted by a marble statue of Cuba's Indian maiden, a symbol of the nation's liberty.

One block west of the plaza, the **Museo de las Parrandas** (Calle Máximo Gómez #71, no tel., Tues.–Sat. 9 A.M.–noon and 1–6 P.M., Sun. 9 A.M.–1 P.M., CUC1 entrance, CUC1 cameras) celebrates the festivals unique to the region. Given the ostentation of the actual *parrandas,* the museum is anticlimactic.

Entertainment and Events

Any time is a good time to visit, but if possible time your visit for Christmas week for the annual *parranda.* By December, the townsfolk

raze it to the ground. They were rebuffed in a pitched battle.

If you have seriously bored kids, consider a brief visit to **Finca La Cabaña** (tel. 042/39-5764, daily 10 A.M.–5 P.M.), one kilometer east of town. This rustic and amateurish re-creation of a peasant farmstead has horseback rides, a mini-zoo, and a cow-milking demo.

Plaza Martí

The town's main square is shaded by tall royal palms beneath which you can sit on marble

FIREWORKS FEVER

The villages and towns due east of Santa Clara are renowned islandwide for *parrandas*, the noisy year-end revels that date back more than a century. The festival apparently began in Remedios on Christmas Eve in 1822, when a zealous priest went through the streets making frightening noises meant to rouse the townspeople and scare them into attending midnight mass. The villagers took the fiesta-like din to heart and gradually evolved a classic Mardi Gras-type carnival celebrated during the days around Christmas and New Year's.

Eventually the *parrandas* spread to the neighboring villages (14 communities now have *parrandas*). Fireworks were introduced and the revels developed into competitions – really, massive fireworks battles – to see who could make the loudest noise. Each of the villages divides into two rival camps represented by mascots: the Carmelitas of Remedios, for example, are represented by a *gavilán* (hawk), and the Sansarices (from San Salvador) by a *gallo* (rooster).

The villagers invest ludicrous emotional value in their wars and spend months preparing in secret. Warehouses are stocked full of explosives and sawhorses studded with fireworks, and the final touches are put on the floats (*trabajos de plaza*) that will be pulled by field tractors around 3 A.M. Spies infiltrate the enemy camp. Even sabotage is not unknown. The rivals take turns parading all through

firework madness during *parrandas*

the night. Rum flows. The singing and dancing gather pace. Conga lines weave through town. Huge banners are waved, to be met by cheers or shouts of derision. *¡Viva la Loma! ¡Viva Guani-jibes!* The excitement builds as each neighborhood stages fireworks displays. The opposing sides alternately present their pyrotechnics. The streets are filled with deafening explosions from stovepipe mortars, rockets, and whirling explosives whizzing overhead and sometimes into the panicked crowd, and the smoke is so thick that you can barely see your way through the streets. Finally, the wildest fireworks are unleashed and the fiesta culminates in an orgy of insane firepower. Pretty fireworks don't earn points. The most relentless, voluminous bombast determines who wins.

are feverishly preparing for their *parranda,* which culminates on December 24. The wild and racket-filled event is a dangerous business, as rockets whiz into the crowd and every year several people are injured. Don't wear flammable nylon clothing. Be sure to check out the midnight mass in the cathedral. Next day the streets are littered with spent drunks and fireworks. On December 26 those citizens who have recovered celebrate the city's "liberation" by Che Guevara's Rebel Army. Pickpockets abound.

There's a good reason that **El Louvre** (tel. 042/39-5639, daily 8 A.M.–2 A.M.), on the plaza's south side, gets packed: It serves draft

Cristal beer. Next door, **Las Leyendas** (tel. 042/39-6131, daily 8 A.M.–2 A.M.) hosts a *cabaret espectéculo* (Fri.–Sun. at 10 P.M., CUC1).

Traditional music and dance is performed at the **Casa de la Cultura** (Gómez, esq. José de Pena, tel. 042/39-5581, Tues.–Sun. 9 A.M.–11 P.M.), one block east of the main square.

The **Teatro Ruben Mártinez** (Cienfuegos #30, tel. 042/39-5346, Mon.–Fri. 8 A.M.–5 P.M.), built in the late 19th century with a triple-tiered horseshoe-shaped auditorium, hosts classical and other performances.

Accommodations

More than 30 homes are licensed as *casas*

particulares. During the end of year *parrandas,* when visitors flood town, restrictions on rentals are lifted and many nonregistered households rent rooms.

For colonial ambience, check into (**Casona Cueto** (Alejandro del Río #72, e/ Enrique Malaret, tel. 042/39-5350, luisenrique@capiro.vcl.sld.cu, CUC20–25), a delightful 18th-century home full of antiques. The owners rent two air-conditioned rooms with fans and modern bathrooms. A courtyard with caged birds and a landscaped rooftop terrace are to the rear.

(**Hostal de Jorge y Gisela** (Brigadier González #29, tel. 042/39-6538, toeva@capiro.ucl.sld.cu, CUC15–25), two blocks south of the plaza, has two rooms in a well-furnished 1950s-style home with a gracious lounge. One room (with an independent entrance) is reached via spiral stairs and has its own sunny lounge and patio, fridge, spacious cross-lit bedroom, and modern bathroom. The second (entered via the house) has fans. There's a rooftop patio for sunbathing. Parking is secure.

Hostal Aponte (Brigadier González #32 altos, e/ Independencia y P. Magalis, tel. 042/39-5398, apontegladys544@yahoo.es, CUC20–25) is upstairs in a spacious colonial home. Eccentric owner Gladys Rojas is a *santera,* so a stay here is a great way of learning something about the religion. She has two air-conditioned rooms, one fairly small, the other much larger and cross-ventilated.

Cubanacán's **Hotel E Mascotte** (Calle Máximo Gómez, tel. 042/39-5341, fax 042/39-5327, reservas@mascotte.vcl.tur.cu, CUC60 s/d year-round including breakfast) is an upgraded 19th-century hotel. It has 14 pleasantly furnished air-conditioned rooms with satellite TV. The bathrooms have marble. A plaque on the outside wall records that here on February 1, 1899, Máximo Gómez met with Robert P. Porter, the special commissioner of U.S. President William McKinley, to negotiate the terms of the Mambí fighters' honorable discharge at the end of the Spanish-Cuban-American War.

By the end of 2010, the **Hotel Barcelona** (www.hotelescubanacan.com) may be open; at last visit the old hotel was being rebuilt behind its original colonial facade on the southeast corner of Plaza Martí.

Food

Start the day with backpackers perusing their Moon guides at **El Louvre** (south side of the plaza, tel. 042/39-5639, daily 8 A.M.–midnight), serving omelets, sandwiches, and burgers.

The **Restaurante La Arcada** (daily noon–3 P.M. and 7 A.M.–10 P.M.), in the Hotel E Mascotte (Calle Máximo Gómez, tel. 042/39-5341), has spiced up its once-boring menu with beef carpaccio (CUC7) and such entrées as pork mignon with creole sauce (CUC8) and grilled fish with parsley, lemon, and butter sauce (CUC8.50). A delightful rustic alternative is **Restaurante El Curujey** (tel. 042/39-5764, daily 10 A.M.–5 P.M.), at Finca La Cabaña, one kilometer east of town. Dishes include a fried banana stuffed with beef hash (CUC2) appetizer, and rabbit in red wine sauce (CUC19).

Beat the heat with ice cream at **Cremería América** (Jesús Crespo, esq. Andres del Río, no tel., daily 9 A.M.–9:45 P.M.), to the northwest side of the plaza.

Information and Services

Remedios is poorly served. It doesn't even have an Etecsa outlet; the nearest *telepunto* is in Caibarién.

Getting There and Away

The bus station (tel. 042/39-5185) is on the road to Santa Clara. The railway station (tel. 042/39-5129) is eight blocks west of the main square. The train linking Santa Clara with Remedios wasn't operating at last visit.

Cubacar (tel. 042/39-5555) has a car rental office at the Oro Negro gas station on the north side of town. **Vía Rent-a-Car** (tel. 042/39-5398) has an office on the west side of the plaza.

Cubanacán in Santa Clara has excursions to the *parranda* (CUC25).

CAIBARIÉN

This sprawling down-at-the-heels coastal town (pop. 39,000), eight kilometers east of Remedios, has some intriguing albeit much-deteriorated colonial structures. There's a 19th-century *trocha* (fort) at the southern entrance to town, where a huge stone crab raises its claws defiantly in the road divide. The main street—Máximo Gómez—leads to **Parque de la Libertad,** surrounded by period edifices. Avenida 5, one block west of Máximo Gómez, is a broad boulevard pinned by the **Monumento José Martí.** On the east side of town, a palm-lined shorefront **Malecón** leads east to a funky fishing fleet.

Caibarién has a year-end *parranda*.

Museo de Agroindustria Azucarera

In 2009, the derelict Central Marcelo Salado sugar-processing factory, at La Reforma, three kilometers west of town, reopened as the Sugar Industry Museum (tel. 042/36-3586, Mon.–Fri. 8 A.M.–4 P.M., CUC3). It does a great job.

First up is an informative video (an English version is offered) on the history of sugar in Cuba, and of sugar production. Then you tour the old mills *(molinos)*.

Eight antique locomotives are on display (the oldest dates from 1904), and 14 were to be added. You can hop aboard a steam train for an excursion from the museum to Remedios (CUC9).

Accommodations and Food

Three blocks from the bayfront, **Pensión Villa Virginia** (Casa #73, Ciudad Pesquera, tel. 042/36-3303, virginiaspension@aol.com, CUC20–25) is a tremendous *casa particular* in a prefab home in a quiet residential area on the east side of town. Take your pick of three nicely furnished rooms. Virginia offers free Internet. And the shaded garden patio is a great place for meals.

In 2009 Islazúl reopened the refurbished, 17-room **Hotel Brisas del Mar** (Rept. Mar Azul, tel. 042/35-1699, brisas@islazulvc.vcl.cyt.cu, CUC20 s, CUC25 d year-round), at the tip of

old steam train at Museo de Agroindustria Azucarera, Caibarién

a peninsula that catches the ocean breezes. The rates are a bargain for this simple, yet charming modern option with a swimming pool.

Caibarién is a culinary desert. Your best bet is **Dino's Pizza** (Av. 9, esq. Calle 10), on the southeast corner of the plaza.

Information and Services

Several banks downtown include **Banco Financiero Internacional** (Av. 7, esq. Calle 6, Mon.–Fri. 8 A.M.–3:30 P.M., Sat. 8 A.M.–1 P.M.).

Etecsa (Av. 11, esq. Calle 10, tel. 042/36-3131, 8:30 A.M.–7:30 P.M.), one block east of the plaza, has Internet and international phone service.

◀ CAYOS DE VILLA CLARA

About five kilometers east of Caibarién, a 50-kilometer-long causeway departs the coast road and leaps from cay to cay, ending at **Cayo Santa María**, 45 kilometers from the mainland. Miles of beaches run along its north shore, shelving into turquoise waters with a coral reef beyond. The cay is in the midst of major development that calls for 10,000 hotel rooms on Cayo Santa María and neighboring **Cayo Las Brujas**. Since 2008, the cays have been rebranded as the "Villa Clara Keys" (www.villaclarakeys.com).

Most of the beaches front hotels; day visitors can buy a day pass (CUC20). Otherwise join the Cubans who get free beach access at La Salinas; the trail is just beyond the airport.

Beyond the hotel zone, you can drive a dirt road to reach **Sendero Ecológico**, a nature trail. The easternmost part of the cay is a military zone with a lighthouse *(faro)* that's off-limits.

You need your passport for a toll booth checkpoint (CUC2 each way).

Recreation

Fishing here is top-notch, notably for tarpon. Excursions are offered (CUC260/350 half/full day). Scuba diving is spectacular: The best site is the wreck of the *San Pascual,* a tanker that ran aground off the west of Cayo Francés;

scuba dives (CUC45 one dive) are offered from **Marina Gaviota** (tel. 042/35-0213, marinasm@enet.cu), adjoining Villa Las Brujas.

A *delfinarium* was under construction at last visit. The marina offers a one-hour visit to dolphin training tanks, including snorkeling (CUC35). It also offers excursions by catamaran (CUC42 half day, CUC72 full day, CUC57 sunset cruise with dinner).

Accommodations and Food

All hotels are operated by Cuba's Gaviota chain and located on the town's one road.

Villas Las Brujas (tel. 042/35-0025, reserva@villa.lasbrujas.co.cu, from CUC61 s, CUC76 d low season, CUC71 s, CUC86 d high season) has 24 spacious *cabinas* atop Punta Periquillo, on Cayo Las Brujas. Nicely appointed, each has two double beds, satellite TV, and modern bathrooms. It has sailcraft on the beach. The **Restaurante El Farallón** (daily 7–10 A.M., noon–3 P.M., and 7–10 P.M.) overlooks the beach but is freezing (what is it with the Cubans and air-conditioning?), and the food wins no prizes.

© CHRISTOPHER P. BAKER

Villas Las Brujas at Cayos de Villa Clara

© CHRISTOPHER P. BAKER

Villa Zaida del Río, Cayos de Villa Clara

Sol Cayo Santa María (tel. 042/35-1500, fax 042/35-1505, www.solmeliacuba.com, from CUC170 s, CUC210 d low season, from CUC252 s, CUC315 d high season) is a deluxe 300-room all-inclusive property run by the Spanish Sol Meliá chain. Its *cabinas,* done up in Meliá's lively trademark pastels, are built on piles and separated by small bridges. It has heaps of facilities, including tennis and a kids' club. The hotel has opened a deluxe extension, the two-bedroom **Villa Zaida del Río** with its own swimming pool and gardens.

A tad more upscale, **Meliá Cayo Santa María** (tel. 042/35-0200, fax 042/35-0550, www.solmeliacuba.com, from CUC190 s, CUC250 d low season, from CUC290 s, CUC360 d high season) has 360 beautifully decorated rooms and a classy elegance to the public areas, which include three swimming pools, and all the water sports you could wish for. In 2008, the near-identical 925-room **Meliá Las Dunas** (tel. 042/35-0100) opened. And 2009 saw Spain's Barceló chain open the mammoth four-star **Barceló Cayo Santa María** (tel. 042/35-0400, www.barcelo.com), with 684 rooms, 21 restaurants, 28 bars, and a mega-spa. This multi-phase hotel will eventually have four hotels in one, with a staggering 2,780 rooms, 21 restaurants, and a golf course!

For top-of-the-line luxe, check into the gorgeous **Occidental Royal Hideaway Ensenachos** (tel. 042/204-3584, www.occidental-hoteles.com, from CUC240 s, CUC320 d), an all-inclusive with three separate sections in English-colonial style, with marble floors throughout. It has 400 rooms, including 10 bungalows, 50 honeymoon rooms, and 10 suites, most a considerable distance from the beach. Every room comes with concierge service. The "Royal Suites" are three kilometers away—a resort within a resort.

Getting There and Around
In early 2010, **AeroGaviota** was the only airline serving the airport on Cayo Las Brujas.

There's a gas station adjacent to the airport, where **Vía Rent-a-Car** (tel. 042/39-5398) has an office.

SANCTI SPÍRITUS

Sancti Spíritus Province is uniquely endowed. No visit to Cuba is complete without a visit to Trinidad—Cuba's best-preserved colonial city. Its unique combination of quintessentially 18th-century architecture, breeze-swept hillside setting, and pickled-in-aspic way of life is irresistibly charming. This UNESCO World Heritage Site lies both in the lee of the Sierra Escambray and within a 10-minute drive of Playa Ancón—the most beautiful beach along the southern shore. Although the Sierra Escambray lies mainly within the provinces of Cienfuegos and Santa Clara, most of the trails and accessible sites of interest lie within Sancti Spíritus's Gran Parque Natural Topes de Collantes, most easily accessed from Trinidad. The town also boasts the broadest range of *casas particulares* in Cuba and happens to be a leading center of *santería* and Afro-Cuban culture, with a tremendous nightlife. Trinidad grew to colonial wealth from sugar, and the nearby and scenic Valle de los Ingenios (Valley of the Sugar Mills) recalls that era.

The eponymous provincial capital struggles to compete. To the north, rolling hills flow down towards the coastal plains, farmed in sugarcane and without beaches of noted appeal. The southern coastal plains are mostly inhospitably marshy, with few villages or roads, although bird-watchers, anglers, and nature lovers are served by a number of wetland reserves.

PLANNING YOUR TIME

A week will barely suffice to enjoy this region, with the bulk of your time centered on

© CHRISTOPHER P. BAKER

HIGHLIGHTS

◖ **Complejo Histórico Comandante Camilo Cienfuegos:** A moving tribute to one of the Revolution's most popular figures, this off-the-beaten-track museum is a must-see on the revolutionary trail (page 329).

◖ **Trinidad's Plaza Mayor:** This is the most complete colonial town center outside Havana, with a fabulous yesteryear ambience and lively Afro-Cuban traditions. There's also a fine choice of *casas particulares* (page 335).

◖ **La Boca and Península de Ancón:** Close to Trinidad, Playa Ancó offers scintillating sands and excellent scuba diving close to shore (page 344).

◖ **Valle de los Ingenios:** Planted in sugarcane, this valley is noted for its ruined colonial sugar mills and is best explored on an antique steam train excursion. Stop at Torre de Manaca-Iznaga, a former sugar estate with a fine restaurant, charming setting, and a 43.5-meter-tall tower that can be climbed for the magnificent views (page 346).

◖ **Gran Parque Natural Topes de Collantes:** This national park hosts magnificent mountain hiking that is great for bird-watching. There are horseback-riding excursions and waterfalls and natural pools good for bathing (page 347).

LOOK FOR ◖ TO FIND RECOMMENDED SIGHTS, ACTIVITIES, DINING, AND LODGING.

Trinidad. The town itself needs two full days for exploring the colonial sites. However, the Trinidad experience is more about slowing down and immersing oneself in the local life, so a full week here should not be considered too much. Budget one day for an excursion to **Topes de Collantes** to hike mountain trails and go birding. You'll want beach time, too, so plan one day for sunning, snorkeling, and perhaps even scuba diving at **Playa Ancón.** If you prefer the company of Cubans, head to La Boca, where locals flock on weekends. A steam-train ride from Trinidad to the **Valle de los Ingenios** is also de rigueur.

Víazul buses operate daily to Trinidad from Havana. Organized excursions are offered from almost every other tourist destination in Cuba.

The city of Sancti Spíritus, which is well served by buses, deserves at least half a day's exploration; you'll be hard-pressed to find more than a full day's worth of things to see and do. Bird-watchers might consider a visit to nearby Embalse Zaza, a vast wetland where the fishing for bass and tarpon is world-class.

The Autopista runs 15 kilometers north of the city and continues east for 20 kilometers before ending abruptly in the middle of nowhere, near the city of Jatibónico. The Circuito Norte cuts across the northern province inland

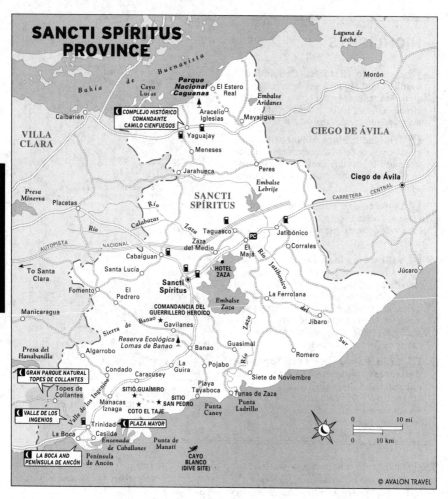

of the coast, which has no beaches of appeal. Nature lovers, however, might get a thrill at Parque Nacional Caguanes, although there are no facilities and getting there is difficult.

Interested in revolutionary history? The Complejo Histórico Comandante Camilo Cienfuegos, nearby at Yaguajay, is one of the better provincial museums.

Sancti Spíritus and Vicinity

SANCTI SPÍRITUS

Sancti Spíritus (pop. 100,000), 390 kilometers east of Havana, is a modern city laid out around a colonial core on a rise above the Río Yayabo. It straddles the Carretera Central, midway between Havana and Santiago.

The settlement of Espíritu Santo was founded in 1514 by Diego Velázquez and Fernández de Cordoba, who conquered the Yucatán. The city began life about six kilometers from its current position but was moved eight years later. The city prospered from cattle ranching and sugar. Its prominence attracted pirates, and during the late 16th and early 17th centuries it was twice ransacked and razed.

In 1895, Winston Churchill arrived in Sancti Spíritus. He loved the cigars but thought the city "a very second-rate place, and a most unhealthy place" (an epidemic of yellow fever and smallpox was raging). It has improved vastly since Churchill passed through. Quaint cobbled streets and venerable houses with iron filigree and wide doors for carriages attest to the city's antiquity, aided by a restoration of much of the central core.

Orientation

The Carretera Central enters town from the north as Bartolomé Masó (connecting the city to the Autopista) and passes down the town's eastern side before arcing east for Ciego de Ávila.

Streets are laid out in a grid, running northwest–southeast and northeast–southwest. The most important east–west thoroughfare, Avenida de los Mártires, runs west from Bartolomé Masó to Plaza Serafín Sánchez (also called Plaza Central), the main square. Avenida Jesús Menéndez runs south from the plaza, crosses the river, and continues to Trinidad. The main street, Independencia, runs south from the square and divides the city into *este* (east) and *oeste* (west). Avenida de los Mártires divides the city into *norte* (north) and *sur* (south).

Plaza Serafín Sánchez

The town's modest Parque Central was laid out in 1522 and named for Serafín Sánchez, a homegrown general in the War of Independence. It

© CHRISTOPHER P. BAKER

Plaza Serafín Sánchez

SANCTI SPÍRITUS

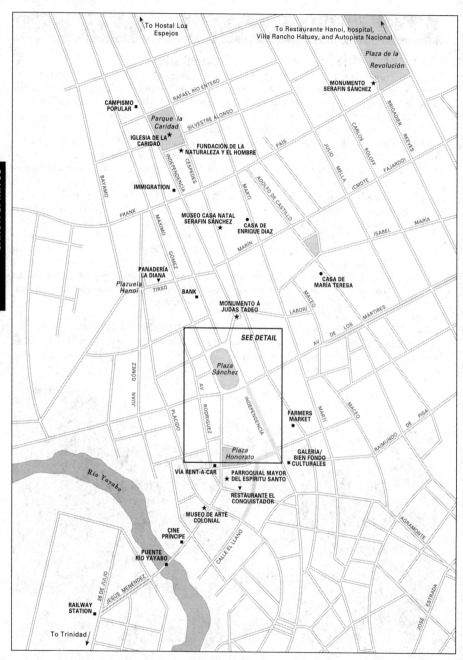

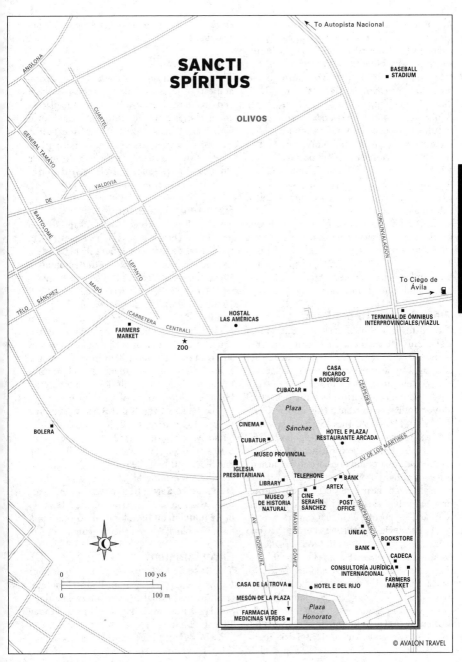

SANCTI SPÍRITUS

To Autopista Nacional

SANCTI SPÍRITUS

OLIVOS

BASEBALL STADIUM

ANGLONA

CUARTEL

GENERAL TAMAYO

VALDIVIA

DE

BARTOLOMÉ

LEPANTO

MASÓ

SÁNCHEZ

TÉLO

(CARRETERA CENTRAL)

CIRCUNVALACIÓN

To Ciego de Ávila

HOSTAL LAS AMÉRICAS

FARMERS MARKET

ZOO

TERMINAL DE ÓMNIBUS INTERPROVINCIALES/VÍAZUL

BOLERA

CASA RICARDO RODRÍGUEZ

CUBACAR

CÉSPEDES

CINEMA

Plaza Sánchez

HOTEL E PLAZA/ RESTAURANTE ARCADA

CUBATUR

MUSEO PROVINCIAL

IGLESIA PRESBITARIANA

TELEPHONE

BANK

AV DE LOS MÁRTIRES

LIBRARY

ARTEX

MUSEO DE HISTORIA NATURAL

CINE SERAFÍN SÁNCHEZ

POST OFFICE

INDEPENDENCIA

AV. RODRÍGUEZ

MÁXIMO

UNEAC

BOOKSTORE

BANK

CADECA

GÓMEZ

CONSULTORÍA JURÍDICA INTERNACIONAL

FARMERS MARKET

0   100 yds

0   100 m

CASA DE LA TROVA

MESÓN DE LA PLAZA

HOTEL E DEL RIJO

Plaza Honorato

FARMACIA DE MEDICINAS VERDES

© AVALON TRAVEL

has none of the charm or grandeur of main plazas elsewhere in Cuba, although it is surrounded by neoclassical buildings, including the impressive *biblioteca* (library) on the west side and the **Teatro Principal** on the south side. The **Museo Provincial General** (tel. 041/32-7435, Mon.–Thurs. and Sat. 9 A.M.–5 P.M., Sun. 8 A.M.–noon, CUC1), next to the library, is full of antiques and has exhibits on local history, sport, music, and more. The **Museo de Historia Natural** (Máximo Gómez Sur #2, tel. 041/32-6365, Mon.–Thurs. and Sat. 9 A.M.–5 P.M., Sun. 8 A.M.–noon, CUC1), half a block south, has a motley collection of stuffed beasts, plus insects, seashells, and more.

To the northeast, the plaza extends one block along Independencia and opens into a tiny square with a statue of local hero Judas Martínez Moles (1861–1915). South of the park, Independencia is pedestrian-only for two blocks and is lined with shops.

Plaza Honorato del Castillo

This diminutive plaza, at the junction of Calle Jesús Menéndez and Honorato, honors a local general in the War of Independence but is pinned by a statue of Rudesindo Antonio García Rojo, an eminent doctor.

On the plaza's south side, the **Parroquial Mayor del Espíritu Santo** (Agramonte Oeste #58, tel. 041/32-4855, Tues.–Sat. 9–11 A.M. and 2–5 P.M.) is well preserved. The church dates from 1680, though the triple-tiered bell tower and cupola are later additions. Relatively austere, it has minimal gilt work and an unimpressive altar, although the ornately carved roof features dropped gables carved and fitted in cross patterns and supporting a circular center.

The **Farmacia de Medicinas Verdes** (Máximo Gómez #38, tel. 041/32-4101, Mon.–Fri. 8 A.M.–noon and 2–6 P.M., Sat. 8 A.M.–noon), on the west side of the plaza, is full of old apothecary jars.

One block southwest of the cathedral, the ornate Palacio del Valle, which belonged to one of the wealthiest families in Cuba, houses the **Museo de Arte Colonial** (Plácido Sur #64, esq. Jesús Menéndez, tel. 041/32-5455, Tues.–Sat. 9 A.M.–5 P.M., Sun. 8 A.M.–noon, CUC2

entrance, CUC1 camera), furnished with period decor.

Calle Llano

The quarter immediately south of the cathedral and east of Jesús Menéndez is the city's oldest and quaintest. Here, Calle Llano and adjacent cobbled streets are closed to traffic and lined with quaint houses graced by fancy wrought-iron balconies, hanging lanterns, and wooden grills.

Jesús Menéndez crosses the Río Yayabo via **Puente Río Yayabo,** a triple-arched bridge built in 1817 of stone and brick.

Parque de la Caridad

This small plaza, three blocks north of Plaza Serafín Sánchez, is graced by a simple church, the **Iglesia de Nuestra Señora de la Caridad.** On the southeast corner, the **Fundación de la Naturaleza y el Hombre** (Calle Cruz Pérez #1, tel. 041/32-8342, funatss@enet.cu, Mon.–Fri. 10 A.M.–4 P.M., CUC0.50) is a museum that honors the 17,524-kilometer journey by a team of Cubans that paddled from the source of the Amazon to the Bahamas in dugout canoes in 1996. The eclectic miscellany displayed ranges from the dugout canoe to models of hominids in various stages of evolution and a copy of Hernán Cortés's medieval suit of armor.

The **Museo Casa Natal Serafín Sánchez** (Céspedes Norte #112, e/ Frank País y Tirso Marín, tel. 041/32-7791, Tues.–Sat. 8:30 A.M.–5 P.M., Sun. 8 A.M.–noon, CUC0.50), one block south of the plaza, is where the patriot-hero was born. He is honored, too, at the **Monumento Serafín Sánchez,** a bronze bas-relief wall on the west side of the **Plaza de la Revolución** on Bartolomé Masó and Frank País, five blocks east of the museum.

Entertainment

The **Casa de la Trova** (Máximo Gómez Sur #26, tel. 041/32-8048), on Plaza Honorato, features traditional performances Tuesday–Sunday 9 P.M.–midnight and a *peña* Sunday 10 A.M.–2 P.M.

Café Artex (Tues.–Sun. 10 P.M.–2 A.M., CUC1), above the Banco Financiero

Internacional on the main plaza, draws youth for karaoke, music, and videos.

Cabaret Los Laureles (Carretera Central, Km 383, tel. 041/32-7016), in the namesake hotel, offers an alfresco *cabaret espectáculo* followed by disco (Fri.–Sat. at 10 P.M., CUC5 entrance, including five beers or a bottle of rum plus two Cokes).

Cine Serafín Sánchez, on the west side of Parque Central, and **Cine Príncipe,** 50 meters east of the old bridge on Jesús Menéndez, show movies.

Bowling? Head to **Bolera** (tel. 041/22339, 24 hours), on Roloff, three blocks south of Avenida de los Mártires. It has bowling lanes (CUC1 for 22 "bowls") and pool tables.

Baseball is played October–May at **Estadio Victoria del Girón,** in Reparto Olivos.

A **zoo** (Tues.–Sun. 9:30 A.M.–3:30 P.M., CUC0.30) on Bartolomé Masó, 100 meters south of Avenida de los Mártires, features lions, monkeys, hyenas, antelopes, etc.

Accommodations

Campismo Popular (Independencia Norte #201, off Parque Maceo, tel. 041/26631) handles bookings for *campismos* throughout the province. All accommodations listed are air-conditioned.

CASAS PARTICULARES

The █ **Hostal Las Américas** (Carretera Central 157 Sur, tel. 041/32-2984, CUC25) wins hands down as best room rental in town and is close to the bus station. This well-kept 1950s modernist home has a large TV lounge plus dining room and garden patio. The two spacious, cross-ventilated bedrooms (the Blue Room and smaller Green Room) are delightful; bathrooms even have hair dryers. Nice!

In the north end of town, **Hostal Los Espejos** (Socorro #56, e/ Céspedes y Martí, tel. 041/32-6261, CUC15–20) is a beautifully kept colonial home that opens to a beautiful rear patio with rockers. Two rooms have private bathrooms. Secure parking.

Casa de María Teresa Lorenzo (Adolfo del Castillo #33 altos, e/ Av. de los Mártires y Valdina, tel. 041/32-4733, CUC15–20) offers two pleasing upstairs rooms with fans and modern hot-water bathrooms.

For a heart-of-affairs option, **Casa de Ricardo Rodríguez** (Independencia #28 altos, tel. 041/23029, CUC20) is a centenarian house on the northeast corner of the main plaza. It has a large lounge with a balcony. Two spacious upstairs rooms are simply furnished and have private bathrooms. Nearby, **Casa de Enrique Díaz** (Martí #111, e/ Sobral y San Cristóbal, tel. 041/27553, CUC20–25) is a spacious colonial home, minimally furnished, but opening to a rear patio with secure parking. It has two pleasant, simply furnished rooms with small private bathrooms.

HOTELS

An ugly duckling turned swan recently upgraded by Cubanacán, the █ **Hotel E Plaza** (tel. 041/32-7102, fax 41/32-8577, aloja@hostalesss.co.cu, CUC60 s/d year-round including breakfast), on the east side of Parque Central, is now one of Cuba's better urban hotels, with 27 handsomely furnished rooms with modern bathrooms. The small lobby bar is a nice spot to tipple, and the once worthless restaurant is now the city's most elegant.

There's a reason Cubanacán's █ **Hotel E del Rijo** (Calle Honorato del Castillo #12, tel. 041/32-8588, fax 041/32-8577, aloja@hostalesss.co.cu, CUC60 s/d year-round including breakfast) is usually booked solid. This 1818 neoclassical structure, entered through soaring carriage doors, combines heaps of yesteryear ambience. Its 16 large rooms (including a suite) surround a patio and boast beamed ceilings, wrought-iron lamps, period art, and modern marble bathrooms.

Islazul's **Villa Los Laureles** (Carretera Central, Km 383, tel. 041/32-7016, fax 041/32-3913, recepcion@loslaureles.co.cu, CUC19 s, CUC28 d low season, CUC21 s, CUC32 d high season) on Bartolomé Masó, about four kilometers north of town, offers 78 modest *cabinas* in meagerly landscaped grounds. All have satellite TV and modern bathrooms. There's a swimming pool, restaurant, and cabaret. Slightly more upscale, nearby **Villa Rancho Hatuey**

(Carretera Central, Km 382, tel. 041/32-8315, fax 041/32-8830, www.islazul.cu, CUC36 s, CUC48 d low season, CUC36 s, CUC53 d high season) has 74 rooms in two-story *cabinas* in contemporary Mediterranean style. There's a squash court and swimming pool.

Food

Don your finest togs to dine at Hotel E Plaza's ❰ **Restaurante Arcada** (tel. 041/32-7102, daily 7:30–10 P.M.), on the east side of Parque Central. Gone are the days when it could barely muster a *bocadito* (sandwich). Now, enjoy a candlelight dinner of chicken in beer with rice (CUC5.25), or pork mignon with creole onion sauce and sour orange (CUC8).

Romance under the stars? Choose the patio of the **Hostal E del Rijo** (Calle Honorato del Castillo #12, tel. 041/32-8588, daily 7:30–10 A.M., 11 A.M.–3 P.M., and 6–10:30 P.M.). The food's pretty good too, although the menu is limited. How about tuna with olive salad (CUC4), pork mignon with creole sauce (CUC9), and caramel pudding (CUC3)?

Mesón de la Plaza (Máximo Gómez #34, tel. 041/28546, daily 9 A.M.–8:30 P.M.), opposite Hostal E del Rijo, is styled as a Spanish *bodega,* with rough-hewn tables and cowhide chairs. Try the *garbanzo mesonero* (garbanzo with bacon, pork, and sausage) or *ensalada de garbanzo* (baked chickpeas, green peas, onions, and peppers, CUC1.50), and baked chicken in orange (CUC4.50), washed down with sangria.

Penny-pinchers might try **Restaurante El Conquistador** (Agramonte Oeste, tel. 041/32-6803, daily noon–2 P.M. and 6–9 P.M.), which serves tortillas (from three pesos) and roast pork (12 pesos), and offers set meals for five pesos.

You can buy produce at the *mercado agropecuario* (Independencia, esq. Honorato, Mon.–Sat. 7 A.M.–5:30 P.M., Sun. 7 A.M.–noon). For baked goodies, try **Panadería La Diana** (Tirso María and Máximo Gómez).

Information and Services

The **post office** (Independencia Sur #8, Mon.–Fri. 8 A.M.–4 P.M.) is one block south of the main plaza; another branch (Bartolomé Masó #167, tel. 041/32-3420) has DHL service. **Etecsa** (Independencia, daily 8:30 A.M.–7:30 P.M.), 50 meters south of Plaza Sánchez, has international telephone plus Internet service.

Banco Financiero Internacional (Independencia Sur #2) is on the southeast corner of Plaza Sánchez; **Banco Popular** is one block south. You can also change foreign currency at **Cadeca** (Independencia Sur #31). Most banks are open Mon.–Fri. 8 A.M.–3:30 P.M. and Sat. 8 A.M.–1 P.M.

Hospital Provincial Camilo Cienfuegos (tel. 041/32-4017) is on Bartolomé Masó, opposite the Plaza de la Revolución. There's a **Farmacia** (Independencia #123, tel. 041/32-4660, 24 hours) on Parque la Caridad, and **Farmacia de Plantas Medicinales** (Máximo Gómez Sur #40, tel. 041/32-4101, Mon.–Fri. 8 A.M.–noon and 2–6 P.M., Sat. 8 A.M.–noon) on Plaza Honorato.

The **Consultoría Jurídica Internacional** (Independencia #39 Altos Sur, e/ Ernesto Valdés Muñoz y Cervantes, tel. 041/32-

Restaurante Arcada in Hotel E Plaza

8448, Mon.–Fri. 8 A.M.–12:30 P.M. and 1:30–5:30 P.M.) provides legal assistance.

Getting There and Away
The **Terminal Provincial de Ómnibus** (tel. 041/32-4142) is at the junction of Bartolomé Masó and the *circunvalación,* east of town. **Víazul** (tel. 041/32-4142) buses traveling Havana, Varadero, and Trinidad to/from Santiago de Cuba stop in Sancti Spíritus. Buses depart Sancti Spíritus for Santiago at 2:25 A.M., 3:10 A.M., 3:20 P.M., and 8:50 P.M.; for Holguín at 1:05 A.M. and 2:15 P.M.; for Havana at 1:55 A.M., 3:05 A.M., 6:45 A.M., 10:45 A.M., 4:30 P.M., and 8:25 P.M.; for Trinidad at 5:25 A.M.; and for Varadero at 5:55 A.M.

Local buses and *camiones* serve nearby towns from the **Terminal Municipal** (Calle Sánchez and Carlos Roloff, tel. 041/22162), one block south of Avenida de los Mártires.

The **train station** (Av. Jesús Menéndez, esq. 26 de Julio, tel. 041/32-9228, or 32-7914 express trains) is 400 meters southwest of Puente Yayabo (ticket office open daily 8 A.M.–4 P.M., until 9 P.M. when there are departures). There is service from Havana every second day at 7:40 P.M. (CUC13.50) and to Havana from Sancti Spíritus at 7:40 P.M., stopping in Santa Clara (CUC3.50). A train to/from Cienfuegos was not operating at last visit.

Trains traveling between Havana and Santiago de Cuba stop at Guayos, 15 kilometers north of Sancti Spíritus. You should be in the front carriage of the train to alight at Guayos; taxis are available to Sancti Spíritus. If departing Sancti Spíritus to catch the *especial* you should buy your ticket at the rail station before departing for Guayos.

Getting Around
Horse-drawn *coches* ply the main streets. Tourist taxis are available on Plaza Serafín Sánchez.

Cubatur (tel. 041/32-8518, cubaturss@enet.cu), on the west side of Plaza Serafín Sánchez, offers excursions.

You can rent cars from **Havanautos** (tel. 0141/28403), in Hotel Los Laureles; **Vía**

(tel. 041/33-6697), on Plaza Honorato; and **Cubacar** (tel. 041/32-8181), on Plaza Serafín Sánchez. There's a Cupet gas station on the Carretera Central, about four kilometers north of downtown.

EMBALSE ZAZA
Six kilometers east of the city, a side road leads south off the Carretera Central to Embalse Zaza, an artificial lake studded with flooded forest and stocked with trout and world-record-breaking bass. Marsh birds flock in from far and wide. Zaza is a favorite spot for bird-watchers and anglers. Lack of rain in 2009 left the lake without water!

EcoTur (tel. 041/54-7419), in Sancti Spíritus, offers fishing (CUC80 per person, eight hours), available at Hotel Zaza.

Accommodations
Islazul's **Hotel Zaza** (tel. 041/32-7015, fax 041/32-8359, recepcion@hzaza.co.cu, CUC14 s, CUC22 d year-round) is a faceless two-story hotel with 124 air-conditioned rooms, most with lake views. It looked deteriorated at my last visit. At least it has a swimming pool.

NORTH OF SANCTI SPÍRITUS
The Circuito Norte coast road parallels the shore some miles inland, connecting Remedios (in Villa Clara Province) and Morón (in Ciego de Ávila Province).

◀ Complejo Histórico Comandante Camilo Cienfuegos
The only sight of interest is in the town of Yaguajay, 40 kilometers east of Caibarién, where a five-meter-tall bronze statue of Camilo Cienfuegos stands one kilometer north of town. Within its base is a museum (tel. 041/55-2689, Mon.–Sat. 8 A.M.–4 P.M., Sun. 9 A.M.–1 P.M., CUC1) dedicated to the revolutionary commander and the battle he led here against Batista's troops in the closing days of December 1958. It displays maps, armaments, models, etc. Camilo's ridiculously stuffed horse is enshrined in its own glass-cased mausoleum.

SANCTI SPÍRITUS

Camilo's tomb at Complejo Histórico Comandante Camilo Cienfuegos

To the rear of the museum, the **Mausoleo Frente Norte de las Villas** has an eternal flame and marble tombs for all Camilo's troops (those still alive, and those dead). They're surrounded by 24 palms symbolizing the date of liberation of Yaguajay. Schoolchildren are bused in each October 28 to toss "a flower for Camilo" into a moat on the anniversary of his death in a mysterious plane crash in 1959.

The hospital opposite the monument was formerly an army barracks, captured by Cienfuegos's Rebel Army in 1958. A small tank (converted from a tractor) used in the assault on the barracks stands outside.

Parque Nacional Caguanas

Northeast of Yaguajay the sugarcane fields meld into the swampy coastal flats, now protected within a national park. The park harbors almost 200 species of fauna, including Cuba's largest colony of cranes—an endemic subspecies of the *Graus canadensis nesiotes* crane. A highlight is the park's 35 or so caves with subterranean galleries and pre-Columbian petroglyphs. Iguanas are found on **Cayo Piedra.** The park is part of the 313,503-hectare

Reserva de la Biosfera Buenavista, enshrining 11 separate protected areas.

Access is via **Mayijagua,** about 15 kilometers east of Yaguajay. Getting there is another matter: The dirt road is fit for four-wheel drive only. **EcoTur** (Carretera Meneses–Yaguajay, Km 1.5, tel. 041/54-7417, ffauna@yag.co.cu) offers excursions here and to the nearby **Área Protegida Jobo Rosado,** also with caves and trails.

Accommodations

Just east of Mayijagua, Islazul's **Villa San José del Lago** (tel. 041/54-6108, fax 041/54-6290, sjlagoscomercial@enet.cu, CUC14 s, CUC22 d year-round) is a modest spa resort with a lagoon with pedal-boats and rowboats, plus three swimming pools (one with thermal water). The 30 simple air-conditioned *cabinas* have satellite TV and modern bathrooms. Massages and mud treatments are offered. It's popular with Cubans and gets lively on weekends.

RESERVA ECOLÓGICA ALTURAS DE BANAO

The road that leads southwest from Sancti Spíritus to Trinidad rises and dips along the foothills of the Alturas de Banao, whose sheer, barren crags remind me of the Scottish highlands.

From the village of **Banao,** 20 kilometers west of Sancti Spíritus, you can follow the valley of the Río Banao seven kilometers into the foothills, where a pristine 3,050-hectare swath is protected in the **Reserva Ecológica Lomas de Banao** (Banao Heights Ecological Reserve, tel. 041/39-9205, CUC4 entrance), also known as El Naranjal. The ecosystems include semideciduous forest, tropical moist forest, and cloud forest. The region is rich in flora, with more than 700 flowering plants (more than 100 are endemic), including over 60 orchid species. Banao is a paradise for bird-watchers. The visitor center, elevation 1,620 meters, offers horseback riding (CUC5) and hikes (from CUC3) to caves and waterfalls. **EcoTur** (tel. 041/54-7419 or 07/641-0306, www.ecoturcuba.co.cu) offers one- to three-day ecotours. Drop-in visitors pay CUC4 entry (CUC8 with lunch).

During the war to oust Batista, Che Guevara

Alturas de Banao, Sancti Spíritus

SANCTI SPÍRITUS

established his headquarters—**Comandancia del Guerrillero Heróico**—near the community of Gavilanes, in the heart of the mountains and reached by a dirt trail; the turnoff from the Trinidad road is at the hamlet of Las Brisas, five kilometers east of Banao. It's a stiff hike (about 10 kilometers) from the trailhead, near Campismo Planta Cantú. There's an obelisk at the *comandancia*.

Accommodations

Reserva Ecológica Lomas de Banao has eight basic cabins (CUC10) with cold water showers, plus a lovely thatched restaurant (8 A.M.–3:30 P.M.).

Campismo Planta Cantú (tel. 041/29698), about five kilometers north of Las Brisas, was not taking foreigners at last visit.

Trinidad and Vicinity

TRINIDAD

Trinidad (pop. 38,000), the crown jewel of Cuba's colonial cities, is 67 kilometers southwest of Sancti Spíritus and 80 kilometers east of Cienfuegos. It was the fourth of the seven cities founded by Diego de Velázquez in 1514. No other city in Cuba is so well preserved or so charming. The entire city is a national monument lent charms by its historical landmarks and its setting of great natural beauty, sitting astride a hill, where it catches the breezes and gazes out over the Caribbean against a backdrop of verdurous Sierra Escambray.

Its narrow, unmarked cobbled streets are paved with stones (*chinas pelonas*) shipped across the Atlantic as ballast or taken from the nearby river. The maze of streets is lined with terra-cotta tile-roofed houses in soft pastel colors. Much of the architecture is neoclassical and baroque, with a Moorish flavor. However, there are no great palaces as in Havana. The exquisite buildings are fronted by mahogany balustrades and massive wooden doors with *postigos* that open to let the breezes flow through cool, tile-floored rooms connected by double-swing half-doors (*mamparas*) topped by *vitrales*.

Mule-drawn carts and cowboys on horseback clip-clop through the cobbled streets. Old folks

© CHRISTOPHER P. BAKER

rock gently beneath shady verandas, serenaded by twittering songbirds in bamboo cages—a Trinidad tradition. At night the town is eerily still. Then the cool air flows downhill, the narrow alleys become refreshing channels, and it's a special joy to stroll the traffic-free streets that make the town feel even more adrift from the 20th century.

Trinidad is steeped in *santería* and Catholicism. Easter and Christmas are good times to visit.

History

The initial settlement, named Villa de la Santísima Trinidad, was founded in 1514 by Diego de Velázquez on a site settled by the Taíno. The Spanish conquistadores found the native Indians panning for gold in the nearby rivers. The Spanish established a lucrative (but short-lived) gold mine that lent vigor to the young township and the wharves of nearby Casilda. Hernán Cortés set up base in 1518 to provision his expedition to conquer the

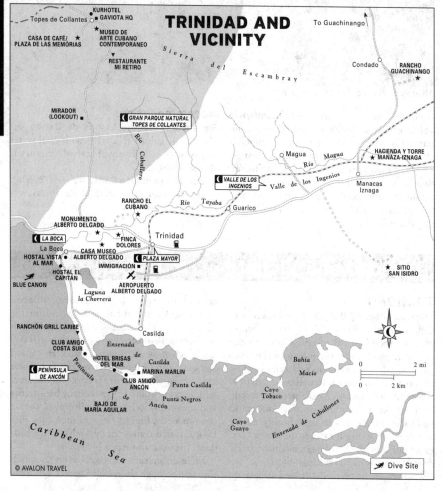

TRINIDAD AND VICINITY

To Guachinango

Topes de Collantes
KURHOTEL
GAVIOTA HQ
CASA DE CAFÉ/
PLAZA DE LAS MEMORIAS
MUSEO DE
ARTE CUBANO
CONTEMPORANEO
RESTAURANTE
MI RETIRO

Sierra   del   Escambray

Condado
RANCHO
GUACHINANGO

MIRADOR
(LOOKOUT)

GRAN PARQUE NATURAL
TOPES DE COLLANTES

Río Cabollero

Magua
Río   Magua
HACIENDA Y TORRE
MANAZA-IZNAGA

VALLE DE LOS
INGENIOS
Valle   de   los   Ingenios
Manacas
Iznaga

RANCHO EL
CUBANO
Río   Tayaba
Guarico

MONUMENTO
ALBERTO DELGADO
LA BOCA
La Boca
HOSTAL VISTA
AL MAR
CASA MUSEO
ALBERTO DELGADO
FINCA
DOLORES
Trinidad
PLAZA MAYOR
IMMIGRACIÓN
SITIO
SAN ISIDRO

HOSTAL EL
CAPITÁN
BLUE CANON
AEROPUERTO
ALBERTO DELGADO
Laguna
la Chorrera

RANCHÓN GRILL CARIBE
Casilda

CLUB AMIGO
COSTA SUR
Ensenada   de
HOTEL BRISAS
DEL MAR
Casilda
PENÍNSULA
DE ANCÓN
MARINA MARLIN
CLUB AMIGO
ANCÓN
Punta Casilda
Bahía
Macío

BAJO DE
MARÍA AGUILAR
Ancón
Punta Negros
Cayo
Tobaco

Caribbean   Sea
Cayo
Guayo
Ensenada   de   Caballones

0   2 mi
0   2 km

© AVALON TRAVEL

Dive Site

musicians and a 1950s Chevrolet on the cobbled streets of Trinidad

© CHRISTOPHER P. BAKER

Aztec empire. Soon fleets bearing the spoils of Mexico gathered, bringing new prosperity and eclipsing Trinidad's meager mines.

Trinidad was just far enough from the reach of Spanish authorities in Havana to develop a bustling smuggling trade. Its position on Cuba's underbelly was also perfect for trade with Jamaica, the epicenter of the Caribbean slave trade. Trinidad grew prosperous importing slaves, many of whom were put to work locally, stimulating the sugar trade. Money poured in from the proceeds of sugar grown in the Valle de los Ingenios. When the English occupied Cuba, in 1762–1763, Trinidad became a free port and prospered even further, entering its golden age.

Wealthy citizens built their sumptuous homes around the main square—Plaza Mayor—and along the adjoining streets. Pianos from Berlin; sumptuous furniture from France; linens, lattices, and silverware from Colombia were unloaded here. Language schools and academies were even set up to prepare the children of the wealthy to complete their studies in Europe. The city's wealth drew pirates. Many citizens prospered as victualers to the sea-roving vagabonds, while some pirates bought property and settled.

By the early 19th century, Cienfuegos, with its vastly superior harbor, began to surpass Casilda, which had begun silting up. Trinidad began a steady decline, hastened by tumult in the slave trade and new competition from more advanced estates elsewhere in Cuba. Isolated from the Cuban mainstream, Trinidad foundered. By the turn of the 20th century, it was a down-at-the-heels little town.

In the 1950s, Batista declared Trinidad a "jewel of colonial architecture." A preservation law was passed. Development was prohibited and the city continued to stagnate in its own beauty. The construction of the Carretera Central on the north side of the Sierra Escambray had already stolen the through traffic, ensuring that Trinidad would be preserved in its past. The town was named a national monument in 1965. A Restoration Committee was established, and the historic core around Plaza Mayor has been completely restored. In 1988 UNESCO named Trinidad a World Heritage Site.

Orientation

Trinidad slopes uphill, to the northeast. The cobbled historical core (*casco histórico*) with most sites of interest takes up the upper quarter

SANCTI SPÍRITUS

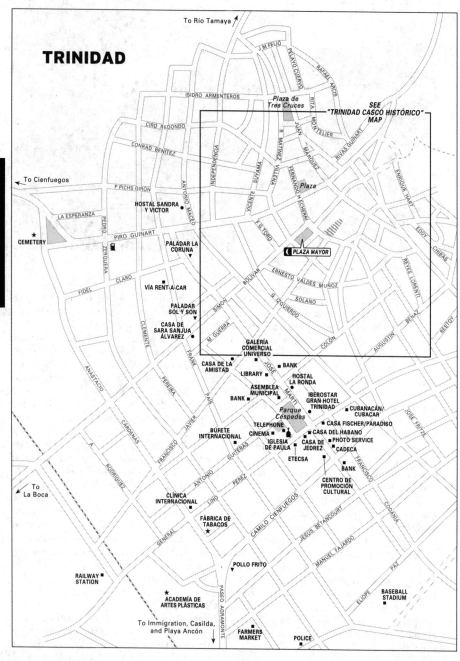

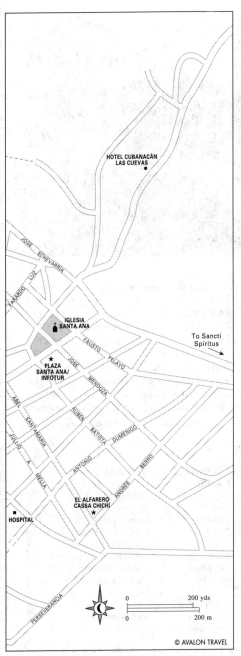

bounded to the south by Calle Antonio Maceo and to the east by Calle Lino Pérez. At its heart is Plaza Mayor, at the top of Calle Simón Bolívar. It's a warren—some streets end at T junctions, while others curl or bifurcate, one leading uphill while another drops sharply to another Y fork or right-angled bend. All this was meant to fool marauding pirates, but it does a pretty good job on visitors, too. The streets are each sloped in a slight V, with gutters in the center (according to legend, the city's first governor had a right leg shorter than the other and could thereby be level when walking the streets by staying on the right-hand side). Many streets are closed to traffic by stone pillars and cannons stuck nose-first in the ground.

Below the touristed core, the streets are paved and laid out on a rough grid with Parque Céspedes at its center. The main street is Calle José Martí, which runs northwest–southeast. Calle Bolívar runs perpendicular and leads northeast to Plaza Mayor. Calle Camilo Cienfuegos, one block southeast of Parque Céspedes, is the major northeast–southwest thoroughfare.

The Circuito Sur road from Cienfuegos bifurcates as it enters Trinidad: Calle Piro Guinart (to the left) leads to the historic core; Anastacio Cárdenas (to the right) skirts the southern end of town and connects with Camilo Cienfuegos (for Sancti Spíritus) and Paseo Agramonte (to Casilda and Playa Ancón).

Most streets have two names: a colonial name and a postrevolutionary name. Locals prefer to use the older names. Thankfully, street signs went up in 2009 with both names.

◖ Plaza Mayor

The graceful plaza lies at the heart of the original settlement. The park at its core is ringed with silver trellises, with shiny white wrought-iron benches beneath the shade of palms and hibiscus bowers. The plaza is adorned with small neoclassical statues, including two bronze greyhounds that would be at home in a Landseer painting.

On the plaza's northeast corner is the modest **Iglesia Parroquial de la Santísima Trinidad**

© CHRISTOPHER P. BAKER

Plaza Mayor, Trinidad

(Mon.–Sat. 11 A.M.–12:30 P.M.). The cathedral was rebuilt in 1894 on the spot where once stood the original parish church. Restored in 1996, it is more English than Spanish inside, with a Victorian-Gothic vaulted ceiling and altar carved from mahogany; there's no baroque extravagance, although the carved statuary is intriguing, as is the 18th-century Cristo de la Vera Cruz (Christ of the True Cross).

On the northwest corner is Palacio Brunet, a beautifully preserved, two-story mansion dating from 1741 and housing the **Museo Romántico** (Calle Fernando Hernández Echerrí #52, esq. Calle Bolívar, tel. 041/99-4363, Tues.–Sun. 9 A.M.–5 P.M., entrance CUC2, cameras CUC2, videos CUC5). The dozen rooms are filled with intriguing artwork and fabulous antiques. Note the solid carved-cedar ceiling, dating from 1770, and the *mediopunto* arches. Upstairs, step out onto

TRINIDAD STREET NAMES

COLONIAL NAME	NEW NAME	COLONIAL NAME	NEW NAME
Alameda	Jesús Menéndez	Jesús María	José Martí
Amargura	Juan Márquez	Lirio	Abel Santamaría
Angarilla	Fidel Claro	Media Luna	Ernesto Valdés Muñoz
Boca	Piro Guinart	Olvido	Santiago Escobar
Carmén	Frank País	Peña	Francisco Gómez Toro
Colón	Colén	Real	Ruben Martínez Villena
Cristo	Fernando H. Echerrí	Reforma	Anastasio Cárdenas
Desengaño	Simón Bolívar	Rosario	Francisco Javier
Encarnación	Vicente Suyama		Zerquera
Gloria	Gustavo Izquierdo	San Procopio	Lino Pérez
Guaurabo	Pablo Pichs Girón	Santa Ana	José Mendoza
Gutiérrez	Antonio Maceo	Santo Domingo	Camilo Cienfuegos

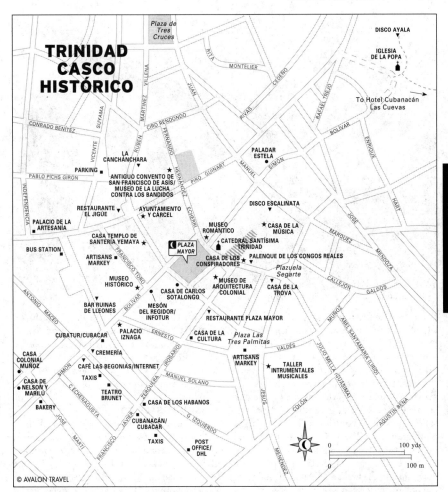

TRINIDAD CASCO HISTÓRICO

© AVALON TRAVEL

the balcony to admire the view down over the square. The stunning wrought-iron bed is the only heirloom of the Brunet family that originates from the house.

During his investigative sojourn in Cuba in 1801, German explorer Alexander von Humboldt stayed here at the impressive Casa Padrón, on the southwest corner of the plaza, at the corner of Bolívar and Mártinez. It is slated to revert to its old function as the Museo de Arqueología y Ciencias Naturales, but don't hold your breath.

On the east side of the square, in the Casa de los Sánchez Iznaga, is the **Museo de Arquitectura Colonial** (tel. 041/99-3208, Mon.–Thurs. and Sat. 9 A.M.–5 P.M., CUC1) with displays and models relating to Trinidad's architectural development.

Museo de la Lucha Contra Los Bandidos

Rising northwest of the plaza is the campanile of the **Antiguo Convento de San Francisco de Asís.** The *torre* (tower) and church are all

Antiguo Convento de San Francisco de Asís

that remain of the original convent, replaced by a baroque structure now housing the Museum of the Fight Against Outlaws (Calle Echerrí #59, esq. Pino Guinart, tel. 041/99-4121, Tues.–Sun. 9 A.M.–5 P.M., CUC1), which traces the campaign against the counterrevolutionary guerrillas (called "bandits" by the Castro government) in the Sierra Escambray in the years following the Revolution. There are maps, photographs, a CIA radio transmitter, a small gunboat the CIA donated to the counter-Castro cause, plus parts of the U-2 spy plane shot down during the Cuban Missile Crisis. Ascend the bell tower for views over the city.

Plazuela Real del Jigüe

This charming triangular plaza (Piro Guinart y Villena), one block west of Plaza Mayor, has a calabash tree in the center. The tree, planted in December 2009, is the youngest in a succession of trees kept alive since 1514, the year the Spanish celebrated their first mass here. Cater-corner to El Jigüe is the **Ayuntamiento y Cárcel** (Piro Guinart #302), the old town hall and jail, with a portion of the original stone-and-lime masonry exposed for view.

Immediately east, the **Casa Templo de Santería Yemayá** (Villena #59) features *santería* altars and hosts occasional religious ceremonies. Jorge Muñoz Fontanills (Simón Bolívar #302, e/ Martí y Maceo) will happily show you his fascinating collection of *orisha* statues.

Museo Histórico

This museum (Simón Bolívar #423, esq. Francisco Toro, tel. 041/99-4460, Sat.–Thurs. and every second Sun. 9 A.M.–5 P.M., entrance CUC2, cameras CUC1, videos CUC5), one block south of Plaza Mayor, occupies the Palacio Cantero. Once the home of the Borrell family, it had a fountain that spouted *eau de cologne* for the ladies and gin for gents. The history of the city is revealed as you move through rooms furnished with rocking chairs, alabaster amphorae, marble-topped tables, and other antiques. Other intriguing exhibits include an antique bell, stocks for holding slaves, banknotes, and a magnificent scale model of the *Andrei Vishinsky*, which entered Trinidad harbor on April 17, 1960—the first Soviet ship to visit Cuba after the Revolution. A watchtower offers fine views.

Entertainment and Events

The **Cine Romelio Cornelio,** on Parque Céspedes, screens movies Tuesday–Sunday at 8 P.M. The local chess club, **Casa de Jedrez** (Lino Pérez #292), is on the east side of the square.

BARS

The atmospheric **Taberna La Canchánchara** (Rubén Martínez, esq. Girón, tel. 041/99-6231, daily 8 A.M.–9 P.M.) is known for its house drink, made from *aguardiente* (raw rum), mineral water, honey, and lime (CUC2).

CABARETS AND DISCOS

Local youth deliver their salsa moves at **Disco Escalinata,** to the rear of **Casa de la Música** (Juan Manuel Marquéz, e/ Bolívar y Menéndez, tel. 041/90-3414, CUC2), while music is also hosted on the steps northeast of Plaza Mayor.

For a uniquely memorable dancing experience, head to **Disco Ayala** (nightly

---

WALKING TOUR OF OLD TRINIDAD

Begin at the northeast corner of **Plaza Mayor** and perambulate the square counterclockwise, taking in all the sights of interest. Back at the northeast corner, immediately east of the cathedral, cobbled Calle Fernando Hernández (Cristo) leads past a wide staircase. At the base of the steps is a handsome ocher-colored house – the **Mansión de los Conspiradores** – with an ornately woodworked balcony. The house is so named because La Rosa Blanca (the secret organization against Spanish colonial rule) met here.

One block east on Cristo brings you to the triangular **Plazuela de Segarta** and Calle Jesús Menéndez, containing some of the oldest homes in the city, among them the **Casa de la Trova,** dating to 1777. Off the northeast corner of the *plazuela* is Calle Juan Manuel Márquez, featuring a trio of houses with wonderfully photogenic elevated galleries.

Turn left on Márquez and walk west one block to Simón Bolívar. To your right, atop the hill, you'll see the near-derelict **Iglesia de la Virgen de la Candelaria de la Popa.** It was built in 1726 and is named for the *popa* (stern) of a ship called the *Virgen de la Candelaria* that sank off Cartagena. The stern washed ashore near Casilda and a chapel was built. Ascend for the views over the city. (You can continue uphill behind the church to the top of the mountain for unsurpassed views.)

Traveling three blocks farther along Márquez delivers you at **Plaza de Tres Cruces,** a bare-earth area pinned by three wooden crosses that for several centuries have formed the terminus of Trinidad's annual Easter procession. Note the houses with metal crosses on their exterior walls: They're way-stops on the procession.

Return along Márquez to Ciro Redondo; turn right. The house at #261 dates to 1754 and was built for Carlos Merlin, a French pirate. Turn left onto Fernando Hernández Echarrí. On your right, at the end of the block, is the **Antiguo Convento de San Francisco de Asís.** After visiting, turn right onto Piro Guinart and walk one block to **Plaza Jigüe,** then walk southeast one block to Playa Mayor and turn right onto Simón Bolívar. The cobbled street leads downhill past the **Museo Histórico.** At Maceo (three blocks), turn right and follow this wide cobbled street for three blocks. Turn right on Lino Pérez, which leads you two blocks downhill to **Parque Céspedes** at Martí. On the southwest side is the **Iglesia de Paula.**

Anyone with an interest in art might follow Lino Pérez south five blocks to the former Antigua Cuartel de Dragones (dragoons' barracks), built in 1844 and now the **Academía de Artes Plásticas** (Prolongación de Camilo Cienfuegos, tel. 041/99-4350, triart@hero. cult.cu, Mon.-Fri. 8 A.M.-5 P.M.). It has seasonal exhibitions of students' work. Although it's not normally open to the public, guides are usually happy to show you the various *talleres* (workshops), from ceramics to computation. It hosts semester-long courses for foreigners.

One block west, the **Fábrica de Tabacos** (Anastacio Cárdenas, e/ Lino Pérez y Cienfuegos) is closed to the public.

10:30 P.M.–2 A.M., CUC3 including one drink), in the caves immediately west of the Hotel Cubanacán Las Cuevas. Flashing lights amid the stalagmites and stalactites? Awesome!

The **Hotel Cubanacán Las Cuevas** (Calle General Lino Pérez final, tel. 041/99-6133) features a small cabaret nightly at 9:30 P.M. (CUC3).

TRADITIONAL MUSIC AND DANCE

The **Palenque de los Congos Reales** (Echerrí #146, esq. Jesús Menéndez, CUC1) has an *espectáculo afrocubano* (daily 1:30 P.M.–midnight). It also hosts dance lessons. Musicians drift in to jam and locals whisk tourists onto the dance floor at **Casa de la Trova** (Echerrí #29, tel. 041/99-6445, daily 10 A.M.–1 A.M., CUC1 after 8 P.M.), one block east of Plaza Mayor. The **Casa de la Cultura** (Zerquera, esq. Ernest Valdes, tel. 041/99-4308, daily 8 A.M.–10 P.M., free) also hosts traditional music, as does **Casa Fischer** (Lino Pérez #312, e/ Codatia y Martí, tel. 041/99-6486, CUC0.50), which posts its weekly medley and hosts daily dance and drumming lessons (CUC5). The ruins of **Teatro Brunet** (Maceo #461, e/ Bolívar y Zerquera, CUC2)

have an *espectáculo campesino* (peasant show) on Wednesday. Teatro Brunet also hosts percussion and dance lessons (Mon.–Sat. 4–8 P.M.).

FESTIVALS AND EVENTS

Trinidad has a tradition for *madrugadas,* early-morning performances of regional songs sung in the streets. Though rarely heard today, *madrugadas* highlight the town's weeklong **Semana de la Cultura** in early January.

Every Easter during **El Recorrido del Vía Crucis** (The Way of the Cross), devout Catholics follow a route through the old city, stopping at 14 sites marked with crosses. The weeklong **Festival de Semana Santa** (Holy Week celebrations) features street processions.

For nine days during Christmas, Trinitarios enact **Fiestas Navideñas,** a street re-creation of Mary and Joseph's journey by donkey. Each night the procession ends at a different house, with a fiesta for children.

Recreation

Horseback riding is offered at **Parque Nacional El Cubano** (tel. 041/99-6611, daily 8 A.M.–4 P.M., CUC6.50 entrance including

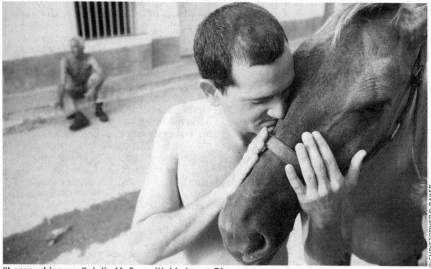

"horse whisperer" Julio Muñoz with his horse Diana

© CHRISTOPHER P. BAKER

PROYECTO DIANA

Local "horse whisperer" Julio Muñoz has a project, **Proyecto Diana** (Calle Martí #401, esq. Santiago Escobar, tel./fax 041/99-3673, www.diana.trinidadphoto. com) to make the world, or at least Cuba, a better place for horses. Despite rural Cuba still being an equine culture, care of horses leaves much to be desired. For example, when horses sicken they are often treated with home remedies that sometimes aggravate the horse's condition; or they're left to die because the owner lacks the means to treat the condition. And the traditional method of breaking in a horse causes pain and damage.

Julio, who started the project after his horse Diana died of colic and has since studied the methods of "horse-whisperer" Monty Roberts, wants to change things by educating local farmers, farriers, and horse-owners. Donations of books, farriers' tools and equipment, and equine medicines are requested.

a drink), one kilometer west of Trinidad. The rides lead to natural pools good for swimming. Cubanacán has an excursion from Trinidad (CUC15).

Tour agencies in Trinidad handle bookings for horseback riding (CUC15, 2 hours including lunch) at **Finca Dolores** (tel. 041/99-6481), a rustic farm turned tourist attraction on the banks of the Río Guaurabo, two kilometers west of Trinidad. A representation of a traditional farm features an aviary, cockfights, milking, and other farm activities during folkloric shows. Your best source for information on horseback riding is Julio Muñoz, the local "horse whisperer" (tel./fax 041/99-3673, www. casa.trinidadphoto.com).

Accommodations

All properties listed are air-conditioned.

CASAS PARTICULARES

Trinidad has about 300 *casas particulares*.

Owners will call around to help you find a place if you don't have a reservation.

My favorite place by far is ((**Casa Colonial Muñoz** (Calle Martí #401, esq. Santiago Escobar, tel./fax 041/99-3673, www.casa. trinidadphoto.com, CUC35), a venerable home built in 1800 and featured in *National Geographic* (Oct. 1999, p. 102). The time-worn house has period furnishings, including swords, old clocks, and centenary prints. Its two lofty-ceilinged bedrooms each have two double beds and fans, and modern, private bathrooms. "You could cook a lobster in the sink," says Julio Muñoz, the English-speaking owner and a professional photographer. There's secure parking, and a stable with horse. Dog-lovers will be in heaven. You can reserve by credit card. Some other *casa particular* owners pretend to be Julio Muñoz to steal his business, and *jineteros* are known to steer you to such houses for a commission.

((**Casa de Carlos Sotalongo** (Calle Ruben Mártinez Villena #33, tel. 041/99-4169, CUC25), on the southeast corner of Plaza Mayor, is another atmospheric winner. Vast front doors open to a cavernous lounge with antiques, modern art, and a colonial tile floor. Local art critic Carlos Sotalongo rents two rooms with terra-cotta floors, metal-frame beds, and private hot-water bathrooms.

The antiquities are even more impressive at ((**Casa Sara Sanjua Álvarez** (Simón Bolívar #266, e/ Frank País y Martí, tel. 041/99-3997, CUC25), a well-kept, beautifully furnished colonial home that opens to an exquisite rose garden with rockers. Two rooms have fans, refrigerators, and modern bathrooms. There's secure parking.

Hostal Sandra y Victor (Antonio Maceo #613, e/ Piro Guinart y Pablo Pichs, tel. 041/99-6444, www.hostalsandra.com, CUC20), just 100 meters from the bus station, has three upstairs rooms with private bathrooms and hot water. A spacious lounge has rockers, and a delightful rooftop terrace features artistic ceramic walls and a bar.

I enjoyed my stay at **Casa de Nelson y Marilú** (Santiago Escobar #172, e/ Frank País y

Martí, tel. 041/99-2899, hostalmarilu@yahoo. es, CUC25), with a pleasant cross-ventilated rooftop chamber with a small modern bathroom. Meals are served on the rooftop terrace with rockers and hammock.

HOTELS

The Instituto Cubano de la Amistad runs the **Casa de la Amistad** (Zerquera, e/ Martí and Francisco Peterson, tel. 041/99-3824, icaptdad@icap.cu, CUC25 s/d), which offers simply furnished rooms with private baths. Normally, it hosts "solidarity" groups, but you might try your luck.

Cubanacán's **Hotel La Ronda** (Calle Martí #239), 50 meters west of Parque Céspedes, had been gutted for a complete renovation as a deluxe Hotel E at my last visit, and Spanish *parador*–style **Mesón del Regidor** (Simón Bolívar #20, tel. 041/99-6572), one block southwest of Plaza Mayor, with four rooms, was also closed for renovation.

The 114 modest air-conditioned rooms at **Hotel Cubanacán Las Cuevas** (Calle General Lino Pérez final, tel. 041/99-6133, fax 041/99-6161, reservas@cuevas.co.cu, CUC54 s, CUC68 d low season, CUC62 s, CUC85 d high season, including breakfast), on the hillside above town, are pricey for what you get. It has a thatched restaurant and bar (the food is mediocre), a swimming pool, car rental, Internet, game room, and nightly cabaret.

Cubanacán's riverside **Horizontes MaDolores** (tel. 041/99-6481, fax 041/99-6579, commercial@dolores.co.cu, CUC37 s, CUC46 d low season, CUC42 s, CUC52 d high season, including breakfast), two kilometers west of Trinidad, enjoys an appealing rustic setting and offers 19 rooms, plus 26 cabins with kitchen. *Criollo* meals are served in an open-sided thatched restaurant. It has a swimming pool.

In 2006, the old Hotel Canada, on Parque Céspedes, metamorphosed into the gorgeous ◖ **Iberostar Gran Hotel Trinidad** (Martí 262, esq. Lino Pérez, tel. 041/99-6070, fax 041/99-6077, commercial@iberostar.trinidad. co.cu, from CUC141 s, CUC172 d year-round),

perhaps the finest urban hotel outside Havana. It mixes colonial elegance with sumptuous contemporary refinements. Highlights include a clubby cigar lounge, game room with pool table, and a chic bar and restaurant.

Food

Most *casas particulares* provide meals.

Only three *paladares* existed at last visit. The best meals in town are served at ◖ **Paladar Estela** (Simon Bolívar #557, tel. 041/99-4329, Mon.–Fri. 6:30–9:30 P.M., and until midnight in winter), one block north of Plaza Mayor, which offers *criollo* meals served in a tree-shaded patio. I recommend the lamb (CUC8) or roast pork (CUC8).

The antique-filled **Paladar Sol y Son** (Simón Bolívar #238, e/ Frank País y José Martí, tel. 041/99-2926, daily 7–11 P.M.) also has courtyard dining and offers a roast chicken special (CUC7). The lesser option is **Paladar La Coruna** (Martí #428, esq. Fidel Claro, tel. 041/99-3838, noon–midnight daily), which serves *criollo* meals on a patio.

Of state-run restaurants, my favorite is **Restaurante El Jigüe** (tel. 041/99-6476, daily noon–10:45 P.M.), facing Plazuela Real del Jigüe, in an atmospheric colonial home with antique chandeliers. The house dish is a filling *pollo el jigüe* (CUC6), with spaghetti and cheese served in an earthenware dish. Wash it down with delicious lemonade (CUC0.65).

Similarly appealing, the **Restaurante Plaza Mayor** (Zerquera, esq. Villena. tel. 041/99-6470, daily noon–10 P.M.) offers the option of dining on the patio or within the colonial mansion. It has an accomplished buffet—the best lunch option in town.

Other *criollo* options aimed at tourists include **Mesón del Regidor** (Simón Bolívar #20, tel. 041/99-6572, daily 7 A.M.–10 P.M.).

Feeling flush? Then dress up to dine at the **Restaurant Gourmet,** in the Iberostar Gran Hotel Trinidad. The creative fare includes smoked salmon appetizer and such entrées as sautéed shrimp over spinach in white wine sauce, and candied tenderloin steak in red wine with mashed potatoes. You can purchase a buffet breakfast (7–10 A.M., CUC15), lunch (12:30–3 P.M.), or dinner (7–10 P.M., CUC20 for appetizer and dessert, or CUC35 for three courses). However, there's no à la carte option, nor can you order an entrée only.

For ice cream, head to the **Cremería** (Antonio Maceo, e/ Bolívar y Zerquera, daily 8 A.M.–10 P.M.).

The best-stocked supermarket is **Galería Comercial Universo** (Martí, e/ Zerquera y Colón). You can buy produce at the *mercado agropecuario* (Pedro Zerquera, esq. Manuel Fajardo, Mon.–Sat. 8 A.M.–6 P.M., Sun. 8 A.M.–noon) and baked goods at the bakery (7 A.M.–7 P.M.) at Simón Bolívar and Martí.

Shopping

All manner of arts and crafts are sold at the **artisans markets** held in Plazuelita Las Tres Palmitas and elsewhere around Plaza Mayor.

For cigars and rum, head to **Casa del Habano** (Maceo, esq. Zerquera, tel. 041/99-6256, daily 9 A.M.–7 P.M.) or **Casa del Habano y Ron** (Martí, esq. Lino Pérez).

The **Casa de la Música** (Juan Manuel Márquez, e/ Bolívar y Menéndez, tel. 041/99-3414) has a wide selection of CDs. Musical instruments can be bought at the **Taller de Instrumentales Musicales** (Menéndez #127-A, e/ Ernesto Valdés y Colón, tel. 041/99-3617), where bongos, *timbales*, etc. are made.

Much of the ceramic work sold locally is made at **El Alfarero Casa Chichí** (Andres Berro Macias #51, e/ Pepito Tey y Abel Santamaría, tel. 041/99-3146, daily 8 A.M.–8 P.M.), where the Santander family carries on a tradition of pottery-making.

Information and Services

Infotur (tel. 041/99-8257, Mon.–Sat. 8:30 A.M.–6 P.M., Sun. 8:30 A.M.–4:30 P.M.) has tourist information bureaus in Plaza Santa Ana and in **Mesón del Regidor** (Simón Bolívar #20).

Banks include **Bandec** (Martí #264, e/ Colón y Zequera), **Banco Popular** (Colón y Miguel Calzada), and **Banco Financiero Internacional** (Cienfuegos, esq. Martí). You can exchange currency at **Cadeca** (Martí

a potter at work at El Alfarero Casa Chichí

#164, e/ Lino Pérez y Céspedes, Mon.–Fri. 8 A.M.–3 P.M.). Most banks are open Mon.–Fri. 8 A.M.–3:30 P.M., Sat. 8 A.M.–1 P.M.

The **post office** (Maceo #418, e/ Zerquera y Colón, tel. 041/99-2443) has DHL service. **Etecsa** (Lino Pérez y Francisco Pettersen, tel. 041/99-6020, daily 8:30 A.M.–7:30 P.M.) has international phone and Internet service. **Café Las Begonias** (Maceo #473, esq. Bolívar, daily 9 A.M.–9 P.M.) also has Internet service (CUC6 per hour).

The **Clínica Internacional** (Lino Pérez #103, esq. Cárdenas, tel. 0419/6492, 24 hours) has a pharmacy as well as a doctor and nurse on hand; it charges CUC25 per consultation, but CUC30 4–7 P.M., CUC50 after 7 P.M., and CUC60 for house calls.

The **police station** (Julio Cuevas Díaz #20, e/ Pedro Zerguera and Cárdenas, tel. 041/99-6900) is two blocks to the northeast.

The **Bufete Internacional** (Frank País, esq. Colón, tel. 041/99-6489, notario@bufete.tdad. cyt.cu, Mon.–Fri. 8 A.M.–5 P.M.) can assist with legal matters.

Getting There and Away
BY AIR
The **Aeropuerto Alberto Delgado** (tel. 041/99-6393) is one kilometer south of town, off Paseo Agramonte. No scheduled air service was offered at last visit.

BY BUS
Buses arrive and depart the **Terminal de Ómnibus** (Izquierda, esq. Piro Guinart, tel. 041/99-6676). **Víazul** buses (tel. 0419/4448, ticket office daily 7 A.M.–7 P.M.) to Trinidad depart Havana at 8:15 A.M. and 1 P.M. (CUC27), and Santiago de Cuba at 7:30 P.M. (CUC20). Buses depart Trinidad for Havana at 7:30 A.M. and 3 P.M., and for Santiago at 8 A.M.

Transtur offers bus transfers between Trinidad and Cienfuegos (CUC6) and Havana (CUC25).

Local buses (tel. 041/99-2404) leave irregularly for Sancti Spíritus (CUC2.10) and Topes de Collantes (CUC1). Eight *camiones* also serve Sancti Spíritus daily.

BY TRAIN
The train station (tel. 041/99-3348, ticket booth open daily 4:30 A.M.–5 P.M.) is at the bottom of Lino Pérez. The only service at last visit was a daily commuter train to Casilda and to Meyer, in the Valle de los Ingenios.

BY CAR
For car rental, try **Cubacar** (Lino Pérez, e/ Martí y Francisco Cadalia, tel. 041/99-6633; and Bolívar, esq. Maceo, tel. 041/99-6257); **Gaviota** (tel. 041/99-6235), which offers house-to-house taxi service between Havana and Trinidad (about CUC110); or **Vía** (Frank País e/ Fidel Claro and Bolívar, tel. 041/99-6388).

The Oro Negro gas station is northeast of town on Fausto Pelayo. A Cupet gas station is one kilometer south of Trinidad on the road to Casilda.

EXCURSIONS
Cubatur (Maceo y Zerquera, tel. 041/99-6314) and **Cubanacán** (Martí, e/ Lino Pérez y Codahia, tel. 041/99-4753) offer excursions, including a city tour (CUC15), steam train ride (CUC10), and to Valle de los Ingenios (CUC25).

Getting Around
Horse-drawn *coches* operate through the new town. **Cubataxi** (tel. 041/99-2340) provides taxi service. *Coco-taxis* (tel. 041/99-2214) cruise the streets (CUC1 minimum).

Paradiso (Lino Pérez, e/ Codania y Martí, tel. 041/99-6486, paradiso@sctd.artex.cu), in Casa Fischer, specializes in cultural tours. A guided city tour costs CUC10.

The **Trinidad Bus Tour** (CUC2) minibus departs Cubatur (Maceo y Zerquera) at 9 A.M., 11 A.M., 2 P.M., 4 P.M., and 6 P.M. and runs to Playa Ancón.

◖ LA BOCA AND PENÍNSULA DE ANCÓN
La Boca, five kilometers west of Trinidad, is a quaint fishing village with traditional tile-roofed *bohíos* and a single coastal road. It appeals for its pocket-scale beaches amid coral coves favored by Trinitarios on weekends. **Casa Museo Alberto Delgado** (tel. 01/5219-9801, Tues.–Sat. 9 A.M.–5 P.M., Sun. 9 A.M.–12:30 P.M., free), two kilometers east of La Boca, honors a Castroite killed during the counterrevolutionary war. It has his pistol, uniform, and some personal effects.

The coast extends south of La Boca to a small point beyond which the long narrow Península de Ancón curls east to **Playa Ancón,** enfolding a mangrove-lined lagoon—the Ensenada de Casilda. The four-kilometer-long beach is fabulous, with sugary white sand and pavonine waters. This beach is the preserve of tourists at the two all-inclusive hotels (you can buy day passes to use the facilities). The sea is perfect for snorkeling, though parts of the beach shelve into rocky waters with sea grasses, and during certain times of year a microscopic sea lice (*agua mala* or *caribe*) can cause all manner of nasty infections.

Recreation

Ancón's offshore reefs have more than 30 dive spots, including sunken vessels. **Cayo Blanco,** nine kilometers southeast of Ancón, is famous for its kaleidoscopic corals and sponges.

Scuba diving is offered at **Club Amigo Ancón** (tel. 041/99-6123, CUC35 per dive, CUC45 night dive), as is snorkeling (CUC10). **Marina Marlin** (tel./fax 041/99-6205, www.nauticamarlin.com) offers "seafari" excursions to Cayo Blanco (CUC45), including snorkeling; a sunset cruise (CUC20, or CUC30 with dinner); speedboat tour (CUC30); fly-fishing (CUC280 up to four people); and deep-sea fishing (CUC300 per person).

Accommodations and Food

Of several *casas particulares* in La Boca, I like **Hostal Vista al Mar** (Calle Real #47, tel. 041/99-3716, CUC20–25), a simply furnished home overlooking the beach and rivermouth. Manolo, the owner, is a gracious and fun host. Choose from three rooms, two with private bathrooms; you rent the whole house. It has parking.

((Hostal El Capitán (Playa La Boca #82, tel. 041/99-3055, captaincasanovatrinidad@yahoo.es, CUC20), 400 meters south of the village, sits above the coral shore. Nice! The two rooms are cross-ventilated and well-lit with louvered windows. Meals are served on a patio. It has parking.

Cubanacán's Soviet-style all-inclusive **Club Amigo Ancón** (tel. 041/99-6123, fax 041/99-6121, reserva@ancon.co.cu, CUC70 s, CUC110 d low season, CU84 s, CUC150 d high season) has been nicely upgraded and is a favorite of Canadian and European charter groups. It has 279 air-conditioned rooms, plus a huge swimming pool and scuba diving.

Fresh from a remake as an all-inclusive, Cubanacán's **Club Amigo Costa Sur** (tel. 041/99-6174, fax 041/99-6172, reservas@costasur.co.cu, from CUC48 s, CUC68 d year-round), is now painted in bright tropical fruit colors. Popular with German tour groups, it has 112 pleasantly furnished rooms and 20 lovely bungalows with contemporary wrought-iron furnishings. There's an intimacy here lacking at the other resorts. Nonguests can buy a pass (CUC15 day, CUC25 night).

The fanciest option is **Brisas Trinidad del Mar** (tel. 041/99-6500, fax 041/99-6565, reservas@brisastdad.co.cu, from CUC74 s, CUC92 d low season, from CUC91 s, CUC114 d high season), adjacent to Club Amigo Ancón. This neocolonial style low-rise is centered on a large freeform pool. The 241 rooms are spacious and have appealing bathrooms. Facilities include three restaurants, live entertainment, water sports, tennis, and even a sauna.

The **Rancho Grill Caribe** (no tel., daily 9 A.M.–10 P.M.), above the coral shore between La Boca and Ancón, is a seafood grill.

Getting There, Away, and Around

The **Trinidad Bus Tour** runs to Playa Ancón. A taxi to/from Trinidad costs about CUC10 one-way.

Marina Marlin (tel./fax 041/99-6205) has moorings but it is *not* an international entry port. Bare-boat and skippered yachts and

Club Amigo Ancón

catamarans can be chartered here; reservations must be made prior to arrival in Cuba (from CUC300 per day up to eight people).

VALLE DE LOS INGENIOS

East of Trinidad, the Carretera de Sancti Spíritus drops spectacularly into the Valley of the Sugar Mills, known more correctly as the Valle de San Luis and declared a UNESCO Cultural Heritage Site. It is named for the many sugar mills, or *ingenios* (43 at its peak), that sprang up over the centuries. The valley was Cuba's most important sugar-producing region into the 19th century. Many of the mills and estate houses remain, albeit mostly in ruin.

Sitio Histórico San Isidro is signed from the highway, about 10 kilometers east of Trinidad. It features a three-story campanile. Most notable is **Sitio Histórico Guaímaro** (daily 7 A.M.–7 P.M.), about 20 kilometers east of Trinidad, which boasts deteriorated wall murals. It has a chapel and well to the rear. Guaímaro is about 600 meters off the highway via a dirt road that continues 11 kilometers (to be attempted in dry season only) to **Sitio Histórico San Pedro,** a rural village of tumbledown wattle-and-daub huts with a couple of restored colonial homes.

You gain a vantage over the valley from the **Mirador del Valle de los Ingenios,** about five kilometers east of Trinidad.

Torre de Manaca-Iznaga

The quaint village of Iznaga is a picture-perfect gem with a prim little railway station. The village, 14 kilometers east of Trinidad, is most famous for **Hacienda Iznaga** (tel. 041/99-7241, daily 9 A.M.–5 P.M.), built 1835–1845 by Alejo María del Carmen e Iznaga, once one of the wealthiest sugar planters in Cuba. The hacienda features a 43.5-meter-tall tower that according to legend was built as a wager. Alejo was to build a tower while his brother Pedro dug a well. The winner would be whoever went highest or deepest (no well has been found). It has seven levels, each smaller than the one beneath. You can ascend the 136 steps (CUC1).

Torre de Manaca-Iznaga

The hacienda is now a restaurant. Lacework, a local specialty, is sold.

Recreation

You can ride horses at **Casa Guachinango** (no tel., daily 9 A.M.–5 P.M.), three kilometers north of Iznaga; a one-hour ride leads to mineral springs good for bathing. This 200-year-old hacienda-turned-restaurant boasts a beautiful setting above the Río Ay. You can also milk cows and be shown how to extract honey from beehives. Lunches are served.

Getting There

A local commuter train departs Trinidad for Meyer via the Valle de los Ingenios at 5 A.M. and 5:20 P.M. (CUC5). It stops at Iznaga and Guachinango. Trains depart Meyer for Trinidad at 6:30 A.M. and 6:40 P.M.

A 1907 steam train also runs an excursion from Trinidad to Guachinango daily at 9:35 A.M., with a lunch stop at Iznaga (CUC10; you pay for lunch separately). Tour agencies make reservations.

STILL PUFFING AWAY

Until a few years ago, Cuba maintained about 200 operating steam trains, projecting yet another surreal image of an island lost in time – what railroad expert Adolf Hungry Wolf calls a "twilight zone in the world of railroading." Most are of U.S. progeny and date from the 1920s (the first Cuban railway was built by the British in 1837). A few are still capable of thundering down the slim tracks with a full load of sugarcane. The trains are kept going because the sugar mills operate only four to five months a year, providing plenty of time to overhaul the engines and keep them in good repair so as to extract a few more thousand miles of hard labor.

However, the drastic closures of sugar mills initiated in 2002 delivered many clunky old engines to the grave. Others have been spruced up for passenger and tourist endeavors. Tourist steam trains currently operate from Trinidad, Morón, and Rafael Freyre.

◖ GRAN PARQUE NATURAL TOPES DE COLLANTES

Five kilometers west of Trinidad, a turnoff from the coast road leads north and begins to climb into the Sierra Escambray, whose slopes swathed in pines and ancient tree ferns, bamboo, and eucalyptus are protected within this national park. The area is tremendous for hiking and birding.

Gran Parque Natural Topes de Collantes is divided into a series of parks, administered by the **Complejo Turístico Topes de Collantes** (tel. 042/54-0330 or 042/54-0117, fax 042/54-0272, www.gaviota-grupo.com, daily 8 A.M.–7 P.M.), located at the entrance to Topes de Collantes. Maps are available, and excursions and guides are booked here or with agencies in Trinidad.

Parque Altiplano is the core park, containing the Topes de Collantes touristic center, is the most developed site.

At its heart, at a refreshingly cool 790 meters, is **Topes de Collantes,** a spa-hotel complex 21 kilometers from Trinidad and dominated by a massive concrete structure—the Kurhotel—designed in 1936, when it served as a sanatorium for victims of tuberculosis. Following the Revolution, the disease was eradicated in Cuba. The structure was then sanitized and turned into a teacher-training facility. The complex, which includes smaller hotels, was developed as a resort area in the late 1970s and now focuses on nature and health tourism. A guide is compulsory.

Parque Altiplano

The Topes de Collantes section is the most developed site. Here is the **Museo de Arte Cubano Contemporáneo** (no tel., daily 8 A.M.–8 P.M., CUC3), in the former home of a Cuban senator; later it served as a "protocol" house for Communist Party members—where VIPs are housed during visits. Its four rooms of stunning art include works by Flora Fong, Esteban Leyra, and other big names in Cuban art.

The **Casa de Café** (7 A.M.–7 P.M.), 400 meters south of the Kurhotel, is a delightfully rustic coffee shop selling locally grown coffee drinks. It has historic photos plus simple tools of the trade, and demonstrations of coffee production. A stone's throw away, nip into the **Plaza de las Memorias** museum (Mon.–Sat. 8 A.M.–5 P.M.) to learn about the history of the Kurhotel and Topes de Collantes. A 10-minute walk leads to the **Jardin de Gigantes** (CUC3), with towering trees.

A trail that begins beside Villa Caburní, east of the Kurhotel, zigzags steeply downhill and leads northeast two kilometers to **Salto de Caburní,** a 75-meter-high waterfall (CUC6.50); in dry season the falls can dry up.

Parque Codina

From the Casa de Café, **Sendero La Batata** (CUC3) leads west to a cave system with underground river and pools good for swimming. From La Batata, **Sendero de Alfombra Mágico** (CUC5) continues to Finca Codina, an erstwhile coffee estate that serves as a post for bird-watchers and hikers. Luncheons are laid on for tour groups, with roast suckling pig. After a couple of toddies, you may feel brave enough to wallow in a pool of medicinal mud. Codina has an orchid garden with trails that lead to waterfalls and caves.

Parque Guanayara

About 10 kilometers northwest of Topes, Parque Guanayara's highlight is the **Sendero Centinelas del Río Melidioso** (CUC7), which follows Melodious River to the **Cascada El Rocío** waterfall, where you can swim in a chilly pool.

Parque El Nicho

El Nicho, reached via the **Sendero El Reino de las Aguas** (CUC5), is perhaps the most beautiful site of all, with its spectacular cascades; a trail leads along the creek above the waterfalls. A 4WD is required to drive there via Crucecitas. Tour groups are often present; opt for an excursion.

Accommodations and Food

The massive, overpriced, **Kurhotel Escambray** (tel. 042/54-0180, from CUC33 s, CUC43 d low season, from CUC38 s, CUC48 d high season) has a Stalinist aesthetic and is reached via a stone staircase on a Siberian scale. The 210 air-conditioned rooms and 16 suites boast the essentials, including modern bathrooms. It has a modest restaurant, gyms, beauty salon, movie theater, and a thermal swimming pool

where massage and therapeutic treatments are offered. But the overriding feel is eerily clinical. Priced similarly, the hotel's **Villa Caburní** has apartment *cabinas* for up to four people.

Hotel Los Helechos (tel. 042/54-0330, fax 042/54-0272, from CUC33 s, CUC43 d low season, from CUC38 s, CUC48 d high season) hides in a cool valley below the Kurhotel. The shocking pink-and-green exterior belies a pleasing restoration inside, with bamboo decor in spacious air-conditioned rooms with satellite TVs and modern bathrooms. Take a room in the front; the rest are poorly lit. It has a swimming pool, restaurant, and bowling alley.

The traditional **Restaurante Mi Retiro** (no tel., daily 10 A.M.–9 P.M.), on a hilltop overlooking a vale about three kilometers south of Topes, is limited to fried chicken or pork.

Getting There

A *camión* runs between Topes and Trinidad. The road rises in a steep, potholed, badly eroded switchback that eventually drops to Manicaragua, on the northern slopes. Drive with utmost caution! Stop at **Mirador de Hanabanilla,** eight kilometers north of Topes, for the spectacular views over Lago Hanabanilla; the roadside café (daily 7 A.M.–7 P.M.) even has beers and cappuccinos.

All other routes through the mountains are suitable for four-wheel drive only.

Tour operators sell excursions by truck to Topes from Trinidad (CUC55). A taxi will cost CUC15 each way.

CIEGO DE ÁVILA AND CAMAGÜEY

These contiguous and geographically similar provinces are dominated inland by rolling savannas and, off the north coast, by the Cayería del Norte, low-lying, sandy coral islands limned by Cuba's most spectacular beaches with sand like confectioner's sugar dissolving into waters of mesmerizing peacock blue hues. Officially called the Archipiélago de Sabana-Camagüey, but known to all Cubans as the Jardines del Rey (King's Gardens), this sea-girt wilderness of coral reefs, cays, islands, and sheltered seas extends for some 470 kilometers in a great line parallel to the coast, between 10 and 18 kilometers from shore. Tourism development is progressing at a steady pace, concentrated on Cayo Coco and Cayo Guillermo.

The islands are mostly covered with low scrub, which forms a perfect habitat for wild pigs and iguanas and birds such as mockingbirds, nightingales, and woodpeckers. The briny lagoons are favored by pelicans, ibis, and as many as 20,000 flamingos. Running along the northern edge of the cays are endless miles of coral reef.

Ernest Hemingway actively pursued German submarines in these seas in the 1940s, immortalizing his adventures in his novel *Islands in the Stream*. It is possible to follow the route of the novel's protagonists as they pursued the Nazis east–west along the cays, passing Confites, Paredón Grande, Coco, Guillermo, and Santa María.

Much of the coastal plain is covered with scrubland and swampy marshland, perfect for bird-watching, and by lagoons, perfect for fishing. Inland, the undulating seas of green

HIGHLIGHTS

◖ Parque Nacional Jardines de la Reina: World-class sportfishing and diving await at this park's way-off-the-beaten-track offshore cays studding crystal-clear shallows (page 358).

◖ Cayo Coco and Cayo Guillermo: Beaches don't get any more gorgeous than at these sibling isles, with turquoise waters, flamingos, and top-class all-inclusive resort hotels to match (pages 362 and 366).

◖ Plaza San Juan de Dios: This square is the most impressive of several atmospheric colonial plazas in the large provincial capital of Camagüey (page 370).

◖ Finca La Belén: There's good hiking and bird-watching at this farm with exotic wildlife and noteworthy accommodations (page 377).

◖ Cayo Sabinal: Coral fringes this lonesome cay with scintillating white sand and peacock blue waters. Its rustic dining and accommodations make for the perfect me-and-only-me getaway (page 379).

◖ Scuba Diving at Playa Santa Lucía: Though the Playa Santa Lucía beach resort is otherwise a dud, the diving is superb (page 380).

LOOK FOR ◖ TO FIND RECOMMENDED SIGHTS, ACTIVITIES, DINING, AND LODGING.

sugarcane merge with cattle country dominated by ranches—*ganaderías*—worked by *vaqueros* with lassoes and machetes lashed to the flanks of their horses.

Pancake-flat Ciego de Ávila (the average elevation of the land is less than 50 meters above sea level) is Cuba's least-populous province, and though it's the nation's leading pineapple producer, almost three-fourths of the province is devoted to cattle. The wedge-shaped province (6,910 square kilometers) forms Cuba's waist, stretching only 50 kilometers from coast

to coast. There are few rivers and no distinguishing features, and few sights of historical interest, even in Ciego de Ávila and Morón, the only two towns of importance. By contrast, the city of Camagüey, capital of the nation's largest province, offers plenty of colonial charm. The surrounding honey-colored rolling plains are reminiscent of Montana, parched in summer by a scowling wind that bows down the long flaxen grasses. These upland plains are bounded to the north by a line of low mountains, the Sierra de Cubitas.

The sparsely populated southern plains are covered almost entirely by marshland and swamps that attract migratory ducks, doves, snipes, quail, and guinea fowl. Bird-watchers will get a thrill, but as yet there are no facilities.

A slender archipelago—the Jardines de la Reina—lies off the southern coast, sprinkled east–west in a straight line across the Gulf of Santa Ana María. This necklace of coral isles boasts fabulous beaches and bird-life, coral formations perfect for scuba diving, and shallow waters that offer angling delights.

PLANNING YOUR TIME

Travel through the provinces is easy. Running through the center of the provinces, the Carretera Central connects Ciego de Ávila and Camagüey cities with Havana and Santiago de Cuba. The cities are also major stops on the main east–west railway, and Vízul buses stop. The paved and less-trafficked Circuito Norte highway parallels the north coast at an average distance of five kilometers inland. Feeder roads connect it with the Carretera Central.

The 400 or so cays of the Jardines del Rey are separated from one another by narrow channels and from the coast by shallow lagoons. However, only three are currently accessible by *pedraplenes* that link Cayo Coco, Cayo Romano, and Cayo Sabinal to the mainland.

Two days is barely sufficient for relaxing on **Cayo Coco** and neighboring **Cayo Guillermo** (connected by another *pedraplén*), the most developed and beautiful of the keys. Visitors can select from a dozen all-inclusive resort hotels. If all you want is to relax with a rum cocktail on fine white sand, with breaks for windsurfing and other water sports, then this could be for you. Don't expect interactions with locals or to glean even an inkling of Cuban life. You can rent cars for forays farther afield.

Gateway to these two cays is Morón, a small-scale town that boasts the excellent Museo Caonabo and the Museo de Azúcar (Sugar Museum), where a steam-train ride is offered.

CIEGO DE ÁVILA & CAMAGÜEY

© CHRISTOPHER P. BAKER

El Bulevar, Ciego de Ávila

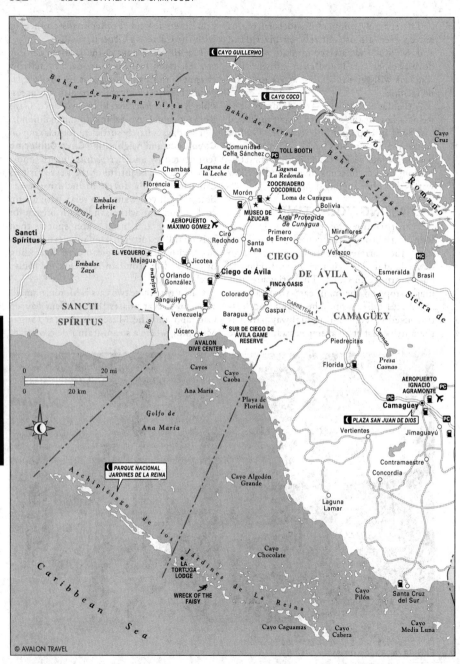

© AVALON TRAVEL

CIEGO DE ÁVILA AND CAMAGÜEY PROVINCES

Cayo Guajaba

Bahía de La Gloria

Cubitas

Sola

Cubitas

CRIADERO DE COCODRILOS
SENADO

Minas
FÁBRICA DE INSTRMENTOS MUSICALES

Crucero de Lugareño

Presa Amistad
Cubano-Bulgara

INGENIO DE SANTA ISABEL
INGENIO EL ORIENTE

Presa La Mañana de Santa Ana

CENTRAL

Siboney
Sibanicú

Cascorro

Sierra del Chorillo
Najasa

FINCA LA BELÉN

Playa Brava

Playa los Pinos

MININT CHECKPOINT

Nuevitas

KING RANCH

Bahía de Nuevitas

San Miguel de Bagá

Camalote

Palo Seco

Guáimaro

LAS TUNAS

FARO COLÓN
Playa Bonita

WRECK OF THE MORTERO

Playa Los Cocos
La Boca
Santa Lucía

SCUBA DIVING

Las Tunas

CAYO SABINAL

Dive Site

Anglers can cast for tarpon, snook, and other game fish in nearby Lago La Redonda. Morón makes a good base for day trips to Cayo Coco and has several *casas particulares.* It is also well served by trains, with direct connection to both Havana and Ciego de Ávila, the provincial capital.

More interesting by far is Camagüey. You could easily justify three days in this colonial city, which boasts several historic plazas. Pity about the *jineteros,* who are more numerous and aggressive here than in other cities. The choice of accommodations includes scores of *casas particulares* and even two fine historic hotels.

Camagüey is a gateway to **Playa Santa Lucía.** This second-rate beach resort is touted in tourist literature but appeals mostly to budget-minded Canadians and Europeans, with second-rate hotels and a desultory nightlife to suit. Sure, the diving is exceptional, but that's about it (even the beach pales in comparison to Cayo Coco). To make matters worse, the hinterland is physically unappealing, although a worthwhile excursion is to **Cayo Sabinal,** with spectacular beaches and waters touted for future development. Consider Santa Lucía a place to lay your head while traveling the Circuito Norte.

Opportunities abound for bird-watchers, not least on the cays, but also at **Finca La Belén,** a wilderness area southeast of Camagüey city. Set amid scenic terrain, it provides a rare opportunity for hiking and is served by a delightful hotel.

Divers, anglers, and yachters should set their sights on the **Parque Nacional Jardines de la Reina.** This necklace of cays off the southern coast is accessed solely from the funky fishing village of Júcaro, south of Ciego de Ávila. This is pristine terrain. Visitation is controlled exclusively through a single agency, based in Júcaro.

CIEGO DE ÁVILA & CAMAGÜEY

Ciego de Ávila and Vicinity

CIEGO DE ÁVILA

The provincial capital city (pop. 85,000), 460 kilometers east of Havana, always struck me as the least inspirational of Cuba's provincial capitals. What a surprise in late 2009 to discover that the colonial core has been improved immensely and the city is worth a day's browse in passing.

The first land grants locally were given in the mid-16th century. Gradually cattle ranches were established. Local lore says that one of the earliest hacienda owners was named Jacomé de Ávila. His property, established in 1538, occupied a large clearing, or *ciego*, and was used as a way station for travelers. A small settlement grew around it, known locally as Ciego de Ávila.

The streets are laid out in a grid. The Carretera Central (Calle Chicho Valdés) runs east–west through the city center. The main street is Independencia, running east–west two blocks north of Chicho Valdés; Independencia divides the city into *norte* (north) and *sur* (south) sections; Marcial Gómez, the main north–south street, divides the city into *este* (east) and *oeste* (west).

Parque Martí and Vicinity

The central plaza, between Independencia and Libertad, and Marcial Gómez and Honorate del Castillo, has a bust of the hero at its center. Victorian-era lampposts surround the square. On the south side, the **Poder Popular,** the town hall, dating from 1911, adjoins **Iglesia San Eugenia,** a modernist church built in 1951. On the southeast corner, the **Museo de Artes Decorativos** (Marcial Gómez #2, esq. Independencia, tel. 033/20-1661, Mon.–Fri. 9 A.M.–6 P.M., Sat. 9 A.M.–4 P.M., Sun. 9 A.M.–noon, entrance CUC1, cameras CUC1) is housed in a restored colonial mansion replete with priceless antiques, with rooms set out as if the occupants were still there.

After perusing the antiquities, catch up on the city's history at **Museo de Historia**

Simón Reyes (Honorato de Castillo, esq. Máximo Gómez, tel. 033/20-4482, Tues.–Fri. 9:30 A.M.–5 P.M., Sat. 9 A.M.–9 P.M., Sun. 9 A.M.–noon, CUC1).

The **Teatro Principal** (Joaquín Agüera, esq. Honorario del Castillo, tel. 033/22-2086), one block south of Martí, was built at the whim of a local society figure. Its enormous hand-carved wooden doors open onto an elaborately decorated interior.

Calle Independencia, west of Plaza Martí, is now a lovely landscaped pedestrian-only boulevard. Check out the local art at the **Galería de Arte** (e/ Simón Reyes y Antonio Maceo, Tues.–Fri. 10 A.M.–8 P.M. and Sat. 4:30–11 P.M.).

Plaza Máximo Gómez

This small plaza, four blocks west of Parque Martí, is worth a visit to view the bronze statue of the hero-general, sword raised.

An old Spanish fort—**Fortín de la Trocha**—stands on the park's east side. It is the only

Fortín de la Trocha, Ciego de Ávila

© CHRISTOPHER P. BAKER

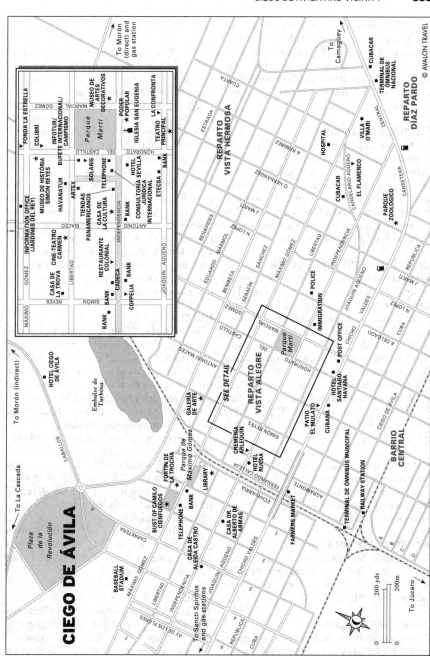

CIEGO DE ÁVILA

CIEGO DE ÁVILA & CAMAGÜEY

one still standing of seven military towers built during the Ten Years War (1868–1878), when a wooden barricade—*La Trocha*—was built by the Spanish to thwart a westward advance by the rebels. The line, which extended from coast to coast, featured 43 forts. Today the fort houses a restaurant.

Parque Zoológico

As Cuba's deplorable zoos go, this one (Hernández, one block north of Chicho Valdés, no tel., Wed.–Sun. 9 A.M.–4:30 P.M., one peso) is just about acceptable in terms of animal conditions. Opened in 2008, it stocks hippos, lions, ostriches, baboons, etc. Yes, mostly African animals, with a token assortment of local beasts, such as *jutías.*

Entertainment and Events

Artex El Patio (Libertad #162) hosts live music on its patio (Wed.–Mon. 9 P.M.–3 A.M.). The **Casa de la Trova** (Libertad #130, Tues.–Thurs. noon–6 P.M. and 9 P.M.–1 A.M., Fri.–Sat. until 2 A.M., Sun. 10 A.M.–2 P.M. and 9 P.M.–2 A.M., CUC3 including one drink) hosts traditional music, as does the **Casa de la Cultura** (Independencia #76, tel. 033/72-3974).

The happening dance spot at last visit was the **Casa de la Música Colibrí** (Tues.–Sat. 9 P.M.–3 A.M., Sun. 4–10 P.M., CUC1–5 per pair), which has a tiny *cabaret espectáculo* followed by disco.

Gotta get your cabaret kicks? **Patio El Mulato** (Antonio Maceo, esq. Chicho Valdés) has a tiny open-air cabaret.

The pirate-themed **Taberna Bucanero** (República #420, tel. 033/25-3413, 24 hours) serves draft Bucanero.

Accommodations

Reservations for *campismos* throughout the province are handled by **Campismo Popular** (tel. 033/22-2501, 8 A.M.–4 P.M.), on the west side of Parque Martí.

CASAS PARTICULARES

Ciego has some first-rate room rentals. Tops in my book is ◖ **Casa de Aleida Castro** (Calle 3 #16, e/ Independencia y Joaquín de Agüero, tel. 033/22-8355, CUC20–30), a well-preserved 1959 middle-class home with a double garage and two air-conditioned rooms; the spacious upstairs wood-paneled room has retro furnishings and opens to a vast rooftop terrace.

◖ **Casa de Dr. Alberto de Armas** (Independencia #317, e/ 1 y 2, tel. 033/22-8451, CUC20) is another delightful yesteryear modernist home. Alberto rents one spacious and handsome room, which opens to a huge patio with arbor and swing seat.

Villa O'Mari (Máximo Gómez #352, e/ 4ta y 5ta Este, tel. 033/22-3267, CUC20) is another marvelous option. This two-story house is smothered in bougainvillea and has a garden patio with rockers, a lounge with TV and stereo system, plus two air-conditioned rooms with modern bathrooms. One has a kitchen and its own entrance via a spiral staircase; the other has a terrace.

HOTELS

Islazul's **Hotel Ciego de Ávila** (Carretera Caballos, tel. 033/22-8013, recepcion@hca. co.cu, CUC17 s, CUC25 d low season, CUC22 s, CUC30 d high season, including breakfast), two kilometers northwest of downtown, is a faceless four-story building with 144 pleasantly furnished air-conditioned rooms. Locals flock to the swimming pool on weekends.

Downtown, Islazul's **Hotel Santiago-Havana** (Independencia y Honorario del Castillo, tel. 033/22-5703, administracion@hshca.cav.co.cu, CUC11 s, CUC16 d year-round) dates back to 1957 and has 76 dourly furnished air-conditioned rooms, plus a bar and cabaret disco.

In early 2010, the old **Hotel Rueda** (Independencia Oeste, esq. Agramonte) was being restored. It promises to be the best place in town when completed.

Food

The only legal *paladar* in town, **El Flamenco** (Candelario Agüero #244, tel. 033/22-5429, daily 7–10 P.M.) offers filling *criollo* dinners.

I'm partial to the colonial ambience at **La**

Confronta (Marcial Gómez, esq. Joaquín Agüeno, tel. 033/20-0931, noon–3 P.M. and 7 P.M.—midnight), in a restored colonial mansion. Pork dishes are the name of the game here. Even foreigners pay in pesos. Pork for pennies!

For a seat with a view, slide into a red leather banquette at the modestly elegant **Restaurante Solaris** (tel. 033/22-2156, daily 12:30 P.M.–10 P.M.), atop the Doce Plantas building on the west side of Parque Martí; the elevator is to the rear of the building. No shorts are allowed. It has the standard *criollo* menu, but a pianist entertains.

For colonial ambience check out **Fonda La Estrella** (Máximo Gómez, esq. Honorato Castillo, tel. 033/26-6186, daily 11:30 A.M.–midnight), with a wooden bar, murals, wrought-iron seating, and live music. I recommend the *ropa vieja* (CUC3.25) or paella (CUC3.50).

The **Restaurante Colonial** (Independencia Oeste #110, tel. 033/22-3595, daily 6 P.M.–midnight) replicates a Spanish *bodega* and is lent character by its contemporary statues of flamenco dancers, a bull's head over the bar, and cowhide chairs. Alas, the menu offers the usual *criollo* staples.

Stalls outside the train station sell pizzas and other snacks, *refrescos,* and *batidos.*

For ice cream, join the line at **Coppelia** (Independencia Oeste, esq. Simón Reyes, Tues.–Sun. 10 A.M.–2:30 P.M. and 5–10 P.M.) or, one block west, **Cremería Arlequin** (esq. Agramonte, Mon. and Wed.–Fri. 10 A.M.–5 P.M. and 7–10 P.M., and Sat.–Sun. until 11 P.M.).

You can buy produce at the *mercado agropecuario* (Mon.–Sat. 6 A.M.–6 P.M.), beneath the overpass at Chicho Valdés and Fernando Calleja, and baked goods at **Panadería Doña Neli** (daily 9 A.M.–9 P.M.), on the northwest corner of Parque Martí.

Information and Services

Infotur (Honorato del Castillo, e/ Libertad y Independencia, tel. 033/20-9109, Mon.–Fri. 8:15 A.M.–4:30 P.M., Sat. 8:30 A.M.–12:30 P.M.) provides tourist information.

The **post office** (Marcial Gómez, esq. Chico Valdés, tel. 033/22-2096), two blocks south of Parque Martí, has DHL service. **Etecsa** (Joaquín Agüera, e/ Honorato y Maceo, daily 8:30 A.M.–7:30 P.M.) has international phone and Internet service.

Bandec (Independencia Oeste, esq. Simón Reyes, and Independencia Oeste, esq. Antonio Maceo) and **Banco Popular** (Independencia, e/ Simón Reyes y Maceo) have branches. You can also change foreign currency at **Cadeca** (Independencia Oeste #118, e/ Maceo y Simón Reyes). Most banks are open Mon.–Fri. 8 A.M.–3:30 P.M., Sat. 8 A.M.–1 P.M.

The **hospital** (Máximo Gómez, tel. 033/22-2429) is at the east end of town.

The **Consultoría Jurídica Internacional** (Independencia, e/ Honorato y Maceo, tel. 033/26-6238, Mon.–Fri. 8:30 A.M.–5 P.M.) offers legal aid; the **police station** (Delgado, e/ Libertad and Independencia) is one block east of the main square.

Getting There and Around
BY AIR
The **Aeropuerto Máximo Gómez** (tel. 033/22-5717) is 22 kilometers north of town. **Cubana** (Chicho Valdés #83, e/ Maceo y Honorario, tel. 033/22-1117, Mon.–Fri. 8:30 A.M.–3 P.M.) flies from Havana.

BY BUS
The **Terminal de Ómnibus Nacional** (tel. 033/22-2407) is on the Carretera Central, 1.5 kilometers east of town. **Víazul** buses (tel. 033/22-2514) stop here. Eastbound buses depart Ciego de Ávila for Santiago at 3:45, 4:25, and 10:50 A.M. and 4:35 and 10:10 P.M., and for Holguín only at 2:20 A.M. and 3:35 P.M. Westbound buses depart Ciego de Ávila for Havana at 12:35, 1:55, and 5:25 A.M. and 3:10 and 6:20 P.M., for Trinidad at 4:05 A.M., and for Varadero at 4:40 A.M.

The **Terminal de Ómnibus Municipal** (tel. 033/22-3076), next to the railway station, serves towns within the province.

BY TRAIN
The **Estación Ferrocarril** (tel. 033/22-3313)

is at the base of Agramonte, three blocks west and six blocks south of Parque Martí. Ciego de Ávila is on the main railroad between Havana and Santiago and all trains stop here. Westbound trains depart Ciego de Ávila for Havana at 2:24 A.M. (CUC22 *especial*) and at 9:17 A.M., 5:54 P.M., and 10:12 P.M. (CUC16 *regular*). Eastbound trains depart Ciego de Ávila for Bayamo at 7:29 A.M., for Santiago de Cuba at 1:15 A.M. (CUC21 *especial)* and at 5:24 A.M. (CUC14.50 *regular*). Trains also depart for Morón. Horse-drawn **coches** are outside the train station.

BY CAR AND TAXI

You can rent cars at **Cubacar** (tel. 033/20-7133), on Candelario Agüero and at the bus station (tel. 033/20-5105). There are gas stations at the junction of the *circunvalación* and Carretera Morón (northeast of town); on Chicho Valdés and Martí; and two blocks east at Chicho Valdés and Independencia. For a taxi, call **Cubataxi** (tel. 033/22-7636).

FLORIDA

East of Ciego de Ávila, the Carretera Central continues almost ruler-straight to Camagüey. The only town of significance is Florida, surrounded by sugarcane fields and dominated by the Central Argentina sugar mill.

It's a good place to bed down on the long journey. **Casa de Teresa** (Máximo Gómez #504, tel. 032/51-6189, CUC10–12) is a pleasant private room rental with two bedrooms; the rear room has a sunny patio balcony. The owners have a fascinating antique clock and watch collection. Alternatively, the Bauhaus-style **Hotel Florida** (Carretera Central, Km 536, tel. 032/51-3011, reservas@hflorida.co.cu, CUC15 s, CUC20 d) offers modest rooms.

◖ PARQUE NACIONAL JARDINES DE LA REINA

The Garden of the Queens archipelago comprises around 660 deserted coral cays in a long chain that extends east–west for some 350 kilometers off the southern coast of Ciego de Ávila and Camagüey Provinces. Flamingos

wade in the briny shallows of the Golfo de Ana María. An extensive coral reef runs along the chain's southern shore, which is lined by white-sand beaches. In November 2008, Hurricane Paloma struck, doing extensive damage.

There's a fishing lodge on **Cayo Bartolo.** Otherwise this is virgin terrain.

Recreation

The cays are nirvana for sportfishing and diving. Reservations are handled by an Italian company, **Avalon Dive Center/Press Tours** (tel. 033/20-6111 Júcaro, www.divingincuba.com and www.avalons.net), which has exclusive permits to the Jardines de la Reina and offers six-day/seven-night diving and fishing packages, mid-October through August. Prices are given on request.

There are 26 dive sites. Diving is permitted only with a guide provided by Avalon, even if you arrive on your own yacht. Professional scuba instructors even stage shark-riding—yes, riding silky sharks like cowboys do horses!

Accommodations

Participants on fishing and diving packages are accommodated aboard the *La Tortuga Lodge,* a former barge turned permanently moored hotel that can accommodate 22 people in seven air-conditioned cabins; the *Halcon,* a 75-foot cruise yacht with six cabins; the 69-foot, four-cabin *La Reina;* and the four-cabin *Caballones.* Non-divers and non-fishers are given rates upon request.

Getting There

All visits to the cays are handled through **Avalon Dive Center/Press Tours** (tel. 033/20-6111, www.divingincuba.com and www.avalons.net) in the browbeaten fishing village of Júcaro, 20 kilometers south of Ciego de Ávila.

Private vessels must report to Avalon, which has exclusive use of **Marina Júcaro.** Yachts can moor at the cays only with prior permission.

MORÓN

Morón (pop. 50,000), 37 kilometers due north of Ciego de Ávila, is the main gateway to Cayo

Coco and Cayo Guillermo and is perfectly positioned for day excursions to the cays. It is known as the City of the Rooster, a name bequeathed in the 18th century by settlers from Morón de la Frontera, in Andalusia, Spain. In the 1950s, Morón's city fathers erected a rooster at the entrance to town. Fulgencio Batista was present for the unveiling. After the Revolution, an officer in the Rebel Army ordered the monument's destruction. In 1981, the city government decided to erect another cockerel in bronze at the foot of a clock tower fitted with an amplifier so that citizens could hear the rooster crow daily at 6 A.M. and 6 P.M. It stands outside the entrance to the Hotel Morón.

Morón featured prominently during the Wars of Independence. The town was captured by rebel troops in 1876. The Spanish colonial army built the 50-kilometer-long wooden barricade—La Trocha—from Morón to Júcaro, on the south coast.

Sights

The only worthwhile site in town is **Museo Caonabo** (Martí #115, tel. 0335/50-4501,

© CHRISTOPHER P. BAKER
cock and clock tower, Morón

Tues.–Fri. 10 A.M.–6 P.M., Sat. 2–10 P.M., Sun. 8 A.M.–noon, CUC1), occupying a three-story neoclassical former bank. Downstairs is dedicated to pre-Columbian culture. Upstairs the historical artifacts range from Spanish swords and *mantillas* to Revolutionary icons, all thoughtfully displayed and labeled.

The defunct Central Patria o Muerte sugar mill at Patria, five kilometers southeast of town, has been turned into the **Museo de Azúcar** (tel. 0335/50-3309, open only to excursion groups), a Sugar Museum describing sugarcane cultivation and refining. There's a model of the *central,* where much of the original machinery is in place within the near derelict building. To the rear are three steam trains; rides are offered on a 1917 Baldwin.

The city is enclosed to the north and east by a vast quagmire of sedges, reeds, and water. **Laguna de la Leche,** five kilometers due north of Morón, is named for its milky complexion, which derives from deposits of gypsum. Bird life includes flamingos. Boat tours are offered (daily 10 A.M.–5:30 P.M., CUC2) from La Cueva, on the west shore.

Northeast of Morón, **Lago La Redonda** claims the largest concentrations of bass in Cuba. **Centro Turístico La Redonda** (tel. 033/30-2489, daily 9 A.M.–7 P.M.), 14 kilometers north of Morón, offers fishing (CUC35 for four hours), Jet Ski rental (CUC1 per minute), and boat trips (CUC4). Yes, there are crocodiles in the water, although you'll have a better chance of seeing them at the **Zoocriadero Cocodrilo** (daily 9 A.M.–7 P.M., CUC2), five kilometers east of Morón and at **Área Protegida de Cunagua** (daily 6 A.M.–6 P.M., CUC1) about 10 kilometers east of town. The latter has hiking trails and a mountaintop restaurant, and horses can be rented.

Entertainment and Events

Each July, the **Carnival Acuático** (Water Carnival) takes place in a canal leading to Laguna de la Leche. Musicians serenade the crowd while the city's prettiest young maidens row boats decorated with garlands of flowers.

The **Casa de la Trova** (Libertad #74, e/

CIEGO DE ÁVILA & CAMAGÜEY

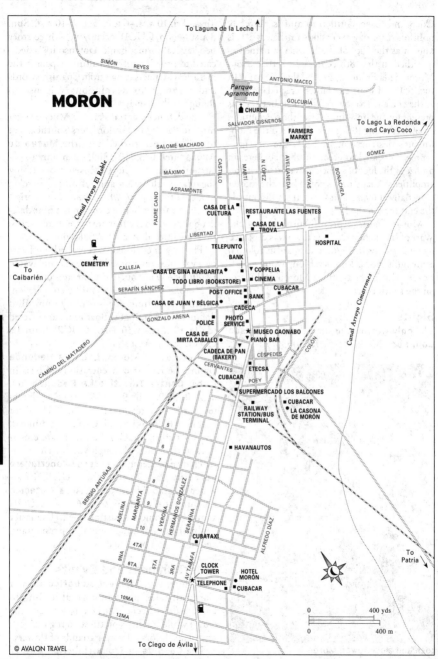

To Laguna de la Leche

SIMÓN REYES

ANTONIO MACEO

MORÓN

Parque Agramonte

GOLCURÍA

CHURCH

SALVADOR CISNEROS

To Lago La Redonda and Cayo Coco

FARMERS MARKET

SALOMÉ MACHADO

GÓMEZ

CASTILLO

MARTÍ

N LÓPEZ

AVELLANEDA

ZAYAS

BONACHEA

MÁXIMO

Canal Arroyo El Roble

PADRE CANO

AGRAMONTE

CASA DE LA CULTURA

RESTAURANTE LAS FUENTES

CASA DE LA TROVA

LIBERTAD

HOSPITAL

TELEPUNTO

CEMETERY

BANK

To Caibarién

CALLEJA

COPPELIA

CASA DE GINA MARGARITA

SERAFÍN SÁNCHEZ

TODO LIBRO (BOOKSTORE)

CINEMA

CUBACAR

POST OFFICE

BANK

CADECA

CASA DE JUAN Y BÉLGICA

GONZALO ARENA

POLICE

PHOTO SERVICE

MUSEO CAONABO

CASA DE MIRTA CABALLO

PIANO BAR

Canal Arroyo Cimarrones

CADECA DE PAN (BAKERY)

CÉSPEDES

COLÓN

CAMINO DEL MATADERO

CERVANTES

ETECSA

CUBACAR

POEY

SUPERMERCADO LOS BALCONES

CUBACAR

RAILWAY STATION/BUS TERMINAL

LA CASONA DE MORÓN

4

5

6

HAVANAUTOS

7

SERGIO ANTUNAS

8

ADELINA

MARGARITA

9

E VERONA

HERMANOS GONZÁLEZ

SERAFINA

ALFREDO DÍAZ

10

To Patria

CUBATAXI

4TA

9NA

6TA

5TA

3RA

AV TARAFA

CLOCK TOWER

HOTEL MORÓN

8VA

TELEPHONE

CUBACAR

10MA

12MA

0   400 yds

0   400 m

To Ciego de Ávila

© AVALON TRAVEL

Martí y Narciso López) hosts traditional music, as does the **Casa de la Cultura** (Martí #224, tel. 033/50-4309), which offers dance lessons.

La Casona de Morón (Cristóbal Colón #41) has pool tables and hosts an outdoor disco (Tues.–Sun.). **Disco La Cueva,** three kilometers north of town on the road to Laguna de la Leche, offers karaoke, *cabaret espectáculo,* and disco (CUC1).

The **Piano Bar** (Martí #111, tel. 033/50-2045, daily 1–10 P.M.) has live music nightly, but the garish lighting kills any romantic ambience.

Accommodations

Casa de Gina Margarita (Callejas #89, e/ Martí y Castillo, tel. 5295-6585, CUC20) is an attractive 1950s home full of antiques and kitsch. It has two modestly furnished, cross-ventilated air-conditioned rooms with small private bathrooms and independent entrance. There's parking and a delightful patio. Almost identical, **Casa de Mirta Caballo** (Dimas Daniel #19, e/ Castillo y Serafina, tel. 033/50-3036, CUC20) is a smallish, simply furnished home that rents two rooms off the rear patio with rockers. Each has an independent entrance and parking.

I've twice stayed at **Casa de Juan y Bélgica** (Castillo #189, e/ San José y Serafín Sánchez, tel. 033/50-3823, juanclen@enet.cu, CUC20), a well-kept home with two air-conditioned rooms with fans and modern bathrooms. Meals are served on a nice patio with planters. There's even a computer; guests get free email use.

Islazul's modest two-story **Hotel Morón** (Av. Tarafa, tel. 033/50-2230, fax 033/50-2133, www.islazul.cu, CUC15 s, CUC22 year-round) offers no frills in its 136 rooms and eight junior suites, but they're adequate, and facilities include a massage salon, barber shop, swimming pool, and disco.

La Casona de Morón (Cristóbal Colón #41, Ciego de Ávila, tel. 0335/50-2236), a colonial mansion that has traditionally catered to anglers, was closed for restoration at last visit.

Food

Pickings are slim. I like the nautically themed (think ships' wheels for ceiling lamps and waitresses in naval costume) **(Restaurante La Atarralla** (tel. 033/50-5351, Tues.–Sun. 2:30–6 P.M.), on a pier overhanging Laguna de la Leche. It serves paella (CUC5), oyster cocktail (CUC2.50), and grilled lobster (CUC7).

Opening to a patio, **Restaurante Las Fuentes** (Calle Martí, e/ Libertad y Agramonte, tel. 033/50-5758, Wed.–Mon. 9 A.M.–11 P.M.) dishes out simple *criollo,* Chinese, and continental plates for CUC2–6.

You can buy bread at **Panadería Doña Neli** (Serafín Sánchez #86, e/ Narciso López y Martí), produce at the *mercado agropecuario* (Machado, esq. Avellaneda), and groceries at **Supermercado Los Balcones** (Avenida Tarafa y Calle 3).

Services

Etecsa (Céspedes, esq. Martí, tel. 033/50-2399, daily 8:30 A.M.–7:30 P.M.) offers phone, Internet, and Cubacel service. **Bandec** (Martí e/ Serafín Sánchez and Gonzalo Arena) has a branch, and you can change foreign currency at **Cadeca** (Martí, esq. Gonzalo Arena, Mon.–Sat. 9 P.M.–4:30 P.M. and Sun. 9 P.M.–noon), immediately south. The **hospital** (tel. 033/50-3530) is at the east end of Libertad.

Getting There and Away

The **bus station** (tel. 033/50-3398) and **railway station** (tel. 033/50-5398) are next to each other on Avenida Tarafa. Eight buses daily connect Morón with Ciego de Ávila.

Trains depart for Morón from Havana daily at 5:10 P.M. (CUC24), from Camagüey at 3:30 P.M. (CUC4.20), and from Ciego de Ávila at 8:10 A.M. and 2:10 P.M. (CUC1). Trains depart Morón for Havana at 12:05 A.M., for Camagüey at 3:15 A.M., for Ciego at 6:10 and 12:15 A.M., and for Santa Clara on alternate days at 12:40 P.M.

Getting Around

Horse-drawn *coches* congregate outside the railway station and ply the main streets.

Cubacar (tel. 033/50-2152) has four outlets in town, including at the Hotel Morón. The Cupet gas station is one block south of the Hotel Morón.

COMUNIDAD CELIA SÁNCHEZ

Much has been made of this community at Turiguanó, 28 kilometers north of Morón, known locally as the Pueblo Holandés because it was modeled on a "Dutch village" (coincidentally, Cuba's first wind-turbine scheme was built here; three giant turbines loom to the east of the village). The 59 gable-roofed houses supported by timber-beam facades transport you lyrically back to Holland, except they are in a sad state of disrepair. The village is named for a revolutionary heroine. Turiguanó was a U.S.-owned private cattle estate before the Revolution. In 1960–1961, the land was expropriated and modern houses in Dutch style built for the 30 or so families who live here and raise the island's native beef breed, the Santa Gertrudis.

Agroturístico Rodeo, the breeding center, has rodeos for tour excursions from the cays.

Cayo Coco and Cayo Guillermo

These two contiguous islands, separated from the mainland by the Bahía de Perros (Bay of Dogs) and joined to it by a manufactured *pedraplén,* are the third-largest tourist destination in Cuba, after Havana and Varadero. Boasting the finest beaches in Cuba and some of the most beautiful jade-colored waters, these cays offer the finest beach experience for sand, sea, and sun hounds who enjoy hotels with a little luxe. Two small facilities cater to budget travelers. All the resort hotels operate on an all-inclusive basis, but there are some motley budget options. Long-term plans call for 22,000 rooms for the twin islands, with heaven knows what ecological consequences. (The 27-kilometer *pedraplén* is made of solid landfill and cuts the Bahía de Perros in two. There are only two sluices, preventing sufficient flow of currents, resulting in significant damage to the mangrove systems.) Soupy mangroves line the southern shores—breeding grounds for hordes of mosquitoes. *Bring repellent!*

There's a toll booth (CUC2 each way, passport required) and security checkpoint at the entrance to the *pedraplén.* Drive carefully; there are no barriers on the sides of the narrow road, which is deteriorated. Eventually, you reach a traffic circle. The road straight ahead leads to the hotel complex and main beaches of Cayo Coco. That to the left leads to Cayo Guillermo.

In 2008, the cays were opened to Cubans, who must buy a prepaid package (CUC8) from **Cubatur** at Agroturístico Rodeo, two kilometers southwest of the checkpoint.

◖ CAYO COCO

This 364-square-kilometer cay is a stunner on account of its 21 kilometers of superlative beaches. Most hotels front the sands of Playa Larga and Playa Flamenco, and, between them, Playa Palma Real. Huge sand dunes—Las Dunas de los Puertos—rise over the west end of Playa Flamingo, offering fabulous views along the coast and an inland lagoon.

Scrub-covered Cayo Coco, which is named for the roseate ibis, or *coco,* was immortalized by Ernest Hemingway. In *Islands in the Stream,* his protagonist, Thomas Hudson, sets foot on the beach at Puerto Coco seeking traces of Nazi soldiers. Farther inland, he discovers the lagoon where flamingos come to feed at high tide. Cayo Coco has one of Cuba's largest flamingo colonies. Every day, they fly over the north end of the *pedraplén* shortly after sunrise and again at dusk.

The 158 bird species here also include migratory waterfowl. The most prominent animals are *jabelis*—wild pigs—and endemic iguanas. There are even deer. The 769-hectare **Parque Nacional El Bagá** (tel. 033/30-1063, daily

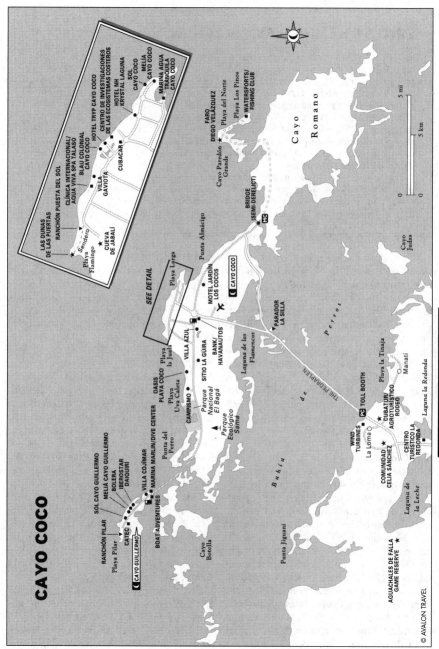

CAYO COCO

CIEGO DE ÁVILA & CAMAGÜEY

Detail inset:
- LAS DUNAS DE LAS PUERTAS
- RANCHÓN PUESTA DEL SOL
- CLÍNICA INTERNACIONAL/ AGUA VIVA SPA TALASO
- BLAU COLONIAL CAYO COCO
- HOTEL TRYP CAYO COCO
- CENTRO DE INVESTIGACIONES DE LAS ECOSISTEMAS COSTEROS
- HOTEL NH KRYSTAL LAGUNA
- SOL CAYO COCO
- MELIÁ CAYO COCO
- MARINA AGUA TRANQUILA CAYO COCO
- CUBACAR
- VILLA GAVIOTA
- CUEVA DE JABALÍ
- Playa Flamingo
- Sendero

Main map labels:
- Cayo Romano
- FARO DIEGO VELÁZQUEZ
- Playa del Norte
- Playa Los Pinos
- WATERSPORTS/ FISHING CLUB
- Cayo Paredón Grande
- BRIDGE (SEMI-DERELICT)
- Cayo Judas
- SEE DETAIL
- Playa Larga
- Punta Almácigo
- MOTEL JARDÍN LOS COCOS
- CAYO COCO
- PARADOR LA SILLA
- Perros
- VILLA AZUL
- BANK/ HAVANAUTOS
- SITIO LA GÜIRA
- Playa la Jaula
- OASIS PLAYA COCO
- Playa Uva Caleta
- CAMPISMO
- Parque Nacional El Bagá
- Parque Ecológico Samá
- Punta del Perro
- Laguna de los Flamencos
- THE PEDRAPLÉN
- TOLL BOOTH
- Playa la Tinaja
- Manatí
- CUBATUR/ AGROTURÍSTICO RODEO
- WIND TURBINES
- La Loma
- COMUNIDAD CELIA SÁNCHEZ
- CENTRO TURÍSTICO LA REDONDA
- Laguna la Redonda
- Bahía de Perros
- SOL CAYO GUILLERMO
- MELIÁ CAYO GUILLERMO
- BOLERA
- IBEROSTAR DAIQUIRÍ
- RANCHÓN PILAR
- Playa Pilar
- CAYO GUILLERMO
- CATEC
- VILLA COJÍMAR
- MARINA MARLIN/DIVE CENTER
- BOAT ADVENTURES
- Cayo Botella
- Punta Jiguaní
- Laguna de la Leche
- AGUACHALES DE FALLA GAME RESERVE

5 mi
5 km
0

© AVALON TRAVEL

ERNEST HEMINGWAY, NAZI HUNTER

In May 1942, Ernest Hemingway showed up at the U.S. embassy in Havana with a proposal to fit the *Pilar* out as a Q-boat, with .50-caliber machine guns and a trained crew with himself at the helm. The boat would navigate the cays off the north coast of Cuba, ostensibly collecting specimens on behalf of the American Museum of Natural History, but in fact on the lookout for Nazi U-boats, which Hemingway intended to engage and disable.

Hemingway's friend Col. John W. Thomason Jr. was Chief of Naval Intelligence for Central America and pulled strings to get the plan approved. The vessel was "camouflaged" and

duly set out for the cays. Gregorio Fuentes – who from 1938 until the writer's death was in charge of the *Pilar* – went along and served as the model for Antonio in *Islands in the Stream*, Hemingway's novel based on his real-life adventures.

They patrolled for two years. Several times they located and reported the presence of Nazi submarines that the U.S. Navy or Air Force were later able to sink. Only once, off Cayo Mégano, did Hemingway come close to his dream: A U-boat suddenly surfaced while the *Pilar* was at anchor. Unfortunately, it dipped back below the surface before Hemingway could get close.

9:30 A.M.–5:30 P.M.) protects the west end of Cayo Coco, though Jet Ski tours through the mangroves harass the bird and fish colonies, and dynamiting for hotel development does the same. The park's facilities (a cultural center and a re-creation of a native Taíno village) were trashed at my last visit. Guided tours of the trails are available, ostensibly; ask at the **Centro de Investigaciones de las Ecosistemas Costeros** (tel./fax 033/30-1151, ciec@ciec.fica. inf.cu), immediately east of the Hotel Tryp Cayo Coco. Charged with responsibility for protecting the local ecology, it was due to open an educational center for visitors in 2010.

Cayo Romano

From the traffic circle, you can follow a rugged road east past the service area (with workers complex and warehouses) to a channel separating Cayo Coco from Cayo Romano. Cross the semi-derelict bridge (it would be condemned anywhere other than Cuba) and ask the military personnel in tatterdemalion uniforms to lift the rope that serves as a barrier. You can follow the road around to **Cayo Paredón,** where the cay's northern tip is studded by a lighthouse—**Faro Diego Velázquez**—built in 1859. A side road fit for jeeps only leads to **Playa Los Pinos,** popular for day excursions by catamaran from Cayo Coco.

Entertainment

All the hotels offer theme parties, cabarets, and discos. A *cabaret espectáculo* is offered at the **Cueva del Jabalí** (tel. 033/30-1206, Tues.–Wed. and Fri. 8:30 P.M.–midnight, CUC15). Excursions are available from the hotels. Bring repellent.

Recreation

All the hotels have water sports. Nonguests can pay for banana-boat rides and water skiing, snorkeling, and Hobie Cat rental, plus kite-surfing at Meliá Sol Club.

Diving (CUC40 one dive) is available at the Hotel Tryp Cayo Coco and Hotel Blau Colonial Cayo Coco, and through **Blue Diving** (tel. 033/30-8179, www.bluediving.com), between the Sol Cayo Coco and Meliá Cayo Coco.

Horseback riding (CUC10 per hour) is offered at **Sitio La Güira** (tel. 033/30-1208, CUC2 cover), a rather hokey facility inland, about six kilometers west of the roundabout. You can even ride a water buffalo. It displays farm animals and hosts a weekly **Fiesta Campesino** (folkloric country show).

Sportfishing (CUC270 half day, CUC410 full day, up to six people), plus fly-fishing at Cayo Paredón (CUC129 half day, CUC179 full-day), is offered from **Marina Marlin Aguas Tranquilas** (tel. 033/30-1328), east of the main roundabout. **EcoTur** (tel. 033/30-8163 or 07/641-0306, www.ecoturcuba.co.cu) offers fishing trips.

You can pilot a speedboat on guided two-hour convoy tours of the mangroves with **Cayo Guillermo Boat Adventure** (tel. 033/30-1515, CUC41), with departures at 9 A.M., 11 A.M., 1 P.M., and 3 P.M.

Catamaran cruises include snorkeling (CUC20 adult, CUC10 child), sunset trips (CUC30 adult, CUC15 child), and a full-day safari (tel. 033/30-1323, CUC75 adult, CUC38 child) with snorkeling and a lobster lunch. Tours are available through most hotels.

Accommodations

Campismo Cayo Coco (tel. 033/30-1039, CUC13 s/d), at Playa Uva Caleta, 15 kilometers west of the Cupet gas station, serves Cubans. No foreigners have been accepted here for years. However, budget hounds have three options: Islazul's 142-room **Villa Azul** (tel. 033/30-1278, fax 033/30-1256, carpeta@villazul.cav.co.cu, CUC19 s/d including breakfast, year-round, CUC35 with beach transfers and all meals) was built to house workers in three-story blocks two kilometers from the beach. All units are simply furnished suites. Price aside, I don't see any upside to staying here. The same goes for Islazul's **Motel Jardín Los Cocos** (tel. 033/30-8121, carpeta@jcocos.cco.tur.cu, CUC15 s, CUC20 d year-round), four kilometers inland. Serving Cubanacán staff and tourists, it offers 24 air-conditioned no-frills rooms with satellite TVs and modern bathrooms. It has a café-bar and swimming pool. And **Sitio La Güira** (tel. 033/30-1208, CUC16 s/d including breakfast), about six kilometers west of the roundabout, has four very rustic huts with private baths, plus a thatched restaurant.

Oasis Villa Gaviota (tel. 033/302180, fax 033/302190, recepcion@villagaviota.co.cu, CUC60 s, CUC80 d low season, CUC80 s, CUC100 d high season) has 48 air-conditioned rooms in two-story blocks arrayed around a handsome pool with bar, plus eight seafront *cabinas*. All are nicely furnished, with satellite TVs. Facilities include a water sports club, gym, and sauna.

Meliá Cayo Coco

When I stayed here in 1996, the **Hotel Blau Colonial Cayo Coco** (tel. 033/30-1311, fax 033/30-1384, www.blau-hotels.com, from CUC76 per person low season, CUC146 s, CUC 242 d high season) impressed. Now this 485-room resort appears dowdy, but it has most amenities you would want.

An elevated contemporary lobby with bar and shopping arcade overlooking a a serpentine swimming pool—one of four on-site—makes a great first impression at the **Hotel Tryp Cayo Coco** (tel. 033/30-1300, fax 033/30-1386, www. solmeliacuba.com, from CUC95 s, CUC140 d low season, from CUC180 s, CUC280 d high season). The food at this sprawling all-inclusive Sol Meliá property is OK at best, but the 508 rooms are nicely furnished and have cavernous marble bathrooms.

Up a rung, **Sol Cayo Coco** (tel. 033/30-1280, fax 033/30-1285, www.solmeliacuba. com, from CUC150 s, CUC200 d low season, from CUC180 s, CUC240 d high season), also managed by Sol Meliá, is a compact all-inclusive with 266 handsome rooms and four suites in condo-style units around a long, sinuous swimming pool. Rooms are equipped to international standard, and the hotel is brimful with facilities.

◖ Meliá Cayo Coco (tel. 033/30-1180, fax 033/30-1381, www.solmeliacuba.com, from CUC145 s, CUC220 d low season, from CUC230 s, CUC345 d high season), adjoining Sol Club, is a more gracious all-inclusive nestled between the beach and a lagoon, with lush landscaping. The 250 spacious rooms are done up in a subdued contemporary take on traditional Spain. A specialty seafood restaurant is suspended over the lagoon, as are two-story villas.

Now under Dutch management, the 690-room **NH Krystal Laguna** (tel. 033/30-1470, fax 033/30-1498, www.nhhotels.com) offers a similarly priced alternative and even has a roller-skating rink.

Another alternative all on its lonesome at Playa Uva Caleta, the 306-room **Oasis Playa Coco** (tel. 033/30-2250, fax 033/30-2255, CUC80 s, CUC120 d year-round) is a two-star hotel billed as a four-star.

Food

Nonguests can purchase a day or night pass to the all-inclusive hotels. If you wish to escape the resorts, your choices are limited to **Parador La Silla** (tel. 033/30-2137), a simple thatched café on one of the cays that precede Cayo Coco; and **Ranchón Puesta del Sol** beach grill at Playa Flamingo.

Information and Services

Infotur (tel. 033/30-9109, aeroinfotjr@enet.cu, Mon.–Sat. 8 A.M.–5 P.M.) has a tour info desk in the airport.

Etecsa (daily 8:30 A.M.–5:30 P.M.) has a telephone center; it's far cheaper to call from here than from the hotels. **DHL** (tel. 033/30-1300, Mon.–Fri. 8 A.M.–5 P.M., Sat. 8 A.M.–1 P.M.) has an office in the Hotel Tryp Cayo Coco.

Clínica Internacional (tel. 033/30-2158, 24 hours), adjacent to Villa Gaviota, has it all: dental clinic, clinical lab, high-pressure oxygen chamber, plus massage and hydrotherapy at the adjoining **Acuavida Spa Talaso.**

Getting There and Away

International flights serve **Cayo Coco International Airport** (tel. 033/30-9165). Some flights arrive at Máximo Gómez International Airport in Ciego de Ávila, from where arrivals are bused to Cayo Coco.

There is no bus service to Cayo Coco.

Skippers can berth at **Base Naútica Cayo Coco** (tel./fax 033/30-2246).

Getting Around

Cubataxi (tel. 033/50-3290) charges CUC25–30 for an island tour in a classic car. A 45-minute tour by horse-drawn *coche* costs CUC5 per person. And *tren* shuttles (open-sided faux trains) run between the hotels (CUC2).

You can hire bicycles, scooters, and cars at most hotels, and cars from **Havanautos** (tel. 033/30-1371), at the airport and at the Cupet gas station; and **Rex** (tel. 033/30-2244), at the airport.

◖ CAYO GUILLERMO

This 18-square-kilometer cay lies west of Cayo Coco, to which it is joined by an umbilical

© CHRISTOPHER P. BAKER

Ranchón Pilar, at Playa Pilar on Cayo Guillermo

pedraplén. Hotels are laid out along chalky, five-kilometer-long **Playa El Paso.** Other beaches unspool westward, ending at **Playa Pilar,** where sand dunes pile up 15 meters high (the road is a potholed *piste*) and a thatched restaurant, **Ranchón Pilar** (noon–3 P.M. serves seafood and *criollo* dishes and has lounge chairs and shade umbrellas.

Inshore fishing is excellent, including for bonefish. Farther out, marlin run through the Old Bahama Channel—Hemingway's "great blue river." **Marina Marlin** (tel. 033/30-1718, commercial@marlin.cco.tur.co), at the east end of Cayo Guillermo, offers sportfishing.

Scuba diving, paragliding, and kite-surfing are available at the **Green Moray Dive Center** (tel. 033/30-1627, greenmoray@marlin.cco.tur.cu), at Meliá Cayo Guillermo.

Horse-riding is offered at CATEC, on the road to Playa Pilar.

Accommodations

Villa Cojímar (tel. 033/30-1712, fax 033/33-1727, ventas@cojimar.gca.tur.cu, CUC51 s, CUC82 d low season, CUC82 s, CUC115 d high season), on Playa El Paso, is a beautiful low-rise all-inclusive property with spacious lawns, 211 rooms, and one suite in small one- and two-story air-conditioned *cabinas.* Facilities include tennis, soccer, and car rental.

More upscale, the 312-room all-inclusive **Iberostar Daiquirí** (tel. 033/30-1560, fax 033/30-1645, ventas@ibsdaiq.gca.tur.cu, CUC110 s, CUC160 d low season, CUC130 s, CUC200 d high season) has a contemporary Spanish vogue and lush landscaping. It has excellent children's facilities, a panoply of water sports and land activities, plus entertainment nightly. There's little to choose between the Iberostar and slightly higher priced, 264-room **Sol Cayo Guillermo** (tel. 033/30-1760, fax 033/30-1748, www.sol-meliacuba.com), managed by Spain's Sol Meliá.

The top hotel is the ❰ **Meliá Cayo Guillermo** (tel. 033/30-1680, fax 033/30-1685, www.solmeliacuba.com, from CUC190 s, CUC250 d low season, from CUC220 s, CUC290 d high season), with 314 air-conditioned rooms in the company's trademark turquoise and Caribbean pastels.

Services
There's a **Banco Financiero Internacional** (Mon.–Fri. 8 A.M.–noon and 1–3 P.M.) outside the Cupet gas station.

Getting There and Around
Transtur operates a shuttle between Cayo Coco and Cayo Guillermo five times daily, calling at all the hotels (CUC5).

The **Trencito** (faux-train) shuttle runs to Playa Pilar from Villa Cojímar at 8:40 A.M. and 1:40 P.M. Horse-drawn *coches* await custom outside the hotels.

Camagüey and Vicinity

CAMAGÜEY
Camagüey (pop. 270,000), 570 kilometers east of Havana and 110 kilometers east of Ciego de Ávila, sits in the center of the namesake province on a bluff above the vast plains. Cuba's third-largest city is full of beautifully restored plazas that lend the city one of its nicknames, "City of Squares." The historic core is a national monument.

Camagüey can be explored in one day but is deserving of two.

Camagüey lacks the heavy baroque architecture of Havana. Its style is simpler, more discreet. The bourgeoisie built their homes with eaves supported by unembellished wooden columns. Always there was a *tinajón*, the big earthenware jars unique to the city and which lent it another nickname: "City of the Tinajones."

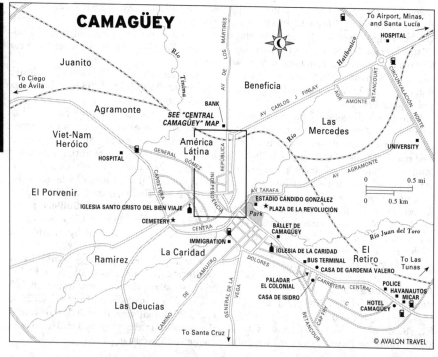

© AVALON TRAVEL

It's a pleasure to walk the colonial streets, especially in late afternoon, when the sun gilds the facades like burnished copper, and at night, too, when light silvers the Spanish grills and facades of the poorly lit streets, full of impending intrigue. In the dark, full of shadows, it is easy to imagine yourself cast back 200 years.

History

Camagüey was one of the original seven settlements founded by Diego Velázquez, though the first buildings were erected in 1515 miles to the north, on the shores of Bahía de Nuevitas. The site lacked fresh water and came under constant attack from local Indians. It was finally moved to its present location, where it was built on the site of an Indian settlement.

The early settlers were beset with water shortages. The town's Catalonian potters therefore made giant earthenware amphorae called *tinajones* to collect rainfall. Soon the jars (up to 2.5 meters tall and 1.5 meters wide) were a standard item outside every home, partly buried in the earth to keep them cool, but always under the gutters that channeled the rain from the eaves. Citizens began to compete with each other to boast the most *tinajones* and demonstrate their wealth. According to local legend, an outsider offered water from a *tinajón* will fall in love and never leave.

The city prospered from cattle raising and, later, sugar, which fostered a local slave-plantation economy. Descendants of the first Spanish settlers evolved into a modestly wealthy bourgeoisie that played a vital role in the national culture. The wealth attracted pirates. The unfortunate city was sacked and almost destroyed twice during the 17th century—in 1688 and 1679. Many Camagüeyans were themselves notorious smugglers who went against the grain of Spanish authority. "This town has always been looked upon with suspicion by the authorities on account of the strong proclivities its people had for insurrection," wrote Samuel Hazard in 1871. U.S. Marines even occupied the city in 1917–1923 to quell antigovernment unrest. Its citizens vigorously opposed the Machado and Batista regimes, when student

CAMELS IN CUBA?

Yes, camels roam the streets of Camagüey and other provincial cities of Oriente. These giant buses – *camellos* – were designed locally to save the day in Havana during the gasoline crisis, when bodies were added to articulated flatbed trucks. They're so named for the shape of the coach: sagging in between two humps like a bactrian camel.

The "camel" is a warehouse on wheels: officially a *supertrenbus*. Designed to carry 220 people, they are usually stuffed with more than 300, so many that the true number can't be untangled. As a popular Cuban joke goes, the always-packed and chaotic *camellos* are like the Saturday-night film on state TV, "because they contain sex, violence, and swear words!" Beware pickpockets!

and worker strikes often crippled the city. They supported the armies of Che Guevara and Camilo Cienfuegos when they entered the city in September 1958. But the province had been one of the most developed before the Revolution, and Fidel's turn to Communism received little support from the independent-minded people of Camagüey.

Following the Revolution, the town and its hinterlands were administered by Huber Matos, the popular Camagüeyan military commander, who challenged Castro's increasingly Communist turn. He was arrested for treason and sentenced to 20 years in prison. (Camilo Cienfuegos, whom Fidel sent to arrest Matos and reorganize the military command, mysteriously died when his plane disappeared on the return trip to Havana).

Orientation

Camagüey is bisected by the Carretera Central, which arcs around the southern side of the labyrinthine historic core, north of the Río Hatibónico. República runs north from the Carretera Central through the heart of the historic quarter and eventually

CIEGO DE ÁVILA & CAMAGÜEY

becomes Avenida de los Mártires. South of the river, Avenida de la Libertad links with the Carretera Central Este (one-way west-bound), linking Camagüey with Las Tunas. Calle Martí bisects the city east–west, link-ing Parque Agramonte—the main square, two blocks west of República—to the Carretera Central westward. The city is encircled by a *circunvalación*, a four-lane freeway.

Many streets have a modern (official) name and an original (now colloquial) name.

Parque Agramonte

This attractive plaza—a parade ground in colonial days—is bounded by Cisneros (west), Independencia (east), Martí (north), and Luaces (south). At its center is a life-size bronze **Monumento Major General Ignacio Agramonte** showing the Mambí general mounted atop his steed, machete in hand. Born in Camagüey, he rose to become a sugar es-tate owner and head of the Camagüeyan rebel forces during the first War of Independence. He was killed in May 1873 at the Battle of Las Guasimas.

The **Catedral de Nuestra Señora de Candelaria Santa Iglesia** (tel. 032/29-4965), on the south side, was built in 1864 atop a pre-decessor established in 1530. In 1688, the pirate Henry Morgan locked the city fathers in the church and starved them until they coughed up the location of their treasures. It's worth a peek for its statuary and beamed roof.

Afro-Cuban poet Nicolás Guillén (1902–1989) was born in the house now called **Casa Natal de Nicolás Guillén** (Hermano Agüiro #57, e/ Cisneros y Principe, tel. 032/29-3706, Mon.–Fri. 8 A.M.–4:30 P.M., free), one block north of the plaza. A loyal nationalist and rev-olutionary, Guillén served as chairman of the National Union of Cuban Writers and Artists (UNEAC), which he helped found. The house contains some of his personal possessions and hosts the **Instituto Superior de Arte,** where music is taught.

Casa Natal de Carlos Finlay (Cristo #5, tel. 032/29-6745, Mon.–Sat. 9 A.M.–5 P.M., CUC1), 50 meters west of the plaza, is the birthplace of the scientist who discovered the vector for yellow fever. It has apothecary jars.

Plaza del Carmen

This intimate cobbled square (Martí and 10 de Octubre), six blocks west of Parque Agramonte, features life-size ceramics figures: an old man pushing a cart, three women sipping *tazas* of coffee, two elderly lovers sharing gossip. Marvelous! The tiny plaza is surrounded by venerable houses in bright pastels. On the west side, the former **Convento de Nuestra Señora del Carmen**, built in 1825, today houses the **Galería de Arte Fidelio Ponce de León** (tel. 032/25-7577, Tues.–Sat. 8 A.M.–5 P.M., Sun. 8 A.M.–noon, CUC1).

◖ Plaza San Juan de Dios

The most impressive square is hidden away two blocks south of Parque Agramonte, one block west of Cisneros. The plaza is a national mon-ument boasting 18th-century buildings with huge doorways and beautifully turned win-dow bars. On the west side is a beautiful blue-and-white house, still privately owned, where once lived poet and songwriter Antón Silvio Rodríguez. A bronze plaque on the wall has the words of his famous "El Mayor," which cel-ebrates Ignacio Agramonte in song.

On the east side, the Moorish **Antiguo Hospital de San Juan de Dios,** a former military hospital dating from 1728, has ar-caded cloisters. Today it houses the **Museo de Arquitectura Colonial** (tel. 032/29-1388, Tues.–Sat. 9 A.M.–5 P.M., Sun. 9 A.M.–noon, CUC1). Adjoining it is the **Iglesia de San Juan de Dios** (open Monday), featuring a splendid mahogany ceiling and a bell tower.

Plaza de los Trabajadores

The Workers' Plaza, three blocks north of Parque Agramonte and two blocks west of República, is a triangular piazza with a vener-able ceiba tree at its heart.

On the east side is the deteriorated **Catedral Nuestra Señora de la Merced** (tel. 032/29-2740), dating to 1748 and boasting an elaborate gilt altar beneath a barrel vaulted ceiling with faded murals. The devout gather to request favors at a silver coffin, the Santa Sepulcro, in a separate chapel. Check out the catacombs, with skeletons in situ.

Ignacio Agramonte was born here on September 23, 1841, at **Casa Natal Ignacio Agramonte** (Agramonte #459, esq. Candelaria, tel. 032/29-7116, Tues.–Sat. 9 A.M.–5 P.M., Sun. 9–11:30 A.M., CUC2), on the south side of the square. Beautifully restored, it is now a museum containing an important art collection, plus mementos and colonial furniture.

One block east of the plaza, the red-brick **Iglesia Nuestra Señora de la Soledad** (República, esq. Agramonte) dates from 1755. It was recently restored and has interior frescos, an elaborate gilt altar, and beamed ceiling.

Other Sights

Pinned by a small statue of José Martí, **Parque Martí,** four blocks east of Parque Agramonte, is worth the visit to admire the neo-Gothic **Iglesia Sagrado Corazón de Jesús.** Dating from 1920, it features beautiful trompe l'oeils.

Casino Campestre, a park on the south side of the river and accessed from the historic center via the stone-and-metal **Puente Hatibónico** bridge dating from 1773, draws locals to gossip and flirt. It has prerevolutionary statues plus a small and dispiriting **zoo** (daily 7:30 A.M.–6 P.M., 0.50 peso), with African animals. On its west, across the Carretera Central, rises the imposing neoclassical **Instituto de Segunda Enseñanza** (Institute of Secondary Education).

To the east of the park, the **Plaza de la Revolución** features an impressive marble and granite **Monumento Ignacio Agramonte** inscribed with 3-D sculptures of Fidel, Che, and other revolutionaries.

The **Museo Provincial Ignacio Agramonte** (Av. de los Mártires #2, tel. 032/28-2425, Tues.–Sat. 10 A.M.–5 P.M., Sun. 10 A.M.–1 P.M., CUC2), at the north end of town, occupies a former garrison for Spanish cavalry. It exhibits an eclectic array of Cubana, from archaeology exhibits and stuffed flora and fauna to historical records up to the Revolution. Nearby, the

Sitio Histórico Asalto al Carro Celular, at the corner of Rosario and Quinones, preserves a bullet-riddled prison van assaulted by revolutionaries on 16 September 1958. It's enshrined in glass.

Entertainment and Events

In early February, the **Jornadas de la Cultura Camagüeyana** celebrates the city's founding. The **Festival del Teatro de Camagüey** is a September biennial. A religious festival is held on September 8 to honor Nuestra Señora de la Caridad, the city's patron saint.

On Saturday nights, República is closed to traffic for a rum-soaked fiesta.

The **Casa de la Trova** (Cisneros #171, tel. 032/29-1357, Mon.–Fri. noon–6 P.M. and 9 P.M.–midnight, Sat. 11 A.M.–6 P.M. and 9 P.M.–2 A.M., and Sun. 11 A.M.–3 P.M., CUC3), on the west side of Parque Agramonte, hosts traditional music, as does **Galería UNEAC** (Cisneros #159, daily 9 A.M.–6 P.M.).

It's not much by Cuban standards, but the small open-air cabaret at **Centro Nocturno El Colonial** (Agramonte, esq. República, tel. 032/78-5239, daily 10 P.M.–2 A.M., CUC1–2) is followed by disco and is the most popular place in town.

The **Gran Hotel** (Calle Maceo #67, tel. 032/29-2314) hosts a *ballet acuático* at 9 P.M. when there are sufficient guests (free). You half expect the Rat Pack to show up at the hotel's moody piano bar (daily 4 P.M.–2 A.M.). The **Hotel Colón** has a gracious bar, but you'll likely be the only tippler.

Be warned: **El Cambio** (daily 10 A.M.–2 A.M.), on the northeast corner of Parque Agramonte, attracts *jineteros* and *jineteras* on the scrounge.

Live jazz! How cool! The venue is **La Bigonia** (República, esq. Santa Rica, no tel., 8:30 P.M.–2 A.M.), a cheery open-air bar with jazz on Saturday nights (CUC3) and recorded music on other nights.

The world-acclaimed Ballet de Camagüey performs at the **Teatro Principal** (Padre Valencia #64, tel. 32/29-3048), dating to 1850 and where notables such as Enrico Caruso once sang.

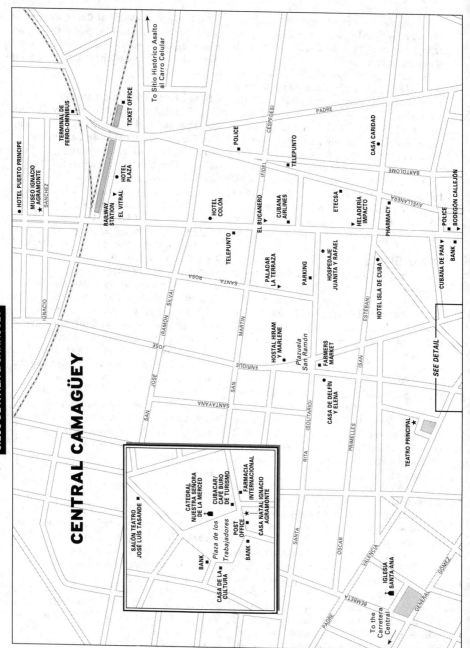

CENTRAL CAMAGÜEY

CIEGO DE ÁVILA & CAMAGÜEY

To Sitio Histórico Asalto al Carro Celular

TERMINAL DE FERRO-ÓMNIBUS

TICKET OFFICE

HOTEL PUERTO PRINCIPE

MUSEO IGNACIO AGRAMONTE ★

SANCHEZ

RAILWAY STATION

EL VITRAL ▼

HOTEL PLAZA

HOTEL COLON

PADRE

CESPEDESI

POLICE ■

CASA CARIDAD

TELEPUNTO ■

FIDEL

EL BUCANERO ■

CUBANA AIRLINES ■

ETECSA ■

HELADERÍA IMPACTO ▼

BARTOLOME

AVELLANEDA

PHARMACY ▼

POLICE ■

BODEGÓN CALLEJÓN ■

IGNACIO

TELEPUNTO ■

SANTA ROSA

RAMON SILVA)

JOSE

PALADAR LA TERRAZA ■

PARKING ■

HOSPEDAJE JUANITA Y RAFAEL ■

HOTEL ISLA DE CUBA ●

CUBANA DE PAN ▼

BANK ■

MARTIN

ENRIQUE

SAN

HOSTAL HIRAM Y MARLENE ■

Plazuela San Ramón

FARMERS MARKET ■

ESTEBAN

SAN

SEE DETAIL

SANTAYANA

JOSE

SAN

RITA (SOLITARIO)

CASA DE DELFIN Y ELENA ●

PRIMELLES

SAN

TEATRO PRINCIPAL ★

SALÓN TEATRO JOSÉ LUÍS TASANDE ■

CASA DE LA CULTURA ■

BANK ■

Plaza de los Trabajadores

POST OFFICE

BANK ■

CATEDRAL NUESTRA SEÑORA DE LA MERCED ■

CUBACAR/ CAFÉ BURÓ DE TURISMO

FARMACIA INTERNACIONAL

CASA NATAL IGNACIO AGRAMONTE ★

SANTA

OSCAR

VALENCIA

GOMEZ

BEMBETA

PADRE

IGLESIA SANTA ANA ♦

GENERAL

To the Carretera Central

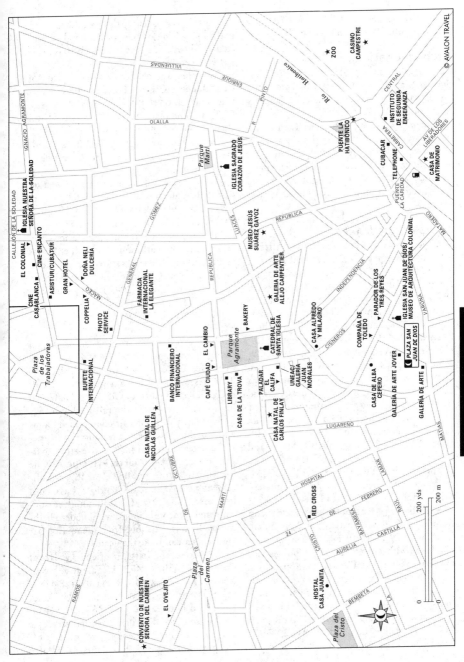

CIEGO DE ÁVILA & CAMAGÜEY

Baseball games are held at the **Estadio Cándido González** October–May.

Accommodations

No *campismos* in the province were taking foreigners at my last visit; check with **Campismo Popular** (Av. de la Libertad #208, e/ Pancha y Agramonte, tel. 032/29-6855).

Warning: Jineteros on bicycles (and scooters) accost tourists arriving in the city and will pursue you relentlessly to guide you to *casas particulares,* in which case you'll have to pay a commission. If you have this guidebook, you don't need them, but they're as hard as fleas to get rid of.

CASAS PARTICULARES

I enjoyed a stay at **Casa Particular Alfredo y Milagro** (Cisneros #124, e/ Raúl Lamar y Padre Olallo, tel. 032/29-7436, allan.carnot@ gmail.com, CUC20), a huge, nicely furnished 1950s house with a pleasant host. Two spacious rooms open to a patio. The son offers massage. A lush patio garden is also a highlight at **Casa Caridad** (Calle Oscar Primelles #310A e/ Bartolomé Masó y Padre Olallo, tel. 032/29-1554, abreucmg@enet.cu, CUC20), where two identical bedrooms with private bathrooms open to an atrium corridor. Hostess Caridad treated me as if she were a doting mom.

Hospedaje Juanita y Rafael (Santa Rita #13, e/ República y Santa Rosa, tel. 032/28-1995, CUC15–20) is beautifully kept and offers a sunlit, breezy lounge filled with contemporary art. The owners rent two spacious, modestly furnished rooms with modern bathrooms.

A standout, **◖ Hostal Hiram y Iraida** (San Ramón #216, e/ Santa Rita y San Martín, tel. 032/24-1662, CUC20) is a charming colonial home with a nicely furnished lounge with modern sofa set and TV, and that opens to a handsome garden with *tinajones*. Two spacious air-conditioned rooms face the garden and have modern bathrooms. It has parking. I enjoyed a stay at **Casa de Delfín y Elena** (San Ramón #171, e/ Primelles y Solitario, tel. 032/29-7262, casadelfinyelena@yahoo.es, CUC20–25), with

two spacious rooms with fans and modern bathrooms. The owner speaks English and Italian; ask Elena to make her delicious *arroz dulce* (sweet rice dessert).

Two other colonial homes I like are **Hostal Casa Juanita** (Cristo #186, e/ Bembeta y Santa Catalina, tel. 032/28-5620, yokivis@terra.es, CUC20), one block east of Plaza Cristo, and **Casa de Alba Cepero** (San Juan de Dios #63, e/ Ángel y San Domingo, tel. 032/29-2572, albita_cepero@yahoo.es, CUC20–25), off Plaza San Juan de Dios.

Handily close to the bus station, **Casa de Gardenia Valero** (Carretera Central #515, e/ Argentina y 2da, tel. 032/27-1203, CUC20) is a splendid middle-class home with two air-conditioned rooms with fans and private hot-water bathrooms; one bathroom is a stunner. It has secure parking. **Casa de Isidro** (Calle Victoria #6, e/ Carretera Central Este y General Reeve, tel. 032/27-1614, CUC20–25) is a virtual carbon copy.

HOTELS

All hotels in town are run by Islazul. Good enough for a night, **Hotel Plaza** (Van Horne #1, e/ República y Avellaneda, tel. 032/28-2413, reservas@hplaza.camaguey.cu, CUC19 s, CUC28 d low season, CUC21 s, CUC30 d high season), opposite the rail station, offers 67 adequately furnished air-conditioned rooms with satellite TVs. It has a restaurant.

Refurbished in 2008, the five-story, bargain-priced **Hotel Puerto Principe** (Av. de los Mártires #60, tel. 032/28-2469, rpublicas@hpp.camaguey.cu, CUC16 s, CUC24 d low season, CUC21 s, CUC30 d high season) has simple yet comfy rooms with modern bathrooms. Be warned: Noise from the rooftop bar and cabaret can wake the dead.

Far better, the bargain-priced **◖ Hotel Colón** (República #472, e/ San José y San Martín, tel. 032/25-4878, fax 032/28-1188, reservas@hcolon.camaguey.cu, CUC32 s, CUC38 d low season, CUC36 s, CUC40 d high season including breakfast) has served as a hotel since 1927. Splendidly restored, it offers gleaming hardwoods, colonial tiles, lofty ceilings, and elegant furnishings. The 48 air-conditioned rooms (one is for travelers with disabilities) have satellite TVs and modern bathrooms. It has an atmospheric lobby bar and fine restaurant.

For location, you can't beat the **Gran Hotel** (Calle Maceo #64, e/ Gómez y Agramonte, tel. 032/29-2314, fax 032/29-9333, reserva@hgh. camaguey.cu, CUC29 s, CUC38 d low season, CUC38 s, CUC48 d high season, including breakfast). This restored 18th-century hotel features dark antiques and has 72 lofty-ceilinged rooms with modern bathrooms. A swimming pool and piano bar are highlights.

The Soviet-style, 142-room **Hotel Camagüey** (Carretera Central Este, Km 4.5, tel. 032/28-7267, jcarpeta@hotelcamaguey. co.cu, CUC21 s, CUC30 d low season, CUC25 s, CUC40 d high season), although nicely refurbished, can't compete for location. It's there if you need it, as is **Hotel Isla de Cuba** (Oscar Primelles #453, esq. Popular, tel. 032/29-2248, fax 032/25-7023, recepcion@ islacuba.co.cu).

Food

The powers that be have been busy opening new restaurants the past few years. Thank goodness! The best newcomer is **Restaurant Isabella** (Ignacio Agramonte, tel. 032/24-2925, Mon.–Fri. 11 A.M.–10 P.M. and Sat.–Sun. 11 A.M.–11 P.M.), 50 meters east of Plaza de los Trabajadores. Stylishly contemporary, this Italian restaurant plays up the movie theme with posters. The menu has spaghetti, prosciutto, and other staples, all below CUC5.

Prefer Spanish? Head to **Bodegón Callejón** (República, esq. Callejón de la Soledad, tel. 032/29-1961, daily 11 A.M.–11 P.M.), where Spanish flags, thick *taberna* benches and tables, plus tapas (below CUC2) and paella (CUC6.50) whisk you allegorically to Iberia.

The **Restaurante Santa María** (República #472, tel. 032/28-3368, daily 7–9:45 A.M., noon–2:30 P.M., and 7–9:30 P.M.), in the Hotel Colón, offers a modicum of elegance by which to enjoy (perhaps) spaghetti or roast chicken. Another good bet is the elegant rooftop restaurant of the **Gran Hotel** (Calle Maceo #64, e/

© CHRISTOPHER P. BAKER

El Ovejito restaurant, Camagüey

Gómez y Agramonte, tel. 032/29-2314, 7 A.M.– 9:30 P.M.), where a lobster enchilada costs CUC6 and a buffet dinner costs CUC10.

The only *paladar* of note is the atmospheric **Paladar La Terraza** (Santa Rosa #8, e/ San Estebán y San Martín, tel. 032/29-8705, 11 A.M.–midnight daily), which has a wood-paneled bar and, upstairs, an breeze-kissed open-sided eatery serving *criollo* fare.

Although it caters to tour groups, **Campaña de Toledo** (Plaza San Juan de Dios, tel. 032/28-6812, daily 10 A.M.–10 P.M.) is lent colonial ambience by terra-cotta tile floors and rustic furniture. Try the lamb soup (CUC1.20) and the house dish, *boliche mechado,* of beef stuffed with bacon (CUC6). Equally atmospheric **El Ovejito** (Hermano Aguero #280, tel. 032/29-2524, Wed.–Sun. noon–9:30 P.M.), on Plaza del Carmen, specializes in lamb and pork dishes (CUC7–15).

Penny pinching? Pork dishes will cost you mere pennies in *moneda nacional* at **El Bucanero** (República e/ San Martín y Santa Rita, tel. 032/25-3413, 24 hours), a pirate-themed bar-restaurant.

Coppelia (Independencia, e/ Agramonte y Gómez, Mon.–Fri. 9 A.M.–9 P.M., Sat.–Sun. 10 A.M.–10 P.M.) serves ice cream for pesos.

Showing Starbucks a thing or two, the **((Café Ciudad** (tel. 032/25-8512, daily 10 A.M.–10 P.M.) is on the northwest corner of Plaza Agramonte. This lovely coffee shop occupies a marvelous colonial building adorned with massive sepia lithographs—a tremendous venue for cappuccinos (CUC1.20), hot chocolate, coffees, and teas.

You can buy baked goods for dollars at **Panadería Doña Neli** (Maceo, daily 8 A.M.–9 P.M.), opposite the Gran Hotel. You can buy produce from the *mercado agropecuario* (Matadero, daily 7 A.M.–6 P.M.).

Information and Services

Infotur (tel. 032/26-5807, infocmg@enet.cu) has an impressive tour bureau at the airport.

The **post office** (Agramonte #461, esq. Cisneros, tel. 032/29-3958, 8 A.M.–5 P.M.), on the south side of Plaza de los Trabajadores, has

DHL service. Etecsa (Avellada, e/ San Martín y Primelles, daily 8:30 A.M.–7:30 P.M.) has international telephone and Internet service.

Banks include **Bandec** (Plaza de los Trabajadores; and República, one block north of Ignacio Agramonte) and **Banco Financiero Internacional** (Independencia, on Parque Maceo). You can also change foreign currency at **Cadeca** (República #353, e/ Primelles y Solitario, Mon.–Sat. 8:30 A.M.–6 P.M., Sun. 8:30 A.M.–1 P.M.). Most banks are open Mon.–Fri. 8 A.M.–3:30 P.M., Sat. 8 A.M.–1 P.M.

Hospital Provincial (Carretera Central, Km 4.5, tel. 032/28-2012) is west of town. **Farmacia Internacional** (Agramonte, 20 meters east of Plaza de los Trabajadores; and Maceo, e/ Gómez y Parque Maceo, Mon.–Fri. 9 A.M.–5 P.M., Sat. 9 A.M.–1 P.M.) stocks imported medicines, but hours are unreliable.

Consultoría Jurídica Internacional (Joaquín de Agüero #166, e/ Tomás Betancourt y Julio Sanguily, Rpto. La Vigía, tel. 032/28-3159) offers legal assistance. **Asistur** (Agramonte #449, e/ López Recio e Independencia, tel. 032/28-6317, asisturcmg@enet.cu, Mon.–Fri. 8 A.M.–5 P.M., Sat. 8 A.M.–1 P.M.) assists travelers in distress.

Getting There and Away
BY AIR

The **Ignacio Agramonte Airport** (tel. 032/26-1000 and 032/26-7154) is 14 kilometers northeast of the city. A taxi costs about CUC8. **Cubana** (República #400, esq. Correa, Camagüey, tel. 032/29-2156) flies from Havana.

BY BUS

The **Terminal de Ómnibuses Intermunicipales** (Carretera Central Oeste, esq. Perú, tel. 032/27-2480) is two kilometers southeast of town. **Víazul** buses (tel. 032/27-0396) between Havana and Santiago de Cuba stop at Camagüey. Eastbound buses depart Camagüey for Holguín at 4 P.M. and 5:25 P.M., for Santiago de Cuba at midnight, 1:25, 5:35, and 6:16 A.M., and 1:20 and 6:25 P.M. Westbound buses depart Camagüey for Havana at 12:10

and 3:25 A.M., and 12:35, 4:30, 10:45, and 11:20 P.M., for Trinidad at 2:15 A.M., and for Varadero at 2:50 A.M.

Buses and *camiones* to provincial destinations depart from the **Terminal de Municipales** (tel. 0322/28-1525), adjoining the train station.

BY TRAIN

The railway station is at the north end of Avellaneda; the ticket office (tel. 032/28-5937) is at the east end of the station. All trains on the Havana–Santiago de Cuba route stop in Camagüey. In addition, train #23 departs Havana for Camagüey at noon, and #9 departs at 10:15 P.M. Trains depart Morón for Camagüey at 3:15 A.M. and 12:55 P.M. Westbound trains depart Camagüey for Havana (CUC32 *especial,* CUC19 *regular*) at 12:27 A.M. (express), 6:10 A.M., 6:37 A.M., 3:38 P.M., and 8:25 P.M., and for Morón at 3:20 P.M. and 6:15 P.M. Eastbound trains depart Camagüey for Bayamo at 10:35 P.M., Guantánamo at 4:35 A.M., and Santiago de Cuba (CUC16 *especial,* CUC11 *regular*) at 3:09 A.M. and 7:59 A.M.

The **Terminal de Ferro-Ómnibus** (tel. 032/28-7525), adjacent to the main station, serves local destinations. Trains depart for Santa Cruz del Sur (CUC3) at 5:45 A.M. (return trains depart Santa Cruz at 3:15 P.M.).

Getting Around

You'll find *coches* outside the rail station and on República; *bici-taxis* ply the streets. For a taxi, call **Cubataxi** (tel. 032/28-1245).

You can rent cars from **Havanautos** (Independencia, esq. Martí, tel. 032/27-2239, and at the airport, tel. 032/28-7067); **Cubacar** (tel. 032/28-5327, in the Café Buro de Turismo on the southeast side of Plaza de los Trabajadores and on the Carretera Central, esq. Av. de los Libertadores); and both **Rex** (tel. 032/26-2444) and **Vía** (tel. 032/24-2498) at the airport.

There are gas stations on the Carretera Central, just west of Puente La Caridad; outside town, on the road to Nuevitas; and at Carretera Central, corner of General Gómez.

Both **Cubatur** (Agramonte #421, e/ Independencia y República, tel. 032/25-4785) and **Havanatur** (tel. 0322/28-8604) offer excursions. **EcoTur** (Calle Céspedes, e/ C y Carretera Central, tel. 032/27-4951, ecotur@ caonao.cu) offers ecotourism excursions.

ÁREA PROTEGIDA DE RECURSOS MANEJADOS SIERRA DEL CHORRILLO

Southeast of Camagüey is an upland area—the Sierra Chorrillo—marked by *mogotes.* The formations lie within the 4,115-hectare Sierra del Chorrillo Managed Resources Protected Area, about 13 kilometers south of the community of Najasa, 43 kilometers southeast of Camagüey. The reserve has two distinct regions: semideciduous woodland and tropical montane forest, plus Cuba's only fossil forest. It protects 110 species of higher plants, a rare endemic cactus, large numbers of *jutías,* and at least 80 bird species, including parrots and *tocororos.*

◖ Finca La Belén

From the entrance, on the south side of the community of El Pilar, a dirt track winds two kilometers uphill to this working farm, where zebu and other exotic cattle species are raised. There are even zebras and various species of antelope (previously raised for the hunting pleasure of Communist bigwigs). Hiking trails lead to mineral springs with pools. Horseback riding (two hours CUC5), show-jumping (CUC7), and guided bird-watching (CUC17) to "Casa Perico" (a peasant home with animals) are offered.

ACCOMMODATIONS

The reserve has a surprisingly modern hotel, ◖ **Motel La Belén** (tel. 032/86-4349, CUC28 s, CUC40 d including breakfast), with a swimming pool, TV lounge, and 10 modern and spacious air-conditioned rooms with modern bathrooms. Its rustic restaurant specializes in meals of antelope. A tent-camp is to be added.

Tours and reservations are handled through **EcoTur** (tel. 032/27-4995, ecotur@caonao.cu).

zebras at Finca La Belén, Camagüey

GUÁIMARO

This small town, straddling the Carretera Central 65 kilometers east of Camagüey, has an intriguing granite column in the town square, **Parque Constitución.** The monument—with bronze bas-reliefs of various heroes of the Wars of Independence—commemorates the opening in April 1869 of the Constitutional Assembly, where the first Cuban constitution was drafted, Carlos Manuel de Céspedes was elected president of the Free Republic of Cuba, and the abolition of slavery was decreed. The building where the 1869 Assembly was held today houses the **Museo Histórico de Guáimaro.**

Between Camagüey and Guáimaro, **Sitio Histórico Ingenio Oriente,** an old sugar mill where General Ignacio Agramonte launched his first attack of the War of Independence in 1868, is promoted along the Carretera Central. Beginning two kilometers east of Sibanicú and eight kilometers west of Guáimaro, it's a 14-kilometer drive along a dirt track to the community of Oriente Rebelde, but the site is of interest only to serious historians.

MINAS

The small town of Minas, 37 kilometers northeast of Camagüey, is known for its **Fábrica de Instrumentos Musicales** (tel. 032/69-6232, Mon.–Fri. 7 A.M.–2 P.M., Sat. 7–11 A.M., free), at the south end of town. Workers turn native hardwoods into elegantly curved violins, violas, cellos, and guitars. The quality isn't the best, but it's a fascinating visit.

There's a **Criadero de Cocodrilos** (daily 7 A.M.–4 P.M., CUC2), or crocodile farm, outside Senado, about 10 kilometers northwest of Minas, on the road to Sola. This farm raises the American crocodile for leather. Divert in Senado to the derelict sugar factory, where a 19th-century steam train—*Elizabet*—stands outside.

Ingenio de Santa Isabel, roadside about 15 kilometers east of Minas on the road to Santa Lucía, is the ruins of a historic sugar mill; it has a pleasant café under shade trees.

The Camagüey–Nuevitas trains stop at Minas.

North Coast of Camagüey

The Circuito Norte coast road runs west–east about 10 kilometers inland of the coast. Floating offshore, **Cayo Romano** is the largest cay in the Archipiélago de Camagüey. It and dozens of other cays sprinkled like stardust offshore are deserted and have no facilities, despite translucent waters and reefs that provide some of the best snorkeling and diving in the hemisphere. The government's tourism master plan contemplates 4,700 hotel rooms.

Cayo Romano is accessed via the town of Brasil, from where a road leads north 5 kilometers to a 12-kilometer-long *pedraplén* that leapfrogs to Cayo Romano and, beyond, Cayo Cruz. There's a military checkpoint. You'll need your passport. Permission to access the cay is never guaranteed. **EcoTur** (tel. 032/27-4995 or 07/641-0306, www.ecoturcuba.co.cu) offers guided fishing trips to Cayo Cruz.

■ CAYO SABINAL

Cayo Sabinal is the easternmost cay in the archipelago and one of my favorites. It is attached to the north coast of Camagüey by a hair's-breadth isthmus and encloses the flask-shaped Bahía de Nuevitas. This virginal isle has 33 kilometers of beaches protected by coral reefs, within one kilometer of shore; the turquoise shallows can be waded.

In all your explorations, you will pass only a couple of military posts (these cays are favored as a drop-off and pickup point by international drug smugglers; visitors usually receive a thorough search by the Guardia Frontera) and no more than a half dozen humble *bohíos* belonging to impoverished charcoal-burners and fisherfolk. There are plenty of birds and iguanas, and wild pigs called *jabalí*, a relative of the peccary. Flamingos wade in the shallows of **Laguna de los Flamencos.**

At the far eastern end of Cayo Sabinal is a lighthouse—**Faro Colón**—built in 1850, and an even older fortress—**Fuerte San Hilario**—built to protect the entrance to Bahía de Nuevitas.

The best place to spend your time is the fantastically lonesome **Playa Los Pinos.** Occasionally a small tour group may arrive for a day visit from Santa Lucía, but it's more likely you will have the place to yourself.

Bring insect repellent!

Accommodations and Food

The Cuban government reckons Sabinal has a potential capacity for 12,000 hotel rooms. Ouch! For now, there is nowhere to stay. Rustic huts at ■ **Restaurante Playas Los Pinos** were destroyed by a hurricane in 2008. Simple seafood dishes are made to order.

Your only option for miles is Islazul's no-frills **Hotel Caonaba** (tel. 032/24-4803, CUC14 s, CUC19 d low season, CUC19 s, CUC24 d high season), 100 meters east of the gas station at the entrance to Nuevitas.

Getting There

Cayo Sabinal is reached via a bridge over the Ensenada de Sabinal, where there's a military checkpoint (you'll need your passport). The gate is usually locked; honk your horn to summon the guard, or retreat 200 yards and drive down to the guard post visible on the flat. Your car will be thoroughly searched coming and going. A CUC5 entrance charge is collected about 600 meters beyond the gate. After a few miles you reach a crossroad. Playa Brava is straight ahead; Playa Los Pinos is about six kilometers to the right (alternatively, drive straight to the shore and turn right for Playa Los Pinos). In places, the narrow tracks are smothered in sand. The going can be challenging after heavy rains, when a four-wheel drive would be wise.

Driving, you'll have to route through the port town of Nuevitas, 12 kilometers north of the Circuito Norte and 65 kilometers northeast of Camagüey. Nuevitas is linked to Sabinal via a road of hard-packed dirt and rock that runs along the western shore of the Bahía de Nuevitas.

Trains depart Camagüey for Nuevitas.

PLAYA SANTA LUCÍA

Popular with budget-oriented German, Italian, and Canadian charter groups, Playa Santa Lucía, 110 kilometers east of Camagüey, 85 kilometers north of Las Tunas, and 20 kilometers north of the Circuito Norte (the turnoff is just north and west of Camalote, about 30 kilometers east of Nuevitas), is touted as a major resort destination. Forget the hype! Santa Lucía is a tacky ugly duckling with minimal infrastructure and zero pizzazz. The meager facilities spread out over several kilometers, with stretches of grassy nothingness between them. What Santa Lucía *does* have is an astounding 20 kilometers of beach protected by an offshore coral reef. *The only reason to visit is for the diving.*

The shorefront road extends west of Santa Lucía to a funky fishing hamlet—**La Boca**— with its own beach, **Playa Los Cocos,** with atmospheric restaurants, plus toilets and showers. The mood is far superior to that of Santa Lucía. The dirt road to La Boca is full of deep pools and mud; a four-wheel drive is recommended.

Mangrove-lined **Laguna Daniel** and **Laguna El Real** form a swampy morass inland of the shore. Flamingos occasionally flock to wallow by day, then take off in a flash of bright pink at dusk.

In 2008, Hurricane Ike trashed Rancho King, a cattle ranch on the Circuito Norte about seven kilometers west of the junction for Santa Lucía. It was once owned by the owners of the famous King Ranch in Texas. The Castro regime expropriated the property, which previously offered horseback riding and let you watch *vaqueros* herding cattle and riding bucking broncos. It remained closed at last visit.

Entertainment and Events

Major hotels have theme night *animaciones* (entertainment); you can buy a night pass for most hotels (about CUC25). To shake some booty, head to **La Jungla** (daily 11:30 P.M.–2 A.M., CUC5), a little thatched beachside disco at

Oasis Brisas Santa Lucía, or to **Mar Verde** (daily 10:30 P.M.–2 A.M., CUC1), where you can mingle with Cubans.

◖ Scuba Diving

Scuba diving is superb. The warm waters support dozens of coral and fish species. And the mouth of the Bahía de Nuevitas is a graveyard of ships, including the steamship *Mortera,* which sank in 1898, its prow resting at a depth of 20 feet. Diving (including resort, certification, and specialized courses) is offered from **Shark's Friend Dive Center** (tel./fax 032/36-5182, shark_friend@nautica. stl.tur.cu), between Brisas and Hotel Club Santa Lucía, with dive trips daily at 9 A.M. and 1 P.M. (CUC30, CUC40 night dive). It has a "shark show" in which you can witness sharks being hand fed (CUC65), plus snorkeling trips (CUC20).

Other Recreation

Marlin Náutico (tel. 032/33-6404), at the west end of the beach, offers fishing (three hours, CUC204 for four people) and catamaran rentals.

Horseback rides are offered at Playa Los Cocos.

Accommodations

Cubanacán runs most hotels (and badly at that), all having air-conditioned rooms with satellite TV.

Campismo Popular Punta de Ganado (tel. 032/36289), about three kilometers east of the roundabout at the entrance to Santa Lucía, is a basic facility for Cubans. It is often closed. Inquire through the **Campismo Popular** (Av. de la Libertad #208, e/ Pancha y Agramonte, tel. 032/29-6855) in Camagüey.

Basic and barebones describes Formatur's overpriced **Hotel Escuela Santa Lucía** (tel. 032/33-6310, fax 032/36-5166, CUC25 s, CUC35 d year-round), a motel-style training hotel. Sure, the 31 air-conditioned rooms have satellite TVs and small modern bathrooms, but that's the best that can be said for this sadly deteriorated place.

Far better is Islazul's **《 Hotel Costa Blanca** (Rpto. Residencial district, tel. 032/33-6373), two kilometers east of the main hotel zone. Opened only in 2009, it has 12 rooms (CUC14 s, CUC22 d year-round) and 16 one-to four-room villas (CUC20–43), all with modern bathrooms and accoutrements, plus a pleasant restaurant. Talk about a bargain!

The ho-hum, Soviet-style, all-inclusive **Club Amigo Mayanabo** (tel. 032/36-5168, fax 032/36-5176, www.hotelescubanacan. com, from CUC45 s, CUC56 d low season, from CUC78 s, CUC98 d high season) has 213 rooms and 12 suites with balconies (first floor only) and king-size or twin beds. There's a tennis court, attractive swimming pool, water sports, plus a nightclub. Its equally undatable Siamese twin is the **Club Amigo Caracol** (tel. 032/36-5158).

Hotel Gran Club Santa Lucía (tel. 032/33-6109, fax 032/36-5153, www.hotelescubanacan.com, from CUC45 s, CUC90 d low season, from CUC65 s, CUC115 d high season) has 252 minimally furnished air-conditioned rooms spread around unkempt grounds. The raised pool with thatched bar is attractive, however, and the elegant buffet restaurant has reasonable fare.

The classiest option, albeit still only two-star in my book, is the overpriced **Oasis Brisas Santa Lucía** (tel. 032/33-6317, fax 032/36-5142, aloja@brisas.stl.cyt.cu, CUC70 s, CUC90 d low season, CUC96 s, CUC120 d high season), a modern, 214-room all-inclusive low-rise combining a contemporary design with traditional thatch. At its heart is a pleasant swimming pool, and it has entertainment, water sports, etc.

Food

There are few other options beyond the dismal hotel restaurants. The Italian-themed beachfront **Restaurante Luna Mar,** in the Centro Comercial Villa Vientos, serves spaghetti and pizzas (CUC4–9) plus seafood.

At Playa Los Cocos, **Bar y Restaurante Bucanero** (daily 9 A.M.–6 P.M.) plays on a pirate theme and serves seafood and *criollo* fare, including lobster (CUC12).

Information and Services

Etecsa (tel. 032/33-6126, daily 8:30 A.M.–7:30 P.M.), next to the gas station at the east end of Santa Lucía, has international telephone and Internet service.

Bandec (Mon.–Fri. 8 A.M.–3:30 P.M., Sat. 8 A.M.–1 P.M.) has a branch on the coast road, 1.5 kilometers east of the tourist center. A **Clínica Internacional** (tel. 032/33-6370, 24 hours) is 200 meters farther east; the Gran Club and Brisas hotels have pharmacies. The police station is 400 meters west of the bank.

Getting There and Around

International charter flights arrive at the Camagüey and Las Tunas airports. A taxi from Camagüey will cost about CUC50 one-way.

Buses operate from Las Tunas and Camagüey (CUC10).

You can rent cars at the hotels and from **Cubacar** (tel. 032/36368), next to Oasis Brisas Santa Lucía.

Cubatur (tel. 032/33-5383) and **Cubanacán** (tel. 032/33-6404) offer excursions, including catamaran trips and to Santiago (CUC20) and Bayamo (CUC18).

Coches ply the shorefront strip (CUC2 between points, or CUC5 one hour). You can rent bicycles and scooters at the hotels.

CIEGO DE ÁVILA & CAMAGÜEY

LAS TUNAS AND HOLGUÍN

Rich in history, physically diverse, and on the cusp of major tourist development, this region is as interesting as any in the nation. Holguín, rather than Las Tunas, steals the show.

Las Tunas Province forms a flat, narrow band across the island, broadening to the northeast. The capital city occupies a low-lying ridge on the eastern edge of the great plains that dominate central Cuba. It is dull, unvarying terrain, mostly farmed for cattle. The scenery begins to grow more lush and interesting eastward. The province has few beaches (at last visit, only Playa Covarrubias had a hotel), and there are few sites of interest other than a modicum of historic buildings in the eponymous provincial capital.

Holguín, by contrast, is chock-full of things to see and do. The capital city itself boasts several colonial plazas and an active nightlife, and

the hinterlands have several unique sites, foremost among them Fidel Castro's birthplace. Holguín's north-central shore is in the throes of touristic development, centered on Playas Guardalavaca and Pesquero. Long-term plans call for a golf course, cruise port, and even a theme park. Inland, the dramatic formations of the Grupo de Maniabon will have you reaching for your camera, and there are pre-Columbian museums and archaeological sites to explore.

East of Holguín city, the coastal plain narrows down to a panhandle extending along the shore at the base of the Sierra de Nipe, Sierra del Cristal, Cuchillas del Toa, and Alturas de Moa. These mountains are nirvana to bird-watchers and hikers. The color of heated chrome, the mountains are also rich in cobalt, manganese, and nickel. The ores are processed at the

© CHRISTOPHER P. BAKER

HIGHLIGHTS

Plaza Calixto García: The largest of Holguín's three plazas, this one is home to two museums of note (page 392).

Gibara: This laid-back fishing town with fine colonial architecture makes a cool place to steep in Cuban culture (page 401).

Guardalavaca: The scorching beaches, magnificent teal-blue waters, and fabulous diving offshore could keep you plenty happy, but be sure to make time for Museo Aborigen Chorro de Maíta, an excellent small museum

and archaeological site recording pre-Columbian culture (page 403).

Museo Conjunto Histórico Birán: Fidel's birthplace and childhood home provides fascinating insight into the boyhood background of Cuba's enigmatic leader (page 408).

Pinares de Mayarí: Crisp mountain air, pine forests, and gorgeous waterfalls tempt birders and hikers to this alpine retreat formerly reserved for the Communist elite (page 409).

LOOK FOR ◖ TO FIND RECOMMENDED SIGHTS, ACTIVITIES, DINING, AND LODGING.

coastal town of Moa, in the far east of Holguín Province; the immediate area is blighted by the mineral extraction industry, which may be the main reason for the prohibition on photography hereabouts.

The southern coastal plains of Las Tunas are farmed in sugar, merging eventually into mangrove swamplands. Southern Holguín Province is flat as a lake, with savanna and sugar sharing the landscape.

In November 2009, Hurricane Ike came ashore near Gibara, devastating much of the region (more than 70 percent of homes in the area were damaged).

PLANNING YOUR TIME

Basically, Las Tunas is a place to pass through en route to Holguín and Oriente. That said, the city of Las Tunas is worth a quick browse, although one day is more than sufficient. All routes through the province pass through the capital, which has several decent *casas particulares*.

The larger city of Holguín offers considerably more to see, including three plazas and, outside town, the Mirador de Mayabe, where you can buy a beer for a suds-supping donkey. Holguín also has a well-developed cultural scene, with everything from an excellent Casa

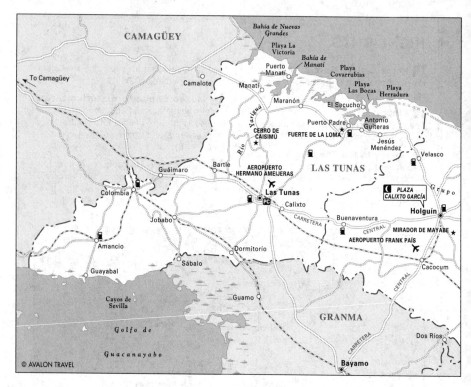

de la Cultura to a bargain-priced cabaret. I recommend a two-day minimum stay.

The seafront town of **Gibara** appeals for its marvelous setting, laid-back lifestyle, and bracing ocean airs. It has an excellent natural history museum and colonial-era *casas particulares.*

The Parque Monumento Nacional Bariay, where Christopher Columbus supposedly first set foot on Cuban soil in 1492, is strongly touted for a half-day visit, with most participants buying into package excursions from the nearby beach resorts. I consider it a waste of money. Far more rewarding is the Museo Aborigen Chorro de Maíta, a pre-Columbian archaeological site; and the similarly focused Museo Indocubano, in Banes. And how about **Museo Conjunto Histórico Birán,** Fidel Castro's birthplace and childhood home?

The beach resort of **Guardalavaca** and

nearby Playa Pesquero are imbued with all-inclusive resorts plus plenty of facilities for trippers on day visits from Holguín. Scuba diving, a dolphin show, and bird-watching, horseback riding, kayaking, and similar activities in Bioparque Rocazul are among the things to do here. You can even take a ride into the Grupo de Maniabon in a 1920 Baldwin steam train.

Birders and hikers should head for **Pinares de Mayarí,** a crisp alpine retreat in the Sierra de Nipe, where the Salto El Guayabo waterfall is not to be missed; or to Cayo Saetía, where the wildlife-viewing is surreal (think camels and zebra).

The Carretera Central cuts through the center of the provinces. At Holguín, it turns southwest for Bayamo, in Granma Province. If heading from Camagüey direct to Granma Province and Santiago, you can bypass Holguín via a paved road that leads southeast from Las

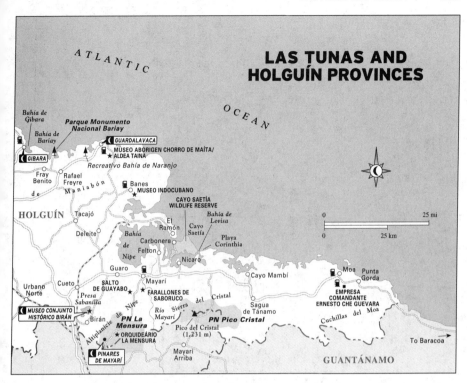

LAS TUNAS AND HOLGUÍN PROVINCES

Tunas to Bayamo and cuts across the Río Cauto plains via the town of Jobabo.

The Circuito Norte runs inland of the Las Tunas coast road and, east of Jesús Menéndez, turns inland for Holguín, beyond which it continues east along the coast for Baracoa and Guantánamo Province. Other roads radiate out from Holguín to Gibara, Guardalavaca, and Banes. East of Moa, much of the Circuito Norte is badly deteriorated.

Víazul buses and Havana–Santiago trains call at Las Tunas and Holguín.

Las Tunas and Vicinity

LAS TUNAS

Las Tunas (pop. 80,000) is a small-time capital of a small-time province. The town is officially known as La Victoria de las Tunas, a name bequeathed by the Spanish governor in 1869 to celebrate a victory in the War of Independence. Patriots under General Vicente García recaptured the town in 1895. Two years later, it was put to the torch by rebels as Spanish forces attempted to retake it. Alas, the fire destroyed many buildings and the town today lacks edifices of architectural note.

Las Tunas (nicknamed "City of Sculptures") is famed for its terra-cotta ceramics, expressed in contemporary art scattered all over the city. Look for works by some of Cuba's leading artists, such as *Liberation of the People* by Manuel Chong, opposite the Asamblea Provincial.

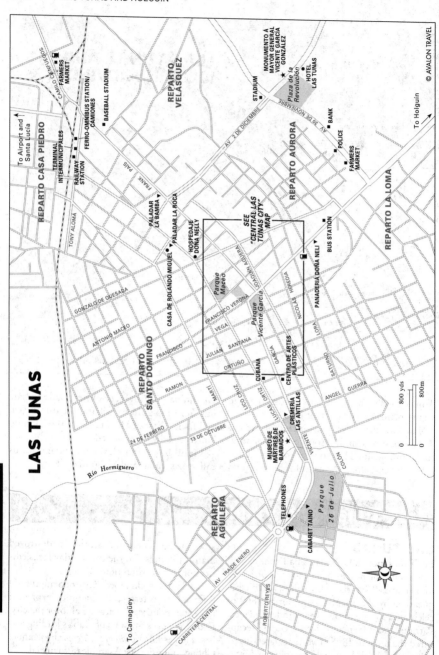

LAS TUNAS

© AVALON TRAVEL

LAS TUNAS & HOLGUÍN

Orientation

The town sits astride the Carretera Central, which enters from the west along Avenida 1ro de Enero, becomes Avenida Vicente García, and slopes up to the central square—Parque Vicente García—where it turns 90 degrees and runs southeast for Holguín as Calle Francisco Verona. A *circunvalación* bypasses the town.

The historic core is laid out in a grid centered on Parque García, at the top of Vicente García, between Calles Francisco Varona and Francisco Vega. Ángel de la Guardia runs northeast to the railway station, where it forks for the airport and Puerto Padre, on the north coast.

Museo de Mártires de Barbados

The Museum to the Martyrs of Barbados (Luca Ortíz #344, tel. 031/34-7213, Tues.– Sat. 11 A.M.–7 P.M., Sun. 8 A.M.–noon, free), at the base of Vicente García, occupies a small wooden house where lived Carlos Leyva González, Cuba's champion *florete* (fencer). Leyva died, along with his brother and the entire Cuban fencing team, when Cubana flight CUT-1201 was destroyed by a bomb en route to Georgetown, Barbados, on October 6, 1976. In all, 73 people died, including 57 Cubans, 5 Koreans, and 11 Guyanese. Right-wing Cuban-American exile Otto Bosch was convicted, but he was pardoned by President George H. W. Bush and is hailed as a hero by extremist Cuban-Americans.

The museum displays a dramatic sculpture of an arm and clenched fist (like a fencer's clutching a foil) made from wreckage of the doomed aircraft.

Parque Vicente García

The town's main square, at the top of Avenida Vicente García, features a marble statue of the local hero, Major General Vicente García González, who burned the city rather than let it fall into Spanish hands. On the southwest corner is a small church. On the park's northeast corner, separated by Calle Colón, is the petite **Plaza Martiana de las Tunas,** with a contemporary sculpture of José Martí and a massive sundial.

The **Centro Histórico** (Francisco Verona, esq. Vicente García, tel. 031/34-8201), on the northwest corner, features meager exhibits on local history. Note the ceramic bas-relief map of the city on its wall. Cater-corner, the **Museo Provincial** (Francisco Varona and Vicente García, tel. 031/34-8201, Tues.–Sat. 1–9 P.M., Sun. 8 A.M.–noon, free) has an exhibition about Juan Cristóbal Nápoles Fajardo (1829–1862), nicknamed "El Cucalambé," a 19th-century poet known for his 10-syllable rhyming songs called *décimas.*

One block south of the park, **Casa del Vicente García González** (Vicente García #5, tel. 031/34-5164, Tues.–Sat. 9 A.M.–6 P.M., Sun. 8 A.M.–noon, CUC1) is where, on September 26, 1876, General Vicente García purportedly began the fire that burned the city. The building, which miraculously survived, is now a museum commemorating the Wars of Independence, the story of García, and the battles for Las Tunas.

Plaza de la Revolución

The ungainly Revolution Plaza, on the northeast side of town, is dominated by the huge **Monumento a Mayor General Vicente**

© CHRISTOPHER P. BAKER

LAS TUNAS & HOLGUÍN

monument of Vicente García, Las Tunas

LAS TUNAS & HOLGUÍN

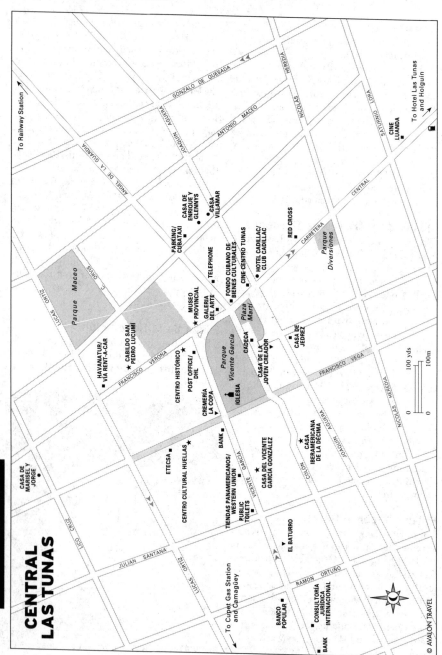

CENTRAL LAS TUNAS

To Railway Station

To Hotel Las Tunas and Holguín

GONZALO DE QUESADA

ANTONIO MACEO

ÁNGEL DE LA GUARDIA

JOAQUÍN AGÜERA

NICOLÁS

HEREDIA

SATURNINO LORA

CINE LUANDA

CENTRAL

CARRETERA

RED CROSS

Parque Diversiones

CASA DE ENRIQUE Y GLENNYS

CASA VILLAMAR

PARKING/ CUBATAXI

TELEPHONE

FONDO CUBANO DE BIENES CULTURALES

CINE CENTRO TUNAS

HOTEL CADILLAC/ CLUB CADILLAC

LUCAS ORTIZ

SIANO 3

Parque Maceo

MUSEO PROVINCIAL

GALERIA DEL ARTE

Plaza Martí

HAVANATUR/ VÍA RENT-A-CAR

CABILDO SAN PEDRO LUCUMÍ

FRANCISCO VERONA

CENTRO HISTÓRICO

POST OFFICE/ DHL

Parque Vicente García

CADECA

CASA DE JEDREZ

CREMERÍA LA COPA

IGLESIA

CASA DE LA JOVEN CREADOR

FRANCISCO VEGA

NICOLÁS

HEREDIA

BANK

ETECSA

CENTRO CULTURAL HUELLAS

TIENDAS PANAMERICANOS/ WESTERN UNION

PUBLIC TOILETS

VICENTE GARCÍA

CASA DEL VICENTE GARCÍA GONZÁLEZ

CASA IBEROAMERICANA DE LA DÉCIMA

COLÓN

JOAQUÍN AGÜERA

CASA DE MARISEL Y JORGE

LUCAS CRUZ

LUCAS ORTIZ

JULIAN SANTANA

EL BATURRO

RAMON ORTUÑO

To Cupet Gas Station and Camagüey

BANCO POPULAR

CONSULTORIA JURÍDICA INTERNACIONAL

BANK

0   100 yds

0   100m

© AVALON TRAVEL

García González, hewn in pink concrete with bas-reliefs showing the local hero of the Wars of Independence with his sword held high. Beneath the monument, the **Salón de los Generales** features bronze busts of other generals in the wars.

Entertainment and Events

Las Tunas hosts the **Jornada Cucalambeana** (Cucalambé Folkloric Festival, tel. 031/34-7770), when songsters from all parts of Cuba honor Nápoles Fajardo. It takes place at Motel El Cornito (tel. 031/34-5015), 10 kilometers west of town, each June or July. At all times of year, the **Casa Iberoamaricana de la Décima** (Calle Colón #161, e/ Francisco Vega y Julian Santana, tel. 031/34-7380, cdecima@tunet.cult.cu) has daily poetry recitals and *peñas.*

The **Feria Interprovincial** agricultural fair in mid-February features rodeos in Parque 26 de Julio, at the base of Vicente García.

Culture vultures can also get a fix of poetry and live music at **Centro Cultural Huellas** (Mon.–Fri. 9 A.M.–5 P.M., Sat. 9 A.M.–noon). The **Cabildo San Pedro Lucumí** (Francisco Verona, e/ Angel Guardia y Lucas Ortíz, tel. 031/34-6461, free) celebrates Afro-Cuban tradition with drumming and dance on Sunday at 9 P.M.

Cabaret Taíno (tel. 031/34-3823), at the base of Vicente García, hosts a *cabaret espectáculo* with crooners and plenty of boas and behinds Saturday at 9 P.M. (35 pesos).

The hottest salsa scene is **Cine Disco Luanda** (Carretera Central, esq. Saturno Lora, tel. 031/34-8671, nightly 10 P.M.–2 A.M., CUC3–5, including drinks), a Western-style disco featuring laser lights. It also has a cinema.

From October to May you can catch a baseball game at **Estadio Julio Antonio Mella,** at the north end of Avenida 2 de Diciembre.

Accommodations

CASAS PARTICULARES

Near the center, **Hospedaje Doña Nelly** (Lucas Ortíz #111, e/ Gonzalo de Quesada y Coronel Fonseca, tel. 031/34-2526, CUC20–25) is a large colonial home with a piano in the lounge, plus an air-conditioned room with a private bathroom. Laundry service is offered.

Casa de Rolando Miguel (Villalón #13, e/ Lucas Ortíz y Lico Cruz, tel. 031/34-2264, CUC15–20) is a pleasant middle-class home with two upstairs air-conditioned rooms, each with fridge and private hot-water bathroom.

Casa de Enrique y Glennys (Villamar #30A altos, e/ Agüero y Guardia, tel. 031/45596, CUC15–25), accessed by a spiral staircase, has a lounge with TV and stereo system, plus a pleasing air-conditioned room with 1950s hardwood furnishings, fridge, and a modern bathroom. There's parking adjacent. If it's full, try **Casa Villamar** (Villamar #30, tel. 031/47245, CUC20), next door.

Casa de Marisel y Jorge (Lico Cruz #188, e/ Francisco Varona y Francisco Vega, tel. 031/34-5533, CUC20–25) has two well-lit, air-conditioned rooms with fans, TVs, and modern bathrooms.

HOTELS

If nondescript neo-Stalinist prefab hotels are your thing, check into Islazul's **Hotel Las Tunas** (tel. 031/34-5014, fax 031/34-3336, reservas@hotellt.co.cu, CUC15 s, CUC20 d low season, CUC23 s, CUC30 d high season), one kilometer east of town on Avenida de 2 Diciembre. It has 142 no-frills air-conditioned rooms.

In 2008, the town finally got a worthwhile hotel. The art deco 【 **Hotel E Cadillac** (Joaquín Agüera esq. Francisco Verona, tel. 031/37-2791, www.islazul.cu, CUC25 s, CUC35 d low season, CUC40 s, CUC50 d high season), built in 1945 in the shape of a slanting, rounded prow with pothole windows, has been rehashed and has eight rooms and two suites with—gasp!—plasma TVs, sleek modern bathrooms, and stylish (albeit cheap) modern furniture.

Food

The best private dining option is **Paladar El Balcón** (Calle Fernando Suárez #14, tel. 031/34-9312, daily 8 A.M.–midnight, CUC5), with huge portions served on a shaded patio or in charmless rooms. **Paladar La Bamba** (Ángel de la Guardia y 2 de Diciembre, no tel., daily 8 A.M.–10 P.M.) has dining under thatch. I recommend the rabbit enchilada (CUC3.50).

I like the Spanish-themed **Restaurante El Baturro** (Vicente García, e/ Santana y Ortuño, tel. 031/34-6270, ext. 108, daily 2–10 P.M.) for its cozy ambience and excellent shrimp enchilada (CUC5). It also offers paella, grilled fish, and *criollo* staples.

The modern-themed snack bar of the **Hotel E Cadillac** (daily 7:30 A.M.–11:30 P.M.) serves sandwiches and *criollo* dishes and is the town's main venue for boy (middle-aged foreign males) meets girl (*jineteras*).

You can buy ice cream for pesos at **Cremería La Copa** (daily 10 A.M.–10 P.M.), on the west side of Parque Vicente García, and **Cremería Las Antillas** (Vicente García, esq. Ángel Guerra, Mon.–Fri. 10 A.M.–10 P.M., Sat.–Sun. 10 A.M.–midnight).

For baked goods, head to **Panadería Doña Neli** (Carretera Central, daily 7 A.M.–10 P.M.), next to the Oro Negro gas station. The *mercado agropecuario* on Camilo Cienfuegos, 200 meters north of the railway station, sells produce.

Information and Services

Bandec (Av. 30 de Noviembre; and Vicente García #69), **Banco Financiero Internacional** (Vicente García, esq. 24 de Octubre), and **Banco Popular** (Vicente García, esq. Francisco Vega) have branches. Most are open Mon.–Fri. 8 A.M.–3:30 P.M., Sat. 8 A.M.–1 P.M.

The **post office** (Vicente García #6, tel. 031/34-3863), on the west side of Parque García, has DHL service.

Etecsa (Francisco Varona, e/ Lucas Ortí and Vicente García, daily 8:30 A.M.–7:30 P.M.) has international telephone and Internet service.

Hospital Che Guevara (Av. Carlos J. Finlay, esq. Av. 2 de Diciembre, tel. 031/34-5012) is 400 meters east of Plaza de la Revolución.

The **Consultoría Jurídica Internacional** (Vicente García, e/ 24 de Febrero y Ramón Ortuño, tel./fax 031/34-6845, Mon.–Fri.

8:30 A.M.–noon and 1:30–5:30 P.M.) offers legal assistance.

Getting There and Around

BY AIR

The **Aeropuerto Hermano Ameijeras** (tel. 031/34-2484) is three kilometers north of town. **Cubana** (Lucas Ortíz, esq. 24 de Febrero, tel. 031/34-6872) serves Las Tunas from Havana twice weekly (CUC94).

BY BUS

The **Terminal de Ómnibus** (tel. 031/34-3060 interprovincial buses, tel. 031/34-2117 intermunicipal buses) is on the Carretera Central, one kilometer east of Parque Vicente García. **Víazul** buses (tel. 031/43060) depart Las Tunas for Holguín at 5:55 A.M. and 7:25 P.M.; for Santiago de Cuba at 2, 7:50, and 8:30 A.M., and 3:20 and 9:05 P.M.; for Havana at 1:30 and 10:35 A.M., and 1:45, 8, and 10:15 P.M.; for Trinidad at 6:45 A.M.; and for Varadero at 12:55 A.M.

Camiones depart for destinations within Las Tunas Province from the railway station.

BY TRAIN

The train station is at Terry Alomá (e/ Lucas Ortíz y Ángel de la Guardia, tel. 031/34-8146). All trains between Havana and Santiago de Cuba stop in Las Tunas (CUC23 to/from Havana, CUC7 to/from Santiago). Westbound trains depart Las Tunas for Havana at 11:30 A.M. (bus), 5:41 P.M. and 12:50 P.M. Eastbound trains depart Las Tunas for Holguín at 11 P.M. (bus) and 12:45 P.M., Santiago de Cuba at 10:41 A.M., and Guantánamo at 7:10 A.M. A two-car commuter train—*ferro-ómnibus*—runs to towns throughout the province.

Horse-drawn *coches* gather outside the train station.

BY CAR AND TAXI

You can rent cars from **Havanautos** (tel. 031/34-6228), in the Hotel Las Tunas, and **Cubacar** (Francisco Verona, esq. Lucas Ortíz, tel. 031/37-1505). There are gas stations on the Carretera Central: one about 400 meters west of Parque Lenin, and one four blocks east of Parque Vicente García.

Taxis are available outside the Hotel Las Tunas (CUC2 to downtown), or call **Cubataxi** (tel. 031/34-2036).

PUERTO PADRE

This pleasant port town, about 30 kilometers northeast of Las Tunas, is one of Cuba's oldest. Locals claim that Christopher Columbus made his first landfall in Cuba in the bay on October 28, 1492, and the settlement first appeared, as Portus Patris, on early 16th-century maps of the New World. During the 19th century, Puerto Padre grew to become Cuba's most important port for sugar export. It featured prominently in the Wars of Independence, when the Spanish built a fortress, **Fuerte de la Loma** (Tues.–Sat. 9:30 A.M.–4:30 P.M. and Sun. 8:30–11:30 A.M., CUC1), built in 1875 in medieval style to protect the southern entrance to town. Well-preserved, it still stands atop the hill at the end of Puerto Padre's La Rambla-style central boulevard (Avenida Libertad), pinned by the **Monumento Máximo Gómez.**

Playa Covarrubias

Las Tunas's north coast is lined with beautiful beaches, although the only one with a resort hotel is Playa Covarrubias, a four-kilometer-long strip of white sands with turquoise waters protected by a coral reef. The beach is 22 kilometers north of the rural community of Marañon, 15 kilometers west of Puerto Padre; it's virtually all scrub and briny pools to each side the whole way. You can buy a day pass (CUC25) to utilize the hotel facilities.

Playas La Herradura and Las Bocas

About 10 kilometers east of Puerto Padre, you pass through Jesús Menéndez and Loma, where

a road leads north eight kilometers to **Playa La Herradura** and, eight kilometers farther west, **Playa Las Bocas.** Both are popular with locals on weekends. A boat for Las Bocas (one peso) leaves from the wharf at El Secucho, 16 kilometers north of Puerto Padre.

Accommodations
CASAS PARTICULARES
Puerto Padre has several private room rentals. Options include **Casa de Leonardo Silva Gómez** (Mártires de la Herradura #98, tel. 031/35-3446, CUC15–20), with two rooms: The ground floor room has a private bath; the upstairs room shares a bathroom.

At Playa Las Bocas, the beachfront **Hospedaje Familiar** (Calle 2 #46, La Playa, tel. 031/53243, CUC20) has two simply furnished rooms.

Playa Herradura also has several *casas particulares.*

HOTELS
Repaired in 2008 after being trashed by Hurricane Ike, Cubanacán's **Brisas Covarrubias** (Playa Covarrubias, tel. 031/51-5530, fax 031/51-5352, www.hotelescubana-can.com, from CUC60 s, CUC80 d low season, from CUC80 s, CUC100 d high season) is a tranquil property with 180 spacious rooms furnished in contemporary style; some have king-size beds. The huge freeform pool has a thatched bar and theater, plus there's a kids' playground, disco, gym, water sports, and diving. However, you're out on a limb here!

Services
Etecsa (Av. Libertad #144, e/ Masó y Flor Crombet, tel. 031/51-5316, 8:30 A.M.–7:30 P.M.) has international telephone and Internet service. The Cupet gas station is one block farther south.

Holguín and Vicinity

HOLGUÍN

Holguín (pop. 320,000), 775 kilometers east of Havana and 200 kilometers northwest of Santiago de Cuba, is the fourth-largest city in Cuba. When Columbus landed nearby in 1492, believing he had arrived in Asia, he sent an expedition inland to carry salutations to the Japanese emperor's court. The explorers came across a large Indian village called Cubanacán. Three decades later, a land grant was made to Capitán García Holguín, who built a settlement immodestly named for himself.

The colonial core contains many fine houses of Spanish origin. Holguín is renowned for one of the most vibrant cultural scenes in Cuba. Nonetheless, Holguín is an industrial city, and Cuba's major breweries are here.

Orientation

The Carretera Central enters from the west and swings south for Granma Province, skirting the city center. Aguilera (eastbound) and Frexes (westbound) link the Carretera Central to the city center. At its heart is Parque Calixto García, bounded by Calles Frexes (north), Martí (south), Libertad (also known as Manduley; east), and Maceo (west).

Martí runs east from the square and merges to the east with Avenida de los Libertadores, which leads through the modern Plaza de la Revolución district and continues to Moa and Baracoa. The city is bypassed to the south by a *circunvalación* linking the Carretera Central with the road to Moa.

Libertad runs north from Parque Calixto García to Avenida Capitán Urbino, which leads northeast to Gibara. Avenida XX Aniversario leads north from Avenida de los Libertadores for Guardalavaca.

Loma de la Cruz

Looming over Holguín to the north is the Hill of the Cross, named for the cross that has stood here since 1790. From here you can look out over the city and across the plains towards the mountain formations of the Grupo de Maniabon.

To get there, climb the 450 or so steps that begin at the north end of Calle Maceo, 10 blocks north of Plaza San José, or drive via Avenida Capitán Urbino.

◖ Plaza Calixto García

The city's expansive main square has at its heart a marble **Monumento General Calixto García.** Holguín's most famous son was born in the simple **Casa Natal de Calixto García** (Miró #147, tel. 024/42-5610, Tues.–Sat. 9 A.M.–9 P.M., CUC1), one block east of the square. Some of his personal effects are on view inside the museum.

On the north side, the **Museo Provincial de Historia** (Frexes #198, tel. 024/46-3395, Tues.–Sat. 8 A.M.–4 P.M., Sun. 8 A.M.–noon, entrance CUC1, cameras CUC1), with an eclectic range of historical artifacts. It was built in 1860–1868 as the Casino Español, where Spanish gentry caroused. It is colloquially known as La Periquera—the Parrot's Cage—supposedly after Spanish troops in their garish yellow, blue, and green uniforms were trapped inside the building, with its cage-like barred windows, when the town was besieged in 1868 by García's troops. The museum's pride and joy is a 35-centimeter-long pre-Columbian axe (the *hacha de Holguín*) carved in the shape of a human. The axe is the provincial symbol.

The **Museo de la Historia Natural Carlos de la Torre** (Maceo #129, tel. 024/42-3935), one block south of the square, is housed in a neoclassical building that was closed for a lengthy restoration at last visit. The museum features an eclectic array of flora and fauna, including a collection of over 4,000 colorful polymite (snail) shells.

Art lovers should pop into **Galería Holguín** (Tues.–Sun. 8 A.M.–10 P.M.), on the southwest corner.

© CHRISTOPHER P. BAKER

bas-relief on Plaza Julio Graves de Peralta, Holguín

Plaza Julio Graves de Peralta

This small square, four blocks south of Parque Calixto García, is anchored by a marble statue of General Graves de Peralta (1834–1872), who led the rebel assault on October 30, 1868, that captured Holguín from the Spanish.

On the east side, the **Iglesia San Isidro** dates from 1720 and is named for the town's patron saint. The wooden ceiling is noteworthy. A bronze statue of Pope John Paul II stands outside.

The dramatic bas-relief of famous local citizens, on the park's west side, forms the facade of **Combinado Deportivo Henry García Suárez,** where you're welcome to pop in to see boxers sparring.

Plaza de la Marqueta

This tiny plaza, between Máximo Gómez and Mártires, and Martí and Luz Caballero, occupies the site of a now derelict market and candle factory (*marqueta* refers to the molds). Surrounding buildings have been brought back to life, and deteriorated life-size figures of local personalities shown in everyday activities dot the square.

The **Instituto Cubano de Libros** print shop (Callejón de Mercado #2, tel. 024/42-4051), on the south side, still makes books using Linotype.

Other Plazas

The antique cobbled **Plaza San José,** two blocks north of Parque Calixto García, is surrounded by colonial buildings and has a statue to local patriots executed during the Wars of Independence. On its east side, the beautiful **Iglesia de San José** is topped by a domed neoclassical clock tower. The church dates from 1820 and features baroque innards. The **Museo de Historia** (tel. 024/46-2121, Mon.– Fri. 8 A.M.–noon and 1–4:30 P.M., free), on the north side, has a motley display relating to the city's past.

The huge **Plaza de la Revolución,** on Avenida XX Aniversario, is dominated by

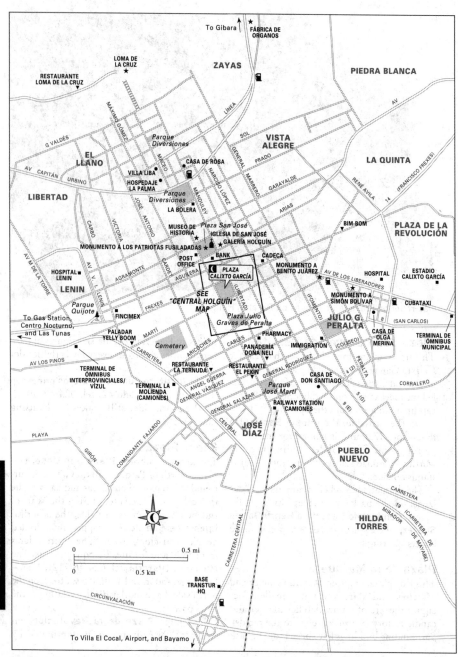

To Gibara
FÁBRICA DE ORGANOS

ZAYAS

PIEDRA BLANCA

LOMA DE LA CRUZ

RESTAURANTE LOMA DE LA CRUZ

LINEA

VISTA ALEGRE

LA QUINTA

G VALDES

MÁXIMO GÓMEZ

SOL

PRADO

EL LLANO

Parque Diversiones

CASA DE ROSA

GENERAL MARRERO

GARAYALDE

(FRANCISCO FREXES)

14

RENE AVILA

AV CAPITÁN URBINO

VILLA LIBA

HOSPEDAJE LA PALMA

MANDULEY

NARCISO LÓPEZ

ARIAS

PLAZA DE LA REVOLUCIÓN

LIBERTAD

Parque Diversiones

LA BOLERA

JOSÉ ANTONIO

MUSEO DE HISTORIA

Plaza San José

IGLESIA DE SAN JOSÉ

GALERÍA HOLGUÍN

BIM-BOM

MONUMENTO A LOS PATRIOTAS FUSILADADAS

VICTORIA

CARBO

POST OFFICE

BANK

CADECA

AV M DE LA TORRE

HOSPITAL LENIN

AGRAMONTE

AGUILERA

PLAZA CALIXTO GARCÍA

MONUMENTO A BENITO JUÁREZ

AV DE LOS LIBERADORES

HOSPITAL

ESTADIO CALIXTO GARCÍA

AV V.I. LENIN

LENIN

Parque Quijote

FREXES

SEE "CENTRAL HOLGUÍN" MAP

(LIBERTAD)

(FOMENTO)

MONUMENTO A SIMÓN BOLÍVAR

8

CUBATAXI

(SAN CARLOS)

To Gas Station, Centro Nocturno, and Las Tunas

FINCIMEX

Plaza Julio Graves de Peralta

JULIO G. PERALTA

CASA DE OLGA MERINA

TERMINAL DE ÓMNIBUS MUNICIPAL

PALADAR YELLY BOOM

MARTI

Cemetery

CABLES

ARICOCHES

PHARMACY

IMMIGRATION

(COLISEO)

PERALTA

AV LOS PINOS

CARRETERA

PANADERÍA DOÑA NELI

GENERAL RODRÍGUEZ

4 (2)

CORRALERO

TERMINAL DE ÓMNIBUS INTERPROVINCIALES/ VÍZUL

RESTAURANTE LA TERNUDA

ANGEL GUERRA

RESTAURANTE EL PEKIN

CASA DE DON SANTIAGO

5 (G)

TERMINAL LA MOLIENDA (CAMIONES)

GENERAL VÁSQUEZ

Parque José Martí

9 (E)

GENERAL SALAZAR

RAILWAY STATION/ CAMIONES

PLAYA

GIRÓN

COMANDANTE FAJARDO

CENTRAL

JOSÉ DÍAZ

PUEBLO NUEVO

13

18

19 (CARRETERA DE

CARRETERA

MIRADOR

HILDA TORRES

DE MAYABE)

0   0.5 mi
0   0.5 km

BASE TRANSTUR HQ

CARRETERA CENTRAL

CIRCUNVALACIÓN

To Villa El Cocal, Airport, and Bayamo

a huge frieze depicting important events in Cuba's history; Fidel is most prominent, of course. Calixto García's mausoleum is here; his mother (also a patriot) is buried east of the plaza beneath a copse. The **Estadio Calixto García** baseball and sports stadium, 200 meters south of the plaza, contains the **Museo del Estadio Calixto García** (tel. 024/46-2606, Mon.–Fri. noon–8 P.M., Sat.–Sun. 8 A.M.–noon, CUC1), a tiny baseball museum featuring sports memorabilia.

Other Sites

Avenida de los Libertadores is lined with monuments to South American "liberators" and revolutionary heroes: Benito Juárez (esq. Aricoches), Simón Bolívar (esq. Cables), Máximo Gómez (esq. San Carlos), Antonio Maceo (400 meters west of Av. de los Internacionalistas), and Che Guevara (esq. Av. de los Internacionalistas).

Still manufacturing mechanized *órganos pneumáticos* (air-compression organs) in traditional manner, **Fábrica de Órganos** (Carretera de Gibara #301, tel. 024/42-6616, Mon.–Fri. 8 A.M.–3:30 P.M., free), on the Gibara road about one kilometer east of General Marrero, provides a fascinating peek at age-old Cuban craftsmanship in rather Dickensian conditions.

Entertainment and Events

A fashion show is hosted at **Salon 1720** (Frexes #190, e/ Manduley y Miró, tel. 024/45-8150) each Friday and Saturday at 9 P.M.

You can schmooze with intellectuals at **UNEAC** (National Union of Cuban Writers and Artists, Libertad #148, tel. 024/46-4066, daily 8 A.M.–midnight), which hosts cultural events.

For 10-pin bowling, head to **La Bolera** (Habana, esq. Libertad, tel. 024/46-8812, daily 10 A.M.–2 A.M., CUC1).

Teatro Comandante Eddy Suñol (Martí #111, tel. 024/46-3161), on Parque Calixto García, hosts ballet, classical, and theatrical performances.

Cine Martí, on the north side of Parque Calixto García, shows movies.

LAS TUNAS & HOLGUÍN

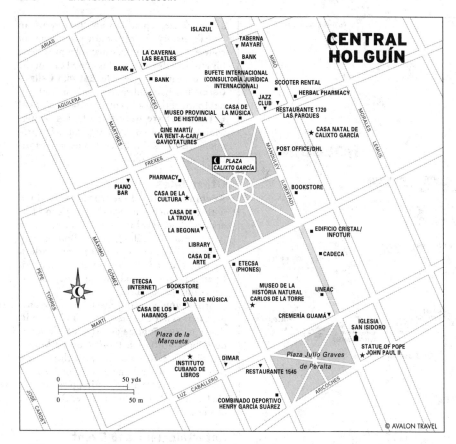

CENTRAL HOLGUÍN

ISLAZUL
TABERNA MAYARÍ
LA CAVERNA LAS BEATLES
BANK
BANK
ARIAS
MIRÓ
BANK
BUFETE INTERNACIONAL (CONSULTORÍA JURÍDICA INTERNACIONAL)
SCOOTER RENTAL
MACEO
HERBAL PHARMACY
AGUILERA
JAZZ CLUB
MUSEO PROVINCIAL DE HISTÓRIA
CASA DE LA MÚSICA
RESTAURANTE 1720 LAS PARQUES
MARTIRES
CINE MARTÍ/ VÍA RENT-A-CAR/ GAVIOTATURES
CASA NATAL DE CALIXTO GARCÍA
MORALES
LEMUS
FREXES
POST OFFICE/DHL
PLAZA CALIXTO GARCÍA
PHARMACY
PIANO BAR
CASA DE LA CULTURA
MANDULEY
LIBERTAD
BOOKSTORE
CASA DE LA TROVA
LA BEGONIA
MÁXIMO
GÓMEZ
LIBRARY
CASA DE ARTE
EDIFICIO CRISTAL/ INFOTUR
CADECA
ETECSA (PHONES)
ETECSA (INTERNET)
BOOKSTORE
MUSEO DE LA HISTÓRIA NATURAL CARLOS DE LA TORRE
UNEAC
PEPE TORRES
CASA DE MÚSICA
CASA DE LOS HABANOS
CREMERÍA GUAMÁ
IGLESIA SAN ISIDORO
MARTÍ
Plaza de la Marqueta
INSTITUTO CUBANO DE LIBROS
DIMAR
Plaza Julio Graves de Peralta
STATUE OF POPE JOHN PAUL II
0   50 yds
0   50 m
LUZ CABALLERO
RESTAURANTE 1545
ARICOCHES
JOSÉ CARDET
COMBINADO DEPORTIVO HENRY GARCÍA SUÁREZ

© AVALON TRAVEL

Wooing a lover? Hire the **Mariachi de Holguín** (tel. 024/47-4914), a suitably attired mariachi group that plays at Casa Natal Galixto each alternate Thursday at 8:30 P.M. (CUC1).

You can catch a baseball game October–May at **Estadio Calixto García** (Avenida XX Aniversario, tel. 024/46-2606).

NIGHTLIFE

It's appropriate the Cuba's main brewing city serves serious sudsters with draft Mayabe beer served in ceramic mugs at the German-style **Taberna Pancho** (Av. Dimitrov, tel. 024/48-1868, daily noon–2 P.M., 2:15–4:15 P.M., 6–8 P.M., and 8:15–10:15 P.M.), next to Hotel Pernik, and **Taberna Mayabe** (Libertad, esq. Aguilera, tel. 024/46-1543, 3–6 P.M. and 8 P.M.–midnight).

Islazul's titillating **Cabaret Nocturno** (tel. 024/42-5185, Wed.–Mon. at 10 P.M., CUC10 including one drink), on the Carretera Central two kilometers west of town, is open-air; no performances during rains. You need your ID.

Timeworn crooners perform at the **Casa de la Trova "El Guayabero"** (Maceo #174, tel. 024/45-3104, Tues.–Sun. 11 A.M.–6 P.M. and 8 P.M.–1 A.M., CUC1), on the west side of Parque Calixto García.

For contemporary sounds, the new hot spot is **Casa de la Música** (Libertad, esq. Frexes), with a medley of venues. Upstairs,

Taberna Mayabe, Holguín

musicians tickle the ivories of the **Piano Bar** (4 P.M.–2 A.M., CUC3); bands perform live downstairs in the air-conditioned **Salon Santa Palabra** (nightly 9 P.M.–2 A.M., CUC3–5); and **Taberna Bucanero** serves draft beer.

There's even live jazz, at the **Jazz Club** (Libertad, esq. Frexes, tel. 024/47-4312, nightly 3 P.M.–2 A.M., CUC5). And, would you believe Beatles music at **La Caverna The Beatles** (tel. 024/45-3440, nightly 4 P.M.–2 A.M., 25 pesos), which attempts to recreate The Cavern with graffiti-strewn walls, posters, and even life-size figures of the Fab Four.

To hear silky *música filin* head to the overly air-conditioned **Piano Bar** (Frexes, esq. Mártires, tel. 024/42-4322, daily noon–2 A.M.), with live music nightly.

FESTIVALS AND EVENTS

Mid-January bursts with cultural events during **Semana de Cultura Holguinera.** Every May 3, a religious procession—**Romería de Mayo**—ascends to the top of Loma de la Cruz. The **Festival Internacional de Ballet**

is held in November every even-numbered year, and the **Fiesta Iberoamericana de la Cultura** in October celebrates the Spanish heritage in music, dance, and theater. And transvestites flock from throughout Cuba for the **Festival de Transvesti.** News of upcoming cultural happenings is posted throughout the city.

Accommodations

You can book Islazul hotels throughout Cuba at its office (Calle Libertad, esq. Aguilera, tel. 024/42-2354, Mon.–Fri. 8:15–11:30 A.M. and 1–4:30 A.M.). All accommodations listed are air-conditioned.

CASAS PARTICULARES

At last count, the city had 168 private rentals. My favorite is **Villa Liba** (Maceo #46, esq. 18, Rpto. El Llano, tel. 024/42-3823, CUC25), a 1950s home replete with period furnishings. Two cross-ventilated rooms have private bathrooms. Erudite and gracious owners Jorge and Marilena (she gives massages) make wholesome meals served on a patio with a vine arbor. There's secure parking.

Hospedaje La Palma (Maceo #52, tel. 024/42-4683, CUC25–30) is another marvelous 1950s home in Southern California style. One of the two large rooms has a soaring beamed ceiling and a marvelous bathroom with piping hot water. The second room has more classical furniture. The place is festooned with art, including a dramatic terracotta bust of Che Guevara. The huge back garden was being turned into a sports venue at last visit.

Casa de Rosa (Libertad #35, esq. 24, tel. 024/42-4630, rosama@telecristal.icrt.cu, CUC25) is a beautifully maintained, cross-ventilated 1940s home with pleasant furnishings and spirited artwork. It has two large rooms with clinically clean bathrooms. There's parking.

Casa de Olga Medina (Calle 12 #12, e/ 7 y 9, Rpto. Peralta, tel. 024/42-5791) is close to the immigration office. Olga's modern upstairs apartment is spacious and has a microwave, ceiling fan, and secure parking.

LAS TUNAS & HOLGUÍN

You won't regret staying at **Casa de Don Santiago** (Narciso López #25, Apto. 3, e/ Coliseo y 2da, tel. 024/42-6146, CUC20–25), on the second floor of a Soviet prefab apartment complex. The single bedroom has a TV, DVD, ceiling fan, but the main reason to stay here is your friendly hosts, who are educated conversationalists.

HOTELS

The Soviet-style **Hotel Pernik** (Av. Dimitrov, tel. 024/48-1011, fax 024/48-1667, www.islazul.cu, CUC20 s, CUC30 d low season, CUC30 s, CUC40 d high season), near the Plaza de la Revolución, has 202 pleasantly refurbished rooms (some have modems), plus a swimming pool, tennis court, and a surprisingly good restaurant.

The yin to the Pernik's yang, the more intimate and similarly priced **Villa El Bosque** (tel. 024/48-1012, fax 024/48-1140, www.islazul.cu, CUC20 s, CUC30 d low season, CUC30 s, CUC40 d high season), 400 meters farther east, has 69 lovely new rooms in cabins, with modern bathrooms, in uninspired, sprawling grounds.

Two new Cubanacán properties, **Hotel Libertad** and **Hotel E La Caballeriza** are slated to open soon as luxury boutique hotels.

Food

The best private dining in town is the air-conditioned 🎧 **Restaurante La Ternuda** (José Cardet #293, daily 6–11 P.M.), hidden upstairs off a narrow street, with a charming and elegant ambience. The menu features soups (CUC1), lamb (CUC5), and *criollo* staples. Lunch is sometimes served by reservation. If La Ternuda is full, consider **Paladar Yelly Boom** (Martí #180, e/ Carretera Central y Antonio Guiteras, tel. 024/42-4096, daily 11 A.M.–11 P.M.) in the converted garage of a modern home.

🎧 **Restaurante 1720 Las Parques** (Frexes #190, e/ Manduley y Miró, tel. 024/45-8150, daily noon–10:30 A.M.) offers classical elegance in a restored colonial mansion. The menu includes onion soup, smoked salmon (CUC6), creole shrimp in brandy (CUC13), and paella (CUC5). Reservations recommended. Penny-pinchers can look out on Plaza Julio Graves at the similarly atmospheric **Restaurant 1545** (Maceo, esq. Luz Caballero, no tel., daily noon–4 P.M. and 6 P.M.–midnight), serving *criollo* fare for pesos. A dress code applies at both restaurants.

Taberna Pancho (Av. Dimitrov, tel. 024/48-1868, noon–10 P.M.) serves set meals, including decent shrimp and pork dishes (CUC2.50–5, including two beers).

For views over town, ascend the Loma de la Cruz to the open-air **Restaurante Loma de la Cruz** (tel. 5285-5647, daily noon–9:30 P.M.), although the menu is limited to *criollo* staples.

The **La Begonia** (daily 8 A.M.–2 A.M.) patio snack bar, on the west side of Parque Calixto García, is *the* unofficial meeting spot for foreign travelers.

The wait is worthwhile for ice cream at **Cremería Guamá** (daily 10 A.M.–10 P.M.), on Plaza Julio Graves. The air-conditioned **Bim-Bom** (Frexes, daily 11 A.M.–11 P.M.) charges an outrageous CUC1 per scoop.

For baked goods head to **Panadería Doña Neli** (Manduley #285, 8 A.M.–8 P.M.), two blocks south of Plaza Julio Graves. You can buy fresh produce at the *mercado agropecuario* at the east end of Coliseo.

Information and Services

Infotur (tel. 024/42-5013, holgdir@enet.cu, Mon.–Fri. 8 A.M.–5 P.M., Sat. 8 A.M.–1 P.M.) has a tourist information bureau upstairs in Edificio Cristal and another at the airport (tel. 024/47-4774, open only when flights arrive).

The **post office** (Máximo Gómez, e/ Aguilera y Arias) is on the east side of Parque Calixto García. **DHL** (Manduley, esq. Frexes, tel. 024/46-8254, Mon.–Fri. 9 A.M.–6 P.M., Sat. 8:30 A.M.–noon) has an office in the Edificio Cristal.

Etecsa (Martí, e/ Mártires y Máximo Gómez, daily 8:30 A.M.–7:30 P.M.) has international telephone and Internet service.

Banks include **Bandec** (on the south side

bici-taxis await customers in Holguín

of Plaza San José; and Maceo, esq. Aguilera); **Banco Financiero Internacional** (Aguilera, esq. Maceo); and **Banco Popular** (Maceo, e/ Aguilera y Arias; and one block south of the Villa El Bosque). You can change currency at **Cadeca** (Libertad e/ Martí y Luz Caballero, Mon.–Sat. 8 A.M.–5 P.M.). Most banks are open Mon.–Fri. 8 A.M.–3:30 P.M., Sat. 8 A.M.–1 P.M.

Hospital Lenin (Av. Lenin, tel. 024/42-5302) is on the west side of town.

Consultoría Jurídica Internacional (Peralta #46, e/ Coliseo y Segunda, Rpto. Peralta, tel. 024/46-8299, Mon.–Fri. 8 A.M.–5 P.M., Sat. 8 A.M.–1 P.M.) and **Bufete Internacional** (Manduely, e/ Frexes y Aguilera, tel. 024/46-8133) provide legal services.

Getting There and Around
BY AIR
The **Aeropuerto Frank País** (tel. 024/46-2512) is 10 kilometers south of town, on the Carretera Central. The domestic terminal is served by a bus from Calle Rodríguez, near the train station six blocks south of Parque Calixto García. **Cubana** (Edificio Cristal, tel. 024/46-8111) and **Aero Caribbean** (Edificio Cristal, tel. 024/46-8556) fly between Havana and Holguín daily.

BY BUS
The **Terminal de Ómnibus Interprovinciales** (Carretera Central #19, e/ 20 de Mayo e Independencia) is on the west side of town. **Víazul** (tel. 024/42-2111) buses depart Havana for Holguín at 7:05 A.M. and 10:35 P.M. (CUC44). Eastbound buses depart Holguín for Santiago de Cuba at 3:15 and 9:05 A.M., and 4:35 P.M. Westbound buses depart Holguín for Havana at 9:20 A.M., and 12:30, 6:45, and 9 P.M.; for Trinidad at 6:45 A.M.; and for Varadero at 11:40 P.M.

Buses to/from Guardalavaca and towns east of Holguín arrive and depart the **Terminal de Ómnibus Municipales** (Av. de los Libertadores, tel. 024/48-1170), opposite the baseball stadium. West and southbound trucks leave from **Terminal La Molienda** (Carretera Central y Comandante Fajardo, tel. 024/42-2322), on the west side of town. Bus #16 connects the Hotel Pernik with downtown.

LAS TUNAS & HOLGUÍN

BY TRAIN

Cuba's main railway line serves **Cacocum** train station (tel. 024/32-7194), 15 kilometers south of town; an hourly bus connects Holguín's **Estación de Ferrocarriles** (Calle Pita, tel. 024/42-2331), eight blocks south of Plaza Calixto García.

From Havana, train #7 arrives Cacocum at 12:06 P.M. and departs for Santiago de Cuba at 12:21 P.M.; train #5 arrives at 8:12 A.M. Train #8 arrives from Santiago de Cuba at 10:59 A.M. and departs for Havana at 11:14 A.M.; train #6 departs for Havana at 4:35 P.M.

BY CAR AND TAXI

You can rent cars through **Cubacar** (tel. 24/42-8196, Hotel Pernik, tel. 024/46-8414 at the airport, com.renta.hlg@transtur.cu), **Havanautos** (tel. 024/46-8412, domestic terminal), **Rex** (tel. 024/46-4644, international terminal) at Aeropuerto Frank País, and **Vía** (tel. 024/42-1602) in, of all places, the Cine Martí.

Excursions are offered by **Cubatur** (Edificio Cristal, tel. 024/42-1679, Mon.–Fri. noon–8:45 P.M. and Sat. noon–4 P.M.).

There are gas stations on Carretera a Gibara, on Avenida de los Libertadores, on Avenida de los Internacionalistas, and at the junction of the Carretera Central and *circunvalación*.

Horse-drawn *coches* and *bici-taxis* (which, uniquely in Holguín, have sidecars and umbrellas) are ubiquitous. **Cubataxi** (tel. 024/42-3290) offers taxi service and **Palmares** (Miró e/ Aguilera and Frexes, tel. 024/46-8150) rents scooters.

MIRADOR DE MAYABE

The Mayabe Lookout (daily 10 A.M.–6 P.M., CUC2 entrance) is high above the Mayabe Valley, eight kilometers southeast of town. The facility includes a fine restaurant and swimming pool and sundeck with views. The place draws locals on weekends.

Adjoining, Finca Mayabe is an ersatz farmstead with turkeys, geese, and other farm animals, a *galleria*—a cock pit—where you can watch cockfights, plus horseback riding.

COCKFIGHTING

Whatever you think about cockfighting – undoubtedly a cruel and vicious "sport" – it is an integral part of macho Cuban culture, particularly in the countryside. The Cuban government even supports the sport and breeds gaming cocks for export.

Gaming cocks are trained to fight beginning when they are about eight months. They are exercised to strengthen their wings, legs, and claws, and to build up stamina. Before combat, their wattles, ears, and crests are removed, as they bleed and could otherwise be seized by their opponents. Feathers are also plucked from the lower body and the birds are shaved. Owners rub their birds down with rum, like seconds massaging prizefighters. The cocks, which fight in weight categories, are fitted with artificial spurs. Fights are to the death.

Fights take place at *vallas* (rings), where the all-male crowd gets excited to the point of hysteria. Though gambling is ostensibly prohibited, it happens anyway.

The Mirador's claim to fame was a beer-loving burro called Pancho (1960–2002), who consumed over 45,000 bottles of beer before dying of cirrhosis! Pancho's equally thirsty young sidekick Panchito keeps the tradition alive. He is given Monday off, presumably to sleep off his weekend hangover. Panchito lives in a stall next to the bar, appropriately named Bar Burro.

Accommodations and Food

Islazul's **Villa Mirador de Mayabe** (tel. 024/42-2160, carpeta@mmayabe.co.cu, CUC20 s, CUC30 d low season, CUC30 s, CUC40 d high season) has 24 nicely furnished hilltop *cabinas*. There's also a fully-staffed four-bedroom house—**Casa de Pancho.** The facility includes a pleasant thatched restaurant and bar (daily 7 A.M.–9 P.M.).

North of Holguín

◖ GIBARA

Gibara (pop. 20,000), 28 kilometers north of Holguín, is a dusty, time-encrusted fishing port that overlooks the Bahía de Gibara. It was a major sugar-trading port in colonial days, when it was known as Villa Blanca and colloquially as La Perla del Oriente (Pearl of the Orient). It has no shortage of intriguing colonial structures, though only remnants remain of the original 18th-century city walls. Its seafront promenade, the **Malecón,** boasts a patinated **statue of Camilo Cienfuegos.**

The town was devastated by Hurricane Ike, which in November 2008 came ashore near here, damaging 70 percent of homes (2,000 homes in Gibara were totally destroyed). In late 2009, the town had been given a fresh coat of paint and was on its way to recovery.

The streets rise steeply south and west of the main plaza. Follow Independencia west, uphill past charming little **Plaza Colón,** and turn right at Calle Cabada to reach the paltry ruins of **Fuerte del Cuartelón,** a 30-minute hike. Go for the view.

You can hire a boat to **Playa Blanca,** a beach on the east side of the bay (CUC5 roundtrip), or drive the 15 kilometers northwest to **Playa Caletones** via a modern wind farm with five turbines (this road connects to Playa Herradura, in Las Tunas Province).

To the southeast of Gibara is a flat-topped mountain, the **Silla de Gibara** (Saddle of Gibara), considered to be the hill described by Christopher Columbus when he landed in Cuba on October 28, 1492.

Parque Calixto García

The pretty main plaza is framed by African oaks (*Robles africanos*) and is pinned by a **Monumento a Los Libertadores de la Patria** (Liberators of the Fatherland), commemorating those who fought in the Wars of Independence. The restored **Iglesia de San Fulgencio** church, with Byzantine-style cupolas, dates from 1850.

The excellent **Museo de Historia Natural** (Luz Caballero #23, tel. 024/84-4458, Mon. 1–4 P.M., Tues.–Sat. 9 A.M.–noon and

© CHRISTOPHER P. BAKER

Gibara, with the Silla de Gibara in the distance

LAS TUNAS & HOLGUÍN

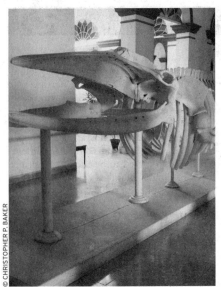

© CHRISTOPHER P. BAKER

whale skeleton, Museo de Historia Natural

1–5 P.M., Sun. 9 A.M.–noon, entrance CUC1, cameras CUC1, videos CUC5) displays stuffed animals and other exhibits on a natural history theme.

The **Museo de Arte Decorativo** (Independencia #19, tel. 024/84-4687, Tues.–Sat. 9 A.M.–noon and 1–5 P.M., Sun. 8 A.M.–noon, entrance CUC2, cameras CUC1, videos CUC5), in a restored neoclassical mansion 50 meters southwest of the square, boasts period furniture and paintings upstairs.

Batería Fernando 7mo, one block east of the square, preserves an old fortress with cannons.

Entertainment

The open-air **Centro Cultural El Colonial** (Peralta, esq. Sartorio, CUC2) has live music Tuesday–Sunday nights.

Gibara is famed nationwide for its love of cinema. The **Cine Jiba** (Luz Caballero #17), on the main plaza, hosts Cuba's annual **Festival Internacional de Cine Pobre** (International Low-Budget Film Festival, tel. 07/838-3657, www.cubacine.cu/cinepobre), drawing rising

movie stars and producers to this unlikely venue each April. A fitting counterpoint to the glitz of Cannes! The festival is a big deal, and the town goes wild with carnival-like celebrations that include fireworks.

Accommodations and Food

There are several excellent *casas particulares* from which to choose. The unbeatable standout is the antique-filled (**La Casa de los Amigos** (Céspedes #15 e/ Luz Caballeros y Peralta, tel. 024/84-4115, lacasadelosamigos@ yahoo.fr, CUC25), where the walls are covered in fabulous murals (some erotic). The gorgeous air-conditioned bedrooms (choose a blue, orange, red, or green room) open to a patio with thatched bar-dining space and have fans, stone-lined walls, batik spreads and linens, and exquisite bathrooms. Alex (Cuban) and Chantal (French) are your delightful hosts.

You'll fall in love with (**Villa Caney** (Sartorio #36, e/ Peralta y Luz Caballero, tel. 024/84-4552, CUC20–25), a colonial gem full of period pieces. It opens to a garden terrace with hammocks, palms, and a thatched restaurant—a delightful space! The owners rent two air-conditioned rooms with fans and private bathrooms with hot water. Next door, and a virtual carbon-copy, is **La Casa de los Hermanos** (Céspedes #13, e/ Peralta y Luz Caballero, tel. 024/34542, CUC20).

Palmares's (**Hostal Buena Vista** (Calle Independencia Final, tel. 024/84-4596, faro-gib@enet.cu, CUC25 s, CUC40 d) opened in April 2009. Overhanging a tiny beach, this modern hotel has ritzy rooms with antique repro furnishings. Nice! A pity about the open sewer smells!

The Hotel Ordoñez was due to open by 2010.

The best of few eateries is the Hotel Buena Vista's **Restaurante El Faro** (Calle Independencia Final, daily 10:15 A.M.–8:15 P.M.), with glass walls fronting the ocean. It serves *criollo* and seafood dishes, including paella. The bar in **Batería Fernando 7mo** (one block east of the square, no tel., daily 10 A.M.–1 P.M.) serves snacks.

Six pesos (25 cents) will buy you a garlic shrimp dish at the no-frills hilltop **Restaurante El Mirador** (tel. 024/84-5259, daily noon–8 P.M.), with views over town.

Getting There and Away

The bus station (tel. 024/84-4215) is at the entrance to town. Buses depart Holguín for Gibara at 6 A.M. and 5:40 P.M., and Gibara for Holguín at 5 A.M. and 4 P.M. *Camiones* also make the journey.

Cubacar (Calle Independencia Final, tel. 024/84-4222) has a rental agency at Restaurante El Faro in Hotel Buena Vista.

There's a gas station at the entrance to town.

RAFAEL FREYRE AND VICINITY

This small town, about 35 kilometers northeast of Holguín, is dominated by the now-defunct Central Rafael Freyre sugar mill. The *central* is the setting for what is touted as the **Museo de Locomotora de Vapor** (Steam Train Museum, tel. 024/85-0493, Mon.–Fri. 9:30 A.M.–11:30 P.M.). Despite years of promise, the museum has yet to emerge. What visitors find are six engines (the oldest dates from 1882) in derelict sheds. Entry is solely by either of two steam-train excursions—"Choo Choo Train" (CUC10) and "Cuba Inside" (CUC7)—offered by Cubatur and Gaviota in Guardalavaca.

The town, also known as Santa Lucía (not to be confused with the resort of that name), lies a few kilometers inland of Bahía de Bariay. If you zigzag through Rafael Freyre and go past the *central,* the road north will take you to the bay and **Playa Blanca,** a gorgeous beach with a commemorative plaque to Columbus that declares this the "site of the first landing of Christopher Columbus in Cuba."

Parque Monumento Nacional Bariay

Created in 2002 to honor Columbus's landing, this 206-hectare park (tel. 024/43-4810, daily 9 A.M.–5 P.M., CUC8 entrance including cocktail, cameras CUC1, videos CUC2) is within the broader Parque Cristóbal Colón. This meager facility features a re-created Indian village—**Aldea Aborigen**—where rather strained reenactments of Taíno life take place, with Cubans in Indian garb; an archaeological site with a small museum; and the uninspired **Monumento al Medio Milenio** commemorating Columbus's landing.

One-hour horseback rides are offered (CUC4 adult, CUC2 children).

To get there, turn north at Frey Benito, four kilometers west of Rafael Freyre. The Rafael Freyre–Frey Benito road continues west to Gibara, passing en route the Silla de Gibara, or saddle-shaped mountain, that Columbus recorded during his visit. CUC2 buys you entry to trails at Campismo Silla, four kilometers west of Frey Benito. It also has horseback riding.

Accommodations

Campismo Silla de Gibara (tel. 5219-4557, CUC5 per person), enjoying a fabulous location at the base of a *mogote,* is a simple holiday camp with 42 basic cabins (some air-conditioned) with cold-water showers. It has a swimming pool, café, volleyball, horseback rides, and trails.

At Playa Blanca, the **Hotel Don Lino** (tel. 024/43-0308, fax 024/43-0310, reservas@don-lino.co.cu, CUC24 s, CUC35 d low season, CUC 60 s, CUC80 d high season) looks over its own small beach. It was recently renovated and has 36 pleasantly furnished air-conditioned rooms in bungalows (18 are oceanview).

G GUARDALAVACA

Guardalavaca (the name means "Guard the Cow") is a resort about 55 kilometers northeast of Holguín. The beaches are gorgeous. Scuba diving and snorkeling are excellent. Most hotels are all-inclusive and cater almost exclusively to package charter groups. Still, although every year sees new amenities, it's small fry compared to Varadero or Cayo Coco, and a stay here may come as a disappointment to

GUARDALAVACA
AND VICINITY

ATLANTIC OCEAN

BLAU COSTA
VERDE BEACH

Playa
Pesquero   HOTEL PLAYA
COSTA VERDE

Playa
El Estero

HOTEL PLAYA
PESQUERO   GAVIOTATOURS

Parque
Monumento
Nacional
Bariay

HOTEL
DON LINO

Playa
Blanca

MONUMENTO
CRISTÓBAL COLÓN

PLAQUE TO
COLUMBUS LANDING

MARINA
INTERNACIONAL
PUERTO DE VITA

STABLES

SITIO ARQUEOLÓGICO

ALDEA
ABORIGEN

PARK
ENTRANCE

MUSEO DE
LOCOMOTORA
DE VAPOR

To Gibara

Rafael
Freyre

To Holguín

SCALE NOT AVAILABLE

© AVALON TRAVEL

sun-sea-and-sand-loving tourists who are expecting the scope of Cancún.

The original resort, comprising Guardalavaca proper, is at the twin-beach strip of **Playa Mayor** and **Playa Las Brisas.** Recent development has focused farther west at **Playa Esmeralda, Playa Pesquero** and **Playa Yuraguanal,** midway between Guardalavaca and Rafael Freyre.

Museo Aborigen Chorro de Maíta

This museum (tel. 024/43-0421, daily 9 A.M.–5 P.M., entrance CUC2, cameras CUC1, videos CUC5), on a hilltop seven kilometers east of Guardalavaca and two kilometers south from the highway, is on a large aboriginal burial site (almost 200 skeletons have been unearthed). A gallery surrounds the burial ground within a building where the skeletons lie in peaceful repose. Pre-Columbian artifacts are displayed. A life-size model Indian village—**Aldea Taína**—has been re-created across the road (CUC3 additional) with an ensemble of locals dressed like Taíno.

Recreativo Bahía de Naranjo

This huge flask-shaped bay, about four kilometers west of Guardalavaca, is fringed by mangroves and dry forest. The eastern headland is accessible via **Las Guanas Sendero Eco-Arqueológico** (daily 8:30 A.M.–5:30 P.M., CUC3), where trails lead to archaeological

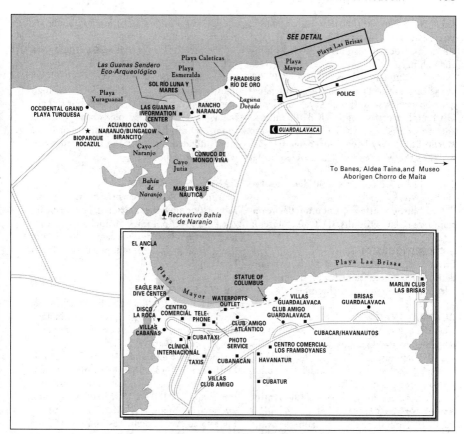

sites and Cueva Ciboney, a funerary cave with petroglyphs. Lookout towers provide a bird's-eye view. An interpretive center offers introductions to the flora and fauna.

Acuario Cayo Naranjo (tel. 024/43-0132, daily 9 A.M.–9 P.M., CUC2 cameras, CUC5 videos) occupies a natural lagoon on the tiny island in the middle of the bay. Sea lions and dolphins perform acrobatics at noon. The hotels offer excursions (CUC40 including boat tour; CUC99 adult, CUC48 children to swim with dolphins).

Entertainment
The hotels all have nightly *animaciones* (cabarets). *The* place to be on weekends is the open-air **Disco La Roca** (tel. 024/43-0167, Fri.–Sun. 11 P.M.–2 A.M., CUC6), overlooking the beach at the west end of Guardalavaca. A *cabaret espectáculo* precedes the disco.

The **Arcada de Juegos** in the Centro Comercial Los Flamboyanes has electronic games.

Recreation
Horseback riding is offered at **Centro Hípico Rancho Naranjo** (Playa Esmeralda) and **Bioparque Rocazul** (daily 9 A.M.–5 P.M., entrance CUC8, cameras CUC1, videos CUC2), a 1,487-hectare recreational facility on the west side of the bay. Trails lead through the scrub and mangroves, and to **Finca Monte Bello**

(CUC16), a faux farm hosting rodeos (Mon., Wed., and Fri. 10:30 A.M., CUC9 adult, CUC5 children). Rocazul also offers guided hiking and fishing.

Marlin Club Las Brisas (tel. 024/43-0774), at the east end of Playa Las Brisas, offers banana-boat rides, waterskiing, kayak and Hobie Cat rental, sportfishing (CUC310), and catamaran excursions (CUC79). The base, and **Marlin Eagle Ray Dive Center** (tel. 024/33-6702) at the west end of Playa Mayor, offer scuba diving (CUC45 one dive) at 11 A.M. and 2 P.M. There are more than 30 dive sites, including wrecks.

Gaviotatours offers a **Locomotur** steam-train ride (CUC49 adults, CUC30 children).

Accommodations

Private room rentals are banned. All accommodations are air-conditioned, with satellite TVs, telephones and modern bathrooms.

GUARDALAVACA

Islazul's **Villas Cabañas** (tel. 024/43-0314, jalojamiento@vcabanas.gvc.cyt.cu, CUC20 s, CU30 d low season, CUC25 s, CUC40 d high season), at the west end of Guardalavaca, offers simple three-person *cabinas*.

Cubanacán's all-inclusive **Club Amigo Atlántico-Guardalavaca** (tel. 024/43-0180, fax 024/43-0200, reserva@clubamigo.gcv.tur.cu) incorporates 747 rooms in four properties. **Club Amigo Guardalavaca** (CUC40 s, CUC50 d low season, CUC88 s, CUC110 d high season), 100 meters inland from the beach, has 234 standard rooms. Activity revolves around a huge swimming pool with a water slide, and there's tennis and volleyball. The beachfront **Club Amigo Atlántico** (CUC56 s, CUC70 d low season, CUC104 s, CUC30 d high season) has more upscale "Tropical" rooms, though not all have ocean views. The contemporary **Villas Club Amigo** (CUC64 s, CUC80 d low season, CUC112 s, CUC140 d high season) has 136 rooms in gracious two-story villas around a swimming pool in landscaped grounds. Last but not least, the beachfront **Villas Guardalavaca** (CUC80 s, CUC100 d low season, CUC120

s, CUC150 d high season) has 144 beachside *cabinas* including four mini-suites.

The nicest place is **Brisas Guardalavaca** (tel. 024/43-0218, fax 024/43-0418, www.brisasguardalavaca.com, from CUC75 s, CUC94 d low season, from CUC96 s, CUC120 d high season), on Playa Las Brisas. This four-star all-inclusive resort has 357 pleasantly furnished rooms, 80 mini-suites, and four junior suites and is divided into villa and hotel complexes with two large pools.

BAHÍA DE NARANJO

Marlin Base Náutica rents the charming two-room **Bungalow Birancito** (tel. 024/43-0132, fax 024/43-0433, CUC50 including breakfast) on Cayo Naranjo, adjacent to the Acuario Cayo Naranjo. It sleeps four people. Meals can be arranged.

PLAYA ESMERALDA

All the following all-inclusive hotels are run by Gaviota (www.grupo-gaviota.cu) and include entertainment, water sports, and most amenities you could want of a beach

The **Sol Río de Luna y Mares** (tel. 024/43-0030, fax 024/43-0065, www.solmeliacuba.com, from CUC150 s, CUC200 d low season, from CUC180 s, CUC230 d high season), operated by Spain's Sol Meliá and comprising two adjacent hotels, has 564 rooms done up in eye-pleasing Caribbean pastels and set in beautifully landscaped grounds. It was refurbished in 2008 and has concierge service. Also managed by Sol Meliá and refurbished in 2008, **Paradisus Río de Oro** (tel. 024/43-0090, fax 024/30095, www.solmeliacuba.com, from CUC170 s, CUC250 d low season, from CUC220 s, CUC300 d high season) is a more upscale 300-room option with similarly lively tropical decor and an exquisite contemporary vogue. A highlight is its Japanese restaurant.

PLAYAS PESQUERO AND YURAGUANA

The 309-room **Blau Costa Verde Beach** (tel. 24/43-3510, fax 24/43-3515, www.blau-hotels.com, from CUC77 s, CUC124 d low season, CUC100 s, CUC170 d high season)

is handsome within, despite its ungainly exterior and awkward layout. The vast freeform pool with swim-up bar is a nice feature. There's not much to choose between the Blau and the similarly priced **Hotel Playa Costa Verde** (tel. 024/43-3520, fax 024/43-3525, sales@playacostaverde.co.cu), with 464 rooms and 16 suites.

Billed as a five-star (it barely meets four-star international standards), the delightful **Hotel Playa Pesquero** (tel. 024/43-3530, fax 024/43-3535) has a vast Asian-style lobby with fish ponds. The 928 junior suites (eight equipped for guests with disabilities) and 16 suites feature lively Caribbean colors and a contemporary neoclassical chic.

Top billing goes to the classy, 520-room **◖ Occidental Grand Playa Turquesa** (tel. 024/43-3540, fax 024/43-3545, www.occidental-hoteles.com, from CUC150 s, CUC200 d) at Playa Yaraguanal. It has six restaurants, and seven pools connected by cascading waterfalls.

Food

◖ El Ancla (tel. 024/43-0381, daily 10 A.M.–10 P.M.), atop a coral outcrop at the west end of Playa Mayor, specializes in seafood; it serves fish dishes for CUC8 and up (lobster costs a ludicrous CUC31).

Conuco de Mongo Viña (no tel., daily 8 A.M.–3 P.M., under CUC5), on the east shore of Bahía de Naranjo, serves *criollo* meals in its thatched restaurant. It has a small zoo and cactus garden.

Most hotels sell day and evening passes (CUC35–50), which include all-inclusive use of their restaurants and other facilities.

Information and Services

The post office and DHL service are in the Las Brisas resort. International calls from hotels are expensive; use the *minipuntos* (telephone kiosks) roadside at Playa Mayor and Playa Esmeralda.

There's a **bank** (Mon.–Fri. 8 A.M.–3:30 P.M., Sat. 8 A.M.–1 P.M.) at Club Amigo Guardalavaca and a **Clínica Internacional** (tel. 024/43-0312, 24 hours) at the west end of Guardalavaca.

Asistur (tel. 024/43-0148, Mon.–Fri. 8:30 A.M.–5 P.M.), in the Centro Comercial Guardalavaca, offers emergency assistance.

Getting There and Away

Guardalavaca has no airport. Vacationers on package tours land at Holguín.

Buses operate between Holguín and Banes, but service is unreliable. A taxi from Holguín will cost about CUC45 one-way.

You can rent cars from **Cubacar** (tel. 024/43-0389), adjacent to Club Amigo Guardalavaca.

Excursions can be purchased at hotel tour desks or direct with **Cubatur** (tel. 024/43-0170), 50 meters south of Centro Comercial Los Framboyantes; **Havanatur** (tel. 024/43-0406, noryuan@havanatur.cu), at the west end of Guardalavaca; or **Gaviota** (tel. 024/43-0903, fax 024/30908, travel.hog@gaviota-tours.co.cu).

Marina Puerto de Vita (tel. 024/43-0445, marvita@enet.cu), one kilometer west of Playa Pesquero, has 38 slips.

Getting Around

Horse-drawn *coches* charge CUC3 for a tour around Guardalavaca (CUC15 to the *acuario*).

You can hop on and off Transtur's **Guardalavaca Beach Tour** (CUC5), which plies between Guardalavaca and Acuario Cayo Naranjo and other beaches three times daily. The **Holguín Bus Tour** (CUC15) departs Guardalavaca at 9:20 A.M. and Holguín at 1 P.M.

Bicycles and scooters (CUC10 one hour, CUC14 two hours, CUC27 per day) can be rented at most hotels.

Taxis await custom west of Villa Turey, or call **Cubataxi** (tel. 024/43-0330).

The gas station is one kilometer west of town.

BANES

Banes (pop. 84,000), about 34 kilometers southeast of Guardalavaca and 70 kilometers northeast of Holguín, is a sleepy provincial sugar town. This is the real Cuba, with all the sundry life that Guardalavaca lacks. For much of the past century, the town was run by the United Fruit Company, which owned virtually all the land hereabouts and had a massive (and now defunct) sugar mill called Boston (since renamed Nicaragua) five kilometers south of town. "El Panchito," a 1888 steam locomotive made in Philadelphia, now stands idle in **Plaza del Panchito,** in the center of town.

Fulgencio Batista was born here in 1901. His future archenemies, Fidel and Raúl Castro, were born nearby at Birán. As youths the brothers would come into town in a red convertible to party at the American Club. On October 12, 1948, Fidel married Mirta Díaz-Balart, daughter of the mayor of Banes, in the art deco **Iglesia de Nuestra Señora de la Caridad,** on Parque Martí (the marriage dissolved five years later but produced a son, Fidelito).

The **Museo Indocubano** (Museum of Indian Civilization, General Marrero #305, tel. 024/80-2487, Tues.–Sun. 8 A.M.–4 P.M., CUC1) exhibits a collection of more than 20,000 pre-Columbian artifacts, most importantly a small gold fertility idol wearing a feather headdress.

Entertainment

On Sundays it all happens at **Café Cantante** (General Marrero #320, no tel.), with afternoon *trova* (2–7 P.M., free) and evening music and dancing, from Buena Vista Social Club–style *son* to salsa. The **Casa de la Cultura** (tel. 024/80-2111, CUC1), next door, competes with its own Sunday-afternoon *trova,* and broad-ranging evening sessions from *bolero* to reggaeton.

Accommodations and Food

Casas particulares include **Casa Evelyn Feria Diesquez** (Bruno Merino #3401-A, e/ Delfín Pepo y Heredia, tel. 024/80-3150, CUC15), with two upstairs rooms opening to a terrace. Each has private bathroom. The hostess is a delight. There's secure parking. If she's full, Evelyn will call around for alternatives.

The best dining, which isn't saying much, is at **Restaurante El Latino** (General Marrero #720, tel. 024/80-2298, daily 11 A.M.–11 P.M.), offering creole dishes to live music accompaniment.

Getting There and Away

Buses operate between Holguín and Banes; the terminal is at Calle Los Angeles and Tráfico. You can also take a *camion* (six times daily).

Holguín to Guantánamo Province

◖ MUSEO CONJUNTO HISTÓRICO BIRÁN

Fidel Castro was born on August 13, 1926, at Finca Las Manacas, at Birán, below the western foothills of the Altiplanici de Nipe, 60 kilometers southeast of Holguín. Castro's father, Ángel, began leasing land from the United Fruit Company in 1910, farmed sugarcane to sell to the mills, and grew wealthy on the proceeds of his 26,000-acre domain. Eventually, he acquired forests, a sawmill, and nickel mine, and was the most important man in the region. Fidel, however, has worked to downplay his social privilege and prefers to exaggerate the simplicity of his background. "The house was made of wood. No mortar, cement or bricks," he told Brazilian theologian Frey Beto in *Fidel: My Early Years.* In truth it's a substantial house—clearly the home of a well-to-do man. The two-story house on wooden pilings with a cattle barn underneath is a replica—the original apparently burned to the ground in 1954. The property also contained a slaughterhouse, repair shop, store, bakery, and other facilities. The handsome *finca* looks out over a large lake.

In 2002 the *finca* (tel. 024/28-6114, Tues.–Sat. 8 A.M.–4 P.M., Sun. 8 A.M.–noon,

poster of the Castro brothers, Birán

entrance CUC10, cameras CUC10, videos CUC10) opened to the public as a National Historic Site. There are enough armed soldiers to repel an invasion! A guide will accompany you as you're shown the graves of Castro's parents, Ángel and Lina (the family housemaid); the simple schoolhouse that Fidel attended (his desk is front row, center, of course); and the local post office and telegraph office. The huge main house has many original furnishings, plus Fidel's personal effects (including his baseball glove and basketball), and the bed in which it is claimed he was born. (In *After Fidel,* author and former CIA analyst Brian Latell cites convincing evidence that Fidel, who was born illegitimate and not legally acknowledged by his father until he was 17, lived his first few years with his mother and apart from his father and his formal wife.)

From Holguín, take the Cueto road (6-123). Turn south five kilometers west of Cueto to Loynaz Echevarría. Turn east (left) just beyond the *central.* The community of Birán is seven kilometers farther, and Finca Las Manacas is two kilometers to the north.

PINARES DE MAYARÍ

From the small town of **Mayarí Abajo,** 80 kilometers east of Holguín, a road climbs sharply onto a broad *altiplano* (plateau) high in the Sierra Cristal, where mists drift languidly through the pine forest. It's a great place to beat the heat and for bird-watching and hiking, centered on Pinares de Mayarí, an eco-focused hotel at the mountain peak of **Loma de Mensura** (995 meters), 20 kilometers south of Mayarí. Much of the region is enshrined in **Parque Nacional La Mensura.** About three kilometers south of Mayarí, you'll pass an unmarked turnoff for the **Farallones de Seboruco** (no tel., daily 8 A.M.–5 P.M., CUC2), a cavern system where indigenous Indian artifacts dating back 5,000 years have been found. It has trails.

At Loma de Mensura, the Cuban Academy of Sciences' **Estación de Investigación Integral de la Montaña** includes an **Orquideario La Mensura** (Mon.–Sat. 8 A.M.–5 P.M., no tel.), an orchid garden, and the 2.4-kilometer-long **Sendero La Sabina** self-guided nature trail named for a local juniper species. You must pay in the hotel (CUC2 entrance and guided tour).

© CHRISTOPHER P. BAKER

Salto El Guayabo

Two kilometers north of the Orquideario is **La Plancha,** another lovely garden set amid eucalyptus and where an old lady demonstrates traditional coffee-grinding in a *pilón* (pestle).

You may need a 4WD vehicle to reach **Finca Los Exóticos** (8 km west of the Pinares road), where elk, nilgai, and deer are bred (originally for the hunting pleasure of the Communist elite).

Salto El Guayabo

The high point of the altiplano is this not-to-be-missed site (7 A.M.–6 P.M., CUC5), 17 kilometers north of Villa Pinares de Mayarí. The *salto* is a twin waterfall (120 and 140 meters, respectively). A *mirador* offers sensational views of the cascade and forested river canyon, and far out to the Atlantic. It has a delightful restaurant in a garden of ferns and poincianas. You can hike two trails: one descends to the base of the falls, the second leads to the top.

Accommodations and Food

Casa de Elin y Ilsïa (Calle Moncada #89, tel.

5291-0845, CUC20 downstairs, CUC25 upstairs, including breakfast), 200 meters south of the Cupet gas station in Mayarí, is the only *casa particular* for miles. Stone walls enhance the pleasing effect in the two air-conditioned guest rooms (one upstairs), each with private bathroom. Meals are served in a thatched *rancho* in the garden. There's secure parking.

At 680 meters above sea level, **Villa Pinares de Mayarí** (tel. 024/50-3308, commercial@vpinares.co.cu, CUC26 s, CUC43 d low season, CUC32 s, CUC46 d high season) is a mountain eco-resort operated by Gaviota. It has 29 spacious yet rustic wooden one-, two- and three-bedroom cottages, all with local TV and private bathrooms. There's a swimming pool and huge restaurant.

CAYO SAETÍA

This 42-square-kilometer cay (CUC10 entrance), 18 kilometers north of the coast highway, is separated from the mainland by a hair's-breadth waterway and forms the easternmost side of the Bahía de Nipes. Its ecosystems range from mangrove swamps to evergreen forests harboring endangered species, including *jabalí* (wild boar), plus exotic animals—ostrich, zebra, camels, and water buffalo, etc.—originally imported for the hunting pleasure of top Communist officials, for whom Cayo Saetía was once a private vacation spot.

One-hour jeep safaris (CUC9) and horseback riding (CUC6 per hour) are available. There are beaches for sunning.

If driving, note that many maps show a non-existent road direct from the Carretera Costa Norte to Cayo Saetía. The real road leads to Felton, a T junction with an unmarked turnoff to the right for Cayo Saetía.

Accommodations and Food

Villa Cayo Saetía (tel. 024/51-6900, director@cayosaetia.co.cu, CUC49 s, CUC60 d low season, CUC54 s, CUC65 d high season) has 12 handsome yet rustic *cabinas* and suites with satellite TVs. The eyes of animals that wandered between crosshairs glower eerily as you dine in the restaurant.

BIG FRUIT

After the Wars of Independence, the vast sugarcane fields of Holguín gradually fell into the hands of U.S. corporations, especially the United Fruit Company (UFC), which bought the land for a pittance and came to dominate economic and political life in the region. While the UFC was also a philanthropic agent of good deeds locally, paying, for example, for a sewer system for the town of Banes, Tad Szulc explains that it was "emblematic of almost everything that was wrong in Cuba's relationship with the United States: the powerlessness, the degree to which the mill constituted a world unto itself in which Cubans had no rights except those conceded by the company." One of the few Cubans who benefited economically from the UFC arrangement was Fidel Castro's father, Ángel Castro, who leased lands from UFC and grew to be both prosperous and powerful. The pitiful existence of many among the Cuban peasantry was not lost on the young Fidel, who, it is claimed, first agitated on workers' behalf as a boy – and on his father's estate.

MOA

East of Mayarí, the Circuito Norte coast road leads past a series of port towns that rely on the mineral ore industries. Tall chimneys belching out smoke announce your arrival at the coastal town of Moa. The town is smothered with red dust from the nearby processing plants. It has been claimed (probably in jest) that Cuban engineers would rather sacrifice their careers than work here. Nonetheless, Moa has the only accommodations in the many lonesome miles between Mayarí and Baracoa. Passing through Sagua de Tanamo (30 kilometers west of Moa), note the **Caballo de Troya** (Trojan Horse), a homemade armored carrier used by revolutionaries against Batista's troops.

Two kilometers east of Moa you'll pass **Empresa Comandante Ernesto Che Guevara,** a huge smelting plant guarded by a statue of Che towering over the gates. The environment has been hammered and sickled into a grotesque gangue pitted with pestilential lagoons. Gnarled, splintered trees add to the dramatic effect, like the aftermath of a World War I bombardment.

Photography is prohibited—one suspects more because the government is embarrassed by the horrendous blight than for any strategic reason!

Accommodations

Islazul's Soviet-era **Hotel Miraflores** (Av. Amistad, tel. 024/66-6103, jcarpeta@miraflores.co.cu, CUC15 s, CUC20 d year-round) has 148 modestly furnished rooms, plus a swimming pool, restaurant, disco, and car rental.

Getting There and Away

Cubana (tel. 024/66-7916) flies from Havana on Monday to Moa's **Orestes Acosta Airport** (tel. 024/66-7012), three kilometers east of town.

A bus departs Holguín for Moa daily, but no bus operates between Moa and Baracoa (70 kilometers farther east); *camiones* make the journey.

There's a gas station one kilometer west of town (**Cubacar,** tel. 024/60-2232, rents cars here) and another at the entrance to Empresa Comandante Ernesto Che Guevara.

GRANMA

Cuba's southwesternmost province abounds with sites of historical importance. Throughout Cuba's history, the region has been a hotbed of rebellion, beginning in 1512 when Hatuey, the local Indian chieftain, rebelled against Spain. The citizens of Bayamo were from the outset at the forefront of the drive for independence, and the city, which became the capital of the provisional republic, is brimful of sites associated with the days when Cuba's *criollo* population fought to oust Spain. Nearby, at La Demajagua, Carlos Céspedes freed his slaves and proclaimed Cuba's independence. And Dos Ríos, in the northeast of the province, is the site where José Martí chose martyrdom in battle in 1895.

The region also became the first battleground in the revolutionary efforts to topple the Batista regime, initiated on July 26, 1953, when Castro's rebels attacked the Bayamo garrison in concert with an attack on the Moncada barracks in Santiago. In 1956, Castro, Che Guevara, and 80 fellow revolutionaries came ashore at Las Colorados to set up their Rebel Army. The province is named for the vessel— the *Granma*—in which the revolutionaries traveled from Mexico.

Several sites recall those revolutionary days, not least La Comandancia de la Plata (Fidel Castro's guerrilla headquarters), deep in the Sierra Maestra. An enormous swath is protected within Gran Parque Nacional Sierra Maestra, fabulous for bird-watching and hiking. You can even ascend the trail to Pico Turquino, Cuba's highest mountain.

For physical drama, Granma Province is

HIGHLIGHTS

Parque Céspedes: Setting of important events in Cuban history, Bayamo's main plaza has two fine museums and other buildings of import. It adjoins Plaza del Himno, an intimate cobbled square with one of the nation's finest and most important churches (page 417).

La Comandancia de la Plata: The ridgetop trail to Castro's former (and well-preserved) guerrilla headquarters is a splendid hike (page 423).

Hiking to Pico Turquino: For the ultimate high, this overnight guided hike to the summit of Cuba's highest peak is strenuous but richly rewarding (page 424).

Parque Nacional Desembarco del Granma: Trails through tropical dry forest provide ample opportunities for spotting rare birds. Caves with dripstone formations are a bonus (page 431).

Marea del Portillo to Santiago de Cuba: The ultimate scenic drive is also an adventure (not least due to a badly deteriorated road). Break out the camera (page 433)!

LOOK FOR **(** TO FIND RECOMMENDED SIGHTS, ACTIVITIES, DINING, AND LODGING.

hard to beat. The province is neatly divided into plains (to the north) and mountains (to the south). The Río Cauto—Cuba's longest river—runs north from these mountains and feeds the rich farmland of the northern plains. The river delta is a vast mangrove swampland. Whereas the north side of the Sierra Maestra has a moist microclimate and is lushly foliated, the south side lies in a rain shadow. Greenery yields to cacti-studded semi-desert.

PLANNING YOUR TIME

Most sites of interest can be discovered by following a circular route along the main highway that runs west from Bayamo, encircles the Sierra Maestra, and runs along the south coast.

If you're into the urban scene, concentrate your time around Bayamo, the provincial capital. Its restored central plaza—**Parque Céspedes**—and adjoining Plaza del Himno have a delightful quality and several historic buildings worth the browse, among them the Casa Natal de Carlos Manuel de Céspedes and the Iglesia Parroquial del Santísima Salvador. If you're in a rush to get to Santiago de Cuba, it's a straight shot along the Carretera Central, perhaps with a short detour to Dos Ríos (with a

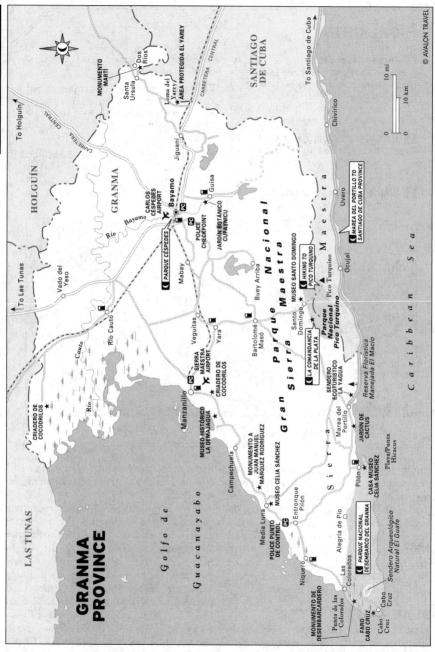

© AVALON TRAVEL

GRANMA
PROVINCE

LAS TUNAS

To Holguín

To Las Tunas

HOLGUÍN

GRANMA

SANTIAGO
DE CUBA

To Santiago de Cuba

CARRETERA CENTRAL

CARRETERA CENTRAL

MONUMENTO MARTÍ
Dos Ríos
Santa Ursula
Loma del Yarey
ÁREA PROTEGIDA EL YAREY

Jiguaní

Chivirico

Bayamo
CARLOS CÉSPEDES AIRPORT
POLICE CHECKPOINT
Guisa
JARDÍN BOTÁNICO CUPAYNICU

Río Bayamo

PARQUE CÉSPEDES

MAREA DEL PORTILLO TO SANTIAGO DE CUBA PROVINCE

Vado del Yeso

Mabay

Buey Arriba

Uvero

Río Cauto

Cauto

Veguitas
SIERRA MAESTRA AIRPORT
Yara
CRIADERO DE COCODRILOS

Bartolomé Masó

MUSEO SANTO DOMINGO

HIKING TO PICO TURQUINO

Pico Turquino

Ocujal

Sierra Maestra

Parque Nacional Gran Sierra Maestra

Santo Domingo

Parque Nacional Pico Turquino

LA COMANDANCIA DE LA PLATA

SENDERO ECOTURÍSTICO LA YAGUA

Reserva Florística Manejada El Macio

Caribbean Sea

CRIADERO DE COCODRILOS

Río

Manzanillo

MUSEO HISTÓRICO LA DEMAJAGUA

MONUMENTO A JUAN MANUEL MÁRQUEZ RODRÍGUEZ
MUSEO CELIA SÁNCHEZ

Campechuela

Marea del Portillo

JARDÍN DE CACTUS

Sierra

Golfo de
Guacanayabo

Media Luna
POLICE PUNTO DE CONTROL
Entronque Pilón
Pilón
CASA MUSEO CELIA SÁNCHEZ
Playa/Punta Hicacos

Alegría de Pío

PARQUE NACIONAL DESEMBARCO DEL GRANMA

Niquero

Las Coloradas

Sendero Arqueológico Natural El Guafe

MONUMENTO DE DESEMBARCADERO
FARO CABO CRUZ
Cabo Cruz
Punta de las Coloradas
Cabo Cruz

0   10 km
0   10 mi

monument commemorating José Martí's martyrdom here in 1895).

Fancy some mountain hiking? Then the Sierra Maestra calls. This vast mountain chain runs about 140 kilometers west–east from the southwest tip of the island (Cabo Cruz) to the city of Santiago de Cuba. The only area developed for ecotourism is at Santo Domingo, gateway to the trailhead to **Pico Turquino** (overnight hike) and **La Comandancia de la Plata** (same-day hike). A guide is compulsory. The access road to Santo Domingo is not for the faint of heart; hill grades appear like sheer drops.

The town of Manzanillo has few sites of interest. The coast road south of Manzanillo, however, has sites sufficient for a day's browsing. Of modest interest are the Criadero de Cocodrilos (croc farm) and Museo Histórico La Demajagua, the former farm where Carlos Manuel de Céspedes became the first landowner to free his slaves. Students of revolutionary history might check out the Museo Celia Sánchez (in Media Luna) and **Parque Nacional Desembarco del Granma,** where Castro and his guerrillas landed to pursue the Revolution. The latter makes for a fleeting visit unless you care to hike the trails that provide spectacular bird-watching on the western slopes of the Sierra Maestra.

A singular reason to visit this region is the spectacular drive between Marea del Portillo and Santiago de Cuba. Running along the coastline for more than 100 kilometers, with the Sierra Maestra rising sheer from the shore, this roller-coaster ride turns a scenic drive into a fantastic adventure. There are virtually no communities en route. You'll need your own wheels; public transport is extremely limited. Hurricane Dennis roared ashore here in July 2005. Much of the road was washed out, and it remains dangerously deteriorated. You can push on from Manzanillo to Santiago de Cuba in a single day. If you plan on visiting all the sites en route, break the drive at Marea del Portillo, a ho-hum beach resort used by budget charter groups (why I don't know; there are very few sights to see around this landlocked locale and the mediocre beach and modicum of activities wear thin very quickly).

Accommodations are limited.

Bayamo and Vicinity

BAYAMO
Bayamo (pop. 130,000) lies at the center of the province, on the Carretera Central, 130 kilometers northwest of Santiago and 95 kilometers southwest of Holguín. The town was the setting for remarkable events during the quest for independence from Spain. The city is called the "Birthplace of Cuban Nationality" and has earned the nickname "La Heróica." Much of the historic core is a national monument.

History
Bayamo, the second settlement in Cuba, was founded in 1513 as Villa de San Salvador de Bayamo by Diego Velázquez on a site near contemporary Yara. It was later moved to its present site. Almost immediately Diego Velázquez set to enslaving the aboriginal population.

Slaves began to arrive from Africa as sugar was planted, fostering to a flourishing slave trade through the port of Manzanillo.

By the 19th century, Bayamo's bourgeoisie were at the forefront of a swelling independence movement. In 1867, following the coup that toppled Spain's Queen Isabella, Carlos Manuel de Céspedes and the elite of Bayamo rose in revolt. The action sparked the Ten Years War that swept the Oriente and central Cuba. Other nationalists rallied to the cause, formed a revolutionary junta, and in open defiance of Spanish authority, played in the parochial church the martial hymn that would eventually become the Cuban national anthem, "To the battle, Bayameses!" With a small force of about 150 men, Céspedes seized Bayamo from Spanish forces on October 20.

GRANMA

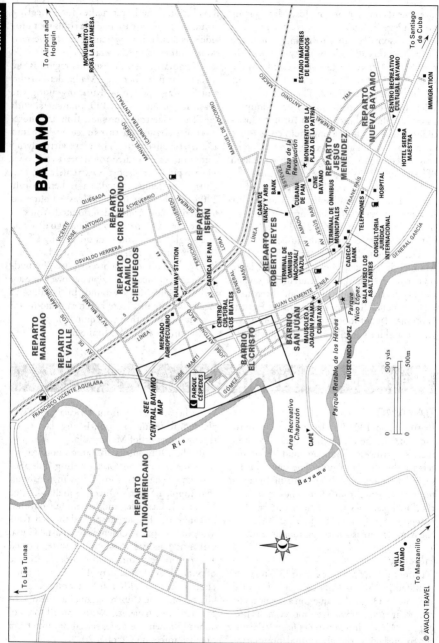

BAYAMO

To Airport and Holguin

MONUMENTO Á ROSA LA BAYAMESA

To Santiago de Cuba

ESTADIO MÁRTIRES DE BARBADOS

MANUEL DE SOCORRO

ANTONIO MACEO

REPARTO NUEVA BAYAMO

CENTRO RECREATIVO CULTURAL BAYAMO

IMMIGRATION

7MA

MONUMENTO DE LA PLAZA DE LA PATRIA

HOTEL SIERRA MAESTRA

REPARTO JESÚS MENÉNDEZ

GENERAL

MANUEL CODEGO (CARRETERA CENTRAL)

QUESADA

REPARTO CIRO REDONDO

JOSE ANTONIO

VICENTE

ECHEVERRIO

FIGUEREDO

Plaza de la Revolución

CINE BAYAMO

CASA DE NANCY Y ARIS

ESTEVEZ

BANK

CUBANA DE PAN

HOSPITAL

AV FRANK PAÍS

OSVALDO HERRERA

REPARTO CAMILO CIENFUEGOS

REPARTO ISERN

LINEA

LORA

REPARTO ROBERTO REYES

AV AMADO

AV JESÚS RABÍ

TERMINAL DE OMNIBUS MUNICIPALES

TELEPHONES

CONSULTORIA JURÍDICA INTERNACIONAL

GENERAL GARCÍA

RAILWAY STATION

CADECA DE PAN

PERUCHO

MASÓ

GENERAL

TERMINAL DE OMNIBUS NACIONAL/ VIAZUL

CADECA BANK

REPARTO MARIANAO

REPARTO EL VALLE

AV DE MILANÉS (LOS) MARTÍ

AV 30

AV 6

LINEA

MERCADO AGROPECUARIO

CENTRO CULTURAL LOS BEATLES

AV SACO

JOSE ANTONIO SACO

ZENEA

JUAN CLEMENTE ZENEA

CUBATAXI

BARRIO SAN JUAN

MAUSOLEO A JOAQUÍN PALMA

Parque Nico López

SALA MUSEO LOS ASALTANTES

FRANCISCO VICENTE AGUILAR

JOSE MARTÍ

GÓMEZ

SEE "CENTRAL BAYAMO" MAP

PARQUE CÉSPEDES

BARRIO EL CRISTO

Parque Retablo de los Héroes

MUSEO NICO LÓPEZ

500 yds

500m

Río

Area Recreativo Chapuzón

CAFÉ

To Las Tunas

REPARTO LATINOAMERICANO

Bayamo

N

VILLA BAYAMO

To Manzanillo

© AVALON TRAVEL

In January 1869, as Céspedes's army of mulattoes, freed slaves, and poor whites was attacking Holguín, Spanish troops were at Bayamo's doorstep. The rebellious citizens burned Bayamo to the ground rather than cede it to Spanish troops. Alas, internal dissent arose among the revolutionary leadership and the Ten Years War fizzled. Spanish troops left Bayamo for a final time on April 28, 1898, when the city was captured by rebel leader General Calixto García during the War of Independence.

Orientation

Bayamo is laid out atop the eastern bluff of the Río Bayamo, which flows in a deep ravine. The historic core sits above the gorge.

The Carretera Central (Carretera Manuel Cedeño) from Holguín enters Bayamo from the northeast and skirts the historic core as it sweeps southeast for Santiago. Avenida Perucho Figueredo leads off the Carretera Central and runs due west to Parque Céspedes. Calle General García—the main commercial street and a pedestrian precinct—leads south from Parque Céspedes, paralleled by Calles José Martí and Juan Clemente Zeneo, which merge south with the Carretera Central. To the north they merge into Avenida Francisco Vicente Aguilera, which begins one block north of Parque Céspedes and leads to a Y fork for Las Tunas and Manzanillo.

El Bulevar

This pedestrian street (General García) runs south from Parque Céspedes for six blocks. In 2009, local artists graced it with ceramic tiles, a grassy median, and sculptures, including turning lampposts into odd works of arts, such as faux trees and bottles.

At Masó, four blocks south of the square, are four key sites. First up, the **Gabinete de Arqueología** (tel. 023/42-1591, Tues.–Fri. 9 A.M.–noon and 1:30–5 P.M., Sat.–Sun. 9 A.M.–1 P.M., CUC1) displays pre-Columbian stoneware and other artifacts. Next door, the **Acuario** (no tel., Tues.–Sat. 9 A.M.–5 P.M. and Sun. 10 A.M.–1 P.M., free) has two dozen

tanks with tropical fish, including endemic garfish.

The **Museo de Cera** (Calixto García #254, tel. 023/42-5421, Mon.–Fri. 9 A.M.–5 P.M., Sat. 10 A.M.–1 P.M. and 7–10 P.M., Sun. 9 A.M.–noon, CUC1 entrance, CUC5 camera), Cuba's only wax museum, displays 10 life-size waxworks, from world-renowned Cuban musician Compay Segundo to Ernest Hemingway and Fabio di Celmo, the Italian tourist killed by a terrorist bomb in a Havana hotel in 1997. The figures are the work of self-taught artists Rafael Barrios Madrigal and his son Leander Barrios Milan.

Next, cross the street to admire **La Maqueta** (tel. 023/42-3633, Mon.–Fri. 9 A.M.–noon and 1:30–5 P.M.), displaying scale models of the city and individual buildings of note.

Ⓒ Parque Céspedes

This beautiful square is surrounded by important buildings. At its center is a granite column topped by a larger-than-life bronze statue of Carlos Manuel de Céspedes. There's also a bust of local patriot Perucho Figueredo (1819–1870), inscribed with the words (in Spanish) he wrote for the *himno nacional*, "La Bayamesa":

To the battle, run, Bayamases
Let the fatherland proudly observe you
Do not fear a glorious death
To die for the fatherland is to live.

Céspedes was born on April 18, 1819, in a handsome two-story dwelling on the north side of the square. The house, **Casa Natal de Carlos Manuel de Céspedes** (Maceo #57, tel. 023/42-3864, Tues.–Sat. 9 A.M.–5 P.M., Sun. 9 A.M.–3 P.M., CUC1) was one of only a fistful of houses to survive the fire of January 1869. Downstairs are letters, photographs, and maps, plus Céspedes' gleaming ceremonial sword. The ornately decorated upstairs bedrooms are full of his mahogany furniture. His law books are there, as is the printing press on which Céspedes published his *Cubana Libre,* the first independent newspaper in Cuba.

Next door is the **Museo Provincial** (Maceo

CENTRAL BAYAMO

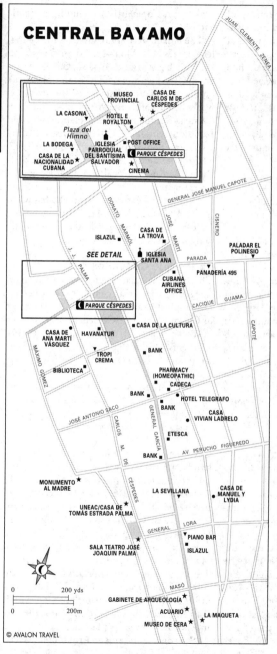

© AVALON TRAVEL

#58, tel. 023/42-4125, Wed.–
Mon. 9 A.M.–5 P.M., Sat.–Sun.
9 A.M.–1 P.M., CUC1 entrance,
CUC5 cameras), in the house
where Manuel Muñoz Cedeño,
composer of the *himno nacional,*
was born.

On the east side is the house
(now the Poder Popular) where
Céspedes, as president of the
newly founded republic, announced the abolition of slavery.

Parque Céspedes opens to
the northwest onto the charming **Plaza del Himno,** dominated by the beautifully restored
**Iglesia Parroquial del Santísima
Salvador** (tel. 023/42-2514,
Mon.–Fri. 9 A.M.–noon and
3–5 P.M., Sat. 9 A.M.–noon), a national monument also known as
the Parroquial Mayor. The revolutionary national anthem was sung
for the first time in the cathedral
(by a choir of 12 women—the
Bayamesas) during Corpus Christi
celebrations on June 11, 1868, with
the dumbfounded colonial governor in attendance. Its most admirable feature is the beautiful mural
of Céspedes and the Bayamesas
above the altar. The church occupies the site of the original church,
built in 1516, rebuilt in 1733, and
rebuilt again following the fire of
1869. On the north side of the cathedral is a small chapel—**Capilla
de la Dolorosa**—that dates back
to 1630 and miraculously survived
the fire. It has a Mudejar ceiling
and a baroque gilt altarpiece.

The quaint **Casa de la
Nacionalidad Cubana** (tel.
023/42-4833, Mon.–Fri. 8 A.M.–
noon and 1–4 P.M., free), on the
west side, houses the town historian's office and displays period
furniture.

© CHRISTOPHER P. BAKER

Iglesia Parroquial del Santísima Salvador, Bayamo

Parque Ñico López

Also known as Plaza de la Patria, this small plaza is named for a revolutionary hero who, along with 24 other members of Fidel Castro's rebels, attacked Batista's army barracks on July 26, 1953. López survived, fled to Mexico, and was with Fidel aboard the *Granma* (he was killed shortly after landing in Cuba in 1956).

López is honored on the **Retablo de los Héroes** (Calles Martí and Amado Éstevez), a bas-relief in the center of the square; in the **Museo Ñico López** (Abihail González, Tues.–Sat. 9 A.M.–noon and 1:30–5 P.M., Sun. 9 A.M.–1 P.M., free), in the former medieval-style barracks, 100 meters west of the square; the tiny **Sala Museo Los Asaltantes** (Agusto Marquéz, tel. 023/42-3181, Tues.–Fri. 9 A.M.–5 P.M., Sat. noon–8 P.M., and Sun. 8 A.M.–noon, CUC0.50), 50 meters southeast of the square; and on the **Plaza de la Revolución** (Av. Jesús Rabi, east of the Carretera Central), where the **Monumento de la Plaza de la Patria** features a bas-relief of heroes of the *Granma* landing.

Entertainment and Events

Fireworks and candles are lit each January 12 on Parque Céspedes to commemorate the burning of the town in 1869, and a procession of horses symbolizes its abandonment.

The lively **Casa de la Trova** (Martí, esq. Maceo, tel. 023/42-5673, Tues.–Sat. 10 A.M.–1 A.M., free by day, CUC1 at night) is fabulous for hearing traditional music. And *bolero* is performed each Saturday at 4 P.M. at **UNEAC** (Céspedes #158, tel. 023/42-3670, www.uneac.com, free), in the Casa de Tomás Estrada Palma, where in 1835 Tomás Estrada Palma was born (he became the first president of Cuba following independence). It hosts jazz each third Thursday of the month (8:30 P.M., free).

The **Sala Teatro José Joaquín Palma** (Céspedes, tel. 023/42-4423) hosts drama, children's theater, and folkloric performances. And the **Casa de la Cultura** (tel. 023/42-5917, daily 8 A.M.–8 P.M.), on the east side of Parque Céspedes, hosts cultural programs.

For charm, check out **La Bodega** (Plaza del Himno, tel. 023/42-1011, Fri.–Sun. 10 P.M.–1 A.M.), a Spanish-style *bodega* with seats made of barrels and cart wheels. It has music in a patio overhanging the river canyon. A less lively but similar alternative is the nearby **La Casona** (Plaza del Himno, Sat. 11 A.M.–11 P.M., Sun.–Mon. 10 A.M.–10 P.M.).

Local group Cubayam sings Beatles songs on weekends at **Centro Cultural Los Beatles** (Zenea e/ Saco y Figueredo, tel. 023/42-1799, Tues.–Sun. 7 A.M.–midnight, 5–10 pesos). This open-air venue is dead during the week. Life-size figures of the Fab Four greet you at the doorway.

You can get your kicks at **Centro Recreativo Cultural Bayamo** (tel. 023/48-6918), opposite the Hotel Sierra Maestra, with a *cabaret espectáculo* Fri.–Sun. at 10:30 P.M. (CUC5 per pair).

Accommodations

You can book *campismos* in the province through **Campismo Popular** (General García #112 e/ Saco y Figueredo, tel. 023/42-4425, Mon.–Fri. 8–11 A.M. and 3–7 P.M., Sat. 9 A.M.–noon).

Museo Ñico López, Bayamo

CASAS PARTICULARES

Among the better town-center options is **Casa de Ana Martí Vázquez** (Céspedes #4, e/ Maceo y Canducha, tel. 023/42-5323, CUC20–25), a gracious home beautifully furnished throughout with antiques and chandeliers. The lounge opens to a shady stone patio. Ana hosts two rooms: One, in a loft, is like a honeymoon suite.

I enjoyed my stay with wonderful hosts at **Casa de Manuel y Lydia** (Donato Mármol #323, e/ Figueredo y Lora, tel. 023/42-3175, nene19432001@yahoo.es, CUC20), with a simply furnished, air-conditioned room with fan, shared hot-water bathroom, opening to a spacious patio with a hammock and rockers. If it's full, try **Casa Vivian Ladrelo** (Donato Mármol #266 e/ Saco y Figueredo, tel. 024/42-1413, CUC20), one block north.

I also enjoyed a stay at **Casa de Nancy y Avis** (Calle Amado Ésteves #67, e/ 8 y 9, Rpto. Jesús Menéndez, tel. 023/42-4726, CUC20), a short walk from downtown. The delightful owners offer one small but pleasing air-conditioned room with fan and private bathroom; the mattress is soft, however. It has secure parking.

HOTELS

The **Hotel E Royalton** (Maceo #53, tel. 023/42-2290, fax 023/42-2268), on the west side of Parque Céspedes, has an all-marble staircase leading to 33 small rooms with firm mattresses and modern bathrooms. At last visit, it was being refurbished to open as a luxury boutique Hotel E, in the Cubanacán chain.

Formatur's pleasing **Hotel Telégrafo** (Saco #108, e/ García y Marmól, tel. 023/42-5510, fax 023/42-7389, www.ehtgr.co.cu, CUC15 s, CUC20 d, CUC30 suite year-round) functions as a hotel school. It has 12 air-conditioned rooms with contemporary furnishings and modern bathrooms. It has a bar and restaurant.

If Hotel Royalton and Hotel Telégrafo are full, try Islazul's **Villa Bayamo** (Carretera de Manzanillo, tel. 023/42-3102, fax 023/42-4485, jservicio@villagrm.co.cu, CUC15 s, CUC24 d year-round), two kilometers west of Bayamo. It has 12 uninspired air-conditioned rooms and 10 two-bedroom cabins, plus a swimming pool and small nightclub.

Cubanacán's Soviet-style **Hotel Sierra Maestra** (Carretera Central, Km 7.5, tel. 023/42-7970, fax 023/42-7973, commercial@hsierra@grm.tur.cu, CUC19 s, CUC30 d year-round), three kilometers southeast of the city center, reopened to tourists in 2009 after being refurbished. Modern bathrooms are the high point of its 114 simply furnished rooms, and it has a swimming pool and disco.

Food

New restaurants deteriorate rapidly in Cuba. Proof in point, Spanish-themed **La Sevillana** (Calixto García #171, e/ Perucho Figueredo y General Lora, tel. 023/42-1472, daily noon–2 P.M. and 6–10 P.M.) is now serving only simple *criollo* dishes for pesos. It has dinner sittings 6–8 P.M. and 8–10 P.M.

Paladar El Polinesio (Parada #125, e/ Cisnero y Pío Rosaro, tel. 023/42-3860, daily noon–11 P.M.) has alfresco dining beneath the stars on an upstairs patio. The house dish is *pollo polinesio* (chicken with pineapple, CUC8).

Otherwise your best bets are the hotel restaurants.

Tropi Crema (daily 10 A.M.–10 P.M.), on Parque Céspedes, serves ice cream for pesos.

For fresh-baked bread, try **Panadería 495** (Cisnero, esq. Parada, daily 6 A.M.–10 P.M.).

© CHRISTOPHER P. BAKER

swimming pool at Hotel Sierra Maestra

Information and Services

The **post office** (tel. 023/42-3305, Mon.–Sat. 9 A.M.–6 P.M.), on the west side of Parque Céspedes, has **DHL** service. **Etecsa** (Marmól e/ Saco y Figueredo, tel. 023/42-8353, daily 8:30 A.M.–7:30 P.M.) has international telephone and Internet service.

Banks include **Bandec** (General García, esq. Saco; and García, esq. Figueredo) and **Banco Popular** (General García, esq. Saco). You can also change foreign currency at **Cadeca,** on the Carretera Central, next to the bus station.

Hospital Carlos Manuel de Céspedes (Carretera Central, Km 1.5, tel. 023/42-5012) is west of the Hotel Sierra Maestra, which has a **Farmacia Internacional** (Mon.–Fri. 8:30 A.M.–noon and 1–5 P.M., Sat. 8:30 A.M.–noon).

The **Consultoría Jurídica Internacional** (Carretera Central, e/ Av. Figueredo y Calle Segunda, tel. 023/42-7379, Mon.–Fri. 8:30 A.M.–noon and 1:30–5:30 P.M.) provides legal services.

Getting There and Around

BY AIR

The **Aeropuerto Carlos Céspedes** (tel. 023/42-7506) is four kilometers northeast of town. A bus operates between the airport and the Terminal de Ómnibus. **Cubana** (Martí, esq. Parada, tel. 023/42-7511, or 023/42-3695 airport) flies between Havana and Bayamo twice weekly.

BY BUS

Buses arrive and depart the **Terminal de Ómnibus** (Carretera Central, esq. Augusta Márquez, tel. 023/42-4036). **Víazul** buses depart Bayamo for Santiago de Cuba (CUC7.56) at 4:35, 4:45, 9:50 and 10:25 A.M., and 5:55 and 10:25 P.M.; westbound for Havana (CUC47.52) at 12:10 and 11:10 A.M., and 5:25 P.M.; for Trinidad (CUC28.08) at 9:40 P.M.; and Varadero (CUC45.36) at 10:25 P.M.

BY TRAIN

The railway station (Saco, esq. Línea, tel. 023/42-4955) is one kilometer west of the

Carretera Central. Train #9 departs Havana for Bayamo daily at 10:15 P.M. (14 hours, CUC25.40) and continues to Manzanillo. Train #10 departs Bayamo for Havana at 12:55 A.M. Other trains serve Santiago de Cuba and Guantánamo, and there are additional trains to Manzanillo and Havana.

BY CAR AND TAXI
You can rent cars from **Havanautos** (tel. 023/42-7375), in the Hotel Sierra Maestra.

Havanatur (tel. 023/42-7662), on the west side of Parque Céspedes, offers excursions (including city tours by horse-drawn *coche*), as does eco-focused **EcoTur** (tel. 023/42-7970 ext. 535), in the Hotel Sierra Maestra.

Horse-drawn *coches* and *bici-taxis* are everywhere. For a taxi, call **Cubataxi** (tel. 023/42-4313).

SOUTH AND EAST OF BAYAMO
The Carretera Central runs east from Bayamo across the Río Cauto floodplain.

Dos Ríos
At Jiguaní, a nondescript town 26 kilometers east of Bayamo, a road leads north to Dos Ríos (Two Rivers), the holy site where José Martí gave his life for the cause of independence.

On April 11, 1895, Martí had returned to Cuba from exile in the United States. On May 19, General Máximo Gómez's troops exchanged shots with a small Spanish column. Martí, as nationalist leader, was a civilian among soldiers. Gómez halted and ordered Martí and his bodyguard to place themselves to the rear. Martí, however, took off down the riverbank towards the Spanish column. His bodyguard took off after him—but too late. Martí was hit in the neck by a bullet and fell from his horse without ever having drawn his gun. Revolutionary literature describes Martí as a hero who died fighting on the battlefield. In fact, he committed suicide for the sake of martyrdom.

Monumento Martí is a simple 10-meter-tall obelisk of whitewashed concrete in a trim garden of lawns and royal palms. White roses surround the obelisk, an allusion to his famous poem, *Versos Sencillos: "Cultivo una rosa blanca en julio como enero..."* A stone wall bears a 3-D bronze visage of Martí and the words, "When my fall comes, all the sorrow of life will seem like sun and honey." A plaque on the monument says simply, "He died in this place on May 19, 1895."

A tribute is held each May 19.

The **Loma el Yarey,** a massif offering 360-degree views over the plains and towards the Sierra Maestra, is the core of **Área Protegida el Yarey.** However, at last visit it was closed to visitors, as was **Villa el Yarey** (tel. 042/7684), a hilltop lodge that is now a drug rehab center run by Cubanacán. To get here, take the road that leads north from the Carretera Central, seven kilometers east of Jiguaní.

Jardín Botánico Cupaynicu
A turnoff from the Carretera Central about two kilometers east of Bayamo leads south to **Guisa,** a charming town in the foothills of the Sierra Maestra. About one kilometer north of Guisa you'll pass a Saracen armored car roadside: it's now the **Monumento Nacional Loma de Piedra,** recalling the battle for the town that took place on November 20, 1958.

Two kilometers before reaching Guisa, a sign at La Nieñita points the way to the Cupaynicu Botanical Garden (tel. 023/39-1330, Tues.–Sun. 8 A.M.–4:30 P.M., CUC2), at Los Mameyes. It's named for a local palm, one of 2,100 species of flora found here. Two-hour guided trips are offered of the 104-hectare garden, divided into 14 zones, including palms (72 species, of which 16 are Cuban), cacti (268 species), rock plants, tropical flowers, etc., accessed via a 1.8-kilometer loop trail. The main area pertains to local endemic species. Birds abound. It also has a greenhouse or ornamentals, plus an herbarium. Local tour companies offer excursions to the garden.

The Sierra Maestra

The Sierra Maestra hangs against the sky along the entire southern coast of Oriente, from the western foothills near Cabo Cruz eastward 130 kilometers to Santiago de Cuba. The towering massif gathers in serried ranges that precede one another in an immense chain rising to Pico Turquino. It is forbidding terrain creased with steep ravines and boulder-strewn valleys. These mountains were the setting for the most ferocious battles in the fight to topple Batista.

Cut off from civilization down on the plains, the hardy mountain folk continue to eke out a subsistence living, supplemented by a meager income from coffee.

PARQUE NACIONAL PICO TURQUINO

This 17,450-hectare national park is named for Pico Turquino, Cuba's highest mountain (1,974 meters). Hiking to the summit is popular with Cubans, almost like a pilgrimage. Fidel Castro had his guerrilla headquarters amid these slopes; the hike to La Comandancia is richly rewarding. So, too, the challenging hike up Pico Turquino.

These mountains are also important for their diversity of flora and fauna. At least 100 species of plants are found nowhere else, and an additional 26 are peculiar to tiny enclaves within the park. Orchids cover the trunks of semideciduous montane forest and centenarian conifers. Higher up is cloud forest, festooned with old man's beard, bromeliads, ferns, and vines, fed by mists that swirl through the forest primeval. Pico Turquino is even tipped by sub-*páramo* (marshy grassland) above 1,900 meters, with wind-sculpted, contorted dwarf species on exposed ridges.

The calls of birds explode like gunshots in the green silence of the jungle. Wild pigs and *jutías* exist alongside three species of frog found only on Pico Turquino, which looms over the tiny community of **Santo Domingo,** on the east bank of the Río Yara, 20 kilometers south of the sugarcane processing town of

Bartolomé Masó (60 kilometers southwest of Bayamo). The road requires first-gear ascents and descents.

Santo Domingo was the setting for fierce fighting June–July 1958. The small **Museo Santo Domingo** (open by request, CUC1) features a 3-D model of the Sierra Maestra with a plan of the battles. Small arms and mortars are displayed.

Entry to the park is permitted 7:30 A.M.–2:30 P.M. only (10 A.M. is the latest you are allowed to set off for Pico Turquino). A guide is compulsory, arranged through the **Centro de Visitantes** (daily 7–10 A.M.) at Santo Domingo. You can book in advance through **Flora y Fauna** (tel. 023/56-5349 in Masó, tel. 023/42-4875 in Bayamo).

From Santo Domingo the corrugated cement road is inclined 40 degrees in places—a breathtakingly steep climb with hairpin bends. After five kilometers the road ends at Alto del Naranjo (950 meters elevation), the trailhead to Pico Turquino and La Comandancia de la Plata. The drive is not for the fainthearted, and not all rental cars can make it! Hire a jeep taxi (CUC5). To hike from Santo Domingo to Alto del Naranjo is a relentless four-hour ascent.

(La Comandancia de la Plata

Fidel named his Rebel Army headquarters in the Sierra Maestra after the river whose headwaters was near his camp on a western spur ridge of Pico Turquino. The 16 buildings were dispersed over one square kilometer on a forested ridgecrest, reached by a tortuous track from Alto de Naranjo (CUC20, plus CUC5 cameras, CUC5 videos) that's a scramble over rocks and mud. The wooden structures were hidden at the edge of the clearing and covered with hibiscus arbors to conceal them from air attacks. Castro's house was built against the ravine, with no visible entrance (it's hidden) and an escape route into the creek. You'll also see the small hospital (run by Che Guevara, who was a qualified doctor) and guest house that

La Comandancia de la Plata

© CHRISTOPHER P. BAKER

is now a small museum with a 3-D model of the area, plus rifles, machine guns, and other memorabilia. Plata was linked by radio to the rest of Cuba (a transmitter for Radio Rebelde loomed above the clearing); it's a steep and slippery ascent to the hut.

Hiking to Pico Turquino

From Alto de Naranjo it's 13 kilometers to the summit. Even here you cannot escape the Revolution. In 1952 soon-to-be revolutionary heroine Celia Sánchez and her liberal-minded father, Manuel Sánchez Silveira, hiked up Turquino carrying a bronze bust of José Martí, which they installed at the summit. In 1957 Sánchez made the same trek with a CBS news crew for an interview with Fidel beside the bust. Che Guevara recorded how El Jefe checked his pocket altimeter to assure himself that Turquino was as high as the maps said it was.

The **Sendero Pico Turquino** begins at Alto de Naranjo (a 7 A.M. departure from Santo Domingo is recommended). En route you'll pass through the remote communities of Palma Mocha, Lima, and Aguada de Joaquín. Hikers normally ascend the summit the same day, then descend to overnight at Aguada de Joaquín.

From the summit, you can continue down the south side of the mountain to Las Cuevas by prearrangement; a second guide will meet you at the summit.

Hikers need to take their own food and plenty of water. You can buy packaged meals (CUC10) at Villa Santo Domingo. There are no stores hereabouts. Warm clothing and waterproof gear are essential (the mountain weather is fickle and can change from sunshine to downpours in minutes), as are a flashlight and bed roll.

Permits (CUC45) include a guide and dorm at Aguada camp. Tip your guide!

Cubanacán (tel. 07/208-9920, www.cubanacanviajes.cu) and **EcoTur** (tel. 023/42-4875 or 07/641-0306, www.ecoturcuba.co.cu) offer two- and three-day guided hikes to the summit.

Accommodations and Food

Serving Cubans and backpackers, the riverside **Campismo La Sierrita** (tel. 023/56-5594, CUC19 per person), six kilometers south

THE WAR IN THE MOUNTAINS

Between 1956 and 1959, the Sierra Maestra was the headquarters for Castro's Rebel Army. Fidel and Raúl Castro, Che Guevara, and a ragged band of survivors from the ill-fated *Granma* landing stumbled into the Sierra Maestra in December 1956. "The story of how Castro was able to recover from a terrible initial defeat, regroup, fight, start winning against Batista units, and form an ultimately victorious Rebel Army is the story of the extraordinary support he received from Sierra Maestra peasants," writes Tad Szulc in *Fidel: A Critical Portrait.*

GAINING GROUND

The initial year in the mountains was difficult. The tiny rebel band won small skirmishes with Batista's troops, but gained their major coup on February 16, 1957, when Herbert L. Matthews of the *New York Times* was led into the mountains to meet the next day with Castro. Matthews's report hit the newsstands on February 24. It began, "Fidel Castro, the rebel leader of Cuba's youth, is alive and fighting hard and successfully in the rugged, almost impenetrable vastness of the Sierra Maestra." Batista had lifted censorship the week before, and Matthews's story created a sensation that Castro milked by releasing a manifesto calling for violent uprising against the regime.

The Rebel Army consolidated its control of the mountains throughout 1957 from its base at La Plata, on the northwest slope of Pico Turquino. The first real battle occurred on May 28, when Castro and a force of 80 men attacked a garrison at El Uvero, on the coast. They lost six men but gained two machine guns and 46 rifles.

In early 1958, the Rebel Army split into four separate units. Castro continued to lead from La Plata, Che Guevara held the northern slopes, Camilo Cienfuegos led a group on the plains near Bayamo, and Raúl Castro opened a new front near Santiago. By spring the Rebel Army had control of most of the mountain regions of Oriente. The enemy was being denied more and more territory. And a radio station – Radio Rebelde – was set up to broadcast revolutionary messages to the nation. All the while, Castro worked assiduously to maintain control of rival groups in Havana.

VICTORY

In May 1958 Batista launched an all-out attack – Operation FF (Fin de Fidel) – using air strikes and 10,000 troops. However, Fidel's peasant-based Rebel Army knew "every path in the forest, every turn in the road, and every peasant's house in the immensely complicated terrain."

For three months they skirmished. By June 19, Castro's troops were virtually surrounded atop their mountain retreat. The rebels rained mortars down into the valley, along with a psychological barrage of patriotic songs and exhortations blasted over loudspeakers to demoralize Batista's tired troops. Then at the battle of Jigüe, which lasted 10 days, Castro's rebels defeated a battalion whose commander, Major José Quevedo, joined the rebels. Batista's army collapsed and retreated in disarray.

Castro then launched his counteroffensive. In August 1958 Castro's troops came down out of the mountains to seize, in swift order, Baire, Jiguaní, Maffo, Contramaestre, and Palma Soriano. On January 2, 1959, the Rebel Army entered Santiago de Cuba. Castro walked up the stairs of the Moncada barracks to accept the surrender of Batista's army in Oriente at the very site where he had initiated his armed insurrection six years before.

of Bartolomé Masó, has 27 simple two- and four-person cabins, plus a basic restaurant. You can make reservations c/o **Campismo Popular** (General García #112, tel. 023/42-4425) in Bayamo.

Islazul's **Villa Balcón de la Sierra** (tel. 023/56-5513, vbasi@islazulgrm.co.cu, CUC14 s, CUC18 d year-round), on a windswept hillock 800 meters south of Bartolomé Masó, is a basic facility with 20 air-conditioned *cabinas* with meager furniture. However, the "suite" (merely a large room) above the restaurant is nicely furnished; a balcony offers spectacular views. **Restaurant Los Pinos** (daily 7 A.M.–10 P.M.) overlooks a swimming pool.

The best option is Islazul's **Villa Santo Domingo** (tel. 059/56-5635, comercial@islazulgrm.co.cu, CUC29 s, CUC34 d low season, CUC32 s, CUC37 d high season including breakfast), on the banks of the river in Santo Domingo. It has 20 air-conditioned cabins, each with TV and modern bathrooms. For a sense of adventure, opt for two-person tents pitched on a canopied deck (CUC3 per person). An open-air riverside restaurant serves *criollo* staples.

Getting There

A *camión* departs Masó for Santo Domingo on Thursday at 8:45 A.M. and 4 P.M. and departs Santo Domingo for Masó at 8 A.M. and 6 P.M.

A jeep-taxi from Bayamo costs about CUC35 each way, CUC10 from Masó.

Manzanillo to Cabo Cruz

MANZANILLO

Manzanillo (pop. 105,000) extends along three kilometers of shorefront on the Gulf of Guacanayabo. In colonial days, it was a smuggling port and center of slave trading. Later the city became the main underground base for Castro's Rebel Army in the late 1950s (Celia Sánchez coordinated the secret supply routes, under the noses of Batista's spies). Today the weatherworn town functions as a fishing port. Many buildings have been influenced by Moorish design. In Barrio de Oro, the cobbled streets are lined with rickety wooden houses with cactus growing between the faded roof tiles.

The **Malecón** seafront boulevard features a life-size bronze statue of Cuban crooner Benny Moré. Offshore, the easternmost cays of the Jardines de la Reina archipelago float on the horizon.

Orientation

The road from Bayamo enters Manzanillo from the east as Avenida Rosales, which runs west to the shore, fronted by Avenida 1 de Mayo and the Malecón and paralleled five blocks inland by Avenida Martí. These roads run west to Avenida Jesús Menéndez. The old city lies within this quadrangle.

To the east the city Avenida Camilo Cienfuegos (the *circunvalación*) runs south from Avenida Rosales, intersects Avenida Jesús Menéndez, and drops to the Malecón.

Parque Céspedes

City life revolves around this handsome square bounded by Martí, Maceo, Marchen, and Masó. The square has little stone sphinxes at each corner and is ringed by royal palms and Victorian-era lampposts. The most notable feature is an Islamic-style *glorieta* (bandstand) inlaid with cloisonné.

The 19th-century **Iglesia Parroquia Purísima Concepción,** on the north side, has a beautiful barrel-vaulted ceiling and elaborate gilt altar.

The **Casa de la Cultura** (Masó #82, tel. 023/57-4210, daily 8 A.M.–6 P.M., free), on the south side, in an impressive colonial building with mosaics of Columbus's landing and Don Quixote tilting at windmills.

On the east side, the **Museo Histórico** (Martí #226, tel. 023/57-2053, Tues.–Fri. 9 A.M.–5 P.M., Sat.–Sun. 9 A.M.–noon and 6–10 P.M., free) displays cannons and antiques.

Worth a peek, too, the **Farmacia Natural** (tel. 023/57-2211, Mon.–Fri. 8 A.M.–noon and 2–6 P.M., Sat. 8 A.M.–noon), on Maceo, 50 meters north of the plaza, has homeopathic remedies and a cash register dating from 1886. To its northeast, the restored **Teatro Manzanillo** (Villuendas, esq. Maceo, tel. 023/57-2973, 5 pesos), dates to 1856.

Monumento Celia Sánchez

Manzanillo's main attraction takes up two entire blocks along Caridad (e/ Martí y Luz

Caballero), where a terra-cotta tile staircase is graced to each side with ceramic murals. At the top is the monument to Celia Manduley Sánchez and a tiny room with portraits and personal effects (Mon.–Fri. 8 A.M.–noon and 2–6 P.M., Sat. 8 A.M.–noon, free) dedicated to the memory of *"La más hermosa y autóctona flor de la Revolución"* (the most beautiful native flower of the Revolution).

The **Plaza de la Revolución** (Av. Camilo Cienfuegos) has a bas-relief mural of Celia Sánchez and other revolutionary heroes.

Entertainment and Events

The town hosts a carnival in August.

The **Casa de la Cultura** (tel. 023/57-4210) and **Casa de la Trova** (Merchan #213, esq. Masó, tel. 023/57-5423), both on the main square, host music performances and cultural events. Both were closed for renovation at last visit.

Piano Bar Mi Manzanillo (J. M. Gómez, esq. Calixto García, tel. 023/57-5312, Tues.–Sun. 2 P.M.–2 A.M., free) applies a dress code. A quartet plays jazz, *música filin,* and even salsa. And music videos, live music, even karaoke,

© CHRISTOPHER P. BAKER

Monumento Celia Sánchez

draw young adults to **Artex Centro Cultural** (Wed.–Mon. 10 P.M.–3 A.M.), on the north side of the plaza.

Flamboyantly gay dancers in skin-tight Lycra wooing female dancers in g-string bikinis and torn fishnets add notes of comedy to the endearing open-air *cabaret espectáculo* at **Costa Azul** (Av. 1ra de Mayo, esq. Narciso López, tel. 023/57-3158, Fri.–Sun. 10 P.M., CUC1). It's followed by a disco. The bar is in a ship hauled ashore! Friday–Sunday it competes with the **Centro Nocturno Los Delfines** in the Hotel Guacanayabo (Av. Camilo Cienfuegos, 10 pesos per couple) and **Centro Nocturno Brisas del Mar** (Ave. Masó), both with disco music.

Teatro Manzanillo (Villuendas, esq. Maceo, tel. 023/57-2973, 5 pesos) hosts cultural programs.

Baseball games are hosted October–May at **Estadio Wilfredo Pages,** off Avenida Céspedes.

Accommodations

There were only seven *casas particulares* in town. My favorite is **(Casa de Adrian y Tonia** (Mártires de Vietnam #49, esq. Caridad, tel. 023/57-3028, CUC20–25), a delightful house with a nice TV lounge with rockers and a balcony overlooking the stairs to the Monumento Celia Sánchez. The owners rent a splendid independent cross-ventilated, air-conditioned apartment upstairs with fans and a modern bathroom plus roof terrace with an arbor and a tiny inflatable plunge pool.

You get a spacious, nicely furnished, air-conditioned upstairs room at **Casa de Eldris y Yosdanis** (Miguel Gómez #347, esq. León, tel. 023/57-2392, nayabo1@yahoo.com, CUC15–25). The hostess is a delight.

Islazul's **Hotel Guacanayabo** (Av. Camilo Cienfuegos, tel. 023/57-4012, fax 023/57-7782, commercial@hguac.co.cu, CUC15 s, CUC20 d year-round) reopened to guests in 2008. Its 108 rooms remain uninspired. At least you get satellite TV, modern bathrooms, a swimming pool, and services. Noise from the disco reverberates on weekends.

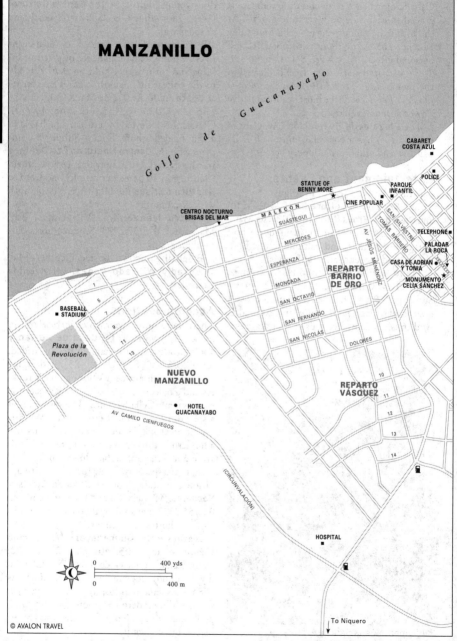

MANZANILLO

Golfo de Guacanayabo

CABARET
COSTA AZUL

POLICE

STATUE OF
BENNY MORE

PARQUE
INFANTIL

CINE POPULAR

CENTRO NOCTURNO
BRISAS DEL MAR

TELEPHONE

MALECÓN

SUÁSTEGUI

PALADAR
LA ROCA

MERCEDES

CASA DE ADRIÁN
Y TONIA

ESPERANZA

REPARTO
BARRIO
DE ORO

MONUMENTO
CELIA SÁNCHEZ

MONCADA

SAN OCTAVIO

SAN SILVESTRE

TOMÁS BARRERO

AV JESÚS MENÉNDEZ

BASEBALL
STADIUM

1

5

7

9

11

13

SAN FERNANDO

SAN NICOLÁS

DOLORES

Plaza de la
Revolución

NUEVO
MANZANILLO

REPARTO
VÁSQUEZ

10

11

12

13

14

HOTEL
GUACANAYABO

AV CAMILO CIENFUEGOS

(CIRCUNVALACIÓN)

HOSPITAL

0   400 yds

0   400 m

To Niquero

© AVALON TRAVEL

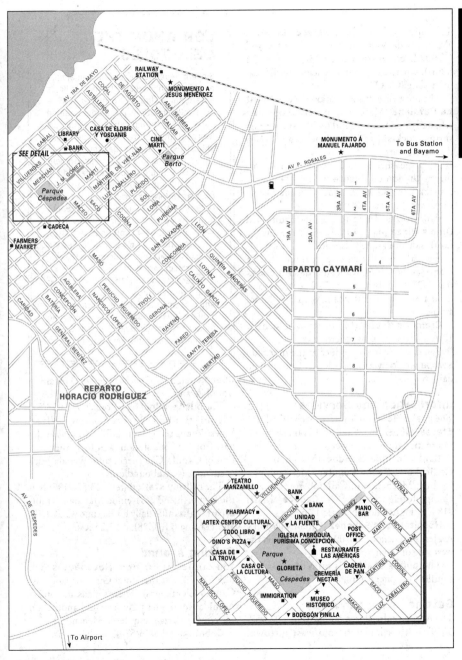

RAILWAY STATION

MONUMENTO A JESÚS MENÉNDEZ

LIBRARY

CASA DE ELDRIS Y YOSDANIS

BANK

CINE MARTÍ

SEE DETAIL

Parque Berto

MONUMENTO Á MANUEL FAJARDO

To Bus Station and Bayamo

AV. TRA DE MAYO

SARIAL

COCAL

ASTILLEROS

1O DE AGOSTO

ANA SEGRERA

TITO CALVAR

VILLUENDAS

MERCHÁN

J. M. GOMEZ

MARTÍ

MÁRTIRES DE VIET-NAM

LUZ CABALLERO

PLÁCIDO

SOL

LOMA

PURÍSIMA

SAN SALVADOR

LEÓN

CONCORDIA

QUINTÍN BANDERAS

LOYNAZ

CALIXTO GARCÍA

GERONA

RAVENO

PARED

SANTA TERESA

LIBERTAD

Parque Céspedes

MACEO

SACO

CODINA

CADECA

FARMERS MARKET

MASÓ

AGUILERA

CONCEPCIÓN

PERUCHO FIGUEREDO

NARCISCO LOPEZ

TIVOLI

BATERIA

CARIDAD

GENERAL BENÍTEZ

AV. P. ROSALES

1RA AV

2DA AV

3RA AV

4TA AV

5TA AV

6TA AV

1
2
3
4
5
6
7
8
9

REPARTO CAYMARÍ

REPARTO HORACIO RODRÍGUEZ

AV. DE CÉSPEDES

To Airport

TEATRO MANZANILLO

BANK

BANK

PHARMACY

PIANO BAR

ARTEX CENTRO CULTURAL

UNIDAD LA FUENTE

TODO LIBRO

POST OFFICE

DINO'S PIZZA

IGLESIA PARRÓQUIA PURÍSIMA CONCEPCIÓN

RESTAURANTE LAS AMÉRICAS

CASA DE LA TROVA

Parque

CADENA DE PAN

CASA DE LA CULTURA

GLORIETA

CREMERÍA NECTAR

Céspedes

IMMIGRATION

MUSEO HISTÓRICO

BODEGÓN PINILLA

VILLUENDAS

SARIAL

MERCHÁN

J. M. GOMEZ

CALIXTO GARCÍA

LOYNAZ

MARTÍ

MÁRTIRES DE VIET-NAM

CODINA

SACO

MACEO

LUZ CABALLERO

NARCISCO LOPEZ

PERUCHO FIGUEREDO

MASÓ

Food

The only legal *paladar* is **Paladar La Roca** (Mártires de Vietnam #68, e/ Benítex and Caridad, c/o Adrian tel. 023/57-3028, 24 hours), where I enjoyed a delicious garlic seafood plate (CUC7).

The most elegant state option is **Restaurant La Catalana** (Martí, esq. Narciso López, no tel., daily noon–2 P.M. and 6–10 P.M.), serving shrimp cocktail, garbanzo, paella, and *criollo* dishes in pesos.

It's a pleasure to sit beneath shade canopies at **Unidad La Fuente** (no tel., 24 hours), a snack bar and ice creamery on the plaza's northwest corner.

Fancy pizza? Head to the air-conditioned **Dino's Pizza** (daily 10 A.M.–10 P.M.), on the north side of Parque Céspedes.

Several no-frills eateries around Parque Céspedes include **Restaurante Las Américas** (tel. 023/57-3043, daily 7–9 A.M., noon–2:30 P.M., and 7–10 P.M.), with a colonial ambience.

Cremería Nectar (Martí, esq. Maceo, daily 10 A.M.–10 P.M.) sells ice creams.

You can buy fresh produce at the **mercado agropecuario** (Martí, e/ Batería y Concepción, daily 6 A.M.–5 P.M.).

Information and Services

The **post office** is on Martí (e/ Saco y Codina). **Etecsa** (Gímez, esq. Codina) has Internet and international phone service.

Banks include **Bandec** (Marchan, esq. Codina) and **Banco Popular** (Marchan, esq. Codina; Machan, esq. Calixto). You can also change foreign currency at **Cadeca** (Martí #184, e/ Figueredo y Narciso López).

Hospital Celia Sánchez (Circunvalación y Av. Jesús Menéndez, tel. 023/57-4011) is on the west side of town.

The **police station** is on Villimedas (e/ Aguilera y Concepción).

Getting There and Away

The **Aeropuerto Sierra Maestra** (tel. 023/57-3019) is 10 kilometers southeast of town.

Cubana (tel. 023/57-4984) flies to Manzanillo from Havana.

The **bus terminal** (Av. Rosales, tel. 023/57-3404) is two kilometers east of town. Víazul buses do not serve Manzanillo. *Camiones* depart from the bus station, and from the junction of Camilo Cienfuegos and Avenida Jesús Menéndez (southbound only).

The **railway station** (tel. 023/57-2195) is at the far north end of Avenida Marchan. Trains depart Manzanillo daily for Bayamo (CUC1.70) and Havana (CUC28) at 10:25 P.M.

Getting Around

You can rent a car from **Havanautos** (tel. 023/57-7737) at the Hotel Guacanayabo (Av. Camilo Cienfuegos). There's a gas station on Avenida Rosales (esq. Av. 1ra) and another on the *circunvalación* (esq. Jesús Menéndez).

Cubataxi (tel. 023/57-4782) has taxis.

MANZANILLO TO NIQUERO

The coastal plains south of Manzanillo are awash in lime-green sugarcane. Five kilometers south of Manzanillo you'll pass a turnoff for the **Criadero de Cocodrilos** (tel. 023/57-8606, Mon.–Fri. 7 A.M.–6 P.M., Sat. 7–11 A.M., CUC5), a crocodile farm with more than 1,000 American crocodiles in algae-filled ponds. Tip the guide.

Reaching the sugar-processing town of Media Luna, 50 kilometers southwest of Manzanillo, divert to view the **Museo Celia Sánchez** (Av. Podio #11, tel. 023/59-3466, Tues.–Sun. 9 A.M.–5 P.M., CUC1), in a simple green-and-white gingerbread wooden house where revolutionary heroine Celia Sánchez was born on May 9, 1920. Media Luna's town park has a fountain with a **statue of Celia Sánchez** sitting atop rocks with her shoeless feet in the trickling water.

The **Monumento a Juan Manuel Márquez Rodríguez,** eight kilometers north of Media Luna, honors the second-in-command of the *Granma,* killed here on December 15, 1956, shortly after the vessel's landing.

Niquero, about 60 kilometers southwest of Manzanillo, is unique for its ramshackle buildings in French-colonial style, lending it a similarity to parts of New Orleans and Key West. The **Communist Party headquarters,** one block from the main square, in a fabulous art nouveau building.

Museo Histórico La Demajagua

La Demajagua (tel. 5219-4080, Mon.–Sat. 8 A.M.–noon and 1–5 P.M., Sun. 8 A.M.–1 P.M., CUC1), 13 kilometers south of Manzanillo, was the sugar estate owned by Carlos Manuel de Céspedes, the nationalist revolutionary who on October 10, 1868, unilaterally freed his slaves and called for rebellion against Spain. His house (of which only the original floor remains) is now a museum with eclectic displays that include period weaponry.

A path leads to a monument of fieldstone in a walled amphitheater encircling remnants of the original sugar mill. Inset in the wall is La Demajagua bell, the Cuban equivalent of the American Liberty Bell, which Céspedes rang to mark the opening of the 1868 War of Independence.

Accommodations and Food

Islazul's pleasant **Hotel Niquero** (Calle Martí, esq. Céspedes, tel. 023/59-2367, hniquero@islazulgrm.co.cu, CUC14 s, CUC18 d year-round), on the main street of Niquero, offers 26 rooms with satellite TV and modern bathrooms; some have king beds. It has an appealing restaurant (7–9:45 A.M., noon–2:45 P.M., 7–9:45 P.M.).

◖ PARQUE NACIONAL DESEMBARCO DEL GRANMA

This UNESCO World Heritage Site (CUC5, passport required), one kilometer south of the hamlet of Las Colorados, about 20 kilometers south of Niquero, protects the southwesternmost tip of Cuba, from Cabo Cruz to Punta Hicacos. The land stair-steps toward the Sierra Maestra in a series of marine terraces left high and dry over the eons. More than 80 percent of the park is covered by virgin woodland. Floral and fauna species are distinct. Drier areas preserve cacti more than 400 years old. Two endemic species of note are the blue-headed quail dove and the Cuban Amazon butterfly. Even endangered manatees inhabit the coastal lagoons.

Two trails are signed on the road. The **Sendero Morlotte-Fustete** leads to cavern systems. The more popular **Sendero Arqueológico Natural El Guafe,** about eight kilometers south of the entrance, also leads through mangroves and scrub to caverns containing dripstone formations. One—the Idolo del Agua—is thought to have been shaped by pre-Columbian Taínos. You can hire guides (CUC5) or hike solo. **EcoTur** (tel. 023/42-4875 or 07/641-0306, www.ecoturcuba.co.cu) offers guided hikes.

The park is named for the spot where Fidel and his band of 79 revolutionaries came ashore at Playa las Coloradas on December 2, 1956. The exact spot where the *Granma* ran aground is one kilometer south of the hamlet of Las Colorados.

Here, the **Monumento de Desembarcadero** consists of a replica of the *Granma* and a tiny museum (entrance CUC2) with a few photos, rifle, and a map showing the route of the *desembarcaderos* into the Sierra Maestra.

A concrete pathway leads 1.8 kilometers through the mangroves to the exact spot where the *Granma* bogged down.

Cabo Cruz

The lonesome, badly potholed road south from Las Colorados dips and rises through dense scrubland; twists around **Laguna Guafes;** and ends at the ramshackle fishing village of Cabo Cruz, the southwesterly tip of Cuba. The **Faro Cabo Cruz** lighthouse (off-limits; it's a military zone), built in 1871, rises 33 meters above a shrimp farm.

A plaque atop the cliff states that Christopher Columbus arrived here in May 1494.

Accommodations and Food

Cubamar's **Campismo Villas Las Colorados** (tel. 023/90-1126, CUC6 per person), at Playa Las Colorados, has 28 basic air-conditioned cabins with cold-water showers that might appeal to hardy backpackers. More comfy options were being prepared at last visit.

The only eatery for miles is **Restaurante El Cabo** (tel. 023/90-1317, 7–9 A.M., noon–2 P.M., and 6–9 P.M.), a seafood restaurant beside the lighthouse in Cabo Cruz.

The South Coast

From Entronque Pilón, five kilometers north of Niquero, a scenic road cuts east through the foothills of the Sierra Maestra and drops down through a narrow pass to emerge on the coastal plains near Pilón, where a gas station is the last before Santiago de Cuba, 200 kilometers to the east.

PILÓN AND MAREA DEL PORTILLO

The flyblown fishing (and, until recently, sugar-processing) town of Pilón is ringed on three sides by mountains and on the fourth by the Caribbean Sea. The land west of Pilón is smothered in now-dying sugarcane. East of Pilón, the land lies in the rain shadow of the Sierra Maestra and is virtually desert. Cacti appear, and goats graze hungrily amid stony pastures. The town's sole attraction, **Casa Museo Celia Sánchez** (Conrado Benítez #20, tel. 023/59-4507) was closed at last visit, still awaiting restoration after being trashed by a hurricane in 2005. This clapboard house was used by Celia Sánchez as a base for her underground supply network for Castro's Rebel Army.

Fifteen kilometers east of Pilón the mountains shelve gently to a wide bay at **Marea del Portillo,** rimmed by a beach of pebbly gray-brown sand. Marea del Portillo is favored by budget-minded Canadian and European charter groups, but facilities are limited to the two resorts and you're out on a land-locked limb. As a vacation spot it's a dud.

Recreation

Water sports and scuba diving (CUC30) are offered at **Marlin Albacora Dive Center** (tel. 023/59-7034), at Club Amigo. Dive sites include the wreck of the *Cristóbal Colón,* a Spanish warship sunk in the war of 1898.

Excursions include horseback rides (from CUC5), a "seafari" with snorkeling at Cayo Blanco, city tours of Niquero and Manzanillo (from CUC12), a hike to La Comandancia de la Plata (CUC95), and a jeep tour to Las Yaguas waterfall (CUC55).

Accommodations

Cubanacán operates three hotels at Marea del Portillo. **Villa Punta Piedra** (tel. 023/59-7062, CUC24 s, CUC30 d year-round, including breakfast), five kilometers west of Marea, was looking down-at-the-heels at last visit. It has 13 spacious air-conditioned villas, plus a restaurant and bar.

The all-inclusive beachfront **Club Amigo Marea del Portillo** (tel. 023/59-7102, fax 023/59-7081, reservas@marea.co.cu, from CUC40 s, CUC50 d) is divided into a beachfront property and a much nicer hilltop facility, 600 meters apart. Together they have 283 rooms and suites, including 56 *cabinas,* all pleasantly furnished (however, the bathrooms are tired, the food dismal, and TV reception awful). Each facility has a restaurant, bar, and swimming pool. A simple cabaret is offered, and the hilltop facility has a disco, but the constant need to walk between the hotels soon grows old.

Getting There, Away, and Around

A *camión* runs between Pilón and Santiago de Cuba on alternate days.

You can rent cars and scooters at the Club Amigo properties through **Cubacar** (tel. 023/59-7185). Horse-drawn *coches* charge CUC3 for a tour of the nearby fishing village.

A rugged mountain road links Bartolomé Masó and Marea; a jeep is required.

◖ MAREA DEL PORTILLO TO SANTIAGO DE CUBA

The rugged coast that links Marea del Portillo and Santiago de Cuba is an exhilarating drive. The paved but dangerously deteriorated road hugs the coast the whole way, climbing over steep headlands and dropping through river valleys. The teal blue sea is your constant companion, with the Sierra Maestra pushing up close on the other side. There are no villages or habitations for miles, and no services whatsoever. Landslides occasionally block the road, much of which has been washed away; near La Cueva you have to run along the shingle beach. It may be impassable at high tide and in storms.

In springtime, giant land crabs march across the road in fulfillment of the mating urge. Amazingly, the battalions even scale vertical cliffs.

The derelict bridge over the Río Macio, 15 kilometers from Marea, marks the border with Santiago de Cuba Province.

© CHRISTOPHER P. BAKER

revolutionary murals near Pilón

SANTIAGO DE CUBA

Santiago de Cuba Province is one of the most historically important regions in the country and claims to be the Cradle of the Revolution. The first charge of machete-wielding Mambí was at Baire in 1868. And in 1953 Fidel Castro's attack on Batista's barracks took place at Moncada, in the city of Santiago, initiating the Revolution that six years later brought him to power.

The namesake capital city, second only to Havana in size, is distinctive in mood and teems with sites of historical and cultural interest, from a castle and the 16th-century house where Diego Velázquez governed Cuba to a notable cathedral and the Moncada barracks. Nearby there are beaches, the holy shrine of El Cobre, Reserva Baconao (featuring a cactus garden, aquarium, crocodile farm, and more); and Parque Nacional Gran Piedra, reached by a circuitous road that leads through cool pine forest to a splendid garden perched atop a peak at over 1,200 meters.

The Santiagüeros carry themselves with a certain lassitude and speak in a lilting tongue with a musical tone. French and African words appear, a legacy of the many French and Haitian families that settled here in the late 18th century. Santiago has the highest percentage of African blood in Cuba. Though the traditional architecture is mostly Spanish, the faces are mostly black. Such musical forms as *son* were birthed here, and the city remains Cuba's most vital center of Afro-Cuban culture.

Most of the province is mountainous. The Sierra Maestra rises west of Santiago. East of the city, an elevated plateau extends for miles, slanting gradually to the sea, with the

© CHRISTOPHER P. BAKER

HIGHLIGHTS

◖ **Casa de Don Diego Velázquez:** The house where Diego Velásquez ruled Cuba is the island's oldest house. In superb condition, it houses a fine museum (page 443).

◖ **Museo Municipal Emilio Bacardí Moreau:** The museum begun by a member of the famous rum family holds his eclectic and fascinating collection inside a beautiful neoclassical edifice (page 443).

◖ **Cuartel Moncada:** This is where it all began: The scene of the attack by Castro & Co. that launched the Revolution is now a school with a gory Museum of the Revolution (page 446).

◖ **Parque Histórico El Morro:** An enormous restored 17th-century castle with a dramatic clifftop setting holds a nightly cannon-firing ceremony (page 448).

◖ **Cementerio de Santa Ifigenia:** Important figures in Cuban history, not least José Martí, are buried in this cemetery (page 450).

◖ **Basílica de Nuestra Señora del Cobre:** A pilgrimage here is de rigueur to see the Cubans praying and making offerings to the Black Virgin (page 458).

◖ **Museo de la Guerra Hispano-Cubano-Americano:** This small yet excellently arranged museum displays maps, artillery pieces, and other articles relating to the Spanish-American War (page 464).

SANTIAGO DE CUBA

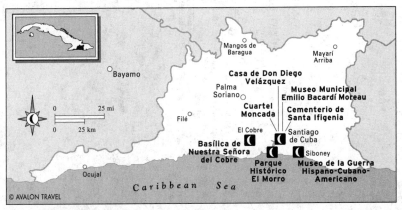

LOOK FOR ◖ TO FIND RECOMMENDED SIGHTS, ACTIVITIES, DINING, AND LODGING.

serrated Cordillera de la Gran Piedra behind. Behind these rise the Sierra de Baracoa and Sierra Cristal, extending into Holguín and Guantánamo Provinces. Together, they lure hikers and bird-watchers, as well as fans of revolutionary history.

PLANNING YOUR TIME

Santiago has enough to keep you intrigued and engaged for three or four days. Downtown,

plan on walking the narrow, sometimes traffic-clogged streets. The list of must-sees includes the **Casa de Don Diego Velázquez** (reputedly the oldest building in Cuba); the excellent **Museo Municipal Emilio Bacardí Moreau,** which while honoring this member of the famous rum family is actually a broad-ranging museum spanning arts, history, and culture; the **Cuartel Moncada,** now the Museo de la Revolución; and the Plaza de

SANTIAGO DE CUBA

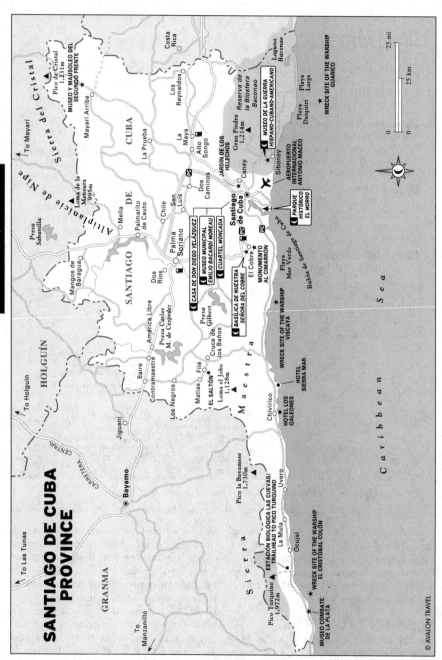

SANTIAGO DE CUBA PROVINCE

To Las Tunas

To Manzanillo

GRANMA

HOLGUÍN

To Holguín

To Mayarí

Sierra del Cristal

Pico de Cristal 1,231m

MUSEO Y MAUSOLEO DEL SEGUNDO FRENTE

Mayarí Arriba

Altiplanicie de Nipe

Loma de la Mensura 905m

Costa Rica

Los Reynaldos

Laguna Baconao

WRECK SITE OF THE WARSHIP GUARICO

CUBA

La Prueba

Reserva de la Biosfera Baconao

MUSEO DE LA GUERRA HISPANO-CUBANO-AMERICANO

Playa Larga

Playa Daiquirí

Presa Subanilla

Mangos de Baragua

Mella

Palmarito de Cauto

SANTIAGO

DE

Dos Ríos

América Libre

Dos Caminos

San Luís

Chile

Palma Soriano

La Maya

Alto Songo

JARDÍN DE LOS HELECHOS

Gran Piedra 1,214m

Caney

Siboney

Playa Verde de Cuba

AEROPUERTO INTERNACIONAL ANTONIO MACEO

Bahía de Santiago de Cuba

Santiago de Cuba

CASA DE DON DIEGO VELÁZQUEZ

MUSEO MUNICIPAL EMILIO BACARDÍ MOREAU

CUARTEL MONCADA

PARQUE HISTÓRICO EL MORRO

BASÍLICA DE NUESTRA SEÑORA DEL COBRE

El Cobre

MONUMENTO AL CIMARRÓN

Presa Carlos M. de Céspedes

Presa de Gilbert

Cruce de los Baños

Baire

Contramaestre

Jiguaní

Bayamo

CARRETERA CENTRAL

Los Negros

Matías

Filé

EL SALTÓN

Loma el Jobo 1,128m

Chivirico

Playa Mar Verde de Cuba

WRECK SITE OF THE WARSHIP VISCAYA

HOTEL SIERRA MAR

HOTEL LOS GALEONES

Maestra

Sierra

Pico la Bayamese 1,730m

ESTACIÓN BIOLÓGICA LAS CUEVAS/ TRAILHEAD TO PICO TURQUINO

La Mula

Uvero

Ocujal

WRECK SITE OF THE WARSHIP EL CRISTÓBAL COLÓN

Pico Turquino 1,972m

MUSEO COMBATE DE LA PLATA

Caribbean Sea

25 mi

25 km

© AVALON TRAVEL

la Revolución, with its humongous statue of General Antonio Maceo. A walk through the once-wealthy Reparto Vista Alegre district is rewarding for its eclectic albeit tatterdemalion buildings; a highlight is the Museo de las Religiones Populares, where you can learn about Afro-Cuban religions.

You'll want wheels to reach sites of interest on the outskirts. These include the **Cementerio de Santa Ifigenia,** where José Martí heads a long list of illustrious figures buried here, and the **Parque Histórico El Morro,** the castle guarding the entrance to Santiago bay (time your arrival for the nightly *cañonazo*).

Use the city as a base for excursions elsewhere in the province. A visit to the basilica and pilgrimage site of El Cobre is de rigueur and might be combined with the rugged drive to El Saltón, a mountain resort that is a good base for bird-watching and hiking. For a scenic drive, head west from Santiago to Chivírico, beyond which lies the trailhead to Pico Turquino, Cuba's highest mountains (a guided overnight hike is easily arranged).

The Reserva de la Biosfera Baconao, a short distance east of Santiago, is an eco-reserve only in name. Still, it's worth a full-day's excursion. Here, the highlight not to miss is the **Museo de la Guerra Hispano-Cubano-Americano,** with superb displays recalling the Spanish-American

War. Most other sites are rather hokey, but the drive is scenic enough. Budget a couple of hours for beachtime at Playa Siboney, where *casas particulares* can be rented.

Santiago's entertainment scene is robust. The city's world-famous Casa de la Trova is still the heartbeat of *son* in the nation. The yang to the Casa de la Trova's yin is the open-air Tropicana, second only to Havana's Tropicana for its sexy Las Vegas–style cabaret. If you're planning a mid-year visit, consider July, when the city erupts for Carnaval, Cuba's most colorful street fiesta. Though a far cry from those in Trinidad or Rio de Janeiro, this colorful festival is a marvelous expression of Afro-Cuban rhythms and of Santiagüerans let-loose sense of fun.

Santiago is well served by trains and buses from elsewhere in Cuba. Dozens of *casas particulares* offer an excellent range of accommodations beyond the state-run hotels, which here include some of the best in the country. Options elsewhere in the province are limited.

Santiago sits within a bowl surrounded by mountains that form windbreaks, and in summer it can feel like an oven. The rainiest season is May–October. Relief may be found in the mountains and at beaches where breezes ease the heat.

Santiago

Santiago (pop. 375,000), home of rum and revolution, has a unique, enigmatic appeal. Older even than Havana, the historic center is a potpourri of rustic, tile-roofed dwellings graced by forged-iron railings, weathered timbers, Moorish balustrades, facades painted in faded pastels, and cacti growing from red-tile roofs, fulfilling an Oriente superstition that a cactus will keep away the evil eye. If a Santiagüero lets his or her cactus die, a year of bad luck will follow.

It is sometimes referred to as "Cuba's most Caribbean city." The majority of the 30,000

or so French planters and merchants who fled Haiti following the Revolution in 1791 settled in and around Santiago, stitching their habits and customs onto the cultural quilt of the city. Eventually black Haitians and Jamaicans came also, as workers. The rich racial mixture has produced some of the most exciting music, art, and architecture in the Caribbean.

Proud Santiagüeros tout their city as the "Hero City," or the *capital moral de la Revolución,* though this is belied by the extreme degree of *jineterismo* and begging, although a police crackdown has improved the situation immeasurably.

SANTIAGO DE CUBA

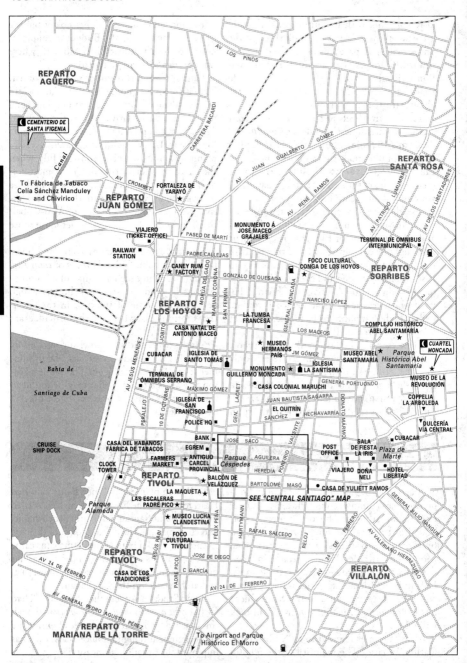

SANTIAGO DE CUBA

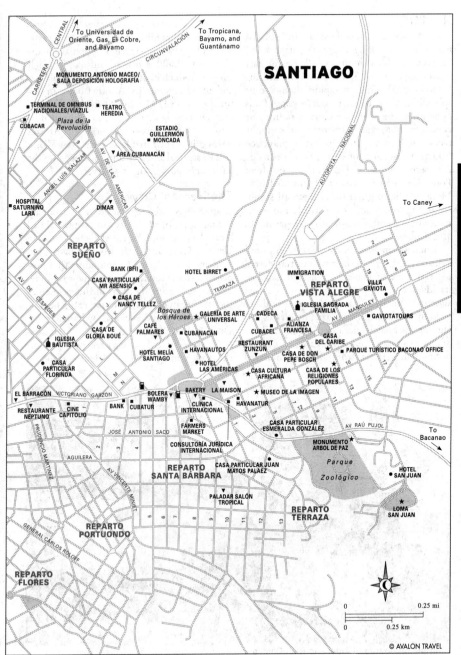

SANTIAGO

To Universidad de Oriente, Gas, El Cobre, and Bayamo

To Tropicana, Bayamo, and Guantánamo

CARRETERA CENTRAL

CIRCUNVALACIÓN

MONUMENTO ANTONIO MACEO/
SALA DEPOSICIÓN HOLOGRAFÍA

TERMINAL DE OMNIBUS
NACIONALES/VÍAZUL

TEATRO
HEREDIA

CUBACAR

*Plaza de la
Revolución*

ESTADIO
GUILLERMÓN
MONCADA

ÁREA CUBANACÁN

AV DE LAS AMÉRICAS

ANGEL LUIS SALAZAR

HOSPITAL
SATURNINO
LARA

DIMAR

AUTOPISTA NACIONAL

To Caney

REPARTO
SUEÑO

AV DE CÉSPEDES

BANK (BFI)

CASA PARTICULAR
MR ASENSIO

CASA DE
NANCY TELLEZ

HOTEL BIRRET

TERRAZA

IMMIGRATION

REPARTO
VISTA ALEGRE

VILLA
GAVIOTA

CASA DE
GLORIA BOUÉ

IGLESIA
BAUTISTA

CASA
PARTICULAR
FLORINDA

*Bosque de
los Héroes*

CAFÉ
PALMARES

HOTEL MELIÁ
SANTIAGO

GALERÍA DE ARTE
UNIVERSAL

CUBANACÁN

HAVANAUTOS

CADECA

CUBACEL

RESTAURANT
ZUNZÚN

HOTEL
LAS AMÉRICAS

IGLESIA SAGRADA
FAMILIA

AV MANDULEY

GAVIOTATOURS

ALIANZA
FRANCESA

CASA
DEL CARIBE

PARQUE TURÍSTICO BACONAO OFFICE

CASA DE DON
PEPE BOSCH

CASA CULTURA
AFRICANA

CASA DE LOS
RELIGIONES
POPULARES

EL BARRACÓN

VICTORIANO GARZON

RESTAURANTE
NEPTUNO

CINE
CAPITOLIO

BANK

CUBATUR

JOSÉ ANTONIO SACO

BOLERA
WAMBY

BAKERY LA MAISON

CLÍNICA
INTERNACIONAL

FARMERS
MARKET

CONSULTORÍA JURÍDICA
INTERNACIONAL

MUSEO DE LA IMAGEN

HAVANATUR

CASA PARTICULAR
ESMERALDA GONZÁLEZ

AV RAÚ PUJOL

To
Bacanao

MONUMENTO
ARBOL DE PAZ

*Parque
Zoológico*

HOTEL
SAN JUAN

AGUILERA

PRUDENCIO MARTÍNEZ

REPARTO
SANTA BÁRBARA

CASA PARTICULAR JUAN
MATOS PALÁEZ

AV VINCENTE MINIET

PALADAR SALÓN
TROPICAL

REPARTO
TERRAZA

LOMA
SAN JUAN

GENERAL CARLOS RÓLOEF

REPARTO
PORTUONDO

REPARTO
FLORES

0   0.25 mi

0   0.25 km

© AVALON TRAVEL

HISTORY

Diego Velázquez founded the city in 1514 and named it for the king of Spain's patron saint, St. Jago. The city, built on hills on the east side of the Bahía de Santiago, was named the Cuban capital and grew rapidly thanks to its splendid harbor. Its first *capitán-general* was none other than Hernán Cortés, soon to be conqueror of Mexico. Other famous conquistadores resided here, too, including Francisco Pizarro (conqueror of Peru), Don Pedro de Alvarado (founder of Guatemala), and Juan Ponce de León (colonizer of Puerto Rico). Many of the original buildings still stand, including Velázquez's own sturdy home, financed by wealth from nearby copper mines at El Cobre.

Santiago remained capital of Cuba only until February 1553, when the governor transferred his residence to Havana. Santiago had lost its advantage and the El Cobre mines closed shortly thereafter. It was subsequently damaged by earthquakes and razed by pirates, including the French buccaneer Jacques de Sores and Welsh pirate Henry Morgan.

Spanish settlers from Jamaica boosted Santiago's numbers when that island was seized by the English in 1655. At the close of the century, when Santiago's population approached 10,000, a massive influx of French émigrés from Haiti doubled the city population and added new vitality. Another boost in fortunes came in 1793, when Spanish authorities granted Santiago an *asamiento* (unlimited license) to import slaves. Countless West African slaves gained their first look at the New World as they stepped shackled and confused into the harsh light on Santiago's wharves.

The Heroes' City

Santiago has had a reputation as a liberal city dating to 1836, when city fathers proclaimed local elections in defiance of the governor in Havana. Governor Tacón won the battle, but Santiago had asserted an autonomy that propelled it to the forefront in the quest for independence. During the Wars of Independence, the city became a concentration camp held by Spanish troops and enclosed by barbed wire. On July 1, 1898, after the United States entered the fray, U.S. troops reached the outskirts of Santiago and the defenses atop San

multiple billboards of Fidel and Raúl Castro

Juan Hill that protected the city. Throughout the morning, the U.S. artillery softened up the Spanish defenders before 3,000 U.S. and Cuban troops (including Teddy Roosevelt and his Rough Riders) stormed the hill under cover of punishing fire. Though Roosevelt's part has been vastly overblown by U.S. history texts, the victory sealed the war. The Spanish navy, meanwhile, had sheltered in Santiago harbor. On July 3, it attempted to escape. A battle ensued and the Spanish fleet was destroyed.

The Spanish surrender was signed on San Juan Hill on July 17. The Spanish flag came down and up went the Stars and Stripes.

Hotbed of Revolution

During the 20th century the city became a hotbed of revolutionary activity during the decades before 1950. The opening shots in Castro's revolution were fired here on July 26, 1953, when the 26-year-old lawyer and his followers attacked the Moncada barracks at dawn in an attempt to inspire a general uprising.

Assassinations by Batista's thugs were common. The terror and turmoil reached a crescendo on November 30, 1956, when a 22-year-old Santiago teacher named Frank País led a group of Castro's 26th of July Movement (M-26-7) rebels in a daring attack on the police headquarters in Santiago, timed to coincide with the landing of the *Granma* bringing Castro and other revolutionaries from exile in Mexico. País's attack was ill-fated, and after the fiasco Batista's henchmen initiated a campaign of indiscriminate murders. Frank País was shot on the street on July 30, 1958. His funeral erupted into a massive protest led by Santiago's mothers while the city workers went on strike, inspiring similar protests throughout Cuba.

On January 2, 1959, two days after Batista fled the island, Fidel Castro and his Rebel Army arrived in Santiago to accept the surrender of Batista's general. Castro gave his victory speech in Parque Céspedes before setting off on a victory parade for Havana.

The postrevolutionary years have seen massive construction. An oil refinery was built,

along with a power-generating plant, textile mill, and cement factory.

ORIENTATION

The Carretera Central from Bayamo enters Santiago from the north, descends to Plaza de la Revolución, and runs into the heart of the city as Avenida de los Libertadores. The coast road from Marea del Portillo enters the city from the west as Paseo de Martí, which rises to Avenida de los Libertadores. The road from Guantánamo enters the city from the east as Avenida Raúl Pujol.

The historic core (*casco histórico*) is roughly arranged in a grid. At its heart is Parque Céspedes, bounded by Félix Pena and Lacret (north–south) and Aguilera and Heredia (east–west). Most sights of interest are within a few blocks of the park. Aguilera leads east from Parque Céspedes uphill to Plaza de Marte, a major hub on the eastern edge of the historic quarter. From here, Avenida 24 de Febrero leads south to the airport and Parque Histórico El Morro. Avenida Victoriano Garzón leads east from Plaza de Marte to the residential Reparto Sueño and Vista Alegre districts, also accessed from Plaza de la Revolución via Avenida de las Américas.

The Autopista Nacional begins in Vista Alegre and extends only 45 kilometers before petering out in the middle of nowhere near Palma Soriano.

A *circunvalación* circles the east and south sides of the city.

PARQUE CÉSPEDES AND VICINITY

Formerly known as Plaza de Armas, this square at the heart of the city is ringed with gas lamps and shade trees. At its heart is a stone statue of the square's namesake hero.

Ayuntamiento

The beautiful building on the north side is the town hall (Aguilera, e/ Genera Lacret y Felix Peña; not open to the public), former headquarters of the Spanish colonial governor. The original building was first occupied by Hernán

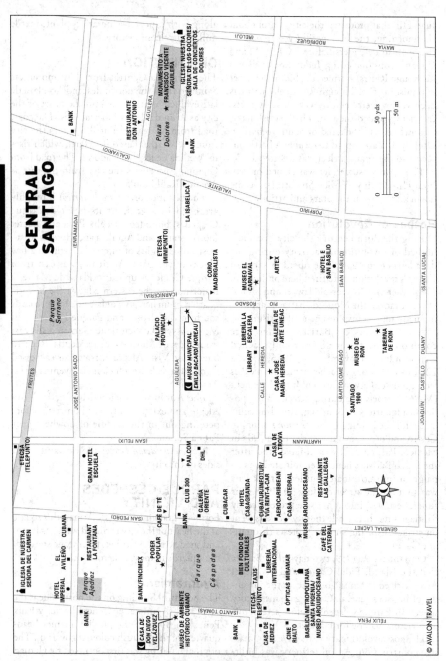

CENTRAL SANTIAGO

Cortés; the current structure dates from the 1950s and is based on a design from 1783. Its antecedent, built in 1855, was toppled by an earthquake and had housed the U.S. military during its occupation of Cuba. It was from the overhanging balcony that Fidel Castro gave the victory speech on January 2, 1959, after he entered town following Batista's flight from Cuba.

Basílica Metropolitana Santa Ifigenia

Raised on a pedestal on the southern side of the plaza, which it dominates, is the cathedral (open for mass Mon. and Wed.–Fri. 6:30 P.M., Sat. 5 P.M., Sun. 9 A.M. and 6:30 P.M.), otherwise known as the Catedral de Nuestra Señora de la Asunción. The cathedral is the fourth building to occupy the site (the original was begun in 1528). The current edifice dates to 1922, although its nave is held aloft by walls erected in 1810. The restored interior includes exquisitely hand-carved choir stalls. The remains of Diego Velázquez are entombed within. Between the church's twin towers is a statue of the Angel of the Annunciation holding a trumpet. The entrance is on Felix Peña.

The east side of the cathedral contains the **Museo Arquidiocesano** (tel. 022/65-4586, Mon.–Sat. 9:30 A.M.–5:30 P.M., entrance CUC1, cameras CUC1, videos CUC3), a cramped space full of religious antiques.

◖ Casa de Don Diego Velázquez

On the park's west side is the former home of Cuba's first colonizer. It dates from 1516 and is supposedly the oldest house in Cuba. The somber Spanish mansion is fronted by dark wooden Moorish window grills and shutters. Velázquez lived upstairs. A gold foundry was maintained downstairs (it is still there, in the rear). The house today contains the **Museo de Ambiente Histórico Cubano** (Felix Peña #602, tel. 022/65-2652, Mon.–Thurs. and Sat. 9 A.M.–4:45 P.M., Fri. 2–4:45 P.M., Sun. 9 A.M.–12:45 P.M., entrance CUC2, cameras CUC1, videos CUC5), with rooms full of period furnishings and artwork. Magnificent!

Basílica Metropolitana Santa Ifigenia

© CHRISTOPHER P. BAKER

SANTIAGO DE CUBA

◖ Museo Municipal Emilio Bacardí Moreau

This museum (Pío Rosado, e/ Aguilera and Heredia, tel. 022/62-8402, Tues.–Sat. 9 A.M.–9 P.M., Sun. 9 A.M.–1 P.M., CUC2 entrance, CUC1 camera) was founded by Emilio Bacardí Moreau (1844–1922) in 1899 and contains his astounding collection. A member of the expatriate and anti-Castroite Bacardí rum family, Emilio, patriot writer and mayor of Santiago, is in good graces; he was imprisoned in the Morro Castle for revolutionary activities. The museum is housed in a huge neoclassical edifice with Corinthian columns.

The first floor contains colonial artifacts, from slave shackles and stocks to antique weapons. The second floor art gallery includes 19th-century and contemporary works. Also here: a small but impressive display of pre-Columbian artifacts from throughout the Americas, including a shrunken head (*cabeza reducida*) and Peruvian mummies. Only three specific items can be photographed: a statue of Che Guevara and one of Santiago Aposto, plus the rear patio.

SANTIAGO STREET NAMES

Most historic streets have both modern and older names.

OLD NAME	NEW NAME
Alameda	Jesús Menéndez
Calvario	Porfirio Valiente
Carnicería	Pío Rosado
Clarín	Padre Quiroga
Corona	Mariano
Enramada	José Antonio Saco
Marina	Aguilera
Reloj	Mayía Rodríguez
San Agustín	Donato Marmól
San Basilio	Bartolomé Masó
San Félix	Hartmann
San Pedro	General Lacret
Santa Lucía	Joaquín Castillo Duany
Santo Tomás	Féliz Peña
Trinidad	General Portuondo
Trocha	24 de Febrero

On the museum's north side rises the 1920s neoclassical **Palacio Provincial,** seat of local government.

CALLE HEREDIA TO PLAZA DOLORES

Calle Heredia, which leads east from Parque Céspedes, has traditionally been closed to traffic on weekend evenings for a cultural fair.

First stop should be the **Casa de la Trova** (Heredia #208, tel. 022/65-2689, daily noon–1 A.M.), formerly the home of revered composer Rafael Salcedo (1844–1917). Most afternoons and evenings the haunting melodies and plaintive *boleros* of the *trova* reverberate down the street.

Casa José María Heredia (Heredia #260, tel. 022/62-5350, Tues.–Sat. 9 A.M.–7 P.M., Sun. 9 A.M.–2 P.M., CUC1) is the birthplace of the 19th-century nationalist poet José María Heredia (1803–1839). The house is furnished in colonial fashion.

Break out your camera at **La Librería La Escalera** (Heredia #265), a tiny bookstore festooned with intriguing bric-a-brac. The **Galería de Arte UNEAC** (Heredia, e/ Hartmann y Pio Rosada, tel. 022/65-3465, ext. 106, www.uneac.com) is worth a peek for its superb art. Take the stairs to the **Museo El Carnaval** (Heredia #304, tel. 022/62-6955, Tues.–Sat. 9 A.M.–5:15 P.M., entrance CUC1, cameras CUC1, videos CUC5), which tells the history of Santiago's colorful carnival. Some of the outlandish costumes are on display. Folkloric shows are held at 4 P.M.

At the junction of Heredia and Valiente, turn north and walk one block into **Plaza Dolores,** a delightful little plaza with wrought-iron seats surrounding a larger-than-life bronze statue of Francisco Vicente Aguilera (1821–1877), a revolutionary leader in the Ten Years War. The **Iglesia Nuestra Señora de los Dolores,** on the east side, is now a concert hall and adjoins the **Colegio Jesuita Dolores,** where Fidel Castro was educated as a youth.

REPARTO TIVOLI

The hilly 17th-century Tivoli district southwest of Parque Céspedes is full of sites associated with figures in the revolutionary pantheon.

Beginning at the park's southwest corner, follow Felix Peña south one block to Masó. Turn left. One block along, at the corner of Calle Corona, you'll pass the **Balcón de Velázquez** (daily 9 A.M.–5 P.M.), a small plaza atop an old Spanish fort. Continue west 100 meters to Calle Padre Pico. Turn left. The broad steps ahead are known as **La Escalanita.** Here, three members of the 26th of July Movement were killed on November 30, 1956, while attacking a nearby police station. To learn more, ascend the steps to the former station, now the **Museo Lucha Clandestina** (Museum of the Underground Fight, Jesús Rabi #1, tel. 022/62-4689, Tues.–Sun. 9 A.M.–5 P.M., CUC1), which tells the tale of Castro's 26th of July Movement (M-26-7). Fidel Castro lived across the street (Jesús Rabi #6) as a youth and, following the attack on Moncada, was imprisoned in the **Antiguo Carcel Provincial** (Aguilera #131), two blocks north.

Three blocks south of the museum is **La**

Casa de los Tradiciones (Rabí #154, e/ Princesa y San Fernando, tel. 022/65-3892, Sun.–Fri. 11:30 A.M.–midnight, Sat. noon–midnight), an old wooden home with gingerbread trim. Inside, this traditional music forum is festooned with photos of famous musicians.

La Maqueta de Santiago

A must-visit, the Model of Santiago (Mariano Corona e/ Masó y Duany, tel. 022/65-2095, Tues.–Sun. 9 A.M.–9 P.M., CUC1 including guide) opened in 2009. Still in construction, this huge 3-D scale-model of the city shows every single building in detail and covers the entire bay from the Morro Castle. Various maps edify on the city's evolution, geography, and future development.

REPARTO LOS HOYOS

The Los Hoyos district north of Parque Céspedes is known for its 18th-century churches. Clerics on a busman's holiday might visit the **Iglesia de Nuestra Señora del Carmen** (Félix Peña #505, esq. Tamayo Freites), known for its statuary; **Iglesia de San Francisco** (Sagarra #121, esq. Mariana Corona), with its triple nave; **Iglesia de Santo Tomás** (Félix Peña #308, esq. General Portuondo); and **Iglesia de la Santísima Trinidad** (General Portuondo, esq. General Moncada), overlooking a tiny plaza dedicated to Guillermo Moncada (1840–1895), a Liberation Army general who was born nearby.

Avenida Sánchez Hechavarría, three blocks north of Parque Céspedes, is lined with houses used by revolutionaries during the effort to topple Batista; concentrated between Hartmann and Valiente, they're marked by bronze plaques. The former home of Vilma Espín, an M-26-7 member who later married Raúl Castro and led the Women's Federation of Cuba, today is **El Quitrín** (Hechavarría #473, e/ Porfirio Valiente y Pío Rosada, tel. 022/62-2528), a store selling lace fashionwear.

The **Museo Hermanos País** (Banderas #266, e/ General Portuondo y Habana, tel. 022/65-2710, Mon.–Sat. 9 A.M.–5 P.M., CUC1) is the birthplace of brothers Frank and José País, who headed the Santiago M-26-7 organization and were killed by Batista's police. The **Museo Casa Natal de Antonio Maceo** (Maceo #207, e/ Corona y Rastro, tel. 022/62-3550, Mon.–Sat. 9 A.M.–5 P.M., closed during rains, CUC1) occupies the birthplace of Antonio Maceo Grajales, the mulatto who rose to become second in command of the Liberation Army during the Wars of Independence.

Four blocks west is the waterfront Avenida Jesús Menéndez. Follow the boulevard north to the railway station to admire the west-facing wall across the street. Painted with a colorful revolutionary mural depicting Fidel leading the Revolution, this is the warehouse of **Fábrica de Ron Caney** (Av. Peralejo, e/ Gonzalo de Quesada y Padre Callejas), one block east. The oldest rum factory in Cuba, it was built in 1868 by the Bacardí family and nationalized in 1959, after which the Cuban government continued to make rum while Bacardí set up shop in Puerto Rico. It is not open to view, but you can sample the goods in the tasting room (Av. Peralejo #103, tel. 022/62-5575, Mon.–Sat. 9 A.M.–5 P.M., Sun. 9 A.M.–noon).

REPARTO SUEÑO

This 19th-century district lies northeast of the old city and **Plaza de Marte,** a small plaza built in 1860 as the Spanish parade ground and execution spot for Cuban patriots. Busts of Cuban patriots speckle the square.

The district is framed by Avenida Victoriano Garzón, Avenida de las Américas, and **Avenida de los Libertadores,** a broad boulevard lined with bronze busts of revolutionary heroes.

In December 2009, city fathers began laying new water pipes for every home. The streets were dug up. Pipes laid. Alas, no thought was given to filling in the troughs. Five square kilometers cross-hatched with trenches!

Complejo Histórico Abel Santamaría

This plaza (General Portuondo, esq. Av. de los Libertadores) features a huge granite cube carved with the faces of Abel Santamaría

THE ATTACK ON MONCADA

At 5 A.M. on Sunday, July 26, Fidel Castro and 122 young followers sang the national anthem. Then, dressed in brown Cuban Army uniforms, they set out from Granjita Siboney crammed inside 16 cars, with Castro in the fifth car – a brand-new 1953 Buick sedan. The third car, containing Raúl (leading a second unit), took a wrong turn and arrived at his target – the Palace of Justice – after the fighting had begun. Another car had a flat tire and yet another car took a wrong turn, which reduced the fighting force to 105 men, who attacked Moncada with a few Winchester rifles, hunting shotguns, a single M-1 rifle, a single Browning submachine gun, and assorted sporting rifles.

Castro had concluded that the fort could be rushed through the southeastern gate. The commandos would then fan out through the barracks with newly seized weapons. At first,

the attack went according to plan. The sentinels were taken by surprise and disarmed. As the commandos rushed into the barracks, an Army patrol appeared. Gunfire erupted. The alarm bells were sounded. Then a volley of machine-gun fire sprayed the rebels, who were forced to retreat. The battle lasted less than 30 minutes. Only eight rebels were killed in combat, but 61 others were caught and tortured to death.

Batista's army, which lost 19 soldiers, claimed that Moncada was attacked by "between 400 and 500 men, equipped with the most modern instruments of war," and that Castro's men had been gunned down at Moncada. A photographer, however, managed to get photos of the tortured *fidelistas*. The gruesome photos were printed, exposing Batista's lie and unleashing a wave of disgust.

and José Martí. A fountain seems to hold the cube aloft. To its north, the **Museo Abel Santamaría** (tel. 022/62-4119, Mon.–Sat. 9:30 A.M.–5 P.M., CUC1) occupies the former hospital where Abel Santamaría and 22 fellow rebels fired at the Moncada barracks and where they were later captured, tortured, and killed. Here, too, Fidel Castro gave his famous "History Will Absolve Me" speech while being judged by an emergency tribunal. Seven rooms house exhibits relating to the event and to the life of Abel Santamaría.

Immediately south, across the street, is the **Palacio de Justicia,** still functioning as a courthouse. It was attacked by Raúl Castro's rebels.

◖ Cuartel Moncada

This former military barracks (General Portuondo, e/ Av. de los Libertadores y Carlos Aponte), with castellated walls and turrets, is renowned for the fateful day on July 26, 1953, when Fidel Castro and his poorly armed cohorts stormed the barracks. After the Revolution, Moncada was turned into a school, the Ciudad Escolar 26 de Julio. A portion of

the building near the entrance gate is riddled with bullet holes. They're not the originals; Batista's troops filled those in. Castro had the holes redone using photographs. This section houses the **Museo Histórico 26 de Julio** (also known as the Museo de la Revolución, tel. 022/62-0157, Tues.–Sat. 9:30 A.M.–5:15 P.M., Sun. 9:30 A.M.–noon, entrance CUC2, cameras CUC1, videos CUC5), which tells the tale of the attack and subsequent revolutionary history. Prolific weaponry includes Castro's personal sharpshooter rifle.

Plaza de la Revolución

This huge plaza at the junction of Avenida de las Américas and Avenida de los Libertadores is dominated by the massive **Monumento Antonio Maceo,** dedicated to the homegrown son of a local merchant who rose to become the hero-general of the War of Independence as second-in-command of the rebel forces. Maceo was nicknamed the "Bronze Titan"—the mammoth statue of the general on a rearing horse is cast in bronze. On the north side, an eternal flame flickers in a marble-lined bowl cut into the base by the entrance to the **Sala Deposición Hológrafía** (Mon.–Sat. 8 A.M.–4 P.M., free) with holograms telling of Maceo's life and of the War of Independence.

REPARTO VISTA ALEGRE

This leafy residential district is bounded on the west by Avenida de las Américas and on the south by Avenida Pujol (Carretera Siboney). Avenida Manduley runs east–west through the center of Vista Alegre and is lined with villas. Many were confiscated after the Revolution and turned into government offices, clinics, and schools.

Museo de la Imagen

This museum (Calle 8 #106, esq. 5, tel. 022/64-2234, Mon.–Sat. 9 A.M.–5 P.M., CUC1) was established by cameraman Bernabá Muñiz, who filmed Fulgencio Batista's coup d'état in 1952, the surrender of the Moncada barracks to the revolutionaries in 1959, and Fidel's victory parade from Santiago to Havana. The Museum of Images features almost 500 photographic, film, and TV cameras—from CIA espionage cameras to a stereoscopic viewfinder from 1872—plus a library of feature films and documentaries dating back to 1926.

Parque Histórico Loma de San Juan

Every U.S. schoolchild knows that Teddy Roosevelt and his Rough Riders defeated the Spanish at San Juan Hill, which rises on the south side of Avenida Pujol to a palm-shaded park. The park contains a replica fort, plus monuments and cannons, including a Tomb of the Unknown Mambí, Cuba's independence fighters. One memorial is dedicated to "the generous American soldiers who sealed a covenant of liberty and fraternity between the two nations." There is no monument, however, to Roosevelt and his Rough Riders, because the Cuban liberationists who helped storm the hill weren't even invited to the surrender ceremony on July 16, 1898, beneath a huge ceiba tree.

A WALK THROUGH VISTA ALEGRE

Leafy Vista Alegre makes for a shaded walking tour.

Begin at the Hotel Meliá Santiago, on Avenida de las Américas. Cater-corner, on the east side of the boulevard, the **Bosque de los Mártires de Bolivia** (esq. Calle 2) features bas-relief tableaux of Che Guevara and his band of revolutionaries who died in Bolivia. The **Galería de Arte Universal** (Calle 1, esq. M, tel. 022/64-1198, Mon.-Sat. 9 A.M.-5:30 P.M.), on the east side of the park, is worth a peek before continuing south along Calle 1 three blocks to Avenida Manduley, where facing you is **La Maison** (Manduley #52, esq. Calle 1), a mansion hosting a nightly fashion show.

Eastward, on the next block, the **Casa Cultura Africana Fernando Ortíz** (Manduley, esq. Calle 5, tel. 22/64-2487, closed for restoration at last visit) displays African masks, carvings, and musical instruments.

Three blocks farther along Manduley brings you to **Casa de Don Pepe Bosch** (esq. Calle 11), a grand neo-baroque mansion now the **Palacio Provincial de Pioneros** (Young Pioneers' School), with a Soviet MiG fighter jet in the playground. If you're into churches, cross Manduley and walk uphill one block to **Iglesia Sagrado Familia** (Calle 11, e/ 4 y 6, open for mass only, Mon. and Fri. at 5 P.M. and Sun. at 10:30 A.M.), a Gothic-style Catholic church built in 1898 with fine stained-glass windows.

Continuing along Manduley to Calle 11; turn right. One block away, at the corner of Calle 8, awaits the **Casa del Caribe** (Calle 13 #154, tel. 022/64-3609, caribe@cultstgo.cult.cu), with exhibits honoring Caribbean cultures. One block south, the **Museo de las Religiones Populares** (Calle 13 #206, e/ 8 y 10, tel. 022/64-2285, ext. 114, daily 9 A.M.-5:30 P.M., CUC1 entrance, CUC1 guide) is dedicated to the *santería* religion and related Afro-Cuban sects.

© CHRISTOPHER P. BAKER

Jardín de los Helechos

The **Monumento Arbol de Paz,** in its own little park off Avenida Pujol 100 meters west of San Juan Hill, occupies the site of the original "peace tree." Cannons and howitzers surround giant bronze plaques (shaped as open books) inscribed with the names of all the U.S. soldiers killed in the war.

Jardín de los Helechos

For an escape from the frenetic bustle, head to this Fern Garden (Carretera de la Caney #129, tel. 022/64-8335, manolito@bioeco.siess.info.cu, Mon.–Sat. 9 A.M.–5 P.M., CUC1), in the colonial village of Caney, three kilometers northeast of Reparto Vista Alegre. What began as a private collection in the mansion of Manuel G. Caloff now boasts more than 360 fern species plus orchids and about 1,000 other plant species divided into zones and specialties, such as miniatures and medicinal plants. It's best visited in winter, when the orchid blooms are profuse. Take bus #15 from Plaza de Marte.

SOUTHERN SUBURBS
◖ Parque Histórico El Morro

The **Castillo de San Pedro del Morro** (tel. 022/69-1569, 8:30 A.M.–7 P.M., entrance CUC4, cameras/videos CUC1) is an enormous piece of military architecture poised atop the cliffs at the entrance to Santiago Bay, about 14 kilometers south of the city. Begun in 1638, the Morro castle was rebuilt in 1664 after Henry Morgan's pirates reduced it to rubble. Cannons are everywhere, and the views from the battlements are spectacular! Exhibits include old

cañonazo, El Morro

© CHRISTOPHER P. BAKER

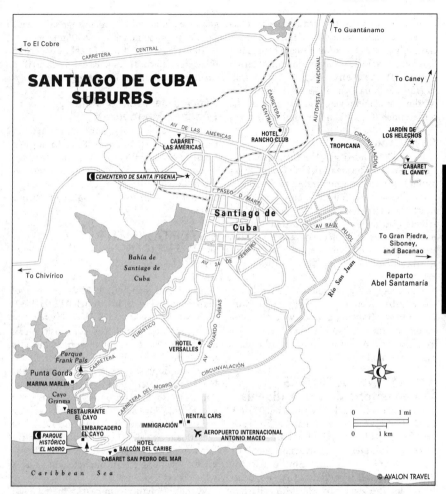

muskets, cutlasses, and more. A **cañonazo** ceremony is held at sunset, when soldiers in period costume put a torch to a cannon in a time-honored tradition that once announced the nightly sealing of the harbor.

The cliff is pinned by the **Faro del Morro** lighthouse built in 1920 and still using the original hand-wound Fresnel lens. Part of a military complex, it's off-limits.

Do call in at the clifftop **Restaurante El Morro** (tel. 022/69-1576, daily noon–10 P.M.), where the mediocre *criollo* dishes are excelled

by fabulous views. The goat-hide chair hanging on the wall is there because Paul McCartney sat on it when he dined here.

Bus #212 runs from downtown to Embarcadero Cayo Granma, from where you can hike up to the castle. If driving, follow Avenida 12 de Agosto south from Plaza de Marte; this leads to Carretera del Morro. Alternatively, you can drive the Carretera Turística, which begins at the southern end of Avenida Jesús Menéndez, following the bayshore to emerge atop the cliffs by the castle. En route, you'll pass **Punta Gorda,** a slender peninsula once fashionable with Santiago's upper class. A large statue of revolutionary hero Frank País looms over the point overlooking Marina Marlin. **Restaurante Punta Gorda** (tel. 022/69-9790, daily noon–3 P.M.), in Marina Marlin, has fabulous views; stop by to enjoy the buffet lunch (CUC8) and seafood dishes.

Cayo Granma
This small island sits in the bay offshore of Punta Gorda. The small fishing colony looks as if it has been magically transferred from the Mediterranean, with its rowboats berthed beneath the eaves of waterfront houses. Narrow streets lead up to a hilltop church, **Iglesia de San Rafael.** The **Restaurante El Cayo** (tel. 022/69-0109, daily noon–5 P.M.), on the northeast side of the cay, serves seafood and *criollo* dishes.

A passenger ferry (20 centavos) serves the cay from Embarcadero Cayo Granma and continues to **Playa Socapa,** a beach with a cannon battery on the headland facing El Morro. An excursion boat runs from Marina Marlin (daily 8:30 A.M.–4:30 P.M., CUC3).

NORTHERN SUBURBS
◖ Cementerio de Santa Ifigenia
This cemetery (Calzada Crombet, tel. 022/63-2723, 8 A.M.–6 P.M., entrance CUC1, cameras CUC1, videos CUC5) is the final resting place of key figures in Cuban history: not least, Carlos Manuel Céspedes, Emilio Bacardí, Tomás Estrada Palma (Cuba's first president), heroes of the attack on the Moncada barracks (look for the red and black flags on their graves), and heroes of the War of Independence, who are entombed in a tiny castle. The grand gateway is dedicated to Cuban soldiers who died fighting in Angola.

The main draw is the **Mausoleo de Martí,** the tomb of José Martí, beneath a crenellated hexagonal tower (each side represents one of the six original provinces of Cuba). Marble steps lead down to a circular mausoleum, designed so that the sun would always shine on his coffin, draped with the Cuban flag. Military

guards stand duty 24/7 and change shifts with a goose-stepping march every 30 minutes.

To get here, you'll pass **Fuerte de Yarayó** (Carretera Bacardí, esq. Paseo de Martí), a small fort built in the late 19th century.

Fábrica de Tabaco Celia Sánchez Manduley
You can watch cigars being hand-made at this factory (tel. 022/63-0872, Mon.–Fri. 8 A.M.–3 P.M.), locally called Fábrica Textilera (it once made textiles). Guided tours are offered. Visits are permitted only with a voucher (CUC3) sold at **Cubatur** on Parque Céspedes.

ENTERTAINMENT AND EVENTS
Nightlife
BARS
The dark and moody **Club 300** (Aguilera, e/ Hartmann y General Lacret, tel. 022/65-3532, nightly 8:30 P.M.–2 A.M., CUC2) is a hot spot for foreign boy meets local gal. Music videos are screened. It's a free-for-all to enter, but a tip usually does the trick.

Serving sophisticates, the **Pico Real** lobby bar, in the Hotel Meliá Santiago (Av. de las Américas, esq. M, daily 6 P.M.–2 A.M.), is a chic spot for enjoying cocktails. A pianist plays most nights, and live jazz is hosted on Friday. For sensational city views, take the elevator to the hotel's top-floor **Bello Bar** (daily 6 P.M.–2 A.M., CUC5 including one drink; hotel guests free), which hosts live music.

A shot of quality rum costs a mere CUC1 at the **Taberna del Ron** (Pío Rosado, esq. Bartolomé Masó, tel. 022/64-1705, daily 10 A.M.–10 P.M.), a simple *bodega*-style bar beneath the Museo de Ron (Bartolomé Masó #358, esq. Carnecería).

TRADITIONAL MUSIC AND DANCE
Santiago's **Casa de la Trova** (Heredia #208, tel. 022/65-2689, noon–1 A.M., CUC1 by day, CUC5 at night) is the island's most famous "house of *trova*." The *trova* tradition of romantic ballads was born here, and

famous Cuban musicians perform. **Patio de Artex** (Heredia #304, tel. 022/65-4814, daily 11 A.M.–1 P.M., 4–7 P.M., and 9:30 P.M.–2 A.M., CUC2), packs in a younger crowd for traditional music performed live. Even livelier, **La Casa de los Tradiciones** (Rabí #154, e/ Princesa y San Fernando, tel. 022/65-3892, daily 8:30 P.M.–midnight and Sat. noon), an old wooden home where even the beer bottles get up and dance.

Coro Madrigalista (Pío Rosada #555, esq. Aguilera, CUC1) is a similar, simpler venue with *son* and *bolero* nightly at 9 P.M. And the **Museo de Ambiente Histórico Cubano** (Felix Peña #602, tel. 022/65-2652) hosts traditional music and other cultural activities, including a fabulous female guitar duet (Wed.–Sat. at 10:30 A.M.).

The following Afro-Cuban *comparsas* (folkloric associations) have workshops where you can watch, and even participate in, practice sessions: **La Tumba Francesa** (Calle Los Maceos #501, esq. General Bandera, no tel., Tues. and Fri. at 9 P.M.), **Foco Cultural El Tivoli** (Desiderio Mesnier #208, tel. 022/62-0142, Mon., Wed., and Fri. at 8:30 P.M. and Sun. at 2 P.M.), and **Ballet Folklórico Cutumba** (Saco, e/ Corona y Padre Pico, tel. 022/62-5860, Tues.–Sun.).

CABARETS AND DISCOS

The **Tropicana** (Autopista Nacional, Km 1.5, tel. 022/68-7020, fax 022/68-7090, Mon. and Fri.–Sat. 10 P.M., CUC20 including one drink), four kilometers northeast of town, hosts a colorful show tracing Caribbean history and culture. This is saucy Las Vegas–style *cabaret espectáculo* at its best.

You'll be the only non-Cuban at the alfresco **Cabaret Las Américas** (Av. Las Américas, tel. 022/63-4658, Tues.–Sun. 8 P.M.–2:30 A.M., 40 pesos), two kilometers northwest of Plaza de la Revolución, in Reparto José Martí. It packs in locals, who break out dancing beneath the stage. Chicken dinners are served. Cabaret junkies can get up close and personal at the bargain-priced **Cabaret Son Caney** (off Carretera de la Caney, tel. 022/64-8292, Tues.–Sun. 10:45 P.M., 40

CARNAVAL!

Carnaval in Santiago de Cuba has been performed since the 19th century, when it was an Easter celebration. Originally it was called the Fiesta de las Mamarrachos (Festival of the Nincompoops), when slaves were given time to release their pent-up energies and frustrations in a celebration full of sexual content. The celebration was bound irrevocably to the secret societies of ancient Africa, transformed in Cuba into neighborhood societies called *carabalí* that vied with one another to produce the most elaborate processions (*comparsas*).

The hourglass drums of the ancestors pound out their *tun q'tu q'tu q'tun* rhythm. The wail of Chinese cornets adds to the racket. And young and old alike rush to join the conga lines full of clowns and celebrants in colonial period dress. The conga lines are followed by floats graced by girls (*luceros* – morning stars) in riotous feathers and sequined bikinis or outrageous dresses. Huge papier-mâché heads supported by dancing Cubans bash into each other. There are representations of the *orishas* in the *comparsas*, and characters representing the various gods lead the way. Every year there's a different theme, and contestants are judged on originality and popularity.

pesos), with a small but fun 40-minute show popular with a gay crowd.

Gays have taken a liking to **Cabaret San Pedro del Mar** (Carretera del Morro km 7.5, tel. 022/69-1287, Fri.–Sun. 10 P.M.–2 A.M., CUC10), near El Morro castle, eight kilometers south of town. Its small *espectáculo* precedes a disco. And the Hotel San Juan hosts the tiny **Cabaret Terraza San Juan** (Av. Siboney y Calle 13, Thurs.–Sun., CUC4 per couple).

The colonial-themed **Santiago Café** (Fri.–Sat. 10 P.M.–2 A.M., CUC5), in the Hotel Meliá Santiago (Av. de las Américas, esq. M), features a small cabaret followed by disco.

La Maison (Manduley #52, tel. 022/64-

1117, daily at 10:30 P.M., CUC5 including one drink) offers an alfresco fashion show followed by a cabaret. Diners get free entry.

The Arts
CLASSICAL PERFORMANCES
The **Teatro Heredia** (Av. de las Américas, esq. Av. de los Desfiles, tel. 022/64-3190), by the Plaza de la Revolución, hosts classical performances, as does the **Conservatorio Estaván Salas** (Santa Lucía #304, tel. 022/62-6167), a music school that also has public concerts.

CINEMA
Cine Rialto (Félix Peña, e/ Heredia y Bartolomé Masó, tel. 022/62-3035) is the city's main movie house.

Festivals and Events
Noche Santiaguera (also called the Festival de Rumba) is held on January 12, featuring a mini-carnival centered on Calle Heredia. The Big Enchilada, however, is the week-long **Carnaval** (Fiesta del Caribe) in late July, when everyone in town gets caught up in the street rumbas and conga lines. The node is the southern end of Avenida Jesús Menéndez, around Avenida 24 de Febrero.

In August, people converge in Parque Céspedes for the **Festival de Pregón,** arriving in carriages smothered with flowers and dressed in traditional costume to compete in traditional verse and song.

Every Friday and Saturday night, local youth gather at Area Cubanacán, on Avenida de las Américas, to hear live bands and watch big-screen music videos.

SPORTS AND RECREATION
Marina Marlin (tel. 022/69-1446, 10 A.M.– 10 P.M. Tues.–Sun.), at Punta Gorda, offers water sports and sportfishing. You can rent watercraft. The **Sala Juegos,** at Hotel San Juan (Av. Siboney y Calle 13), has two mini bowling lanes plus pool tables. And **Bolera Wamby** (Garzón, esq. 7) is a bowling alley due to open at last visit.

Bored kids might enjoy the **Parque**

Zoológico (Av. Pujol, Tues.–Fri. 10 A.M.–5 P.M., Sat.–Sun. 9 A.M.–5 P.M., CUC1 adults, CUC0.50 children), immediately west of Hotel San Juan. Conditions aren't the best.

Estadio Guillermo Moncada (Av. de las Américas y Calle E, tel. 022/64-2640) hosts baseball games October–March.

ACCOMMODATIONS
Casas Particulares
There are more than 400 *casas particulares* in Santiago, a noisy city; you'll want a room to the rear. All are air-conditioned.

DOWNTOWN
The **Casa Catedral** (San Pedro #703 altos, e/ Heredia y San Basilio, tel. 022/65-3169, CUC20–25) has views over Parque Céspedes from a breeze-swept, marble-floored lounge with balcony. The owners rent two simply furnished rooms. One has a huge, tiled colonial bathroom that is a feature in itself. The second has a small modern bathroom, kitchenette, and private entrance.

Justifiably popular, **Casa Colonial Maruchi** (San Felix #357, e/ Trinidad y San Germán, tel. 022/62-0767, maruchib@yahoo.es, CUC25–30) is a beautiful colonial house filled with antiques and *santería* icons. The two rooms (one with brass bed) with private hot-water bathrooms open to a lush patio. The owner, Maruchi Berbes, an expert on Afro-Cuban culture, hosts dance and drumming classes.

My favorite place, a true standout, is ◖ **Casa de Yuliett Ramos** (San Basilio #513 e/ Clarin y Reloj, tel. 022/62-6635, CUC15–25). Yuliett's home is endearingly decorated with stone walls and wood paneling. One of the two rooms opens to a patio balcony; the other has a quaint sundeck. Join the family in the TV lounge with red leather sofa.

REPARTO SUEÑO
One of the nicest houses in town is **Casa de Florinda Chaviano Martínez** (Calle I #58, e/ 2da y 3ra, tel. 022/66-3660, CUC25), with a modern lounge and a single, well-lit room with modern hot-water bathroom. A handsome patio

with grapevine arbor proves perfect for enjoying breakfast. The hosts are liberal and attentive.

Similar alternatives include **Casa de Gloria Boué** (Calle J #212, e/ 5ta y 4ta, tel. 022/64-4949, CUC25) and **Casa Particular Nancy Téllez** (Calle J #265, e/ 6ta y 5ta, tel. 022/62-5109, juanmatos78@yahoo.es, CUC20–25), each with two nicely furnished rooms.

For a self-contained option try 【 **Casa de Mr. Asensio** (Calle J #306, e/ Av. de las Américas y 6ta, tel. 022/62-4600, manuel@medired.scu.sld.cu, in Italy tel. 019/692-067, CUC20–25). The air-conditioned upstairs apartment has lively 1950s decor, cross-ventilation, and fans, plus small kitchen, a rooftop patio, and private garage.

REPARTOS VISTA ALEGRE AND TERRAZA

These leafy residential suburbs offer some of the nicest middle-class houses in town. Two of my favorites are **Casa Particular Esmeralda González** (Av. Pujol #107, esq. 5ta, tel. 022/64-6341, rachelbarreiro@yahoo.es, CUC20–25), where Esmeralda rents a spacious, well-lit, cross-ventilated room with fans, kitchenette, TV, independent entrance, marvelous period bathroom, and parking; and 【 **Casa Particular Juan Matos Palaez** (Calle Bitirí #102, esq. Taíno, tel. 022/64-1427, cmatos@eccs.ciges.inf.cu, CUC25–30), a beautiful 1950s-style home with two nicely furnished rooms with exquisite tiled hot-water bathrooms, plus huge patios to the front and rear.

Hotels

All hotels listed have air-conditioned rooms and satellite TV unless noted. Expect the **Hotel Imperial** (Enramada, esq. Felix Peña) to shine when it opens anew in 2011 after restoration; it boasts a lovely baroque facade.

UNDER CUC50

The impecunious might try **Hotel Birret** (Calles L y 7, tel. 022/64-2047, CUC8 s, CUC10 d), in Reparto Vista Alegre. Run by the Universidad del Oriente, it offers basic rooms with shared bathrooms with cold water only.

The cheapest digs are at **Hotel Gran Hotel Escuela** (Saco, esq. Hartmann, tel. 022/65-3020, fax 022/68-7123, www.granhotelstgo.cu, CUC12 s, CUC18 d year-round), a training hotel with 15 functional rooms with safes and simple bathrooms. It has a bar, café, and restaurant.

Islazul's **Hotel Libertad** (Aguilera #658, tel. 022/62-3080, fax 022/62-8394, reserve@libertad.tur.cu, CUC26 s, CUC32 d low season, CUC32 s, CUC38 d high season, including breakfast), on the south side of Plaza de Marte, has a classical motif and exquisite tilework and hardwoods throughout. It offers 42 smallish but amply furnished rooms with small modern bathrooms. It has a lobby bar, elegant restaurant, and Internet.

Villa Gaviota (Manduley #502, e/ 19 y 21, tel. 022/64-1370, fax 022/68-7106, reservas@gaviota.co.cu, from CUC34 s, CUC48 d low season, from CUC40 s, CUC48 d high season), in Vista Alegre, features 46 modestly furnished rooms and bargain-priced villas in a quiet residential district. There's a swimming pool, a store, and a restaurant and disco.

If all else in town is full, try Islazul's lackluster **Hotel Balcón del Caribe** (Carretera del Morro, Km 7.5, tel. 022/69-1506, fax 022/69-2398, carpeta@bcaribe.scu.tur.cu, CUC16 s, CUC24 d low season, CUC19 s low season, CUC30 d high season), atop the cliffs near the Morro Castle; and **Hotel Rancho Club** (Carretera Central, Km 4.5, tel. 022/63-3202, fax 022/62-2049, direccion@rancho.scu.tur.cu), on the hillside four kilometers north of town.

East of town, Gaviota's **Hacienda El Caney** (Carretera de Caney, tel. 022/68-7134, commercial@gaviota.co.cu, CUC 24 s, CUC33 d low season, CUC28 s, CUC35 d high season) rents three pleasant rooms, perfect for a family or group seeking out-of-town quietude (although you're on a busy road).

CUC50-100

Cubanacán's 【 **Hotel E San Basilio** (San Basilio #403, e/ Calvario y Carnicería, tel. 022/65-1702, fax 022/65-6039, hotelesanbasilio@tur.cu, CUC60 s/d year-round) has turned a former colonial mansion into a delightful eight-room hotel (an extension of the Hotel Versalles). Rooms are regally decorated and have and beautiful modern bathrooms. It has a small restaurant and 24-hour lobby bar.

Wow! Cubanacán's 72-room 【 **Hotel Versalles** (Alturas de Versalles, Km 1.6, Carretera del Morro, tel. 022/69-1016, fax 022/68-6039, reservas@hotelversalles.co.cu, from CUC51 s, CUC64 d low season, CUC61 s, CUC76 d high season) recently refurbished and is now striking, not least for its stylish contemporary furnishings, lovely bathrooms, and large balconies with city views. Its elegant restaurant has a stunning stained-glass window, plus the pool deck is a great place to lounge.

Islazul's **Hotel San Juan** (Av. Siboney y Calle 13, tel. 022/68-7200, fax 022/68-7134, jcarpeta@sanjuan.co.cu, CUC29 s, CUC40 d low season, CUC35 s, CUC60 d high season, including breakfast), on San Juan Hill, has 110 modestly furnished rooms in villa-style blocks—take an upstairs room with a lofty ceiling to help dissipate the heat. Facilities include a swimming pool and nightclub, but you're a long way from the center. Islazul's **Hotel Las Américas** (Av. de las Américas y General Cebreco, tel. 022/64-2011, fax 022/68-7075, comerc@hamerica.hor.tur.cu, CUC29 s, CUC40 d low season, CUC35 s, CUC60 d high season, including breakfast) is an uninspired 70-room property, albeit closer to the center.

CUC100-150

Gran Caribe's 58-room 【 **Hotel Casagranda** (Heredia #201, e/ Lacret y Hartman, tel. 022/68-6600, fax 022/68-6035, reserva@casa-gran.gca.tur.cu, from CUC67 s, CUC96 d low season, from CUC76 s, CUC112 d high season, including breakfast), on Parque Céspedes, is the place to be. Many rooms have antique reproductions; suites even have gold silk fabrics. It has an upscale restaurant, and you can sit on its first-floor veranda and sip a Cuba libre, smoke a *puro,* and watch the flood of life through the colonial plaza. Ostensibly, it is to

be refurbished and come under the wings of England's Esencia hotel group.

Setting the gold standard in Santiago is Cubanacán's 【 **Hotel Meliá Santiago** (Av. de las Américas, esq. M, tel. 022/68-7070, fax 022/68-7170, www.meliasantiagodecuba.solmelia.com, from CUC110 s/d low season, from CUC140 s/d high season), a 15-story modernist structure with 270 rooms, 30 junior suites, and three suites (with free wireless Internet), all done up with contemporary furniture. It has heaps of facilities, including two of the best restaurants in town, plus sauna, gym, swimming pool, boutiques, beauty parlor, barber shop, business center, and nightclub. Nonguests can buy a day pass (CUC10).

FOOD

For breakfast, head to one of the hotels, such as the terrace of the Hotel Casagranda (Heredia #201, e/ Lacret y Hartman), or to **Pan.Com** (Hartmann, esq. Aguilera, no tel., daily 9 A.M.–9 P.M.), selling sandwiches, omelets, etc.

The city has exploded with new options in recent years. Here's the pick of the litter.

Paladares

At last visit, only two *paladares* were in existence. The best is **Paladar Salón Tropical** (Fernández Marcané #310, e/ 9 y 10, tel. 022/64-1161, daily noon–midnight), offering rooftop dining beneath an arbor or a romantic cross-ventilated room with stained-glass windows. The menu ranges from pizzas (CUC4) to fricasséed lamb (CUC8).

Downtown, and much the lesser option, **Paladar Las Gallegas** (Bartolomé Masó #305 altos, e/ Hartman y General Lacret, tel. 022/62-4700, daily noon–midnight, CUC3–5) offers *criollo* fare.

Criollo

【 **El Barracón** (Av. Garzón, esq. Prudencio Martínez, tel. 022/66-1877, noon–11 P.M.) plays up the runaway slave theme wonderfully with life-size models, medieval-style tables and chairs, and wrought-iron lanterns.

The pork-focused menu also has lamb stew (CUC5).

Plaza Dolores has a fistful of unremarkable eateries, popular for their tables laid out on the square. Although closed for renovation at last visit, **Santiago 1900** (Bartolomé Masó #354, e/ Pío Rosado y Hartmann, tel. 022/62-3507), the former home of the Bacardí family, promises a fine colonial ambience when complete.

Continental

Despite its ritzy elegance and exceptional cuisine at reasonable prices, not many folks dine at **(Restaurant La Isabelica** (tel. 022/68-7070, daily 7–11 P.M.), in the Hotel Meliá Santiago (Av. de las Américas, esq. M). I savored a pumpkin curried soup (CUC3) and jumbo shrimp flambéed with rum (CUC16), plus profiteroles (CUC3). And the Hotel Meliá Santiago's stylishly contemporary **(Restaurant La Fontana** (daily noon–11 P.M.) justifiably draws Santiago's moneyed elite and Italian males intent on impressing their Cuban girlfriends. It serves Italian dishes, although my fave is a tasty fish fillet with capers in white wine sauce (CUC12). Pity about the mangy cats underfoot!

For cheap and basic Italian, head to **Ristorante Fontana di Tresi** (Saco, e/ General Lacret y Felix Peña, daily noon–5 P.M. and 6–11 P.M.), serving pizzas and spaghetti.

Some of the best cuisine is served at the stylish yet stiffly formal and expensive **(Restaurante Casa Grande** (daily 7–10 A.M., noon–3 P.M., and 7:30–10 P.M.), in the Hotel Casagranda; cuisine is *criollo* with a hint of the Continent. The same dishes can be ordered on the hotel's terrace bar.

Restaurant Zunzún (Av. Manduley #159, tel. 022/64-1528, daily noon–10 P.M.), in a mansion in Vista Alegre, has a varied menu ranging from *tapas* (CUC2) to lobster enchiladas (CUC25).

Worth the drive, the elegant **Restaurante Los Vitrales** (Alturas de Versalles, Km 1.6, Carretera del Morro, tel. 022/69-1016, daily 7–10 A.M., noon–2 P.M., and 7–10 P.M.), in the Hotel Versalles, has a gorgeous setting with city view. The house dish is a fish fillet stuffed with shrimp (CUC9).

Seafood

If you don't mind the passing traffic, you'll be more than satisfied with **Dimar** (Av. de las Américas, esq. D, tel. 022/69-1889, daily 8 A.M.–11 P.M.), a clean, glass-enclosed restaurant serving seafood dishes for below CUC10, as does the modestly elegant **Restaurante Neptuno** (Av. Garzón, esq. Prudencia Martínez, no tel., daily 11 A.M.–11 P.M.).

Cafés and Desserts

After exploring the frenetic streets, head to the **Café de Té** (Calle Aguilera, esq. General Lacret, Tues.–Sun. 9:15 A.M.–8:45 P.M.), which sells herbal and flavored teas; **La Isabelica** (Aguilera, esq. Valientes, no tel., 7 A.M.–11 P.M.), a 300-year-old coffeehouse favored by locals; or the air-conditioned **Dulcería Vía Central** (Av. Garzón, esq. Av. de los Presidentes, no tel., daily 7 A.M.–11 P.M.), above a bakery. Fresh-baked goodies are also sold at **Doña Neli** (no tel., Mon.–Sat. 7 A.M.–7 P.M. and Sun. 7 A.M.–2 P.M.), on the southwest corner of Plaza de Marte.

Women in 1950s-style uniforms roam the colonial streets and sell coffee from thermoses (0.40 centavos).

For ice cream, head to **Coppelia** (Av. de los Libertadores, esq. Av. Garzón, tel. 022/62-0435, Tues.–Sun. 9 A.M.–11:40 P.M.), a temple of delight with long lines to get in.

Self-Catering

You can buy fresh produce and meats at the *mercado agropecuario* (Aguilera and Padre Pico, Mon.–Sat. 6 A.M.–5 P.M.) and the squeaky-clean **El Avileño** market (Saco e/ Felix Peña y General Lacret, Tues.–Sat. 8 A.M.–noon and 4–7 P.M., Sun. 8 A.M.–noon).

SHOPPING

Calle Heredia, east of Parque Céspedes, is lined with crafts stalls. For fine art head to **Galería de Arte UNEAC** (Heredia, e/ Hartmann y Pio Rosada, tel. 022/65-3465, ext. 106).

coffee-hostesses on Calle Aguilera

Egrem (Hartmann, e/ Máximo Gómez and Portuondo, tel. 022/65-2227) has a large CD selection and musical instruments.

The tasting room adjoining **Fábrica de Ron Caney** (Av. Peralejo #103, tel. 022/62-5575, daily 9 A.M.–5 P.M.) sells a wide range of national rums, including rare 25-year-old Ron Paticruzado. It is also well-stocked with cigars, as are the **Casa del Habano** (Aguilera, esq. Jesús Menéndez, tel. 022/65-4207, Mon.–Sat. 9 A.M.–5 P.M., Sun. 9 P.M.–noon) and **Casa del Tabaco** (daily 8 A.M.–8 P.M.) in the Hotel Meliá Santiago (Av. de las Américas, esq. M).

For a genuine hand-embroidered blouse or *guayabera,* head to **El Quitrín** (Hechavarría #473, e/ Porfirio Valiente y Pio Rosada, tel. 022/62-2528, Mon.–Fri. 7:30 A.M.–4 P.M.).

INFORMATION AND SERVICES

You'll find an **Infotur** booth in the airport car park (tel. 022/69-2099) and on the southeast corner of Parque Céspedes (Lacret, esq. Heredia, tel. 022/66-9401, daily 8 A.M.–7 P.M.).

Money

There are branches of **Banco Financiero Internacional** on Félix Pena one block north of Parque Céspedes, and on Saco, at the corner of Porfirio Valiente; there are more than a dozen other banks. You can exchange foreign currency at **Cadeca** (Aguilera #508, tel. 022/65-1383).

Communications

The **post office** (Aguilera #310, esq. Padre Quiroga) adjoins **DHL** (tel. 202/68-6323 or 65-4750). **Etecsa** (Freites, esq. Hartmann, tel. 022/65-7524; and Heredia, e/ Félix Pena y General Lacret, tel. 022/65-7524, daily 8:30 A.M.–7:30 P.M.), on the south side of Parque Céspedes, has international telephone and Internet service, as do the tourist hotels.

Medical Services

The **Clínica Internacional** (Av. Raúl Pujol, esq. Calle 8, tel. 022/64-2589, 24 hours) charges CUC25 per consultation, or CUC30 between 4 P.M. and 7 A.M. and for hotel visits. The clinic has a modestly stocked pharmacy, as does the Hotel Meliá Santiago (Av. de las Américas, esq. M). **Ópticas Miramar** (Calle Santo Tomás e/ Aguilera y Heredia, tel. 022/62-5259) has optical services.

Legal Aid and Safety

In trouble? **Asistur** (Calle 4, e/ 7 y 9, tel. 022/68-6128, asisturstago@enet.cu, Mon.–Sat.

8 A.M.–5 P.M.), on Parque Céspedes, provides travelers' emergency assistance. The **Consultoría Jurídica Internacional** (Calle 8 #54, e/ 1 y 3, Rpto. Vista Alegre, tel. 022/64-4546) provides legal services.

GETTING THERE AND AWAY
By Air
Aeropuerto Internacional Antonio Maceo (tel. 022/69-1014), off Carretera del Morro, is eight kilometers south of Santiago. Buses #212 and 213 (via Punta Gorda) operate between the airport and Avenida de los Libertadores, downtown. A taxi costs CUC7 one-way.

Cubana (Enramada, esq. San Pedro, tel. 022/65-1577, airport tel. 022/69-1214) serves Santiago from Europe, plus daily from Havana, and from Varadero, Camagüey, and Baracoa.

By Bus
Víazul buses (tel. 022/62-8484) for Santiago arrive and depart the **Terminal de Ómnibus Nacional** (Av. de los Libertadores, esq. Av. Juan Gualberto Gómez, tel. 022/62-3050). Buses depart Santiago daily for Havana at 9 A.M. and 3:15, 6 (express), and 10 P.M.; for Baracoa at 7:45 A.M.; for Trinidad at 7:30 P.M.; and for Varadero at 10:15 P.M.

Local buses and *camiones* operate to outlying destinations from the **Terminal de Ómnibus Municipales** (Av. de los Libertadores y Calle 4, tel. 022/62-4329). *Camiones* for Bayamo and Guantánamo leave from the **Terminal de Ómnibus Intermunicipales Serrano** (Av. Jesús Menéndez, e/ Máximo Gómez y Juan Bautista Sagarra, tel. 022/62-4325).

By Train
Trains arrive and depart the railway station (Av. Jesús Menéndez y Martí, tel. 022/62-2836). Buy your tickets at the **Viajero** (tel. 022/65-1381, 9 A.M.–6 P.M.) ticket office on the station's north side; you must go the same day for travel on the Tren Francés express to Havana and 24 hours beforehand for the regular train. The Viajero office at Aguilera #565 (tel. 022/65-2143) was not selling tickets to foreigners at last visit.

By Sea
Ships berth at the cruise terminal (Av. Jesús Menéndez, tel. 022/65-1763).

Marina Marlin (tel. 022/69-1446), at Punta Gorda, has moorings for 60 yachts.

By Car
All tourist hotels have rental agencies. **Havanautos** (Hotel Las Américas, tel. 022/68-7160), **Cubacar** (Hotel San Juan, tel. 022/68-7206; Av. de los Libertadores, esq. Av. Juan Gualberto Gómez, tel. 022/62-3884; Plaza de Marte, tel. 022/62-9194; beneath the Hotel Casagranda, tel. 022/68-6170), **Vía** (on the southeast corner of Parque Céspedes), and **Rex** (tel. 022/68-6445 downtown; tel. 022/68-6446 airport) all have offices at the airport.

GETTING AROUND
By Bus
Crowded buses serve most of the city (20 centavos). Bus #1 runs between Parque Céspedes and both the interprovincial and intermunicipal bus terminals. Most people get around on *camiones,* penned in shoulder-to-shoulder like cattle.

By Taxis and Scooter
Taxis hang out on the south side of Parque Céspedes and outside the tourist hotels. **Cubataxi** (tel. 226/65-1038) has taxis on call. **Grantaxi** (tel. 022/62-4328) offers rides in classic Yankee autos.

You can rent scooters at the **Hotel San Juan** (Av. Siboney y Calle 13).

Organized Excursions
City tours are offered by **Cubatur** (Heredia, esq. General Lacret, tel. 022/68-6033, and Garzón e/ 3ra y 4t, tel. CUC54, including the Morro castle); **Cubanacán** (Av. de las Américas y M, tel. 022/64-2202); **Gaviotatour** (Av. Manduley #456, tel. 022/68-7135); and **Paradiso** (Heredia #305, tel. 022/62-7037), which specializes in cultural tours.

Marina Marlin (tel. 022/69-1446) offers a hour-long bay excursion (CUC12 including cocktail) with a 10-passenger minimum.

North and West of Santiago

EL COBRE

The village of El Cobre, on the Carretera Central, 20 kilometers northwest of Santiago, takes its name from the copper mine that the Spanish established in the mid-1500s. In 1630, it was abandoned, and the African slave-miners were unilaterally freed. A century later it was reopened by Colonel Don Pedro Jiménez, governor of Santiago, who put the slaves' descendants back to work. The slaves were officially declared free in 1782, a century before their brethren in the cane fields. Although the mine closed in 2000, the pit (filled with a turquoise lagoon) can be seen from the **Monumento al Cimarrón,** beyond the village. This monument, reached by steep stairs, is dedicated to the slaves who rebelled.

◖ Basílica de Nuestra Señora del Cobre

Dominating the village is the ocher-colored, red-domed, triple-towered hilltop Basílica del Cobre (tel. 022/34-6118, daily 6:30 A.M.–6 P.M.). The church—Cuba's only basilica—was erected in 1927 (a hermitage has occupied the site since 1608, however) and is a national shrine dedicated to the Virgin of Charity, the patron saint of Cuba to whom miraculous powers are ascribed (she is synonymous with Ochún, the sensual goddess of love in *santería*).

The front entrance is reached via a steep staircase. More usual is to enter at the rear, from the parking lot, where the **Sala de Milagros** (Salon of Miracles) contains a small chapel with a silver altar crowded with votive candles and flowers. To left and right are tables with miscellaneous objects placed in offering. On the walls hang scores of silver *milagros;* the two centuries of ex-votos include a small gold figure left by Castro's mother, Lina Ruz, to protect her two sons, Fidel and Raúl, during the war in the Sierra Maestra.

Steps lead up to a separate altar where the

Virgen de la Caridad del Cobre resides in effigy in an air-conditioned glass case. Clad in a yellow cloak and crown (Ochún's color is yellow), she is surrounded by a sea of flowers and the entire shrine is suffused with narcotic scents. Once a year thousands of devotees make their way along the winding road, many crawling painfully uphill to fulfill a promise made to the saint at some difficult moment in their lives. The unlucky angler in Ernest Hemingway's *Old Man and the Sea* promises to "make a pilgrimage to the Virgin de Cobre" if he wins his battle with the massive marlin. In 1952, Hemingway

---

THE LEGEND OF THE BLACK VIRGIN

All Cubans know the legend of the Virgen de la Caridad (colloquially known as the Virgen del Cobre), the most revered religious figure in Cuba. According to folklore, in 1608, two mulatto brothers, Rodrigo and Juan de Hoyos, and a young black boy, Juan Moreno, were fishing in the Bay of Nipes, off the north coast of Cuba, when they were caught in a storm. As their boat was about to capsize, a small raft appeared bearing a statue of a black Virgin Mary holding a black baby Jesus and a cross. The statue was inscribed with the words *Yo soy la Virgen de la Caridad* (I am the Virgin of Charity). At that moment the seas calmed.

The story gained popularity and miracles were ascribed to the virgin. In time a shrine was built near the copper mine at El Cobre. Pope Benedicto XV declared her the patron saint of Cuba on May 10, 1916.

Today, the black Virgin is associated with Ochún, the *santería* goddess of love and water. She is usually depicted in a yellow gown, standing atop the waves with the three fishermen in their little boat at her feet.

© CHRISTOPHER P. BAKER

Sala de Milagros at El Cobre

dedicated his Nobel Prize for Literature to the Virgin, placing it in her shrine.

Masses (*misas*) are offered Monday–Saturday (except Wed.) at 8 A.M. and Sunday at 8 and 10 A.M. and 4:30 P.M.

Touts will rush forward to sell you flower wreaths, miniature *chacitas* (images of the Virgin), and iron pyrite—fool's gold—culled from the residue of the nearby mine. "*Es real!*" they say, attempting to put a small piece in your hand. A firm "No gracias!" should suffice.

Accommodations and Food

The **Hospedaje El Cobre** (tel. 022/34-6246), behind the church, serves pilgrims and has 16 basic rooms where foreigners are welcome when space allows; each room has three single beds and a private bathroom (25 pesos s, 40 pesos d). Couples must be married and show ID with the same address. A refectory serves basic fare at 7:30 A.M., noon, and 6 P.M. For reservations, write Hermana Elsa Aranda, Hospedaje El Cobre, El Cobre, Santiago.

Getting There

Bus #202 operates four times daily to El Cobre from Santiago's Terminal de Ómnibus Intermunicipales. *Camiones* run from Avenida de las Américas, esq. Calle M, and from Avenida de los Libertadores y Calle 4. A taxi will cost about CUC25 round-trip. Tour operators offer excursions.

EL SALTÓN

The easternmost spurs of the Sierra Maestra rise west of Santiago. Nestled in a valley, El Saltón is touted as a mountain health resort, with picture-perfect cascades. It's excellent for bird-watching. The lodge offers massage, sauna, and whirlpool, as well as horseback rides (CUC2 per hour) and guided hikes.

Accommodations

Cubanacán's **Horizontes Villas El Saltón** (Carretera Puerto Rico a Filé, III Frente, tel. 022/56-6326, fax 022/56-6492, salton@enet. cu, CUC25 s, CUC30 d low season, CUC30 s, CUC40 d high season) is an eco-lodge built in the 1970s as an anti-stress center for the Cuban elite. Accommodations are in 22 modestly appointed double rooms in four separate buildings. An open-sided, thatched restaurant overlooks the river.

Getting There

El Saltón is reached from Contramaestre, on the Carretera Central about 70 kilometers northwest of Santiago, then 27 kilometers south to the village of Cruce de los Baños, where the paved road gives out. El Saltón is eight kilometers west of Cruce via the community of Filé.

Camiones operate to Cruce de los Baños from Santiago.

SANTIAGO TO CHIVÍRICO

The bone-rattling drive west along the coast from Santiago is magnificent, with the Sierra Maestra plummeting to a crashing sea. The road becomes gradually more lonesome as you pass rustic fishing villages and pocket-size beaches. The section between Palma Mocha and La Plata is frequently washed out by storms; don't be surprised to find the road impassable, or to find heavy-duty trucks ferrying passengers across washed-out sections.

The only settlement is Chivírico, a fishing village about 80 kilometers west of Santiago. Here you'll find two foreign-operated hotels with knockout views. Nearby **Las Cuevas de Murciélagos** is full of bats, while about 22 kilometers farther west of Chivírico, at **Uvero** and reached via a glade of palms, is a monument marking the site where Castro's Rebel Army won its first major victory against Batista's troops on May 28, 1957.

About 12 kilometers west of Ocujal (48 kilometers west of Chivírico), you cross the mouth of the Río La Plata. It was here, on January 17, 1957, that Castro's Rebel Army first came down from the Sierra Maestra to attack a small garrison of Batista's Rural Guard. The **Museo Combate de la Plata** (Tues.–Sat. 9 A.M.–noon and 2–6 P.M., Sun. 9 A.M.–noon, CUC1) is 400 meters off the road, beside the river, on the west side of the bridge. Three thatched huts exhibit uniforms, maps, small arms, and more. There's no sign when traveling eastbound.

Hiking to Pico Turquino

Just as Edmund Hillary climbed Everest "because it was there," so Pico Turquino lures the intrepid who seek the satisfaction of reaching the summit of Cuba's highest peak, heart of the 17,450-hectare Parque Nacional Pico Turquino. Most hikers set off from Santo Domingo, in Granma Province, on the north side of the mountain. On the south side, a dauntingly steep 13-kilometer trail begins at **Estación Biológica Las Cuevas del Turquino,** at Las Cuevas, 55 kilometers west of Chivírico. A guide is compulsory (CUC20 per person, plus CUC5 for cameras, plus mandatory tip).

You'll need to set off around 4 A.M. to summit before clouds set in (no departures are permitted after 7 A.M.). You normally ascend and return in one day, a 10-hour feat, although you can shelter at 1,650 meters on Pico Cuba (with a rudimentary kitchen with stove) and at La Esmajagua, midway between Pico Cuba and Las Cuevas (CUC30 for a two-day hike). If you want to cross the Sierra, you can hike all the way to Alto del Naranjo, on the north side of the mountain, a two-night/three-day journey (CUC48). You'll need two sets of guides—one for each side of the mountain—arranged in advance.

You'll need to be self-sufficient (bring all the food and water you need). The weather is unpredictable; dress accordingly. Cold winds often kick up near the summit; the humidity and wind-chill factor can drop temperatures to near freezing. Rain is always a possibility, downpours are common, and fog is almost a daily occurrence at higher elevations by mid-morning.

Book through the Centro de Visitantes in Santo Domingo or **EcoTur** (Masó #352, tel. 022/62-5438 or 5289-3558, www.ecoturcuba. co.cu) in Santiago, which offers personalized guided tours, including round-trip jeep transfers. You need to carry your own gear. No sleeping bags or blankets are available.

A shorter, four-hour hike to La Esmajagua and back costs CUC13 (plus CUC5 camera).

Recreation

Brisas Sierra Mar (Carretera de Chivírico, Km 60, tel. 022/32-9110) offers **scuba diving** (CUC30, or CUC60 for a wreck dive, CUC365 for a certification course). The most popular dive site is the wreck of the Spanish cruiser *Colón,* sunk on July 3, 1898, by the U.S. Navy. It rests just 20 meters below the surface, 35 meters from shore just east of Ocujal. Offshore from Km 24.7 is the wreck of the Spanish-American warship *Juan González,* and off Asseredero, at Km 32, lies the wreck of the cruiser *Viscaya.*

Accommodations and Food

Planning to hike Pico Turquino? You can camp (you'll need to be self-sufficient) at Estación Las Cuevas, which has a basic dormitory with three beds (CUC5 per person). Alternatively, **Campismo La Mula** (reservations: Campismo Popular, Jagüey #163, e/ Mariano Corona y Padre Pico, Santiago, tel. 022/62-9000, CUC5 per person) at the mouth of the Río La Mula, 12 kilometers east of Las Cuevas, has basic cabins with cold showers, plus a simple restaurant. Many of the Cubans here will probably be hiking to Pico Turquino. Mosquitoes abound.

    Campismo Caletón Blanco (c/o Campismo Popular), 30 kilometers west of Santiago, also has simple cabins and accepts foreigners.

    Cubanacán's clifftop **Brisas Sierra Mar** (Carretera de Chivírico, Km 60, tel. 022/32-9110, fax 022/32-9116, reservat@smar.scu.

swimming pool at Brisas Sierra Mar

tur.cu, from CUC45 s, CUC56 d low season, from CUC55 s, CUC74 d high season) is a beautiful all-inclusive 10 kilometers east of Chivírico. The 200 nicely furnished rooms have modern accoutrements. Its heaps of facilities include water sports and a swimming pool high above the beach. It shares facilities with the more intimate 34-room **Brisas Los Galeones** (Carretera de Chivírico, Km 60, tel. 022/32-6160, fax 022/32-6435, from CUC32 s, CUC40 d low season, CUC64 s, CUC80 d high season), perched atop a headland about 10 kilometers east of Brisas Sierra Mar; a shuttle connects the two. The spacious rooms have king-size beds and balconies. A charming restaurant overlooks a pool, and it has a game room, tiny gym, and sauna. A 296-step staircase leads to a beach.

    Nonguests can buy day passes to the Brisas hotels (CUC19 per person 9 A.M.–6 P.M., CUC25 7–11 P.M. including all meals and drinks, or CUC9 dinner only).

MAYARÍ ARRIBA

This small town squats in the rugged Sierra del Cristal rise northeast of Santiago. Carlos Manuel de Céspedes established his revolutionary government here in the 1860s, and Raúl Castro established his military headquarters here when he opened the Second Front in 1958. Access is via the crossroads village of Alto Songo, 23 kilometers northeast of Santiago.

    The **Museo Comandancia del Segundo Frente** (Museum of the Second Front, Av. de los Mártires, tel. 022/42-5749, Tues.–Sun. 8 A.M.–3:30 P.M., one peso) displays photos, maps, and military hardware, including a helicopter and even full-scale models of a P-51 Mustang and other U.S. warplanes.

    Uphill, a palm-lined boulevard leads to the **Mausoleo del Segundo Frente** (daily 8 A.M.–3:30 P.M., free), a dramatic marble mausoleum set in an arc of royal palms, surrounded by red *califo rojo* plants (they represent the blood of revolutionary martyrs). A ceremony is held here each March 11.

    The plaza by the Cupet gas station features a life-size lion and rhino carved in stone.

Reserva de la Biosfera Baconao

The 32,400-hectare Baconao Biosphere Reserve extends 40 kilometers from the eastern suburbs of Santiago to the border with Guantánamo Province. The park was named a biosphere reserve by UNESCO for its biodiversity, including many species endemic to the region. A full day is barely sufficient. It is reached from Santiago via the Carretera Siboney, lined with 26 **monuments** to the heroes of the Moncada attack.

The region has beaches popular with locals on weekends. Few are inspiring (except Playa Daiquirí, which is exclusively for the use of the Cuban military and their families; it was here that Teddy Roosevelt and his Rough Riders disembarked in 1898 during the Spanish-American War, and where U.S. Marines landed in 1912 and 1917 to quell a series of strikes in Santiago and Guantánamo). The unremarkable hotels appeal principally to undiscriminating budget package vacationers.

The administrative office in Santiago (Av. 8 #354, Rpto. Vista Alegre, tel. 022/64-1932) has no tourist info.

Getting There and Away

Buses depart Santiago's Terminal de Ómnibus Municipales (Av. de los Libertadores, esq. Calle 4) to Playa Siboney and Baconao, which are also served by *camiones*.

A taxi from Santiago will cost about CUC35 round-trip to Siboney (about CUC50 to Baconao; be sure to prearrange a return pickup).

If driving, slow for the *punto de control* (police checkpoint) about 10 kilometers east of Santiago. The only gas station (24 hours) is 26 kilometers east of Santiago.

PARQUE NACIONAL GRAN PIEDRA

This park encompasses the Cordillera de la Gran Piedra, a lush mountain environment for bird-watching and hiking. Access is from a T junction at Las Guasimas, 13 kilometers from Santiago, where the **Prado de las Esculturas** (daily 8 A.M.–4 P.M., CUC1) is a sculpture garden with about 20 uninspired contemporary works lining a trail.

The deteriorated road winds up through

RESERVA DE LA BIOSFERA BACONAO

ravines, growing ever steeper and more serpentine until it deposits you at **Pico Gran Piedra** (1,234 meters), a distance of 14 kilometers, on a ridge with a view down the mountains. It's noticeably crisper and cooler up here, where clouds swirl through the tall pines and bamboo.

A restaurant and hotel sit at 1,150 meters elevation, where guides can be hired to hike four trails (CUC2 per person). A 454-step stairway leads up to the **Gran Piedra** (Great Rock), where you can climb a steel ladder onto the massive boulder for a spectacular view. On a clear day you can see the Blue Mountains in Jamaica.

A bus from Santiago runs weekly.

Jardín Ave de Paraíso

This 45-hectare garden (daily 7 A.M.–4 P.M., CUC1), 800 meters west of Villa Gran Piedra, was created in 1960 on a former coffee plantation to raise flowers. The garden is a riot of color and scents, difficult to dampen in even the wettest of weather. Guides will show you around a series of juxtaposed gardens, surrounded by topiary hedges. Amaryllises grow with carnations, *salvia roja* spring up beside daisies, blood-red dahlias thrive beside the garden's namesake "birds of paradise." There are potting sheds, too, full of begonias and anthuriums, and a prim courtyard with a café.

Visits are permitted only with a voucher sold by **Cubanacán** (Av. de las Américas y M, tel. 022/64-2202, CUC5) in Santiago.

Cafetal La Isabelica

Two kilometers east of Gran Piedra via a rutted dirt road are the remains of a coffee plantation built by Victor Constantin Couson, a French immigrant who fled Haiti in 1792. Now a museum (daily 8 A.M.–4 P.M., CUC1), the ruins of the two-story *finca* exhibit farming implements and furniture. The coffee-crushing wheel can still be seen. Trails lead through the estate and forests.

Accommodations

Islazul's **Villa Gran Piedra** (Carretera de la Gran Piedra, Km 14, tel. 022/68-6147, reception@gpiedra.scu.tur.cu) has 22 rustic, modestly furnished red-brick cottages atop the ridge crest—a spectacular setting at a crisp 1,225 meters! An atmospheric restaurant and bar offer views.

SIBONEY

The little village of Siboney, replete with wooden French-style Caribbean homes, lies in a sheltered bay with a mediocre beach, **Playa Siboney.** Being the closest beach to Santiago, it's popular with Cubans who flock on weekends. A war memorial recalls the landing of U.S. troops on June 24, 1898.

Granjita Siboney

This red-tile-roofed farmhouse, one kilometer inland of Siboney, is the site from which Fidel Castro and his loyal cohorts gathered for their attack on the Moncada barracks: They sang the national anthem in whispers, and at five o'clock on the morning of Sunday, July 26, 1953, the 124 rebels set out in a convoy of 26 cars. Today it is a museum (tel. 022/39-9168, daily 9:15 A.M.–4:45 P.M., entrance CUC1, cameras CUC1, videos CUC5) displaying weapons and bloodstained uniforms. Newspaper clippings

SANTIAGO DE CUBA

tell the tale of horrific torture. Six of the attackers died in the attack; 61 others died in captivity. Batista's henchmen then took the already-dead revolutionaries to Granjita Siboney, where he blasted them with gunfire to give the impression that they had been caught plotting and were shot in a battle.

◖ Museo de la Guerra Hispano-Cubano-Americano

This excellent little museum (tel. 022/39-9119, Mon.–Sat. 9 A.M.–5 P.M., CUC1), 100 meters east of Granjita Siboney, is dedicated to the Spanish-Cuban-American War of 1898 and does a good job of it, too. Its thoughtful and detailed presentations include huge historical photos, superb maps, scale models of warships and the battles, and original cannons and other weaponry, including two Spanish torpedoes.

Accommodations and Food

Every second family here rents a *casa particular*. Filling meals are a highlight at **Casa de Ovidio González Sabaldo** (Av. Serrano y Calle del Barco, tel. 022/39-9340, CUC20–50), a splendid three-story wooden home with two modestly furnished rooms with private hot-water bathrooms.

For a shorefront locale, try **Casa de María Elena González** (Obelisco #10, tel. 022/39200, CUC20), a clean, cross-ventilated modern three-story house with a swimming pool in the stone patio. One of its two rooms opens to a breeze-swept terrace with fabulous views; the second, atop the roof, has floor-to-ceiling louvered glass windows.

About the only eatery here is **Restaurante La Rueda** (tel. 022/39-9325, Mon.–Tues. 9 A.M.–6 P.M., Thurs.–Sun. 9 A.M.–midnight), which serves *criollo* fare (less than CUC5) and has ocean views. The place was once owned by Compay Segundo (real name Francisco Repilado), of Buena Vista Social Club fame.

SIBONEY TO LAGUNA BACONAO

From a T junction at Granjita Siboney, a spur road leads east through the park. First up is

Comunidad Artística Oasis, a pretty little hamlet of fieldstone cottages, about three kilometers from the T junction. The entire community, comprising 10 families, works as artists and has open studios. Horseback rides are offered at **Finca Guajira Rodeo,** where rodeos are held. The side road through the hamlet continues to **Playa Bucanero,** the private reserve of the Hotel Bucanero.

Beyond Verraco, a massive limestone plateau shoulders up against the coast, with the road running between them. The Carretera Baconao ends just beyond the hamlet of Baconao, where there's a military barrier.

Valle de la Prehistoria

It's a shock to find a *Tyrannosaurus rex* prowling the Prehistoric Valley (Carretera de Baconao, daily 8 A.M.–5 P.M., entrance CUC1, cameras CUC1, videos CUC5), about six kilometers east of El Oasis. The beast is one of dozens of life-size dinosaurs that lurk in a natural setting. An *Apatosaurus* (alias brontosaurus) wallows in a pool. There are even woolly mammoths, and a pterodactyl atop a hillock. Real-life goats nibble amid the make-believe beasts made of concrete. A **Museo de Ciencias Naturales** (daily 8 A.M.–4:45 P.M., CUC1) displays polymite snails and other exhibits of flora and fauna.

Museo Nacional de Transporte Terreste

Dowagers from the heyday of Detroit and Coventry are on view at this auto museum (tel. 022/39-9197, daily 8 A.M.–5 P.M., entrance CUC1, cameras CUC1, videos CUC2), behind the Cupet gas station, two kilometers east of the Valle de la Prehistoria. Custodians put the spit and polish to about three dozen cars, from a 1912 Model-T Ford to a 1960 Lincoln Continental, a 1954 MG sports car, and singer Benny Moré's Cadillac. The **Museo de Autos Miniaturas** (Miniature Car Museum) contains more than 2,500 tiny toy cars, from the earliest models to modern-day productions.

Playa Verraco

Passing the turnoff for Playa Daiquirí (off-limits), you'll come to a bend in the road with a huge mosaic of a *tocororo,* the national bird of Cuba, inlaid in the hillside. A few kilometers beyond is **Comunidad Artística Los Mamoncillas,** at Playa Verraco. Here, the entire community is engaged in arts. You can browse open studios.

Farther east the land grows more arid. Inland of Playa Sigua you'll pass the **Jardín de Cactos** (daily 8 A.M.–3 P.M., CUC5), displaying about 200 species from around the world. **Expo Mesoamérica** is another cactus garden containing Mesoamerican sculptures at the base of cliffs opposite the Club Amigo Los Corales.

Acuario Baconao

This aquatic park (tel. 022/35-6264, Tues.–Sun. 9 A.M.–5 P.M., CUC5), about 50 kilometers east of Santiago, has a small yet impressive museum on nautical miscellany and marine life. The real-life exhibits, which include moray eels, marine turtles, and a shark tank with walk-through glass tunnel, are dismal. The highlights are the daily dolphin shows at 10:30 A.M. and 3 P.M.; you can even get in the water with these endearing beasts.

Laguna Baconao

The large Laguna Baconao, immediately west of the hamlet of Baconao, is edged by mountains at the far east end of Baconao reserve. There are a few dolphins (and crocodiles, apparently) in the lake. Boat excursions are offered (CUC2) at **Complejo Turístico Laguna Baconao** (Carretera Baconao, Km 53, daily 8:30 A.M.–4:30 P.M.), where crocs are bred as a tourist attraction.

Accommodations and Food

With its own sculpture garden, **C Casa de Enrique y Rosa** (Carretera de Baconao, Km 17.5, Comunidad Artística Los Mamoncillas, Playa Verraco, tel. 022/35-6205, CUC20) is the home of a family of ceramists who rent one spacious air-conditioned room with fan, refrigerator, and a delightful tiled bathroom. It has secure parking.

Gran Caribe's **Hotel Club Bucanero** (Carretera de Baconao, Km 4, Arroyo La Costa, tel. 022/68-6363, fax 022/68-6070, commercial@hbucanero.co.cu, CUC25 s, CUC40 d low season, CUC84 s, CUC120 d high season) was refurbished in 2009 after being trashed by Hurricane Dennis. This clifftop option has a dramatic location. The hotel has 200 pleasant rooms featuring natural stone. The tiny beach has water sports and a bar-restaurant.

A carbon copy of the Hotel Bucanero, Islazul's 115-room, stone-lined **Hotel Costa Morena** (Playa Larga, Carretera de Baconao, Km 38.5, tel. 022/35-6126, fax 022/35-6160, recepcion@cmorena.co.cu, CUC25 s, CUC40 d low season, CUC84 s, CUC120 d high season) sits in ungainly grounds that overlook a narrow pebble beach. The high point is its atmospheric **Restaurant Las Orquideas** (daily 7:30–9:30 A.M., 12:30–2 P.M., and 6:30–9 P.M.)

Cubanacán's **Club Amigo Carisol-Los Corales** (tel. 022/35-6155, fax 022/35-6177, reserva@carisol-loscorales.co.cu, from CUC75 s, CUC100 d all-inclusive) is divided into two adjoining properties: Carisol is for adults only; Caracol caters to families. Together they offer 310 rooms, including 46 junior suites. Nothing scintillating here, but the large pool area appeals and you get your cocktails, water sports, and buffets included. You can rent scooters for exploring.

The thatched **La Casa Rolando** (tel. 022/62-2252, daily 9 A.M.–4 P.M.), at Complejo Turístico Laguna Baconao, serves *criollo* dishes. You can buy a day pass (CUC15) to Club Amigo Carisol-Los Corales.

GUANTÁNAMO

Guantánamo. The name reverberates around the world. Everyone knows it as a U.S. naval base and a humiliating thorn in the side of Castro's Cuba. In fact, Guantánamo is also both a city and province, which tapers eastward to Punta de Maisí, the easternmost point of the island. The province is almost wholly mountainous. Except for a great scalloped bowl surrounding the town of Guantánamo, the uplands push up against a barren coastal plain.

The wild eastern shore and secluded mountains offer fantastic opportunities for hiking. Uniquely, traces of indigenous culture linger, notably around Baracoa, Cuba's oldest city, near where a ball court similar to those of the Mayan culture has been discovered. Baracoans claim that Columbus first set foot in Cuba here and left a wooden cross (now on view in the town's cathedral) as a memento. Whatever the truth, it's undisputed that the Spanish conquistadores who came on Columbus's heels established the first town in Cuba at Baracoa. The town retains an aged colonial feel in a setting that any other city would die for.

Today a great part of the mountain region is protected within a system of reserves slowly being developed for ecotourism. These wildlife-rich mountains harbor rare plant and bird species and polymites (snails that haul fabulously colored shells on their backs).

The northeast coast and north-facing mountains around Baracoa are the rainiest region in Cuba. By contrast, valleys along the southern coast are pockets of aridity, and cacti grow in the lee of Cuba's wettest slopes.

Alas, Baracoa took a brutal beating at the

HIGHLIGHTS

◖ Zoológico de Piedra: There's no question that a mountainside zoo where the life-size critters are hewn from boulders is one of a kind (page 476).

◖ La Farola: A steep mountain road snaking into the pine-clad Sierra Cristal offers fabulous vistas, but watch those bends (page 477)!

◖ Museo Arqueológico Cueva del Paraíso: This fascinating albeit simple museum of Taíno culture is set in hillside funerary caverns with pre-Columbian skeletons still in situ (page 479).

◖ Parque Natural Duaba and El Yunque: Rugged mountain terrain provides a challenging but rewarding hike to the top of the famous rock formation El Yunque, with incredible views as an added bonus (page 484).

◖ Parque Nacional Alejandro de Humboldt: Wilderness supreme! This park provides great opportunities for bird-watching and hiking into the mountains, and manatees can be spotted along the shore (page 485).

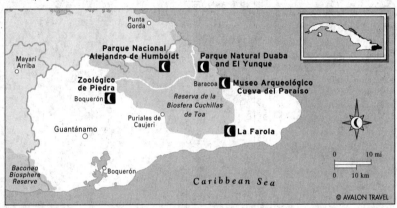

LOOK FOR ◖ TO FIND RECOMMENDED SIGHTS, ACTIVITIES, DINING, AND LODGING.

hands of Hurricane Ike, which came ashore here in September 2008, devastating the town.

PLANNING YOUR TIME

A single badly deteriorated road hugs the north coast, linking Holguín and Baracoa (and on to Guantánamo and Santiago de Cuba—public transport along this route is infrequent). Hence, you don't need to backtrack if you have your own car. For scenery, you should definitely plan on the Guantánamo city to Baracoa route via **La Farola,** a wheezing mountain switchback that has some nerve-wracking bends and slingshots you over the Sierra Cristal. Trains

connect Guantánamo city to Santiago de Cuba and Havana. Víazul also offers daily bus service from Santiago de Cuba to Guantánamo and Baracoa, but demand is tight and advance reservations are recommended.

The town of Guantánamo is more a place to overnight in passing; despite its size it has very little in the way of sightseeing. The music scene, however, is another matter. Guantánamo has more traditional Afro-Cuban cultural centers than you can shake a stick at.

The hinterlands of Guantánamo township boast two sites of unique appeal. First, the U.S. naval base holds a fascination that many

GUANTÁNAMO

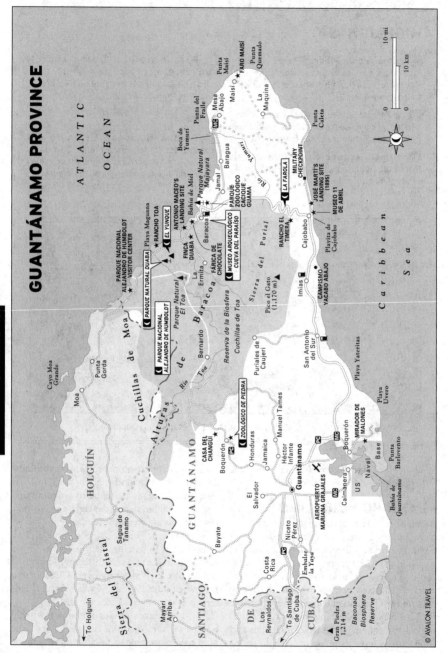

GUANTÁNAMO PROVINCE

ATLANTIC

OCEAN

Cayo Moa Grande

Punta Gorda

Moa

HOLGUÍN

Sagua de Tanamo

Mayarí Arriba

Sierra del Cristal

SANTIAGO

DE

CUBA

Los Reynaldos

Gran Piedra 1,214 m

Baconao Biosphere Reserve

To Holguín

To Santiago de Cuba

Cuchillas de Moa

Alturas

GUANTÁNAMO

Bayate

Costa Rica

Niceto Pérez

Embalse la Yaya

El Salvador

Boquerón

Jamaica

Héctor Infante

Honduras

Manuel Tames

CASA DEL CHANGÜÍ ★

⊂ ZOOLÓGICO DE PIEDRA

PC

Puriales de Caujerí

San Antonio del Sur

Pico el Gato (1,170 m) ▲

Imías

Sierra del Purial

CAMPISMO YACABO ABAJO

Playita de Cajobabo

Cajobabo

MUSEO 11 DE ABRIL

JOSÉ MARTÍ'S LANDING SITE (1895)

RANCHO EL TIMERA

◀ LA FAROLA

MILITARY CHECKPOINT

MC

FARO MAISÍ ◀

Punta Maisí

Punta Quemado

Punta Caleta

La Maquina

Maisí

Mesa Abajo

MC

Punta del Fraile

Boca de Yumurí

La Maquina

Baragua

Jamal

Río Yumurí

Barahua

Parque Natural Majayara

PARQUE ZOOLÓGICO CACIQUE GUAMA

Baracoa

Bahía de Miel

ANTONIO MACEO'S LANDING SITE ★

EL YUNQUE ◀

RANCHO TOA ★

Playa Maguana

PARQUE NACIONAL ALEJANDRO DE HUMBOLDT VISITOR CENTER

⊂ PARQUE NATURAL DUABA

FINCA DUABA ★

La Ermita

FÁRICA DE CHOCOLATE

⊂ MUSEO ARQUEOLÓGICO CUEVA DEL PARAÍSO

FÁBRICA DE CHOCOLATE

⊂ PARQUE NACIONAL ALEJANDRO DE HUMBOLDT

Parque Natural El Toa

Baracoa

Reserva de la Biosfera

Cuchillas de Toa

Río Toa

Bernardo

Río Toa

Caribbean

Sea

San Antonio del Sur

Playa Yacabritas

Playa Uvero

MIRADOR DE MALONES

MC

Boquerón

Base Naval

Punta Barlovento

US Naval Base

Bahía de Guantánamo

Caimanera

MC

AEROPUERTO MARIANA GRAJALES

Guantánamo

PC

✈

CUBA

© AVALON TRAVEL

Punta del Fraile

10 mi

10 km

© CHRISTOPHER P. BAKER

1959 Imperial Crown in Guantánamo

travelers can't resist. While the chances of visiting the base are actually less than you winning the lottery, you *can* get to see it from the most unlikely place imaginable: a Cuban military lookout at Caimanera, where foreign visitors are treated almost like VIPs. You'll need to set things up in advance, but the Cubans make it easy by offering prearranged tours handled through the Gaviota tour agency. Not to be missed is the **Zoológico de Piedra.** Within a one-hour drive of the city, this "stone zoo" features more than 200 life-size animals hewn from rock. Plan a half-day visit, timed to coincide with a music performance at the nearby Casa de Changüí.

History buffs on the trail of José Martí should make a pilgrimage to Cajobabo, with its Museo Municipal 11 de Abril honoring Martí's landing at nearby Playitas, where a clamber over beach boulders reveals a marble monument at the exact spot where the nationalist hero stepped ashore. You can take in both the stone zoo and Cajobabo in one day's leisurely drive between Guantánamo and Baracoa.

Baracoa deserves two days minimum. One day is more than sufficient for sightseeing, with the highlights being the Catedral Nuestra Señora de la Asunción and the not-to-miss **Museo Arqueológico Cueva del Paraíso.** The second day you'll want to hike to the top of **El Yunque,** perhaps combined with horseback riding nearby or kayaking in search of manatees in **Parque Nacional Alejandro de Humboldt.** Day three is for a drive to Yumurí for a boat trip upriver. Many visitors choose to linger to simply kick back and steep in the sense of having been transported to Gabriel García Marquez's Macondo (the surrealistic village in *One Hundred Years of Solitude*).

GUANTÁNAMO

Guantánamo and Vicinity

GUANTÁNAMO

Guantánamo, 82 kilometers east of Santiago de Cuba, is a large city (pop. 180,000) at the head of a deep bay of the same name and some 25 kilometers inland of the U.S. naval base, which lies at the mouth of the bay. The colonial heart of the otherwise ungainly city has been spruced up and enlivened in recent years. Much of the population is descended from Haitian and English-speaking Caribbean immigrants who arrived in the 1920s to work in the sugar fields. The connections are strong: A British West Indian Welfare Center (an association for English-speaking descendants, locally called *ingleses*—Englishmen) and a Haitian cultural center,

Tumba Francesa, work to keep alive the traditions and anomalous culture (Haitians are called *franceses*—Frenchmen).

Given the proximity of the U.S. naval base, there's a strong Cuban military presence (when serious friction occurs between Cuba and the United States, the city gears up for a worst-case scenario). U.S. Marines first arrived here in June 1898 during the Spanish-Cuban-American War, following which the town developed a near-total economic dependency on the base, which employed hundreds of Cuban workers. Prostitution was also a major industry. Says an early guidebook, "The flourishing prostitution business passed from generation to generation like titles to land, and it was

© AVALON TRAVEL

not unusual to find three generations of women in service to the base."

Orientation

Guantánamo is laid out in a grid and approached from Santiago de Cuba by a four-lane highway that enters town from the northwest. The historic district is accessed by Paseo (Avenida Estudiantes), and further south by Avenida Camilo Cienfuegos, a wide boulevard that runs along the southern edge of downtown. North of Paseo is Reparto Caribe, where the Hotel Guantánamo overlooks Plaza de la Revolución. The center of town is Parque Martí, six blocks north of Camilo Cienfuegos and four blocks south of Paseo. Flor Crombet (colloquially called El Bulevar), to the park's southeast, and Aguilera, on the park's north side, are lively pedestrian precincts.

Calle 5 de Prado (one block north of Parque Martí) leads east across the Río Bano for Baracoa. A *circunvalación* (ring road) runs north of the city.

Parque Martí and Vicinity

What little there is to see surrounds this attractive square with a beautifully restored church—**Iglesia Parroquial de Santa Catalina**—on the north side; note its impressive *alfarje* ceiling. A **monument of José Martí** is on the west side of the church.

Built in Parisian fashion and topped by a cupola—La Fama—bearing a herald with trumpet, the exquisite turn-of-the-century **Palacio Salcido** one block northwest of the square houses

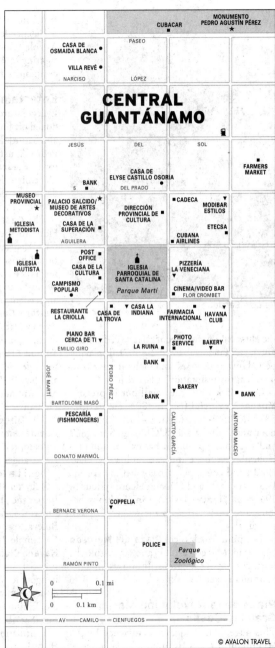

CENTRAL GUANTÁNAMO

GUANTÁNAMO

© AVALON TRAVEL

Palacio Salcido

the **Museo de Artes Decorativos** (Pedro Pérez #804, esq. Prado, tel. 021/32-4407), displaying period furniture, vases, and more. It was closed for a lengthy restoration at last visit.

One block west, the small but impressive **Museo Provincial** (Martí #804, tel. 021/32-5872, Mon. 2–5 P.M., Tues.–Sat. 8:30 A.M.–noon and 2:30–5 P.M., CUC1) dates from 1862 and was once a prison. It has exhibits on pre-Columbian culture and natural history; cigar bands; and coins; plus a bas-relief map of the U.S. naval base and Cuban defense system. A 1940s-era Harley-Davidson in the lobby belonged to a revolutionary messenger, Capitán Asdrúbal.

The pink neoclassical **Plaza del Mercado** (Antonio Maceo, esq. Prado), two blocks northeast of the square, still houses an agricultural market.

Plaza de la Revolución Marian Grajales Coello

This huge, barren square is enlivened by the **Monumento a los Héroes,** a huge concrete structure with the faces of heroes from the War of Independence. The bones of Los Mártires de Angola (Cuban military personnel who died fighting in Angola) are interred here. Military ceremonies are often held.

Entertainment and Events

Every Saturday evening, Pedro Pérez is cordoned off for a street party, while every Friday and Saturday night, local youth gather at Plaza Pedro Agustín Pérez to hear live bands perform. **Fiesta a la Guantanamera,** in early December, highlights traditional music and dance, as does the **Festival Nacional de Changüí** in mid-December.

The **Casa de la Trova** (Pedro Pérez, esq. Flor Crombet, no tel., daily 9 A.M.–midnight, CUC1 entrance) is a great spot to hear traditional music performed live. Watch for performances by Orquestra Revé, a local (and world-famous) exponent of *son-changüí* (an antecedent of *son*). The **British West Indian Welfare Center** (Serafín Sánchez #663, e/ Paseo y Narciso López, tel. 021/32-5297) hosts music and dance sessions featuring *changüí.* **Tumba Francesa** (Serafín Sánchez #715, e/ Jesús del Sol y Narciso López, Tues., Thurs., and Sat. 9:30 A.M.–1 P.M.) is a great place to hear the music and dance styles evolved by Haitians.

The **Dirección Provincial de Cultura de Guantánamo** (Calixto García #806, e/ Aguilera y Prado, tel. 021/33-3210, milene@gtmo.cult.cu) arranges music and dance events.

Beer? **La Ruina** (Calixto García, e/ Crombet y Gulo, tel. 021/92-9565, daily 9 A.M.–1 A.M., free) is the place to sip suds in a colonial structure run *bodega*-style with wooden benches. El Bulevar sprouted several bars in 2009, such as the simple 24-hour **La Reyna** (for rum) and **Havana Club** (Sun.–Thurs. 10 A.M.–midnight, Fri.–Sat. until 2 A.M.), *the* in-spot, but also a hangout for *jineteros* and *jineteras.* There's now even a **Piano Bar Cerca de Ti** (Pedro Pérez, esq. Emilio Giro, tel. 021/32-8191), with a pianist (Sat.–Sun. 9 P.M.–midnight).

If titillation is your thing, head to **Cabaret Hanoi** (tel. 021/38-2901, CUC1), four

GUANTANAMERA . . .

Everywhere in Cuba you'll hear "Guajira Guantanamera" played by troubadours. It's become a kind of signature tune. The melody was written in 1928 by Joseito Fernández (1908-1979), who at the time was in love with a woman from Guantánamo. When the song was first played on the radio in 1934, it became an overnight hit. In 1962, Cuban classical composer Julian Orbon (1925-1991) added the words of José Martí's *Versos Sencillos* (simple verses) to Fernández's melody and played it to friends and family, including Hector Angulo, one of his students. In the early 1960s, Angulo taught the song to folk singer Pete Seeger, who transcribed it for guitar. Angulo and Seeger launched it to international fame.

kilometers northeast of town, where a *cabaret espectáculo* is followed by a disco (Sat.–Sun. 10 P.M.). The **Hotel Guantánamo** (Calle 13, e/ Ahogado y Oeste, tel. 021/38-1015, CUC5) also has disco nightly (8 P.M.–1 A.M.). The modish **Modibar Estilos** (Maceo y 5 del Prado, tel. 021/35-1314) has a catwalk—a venue for a small cabaret (Sat.–Sun. 10 P.M.), "bodyart" show (Fri. 10 P.M.), and other nightly events.

Movies are shown at the **cinema** and adjoining **Video Bar La Esquina del Cine** (2 pesos), on the southeast corner of Parque Martí.

Accommodations

You can make reservations for *campismos* in the province at **Campismo Popular** (Flor Crombet #410, tel. 021/32-7356, Mon.–Fri. 8 A.M.–noon and 2–4 P.M.).

CASAS PARTICULARES

One block northeast of Plaza de la Revolución and handy for services at the Hotel Guantánamo, **Casa Doña Mimi** (Ahogados #3106, e/ 14 y 15 Norte, Rpto. Caribe, tel. 021/38-4161, CUC20) is good value. This modern bungalow has one cool, spacious room

with local TV and large hot-water bathroom, plus secure parking.

Although it's on the outskirts of town, my favorite place is (**C** **Casa de Norland Pérez** (Carretera de Santa María #301, esq. 7 Norte, Rpto. Rí Guaso, tel. 021/32-1532, CUC20–25), the 1953 modernist home of accomplished artist Miguel Ulria Noa and his equally gifted son Yismichael. Two identical bedrooms have TVs and fridges (and street noise). A thatched restaurant and game room were being built in the patio garden.

Downtown there are half a dozen options. **Villa Reve** (Pedro Pérez #670A, e/ Paseo y Narcisco López, tel. 021/32-2159, reve@infosol.gtm.sld.cu, CUC15–20) is a colonial home with airy patio and eight rooms to choose from. Interior rooms downstairs are gloomy. Upstairs rooms are well lit and cross-ventilated, and have modern bathrooms. Worthy and similar alternatives include **Casa de Osmaida Blanca** (Pedro Pérez #664, e/ Paseo y Narciso López, tel. 021/32-5193, CUC15–20), with a splendid rooftop terrace with bar; **Casa de Elsye Castillo Osoria** (Calixto García #766, e/ Prado y Jesús del Sol, tel. 021/32-3787, CUC20); and **Casa Señor Campos** (Calixto García #718 e/ Jesús del Sol y Nico López, tel. 5290-0847, CUC20).

HOTELS

Islazul's **Villa Turística La Lupe** (tel. 021/38-2602, recepcion@lupegtm.co.cu, CUC15 s, CUC20 d year-round), four kilometers north of town on the banks of the Río Bano, draws Cubans to the noisy poolside bar on weekends. It has 50 lovely rooms with modern bathrooms in two-story units. In town, Islazul's **Hotel Guantánamo** (Calle 13, e/ Ahogado y Oeste, tel. 021/38-1015, fax 021/38-2406, jrecephotel@hotelgtmo.cu.cu, CUC15 s, CUC20 d year-round) has simpler, no-frills rooms with modern bathrooms, plus most services you could want, from disco to car rental.

Food

Guantánamo's dire dining scene has improved in recent years, although it has no *paladares*, and the short-lived Restaurante Vegetariano is now the lackluster **La Criolla** (Pedro Pérez, esq. Flor Crombet, daily noon–2:30 P.M. and 5–10:30 P.M.), serving basic *criollo* fare.

For romance, head to ◖ **Restaurante Los Girasoles** (Ahogados #6501, esq. a 15 Norte, Rpto. Caribe, tel. 021/38-4178, daily noon–9:30 P.M.), offering candlelit dinners, including shrimp cocktail (CUC2), in an elegant 1950s home. The night I dined here, however, it had only pork and fried chicken (CUC3). Reservations advised. Alternatively, try **Ranchón Río Bano** (daily 11 A.M.–6 P.M.), a thatched riverside restaurant at Villa Turística La Lupe (four kilometers north of town).

Five pesos will buy you a slice of what passes for pizza at **Pizzería La Veneciana** (Mon.–Sat. 10 A.M.–2:45 P.M. and 5:30–10:45 P.M.), on the east side of Parque Martí. At least the coffee is good at **Casa La Indiana** (24 hours), on the south side of Parque Martí. And **Coppelia** (Pérez, esq. Bernace Verona, daily 9 A.M.–10 P.M.) serves delicious ice cream for pesos.

You can buy produce at the *mercado agropecuario* (Antonio Maceo, esq. Prado, Mon.–Sat. 8 A.M.–6 P.M., Sun. 8 A.M.–2 P.M.).

Information and Services

Infotur (tel. 021/38-5838, 8 A.M.–5 P.M.) has an tourist info bureau in the Hotel Guantánamo.

The **post office** (Pérez, esq. Aguilera, tel. 021/32-4668) has DHL service. **Etecsa** (Maceo e/ Aguilera y Prado, tel. 021/32-7878, daily 8:30 A.M.–7:30 P.M.) has international phone and Internet service.

The **Farmacia Internacional** (Flor Crombet e/ Calixto García y Maceo, tel. 021/35-1129, Mon.–Fri. 9 A.M.–5 P.M., Sat. 9 A.M.–4 P.M.) is relatively well-stocked. **Hospital Agostinho Neto** (Carretera El Salvador, Km 1, tel. 021/35-5450) is half a kilometer south of town.

Getting There and Away

Aeropuerto Mariana Grajales (tel. 021/32-3564), 12 kilometers east of town, is not served by international flights. **Cubana** (Calixto García #817, e/ Prado y Aguilera,

tel. 21/32-4533) flies between Havana and Guantánamo.

The **bus terminal** (tel. 021/32-5588) is two kilometers south of town. **Víazul** (tel. 021/80121) buses for Guantánamo depart Santiago de Cuba at 7:45 A.M. (CUC6.48) and Baracoa at 2:15 P.M. (CUC10.80). Buses depart Guantánamo for Santiago de Cuba at 5:25 P.M. and for Baracoa at 9:30 A.M.

The **train station** (tel. 021/32-5518) is on Pedro Pérez, one block east of Paseo. Trains depart for Guantánamo from Havana at 6:25 P.M. (#5, CUC43 *especial*) and 8:20 P.M. (#720, CUC32, *regular*), and from Holguín at 2:20 P.M. (CUC6.50). They depart from Guantánamo for Havana at 12:30 P.M. (#6) and 1:50 A.M., and for Holguín at 5:30 A.M.

Getting Around

Horse-drawn *coches* abound. Bus #9 runs past the Hotel Guantánamo from Paseo.

Cubataxi (tel. 021/32-3636) offers taxi service. **Cubacar** (tel. 021/35-5515) has car rental in the Hotel Guantánamo (Calle 13, e/ Ahogado y Oeste).

You can rent scooters from **Palmares Motoclub** (Calixto García e/ Crombet y Giro, tel. 021/32-9565).

U.S. NAVAL BASE AND VICINITY

The U.S. naval base (www.nsgtmo.navy.mil), which is colloquially referred to as Gitmo, for the official airport code, GTMO, occupies both sides of the entrance to Guantánamo Bay, which is inhabited by endangered manatees and marine turtles (iguanas, the unofficial Gitmo mascot, roam on land). The Naval Air Station (NAS), on the western side of the bay, is separated by four kilometers of water from the naval station, on the east side. Hence, the bay is crisscrossed by helicopters, boats, and an hourly ferry, while Cuban vessels also pass to and fro (the treaty guarantees free access to the waters to Cuban vessels and those of Cuba's trading partners heading in and out of the Cuban port of Boquerón; an Anti-Air Warfare Center monitors Cuban traffic).

GUANTÁNAMO NAVAL BASE

Guantánamo (Gitmo) is the only U.S. overseas military base located in a Communist country. It's also a constant thorn in the side of Cuban-U.S. relations. Since 1903 the United States has held an indefinite lease on the property, which it claimed as a prize at the end of the Spanish-American War. The 45 square miles of land and water were formally handed over to the United States in ceremonies aboard the USS *Kearsarge*, anchored in the bay, on December 10, 1903.

The Platt Amendment, which "granted" use of the base to Uncle Sam, was dropped in 1934, and a new treaty was signed. Although it confirmed Cuba's "ultimate sovereignty," the treaty stipulated that the lease would be indefinite and could be terminated only by agreement of both parties (or if the United States decides to pull out). In the original lease, the United States agreed to pay Cuba the sum of US$2,000 in gold per year. In 1934, when gold coins were discontinued, the rent was upped to US$4,085, payable by U.S. Treasury check. The first rent check that Uncle Sam paid to Castro's regime, in 1959, was cashed. Since then Fidel, who refuses to accept the legitimacy of the treaty, has refused to cash the checks.

The gates were closed on January 1, 1959, and have not been reopened.

LIFE ON THE BASE

Today, 9,500 U.S. servicemen live here amid all the comforts of a small Midwestern town. There are five swimming pools, four outdoor movie houses, 400 miles of paved road, and a golf course. McDonald's, KFC, Pizza Hut, and Taco Bell even have concessions – the only ones in Cuba. Another 7,000 civilians also work here, including a small number of Cubans who chose to remain following the Revolution, while a dwindling number of Cubans also "commute" to work daily through the base's Northeast Gate.

In 1964 the Cuban government cut off the base's water supply. It was replaced with a seawater desalinization plant that today provides 3,000,000 gallons of fresh water daily, along with electrical power.

The facility was until recently ringed by the largest U.S. minefield in the world, laid down during the Cuban Missile Crisis of 1962 but dug up and disarmed in 1999. The Cuban mines remain, as does a "cactus curtain" meant to deter defectors from Cuba from reaching the base. Nonetheless, each year many Cuban "fence-jumpers" risk death to reach a "paradise" promised by radio and television stations broadcasting from the base.

Since 2002, the base has been used to house suspected Taliban and Al Qaeda terrorists.

Castro has proposed to make the base a regional medical center for all of the Caribbean if Uncle Sam relinquishes his hold.

The bay is ringed by Cuban military bases, two Cuban naval facilities (Glorieta and Boquerón) and **Mirador de Malones** (U.S. marines call it "Castro's Bunker"), a command center buried deep beneath the mountain on the east side of the bay. Unbelievably, visits to the bunker have been permitted in past years, but no longer. Check with Infotur in town.

The main gate (permanently closed since 1959) is at **Caimanera,** 22 kilometers south of Guantánamo. This small Cuban town is surrounded by salt flats; its economy is based on salt, fishing, and a Frontera Brigada military complex. Before the Revolution, many *caimaneros* worked on the U.S. naval base, while *caimaneras* worked in the strip joints and brothels that were the town's staple industry.

Caimanera is a restricted military zone, and visits by foreigners are limited to excursions offered by **Habanatur** (Fri.–Sun. 8 A.M.–5 P.M. for individuals, Sat.–Sun. for groups, CUC12 per person with cocktail and lunch); 24 hours notice is required. Individuals may be able to get a pass from Infotur or Habanatur after MININT checks you out. The situation is fluid and depends on the state of international relations. If you visit, from the three-story observation tower of the Hotel Caimanera you can look out past Cuban watchtowers to the naval base that Castro has called "a dagger plunged

stone gorilla at the Zoológico de Piedra

© CHRISTOPHER P. BAKER

in the heart of Cuban soil," and that blazes brightly at night like a mini–Las Vegas.

Accommodations

Islazul's **Hotel Caimanera** (Loma Norte, Caimanera, tel. 021/49-9414, CUC12 s, CUC16 d) is open only to groups prearranged through Habanatur or otherwise issued passes. It has 17 air-conditioned rooms plus a swimming pool.

Getting There

Prior permission to visit Gitmo is required from the U.S. military and isn't granted to your average Joe. **Air Sunshine** (tel. 954/434-8900 or 800/327-8900, http://airsunshine.com) flies between Fort Lauderdale and Gitmo (Sun.–Thurs., US$250 each way).

Trains run to Caimanera from Guantánamo four times daily.

NORTH OF GUANTÁNAMO

North of the city, sugarcane fields merge into mountains. You need your passport for a police *punto de control* one kilometer before the Zoológico de Piedra, beyond which a security zone is off-limits.

◖ Zoológico de Piedra

The "stone zoo" (no tel., daily 8 A.M.–5 P.M., entrance CUC1, cameras CUC1, videos CUC5), in the mountains 25 kilometers northeast of Guantánamo, features a menagerie of wild animals from around the world—lions, tapirs, hippopotamuses, elephants, and other species—hewn from huge calcareous rocks with hammer and chisel by a coffee farmer, Ángel Iñigo. Iñigo has carved more than 426 animals that he had seen only in photographs in books, representing more than 30 years of work. Over a kilometer of stone pathways lead through the thick foliage, revealing such carved scenes as a buffalo being attacked by mountain lions, two monkeys picking fleas from each other, and Stone Age figures killing a wild boar. The zoo is a work in progress.

The thatched **Restaurante Mirador La Piedra** (Tues.–Sun. 11 A.M.–midnight), at the zoo, has fantastic views, but don't count on food being available.

Guantánamo to Baracoa

About 20 kilometers east of Guantánamo city, the coast road rises up a two-kilometer-long hill where you have your views back down over the milky bay. Beyond the crest, the road drops to the coast and you emerge at **Playa Yateritas,** a golden beach popular with residents of Guantánamo on weekends. For the next few miles, you'll pass little coves cut into the raised coral shore.

Beyond the hamlet of **Imias,** the terrain turns to semi-desert, with valley bottoms filled with orchards and oases of palms. **Campismo Yacabo Abajo** (tel. 021/88-0289, CUC6 per person), about five kilometers west of Imias, has modern yet basic beachfront cabins. There's a café and horseback rides (CUC3). Check ahead with *campismo popular* offices in Baracoa or Guantánamo.

CAJOBABO

The community of Cajobabo, 45 kilometers east of Guantánamo, is hallowed ground. Here, at **Playitas,** two kilometers further east, José Martí, Máximo Gómez, and four other prominent patriots put ashore in a small rowboat on April 11, 1895, after years of exile. The tiny beachfront **Museo Municipal 11 de Abril** (no tel., daily 8:30 A.M.–noon and 1–5:30 P.M., CUC1) honors Martí. A replica of the boat sits outside the museum and is used each April 11, when the landing is reenacted and cultural activities are hosted. A guide will lead you along a three-kilometer trail via Playitas (CUC1), reached via a steep headland. Beyond the rocks at the far east end of the beach hides a tiny cove with a **marble monument** inset into the cliff face, laid in 1947 with a base resembling the prow of a boat.

The shorefront road continues east to Punta Maisí at the eastern tip of Cuba. One of the most dramatic drives in all Cuba is, alas, off-limits to foreigners: A military checkpoint bars the way.

◖ LA FAROLA

Immediately beyond Cajobabo, the highway turns north and climbs into the Sierra del Purial along La Farola, initiated during

© CHRISTOPHER P. BAKER

La Farola, Guantánamo

GUANTÁNAMO

the Batista era (it was called the Vía Mulata) and completed since the Revolution to link Baracoa with the rest of Cuba. This highway spirals uphill through the valley of the Ríos Yumurí and Ojo. The road narrows with the ascent, the bends growing tighter, the views more dramatic and wide-ranging. Soon you are climbing through pine forests amid the most non-Cuban landscapes in Cuba.

The summit (Alto de Coltillo) hosts a tiny café, beyond which the road drops through a moist valley until you emerge by the sea at Baracoa. The unlit road is subject to landslides. *Drive with care!*

Baracoa and Vicinity

BARACOA

Baracoa (pop. 65,000) lies 200 kilometers east of Santiago, 120 kilometers east of Guantánamo, and is really miles from anywhere. The somnolent town nestles hard up against the ocean beneath the great hulking flat-topped mass of El Yunque. Baracoa curves around the wide Bahía de Miel (Honey Bay), lined with black-sand beaches.

Isolation breeds individuality, and Baracoa is both isolated and individual. The town looks and feels antique, with its little fortresses and streets lined with venerable wooden edifices, rickety and humbled with age.

Baracoans have a good deal of Indian blood, identified by their short stature, olive-brown skins, and squared-off faces.

History

On October 27, 1492, approaching Cuban shores for the first time, Christopher Columbus saw "a high, square-shaped mountain, which looked like an island." For centuries, it was widely accepted that the mountain he saw was El Yunque. It is now thought that Columbus was actually describing a similar flat-topped mountain near Gibara, many miles to the west (Baracoans, however, are staunchly partisan on the subject).

In 1510, Don Diego Velázquez de Cuellar arrived fresh from Spain with 300 men and founded La Villa de Nuestra Señora de la Asunción, the first of the original seven cities founded by Velázquez. As such, it is the oldest colonial city in the Americas. The indigenous Taíno population resisted the strange cutthroat proselytizers. A Dominican-born chief named Hatuey rallied the Indians in a rebellion against Spanish enslavement. The Spanish repelled the Indians and captured Hatuey. The noble "savage" was burned at the stake.

Baracoa's remote geographical circumstance did little to favor the settlement. After five years, Santiago de Cuba, with its vastly superior harbor, was proclaimed the new capital. Baracoa languished in limbo for the next two centuries, without road or rail link to the rest of Cuba until La Farola was completed in the early 1960s.

In September 2008, Hurricane Ike came ashore here, tearing up Baracoa pretty badly; many of the houses along the Malecón were demolished.

Orientation

La Farola enters town from the east as Calle José Martí. The town is only a few blocks wide, with narrow roads running parallel to the shore. The wind-swept Malecón runs along the seafront, two blocks north of Martí. From Holguín, the town is accessed via Avenida Primero de Abril, which curls around the western harbor.

Fortresses

Dominating the town is **El Castillo,** a fortress—Castillo Seboruco—atop the rocky marine terrace that looms above Baracoa, offering a bird's-eye view. It was built during the War of Jenkins' Ear (1739–1741) between Spain and Britain, when the two nations' navies battled it out over the issue of trading rights in the New World. It has metamorphosed as the Hotel El

Castillo and is accessed by a steep staircase at the southern end of Frank País.

Tiny **Fuerte Matachín,** at the east end of Martí and the Malecón, dates to 1802 and guards the eastern entrance to the old town. A bronze bust of General Antonio Maceo stands outside the fortress, with its thick walls topped with cannons. The storehouse houses the **Museo Matachín** (tel. 021/64-2122, daily 8 A.M.–noon and 2–6 P.M., CUC1 entrance, CUC1 camera), tracing the history of the region since pre-Columbian days. It also displays polymites (the local polychromatic snails). The round tower—**Torreón de Toa**—immediately south of the fort served as a Spanish customs checkpoint.

The semicircular **Fortaleza de la Punta,** at the far west end of Martí, was built in 1803 to guard the harbor entrance. It's now a restaurant.

Plaza Independencia

This triangular plaza (Antonio Maceo, e/ Frank País y Ciro Frias) is the town hub and is pinned by a **bust of Hatuey,** the Indian chief. It is dominated by the near-derelict **Catedral Nuestra Señora de la Asunción** (it was trashed by Hurricane Ike and will likely remain closed for some time), dating from 1805 on the site of an earlier church destroyed by pirates in 1652. The church is famous for the "Cruz de la Parra," a dark, well-worn, meter-tall cross (supposedly the oldest European relic in the Americas). Baracoans believe that Columbus left the cross upright amid stones at the harbor entrance in 1492. Carbon-dating analysis confirms that it is indeed about 500 years old, although scientific study by experts determined that the cross was made of *Coccoloba diversifolia,* a native New World hardwood that grows abundantly around Baracoa. Perhaps Columbus whittled the cross himself in Cuba!

◖ Museo Arqueológico Cueva del Paraíso

The highlight of Baracoa is this archaeological museum (no tel., Mon.–Fri. 8 A.M.–5 P.M.,

Sat.–Sun. 8 A.M.–noon, CUC2), inside a cave on the southern side of town. Aboriginal artifacts, carvings, and jewelry, plus skeletons (one possibly being the *cacique* Guamá, who rebelled against Spain) are displayed within floodlit glass cases ensconced within crevices between the dripstone formations. A funerary cave has skeletons in situ; access is via makeshift wooden scaffolding: *you clamber at your own risk!* Follow Calle Moncada uphill to a tiny traffic circle; the museum is signed from here.

Other caves with dripstone formations and Taíno petroglyphs (one of which local archaeologists purport represents Columbus's three caravels) are protected in **Parque Natural Majayara,** east of town. It was closed to visitors at last visit.

Parque Zoológico Cacique Guamá
This small zoo (tel. 021/64-3409, Tues.–Sun. 8 A.M.–4 P.M., 20 centavos), seven kilometers east of Baracoa, displays monkeys, a hippo, a lion, birds, crocodiles, rodent-like *jutías,* and a near-extinct relative, the *almique,* indigenous to eastern Cuba.

Entertainment and Events
The **Semana de la Cultura** is a week-long cultural festival kicked off on April 1 to celebrate Antonio Maceo's landing at nearby Duaba in 1895.

Every Saturday night, a street party—*fiesta callejera*—is set up on Calle Maceo, which is cordoned off and lit with Christmas lights, while the boom-box music reverberates until well past midnight, and only the dead can sleep.

The **Casa de la Trova** (Maceo #149, e/ Ciro Frías y Pelayo Cuervo, no tel., daily 9 P.M.–2 A.M., 10 pesos) is one of the liveliest and most intimate venues in Cuba for savoring traditional music, such as local adaptations of Cuban *son* known as *el nengen* and *el kiriba.* Likewise, **Casa de la Cultura** (Maceo, e/ Frank País y Maraví, tel. 021/64-2364) and **Fondo de Bienes Culturales** (Mon.–Sat. 5 P.M.–12:30 A.M. and Sun. 8:30 P.M.–12:30 A.M.), 50 meters west.

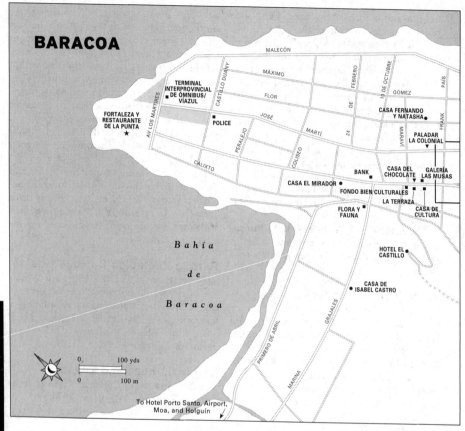

BARACOA

Bahía de Baracoa

To Hotel Porto Santo, Airport, Moa, and Holguín

For a quiet sip, relax at the open-air bar in the **Hotel El Castillo** (Calle Calixto García, Loma del Paraíso). For boy-meets-girl, it all happens at the open-air **Café El Parque** (24 hours) on the south side of Plaza Independencia, where live music is offered. Foreigners who don't pick up a Cuban partner here can surely do so at the hilltop **El Ranchón** (no tel., 9 P.M.–2 A.M., CUC1), 800 meters east of the Hotel El Castillo (you can also ascend the dark staircase at the south end of Coroneles Gajano); music videos draw everyone onto the dance floor.

The rooftop **La Terraza** (Maceo, e/ Maraví y Frank País) has a middling *cabaret espectáculo* featuring saucy showgirls (Tues.–Sun. at 11 P.M., CUC1).

Estadio Manuel Fuentes Borges, east of town, hosts baseball games October–May.

Accommodations

Book local *campismos* at **Campismo Popular** (Martí #225, e/ Galano y Reyes, tel. 021/64-2776).

CASAS PARTICULARES

There are scores of private rooms for rent. All are air-conditioned and most serve meals. Here are a few of my faves.

For an independent apartment, try **Casa Fernando y Natasha** (Flor Crombet #115 e/ Frank País y Maraví, tel. 021/64-3820, CUC20), taking up the ground floor below the owners'

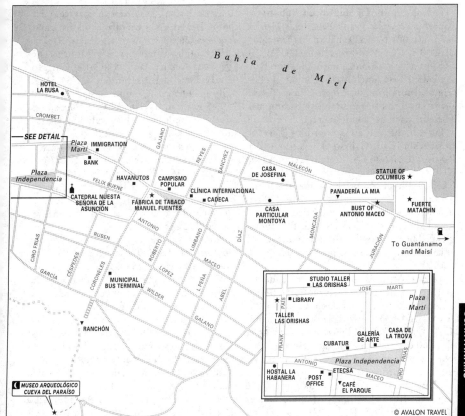

© AVALON TRAVEL

home. You get a TV lounge and modern bathroom. The friendly owners were tremendously attentive when I stayed here in 2009.

I also enjoyed my stay at **Casa de Josefina** (Flor Crombet #269, c/o tel. 021/64-1928, CUC15–20), where the pleasant hosts offer one room with a firm mattress, fan, private bathroom, and terrace.

(**Casa Particular El Mirador** (Maceo #86, e/ 24 de Febrero y 10 de Octubre, tel. 021/64-2647, ilianacu09@gmail.com, CUC15–20) is one of the best room rentals. Hostess Iliana Sotorongo Rodríguez's attractive colonial home has two spacious upstairs rooms with fans and lofty ceilings that open to a balcony with rockers and views.

An excellent and similar alternative, (**Casa de Isabel Castro** (Marian Grajales #35, tel. 021/64-2267, CUC15–20) has 1950s retro decor. The patio to the rear gets the sun and opens to a large garden with fruit trees. It has secure parking.

Casa de William Montoya (Martí #287, e/ Abel Díaz y Glicerio Blanco, tel. 021/64-1917, CUC20–25) is a lofty-ceilinged colonial home with a pleasant lounge, two rooms with private bathrooms, plus secure parking.

HOTELS

All hotels are operated by Gaviota (reservasps@ gaviota.co.cu) and have air-conditioned rooms with satellite TV.

Thumbs up for ◖ **Hostal La Habanera** (Maceo #126, esq. Frank País, tel. 021/64-5273, fax 021/64-5339, habanabc@enet.cu, CUC30 s, CUC35 d low season, CUC35 s, CUC40 d high season), a splendid restoration of a colonial-era hotel. Its 10 rooms around a central atrium patio have high ceilings, pleasant rattan furniture, and modern bathrooms. There's a small bar and restaurant.

For a room with a view opt for ◖ **Hotel El Castillo** (Calle Calixto García, Loma del Paraíso, tel. 021/64-5106, fax 021/64-5339, CUC42 s, CUC56 d low season, CUC44 s, CUC60 d high season), built atop the foundations of El Castillo. It has 62 rooms (28 are in a new block opened in 2010) furnished colonial style, with balconies with El Yunque views. The restaurant is the best in town, but at last visit the swimming pool was jade-green with algae.

If El Castillo is full, a lesser yet identically priced alternative is **Hotel Porto Santo** (Carretera del Aeropuerto, tel. 021/64-5106, fax 021/64-5339, www.gaviota-grupo.com, CUC42 s, CUC56 d low season, CUC44 s, CUC60 d high season) on the west side of the bay. Its 36 rooms and 24 *cabinas* surround an amoeba-shaped pool, and it has tennis.

Warning: You"ll regret booking into the 12-room **Hotel La Rusa** (Máximo Gómez #161, tel. 021/64-3011, fax 021/64-5339, larusa@enet.cu, CUC20 s, CUC25 d low season, CUC25 s, CUC30 d high season), facing the Malecón. (It once belonged to a Russian woman, Mima Rubenskaya, who fled the Soviet Union in 1917 and settled in Baracoa long before it turned Communist; if you want to know more about her, check out the museum in the Fuerte Matachín.) It was totally drenched during Hurricane Ike in 2008 and despite being refurbished, is so mildewed (water was even running out of the walls and down the stairs at my last visit) that it should be condemned.

Food

The only *paladar,* ◖ **La Colonial** (Martí #123, e/ Maraví y Frank País, tel. 021/64-5391, daily 10 A.M.–11 P.M.), has heaps of cozy colonial charm. It even serves swordfish and shark and *dorado* in huge portions (most dishes CUC7).

Although it has its off nights, the ◖ **Restaurant Duaba** (Calle Calixto García, Loma del Paraíso, tel. 021/64-5165, daily 7–9:45 A.M., noon–2:30 P.M., and 7–9:45 P.M.), in the Hotel El Castillo, serves creative local dishes such as seafood prepared in coconut sauce with herbs (CUC8), and a delicious rice in sweet coconut sauce dessert (CUC2). **Restaurante La Punta** (tel. 021/64-1480, daily 10 A.M.–10 P.M.), in Fortaleza de la Punta, can't be beat for its airy patio setting and colonial ambience. The limited *criollo* menu includes a fish, crab, and shrimp special (CUC9).

Another winner is the modestly elegant **Restaurante La Habanera** (Maceo #68, esq. Frank País, tel. 021/64-5273, daily 7 A.M.–9:45 P.M.), in the Hostal La Habanera. Try the house special appetizer of corn tamale with bacon and sausage with garlic, herbs, and *criollo* sauce (CUC3).

You can buy a chocolate drink, *natilla* (a kind of chocolate mousse), and chocolate bars for pesos at the **Casa del Chocolate** (Antonio Maceo #121, esq. Maraví, tel. 021/64-1553, daily 7:30 A.M.–10:20 P.M.).

For baked goods, head to **Panadería La Mia** (Martí #335), one block west of Fuerte Matachín. You can buy produce at the *mercado agropecuario* (24 de Febrero y Malecón).

Shopping

Galería Eliseo Osoris (Félix Ruenes #25, Mon.–Fri. 9 A.M.–noon and 4–9 P.M., Sat.–Sun. 4–10 P.M.), on the north side of Plaza Independencia, sells paintings and sculptures. Also try the **Bien Fondo Culturales** (Maceo #120); the **Taller la Musa** (Calle Maceo #124, e/ Maraví y Frank País), where noted artists Roel Caboverde and Orlando Piedra sell original paintings; and **Studio Taller Las Orishas** (Martí #131, e/ Frank País y Pelayo Cuervo, www.luiseliades.com), cater-corner to **Taller las Orishas** (Ciro Frías #48, e/ Ruber López y Calixto García), which makes dolls.

THE LOCAL FLAVOR

Baracoa is acclaimed for its original cuisine based on the coconut, which finds its way into such local delicacies as *calalú*, a spinach-like vegetable simmered in coconut milk; *bacán*, a tortilla made of baked plantain paste mixed with coconut milk, wrapped in banana leaves, and filled with spiced pork; *cucurucho*, an ambrosial sweet made of shredded coconut mixed with papaya, orange, nuts, and sugar or honey, served wrapped in folded palm leaves; delicious *turrón de coco*, a baked bar of grated coconut mixed with milk and sugar; and *frangollo*, a dish of green bananas toasted and mashed.

For drinks, try *chorote*, a tasty chocolate drink thickened with cornstarch; *sacoco*, a concoction of rum and coconut milk served in green coconuts; *sambumbia*, made of honey, lemon, and water; and *pru*, made from pine needles and sugar syrup.

Cuban chocolates come from here too. They're made at the **Fábrica de Chocolate** (not open to visits), two kilometers west of Baracoa.

Fisherfolk also net a local oddity, *tetí*, a tiny red fish that migrates like salmon up the Río Toa. The fish arrive at the mouth of the river enveloped in a gelatinous cocoon that splits apart on contact with fresh water. *Tetí* is eaten raw with cocktail sauce.

Information and Services

Infotur (Maceo #129-A e/ Maravi y Frank País, tel. 021/64-1781, Mon.–Sat. 8:30 A.M.–4:45 P.M., Sun. 8:30 A.M.–noon) has a helpful tourist information bureau.

The **post office** (daily 8 A.M.–8 P.M.) is on Plaza Independencia. Next door, **Etecsa** (Maceo #134, tel. 021/64-2543, daily 8:30 A.M.–7:30 P.M.) has international telephone and Internet service.

Bandec has two branches (Maceo, esq. Marina Grajales; and on Plaza Martí).

Hospital General Docente (tel. 021/43014,

021/42568 for emergencies) is two kilometers east of town. The **Clínica Internacional** (Martí, esq. Reyes, tel. 021/64-1038, 24 hours) has a nurse on duty 24/7 and a pharmacy.

The police station is on Martí e/ Duany y Coliseo.

Getting There and Away

Aeropuerto Gustavo Rizo (tel. 021/64-2216) is on the west side of the bay. **Cubana** (Martí #181, tel. 021/64-5374) connects Baracoa with Havana twice weekly and with Santiago de Cuba once weekly.

Buses arrive and depart the **Terminal Interprovincial** (Los Mártires, esq. Martí, tel. 021/64-3880). A **Víazul** bus (tel. 021/64-3093) departs Baracoa for Guantánamo and Santiago de Cuba at 2:15 P.M.

Camiones serve Moa and Guantánamo from the **Terminal Municipal** (Coroneles Galano, esq. Rubio López).

You can rent cars from **Cubacar** at the airport (tel. 021/64-5343) and Hotel La Habanera (tel. 021/64-5212); and **Vía** (tel. 021/64-5135) at the Hotel Porto Santo and Hotel El Castillo.

Getting Around

For a 56-kilometer loop tour of town and the environs, hop aboard the **Baracoa Bus Tour** (Calle Maceo #132, tel. 021/64-5212, CUC5), offered four times daily in a minibus. You can hop on and off along the route, which begins in Parque Central.

Horse-drawn *coches* and pedal-powered *bici-taxis* ply the main streets. For a taxi, call **Cubataxi** (tel. 021/64-3737).

You can rent **scooters** at the Hotel El Castillo (Calle Calixto García, Loma del Paraíso, CUC6 first hour, CUC26 per day).

Cubatur (Martí #181, tel. 021/64-5306, cubatourbaracoa@enet.cu) and **Gaviotatours** (Calle Calixto García, Loma del Paraíso, tel. 021/64-5165), in the Hotel Castillo, offer excursions. **EcoTur** (Calixto García, esq. Marina Grajales, tel. 021/64-3665, ecoturbc@enet.cu, Mon.–Sat. 8 A.M.–6 P.M.) handles excursions into the nearby national parks.

There are gas stations beside Fuerte Matachín and one kilometer east of town.

RESERVA DE LA BIOSFERA CUCHILLAS DE TOA

West of Baracoa, the 208,305-hectare Cuchillas de Toa Biosphere Reserve encompasses most of the Alturas de Sagua-Baracoa, Cuchillas de Toa, and Cuchillas de Moa mountain ranges, and rises from sea level to 1,139 meters in elevation. The reserve has diverse climate types and ecosystems and protects the richest flora and fauna in Cuba, including more endemic species than anywhere else on the island, not least the polymite (a colorful snail species).

Much of the area is forested in Cuban pine, a perfect habitat for the ivory-billed woodpecker and its cousin, the endemic and endangered royal woodpecker. (The ivory-billed woodpecker was once common throughout the American South, but they have not been seen in the United States since the 1940s. The bird was considered extinct until the mid-1980s, when it was identified in these mountains. The sightings resulted in the Cuban government's establishing a 220-square-kilometer protection area. However, no sightings have since been made.)

The reserve, under the aegis of **CITMA** (Ciencias Tecnología de Ambiente, Martí #133, esq. Frank País, tel. 021/64-3300, conservacion@toa.gtm.sld.cu), is divided into several national parks. Visits are coordinated through **EcoTur** (Calixto García, esq. Marina Grajales, tel. 021/64-3665, ecoturbc@enet.cu).

〖 Parque Natural Duaba and El Yunque

At the mouth of the Río Duaba, five kilometers west of Baracoa, is **Playa Duaba,** a black-sand beach where general Antonio Maceo and 22 compatriots landed in April 1895 to fight the War of Independence. Immediately beyond is the site where he fought his first battle. He is honored by a roadside bust.

You can turn inland here and follow a dirt road one kilometer to **Finca Duaba** (no tel., daily 8 A.M.–7 P.M.), a fruit farm with a restaurant serving *criollo* meals. Guided tours are offered (CUC1), as are boat trips to the rivermouth (CUC2). **EcoTur** offers excursions from Baracoa (CUC12).

El Yunque, Baracoa

© CHRISTOPHER P. BAKER

The park enfolds El Yunque ("the anvil"), the spectacular table-top mountain (575 meters) that dominates the landscape west of Baracoa. This sheer-sided giant—the remains of a mighty plateau that once extended across the entire area—was hallowed according to the Taíno Indians. Mists flow down from the summit in the dawn hours, and it glows like hot coals at dusk, when the setting sun pours over the red rocky walls like molten lava. Waterfalls pour from its summit, washing away soil and mineral nutrients. The soils are thin, and the oases of orchids, lichen, mosses, and forest seem to survive on water and air alone.

You can hike to the summit (four hours round-trip, CUC13 from Campismo El Yunque, CUC15–182 from Baracoa, with compulsory guide). From the coast highway, take the signed turnoff for Finca Duaba, then keep left at the Y fork (the *campismo* is to the left; Finca Duaba is to the right). **Sendero El Jutiero** from the *campismo* leads to cascades.

Parque Natural el Toa

This park, immediately west of Parque Natural Duaba, extends into the interior mountains. The seven-kilometer-long **Sendero Juncal Rencontra** trail transcends the mountains, leading from the Río Duaba to the Río Toa; guided hikes (CUC22 from Baracoa) end with a boat or jeep return. Visits need to be coordinated with EcoTur or Gaviota.

🅲 Parque Nacional Alejandro de Humboldt

This 70,835-hectare park extends into Holguín Province. A guide is compulsory. There's a two-meter-tall statue of the German explorer roadside near the **visitor center** (daily 8 A.M.–7 P.M.), with 3-D map of the park, on the east side of Recreo, five kilometers west of the Río Nibujón. The **Sendero Balcón de Iberia** leads inland to waterfalls and natural swimming pools (five hours, last departure at 11 A.M., CUC10, or CUC22 with transport from Baracoa). The shorter **Sendero El Recreo** (CUC10) hugs the shore of **Parque Natural Bahía de Taco,** incorporated within

---

POLYMITES

Polymita pictas is a species of tiny snail unique to the Baracoa region. This diminutive critter is much sought by collectors for its Joseph's coat of many colors, which are as unique to each individual polymite as fingerprints are to humans. *However, the species is endangered and it is illegal to catch, buy or export them.*

According to an Indian legend, the snails' shells were originally colorless. One snail, while slowly roaming the region, was taken by the area's lush beauty and asked the mountains for some of their green. Then he admired the sky and asked for some blue. When he saw the golden sands, he asked for a splash of yellow, and for jade and turquoise from the sea.

Parque Nacional Alejandro de Humboldt, and protecting 2,263 hectares of marine ecosystems, including mangroves, an offshore cay, and white-sand beaches shelving to a coral reef. Manatees are often seen. The **Sendero Bahía de Taco** includes a boat excursion (CUC5). EcoTur and Gaviota offer excursions from Baracoa.

Accommodations and Food

Campismo El Yunque (tel. 021/64-5262), midway between Finca Duaba and the summit of El Yunque, has 16 basic huts, each sleeping up to six people. It was planning to accept foreigners, perhaps in 2011.

In 2009, EcoTur opened the simple **Finca La Esperanza** (CUC20 per person, including meals and boat tour) at the mouth of the Río Toa. Each of four rooms has four beds and fans.

Exuding international appeal, Gaviota's 🅲 **Villa Maguana** (Carretera de Moa, Km 20, tel. 021/64-5106, fax 021/64-5339, CUC57 s, CUC73 d low season, CUC66 s, CUC83 d high season, including meals), 28 kilometers west of Baracoa, nestles in its own cove with a white-sand beach and turquoise waters.

GUANTÁNAMO

© CHRISTOPHER P. BAKER

Playa Maguana, near Baracoa

Upgraded and expanded, it has 16 lovely rooms with modern bathrooms in two-story fourplex wooden structures.

BARACOA TO PUNTA MAISÍ

The coast road east from Baracoa follows a winding course inland via the hamlet of Jamal, touching the coast again 20 kilometers east of Baracoa at **Playa Baragua,** famous for its long, ruler-straight silver-sand beach with a fabulous view towards El Yunque. Break out the camera!

Beyond Baragua, the road eventually passes through a cleft in the vertical cliffs spanned by a natural arch called Túnel de los Alemanes (Germans' Tunnel). Beyond, you emerge at **Boca de Yumurí,** where the Río Yumurí cuts through a deep canyon to meet the Atlantic breakers. You can rent pedal boats at **Café Yumurí** (daily 10 A.M.–6 P.M.), and locals will accost you as you step from your car to lasso you into a boat ride upriver (CUC2 round-trip).

Punta Maisí

Immediately east of the Río Yumurí, the road begins a daunting first-gear switchback ascent and beyond Mesa Abajo deteriorates to a rutted dirt road that leads to **La Máquina,** the center of a coffee growing region on the cooler eastern slope of the Meseta de Maisí, 22 kilometers beyond the rivermouth.

La Máquina looks down over a vast plain studded with cacti. Far below, a *faro* built in 1862 at Punta Maisí pins the easternmost tip of Cuba, where day breaks 40 minutes before it occurs in Havana. A rugged track descends from La Máquina to the lighthouse, 12 kilometers away. You have reached land's end, 1,280 kilometers from Havana.

Access to La Máquina is closed to foreigners; military checkpoints on the east side of the Río Yumurí and east of Cajobabo bar the way. However, guided group tours can be arranged through **Havanatur** (Calle Marti #202 e/ Céspedes y Galano, tel. 021/64-5358, laffita@ havanatur.cu), in Baracoa.

BACKGROUND

The Land

Cuba lies at the western end of the Greater Antilles group of Caribbean islands, which began to heave from the sea about 150 million years ago. Curling east and south like a shepherd's crook are the much younger and smaller mostly volcanic Lesser Antilles, which bear little resemblance to their larger neighbor.

Cuba is by far the largest of the Caribbean islands at 110,860 square kilometers. It is only slightly smaller than the state of Louisiana and half the size of the United Kingdom. It sits just south of the Tropic of Cancer at the eastern perimeter of the Gulf of Mexico, 150 kilometers south of Key West, Florida, 140 kilometers north of Jamaica, and 210 kilometers east of Mexico's Yucatán Peninsula. It is separated from Hispaniola to the east by the narrow, 77-kilometer-wide Windward Passage.

Cuba is actually an archipelago with some 4,000-plus islands and cays dominated by the main island (104,945 square kilometers), which is 1,250 kilometers long—from Cabo de San Antonio in the west to Punta Maisí in the east—and between 31 and 193 kilometers wide. Plains cover almost two-thirds of the island. Indeed, Cuba is the *least* mountainous of the Greater Antilles, with a median elevation of less than 100 meters above sea level.

Slung beneath the mainland's underbelly is Isla de la Juventud (2,200 square kilometers),

© CHRISTOPHER P. BAKER

CUBA'S VITAL STATISTICS

Area: 110,860 square kilometers (42,804 square miles)
Population: 11,240,000 (2008 est.)
Annual Population Growth: 0.33 percent
Urbanization: 75.9 percent
Capital: Havana, pop. 2,200,000
Principal Cities: Camagüey, pop. 740,000; Ciego de Ávila, 365,000; Cienfuegos, 370,000; Guantánamo, 495,000; Holguín, 985,000; Las Tunas, 420,000; Matanzas, 610,000; Pinar del Río, 695,000; Sancti Spíritus, 435,000; Santa Clara, 810,000; Santiago de Cuba, 990,000
Literacy: 99.8 percent
Life Expectancy: 77.7 years
Annual Birth Rate: 12.03 per 1,000
Mortality Rate: 7.19 per 1,000
Infant Mortality Rate: 6.33 per 1,000

the westernmost of a chain of smaller islands—the Archipiélago de los Canarreos—which extends eastward for 110 kilometers across the Golfo de Batabanó. Farther east, beneath east-central Cuba, is a shoal group of tiny coral cays—the Archipiélago de los Jardines de la Reina—poking up a mere four or five meters from the sapphire sea. The central north coast is rimmed by a necklace of coral jewels limned by sand like crushed sugar shelving into bright turquoise shallows, with surf pounding on the reef edge.

TOPOGRAPHY
Cuban Highs

The fecund flatlands are disjoined by three mountain zones, where the air is cool and inviting and the roads dip and rise through very untropical-looking countryside. The westernmost mountains are the slender, low-slung Sierra del Rosario and Sierra de los Órganos, which together constitute the Cordillera de Guaniguanico, forming a backbone along the length of northern Pinar del Río Province. In their midst is the striking Valle de Viñales, a classic karst landscape of limestone formations called *mogotes*.

The Sierra Escambray rises steeply over west-central Cuba, dominating eastern Cienfuegos and southern Villa Clara Provinces.

A third mountain zone, incorporating several adjacent ranges, overshadows the provinces of Granma, Santiago de Cuba, and Guantánamo and spills over into Holguín Province. To the west, the precipitous Sierra Maestra rises steeply from the sea, culminating atop Pico Turquino (1,974 meters), Cuba's highest mountain. To the east are the Cuchillas de Toa, Sierra de Puriscal, and Sierra de Cristal.

Down by the Shore

Cuba has more than 400 beaches in shades of oyster white, chocolate brown, gold, and taupe. The most beautiful line the ocean side of the innumerable coral cays beaded like pearls off the north coast. Most beaches along the south coast can't compare; exceptions include Playa Ancón and Cayo Largo.

The north coast is indented by huge, flask-shaped bays, not least Bahía de Habana, on whose western shores grew Havana.

Rivers

Cuba has over 500 rivers, most of them short, shallow, and unnavigable. The principal river, the 370-kilometer-long Río Cauto, which originates in the Sierra Maestra and flows northwest, is navigable by boat for about 80 kilometers. Most rivers dwindle to trickles in the dry season, then swell to rushing torrents, flooding extensive areas on the plains when the rains come in summer. Cuba is studded with huge artificial reservoirs.

CLIMATE

Cuba lies within the tropics, though its climate—generally hot and moist—is more properly semi- or subtropical. There are

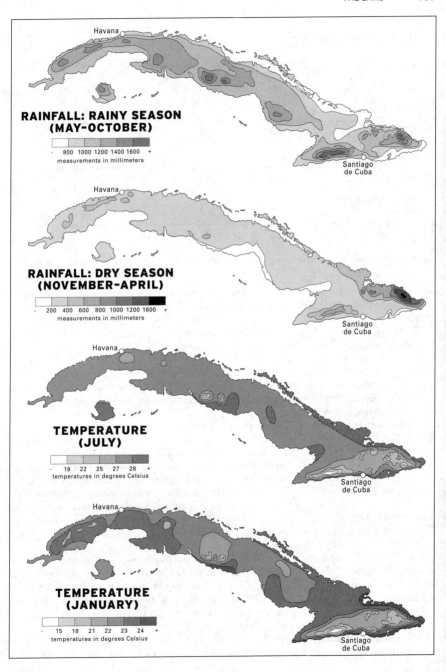

**RAINFALL: RAINY SEASON
(MAY–OCTOBER)**

- 800 1000 1200 1400 1600 +
measurements in millimeters

**RAINFALL: DRY SEASON
(NOVEMBER–APRIL)**

- 200 400 600 800 1000 1200 1600 +
measurements in millimeters

**TEMPERATURE
(JULY)**

- 19 22 25 27 28 +
temperatures in degrees Celsius

**TEMPERATURE
(JANUARY)**

- 15 18 21 22 23 24 +
temperatures in degrees Celsius

Havana

Santiago
de Cuba

CUBA'S CLIMATE

Average temperatures are listed in degrees Celsius.

	Jan.	Feb.	Mar.	April	May	June	July	Aug.	Sept.	Oct.	Nov.	Dec.
National Average												
	26	26	27	29	30	31	32	32	31	29	27	26
Havana												
	22	22.5	23	25	26	27	28	28	27.5	26	24	22.5
DAYS WITH RAINFALL **Havana**												
	6	4	4	4	7	10	9	10	11	11	7	6

only two seasons: wet (May to November) and dry (December to April), with regional variations.

The island is influenced by the warm Gulf Stream currents and by the North Atlantic high-pressure zone that lies northeast of Cuba and gives rise to the near-constant *brisa,* the local name for the trade winds that caress Cuba year-round. Indeed, despite its more southerly latitude, Havana, wrote Ernest Hemingway, "is cooler than most northern cities in those months [July and August], because the northern trades get up about ten o'clock in the morning and blow until about five o'clock the next morning." Summer months, however, can be insufferably hot and humid.

Temperatures

Cuba's mean annual temperature is 25.2°C, with an average of eight hours of sunshine per day throughout the year. There is little seasonal variation, with an average temperature in January of 22°C, rising (along with humidity) to an average of 27.2°C in July. Nonetheless, in summer the temperature can rise to 32°C or more, and far higher in the Oriente, especially the lowlands of Guantánamo Province (the hottest part of

the country). The southern coast is generally hotter than the north coast, which receives the trades. Winds sometimes rip across the central plains in summer, drawn by the rise of hot air off the land.

Midwinter temperatures can fall below 10°C, when severe cold fronts sweep down into the Gulf of Mexico. Atop the higher mountains temperatures may plunge at night to 5°C.

Rainfall

Rain falls on Cuba an average of 85–100 days a year, totaling an annual average of 132 centimeters. Almost two-thirds falls during the May–October wet season, which can be astoundingly humid. Summer rain is most often a series of intermittent showers (or dramatic, short-lived deluges), but downpours and lingering storms are common. Years of relative drought are common.

Central and western regions experience a three- to five-month dry period known as La Seca. February through April and December are the driest months. Nonetheless, heavy winter downpours are associated with cold fronts sweeping south from North America.

The Atlantic coast tends to be slightly rainier than the southern coast. The mountains receive the highest rainfall, especially the uplands of eastern Oriente (up to 400 centimeters fall in the Cuchillas de Toa). The mountains produce regional microclimates, forming rain shadows along the southeast coast, so that pockets of cacti and parched scrub grow in the lee of thick-forested slopes.

Hurricanes

Cuba lies within the hurricane belt. August through October is hurricane season, but freak tropical storms can hit Cuba in other months, too. Most hurricanes that strike Cuba originate in the western Caribbean during October and move north over the island. Cuba has been struck by several hurricanes in recent years. In fact, 2008 was one of the worst years in history, with three direct hits in two months: Gustav came ashore on August 30; Ike blasted the country September 7–9, and Paloma hit on November 8. Gustav and Ike displaced two million people and inflicted an estimated US$8 billion in damage (Cuba turned down the U.S.'s offer of US$6 million in rebuilding supplies).

The country has a highly developed disaster preparedness and exemplary civil defense network for evacuations.

Flora

Cuba's ecosystems tout the most impressive species diversity of any Caribbean island. Despite four centuries of devastating deforestation, extensive tracts remain cloaked in a dozen shades of tropical green. Coastal mangrove and wetland preserves, dry forest, scrubby pine forest, pockets of rainforest and even montane cloud forest, almost desert-dry terrain supporting cacti, and other wild places are strewn like isles within an isle.

Cuba boasts more than 6,700 higher-plant species, of which some 3,180 are endemic and about 950 are endangered.

TREES

Indigenous tree species include mahogany, cedar, pine, rosewood, ebony, lignum vitae, cottonwood, logwood, *majagua,* and the deciduous, silvery *yagruma,* which shimmers as if frosted and bursts forth with huge lily-like blooms. Many species are in short supply following centuries of logging to supply the furniture makers of Europe and to clear the land for King Sugar. The mountain ranges still have ecosystems typical of original Antillean vegetation.

Archetypal species include the swollen baobab, which looks as if it has its roots in the air (for which it is sometimes called the "upside-down tree"), and the silver-trunked *kapok,* or silk-cotton, better known in Cuba as the revered *ceiba* (*Ceiba pentandra*), with broad trunk and wide-spreading boughs. It is considered sacred by adherents of *santería.* Other species are exotics, imports from far-off lands, such as eucalyptus from Australia.

The bully of trees is the *jagüey,* a species of strangler fig. It sprouts from the tops of trees from seeds dropped by birds or bats. It then sends roots to the ground, where they dig into the soil and provide a boost of sustenance. Slowly—it may take a full century—the roots grow and envelop the host tree, choking it until it dies and rots away, leaving the hollow, free-standing fig tree.

There are fruit trees, too, such as the alligator pear tree; the big, dark green *aguacates;* and the *zapote,* whose pulpy red fruit is the queen of Cuban fruits. One of Sierra del Rosario's endemic species, *Psidium guayabita,* produces a berry from which sweet *licor de guayabita* and dry *guayabita seca* brandy are made. Sea grape trims the island's shores, as does the coastal manchineel, whose poisonous sap and tiny apple-like fruits should be avoided.

Palms and large-leafed undergrowth such as the "everlasting plant," whose large leaves form habitats for other plants, give way to ferns, bracken, pine trees, feathery-leafed *palo de cotorra* (parrot tree), and parasitic *conde de pino* (count of the pine) vine. Above 2,000 meters, the vegetation changes abruptly to cloud forest. Some wind-battered elfin woods on exposed ridges are dwarfed, whereas more protected areas have majestically tall trees festooned with bromeliads, lichens, mosses, yellow-flowering *palo de cruz* vines, and all manner of lianas and creepers.

Many trees host epiphytes, arboreal nesters ("epiphyte" comes from the Greek, "upon plants") that attach themselves to tree trunks or branches. The epiphytic environment is a kind of nutrient desert. Thus bromeliads—brilliantly flowering, spiky leafed "air plants" up to 120 centimeters across—have developed tanks or cisterns that hold great quantities of rainwater and decaying detritus in the whorled bases of their stiff, tightly overlapping leaves. The plants gain nourishment from dissolved nutrients in the cisterns. Known as "tank epiphytes," they provide trysting places and homes for tiny aquatic animals high above the ground.

royal palms, Cuba

© CHRISTOPHER P. BAKER

Palms

Visually, the predominant species are the palms, of which Cuba has more than 30 types, including the rare cork palm, found in the western part of Cuba. Those palms with the swollen *lower* trunks are not mutations but *barrigonas,* or belly palms, so named because of their remarkable ability to store water. The coconut palm is severely outnumbered, although it holds its own in northeast Cuba around Baracoa.

The king of palms is the ubiquitous silver-sheathed *Roystonea regia,* the royal palm, which grows singly or in great elegant clumps. Its smooth gray trunk, which can tower 25 meters, resembles a great marble column with a curious bulge near the top. Its fronds (*pencas*) make good thatch, and the thick green base—the *yagua*—of the *penca,* being waterproof, also makes an excellent roof or siding material. The trunk itself makes good timber. Bees favor palm honey. The seeds are used for pig feed.

And birds love its black fruit and carry the seeds (*palmiche*) all over the country. As part of the national emblem, it is protected by law, despite its ability to thrive almost anywhere.

Mangroves

Cuba's shorelines are home to five species of mangrove. Mangroves are halophytes, plants that thrive in salty conditions. Although they do not require salt (in fact they grow better in fresh water), they thrive where no other tree can. These pioneer land builders thrive at the interface of land and sea, forming a stabilizing tangle that fights tidal erosion and reclaims land from the water. The irrepressible, reddish-barked, shrubby mangroves rise from the dark water on interlocking stilt roots. Small brackish streams and labyrinthine creeks wind among them like snakes.

Their sustained health is vital to the health of other marine ecosystems. Cuba's rivers carry silt out of the mountains onto the coastal alluvial plains, where it is trapped by mangroves. The nutrient-rich mud fosters algae and other small organisms that form the base of the marine food chain. A look down into the water reveals luxuriant life: oysters and sponges attached to the roots, small stingrays flapping slowly over the bottom, and tiny fish in schools of tens of thousands. Baby sharks and other juvenile fish spend much of their early lives among mangrove roots, which keep out large predators. High tide brings larger diners—big mangrove snappers and young barracudas hang motionless in the water. Mangrove swamps are esteemed as nurseries of marine life and havens for water birds—cormorants, frigate birds, pelicans, herons, and egrets—which feed and nest here by the thousands, producing guano that makes the mangroves grow faster.

Mangroves build up the soil until they strand themselves high and dry. In the end they die on the land they have created.

FLOWERS AND GARDENS

The forests and grasslands flare with color. Begonias, anthuriums, "Indian laburnum," oleander, and poinsettia are common, as are mimosa, hibiscus, blossoming hydrangea, bright-pink morning glory, and bougainvillea in its rainbow assortment of riotous colors. Trees such as the vermilion flame-of-the-forest, purple jacaranda, blue rosewood, and almost fluorescent yellow *corteza amarilla* all add their seasonal bouquet to the landscape.

Cuba's national flower is the brilliant white, heady-scented *mariposa*, a native species of jasmine that became a symbol of rebellion and purity at the time of the Wars of Independence.

African golden trumpet is found everywhere. Water hyacinths, with their white and purple blooms, crowd freshwater lakes. Scarlet Cupid's tears (*lágrimas de Cupido*) speckle green meadows. Fence posts cut from the piñon tree grow from a stick in the ground and burst into bright-pink efflorescent blossom. And jasmine, orange *jubia d'oro*, and azalea flank major thoroughfares and run down the central divides.

Cuba has several hundred known species of orchids, and countless others await discovery. At any time of year dozens of species are in bloom, from sea level to the highest reaches of the Sierra Maestra. Poke around with magnifying glass in hand and you'll come across species with flowers less than one millimeter across. Others have pendulous petals that can reach more than half a meter. Some flower for only one day. Others will last several weeks. The greatest diversity exists in humid midelevation environments, where they are abundant as tropical epiphytes, although not all orchids lead epiphytic lives.

Fauna

The majority of Cuba's fauna species are invertebrates (mostly insects), with a great many species endemic to specific regions. Unique species and subspecies include the world's smallest frog (*Sminthillus limbatus*) and smallest bird (the bee hummingbird, or *zunzuncito*); an endemic crocodile species; and unique, beautifully colored snails of the genus *Polymita*.

BIRDS

Cuba has 354 recorded species of birds, of which 149 species breed on the island and 21 are native to Cuba. Birds that have all but disappeared in other areas still find tenuous safety in protected pockets of Cuba, although some 37 species are listed as threatened due to habitat destruction, pesticide pollution, and hunting (a popular Cuban pastime).

Cuba is a major stopover for migratory waterfowl. Spoonbills and flamingos are also common on the cays and coastal lagoons. White egrets (*coco blanco*) are found around cane fields and water flats, and their cousins the ibis (*coco negro*) and blue heron (*garza*) can be seen picking at a buffet that extends for miles. Frigate birds, with their long scimitar wings and forked tails, hang like sinister kites in the wind. *Gaviotas,* or gulls, also prefer maritime regions, as does the *gincho* (the sea osprey).

Of terrestrial species, the wood stork can be seen in scrub areas, also favored by the *cararia,* a relative of the Senegalese snakebird. Tanagers and woodpeckers brighten the forests. Listen at night for the hoot of the barn owl and pygmy owls. The *tocororo* (a member of the trogon family) is the national bird, perhaps because its brilliant blue, white, and red plumage copies the colors of the national flag. It wears a scarlet sash across its breast. Listen for its tell-tale call: *có-co-có-co-có-có.*

There were so many parrots and macaws in the New World 500 years ago that the Americas were shown on maps as Terra Psittacorum, land of the free parrot. Even Columbus took as a pet a Cuban parrot. These are now on the road to extinction (the Cuban macaw became extinct in the 19th century). The best place to spot parrots is the Los Indios forest reserve on Isla de la Juventud, inhabited by 153 species of birds, including the Cuban *grulla* or sand-bill crane.

Cuba also has three species of hummingbirds, whose magnificent emerald and purple liveries shimmer iridescent in the sunlight as they sip nectar from the blooms and twirl in midair, their wings a filmy blur. Hummers earned a place in the mythology of the Taíno, who called them *colibrí,* meaning "god bird." They symbolized rebirth, since the Indians believed that the creature died when the weather turned dry and was born again when the rains came. They worshipped the bird as a *zemi,* a fetish idol.

One of Cuba's hummingbirds is the smallest bird in the world: the bee hummingbird or *zunzuncito,* also called the *pájaro mosca*—fly bird—for its diminutive size. It weighs less than a penny.

AMPHIBIANS AND REPTILES

The most common reptiles you'll see are any of 46 lizard species, especially the bright green *lagartilla* lizard with its vermilion wattle, the comical curly-tailed lizard, and geckos. Dragonlike iguanas, which can grow to two meters in length, can be seen on the cays crawling through moist deciduous forest leaf litter or basking on branches that hang over water—its preferred route of escape when threatened. Its head is crested with a frightening wig of leathery spines, its heavy body encased in a scaly hide, deeply wrinkled around the sockets of its muscular legs. Despite its menacing *One Million Years B.C.* appearance, it is a nonbelligerent vegetarian.

Aquatic turtles (terrapins) are also common, particularly in the Zapata Peninsula.

The amphibians are primarily represented by the frogs and toads, most of which you're probably more likely to hear than to see. Spelunkers might spot the axolotl, a blind, albino cave-dwelling newt.

Cuba is also home to 14 species of neotropical snakes. None is venomous. Among the more common snake species are the wide-ranging boas. The *majá,* or Cuban boa, can grow to four meters in length and proves adept at slithering up trees. Its converse is the 20-centimeter-long pygmy boa, found solely in the caves of the Valle de Viñales.

Crocodiles and Caimans

The speckled caiman is common in lowland wetlands and can grow to more than two meters long. Another species, the nonnative caiman or *babilla,* is found on the Isla de la Juventud. Its scales take on the blue-green color of the water it slithers through.

The endemic yellow and black *Crocodylus rhombifer* is found only in the Zapata Peninsula but is being reintroduced to the Lanier swamps, Río Cuato estuary, and other native areas. The crocodile was hunted to near extinction during colonial days and today has the most restricted geographical range of any crocodile species in the world. *Lagarto criollo* (as the Cuban croc is colloquially known) is much more aggressive than its cousin, the American crocodile, which inhabits many of the estuaries and coastal mangroves around the island and which interbred with the Cuban crocodile. Since the Revolution, Cuba has had an active and highly successful breeding program to save

© CHRISTOPHER P. BAKER

Cuban crocodile

the indigenous species. Today the population is abundant and healthy (about 6,000 exist in the wild). In 1995, the Cuban government was authorized by the Convention of International Trade in Endangered Species to market the skins of the animals worldwide to be turned into shoes and handbags, with the money to be plowed back into conservation—only crocs in the captive-breeding program are culled.

The creatures, which can live 80 years or more, spend much of their days basking on mud banks. At night, they sink down into the river for the hunt. While the American species is a fish eater, the omnivorous Cuban crocodile occasionally likes meat—wild boars, deer, unsuspecting anglers. Crocs cannot chew. They simply snap, tear, and swallow. Powerful stomach acids dissolve everything. A horrible way to go!

Marine Turtles

Marine turtles, notably the hawksbill and, to a lesser degree, the green, nest on Cuban beaches, mostly on Isla de la Juventud and southern cays. Most of the important nesting sites in Cuba are now protected, and access to some is restricted. Despite legislation outlawing the taking of turtle eggs or disturbance of nesting turtles, however, adult turtles continue to be captured for meat by Cuban fishermen. Hawksbills are also hunted illegally in Cuba (which lobbies to reopen international trade in hawksbill shell products) for the tourist trade—one often sees stuffed turtle specimens for sale, and shells are used in jewelry and ornaments.

Of the hundreds of eggs laid by a female in one season, only a handful survive to maturity. Cayo Largo has Cuba's only turtle farm.

FISH AND SHELLFISH

The warm waters off Cuba's coast are populated by more than 900 species of fish and crustaceans—from octopus, crabs, turtles, and lobsters the size of house cats to sharks, tuna, and their cousins the billfish, which aerodynamically approach swimming perfection. The sailfish (a type of billfish) has been timed swimming over short distances at 110 kilometers per hour—faster than the cheetah. Unlike other fish, they are also warm-blooded, with temperatures considerably higher than those of the water around them.

The lucky diver may also spot whale sharks (the largest fish in the world) and manta rays up to seven meters across.

Fish to avoid include the fatally toxic and heavily camouflaged stonefish and the beautiful orange-and-white-striped lionfish, whose long spines can inflict a killer sting. The bulbous puffer, which can blow itself up to the size of a baseball, is also poisonous. Jellyfish are common, too, including the lethal Portuguese man-o'-war. And don't go probing around inside coral, where moray eels make their home—their bite can take your fingers off.

Inland, the waters of Zapata harbor the rare *manjuarí,* the Cuban "alligator gar" (*Atractosteus tristoechus*), a living fossil.

Coral Reefs

Coral reefs—the most complex and variable community of organisms in the world—rim much of Cuba at a distance of usually no more than one kilometer offshore. The reefs are an aquatic version of the Hanging Gardens of Babylon. On the sea floor sit the massive brain corals and the delicate, branching sea fans and feathers; nearer the surface are elkhorn corals, frond-like gorgonians spreading their fingers upward toward the light, lacy outcrops of tubipora like delicately woven Spanish mantillas, and soft flowering corals swaying to the rhythms of the ocean currents.

Corals are animals that secrete calcium carbonate. Each individual soft-bodied coral polyp resembles a small sea anemone and is surrounded by an intricately structured calyx of calcium carbonate, an external skeleton that is built upon and multiplied over thousands of generations to form fabulous and massive reef structures. Though stinging cells protect it against some predators, coral is perennially gnawed away by fish, surviving by its ability to repair itself and at the same time provide both habitat and food for other fauna.

MAMMALS

Given the diversity of Cuba's ecosystems, it may come as a surprise that only a few dozen mammal species live here, half of them bats. Wild boar (*jabalí*) are common in many wild regions, including the cays of Jardines de la Rey, the Lanier swamps of Isla de la Juventud,

and the Península de Guanahacibibes, all areas where a small species of deer is also found.

Much of the wildlife is glimpsed only as shadows, such as the *jutía* (*Capromyys*), a large forest rodent related to the guinea pig and coypu of South America. It is edible and has been hunted for meat since indigenous times. Today it is endangered though found island-wide. A well-known indigenous animal that you are *not* likely to see is the solenodon, a rare and primitive insectivorous mammal. The solenodon was thought to have become extinct early this century, but a sole female was spotted in the 1970s, prompting creation of a protected reserve in the Cuchillas de Toa mountains. This ratlike mammal (also called the *almiqué*) has large padded feet and claws and a long proboscis good for sucking up ants.

Bats are by far the most numerous mammals: Cuba has 27 species. You may come across them slumbering by day halfway up a tree or roosting in a shed. Most species—like the Cuban flower bat and the giant Jamaican fruit bat, with a wingspan of more than 51 centimeters—are frugivores or insectivores. Weighing in as the smallest bat in the world is Cuba's butterfly bat, also known as the moth bat. There are no vampire bats in Cuba.

Marine Mammals

Cuba, like most neotropical countries, has few marine mammals, though several species of dolphins are common and seven species of whales are occasionally seen in Cuban waters. The West Indian manatee inhabits coastal lagoons. This herbivorous, heavily wrinkled beast looks like a tuskless walrus, with small beady eyes, fleshy lips, and no hind limbs—just a large, flat, spatulate tail. The creature can weigh up to 900 kilograms and reach 4.3 meters in length. Now endangered, only a few remain in the most southerly waters of the United States and isolated pockets of the Caribbean. Zapata, where the animals are legally protected, has one of the few significant populations, and they are often seen off the northeast coast near Baracoa.

INSECTS

With almost 200 identified species of butterflies and moths (at least 28 endemic), Cuba is a lepidopterist's paradise. You can barely stand still for one minute without checking off a dozen dazzling species: the transparent Cuban clear-wing butterfly, metallic gold monarch, delicate black-winged heliconius splashed with bright red and yellow, the scintillating yellow orange-barred sulphur, and huge swallowtails fluttering and diving in a ballet of stupendous color. At dusk the air trills with the sound of cicadas (*cigarras*), while fireflies flit by all a-twinkle with phosphorescence.

Hosts of unfriendly bugs also exist: chiggers, wasps and bees, mosquitoes, and the famous "no-see-ums" (*jejenes*).

Conservation

Cuba is likened by socialists to the setting of Ernest Callenbach's novel *Ecotopia,* about an egalitarian and environmental utopia where the streets are clean, everything is recycled, and nothing is wasted; where there are few cars and lots of bicycles; where electricity is generated from methane from dung; where free health and education services reach the farthest rural outpost; and where city dwellers tend agricultural plots designed to make the island self-sufficient in food and break its traditional dependence on cash crops for export.

Though simplistic, there's truth in this vision. The Cubans are ahead of the times in coping with problems the entire world will eventually face. Indeed, during the Rio Earth Summit in Brazil in 1993, Cuba was one of only two countries worldwide to receive an A+ rating for implementation of sustainable development practices.

Much of the self-congratulatory hype is propagandist rhetoric. Cuba's advances are recent, necessitated by the collapse of the Soviet bloc. The fuel shortage caused Cubans to relinquish their cars in favor of bicycles. Everything from solar power (neglected, despite the perfect climate) to windmills is now being vaunted as alternative energy. Three wind farms were in operation nationwide in 2009, when work on a fourth began; solar panels are also being installed. Meanwhile, most of Cuba's sugar mills are now powered by *bagazo* (waste from cane processing). By necessity, Cuba began to edge away from debilitating farming systems based on massive inputs of pesticides and fertilizers. It initiated sustainable organic farming techniques and soil conservation program, while experiments were undertaken to determine which plants had medicinal value. Herbal medicine is today a linchpin in the nation's besieged health system.

Nonetheless, there is a lack of public education about ecological issues and few qualified personnel to handle them. And despite much-touted environmental laws, Cuba suffers from horrific waste and pollution. (In 1978 the government established the National Committee for the Protection and Conservation of Natural Resources and Environment. It has done a poor job.) Industrial chimneys cast deathly palls over parts of Havana, Moa, and other nickel-processing towns of Holguín Province. The cement works at Mariel smother the town in a thick coat of dust. And heaven knows what cancer statistics can be culled among the workers at the asbestos works at Jatibónico. *Asbestos!* You see it still in construction use everywhere! Then there are the decades-old Yankee automobiles and the Hungarian-made buses that, in Castro's words, "fill the city with exhaust smoke, poisoning everybody. We could draw up statistics on how many people the Hungarian buses kill." In townships nationwide, rivers and streams are polluted like pestilential sewers, which, in many cities, are often broken.

Deforestation and Conservation

When Christopher Columbus arrived in Cuba, more than 90 percent of the island was covered in forest. On the eve of the Revolution, only 14 percent of the land was forested. The revolutionary government undertook a reforestation program in the mid-1960s. Following the collapse of the Soviet bloc, the government announced a second reforestation plan; it claims to have planted 137 million saplings in 2007 alone! Virtually the entire reforestation program, however, is in firs, not diverse species. There is little effort to regenerate primary forest.

Recent engineering projects to promote tourism in the northern cays have been ecological disasters. Construction of the *pedraplén* linking Cayo Coco to mainland Ciego de Ávila Province cut off the flow of tidal waters, to the severe detriment of local ecology. Dynamiting for hotel construction has scared away flocks of flamingos, while previously protected areas are gerrymandered to make way for massive new all-inclusive hotels. Meanwhile, coral reefs have suffered from turbidity from land-generated sediments and by agricultural runoff of poisonous pesticides used in the sugarcane fields.

Although Cuba has had notable success in bringing the Cuban crocodile back from the dead, the Cuban government has shown little concern for international conservation laws.

Cuba campaigns to get sales of hawksbills legalized again internationally. Endangered black coral is the staple of Cuba's jewel industry. And lobsters, conch, and shrimp are becoming endangered in Cuban waters to cater to the tourist market and for export.

National Parks

Cuba officially claims 13 national parks, 23 ecological reserves, 5 nature reserves, 11 fauna refuges, 9 flora reserves, and 17 other protected areas. In addition, UNESCO has declared six regions to be biosphere reserves: Reserva de la Biosfera Sierra del Rosario and Reserva de la Biosfera Península de Guanahacabibes in western Pinar del Río; Reserva de la Biosfera Ciénaga de Zapata in Matanzas; Reserva de la Biosfera Buenavista, in north-central Cuba; and Reserva de la Biosfera Cuchillas del Toa and Reserva de la Biosfera Baconao in eastern Cuba. The **Ministerio de Ciencia, Tecnología y Medio Ambiente** (Ministry of Sciences, Technology, and Environment, or CITMA, www.medioambiente.cu) has responsibility for the environment; its **Agencia de Medio Ambiente** (Environmental Agency, www.ama.cu) administers parks and reserves.

History

Cuba has a sunny geography shadowed by a dark, brooding history. A sound knowledge of the island's history is integral to understanding Cuba today. It is as fascinating a tale of pathos as that of any nation on earth—perhaps keener, suggests Frank Tannebaum, "because nature has been kind to the island."

PRE-COLUMBIAN HISTORY

The aborigines numbered no fewer than 100,000 when Christopher Columbus chanced upon the island in 1492. The Spaniards who claimed the island lent the name Arawaks to the indigenous peoples, but there were several distinct groups that had left the Orinoco basin

of South America and island-hopped their way up Caribbean islands over centuries.

The earliest to arrive were the Gauanajatabeys, hunter-gatherers who lived in the west, in what is now Pinar del Río Province. They were followed by the Ciboneys, who settled along the south coast, where they established themselves as farmers and fishermen. Little is known of these pre-Ceramic peoples (3500 B.C.–A.D. 1200). The pre-Ceramic tribes were displaced by the Taíno, who first arrived from Hispaniola around A.D. 1100 and, in a second wave, in the mid-15th century, when they were driven from their homeland on Hispaniola by the barbarous Caribs.

A Peaceable Culture

The Taíno lived in *bohíos,* thatched circular huts. Villages, which allied with one another, consisted of 15 or so families who shared property and were governed by a *cacique,* or clan leader. Since the land produced everything, the indigenous peoples were able to live well and peaceably. The indigenous peoples culled fish from the rivers (often using *guaicán,* or sucker fish, tethered on lines to bait larger fish) and birds from the trees, which also produced tropical fruits and nuts in abundance. The Taíno also used advanced farming techniques to maximize yields of yucca (also called manioc) and corn (*mahis,* or maize).

Although they went naked, the Taíno were skilled weavers who slept in tightly woven cotton nets (a precursor to today's hammocks) strung from poles—the Spaniards would later use native labor to weave sailcloth. They were also skilled potters and boat builders who hewed canoes from huge tree trunks. It seems they had evolved at least basic astronomical charts, painted on the walls of caves.

Columbus "Discovers" Cuba

After making landfall in the Bahamas in 1492 during his first voyage to the New World, Columbus took on indigenous guides and threaded the maze of islets that lay to the southwest. On the evening of October 27, 1492, Columbus first set eyes on Cuba. He voyaged along the north coast for four weeks and finally dropped anchor on November 27, 1492, near today's Gibara.

"They are the best people in the world," Columbus recorded of the Indians, "without knowledge of what is evil; nor do they murder or steal.... All the people show the most singular loving behavior…and are gentle and always laughing." The Spaniards would change that forever.

THE SPANISH TAKE OVER

In 1509 King Ferdinand gave Christopher Columbus's son, Diego, the title of Governor of the Indies with the duty to organize an exploratory expedition led by Diego Velázquez de Cuellar (1465–1524). In 1511 four ships from Spain arrived carrying 300 settlers under Diego Columbus and his wife, María de Toledo (grandniece of King Ferdinand). Also on board was tall, portly, blond Velázquez, the new governor of Cuba, and his secretary, young Hernán Cortés (1485–1547), who later set sail from Havana for Mexico to subdue the Aztecs.

Velázquez founded the first town at Baracoa in 1512, followed within the next few years by six other crude *villas*—Bayamo, Puerto Príncipe (today's Camagüey), San Cristóbal de la Habana, Sancti Spíritus, Santiago de Cuba, and Trinidad—whose mud streets would eventually be paved with cobblestones shipped from Europe as ballast.

A Sordid Beginning

The Spaniards were not on a holy mission. The Spaniards had set out in quest of spices, gold, and rich civilizations. Thus the indigenous island cultures—considered by the Spaniards to be a backward, godless race—were subjected to the Spaniards' ruthless and mostly fruitless quest for silver and gold. A priest named Bartolomé de las Casas (1474–1566) accompanied Velázquez and recorded in his *History of the Indies:*

> The Indians came to meete us, and to receive us with victuals, and delicate cheere… the Devill put himselfe into the Spaniards, to put them all to the edge of the sword in my presence, without any cause whatsoever, more than three thousand soules, which were set before us, men, women and children. I saw there so great cruelties, that never any man living either have or shall see the like.

Slavery was forbidden by papal edict, but the ingenious Spaniards immediately found a way around the prohibition. Spain parceled its new conquests among the conquistadores. The Indians were turned into *peones*—serfs under the guise of being taught Christianity.

Each landowner was allotted from 40 to 200 Indian laborers under a system known as the *encomienda*, from the verb "to entrust." Those Indians not marched off to work in mineral mines were rounded up and placed on plantations. Since the Indians were supposed to be freed once converted, they were literally worked to death to extract the maximum labor.

The Indian resistance was led by Hatuey, an Indian chieftain who had fought the Spanish on the island of Hispaniola and fled to Cuba after his people were defeated. Eventually the Spaniards captured the heroic Indian chief and burned him at the stake on February 2, 1512. Thus the Spaniards, in their inimically cruel fashion, provided Cuba with its first martyr to independence.

The 16th century witnessed the extinction of a race. Those Taíno not put to the sword or worked to death fell victim to exotic diseases. Measles, smallpox, and tuberculosis also cut down the Taínos like a scythe. They had no natural resistance to European diseases. Within 100 years of Columbus's landfall, virtually the entire indigenous Cuban population had perished.

The Key to the New World

The Spanish found little silver and gold in Cuba. They had greater luck in Mexico and Peru, whose indigenous cultures flaunted vast quantities of precious metals and jewels. Cuba was set to become a vital stopover for Spanish galleons and traders carrying the wealth of the Americas back to Europe.

In 1564 a Spanish expedition reached the Philippines. The next year it discovered the northern Pacific trade winds that for the next 250 years propelled ships laden with Chinese treasure to Acapulco, from where the booty was carried overland to Veracruz, on the Gulf of Mexico, and loaded onto ships bound for Havana and Europe. Oriental perfumes, pearls, silks, and ivories passed through Havana. To these shipments were added silver from Bolivia, alpaca from Peru, and rare woods from Central America, plus Cuban tobacco, leather, fruit, and its own precious woods. To supply the fleets, the forests were felled, making room for meats, hides, tobacco (and, later, sugar) for sale in Europe.

With the Indian population devastated, the Spanish turned to West Africa to supply its labor. By the turn of the century, an incredibly lucrative slave trade had developed. Landowners, slave traders, merchants, and smugglers were in their heyday—the Spanish Crown heavily taxed exports, which fostered smuggling on a remarkable scale. The Spaniards tried to regulate the slave trade, but it was so profitable that it resisted control.

The Period of Piracy

As early as 1526, a royal decree declared that ships had to travel in convoy to Spain. En route, they gathered in Havana harbor. The crown had a vested interest in protecting the wealth from pirates; it received one-fifth of the treasure. In 1537, Havana itself was raided. One year later, French pirate Jacques de Sores sacked the capital; when a bid by the Spaniards to retake the city faltered, de Sores razed it.

Soon, pirates were encouraged (and eventually licensed) by the governments of France, Holland, and England to prey upon Spanish shipping. In 1587 King Philip of Spain determined to end the growing sea power of England and amassed a great armada to invade her. Sir Francis Drake, John Hawkins, and Sir Walter Raleigh assembled a fleet and destroyed the armada, breaking the power of Spain in the Old World.

Now, no city was safe. There were hundreds of raids every year. Spain was impotent. In 1662, Henry Morgan, a stocky Welshman and leader of the Buccaneers, a motley yet disciplined group of pirates that would later operate under British license from Port Royal in Jamaica, ransacked Havana, pilfered the cathedral bells, and left with a taunt that the Spanish weren't equal to the stone walls that Spain had built: "I could have defended Morro Castle with a dog and a gun."

The Spanish Crown treated Cuba as a cash cow to milk dry as it pleased. For example, it had monopolized tobacco trading by 1717. The restriction so affected farmers' incomes that the *vegueros* (tobacco growers) marched on Havana. The rebellion, the first against Spain, was brutally crushed. In 1740, Spain created the Real Compañía, with a monopoly on all trade between Cuba and Spain. It bought Cuban products cheaply and sold necessities from Europe at inflated prices.

England Takes Over

On January 4, 1762, George III of England declared war on Spain. On June 7, a British fleet of 200 warships carrying 11,000 troops put ashore and Havana erupted in panic. The Spanish scuttled three ships in the harbor mouth, ineptly trapping their own warships inside the harbor. That night, when Spanish guards atop the Cabaña began firing at British scouts, the Spanish warships began blasting the ridge, causing their own troops to flee. The British took the ridge and laid siege to Havana. On July 29 sappers blew an enormous hole in the Castillo de Morro, and the flag of St. George was raised over the city.

The English immediately lifted Spain's trade restrictions. Foreign merchants flocked, and Cuba witnessed surging prosperity. Jamaican sugar planters, however, pressured England to cede back to Spain what would otherwise become a formidable rival for the English sugar market. On February 10, 1763, England exchanged Cuba for Florida in the Treaty of Paris. In the interim, Spain had acquired a more enlightened king, Charles III, who continued the free-trade policy. The boom continued, encouraged a decade later when the United States began trading directly with Cuba.

KING SUGAR RULES

North Americans' collective sweet tooth fostered the rapid expansion of sugar plantations in Cuba. Wealthy Cuban and U.S. slave merchants funded planting of new lands by granting loans for capital improvements, all meant to foster an increasing need for slaves. Land planted in sugar multiplied more than tenfold by the end of the 18th century and was boosted with the Saint Domingue (Haiti) rebellion in

1791. About 30,000 French planters washed up in Cuba, bringing their superior knowledge of sugar production.

These events sent the slave trade soaring. In 1713, the Treaty of Utrecht, which ended the War of the Spanish Succession, had granted the British sole rights to the Spanish-American slave trade. The trade grew throughout the century: As many as 200 slaving ships called into Havana annually during the 1830s. Although in 1817 Spain signed a treaty with England to abolish the trade, Cuban officials were so enriched by bribes that the industry continued unabated. Only in 1888 was slavery in Cuba abolished.

By 1760 Havana was already larger than New York or Boston. The first University of Havana had been established in 1728, the first newspaper in 1763, and the postal service in 1764. Spanish ships unloaded builders and craftsmen, hired to help citizens display their earnings in an outpouring of architectural sophistication. They brought with them a Moorish aesthetic, which they translated into what Juliet Barclay calls a unique "tropical synthesis of column, courtyard, and chiaroscuro." Monuments and parks were erected, along with public libraries and theaters. Streets were paved, and beautiful colonial homes were erected. In 1790 street lamps went up in Havana. While the British went out to their colonies to grow rich and return, the Spanish went to grow rich and stay. They brought a permanence of design and planning to their New World cities that other colonial powers never achieved.

THE REVOLUTIONARY ERA

Spain, however, continued to rule Cuba badly. Spain's colonial policy, applied throughout its empire, was based on exploitation, with power centralized in Madrid, and politics practiced only for the spoils of office and to the benefit solely of *peninsulares*—native-born Spaniards. "The Spanish officials taxed thrift right out of the island; they took industry by the neck and throttled it," thought Frederic Remington on his visit in 1899. Cuban-born *criollos* resented the corrupt *peninsulares* who denied them self-

SLAVE SOCIETY

Black slavery in Cuba began in 1513 with the arrival of slaves from Hispaniola, and it wasn't abolished until 1886. At the peak of the trade, in the 1840s, slaves formed about 45 percent of Cuba's population.

The majority of slaves who were shipped to Cuba came from highly developed West African tribes such as the Fulani, Hausa, and Yoruba. They came mostly from Senegal, Gambia, and Guinea at first, and later from Nigeria and the Congo. Distinct ethnic groups were kept together, unlike in North America. As a result, their traditions and languages have been retained and passed down.

After being rounded up and herded to African ports, slaves were loaded onto ships, where they were packed like sardines. Chained together body-to-body in the airless, dark, rancid hold, they wallowed in their own excrement and vomit on the nightmare voyage across the Atlantic. Dozens died. They arrived in Cuba diseased and half-starved. Once ashore, the Africans were sold to plantation owners or to work in grand mansions (only about one-third worked the plantations; most were domestics who lived in the cities). No attention was paid to family relationships. Parents, children, and siblings were torn asunder forever.

Understandably, rebellion was always around the corner. The first slave revolt occurred in 1532 in Oriente. A few years later, Havana was sacked by slaves in the wake of an attack by French pirates. Other slaves fled to the mountains. To track down runaways, the authorities used posses with specially trained hunting dogs. When a slave was caught, it was standard procedure to cut off one ear as a warning to other slaves.

Nonetheless, slaves had the legal right to buy their own and their relatives' freedom. Slaves could keep a percentage of whatever fee their masters charged for hiring them out as labor and apply it toward buying their manumission. Free blacks formed a significant part of Havana's populace: "In no part of the world, where slavery exists, is manumission so frequent as in the island of Cuba," noted Alexander von Humboldt. Once free, they could even own and sell property. Many free blacks set up small businesses or worked as artisans, while women hired out as domestics. Some rose to positions of wealth and prominence, and there evolved a significant slave-owning black middle class. An overseer called the *síndico* existed to ensure that slaves' rights were enjoyed: For example, if a slave wished to change his mas-

determination: No Cuban could occupy a public post, set up an industry or business, bring legal action against a Spaniard, or travel without military permission.

Following the Napoleonic wars in Europe, Spain's New World territories were wracked by wars of independence led by Simón Bolívar. By 1835 only Cuba and Puerto Rico had not gained independence from Spain. Meanwhile, a new generation of young Cuban intellectuals and patriots began to make their voices heard. In 1843, Miguel Tacón became governor. He suppressed patriotic sentiment and executed or exiled leading nationalists. Meanwhile, the island, says historian Louis A. Pérez Jr., "had achieved a level of modernity that far surpassed Spain's, emphasizing the gap between

the Cuban potential and Spanish limitations. Spain could not provide Cuba with what it did not itself possess." Spain clung to its colony with despairing strength and the support of wealthy *criollos* (concentrated in western Cuba), who feared that abolitionist sentiments in Europe would lead to abolition of slavery in Cuba.

Uncle Sam Stirs

Annexation sentiment in the United States had been spawned by the Louisiana Purchase of 1803. The Mississippi River became the main artery of trade, and Cuba's position at the mouth of the Gulf of Mexico took on added strategic importance. Thus in 1808 Thomas Jefferson attempted to purchase Cuba from

ter, the *síndico* could force an owner to grant a slave three days absence to look for one; he could also ask the owner to value the price, after which that sum could not be raised.

Slaves were rarely allowed to marry and raise families. Certain slave owners bred slaves like cattle for sale. Strong males were picked out to mate with the healthiest women, who were expected to produce healthy babies every year. Wet nurses looked after the *criollitos*, who sometimes never saw their parents again. It was common for white men to take a black mistress, and their offspring usually received their freedom. Occasionally, a black mistress would be particularly favored and treated well. There were limits to their upward mobility, as with Cecilia Valdés, the heroine of the eponymous novel by Cirilo Villaverde about a mulatta who cherishes the idea of rising to become accepted by Havana's upper social stratum, but whose ambition ends in a violent denouement.

PLANTATION LIFE

Plantation slaves lived in *barracoons*, which were primitive barracks. They had only mud floors and little ventilation. A hole in the ground served as a communal toilet. The slaves were awakened at 4:30 A.M. By 6 A.M. they were marching in file to the fields, where they worked until sunset. At 8:30 P.M., the silence bell was rung, and everyone had to go to sleep. Slaves stopped working when they reached 60 years of age. Sunday was rest day.

Men were issued sturdy, coarse linen clothes, and the women blouses, skirts, and petticoats. The women also wore gold jewelry and earrings bought from Moorish tinkers who traveled between plantations. Chinese peddlers also made the rounds, selling sesame seed cakes and other items. Small private plots were the slaves' salvation. Here, they could grow vegetables and raise livestock, which they often sold to whites who came out from the villages. Some plantation owners even allowed slaves to visit nearby taverns. All in all, slaves fared better in Cuba than on neighboring islands, and far better than in the United States.

House slaves, while treated poorly, experienced better conditions than slaves in the country. Even so, urban slaves were not spared harsh punishment, which was carried out in public by trained experts.

The most comprehensive account of plantation life is *Autobiography of a Runaway Slave*, by Estefan Montejo, who related his life as a slave and runaway (*cimarron*) in 1963 at the age of 105.

Spain (he was the first of four presidents to do so). John Quincy Adams thought Cuba a fruit that would ripen until it fell into the lap of the United States. Sentiment didn't come into it. By 1848, 40 percent of Cuba's sugar was sold to the U.S. market; manufactures began flowing the other way. Yankees yearned for expanded trade. Thus President James Polk (1845–1849) offered Spain US$100 million for Cuba. President Franklin Pierce (1853–1857) upped the ante to US$130 million. His successor, James Buchanan, tried twice to purchase Cuba for the same price. But Spain wasn't selling.

The American Civil War changed the equation. With slavery in the United States ended, it became impossible for Spain to keep the lid on Cuba. In 1868 the pot boiled over.

The Ten Years War

The planters of western Cuba were determined to forestall the abolition of slavery in Cuba. But the relatively poor, backward, and *criollo* eastern planters had little to lose. Their estates were going bankrupt and falling into the hands of rapacious Havana moneylenders.

On October 10, 1868, a planter named Carlos Manuel de Céspedes freed the slaves on his plantation at La Demajagua, near Manzanillo, in Oriente. Fellow planters rushed to join him, and as the dawn broke over the dewy plantations of Oriente, they raised the *Grito de Yara* (Shout of Yara). Within a week, 1,500 men had flocked to Céspedes's calling (they called themselves the Mambí, after a freedom fighter in Santo Domingo). For the next

10 years Cuba would be roiled by the first war of independence (the Ten Years War, 1868–1878), a bitter war in which white and black *criollos* fought side by side against 100,000 Spanish volunteers shipped from Spain with a virtual carte blanche to terrorize the people of Cuba.

Guerrilla warfare seized the island. Led by two brilliant generals—one a white, General Máximo Gómez, and the other a mulatto, Antonio Maceo—the rebels liberated much of the island and seemed on the verge of victory. However, the movement collapsed, and in 1878 the forces signed the Pact of Zanjón. The rebels were given a general amnesty, and slaves who had fought with the rebels were granted their freedom.

The Cuban economy had been devastated. Huge tracts of land lay abandoned. Amid the chaos, North American investors bought up ravaged sugar plantations and mills at ludicrously low rates. Meanwhile, the Spanish reverted to the same old recipe of tyranny. Independence, the one dignified solution refused the *criollos,* was the cause that united the population of Cuba.

The long, bloody war claimed the lives of 250,000 Cubans and 80,000 Spaniards. At least 100,000 Cubans were forced to flee; their lands were expropriated and given to loyalists. Among those arrested was a teenager named José Martí y Pérez. After a brief imprisonment, the young gifted orator, intellectual, poet, and political leader was exiled to Spain.

Martí's Martyrdom

Following his exile, José Martí traveled to the United States, where he settled. Through his writings and indefatigable spirit he became the acknowledged "intellectual author" of independence. In 1892 he formed the Cuban Revolutionary Party and led the independence movement.

In 1895 Martí joined General Máximo Gómez in the Dominican Republic. Together they sailed to Cuba. On April 11, they landed at Cajobabo at the eastern end of the island. Martí kissed the Cuban soil he had not seen for 16 years. From here, they linked up with the great Cuban general Antonio Maceo and his ragtag army. Together they launched the War of Independence (1895–1898).

Barely one month after returning from exile, Martí martyred himself on May 19, 1895, at the age of 42. His motto was, "To die for the fatherland is to live." Martí's death left Cuba

bust of José Martí

without a spiritual leader. But the Cubans were determined to seize their freedom. Generals Gómez and Maceo led an army of 60,000 the full length of Cuba, smashing Spanish forces en route. Maceo's brilliant tactics earned worldwide acclaim until he was finally killed in battle in December 1896.

After Maceo's death, the struggle degenerated into a destructive guerrilla war of attrition. In a desperate bid to forestall independence, the ruthless Spanish governor, Valeriano Weyler, herded virtually the entire campesino population into concentration camps. The *reconcentración* campaign claimed the lives of 10 percent of Cuba's population. In turn, the rebels torched the sugarcane fields until the conflagration licked at the fringe of Havana.

THE SPANISH-CUBAN-AMERICAN WAR

The ideal of *¡Cuba libre!* (Free Cuba!) had support among the U.S. populace, which saw echoes of its own struggle for independence a century earlier. The public hungered for information about the war. The *New York World* and *New York Journal,* owned by Joseph Pulitzer and William Randolph Hearst respectively, started a race to see which newspaper could first reach one million subscribers. While Hearst's hacks made up stories from Cuba, the magnate himself worked behind the scenes to orchestrate dramatic events. He sent the photographer Frederic Remington to Cuba in anticipation of the United States entering the war. At one point Remington wired Hearst: "There will be no war. I wish to return." Hearst hastily replied: "Please remain. You furnish the pictures and I'll furnish the war."

Remember the *Maine!*

Responding to public pressure, President McKinley sent a warship—the USS *Maine*—to Havana to protect U.S. citizens living there. On February 5, 1898, the ship mysteriously exploded and sank in Havana Harbor, killing 258 people. Evidence suggests this was an accident, but Hearst had his coup and rushed the news out in great red headlines, beating the *World* to the one million mark. He blamed the Spanish, and so did the public. His *New York Journal* coined the phrase "Remember the *Maine,* to hell with Spain." Theodore Roosevelt, then Assistant Secretary of the Navy, also fanned the flames, seeing the venture as "good for the navy." On April 25, 1898, Congress declared war against Spain.

The Cuban general, Máximo Gómez, did not want U.S. troops. His guerrilla army—the Mambí—was on the verge of victory and would have undoubtedly won independence before the close of the century. However, Cuba's freedom fighters soon found themselves forced into the back seat.

The Yanks thought the Cubans a dirty and decrepit lot—most of whom weren't even *white!* Where the Mambí did fight, heroically, their part was dismissed, as at the pivotal engagement at San Juan Hill in Santiago de Cuba, where, on July 1, 1898, a cavalry charge ostensibly led by Theodore Roosevelt sealed the war. In a decisive naval battle on July 3, the U.S. Navy decimated the Spanish fleet as it attempted to escape Santiago harbor. On July 17, Spain surrendered. The Spanish flag was lowered and the Stars and Stripes raised, ending one of the most foolishly run empires in the world. Cuba ended the century as it had begun—under foreign rule.

Uncle Sam Takes Over

Washington "granted" Cuba "independence"—at the end of a short leash. The U.S. military occupation formally began on January 1, 1899, when 15 infantry regiments, one of engineers, and four of artillery arrived to "pacify" Cuba. They would remain for four years. Washington dictated the peace terms embodied in the Treaty of Paris, signed on April 11, 1899. Even the Cuban constitution was written by Washington in 1901, ushering in a period known as the Pseudo-Republic. Rubbing salt in the wound of Cuban sensibilities was a clause called the Platt Amendment, named for Senator Orville H. Platt of Connecticut but written by Elihu Root, Secretary of War. Through it, Uncle Sam acquired the Guantánamo naval

HEROES OF THE WARS OF INDEPENDENCE

CARLOS MANUEL DE CÉSPEDES

Céspedes (1819–1874), known as "Father of Our Country," was a sugar planter in Oriente. As a young and ardent nationalist, he published *Cubana Libre*, the first independent newspaper in Cuba, and was arrested for revolutionary activity. On October 10, 1868, he freed his slaves, enrolled them in an army, and, in an oration known as the *Grito de Yara* (Shout of Yara), declared an open revolt against Spain. Céspedes was named head of the Revolutionary government. When Spanish troops captured Céspedes's son Oscar and offered to spare his life in exchange for the father's surrender, the father claimed that all Cubans were his sons and that he could not trade their freedom for that of one person. His son was promptly shot. In 1873 Céspedes was removed from his position as president of the Republic in a meeting to which no one had bothered to invite him. He was cut down in a hail of bullets a year later – ambushed by the Spanish at San Lorenzo, where he had retreated to await a ship to take him to a life in exile.

CALIXTO GARCÍA

Calixto García Iñiguez (1840–1898) was born in Holguín of a Spanish noble family and rose to become top commander of the rebel army in the Oriente in the Ten Years War (1868–1878), during which he was captured by the Spanish. García attempted suicide rather than be captured, but the bullet miraculously exited his forehead without killing him. He was held under supervision in Spain, where he lived for 15 years. In March 1896, García escaped from Spain and returned to Cuba. As second-in-command of the rebel Mambí army during the War of Independence (1895–1898) he led a brilliant campaign in which his army liberated many Spanish-held cities. His troops participated alongside U.S. troops in the assault on Santiago de Cuba that sealed Cuba's independence from Spain. García and fellow Mambí leaders were barred from the victory ceremony. Nonetheless, García, who died of pneumonia, was buried with full U.S. military honors in Arlington National Cemetery.

MÁXIMO GÓMEZ

Máximo Gómez y Baez (1836–1905) was born in Santo Domingo, Dominican Republic. He joined the Spanish Army in 1856 and commanded Spanish reserve troops in Cuba before switching sides. He was immediately named a general at the outbreak of the Ten Years War

---

base and the right to intervene whenever the United States deemed it necessary.

On May 20, 1902, the U.S. flag was lowered and the lone-star flag of Cuba rose into the sunny sky. "It's not the republic we dreamed of," said Máximo Gómez.

THE PSEUDO-REPUBLIC

The Pseudo-Republic was an era of Yankee colonization and domestic acquiescence. Economically, North America held sway. Politically, Washington called the shots. United States officers who spoke no Spanish, had never lived in a hot country, and had no notion of Spanish or Cuban history and ideals found themselves in charge of a tired, starving people and a devastated land wrecked by war. As Hugh Thomas suggests: "This continuous U.S. presence, benevolent though it often set out to be, paternalistic though it usually was in practice, fatally delayed the achievement of political stability in Cuba."

Nonetheless, the United States pumped millions of dollars into reconstruction. Under General Wood, the U.S. authorities set up schools, started a postal system, established a judiciary and civil service, organized finances, paved roads in cities throughout the nation, and managed to eradicate yellow fever.

The United States installed its first president, Tomás Estrada Palma, who received his salary and instructions directly from Washington. Palma, though reelected in

and rose to become commander-in-chief of the liberation army before retiring to his plantation in the Dominican Republic. He returned to Cuba alongside José Martí on April 11, 1895, as supreme commander of the Army of Liberation. His brilliant guerrilla tactics were instrumental in weakening the Spanish forces that eventually surrendered to U.S. forces in 1898. Prominent Cuban leaders invited Gómez to run for the presidency of the newly independent republic, but he declined. He died in Havana.

ANTONIO MACEO GRAJALES

Maceo (1845-1896), a mulatto of mixed African and Spanish descent, hailed from Santiago and rose from the rank of private to that of a general in the rebel army in the Ten Years War. A brilliant guerrilla strategist, Maceo was known for his whirlwind strikes against superior forces. He fought in over 900 battles and was wounded 24 times, earning the nickname the "Bronze Titan." Maceo also survived a slander campaign by white commanders, who charged him with seeking a "Black Republic." His father died in battle in Maceo's presence, as did two of his brothers, one of whom died in his arms. The fearless leader refused to accept the treaty ending the war in 1878 and fought on for several months until fleeing into exile – his act is known as the Protest of Baraguá. He returned on March 30, 1895, to help lead the War of Independence; as a commander of the Army of Liberation he led an army all the way to Pinar del Río before being killed in battle near Havana on December 7, 1896.

JOSÉ MARTÍ

José Martí (1853-1895) is the single most important person in colonial Cuban history. Martí was born in Habana Vieja and was 15 years old when the Ten Years War erupted, and he sympathized with the nationalist cause. Publishing his first newspaper, La Patria Libre (Free Fatherland), at the age of 16, he became one of the most prolific and accomplished Latin American writers of his day – his writing helped define the school of modern Latin American poetry. He was also the political leader of the independence cause, credited with having "brought the republic to birth." Martí was able to meld exiled factions together and integrated the cause of Cuban exile workers into the crusade. He also founded a revolutionary center, Cuba Libre (Free Cuba), and La Liga de Instrucción, which trained revolutionary fighters.

1905, was too honest and weak to hold greedy politicians in check. Each Cuban president forged new frauds of his own and handed out sinecures (which the Cubans called *botellas*—milk bottles given to babies) to cronies. The U.S. government was constantly influenced to support this or that Cuban who had given, or would give, opportunities to U.S. investors or had borrowed from North American banks. When U.S. economic interests were threatened, Uncle Sam sent in troops—"dollar diplomacy" it was called, a phrase coined by President Howard Taft. The United States landed Marines in 1906, 1912, and 1917. Dollar diplomacy was blind to the corruption, state violence, and poverty plaguing the country.

A U.S. Colony

The opening years of the Cuban republic were a time of great opportunity for everyone except Cubans. Everything was up for grabs. Cuba witnessed a great influx of capital as U.S. companies invested in every major industry—tobacco, railroads, utilities, mining, and, above all, sugar. Several thousand U.S. citizens settled, bringing their North American style and sensibilities to the city. In short order, every major industry was U.S.-owned. U.S. interests in the sugar industry increased almost overnight from 15 percent to 75 percent. Cuba had become a giant Monopoly board controlled by Uncle Sam.

Thanks to billions of dollars of investment, the Cuban economy bounced back with vigor, though the mass of rural families struggled to survive. Although the sugar workers had no other way of earning a living, the sugar companies paid them wages for only half a year. Employment lasted only as long as the dry season, when the downtime began. Most workers and their families lived in squalor and suffered miserably for half the year. (Not all estates were of this model. For example, the Hershey company built modern homes for its Cuban employees and provided clinics, schools, and social services.)

Profits from sugar were so great that Cubans sold out their other properties and poured their money into the industry, deriving dividends from sweetening the desserts of the world. The peak of the sugar boom—the "dance of the millions"—lasted from 1915 to 1920, when the price of sugar climbed to US$0.22 a pound. Then came the crash. In 1924, Cuba produced more than 4.5 million tons of sugar. The next year it produced a million tons more—but the sugar sold for less than US$0.01 a pound.

Sugar money paid for massive civic constructions and public utilities and for the plush mansions in Beaux-Arts and art deco style then blossoming in cities all over Cuba. Havana—jewel of the Caribbean—wore a new luster. Cuba of the 1920s was far and away the richest tropical country anywhere, with a per capita income equivalent to that of Ireland, two-thirds that of Britain, and half that of the United States. As Prohibition and a wave of morality swept through the United States, Yankees flocked to Havana, which, wrote Juliet Barclay, was filled with "milkshakes and mafiosi, hot dogs and whores. Yanqui Doodle had come to town and was having martini-drinking competitions in the Sevilla Bar."

The Machado Epoch

In 1924, President Alfredo Zayas, having made his millions, declined to run for reelection. General Gerardo Machado y Morales (1871–1939) stepped into the breach. Machado acted on his promises to construct schools, highways, and a health care system, and initiated an ambitious development plan for Cuba. However, he was also a uniquely corrupt man susceptible to *la mordida* (literally, "the bite"—bribes), which undercut law and order. In 1928 Machado manipulated a phony election and became a tropical Mussolini, supported by a personal police force of 15,000. His politics were to make himself rich and to protect U.S. investments. His method was to assassinate anyone who opposed his government.

When the Great Depression hit, Cuba's one-crop economy was dealt a death blow, bringing misery throughout the country. The United States raised its import tariffs on sugar, exacerbating Cuba's plight. The Cuban economy collapsed, and the nation disintegrated into violent mayhem. Havana and other cities were swept by random bombings and assassinations. Machado responded to a growing number of hunger marches, strikes, and antigovernment demonstrations with greater repression. President Calvin Coolidge, of course, thought that "under Machado, Cuba is a sovereign state.... Her people are free, independent, in peace, and enjoying the advantages of democracy." Finally, in the summer of 1933, a general strike brought the whole country to a halt. On August 11, Machado fled the country carrying a suitcase full of gold.

Batista Days

Diplomat Sumner Welles, sent to Cuba earlier that summer by Franklin D. Roosevelt, appointed Carlos Manuel de Céspedes (son of the hero of the Ten Years War) as Cuba's provisional president. Within the month he had been overthrown by an amalgam of students and army officers. In short order, a pivotal 32-year-old sergeant named Fulgencio Batista y Zaldivar (1901–1973) led a *golpe* called the Sergeant's Revolt, which ousted the senior officers. (Batista was born out of wedlock and into dire poverty at Veguitas, near Banes, a backyard region of Oriente. His Chinese father was a sugarfield worker; his mother was black.) They handed power to a five-man civilian commission that named a leftist university professor, Dr. Ramón Grau San Martín, president.

Grau lasted only four months. He was far too reformist for Washington. Batista, self-promoted to colonel and chief of the army, was under no illusions as to the intentions of the United States, which sent 30 warships to Cuba as a warning. On January 14, 1934, Batista ousted Grau and seized the reins of power. Batista would have center stage until driven from power in 1959. Impressed by Batista's fealty to Washington, in 1934 the United States agreed to annul the Platt Amendment—with the exception of the clause regarding the Guantánamo naval base. Following promulgation of a new and progressive constitution in 1940, Batista ran for the presidency himself on a liberal platform. Cuban voters gave him a four-year term (1940–1944) in what was perhaps the nation's first clean election.

Batista at first displayed relative benevolence and good sense. He maintained enlightened attitudes on elections, civil liberties, public welfare, and workers' rights, enacted progressive social reforms and a new, liberal constitution. For pragmatic reasons, Batista legalized the Partido Comunista de Cuba, and two leading Communists—Juan Marinello and Carlos Rafael Rodríguez—became ministers in his 1940–1944 government.

In the 1944 election, Batista's hand-picked successor lost to Ramón Grau San Martín, the president Batista had deposed. Batista retired to Florida a wealthy man, leaving his country in the hands of men who permitted their administrations to again sink into chaos. Assassinations and bombings were once again daily events. Two rival gangster groups—the Socialist Revolutionary Movement (MSR) and Insurrectional Revolutionary Union (UIR)—ruled the streets. The public suicide on August 5, 1951, of Senator "Eddy" Chibás, incorruptible head of the Ortodoxo party, brought together a broad spectrum of Cubans fed up with corruption and student gangsterism.

In 1952 Batista again put himself up as a presidential candidate in the forthcoming elections. It soon became clear that he wouldn't win. On March 10, only three months before the election, he upended the process with a bloodless pre-dawn *golpe*. One of the reform-minded candidates for congress whose political ambitions were thwarted by Batista's coup was a dashing young lawyer named Fidel Castro. (In 1952, the 25-year-old lawyer had risen to prominence as the most outspoken critic of corrupt government and was being hailed as a future president.) Harry Truman immediately recognized Batista's regime. Batista had forsaken his interest in the Cuban people. He had lingered too long in Miami with mafiosi and had come back to commit grand larceny hand in hand with the mob.

Batista initiated massive civic construction work that conjured a tourist boom, spurring economic growth and fueling prosperity. As the Batista epoch progressed, however, gangsters began to take over the hotels and casinos with Batista's blessing—for a cut of the proceeds, of course. It wasn't until the mid-1950s that an infusion of foreign capital built Havana's mobster-run Las Vegas–style hotel-casinos, with which prerevolutionary Cuba will always be associated. North Americans arrived by plane or aboard the *City of Havana* ferry from Key West to indulge in a few days of sun and sin. They went home happy, unaware that behind the scenes chaos and corruption were rife.

In November 1954, Batista won the presidential election. Though the elections were rigged, Washington quickly embraced the "constitutional" regime. Batista maintained his cynical rule with a brutal police force. Many Cubans were disgusted by the depth of repression and depravity into which Havana had sunk, made more wretched by the poverty and destitution endemic in the slums of Havana and by the illiteracy and malnourishment that were part of the rural condition. Batista's secret police tortured suspected opposition members and hung them from trees while "militants of Castro's Twenty-Sixth of July Movement placed phosphorous bombs in movie houses, buses, nightclubs, theaters, and parks," says historian Rosalie Schwartz. "The President's regime was creaking dangerously towards its end," wrote Graham Greene in *Our Man in Havana*.

THE GATHERING STORM

Almost immediately following Batista's *golpe,* Fidel Castro began to plot Batista's downfall. Castro possessed a vision of his place in Cuba's future that seemed preordained. He was also ruthlessly focused. His plan: street protests and legal challenges to the Batista regime and a secret conspiracy simmering underneath. He organized the movement and ran it with military discipline. The secret police came to arrest Castro within 24 hours of Batista's coup, forcing him underground.

Washington's continued support of Batista ostensibly revolved around the issue of Communism—an entirely irrelevant question with regard to Cuba. Castro shunned the Communist Party, whose members were excluded from the Movement. Even Castro's Communist brother, Raúl, was kept out for a time. Instead, political instruction centered on the nationalist philosophy of José Martí.

The Attack on Moncada

Castro, then 26 years old, launched his revolution on July 26, 1953, with an attack on the Moncada barracks in Santiago de Cuba. Unfortunately, everything conspired to go wrong the moment the attack began. It quickly collapsed in a hail of bullets. Batista declared a state of emergency. His propaganda machine went to work to convince the nation that the rebels had committed all kinds of atrocities. Unknown to Batista, however, the torture and assassination of 64 rebels who had been captured had been photographed. When the gruesome photos were published, a wave of revulsion swept the land. The Catholic hierarchy stepped in and negotiated a guarantee of the lives of any future captives.

Castro was eventually captured by an army detachment whose commander—a 53-year-old black lieutenant named Pedro Sarría—disobeyed orders to kill Castro on sight (Batista jailed Sarría, who would go on to become a captain in Fidel's Revolutionary Army). Once in Santiago jail, reporters were even allowed to interview Castro—a public relations coup that sowed the seeds of future victory. Amazingly,

Fidel was allowed to broadcast his story over the national radio to demonstrate how subversive he was. "Imagine the imbecility of these people!" Fidel later said, "At that minute, the second phase of the Revolution began."

History Will Absolve Me

Castro, who acted as his own attorney, was sentenced in a sealed court that opened on September 21, 1953. Castro never attempted to defend against the charges leveled at him and his fellow conspirators. He relied solely on attacking Batista's regime, and proudly defended his own actions in a mesmerizing oratory, citing history's precedents for taking up arms against tyrants and ending with the words, "Condemn me, it does not matter. History will absolve me!" (The Moncada attack parallels in many ways Hitler's failed Rathaus Putsch in 1924. Indeed, Castro had studied and memorized *Mein Kampf,* and his "History Will Absolve Me" speech was closely modeled on the words of Adolf Hitler at the end of his Putsch trial, which ended with the words, "You may pronounce us guilty, [but] history will smile.... For she acquits us!")

Castro was cheered as he was led away to serve 15 years in jail on the Isle of Pines (now Isla de la Juventud). José Martí had also been imprisoned on the Isle of Pines, adding to Castro's symbolic association with the original revolutionary hero. Fidel was imprisoned with 25 other companions of the July 26 attack. The media gave wide coverage to Castro, whose stature increased with each day in jail. In May 1955 Batista bowed to mounting public pressure and signed an amnesty bill passed by congress. Castro and the Moncada prisoners were free. Nonetheless, Castro was forced to move constantly for his own safety. On July 7, 1955, he boarded a flight to Mexico.

Castro's Exile

Castro's goal in exile was to prepare a guerrilla army to invade Cuba. Fidel's enthusiasm and optimism were so great that he managed to talk Alberto Bayo, a hero of the Spanish Civil War, into giving up his business to train his nascent army—now known as M-26-7 (Movimiento Revolucionario 26 Julio)—in guerrilla warfare. (One of the foreigners who signed up was Ernesto "Che" Guevara, an Argentinean doctor and intellectual.)

In a brilliant coup, Fidel sent a powerful message to the congress of the Ortodoxo party, in which he called for the 500 delegates to reject working with Batista through congressional elections and to take the high road of revolution. The delegates jumped to their feet chanting "Revolution!" (The Communists continued to shun him—the "objective conditions" defined by Karl Marx didn't exist.) Castro also authored the movement's manifesto, laying out the revolutionary program in detail: "The outlawing of the *latifundia,* distribution of the land among peasant families.... The right of the worker to broad participation in profits.... Drastic decrease in all rents.... Construction by the state of decent housing to shelter the 400,000 families crowded into filthy single rooms, huts, shacks, and tenements.... Extension of electricity to the 2,800,000 persons in our rural and suburban sectors who have none.... Confiscation of all the assets of embezzlers acquired under all past governments. . . ."

Castro's plan called for a long-term war in both countryside and urban areas, although he eschewed random violence against the public. To raise money for the endeavor, he toured the United States, speechmaking to thousands of Cuban exiles and Yankees alike.

The *Granma* Landing

Shortly after midnight on November 25, 1956, Castro and his revolutionaries set off from Tuxpán, Mexico, for Cuba aboard a 38-foot-long luxury cruiser. The *Granma* had been designed to carry 25 passengers. Battered by heavy seas and with a burden of 82 heavily armed men and supplies, the vessel lurched laboriously toward Cuba. One engine failed and the boat slowed, falling two days behind schedule. At dawn on December 2, it ran aground two kilometers south of the planned landing site at Playa Las Coloradas. The men had to

abandon their heavy armaments and supplies and wade ashore through dense mangroves. Two hours later, just after dawn, Fidel Castro stood on terra firma alongside 81 men, with minimal equipment, no food, and no contact with the movement ashore. "This wasn't a landing, it was a shipwreck," Che Guevara later recalled.

Within two hours of landing, *Granma* had been sighted and a bombardment began. On December 5, the exhausted column was ambushed. Only 16 men survived, including Fidel and Raúl Castro and Che Guevara. On December 13, Castro's meager force finally made contact with a peasant member of the 26th of July Movement, and with that, word was out that Fidel had survived. Aided by an efficient communications network and support from the mountain peasants, the rebel unit moved deeper into the mountains and to safety.

THE CUBAN REVOLUTION

Soon men began joining the Rebel Army, mostly idealists keen to help oust a corrupt regime, but many of them, claims Jon Lee Anderson, were "former rustlers, fugitive murderers, juvenile delinquents, and marijuana traffickers." On January 16, Castro's modestly armed force struck an army post. Batista responded with a ruthless campaign against the local populace, while B-26 bombers and P-47 fighter planes supplied by the United States strafed the Sierra Maestra. Batista managed to alienate the peasantry upon whom Castro's forces relied, while the Rebel Army cemented the support of the *guajiros* by assisting with the coffee harvest.

War in the Cities and Countryside

While the Rebel Army nibbled away at its foes in the mountains, a war of attrition spread throughout the countryside and cities. Sugarcane fields were razed; army posts, police stations, and public utilities were destroyed. On March 13, an attack on the presidential palace in Havana by the Students' Revolutionary Directorate failed, and 35 students died in

REVOLUTIONARY HEROES

CAMILO CIENFUEGOS

Camilo Cienfuegos Gorriarán (1932-1959) was born to Spanish anarchists and became a radical student activist against the Batista regime. In 1956 he joined Castro's guerrilla army in Mexico and was a participant in the *Granma* landing. He was named Chief of Staff and established himself as a brilliant commander in Castro's guerrilla army. Cienfuegos's column occupied Havana immediately following the toppling of Batista. Although not a Communist, Cienfuegos was an influential and popular figure in the early Castro regime. In October 1959, Castro sent Cienfuegos to arrest the Camagüeyan rebel commander, Hubert Matos. While returning to Havana on October 28, Cienfuegos's Cessna disappeared under mysterious circumstances.

JULIO ANTONIO MELLA

Julio Antonio Mella (1903-1929) was born in Havana and was educated in the United States and, later, at the University of Havana, where he led Communist-inspired demonstrations that included a student takeover of the university. He founded the University Students Federation and the periodical *Juventud.* Mella also initiated actions against the corrupt Machado regime. In August 1925, Mella co-founded the Cuban Communist Party and the Anti-Imperialist League of the Americas. He was expelled from the university and later imprisoned. In 1926 he was exiled to Mexico. He became embroiled in infighting within the Mexican Communist Party and was assassinated in 1929.

FRANK PAÍS

Frank País (1935-1958) was born in Santiago de Cuba and became a student activist at the University of Santiago, where he founded the anti-Batista Movimiento Nacional Revolucionario. Later he merged his MNR with Castro's M-26-7 movement, becoming the movement's principal leader in Oriente. País was named head of Cuban-based revolutionary activities during Castro's absence in Mexico. He led the ill-fated attack on the police headquarters in Santiago on November 30, 1956, timed to coincide with the *Granma* landing. País led reprisal assassinations of Batista henchmen. His young

the attack. Castro, far off in the mountains of Oriente, increasingly found himself in a battle for revolutionary leadership with the movement's urban wings and on July 12 committed himself to "free, democratic elections" to assuage the growing leadership crisis.

Castro also affirmed the movement's choice of a respected liberal judge, Manuel Urrutia Lleó, to head a provisional government after Batista's fall. Urrutia promptly left for exile in the United States, where he was instrumental in Eisenhower's pledge to stop arming Batista. However, Washington kept shipping arms secretly (including napalm, which was used to bomb peasant villages) and even re-armed Batista's warplanes at Guantánamo naval base.

Finally Batista decided to launch an all-out offensive in the Sierra Maestra with 10,000 men—Operation FF (Fin de Fidel).

The *fidelistas,* however, beat back the 76-day offensive and even captured two tanks and huge quantities of modern weapons. Radio Rebelde broadcast the victories to the rest of the nation from La Plata, Castro's secret headquarters.

In July Castro and eight leading opposition groups signed an agreement to create a civic coalition. The writing now on the wall, Washington began negotiations with Castro while maneuvering to keep him from power. (Meanwhile, the CIA was channeling funds—at least US$50,000 was delivered between November 1957 and mid-1958—to Castro's movement. The top-secret operation remains classified by the U.S. government.) In September, Castro led an offensive to take Santiago de Cuba. On December 30, Che Guevara captured Santa Clara. The scent of victory was in the air.

brother José was killed by Batista's police in June 1957; Frank was assassinated by agents one month later.

CELIA SÁNCHEZ

Celia Sánchez Manduley (1920-1980) was born in Media Luna, Oriente, and at an early age became a dedicated anti-Batista revolutionary. Later, as a leader in Castro's 26th of July Movement, she set up and ran the networks that smuggled men and munitions to Castro's Rebel Army in the mountains. She also saw combat at the Battle of Uvero. Sánchez was 36 years old when she met Fidel for the first time, on February 16, 1957. She became his secretary and, some say, his lover. For many years she was the most important person in Fidel Castro's life and held various important positions in the Castro government. Celia was his compass and kept Fidel in touch with the people; she helped balance and minimize Fidel's absolutist side and was one of only a handful of people who could give him news and opinions he didn't want to hear. Her death from cancer in January 1980 profoundly shook Castro and removed from his life the only person with whom he could truly relax.

ABEL AND HAYDEE SANTAMARÍA

Brother and sister Abel (1925-1953) and Haydee (1931-1980) Santamaría were born in Havana and were early participants in the efforts to oust Batista. A confidante of Fidel Castro, and his designated successor in the revolutionary movement, Abel Santamaría helped organize the attack on the Moncada barracks. He led a contingent that captured the hospital across the street. Santamaría and his men continued to snipe at the barracks, unaware that the attack had failed. Batista's troops stormed the hospital, where Santamaría and his men had taken to bed, pretending to be patients (Haydee was also one of the attackers and pretended to be a nurse). They were betrayed and ruthlessly tortured: Haydee's fiancé, Boris Luis, was beaten to death on the spot, and Abel died later that day. Following the Revolution, Haydee became head of the Casa de las Américas. She committed suicide in 1980.

The Revolution Triumphs

Washington persuaded Batista to hand over power to a civilian-military junta. At midnight on New Year's Eve 1958, Batista and his closest supporters boarded a plane for the Dominican Republic. (Batista settled in Spain, where he lived a princely life until his death in 1973. The poor cane cutter died as one of the world's wealthiest men—he had milked Cuba of almost US$300 million.) On January 2, the same day that the rebel armies of Camilo Cienfuegos and Che Guevara entered Havana, Castro's army took over Santiago de Cuba. That night he delivered a televised victory speech and the following day the triumphant guerrilla army began a five-day victory march to Havana, with crowds cheering Castro atop a tank, all of it televised to the nation.

Castro was intent from day one on turning the old social order upside down. Fidel moved cautiously but vigorously to solidify his power under the guise of establishing a pluralist democracy, but his aim was clear. Although Manuel Urrutia had been named president and an unusually gifted coalition cabinet had been formed (the U.S. government recognized Urrutia's government on January 4, 1959), Castro—the real power-holder—set up a parallel government behind the scenes. He began secretly negotiating with the Communists to co-opt them and build a Marxist-Leninist edifice (many of his wartime *compadres* who resigned over this issue were jailed for treason).

Castro recognized that the Cuban people were not yet ready for Communism; first he had to prepare public opinion. He also had to avoid antagonizing the United States. Castro manipulated Urrutia by getting himself named prime minister with power to direct government policy. Speaking before large crowds, he molded and radicalized the public mood as a tool to pressure the Urrutia government, which he repeated must obey "the will of the people." Meanwhile, hundreds of Batista supporters and "enemies of the Revolution" were dispatched following summary trials. The executions, presided over by Che Guevara, were halted after international protests.

Uncle Sam Responds

Castro—determined to assert Cuba's total independence—feared the possibility that U.S. Marines would steal his revolution as they had stolen independence at the end of the Spanish-Cuban-American War in 1898. Just as Washington became obsessed with the Communist issue without understanding or taking into account Cuban nationalism, Castro allowed himself to become obsessed with the United States and its Plattist mentality. An antagonistic relationship between a Castroite Cuba and the United States was inevitable. History ordained it. The Revolution was born when the east–west struggle for power was at its zenith. There was no way Uncle Sam could tolerate a left-leaning revolution beyond its control only 90 miles from Florida, especially one that was aligning itself with America's principal enemy.

In March 1959, Castro visited the United States. Vice President Nixon met with him and badly misread the Cuban leader—he considered Castro to be controlled by the Communists. Castro disingenuously promised not to expropriate foreign-owned property and affirmed that elections would *follow* "democracy," which he publicly defined as when all Cubans were employed, well fed, well educated, and healthy. "Real democracy is not possible for hungry people," he said.

Let the Reforms Begin!

On March 6, 1959, all rents in Cuba were reduced by 50 percent. Two months later, Cuba enacted an Agrarian Reform Law acclaimed, at the time, by the U.N. as "an example to follow." Large sugar estates and cattle ranches were seized without compensation by Castro's National Institute of Agrarian Reform, or INRA, headed by the Rebel Army. The agrarian reform significantly upped the ante in the tensions between Cuba and Washington and established a still unresolved grievance: nonpayment for illegally seized land (over time, all claims by Spanish, British, French, Canadian, and Dutch owners were settled).

Understandably, Miami received a flood of unhappy exiles. At first, these were composed of corrupt elements, from pimps to political hacks escaping prosecution. As the reforms extended to affect the upper and middle classes, they, too, began to make the 90-mile journey to Florida. The trickle turned into a flood, including about 14,000 children sent to Miami by their parents in the Operation Peter Pan airlift (1960–1962). About 250,000 Cubans left by 1963, most of them white, urban professionals—doctors, teachers, engineers, technicians, businesspeople, and others with entrepreneurial skills. As Castro's Revolution turned blatantly Communist and authoritarian, many of his revolutionary cohorts also began to desert him. Later, intellectuals and homosexuals joined the flood. (Those who were forced to leave Cuba had to leave their possessions behind. Their houses were confiscated ("donated to the Revolution" is the official verbiage) and divvied up to loyal *fidelistas* and citizens in need of housing, while others became schools, medical facilities, and social centers.

On July 13, 1959, President Urrutia denounced the growing Communist trend. Castro resigned as prime minister, then played a brilliant gambit. Castro had arranged for peasants to be brought to Havana from all over Cuba to celebrate the anniversary of the attack on Moncada. Castro appeared on television and denounced Urrutia. The streets of Havana erupted in calls for the president's resignation and pleas for Castro's return. Urrutia was forced to resign. Castro had carried out the world's first coup d'état by TV!

Into Soviet Orbit

Castro had decided on a profound new relationship. He knew, wrote Lee Anderson, "if he was

"Patriotism or Death" billboard

ever to govern as he saw fit and achieve a genuine national liberation for Cuba, he was going to have to sever [U.S. relations] completely." To the Kremlin, Cuba seemed like a perfect strategic asset, so Castro and Khrushchev signed a pact. Ever fearful of a U.S. invasion and unsure as yet of the depth of Soviet assistance, Castro initiated a massive militia-training program, while emissaries began to purchase arms overseas. The first shipment arrived from Belgium on March 4, 1960, aboard the French ship *Le Coubre.* One week later, the steamship exploded in Havana Harbor, killing 80 Cubans. One school supports Castro's contention that the CIA was responsible; another school believes Castro may have arranged the bombing. Whatever the truth, the event managed to rally the Cuban people around Castro at a time when he was facing increasing opposition at home. During the funeral ceremony for the victims, Castro uttered the rallying cry that would later become the Revolution's supreme motto: *¡Patria o muerte!* (Patriotism or death!). Recalls Nobel Laureate Gabriel García Márquez: "The level of social saturation was so great that there was not a place or a moment

when you did not come across that rallying cry of anger.... And it was repeated endlessly for days and months on radio and television stations until it was incorporated into the very essence of Cuban life."

When Soviet oil began to arrive in May 1960, U.S.-owned refineries refused to refine it. In response, the Cuban government took over the refineries. In July, President Eisenhower refused to honor a purchase agreement for Cuban sugar. Cuba's biggest market for virtually its entire source of income had slammed the door. Washington couldn't have played more perfectly into the hands of Castro and the Soviet Union, which happily announced that it would purchase the entire Cuban sugar stock. Hit with Eisenhower's right cross, Castro replied with a left hook: he nationalized *all* Yankee property. In October the Eisenhower administration banned exports to Cuba. In January 1961 the Kennedy administration broke diplomatic ties with Cuba; in March Kennedy extended the embargo to include Cuban imports—the beginning of a trade embargo that is still in effect. Kennedy pressured Latin American governments to

THE U.S. EMBARGO

Since the 1960s, Washington has clamped a strict trade embargo on Cuba in the expectation that economic distress would oust Castro or at least moderate his behavior. Since 1996 the U.S. embargo has been embodied in law (heretofore it was an executive order). Here's what Uncle Sam says the embargo, enacted on February 3, 1962, by President Kennedy, is about:

> The fundamental goal of U.S. policy toward Cuba is to promote a peaceful transition to a stable, democratic form of government and respect for human rights. Our policy has two fundamental components: maintaining pressure on the Cuban Government for change through the embargo and the Libertad Act while providing humanitarian assistance to the Cuban people, and working to aid the development of civil society in the country.

Critics call it a violation of international law that injures and threatens the welfare of Cuban people. The United Nations General Assembly routinely votes to condemn it (the 2009 vote was 187-3, with only Palau and Israel – which trades with Cuba – joining the United States in voting against the resolution).

Uncle Sam even fines *foreign* companies doing business with Cuba. Talk about shooting oneself in the foot! For example, when Hilton and Sheraton hotels worldwide were banned from accepting Cuban trade delegations, European unions and parliamentarians initiated a boycott of the hotel chains, while the Mexican government even fined Sheraton US$100,000 for expelling Cuban guests in violation of international law. Meanwhile, the ultimate irony and hypocrisy is that although no Cuban goods can be sold to the United States, the U.S. *does* permit sales of "agricultural" and certain other goods to Cuba under a waiver that runs from daiquiri mix to rolls of newsprint (even the Communist rag, *Granma*, is printed on paper from Alabama), to the tune of US$718 million in 2008!

The effects of the embargo (which Castro calls *el bloqueo*, or blockade) are much debated. In 1999, Cuba filed a claim for US$181 billion in reparations. However, in 2000, the International Trade Commission (ITC) determined that the embargo has had a minimal impact on the Cuban economy, citing domestic policies as the main cause of Cuba's economic woes (for three decades, the effects of the embargo were almost entirely offset by massive subsidies from the Soviet Union). As President Carter noted during his visit to Havana in May 2002: "These restraints are not the source of

follow suit. Every Latin American country except Mexico fell in line.

By slamming the door, the United States had severed Cuba's umbilical cord. The island faced economic collapse. During that period of intense Cold War, there were only two routes for underdeveloped nations. One way led West, the other East. Lock one door and there ceases to be a choice. But Castro was ahead of the game.

The Bay of Pigs Fiasco

Meanwhile, internal opposition to Castro was growing as government repression increased. Bands of counterrevolutionary guerrillas had set up a front in the Sierra Escambray. Many former Castro supporters fought against him when they realized that he had turned Communist *caudillo* and that a personality cult was being erected. The Lucha Contra Bandidos (Struggle Against Bandits) lasted until 1966 before finally being eradicated.

Castro, with his highly efficient intelligence operation, knew that the CIA was plotting an invasion of Cuba by exiles. In mid-1960 he began to suppress the press. He also established the Committees for the Defense of the Revolution (CDRs)—a countrywide information network for "collective vigilance." Cuba's State Security began a nationwide sweep

Cuba's economic problems. Cuba can trade with more than 100 countries, and buy medicines, for example, more cheaply in Mexico than in the United States."

The paradox is that the policy achieves the opposite effect to its stated goals: It provides a wonderful excuse for the Communist system's economic failings, and a rationale to suppress dissidents and civil liberties under the aegis of national security for an island under siege. It also permits Fidel Castro to perform the role of Cuba's anti-imperialistic savior that he has cast for himself.

Although State Department officials privately admit that the embargo is the fundamental source of Fidel's hold on power, U.S. presidents are wed to what Ann Louise Bardach calls a "transparently disastrous policy, trading off sensible and enduring solutions for short-term electoral gains [in Florida]" in response to fanatically anti-Castroite Cuban-American interests.

WHAT U.S. CITIZENS CAN DO TO HELP END THE EMBARGO AND TRAVEL BAN

U.S. citizens who oppose the embargo and restrictions on U.S. citizens' constitutional right to travel can make their views known to representatives in Washington.

Contact Your Senator or Representative in Congress (U.S. Congress, Washington, DC 20510, tel. 202/224-3121 or 800/839-5276, www.house.gov and www.senate.gov). Write a simple, moderate, straightforward letter to your representative that makes the argument for ending the travel ban and embargo and requests he/she cosponsor a bill to that effect.

Write or Call the President (The President, The White House, Washington, DC 20500, tel. 202/456-1414, president@whitehouse.gov). Also call or fax the **White House Comment Line** (202/456-1111, fax 202/456-2461, www.whitehouse.gov) and the **Secretary of State** (202/647-4000, www.state.gov/secretary).

Publicize Your Concern. Write a simple, moderate, straightforward letter to the editor of your local newspaper as well as any national newspapers or magazines and make the argument for ending the embargo.

Support the Freedom to Travel Campaign. Contact the **Latin America Working Group** (424 C St. NE, Washington, DC 20002, tel. 202/546-7010, www.lawg.org), which campaigns to lift the travel restrictions and U.S. embargo, monitors legislators, and can advise on how representatives have voted on Cuba-related issues; and sign the **Orbitz Open Cuba** (www.opencuba.org) petition.

against suspected "counterrevolutionaries" and opponents.

On April 15, 1961, Cuban exiles strafed Cuban airfields as a prelude to a CIA-sponsored invasion. Castro turned the funeral for the seven persons killed into a stirring call for defiance: "What the imperialists cannot forgive us for…is that we have made a socialist revolution under the nose of the United States." It was his first public characterization of the Revolution as socialist. The debacle thus created the conditions by which socialism became acceptable to a nation on the brink of invasion.

President Kennedy was assured that the Cuban people would rise up in arms. They

did, and within 72 hours they had defeated the CIA-backed invasion at the Bay of Pigs on April 17, 1961. States ambassador Bonsal declared that the Bay of Pigs "consolidated Castro's regime and was a determining factor in giving it the long life it has enjoyed." As Castro admitted: "Our Marxist-Leninist party was really born at Girón; from that date on, socialism became cemented forever with the blood of our workers, peasants, and students."

The debacle not only solidified Castro's tenure but also provoked a repressive house-cleaning of anyone thought to be too independent or deviant. As Castro saw it, you were either for the Revolution or against it. By 1965, at least

THE CUBAN MISSILE CRISIS

The Cuban Missile Crisis (Cubans call it the October 1962 Crisis) was the result of the escalating tensions of the deepening Cold War. The Soviet Union felt severely threatened by the U.S. deployment of intermediate-range ballistic missiles on Turkey's border with the USSR. To the Soviets, the Bay of Pigs fiasco provided an opportunity to establish bases at equally close range to the United States, which could then be used as bargaining chips for a reduction of U.S. bases in Turkey.

The Soviets told Castro that the United States was planning to invade Cuba. Fidel accordingly requested "strategic defensive weapons." The Soviets began their military build-up in Cuba in early 1962, then pressured the Cuban government to formally request that the Soviet Union install nuclear missiles.

On October 14, a U-2 spy plane over western Cuba discovered missile sites. President Kennedy demanded that they be removed. Khrushchev refused. On October 22, Kennedy went on national TV and announced, "I have directed...initial steps to be taken immediately for a strict quarantine on all offensive military equipment.... It shall be the policy of this nation to regard any nuclear missile launched from Cuba as an attack by the Soviet Union on the United States, requiring full retaliatory response on the Soviet Union." As he began speaking, 54 Strategic Air Command (SAC) bombers took to the air, Polaris submarines

put to sea, and a U.S. naval task force set out to intercept Soviet vessels and blockade Cuba. That day, *Revolución* published the banner headline "U.S. Prepares Invasion of Cuba." (The Cubans remained on combat alert for a month, prepared to face down the atomic bomb with rifles. Maurice Halperin, in *Return to Havana*, recalls living in Havana in October 1962: "Unbelievably, the popular mood was defiance. '¡Patria o Muerte!' Fidel shouted, and the masses seemed almost eager to take on the Yankees. There was an air of celebration in the city.... Havana was throbbing.")

A volatile exchange of messages between Kennedy and Khrushchev followed. Tensions mounted. On October 24 the U.S. military went to DefCon (Defense Condition) 2 – for the first and only time in history. In the middle of the escalating tensions, the destroyer USS *Beale* dropped depth charges on Soviet submarine B-59, not knowing that the sub had nuclear-tipped torpedoes on board. The two superpowers verged on full-scale nuclear war.

ROGUE ELEPHANTS
While Kennedy was looking at the regional implications, Thomas Powers, commander of SAC, and Curtis LeMay, U.S. Air Force Chief of Staff, were hoping for a preemptive war. The United States and USSR had been moving toward a policy of mutual deterrence based

20,000 political prisoners—including homosexuals, practicing Catholics, and other "social deviants"—languished in jails.

The Cuban Missile Crisis
On December 1, 1961, Castro informed Cuba and the world that Cuba was officially a Marxist-Leninist state. The news was a bombshell to the Kennedy administration, which in March 1962 launched Operation Mongoose—a six-phase program to oust Castro. Four hundred CIA agents were assigned full-time to the operation, which was led by Bobby Kennedy.

Kennedy's threat to do away with socialist Cuba virtually obliged Fidel to ask the Soviets for rockets to defend Cuba in the event of a U.S. invasion. In August, Soviet personnel and MiG fighter-bombers began to arrive. Kennedy had warned the Soviets that the United States would not tolerate the installation of missiles. Khrushchev promised Kennedy that no "offensive weapons" were being supplied to Cuba. His deceit had near-calamitous consequences. No direct contact was made with Castro during the crisis, and no one in the administration attempted to

on a pact of "no first-strike," a policy the two figures publicly abhorred. Their missiles would then be a "wasting asset." They pushed Kennedy to bomb Cuba and take out the missiles, believing the Soviets wouldn't dare to respond.

At the height of the crisis, on October 26, Powers ordered a launch of an ICBM from Vandenberg Air Force Base. Although it was launched across the Pacific and hit the missile test range in Kwajalein atoll in the Marshall Islands, it was still a deliberate provocation. After Khrushchev complained that U-2 spy planes flying over Siberia "could be easily taken for a nuclear bomber, which might push us to a fateful step," Powers ordered SAC bombers to deliberately fly past their turnaround points into Soviet airspace. They were recalled at the eleventh hour when Khrushchev relented and ordered the missiles removed.

ROGUE COMANDANTE

Fidel – always the gambler – was equally reckless. According to Carlos Franquí, editor of *Revolución* at the time, Fidel "drove to one of the Russian rocket bases, where the Soviet generals took him on a tour [the missile sites were Russian territory].... At that moment, an American U-2 appeared on a radar screen, flying low over the island.... The Russians showed him the ground-to-air missiles and said that

with a push of a button, the plane would be blown out of the sky.

"Which button?" Fidel reportedly asked.

"This one," a general replied.

At that, says Franquí, "Fidel pushed it and the rocket brought down the U-2. Anderson, the American pilot, was the only casualty in that war. The Russians were flabbergasted, but Fidel simply said, 'Well, now we'll see if there's a war or not.'"

Castro has vigorously denied that he (or any Cuban) shot down the U-2 on October 27. "It is still a mystery how it happened," he claims. However, Soviet ambassador Alexeev had cabled Moscow on October 25 warning that Castro wanted "to shoot down one or two American planes over Cuban territory." He had not only created a potential world catastrophe, he had wanted to pursue it to its most horrific consequences: In another cable sent to Moscow on October 26, he urged the Soviets to make a preemptive nuclear strike at the United States: "However difficult and horrifying this decision may be, there is, I believe no other recourse," he wrote.

Castro learned of Khrushchev's decision to back down over the radio, along with the rest of the world. He was livid. When United Nations Secretary-General U Thant met Castro immediately after the crisis to arrange for verification that the missiles had been removed, Castro refused all cooperation.

consider what Castro's part in the game of Russian roulette might have been.

Castro may have correctly calculated that the threat of nuclear conflict could save him from a non-nuclear attack. The crisis had ended with a guarantee from Kennedy that the United States would not invade Cuba (the non-explicit no-invasion pledge was withdrawn after Castro refused to permit verification). Nonetheless, the Kennedys had initiated another invasion plan for 1964—OPLAN 380-63. Before it could be implemented, the president was dead, shot by Lee Harvey Oswald.

Castro was now free to move forward with his socialist revolution.

MAKING THE REVOLUTION

Cuba in 1959 was comparatively advanced in socioeconomic terms. It had a huge middle class. And the island's per capita rankings for automobiles, telephones, televisions, literacy, and infant mortality (32 per 1,000 live births) were among the highest in the Western hemisphere. But hundreds of thousands of Cubans also lived without light, water, or sewage. Poverty was endemic, and thousands of citizens lived by begging and prostitution.

Castro's government poured its heart and soul into improving the lot of the poor. Castro, for example, dubbed 1961 the Year of Education. "Literacy brigades" were formed of university students and high school seniors, who fanned out over the countryside with the goal of teaching every single Cuban to read and write. Within two years, the regime had added 10,000 classrooms. By the end of its first decade, the number of elementary schools had nearly doubled and the number of teachers had more than tripled. Castro also set up special schools for the indigent, the blind, deaf, and mute, and ex-prostitutes. Electricity, gas, and public transport fees were dramatically lowered, as were rents and other fees. The government poured money into health care. And the Revolution brought unparalleled gains in terms of racism and social relations.

However, Castro's reforms came at the cost of politicizing all private choices and the totalitarian precedence over individual liberties. Havana and other cities were neglected and left to deteriorate. And the free-thinking entrepreneurial middle class was effaced. Cuba's far-reaching social programs also had a price tag that the national economy could not support.

Mismanaging the Economy

The young revolutionaries badly mismanaged the Cuban economy, swinging this way and that as Castro capriciously tacked between Soviet dictate and personal whim. In confusedly searching for "truly original socialism," Castro committed economic errors that were worsened by bureaucratic mismanagement and abrupt reversals in direction. Sound economic decisions were sacrificed to revolutionary principles intended to advance the power of the state over private initiative. Meanwhile, Che Guevara, president of the National Bank of Cuba and Minister of Finance and Industry, replaced trained managers with Communist cadres.

Gradually, inventories of imported goods and cash at hand were exhausted. As machinery broke down, no replacements could be ordered from the United States because of the trade ban enacted in 1961. Raw materials could not be bought. Soon the economy was in appalling shape. In 1962 rationing was introduced. The black market began to blossom.

Sugar monoculture was held to blame. Castro decided to abandon a sugar-based economy and industrialize. When that attempt to failed, Castro switched tack and mobilized the entire workforce to achieve a record sugar harvest: 10 million tons a year by 1970 (the all-time previous record was only 6.7 million tons). Tens of thousands of inexperienced "voluntary" workers left their jobs in the cities and headed to the countryside. Holidays were abolished. Every inch of arable land was turned over to sugar. Nonetheless, only 8.5 million tons were harvested and the severely disrupted economy was left in chaos.

To make matters worse, in 1968 Castro nationalized the entire retail trade still in private hands. More than 58,000 businesses—from corner cafés to auto mechanics—were eliminated in the "Great Revolutionary Offensive." As a result, even the most basic items disappeared from the shelves.

The Soviets saved the day. Bit by bit, Castro was forced to follow Soviet dictates. Castro's zealous experimentations gave way to a period of enforced pragmatism. In 1976, Cuba joined COMECON, the Soviet bloc's economic community. Cuba would henceforth supply sugar to the European socialist nations in exchange for whatever the island needed; sugar was even rationed in Cuba to meet obligations. Meanwhile, that year the First Communist Party Congress initialed a new constitution that recognized Marxist-Leninism as the state's official ideology and the party as the sole representative of the people.

Adventurism Abroad

Castro was committed to exporting his Revolution (he had been complicit in armed plots against several neighboring countries from the moment the Revolution succeeded, including support for a failed invasion of the

Dominican Republic in June 1959). In 1962 Guevara launched a wave of Cuban-backed guerrilla activity throughout Latin America that was endorsed by Castro in his "Second Declaration of Havana"—a tacit declaration of war on Latin American governments. At the Organization of Latin American Solidarity conference in Havana in August 1967, Castro launched his Fifth International, to "create as many Vietnams as possible" in defiance of the Soviet Union's policy of coexistence with the United States. Said Castro: "The duty of every revolutionary is to make the revolution."

Cuban troops had already been sent to countries as far afield as Algeria and Zaire. Soon revolutionary fighters from Angola, Mozambique, and elsewhere were being trained at secret camps on Isla de la Juventud. In Ethiopia and Angola, Cuban troops fought alongside Marxist troops in the civil wars against "racist imperialism," while in Ethiopia they shored up a ruthless regime. In Nicaragua, Cubans trained, armed, and supported the Sandinista guerrillas that toppled the Somoza regime. More than 377,000 Cuban troops were rotated through Angola during the 15-year war (the last troops came home in May 1991), proportionally far greater than the U.S. troop commitment in Vietnam. Tens of thousands of Cuban doctors and technical specialists were also sent to more than two dozen developing nations to assist in development.

(El Jefe launched his international initiatives at a time when Washington was looking at rapprochement with Cuba, beginning with the Ford administration, which worked out several agreements with the Castro government—a gradual lifting of the embargo was approved. Castro's adventurism cooled Uncle Sam's enthusiasm.)

The Mariel Boatlift

In 1980, 12 Cubans walked through the gates of the Peruvian embassy in Havana and asked for asylum. The Peruvians agreed. Carter announced that the United States would welcome Cuban political refugees with "open arms." In a fit of pique, Castro removed the embassy guards, and 11,000 Cubans rushed into the embassy. Castro decided to allow them to leave, along with dissidents and other disaffected Cubans. Many were coerced to leave, while Castro added to the numbers by emptying his prisons of criminals and homosexuals and other "antisocial elements." Thus Castro disposed of more than 120,000 critics and disaffected. The Carter administration was forced to accept the *Marielitos*.

In the 1980s President Ronald Reagan took a much harder line. In 1983, U.S. Marines stormed the Caribbean island of Grenada to topple Maurice Bishop's Cuban-backed socialist regime. The Reagan administration also spawned the Cuban-American National Foundation to give clout to the right-wing Cuban-American voice. In 1985 it established Radio Martí to broadcast anti-Castro propaganda into Cuba.

THE BUBBLE BURSTS

Meanwhile, Mikhail Gorbachev had become leader of the Soviet Union and was initiating fateful reforms—just as Castro turned more sharply toward Communist orthodoxy. (In 1986, for example, Castro closed free farmers markets, a brief fling that had led to an increase in the food supply. He was alarmed at the success of the free-market experiment and railed against "millionaire garlic growers.") The basic structure of Soviet-style planning and management would not be altered. *Glasnost* and *perestroika*, Gorbachev's "heresies," would not be tolerated in Cuba.

In 1989 the Berlin Wall collapsed and the Communist dominoes came tumbling down. However, the news in Cuba was dominated by a political show trial that made it clear that reform was not in the cards. General Arnaldo Sánchez Ochoa, a powerful and charismatic national hero with impeccable credentials going back to the Sierra Maestra, was accused (on false charges) of colluding with the Colombian drug cartel to smuggle drugs to the United States via Cuba. After a closed trial, Ochoa and 13 other high-ranking officers were convicted of treason and corruption. Ochoa and three others were executed. A purge followed, notably of the Ministry of the Interior (MININT), but also of dissidents and private entrepreneurs. Rumors swept the island that Ochoa, who had been espousing reformist discontent, had been conspiring to oust Castro.

The "Special Period"

With the Eastern bloc umbilical cord severed, Cuba's economy collapsed. In January 1990, Castro declared that Cuba had entered a Special Period in a Time of Peace. He also announced a draconian, warlike austerity plan. A new slogan appeared throughout Cuba: *¡Socialismo o muerte!* (Socialism or death!). Inevitably, rising political discontent boiled over on April 21, 1991, when clashes erupted against the police—the first act of spontaneous rebellion since 1959. Then on August 18, 1991, on the last day of the highly successful Pan-American Games in Havana (which Cuba won with 140 gold medals), the Soviet Union began its dizzying unraveling. Reformer Boris Yeltsin took power. Subsidies and supplies to Cuba virtually ceased.

After the last Soviet tanker departed in June 1992, the government began electricity blackouts that soon lasted all day. There were no fans, no air-conditioning, no refrigeration, no lights. Nor fuel for transportation. Buses and taxis gave way to horse-drawn carts. Without oil or electricity to run machines, or raw materials to process, or spare parts to repair machinery, factories closed down and state bureaucracies began transferring laid-off workers to jobs in the countryside. Gaiety on the streets was replaced with a forlorn melancholy.

Harvests simply rotted in the fields for want of distribution. People accustomed to a government-subsidized food basket guaranteeing every person at least two high-protein, high-calorie meals a day were stunned to suddenly be confronting shortages of almost every staple. When East German powdered milk ceased to arrive, Cuba eliminated butter; when Czechoslovakian malt no longer arrived, Cuban beer disappeared. Soaps, detergents, deodorants, toilet paper, clothing, everything vanished. Cubans had to resort to making hamburger meat from banana peels and steaks from grapefruit rinds. Many Cubans began rearing *jutías,* ratlike native rodents. The most desperate resorted to rats. Cuba, the only country in Latin America to have eliminated hunger, began to suffer malnutrition and debilitating diseases. Thousands of people starved to death, while many more committed suicide. Meanwhile, believing that Cuba was on the verge of collapse, Uncle Sam tightened the screws by passing the Cuban Democracy Act, which reduced economic assistance to countries trading with Cuba and prohibited U.S. subsidiary companies abroad from trading with Cuba.

The reformist movement found an unexpected ally in Raúl Castro, who argued for deregulating key sectors of the economy. Market-savvy reformers were elevated to positions of power and cobbled together a recovery plan led by tourism. The Revolution's ideological principles were turned on their head. Possession of the dollar was legalized and private enterprise was permitted.

By 1994 a cautious sense of optimism began to emerge. The awful *apagones* (blackouts) were trimmed. Food crops no longer rotted in the fields. And the legal availability of dollars eased life for those Cubans who had access to greenbacks, while farmers markets eased life for those without.

The Balsero Crisis

On August 5, 1994, crowds gathered along the Malecón in response to a rumor that a major exodus was to be permitted and that a flotilla of boats was en route from Florida. When police attempted to clear the boulevard, a riot ensued, and two police officers were killed. Castro saw a chance to defuse a dangerous situation and benefit. He declared that Cuba would no longer police the U.S. borders: If the United States would not honor its agreement to allow people to migrate legally, then Cuba would no longer try to prevent anyone from going illegally. (Leaving Cuba without an exit permit is illegal; Cubans are rarely granted such visas. Meanwhile, the United States' 1966

Cuban Adjustment Act *guarantees* residency to Cubans who step foot on U.S. soil. The United States had agreed to accept an annual quota of 20,000-plus Cuban immigrants, but most Cubans who petitioned the United States for a visa were rejected. The more difficult the economic circumstances became in Cuba, the fewer legal immigrants were accepted, while the greater the number of *illegals* who were taken in.)

The United States was hoisted on its own petard as thousands of *balseros* (rafters) fled Cuba on makeshift rafts. By September 9, when the two countries agreed to measures "to ensure that migration between the two countries is safe, legal, and orderly," more than 30,000 Cubans had been rescued at sea and shipped to Guantánamo naval base, which was expanded to eventually house up to 65,000 refugees.

Meanwhile, a Miami-based volunteer group called Brothers to the Rescue had been operating rescue missions. When the flood of *balseros* stopped, pilots of the organization began buzzing Havana and dropping "leaflets of a subversive nature." On February 24, 1996, Cuban jet fighters shot two Brothers to the Rescue Cessnas down, killing both pilots. (The Cuban government claimed that the aircraft came down in Cuban territorial waters, but an investigation by the independent International Civil Aviation Organization confirmed that the two Cessnas were downed 10.3 and 11.5 miles *north* of Cuban airspace.) Cuban-American exiles and Republican presidential candidates campaigning for the mid-March Florida primary erupted in fury. The incident scuttled the Clinton administration's carefully calibrated policy on Cuba of promoting democratic change as a prelude to easing the embargo.

Following the Brothers to the Rescue incident, arch-right-wingers Sen. Jesse Helms and Rep. Dan Burton Helms rode the wave of anti-Castro sentiment in Miami and Washington and steered the Cuban Liberty and Democratic Solidarity Act through Congress. Clinton signed the bill, which (among other things) requires that U.S. presidents now seek congressional approval if they seek to modify or lift

the embargo; stipulates that the embargo can only be lifted when a "transition government" is in place in Cuba that meets U.S. criteria; denies entry into the U.S. territory to anyone who has done business with Cuban nationals or the Cuban government; and bars U.S. banks from lending to these companies; and will allow any U.S. citizen whose property was confiscated after the Revolution to sue any foreign corporation that has "benefited" from the property or from its use. (The law really represents the interests of very wealthy Cuban-Americans, such as the Bacardi Corporation, the National Association of Sugar Mill Owners of Cuba, and the Cuban Association for the Tobacco Industry, who clearly benefit while Cuban products are banned.)

The law, which violates international law, has earned the wrath of the United States' leading allies; Canada even enacted retaliatory legislation. It also united Cubans behind the Castro government as nothing had done in years.

Holy Smoke

In January 1998, Pope John Paul II made a highly publicized four-day visit to Cuba. For the occasion, Castro made Christmas an official holiday and festive lights went up in the streets for the first time in decades. Castro had invited the pope in the hope that a papal embrace magnified by television exposure might defuse internal opposition and give the regime new legitimacy. Castro had been counting on air-play from the 4,000 journalists who descended on Havana to cover the event, including the major U.S. media, who promptly turned heel when the Monica Lewinsky scandal broke as the pope touched Cuban soil.

Meanwhile, in 1997, Miami-based Cuban-American exiles launched a bombing campaign against the Cuban tourist industry, killing an Italian tourist. But the real enemy lay within. Serious crime had returned to the streets of Cuba. Cocaine was being sold on the street and at discos. Thousands of young Cuban women had turned to quasi-prostitution. And corruption was becoming entrenched.

Reasserting State Control

On January 1, 1999, Cubans celebrated the 40th anniversary of the Cuban Revolution. The economy was bouncing back, driven by dollars from tourism, and was given a boost in January when President Clinton eased the trade embargo, permitting U.S. citizens to send up to US$1,200 annually to Cuban individuals and non-government organizations. Castro called the move a "fraud."

Meanwhile, Castro announced draconian legislation—the Law for the Protection of Cuba's National Independence and Economy. Thousands of Special Brigade police were deployed on street corners throughout major cities. The policy was officially "a battle against disorder, crime, disrespect for authority, illegal business, and lack of social control." Outlawed, too, were the "supply, search or gathering of information" for and "collaboration" with foreign media. To get the point across, in March 1999 four prominent dissidents received harsh sentences, resulting in the United Nations Commission on Human Rights condemning Cuba. In June 1999 dozens of high officials within the tourism and business sectors were fired and arrested for corruption. The state was also reasserting control throughout the private economy.

INTO THE NEW MILLENNIUM

Cuba saw the millennium in with a new battle with Uncle Sam, this one over a five-year-old boy, Elián González, saved by the U.S. Coast Guard after his mother and 10 other people drowned when their boat sank en route from Cuba to Florida. Miami's anti-Castroite Cubans and right-wing politicians demanded that the boy remain in the United States against his Cuban father's wishes. Castro (who routinely denies permission for the children of Cuban exiles to join their parents abroad) turned the issue into an anti-American crusade by organizing "Free Elián" rallies. Castro vowed that protests would last "10 years, if necessary," while the case wound through the Florida courts. Elián's custodians refused to hand him over to his loving father when he arrived in the

United States in April 2000 to collect his son. In a dawn raid, the INS grabbed Elián and reunited him with his father. In late June Elián and his father returned to Cuba after the U.S. Supreme Court affirmed the father's right to custody of his son.

To Fidel Castro, the battle for Elián was personal, recalling with astonishing parallels an incident that occurred forty-odd years ago when a Cuban father discovered that his estranged wife had left for the United States and taken their five-year-old son with her. The courts awarded custody of the son to the mother. But the father, who was enraged by the thought of his son being raised in Miami by relatives who were his sworn political enemies, refused to acknowledge his loss: "One day I'll get my son and my honor back—even if the earth should be destroyed in the process.... I am prepared to reenact the Hundred Years War. And I'll win it," he wrote to his sister. The man later talked the mother into letting the boy visit him in Mexico on his word "as a gentleman" that the boy would be returned in two weeks. Instead the boy was secreted away, so that the wife had to enlist the Mexican police to get her son back. They did so at gunpoint, seizing him from the father's henchmen while he was being taken for a drive near Mexico City's Chapultepec Park. The mother remarried and returned with the boy to her new home in Havana. But Cuba turned Communist and in 1964 she fled the island for Spain. The father, however, wouldn't let the woman take her son with her. The mother was Mirta Diaz-Balart, whose nephew, Lincoln Diaz-Balart, is a Republican Congressman for Florida, an arch anti-Castroite and champion of the crusade to keep Elián González in the United States. The boy's name was Fidelito. His father is Fidel Castro.

New Battles

In 2001, as the George W. Bush administration initiated an increasingly hard-line approach to Cuba, Castro launched the "Battle of Ideas," an ongoing ideological campaign to shore up flagging support for socialism.

THE "CUBAN FIVE"

The faces of the "Cuban Five" have for the past few years been ubiquitous throughout Cuba, from billboards and daily news items to T-shirts and every website, while massive demonstrations for their cause continue to be held nationwide. Accused by the U.S. government of "espionage," the five Cubans – Fernando González, René González, Antonio Guerrero, Gerardo Hernández, and Ramón Labañino – were convicted in U.S. federal court on June 8, 2001, and sentenced to from 15 years to life terms.

The five "innocents," as they are called in Cuba, were indeed spies. However, the agents of Cuban intelligence weren't spying against the U.S. government. Instead, they had infiltrated extreme right-wing Cuban-American groups, such as Omega 7 and Alpha 66, that continue to plan and perpetrate terrorist acts against moderate Cuban-Americans espousing dialogue with Cuba; against Cuba-bound travelers and Cuba-travel suppliers; and against Cuba, including machine gun raids on Varadero and, in 1997, a bombing campaign in Havana that killed an innocent Italian tourist.

Such groups have acted with impunity for decades, and the U.S. government has basically turned a blind eye to their terrorist acts.

(For example, anti-Castroite, CIA-trained Bay of Pigs operative Orlando Bosch was convicted of conspiring in the bombing of a Cubana airliner on October 6, 1976, that killed 73 passengers, but he was granted a pardon by President Bush. His co-conspirator, Luis Posada, was convicted of the bombing in Venezuela but escaped from jail and returned to Miami, where he has never been prosecuted.) Because the U.S. government refuses to prosecute Cuban-American terrorists, Cuban agents have infiltrated such groups to monitor them and identify future threats.

In 2001, Castro used novelist Gabriel García Marquéz as an emissary to present a dossier to President Bill Clinton with evidence of a plot to bomb a Cuban-bound airliner. The FBI was invited to Havana, where it was given access to files. The FBI uncovered and arrested the "five," but not the Cuban-American plotters. Castro, who surely knew that his agents would be discovered, chose not to recall them, suggesting that he intentionally sacrificed the five to create a new *cause célèbre!*

An effort to free the "five" has garnered the support of leading international figures. For more information, contact **Free the Five** (415/821-6545, www.freethefive.org).

The following spring, Jimmy Carter made a five-day visit to Havana—the first by a U.S. president to Cuba since Calvin Coolidge in 1928. Just days before Carter's arrival, dissidents delivered to the National Assembly a petition presented by a dissident group, Proyecto Varela (Varela Project), containing 11,020 signatures demanding sweeping reforms in Cuba. Amazingly, Fidel permitted Carter to address the nation live on TV. Carter denounced the U.S. embargo, as Fidel no doubt had wished, but focused primarily on the call for greater freedoms in Cuba and mentioned Proyecto Varela by name—the first time most Cubans learned of the organization.

Three weeks later, with Carter safely off the island, Castro sought to stamp out the Varela germ. The Castro regime pulled out of its hat a petition of more than eight million signatures, it claimed, calling for a resolution to make the existing constitution "eternal" and "untouchable." (The government had knocked on everyone's door and confronted individuals face to face, and the names of those who failed to vote were recorded.) In March 2003 Castro initiated a harsh crackdown on dissidents, independent journalists, and librarians. Meanwhile, two Cuban planes were successfully hijacked to the United States, and an attempt to hijack a ferry failed when it ran out of fuel 30 miles from Havana. The Cuban military towed the vessel back to Havana; following a swift trial, three of the hijackers were executed by firing squad.

The Past Few Years

The Bush administration implemented new restrictions aimed at stopping all travel to Cuba as part of a broader attempt to cut the flow of dollars to Cuba. Bush also assigned millions of dollars for anti-Castro activities, including Radio & TV Martí—a boondoggle that the Cuban government has successfully blocked for years.

Castro was buoyed by a major discovery of crude oil offshore of Cuba. Having allied himself ever more closely with Venezuela's Hugo Chávez and increasingly with China (now Cuba's second largest trading partner), Castro stepped up retrenchment of the socialist system. Many foreign companies were ousted. And the U.S. dollar was banned. Meanwhile, the first of tens of thousands of poor patients from Latin America arrived for free eye operations bankrolled by Venezuela; Operación Milagro (Operation Miracle) will eventually treat more than six million patients from developing nations.

On July 31, 2006, Fidel Castro was taken seriously ill and underwent intestinal surgery on the eve of his 80th birthday. In February 2008, an extremely frail Fidel handed power to his brother Raúl Castro, who was duly elected as head of state by the National Assembly (Fidel continues to rant in his frequent editorials for *Granma*). The transition has gone smoothly. Raúl, who stated that he welcomed ways to normalize relations with Uncle Sam, has since enacted minor reforms aimed at increasing economic productivity (primarily in agriculture), but with the recalcitrant Fidel still pulling strings, no major reforms have yet taken place.

The inauguration of President Barack Obama in January 2009 augered possibility of a new thaw between Washington and Havana. In March, President Obama rescinded all restrictions on travel to Cuba for family visits and called for "constructive engagement" with Cuba (Congress inched toward lifting all prohibitions on travel). In June, the Organization of American States voted to re-admit Cuba (which responded that it had no such interest). Meanwhile, Vice President Carlos Lage and Foreign Minister Felipe Pérez Roquez were ousted. Word later leaked that Cuba's intelligence service had recorded them belittling Fidel and casting doubt on Raúl's ability to govern. Raúl also replaced several other high-level officials with his loyalists.

billboard honoring Fidel and Raúl Castro, Granma Province

© CHRISTOPHER P. BAKER

In November 2009, Cuba arrested a U.S. citizen on charges of assisting dissident groups, causing Raúl Castro to launch a venomous attack on President Obama's administration. In February 2010, U.S. and Cuban officials reinstated the first direct talks between the two nations since Bush scrapped them in 2004; however, a background of animosity remains.

Government

Cuba is an independent socialist republic. The Cuban constitution, adopted in 1975, defines it as a "socialist state of workers and peasants and all other manual and intellectual workers." General Raúl Castro Ruz is head of both state and government. In February 2008, Raúl succeeded from his elder brother Fidel, who had served as top dog 1959–2008. Total power is legally vested in Raúl Castro as President of the Republic, President of the Council of State, President of the Council of Ministers, and Commander in Chief of the armed forces. General José Ramón Machado is First Vice President of both the Council of State and the Council of Ministers. (Machado, a doctor and old-guard revolutionary, fought alongside the Castros in the Sierra Maestra, rose to the rank of *comandante*, and later, as Minister of Health, oversaw development of Cuba's health system.)

There are no legally recognized political organizations independent of the Communist Party, which controls the labyrinthine state apparatus and which the constitution (copied largely from the Soviet constitution of 1936) recognizes as "the highest leading force of the society and of the state."

STATE STRUCTURE
The Central Government
The highest-ranking executive body is the Consejo de Ministros (Council of Ministers), headed by Raúl and comprising several vice presidents and ministers. Its Executive Committee administers Cuba on a day-to-day basis and is ostensibly accountable to the National Assembly of People's Power, which "elects" the members at the initiative of the head of state. The council has jurisdiction over all ministries and central organizations and effectively runs the country under the direction of Raúl, who since coming to power has replaced many ministers with loyal military figures.

The 614-member Asemblea Nacional (National Assembly) is invested with legislative authority but exercises little legislative initiative. It is mostly a rubber-stamp legislature, headed since 1993 by Ricardo Alarcón. The Assembly is elected for a five-year term but meets only twice annually. Deputies are elected directly by voters, but candidates (who must be approved by the Communist Party) run unopposed; most are drawn from the party bureaucracy.

The 31-member Consejo del Estado (Council of State) is modeled on the Presidium of the former Soviet Union and functions as the Executive Committee of the National Assembly when the latter is not in session.

The Cuban Communist Party
The sole political party is the Partido Comunista de Cuba (PCC), of which Fidel Castro remains head and his brother Raúl vice secretary. The PCC, whose goal is "to guide common efforts toward the construction of socialism," occupies the central role in all government bodies and institutions. It is led by the Buró Político (Politburo) and steered by the Comité Central (Central Committee), whose members are selected by Castro. It meets every six months and is the principal forum through which the party leadership disseminates party policy.

At the base of the PCC chain is the party cell of 10 members organized at work and educational centers. Youth organizations are the most common avenue for passage into the PCC. Current membership is about 600,000 (about 5 percent of the population).

The Castros have drawn from "the elite of the elite" of the party to maintain their government. Loyalty takes precedence over all other considerations. Although the Council of State and Council of Ministers ostensibly make the decisions, Raúl Castro shapes those decisions, while Fidel pulls the strings from backstage.

Local Government

The country is divided into 14 provinces and 169 municipalities (*municipios*), dominated by the city of Havana, a separate province. Each province and municipality is governed by an Assembly of Delegates of People's Power, representing state bodies at the local level. Members are elected by popular ballot and serve two-and-a-half-year terms.

The organs of *poder popular* (popular power) also serve as forums for citizens' grievances and deal with problems such as garbage collection, housing improvement, and running day-care centers. The PCC closely monitors their performance.

Committees for the Defense of the Revolution

The linchpins in maintaining the loyalty of the masses and spreading the Revolution at the grassroots level are the neighborhood Comités para la Defensa de la Revolución. There are 15,000 CDRs in Havana, and 100,000 throughout the island. Almost every block has one. On one hand, the CDRs perform wonderful work: They collect blood for hospitals, discourage kids from playing hooky, and so on. But they are also the vanguard in watching and snitching on neighbors (the CDRs are under the direction of MININT, the Ministry of the Interior). Above the voluntary CDR head is the *jefe del sector,* the sector boss in charge of four CDRs and who specifically looks for revolutionary delinquency.

Other Mass Organizations

Citizen participation in building socialism is manifested through mass organizations controlled by the PCC. Prominent among them are the Federation of Cuban Women, the Confederation of Cuban Workers, and the Union of Communist Youth. No independent labor organizations are permitted. Membership in mass organizations is a virtual prerequisite for getting on in Cuban society. Promotions, access to university, etc., rely upon being a "good revolutionary" through participation in an organization.

The Judiciary

Courts are a fourth branch of government and are not independent. The individual in Cuba enjoys few legal guarantees. The judiciary is charged with "maintaining and strengthening socialist legality." The Council of State can overturn judicial decisions, and Fidel Castro has frequently done so in political trials. Interpretation of the constitution is the prerogative of the National Assembly, not the courts. Cuba's legal system is modeled on *Alice in Wonderland*'s topsy-turvy world in which defendants are required to prove their innocence, rather than for prosecutors to prove the defendants' guilt. Hence, thousands of Cubans languish in jails for crimes the State finds it convenient to convict them of.

The highest court in the land is the People's Supreme Court in Havana. The president and vice president are appointed by Fidel Castro; other judges are elected by the National Assembly. Private practice of law is not permitted. The penal code accepts a defendant's confession as sufficient proof of his guilt, and there are many cases of individuals pressured into confessing to crimes they did not commit. Capital punishment by firing squad remains for 112 offenses (79 for violations of state security).

Cuba, however, has a policy of criminal rehabilitation for all but political crimes. In meting out punishment, the penal system allows for amends and guarantees an individual's job upon release from prison.

Military and Security

Cuba once boasted a formidable military under the aegis of the Fuerzas Armadas Revolucionarias (Revolutionary Armed Forces,

HUMAN RIGHTS

"It is fair to say that under [Fidel] Castro, Cubans have lost even the tenuous civil and political liberties they had under the old regime," claims Professor Wayne Smith, former head of the U.S. Interests Section in Havana. "Woe to anyone who gets on a soap box in downtown Havana and questions the wisdom of the Castro government." In March 2008, Cuba signed two United Nations international covenants on human rights. Nonetheless, the UN Human Rights Commission places Cuba on its list of worst offenders; Amnesty International also named Cuba the worst offender in Latin America.

The Cuban penal code states that disrespect for authorities is good for one to seven years in prison. As a result, Cubans talk in whispers when discussing the government and live generally in a state of fear about police informers. People face harsh retribution if they cross the line into political activism. The regime is not above jailing even its most loyal supporters if they renege on the Revolution. Carlos Franquí, leading revolutionary, founder of Radio Rebelde, and editor-in-chief of *Revolución*, was even expunged from photos and made a nonperson until he was forced to flee surreptitiously to France.

Contemporary Cuba, however, is a far cry from the 1960s, when crushing sentences were imposed en masse following secret, often puppet, trials. In 1965 when the CIA was doing its best to overthrow the Cuban government, Castro admitted that there were 20,000 "counterrevolutionary criminals" in Cuban jails, including cultural and political dissidents. The true numbers were unquestionably higher. The repression runs hot and cold. In 2002, dissidents led by Oswaldo Payá Sardiña (winner of the 2002 Sakharov Prize for Freedom of Thought) formed Proyecto Varela, which presented a petition signed by 11,000 Cubans urging reform. In response, 75 dissident leaders were brutally sentenced in the harshest crackdown in memory (the mock trials exposed that the dissident leadership is riddled with government spies). Their spouses formed the Damas de Blancos (Women in White), who each Sunday attend mass then stage a silent street protest along Havana's 5ta Avenida to demand their husbands' release. They are occasionally harassed by MININT's Rapid Response Detachments, who deal with public expressions of dissent through *actos de repudios*, beating up dissidents, much as did Hitler's Blockwarts.

Since succeeding his brother, Raúl has released several dozen dissidents. In 2008, the Cuban Commission of Human Rights listed 219 political prisoners in jail. *Plantados* (dissidents who remain firm) report physical abuses. On February 22, 2010, dissident Orlando Zapata Tamaya died following a hunger strike to protest repeated abuses at his Kilo 7 prison in the eastern province of Camagüey. Cuba is one of the few countries that do not allow the Red Cross or other international organizations to inspect their prisons.

The government refers to dissident organizations as "mercenaries," after the U.S. Interests Section began offering radios (to tune in to Radio Martí) and financial support, effectively turning dissidents – most of whom decry the U.S. efforts – into paid agents of a foreign government.

or FAR, www.cubagob.cu/otras_info/minfar), commanded by Raúl Castro. However, the number of men and women on active duty has shrunk from over 180,000 in 1993 to about 55,000 in 2009. In addition, Cuba has more than 100,000 reservists supplemented by about 1.3 million in the territorial militias. (All males between the ages of 16 and 45 are subject to conscription; women between 17 and 35 may volunteer.) The key to defense is the "Guerra de Todo el Pueblo" (War of All the People): In the event of an attack, the *entire* population of Cuba will be called into action.

In 1991 the military was re-engineered to help the economy and now earns its way by investments in tourism, agriculture, and industry, and today employs 20 percent of all workers in Cuba. High-ranking military figures hold key positions throughout the economy and government.

State security is the responsibility of the Ministry of the Interior, which operates a number of intelligence-related services, plus the National Revolutionary Police (PNR). Other intelligence units—most notoriously, the much-feared Seguridad del Estado or G-2—are

HOW CUBANS FEEL ABOUT THE REVOLUTION

A large segment of Cubans see Fidel Castro as a ruthless dictator who cynically betrayed the democratic ideals that he used to rally millions to his banner. To Miami exiles especially, Fidel is just a common tyrant. Nonetheless, Fidel retains the admiration of many among the Cuban people to whom he was and remains a hero. There persists an adulation for *el máximo* or *el caballo* (the horse – an allusion to the Chinese belief that dreaming of certain figures represents numbers to place bets on, and that the horse is number one). Traveling through Cuba you'll come across families who keep a framed photograph of him, though many do so to keep in Fidel's good books.

Many of the same Cubans who complain about harrowing privation and the ubiquitous and oppressive presence of the state will, in almost the same breath, profess loyalty to Fidel, who still retains a substantial base of popular support among the Cuban public. Those with a hate-hate relationship are resigned to sullen silence, prison, or exile. Most Cubans, however, have a love-hate relationship with Fidel, a result of the unifying power of national pride, the very real achievements of the Revolution, and above all, Fidel's unique charisma and the way he has been able to shape the minds of *cubanos* like a hypnotist.

TANGIBLE GAINS
Cuba has invested 50 years of resources to become one of the few underdeveloped nations that protect virtually all members of society from illiteracy and ill health. This, plus tremendous advances in racial and sexual equality and the fact that Cuba's culture is nourished and its independence affirmed, has produced mammoth goodwill, especially in the countryside, where support for the Revolution is strongest.

Many among the party faithful, of course, espouse support because they're the beneficiaries of the system, which nurtures its own social elite with access to cars and other privileges (most high-ranking Communist officials are A-type personalities who would be equally at home in a Fascist regime). For loyalists, defending the system is a knee-jerk reaction. The party faithful are so defensive of their system that, says Isadora Tattlin, "if you mention material hardship, they will launch right into education and health care, as if no other country in the world offered free education and health care."

WHOLESALE DISCONTENT
Despite the gains, the majority of urbanites long ago lost faith in the Castro government. The mood on the streets is one of frustration. Most Cubans are pained by their own poverty and the political posturing to disguise it. Urbanites, especially, are anxious for a return to the market economy and a chance to control and improve their own lives. Most Cubans are tired of the inefficiencies, the endless hardships, the constant sacrifices to satisfy the Castro brothers' pathological battle with Uncle Sam. They hate being answerable to the state for their every move; being forced to break the law constantly to survive; and living under the stress of being caught for the slightest transgression.

When you ask these Cubans how change will come, most roll their eyes and shrug. Silence, congruity, and complicity – pretending to be satisfied and happy with the system – are cultural reflexes deeply ingrained in the Cuban culture. As James Michener wrote of Havana, perhaps "Only the kindness of the climate prevents the smoldering of revolt that might accompany the same conditions in a cold and relentless climate."

operated by the Department of State Security and the General Directorate of Intelligence. There are more security-linked officials than meet the eye.

GOVERNMENT BY WHIM

Cuba is really a *fidelista* state in which Marxist-Leninism has been loosely grafted onto Cuban nationalism, then tended and shaped by one man. Today Cuba is in transition from the domineering role of Fidel to the less-defined commanding rule of his younger brother, Raúl. Fidel preferred to leave his development choices open, allowing a flexible interpretation of the correct path to socialism. Ideological dogma was subordinated to tactical considerations. Fidel's *caudillo* temperament (that of a modernizing but megalomanical political strongman) are powerful factors in his decision-making, which have involved the minutest aspects of government. Fidel even chose Miss Cuba every year!

Government officials had to study Castro's speeches intently to stay tuned with his forever-changing views. The fear of repercussions from on high is so great that the bureaucracy—Cubans call it a "*burro*cracy"—has evolved as a mutually protective society. Bureaucratic incompetence affects nearly every aspect of daily life: In a speech in early 1987, Fidel said, "We must correct the errors we made in correcting our errors." Fidel and Raúl blame the shortcomings on irresponsible managers, lack of discipline, and corruption, making the noticeable exception of their own performance.

Nonetheless, the past decade has seen the rise of a new generation with greater decision-making powers in the upper echelons of Cuba's self-supporting state enterprises.

Fidel Castro has run Cuba as much by charisma as through institutional leadership: *personalismo* is central in *fidelismo*. Fidel has called Western democracies "complete garbage." He preferred "direct democracy"—his appeals ("popular consultations") to the people, relying on his ability to whip up the crowds at mass rallies with persuasive arguments to keep revolutionary ardor alive. Although a less gifted orator than his elder brother, Raúl has continued the style.

A State of Acquiescence

The Castros have engineered a state where an individual's personal survival requires a display of loyalty and adherence to the Revolution. The state maintains control through intimidation and repressive laws. According to Wayne Smith, "A margin of public criticism is allowed, to vent political pressure. The headiest steam is periodically allowed to leave for Florida on rafts and inflated inner tubes."

The government maintains a file on *every* worker, a labor dossier that follows him or her from job to job. Cubans have to voice—or fake—their loyalty. Transgressions are reported in one's dossier. If "antisocial" comments or behavior are noted, the worker may be kicked out of his or her job, or blackballed, or one's child might be put on the slow track in education. Most Cubans have accommodated themselves to the parameters of permissible behavior set out years ago.

FIDEL CASTRO

Born and dispatched into this world with the engine of an athlete, Castro has the discipline of a warrior, the intellect of a chess master, the obsessive mania of a paranoiac, and the willfulness of an infant.

– Ann Louise Bardach

Whatever you think of his politics, Fidel Castro is unquestionably one of the most remarkable and enigmatic figures of this century, thriving on contradiction and paradox like a romantic character from the fiction of his Colombian novelist friend Gabriel García Márquez.

Fidel Castro Ruz, child prodigy, was born on August 13, 1926, at Manacas *finca* near Birán in northern Oriente, the fifth of nine children of Ángel Castro y Argiz. Fidel's father was an émigré to Cuba from Galicia in Spain as a destitute 13-year-old. In Cuba, he became a wealthy landowner who employed 300 workers on a 26,000-acre domain; he owned 1,920 acres and leased the rest from the United Fruit Company, to whom he sold cane. Fidel's mother was the family housemaid, Lina Ruz González, whom Ángel married after divorcing his wife. Fidel weighed 10 pounds at birth—the first hint that he would always be larger than life. Fidel, who seems to have had a happy childhood, likes to obfuscate the true details of his illegitimacy and early years.

As a boy Fidel was extremely assertive and combative. He was a natural athlete. He was no sportsman, however; if his team was losing, he would leave the field and go home. Gabriel García Márquez has said, "I do not think anyone in this world could be a worse loser." It became a matter of principle to excel at everything.

Star Rising

In October 1945 Fidel enrolled in Havana University's law school, where he plunged into politics as a student leader. Fidel earned his first front-page newspaper appearance following his first public speech, denouncing President Grau, on November 27, 1946. In 1947, Fidel was invited to help organize Edward Chibás's Ortodoxo party. He stopped attending law school and rose rapidly to prominence, including as head of his revolutionary group, Orthodox Radical Action.

The period was exceedingly violent and Fidel never went anywhere without a gun. Fidel was soon on the police hit list, and several attempts were made on his life. In February 1949, Fidel was accused of assassinating a political rival. After being arrested and subsequently released on "conditional liberty," he went into hiding. In March, he flew to Bogotá to attend the Ninth Inter-American Conference, where foreign ministers were to sign the charter of the Organization of American States. Soon enough, Fidel was in the thick of demonstrations opposing the organization as a scheme for U.S. domination. One week later, while he was on his way to meet Jorge Eliécer Gaitán (leader of the opposition Progressive Liberal Party), Gaitán was assassinated. Bogotá erupted in

riots. Fidel was drawn in and, arming himself with a tear-gas shotgun, found himself at the vanguard of the Revolution. Inevitably, he made headline news.

On October 12, 1949, Fidel married a philosophy student named Mirta Díaz-Balart. They honeymooned extravagantly—even staying in the Waldorf-Astoria—for several weeks in the United States. Fidel, the consummate opportunist, may have married for political gain: Mirta's father was mayor of Banes, a Cuban congressman, and a close friend of Fulgencio Batista, who gave the couple US$1,000 for their honeymoon. (Mirta's brother, Rafael, headed Batista's youth organization and would later be named Batista's Minister of the Interior, in charge of the secret police. He fled Cuba after the Revolution; his son keeps the right-wing flame burning as a U.S. congressman from Florida.)

In November, Fidel gave a suicidal speech in which he admitted his past associations with gangsterism then named all the gangsters, politicians, and student leaders profiting from the "gangs' pact." In fear for his life, Fidel left Cuba for the United States. He returned four months later to cram for a multiple degree. In September 1950, Fidel graduated with the title of Doctor of Law.

Congressional Candidate

By 1951, Fidel was preparing for national office. His personal magnetism, his brilliant speeches, and his apparent honesty aroused the crowds. Batista, who had returned from retirement in Florida to run for president, even asked to receive Fidel to get the measure of the young man who in January 1952 shook Cuba's political foundation by releasing a detailed indictment of President Prío. (According to Ann Louise Bardach, Fidel perused Batista's library. "You have many books here but you don't have a very important book, Curzio Malaparte's *The Technique of the Coup d'État*. I'll send you a copy," he apparently said. Fidel later studied the writings of Hitler and Mussolini and modeled their coup attempts in his own quest for power.)

Fidel Castro's boyhood sniper rifle at Museo Conjunto Histórico Birán

Fidel was certain to be elected to the Chamber of Deputies. It was also clear that Batista was going to be trounced in the presidential contest, so at dawn on March 10, 1952, he effected a *golpe*. Says Tad Szulc: "Many Cubans think that without a coup, Fidel would have served as a congressman for four years until 1956, then run for the Senate, and made his pitch for the presidency in 1960 or 1964. Given the fact that Cuba was wholly bereft of serious political leadership and given Fidel's rising popularity…it would appear that he was fated to govern Cuba—no matter how he arrived at the top job."

A Communist *Caudillo*

At 30 years old, Fidel was fighting in the Sierra Maestra, a disgruntled lawyer turned revolutionary who craved Batista's job. At 32, he had it. He was determined not to let go. Fidel used the Revolution to carry out a personal *caudillista* coup. "Communist or not, what was being built in Cuba was an old-fashioned personality cult," wrote Jon Lee Anderson.

Fidel has since outlasted 10 U.S. presidents, each of whom predicted his imminent demise and plotted to hasten it by fair means or foul.

He said he would never relinquish power while Washington remains hostile—a condition he has thrived on and worked hard to maintain. Fidel—who knew he could never carry out his revolution in an elective system—is consummately Machiavellian: masking truth to maintain power. Says Guillermo Cabrera Infante, "Fidel's real genius lies in the arts of deception, and while the world plays bridge by the book, he plays poker, bluffing and holding his cards close to his olive-green chest." Adds historian Hugh Thomas: "Often the first person he deceived was himself."

Nonetheless, Fidel genuinely believes that disease, malnutrition, and illiteracy are criminal shames and that a better social order can be created through the perfection of good values. Despite the turn of events, Fidel clings to the thread of his dream: "If I'm told 98 percent of the people no longer believe in the Revolution, I'll continue to fight. If I'm told I'm the only one who believes in it, I'll continue." But he is far from the saint his ardent admirers portray.

A Hatred of Uncle Sam

Fidel turned to Communism for strategic not ideological reasons, but his bitterness toward the United States also shaped his decision. He has been less committed to Marxism than to anti-imperialism, in which he is unwavering. He has cast himself in the role of David versus Goliath, in the tradition of José Martí. Fidel sees himself as Martí's heir, representing the same combination of New World nationalism, Spanish romanticism, and philosophical radicalism. His trump card is Cuban nationalist sentiment.

His boyhood impressions of destitution in Holguín Province under the thumb of the United Fruit Company and, later, the 1954 overthrow of the reformist Arbenz government in Guatemala by a military force organized by the CIA and underwritten by "Big Fruit" had a profound impact on Fidel's thinking. Ever since, Fidel has viewed world politics through the prism of anti-Americanism. During the war in the Sierra Maestra, Fidel stated, "When this war is over, it will be the beginning, for me, of a much wider and bigger war; the war I'm going to wage against [the Americans]. I realize that that's going to be my true destiny."

He brilliantly used the Cold War to enlist the Soviet Union to move Cuba out of the U.S. orbit, and was thus able—with Soviet funds—to bolster his stature as a nationalist redeemer by guaranteeing the Cuban masses substantial social and economic gains while exerting constant energy and creativity to keep the United States at a distance.

Many Talents

Fidel has a gargantuan hunger for information, a huge trove of knowledge, and an equally prodigious memory. He never forgets facts and figures, a remarkable asset he nourished at law school, where he forced himself to depend on his memory by destroying the materials he had learned by heart. He is a micromanager. There is a sense of perfection in everything he does, applied through a superbly methodical mind and laser-clear focus. He has astounding political instincts, notably an uncanny ability to predict the future moves of his adversaries (Fidel is a masterly chess player). Fidel's "rarest virtue," says his intimate friend Gabriel

García Márquez, "is the ability to foresee the evolution of an event to its farthest-reaching consequences."

Fidel is also a gambler of unsurpassed self-confidence. He has stood at the threshold of death several times and loves to court danger. "Fidel has to manufacture the danger that lets him feel alive," notes journalist Eugene Robinson. Above all, Fidel has an insatiable appetite for the limelight, and a narcissistic focus on his theatrical role: The one thing that infuriates Fidel is to be ignored. Says Walter Russell Mead: "Fidel needs international celebrity the way a fire needs oxygen." His beard is also more than a trademark; he likes to hide his double chin; likewise, he wears false teeth, and his long fingernails are lacquered and filed. He never laughs at himself unless he makes the joke. And he assiduously avoids singing or dancing—he is perhaps the only male in Cuba who has never been seen to dance.

Fidel nurtures his image with exquisite care, feigning modesty to hide his immense ego. He sees himself as a leader of vast international significance, and the "absolute patriarch" of his country, suggests Bardach. He also claims that his place in history does not bother him. Yet in the same breath he likens himself to Jesus Christ: Fidel has carefully cultivated the myth of Fidel the Christ-like redeemer figure.

Fidel's revolutionary concept has been built on communicating with the masses through public speeches, televised in entirety. Fidel is masterfully persuasive, an amazingly gifted speaker who in his better days could hold Cubans spellbound with oratory, using his flattery and enigmatic language to obfuscate and arouse. His speeches lasted for hours. Fidel's loquaciousness is legendary. He is not, however, a man of small talk; he is deadly serious whenever he opens his mouth. His digressive repertoire is immense: "Fidel, the former lawyer, can argue anything from any side at any time," writes Bardach. He also listens intently when the subject interests him; he is a great questioner, homing immediately to the heart of the matter.

Dilettante Extraordinaire

Cubans' bawdy street wisdom says that Fidel had various domiciles so that he could attend to his lovers. When he was in better health, Fidel was an avid consumer of Cuba's anti-cholesterol drug, PPG, renowned for its Viagra-like side effects. He has admitted to having at least 12 children, but acknowledges there may be others; "almost a tribe!"

Many highly intelligent and beautiful women have dedicated themselves to Fidel and his cause. But Fidel saves his most ardent passions for the Revolution, and the women (and children) in his life have been badly treated. Meanwhile, Delia Soto del Valle, Fidel's second wife, with whom he has five sons, is rarely seen in public, and never with her husband. The average Cuban in the street knows virtually nothing of the private life of their secretive leader. The Cuban media are prohibited from reporting on Fidel's personal life, and photos of Soto del Valle and their children have only recently been published in Cuba.

Fidel was a "dilettante extraordinaire" in esoteric pursuits, notably gourmet dining (but not cigars; Fidel quit smoking in 1985). His second love was deep-sea fishing. He was also a good diver and used to frequently fly down to spearfish at his tiny retreat on Cayo Piedra.

Fidel retains the loyalty of millions of Cubans, but he is only loyal to those who are loyal to him. His capacity for Homeric rage is renowned, and it is said that no official in his right mind dares criticize him. Paradoxically, he can be extremely gentle and courteous, especially towards women, in whose company he is slightly abashed. Cubans fear the consequences of saying anything against him, discreetly stroking their chins—an allusion to his beard—rather than uttering his name (he is also known as *el que no debe ser nombrado,* "he whose name can't be spoken"). In 1996 his biographer Tad Szulc wrote, "He is determined not to tolerate any challenge to his authority, whatever the consequences." Fidel does not forget, or pardon, and never apologizes as a matter of policy. Beneath the gold foil lies a heart of cold steel. Thus, he is prepared to

RAÚL CASTRO

Born at Birán on June 3, 1931, Raúl is the youngest of the three Castro brothers (Cubans refer to him as *el chino* and slant their eyes to denote him – an allusion to the belief that he was fathered by a Chinaman, Batista loyalist Felipe Miraval). Although a mediocre student, he proved a capable commander in Fidel's guerrilla army and has been at the forefront of government since 1959.

Although an immensely capable manager, Raúl has none of his brother's charisma and is far less popular than Fidel, from whom he derived his political strength. He enjoys the absolute loyalty of the army, however, which he has led with skill and savvy.

Raúl has been a Communist since youth. Although he seems absolutely devoted to preserving the socialist revolution and one-party state, he is more pragmatic than Fidel and shows signs of wishing to step up the pace of economic reform while keeping a tight lid on political dissent. He is also a delegator, not the obsessive micro-manager that Fidel is. Nor is he filled with his brother's vast ego. Until Fidel dies, Raúl won't do anything to embarrass Fidel.

The real test will come with Raúl's passing (he is said to have an alcohol problem), when the true power struggle begins. But who knows? Perhaps Fidel will outlast him!

eliminate anyone, no matter who, if it serves him. His policies have divided countless families, and Fidel's family is no exception. His sister, Juanita, left for Miami in 1964 and is an outspoken critic of her brother's policies (in her 2009 autobiography, *Fidel and Raúl, My Brothers: The Secret History,* she revealed that she even worked for the CIA against her brother before fleeing Cuba). His tormented daughter, Alina Fernández Revuelta, fled in disguise in 1993 and vilifies her father from her home in Miami. Fidel's former wife, Mirta

Díaz-Balart, lives in Spain but makes regular visits (it is Raúl Castro, however, who tends to her).

Fidel—and now Raúl—have denied that a personality cult exists. Yet everywhere monuments, posters, and billboards are adorned with their quotations and faces. Fidel's visage is the banner of the daily newspaper, *Granma*, while the front pages of newspapers and television news are dominated by the brothers' public acts or speeches. And at rallies around the country, stooges work the crowds with chants of "Fee-del!" and "Raúl!"

The indefatigable Cuban leader, who turned 84 in 2010 and has outlasted all other leaders of his time, was taken life-threateningly ill in July 2006 and underwent emergency surgery for diverticulitis (in Cuba, his illness is a state secret). In 2010, he had aged markedly and looks like the frail old man that he is. Still, he remains First Secretary of the Communist Party, and although Raúl is officially in charge, Fidel clearly exercises veto power behind the scenes. Nonetheless, he hasn't been seen in public since having taken ill. At press time, the latest proof that he was still alive was photographs showing Fidel meeting with Brazilian president Lula Da Silva on February 24, 2010.

The Economy

One may wait fifteen minutes to buy a pound of rice, or thirty minutes for a bus that never shows. Another may wait four days in a provincial terminal for an airplane that's sitting in a hangar in some other province waiting for repairs from a mechanic who happens to be waiting in line at the doctor's office, but the doctor is late, still waiting for a permission slip from a government functionary who's behind schedule because she, too, had to wait in line all morning trying to reschedule her daughter for an eye exam that was delayed because the optometric lens was waiting to be repaired by the technician who was busy waiting at the train station for his relatives to arrive.

— Ben Corbett, *This Is Cuba*

HOW IT WAS

For several decades prior to the Revolution, U.S. corporations virtually owned the island. Most of the cattle ranches, more than 50 percent of the railways, 40 percent of sugar production, 90 percent of mining and oil production, and almost 100 percent of telephone and utility services were owned by U.S. companies. Every year, beginning in 1934, the U.S.

Congress established a preferential quota for Cuban sugar. In exchange for a guaranteed price, Cuba had to guarantee tariff concessions on U.S. goods sold to Cuba. The agreement kept Cuba tied to the U.S. as a one-commodity economy and to U.S. goods.

Nonetheless, despite immense poverty

WHAT A JOKE!

After the Revolution, Che Guevara was named president of the bank and Minister of Finance. He loved to regale listeners with the joke of how he'd gotten the job, according to author Jon Lee Anderson. Supposedly, at a cabinet meeting to decide on a replacement of bank president Felipe Pazos, Castro asked who among them was a "good *economista*." Che raised his hand and was sworn in as Minister of Finance and head of the National Bank. Castro said: "Che, I didn't know you were an economist." Che replied, "I'm not!" Castro asked, "Then why did you raise your hand when I said I needed an economist?" To which Guevara replied, "Economist! I thought you asked for a Communist."

throughout the country, Cuba's national income in 1957 of US$2.3 billion was topped only by that of the much larger countries of Argentina, Mexico, and Venezuela.

Castro and Che Guevara, who became the Minister of Industry, might have been great revolutionaries, but they didn't have the skills to run an efficient economy, which they swiftly nationalized. There were few coherent economic plans in the 1960s—just grandiose schemes that almost always ended in near ruin. They replaced monetary work incentives with "moral" incentives, set artificially low prices, and got diminishing supplies in return. Socialism had nationalized wealth but, says Guillermo Cabrera Infante, it "socialized poverty too," leaving Cuba with a ruined economy.

Soviet Largesse

For almost three decades, the Soviet Union acted as Cuba's benefactor, providing aid estimated at around US$11 million per day—the greatest per capita aid program in world history. Says P. J. O'Rourke, "The Cubans got the luxury of running their economy along the lines of a Berkeley commune, and like California hippies wheedling their parents for cash, someone else paid the tab." The Soviet Union also sustained the Cuban economy by buying 85 percent of its foreign exports. In 1989, 84 percent of Cuba's trade was with the Soviet bloc.

After the collapse of the Soviet bloc, Cuba's economy was cut adrift. Between 1990 and 1994, the economy shrank as much as 70 percent. The work force was left idle. To compound the problem, the world market price of sugar, which in the 1980s accounted for 80 percent of Cuba's export earnings, also plummeted, along with Cuba's sugar harvest.

Farewell to Marxism

In October 1991 the Cuban Communist Party Congress adopted a resolution establishing profit-maximizing state-owned Cuban corporations that operate independently of the central state apparatus. In 1995 Cuba passed a law (since rescinded) allowing foreigners to have wholly owned businesses (by 2003, about 800 foreign companies were doing business with Cuba). Cuba began sending its best and brightest abroad for crash courses in capitalist business techniques (you'd hardly know it, however, by the absurd decisions and ineptitude still being made by Cuba's state managers). Havana has even handed over large chunks of the economy to the military, which began sweeping experiments. Today generals in civilian clothes run corporations such as Gaviota, whose resort hotels are built by the army's construction company, Unión de Empresas Constructoras.

In 1993, to soak up foreign currency floating freely in the black market as cash remittances (*remesas* from families in the U.S. topped US$1.4 billion in 2009) or as tips from foreign tourists, the Cuban government legalized possession of the U.S. dollar and opened up "foreign exchange recovery stores" (shops) selling imported items, from toothpaste to Japanese TVs. The government also legalized self-employment: By mid-1995, 210,000 Cubans (about 5 percent of Cuba's labor force) had registered as *cuentapropistas*, subject to taxation up to 50 percent.

Back from the Brink

By 2005, with the economy stabilized (and bolstered by growing economic ties to China and Venezuela), the government began rolling back reforms. By the end of that year, only a handful of foreign investors (the rest were sent packing without their assets) remained. Joint-venture enterprises have lost much of their autonomy. And Cuba's self-employed, who typically earn far more than the average monthly salary of 420 pesos (equivalent to US$18), have also found Cuban-style capitalism bruising in the face of regulations meant to force them back out of business.

In 2004, Castro banned the dollar, forcing Cubans to exchange hoarded greenbacks—or *fula,* as Cubans call it in a reference to the green-gray gunpowder used in *santería* to invoke the spirits—for convertible pesos, resulting in an instant injection of US$1.5 billion into the Cuban economy. Castro also revalued the convertible peso 8 percent against other currencies (Cubans now receive only 83 convertible pesos for every US$100 sent from Florida after the Cuban government skims off commissions).

HOW IT IS

Cuba, with an annual GDP of US$110 billion, is running a massive trade deficit and a foreign debt topping $19 billion as of 2009. The economy, which is in freefall, is kept afloat with substantial aid from Venezuela, which supplies Cuba with oil (US$3.1 billion in 2008) and financial aid. Brazil, China, and Russia have also substantially increased their investments.

The economy suffered a devastating blow in 2008, when a series of hurricanes caused an estimated US$10 billion in damage. Raúl Castro initiated belt-tightening, including restrictions on remittances of profits by foreign corporations doing business in Cuba. Key ministers have been replaced with disciplinarians charged with bringing military-style efficiency to the economy. Several economic entities and ministries have been disbanded or merged. A new salary bonus system that rewards productivity was introduced.

AGRICULTURE

"There must be much hunger," says one of Ernest Hemingway's characters in *Islands in the Stream.* "You cannot realize it," comes the reply. "No I can't," Thomas Hudson thought. "I can't realize it at all. I can't realize why there should ever be any hunger in this country ever." Traveling through Cuba, you'll also sense the vast potential that caused René Dumont, the outstanding French agronomist, to say that "with proper management, Cuba could adequately feed five times its current population."

Before the Revolution, Cuba certainly couldn't feed itself: The best arable lands were planted in sugarcane for export. Alas, since the Revolution, management of agriculture has been inept. First, Castro organized land in a system of centralized, inefficient state farms dedicated to sugarcane monoculture to satisfy the Soviet sweet tooth. (Cuba is the only country in Latin America whose production of rice, for example, hasn't risen since 1958; in 2008, major investment was initiated to increase rice production.) Declining agricultural production was exacerbated in the early 1990s due to a lack of machinery, fertilizers, and alternating droughts and torrential storms. Food distribution is also centralized and highly inefficient.

In September 1993 Cuba established autonomous cooperatives that farm government land but own the crop they harvest (although they must follow state directives and sell their crops to the state at fixed prices). Private owners utilize about 20 percent of Cuba's cultivable land; they, too, must sell 80 percent of their produce to the state at fixed prices. The Cubans also began experimenting with alternative farming in the early 1980s; the demise of the Soviet Union forced them to plunge in headlong. Meanwhile, several thousand community-operated gardens have eased food shortfalls (alongside private farms, these *agropónicos* account for about half the food grown in Cuba).

Since taking over from Fidel, Raúl has initiated significant reforms: More than 45,000 farmers have been given usufruct of vacant state land (more than half of Cuba's arable land lies idle, however); local councils have been given greater autonomy over food production; and the state has supposedly paid its outstanding debts to farmers and increased the prices it pays for produce.

Despite these changes, production remains insufficient to meet domestic needs: In 2007, Cuba imported US$1.6 billion in food, equivalent to 80 percent of what it consumes (35 percent came from the United States, worth US$718 million in 2008, making Uncle Sam Cuba's largest supplier of food).

Cattle, Citrus, and Coffee

Cuba has always had a strong cattle industry, particularly in the provinces around Camagüey, which has been famous for beef and dairy production since before the Revolution. There were 6.5 million head of cattle on the eve of the Revolution, when milk production was 9.6 million liters a year. Following the Revolution, the herds were slaughtered to compensate for falling production of other foods; by 1963, there were only two million head. That year, Castro took a lively interest and made animal husbandry a national priority, resulting in the breeding of Cuba's home-grown Charolais, Santa Gertrudis, and F1 strains. By 1980, Cuba had replenished its herds. Thereafter the industry has again declined. Private farmers are again permitted to raise cattle, but they are severely restricted. (Killing cattle for private consumption or sale of meat is illegal, and farmers are fined for each head of cattle they lose.)

Cuba produces about one million tons of citrus. Most citrus goes to produce juices and extracts, much of it for export to Europe. Effort has been made in recent years to upgrade with investments from Chile and Israel.

Cuba produces excellent coffee. The finest quality is grown in the Sierra Escambray, although most coffee is grown in the mountains of eastern Cuba. Cuba enjoyed modest exports on the eve of the Revolution, following which Fidel initiated a massive and disastrous coffee planting scheme that cordoned lowland Havana with the upland plant. Production has since declined markedly, due, not least, to out-of-date technology and the use of unskilled high school students to bring in the harvest. Production peaked in 2006 at over 8,000 tons. The highest quality coffee is exported. Domestic coffee is adulterated with roasted wheat.

Sugar

¡Azúcar! The whole country reeks of sweet, pungent sugar, Cuba's curse and blessing. The unusual depth and fertility of Cuba's limestone soils are unparalleled in the world for producing sugar. The Cuban landscape is one of endless cane fields, lorded over by the towering chimneys of great sugar mills.

The nation's bittersweet bondsman has been responsible for curses like slavery and the country's almost total dependence on not only the one product, but on single imperial nations:

first Spain, then the United States, and most recently the Soviet Union. Production rose gradually from about five million tons a year in the early 1970s to 7.5 million tons on average in the late 1980s. Three-quarters went to feed the Soviet bear; the rest went to capitalist markets to earn hard currency. The collapse of the Soviet bloc rendered a triple whammy to Cuba's obsolete sugar industry. Cuba had to produce more and more sugar to generate the same income while facing growing competition from new producers such as India and

THE *ZAFRA*

With the onset of the dry season, Cuba prepares for the *zafra*, the sugar harvest, which runs from November through June. Then *macheteros* (cane-cutters) are in the fields from dawn until dusk, wielding their blunt-nosed machetes after first burning the cane stalks to soften them for the cut. The *macheteros* grab the three-meter-tall stalks, which they slash close to the ground (where the sweetness concentrates). Then they cut off the top and strip the dry leaves from the stalk.

Today, three-quarters of the crop is harvested mechanically. The Cuban-designed combine-harvester can cut a truckload of cane (close to seven metric tons) in 10 minutes, three times more than the most skilled *macheteros* can cut by hand in a day.

The cut cane is delivered to one of the approximately 44 sugar mills in Cuba (reduced from about 150), which operate 24 hours a day, pouring black smoke into the air. Here the sugarcane is fed to the huge steel crushers that squeeze out the sugary pulp called *guarapo*, which is boiled, clarified, evaporated, and separated into molasses and sugar crystals. The molasses makes rum, yeast, and cattle feed. *Bagazo*, the fiber left after squeezing, fuels boilers or is shipped off to mills to be turned into paper and wallboard. The sugar is shipped by rail to bulk shipping terminals for transport to refineries abroad.

tobacco curing at Finca El Pinar San Luís, Pinar del Río

increasingly more efficient sugar beet producers. From seven million tons in 1991, the harvest plummeted to 1.4 million tons in 2009, worth a relatively paltry US$220 million.

In 2002, the government announced that more than 3.1 million acres of canefields were to be converted to food crops. All but 44 of the nation's 156 sugar mills have since been closed and 100,000 sugar workers made redundant. Then, remarkably, in another turnabout in 2006, the government announced that it intended to revive the sugar industry and expand production!

Tobacco

About 50,000 hectares are given to tobacco, Cuba's second most important agricultural earner of foreign exchange. It is grown predominantly in a 90-mile-long, 10-mile-wide valley—Vuelta Abajo—in Pinar del Río, on small properties, principally privately owned; the average holding is only 10 hectares (about 25 acres).

The tobacco industry has been devastated by hurricanes in recent years, causing massive devastation and losses within the industry.

Cuba's state-run Habanos S.A. has struggled to maintain quality, not least due to overproduction in some years. Production fell 8 percent in 2009, when Cuba sold about 150 million cigars, worth US$306 million.

INDUSTRY

Cement, rubber, and tobacco products, processed foods, textiles, clothing, footwear, chemicals, and fertilizers are the staple industries. Cuba has also invested in metal processing, spare parts industries, and factories turning out domestic appliances, albeit often of shoddy quality. It also has steel mills, bottling plants, paper-producing factories, and animal feed factories. Even Sony TVs, Cuban-designed computers, and vehicles are assembled from foreign parts.

Many factories date from the antediluvian dawn. An exception is in pharmaceuticals, where its investments in biotechnology generate more than US$300 million a year.

Mining

Cuba boasts large resources of chromite, cobalt, iron, copper, manganese, lead, and zinc,

CIGARS

FROM LEAF TO CIGAR

The tobacco leaves, which arrive from the fields in dry sheets, are first moistened and stripped. The leaves are then graded by color and strength (each type of cigar has a recipe). A blender mixes the various grades of leaves, which then go to the production room, where each *tabaquero* and *tabaquera* receives enough tobacco to roll approximately 100 cigars for the day.

The rollers sit at rows of *galeras* (workbenches) with piles of loose tobacco leaves at their sides. The rollers' indispensable tool is a *chaveta,* a rounded, all-purpose knife for smoothing and cutting leaves, tamping loose tobacco and circumcising the tips. While they work, a *lector* (reader) reads aloud from a strategically positioned platform or high chair. Morning excerpts are read from the *Granma* newspaper; in the afternoon, the *lector* reads from historical or political books, or short stories and novels. Alexandre Dumas's novel *The Count of Monte Cristo* was such a hit in the 19th century that it lent its name to the famous Montecristo cigar.

The *torcedor* (cigar roller) fingers his or her leaves and, according to texture and color, chooses two to four filler leaves, which are laid end to end and gently yet firmly rolled into a tube, then enveloped by the binder leaves to make a "bunch." The rough-looking "bunch" is then placed with nine others in a small wooden mold that is screwed down to press each cigar into a solid cylinder. Next, the *tabaquera* selects a wrapper leaf, which she trims to size. The "bunch" is then laid at an angle across the wrapper, which is stretched and rolled around the "bunch," overlapping with each turn. A tiny quantity of flavorless tragapanth gum (made from Swiss pine trees) is used to glue the *copa* down. Now the *torcedor* rolls the cigar, applying pressure with the flat of the *chaveta*. Finally, a piece of wrapper leaf the size and shape of a quarter is cut to form the cap; it is glued and twirled into place, and the excess is trimmed. The whole process takes about five minutes.

Cigar rollers serve a nine-month apprenticeship, and each factory has its own school. Those who succeed graduate slowly from making petit corona cigars to the larger and specialized sizes. Rollers are paid piece rates based on the number of cigars they produce. They can puff as much as they wish on the fruits of their labor while working. The majority of rollers are women. Prior to the Revolution, only men rolled cigars; the leaves were selected by women, who often sorted them on their thighs, giving rise to the famous myth about cigars being "rolled on the dusky thighs of Cuban maidens."

AND SO TO MARKET

The roller ties cigars of the same size and brand into bundles – *media ruedas* (half-wheels) – of 50 using a colored ribbon. These are then fumigated in a vacuum chamber. Quality is determined by a *revisador* (inspector), according to eight criteria, such as length, weight, firmness, smoothness of wrappers, and whether the ends are cleanly cut. *Catadores* (professional smokers) then blind test the cigars for aroma, draw, and burn, the relative importance of each varying according to whether the cigar is a slim panatela (draw is paramount) or a fat robusto (flavor being more important). The *catadores* taste only in the morning and rejuvenate their taste buds with sugarless tea.

Once fumigated, cigars are placed in cool cabinets for three weeks to settle fermentation and remove any excess moisture. The cigars are then graded according to color and then shade within a particular color category. A trademark paper band is then put on. Finally, the cigars are laid in pinewood boxes, with the lightest cigar on the right and the darkest on the left (cigars range from the very mild, greenish-brown *doble claro* to the very strong, almost black *oscuro*). A thin leaf of cedar wood is laid on top to maintain freshness, and the box is sealed with a green-and-white label guaranteeing the cigars are genuine Havanas, or *puros habanos* (today the terms *puro* and *habano* are synonyms for cigar).

all concentrated in northeastern Cuba. Cuba is also the world's sixth-largest producer of nickel and has about 37 percent of the world's estimated reserves. Nickel exports earned US$1.5 billion in 2008, down from US$2.2 billion in 2007.

Oil

In April 1960 the Soviet ship *Chernovci* arrived with a 70,000-barrel load of oil—the beginning of a 10,000-kilometer petroleum pipeline that was maintained for three decades. Cuba traded nickel, citrus, and sugar to the Soviet Union in return for 10–12 million tons of crude oil and petroleum per year. As much as half of this was re-exported for hard currency to purchase necessities on the world market (by the mid-1980s, oil surpassed sugar as the island's major money-maker). Today, Cuba meets the bulk of its needs with some 100,000 barrels a day of discounted Venezuelan oil, paid for in part in medical and other services.

Cuba *does* have oil, and crude is currently being pumped from 20 oil fields concentrated near Varadero. Production rose to 75,000 barrels per day in 2007—enough to cover 50 percent of the island's needs. However, Cuba's crude oil is heavy, with a high sulfur content. Seeking higher-quality oil, the Cuban government has opened up a 112,000-square-kilometer zone of the Gulf of Mexico for deep-water exploration by foreign companies. In December 2004, Fidel announced discovery of a crude oil deposit (he claims that as much as 20 billion barrels are to be found off Cuba's northwest coast). Venezuela funded a new refinery, which opened at Cienfuegos, in 2008.

TOURISM

Before 1959 Cuba was one of the world's hottest tourist destinations. When Batista was ousted, most foreigners stayed home. Apart from a handful of Russians, the beaches belonged to the Cubans throughout the 1960s, '70s, and '80s, when tourism contributed virtually

nothing to the nation's coffers. Havana's view of tourism profoundly shifted with the demise of the Soviet Union. Cuba set itself an ambitious long-term goal of five million tourists annually by 2010. Tourism, however, peaked in 2005 at 2.3 million visitors, before falling off in 2006 and 2007, then recuperating to 2.43 million in 2009 (some 10 percent of all Caribbean arrivals, not bad considering that U.S. travelers are barred by their own government). Tourism earned Cuba US$2.4 billion in 2008, but fell 11 percent in 2009.

Canada accounted for 50 percent of arrivals in 2009 (almost all of it at all-inclusive beach resorts), followed by Great Britain, Italy, then Spain. Cuba is currently focusing on the former Soviet bloc market.

Despite having upgraded most of its hotel infrastructure to international standards, Cuba has failed to establish a significant level of repeat business because of poor service, lousy food, state-sponsored rip-offs, and outrageous prices. In March 2008, Cuba announced that it would build 30 new hotels by 2014 (including 10 in Havana)—ostensibly in the event that U.S. travel restrictions are lifted—complementing by 22 percent an existing crop of 47,000 hotel rooms that, in high season, is barely sufficient to keep up with existing demand. (Speculation that tourism infrastructure will buckle under the weight of a U.S. stampede seems misplaced. The Cuban government will likely opt to regulate the influx—by limiting aircraft landing rights and perhaps even introducing a visa system—until it can get its new infrastructure in place.)

The Ministry of Tourism oversees tourism development and acts as watchdog over state-owned agencies that operate autonomously with the authority to form joint-management agreements with foreign tourism companies. Since 2005 it has been run by a military figure, Manuel Marero Cruz, and has restructured hotel groups and taken over many tourism-related businesses under its own direction.

Cuban Society

I was at that hallucinatory early stage in my encounter with this new country, the stage at which a perfect descriptive framework emerges, distinct and complete, and all that seems left to do is fill in a few blanks and add a bit of ornament. From that golden and illusion-filled moment, ignorance always increased geometrically. For the next week or month or decade, each day adds a bit of understanding about the place. But if you're paying attention, each day also takes a bit of understanding away.

– Eugene Robinson, Last Dance in Havana

DEMOGRAPHY

According to Cuba's National Statistic Office (www.one.cu), the population in July 2009 was estimated at 11,235,000, of which 75.9 percent were classified as urban; 19.9 percent live in the city of Havana, with a population of about 2,200,000. Santiago de Cuba, the second-largest city, has about 350,000 people. The annual average growth rate is 0.23 percent and declining.

The low birth and mortality rates and high life expectancy also mean a rapidly aging population. About 16.2 percent of the population is 60 years or older—an enormous social security burden for the beleaguered government.

The United Nations Human Development Index ranks Cuba third in the Caribbean (behind the Bahamas and Barbados) and fifth in Latin America (behind Argentina, Chile, Uruguay, and Costa Rica).

Ethnicity and Race Relations

Officially about 37 percent of the population is "white," mainly of Spanish origin. About 11 percent is black, and 53 percent is mulatto of mixed white-black ethnicity—Cuban lore claims there is some African in every Cuban's blood. Chinese constitute about 0.1 percent.

After emancipation in 1888, the island was spared the brutal segregation of the American South, and a black middle class evolved alongside a black underclass, with its own social clubs, restaurants, and literature. "Cuba's color line is much more flexible than that of the United States," recorded black author Langston Hughes during a visit in 1930: "There are no Jim Crow cars in Cuba, and at official state gatherings and less official carnivals and celebrations, citizens of all colors meet and mingle." Gradually, U.S. visitors began to import Southern racial prejudice to their winter playground. To court their approval, hotels that were formerly lax in their application of color lines began to discourage even mulatto Cubans. Cuba on the eve of the Revolution had adopted discrimination. When dictator Fulgencio Batista—who was a mixture of white, black, and Chinese—arrived at the exclusive Havana Yacht Club, they turned the lights out to let him know that although he was president, as a mulatto he wasn't welcome.

The Castro government swiftly outlawed institutionalized discrimination and vigorously enforced laws to bring about racial equality. The social advantages that opened up after the Revolution have resulted in the abolition of lily-white scenes. Cuban society is as intermixed as any other on earth. Racial harmony is everywhere evident. Mixed marriages raise no eyebrows in Cuba. Black novelist Alice Walker, who knows Cuba well, has written, "Unlike black Americans, who have never felt at ease with being American, black Cubans raised in the Revolution take no special pride in being black. They take great pride in being Cuban. Nor do they appear able to feel, viscerally, what racism is." Hence, blacks are, on the whole, more loyal to Castro than whites.

Nonetheless, the most marginal neighborhoods still have a heavy preponderance of blacks. Most Cuban blacks still work at menial jobs and earn, on average, less than whites. And blacks are notoriously absent from the upper echelons of government. (Since 1994, when Havana witnessed what were essentially race riots, the government has been promoting black officials and elevating blacks to more prominent positions in tourism.) Nor has the Revolution totally overcome stereotypical racial thinking and prejudice. Black youths, for example, claim to be disproportionately harassed by police (though, ironically, blacks are well represented among the uniformed police). And you still hear racist comments, though most racial references—and Cuba is full of them—are well-meaning.

CHARACTER, CONDUCT, AND CUSTOMS

Although a clear Cuban identity has emerged, Cuban society is not easy to fathom. Cubans "adore mystery and continually do their damnedest to render everything more intriguing. Conventional rules do not apply," thought author Juliet Barclay. The Cubans value context, and the philosophical approach to life differs markedly from North America or northern Europe. Attempts to analyze Cuba through the North American value system are bound to be wide of the mark.

In the decades since the Revolution, most Cubans have learned to live double lives. One side is spirited, inventive, irrepressibly argumentative and critical, inclined to keep private shrines at home to both Christian saints and African gods, and profit however possible from the failings and inefficiencies of the state. The other side commits them to be good revolutionaries and to cling to the state and the man who runs it. When loyalists (those faithful to Fidel) speak of the "Revolution," they don't mean the toppling of Batista's regime, or Castro's seizure of power, or even his and the country's conversion to Communism. They mean the ongoing process of building a society where everyone supposedly benefits. Despite a pandemic of disaffection, many Cubans seem happy to accept the sacrifice of individual liberties for the abstract notion of improving equality.

The Cuban people are committed to social justice. The idea that democracy includes every person's right to guaranteed health care and education is deeply ingrained in their

SPANISH SURNAMES

Spanish surnames are combinations of the first surname of the person's father, which comes first, and the mother's first surname, which comes second. Thus, the son of Ángel Castro Argiz and Lina Ruz González is Fidel Castro Ruz.

After marriage, women do not take their husbands' surnames; they retain their maiden names. A single woman is addressed as *señorita* if less than 40 years old, and *señora* if above 40.

consciousness. True, city folk crave the opportunity to better their lives materially, but few Cubans are concerned with the *accumulation* of material wealth. Most Cubans are more interested in sharing something with you than getting something from you. They are unmoved by talk of your material accomplishments.

The traditional Afro-Cuban tropical culture has proved resistant to puritanical revolutionary doctrine. Cubans are sensualists of the first degree. Judging by the ease with which couples neck openly and spontaneously slip into bed, the dictatorship of the proletariat that transformed Eastern Europe into a perpetual Sunday school has made little headway in Cuba. The state may promote the family, but Cubans have a notoriously indulgent attitude towards casual sex. Infidelity is "as Cuban as sugarcane," suggests Ann Louise Bardach.

Cubans are also notoriously toilet- and fashion-conscious. Even the poorest Cuban manages to keep fastidiously clean and well dressed.

The struggles of the past decades have fostered a remarkable sense of confidence and maturity. As such, there's no reserve, no emotional distance, no holding back. Cubans are self-assured and engage you in a very intimate way. They're not afraid of physical contact; they touch a lot. They also look you in the eye: They don't blink or flinch but are direct and assured.

And free of social pretension. They're alive and full of emotional intensity, and chock-full of *chispas* (sparks).

Social Divisions

The Revolution destroyed the social stratification inherited from Spanish colonial rule. Distinct delineations among the classes withered away. Not that prerevolutionary Cuba was entirely rigid—it was unusual in Latin America for its high degree of "social mobility." There was a huge middle class.

As an agrarian-populist movement, *fidelismo* destroyed the middle class, eradicating their hard-earned wealth and tearing families asunder. The "privileged" classes were replaced by a new class of senior Communist Party members and army officials who control everything and enjoy benefits unavailable to other Cubans.

Cubans lack the social caste system that makes so many Europeans walk on eggshells. There is absolutely no deference, no subservience. Cubans accept people at face value and are slow to judge others negatively. They are instantly at ease, and greet each other with hearty handshakes or kisses. Women meeting for the first time will embrace like sisters. A complete stranger is sure to give you a warm *abrazo,* or hug. Cubans call each other *compañero* or *compañera,* which Martha Gellhorn described as having a "cozy sound of companionship." As a foreigner, you'll meet with the warmest courtesies wherever you go. Cubans can't understand why foreigners are always saying, "Thank you!" Doing things for others is the expected norm.

In the past few decades, however, a stratified society has emerged. The values and ethics are becoming strained. Prostitution is once again rampant. An economic elite of *masetas* (rich Cubans) has become visible, as has a class of desperately impoverished. And low-level corruption, long a necessity for getting around Cuba's socialist inefficiencies, has blossomed into more insidious high-level graft and racketeering. Many people are alternately sad and high-spirited (Cuba's suicide rate is almost double that of the United States and is the greatest cause of death between the ages of 15 and 45).

The *jineteras,* the petty thieves on the streets, the children who now resort to begging: all these things are the result of Cuba's poverty.

Many families are torn by divided feelings towards the Revolution and Castro and don't even talk with one another. The worst divisions are found among families split between those who departed for Miami and those who stayed. *Se fue* (he/she left) and *se quedó* (he/she stayed) carry profound meaning. Every year tens of thousands plot their escape to Miami, often without telling their relatives, and sometimes not even their spouses. Cubans thus tend to evolve speedy relationships and/or grasp at opportunity. "All the Cubans' experience tells them that there is no time to go slow, that pleasures and love must be taken fast when they present themselves because tomorrow…*se fue,*" wrote Claudia Lightfoot.

Cuban Curiosity

A sense of isolation and a high level of cultural development have filled Cubans with intense curiosity. Many will guess your nationality and quiz you about the most prosaic matters of Western life, as well as the most profound. Issues of income and cost are areas of deep interest.

Cubans are starved of much information. They watch Hollywood movies and often converse with a surprising mix of worldly erudition and astounding naïveté. If you tell them you are a *yanqui,* most Cubans light up. They are genuinely fond of U.S. citizens. However, although Cubans thrive on debate, they are hesitant to discuss politics openly except behind closed doors. Only in private, and once you have earned their trust, will you be able to gauge how they really feel about Cuba and Castro.

Humor

Despite their hardships, Cubans have not lost the ability to laugh. Stand-up comedy is a tradition in Cuban nightclubs. Cubans turn everything into a *chiste* (joke), most of which are aimed at themselves. Their penetrating black humor spares no one—the insufferable bureaucrat, *jineteras,* the Special Period. Not even

THE CUBAN-AMERICANS

There are more than one million Cuban-born people in the United States, half of them naturalized citizens, according to the U.S. Census Bureau. They are concentrated in Dade County, Florida, and New Jersey. Their capital is Miami, just 140 miles from Havana – a distance protracted by a generation of despair, hubris, and bile. Even Fidel has family in exile, and not just his daughter Alina, who has called her father a "tyrant" and "mediocrity," but also his sister Juanita, who fled to Miami in the early 1960s and speaks out against the pain and turmoil her brother has caused.

The "old guard" (Fidel calls them *gusanos* – worms) were forced to flee Cuba, where they formed the wealthy and middle classes, shortly after the Revolution. Many were corrupt *batistianos* who have grown inordinately powerful, infusing Miami politics and business with their repressive, anti-democratic ways. Many of these Cuban-Americans have grown militant with distance and time, cultivating delusion "like hothouse orchids," in the words of Cristina García. They can't get over their bitterness, not least because Fidel Castro won't let them. Says Walter Russell Mead: "Castro destroyed the world the exiles knew and loved...over the decades, he has showered them with infamy and filth and done his best to offend every patriotic, religious, and personal sensibility they have. Miami is furious, and Castro knows how to twist the knife to keep the wounds always fresh."

The extremist Cuban-American lobby is so caught up in desire for vengeance that it has been blinded by its own rage. Says columnist Mead: "Time after time, [Castro] plays them like a violin. He can provoke them into paroxysms of gibbering rage, he can lock them into self-destructive political opinions, he can even turn their greatest strength – their ability to monopolize the American political debate over Cuba policy – into a pillar propping up his regime."

HARDBALL POLITICS

Contemporary U.S. policy toward Cuba is largely shaped by the hard-nosed right-wing constituency, whose U.S.-Cuba Democracy Political Action Committee has made over US$10 million in campaign donations since 2004. The lobby works hard to keep Washington from cutting a deal.

Why do Cuban-Americans themselves remain vested in the embargo if it helps keep the Castros in power?

First, consider the large Cuban-American companies that were dispossessed of their properties in Cuba: the exiled Fanjul family has become Florida's largest sugar producer; Bacardi is the world's largest rum producer. It's hardly conceivable that they would welcome the U.S. market being opened to Cuban

Fidel is spared the barbs, although his name is never used, and no one in his right mind would tell such a joke in public.

Cubans also boast a great wit. They lace their conversations with double entendres and often risqué innuendo.

The Nationalist Spirit

Cubans are an intensely passionate and patriotic people united by love of country. Cubans are nationalists before they are socialists or even incipient capitalists. The revolutionary government has engaged in consciousness-raising on a national scale, instilling in Cubans that they can have pride as a nation. Primary school children not only lisp loyalty to the flag daily at school, they recite their willingness to *die* for it.

Cubans had not expected socialism from the Revolution, but those who could accept it did so not simply because so many benefited from the social mobility the Revolution had brought but because, as Maurice Halperin suggests, "it came with nationalism; that is, an assertion of economic and political independence from the United States, the goal of Cuban patriots for a half century." This provides Cubans with a different perspective and viewpoint on history.

rum and sugar, especially when produced by factories and on land they once owned. Both companies are major players in Miami and Washington politics and are steadfast in their effort to maintain the embargo

Second, a small group of rich and powerful Cuban-Americans don't want to see a change for reasons of power and personal gain. Anti-Castroism has become a linchpin of their domestic clout, including control over the financially lucrative Radio and TV Martí, a Cuban-American administered entity that beams propaganda into Cuba and is funded to the tune of some US$34 million a year. The Cubans manage to jam the transmissions, which virtually no Cuban sees or hears. Yet this absurd waste continues, despite General Accounting Office audits that have found that much of the annual largesse can't be accounted for (Republican Congressional representatives Lincoln Diaz-Balart and Ileana Ros-Lehtinen have had shows on Radio Martí, which also helps explain why this boondoggle continues.)

The Cuban-American National Foundation (CANF), the most powerful of the exile groups, considers itself the Cuban government in exile and has been more or less treated as such by U.S. administrations. Moderates, such as Cambio Cubano (Cubans for Change), the Cuban Committee for Democracy, and the Cuban-American Alliance Education Fund, have limited influence; they can't get Washington's ear because the right-wing has out-organized and outspent them.

However, the moderate voice is getting stronger and was undoubtedly assisted by the Elian González debacle. Florida's Cuban community is now divided between the hard-line old guard and younger, American-born second-generation Cuban-Americans who hold less passionate political views. A 2009 poll of Cuban-Americans showed that the mood had shifted, with 67 percent in favor of lifting travel restrictions.

THE VIEW FROM CUBA

The Cuban government portrays the rightist exiles (which it calls the "Miami Mafia") as the top rung of a class structure that left a racist society and carried their prejudice with them – "had Elián González been black, they would have tossed him back into the sea," suggests Ann Louise Bardach. No Cubans see the CANF leadership defending free health or education or the interests of the elderly and poor. They also fear that their homes and land will be sold from under them if the ultraconservative exiles ever return to power. It's a well-founded fear. Many Cuban-Americans are determined to gain back what they left behind, while others seem eager to make money from selling off Cuban assets.

Labor and the Work Ethic

Cubans combine their southern joy of living with a northern work ethic. Through the centuries, Cuba has received a constant infusion of the most energetic people in the Caribbean. The entrepreneurial spirit isn't dead, as attested by the success of the self-employed that sprang up in 1993 before being quashed by crippling taxation and state harassment.

The vast majority of Cubans work for the state, which with few exceptions dictates where an individual will work. However, a huge proportion of the adult population is unemployed or has no productive work, despite official figures. Thus the degree of anomie is great. Many Cubans ask their doctor friends to issue *certificados* (medical excuses) so that they can take a "vacation" from the boredom of employment that offers little financial reward and little hope of promotion. *Socio* is the buddy network, used to shield you from the demands of the state. *Pinche* and *mayimbe* are your high-level contacts, those who help you get around the bureaucracy, such as the doctor who writes a false note to relieve you of "voluntary" work in the countryside. Meanwhile, so many teachers have left their profession to work in tourism that tourism companies are now forbidden from hiring teachers.

The improvements in the living standards among rural families in the early decades of the Revolution have not been enough to keep the younger generation on the land. There has been a steady migration from the *campos,* despite the government having banned such freedom of movement. To make up for the labor shortfall, Castro invented "volunteer" brigades. Urban workers, university students, and even schoolchildren are shipped to the countryside to toil in the fields as *microbrigadistas.* Although the legal minimum working age is 17, the Labor Code exempts 15- and 16-year-olds to allow

them to fill labor shortages. Volunteer workers get an *estímulo,* a reward, such as priority listing for apartments.

Wages are according to a salary scale of 22 levels, with the top level getting six times that of the lowest. Highly trained professionals share the same struggles as unskilled workers. Life is little different for those who earn 250 pesos (US$10) a month and those who earn 1,000 (US$40). Such wages don't go far in contemporary Cuba. In 2008, Raúl announced that wage caps would be lifted. Nonetheless, the Cuban government is not about to let anyone get rich. (For example, the state agency charges foreign entities in Cuba US$450 per

PROSTITUTION, OR MERELY PERMISSIVE?

Before the Revolution, Batista's Babylon offered a tropical buffet of sin: Castro declared that there were 100,000 prostitutes in Havana, about 10 times the true figure. In 1959, the revolutionary government closed down the sex shows and porn palaces and sent the prostitutes to rehabilitative trade schools, thereby ostensibly eliminating the world's oldest trade. Prostitution reappeared, however, within a few years. Fred Ward recorded in 1977 how "a few girls have been appearing once again in the evenings, looking for dates, and willing to trade their favors for goods rather than money."

jineteras – the word comes from *jineta,* horsewoman, or jockey – have always been part of the postrevolutionary landscape, especially at embassy functions (the Cuban government, claimed Guillermo Cabrera Infante, has always made "state mulattas" available to foreign dignitaries, for whom it even maintains a "discreet house of select prostitutes" in Jaimanitas, according to journalist Pedro Alfonso). Critics even claim that in the early 1990s, the Cuban government sponsored the island's image as a cheap sex paradise to kickstart tourism. The situation reached its nadir when in 1999 a Mexican company, Cubamor, was accused of operating organized sex tours with official connivance.

THE GOVERNMENT'S RESPONSE
"The state tries to prevent it as much as possible. It is not legal in our country to practice prostitution, nor are we going to legalize it. Nor are we thinking in terms of turning it into a freelance occupation to solve unemployment problems. We are not going to repress it either," Castro told *Time* magazine, while boasting that Cuba had the healthiest and best-educated prostitutes in the world.

However, the Cuban government was clearly stung by foreign media reports on the subject. In 1996, Cuban women were barred from tourist hotels, and the police initiated a crackdown. A mandatory two-year jail term (since increased to four years) was imposed for any female the government considers a "prostitute." Thousands of young women (many of them innocent females) were picked up on the streets and jailed, while anyone without an official Havana address was returned to her home in the countryside. Several provinces temporarily banned sexual relations between Cubans and tourists entirely. (Foreigners may once again legally bed with Cubans.) Many cabaret showgirls operate a kind of unofficial prostitutes' guild. And *jineteras* continue to work the major tourist discos and bars with the complicity of the staff (and often of local police). Cuban males, too, tout themselves as

worker monthly, but pockets the hard currency fees and then pays the workers in near worthless pesos.) Denied the means of self-advancement, most Cubans are left treading water (the Communist elite are a clear exception, and many have aggrandized themselves). Tens of thousands are trapped in a poverty from which there is no escape.

Sexual Mores

Cuba is a sexually permissive society. As journalist Jacobo Timerman wrote, "Eros is amply gratified in Cuba and needs no stimulation." A joyous eroticism pervades Cuban men and women alike, transcending the hang-ups

of essentially puritanical Europe or North America. Seduction is a national pastime pursued by both sexes—the free expression of a high-spirited people confined in an authoritarian world. After all, Cubans joke, sex is the only thing Castro can't ration.

Che Guevara's widow, Aleida March, told biographer Jon Lee Anderson that women were "throwing themselves" at the *barbudos* ("bearded ones") after the triumph of the Revolution and that, "Well—with a big smile as if to indicate it was quite a scene—there had been a lot of 'lovemaking' going on." Thus the tone was set early, noted Lois Smith and Alfredo Padula, by a "bacchanal in which the

gigolos and are often warmly received by foreign females seeking Cuban lovers.

Like everything in Cuba, the situation is complex and needs some explaining.

A CHANCE TO GET AHEAD

The women who form intimate relationships with tourists are a far cry from the uneducated prostitutes of Batista days. Most are ordinary Cubans who would laugh to be called *jineteras*. A study by the Federation of Cuban Women (FMC) declared that "what motivates these women...is the desire to go out, to enjoy themselves, go places where Cubans are not allowed to go." A pretty *cubana* attached to a generous suitor can be wined and dined and get her entrance paid into the discos, drinks included, to which she otherwise wouldn't have access. They're seeking a *papiriqui con guaniquiqui* (a sugar daddy) as a replacement for a paternalistic government that can no longer provide even the basics.

Many women become attached to a man for the duration of his visit in the hope that a future relationship may develop. Their dream is to live abroad – to find a foreign boyfriend who will marry them and take them away. It happens all the time, especially for good-looking *negras de pelo* (black women with straight hair). "Italian and German men are *locos* for

negras y mulatas de pelo," says Lety, in Isadora Tattlin's *Cuban Diaries*. "'Ay, being *una negra de pelo* in Cuba is as good as having a visa to Canada or western Europe, guaranteed. And being *una negra* with blue eyes' – Lety shakes her fingers again, like they have been scalded – 'when the girl turns fourteen, people say, "*el norteño* is coming, *chica*, pack your bags!"'"

In a society where promiscuity is rampant and sex on a first date is a given, any financial transaction – assuredly, more in one night in *pesos convertibles* than she can otherwise earn in three months' salary in worthless pesos – is reduced to a charitable afterthought to a romantic evening out. Thus, educated and morally upright Cuban women – doctors, teachers, accountants – smile at tourists passing by on the street or hang out by the disco doorways, seeking affairs and invitations, however briefly, to enjoy a part of the high life.

Sex is legal at the age of 16 in Cuba, but under Cuban and international law foreigners can be prosecuted for sex with anyone under 18 (*menores de edad*). Foreign males intending to have sexual relations with a Cuban female should always be sure to check her *carnet* to determine her age; note that discos permit entry to anyone 15 years of age or older, and many "women" in discos are *menores de edad*.

triumphant revolutionaries and euphoric nation celebrated between the sheets." Cuban sexuality has ever since defied the efforts of the Revolution to tame and control it.

Promiscuity is rampant. So are extramarital affairs ("infidelity is the national sport," says Ann Louise Bardach). Both genders are unusually bold. Long glances—*ojitos*—often accompanied by uninhibited comments, betray envisioned improprieties. Even the women murmur *piropos* (catcalls or courtly overtures) and sometimes comic declarations of love. Regardless of age, one is *expected* to enjoy sex, and as much of it as one can handle, regardless of gender orientation.

Homosexuality

Cuban homosexuals must find it ironic that the heart of the homosexual world is Castro Street in San Francisco. It is assuredly not named in El Jefe's honor, as gays—called *maricones* (queens), *mariposas* (butterflies), *pájaros* (birds), *patos* (ducks), or *gansos* (geese) in the Cuban vernacular (and *tortillas* for lesbians)—were persecuted following the Revolution. Castro (who denies the comment) supposedly told journalist Lee Lockwood that a homosexual could never "embody the conditions and requirements of a true revolutionary." Homosexuals were classified as "undesirable."

Thus gays and lesbians met with "homophobic repression and rejection" in Cuba, just as they did in the United States. In Cuba, however, it was more systematic and brutal. The pogrom began in earnest in 1965; homosexuals were arrested and sent to agricultural work and reeducation camps—UMAP (Units for Military Help to Agricultural Production). Echoing Auschwitz, over the gate of one such camp in Camagüey was the admonition "Work Makes You Men." Many brilliant intellectuals lost their jobs because they were gay or accused of being gay through anonymous denunciation. Homosexuals were not allowed to teach, become doctors, or occupy positions from which they could "pervert" Cuban youth.

Although UMAP camps closed in 1968 and those who had lost their jobs were reinstated and given back pay, periodic purges occurred throughout the 1970s and early '80s. Understandably, many homosexuals left—or were forced to leave—on the Mariel boatlift. However, by the mid-1980s, Cuba began to respond to the gay rights movement that had already gained momentum worldwide. Officially the new position is that homosexuality and bisexuality are no less natural or healthy than heterosexuality. In 1987, a directive was issued to police to stop harassment. And an official atonement was made through the release at the 1993 Havana Film Festival of *Vidas Paralelas* (*Parallel Lives*) and *La Bella de Alhambra* (*The Beauty at the Alhambra*), and the hit movie *Fresa y chocolate* (*Strawberry and Chocolate*).

Although discrimination continues, sexologist Mariela Castro Espín (Raúl's daughter and head of the National Sex Education Center) leads the effort to treat the LGBT community as equals.

Gay Cuba (1995), by Sonja de Vries, and *Dos Patrias, Cuba y la Noche* (2007), by Christian Liffers are documentary films that look candidly at the treatment of gays in Cuba since the Revolution.

LIFE IN CUBA

On the eve of the Revolution, Cuba was a semi-developed country with more millionaires than anywhere south of Texas and an urban labor force that had achieved "the eight-hour day, double pay for overtime, one month's paid vacation, nine days' sick leave, and the right to strike." On the other hand, in 1950, a World Bank study team reported that 40 percent of urban dwellers and 60 percent of rural dwellers were undernourished, while over 40 percent of Cuban people had never gone to school, and only 60 percent had regular full-time employment.

The Revolution has immeasurably improved the condition of millions of Cubans, eliminating the most abject poverty while destroying the middle and wealthy urban classes and imposing a general paucity, if not poverty, on millions of others. At least everyone had the essentials and enjoyed two two-week vacations a year at the beach. And the government provided five crates of beer as a wedding present and birthday cakes for kids under 10. The state even issues a nightgown to brides and pregnant women, "causing some irreverent wags to note that these were exactly the two times when a woman least needed one," says Georgie Ann Geyer.

The Bare Essentials

Rows upon rows of citrus trees grow just 30 miles from Havana, but it is near impossible to find an orange for sale. Vast acres go unfarmed. Cultivated land goes untended. What happens to the food produced is a mystery. Hospitals, schools, and work canteens get priority, but little reaches the *bodegas* (state grocery stores)—almost 40 percent of produce is stolen as it passes through the distribution system known as *acopio*. The average Cuban faces absences of everything we take for granted in life.

The *libreta*—the ration book meant to supply every Cuban citizen with the basic essentials—provides, at best, supplies for perhaps 10 days per month (in 2008, Raúl Castro hinted that the system may be abandoned; potatoes and some other items were deleted). So much is allowed per person per month—six pounds of rice, eleven ounces of beans, five pounds of sugar, four ounces of lard, eight eggs—although the items aren't always available.

The U.S. embargo—*el bloqueo*—is blamed, even though in 2008 Cuba purchased 40 percent of its foods (agricultural goods are permitted by U.S. law) from U.S. suppliers, worth US$870 million! There's no shortage of other U.S. products, from Marlboro cigarettes to Mack trucks, imported through other countries. Cuba has no problem importing whatever it needs (from Dell computers to US$200,000 Mercedes buses) from other countries. The 2009 International Fair of Havana, Cuba's largest trade expo, attracted 1,230 companies from 54 countries, including 35 from the United States.

The real problem is that Cubans are paid virtual slave-labor wages in pesos, but all things worth buying—including daily necessities such as toilet paper, detergent, and soap—are sold by Cuban state enterprises for "convertible pesos" (obtainable only in exchange for foreign currency) at an average markup of 240 percent. Fortunately, rent and utilities are so heavily subsidized that they are virtually free, as is health care.

The Black Market

The black market, known as the *bolsa* (the exchange), resolves the failings of the state-controlled economy. Most Cubans rely on the underground economy—*los bisneros*—doing business illegally; on theft or fortuitous employment; or, for the exceedingly fortunate, a wealthy relative or a lover abroad. Cubans have always survived by *resolviendo*—the Cuban art of barter, the cut corner, or theft. The black market touches all walks of life. Even otherwise loyal revolutionaries are forced to break the law to survive. (In October 2005, after disclosing that half the gasoline in the country was being stolen, Castro fired gas station attendants en masse and replaced them with thousands of university students and young Communist Party supporters.)

A few years ago a peso income had some value. Today it is virtually worthless. Life has become organized around a mad scramble for foreign currency and *pesos convertibles*. The lucky ones have access to family cash, known as *fula,* sent from Miami. Cubans joke about getting by on *fé,* which is Spanish for faith, but today it's an acronym for *familia extranjera*—family abroad. Cuban economists reckon that about 60 percent of the population now has some form of access to *pesos convertibles*. The rest must rely on their wits. The majority of Cubans have to simply *buscar la forma,* find a way. Every morning people prepare to cobble together some kind of normalcy out of whatever the situation allows. Cubans are masters at making the best of a bad situation. *Resolver* (to resolve) is one of the most commonly used verbs on the island. The very elderly with no access to foreign currency, however, fare extremely badly, and thousands are malnourished, existing in abject poverty at a level barely above *sobrevivencia* (mere survival).

True, a large percent of the people now own cellular phones and other contemporary accoutrements. Everything else is a hand-me-down—mummified American cars, taped-together Russian refrigerators, and 45-pound Chinese bicycles. The staple of transport in cities is the horse-drawn cart. The staple for inter-city travel is the open-topped truck, often without any seats.

There's always *la yuma*—the United States (from the 1957 film *3:10 to Yuma* starring Glenn Ford and Van Heflin)—beckoning just 90 miles away (in 1996, when the U.S. Interests Section held a lottery to issue 20,000 visas, it received 541,500 applications by the cut-off date). Cubans lucky enough to receive visas to emigrate to the United States are bilked by the Cuban government (to the tune of almost US$1,000). Meanwhile, the families' possessions are seized by the government; a state inspector takes an inventory, and if anything is missing on the day of departure the *carta blanca* is revoked and with it any chance of leaving.

Simple Pleasures

Cuba has no *fiesta* tradition. The Cubans are too busy playing baseball or practicing martial arts while the others while away the long, hot afternoons playing dominoes or making love. In rural areas pleasures are simple: cockfights, rodeos, cigars, cheap rum, and sex. Urban life is more urbane, offering movies, discos, theater, cigars, cheap rum, and sex.

Cuban social life revolves around the family and friends and neighbors. Cubans are a gregarious people, and foreigners are often amazed by the degree to which Cubans exist in the public eye, carrying on their everyday lives behind wide-open windows open to the streets as if no one were looking.

Nonetheless, for all its musical gaiety and pockets of passionate pleasure, life for the average Cuban is dreary, even melancholy. Socialist equality looks dismal as you contemplate the aged and impoverished walking around inconsolably as if they've been castrated—*jaca* is the local term—and at a loss over their lives, rumi-

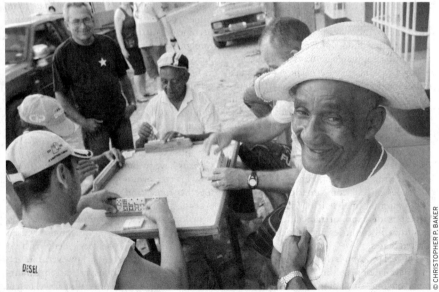

men playing dominoes in Trinidad

© CHRISTOPHER P. BAKER

nating over what has gone terribly wrong with a revolution that held greater promise.

Living Conditions

Half an hour in Havana is enough to cure you of a taste for that distressed look so popular in Crate & Barrel stores.

— P. J. O'Rourke

Until the Revolution, government expenditures were concentrated mostly in and around Havana and the provincial cities. The countryside was neglected and had few sewers or plumbing, few paved roads or electricity. Rural housing was basic. According to the 1953 census, only 15 percent of rural houses had piped water, 54 percent had no toilet whatsoever, and 43 percent had no electricity. Since the Revolution, the government has concentrated its energies on developing the countryside. Most housing built since the Revolution (in both town and country) is concrete apartment block units of a standard Bulgarian design— the ugly Bauhaus vision of uniform, starkly functional workers' housing. Most were built by unskilled volunteer labor and have not been maintained, adding salt to the wound of the aesthetic shortfall.

The typical country house, or *bohío,* is a low, one-story structure with thick walls to keep out the heat, built of adobe or porous brick covered with stucco and roofed with thatch or red tiles. But tens of thousands of rural dwellers still live in slum shacks of scrap tin and wood, with dirt floors. Most have a crude outhouse toilet, an open-air kitchen, and perhaps a well or a hand-pump for water; many houses still have no water, including 8.7 percent that have no toilets whatsoever, according to the 2002 census. However, virtually every house on the island today has electricity (payments are made directly to state authorities), although everyone is subject to occasional blackouts (*apagones*).

Most cities ache with penury and pathos. Havana, sultry seductress of prerevolutionary days, needs a million gallons of paint. Most prerevolutionary housing is deteriorated to a point of dilapidation (a 1999 report by the Havana municipal authorities admitted that 100,000 houses are officially considered unsafe, and 20 percent of the population lives in housing considered to be in "precarious condition"). Many Cubans cling to family life behind crumbling facades festooned with makeshift wiring and inside tottering buildings that should have faced the bulldozer's maw long ago. Many buildings have unpainted walls mildewed by the tropical climate, and stairs so dilapidated one is afraid to step onto them. The worst examples are hidden behind more substantial housing. Everywhere the housing shortage is so critical that many Cubans live in a *barbecue,* a room divided in two. Due to lack of space, the high-ceilinged rooms of many old colonial buildings have been turned into two stories by adding new ceilings and staircases. Several generations are often crowded together unwillingly; there is simply nowhere for the offspring to go. Still, there *are* many fine, well-kept houses, and every city has a section that resembles its middle-class American counterpart.

By law, no renter can pay more than 10 percent of his or her salary in rent, and almost 80 percent of Cubans own their own homes. Martha Gellhorn noted: "Rents pile up like down payments year after year, until the sale price of the flat is reached, whereupon bingo, you become an old-fashioned capitalist owner." Those who owned houses before the Revolution have been allowed to keep them; those who fled Cuba had their property seized by the state. Cubans can swap their houses without state approval but cannot buy or sell them. Cash transactions involving houses are illegal. The laws are full of quicksand. For example, only houses of similar sizes may be swapped. And some neighborhoods have had their populations "frozen" by law, so that if a family of four wants to move out, no more than four may move in. Since there's no such thing as classified ads or websites for real estate, Cubans hang signs outside their homes announcing *se permuta* ("for swap"). A swap can take years to arrange, after which the government must approve it—another year or so. Cubans can have their property seized for any number of seemingly minor infractions while others, after being moved out because the government claims their homes are no longer safe, are powerless when the government then refurbishes the building for its own ends. Nice houses in good neighborhoods are often taken by the government for the political elite or for government offices.

Interiors often belie the dour impression received on the street. Rooms everywhere are kept spick-and-span and furnished with family photos, kitschy ceramic animals, plastic flowers, and other effusive knickknackery—and frequently a photo of Fidel or Che. Virtually every home in Cuba retains its original, tattered prerevolutionary furniture. And usually there's a *perrito* (a small dog), as Cubans are animal lovers.

Supplies for repairs are virtually impossible to find. Nails? Paint? Forget it. The equivalent of Home Depot or Ace Hardware doesn't exist. Everything has to be foraged. Anyone who wants to repair or remodel a home must prove that all building materials were purchased from the state. Hence, merely to fix a falling-down wall can lead to a home being confiscated. Meanwhile, municipal administration is a disaster. When sidewalks collapse, no repairs are made; when pavements buckle, they go unattended. Sewers and electrical boxes aren't maintained, so over time everything is jerry-rigged and/or deteriorates without hope of repair. Meanwhile, idealists at the Florida International University School of Architecture's "Project Havana" are creating guidelines to protect the city's character by renovation while adding 250,000 badly needed houses in a post-Castro transition.

CHILDREN AND YOUTH
One of the simplest pleasures for the foreign traveler is to see smiling children in school uniforms so colorful that they reminded novelist James Michener of "a meadow of flowers. Well nourished, well shod and clothed, they were the permanent face of the land." And well behaved, too!

Children are treated with as much indulgence by the state as by family members. The government has made magnificent strides to improve the lot of poor children—though, to be sure, many are still so poor they go without shoes. And it teaches youngsters magnificent values. Children are sworn in at the age of six to become Pioneros—Communist Pioneers—where they learn the virtues of public service doing duty, such as collecting litter.

After high school has ended, all Cuban males must perform two years of military service while most girls serve two years as *trabajadores sociales* doing social work.

Youth are served by their own newspapers, such as *Juventud Rebelde* (Rebel Youth).

The "I" Generation
More than 65 percent of the Cuban population was born after the Revolution. Where their parents use "we," Cuba's youth use "I"—I want to do so and so. The majority are bored by the constant calls for greater sacrifice. They want to enjoy life like kids the world over, and in much the same way. A worrisome number of students are dropping out of class or playing truant. Many youths realize they can get further on their own and are going into business for themselves as *cuenta propistas* (freelancers), making a buck driving taxis, while their sisters turn to dating foreign tourists. In recent studies to ascertain high school students' goals, almost every student stated a desire to work as a *cuenta propista* or with tourists.

The government worries that the increased association with foreign tourists helps foster nonconformism, such as the growing number of rap fans, Rastafarians, and long-haired youths—*roqueros* and *frikis*—who sport ripped jeans and would look at home at a Metallica concert.

Cuban youth are expressing their individuality—they want to be themselves, which today means showing a marked preference for anything North American, especially in clothing. They wouldn't be caught dead in a *guayabera*, the traditional tropical shirt favored by older men (and considered a sure sign of someone who works for the government). Young women dress in the latest fashion—tight jeans, halter tops, mini-skirts, short shorts. Young men follow suit, though more conservatively, as well as their budgets allow. A cell phone is de rigueur for those with the means to afford one.

FEMINISM AND MACHISMO

The country has an impressive record in women's rights. A United Nations survey ranks Cuba among the top 20 nations in which women have the highest participation in politics and business. Women make up 50 percent of university students and 60 percent of doctors, although they are still poorly represented in the highest echelons of government. A review of the University of Havana yearbooks shows that women were well represented *before* the Revolution also.

Women are guaranteed the same salaries as men and receive 18 weeks of paid maternity leave—six before the birth and the remainder after. Working mothers have the right to one day off with pay each month, or the option of staying home and receiving 60 percent of their full salary until the child reaches the age of six months. And every woman and girl can get free birth control assistance, regardless of marital status. The Cuban Family Code codifies that the male must share household duties.

Despite this, prejudices born of the patriarchal Spanish heritage still exist. Male machismo continues, while the Revolution has not been able to get the Cubanness out of Cuban women who, regardless of age, still adore coquetry.

RELIGION

Cuba was officially atheist from the early 1960s until 1992 (it has since officially been a secular state). Nonetheless, a recent government survey found that more than half of all Cubans are *creyentes,* believers of one sort or another.

Christianity

Cubans have always been relatively lukewarm

SWEET 15

Decades of socialism have killed off many traditional celebrations – but not *fiestas de quince,* the birthday parties celebrating a girl's 15th birthday and her coming of age. There is nothing like a *quince* party (a direct legacy of a more conservative Spanish era) for a young *cubana.*

Parents will save money from the day the girl is born to do her right with a memorable 15th. A whole arsenal might be involved, from the hairdresser and dressmaker (a special dress resembling a wedding gown or a knock-'em-dead Scarlett O'Hara outfit is de rigueur) to the photographer and the classic American car with chauffeur to take the young woman and her friends to the party.

© CHRISTOPHER P. BAKER

Fifteen-year-old girls celebrate their *fiesta de quince.*

about Christianity. In colonial times, there were few churches in rural districts, where it was usual for a traveling priest to call only once a year to perform baptisms and marriages. Moreover, the Catholic Church sided with the Spanish against the patriots during the colonial era and was seen by *criollos* as representing authoritarianism hand-in-hand with the Spanish Crown. Later, the Catholic Church had a quid pro quo with the corrupt Machado, Grau, and Batista regimes. When the Revolution triumphed, many of the clergy left for Miami along with the rich to whom they had ministered.

The Catholic Church grew concerned as the Revolution moved left; when Fidel nationalized the church's lands, it became a focus of opposition. In August 1960, the Catholic bishops issued a pastoral letter formally denouncing the Castro government. Many priests were expelled. Practicing Catholics were banned from the Communist Party. Practitioners were harassed. Religious education was eliminated from the school curriculum, and a scientific understanding of the world was promoted.

In 1986 Fidel Castro performed an about face: Religion was no longer the opiate of the masses. In 1991, the Communist Party opened its doors to believers, and security agents disappeared from churches. It was a timely move, co-opting the shifting mood. The collapse of the Soviet Union and onset of the Special Period left a spiritual vacuum that fed church attendance. Castro attempted to go with the rising tide. In November 1996, he met with Pope John Paul II in Rome. The pontiff's emotionally charged visit to Cuba in January 1998 was an extraordinary event that boosted the influence of the Catholic Church in Cuba and reignited an expression of faith among the Cuban people. (The pope's visit prompted a flood of Protestant missionaries, who seem more fearful of the spread of "papism" than of Communism. Castro has preferred the Protestant church. Protestants are estimated to number about 300,000, with about 23 distinct churches represented.)

The Catholic Church hierarchy has continued to be highly critical of the Castro government. Despite increased tolerance of the church, harassment continues. In December 1999 the pope, disappointed with the meager progress since his visit, urged Castro to respect human rights and display "a more generous opening."

A huge percentage of Cubans remain atheistic, or at least agnostic. A far larger percentage, however, are superstitious and believe to lesser or greater degree in *santería,* to hedge their bets.

Santería

Santería, or saint worship, has been deeply entrenched in Cuban culture for 300 years. The cult is a fusion of Catholicism with the Lucumí religion of the African Yoruba tribes of modern-day Nigeria and Benin. Since slave masters had banned African religious practice, the slaves cloaked their gods in Catholic garb and continued to pray to them in disguise. Thus, in *santería,* Catholic figures are avatars of the Yoruban *orishas* (divine beings, or guardian spirits, of African animism). Metaphorically *orishas* change their identity—even their gender—at midnight. By day, adherents may pray in front of a figure of Santa Barbara and at night worship the same figure as Changó. There are about 400 guardian spirits in the pantheon, but only about 20 are honored in daily life.

It is thought that the *orishas* control an individual's life, performing miracles on a person's behalf. They are thus consulted and besought. A string of bad luck will be blamed on an *orisha,* who must be placated. They're too supreme for mere mortals to communicate with directly: *Santeros* or *babalawos* (priests) act as go-betweens to interpret their commands (for a fee). *Babalawos* use divination to interpret the *obi* and *ifá* (oracles) and solve everyday problems using pieces of dried coconut shells and seashells.

Many a home has a statue of an *orisha* to appease the spirits of the dead. Even Fidel Castro, a highly superstitious person, is said to be a believer. He had triumphed on January 1, a holy day for the *orishas.* The red and black flag of the revolutionaries was that of Eleggúa, god of destiny. Then, on January 8, 1959, as Fidel delivered his victory speech before the nation, two doves flew over the audience and circled the brightly lit podium; miraculously, one of the doves alighted on Fidel's shoulder, touching off an explosion from the ecstatic onlookers: *"Fee-del! Fee-del! Fee-del!"* In *santería,*

SANTERÍA TERMS

babalawo: a high priest of Lucumí

batá: set of three drums of Yoruba origin – *iya, itotele,* and *okonkolo*

Changó: the mighty *orisha* of fire, thunder, and lightning

Elegguá: messenger of all *orishas;* guardian of the crossroads and god of destiny

fundamento: a strict set repertoire of rhythms for each *orisha*

iyawó: *santería* initiate; or "bride" of the *orishas*

Obatalá: *orisha* of peace and purity

obi and ifá: oracles

Ochún: the sensuous black goddess that many Cuban women identify as the *orisha* of love; syncretistically, the Virgen de la Caridad

Ogún: *orisha* represented as a warrior

orishas: deities symbolic of human qualities and aspects of nature

toque: specific rhythm attributed to an *orisha*

doves are symbols of Obatalá, the son of God. To Cubans—and perhaps Fidel himself—the event was a supreme symbol that the gods had chosen Fidel to guide Cuba. It was "one of those rare, magical moments when cynics are transformed into romantics and romantics into fanatics," wrote photojournalist Lee Lockwood.

Nonetheless, following the Revolution, the government stigmatized *santería* as *brujería* (witchcraft) and tried to convert it into a folkloric movement. In the late 1980s, *santería* bounced back. In 1990 the Castro government began to co-opt support for the faith. Reportedly, many *babalawos* have been recruited as agents by MININT, for they above all know people's secrets.

Throughout Cuba, you'll see believers clad all in white, having just gone through their initiation rites as *santeros* or *santeras*. A follower of *santería* may choose at any stage in life to undertake an elaborate initiation that will tear the follower away from his or her old life and set their feet on *la regla de ocha*—the way of

the *orishas*. During this time, the *iyawó* will be possessed by, and under the care of, a specific *orisha* who will guide the initiate to a deeper, richer life. Initiations are highly secret and involve animal sacrifice (usually pigeons and roosters). The rites are complex. They include having to dress solely in white and stay indoors at night for a year, though exceptions are made for employment. And an *iyawó* may not touch anyone or permit him- or herself to be touched, except by the most intimate family members or, this being Cuba, by lovers.

Santería is a sensuous religion—the *orishas* let adherents have a good time. The gods themselves are fallible and hedonistic philanderers, such as the much feared and respected Changó (or Santa Barbara), whose many mistresses include Oyá (or Santa Teresa, patron saint of the ill and dead, and guardian of cemeteries) and Ochún (the Virgen de la Caridad), the sensuous black goddess of love.

Each saint has specific attributes. Changó, for example, dresses in red and white and carries a scepter with a double-headed axe. Followers of Changó wear collars decorated with red and white plastic beads. Ochún wears yellows; thus her followers wear yellow and white beads. Obatalá (the Virgen de la Merced), goddess of peace and creation, dresses in white. Yemayá (the Virgen de Regla), goddess of the sea and of motherhood, wears blue and white. Each saint also has an "altar" where offerings (fruits, rum-soaked cakes, pastries, and coins) are placed. Devout *santeros* even keep a collection of vases in their bedrooms in which one's personal *orisha*, plus Obatalá, Yemayá, Ochún, and Changó live, in that hierarchical order.

African Cult Religions

Other spiritualist cults exist in Cuba. The most important is the all-male Abakuá secret mutual protection society that originated in Nigeria, appearing in Cuba in the early 19th century. It still functions among the most marginalized black communities, where it is known as *ñañiguismo*. The first duty of an adherent is to protect a fellow member. Membership is restricted to "brave, virile, dignified, moral men" who contribute to their communities. It involves worship of ancestral devil figures, called *diablitos* or *iremes,* where dancers dress from head to toe in hooded hessian costumes.

Palo Monte (known also as *reglas congas*) also derives from west-central Africa and is a spirit religion that harnesses the power of the deceased to control supernatural forces. Adherents (called *paleros*) use ritual sticks and plants to perform magic. Initiates receive small incisions in their body into which magical substances are inserted.

EDUCATION

Cuba's education system is a source of national pride. One in every 15 people is a college graduate. And even in the most remote Cuban backwater, you'll come across bright-eyed children laden with satchels, making their way to and from school in pin-neat uniforms colored according to their grades (younger ones wear short-sleeved white shirts, light-blue neckerchiefs, and maroon shorts or mini-skirts; secondary school children wear white shirts, red neckerchiefs, and ocher-yellow long pants or mini-skirts.

Official statistics are contradictory. The Cuban government claims that on the eve of the Revolution, 43 percent of the population was illiterate and half a million Cuban children went without school; however, the U.N. Statistical Yearbook suggests that as much as 80 percent of the population was literate, behind only Argentina, Chile, and Costa Rica for the time.

Private and religious schools are forbidden.

Accomplishments

In December 1960 the government announced a war on illiteracy. On April 10, 1961, 120,000 literacy workers—*brigadistas*—spread throughout the island to teach reading and writing to one million illiterates. The government established about 10,000 new classrooms in rural areas. Today literacy is about 99.8 percent, according to UNESCO, exceeding all other Latin American nations (compared to 96 percent for the United States and 99 percent for the United Kingdom). The statistics also show

that the average Cuban child receives about 11.3 years of schooling—the U.S. equivalent is 15.9; that of the U.K. is 16.6. At age 15 (ninth grade), children are evaluated and graded to determine their future: At 16 most secondary students begin two years at a PRE (for *pre-universitario*), often an *escuela del campo* where they live in boarding schools attached to plots of arable land. Time is equally divided between study and labor, fulfilling José Martí's dictum: "In the morning, the pen—but in the afternoon, the plow." Often, very little work gets done in the fields and youth spend much of their time in dalliance. Children with special talents may opt to attend specialist schools that foster particular skills in art, music, or sports—assuming, of course, that they display the correct behavioral attitudes. Children of the Communist Party and military elite get special treatment.

In 2002, Castro announced a new effort to raise education, with the goal of having one teacher per every 20 students in all elementary classes; installation of computer labs; and a crash course to train "emergency teachers." In 2004, it claimed to have achieved only 12 students per teacher. However, Cubans complain about low-quality teaching; many teachers are barely out of high school themselves.

Cuban children display inordinate literary and mathematical abilities; a UNESCO study of language and mathematics skills throughout Latin America found that Cuba was way ahead of all other nations (the World Bank's *World Development Indicators* data show Cuba as topping virtually all other poor countries in education statistics).

Cuba has four universities. In addition, in 2002 it opened the **Universidad de las Ciencias Informáticas** (Carretera de San Antonio de los Baños, Km 2.5, Torrens, Municipio Boyeros, Havana, tel. 07/837-2548, www.uci.cu), with 10,000 students arranged into teams to develop commercial software.

The Downside

As the Brazilian economist Roberto Campos said, statistics are like bikinis: They show

children in class

what's important but hide what's essential. For one, the hyper-educated population is hard pressed to find books and other educational materials. Few schools have a library or gym or laboratory. Schools have been hit by a shortage of teachers lost to tourism jobs (they have been replaced by student teachers). The entire literary panorama is severely proscribed: Only politically acceptable works are allowed. The state often dictates what university students will study. Students of all ages are monitored for their "political soundness," and their ability to move up into institutions of higher education depends on their demonstrating support for the Revolution (children of "counterrevolutionaries" are often punished along with their parents). Options for adult education are virtually nonexistent. And thousands of qualified Cuban school graduates are denied university places reserved for Venezuelans and other "solidarity" students.

HEALTH

According to the Castro government, in pre-revolutionary Cuba only the monied class could afford good medical care; it also has

claimed that there were only 6,250 physicians in all of Cuba on the eve of the Revolution. True, many people (especially in rural areas) went without medical services. According to the United Nations Statistical Yearbook, however, in 1958 Cuba had an advanced medical system that ranked third in Latin America (behind only Uruguay and Argentina), with 128 physicians and dentists per 100,000 people—the same as the Netherlands, and ahead of the United Kingdom, with 122 per 100,000 people. And Cuba's infant mortality rate of 32 per 1,000 live births in 1957 was the lowest in Latin America and the 13th lowest in the world (today it is the 28th lowest).

From the beginning, health care has assumed an inordinately prominent place in revolutionary government policies (about 12 percent of its budget). Today, 20 medical schools churn out thousands of doctors each year. In 1978, Castro predicted that Cuba would become the bulwark of third world medicine, put a doctor on every block, become a world medical power, and surpass the United States in certain health indices. In all four, he has been vindicated. Moreover, Cuban doctors are inspired by a genuine concern for the Hippocratic oath, without concern for money.

Cuba's life expectancy of 78.3 years is behind only Chile, Costa Rica, Puerto Rico in Latin America and exceeds that of the United States (78.2); it also has one of the highest rates of centenarians per capita in the world. In 2009 Cuba's infant mortality rate of 5.4 per 1,000 births also bettered that of the United States (6.3) and was almost as good as the United Kingdom's (4.8).

Family Doctor Program

The Revolution's accomplishment is due to its emphasis on preventative medicine and community-based doctors. A near 100 percent immunization rate has ensured the total eradication of several preventable contagious diseases. For example, Cuba has the highest rate of immunization against measles in the world, says UNICEF, which uses the measles immunization rate as the most reliable barometer of a country's commitment to bringing basic medical advances to its people.

Castro set out to train doctors en masse. According to the World Health Organization,

Cuba has a doctor for every 170 residents, ahead of the United States with 1:188. (Dental care lags behind, however, with one dentist for about every 1,280 inhabitants.) The idea is for every Cuban to have his or her own doctor trained in comprehensive general medicine close by, living and working in the neighborhood, combining the duties of a family doctor and public health advocate. Every community has a *casa del médico* (family doctor's home), with a clinic. Every town also has a hospital, plus a maternity home and a day-care center for the elderly, and mobile laboratories travel the country. All medical services are free.

Beyond Primary Care

Cuba also commands the kind of technology that most poor countries can only dream about: ultrasound for obstetricians, CAT scans for radiologists, stacks of high-tech monitors in the suites for intensive care. Cuba has performed heart transplants since 1985, heart-lung transplants since 1987, coronary bypasses, pacemaker implantations, microsurgery, and a host of other advanced surgical procedures. Even sex-change operations are

CUBA'S FLYING DOCTORS

Since 1963 when Cuba sent 56 doctors to newly independent Algeria, the country has provided medical assistance to developing countries regardless of its own economic straits. In 1985 the *New York Times* dubbed Cuba's international medical aid program "the largest Peace Corps-style program of civilian aid in the world." Cuba regularly deploys medical brigades to regions struck by disasters, and has donated entire hospitals to developing countries. In 2009 medical personnel were serving in 81 countries around the world; as of 2009, some 134,000 Cuban doctors and paramedics had served abroad. When the Haiti earthquake struck on January 12, 2010, Cuba already had 344 doctors serving there.

Cuba has also offered free medical care in

Cuba for patients from abroad, most famously for 20,000 child victims of the Chernobyl nuclear disaster in the Soviet Union. And since it was initiated in 2005, Cuba's Operación Milagro (Operation Miracle) has performed thousands of free eye operations on indigent people from throughout the Americas and Caribbean.

In November 1999, Cuba converted a naval academy into the Latin American School for Medical Sciences, offering free medical education to students from developing countries (including full scholarships for 250 students from disadvantaged communities in the United States): In May 2009, Cuba claims that more than 24,000 third world students were studying health care in Cuba on scholarships provided by the Cuban state.

provided free of charge. The Pan-American Health Organization stated that the Hospital Hermanos Almeijeiras "conducts research and uses technology at the international cutting edge in the 38 specialties in which services are rendered." *Science* magazine rated the Ibero-Latin American Center for Nervous System Transplants and Regeneration as the world's best for the treatment of Parkinson's disease. And Cuban doctors "have turned mass production eye operations into a fine art," says the BBC's Michael Voss.

Cuba has also made notable leaps in advancing the field of molecular immunology. It even manufactures interferons for AIDS treatment; a meningitis vaccine first "discovered" at the Finlay Institute; even a cure for the skin disease vitiligo.

The Downside

Local pharmacies are meagerly stocked; Cuban pharmaceuticals are exported to obtain foreign funds, and although pharmacies for foreigners are fully stocked, the Cuban government opts not to import pharmaceuticals for Cubans. Resources have also been shifted from primary care toward turning Cuba's medical system into a profit-making enterprise catering to foreigners, notably in the surgical and advanced medicines fields. (Dr. Hilda Molina, founder of Havana's International Center for Neurological Restoration, claims that "foreigners are assigned the highest priority, followed by government functionaries and their families, followed by athletes with good records of performance, then dancers, and lastly, ordinary Cuban patients.") Cubans also complain that the plethora of Cuban medical staff serving abroad has sapped local clinics and hospitals. In 2008, Raúl Castro announced an overhaul of the health system, reducing the number of clinics by half. Outside Havana, conditions in hospitals and clinics are often of third world standard; everywhere, medical equipment is broken. In 2009, a visit to a hospital outside Santa Clara revealed men and women sharing wards with open toilets that lacked doors.

In 2000, the U.S. rescinded restrictions preventing medicines and medical equipment manufactured in the United States or under U.S. patent from being exported to Cuba. In 2001, Cuba began purchasing millions of dollars of U.S. medical products. (Nonetheless, Fidel has consistently refused to accept Uncle Sam's occasional offers of medical relief; in December 1999, he turned away 55,000 pounds of desperately needed U.S. medical supplies meant for pediatric hospitals.)

Arts

Since the Revolution, the government's sponsorship of the arts has yielded a rich harvest in every field. Cuba is one of the few tropical countries to have produced a modern culture of its own. The Centro Nacional de Escuelas de Arte (National Center of Schools of Art), created in 1960, has 41 schools under its umbrella, including the national Escuela de la Música, a national folkloric school, two ballet schools, two fine-arts schools, and a school of modern dance, plus schools at the provincial level. The graduates are superbly trained, despite great shortages of instruments and other materials.

During the first two years of the Revolution, Castro enjoyed being the "bohemian intellectual," and artists and writers enjoyed relative freedom. As the romantic phase of the Revolution passed into an era of more dogmatic ideology, the Culture Council took a hard line. In 1961 the government invited intellectuals to a debate on the meaning of cultural liberty at which Castro offered his "Words to the Intellectuals," which he summed up with a credo: "Within the Revolution, everything. Outside the Revolution, nothing!" The government acquired full control of the mass media. Intellectuals, writers, and artists were intimidated into ideological straitjackets.

Ever since, no politically incorrect works have been allowed.

MUSIC AND DANCE

Author Norman Mailer scolded President Kennedy for the Bay of Pigs defeat by asking, "Wasn't there anyone around to give you the lecture on Cuba? Don't you sense the enormity of your mistake—you invade a country without understanding its music." These days it's Cuba that's invading the United States and the rest of the world. Says *Rhythm Music* magazine: "From Babalu to Bamboleo, a wealth of musicians is pouring out from under the Mango Curtain." The rhythm juggernaut is typified by the explosive 1999 success of the Grammy-winning *Buena Vista Social Club.*

Music—the pulsing undercurrent of Cuban life—is everywhere. Dance, from the earliest *guaguancó* to the mambo craze, has always been a potent expression of an enshrined national tradition: Cuban sensualism. Girls are whisked onto the dance floor and whirled through a flurry of complicated steps and sensuous undulations just a little closer than cheek to cheek. It's a wonder the birth rate isn't higher.

Folkloric Music and Dance

In Cuba, folkloric music (*música folklórica*) usually refers to Afro-Cuban music. The earliest influence was Spanish. The colonists brought the melodies, guitars, and violins from which evolved folk music, or *guajira,* influenced through contact with black culture. The fusion gave rise to *punto campesino* (peasant dances), including the all-important *danzón* (the first dance in Cuba in which couples actually touched each other), the *zapateo,* the slow and sensual *yambú* and the *colombia,* a solo men's dance performed blindfolded with machetes—all popular in past centuries among white country people and accompanied by small accordions, kettledrums, gourds, and calabashes. The melancholic love song *Guantanamera* is undoubtedly the most famous of Cuban *guajiras.*

From Europe, too, came the *trovas,* poetic songs (*canciones*) concerned with great historical events and, above all, with love. *Trovas,* which were descended from the medieval ballad, were sung in Cuba throughout the colonial period. *Trovadores* performed for free, as they still do at *casas de la trova* islandwide. The duty of the *casas* is to nurture the music of the provinces, and their success is one reason why Cuba is today a powerhouse on the international music scene.

This century has seen the evolution of the sultry *bolero* (a fusion of traditional *trovas* with Afro-Cuban rhythms) and more recently *trovas nuevas,* which often include subtle criticism of governmental dogma, as echoed by Pablo Milanés and Silvio Rodríguez.

The African Influence

Almost from the beginning, the Spanish guitar (from the tiny *requinto* to the *tres,* a small guitar with three sets of double strings) joined the hourglass-shaped African *bata* and bongo drum, claves (two short hardwood sticks clapped together), and *chequerí* (seed-filled gourds) to give Cuban music its distinctive form. Slaves played at speakeasies in huts in the slaves' quarters. Their jam sessions gave birth to the *guaguancó,* an erotic rumba—"a vertical suggestion of a horizontal intention," it has been called—in which the man tries to make contact with the woman's genitals and the woman dances defensively, with handfuls of skirt in front of her groin. Later, slaves would take the *guaguancó* a few steps farther to create the sensuous *rumba,* a sinuous dance from the hips from which tumbled most other forms of Cuban music, such as the *tumba francesa,* a dance of French-African fusion, and *son.*

Son, which originated in the eastern provinces of Oriente, derived as a campesino-based form combining African call-and-response verse to Spanish folk tunes using *décima* verses (octosyllabic 10-line stanzas). Popularized on radio by 1920s artists such as Rita Montaner and Ignacio Piñero's Septeto Nacional orchestra, *son* became the national music form.

By the 1930s, *son* was adopted and melded

THE *BUENA VISTA SOCIAL CLUB*

In 1996, Cuban music promoter Juan de Marcos rounded up a clique of legendary but largely forgotten veteran musicians to make a comeback album. Eclectic U.S. slide guitarist Ry Cooder happened to make a musical pilgrimage to Cuba around the same time, struck a deal with Marcos, and gifted to the world the *Buena Vista Social Club,* naming the album for a Havana venue where many of the artists performed in the 1950s. German film director Wim Wenders tagged along with his Beta steadicam to chronicle how Cooder ushered the half-forgotten relics of prerevolutionary Cuba into recording studios, cut an album of sepia-toned tunes, and dispatched them on a world tour and runaway success. The documentary (also called *Buena Vista Social Club*) celebrates the elderly musicians' performance on the world stage and offers a portrait of their life back in an impoverished Cuba.

The tender heart of the movie is crooner Ibrahim Ferrer, a soft-spoken septuagenarian who had been a singer with the legendary Benny Moré band in the 1950s, but who was shining shoes at the time Cooder's team rediscovered him. His weathered yet still nimble voice is supported by the arthritic fingers of 76-year-old pianist Ruben González, creator in the early 1940s of the modern Cuban piano sound, flying into action after long retirement; the slick guitar work of Francisco Repalido, known as "Compay Segundo," the grandfather of *son* music, who plays in his trademark Panama hat; guitarist Eliades Ochoa, a maestro of the *guajira* (country lament), easily recognized in his cowboy hat; and the dulcet voice of Omara Portuondo, who was once one of the leading *bolero* singers in Cuba.

This suave old bunch of codgers wowed the world when the documentary movie, produced by Cooder, was released in 1999, introducing the richness of *son, danzón,* and *bolero* in a style untouched by contemporary trends. The result was a runaway success. The CD won the Grammy for Tropical Music and topped the charts among Latin albums, taking Cuban music international for the first time, selling several million copies worldwide, and creating international nostalgia for the old Havana whose charmingly dilapidated streets are the setting for Wenders's wonderful movie.

Alas, all the main stars except Ochoa and Portuondo (who in 2009 won a Grammy at the age of 69) have since passed away.

with U.S. jazz influences by large band orchestras (*orquestras típicas*) with percussion and horn sections and tall conga drums called *tumbadores,* epitomized by the roaring success of Benny Moré (born Bartolomé Maximiliano Moré, 1919–1963), the flamboyant *bárbaro del ritmo*—the hot man of rhythm—who became a national idol and had his own big band, the Banda Gigante. The success of big band paved the way for the eventual evolution of salsa. Such contemporary salsa groups as Los Van Van have incorporated the *son,* which has its own variants, such as *son changüí* from Guantánamo Province, typified by the music of Orquestra Revé.

The mambo, like the cha-cha, which evolved from *son,* is a derivative of the *danzón* jazzed up with rhythmic innovations. Mambo is a passé but still revered dance, like the jitterbug in the United States, danced usually only by older people. Created in Cuba by Orestes López in 1938, mambo stormed the United States in the 1950s, when Cuban performers were the hottest ticket in town. Though the craze died, mambo left its mark on everything from American jazz to the old Walt Disney cartoons where the salt and pepper shakers get up and dance.

The mix of Cuban and North American sounds created blends such as *filin* music, a simple, honest derivative of the *bolero,* as sung by Rita Montaner and Nat "King" Cole, who performed regularly in Havana; and *Cu-bop,* which fused bebop with Afro-Cuban rhythms, epitomized by Moré, who was considered the top artist of Cuban popular music.

Modern Sounds

Salsa is the heartbeat of most Cuban nightlife and a musical form so hot it can cook the pork. Los Van Van—one of Cuba's hottest big, brassy salsa-style bands—and Irakere have come up with innovative and explosive mixtures of jazz, classical, rock, and traditional Cuban music that have caused a commotion in music. They regularly tour Europe and Latin America. And Bamboleo is a leader in *timba* (high-speed new-wave salsa).

For a long time, the playing of jazz in Cuba was discouraged as "representative of Yankee imperialism." The government began to lighten up in the 1980s. Today, Cuba boasts wonderful jazz players. The undisputed king of contemporary jazz is pianist Chucho Valdés, winner of five Grammy awards for his scorching-hot compositions.

More recently, rap has come to Cuba. Although the rhythms, gestures, and posturing take their cues from U.S. urban ghettoes, Cuban hip-hop is gentler, less dependent on guttural, driving aggression and more based on melodic fusion. Rap-based, reggae-influenced *reggaeton* is now the most universally popular and ubiquitous sound on the island, performed by such groups as Sintesis and Obsesión. Beginning in 2002, the government responded to increasingly critical hip-hop content with a severe yank on the leash, ironically by lending it official support (there's even a Minister of Hip-Hop), permitting the government to usurp and control it. The state decides what music can be played, and when and where. Playing unofficial venues can get performers arrested, and it is not unknown for officials to literally pull the plug on unofficial rehearsals and concerts. The same holds true for rock, which has been lassoed by the Unión Juventud de Cuba (the Young Communists) to corral disaffected youth. Rock was once officially banned. Cuba's *roqueros* (rockers) and *frikis* (freaks, known for their torn clothes and punkish hair) faced a hard time of things for many years, as the government considered them social deviants. Foremost groups include Combat Noise, Zeus, and Garage Hall.

Classical Music and Ballet

It is astounding how many contemporary Cubans are accomplished classical musicians. Everywhere you go, you will come across violinists, pianists, and cellists serenading you for tips while you eat. Cuba also boasts several classical orchestras, notably the Orquestra Sinfónica Nacional. Watch, too, for performances by Frank Fernández, Cuba's finest classical pianist.

Cubans love ballet, which is associated in Cuba with one name above all: Alicia Alonso. Havana got its own ballet company—the Sociedad Pro-Arte Música—in 1931, with a conservatory that produced many outstanding ballet dancers, including Alonso, born to an aristocratic family in Havana on December 21, 1921. Alonso was a prima ballerina with the American Ballet Theater since its inception in the 1940s. She returned to Cuba and, sponsored by Batista (who hated ballet but considered her star status a propaganda bonus), founded the Ballet Alicia Alonso, which in 1955 became the Ballet de Cuba. Alonso was outspoken in her criticism of the "Sordid Era," and she went into exile in 1956 when Batista withdrew his patronage. The Revolution later adopted her (Alonso is a favorite of Fidel), and her ballet company was re-formed and renamed the Ballet Nacional de Cuba. Her company is renowned worldwide for its original choreography and talent. The Camagüey Ballet—founded by Alicia's husband, Fernando Alonso—is also renowned for its innovative streak, as is the Santiago-based Ballet Folklórico de Oriente, which lends contemporary interpretations to traditional themes.

ART

Artists followed classical European prescriptions throughout the early colonial period, and only in the 19th century did a distinctly national school arise, with mulatto artists José Nicolás de la Escalera and Vincente Escobar at the fore. Their *costumbrista* movement presented an idealized vision of *criollo* culture. In 1818, Juan Bautiste Vermay opened the Academía Nacional de Bellas Artes, the

CUBAN POSTER ART

Cuba's strongest claim to artistic fame is surely its unique poster art, created in the service of political revolution and acclaimed as "the single most focused, potent body of political graphics ever produced in this hemisphere." The three leading poster-producing agencies have produced over 10,000 posters since 1959. Different state bodies create works for different audiences: Artists of the Cuban Film Institute (ICAIC), for example, design posters for movies from Charlie Chaplin comedies to John Wayne westerns; Editora Política (the propaganda arm of the Cuban Communist Party) produces posters covering everything from AIDS awareness, baseball games, and energy conservation to telling children to do their homework.

Cuba's most talented painters and photographers rejected Soviet realism and developed their own unique graphic style influenced by Latin culture and the country's geography. The vibrant colors and lush imagery are consistent with the physical and psychological makeup of the country, such as the poster urging participation in the harvest, dripping with psychedelic images of fruit and reminiscent of a 1960s Grateful Dead poster.

See *iRevolución! Cuban Poster Art*, by Lincoln Cushing, for more information.

were instrumental in formation of a Cuban post-impressionist school, while Wilfredo Lam, perhaps the greatest painter to emerge from Cuba during the 20th century, adopted Afro-Cuban mysticism to his exploration of the surrealist style inspired by Picasso. (Lam traveled to Paris and developed close ties with the surrealists and primitivists. Picasso took Lam under his wing.) Lam broke with the traditional rules and created his own style, marrying Cubism and surrealism with Afro-Cuban and Caribbean motifs. The traditions of Afro-Cuban *santería* also influenced the works of René Portacarrero.

The artists who grew up *after* the 1959 revolution have been given artistic encouragement (even entire villages, such as Verraco near Santiago, exist as art communities). In the late 1960s, the government tried to compel Cuban artists to shun then-prevalent decadent abstract art and adopt the realistic style of the party's Mexican sympathizers, such as Diego Rivera and David Alfaro Siqueiros. In 1980 the Cuban government began to loosen up. The artists began shaking off their clichés and conservatism, and began holding unofficial exhibitions in their homes. By the late 1980s they were overstepping their bounds. Armando Hart, then Minister of Culture, decided that the Cuban artists' enthusiasm should be promoted from afar. Mexico City was selected and a community of deported artists has evolved—quixotically, with official Cuban sponsorship. Contemporary Cuban artists express an intense Afro-Latin Americanism in their passionate, visceral, colorful, socially engaged, and eclectic body of widely interpretive works.

Cuba has 21 art schools, organized regionally with at least one per province. The Instituto Superior de Arte, Cuba's premier art school, remains key as an educational center and gateway to the world of Cuban art. The Cuban state fosters academic training in still life, landscape, and figure form. On attaining mastery of these skills, artists are encouraged to experiment in personal expression without overstepping Castro's 1961 dictum to think more of the message than the aesthetic. As

second national arts school in the Americas, which perpetuated the French allegorical, neoclassical stylistic form of painting, marked by a courtly stiffness.

The coming of independence opened Cuba to a wave of new influence, led by Armando García Menocal. Europe's avant-garde movement swept in as painters such as Eduardo Abela and Cabrera Moreno adopted international styles to represent emblematic Cuban themes, such as the figure of the *guajiro*. Victor Manuel García and Marcelo Pogolotti

a result, says critic Tina Spiro, "most Cuban artwork, regardless of its style, is informed by a precision of line and a beautiful technical finish."

Until recent years, artists were employed by various Cuban state institutions and received a small portion of receipts from the sale of their work. In 1991 the government finally recognized that copyright belongs with the artist. It has created independent profit-making, self-financing agencies to represent individual artists on a contractual basis whereby the agency retains 50 percent of sales receipts from the sale or licensing of copyrights abroad, making artists a hugely privileged group (Cuba's few true millionaires are all world-renowned, royalty-earning artists and musicians).

Eroticism—often highly graphic—is an integral component of contemporary Cuban art, as exemplified by the works of Chago Armada, Carlos Alpizar, and Aldo Soler. Much of current art subtly criticizes the folly of its socio-political environment, but usually in a politically safe, universal statement about the irony in human existence, expressing the hardships of daily life in a dark, surreal way.

Among Cuba's most revered contemporary artists is Alfredo Sosabravo, the most versatile and complete artist among those making up the plastic-arts movement in Cuba today. You'll come across his works (and influence) everywhere, including a permanent exhibition at Havana's Museo Nacional and the Palacio de Bellas Artes. He is dramatically present in hotel lobbies and other tourist spots. Look, too, for the works (inspired by nature and *santería*) of Manuel Mendive; the naive works of José Fuster; and the existential works by Alicia Leal.

LITERATURE

Cuba's goals and struggles have spawned dozens of literary geniuses whose works are mostly clenched fists that cry out against social injustice. The most talented Cuban writers all produced their best works in exile. Cirilo Villaverde (1812–1894) fought with the Rebel Army and was imprisoned as a nationalist, and his spellbinding novel *Cecilia Valdés,* written in exile in the 1880s, helped establish Villaverde as Cuba's foremost 19th-century novelist. From exile, too, José Martí, the 19th-century nationalist leader whose works helped define the school of modern Latin American poetry, produced a long list of brilliant works, including the seminal *Versos Sencillos.*

There evolved in the 1930s and '40s a *poesía negra* (black poetry) that drew heavily on the myths and memories of slavery, very socialist in content, as portrayed by the works of mulatto poet Nicolás Guillén (1902–1989). Guillén also spent time in exile during the closing years of the Batista regime, having become a Communist while serving as a journalist covering the Spanish Civil War. Following the Revolution, he helped found the **Unión Nacional de Escritores y Artistas de Cuba** (National Union of Cuban Writers and Artists or UNEAC, Calle 17 #351, esq. H, Vedado, Havana, tel. 07/832-4551, www.uneac.com).

Similarly, Alejo Carpentier (1904–1980), acclaimed as Cuba's greatest latter-day writer, was imprisoned by the dictator Machado but escaped and fled Cuba for Paris on a false passport. He returned to Cuba in 1937 but in 1946, during the violent excesses of the Batista era, fled Cuba for Venezuela, where he wrote his best novels. When the Castro revolution triumphed, Carpentier returned and was named head of the state publishing house. He is known for his erudite and verbally explosive works, which were seminal in defining the surreal Latin American magic-realist style. Following the Revolution, Carpentier became a bureaucrat and sycophant and in 1966 was appointed ambassador to Paris, where he died in 1980.

Freeze and Thaw

In the first two years of the Revolution, literary magazines such as *Lunes de Revolución* attained an extraordinary dynamism. In 1961, however, Castro dictated that only pro-revolutionary works would be allowed. Ever since, the state has determined who gets published, as well as who speaks on radio or television. The ice age lasted for a decade and came to a

tatterdemalion books for sale in Plaza de Armas, Havana

climax in 1970–1976, a period euphemistically called "the gray five years" (*quinquenia gris*). The worst years ended when the Ministry of Culture was founded in 1976, ushering in a period of greater leniency. Most of the boldest and best writers, many of whom had been devoted revolutionaries, left. Among them were Guillermo Cabrera Infante, Carlos Franqui, Huberto Padilla, Reinaldo Arenas, and Virgilio Piñera. Although much of the cream of the crop left Cuba, the country still maintained a productive literary output. Notable examples are Lezama Lima (1912–1976), author of *Paraíso,* which was later made into a successful film; Nicolás Guillén; and Dulce María Loynaz (1902–1997).

The 1990s saw a thaw. The Cuban government began to salvage those artists and writers who, having produced significant works, were never allowed to publish. Many writers previously reduced to nonpersons now see their works published. Cuba's political climate, however, runs hot and cold. In 1996, writers began to feel a sharp tug on the leash. There are no independent publishing houses. Hence, many splendid writers find it difficult to get their books published. Some authors have resorted to sending manuscripts with foreigners, such

as Pablo Juan Gutiérrez, whose blistering *Dirty Havana Trilogy* is an indictment on the hardships of life in contemporary Cuba. Others become "official writers," producing pabulum that panders to the Castro government's self-congratulatory ego.

Reading matter remains severely proscribed by the government, which decides what may or may not be read. Bookstores are few and meagerly stocked, so that tattered antique editions do the rounds until they crumble to dust. Nonetheless, Cubans are avid readers, and not just of home-country writers. The works of many renowned international authors, such as Ernest Hemingway, Gabriel García Márquez, and Isabel Allende are widely read.

FILM

In 1959 Cuba established a high-quality cinema institute to produce feature films, documentaries, and newsreels. All movies in Cuba are under the control of the **Instituto Cubano de Cinematografía** (ICAIC, Calle 23 #1155, e/ 10 y 12, Vedado, Havana, tel. 07/831-3145, www.cubacine.cu), the Cuban Film Institute. Much of ICAIC's works are documentary-style movies in support of the Revolution, perfected by Santiago Álvarez (1919–1998), as in his *Hasta la Victoria Siempre* (1967) and *Mi Hermano Fidel* (1977). Perhaps the most powerful movie in the documentary-style genre is *Soy Cuba* (I Am Cuba), Soviet director Mikhail Kalatozov's black-and-white early-1960s Cold War agitprop made when the idealism and the promise of the Cuban Revolution were genuine.

Undoubtedly the most respected of Cuba's filmmakers was Tomás Gutiérrez Alea (1928–1996), whose works were part of a general questioning of things—part of the New Latin American Cinema. The Film Institute granted a relative laxity to directors such as Gutiérrez, who was instrumental in its formation and whose populist works are of an irreverent picaresque genre. For example, his 1966 *La muerte de un burócrata* (*Death of a Bureaucrat*) was a satire on the stifling bureaucracy imposed after the Revolution; and *Memorias del subdesarrollo* (*Memories of Underdevelopment*), made in 1968, traced the life of a bourgeois intellectual adrift in the new Cuba.

Gutiérrez's finest film is *Fresa y Chocolate* (*Strawberry and Chocolate*), released in 1994. The poignant and provocative movie, set in Havana during the repressive heyday of 1979, explores the nettlesome friendship between a flagrant homosexual and a macho Party member, reflecting the producer's abiding questioning of the Revolution to which he was nonetheless always loyal.

Humberto Solas (born 1941) is another leading director within the New Latin American genre. His *Lucía* (1969), which tells the tale of three women of that name living in different epochs, is considered a classic of feminist sensitivity. Most recently, his *Miel para Oshun* (*Honey for Oshun,* 2001) addresses the story of exiled Cubans returning to the island. As a tale of loss, longing, and rediscovery the movie is a visceral, moving examination of the emotional scars created by the Revolution in Cuba.

Another leading Cuban director is Juan Carlos Tabío (born 1944), who follows in the traditional of Alea, with whom he co-directed *Guantanamera,* a farcical parody on Communist bureaucracy, told through the tale of a cortege attempting to return a body to Havana for burial. Tabío's *Lista de espera* (*The Waiting List,* 2000), another magical-realist whimsy, aims its arrow at the dire state of transportation in Cuba, focusing on a group of disparate Cubans waiting in vain for a bus, eventually transforming the bus station into a kind of socialist utopia in which they themselves find transformation.

The annual **International Festival of New Latin American Cinema** (www.habanafilmfestival.com) is held each December, and the **Festival Internacional de Cine Pobre** (International Low-Budget Film Festival, www.cubacine.cu/cinepobre) is held in April.

ESSENTIALS

U.S. Law and Travel to Cuba

Moon Cuba provides complete travel information for all travelers, regardless of origin. Cuba has no restrictions on international travel. However, the U.S. government does. Most *yanquis* harbor the false impression that it's illegal for U.S. citizens to visit Cuba; it's not, it's merely illegal to spend money there, or to do so in pursuit of travel. The U.S. Supreme Court has affirmed the constitutional right of unrestricted travel; thus the U.S. government invokes the 1916 Trading with the Enemy Act to prohibit travelers from *trading* with Cuba.

To visit Cuba legally you must either spend no money there or qualify for a license issued by the U.S. Treasury Department in order to buy goods or services. Except as specifically licensed by the Office of Foreign Assets Control (OFAC), payments of any kind in connection with travel to Cuba are prohibited, including prepaid tours to companies in third countries. The regulations change frequently and are open to interpretation by OFAC staff. (At press time, the Obama administration had liberalized restrictions for Cuban-Americans, and more liberal interpretation of the laws is evident; more licenses are being granted, and the Bush administration witchhunt of transgressors appears to have been relaxed.)

The regulations apply to: U.S. citizens and permanent residents wherever they are located;

© CHRISTOPHER P. BAKER

all people and organizations physically in the United States (including airline passengers in transit); and all branches and subsidiaries of U.S. companies and organizations throughout the world.

To determine if you or your organization qualifies for a **general license** (which does not require prior authorization) or a **specific license** (which does require prior authorization), contact the Licensing Division, **Office of Foreign Assets Control** (U.S. Department of the Treasury, 1500 Pennsylvania Ave. NW, Washington, DC 20200, tel. 202/622-2480, www.treas.gov/offices/enforcement/ofac/programs/cuba/cuba.shtml).

All licensed U.S. travelers to Cuba must have a visa from the Cuban government prior to reserving their flight.

General Licenses

The following categories of travelers are permitted to spend money for Cuban travel without the need to obtain special permission from OFAC, and they are not required to inform OFAC in advance of their visit to Cuba.

Official government travelers, including representatives of international organizations of which the United States is a member, traveling on official business.

Journalists and supporting broadcasting or technical personnel regularly employed in that capacity by a news reporting organization and traveling for journalistic activities. (The Cuban government requires that you be issued a journalist's visa, not a tourist card.)

Full-time professionals whose travel is directly related to "noncommercial, academic research" in their professional field and whose research will comprise a full work schedule in Cuba and has a likelihood of public dissemination; or whose travel is directly related to attendance at professional meetings or conferences that do not promote tourism or other commercial activity involving Cuba or the production of biotechnological products, so long as such meetings are organized by "qualifying international bodies."

Persons visiting family: People with close relatives in Cuba may visit them as often as desired and for an unlimited period.

Other: As of September 2009, individuals traveling to conduct business in the field of agricultural and medicinal product sales (including marketing, negotiation, delivery, or servicing of exports), and in telecommunications, including conferences and meetings, are required to submit written reports to OFAC 14 days prior to and subsequent to travel.

Fully hosted travel, formerly allowed, is no longer permitted.

Specific Licenses

A specific license requires written government approval. Applicants should write a letter to OFAC (http://cubatravel.ofac.treas.gov) stating the date of the planned visit and the length of stay; the specific purpose(s) of the visit; plus the name(s), title(s), and background(s) of the traveler. Allow two or three months. Special licenses are issued by OFAC on a case-by-case basis authorizing travel transactions in connection with these travel categories:

Humanitarian travel and support for the Cuban people: Persons traveling to Cuba to accompany licensed humanitarian donations or in connection with activities of recognized human rights organizations investigating human rights violations; or travel aimed at promoting "independent activity intended to strengthen civil society in Cuba."

Freelance journalists: Persons with a suitable record of publication who are traveling to do research for a freelance article.

Professional research and meetings: Persons engaging in professional research or attending professional meetings that do not meet the general license requirements.

Educational research: U.S. universities, colleges, and nongovernmental organizations may apply for one-year travel permits to Cuba that will permit students and academic staff to travel to Cuba. Once such a license is approved, the following categories of travelers affiliated with that academic institution are authorized to engage in travel-related transactions without seeking further approval: (1) undergraduate or graduate students participating in a structured educational program lasting at least 10 weeks in Cuba as part of a course offered at a U.S. undergraduate or graduate institution; (2) persons doing noncommercial Cuba-related academic research for the purpose of qualifying academically as a professional (e.g., research toward a graduate degree); (3) students participating in a formal course of study lasting at least 10 weeks at a Cuban academic institution, provided the Cuban study will be accepted for credit toward a degree at the licensed U.S. institution; (4) persons regularly employed as teachers at a licensed U.S. undergraduate or graduate institution who plan to teach part or all of an academic program at a Cuban academic institution for at least 10 weeks; (5) full-time employees of a licensed institution organizing or preparing for the educational activities described above. In all cases, students and teachers planning to engage in such transactions must carry a letter from the licensed institution stating the institution's license number and that the individual meets the specific criteria.

Religious organizations: Specific licenses may be issued by OFAC to religious organizations authorizing individuals affiliated with the organization to engage in travel transactions so long as a full-time program of religious activity is pursued in Cuba. Persons wishing to engage in religious activities that are not authorized pursuant to a religious organization's license may also apply for a specific license, including for multiple trips.

Public performances, athletic or other competitions, and exhibitions: Persons traveling to participate in such events may apply, so long as the event is open to public attendance and any profits go to a U.S.-based charity or independent nongovernmental organization in Cuba. Also, amateur or semiprofessional athletes or teams selected for a competition by the relevant U.S. sports federation may travel to participate in athletic competition held under the auspices of an international sports federation, so long as the event is open to the Cuban public.

Private foundations or research or educational institutions: Persons traveling to Cuba on behalf of private foundations, research institutes, or educational institutes that have an established interest in international relations to collect information related to Cuba for noncommercial purposes.

Export, import, or transmission of informational materials: Persons traveling to engage in exportation, importation, or transmission of informational materials.

What You May Spend, Take, and Return Home With

Licensed travelers, including for family visits, are authorized to spend up to the State Department Travel per diem allowance, which was US$179 in Havana and US$126 for the rest of Cuba at press time. Journalists may spend more than this allowance (the amount is unspecified), and other licensed travelers may spend additional money "for transactions directly related to the activities for which they received a license." Money may be spent only for purchases of items directly related to licensed travel, such as hotel accommodations, meals, and goods personally used by the traveler in Cuba. Credit cards, including those issued by foreign firms, may *not* be used.

Accompanied baggage is limited to 44 pounds.

Regardless of the reason for travel, licensed travelers are not permitted to return to the United States with any Cuban purchases, other than informational material, which may be brought back without limitation (this includes art, CDs, films, etc.). The regulations apply even to foreigners in transit through U.S. airports: Since the U.S. has no transit entry, *all* passengers in transit, say, from Mexico to Europe, must pass through U.S. Immigration and Customs; any Cuban items may be confiscated, whether bought in Cuba or not.

Qualified Travel Service Providers

U.S. law states, "U.S. travel service providers, such as travel agents and tour operators, who handle travel arrangements to, from, or within Cuba must hold special authorizations from the U.S. Treasury Department to engage in such activities." OFAC licenses companies as authorized Travel Service Providers (TSPs), who are legally entitled to make commercial travel arrangements to Cuba. TSPs can only make reservations for individual travel for licensed travelers. You must obtain approval before proceeding with a reservation. (OFAC may issue TSP licenses to certain companies and organizations permitting them to offer pre-packaged group tours, so long as such programs fall within the areas for licensed travel.)

However, referring to non-TSP travel agencies and tour operators, "It is possible to provide travel services to U.S. persons legally able to travel to Cuba for family visits, professional research, or news gathering," says Michael Krinsky, a partner in the law firm of Rabinowitz, Boudin, Standard, Krinsky and Lieberman (740 Broadway, New York, NY 10003, tel. 212/254-1111, fax 212/674-4614, www.rbskl.com/mk.html), which represents the Cuban government in the United States. They may also be able to provide services, such as travel arrangements to Jamaica, from where a traveler makes his or her own arrangements for travel to and within Cuba. Treasury Department regulations do not "show a clear penalty against travel agents who book travel this way." Travel agents should double-check the regulations, however, with OFAC or with Krinsky.

"Illegal" Travel

Individuals who choose to circumvent U.S. law do so at their own risk and the author and publisher accept no responsibility for any consequences that may result from such travel.

Every year, thousands (20,100 in 2007, according to Cuba, down from 84,500 in 2003) of U.S. citizens slip into Cuba through Canada, Mexico, and other third countries to savor the frisson of the forbidden. Cubans play their part by abstaining from stamping passports (however, many travelers report receiving a small stamp, such as a purple square, on page 16 of their passports, familiar to U.S. authorities).

Persons subject to U.S. jurisdiction who travel to Cuba without a license bear a "presumption of guilt" and may be required to show documentation that all expenses incurred were paid by a third party not subject to U.S. law.

Very few people ever have trouble coming back. Nonetheless, if Uncle Sam decides to go after perceived offenders, the latter will first receive a questionnaire and, if OFAC believes the law has been broken, a "pre-penalty notice" listing the amount of the proposed fine. (Trading with Cuba illegally is good for up to a US$55,000 fine under provisions of the Helms-Burton Bill, plus up to US$250,000 under the Trading with the Enemy Act, but most demands for fines have been US$7,500.) If issued a penalty notice, you have 30 days to appeal. If the case is not settled out of court, it ostensibly goes before an administrative law judge, who can uphold or dismiss the penalty, but *no* judges are in place to adjudicate! Thus, anyone receiving a pre-penalty notice can effectively kill the action dead by requesting a hearing. (Only two people have ever been prosecuted: In January 2005 a judge slapped the first-ever such fine—for US$5,250—on a Michigan couple who had traveled in 2001 on a religious mission; the second penalty was for US$780.) If you choose to pay the fine requested in the pre-penalty notice, as many people do, you can negotiate the amount.

HOW TO DEFEND THE RIGHT TO TRAVEL

The **National Lawyers Guild** (132 Nassau St., Suite 922, New York, NY 10038, tel. 212/679-5100, www.nlg.org/cuba/#Travel) has a Cuba subcommittee that can aid in defending against enforcement actions. The **Center for Constitutional Rights** (666 Broadway, New York, NY 10012, tel. 212/614-6464, www.ccr-justice.org) is the primary institutional clearinghouse for legal information about the Cuba travel regulations and represents those who have been accused of violating the ban.

Getting There and Away

BY AIR

About 40 airlines service Cuba. The majority of flights arrive at Havana's José Martí International Airport or Varadero's Juan Gualberto Gómez International Airport. Cuba has eight additional international airports: Camagüey, Cayo Coco, Cayo Largo del Sur, Ciego de Ávila, Holguín, Santa Clara, and Santiago de Cuba.

Cuba's national airline, **Cubana de Aviación** (www.cubana.cu), generally offers lower fares than competing airlines. Cubana has DC-10s and Airbus A-320s that serve Europe and Mexico. However, the workhorses in the stable remain Soviet-made aircraft. The airline is poorly managed, service is charmless, and its safety record is poor.

Fares quoted in this book are based on rates advertised at press time. They are subject to change and should be used only as a guideline.

To get the cheapest fares, make your reservations as early as possible, especially during peak season, as flights often sell out. Low-season and midweek travel is often cheaper, as are stays of more than 30 days.

Most scheduled airlines permit two pieces of checked baggage, although a fee may apply; most charter airlines permit 20 kilos of baggage and charge extra for overweight bags. Cubana (20–40 kilograms, depending on class) charges extortionate rates for each kilo over your limit. Keep any valuable items, such as laptop computers, in your carry-on luggage. Always reconfirm your reservation and return flight within 72 hours of your departure (reservations are frequently cancelled if not reconfirmed; Cubana is particularly bad) and arrive at the airport with plenty of time to spare. Always keep a photocopy of your ticket separate from your ticket and other documents as a safeguard in the event of loss or theft.

ONLINE BOOKINGS

U.S. websites such as www.orbitz.com and www.travelocity.com are barred from displaying Cuba-related flight information and from making reservations for Cuba flights. However, many foreign-based websites, including those of airlines such as Copa and Grupo Taca (but not Air Jamaica or Mexicana), offer reservation services for travel to Cuba. Except as specifically licensed by OFAC, it is illegal for any U.S. citizen or resident to make payments in connection with travel to Cuba through such websites.

All international passengers en route to Cuba via the U.S., say on a round-the-world ticket, must have a separate ticket stock for the Cuba portion and ensure that "Cuba" does not appear on the main ticket stock.

From the United States

No scheduled commercial flights are permitted between the United States and Cuba.

Licensed Flights: About two dozen companies—called Carrier Service Providers (CSPs)—are authorized to fly direct charters to Cuba from the United States, solely for licensed passengers as permitted by the U.S. Treasury Department. Charters use aircraft operated by Continental, Grupo Taca, and United Airlines.

PRIVATE AIRCRAFT

Private pilots must contact the **Instituto de Aeronáutica Civil de Cuba** (Calle 23 #64, e/ Infanta y P, Vedado, tel. 07/834-4949, fax 07/834-4553, www.iacc.gov.cu) at least 10 days before arrival in Cuba and at least 48 hours before an overflight.

U.S. owners of private aircraft, including air ambulance services, who intend to land in Cuba must obtain a temporary export permit for the aircraft from the U.S. Department of Commerce before departure.

HUMANITARIAN COURIERS

You can make tax-deductible donations to the following relief organizations, which are licensed by OFAC to run food, medicine, and other humanitarian aid to Cuba using ordinary U.S. citizens as volunteer couriers.

- **Caribbean Medical Transport** (1393 Cold Hill Rd., Lyndonville, VT 05851, www.cubacaribe.com)

- **Cuba AIDS Project** (P.O. Box 234, Mount Freedom, NJ 07970, tel. 973/462-0702, www.cubaaidsproject.com

- **Operation USA: Cuba Medical Relief Project** (3617 Hayden Av., Suite A, Culver City, CA 90232, tel. 310/838-3455, fax 310/838-3477, www.opusa.org)

- **U.S.-Latin American Medical Aid Foundation** (1215A Castle Hill, Austin, TX 78703, tel. 512/477-2438, www.medaid.org)

In Canada, **Not Just Tourists** (866/426-3695, www.notjusttourists.org) sends suitcases of medicines to Cuba using tourist volunteers.

Why are prices so high? One, the monopolistic nature of the CSP business; two, because Cuba imposes landing rights of US$100–133 per passenger. CSPs and licensed TSPs may also make reservations for authorized or fully hosted travelers on flights between third countries and Cuba for authorized travelers.

The following CSPs are recommended:

- **ABC Charters** (1125 SW 27th Ave., Miami, FL 33174, tel. 305/263-6829 or 866/411-1147, fax 305/263-7187, www.abc-charters.com) has flights from Miami to Havana (US$559 round-trip) and Holguín.

- **C&T Charters** (932B Ponce de Leon Blvd., Coral Gables, FL 33134, tel. 305/445-3337, www.ctcharters.com) has charters to Havana and Camagüey from both Miami (US$559 round-trip) and New York (US$895 round-trip).

- **Cuba Travel Services** (300 Oceangate, Suite 910, Long Beach, CA 90802, tel. 310/772-2822 or 800/963-2822, www.cubatravelservices.com), with offices in Hialeah and San Juan, offers charter flights from Los Angeles to Havana (US$629 round-trip) and from Miami to Havana (US$449 round-trip).

- **Marazul Charters** (8324 SW 40th St., Miami, FL 33155, tel. 305/559-7114 or 800/993-9667, www.marazulcharters.com) operates charters from Miami to Havana.

Via Third Countries: The Treasury Department issues the following advisory: Except as specifically licensed by OFAC, "The Regulations prohibit all transactions relating to travel-related tourist transactions in Cuba, including prepayment in third countries for Cuba-related expenses" for unlicensed travelers. Nonetheless, thousands of U.S. citizens and residents travel to Cuba through Canada, Mexico, the Caribbean, or Central America aboard foreign airlines.

Anyone showing an airline reservation that includes an onward flight to Cuba will be refused boarding on the flight within the United States. *Unlicensed travel therefore requires completely separate reservations and tickets for your travel to/from a third country and to/from Cuba.* Since you *must* make separate reservations for the two legs, you'll need to pick up your checked bags in your third-country destination then check in again for the Cuba flight (and vice versa on the way home). If possible, pack light and carry everything on to the plane.

Travelers should assume a possibility that passenger manifests for flights to Cuba, including reservations made using the Amadeus reservations system, may be shared with and/or monitored by U.S. authorities.

From Canada

Non-licensed U.S. travelers should note that all airlines overflying the U.S. (i.e., between Canada and Cuba) are required to share their passenger manifests with U.S. Homeland Security.

Most flights from Canada land at Varadero and other beach destinations. You can find cheap airfares—about C$400 round-trip—through **Wholesale Travel** (tel. 416/366-0062 or 888/970-3600, www.wholesaletravel.com) and **Travel Cuts** (tel. 866/246-9762, www.travelcuts.com).

A. Nash Travel Inc. (5865 McLaughlin Rd., Unit 2B, Mississauga, ON L5R 1B8, tel. 905/755-0647 or 800/818-2004, fax 905/755-0729, www.nashtravel.com) is a recommended Cuba specialist.

Scheduled Flights: Highly regarded **Air Canada** (tel. 800/247-2262, www.aircanada.com) flies from Calgary to Varadero; from Halifax to Holguín; from Montreal to Cayo Coco, Cayo Largo, Havana, Holguín, Santa Clara, and Varadero; from Ottawa to Havana and Santa Clara; from Toronto to Cayo Coco, Havana, Santa Clara, and Varadero; and from Vancouver to Havana. **Cubana** (675 King St. W. #206, Toronto, tel. 416/967-2822 or 866/428-2262, www.cubana.cu) flies from Montreal to Camagüey, Cayo Largo, Cienfuegos, and Havana; and from Toronto to Camagüey, Cayo Largo, Cienfuegos, Havana, Holguín, Santa Clara, and Santiago de Cuba.

Charter Flights: Most charter flights are designed as beach vacation packages, but charter operators also sell "air-only" tickets.

Air Canada Vacations (tel. 866/529-2079, www.aircanadavacations.com) offers flexible "build-your-own" packages using Air Canada flights.

Air Transat (tel. 866/847-1112, www.air-transat.com) flies from Calgary to Varadero; from Edmonton to Varadero; from Halifax to Varadero; from Montreal to Camagüey, Cayo Coco, Cayo Largo, Holguin, and Varadero; from Ottawa to Holguín, Santa Clara, and Varadero; from Quebec City to Holguín, Santa Clara, and Varadero; from Toronto to Camagüey, Holguín, and Varadero; and from Vancouver to Varadero. **Skyservice** (tel. 800/701-9448, www.skyserviceairlines.com) flies from Calgary to Varadero; from Edmonton to Varadero; from Halifax to Cayo Coco and Holguín; from Montreal to Holguín; from Ottawa to Varadero; from Regina to Varadero; from Toronto to Cayo Coco and Varadero; from Vancouver to Varadero; and from Winnipeg to Holguín and Varadero. **SunWing** (tel. 800/761-1711, www.sunwing.ca) has the most extensive service, with flights to eight Cuban destinations from 19 Canadian airports. **Westjet** (tel. 888/937-8538, www.westjet.com) flies from Halifax to Cayo Coco and Holguín; from Moncton to Varadero; from Montreal to Varadero; from Ottawa to Santa Clara; from Saskatoon to Varadero; and from Toronto to Cayo Coco.

From Europe

Note that if flying aboard a U.S. carrier, you must have your ticket for the Cuban portion issued separately with another carrier.

From France: Havana is served by **Air France** (tel. 0820-320-820, www.airfrance.com), nine times weekly from Paris's Charles de Gaulle airport using Boeing 777s (from about €785 round-trip). **Corsairfly** (tel. 0820-042-042, www.corsairfly.com) flies a Boeing 747 weekly from Paris Orly to Havana. **Cubana** (41 Boulevard du Montparnasse, 75006 Paris, tel. 01/53-63-23-23) flies from Paris Orly airport to Havana via Santiago de Cuba on Sundays using an Ilyushin L-96 (from €532 round-trip). **Air Europa** (tel. 902/401-501 in Spain, www.aireuropa.com) flies between Paris Charles de Gaulle and Havana via Madrid.

From Germany: Charter company **Condor** (tel. 0180/5-70-72-02, www.condor.com) flies from Frankfurt and Munich to Holguín and Cayo Coco. **AirBerlin** (tel. 0180/5-73-78-00, www.airberlin.com), formerly LTU, flies from Berlin to Varadero on Thursday (from €778 round-trip). Tour operator **Reisegalerie** (Gruneburgweg 84, 60323 Frankfurt, tel. 069/9720-6000, www.reisegalerie.com) specializes in Cuba.

From Italy: You can use **Alitalia** (tel. 800/650-055, www.alitalia.it) to connect with Air France, Iberia, or Virgin Atlantic flights. Air France and Iberia fly from Milan to Havana via Paris and Madrid, respectively. **Blue Panorama** (tel. 06/6021-4737, www.blue-panorama.com) carries the bulk of Italian tourists to Cuba with daily flights from Rome to Cayo Largo, Havana, and Santiago de Cuba (from €635 round-trip). **Livingstone** (tel. 0331/267-321, www.lauda.it), formerly Lauda Air, flies charters from Milan to Cayo Largo and from Rome and Milan to Havana and Holguín.

From the Netherlands: Havana is served by **Martinair** (tel. 20/60-11-767, www.martinair.com) from Amsterdam (from €619 round-trip).

From Russia: Russia's **Aeroflot** (tel. 0495/223-5555 or 800/333-5555, www.aeroflot.ru/eng/) flies from Moscow to Havana on Monday and Friday (from US$1,070 round-trip). **Cubana** (tel. 0495/642-9439, www.cubana.ru) operates once a week from Moscow.

From Spain: Havana is served by **Iberia** (tel. 902/400-500, www.iberia.com) from Madrid daily (from €790 round-trip); likewise **Air Europa** (tel. 902/401-501, www.air-europa.com). **Cubana** (tel. 091/758-9750, www.cubana.cu) flies from Madrid to Havana and Santiago de Cuba on Monday and Thursday using a DC-10 (from €560 round-trip).

From the United Kingdom: My favorite airline, **Virgin Atlantic** (tel. 800/821-5438, www.virgin-atlantic.com), flies on Wednesday and Sunday from Gatwick to Havana (from £602 round-trip). **Cubana** (tel. 020/7536-8177, www.cubanacan.cu) flies from Gatwick to Havana via Holguín on Wednesday (from £457 roundtrip). **Air Jamaica** (tel. 020/7590-3600, www.airjamaica.com), which no longer operates from the U.K., has a codeshare agreement with Virgin Atlantic; you can fly the latter to Montego Bay or Kingston and hop over to Havana with Air Jamaica. Good online resources for discount tickets include www.ebookers.com, www.cheapflights.co.uk, and www.travelsupermarket.com, and for charter flights, there's **Charter Flight Centre** (tel. 0845/045-0153, www.charterflights.co.uk).

From the Caribbean

From the Bahamas: As of 2008, **Bahamasair** (tel. 242/377-5505, http://up.bahamasair.com) has Nassau–Havana flights (Tues., Thurs., and Sun. at 12:45 P.M., US$329 round-trip); you cannot book via the website. A **Cubana** charter flight operates to Havana from Nassau (Mon.–Sat. 2:30 P.M., US$329 round-trip, plus US$15 visa and US$7 ticket tax). Book through **Havanatur** (East Bay Shopping Centre, East Bay St., Nassau, tel. 242/393-5281, www.havanaturbahamas.com) or **Majestic Travel** (tel. 242/328-0908). Neither accepts credit card reservations; you'll have to pay through a Western Union wire transfer or by certified check, which has to be mailed. You can pick up your ticket in Nassau or have it delivered to the airport for pickup. Midweek, it's often possible to purchase a ticket at the counter two hours before departure time. *Returning from Cuba, you pass through U.S. Immigration and Customs here; officials are wise to the arrival of flights from Havana.*

From the Cayman Islands: Havana is served three times weekly by **Cayman Airways** (tel. 345/949-8200, www.caymanairways.com) from Grand Cayman (from US$217 round-trip).

From the Dominican Republic and Haiti: Panama's **Copa** (www.copaair.com) flies between Santo Domingo and Havana via Panama City four times daily (from US$284 round-trip). **Cubana** (Av. Tiradentes y 27 de Febrero, Santo Domingo, tel. 809/227-2040, cubana.aviacion@codetel.net.do) serves Havana from Santo Domingo on Thursday and Sunday (from US$395 round-trip). Cuba's **Aero Caribbean** (www.aerocaribbean.cu) supposedly flies on Friday and Sunday between Santo Domingo and Santiago de Cuba (US$510 round-trip).

From Jamaica: Troubled **Air Jamaica** (tel. 800/523-5585 in North America, tel. 888/359-2478 in Jamaica, www.airjamaica.com) flies thrice weekly from Montego Bay and Kingston to Havana (from US$420 round-trip). U.S. travelers cannot book a Cuba leg via Air

Jamaica's website; you must call Jamaica directly and pay for the Jamaica–Cuba leg upon arrival in Jamaica. The airline has a reputation for losing luggage. **Caribic Vacations** (tel. 876/953-9895, www.caribicvacations.com), **Tropical Tours** (tel. 876/953-9100, www.tropicaltours-ja.com), and **Marzouca Marketing & Sales** (tel. 876/971-3859, www.cubaonweb.com) offer charter flights and package excursions from Montego Bay to Havana.

From Central America

Copa and Taca permit reservations and payment by credit card online for flights through Central America.

Copa (tel. 507/217-2672 or 800/359-2672 in the U.S., www.copaair.com) flies to Havana from Panama City four times daily (from US$548 round-trip). **Taca** (tel. 305/870-7500 or 800/400-8222, www.taca.com) has twice-daily flights from El Salvador to Havana (from US$644 round-trip) and daily flights from Costa Rica (from US$413) with connecting flights from the United States. **Cubana** (www.cubana.cu) flies to Havana daily from Costa Rica (tel. 506/2221-7625, cubanaju@racsa.co.cr) and from Guatemala (tel. 502/2367-2288) on Saturday.

From Mexico: The national carrier **Mexicana** and its subsidiary **Click** (tel. 59/9848-5998 in Mexico City, tel. 800/801-2010 from elsewhere in Mexico, tel. 800/531-7921 from the U.S.) have daily flights to Havana from Cancún (from US$297 round-trip), Mexico City (from about US$430 round-trip), and Mérida (from US$402 round-trip). However, U.S. citizens can't book via their website. To make reservations, call the airline and request a special telephone number (tel. 55/5448-0990) that handles Cuba reservations. Credit cards (except American Express) are not accepted; pay in cash at the Mexican gateway airport at least four hours before departure. (*Note:* Mexicana reportedly has a reputation for delaying luggage on this route.) **Cubana** (tel. 52-55/52-506355 in Mexico City, tel. 52-9988/87-7210 in Cancún, reservaciones@cubanamexico.com) also flies from Mexico City five times weekly (from US$430 round-trip) and daily from Cancún (from US$306 round-trip).

Cuban-owned **Viajes Divermex** (Av. Cobá #5, Centro Comercial Plaza América, Cancún, Quintana Roo, México CP 77500, tel. 998/884-5005, www.divermex.com) specializes in Cuba packages.

From Nicaragua: Cuba's **Aero Caribbean** (www.cubajet.com) flies from Managua to Havana on Saturday (US$572 round-trip).

From South America

Lan Chile (tel. 866/435-9526, www.lanchile.com) flies to Havana from Santiago de Chile on Sunday (from US$1,040 round-trip).

Cubana (www.cubana.cu) flies to Havana from Quito, Ecuador; Buenos Aires, Argentina; Sao Paulo, Brazil; Bogota, Colombia; and Caracas, Venezuela.

From Asia

You can fly to Paris, London, Madrid, or Canada and connect with flights to Cuba. Eastbound, flying nonstop to Los Angeles, then to Mexico City or Cancún, is perhaps the easiest route.

STA Travel (www.statravel.com) sells discounted tickets and has a branch in Bangkok (tel. 662/236-0262).

From Australia and New Zealand

The best bet is to fly to either Los Angeles or San Francisco and then to Cuba via Mexico, El Salvador, or Panama; or to Canada and on to Havana. **Air New Zealand** (Australia tel. 132-476, New Zealand tel. 0800/737-000, www.airnewzealand.com), **Qantas** (Australia tel. 131-313, New Zealand tel. 0800/808-767, www.qantas.com.au), and **United Airlines** (Australia tel. 131-777, New Zealand tel. 0800/747-400) offer direct service between Australia, New Zealand, and North America. A route via Santiago de Chile and then to Havana is also possible.

Specialists in discount fares include **STA Travel** (Australia tel. 134-782, www.statravel.com.au; New Zealand tel. 0800/474-400, www.statravel.co.nz). A good online resource for discount airfares is **Flight Centre** (Australia tel. 133-133, www.flightcentre.com.au).

BY SEA
By Cruise Ship

The U.S. embargo has restricted the cruise industry's access to Cuba. Nonetheless, several foreign cruise ships have featured Cuba on their itineraries. None has stood the test of time. In 2005, Castro belittled the cruise industry and said cruise passengers were no longer welcome. Passenger arrivals plummeted from 102,000 in 2005 (generating US$15 million) to 11,000 in 2007.

England's **Fred Olsen Cruise Lines** (tel. 01473/746-175, www.fredolsencruises.co.uk) features a two-day Havana stop-over on its 15-day Caribbean cruises from Bridgetown, Barbados, aboard the *Braemar.* And in December 2009, **Thomson Holidays** (tel. 0871/231-4691, www.thomson.co.uk) launched three Caribbean itineraries featuring Cuba with the new, 1,500-passenger *Thomson Dream.*

Germany's **Aida Cruises** (tel. 0381/2027-0707, www.aida.de) occasionally features Havana on its peak-season programs.

By Freighter

Hamburg-Süd Reiseagentur GMBH (Ost-West 59, 20457 Hamburg, tel. 040/3705-157, fax 040/370-5242, www.freighter-voyages.com) books passage aboard the *Melfi Iberia* sailing from Italy and Spain to Havana on a 38-day journey (from €3,535). Germany's **Hapag Lloyd** (tel. 49/403-0010, www.hapag-lloyd.com) has serviced Cuba in past years.

In the United Kingdom, book through **Strand Voyages** (357 Strand, London WC2R 0HS, tel. 020/7010-9290, www.strandtravel.co.uk). U.S. citizens can book through **Freighter World Cruises** (180 S. Lake Ave. #335, Pasadena, CA 91101, tel. 626/449-3106 or 800/531-7774, www.freighterworld.com).

By Private Vessel

No advance permission is required to arrive by sea. However, it's wise to give at least 72 hours advance warning by faxing details of your boat, crew, and passengers to the six official entry ports operated by Cuba's **Marlin Náutica y Marinas** (tel. 07/273-7912, www.nauticamarlin.com) and **Gaviota** (tel. 07/869-5774, www.gaviota-grupo.com). Only a few are up to international par, although most offer fresh water, 110-volt electrical hookups, plus diesel and gasoline.

For cruising, you'll need to register your boat upon arrival and receive a *permiso especial de navegación* (from CUC50, depending on the length of your boat). You'll need an official clearance (a *despacho*) to depart for your next, and each and every, stop. Authorities will usually ask for a planned itinerary, but insist on flexibility to cruise at random toward your final destination. A *permiso de salida* will be issued listing your final destination and possible stops en route.

Two excellent references are Simon Charles's *Cruising Guide to Cuba* and Nigel Calder's *Cuba: A Cruising Guide.*

Uncle Sam requires that U.S. boaters get pre-authorization from the Coast Guard Marine Safety Office (www.uscg.mil/hq/cg5/cg531/CubaTravel.asp); an export license from the Commerce Department; and a specific license from OFAC. Applications must be made through the Seventh Coast Guard District (tel. 305/415-6920, fax 305/415-6925). All persons subject to U.S. law aboard vessels, including the owner, must be licensed travelers. Vessel owners are prohibited from carrying travelers to Cuba who pay them for passage if the owner does not have a specific license from OFAC authorizing him or her to be a Service Provider to Cuba.

The United States and Cuba do not have a Coast Guard agreement (however, the U.S. Interests Section *has* arranged such assistance to U.S. yachters). There are many reports of Cuban authorities being indifferent to yachters in distress, some of whom have had their vessels impounded; in several cases, foreign yachters have lost their vessels to corrupt officials. In case of emergencies requiring financial transactions, such as repair of vessels, travelers should contact OFAC (tel. 202/622-2480) for authorization.

Haut Insurance (80 Chestnut St., Andover, MA 01810, tel. 978/475-0367, www.john-galden.com) handles insurance coverage to yachters cruising in Cuban waters.

In Havana, **Tienda el Navegante** (Calle Mercaderes #115, e/ Obispo y Obrapía, Habana Vieja, tel. 07/861-3625, VHF channel 16 CMYP3050) sells **nautical charts** of Cuban waters.

BY ORGANIZED TOUR

Joining an organized tour offers certain advantages over traveling independently. However, you'll be almost entirely divorced from the local culture as you are hauled between official tourist sites by guides giving you the "rah-rah-rah" revolutionary spiel. Check the tour inclusions to identify any hidden costs such as airport taxes, tips, service charges, extra meals, etc. Most tours are priced according to quality of accommodations.

Tours from the United States

These organizations offer trips and/or can arrange trips for licensed academic and cultural organizations:

- **Art Quest International** (801 Idaho Ave., Suite 15, Santa Monica, CA 90403, tel. 310/393-3435, www.artquestintl.com), formerly Cuba Cultural Travel.
- **Center for Cuban Studies** (231 W. 29th St., New York, NY 10001, tel. 212/242-0559, www.cubaupdate.org).
- **Global Exchange** (2017 Mission St. #303, San Francisco, CA 94110, tel. 415/255-7296, www.globalexchange.org). This left-wing organization offers "Reality Trips."
- **Marazul Tours** (8328 SW 40th St., Miami, FL 33155, tel. 305/559-7114 or 800/993-9667, www.marazulcharters.com).
- **Ya'lla Tours** (tel. 800/644-1595, www.yallatours.com).

VOLUNTEER PROGRAMS

The Bush administration rescinded the fully hosted travel and person-to-person exchange provisions permitting "solidarity" tours, in which participants perform voluntary work that contributes to the human community while learning some invaluable life lessons. Nonetheless, the following agencies offer programs.

Pastors for Peace (418 W. 145th St., New York, NY 10031, tel. 212/926-5757, fax 212/926-5842, www.ifconews.org), which operates without a license, delivers humanitarian aid to Cuba through the annual U.S.–Cuba Friendshipment Caravan, which travels via Canada or Mexico. The **Venceremos Brigade** (P.O. Box 5202, Englewood, NJ 07631-5202, tel. 212/560-4360, www.venceremosbrigade.net) organizes annual solidarity trips and "work-camp" brigades (also without a license).

Volunteers for Peace (1034 Tiffany Rd., Belmont, VT 05730, tel. 802/259-2759, www.vfp.org) has "International Workcamps" in Cuba for volunteers.

Friendship Force International (34 Peachtree St. NW, Suite 900, Atlanta, GA 30303, tel. 404/522-9490, www.friendshipforce.org) has taken participants to Cuba in past years, as have **People to People Ambassadors** (Dwight D. Eisenhower Bldg., 110 S. Ferrall St., Spokane, WA 99202, tel. 509/568-7000 or 866/794-8309, www.ambassadorprograms.org) and **Witness for Peace** (3628 12th St. NE, Washington, DC 20017, tel. 202/547-6112, www.witnessforpeace.org).

ACADEMIC EXCHANGES AND CULTURAL PROGRAMS

Most entities that held licenses to operate academic and cultural-exchange programs no longer do so. Such programs have in past been offered by the **Cuba Exchange Program** (School of Advanced International Studies at Johns Hopkins University, 1740 Massachusetts Ave. NW, Washington, DC 20036, tel. 202/663-5600, www.sais-jhu.edu); **MacArthur Cuba Scholarly Exchange** (Center for Latin

STUDYING IN CUBA

Thousands of people every year choose to study in Cuba, be it for a month-long dance course or six years of medical training. Be prepared for basic living conditions if signing up for a long-term residential course. Restrictions for U.S. students apply.

UniversiTUR (Calle 30 #768, e/ Kohly y 41, Nuevo Vedado, tel. 07/855-5978, agencia@universitur.get.tur.cu) arranges study at centers of higher learning. For study at the **Universidad de la Habana,** contact the Dirección de Posgrado (Calle J #556, e/ 25 y 27, Vedado, tel. 07/832-4245, www.uh.cu).

Cuba's **Ministerio de Relaciones Exteriores** (MINREX, Foreign Relations Ministry) provides a complete list of Cuban institutions that offer courses to foreigners at http://embacu.cubaminrex.cu/Default.aspx?tabid=1210.

STUDENT VISAS

You can no longer study in Cuba using a tourist visa, however short the duration of study, unless you travel via UniversiTUR. All others require a student visa (CUC80), which can be requested in advance from the Director of Graduate Degrees of the relevant university 20 days prior to your intended arrival date. Visas can ostensibly be picked up at the Cuban consulate in your country. Visas are good for 30 days but can be extended upon arrival in Cuba for CUC25.

You can *arrive* in Cuba with a tourist visa, however. You then have 48 hours to register for your university program and request a change of visa status (CUC65). You'll need six passport photos, your passport and tourist card, plus a license certificate for the *casa particular* where you'll be staying.

ARTS, MUSIC, AND DANCE

The **Cátedra de Danza** (Calzada #510, e/ D y E, Vedado, tel. 07/832-4625, fax 07/833-3117, www.balletcubacult.cu) offers monthlong ballet courses for intermediate- and advanced-level professionals and students.

The **Centro Nacional de Conservación, Restauración y Museología** (Calle Cuba #610, e/ Sol y Luz, Habana Vieja, tel. 07/861-2877, fax 07/866-5696, www.cencrem.co.cu) offers courses for urban planners, conservationists, and architects.

The **Instituto Superior de Arte** (Calle 120 #11110, e/ 9na y 13, Cubanacán, tel. 07/208-

American Studies, University of Chicago, 5848 S. University Ave., Chicago, IL 60637, tel. 773/702-8420, http://clas.uchicago.edu); **Plaza Cuba** (P.O. Box 3083, Berkeley, CA 94703, tel. 510/848-0911, www.plazacuba.com), which specializes in music and dance workshops; and the **Center for Cross-Cultural Study** (446 Main St., Amherst, MA 01002, tel. 413/256-0011, www.cccs.com), which also oversees the **Cuba Academic Alliance** (www.cccs.com/CubaAcademicAlliance), working to challenge restrictions on academic travel.

Tours from Canada

Cuba Education Tours (2278 E. 24th Ave., Vancouver, BC V5N 2V2, tel. 877/687-3817, www.cubafriends.ca) offers "solidarity" and special-interest tours.

Quest Nature Tours (491 King St., Toronto, ON M5A 1L9, tel. 416/633-5666 or 800/387-1483, www.questnaturetours.com) offers birding and nature tours.

Real Cuba (Box 2345, Swan River, MB, R0L 1Z0, tel. 306/205-0977, www.realcuba-online.com) offers special theme trips, including bicycling, walking and bird-watching, and photography workshops.

WowCuba (430 Queen St., Charlottestown, PE, C1A 4E8, tel. 902/368-2453, www.wowcuba.com) specializes in bicycle tours of Cuba, but has other programs, including scuba diving.

Several companies offer air-hotel beach packages, including: **Signature Vacations** (tel. 866/324-2883, www.signaturevacations.com); **Sunquest Vacations** (tel. 877/485-6060,

0288, www.cubarte.cult.cu) offers courses in music, dance, theater, and visual arts.

The **Unión de Escritores y Artistas de Cuba** (Calle 17 #351, esq. H, Vedado, tel. 07/832-4551, www.uneac.org.cu) offers courses in the arts and Cuban culture.

The **Taller Experimental de Gráfica** (Callejón del Chorro #6, Plaza de la Catedral, Habana Vieja, tel. 07/864-7622, tgrafica@cubarte.cult.cu) offers courses in engraving and lithography.

Paradiso: Promotora de Viajes Culturales (Calle 19 #560, esq. C, Vedado, tel. 07/832-6928, www.paradiso.cu) arranges participation in cultural courses and programs, from children's book publishing to theater criticism.

The **Universidad de la Habana** (Dirección de Posgrado, Calle J #556, e/ 25 y 27, Vedado, tel. 07/832-4245, www.uh.cu) has 60-hour courses in Cuban culture beginning the first Monday of every month.

MEDICAL TRAINING

Cuba offers scholarships for disadvantaged and minority students from the U.S. and developing nations to attend the **Escuela Latinoamericana de Medicina** (Latin American School of Medical Sciences, ELACM, Santa Fe, Havana, tel. 07/201-4370, www.elacm.sld.cu). Courses last six years and graduates are full-fledged doctors. U.S. applicants should contact the Cuban Interests Section, 2630 16th St. NW, Washington, DC 20009, tel. 202/797-8518, ext. 109, www.afrocubaweb.com/infomed/medscholarships.htm.

SPANISH-LANGUAGE COURSES

The **Universidad de la Habana** (Dirección de Posgrado, Calle J #556, e/ 25 y 27, Vedado, tel. 07/832-4245, www.uh.cu/infogral/estudiaruh/postgrado/english.html) and provincial universities throughout Cuba offer Spanish-language courses of 20-80 hours (CUC100-300), plus "Spanish and Cuban Culture" courses of 320-480 hours (CUC960-1,392). Courses begin the first Monday of the month, year-round.

The **Centro de Idiomas y Computación José Martí** (José Martí Language and Computer Center, Calle 90 #531, e/ 5ta B y 5ta C, Miramar, Havana, tel. 07/209-6692, fax 07/204-4846) also offers Spanish language courses of 20-80 hours (CUC130-330).

www.sunquest.ca); and **Transat Holidays** (tel. 866/322-6649, www.transatholidays.com).

Tours from the United Kingdom

Captivating Cuba (22 St. Peter's Square, Hammersmith, London W6 9NW, tel. 08444/129-916, www.captivatingcuba.com) offers a wide range of trips.

Journey Latin America (12 Heathfield Terr., London W4 4JE, tel. 020/8747-8315, www.journeylatinamerica.co.uk) offers trips from a "Havana Weekend Break" to self-drive packages.

CubaWelcome (tel. 020/7498-8266, www.cubawelcome.com) offers FIT (fully independent travel) and group packages, from "Cigars & Golf" to photography and even a "Che Guevara Tour."

Regal Holidays (58 Lancaster Way, Ely, Cambs, CB6 3NW, tel. 01353/659-999, www.regal-diving.co.uk) and **Scuba en Cuba** (7 Maybank Gdns., Pinner, Mddx. HA5 2JW, tel. 01895/624100, www.scuba-en-cuba.com) offer dive packages to Cuba. **KE Adventures Travel** (32 Lake Rd., Keswick Cumbria, CA12 5DQ, tel. 017687/73966, www.keadventure.com) has bicycle tours.

San Cristobal UK (2a Eastcheap, London EC3M 1AA, tel. 020/7621-6524, www.scuktravel.com) has sightseeing tours and hotel packages.

The **Cuban Solidarity Campaign** (218 Green Lanes, London N4 2HB, tel. 020/8800-0155, www.cuba-solidarity.org) offers "solidarity" work brigades; and **Caledonia Languages Abroad** (72 Newhaven Rd., Edinburgh,

EH6 5QG, Scotland, tel. 0131/621-7721, www.caledonialanguages.co.uk) offers volunteer work programs plus language study programs. **Cactus Language** (tel. 888/577-8451, www.cactuslanguage.com) has language courses in Cuba.

Tours from Europe
In Germany, contact **Kuba Reisen** (www.reisen-kuba.com) or **Sprachcaffe Cuba Travel** (tel. 069/610-9120, www.sprachcaffe-kuba.com), both with a large range of trips.

In Italy, try **Eden Viaggi** (tel. 039/0721-4421, www.edenviaggi.it), which primarily has hotel packages, or **Lovely Cuba** (tel. 02/4549-8556, www.lovelycuba.com). **Press Tours** (tel. 02/3496-6264, www.presstours.it) offers special-interest trips, including diving.

Tours from Australia and New Zealand
Caribbean Bound (379 Pitt St., Suite 102, Sydney 2000, NSW, tel. 2/9267-2555, www.caribbean.com.au); **Caribbean Destinations** (291 Auburn Rd., Melbourne, VIC 3122, tel. 800/354-104, www.caribbeanislands.com.au); and **Innovative Travel** (P.O. Box 21247, Edgeware, Christchurch, New Zealand, tel. 3/365-3910, www.innovative-travel.com) have packages to Cuba.

The **Australia Cuba Friendship Association** (P.O. Box ZK364, Haymarket NSW 1240, www.sydney-acfs.org) offers work programs.

GETTING AWAY
Cuba charges CUC25 departure tax on international flights. Cuban check-in staff often scam foreigners by attempting to charge an excess baggage fee where none should apply.

Know your legal allowance (which varies between airlines). Try to use a counter with a visible scale screen and check that it is properly zeroed before your bags are put on.

Customs
Cuba prohibits the export of valuable antiques and art without a license.

Returning to the United States: U.S. citizens who have traveled to Cuba are not allowed to bring back any Cuban purchases, regardless of whether or not travel was licensed. The exception is literature and other informational materials. All other Cuban goods will be confiscated, wherever acquired and regardless of value. These restrictions apply to citizens of *any* country arriving from any other country, including in-transit passengers; contact the **U.S. Customs Service** (1300 Pennsylvania Ave. NW, Washington, DC 20229, tel. 703/526-4200, www.cbp.gov/xp/cgov/travel).

Returning to Canada: Canadian citizens are allowed an "exemption" of C$750 for goods purchased abroad, plus 1.14 liters of spirits, 200 cigarettes, and 50 cigars. See www.traveldocs.com/ca/customs.htm.

Returning to the United Kingdom: U.K. citizens may import goods worth up to £340, plus 200 cigarettes, 50 cigars, and one liter of spirits. See www.hmrc.gov.uk/customs/arriving.

Returning to Australia and New Zealand: Australian citizens may import A$900 of goods, plus 250 cigarettes or 50 cigars, and 2.5 liters of spirits. See www.customs.gov.au/site/page.cfm?u=4352. New Zealand citizens can import NZ$700 worth of goods, 200 cigarettes, 50 cigars, and three bottles of spirits. See www.customs.govt.nz/travellers.

Getting Around

BY AIR

Most major Cuban cities have an airport. Cuba's state-owned airlines have a monopoly. Their safety records do not inspire confidence, although many old Soviet planes have been replaced by modern aircraft. Because of hijacking attempts, Cuban authorities restrict the amount of fuel on aircraft on internal flights. Flights are often booked up weeks in advance, especially in peak season. Tickets are normally nonrefundable. If you reserve before arriving in Cuba, you'll be given a voucher to exchange for a ticket upon arrival in Cuba. Arrive on time for check-in; otherwise your seat will be given away. Delays, cancellations, and schedule changes are common. You can book at hotel tour desks.

Cubana (Calle 23, e/ 0 y P, Havana, tel. 07/834-4446, www.cubana.cu) serves most airports. Fares are 25 percent cheaper if booked in conjunction with an international Cubana flight.

Aerocaribbean (Calle 23 #64, Vedado, tel. 07/879-7524) and **Aerogaviota** (Av. 47 #2814, e/ 28 y 34, Rpto. Kohly, Havana, tel. 07/203-0668, fax 07/204-2621, www.aerogaviota.com) also operate flights. Since they're all state-owned, don't be surprised to find yourself flying Aerocaribbean even if you booked with Cubana.

BY BUS
Tourist Buses

Víazul (Av. 26, esq. Zoológico, Nuevo Vedado, Havana, tel. 07/881-1413, www.viazul.cu, daily 7 A.M.–9 P.M.) operates bus services for foreigners to key places on the tourist circuit using modern air-conditioned buses. Children travel at half price. At press time, a 5 percent discount was offered for round-trip tickets to Cienfuegos, Trinidad, Pinar del Río, and Viñales. A 10 percent fee applies for cancellations made more than 24 hours before departure; a 25 percent fee applies if you cancel within 24 hours. A 20-kilo baggage limit applies. Excess baggage is charged 1 percent of your ticket cost per kilo. Bicycles are charged CUC0.80–4, depending on distance.

© CHRISTOPHER P. BAKER

Víazul bus, Viñales

VÍAZUL BUS SCHEDULE

Route	Departure Times	Duration	One-Way Fare
Havana-Santiago	9:30 A.M., 3 P.M., 6:15 P.M. (direct to Camagüey, including dinner), and 10 P.M.	13 hours	CUC51
Santiago-Havana	9 A.M., 3:15 P.M., 7:30 P.M. (via Trinidad), and 10 P.M.	13 hours	CUC51

Stops are made at Entronque de Jagüey (CUC12), Santa Clara (CUC18), Sancti Spíritus (CUC23), Ciego de Ávila (CUC27), Camagüey (CUC33), Las Tunas (CUC39), Holguín (except 10 P.M. departure, CUC44), and Bayamo (CUC44). The 6:15 P.M. departure links with Santiago-Baracoa service.

Havana-Holguín	8:40 A.M., 8:30 P.M.	12.5 hours	CUC44

Stops are made at Sancti Spíritus (8:30 P.M. departure only, CUC23), Santa Clara (8:40 A.M. departure only, CUC18), Ciego de Ávila (CUC27), Camagüey (CUC33), and Las Tunas (8:30 P.M., CUC39).

Havana-Trinidad	8:15 A.M. and 1 P.M.	5.75 hours	CUC25
Trinidad-Havana	7:45 A.M. and 3 P.M.	5.75 hours	CUC25

Stops are made at Entronque de Jagüey (CUC12), Playa Larga and Playa Girón (8:15 P.M. departure only, CUC13), Aguada de Pasajeros (1 P.M. departure only, CUC13), Yaguarama (CUC14), Rodas (CUC15), and Cienfuegos (CUC20).

Transtur (tel. 07/838-3991, www.transtur.cu) operates tourist bus excursions within Havana and Varadero by open-top double-decker bus, and in Matanzas, Viñales, Playa Girón, Trinidad, Cayo Coco, Holguín, Guardalavaca, and Baracoa by minibus.

Public Buses

Since 2005 Cuba has imported more than 5,000 modern Chinese-made Yutong buses to replace its aging, decrepit fleet of hand-me-downs. There are two classes of buses for long-distance travel: *Especiales* are faster (and often more comfortable) than crowded and slow *regulares,* which in many areas are still old and rickety with butt-numbing seats.

LAST IN LINE

Cuban lines (*colas*), or queues, can be confusing to foreign travelers. Cubans don't line up in order in the English fashion. Lines are always fluid, whether in a shop, bank, or bus queue. Follow the Cubans' example and identify the last person ahead of you by asking for ¿el último? ("who's last?"). It's like a game of tag. You're now el último until the next person arrives. Thus you don't have to stand in line, but can wander off to find some shade and then simply follow the person ahead of you onto the bus.

Route	Departure Times	Duration	One-Way Fare
Havana-Varadero	8 A.M., 10 A.M., 3:15 P.M., and 6 P.M.	3 hours	CUC10
Varadero-Havana	8 A.M., 11:25 A.M., 3:30 P.M., and 6 P.M.	3 hours	CUC10
Stops are made at Playas del Este (8 A.M. departure only, CUC6), Matanzas (CUC7), and Aeropuerto de Varadero (by request).			
Havana-Viñales	9 A.M. and 2 P.M.	3.25 hours	CUC12
Viñales-Havana	8 A.M. and 2 P.M.	3.25 hours	CUC12
Stops are made at Las Terrazas (9 A.M. departure only, CUC6) and Entronque de Candelaria (9 A.M. departure only, CUC6), and in Pinar del Río (CUC11).			
Santiago-Baracoa	7:45 A.M.	5 hours	CUC15
Baracoa-Santiago	2:15 P.M.	5 hours	CUC15
Trinidad-Santiago	8:15 A.M.	12 hours	CUC33
Santiago-Trinidad	7:30 P.M.	12 hours	CUC33
Varadero-Trinidad	7:30 A.M.	6 hours	CUC20
Trinidad-Varadero	2:30 P.M.	6 hours	CUC20

Most towns have *two* bus stations for out-of-town service: a Terminal de Ómnibus Intermunicipales (for local and municipal service) and a Terminal de Ómnibus Interprovinciales (for service between provinces). Often they're far apart. *Caution: Pickpockets plague the buses and often work in pairs; foreigners are their first targets.*

INTERPROVINCIAL SERVICES
The state agency **Astro** (Av. Independencia #101, Havana, tel. 07/870-3397) operates all interprovincial services linking cities throughout the island. However, in 2009, it became off-limits to foreigners, except for students signed up at Cuban institutions.

INTERMUNICIPAL SERVICES
You may or may not be denied service; it's a crap shoot. No reservations are available for short-distance services between towns within specific provinces. You'll have to join the queue.

CAMIONES
The staple of travel between towns is a truck, or *camión*. Most travel only to the nearest major town, so you'll need to change *camiones* frequently for long-distance travel. Some are open-sided flatbeds with canvas roofs. Sometimes it's a truck with a container of makeshift windows cut out of the metal sides and basic wooden seats welded to the floor.

TRAIN SCHEDULES AND FARES

FROM HAVANA

Destination	Depart	Train No.	Arrive
Bayamo	8:15 P.M.	9	4:00 P.M.
Camagüey	12:00 P.M. (noon)	23	9:00 P.M.
Guantánamo	6:25 P.M.	5	12:20 P.M.
Morón	12:55 A.M.	29	12:55 A.M.
Sancti Spíritus	7:40 P.M.	25	5:30 A.M.
Santiago de Cuba	5:30 P.M.	3	8:30 A.M. (*especial*)
Santiago de Cuba	6:45 P.M.	7	3:30 P.M.

TO HAVANA

Origin	Depart	Train No.	Arrive
Bayamo	12:55 A.M.	10	8:30 P.M.
Camagüey	6:10 A.M.	24	3:10 P.M.
Guantánamo	12:30 P.M.	6	6:30 A.M.
Morón	12:50 A.M.	30	8:10 A.M.
Sancti Spíritus	7:40 P.M.	26	5:45 A.M.
Santiago de Cuba	6:50 P.M.	4	10:00 A.M. (*especial*)
Santiago de Cuba	8:10 A.M.	8	4:50 A.M.

They depart from designated transportation hubs (often adjacent to bus or railway stations). You pay in pesos (1–10 pesos), depending on distance. Officially, foreigners are banned, so expect to be turned away by the drivers.

WITHIN TOWNS

Provincial capitals have intra-city bus service, which can mean *camiones* or makeshift horse-drawn *coches*. Buses—*guaguas* (pronounced WAH-wahs)—are often secondhand Yankee school buses or uncomfortable Hungarian or Cuban buses. They're usually overcrowded and cost 10–20 centavos (the standard fare). In El Oriente, many cities use *camellos*, uncomfortable and crowded homemade articulated bodies hauled by trucks.

FARES TO/FROM HAVANA

Origin/Destination	Fare
Cacocum (Holguín)	CUC26.50
Camagüey	CUC19 regular/CUC41 especial
Ciego de Ávila	CUC15.50
Cienfuegos	CUC11
Colón	CUC6
Florida	CUC17.50
Guantánamo	CUC32
Holguín	CUC26.50
Jatibínico	CUC14
Jovellanos	CUC5
Las Tunas	CUC23
Matanzas	CUC3
Morón	CUC24
Pinar del Río	CUC6.50
Placetas	CUC11.50
Sancti Spíritus	CUC13.50
Santa Clara	CUC10 regular/CUC21 especial
Santiago de Cuba	CUC30 regular/CUC62 especial

Bus stops—*paradas*—are usually well marked. To stop the bus, shout *¡pare!* (stop!), or bash the box above the door in Cuban fashion. You'll need to elbow your way to the door well in advance (don't stand near the door, however, as you may literally be popped out onto your face; exiting has been compared to being birthed). Don't dally, as the bus driver is likely to hit the gas when you're only halfway out.

BY TRAIN

The **Ünion de Ferrocarriles de Cuba** operates rail service. One main line spans the country connecting all the major cities, with secondary cities linked by branch lines. Commuter trains called *ferro-ómnibus* provide suburban rail service in and between many provincial towns.

Published schedules change frequently: Check departure and arrival times and plan accordingly, as many trains arrive (and depart) in the wee hours of the morning. The carriages haven't been cleaned in years (windows are usually so dirty you can barely see out), and most are derelict in all manner of ways. Few trains run on time, departures are frequently cancelled, and safety is an issue: In February 2009, three people died when two trains collided near Sibanicu, in Camagüey Province, and in October 2007, 28 people were killed when a Manzanillo-bound train from Santiago collided with a bus at a level crossing at Yara, in Granma Province. In 2006, 12 new Chinese diesel trains were shipped to Cuba. In October 2007, 200 new railway cars were ordered from Iran. And in September 2007, Cuba signed a deal with the Venezuelan Economic and Social Development Bank to invest US$100 million to improve rail tracks, signals, and communications, not least, stated Cuban transport minister Jorge Luis Sierra, with a goal of increasing "the [average] speed of our trains from 40 to 100 kilometers per hour." *Yikes!*

Bicycles are allowed in the baggage compartment (*coche de equipaje*). You usually pay (in pesos) at the end of the journey.

Service

Train service has been cut back drastically in the past few years.

The fast *especial* (train #3), also known as the Tren Francés (French train), now operates between Havana and Santiago de Cuba every third day and takes 12.5 hours for the 860-kilometer journey. You can choose *primera especial* (first class), with comfy recliner seats; *primera*, the old second class, has smaller, non-reclining seats. Slower and more basic *regular* trains #5 and #7 run every third day when the Tren Francés isn't running (hence, there's service two out of three days). Expect bone-chilling air-conditioning, TVs showing movies (loudly), a poorly stocked *cafetería* car, and *ferromoza* (rail hostess) meal service. Regardless, take snacks and drinks. Relieve yourself before boarding as toilets are grim (and some have no doors); bring toilet paper!

Additional trains operate between Havana and Sancti Spíritus, Camagüey, and Morón.

Reservations

The state agency **FerroCuba** (Av. de Bélgica, Havana, tel. 07/861-9389 or 861-8540, ferrotur@ceniai.cu) handles ticket sales and reservations for all national train service. Foreigners pay in CUC, for which you get a guaranteed first-class seat. In Havana, tickets for foreigners are sold at the dysfunctional Terminal La Coubre (tel. 07/862-1000), 100 meters south of the main railway station (tel. 07/862-1920). Elsewhere you can normally walk up to the FerroCuba office at the station, buy your ticket, and take a seat on board within an hour. Buy your ticket as far in advance as possible. You should also buy your ticket for the next leg of your journey upon arrival in each destination. Reservations can sometimes be made through Infotur offices (tel. 07/866-3333, www.infotur.cu) and other regional tour agencies. You'll need your passport.

Reservations for local commuter services can't be made.

BY TAXI
Tourist Taxis

Cubataxi operates radio-dispatched *turistaxis*, also found outside tourist hotels nationwide, and at *piqueras* (taxi stands) around the main squares. Few taxi drivers use their meters. *Taxistas* have their own *trampas* or *estafas* (swindles), such as resetting the meter to record a much lower mileage, then charging you the going rate for the journey. Since the dispatcher records the destination, the taxi driver splits the excess with the dispatcher.

In tourist venues, modern Japanese or European cars are used. Beyond tourist areas, Cubataxi's vehicles are usually beat-up Ladas. You put your life at risk in these vehicles, almost none of which have seatbelts. (They're so clapped out; Cuba is the only place in the world I've had to push my own cab to the airport!)

Peso Taxis

Havana and most provincial capitals have peso

taxis serving locals and charging in pesos. Peso-only taxis are not permitted to carry foreigners, but many drivers will run the risk of huge fines.

The workhorses are the *colectivos,* shared cabs that pick up anyone who flags them down (they also hang outside railway and bus terminals), often until they're packed to the gills.

Sometimes called *máquinas* (machines), they run along fixed routes much like buses and charge similar fares. Most are old Yankee jalopies. They usually take as many passengers as they can cram in.

In 2009, the Cuban government began issuing new licenses for the first time in a decade; the number of private taxis has since doubled.

CUBA'S VINTAGE AMERICAN CARS

Automotive sentimentality is reason enough to visit Cuba, the greatest living car museum in the world. American cars flooded into Cuba for 50 years, culminating in the Batista era, when Cuba imported more Cadillacs, Buicks, and DeSotos than any other nation in the world. Then came the Cuban Revolution and the U.S. trade embargo. In terms of American automobiles, time stopped when Castro took power.

Today, Cuba possesses about 450,000 cars, of which perhaps one-sixth are prerevolutionary American autos dating back to the 1920s and '30s. High-finned, big-boned dowagers from Detroit's heyday are everywhere. In certain areas, one rarely sees a vehicle that is *not* a venerable, usually decrepit, classic of yesteryear. Model-T Fords. Chrysler Windsors. Chevy Bel Airs and Impalas. Oldsmobile Golden Rockets. Cadillac Eldorados. Kaisers, Hudsons, and Edsels. They're all there, gleaming in the lyrical Cuban sunlight, inviting foreigners to admire the dashboard or run their fingers along a tail fin.

Lacking proper tools and replacement parts, Cubans adeptly cajole one more year out of their battered hulks. Their intestinally reconstituted engines are monuments to ingenuity – decades of improvised repairs have melded parts from Detroit and Moscow (Russian Gaz jeeps are favorite targets for cannibalization, since their engines were cloned from a Detroit engine). One occasionally spots a shining example of museum quality. The majority, though, have long ago been touched up with house paint and decorated with flashy mirrors and metallic stars, as if to celebrate a religious holiday. Some are adorned with multicolored

flags to invoke the protection of Changó or another *santería* deity.

Owners of prerevolutionary cars can sell them freely to anyone with money to buy, but the chances of owning a more modern car are slim. Virtually all cars imported since 1959 – Polish Fiats, Soviet UAZs, jeep-like Romanian AROs, and more recently Mercedes, Nissans, and Citroëns – are owned by the state. New cars are leased out to high-level workers, and others who work for foreign companies, but the cars must be returned if they lose their jobs. Benighted workers such as sports stars and top artists have been gifted or allowed to buy cars. The cars can only be resold back to the government, which pays a pittance – in pesos.

In *Driving Through Cuba,* author Carlo Gébler drives around the island in quest of a '57 Cadillac Eldorado Brougham; a super-deluxe pillarless sedan with a brushed aluminum roof, two front-end protuberances known as "Dagmar" bumpers (which Cadillac unashamedly advertised as "bosoms"), and "a rear end that would've received an X-rating had it been a movie." Alas, the most sumptuous American car ever made proved elusive – not surprisingly, for only 704 Broughams were produced. But you can bet there's at least one to be found on the island. After all, in the 1950s, Havana bought more Cadillacs than any other city in the world. Reason enough to visit!

My own *Cuba Classics: A Celebration of Vintage American Automobiles* (www.christopherbaker.com) is an illustrated coffee-table book that offers a paean to the cars and their owners.

"Gypsy" Cabs

Illegal cabs driven are usually beat-up Ladas or American jalopies; they're inherently unsafe, and best avoided. Freelance driver-guides hang outside the largest tourist hotels and discos late at night. Your fare is negotiable. Educate yourself about *turistaxi* fares to your destination beforehand, as many drivers attempt to gouge you and you may end up paying more than you would in a tourist taxi. Agree on the fare *before* getting in. Make sure you know whether it is one-way or round-trip.

Coco-taxis

Toys "R" Us doesn't yet have an outlet in Cuba, but you'd never know it. These bright yellow, fiberglass motorized tricycles look like scooped-out Easter eggs on wheels. You'll find them outside major hotels and cruising the tourist zones in major cities. They charge about the same as tourist taxis. However, they have no safety features, and several accidents involving tourists have been reported.

Bici-taxis

Bici-taxis—the Cuban equivalent of rickshaws—patrol the main streets of most Cuban cities. These tricycles have been cobbled together with welding torches, with car-like seats and shade canopies. They offer a cheap (albeit bumpy) way of sightseeing and getting around if you're in no hurry. Some *ciclo-taxis* are only licensed to take Cubans (who pay pesos). Always negotiate a fare before setting off.

Coches

These horse-drawn cabs are a staple of local transport. In Havana, Varadero, and other beach resorts, elegant antique carriages with leather seats are touted for sightseeing. Elsewhere they're a utility vehicle for the hoi polloi and are often decrepit, with basic bench seats. They operate along fixed routes and usually charge one to three pesos, depending on distance.

BY CAR

Cuba is a great place to drive if you can handle the often perilous conditions. There are no restrictions on where you can go. Cuba has 31,000 kilometers of roads (15,500 kilometers are paved), though even major highways are deteriorated to the point of being dangerous (a major upgrade of roads nationwide was launched in 2008).

The main highway, the Carretera Central (Central Highway), runs along the island's

COLOR CODES

In Cuba, car license plates (*chapas* or *placas*) come in different colors, each depicting a specific usage:
black: foreign diplomatic corps
blue: a state-owned vehicle for commercial use, such as a taxi or tractor
brown: lower rank government officials
green (dark): army
green (light): Ministry of the Interior; don't mess with this!
maroon: rental car
orange (dark): foreign business or journalist
orange (light): Cuban business managers and officials
red (dark): a company car that can be driven 24/7
red (light): a company car for use during business hours only
white: high-ranking government official
yellow: private vehicle (the letters HK denote a foreign resident in Cuba)

spine for 1,200 kilometers from one end of the country to the other. This two-laner leads through sleepy rural towns. For maximum speed take the A-1, or Autopista Nacional (National Expressway), the country's only freeway—eight (unmarked) lanes wide and fast. Construction came to a halt with the Special Period; about 650 kilometers have been completed, from Pinar del Río to a point just east of Santi Spíritus, and from Santiago de Cuba about 30 kilometers northwestward. *Warning: It is extremely dangerous!*

Only a few highways are well signed, although things are improving. You can buy the *Guía de Carreteras* road atlas at tour desks and souvenir outlets. It's extraordinary how little Cubans know of regions outside their own locale. Rather than asking, "Does this road go to so-and-so?" (which will surely earn you the reply, *"¡Sí, señor!"*), ask *"¿Dónde va esta ruta?"* ("Where does this route go?").

Traffic Regulations and Safety

To drive in Cuba, you must be 21 years or older and hold either a valid national driver's license or an international driver's license (IDL), obtainable through automobile association offices worldwide (www.aaa.com, United States; www.caa.ca, Canada; www.theaa.com, U.K.; www.aaa.asn.au, Australia; or www.aa.co.nz, New Zealand).

Traffic drives on the right. The speed limit is 100 kph (kilometers per hour) on freeways, 90 kph on highways, 60 kph on rural roads, 50 kph on urban roads, and 40 kph in children's zones. Speed limits are vigorously enforced. Ubiquitous, over-zealous traffic police (*tránsitos* or *tráficos*) patrol the highways. Oncoming cars will flash their lights to indicate the presence of police ahead. Major highways have *puntos de control*—police control points. If you receive a traffic fine, the policeman will note this on your car rental contract, to be deducted from your deposit. The *tráfico* cannot request a fine on the spot, although Cuban police occasionally attempt to extract a subtle bribe. If so, ask for the policeman's name and where you can fight the ticket (this usually results in you being waved on your way).

Seatbelt use is not mandatory, but motorcyclists are required to wear helmets. Note that it's illegal to: 1) enter an intersection unless you can exit; 2) make a right turn on a red light unless indicated by a white arrow or traffic signal (*derecha con luz roja*); or 3) overtake on the right. You must stop at *all* railway crossings before crossing. Headlights by day are illegal, except for emergency vehicles, but you should use yours and be seen.

Road conditions often deteriorate without warning, and obstacles are numerous: everything from wayward livestock to mammoth potholes. Driving at night is perilous, not least because few roads are lit. Sticks jutting up in the road usually indicate a dangerous hole. *Keep your speed down!*

Accidents and Breakdowns

Rental car agencies have a clause to protect against damage to the car from unwarranted repairs. Call the rental agency; it will arrange a tow or send a mechanic.

In the event of an accident, *never* move the vehicles until the police arrive. Get the names, license plate numbers, and *cédulas* (legal identification numbers) of any witnesses. Make a sketch of the accident. Then call the **transit police** (tel. 07/882-0116 in Havana; tel. 116 outside Havana) and rental agency. In case of injury, call for an **ambulance** (tel. 104 nationwide). Do not leave the accident scene; the other party may tamper with your car and evidence. Don't let honking traffic pressure you into moving the cars. If you suspect the other driver has been drinking, ask the policeman to administer a Breathalyzer test—an *alcolemia*.

Accidents that result in death or injury are treated like crimes, and the onus is on the driver to prove innocence. Prison sentences can range 1–10 years. If you are involved in an accident in which someone is injured or killed, you will not be allowed to leave Cuba until the trial has taken place, which can take up to a year. Contact your embassy for legal assistance.

Gasoline

Gasoline (*petróleo*) and diesel (*gasolina*) are sold at Cupet and Oro Negro stations (*servicentros*) nationwide. Most are open 24 hours. Gas stations are supposed to sell only *especial* (usually about CUC0.90 per liter—about CUC3.25 a gallon) to tourists in rental cars, and you may be refused cheaper *regular,* even if that's all that's available. (Local gas stations, *bombas,* serve *regular* to Cubans only.) Electricity blackouts often shut the pumps down. Few stations accept credit cards.

Insurance

If you have your own vehicle, the state-run organization **ESEN** (Calle 5ta #306, e/ C y D, Vedado, Havana, tel. 07/832-2508) insures automobiles and has special packages for foreigners.

Rental

Don't rent a car at the airport; relax for a day or two first.

Demand exceeds supply. During Christmas and New Year, you'll need reservations, which can only be done within 15 days of your arrival; it's no guarantee that your reservation will be honored (ask for a copy of the reservation to be faxed to you and take this with you). There is no national computer database of rental car stock. If one office tells you there are no cars, go to another office (even of the same company). In a worst-case scenario, head to the next town (cars are always in short supply in Havana, but are often available in Matanzas).

Expect to pay CUC50–185 per day with unlimited mileage, depending on vehicle; a two-day minimum applies for unlimited mileage. Added charges apply for one-way rentals, for drivers under 25 years of age, and for second drivers (CUC15). Discounts apply for rentals over seven days. The companies accept cash or credit cards (except those issued by U.S. banks). You must pay a deposit of CUC200–500; the agency will run off a credit card authorization that you will receive back once you return the car, assuming it has no damage. You must pay in cash for the first tank of gas before you drive away, although your contract states that you must return the tank empty (an outrageous state-run rip-off). Check the fuel level *before* setting off; if it doesn't look full to the brim, point this out to the rental agent and demand a refund, or that it be topped off (but good luck!). Clarify any late return penalties, and that the time recorded on your contract is that for your *departure with the car,* not the time you entered into negotiations.

Rental cars are poorly serviced and are often not roadworthy, although in 2009 Transtur

MAKING SENSE OF ADDRESSES

In most Cuban cities, addresses are given as locations. Thus, the Havanatur office is at Calle 6, e/ 1ra y 3ra, Miramar, Havana, meaning it is on Calle 6 between (e/ for *entre* – between) First and Third Avenues (Avenidas 1ra y 3ra).

Street numbers are occasionally used. Thus, the Hotel Inglaterra is at Prado #416, esq. San Rafael, Habana Vieja; at the corner (esq. for *esquina* – corner) of Prado and Calle San Rafael, in Old Havana (Habana Vieja).

Reparto (abbreviated to Rpto.) is a district. *Final* refers to the end of a street, or a cul-de-sac.

Piso refers to the floor level (thus, an office on *piso 3ro* is on the third floor). *Altos* refers to "upstairs," and *bajos* refers to "downstairs."

Most cities are laid out on a grid pattern centered at a main square or plaza, with parallel streets (*calles*) running perpendicular to avenues (*avenidas*).

Many streets have at least two names: one predating the Revolution (and usually the most commonly used colloquially) and the other a postrevolutionary name. On maps, the modern name takes precedence, with the old name often shown in parentheses.

(which parents Cubatur, Havanautos, and Rex) purchased 1,500 new vehicles. Inspect your car thoroughly before setting off; otherwise, you may be charged for the slightest dent when you return. Don't forget the inside, plus radio antenna, spare tire, the jack, and wrench. Don't assume the car rental agency has taken care of tire pressure or fluids. Note the *Aviso Próximo Mantenimiento* column on the rental contract. This indicates the kilometer reading by which you—the renter!—are required to take the car to an agency office for scheduled servicing; you're granted only 100 kilometers leeway. If you fail to honor the clause, you'll be charged CUC50. This scam is a disgrace, as you may have to drive miles out of your way to an agency and then wait hours, or even overnight, for the car to be serviced.

Most agencies offer a chauffeur service (CUC40–90 a day). A four-wheel-drive is recommended only for exploring mountain areas.

RENTAL COMPANIES

Only state-owned car rental agencies operate. **Transtur** (Calle L #456, e/ 25 y 27, Vedado, tel. 7/835-0000, fax 07/273-2277, www.transtur.cu) operates **Cubacar** (Calle 21, e/ N y O, Vedado, Havana, tel. 07/836-4038), **Havanautos** (tel. 7/204-6547, www.havanautos.com), and **Rex** (tel. 7/273-9166, www.rex.cu). There are scores of offices nationwide. There's really no difference between the companies, although rates vary. For example, Havanautos offers 20 types of vehicles—from the tiny Hyundai Atos (CUC411 weekly) to an eight-passenger Hyundai TQ minivan (CUC1,131 weekly), BMW 5-series (CUC1,104 weekly), and Audi A4 convertible (CUC1,729 weekly). Rex Limousine Service has eight models—from the Seat Cordoba (CUC455 weekly) to the Hyundai TQ minivan, BMW 5-series, and Audi A4 convertible. Rates may vary between agencies, but typically include 150 kilometers daily (unlimited on rentals of three days or more).

Gaviota's **Vía Rent-a-Car** (Calle 98 e/ 9ta y 11, Cubanacán, Havana, tel. 07/206-9935, fax 07/207-9502, www.gaviota-grupo.com)

small rental car in Reserva de Biosfera Península de Guanahacabibes

rents Hyundais, Peugeots, and three kinds of Suzuki jeeps.

Gran Car (Calle Marino, esq. Santa María, Nuevo Vedado, tel. 07/855-5567, grancardp@transnet.cu) rents 1950s classic autos with drivers in Havana, Varadero, and Santiago de Cuba.

FLY-DRIVE PACKAGES

"Fly & Drive" packages (6–21 nights) are offered by **WowCuba** (430 Queen St., Charlottestown, PE, Canada CIA 4E8, tel. 902/368-2453 or 800/969-2822, www.wowcuba.com). You simply pick up your vehicle (choose anything from a Hyundai Atos to an Audi A4 or a minivan) at any of 20 locations throughout Cuba and hit the road armed with vouchers good at any of 60-plus hotels islandwide (from CUC641 single or double for six nights).

INSURANCE

It's wise to purchase insurance offered by the rental agency. You have two choices: CDW (Collision Damage Waiver, CUC15–20 daily;

DISTANCES IN CUBA

DISTANCE (KM)	HAVANA	PINAR DEL RÍO	MATANZAS	SANTA CLARA	CIENFUEGOS	SANCT SPÍRITUS
Baracoa	1,168	1,331	1,087	890	957	804
Bayamo	819	984	740	543	610	457
Camagüey	546	711	467	270	337	184
Ciego de Ávila	438	603	359	162	229	78
Cienfuegos	243	419	193	74	–	153
Guantánamo	1,026	1,191	825	750	817	664
Guardalavaca	802	967	723	526	593	440
Havana	–	176	102	276	243	362
Holguín	748	913	699	472	539	388
Las Tunas	670	835	591	394	461	308
Matanzas	102	267	–	197	193	283
Pinar del Río	176	–	267	441	419	527
Sancti Spíritus	362	527	283	86	153	–
Santa Clara	276	441	197	–	74	88
Santa Lucía	658	823	579	382	446	296
Santiago de Cuba	944	1,109	865	668	735	582
Soroa	86	89	188	362	329	448
Trinidad	321	497	271	89	78	67
Varadero	144	309	42	196	177	282
Viñales	193	28	295	469	436	555

with a deductible of CUC200–500) covers accidents, but not theft. Super CDW (CUC20–40) offers fully comprehensive coverage, except for the radio and spare tire. The insurance has to be paid in cash. If you decline, you'll be required to put down a huge cash deposit. If your car is broken into or otherwise damaged, you must get a police statement (a *denuncia*), otherwise you will be charged for the damage. You can also name any licensed Cuban driver on your rental policy. *However, if you (or anyone else driving your rented vehicle) are deemed at fault in an accident, rental agencies will nullify coverage and seek damages to cover the cost of repairs. Another disgrace! Isn't that the point of insurance?* You may be prevented from leaving the country until payment is obtained.

SAFETY

Theft, including of car parts, is a huge problem. Always park in *parqueos,* designated parking lots with a *custodio* (guard). Alternatively, tip the hotel security staff or hire someone to guard your car.

Your car rental contract states that picking up hitchhikers is not allowed. Many tourists have been robbed, and I do not endorse picking up hitchhikers.

Motorcycles and Scooters

You cannot rent motorcycles in Cuba (except, perhaps, from private individuals). Scooters can be rented in Havana and at resort hotels.

Several North American entities have attempted to organize motorcycle tours, without success, due to U.S. law. **Moto Mundo Bike Tours** (Hoejagervej 8, 8544 Moerke, Denmark, tel. 45/8637-7654, http://moto-mundo.com) offers a 20-day motorcycle tour of Cuba. You must supply your own bike, which will be shipped from Copenhagen.

BY BICYCLE

As of 2009, bike rental is no longer available in Cuba (other than feeble beach cruisers at resort hotels); you'll need to bring your own bike. A sturdy lock is essential, as bicycle theft is a pandemic.

HITCHHIKING

Despite the import of 5,000 Chinese buses, *fidelismo* has been so catastrophic on transport that the populace relies on anything that

© CHRISTOPHER P. BAKER

bicyclists near Holguín

THE BICYCLE REVOLUTION

In 1991, when the first shipment of Flying Pigeon bicycles arrived from China, there were only an estimated 30,000 bicycles in Havana, a city of two million people. The visitor arriving in Cuba today could be forgiven for imagining he or she had arrived in Vietnam. Bicycles are everywhere, outnumbering cars, trucks, and buses 20 to 1.

Cynics have dubbed Cuba's wholesale switch to bicycles since the collapse of the Soviet bloc as a socialist failing, a symbol of the nation's backwardness. Others acclaim it an astounding achievement, a two-wheel triumph over an overnight loss of gasoline and adversity. *Granma,* the Cuban newspaper, christened it the "bicycle revolution."

Professor Maurice Halperin, who taught at the University of Havana, does not "recall seeing a single adult Cuban on a bicycle in Havana during the entire period of my residence in the city, from 1962 to 1968." The collapse of the Soviet Union severed the nation's gasoline pipeline. Transportation ground to a halt, along with the rest of the Cuban economy. In November 1990 the Cuban government launched sweeping energy-saving measures that called for a "widespread substitution of oxen for farm machinery and hundreds of thousands of bicycles for gasoline-consuming vehicles," launched as a "militant and defensive campaign" embodied on May 1, 1991, when the armed forces appeared on bicycles in the May Day parade. The government contracted with China to purchase 1.2 million bicycles, and by the end of 1991, 500,000 single-gear Chinese bicycles were in use on the streets of Havana.

Overnight, Cuba transformed itself into the bicycle capital of the Americas. "The comprehensiveness and speed of implementation of this program," said a 1994 World Bank report, "is unprecedented in the history of transportation." The report noted that about two million bicycles were in use islandwide. Most were made in Cuba, which established five bicycle factories to supplement the Chinese imports (each factory produces a different model). Cuba imports parts such as small bolts, chains, spindles, and brakes, but makes the frames, forks, and handlebars.

Most *bicis* are cumbersome beasts (many with only one gear) weighing as much as an elephant. The bikes are made of poor quality parts and, like more modern Chinese bicycles sold at dollar stores throughout Havana, are basically junk. "After two days, the screws are already falling off," says Linda Nauman, director of **Bicycles Crossing Borders** (tel. 416/364-5329, http://bikestocuba.org), a Canadian cooperative that sends new and used bikes to Cuba.

moves. Roadways are lined with thousands of hitchers, many of them so desperate after hours in the sun that they wave peso bills at any passing vehicle—whether it be a tractor, a truck, or a motorcycle. If it moves, in Cuba it's fair game. The state has even set up *botellas* (hitchhiking posts) where officials of the Inspección Estatal, wearing mustard-colored uniforms (and therefore termed *coges amarillas,* or yellow-jackets), are in charge. They wave down virtually anything that comes along, and all state vehicles must stop to pick up hitchers.

It can be excruciatingly slow going, and there are never any guarantees for your safety. Hence, I don't recommend or endorse hitchhiking.

Cubans are officially barred from picking up foreign hitchhikers at the risk of huge fines. If you receive a ride in a private car, politeness dictates that you offer to pay for your ride: *"¿Cuánto le debo?"* after you're safely delivered.

ORGANIZED EXCURSIONS

State-owned companies such as Gaviota and Havanatur offer excursions throughout Cuba. You can book at tour desks in tourist hotels.

Several foreign companies offer tours and have offices in Cuba. I recommend **WowCuba** (Centro de Negocios Kohly, Calle 34 e/ 49 y 49A, Kohly, Havana, tel. 7/272-1777, www.wowcuba.com), with specialist programs.

CUBAN TOUR OPERATORS

Agencía de Viajes San Cristóbal: Oficios #110, e/ Lamparilla y Amargura, Habana Vieja, tel. 07/861-9171, www.viajessancristobal.cu. Tours and excursions within Havana.

Cubamar Viajes: 3ra Av., e/ 12 y Malecón, Havana, tel. 07/832-1116, www.cubamarviajes. cu. Primarily nature- and camping-related programs.

Cubanacán Viajes: Calle 23 #156, e/ O y P, Vedado, Havana, tel. 07/208-9920, www. cubanacan.cu. A major tour operator with excursions nationwide.

Cubatur: Calle 23, esq. L, Vedado, Havana, tel. 07/833-3142, www.cubatur.cu. Major tour information and booking agency.

EcoTur, S.A.: Av. Independencia #116, esq. Santa Catalina, Cerro, Havana, tel. 07/641-0306, www.ecoturcuba.co.cu. Focuses on nature and ecotourism.

Gaviota Tours: Av. 47 #2833, e/ 28 y 34, Rpto. Kohly, Havana, tel. 07/204-5708, www.gaviota-grupo.com. Specializes in nature -based tours, but also offers generic sightseeing.

Havanatur Tour & Travel: Av. Paseo, e/ 27 y 27, Vedado, Havana, tel. 07/201-9800 or 830-8227, www.havanatur.cu. The largest operator, Havanatur has the widest range of tours.

Paradiso: Promotora de Viajes Culturales: Calle 19 #560, esq. C, Vedado, Havana, tel. 07/832-9538, www.paradiso.cu. Cuba's premier specialist in cultural programs.

UniversiTUR: Calle 30 #768, e/ Kohly y 41, Nuevo Vedado, tel. 07/855-5978, agencia@ universitur.get.tur.cu. Arranges programs and lodgings for foreign students and academics.

Visas and Officialdom

DOCUMENTS AND REQUIREMENTS
Cuban Tourist Visas

A passport valid for six months from date of entry is required. Every visitor needs a Cuban visa or tourist card (*tarjeta de turista*) valid for a single trip of 30 days (90 days for Canadians); for most visitors, including U.S. citizens, a tourist card will suffice. No tourist card is required for transit passengers continuing their journey to a third country within 72 hours. Tourist cards are issued outside Cuba by tour agencies or the airline providing travel to Cuba. In some cases, tourist cards are issued at an airport upon arrival within Cuba. They cost US$15 (£15 in the U.K.; flights from Canada include the fee), but commercial agencies sometimes charge US$25 or more (but up to US$75 from Miami).

Don't list your occupation as journalist, police, military personnel, or government employer, as the Cuban government is highly suspicious of anyone with these occupations.

EXTENSIONS

You can request a single 30-day (90 days for Canadians) tourist visa extension (*prórroga*, CUC25, payable in stamps—*sellos*—purchased at Cuban banks) in Havana at **Inmigración** (Desamparados #110 e/ Habana y Compostela, c/o tel. 07/861-3462, Mon.–Wed. and Fri. 8:30 A.M.–4 P.M., Thurs. and Sat. 8:30–11 A.M.), in the Centro de Negocios Alameda de Paula, or at immigration offices in major cities. If you're staying in a *casa particular,* you will need to provide a receipt for the house.

Visitors who overstay their visas may be held in custody until reports are received on their activities in the country. In such an event, you are billed CUC20 daily! Do not overextend your stay.

The U.S. government recommends that its citizens arriving in Cuba register at the U.S.

Interests Section, in Havana. Cuba has no restrictions on U.S. tourists. *However, all U.S. citizens traveling with a U.S. Treasury Department
license are now suspect in the eyes of the Cuban
government, and there are recent reports of innocent U.S. travelers being investigated and even
jailed. Licensed U.S. travelers should assume that
they may be under surveillance and should avoid
any activities that heighten such suspicion.*

CUBAN ÉMIGRÉS
Cuban-born individuals who permanently left
Cuba after December 31, 1970, must have a valid

Cuban passport to enter and leave Cuba (you
will also need your U.S. passport to depart and
enter the United States). Cuban passports can
be obtained from the **Cuban Interests Section**
(2639 16th St. NW, Washington, DC 20009,
tel. 202/797-8518, cubaseccion@igc.apc.org) or
any Cuban consulate in other countries. Cuban
émigrés holding Cuban passports do not need
to apply for a visa to travel to Cuba. Cuba does
not recognize dual citizenship for Cuban citizens
who are also U.S. citizens; Cuban-born citizens
are thereby denied representation through the
U.S. Interests Section in the event of arrest.

REGIONAL IMMIGRATION OFFICES

The following regional offices have varying hours for handling requests for visa extensions (*prórrogas*) and other immigration issues:

- **Baracoa:** Martà #177, Mon.-Wed. and Fri. 8:15 A.M.-noon and 1-4 P.M., and Thurs. 8:15 A.M.-noon

- **Bayamo:** Carretera Central y 7ma, Rpto. Las Caobas, tel. 023/48-6148, Mon.-Tues. and Thurs.-Fri. 9 A.M.-noon and 1:30-4 P.M.

- **Camagüey:** Calle 3ra #156, e/ 8 y 10, Rpto. Vista Hermosa, tel. 032/27-5201, Mon.-Tues. and Thurs.-Fri. 8-11:30 A.M. and 1-3 P.M.

- **Ciego de Ávila:** Independencia Este #14, tel. 033/27-3387, Mon.-Tues. 8 A.M.-noon and 1:30-3:30 P.M., and Wed. and Fri. 8 A.M.-noon

- **Cienfuegos:** Av. 48, e/ 29 y 31, tel. 043/51-8853, Mon.-Thurs. 8 A.M.-noon and 1-3 P.M.

- **Guantánamo:** Calle 1 Oeste, e/ 14 y 15 Norte, one block north of the Hotel Guantánamo, Mon.-Wed. 8:30 A.M.-noon and 2-5 P.M.

- **Holguín:** General Vásquez y General Marrero, tel. 024/40-2321, Mon.-Wed. and Fri. 8:15 A.M.-noon and 1-5 P.M., and Thurs. 8:15 A.M.-noon

- **Las Tunas:** Av. Camilo Cienfuegos, Rpto. Buena Vista

- **Manzanillo:** Martí, esq. Masó, tel. 023/57-2584, Mon.-Tues. and Thurs.-Fri. 9 A.M.-noon and 1:30-4 P.M.

- **Matanzas:** Calle 85 #29408, Mon.-Wed. and Fri. 8 A.M.-4 P.M.

- **Nueva Gerona:** Calle 35 #3216, esq. 34, tel. 046/30-3284, Mon.-Fri. 8:15-11:30 A.M. plus Mon. and Wed. 5-6 P.M., and Sat. 9-11 A.M.

- **Pinar del Río:** Gerardo Medina, esq. Isabel Rubio, tel. 048/77-1404, Mon.-Wed. and Fri. 8 A.M.-3 P.M.

- **Sancti Spíritus:** Independencia Norte #107, tel. 041/32-4729, Mon.-Tues. and Thurs.-Fri. 8:30 A.M.-5 P.M., Sat. 8:30 A.M.-noon

- **Santa Clara:** Av. Sandino, esq. 6ta, three blocks east of Estadio Sandino, tel. 042/20-5868, Mon.-Wed. and Fri. 8 A.M.-noon and 1-3 P.M.

- **Santiago de Cuba:** Calle 13, e/ Carretera de Carey y 14, tel. 022/64-2557, Mon., Tues., Thurs., and Fri. 8:30 A.M.-noon and 1-4 P.M. (There's also an office outside the airport.)

- **Trinidad:** Concordia #20, off Paseo Agramonte, tel. 041/99-6950, Tues.-Thurs. 8 A.M.-4 P.M.

- **Varadero:** Calle 39 y 1ra, tel. 045/61-3494, Mon.-Fri. 8 A.M.-noon and 1-3:30 P.M.

Non-Tourist Visas

If you enter using a tourist visa and then wish to change your visa status, contact the **Ministerio de Relaciones Exteriores** (Ministry of Foreign Affairs; MINREX, Calle Calzada #360, e/ G y H, Vedado, tel. 07/835-7421 or 832-3279, www.cubaminrex.cu). Journalists must enter on a journalist's D-6 visa. Ostensibly these should be obtained in advance from Cuban embassies, and in the United States from the **Cuban Interests Section** (2639 16th St. NW, Washington, DC 20009, tel. 202/797-8518, cubaseccion@igc.apc.org). However, processing can take months. If you enter on a tourist visa and intend to exercise your profession, you must register for a D-6 visa at the **Centro de Prensa Internacional** (International Press Center, Calle 23 #152, e/ N y O, Vedado, Havana, tel. 07/832-0526, cpi@cpi.minrex.gov.cu, Mon.–Fri. 8:30 A.M.–5 P.M.). Ask for an Accreditación de Prensa Extranjera (Foreign Journalist's Accreditation). You'll need passport photos. Here, a journalist's visa (CUC70) can be got in a day, but you might not get your passport back for a week.

A commercial visa is required for individuals traveling to Cuba for business. These must also be obtained in advance from Cuban embassies.

Other Documentation

Visitors need a return ticket and adequate finances for their stay. The law requires that you carry your passport and tourist card with you at all times. Make photocopies of all your important documents and keep them separate from the originals, which you can keep in your hotel safe.

Cuban Embassies and Consulates

Cuba has Cuban embassies and representation in most major nations. For a complete list visit http://embacu.cubaminrex.cu.

- **Australia:** 128 Chalmers St., Surry Hills, NSW 2010, tel. 02/9698-9797, fax 02/8399-1106, asicuba@bigpond.com.au.
- **Canada:** 388 Main St., Ottawa, ON K1S 1E3, tel. 613/563-0141, fax 613/540-0068, cuba@embacubacanada.net (embassy and consulate); 4542 Decarie Blvd., Montreal, QC H4A 3P2, tel. 514/843-8897, fax 514/845-1063, seconcgc@bellnet.ca (consulate); 5353 Dundas St. W. #401, Toronto, ON M9B 6H8, tel. 416/234-8181, fax 416/234-2754, cubacon1@on.aibn.com (consulate).
- **France:** 16 rue de Presles, Paris, tel. 1/45-67-55-35, fax 1/45-67-08-91, conscu@ambacuba.fr.
- **Germany:** Stavangertrasse 20, D-10439 Berlin, tel. 30/9161-1813, fax 30/916-4553, embacuba-berlin@botschaft-kuba.de (embassy). Gotlandstr. 15, 10439 Berlin-Pankow, tel. 030/4473-7023 (consulate).
- **Italy:** Via Pirelli #30, 20121 Milano, tel. 02/6739-1344, fax 02/6671-2694, concubmi@tiscalinet.it (consulate). Via Licinia 7, 00153 Rome, tel. 06/571-7241, fax 06/574-5445, embajada@ecuitalia.it (embassy).
- **Spain:** Paseo de La Habana #194, C.P. 28036, Madrid, tel. 34/359-2500, fax 91/359-6145, secreembajada@ecubamad.com (embassy). Calle Conde de Peñalver #38, 28006, Madrid, tel. 91/401-0579, fax 91/402-1948, ccubamadrid@telefonica.net (consulate).
- **United Kingdom:** 167 High Holborn, London WC1V 6PA, tel. 020/7240-2488, fax 020/7836-2602, http://cuba.embassyhomepage.com.
- **United States:** The Cuban Interests Section (2639 16th St. NW, Washington, DC 20009, tel. 202/797-8518, fax 202/986-7283, cubaseccion@igc.apc.org) is under the aegis of the Swiss embassy.

CUSTOMS

Visitors to Cuba are permitted 20 kilos of personal effects plus "other articles and equipment depending on their profession," all of which must be re-exported. A CUC25 per kilo charge applies for items over 20 kilos. An additional two kilos of gifts are permitted, if packed separately. Visitors are also allowed 10 kilos of medicines, 200 cigarettes, 50 cigars, 250 grams of pipe tobacco, and up to three liters of wine and alcohol. An additional US$200 of "objects and articles for noncommercial use" can be imported, subject to a tax equal to 100 percent of the declared value, but this applies mostly to Cubans and returning foreign residents. Laptops must be declared; you will need to fill out a customs declaration, and the laptop *must* depart Cuba with you. "Obscene and pornographic" literature is banned—the definition includes politically unacceptable tracts. (If you must leave items with customs authorities, obtain a signed receipt to enable you to reclaim the items upon departure.)

For further information, contact the **Aduana** (Customs, Calle 6, esq. 39, Plaza de la Revolución, Havana, tel. 07/883-8282, www.aduana.co.cu).

EMBASSIES AND CONSULATES

The following nations have embassies and consulates in Havana. Those of other countries can be found at the Ministerio de Relaciones Exteriores website (www.cubaminrex.cu/DirectorioDiplomatico/Articulos/Cuba/A.html).

- **Australia:** c/o Canadian Embassy.

- **Canada:** Calle 30 #518, esq. 7ma, Miramar, tel. 07/204-2516, fax 07/204-2044.

- **United Kingdom:** Calle 34 #702, e/ 7ma y 17-A, Miramar, tel. 07/204-1771, fax 204-8104.

- **United States:** The U.S. Interests Section (Calzada, e/ L y M, Vedado, Havana, tel. 07/833-3551 to 07/833-3559, emergency/after hours tel. 07/833-3026, http://havana.usinterestsection.gov, Mon.–Fri. 8:30 A.M.–5 P.M.), the equivalent of an embassy, operates under the protection of the Swiss government. Readers report that it has been helpful to U.S. citizens in distress, and that staff are not overly concerned about policing infractions of travel restrictions.

Recreation

BICYCLING

Bicycle touring offers a chance to explore the island alongside the Cubans themselves. Roads are little trafficked yet full of hazards. Wear a helmet! Most airlines treat bicycles as a piece of luggage and require that bicycles be boxed; Cubana does not. Bring essential spares, plus locks.

If planning an all-Cuba trip, touring is best done in a westerly direction to take advantage of prevailing winds. A good resource is *Bicycling Cuba*, by Barbara and Wally Smith.

In Cuba, **Havanatur** (tel. 07/201-9763, www.havanatur.cu/cicloturismo.asp), **Cubanacán** (tel. 07/208-9920, www.cubanacanviajes.cu), and **WowCuba** (Centro de Negocios Kohly, Calle 34 e/ 49 y 49A, Kohly, Havana, tel. 07/272-1777, www.wowcuba.com) offer bicycle tours.

BIRD-WATCHING

The Zapata Peninsula is one of the best bird-watching areas in the Caribbean (its 203 species include 18 of the nation's 21 endemics), as are Cayo Coco (more than 200 species, including flamingos), Isla de la Juventud (for cranes and endemic parrots), plus mountain zones such as the Sierra del Rosario, Reserva de la Biosfera Baconao and Reserva de la Biosfera Cuchillas de Toa.

Cuba Caribbean Travel (www.cubacaribbeantravel.com/Ppalbird.htm) has numerous birding tours. In Cuba, **Cubanacán** (tel. 07/208-9920, www.cubanacanviajes.cu) has a 10-day guided birding trip.

The **FatBirder** webpage (www.fatbirder.com/links_geo/america_central/cuba.html) is an excellent resource.

ECOTOURISM AND HIKING

Cuba has the potential to be a hiking and ecotourism paradise. Both are relatively undeveloped. Notable exceptions are the trails in the Sierra del Rosario and Parque Nacional Península de Guanahacabibes, in Pinar del Río; and Parque Nacional Pico Turquino and Cuchillas de Toa, in Oriente.

Guides are compulsory. Cuba has very few naturalist guides. Pinares de Mayarí (in Holguín Province), El Saltón (in Santiago Province), and Moka Hotel (in Pinar del Río) are Cuba's three so-called "eco-lodges," although they are really lodges merely set in wilderness areas.

Cubanacán (tel. 07/208-9920, www.cubanacanviajes.cu) has hiking and nature trips, including a guided trek up Pico Turquino. **Cubamar Viajes** (Calle 3ra, e/ 12 y Malecón, Havana, tel. 07/833-2523, fax 07/833-3111, www.cubamarviajes.cu) and **EcoTur, S.A.** (Av. Independencia #116, esq. Santa Catalina, Cerro, Havana, tel. 07/641-0306, www.ecoturcuba.co.cu) offer eco-oriented tours—but include hunting and Jet Skiing!

FISHING
Freshwater and Inshore Fishing

Cuba's freshwater lakes and lagoons boil with tarpon, bonefish, snook, and bass. The star of the show is largemouth bass, which is best at Lago Hanabanilla in the Sierra Escambray; Embalse Zaza in Sancti Spíritus Province; and Lago Redonda, near Morón in Ciego de Ávila Province. As for bonefish and tarpon, few (if any) destinations can compare. This feisty shallow-water gamefish is abundant off Cayo Largo and the Cayos de Villa Clara; in the Jardines de la Reina archipelago south of Ciego de Ávila Province; and in the coastal lagoons of Zapata Peninsula.

The only centers for inshore fishing are **Villas Gran Caribe Ecolodge** on Cayo Largo and liveaboard boats in the Jardines de la Reina.

CubaWelcome (U.K. tel. 020/7731-6871, mike@cubawelcome.com) offers fishing tours and has an office in Havana. In Cuba, **EcoTur** (tel. 07/641-0306, www.ecoturcuba.co.cu) offers fishing trips.

Deep-Sea Fishing

So many game fish stream through the Gulf Stream that Ernest Hemingway called his "great blue river" that hardly a season goes by without some IGFA record being broken. The marlin run begins in May, when they swim against the current close to the Cuban shore. The Cubans aren't yet into tag-and-release, preferring to let you sauté the trophy (for a cut of the steak).

Fishing expeditions are offered from marinas nationwide.

GOLF

Before the Revolution, Cuba had several golf courses. After 1959, they were closed and fell into ruin. The only courses currently open are the nine-hole Havana Golf Club and an 18-hole championship course in Varadero. For years, Cuba has been talking about investing in its future as a golfing destination. Ten new golf course projects are on the books. In May 2010, Cuba announced it would finally approve financing the resorts through residential real estate sales to foreigners—a prerequisite for foreign investors.

ROCK CLIMBING AND SPELUNKING

Cuba is riddled with caverns, and caving (spelunking) is growing in popularity, organized through the **Sociedad Espeleológica de Cuba** (Calle 9na, esq. 84, Havana, tel. 07/881-5802, http://sec1940.galeon.com), which also has a climbing division (c/o Anibal Fernández, Calle Águila #367, e/ Neptuno y San Miguel, Centro Habana, tel. 07/862-0401, anibalpiaz@yahoo.com). Many climbing routes have been established in Viñales. Climbing routes are open and no permission is necessary. Cuban-American climber Armando Menocal (U.S. tel. 307/734-6034, www.cubaclimbing.com) is a good resource. Fernández and Menocal's superb *Cuba Climbing* (www.quickdrawpublications.com) guidebook is indispensable.

SAILING AND KAYAKING

Most all-inclusive resort hotels have Hobie Cats for hourly rental. Some also have kayaks.

Yachts and catamarans can be rented at most marinas; try **Marlin Naútica y Marinas** (tel. 07/273-7912, www.nauticamarlin.com). You can also charter through German company **Charter Partner** (tel. 089/2736-9150, www.charterpartner.com), and Germany-based **Plattensail** (www.platten-sailing.de) offers yacht charters out of Cienfuegos.

Seakunga Adventures (101 W. Broadway #184, Vancouver, BC V7H 4E3, tel. 800/781-2269) has 10-day kayaking trips in Cuba, plus a four-day yacht cruise out of Varadero.

SCUBA DIVING
Cuba is a diver's paradise. There are dozens of sunken Spanish galleons and modern vessels and aircraft, and the coral formations astound. Visibility ranges from 15 to 35 meters. Water temperatures average 27–29°C.

Cuba has almost 40 dive centers. Most large resort hotels have scuba outlets. Certification courses are usually for the American and Canadian Underwater Certification (ACUC), not PADI. Cuban dive masters are generally well-trained, but equipment is often not up to Western par, and dive shops are meagerly equipped. Spearfishing is strictly controlled. Spearguns and gigs are *not* allowed through customs.

Cuba has four principal dive areas: the Archipiélago de Las Colorados, off the north coast of Pinar del Río; the Jardines de la Rey archipelago, off the north coast of Ciego de Ávila and Camagüey Provinces; the Jardines de la Reina archipelago off the southern coast of Ciego de Ávila and Camagüey Provinces; and Isla de la Juventud and Cayo Largo. The so-called "Blue Circuit" east of Havana also has prime sites, as do the waters off the tip of Cabo de Corrientes, at the westernmost point of Cuba (good for whale sharks). Isla de la Juventud, with many of the best wrecks and walls, is primarily for experienced divers. Varadero is of only modest interest for experienced divers, although it has caves and wrecks.

WIND SPORTS
Surfing hasn't yet come to Cuba, and there are no boards to be rented. (However, there is a small group of Cuban aficionados using home-made boards fashioned from polystyrene ripped from discarded refrigerators and waxed with melted candles!) The north coast shores offer great possibilities, notably December–April, when the trade winds kick up good breaks. The south shore is generally placid except during summer, when frequent but unpredictable storms push the rollers ashore. Airlines will let you check your board as baggage, but some surfers have reported having boards confiscated by Cuban customs. A good starting point is the website www.havanasurf-cuba.com.

Sailboards and kitesurfing are available at Varadero, Cayo Coco, Guardalavaca, and other resorts.

Entertainment and Events

Cuba pulsates with the Afro-Latin spirit, be it energy-charged Las Vegas–style *cabarets* or someone's home-based celebration (called *cumbanchas*, or rumbas), where drummers beat out thumping rhythms and partners dance overtly sexual *changüí* numbers. And *noches cubanas* take place in most towns on Saturday nights, when bars and discos are set up alfresco and the street is cleared for dancing.

That said, Cuba's nocturnal entertainment scene is a far cry from days of yore, and in many locales you are hard-pressed to find any signs of life.

Paradiso (Calle 19 #560, esq. C, Vedado, Havana, tel. 07/832-9538, www.paradiso.cu) promotes artistic and cultural events, festivals, courses, and workshops.

NIGHTLIFE
Bars and Discos
Cuba's bar scene is anemic. Cuban cities are relatively devoid of the kind of lively sidewalk

CONSUMO MÍNIMO

You'll come across this term everywhere for entry to nightclubs and many other facilities. The term means "minimum consumption." Basically, it means that patrons have a right to consume up to a specified amount of food and/or beverage with a cover charge. For example, entry to the swimming pool at the Hotel Sevilla costs CUC20 but includes a *consumo mínimo* of up to CUC16 of food and beverage. There are no refunds for unused portions of the fee. The system is rife with *estafas* (swindles).

bars that make Rio de Janeiro buzz and South Beach hum. Tourist-only hotel bars are with few exceptions pretty dead, while those serving locals are run-down to the point of dilapidation (and often serving beer or rum in sawn-off beer bottles).

The dance scene is much livelier. Most towns have at least one disco or *centro nocturno* (nightclub or open-air disco) hosting live music from salsa bands to folkloric trios. Romantic crooners are a staple, wooing local crowds with dead-on deliveries of Benny Moré classics. Western-style discos are few. Foreign males can expect to be solicited outside the entrance: Cuban women beg to be escorted in because the cover charge is beyond their means and/or because the venue only permits couples to enter. Drink prices can give you sticker shock: it's cheaper to buy a bottle of rum and a Coca-Cola. Few discos get their groove on before midnight.

Many clubs apply a *consumo mínimo* (minimum charge) policy that covers entry plus a certain value of drinks.

Folkloric Music Venues

Every town has a Casa de la Trova and a Casa de la Cultura where you can hear traditional *música folklórica* (folkloric music), including ballad-style *trova* (love songs rendered with the

aid of guitar and drum), often blended with revolutionary themes. UNEAC (National Union of Cuban Writers and Artists, www.uneac.co.cu) also has regional outlets hosting cultural events.

Look for performances by the Conjunto Folklórico Nacional (National Folklore Dance Group), founded in 1962 to revive Cuban folk traditions.

Cabarets

One of the first acts of the revolutionary government was to kick out the Mafia and close down the casinos and brothels. "It was as if the Amish had taken over Las Vegas," wrote Kenneth Tynan in a 1961 edition of *Holiday.* Not quite! Sure, the strip clubs and live sex shows are gone. But sexy Las Vegas–style cabarets (called *espectáculos,* or shows) remain a staple of Cuban entertainment; every town has at least one. They're highlighted by long-legged dancers wearing high heels and g-strings, with lots of feathers and frills. Singers, magicians, acrobats, and comedians are often featured. Cuban couples delight in these razzmatazz spectacles and shake their heads at any puritan's concept that they are sexist.

Outshining all other venues is the Tropicana, with outlets in Havana, Matanzas, and Santiago de Cuba.

THE ARTS

Theater is the least developed of Cuba's cultural media. Theater was usurped by the Revolution as a medium for mass-consciousness-raising. As such it became heavily politicized. In recent years, however, an avant-garde theater has evolved. The run-down theaters are used mostly for operatic, symphonic, and comic theater. However, you'll need to be fluent in Spanish to get many giggles out of the comedy shows, full of burlesque and references to politically sensitive third-rail issues.

CINEMA

Cubans are passionate moviegoers, although most cinemas are extremely run-down. Entrance usually costs a peso and the menu is surprisingly varied and hip. Movies are often subtitled in Spanish (others are dubbed; you'll need to be fluent in Spanish). No children under 16 are admitted; most towns have special children's screenings.

Many cinemas also have *salas de videos*—tiny screening rooms.

FESTIVALS AND EVENTS

The annual calendar is filled with cultural events ranging from "high culture," such as the International Ballet Festival, to purely local affairs, such as the year-end *parrandas* of Villa Clara Province, where the townsfolk indulge in massive fireworks battles. A highlight is Carnaval, held in Havana (August) and Santiago (July). Religious parades include the Procession of the Miracles (December 17), when pilgrims descend on the Santuario de San Lázaro, at Rincón, on the outskirts of Santiago de las Vegas in suburban Havana. The old Spanish holiday El Día de los Reyes Magos (Three Kings' Day), on January 6, is the most important religious observance.

For a list of events, contact the **Buró de Convenciones** (Hotel Neptuno, 3ra y 70, Miramar, Havana, tel. 07/204-8273, www.cubameeting.travel).

MAJOR FESTIVALS

FESTIVAL/EVENT	MONTH	LOCATION
Habanos Festival (Cigar Festival)	February	Havana
Festival Internacional de Jazz (International Jazz Festival)	February	Havana
Festival de Semana Santa (Easter)	April	Trinidad
Festival Internacional de Percusión (International Percussion Festival)	April	Havana
Festival Internacional de Cine Pobre (International Low-Budget Film Festival)	April	Gibara
Carnaval de la Habana	August	Havana
Fiesta del Caribe (Carnaval)	July	Santiago de Cuba
Festival de la Habana de Música Contemporánea (Havana Festival of Contemporary Music)	October	Havana
Fiesta Iberoamericana de la Cultura (Festival of Latin American Culture)	October	Holguín
Festival Internacional de Ballet (International Ballet Festival)	October	Havana
Festival del Nuevo Cine Latinoamericano (Festival of New Latin American Cinema)	November	Havana
Festival Internacional de Música Benny Moré (Benny Moré International Music Festival)	December	Cienfuegos

LOCO POR BÉISBOL

Béisbol (or *pelota*) is as much an obsession in Cuba as it is in the United States – more so, in fact. Just watch Cuban kids playing, writes author Randy Wayne White, "without spikes, hitting without helmets, sharing their cheap Batos gloves, but playing like I have never seen kids play before. It wasn't so much the skill – though they certainly had skill – as it was the passion with which they played, a kind of controlled frenzy." No wonder Cuba traditionally beats the pants off the U.S. team in the Olympic Games.

Baseball was introduced to Cuba in the 1860s, the island's first professional team – the Habana Baseball Club – was formed in 1872, and the first league was formed six years later. In 1909, Ralph Estep, a salesman for Packard, journeyed through Cuba and found the country to be "baseball crazy." Baseball terminology found its way into the Cuban lexicon, while many aspiring young Cubans fulfilled their dreams of making it to the big leagues; prior to the Revolution, many Cubans found positions in the U.S. leagues. The flow went both ways. Babe Ruth and Willie Mays played for Cuban clubs, for example, as did Tommy Lasorda, who played five seasons in Cuba.

Players who make the Cuban national team and barnstorm the Olympics earn about 400 pesos a month – about the same as the average laborer. It's not surprising that many are tempted by the prospect of riches in the U.S. professional leagues. More than 40 Cuban baseball stars have fled Cuba since 1991, when Rene Arocha (who became a star pitcher for the St. Louis Cardinals) split from the Cuban national team during a stopover in Miami. In 1996, the defection of Livan Hernández (who was snatched up for US$4.5 million by the Florida Marlins) so rankled Castro that in a fit of spite, Livan's half-brother, Orlando "El Duque" Hernández, one of the world's greatest pitchers, was barred from playing and relegated to work in the Havana Psychiatric Hospital. Understandably, in January 1998 he fled Cuba on a homemade raft and was signed by the Yankees for US$6.6 million.

Still, not every player is eager to leave. In 1995, Omar Linares, slugging third baseman for the Pinar del Río team and considered to be one of the best amateur baseball players in the world, rejected a US$1.5 million offer to play for the New York Yankees. In 2002, however, Linares and third baseman Omar Kindelan signed to play with Japanese teams for US$4,000 monthly, with the Cuban government taking a slice of the salary.

Cuba is led by a sports fanatic. In the early years of power, Castro would often drop in at Havana's Gran Stadium (in 1971 it was renamed Estadio Latinoamericano) to pitch a few balls at the Sugar Kings' batters. And everyone knows the story of how Castro once tried out as a pitcher for the old Washington Senators. Who knows? Had the story been true, Fidel might have become a Senator and not a dictator.

Cuba's stars play more than 100 games a season on regional teams under the supervision of the best coaches, sports doctors, and competition psychologists outside the U.S. big leagues. Each province has a team on the national league (Liga Nacional), and two provinces and the city of Havana have two teams each, making 16 teams in all. They're divided into two zones – Occidente and Oriente – with two groups of four teams each. The last game of every three-game series is played in a *pueblo* away from the provincial capital so that fans in the country can see the teams live. The season runs October–March. The teams play a 39-game season, with the top seven teams going on to compete in the 54-game National Series, culminating when the top Oriente team battles the top Occidental team in a seven-game series.

Stadiums are oases of relaxation and amusement. There are no exploding scoreboards or dancing mascots, and beer and souvenir hawkers are replaced by old men wandering among the seats selling thimble-size cups of sweet Cuban espresso. Spam sandwiches replace hot dogs in the stands, where the spectators, being good socialists, also cheer for the opposition's base-stealers and home-run hitters. Balls (knocked out of the field by aluminum Batos bats made in Cuba) are even returned from the stands, because fans understand they're too valuable to keep as souvenirs.

Cubaball Tours (4772 Narvaez Dr., Vancouver, BC V6L 2J2, Canada, tel. 604/266-4664, www.cubaballtours.com) offers baseball trips to Cuba.

TURNING OUT CHAMPIONS

Tiny Cuba is one of the top five sports powers in the world, excelling in baseball, volleyball, boxing, and track and field. Cuba is by far the strongest Olympic power in Latin America, and took 12th place at the 2008 Olympic Games in Beijing.

Cuba's international success is credited to its splendid sports training system. When the Revolution triumphed, sports became a priority alongside land reform, education, and health care. In 1964 the Castro government opened a network of sports schools – Escuelas de Iniciación Deportiva (EIDE) – as part of the primary and secondary education system, with the job of preparing young talent for sports achievement. There are 15 EIDE schools throughout Cuba. The island also has 76 sports academies and an athletic "finishing" school in Havana, the Escuela Superior de Perfeccionamiento Atlético.

Sports training is incorporated into every school curriculum. School Games are held islandwide every year and help identify talent to be selected for specialized coaching. For example, María Colón Rueñes was identified as a potential javelin champion when she was only seven years old; she went on to win the gold medal at the Moscow Olympics. Many of Cuba's sports greats have passed through these schools – track-and-field stars such as world-record-holding high jumper Javier Sotomayor, world-record sprinters Leroy Burrel and Ana Fidelia Quirot, and volleyball legends such as Jel Despaigne and Mireya Luis.

Sports figures are considered workers and "part of the society's productive efforts." As such, sports stars are paid a salary on a par with other workers, although most national team members also receive special perks, such as new cars. Not surprisingly, almost every international competition outside Cuba results in at least one defection.

SPECTATOR SPORTS

Cuba is a world superstar in sports and athletics, as it was even before the Revolution, especially in baseball and boxing. Following the Revolution, professional sports were abolished and the state took over all sports under the **Instituto Nacional del Deportivo y Recreo** (National Institute for Sport, Physical Education, and Recreation, INDER).

The Cuban calendar is replete with sporting events. **Cubadeportes** (Calle 20 #706, e/ 7 y 9, Miramar, tel. 07/204-0945, www.cubadeportes.cu) specializes in sports tourism and arranges visits to sporting events and training facilities.

Shopping

Department stores and shopping malls can be found in Havana. These, and smaller outlets in every town, sell Western goods from toiletries, Levis, and Reeboks to Chinese toys and Japanese electronics sold for CUC at vastly inflated prices. If you see something you want, *buy it!* If you dally, it most likely will disappear. Most stores selling to tourists accept foreign credit cards except those issued by U.S. banks. Peso stores are meagerly stocked with crap no one will ever buy.

Shipping from Cuba is problematic. If you can afford it, use an express courier such as DHL (www.dhl.com), rather than **Cubapost** (Calle P #108, Vedado, tel. 07/836-9790) or **Cubapacks** (Calle 22 #4115, e/ 41 y 47, Miramar, tel. 07/204-2742).

Note: U.S. residents are not allowed to bring back or mail any item from Cuba, except art and literature.

ARTS AND CRAFTS

For quality arts and crafts, Cuba is unrivaled in the Caribbean. Arts and crafts are sold by artisans at street stalls and in state agency stores such as the Fondo Cubano de Bienes Culturales and ARTEX. The best stuff is sold in upscale hotels, which mark up accordingly. Tourist venues are overflowing with kitschy paintings, busty cigar-chomping ceramic mulattas, erotic carvings, and papier-mâché vintage Yankee cars. There is also plenty of true-quality art, ranging from paintings to hand-worked leather goods. You'll also see *muñequitas* (dolls) representing the goddesses of the *santería* religion.

Most open-air markets offer silver-plated jewelry at bargain prices (a favorite form is old cutlery shaped into bracelets), while most upscale hotels have *joyerías* (jewelry stores) selling international-quality silver jewelry, much of it in a distinctly Cuban contemporary style. *Avoid buying black coral, turtle shell jewelry, and other animal "craft" items.* The Cuban government doesn't seem conscientious in this regard, but European and North American customs officials may seize these illegal items.

A limited amount of bargaining is normal at street markets. However, most prices are very low to begin with. If the quoted price seems fair, pay up and feel blessed that you already have a bargain.

Exporting Arts and Antiques

In 2003, the government stopped issuing permits for antiques, including antiquarian books, stamp collections, furniture, and porcelain. An export permit is required for all quality artwork; the regulation doesn't apply to kitschy tourist art. State-run commercial galleries and *expo-ventas* (galleries representing freelance artists) will issue an export permit or arrange authorization for any items you buy.

Export permits for items for which you have not received an official receipt may be obtained from the **Registro Nacional de Bienes Culturales** (National Registry of Cultural Goods, Calle 17 #1009, e/ 10 y 12, Vedado, Havana, tel. 07/831-3362, www.cnpc.cult. cu, Mon.–Fri. 9 A.M.–noon), in the Centro de Patrimonio Cultural, or at regional offices in provincial capitals. A single work costs CUC10,

handmade jewelry

CUBAN CIGARS

It seems ironic that Cuba – scourge of the capitalist world – should have been compelled by history and geography to produce one of the most blatant symbols of capitalist wealth and power. Yet it does so with pride. The unrivaled reputation of Cuban cigars as the best in the world transcends politics, transubstantiating a weed into an object capable of evoking rapture. Cubans guard the unique reputation scrupulously.

Cuban cigars – *habanos* or *puros* – are not only a source of hard currency; they're part and parcel of the national culture. Although Fidel gave up smoking in 1985, Cubans still smoke 250 million cigars domestically every year. Another 160 million or so are exported annually. Although some 20 percent of Cuban cigars are machine-made, the best are still hand-rolled.

HOW CIGARS GOT THEIR START

The cigar tradition was first documented among the indigenous tribes by Christopher Columbus. The Taíno made monster cigars – at the very least, they probably kept the mosquitoes away – called *cohibas*. The word "cigar" originated from *sikar*, the Mayan word for smoking, which in Spanish became *cigarro*.

The popular habit of smoking cigars – as opposed to tobacco in pipes, first introduced to Europe by Columbus – began in Spain, where cigars made from Cuban tobacco were first made in Seville in 1717. Demand for higher-quality cigars grew, and *Sevillas* (as Spanish cigars were called) were superseded by Cuban-made cigars. Soon, tobacco was Cuba's main export and received a boost after the Peninsula Campaign (1806-1812) of the Napoleonic wars, when British and French veterans returned home with the cigar habit, creating a fashion in their home countries. "No lover of cigars can imagine the voluptuous pleasure of sitting in a café sipping slowly a strong magnificent coffee and smoking rhythmically those divine leaves of Cuba," wrote American pianist Arthur Rubinstein.

BUNDLED, BOXED, AND BOYCOTTED

The banking firm of H. Upmann initiated export in cedar boxes in 1830, when it imported cigars for its directors in London. Later, the bank decided to enter the cigar business, and introduced the embossed cedar box complete with colorful lithographic label for each specific brand.

The Montecristo was the fashionable cigar of choice. In the 1930s, any tycoon or film director worth the name was seen with a whopping Montecristo A in his mouth. Half of all the Havanas sold in the world in the 1930s were Montecristos, by which time much of Cuba's tobacco industry had passed into U.S. ownership. Among the devotees of Cuban cigars was President Kennedy, who smoked Petit Upmanns. In 1962, at the height of the Cuban Missile Crisis, Kennedy asked his press secretary, Pierre Salinger, to obtain as many Upmanns as he could. Next day, reported Salinger, Kennedy asked him how many he had found. Twelve hundred, replied his aide. Kennedy then pulled out and signed the decree establishing a trade embargo with Cuba. Ex-British premier Winston Churchill also stopped smoking Havanas and started smoking Jamaican cigars, but after a time he forgot about politics and went back to Havanas. His brand was Romeo y Julieta.

The embargo dealt a crushing blow to Cuba's cigar industry. Castro nationalized the industry and founded a state monopoly, Cubatabaco. Many dispossessed cigar factory owners immigrated to the Dominican Republic, Mexico, Venezuela, and Honduras, where they started up again, often using the same brand names they had owned in Cuba. Today, the Dominican Republic produces 47 percent of the handmade cigars imported into the United States.

but CUC30 is good for up to 50 works of art. You must bring the object for inspection, or a photo if the object is too large. Allow up to two days for processing.

CIGARS

Cuba produces the world's best cigars (*habanos*, *tabacos*, or *puros*) at perhaps one-half the price of similar cigars in London.

Since 1985, handmade Cuban cigars have carried the Cubatabaco stamp plus a factory mark and, since 1989, the legend *"Hecho en Cuba. Totalmente a Mano."* (Made in Cuba. Completely by Hand.). If it reads *"Hecho a Mano,"* the cigars are most likely hand *finished* (i.e., the wrapper was put on by hand) rather than hand *made*. If it states only *"Hecho en Cuba,"* they are assuredly machine made. As of 2005, all boxes feature a holographic seal (any other boxes are subject to seizure by Cuban customs).

There are about 40 brands, each in various sizes and even shapes; sizes are given specific names, such as Corona (142mm) and Julieta (178mm). Fatter cigars—the choice of connoisseurs—are more fully flavored and smoke more smoothly and slowly than those with smaller ring gauges. As a rule, darker cigars are also more full-bodied and sweeter.

All cigar factories produce various brands. Some factories specialize in particular flavors, others in particular sizes. Several factories might be producing any one brand simultaneously, so quality can vary markedly even though the label is the same. Experts consider cigars produced in Havana's El Laguito factory to be the best. As with fine wines, the quality of cigars varies from year to year. The source and year of production are marked in code on the underside of the box. The code tells you a lot about the cigars inside. Even novices can determine the provenance and date of cigars if they know the codes. However, the code system keeps changing to throw buyers off, so that cigars of different ages have different codes. The first three letters usually refer to the factory where the cigars were made, followed by four letters that give the date of manufacture.

THE *GUAYABERA*

The traditional *guayabera*, Cuba's all-purpose gift to menswear, was created in central Cuba more than 200 years ago and is the quintessential symbol of Latin masculinity. Despite the infusion of New York fashion, this four-pocket, straight-bottom shirt remains the essence of sartorial style. The *guayabera*, thought Kimberley Cihlar, "is possessed of all the sex appeal any Latin peacock could want." Nonetheless, younger Cubans shun the shirt as a symbol of someone who works for the government.

The *guayabera*, which comes short sleeved or long, is made of light cotton perfect for weathering the tropical heat. In shape, it resembles a short-sleeved jacket or extended shirt and is worn draped outside the pants, usually as an outer garment with a T-shirt beneath. Thus it fulfills the needs of summertime dressing with the elegance of a jacket and the comfort of, well, a shirt. It is embellished with patterned embroidery running in parallel stripes down the front and is usually outfitted with pockets – with buttons – to stow enough *habanos* for a small shop.

The expertise and care expressed in the factory determine how well a cigar burns and tastes. Cigars, when properly stored, continue to ferment and mature in their boxes—an aging process similar to that of good wines. Rules on when to smoke a cigar don't exist, but many experts claim that the prime cigars are those aged for 6–8 years. Everyone agrees that a cigar should be smoked either within three months of manufacture or not for at least a year; the interim is known as a "period of sickness." Cigars should be slightly soft when gently squeezed; have a fresh, robust smell (a stale smell may indicate a fake, low-quality, or poorly stored cigar); be tightly rolled, smooth and silky in texture, and free of any protuberances or air pockets. The cigars should be of near identical color and shape.

You may leave Cuba with up to CUC2,000 worth of cigars with purchase receipts, which you also need for any more than 23 loose or unwrapped cigars. You can buy additional cigars in the airport duty-free lounge after passing through customs controls. Cigars can be bought at virtually every tourist hotel and store, or at dedicated Casas del Habano or Casas del Tabaco nationwide. Most shop clerks know little about cigars. Prices can vary up to 20 percent from store to store. If one store doesn't have what you desire, another surely will. Inspect your cigars before committing to a purchase.

In cities, *jineteros* (street hustlers) will offer you cigars at what seems the deal of the century. *Forget it!* The vast majority are low-quality, machine-made cigars sold falsely as top-line cigars to unsuspecting travelers. The hustlers use empty boxes and seals stolen by colleagues who work in the cigar factories, so the unknowing buyer is easily convinced that this is the real McCoy.

LITERATURE

Books are severely restricted by the government, which maintains an iron fist over what may be read. There are *no* newsstands or newsagents. A few foreign periodicals are not for sale except in upscale tourist hotels.

Most tourist outlets sell a limited range of English-language coffee-table books, travel-related books, and political treatises that have been approved by the censors. Otherwise the few bookstores that exist stock mostly Spanish-language texts, mostly socialist texts glorifying the Revolution. Castro's own writings are the most ubiquitous works, alongside those of Che Guevara and José Martí. A new book chain, **Todo Libro,** was created in 2008 and has stores in half a dozen cities.

Accommodations

RESERVATIONS

Since January 2008, new tourism cards no longer ask for proof of three nights' pre-booked accommodation upon arrival; however, it's wise to have pre-booked rooms or, at least, the address of a hotel or *casa particular* (private room rental) in mind in case you're questioned.

Christmas and New Year's are particularly busy, as are major festivals. Book well ahead; call direct, send a fax or email, or have a tour operator abroad make your reservation (the latter are sometimes cheaper thanks to wholesalers' discounts). Insist on written confirmation and take copies with you, as Cuban hotels are notorious for not honoring reservations. Pay in advance for all nights you intend to stay; otherwise you might be asked to check out to make room for someone else.

Charter package tours with airfare and hotel included may offer the cheapest rates, although the less notable hotels are often used.

PRICES

The Cuban government has a monopoly, and it jacks up and reduces prices nationwide according to market trends. Rates also vary for low (May–June and September–November) and high season (December–April and July–August). Cuba has no room tax or service charge.

Often it's cheaper to pay as you go rather than prepaying. The same goes for meals. A "modified American plan" (MAP; room rate that includes breakfast and dinner) can be a bargain at beach resorts, where ordering meals individually can be a lot more expensive. In Havana, you're better off with a European plan (EP; room with breakfast only). If you're not intent on exploring beyond your resort, consider an all-inclusive property, where the cost of all meals, drinks, and activities is included in the room rate.

TYPES OF ACCOMMODATION
Camping
Cuba is not geared for camping. Tent sites don't exist and you need permission to camp "wild." The government is paranoid about foreigners

```
FAWLTY
TOWERS?
```

Cuba's hotel foibles conjure up déjà vu for viewers of *Fawlty Towers*, the BBC's hilarious sitcom. Most hotels have a few petty annoyances. For example, after a hot, sticky day, you return to your room to find no hot water — for which you're supposed to get 10 percent off your bill. No running water at all? Twenty percent off. In theory, you're entitled to a well-defined refund for each such contingency. A sorry mattress is worth a 10 percent discount, according to the State Prices Commission. *Good luck!*

The number of faults in hotels is generally in inverse proportion to price. At the cheapest places, you'll find gurgling pipes, no sinkplugs, and tired mattresses and sheets too short for the bed. "Staying in less-than-two-star hotels...means passing below the rock bottom of comfort, to the point where involuntary abuse of guests begins," wrote Isadora Tattlin.

Far too many hotels have abysmal service. Castro agreed: "Cubans are the most hospitable, friendly, and attentive people in the world. But as soon as you put a waiter's uniform on them, they become terrible." To be fair, things are improving. Cuba has set up hotel-management training schools run by Austrians.

Hotels under foreign management are generally of a higher standard than their purely Cuban equivalents. That said, even the best hotels are not entirely free of Cuban quirks. Even in top hotels, no one thinks to clean the fixtures, for example, so that hotels only one or two years old quickly become grimy. It's enough to make you wonder if Basil Fawlty is running the show.

on the loose. While urbanites are savvy about the rules, rural folks may not be; you potentially expose farmers to ruinous fines merely for having you on their land. The system assumes guilt unless the farmer can prove that he or she has not, or was not going to, accept money.

Cuba has 84 *campismos,* simple holiday camps with basic cabins and facilities operated by **Campismo Popular** (Calle 13 #857, e/ 4 y 6, Vedado, Havana, tel. 07/831-0080 or 830-9044), which has booking offices island-wide. Some have been upgraded for tourists. Often camps are closed Monday–Thursday and off-season; during summer they're often full with Cubans.

Peso Hotels
Peso hotels cater to Cubans and are extremely cheap—usually the equivalent of less than CUC1. A few properties off the tourist path may accept foreigners in a pinch. You cannot book peso hotels; you will have to do this face-to-face in Cuba. Most are dour. Check the room for running water, functioning electricity, etc. before agreeing to a reservation.

Tourist Hotels
In 2009, Cuba claimed 46,500 hotel rooms, of which 62 percent were declared to be four- or five-star. All hotels in Cuba are owned by five state-run Cuban hotel entities that ostensibly compete for business, some in cooperative management agreements with foreign (mostly Spanish) hotel groups. However, hotels frequently juggle between the following entities:

- **Cubanacán** (Calle 23 #156, e/ O y P, Vedado, Havana, tel. 07/833-4090 or 208-9920, www.cubanacan.cu) has more than 50 hotels. Its Hoteles Brisas and Hoteles Club Amigo are (supposedly) four-star and three-day all-inclusive beach resorts. Its Hoteles Horizontes are urban hotels (usually lackluster two- or three-star ones). Hoteles 'E' are small boutique hotels. It also has Hoteles Cubanacán.

- **Gaviota** (Calle 70, e/ 5ta y 7ma, Miramar, Havana, tel. 07/206-9595, fax 07/206-9912, www.gaviota-grupo.com) owns eco-lodges, deluxe city hotels, and all-inclusive beach resorts.

- **Gran Caribe** (7ma Av. #4210, e/ 42 y 44, Miramar, Havana, tel. 07/204-9201, fax 07/204-0238, www.gran-caribe.com), once managed deluxe hotels; today it has some three dozen hotels ranging from two to five stars.

- **Hoteles Habaguanex** (Calle Oficios #110, e/ Lamparilla and Amargura, Habana Vieja, tel. 07/867-1039, fax 07/860-9761, www.habaguanexhotels.com) operates historic hotels in Habana Vieja.

- **Islazul** (Calle 19 e/ Paseo y A, Vedado, tel. 07/832-7718, fax 07/833-3458, www.islazul.cu) operates inexpensive hotels catering primarily to Cubans (who pay in pesos). Some of its properties are splendid bargains.

The ratings Cuba gives its hotels are far too generous; most fall one or two categories below their international equivalents. Most towns have one or two historic hotels around the central park and a concrete Bauhaus-era Soviet hotel on the outskirts. Hotels built in recent years are constructed to international standards, although even the best suffer from poor design, shoddy construction, apathetic (and unethical) staff, and poor management. Only top-line hotels provide shampoo, toiletries, sink plugs, or face cloths—but don't count on it.

Many hotels use both 220-volt and 110-volt outlets (usually marked), often in the same room. Check before plugging in any electrical appliances, or you could blow a fuse. Note that "minibars" in most hotel guest rooms are actually small (and empty) refrigerators.

Upon registering, you'll be issued a *tarjeta de huésped* (guest card) at each hotel, identifying you as a hotel guest. Depending on your hotel, the card may have to be presented when ordering and signing for meals and drinks, changing money, and often when entering the elevator to your room.

Many hotels open their swimming pools to Cuban locals; most all-inclusive hotels sell day-passes to nonguests wishing to use the facilities.

APARTHOTELS AND *PROTOCOLOS*

Aparthotels offer rooms with kitchens or kitchenettes. Most are characterless. Many are linked to regular hotels, giving you access to broader facilities.

Cubanacán and Gran Caribe handle reservations for *protocolos*—special houses reserved for foreign dignitaries. Most are in mansions in the Cubanacán region of Havana (they include Frank Sinatra's former home), but most other towns have at least one.

ALL-INCLUSIVE RESORTS

Most beach resorts are run as all-inclusives: cash-free, self-contained properties where your room rate theoretically includes all meals and beverages, entertainment, and water sports at no additional fee. Standards vary. Properties managed by international name-brand hotel chains are preferred to the purely Cuban-run affairs.

NATURE LODGES

About half a dozen quasi-"ecotourism" properties can be found in mountain areas or close to nature reserves. Cuba has no eco-lodges to international standards. The most prominent is La Moka (Pinar del Río), though it's an eco-lodge only in name; others include Villa Soroa (Pinar del Río), Pinares del Mayarí, and Villa El Salton (Santiago de Cuba).

SECURITY

All tourist hotel lobbies have security staff, posted following the spate of bombs planted in Havana's hotels in 1997. They serve to prevent a repeat performance, but also do double duty to keep out unsavory characters (and Cubans slipping upstairs with foreign guests).

Theft is an issue in hotels. If your hotel has a safe deposit box, use it. Before accepting a room, ensure that the door is secure and that someone can't climb in through the window. *Always* lock your door. Keep your suitcase locked when you're not in your room, as maids frequently make off with clothing and other items. (One trick is to spread your items around drawers so you don't know where anything is.)

Casas Particulares

My favorite option is a *casa particular* (private house)—a room in a family home, granting you a chance to gain a perspective on Cuban life. This can be anything from a single room with a live-in family to a self-sufficient apartment. The going room rate in Havana is CUC20–40 (but up to CUC300 for entire houses), and CUC10–35 outside Havana. Many more *casas particulares* exist than I can list in this book.

Legally licensed houses post a blue Arrendador Divisa sign, like an inverted anchor, on the front door (those with a red sign are licensed to rent only to Cubans, in pesos). Avoid illegal, unlicensed *casas particulares*.

Check to see if hot water is available 24 hours, or only at specific times. Avoid rooms facing streets, although even rooms tucked at the backs of buildings can hold an unpleasant surprise in pre-dawn hours, when all manner of noises can intrude on your slumber.

Reservations are recommended during high season. If you arrive in a town without a reservation, owners of *casas particulares* are happy to call around on your behalf. Touts do a brisk business trying to steer travelers to specific *casas,* and are not above telling independent travelers lies, such as that a particular house you might be seeking has closed. The tout's commission will be added to your rent. Many touts pose as hitchhikers on roads into major cities; others chase you around by bicycle.

Spell out all the prices involved before settling on a place to stay. Remember, most home owners have cut their rates to the bare bones while facing punitive taxes. Most serve meals: breakfasts usually cost CUC3–5, dinners typically cost CUC5–10. Many homes have shower units with electric heater elements, which you switch on for the duration of your shower. Beware: It's easy to give yourself a shock.

Your host must record your passport details, to be presented to the Ministry of the Interior within 24 hours (hence, MININT is always abreast of every foreigner's whereabouts). Honor regulations and avoid attracting undue attention to your host's home, as the legal repercussions of even the hint of an infraction can be serious.

CASA PARTICULAR OWNERS' BURDENS

Since the triumph of the Revolution, the Urban Reform Law explicitly prohibited the rental of housing, despite which *casas particulares* (or *hospedajes*) began to blossom in the mid-1990s following a ban on having Cuban guests in hotel rooms – foreign guests turned to renting private rooms for their liaisons. With tourism booming, the government faced a room shortage. Hence, in 1996 the law was begrudgingly reformed: Cubans are now permitted to rent out up to two rooms, albeit under rigid and ever-tighter state regulations.

The government frowns upon the businesses and seemingly wants to squeeze *casas particulares* out of business. In 2004 it stopped granting licenses and began taking many away, while a stiff tax code is intended to sting *casas particulares* as much as possible. The tax varies according to district – in Havana, it's CUC150 monthly in a nontourist zone and CUC325 in a tourist zone – and is payable whether the homeowner receives guests or not. An additional tax on income is paid at the end of the year, and additional fees apply for signs outside the house, on-site parking, and miscellaneous attributes.

The owner of a *casa particular* may not operate any other business, including car rental or guide services. And the owner must remain open 365 days a year; no vacation is permitted. Nor can they close in slow season, when they must continue to pay set taxes; if they close, they lose their license.

Inspectors visit regularly to check the books and property. The slightest infractions are dealt with harshly: a CUC1,500 fine is standard. And a three-strike rule applies: After three infractions, the house is seized by the government!

Unauthorized Accommodations

Tourists must receive written permission from immigration authorities to stay anywhere other than a hotel or *casa particular*. If you wish to stay with Cuban friends, you must go to the nearest immigration office within 24 hours to convert from a tourist visa to an A2 visa (CUC25). You must be accompanied by the person you wish to stay with. If an unregistered foreigner is found staying in a house (or camping), the Cuban host must prove that the foreigner is not a paying guest—an almost impossible situation. Thus, the Cuban is automatically found guilty of renting illegally. The regulations are strictly enforced, and fines are ruinous!

Posadas

The government runs 24-hour "love hotels," also known as *posadas* (or "motels"), which exist so that couples can enjoy an intimate moment together. In most, conditions are modest to say the least. Rooms are usually rented for three hours, typically for five pesos (US$0.25), for which the state thoughtfully provides a bottle of rum by the bed. Foreigners are usually turned away if accompanied by Cuban partners.

Cuban Guests

Since 2008, Cubans have been allowed to room in "tourist" hotels, although few can afford it. The new rulings also permit foreigners and Cubans to share a hotel room (previously, staff went to sometimes absurd lengths to prevent Cuban guests from entering the rooms of foreign hotel guests, and vice versa). Foreigners staying in *casas particulares* are also permitted to share their room with Cubans of either gender; in all cases, your host must record your guest's *cédula* (ID) details for presentation to MININT within 24 hours. MININT runs the Cuban guest's name through a computer database; if the name of a woman appears three times with a different man, she is arrested as a "prostitute" and gets a mandatory four-year jail term (in Varadero, a single "offense" is good for a jail term).

The rules keep changing. A foreigner is permitted to host only one Cuban partner during his or her stay in a hotel. Multiple partners are permitted, however, in *casas particulares*. Woe betide any *casa particular* owner whose guest is discovered with an unrecorded Cuban in his or her room, let alone underage. In such cases, the owner of the *casa particular* can lose his or her license and receive a jail term.

Food and Drink

A standing joke in Cuba is: What are the three biggest failures of the Revolution? Breakfast, lunch, and dinner. The poor quality of food is a constant source of exasperation. Before the Revolution, Cuba boasted many world-class restaurants. Alas, after 1959 many of the middle- and upper-class clientele fled Cuba along with the restaurateurs and chefs, taking their knowledge and entrepreneurship with them. In 1967 all remaining restaurants were taken over by the state. It was downhill from there.

The blasé socialist attitude to dining, tough economic times, and general inefficiencies of the system is reflected in boring (usually identical) menus, abysmal standards (tablecloths rarely get washed), and lack of availability. Some of the lousiest service and dishes can be had for the most outrageous prices. And don't assume that a restaurant serving good dishes one day will do so the next. Restaurants rely upon the dysfunctional state distribution system to deliver daily supplies.

In the provinces eating can be a real challenge. Shortages are everywhere: A refrigerator in Cuba is called a *coco* because it has a hard shell on the outside and nothing but water inside. It can be a wearying experience trying to find somewhere with palatable food. After a while you'll be sick to death of fried chicken, *bocaditos,* and vegetables of dubious quality. As a foreign visitor, you're privileged to get the best that's available. Plan ahead. Stock up on sodas, biscuits, and other packaged snacks at CUC-only stores before setting out each day.

Most restaurants serve *criollo* (traditional Cuban) food, but only a few truly excel. Still, Cuba has begun to invest in culinary (and management) training, and many commendable restaurants have opened, with more being added. In general, the best meals are served in the upscale hotels and tend toward "continental" cuisine. Few places other than hotel restaurants serve breakfast; most offer variations on the same dreary buffets. The variety is usually limited, and presentation often leaves much to be desired. Top-class hotels under foreign management usually do a bit better.

Many restaurants crank up air-conditioning to freezing. Sometimes service is swift and friendly, sometimes protracted and surly. You're likely to be serenaded by musicians, who usually hit up any available tourists for a tip (or to sell a CD or cassette recording). Eating in Cuba doesn't present the health problems associated with many other destinations in Latin America. However, hygiene at streetside stalls is often questionable.

Peso Eateries

Pesos-only restaurants are for Cubans. Food availability tends to be hit or miss and the cuisine undistinguished at best. Many restaurants offer an *oferta especial* (special offer), usually a set meal of the day. Some sell *cajitas,* bargain-priced boxed take-out meals for a few pesos.

State-run *merenderos* and private roadside snack stalls—the staple for local dining—display their meager offerings in glass cases. A signboard indicates what's available, with items noted on strips that can be removed as particular items sell out. These stalls are an incredibly cheap way of appeasing your stomach with snacks. The "$" sign at peso eateries refers to Cuban pesos, not U.S. dollars.

The staple of street stalls is basic *pizzeta* (pizza), usually five pesos per slice. Pizzas are dismal by North American standards—usually a bland doughy base covered with a thin layer of tomato paste and a smattering of cheese and ham. Other staples are fatty pork *bocaditos, pan con queso* (basic but tasty cheese sandwich), *fritura de maíz* (corn fritters), and *pay de coco* (coco flan).

Paladares

Private restaurants—*paladares*—have been permitted since September 1994 to help resolve the food crisis. The word means "palate," and comes from the name of the restaurant of the character Raquel, a poor woman who makes her fortune cooking, in a popular Brazilian TV soap opera, *Vale Todo.* Here you can fill up for CUC5–15, usually with simple, albeit huge meals that usually include a salad and dessert. The owners often display an inventiveness and good service lacking in state restaurants. Some are open 24 hours. Not all owners are honorable, however; lack of a written menu listing prices can be a warning sign. Don't ever order food without seeing the menu, or the price is likely to be jacked up.

Paladares are fettered by onerous taxation and rigorous restrictions that are usually honored in the breach. For example, they are not allowed to sell shrimp or lobster (a state monopoly) or potatoes! Nonetheless, most do, so ask: It's easy enough to find a huge lobster meal for CUC10, including beer or soft drink, although such meals are often served in a second dining room hidden at the rear of the house. Beef is also illegal: The state maintains a monopoly and anyone found selling beef can face a lengthy spell in jail. Though relatives can assist, owners cannot hire salaried workers. And they may serve only up to 12 people at one seating (politically favored owners brazenly cram far more guests in than are legally allowed).

No new licenses for *paladares* have been issued since 2004, and inspections, the crippling monthly licensing fee, and taxes have put many out of business.

Taxi drivers and *jineteros* may offer recommendations. Their commission will be added to your bill.

Food Chains

There are as yet no McDonald's or KFCs in Cuba (except at the Guantánamo U.S. military base). However, the Cuban government has established a chain of tacky equivalents, including KFC-style fried-chicken joints called El Rápido. Food often runs out or is severely limited, and the quality is usually awful. Cuba's answer to McDonald's is Burgui, open 24 hours. Are you sure that's *meat*?

The government has done a better job with seafood. The Dimar chain has roadside restaurants in major cities selling seafood at fair prices. The Baturro chain of Spanish-style *bodegas* has outlets in major cities, with charming ambience and *criollo* fare of acceptable standard.

Self-Catering

For the average Cuban, shopping for food is a dismal activity. There are scant groceries and no roadside 7-Eleven equivalents. The state-run groceries, called *puestos,* where fresh produce—often of questionable quality—is sold, can make Westerners cringe. Cuba's best fruits and vegetables are exported for hard currency or turned into juices. Cheese and milk are precious scarcities. As a result, most Cubans rely on the black market.

Private farmers sell their excess produce at *mercados agropecuarios* (or *agros* for short). Every town has at least one *agro*. Carrots, cucumbers, chard, and pole beans are about the only vegetables available year-round; tomatoes disappear about May and reappear around November, when beets, eggplants, cabbages, and onions are also in season. Don't expect to find potatoes, the sale of which is restricted to the *libreta* (ration book). Chicken and pork are sold at *agros,* but not beef. The government-run *pescaderías especiales* sell fish and other seafood.

You can buy imported packaged and canned goods (at inflated prices) at CUC-only stores.

Cafés and Bakeries

Cuba has few sidewalk cafés, and most of the prerevolutionary *cafeterías* (coffee stands) and tea shops (*casas de té* or *casas de infusiones*) have vanished. Most cafés are really snack bars-cum-restaurants; there are few in the purist Parisian tradition, and as of yet, no Starbucks equivalents.

Most towns have bakeries serving sugary confections and Cuba's infamously horrible bread (served as buns or twisted rolls). Cuba's reputation for lousy bread pre-dates the Revolution ("Why can't the Cubans make decent bread?" Che Guevara is reported to have asked). To be fair, some hotels and restaurants serve excellent bread, and the situation has improved following the arrival of French expertise to run the Pain de Paris bakery chain (Monday and Tuesday are usually best; after that the selection diminishes). And Doña Neli bakeries and the Pan.Com snack restaurant chain, in most large cities, offer quality baked goods and sandwiches, respectively.

WHAT TO EAT
Cuban Dishes

Cuban food is mostly peasant fare, usually lacking in sauces and spices. *Cerdo* (pork) and *pollo* (chicken) are the two main protein staples, usually served with *frijoles negros* (rice and black beans) and *plátanos* (fried banana or plantain). *Cerdo asado* (succulent roast pork), *moros y cristianos* (Moors and Christians—rice and black beans), and *arroz congrí* (rice with red beans) are the most popular dishes. *Congrí oriental* is rice and red beans cooked together. *Frijoles negros dormidos* are black beans cooked and allowed to stand till the next day. Another national dish is *ajiaco* (hotchpotch), a stew of meats and vegetables.

Cubans love *pollo frito* (fried chicken) and *pollo asado* (grilled chicken), but above all love roast pork—with ham, pork is the most ubiquitous dish. Beef is virtually unknown outside the tourist restaurants, where filet mignon and prime rib are often on the menu, alongside *ropa vieja* (a braised shredded beef dish). Most steaks tend to be far below Western standards—often overcooked and fatty. Meat finds its way into snacks such as *empanadas de carne,* pies or flat pancakes enclosing meat morsels;

RESTAURANT SCAMS

The creativity that Cubans apply to wheedle dollars from foreigners has been turned into an art form in restaurants. Here are a few tricks:

Added Items: Bread and butter is often served without asking, but you are charged extra. Mineral water and other items often appear on your bill, even though you didn't ask for them, or they never arrived.

Á la Carte Be Damned!: The restaurant has a fixed price for a set menu but your bill charges separately for itemized dishes, which add up to considerably more. Beware menus that don't list prices.

Bait and Switch: You ask for a cola and are brought an imported Coca-Cola (CUC2) instead of Tropicola (CUC0.50), a perfectly adequate Cuban equivalent.

Commissions: The *jinetero* who leads you to a recommended *paladar* gets his commission added to your bill, even if he's merely picked you up outside the *paladar* you've already chosen.

Dollars or Pesos?: The "$" sign is used for both dollars and pesos. In a peso restaurant you may be told that the "$" prices are in dollars. Sometimes this is true. Even so, change may be given in pesos.

¡No Hay!: You're dying for a Hatuey beer but are told *ino hay!* (there is none). The waiter brings you a Heineken. Then you notice that Cubans are drinking Hatuey. You're then told that the Hatueys aren't cold, or that Heineken (which is more expensive) is better.

Overpricing: Compare the prices on your bill against those on the menu. One or two items on your bill may be inflated.

Variable Pricing: Always ask for a printed menu with prices. Some places charge according to how much they think you are worth. If you're dressed in Gucci, expect to pay accordingly.

---

and *picadillo,* a snack of spiced beef, onion, and tomato. Crumbled pork rinds find their way into *fufu,* mixed with cooked plantain, a popular dish in Oriente. And ham and cheese find their way into fish and stuffed inside steaks as *bistec uruguayo.*

Corvina (sea bass), *filet de emperador* (swordfish), and *pargo* (red snapper) are the most common fish. Fish dishes are often zealously overcooked, often with lots of bones for good measure. State restaurants charge CUC10–35 for lobster dishes.

Vegetables

Few Cubans understand the concept of vegetarianism. Since colonial days meat has been at the very center of Cuban cooking. Cubans disdain greens, preferring a sugar and starch-heavy diet. At last visit, Cuba had only *one* true vegetarian restaurant! Only a few restaurants serve vegetarian dishes, and servers in restaurants may tell you that a particular dish is vegetarian, even though it contains chunks of meat. Most beans are cooked in pork fat, and most *congrí* (rice with red beans) dishes contain meat. *"Protein vegetal"* translates as "soy product."

Fresh vegetables rarely find their way onto menus, other than in salads. *Ensaladas mixtas* (mixed salads) usually consist of a plate of lettuce or *pepinos* (cucumbers) and tomatoes (often served green, yet sweet) with oil and vinaigrette dressing. *Palmito,* the succulent heart of palm, is also common. Often you'll receive canned vegetables. Sometimes you'll receive shredded *col* (cabbage), often alone.

Plátano (plantain), a relative of the banana, is the main staple and almost always served fried, including as *tostones,* fried green plantains eaten as a snack. Yucca is also popular: it resembles a stringy potato in look, taste, and texture and is prepared and served like a potato in any number of ways. *Boniato* (sweet potato) and *malanga,* a bland root crop rich in starch, are used in many dishes.

Fruits

Elsewhere in the Caribbean, you can't drive around a bend without having someone selling a bunch of ripe bananas or handfuls of papayas, mangoes, or coconuts. Not so in Cuba. You'll pass fields of pineapples, melons, oranges, and grapefruits, but you won't have easy access to any outside of hotel restaurant buffets or farmers markets. Virtually the entire fruit harvest goes to produce fruit juice.

Local *mercado agropecuarios* sell well-known fruits such as papayas (which should be referred to as *fruta bomba;* in Cuba, "papaya" is a slang term for vagina), plus such lesser-known types as the furry *mamey colorado,* an oval, chocolate-brown fruit with a custardy texture and taste; the cylindrical, orange-colored *marañon,* or cashew-apple; the oval, coarse-skinned *zapote,* a sweet granular fruit most commonly found in Oriente; and the large, irregular-shaped *guanábana,* whose pulp is sweet and "soupy," with a hint of vanilla.

Coconuts are rare, except in sweets and around Baracoa, where coconut forms a base for the nation's only real regional cuisine.

Desserts

Cubans have a sweet tooth, as befits the land of sugar. They're especially fond of sickly sweet sponge cakes (*kek* or *ke*) covered in soft "shaving-foam" icing and sold for a few centavos at *panaderías* (bakeries). *Flan,* a caramel custard, is also popular (a variant is a delicious pudding called *natilla*), as is marmalade and cheese. Also try *tatianoff,* chocolate cake smothered with cream; *chu,* bite-size puff pastries stuffed with an almost-bitter cheesy meringue; and *churrizo,* deep-fried doughnut rings sold at every bakery and streetside stalls, where you can also buy *galletas,* sweet biscuits sold loose.

Coconut-based desserts include *coco quemado* (coconut pudding), *coco rallado y queso* (grated coconut with cheese in syrup), and the *cucurucho,* a regional specialty of Baracoa made of pressed coconut and sugar or honey.

Cubans are lovers of ice cream, sold at *heladerías* (ice-cream stores) and street stalls. Cubans use specific terms for different kinds of scoops. *Helado,* which means "ice cream," also means a single large scoop; two large scoops are called *jimagua;* several small scoops is an *ensalada;* and *sundae* is ice cream served with fruit.

DRINKING
Nonalcoholic Drinks

Water is not always reliable, and many water pipes are contaminated through decay. Stick to bottled mineral water, readily available carbonated (*con gas*) or non-carbonated (*sin gas*). Coca-Cola and Pepsi (or their Cuban-made equivalent, Tropicola), Fanta (or Cuban-made Najita), and other soft drinks are widely available. Malta is a popular nonalcoholic drink that resembles a dark English stout but tastes like root beer.

Far more thirst-quenching and energy-giving, however, are *guarapo,* fresh-squeezed sugarcane juice sold at roadside *guaraperías; prú,* a refreshing soft drink concocted from fruit, herbs, roots, and sugar; *batidos,* fruit shakes blended with milk and ice; and *refrescos naturales,* chilled fruit juices (avoid the sickly sweet water-based *refrescos* and *limonadas*).

No home visit is complete without being offered a *cafecito.* Cubans love their coffee espresso-style, thick and strong, served black in tiny cups and heavily sweetened. Much of Cuban domestic coffee has been adulterated—*café mezclado*—with other roasted products. Stick with export brands sold vacuum packed. *Café con leche* (coffee with milk) is served in tourist restaurants, usually at a ratio of 50:50, with hot milk. Don't confuse this with *café americano,* diluted Cuban coffee.

Alcoholic Drinks

Cuba makes several excellent German-style beers, usually served chilled. One of the best is Bucanero, a heavy-bodied lager that comes light or dark. Cristal (the most commonly available) is lighter. Harder-to-find brews include Hatuey, my favorite. Imported Heineken and Canadian and Mexican brands are sold in CUC stores and hotel bars. Clara is a rough-brewed beer for domestic consumption (typically one peso).

CUBA'S COCKTAILS

Cuba's cocktails are legendary. Many were created in the Roaring Twenties, such as the Mary Pickford (white rum, pineapple juice, grenadine, maraschino cherry, and ice), the *ron collins* (white rum, lemon juice, club soda, sugar, and ice, garnished with a cherry and orange slice), the *presidente* (white rum, vermouth, grenadine, and ice), and *Havana especial* (white rum, pineapple juice, lemon juice, maraschino, and ice).

Dark rums are used in cocktails such as the *mulatta* (rum, cocoa liqueur, lemon juice, and crushed ice), the almost forgotten *sacao* (rum, coconut water, and ice), and the Isla de Pinos (rum, grapefruit juice, and ice).

Refreshing and simple to make, these "big three" are the hit of any party:

CUBA LIBRE

Who can resist the killer kick of a rum and Coke? Supposedly, the simple concoction was named more than a century ago after the war cry of the independence army: "Free Cuba!"

The Perfect Cuba Libre: Place ice cubes in a tall glass, then pour in 2 ounces of seven-year-old Havana Club *añejo* rum. Fill with Coca-Cola, topped off with 1 ounce of lemon juice. Decorate the rim with a slice of lemon. Serve with a stirrer.

DAIQUIRI

The daiquiri is named for a Cuban hamlet 16 miles east of Santiago de Cuba, near a copper mine where the mining firm's chief engineer, Jennings S. Cox, first created the now world-famous cocktail that Hemingway immortalized in his novels. Cox had arrived in 1898, shortly after the Spanish-American War, to find workers at the mines anxious about putatively malarial drinking water. Cox added a heartening tot of local Bacardí rum to boiled water, then decided to give his mixture added snap and smoothness by introducing lime juice and sugar.

The concoction was soon duplicated, and within no time had moved on to conquer every high-life watering hole in Havana. It is still most notably associated with El Floridita and Hemingway's immortal words: *"Mi mojito en La Bodeguita, mi daiquirí en El Floridita."*

Shaved ice, which gave the drink its final touch of enchantment, was added by Constante Ribailagua, El Floridita's bartender, in the 1920s. The frozen daiquiris, "the great ones that Constante made," wrote Hemingway, "had no taste of alcohol and felt, as you drank them, the way downhill glacier skiing feels running through powder snow and, after the sixth and eighth, felt like downhill glacier skiing feels when you are running unroped."

A daiquiri should include all of Cox's original ingredients (minus the water, of course). It may be shaken and strained, or frappéed to a loose sherbet in a blender and served in a cocktail glass or poured over the rocks in an old-fashioned glass. The "Papa Special," which Constante made for Hemingway, contained a double dose of rum, no sugar, and a half ounce of grapefruit juice.

The Perfect Daiquiri: In an electric blender, pour half a tablespoon of sugar, the juice of half a lemon, and 1.5 ounces of white rum. Serve semi-frozen blended with ice (or on the rocks) in a tall martini glass with a maraschino cherry.

MOJITO

The *mojito* supposedly originated as a lowly drink favored by slaves. It is now considered the classic drink of Cuba, favored by tourists today as it has been since the 1940s, when Ángel Martínez, then owner of La Bodeguita del Medio, hit upon the idea of giving credit to writers, who popped in to sup, establishing a bohemian scene that promoted the bar and its drink.

The Perfect *Mojito*: With a stirrer, mix half a tablespoon of sugar and the juice of half a lime in an eight-inch highball glass. Add a sprig of yerba buena (mint), crushing the stalk to release the juice; two ice cubes; and 1.5 ounces of Havana Club Light Dry Cuban rum. Fill with soda water, add a small splash of angostura, then dress with a mint sprig. *¡Salud!*

© CHRISTOPHER P. BAKER

enjoying a beer and cigar at the Taberna de la Muralla, Plaza Vieja, Havana

Most villages have *cervecerías* (beer dispensaries) for the hoi polloi; often these are roadside dispensers on wheels where you can buy beer in paper cups or bottles sawed in half for a few centavos.

About one dozen Cuban rum distilleries produce some 60 brands of rum. They vary widely—the worst can taste like paint thinner. Cuban rums resemble Bacardi rums, not surprisingly, as several factories were originally owned by the Bacardí family. Each brand generally has three types of rum: clear "white rum," labeled *carta blanca,* which is aged three years (about CUC5 a 0.75 liter bottle); the more asserting "golden rum," labeled *dorado* or *carta oro,* aged five years (about CUC6); and *añejo,* aged seven years (CUC10 or more). The best in all categories are Havana Club's rums, topped only by Matusalem Añejo Superior (described by a panel of tasting experts as showing "a distinctive Scotch whisky-like character, with peaty and smoky aromas and flavors accented by orange-peel notes dry on the palate and long in the finish"). A few limited-production rums, such as Ron Santiago 45 Aniversario and the 15-year-old Havana Club Gran Reserva, approach the harmony and finesse of fine Cognacs.

Golden and aged rums are best enjoyed straight. White rum is ideal for cocktails such as a piña colada (rum, pineapple juice, coconut cream, and crushed ice) and, most notably, the daiquiri and the *mojito*—both favorites of Ernest Hemingway, who helped launch both drinks to world fame.

Impecunious Cubans drink *tragos* (shots) of *aguardiente*—cheap, overproof white rum. Beware bottles of rum sold on the street—it may be bootleg crap.

Cuba's rum manufacturers also make liqueurs, including from coffee, crème de menthe, cocoa, guava, lemon, pineapple, and other fruits. Certain regions are known for unique liqueurs, such as *guayabita,* a drink made from rum and guava exclusive to Pinar del Río.

Imported South American, French, and Californian wines (*vinos*) are widely available, although costly and usually "disturbed" by poor storage. Avoid the local and truly terrible Soroa brand, made of unsophisticated Italian wine blended with local grapes from Soroa, Pinar del Río.

Tips for Travelers

PERSONAL CONDUCT

Cubans are respectful and courteous, with a deep sense of integrity. You can ease your way considerably by being courteous and patient. Always greet your host with *"¡Buenos días!"* ("Good morning!") or *"¡Buenas tardes!"* ("Good afternoon!"). And never neglect to say *"gracias"* ("thank you"). Topless sunbathing is tolerated at some tourist resorts, and nude bathing is allowed only on Cayo Largo.

Cubans are extremely hygienic and have a natural prejudice against anyone who ignores personal hygiene.

Smoking is ostensibly prohibited in theaters, stores, buses, taxis, restaurants, and enclosed public areas, but the prohibition is rarely enforced.

Respect the natural environment: Take only photographs, leave only footprints.

ACCESS FOR TRAVELERS WITH DISABILITIES

Cubans go out of their way to assist travelers with disabilities, although few allowances have been made in infrastructure.

In the United States, the **Society for Accessible Travel & Hospitality** (347 5th Ave. #610, New York, NY 10016, tel. 212/447-7284, www.sath.org) and the **American Foundation for the Blind** (11 Penn Plaza #300, New York, NY 10001, tel. 212/502-7600 or 800/232-5463, www.afb.org) are good resources, as is Cuba's **Asociación Cubana de Limitados Físicos y Motores** (Cuban Association for Physically & Motor Disabled People, ACLIFIM, Calle 6 #106, e/ 1ra y 3ra, Havana, tel. 07/202-5070, fax 07/204-8787, www.aclifim.sld.cu).

TRAVELING WITH CHILDREN

Cubans adore children and will dote on yours. Children under the age of two travel free on airlines; children between 2 and 12 are offered special discounts. Children under 16 usually stay free with parents at hotels, although an extra-bed rate may be charged. Children under 12 normally get free (or half-price) entry to museums.

Children's items such as diapers (nappies) and baby foods are scarce in Cuba. Bring cotton swabs, diapers, Band-Aids, baby foods, and a small first-aid kit with any necessary medicines for your child. Children's car seats are not offered in rental cars.

The equivalent of the Boy and Girl Scouts and Girl Guides is the **Pioneros José Martí** (Calle F #352, Vedado, Havana, tel. 07/832-5292, www.somosjovenes.cu), which has chapters throughout the country. Having your children interact would be a fascinating education.

MALE TRAVELERS

The average male visitor soon discovers that Cuban woman have an open attitude towards sexuality. They are also much more aggressive than foreign men may be used to, displaying little equivocation.

Romantic liaisons require prudence. Petty robbery (your paramour steals your sunglasses or rifles your wallet while you take a shower) is common. Muggings by accomplices are a rare possibility, and in 2002 a ring of high-class prostitutes robbed tourists by drugging their drinks. Several tourists have even been murdered during sexual encounters.

Men in "sensitive" occupations (e.g., journalists) should be aware that the femme fatale who sweeps you off your feet may be in the employ of Cuba's state security.

WOMEN TRAVELING ALONE

Cuban men treat women with great respect and, for the most part, as equals. True, Cuba remains a macho society, but post-revolutionary political correctness is everywhere. Sexual assault of women is almost unheard of. If you do welcome the amorous overtures of men, Cuba is heaven. The art of gentle seduction is to Cuban men a kind of national pastime—a sport and a trial of manhood. They will hiss like serpents in appreciation, and call out *piropos*—affectionate and lyrical epithets. Take effusions of love with a grain of salt; while swearing eternal devotion, your Don Juan may conveniently forget to mention he's married. While the affection may be genuine, you are assuredly the moneybags in the relationship. Plenty of Cuban men earn their living giving pleasure to foreign women looking for love beneath the palms or, like their female counterparts, taking advantage of such an opportunity when it arises.

If you're not interested, pretend not to notice advances and avoid eye contact.

Cuba's **Federación de Mujeres Cubanas** (Cuban Women's Federation, Galiano #264, e/ Neptuno y Concordia, Havana, tel. 07/862-4905, www.mujeres.co.cu) is a useful resource. It publishes **Mujeres**, a women's magazine.

STUDENT AND YOUTH TRAVELERS

Foreign students with the **International Student Identity Card** (ISIC) or similar student ID receive discounts to many museums. You can obtain an ISIC at any student union, or in the United States from the **Council on International Educational Exchange** (CIEE, 300 Fore St., Portland, ME 04101, tel. 207/553-4000, www.ciee.org), and in Canada from **Travel Cuts** (tel. 866/246-9762, www.travelcuts.com).

The **Federación Estudiantil Universitario** (Calle 23, esq. H, Vedado, Havana, tel. 07/832-4646, www.almamater.cu) is Cuba's national student federation.

SENIOR TRAVELERS

Cuba honors senior citizens, who receive discounted entry to museums and other sights. This may apply to foreign seniors in a few instances.

A useful resource is the **American Association of Retired Persons** (AARP, 601 E St. NW, Washington, DC 20049, tel. 888/687-2277, www.aarp.org).

Canadian company **ElderTreks** (597 Markham St., Toronto, ON M6G 2L7, tel. 416/588-5000 or 800/741-7956, U.K. tel. 0808/234-1714, www.eldertreks.com) offers 13-day trips to Cuba.

GAY AND LESBIAN TRAVELERS

Cuba is schizophrenic when it comes to homosexuality. The situation blows hot and cold and discrimination still exists, despite recent positive strides. (For example, two people of the same gender may now share the same bed in *casas particulares,* but gay organizations and clubs are illegal.)

Useful resources include the **International Gay & Lesbian Travel Association** (915 Middle River Dr. #306, Fort Lauderdale, FL 33304, tel. 954/630-1637, www.iglta.org).

Coda Tours (12794 Forest Hill Blvd., Suite 1A, W. Palm Beach, FL 33414, tel. 561/791-9890 or 888/677-2632, www.coda-tours.com) has offered gay tours to Cuba in the past.

Cuba's **Centro Nacional de Educación Sexual** (Calle 10 #460, Vedado, Havana, tel. 07/832-5464, www.cenesex.sld.cu) advances gay rights.

GETTING MARRIED IN CUBA

It's fairly easy to get married in Cuba if you have the correct documents in place. Civil marriages are handled by the **Bufete Internacional** (5ta Av. #16202, esq. 162, Rpto. Flores, Havana, tel. 07/273-6824, fax 07/204-6750, www.bufeteinternacional.cu), the "International Lawyer's Office," which has an office in most major cities. The marriage certificate costs CUC525, plus there are other expenses. Foreigners need to produce their birth certificate, proof of marital status if single, and a divorce certificate (if relevant). These need to be translated into Spanish, and authenticated by the Cuban consulate in the country in which they were issued. Marriages in Cuba are recognized in the United States.

Cubanacan (www.cubanacan.cu) offers wedding packages at certain resorts.

Health and Safety

BEFORE YOU GO

Dental and medical checkups are advisable before departing home. Take along any medications; keep prescription drugs in their original bottles to avoid suspicion at customs. I had my spectacles stolen in Cuba—a reminder to take a spare pair (or at least a prescription for eyewear). If you suffer from a debilitating health problem, wear a medical alert bracelet.

A basic health kit should include alcohol swabs and medicinal alcohol, antiseptic cream, Band-Aids, aspirin, diarrhea medication, sunburn remedy, antifungal foot powder, antihistamine, surgical tape, bandages and gauze, and scissors.

Information on health concerns can be answered in advance of travel by the **Department of State Citizens Emergency Center** (tel. 888/407-4747 or 202/501-4444 from overseas, http://travel.state.gov), the **Centers for Disease Control and Prevention** (tel. 800/232-4636, www.cdc.gov), and the **International Association for Medical Assistance to Travellers** (tel. 716/754-4883, www.iamat.org), with offices worldwide.

Travel Insurance

Travel insurance is recommended. Travel agencies can sell you travelers' health, baggage, and trip cancellation insurance. Check to see if policies cover expenses in Cuba.

Swiss-based **Assist-Card** (tel. 305/381-9959 or 800/874-2223 in the U.S., www.assist-card.com, tel. 07/867-1315 in Cuba, assistcuba@assist-card.com) offers travel assistance with everything from tracking lost luggage to emergency transfers and repatriation. You can obtain insurance in Cuba through **Asistur** (Prado #212, e/ Trocadero y Colón, Habana Vieja, tel. 07/866-4499 or 07/866-8527, www.asistur.cu, Mon.–Fri. 9 A.M.–5 P.M.), which represents about 160 insurance companies in 40 countries; **Aseguradora del Turismo La Isla, S.A.** (Calle 14 #301, esq. 3ra Av., Miramar, tel. 07/204-7490, fax 07/204-7494, www.cuba.cu/laisla); and **ESEN** (Calle 5ta #306, e/ C y D, Vedado, tel. 07/832-2508).

Vaccinations

No vaccinations are required to enter Cuba unless you are arriving from areas of cholera and yellow fever infection. Epidemic diseases have mostly been eradicated throughout the country. However, viral meningitis and dengue fever occasionally break out.

Consult your physician for recommended vaccinations. Consider vaccinations against tetanus and infectious hepatitis.

MEDICAL SERVICES

Sanitary standards in Cuba are generally good. As long as you take appropriate precautions and use common sense, you're not likely to incur a serious illness or disease. Cuba's much-vaunted public health system faces severe shortages of medicines and equipment; with few exceptions, facilities and standards are not up to those of North America or northern Europe.

Local pharmacies are meagerly stocked and medicines are hard to find away from key tourist spots. *Turnos regulares* pharmacies are open 8 A.M.–5 P.M.; *turnos permanentes*—also known as *pilotos*—are open 24 hours.

In 2009, Cuba became paranoid about swine flu (H1N1 virus), and several foreigners report having been forcibly hospitalized (for up to four days!) for tests after showing flu-like symptoms.

Facilities for Foreigners

Foreigners receive special treatment through **Servimed** (tel. 07/204-4811, www.servimed-cuba.com), a division of **Cubanacán Turismo y Salud** (Av. 43 #1418, esq. 18, Miramar, Havana, tel. 07/204-4811, www.cubanacan.cu), which promotes health tourism, from "stress breaks" to advanced treatments such as eye, open-heart, and plastic surgery—even breast implants are available.

Most major cities and resort destinations

have 24-hour international clinics (*clínicas internacionales*) staffed by English-speaking doctors and nurses, plus foreigners-only international pharmacies (*farmacias internacionales*) stocked with Western pharmaceuticals. Larger tourist hotels also have nurses on duty and doctors on call, and some have pharmacies. **Óptica Miramar** (7ma Av., e/ 24 y 26, Miramar, tel. 07/204-2269, direccion@opticam.cha.cyt.cu) provides optician services and sells contact lenses and eyeglasses. It has outlets nationwide. See www.servimedcuba.com/es/directorio.php for a complete list of Servimed facilities.

Pay in CUC or by credit card (unless issued on a U.S. bank). Get a receipt with which to make an insurance claim once you return home. You can call your insurance company in advance, however, of medical treatment. If approved, the company can pay direct to Asistur (Prado #208, Havana, tel. 07/866-4499, www.asistur.cu), which then pays the Cuban clinic.

A Canadian company, **Choice Medical Services** (tel. 866/672-6284, www.choice-medicalservices.com), assists North Americans with receiving low-cost health care in Cuba, typically at 80 percent saving over costs in the United States. However, U.S. citizens should note that even if visiting Cuba legally, payment for "nonemergency medical services" is prohibited.

Medical Evacuation

Uncle Sam has deemed that even U.S. emergency evacuation services cannot fly to Cuba to evacuate U.S. citizens without a license from the Treasury Department. The rules keep changing, so it's worth checking the latest situation with such companies as **Traveler's Emergency Network** (tel. 800/275-4836, www.tenweb.com) and **International SOS Assistance** (tel. 215/942-8000, www.internationalsos.com), which provide worldwide ground and air evacuation.

In Cuba, insurance packages sold by **Aseguradora del Turismo La Isla** (Calle 14 #301, esq. 3ra Av., Miramar, tel. 07/204-7490, fax 07/204-7494, www.cuba.cu/laisla)

include US$5,000 coverage for medical evacuation.

Swiss-based **Assist-Card** (tel. 305/381-9959 or 800/874-2223 in the U.S., www.assist-card.com, tel. 07/867-1315 in Cuba) provides emergency services in Cuba, even for U.S. citizens, including emergency evacuation. It works in conjunction with **Asistur** (Prado #212, e/ Trocadero y Colón, Habana Vieja, tel. 07/866-4499 or 07/866-8527, www.asistur.cu, Mon.–Fri. 9 A.M.–5 P.M.).

HEALTH PROBLEMS

Cuba is a tropical country and the health hazards are many: filthy public fixtures, garbage rotting in the streets, polluted watercourses, broken sewer pipes, holes in sidewalks, dilapidated buildings, and so on. In addition, molds, fungus, and bacteria thrive. The slightest scratch can fester quickly. Treat promptly with antiseptic and keep any wounds clean.

Intestinal Problems

Cuba's tap water is questionable. Drink bottled water, which is widely available. Don't brush your teeth using suspect water. Milk is pasteurized, and dairy products in Cuba are usually safe.

Diarrhea: The change in diet may briefly cause diarrhea or constipation. Most cases of diarrhea are caused by microbial bowel infections resulting from contaminated food. Don't eat uncooked fish or shellfish, uncooked vegetables, unwashed salads, or unpeeled fruit. Diarrhea is usually temporary, and many doctors recommend letting it run its course. If that's not preferable, medicate with Lomotil or similar antidiarrheal product. Drink lots of liquid. Avoid alcohol and milk. If conditions don't improve after three days, seek medical help.

Dysentery: Diarrhea accompanied by severe abdominal pain, blood in your stool, and fever requires immediate medical diagnosis. Tetracycline or ampicillin is normally used to cure bacillary dysentery. More complex treatment is required for amoebic dysentery.

Other Infections: Giardiasis, acquired from infected water, causes diarrhea, bloating, persistent indigestion, and weight loss. Intestinal worms can be contracted by walking barefoot on infested beaches, grass, or ground. Hepatitis A can be contracted through unhygienic foods or contaminated water (salads and unpeeled fruits are major culprits). The main symptoms are stomach pains, loss of appetite, yellowing skin and eyes, and extreme tiredness. The much rarer hepatitis B is usually contracted through unclean needles, blood transfusions, or unprotected sex.

Sunburn and Skin Problems

The tropical sun can burn even through light clothing or shade. Use a suncream or sunblock of at least SPF 15. Bring sunscreen; it's not readily available beyond beach resorts in Cuba. Wear a wide-brimmed hat. Calamine lotion and aloe gel will soothe light burns; for more serious burns, use steroid creams.

Sun glare can cause conjunctivitis; wear sunglasses. Prickly heat is an itchy rash, normally caused by clothing that is too tight or in need of washing; this and athlete's foot (a fungal infection) are best treated by airing the skin and washing your clothes. Ringworm, another fungal infection, shows up as a ring, most commonly on the scalp and groin; it's treated with over-the-counter ointments.

Dehydration and Heat Problems

The tropical humidity and heat can sap your body fluids like blotting paper. Leg cramps, exhaustion, dizziness, and headaches are signs of dehydration. Drink lots of water. Avoid alcohol.

Excessive exposure to too much heat can cause potentially fatal heat stroke. Excessive sweating, extreme headaches, and disorientation leading to possible convulsions and delirium are symptoms. Emergency medical care is essential.

The common cold (*gripe,* pronounced GREE-pay, or *catarro cubano*) is a pandemic among Cubans, often brought on by the debilitating effects of constantly shifting from overly air-conditioned interiors to sultry outdoor heat.

Critters

Snakes (*culebras*) are common in Cuba; they're non-venomous. Scorpions (*alacranes*) also exist; their venom can cause nausea and fever but is not usually serious. In the wild, watch where you're treading or putting your hands. Crocodiles are a serious threat in swampy coastal areas and estuaries; don't swim in rivers! Most areas inhabited by crocodiles, such as the Zapata swamps, are off-limits to foreigners without guides.

Mosquitoes abound. Repellent sprays and lotions are a must by day for many areas. Citronella candles, electric fans, and mosquito coils (*espirales,* which are rarely sold in Cuba) help keep mosquitoes at bay at night. Bites can easily become infected in the tropics; avoid scratching! Treat with antiseptics or antibiotics. Antihistamine and hydrocortisone can help relieve itching.

Malaria isn't present in Cuba. However, mosquitoes *do* transmit **dengue fever,** which *is* present. Its symptoms are similar to those for malaria, with severe headaches and high fever and, unlike malaria, additional severe pain in the joints, for which it is sometimes called "breaking bones disease." It is not recurring. There is no cure; dengue fever must run its course. The illness can be fatal (death usually results from internal hemorrhaging).

Chiggers (*coloradillas*) inhabit tall grasslands. Their bites itch like hell. Nail polish apparently works (over the bites, not on the nails) by suffocating the beasts.

Tiny, irritating *jejenes* (known worldwide as "no-see-ums"), sand flies about the size of a pinpoint, inhabit beaches and marshy coastal areas. This nuisance is active only around dawn and dusk, when you should avoid the beach. They are not fazed by bug repellent, but Avon's Skin-So-Soft supposedly works.

Jellyfish (*agua mala*) are common along the Atlantic shore, especially in winter and spring. They can give a painful, even dangerous, welt that leaves a permanent scar. Dousing in vinegar can help neutralize the stingers, while calamine and antihistamines should be used to soothe the pain. In Caribbean waters, a microscopic mollusk that locals call *caribe* can induce all manner of illnesses, from diarrhea and severe fever to itching. It, too, is more frequent in winter.

Sea urchins (*erizos*) are common beneath the inshore water line and around coral reefs. These softball-size creatures are surrounded by long spines that will pierce your skin and break off if you touch or step on them. Excruciatingly painful! You'll have to extract the spines.

Rabies, though rare in Cuba, can be contracted through the bite of an infected animal. It's always fatal unless treated.

Sexually Transmitted Diseases

Cubans are promiscuous, and sexually transmitted diseases are common, although the risk of contracting AIDS in Cuba is extremely low (the rate of infection is among the world's lowest). Use condoms (*preservativos*), widely available in Cuba.

Travel, hot climates, and a change of diet or health regimen can play havoc with your body, leading to yeast and other infections. For women, a douche of diluted vinegar or lemon juice can help alleviate yeast infections. Loose, cotton underwear may help prevent infections such as candida, typified by itching and a white, cheesy discharge. A foul-smelling discharge accompanied by a burning sensation may be trichomoniasis, usually caught through intercourse.

SAFETY
Crime and Hustling

All the negative media hype sponsored by Washington has left many people with a false impression that Cuba is unsafe. Far from it. In rural areas many residents still say they can hardly remember the last time a crime was committed. However, the material hardships of Cubans combined with the influx of wealthy tourists *has* fostered crime. Pickpockets (*carteristas*) and purse slashers work the streets and buses. Chambermaids pilfer items from guests' luggage. Theft from luggage occurs at the airport, where bogus tour operators and taxi drivers also prey on tourists (the British embassy also reports attempted robberies from vehicles on the Havana airport road). Muggings have

CUBA'S WAR ON AIDS

Cuba has one of the world's most aggressive and successful campaigns against AIDS. The World Health Organization (WHO) and the Pan-American Health Organization have praised as exemplary Cuba's AIDS surveillance system and prevention program. The program has stemmed an epidemic that rages only 50 miles away in Haiti and kept the spread of the disease to a level that no other country in the Americas can equal. As of January 2008, about 1,582 people had died of AIDS in Cuba, which has an adult prevalence rate of 0.1 percent, the lowest in the Americas. Although in Cuba in the early years it was predominantly a heterosexual disease, today about 70 percent of AIDS sufferers are gay men (the number of HIV positive cases has tripled since 1998).

Cuba's unique response to the worldwide epidemic that began in the early 1980s was to initiate mass testing of the population and a "mandatory quarantine" of everyone testing positive. Twelve AIDS sanatoriums were developed throughout the island. By 1994, when the policies of mandatory testing and confinement were ended, about 98 percent of the adult population had been tested. Voluntary testing continues. An outpatient program was implemented so that sufferers could continue to lead a normal life; residents live in small houses or apartments, alone or as couples.

Cuba's biogenetic engineering industry has been at the forefront of research for an AIDS vaccine and cure.

The **Cuba AIDS Project** (P.O. Box 234, Mount Freedom, NJ 07970, tel. 973/462-0702, www.cubaaidsproject.com) delivers medications to Cuba.

escalated. Car-related crime is on the increase, notably by bogus hitchhikers and staged punctures (if you get a puncture, drive on several kilometers, preferably to a town, before stopping). Sexual assault appears to be rare.

There have been several unreported murders of tourists in recent years. Most, but not all, have involved sexual relations between foreigners and Cubans. *Never* go to a *casa clandestina* (an illegal room rental, usually rented by the hour), and *always* check a Cuban partner's *carnet* (ID) and leave a copy with someone you trust if possible.

Most crime is opportunistic snatch-and-grab. Caution is required when walking city streets (especially at night) and in crowded places. If you sense yourself being squeezed or jostled, elbow your way out of there immediately.

The **U.S. State Department** (888/407-4747, or 202/501-4444 from overseas, www.travel.state.gov) and **British Foreign and Commonwealth Office** (tel. 020/7008-1500, from overseas 020/7008-0210, www.fco.gov.uk) publish travel advisories.

HUSTLING AND SCAMS

Your biggest problem will probably be hustling by *jineteros* (street hustlers), plus scams pulled by restaurants, hotels, and other tourist entities. And the *consumo mínimo* charge in many bars and nightclubs is an invitation to fleece you. Be prepared for charges for things you didn't consume or which didn't materialize, and for higher charges than you were quoted. Insist on an itemized bill at restaurants, add it up diligently, and count your change.

Car rental companies and tour agencies (and their employees) are adept at scams. You pay for a deluxe hotel, say, on a package to Cayo Largo, but are told when you arrive that the hotel in question doesn't honor such packages. You're then fobbed off to the cheapest hotel. When you return to Havana to request a refund, the documents relating to your trip can't be found. Rarely is there a manager available, and usually they say there's nothing that can be done. If the scam amounts to outright theft, take the staffer's name and threaten to report

him or her to the head office and police. Don't pay cash in such conditions. Pay with a credit card and challenge the bill. Or simply refuse to pay. Good luck! Once it has your money, the Cuban government is not about to give refunds under virtually any condition.

COMMON-SENSE PRECAUTIONS

Make photocopies of all important documents. Carry the photocopies with you, and leave the originals along with your other valuables in the hotel safe. Prepare an "emergency kit" to tide you over if your wallet gets stolen.

Never carry more cash than you need for the day. Never carry your wallet in your back pocket; wear a secure money belt. Spread your money around your person. Thread fanny pack straps through the belt loops of your pants, and never wear your purse or camera loosely slung over your shoulder. Wear an inexpensive watch. Don't flaunt jewelry. Be wary when cashing money at a bank. Do *not* deal with *jineteros*. Insist that credit card imprints are made in your presence. And make sure any imprints incorrectly completed are torn up; destroy the carbons yourself.

JINETERISMO

Jineteros (male hustlers) and *jineteras* (females who trade sex for money) are a persistent presence in tourist zones, where they pester foreigners like flies around fish.

Jineteros try to sell you cigars, tout places to stay or eat, or even a good time with their sisters. In provincial cities, touts on bicycles descend on tourists at traffic lights and will trail you through town, sometimes merely in the hope that you'll give them money to go away. If you're a female tourist, expect to be hustled by Cuban males ingratiating themselves as potential boyfriends.

The best defense is to completely ignore them. Don't say a word. Don't look them in the eye. Don't even acknowledge their presence. Just keep walking.

BITE YOUR TONGUE!

As Pico Iyer wrote in *Cuba and the Night:* "The whole city is a circle of informers." Cubans are a paranoid people, never sure who might be a *chivato,* a finger pointer for the CDR or MININT, the much-loathed Ministry of the Interior. In this regard, Cuba doesn't seem to have changed much since the 1930s, when Hemingway told Arnold Samuelson, "Don't trust anybody. That fellow might have been a government spy trying to get you in bad. You can never tell who they are."

Many visitors take the fact that you never hear a bad word about the system or the Bearded One expressed in public as a tacit expression that Cubans overwhelmingly support their government. In fact, no one in his or her right mind would dare to criticize the government or the Castros in public. With so many people employed as informers, there is a culture of mistrust summed up in the Cuban saying: "You can swim safely if you keep your mouth closed." If you open your mouth, you might swallow water and drown.

Sometimes a diatribe against the government (usually offered in hushed tones) will end in mid-stream as the speaker taps his two fore-fingers on his opposite shoulder, signifying the presence of a member of State Security. Hence, Cubans have developed a cryptic, elliptical way of talking where nuance and meaning are hidden from casual tourists.

Even foreigners are not above surreptitious surveillance; those in sensitive occupations, such as embassy staff, are *muy bien acompañados* (well accompanied) by agents of State Security, sometimes identifiable by their imitation Lacoste shirts or *guayaberas,* pressed pants or stonewashed jeans, mirrored glasses, and well-groomed moustaches. Foreign journalists may even be assigned specific hotel rooms (which may be bugged) while journalists staying in *casas particulares* are sure to be kept an eye on. Be wary, too, of the beautiful *cubana* or *cubano* too eager to be your lover and of what you say to drivers of tourist taxis or to hotel staff, as they may report to the General Directorate for State Security (DGSE).

Fortunately, tourists are free to roam wherever they wish without hindrance or a need to look over their shoulder. That said, nay-saying the Revolution or you-know-who in public can swiftly land you in trouble. Cuban authorities have zero tolerance for foreigners who become involved in political activity, especially with known dissidents. (The Cuban government now looks with suspicion on U.S. travelers entering on religious or humanitarian licenses.) In some cases, individuals have been detained in Cuba or deported without any reason given. Be circumspect about what you say, especially to anyone you do not implicitly trust. Avoid making inflammatory or derogatory comments; otherwise you could well find yourself on the next plane home.

Never leave items unattended. Always keep an eye on your luggage on public transportation. Don't carry more luggage than you can adequately manage. And have a lock for each luggage item. Always keep purses fully zipped and luggage locked, even in your hotel room. Don't leave *anything* within reach of an open window or in your car, which should always be parked in a secure area overnight.

Drugs

Few countries are so drug free. You may occasionally come across homegrown marijuana, but serious drug use is unknown in Cuba. Nonetheless, drug use has increased in recent years with the blossoming of tourism and as Colombian and Jamaican drug lords take advantage of Cuba's remote, scattered cays to make transshipments en route to the United States. In January 2003, the Cuban government initiated a nationwide campaign against possession and trafficking in drugs. Draconian laws are strictly enforced and foreigners receive no special favors. Cuban law allows for the death penalty, and sentences in excess of 20 years are the norm.

Traffic and Pedestrians

Be wary when crossing streets. Stand well away from the curb—especially on corners, where buses often mount the sidewalk. Watch your step! Sidewalks are full of gaping potholes and tilted curbstones. And drive with extreme caution. Driving in Cuba presents unique dangers, from treacherous potholes and wayward bicyclists to cattle and ox-drawn carts wandering across four-lane freeways. Use extra caution when passing tractors and trucks, which without warning tend to make sweeping turns across the road.

Racial Discrimination

Despite all the hype about Cuba being a color-blind society, racial discrimination still exists. Non-white tourists can expect to be mistaken for Cubans and hassled on the streets by police requesting ID. Likewise, tourists of non-European descent are more likely to be stopped at the entrances to hotel lobbies and other tourist venues. Mixed-race couples can expect to draw unwanted attention from the police.

Officialdom

Cuba has an insufferable bureaucracy, and working with government entities can be a perplexing and frustrating endeavor. Very few people have the power to say, "Yes," but everyone is allowed to say, "No!" Finding the person who can say "Yes" is the key. Logic and ranting get you nowhere. Charm, *piropos* (witty compliments), or a gift of chocolate works better.

The Policía Revolucionario Nacional (National Revolutionary Police, or PNR) is a branch of the Ministry of the Interior (MININT) and a major role is to enforce revolutionary purity. Uniformed police officers also perform the same functions as in Western countries, although with far less professionalism than you may be used to in the United States or Europe. Cuban police officers tend to treat foreigners with disdain (they're trained to be paranoid about Western imperialists). Never attempt to photograph police or military without their permission.

If a police officer wants to search you, insist on it being done in front of a neutral witness—*"solamente con testigos."* If at all possible, do *not* allow an official to confiscate your passport. Tell as little as circumspection dictates—unlike priests, policemen rarely offer absolution for confessions. If a police officer asks for money, get name and badge number and file a complaint with the Ministry of Foreign Relations.

If Trouble Strikes

In emergencies, call:

- 104 for an ambulance
- 105 for fire
- 106 for police

If things turn dire, contact **Asistur** (Prado #212, e/ Trocadero y Colón, Habana Vieja, tel. 07/866-4499 or 866-8527, www.asistur.cu, Mon.–Fri. 9 A.M.–5 P.M.), which provides assistance to tourists in trouble. It has a 24-hour "alarm center," plus outlets in Camagüey, Ciego de Ávila, Cienfuegos, Guardalavaca, Santiago de Cuba, and Varadero. You should also contact your embassy or consulate. It can't get you out of jail, but can help locate a lawyer or arrange for funds (the U.S. State Department hates to admit this, but even U.S. citizens in Cuba can request help in an emergency).

If you're robbed, immediately file a police report with the **Policía Revolucionaria Nacional** (PNR, in Havana, Calle Picota, e/ Leonor Pérez y San Isidro, tel. 07/867-0496 or 07/862-0116). You'll receive a statement (*denuncia*) for insurance purposes. Proceedings can take hours (readers report Kafkaesque experiences). If you're involved in a car accident, call the ***tránsitos*** (transit police, tel. 07/862-0116 in Havana, 106 outside Havana).

If you're charged with a crime, request that a representative of your embassy be present, and that any deposition be made in front of an independent witness (*testigo*).

There are reports of Cuban police jailing victims of passport theft while the crime and

AREA CODES AND EMERGENCY NUMBERS

Cuba is slowly introducing uniform numbers for emergencies.

	AREA CODE	AMBULANCE	FIRE	POLICE
HAVANA	07	104	105	106
HAVANA PROVINCE	047			
Artemisa	047	36-2597	105	106
Batabanó	047	58-5335	105	106
San Antonio de los Baños	047	38-2781	105	106
CAMAGÜEY	032	104	105	106
CIEGO DE ÁVILA	033	104	105	106
Cayo Coco	033	104	30-9102	30-8107
CIENFUEGOS	043	104	105	106
GRANMA	023	104	105	106
Pilón	023	104	105	59-4493
GUANTÁNAMO	021	104	105	106
HOLGUÍN	024	104	105	106
Banes	024	80-3798	105	106
ISLA DE LA JUVENTUD	046			
Cayo Largo	046	24-8238	24-8247	39-9406
Nueva Gerona	046	32-2366	105	106
LAS TUNAS	031	104	105	106
MATANZAS	045			
Cárdenas	045	52-7640	105	106
Jagüey Grande	045	91-3046	105	106
Matanzas	045	28-5023	105	106
Playa Girón	045	98-7364	105	106
Varadero	045	66-2306	105	106
PINAR DEL RÍO	048			
Pinar del Río City	048	76-2317	105	106
Viñales	048	–	105	106
SANCTI SPÍRITUS	041			
Sancti Spíritus	041	32-4462	105	110
Trinidad	041	99-2362	105	106
SANTIAGO DE CUBA				
Santiago de Cuba	022	185, 62-3300	105	106
VILLA CLARA	042	104		
Caibarién	042	36-3888	105	106
Remedios	042	39-5149	105	106
Santa Clara	042	20-3965	105	106

victim are investigated. Report to your embassy *before* reporting ID theft to the police.

HELP FOR U.S. CITIZENS
Travelers report that the **U.S. Interests Section** (Calzada, e/ L y M, Vedado, tel. 07/833-3551, emergency/after hours tel. 07/833-2302, http://havana.usinterestsection. gov, Mon.–Fri. 8 A.M.–4:30 P.M.) has a good record in helping U.S. citizens in need in Cuba. The U.S. Department of State has a **Hotline for American Travelers** (tel. 202/647-5225), and you can call the **Overseas Citizen Service** (tel. 888/407-4747, from overseas tel. 202/501-4444 for after-hours emergencies, http://travel. state.gov, Mon.–Fri. 8 A.M.–8 P.M.) if things go awry. However, the United States does not have full diplomatic representation in Cuba. If arrested, U.S. citizens should ask Cuban authorities to notify the U.S. Interests Section. A U.S. consular officer will then try to arrange regular visits. Cuba does not recognize dual citizenship for Cuban citizens who are also U.S. citizens; Cuban-born citizens are denied representation through the U.S. Interests Section.

LEGAL ASSISTANCE
Consultoría Jurídica Internacional (CJI, International Judicial Consultative Bureau, Calle 16 #314, e/ 3ra y 5ta, Miramar, tel. 07/204-2490, fax 07/204-2303, www.cji.co.cu) provides legal advice and services. It can assist travelers, including those who lose their passports or have them stolen.

The **Bufete Internacional** (Av. 5ta #16202, esq. 40, Miramar, Havana, tel. 07/204-5126, bufete@bufeteinternacional.cu) offers similar services. Both have branches in major cities.

Communications

POSTAL SERVICE
Correos de Cuba (Av. Rancho Boyeros, Havana, tel. 07/879-6824, Mon.–Sat. 8 A.M.–6 P.M.) operates the Cuban postal service, which is slow, and delivery is never guaranteed. (Mail between the U.S. and Cuba travels via Canada or Mexico; fortunately, in early 2010 the two governments met to discuss renewing direct service, which ended in 1961.) Mail is read by Cuba's censors; avoid politically sensitive comments. *Never* send cash. Post offices (*correos*) usually open weekdays 10 A.M.–5 P.M. and Saturday 8 A.M.–3 P.M., but hours can vary widely. Most tourist hotels accept mail for delivery.

International airmail (*correo aereo*) averages one month (savvy Cubans usually hand their letters to foreigners to mail outside Cuba). When mailing from Cuba, write the country destination in Spanish: Inglaterra (England, Scotland and Wales), Francia (France), Italia (Italy), Alemania (Germany), España (Spain), Suiza (Switzerland), and Estados Unidos (United States, often referred by "EE.UU.").

International postcards, including prepaid ones, cost CUC0.50 (to all destinations); letters cost CUC0.80. Within Cuba, letters cost from 15 centavos (20 grams or less) to 2.05 pesos (up to 500 grams); postcards cost 10 centavos. Stamps are called *sellos* (SAY-yos).

Parcels from Cuba must be *unwrapped* for inspection. It is far better to send packages through an express courier service, although the same regulation applies.

You can receive mail in Havana by having letters and parcels addressed to you using your name as it appears on your passport or other ID for general delivery to: "c/o Espera [your name], Ministerio de Comunicaciones, Avenida Independencia and 19 de Mayo, Habana 6, Cuba." To collect mail, go to the **Correos de Cuba** (Av. Rancho Boyeros, Havana, tel. 07/879-6824, Mon.–Sat. 8 A.M.–6 P.M.) for pickup. Also consider having incoming mail addressed "Espera [your name] c/o [your embassy]."

Express Mail

DHL Worldwide Express (www.dhl.com) has offices in major cities. The main office is in Havana (1ra Av., esq. 26, Miramar, tel. 07/204-1578, fax 07/204-0999, commercial@dhl.cutisa.cu).

Cubapost (Calle P #108, Vedado, tel. 07/836-9790) and **Cubapacks** (Calle 22 #4115, e/ 41 y 47, Miramar, tel. 07/204-2742) offer international express mail and parcel service.

Restrictions

Letters and literature can be mailed from the United States without restriction. Gift parcels can be "sent or carried by an authorized traveler" to an individual or religious or educational organization if the domestic retail value does not exceed US$200 (food items have no limit). Only one parcel per month is allowed, and contents are limited to food, vitamins, seeds, medicines, medical supplies, clothing, personal hygiene items, and a few other categories. All other parcels are subject to seizure.

TELEPHONE SERVICE

Cuba's modern digital telephone system is the responsibility of the **Empresa de Telecomunicaciones de Cuba** (Etecsa, tel. 07/266-6666 or 118, www.etecsa.cu), headquartered in the Miramar Trade Center in Havana. It has a central office (*telepunto*) with international phone and Internet service in all major towns.

There are still quirks, with some days better than others. And phones are scarce: Cuba has one of the lowest rates of telephones per capita in Latin America: only 12.6 per 100 people in 2008 (the lowest in the region, trailing even Haiti).

Call 113 for directory inquiries. The national telephone directory is available online at www.pamarillas.cu, and on CD-rom (Grupo Directorio Telefónico, tel. 07/266-6305). Etecsa also publishes a dandy little *Yellow Pages for Tourists* (*Páginas Amarillas Para el Turista*). Telephone numbers change often. Trying to determine a correct number can be problematic because many entities have several numbers and rarely publish the same number twice.

colonial-era brass postbox, or *buzón*, Plaza San Francisco, Havana

© CHRISTOPHER P. BAKER

Most commercial entities have a switchboard (*pizarra*).

Public Phone Booths

Etecsa operates glass-enclosed telephone kiosks called *micropuntos* (*telecorreos* where they combine postal services). They use phone cards, sold on-site and at tourist hotels and miscellaneous other outlets. There are two types of phone cards: Propia and Chip.

Propia cards use a number specific to each card that is keyed into the telephone when prompted. Propia cards are for local and national calls (blue, 5 pesos and 10 pesos) and for international calls (green, CUC5, CUC10, and CUC15). You can add value to the same card at *telepuntos*. At last visit, per-minute rates using Propia were: CUC1.40 6 P.M.–6 A.M. and CUC1.95 6 A.M.–6 P.M. to the United States and Canada; CUC1.65 and CUC2.35 to Mexico, Central America, and Caribbean; CUC2.10 and CUC3.05 to South America; CUC2.55 and CUC3.65 to Europe and the rest of the world.

Chip cards (CUC5, CUC10, and CUC20) are used for local, national, and international calls. They are inserted into the phone and the cost of the call is automatically deducted from the card's value. If the card expires during your call, you can continue without interruption by pushing button C and inserting a new card. At last visit, per-minute rates using Chip were: CUC2 to Canada; CUC2.25 to the United States; CUC2.60 to Mexico, Central America, and Caribbean; CUC3.40 to South America; CUC4 to Europe and the rest of the world.

Stand-alone public phones tend to be on noisy street corners. Some still accept 5- and 20-centavo coins, which can only be used for local and national calls. When you hear a short "blip," *immediately* put in another coin to avoid being cut off.

Public phones do not accept collect or incoming calls.

International Calls

When calling Cuba from abroad, dial 011 (the international dialing code), then 53 (the Cuba country code), followed by the city code and the number. For direct international calls from Cuba, dial 119, then the country code (for example, 44 for the U.K.), followed by the area code and number. For the international operator, dial 012 (Havana) or 180 (rest of Cuba).

In April 2009, the Obama administration announced that U.S. telecommunications companies would be allowed to establish direct connections with Cuba; at press time, the Cubans had not yet agreed.

Cost per minute varies depending on time of day and location of the call. Calls from domestic phones cost CUC1.20 6 P.M.–6 A.M. and CUC1.80 6 A.M.–6 P.M. to the United States and Canada; CUC1.70 and CUC2.50 to Mexico, Central America, and Caribbean; CUC2.20 and CUC3.25 to South America; CUC2.55 and CUC3.80 to France, Germany, Italy, and Spain; and CUC2.80 and CUC4.20 to the rest of the world. Rates are much higher for operator-assisted calls and from tourist hotels, most of which have direct-dial telephones in guest rooms.

Domestic Calls

For local calls in the same area code, simply dial the number you wish to reach. To dial a number outside your area code, dial 0, then wait for a tone before dialing the local city code and the number you wish to reach. For the local operator, dial 0. Local calls in Havana cost approximately 5 centavos (about a quarter of a cent). Rates for calls beyond Havana range from 30 centavos to 3 pesos and 15 centavos for the first three minutes, depending on zone—tourist hotels and Etecsa booths charge in CUC equivalent.

Cellular Phones

Cubacel (Calle 28 #510, e/ 5 y 7, Miramar, tel. 05/264-2266 or 07/880-2222, www.cubacel. com, daily 8:30 A.M.–7:30 P.M., Sat. 8 A.M.–noon) provides cellular phone service and has offices in most major cities. Cuba has roaming agreements with several countries, and in April 2009, President Obama granted permission for U.S. companies to do deals with Cuba. If your service provider doesn't have an agreement you may still be able to use your own cellular phone in the country. Cubacel can activate most phones (except fixed service provider phones, such as Verizon) and can provide you with a local line: CUC40 for Cubans and residents; tourists pay CUC3 daily plus usage (CUC0.30–0.50 per minute). They also sell cell phones (from CUC49 Motorolas to CUC331 Samsungs).

Cell phone numbers in Cuba have eight digits, beginning with 5, and omit the provincial area codes.

ONLINE SERVICE IN CUBA

Computer communications are tightly controlled, and access for the average Cuban is severely restricted. Only since 2008 have Cuban citizens (other than doctors and a few other approved individuals) been permitted to own computers. Cubans are permitted to send and receive emails, but government authorization is needed to access the Internet; everyone else is limited to the Intranet of local, government-sanctioned websites. The Cuban government has stated that ordinary Cubans will be granted Internet access following completion of an optic cable from Venezuela (but don't hold your breath).

Etecsa has a monopoly on Internet service, which it offers at most *telepuntos* (prepaid cards cost CUC6, one hour). You need to present your passport, which will be recorded, along with the number of your prepaid card (assume that all emails are read directly off the server by security personnel). Tourist hotels also have Internet service using Etecsa's system (CUC6–10 per hour, depending on hotel). Some hotels have dataports and wireless Internet in guest rooms.

You can save money on Internet time by typing emails in advance then saving them to a disc; use the disc to copy and paste messages into an email.

Media

NEWSPAPERS AND MAGAZINES
Before You Go
Take all the reading matter you can with you, as there are no newsagents or newsstands in Cuba. The best English-language magazine is the lavishly illustrated U.K.-published **Cuba Absolutely** (www.cubaabsolutely.com/contact.html), a slick annual that also maintains a superb website. Its near-identical rival is the Canadian-published **CubaPlus** (www.cubaplus.ca).

Serving investors are **CubaNews** (P.O. Box 1345, Wheaton, MD 20915, tel. 301/452-1105, www.cubanews.com) and **Cuba Trade & Investment News** (P.O. Box 13752, Tampa, FL 33681, tel. 813/839-6988, www.cubatradenews.com).

In Cuba
A small selection of international newspapers and carefully selected consumer publications are sold in some tourist hotels. Foreign publications are distributed in Cuba through **World Services Publications** (5ta Av. #1808, Flores, Havana, tel. 07/273-3066).

Pre-Castro Cuba had a vibrant media sector, with 58 daily newspapers of differing political hues. The Castro government closed them all down. Today domestic media is entirely state controlled and subject to what Maurice Halperin refers to as "the self-righteous and congratulatory monotony of the Cuban propaganda machine." There is no independent press.

The most important daily—and virtually the sole mouthpiece of international news—is *Granma* (www.granma.cu), the cheaply produced official outlet of the Communist Party. This eight-page rag focuses on denigrating the United States and profiling socialist victories. (No negatives are reported about domestic affairs; instead, *habaneros* rely for news on *radio bemba,* the fast-moving street gossip or grapevine.) *Granma* is sold on the street but rapidly sells out as many Cubans buy it to use as toilet paper. A weekly edition published in Spanish, English, and French is sold in hotels.

Juventud Rebelde, the evening paper of the Communist Youth League, echoes *Granma.* Similar mouthpieces include the less easily found *Trabajadores* (*Workers,* weekly), *Mujeres* (a monthly magazine for women), and such arts and culture magazines as *Habanera* (monthly) and *Bohemia* (weekly).

LIBRARIES
Cuba's *bibliotecas* have been neglected since the Revolution and are poorly stocked. In some, books—most of which are in tatterdemalion condition—are stocked in closed areas, with library access limited to a few privileged Cubans who are granted special permits. Access for foreigners can be difficult to obtain. The state monitors borrowers.

RADIO AND TELEVISION
All broadcast media in Cuba are state-controlled.

INDEPENDENT LIBRARIES

Fidel Castro's statement, at the International Book Fair in Havana City in February 1998, that "In Cuba no books are forbidden, there is just no money to buy them," sparked several Cubans with a passion for literature and learning to create an independent library system to offer publications that are not available in state-run bookstores or libraries. By 2003 the initiative had grown to more than 100 independent libraries nationwide, consisting of small collections of books housed in private homes. The libraries are entirely dependent on donations from abroad. The government considers them counterrevolutionary and has referred to the librarians as "mercenaries" since the U.S. Interests Section has provided assistance.

The founders of the **Independent Libraries of Cuba** (www.bibliocuba.org), Berta Mexidor Vázquez and her husband, Dr. Ramón Humberto Colas Castillo, were fired from their jobs and then evicted from their home (Amnesty International adopted Colas as a prisoner of conscience) and eventually forced to leave Cuba. Other librarians have been imprisoned and/or received beatings, and their books and magazines have been confiscated. Ironically, prohibited material includes copies of the United Nations Universal Declaration of Human Rights.

For further information, contact **Friends of Cuban Libraries** (www.friendsofcubanlibraries.org), which provides books to people traveling to Cuba for delivery to the libraries. *Note: Foreigners who visit the libraries face potential consequences: One reader who visited wrote to report "a suspicious brush with the police wanting to question [him] on a 'drug' charge."*

Television

Most tourist hotel rooms have satellite TVs showing international channels such as HBO, ESPN, CNN, and so on (the Cuban government pirates the signals). No Cuban (except the Communist elite) is permitted access to satellite TV; a few illegal and jerry-rigged dishes festoon Cuban rooftops, risking the wrath of authorities. Ordinary Cubans must make do with the four national TV networks: Canal 6: CubaVisión and Canal 2: Tele Rebelde, plus Canal Educativo and Canal Educativo-Dos, two educational channels. There is also one provincial station in Oriente.

Programming is dominated by dreary reports on socialist progress; Fidel's lengthy speeches (which take precedence over all other programming); and the daily *mesa redonda* (roundtable), a political "discussion" that is merely a staged denunciation of wicked Uncle Sam. However, Tele Rebelde features selections from CNN España international news coverage. Cuban television also has some very intelligent programming, emphasizing science and culture (often culled for the Discovery Channel, etc.), plus sports and foreign movies. There are no advertisements, but five-minute slots might inveigh against abortions or exhort Cubans to work hard, while cartoons aim to teach Cuban youth sound morals. Cubans are so addicted to Latin American *telenovelas* (soap operas) that you can walk through Havana when the *novela* is showing and follow the show as you walk.

Radio

Cuba ranked eighth in the world in number of radio stations in 1958. Today it has only five national radio stations: Radio Enciclopedia (94.1 FM) and Radio Musical Nacional (590 AM and 99.1 FM) offer classical music; Radio Rebelde (640 and 710 AM, and 96.7 FM) and Radio Reloj (950 AM and 101.5 FM) both report news; and Radio Progreso (640 AM and 90.3 FM) features traditional music. Radio Taíno (1290 AM and 93.3 FM) caters to tourists with programs in English, French, and Spanish.

There are also provincial and local stations. However, in much of the countryside you can put your car radio onto "scan" and it will just go round and round without ever coming up with a station.

Information and Services

MONEY

Currency

CONVERTIBLE PESOS

All prices in this book are quoted in Cuban Convertible Pesos (*pesos convertibles*), denominated by "CUC" (pronounced "say-ooh-say") and often, within Cuba, by "$." Foreigners must exchange their foreign currency for convertible pesos (at press time 1 dollar was worth CUC0.89), issued in the following denominations: 1, 3, 5, 10, 20, 50, and 100 peso notes; and 1, 5, 10, 25, and 50 centavo plus CUC1 and CUC5 coins. Euros are acceptable tender in Varadero, Cayo Coco, and Havana.

Always carry a wad of small bills; change for larger bills is often hard to come by.

CUBAN CURRENCY

The Cuban currency (*moneda nacional*), in which state salaries are paid, is the peso, which is worth about US$0.04 (the exchange rate at press time was about 25 pesos to the dollar). It is also designated "$" and should not be confused with the CUC or U.S. "$" (to make matters worse, the dollar is sometimes called the peso). The peso is divided into 100 centavos.

There is very little that you will need pesos for. Exceptions are if you want to travel on local buses or buy snacks from street stalls.

In 2008, the government announced that it is planning to do away with the two-currency system.

EXCHANGING CURRENCY

Foreign currency can be changed for CUC at tourist hotels, banks, and official *burós de cambios* (exchange bureaus) operated by **Cadeca** (Av. 26, esq. 45, Nuevo Vedado, tel. 07/855-5701), which has outlets throughout Cuba. They can also change CUC or foreign currency for *moneda nacional*. A 10 percent commission is charged for exchanging U.S. dollars; other foreign currencies are not charged. To avoid the surcharge, U.S. visitors should change their dollars into Canadian dollars or euros *prior* to arriving in Cuba. Check the current exchange

---

NATIONAL HOLIDAYS

January 1: Liberation Day (Día de la Liberación)

January 2: Victory Day (Día de la Victoria)

January 28: José Martí's birthday

February 24: Anniversary of the Second War of Independence

March 8: International Women's Day (Día de la Mujer)

March 13: Anniversary of the students' attack on the presidential palace

April 19: Bay of Pigs Victory (Victoria del Playa Girón)

May 1: Labor Day (Día de los Trabajadores)

July 26: National Revolution Day (anniversary of the attack on the Moncada barracks)

July 30: Day of the Martyrs of the Revolution

October 8: Anniversary of Che Guevara's death

October 10: Anniversary of the First War of Independence

October 28: Memorial day to Camilo Cienfuegos

December 2: Anniversary of the landing of the *Granma*

December 7: Memorial day to Antonio Maceo

rates at the **Banco Central de Cuba** website (www.bc.gov.cu).

Jineteros may offer to change currency illegally on the streets. Many tourists are ripped off and muggings have been reported.

BANKS

All banks in Cuba are state entities. No foreign banks are present. The most important of the banks catering to foreigners is the **Banco Financiero Internacional,** which offers a full range of banking services. Branches nationwide are open Monday–Saturday 8 A.M.–3 P.M. (but 8 A.M.–noon only on the last working day of each month). **Banco de Crédito y Comercio** (Bandec) is the main commercial bank, with outlets islandwide (most are open weekdays 8:30 A.M.–3 P.M.). **Banco Popular** and **Banco Metropolitano** also provide foreign transaction services.

Cuban banks have been known to pass off counterfeit CUC50 and CUC100 bills to foreigners. When receiving such bills, always check for watermarks.

CREDIT CARDS AND ATMS

Most hotels, larger restaurants, and major shops accept credit cards, as long as they are not issued or processed by U.S. banks (British travelers should check that their cards can be used, as about 20 percent of British-issued cards are outsourced to U.S. companies). Credit card transactions are charged 11 percent commission (comprising an 8 percent levy on currency exchange, plus a 3 percent conversion fee).

You can use your non-U.S. credit card to obtain a cash advance up to CUC5,000 (CUC100 minimum). U.S. citizens must travel on a cash-only basis as they are legally prohibited from using credit cards in Cuba—period—including those issued by foreign banks.

Automated teller machines (ATMs) at major banks dispense CUC to Cubans with cash cards. Many ATMs are linked to international systems such as Cirrus (non-U.S. Visa designated cards work, but not MasterCard). Use them only during bank hours, as they often eat your card.

Problem with your card? Contact **Fincimex** (Calle L, e/ 23 y 25, Vedado, Havana, tel. 07/835-6444, Mon.–Thurs. 8:15 A.M.–noon and 1–4:30 P.M. and Fri. 8:15 A.M.–noon and 1–3:30 P.M.), which has branches in major cities.

TRAVELERS CHECKS

Travelers checks (unless issued by U.S. banks) are accepted in some tourist restaurants, hotels, and foreign-goods stores. They can also be cashed at most hotel cashier desks, as well as at banks. You should *not* enter the date or the place when signing your checks—a quirky Cuban requirement.

MONEY TRANSFERS

Western Union (tel. 800/325-6000 in the U.S., www.westernunion.com) is licensed to handle wire transfers to Cuba for Cuban-American residents only. Only certain designated offices are permitted to handle such transactions.

For foreigners, Cuba's **TransCard** (Canada tel. 416/840-1466, www.smart-transfer.com) and **Caribbean Transfers Travel Card** (www.caribbeantransfers.com) operate much like a debit card. The user deposits funds into a secure account abroad (you can do so online), then uses that account to withdraw cash at ATMs, banks, and Cadeca, or to pay for goods and services at locations in Cuba. Caribbean Transfers Travel Card has offices in nine countries, including the U.S. (tel. 877/283-6842), for Cuban-American families wishing to send remittances. You can apply either online or in Cuba through **Fincimex** (Calle L, e/ 23 y 25, Vedado, Havana, tel. 07/835-6444, Mon.–Thurs. 8:15 A.M.–noon and 1–4:30 P.M., Fri. 8:15 A.M.–noon and 1–3:30 P.M.). An alternative for Cuban-Americans is Cuba's **Dinero a Cuba** (tel. 305/359-4493, www.dineroacuba.com).

Options for non U.S.-citizens include the Swiss company **AWS Technologies** (www.aws-transaction.com).

COSTS

Prices rise and fall like a yo-yo, according to the Cuban government's whim. After overpricing almost everything, since 2006 the Cuban government has slashed prices for hotels and many tourist services.

If you use public transport, rent *casas particulares,* and dine on the street and at peso snack bars, you may be able to survive on as little as CUC25 a day (more in Havana). For a modicum of comforts, budget at least CUC60 a day.

TIPPING
Cubans receive slave-rate wages. Your waiter dressed in a tux probably lives in a slum and is being paid less than CUC1 per day. Waiters expect to be tipped 10 percent, even where a service charge has been added to your bill (waiters and staff see only a small fraction of this, if any). Alas, many waiters haven't figured out that a tip is meant to reward good service.

Museum guides often follow you around in the hope of soliciting a tip. If you don't welcome the service, say so upfront. Musicians in bars and restaurants will usually hover by your table until tipped, after which they usually move on to the next table.

MAPS AND TOURIST INFORMATION
Tourist Bureaus
Cuba's **Ministerio de Turismo** (Av. 3ra y F, Vedado, Havana, tel. 07/836-3245 or 832-7535, www.cubatravel.cu) is in charge of tourism. It has offices in a dozen countries, including Canada (1200 Bay St., Suite 305, Toronto, ON M5R 2A5, tel. 416/362-0700, fax 416/362-6799, www.gocuba.ca; and 2075 rue University, Bureau 460, Montreal, QC H3A 2L1, tel. 514/875-8004, fax 514/875-8006), Germany (Kaiserstrasse 8, Frankfurt D-60313, tel. 069/6860-2908, www.cubainfo. de), Italy (Vía General Fara #30, Milano 20124, tel. 02/6698-1463, www.cuba-si.it), and the United Kingdom (154 Shaftesbury Ave., London WC 2H8JT, tel. 020/7240-6655, director@cubasi.info). There is no office in the U.S.; however, the Canadian offices will mail literature to U.S. citizens.

Publicitur (Calle 19 #60, e/ M y N, Vedado, tel. 07/838-2826, www.publicitur.com) is responsible for publishing and disseminating tourism literature.

Cuba is a member of the **Caribbean Tourism Organization** (CTO, 80 Broad St., 32nd Floor, New York, NY 10004, tel. 212/635-9530, www.doitcaribbean.com), which is a handy information source; and the **Caribbean Hotel Association** (CHA, 2655 LeJeune Rd., Suite 910, Coral Gables, FL 33134, tel. 305/443-3040, www.caribbeanhotelassociation.com), both of which are barred under U.S. law from promoting tourism to Cuba in the United States. The CTO has offices in Canada (130 Bloor St. W., Suite 301, Toronto, ON M5S 1N5, tel. 416/935-0767, ctotoronto@caribtourism.com) and the U.K. (22 The Quadrant, Richmond, Surrey TW9 1BP, tel. 0208/948-0057, ctolondon@caribtourism.com).

Infotur (5ta Av. y 112, Miramar, tel. 07/204-3977, www.infotur.cu), the government tourist information bureau, operates Palacios de Turismo (tourist information booths) in Havana and most major cities and tourist venues nationwide. Every tourist hotel has a *buró de turismo.*

Other Information Bureaus
Agencia de Información Nacional (Calle 23 #358, esq. J, Vedado, Havana, tel. 07/832-5541, www.ain.cubaweb.cu) dispenses information about virtually every aspect of Cuba, but serves primarily as a "news" bureau. The **Oficina Nacional de Estadísticas** (Paseo #60, e/ 3ra y 5ra, Vedado, Havana, tel. 07/830-0053, www. one.cu) provides statistics on Cuba.

Maps
A 1:250,000 topographical road map produced by Kartografiai Vallalat, of Hungary, and a similar map by Freytag and Berndt are recommended. Likewise, Cuba's own Ediciones Geo produces a splendid 1:250,000 *La Habana Tourist Map,* plus a 1:20,000 *Ciudad de la Habana* map, sold in Cuba. The pocket-sized

© CHRISTOPHER P. BAKER

Infotur office, Baracoa

Guía de Carreteras Cuba road atlas can be purchased at souvenir outlets.

The **Tienda de las Navegantes** (Calle Mercaderes #115, e/ Obispo y Obrapía, Habana Vieja, tel. 07/861-3625, Mon.–Fri. 8 A.M.–5 P.M., Sat. 8 A.M.–1 P.M.) has a wide range of tourist maps.

WEATHER FORECASTS

The daily *Granma* and weekly *Cartelera* newspapers print weather forecasts. Cuban TV newscasts have daily forecasts (in Spanish). The **Instituto de Meteorología** (Meteorological Institute, www.met.inf.cu) provides weather information in Spanish online.

PHOTOGRAPHY

You can take photographs freely (except of military and industrial installations, airports, officials in uniform, and sometimes hotels). Most museums charge for photography.

Visitors are allowed to bring one camera plus a video camera, which will be X-rayed (hand inspection is not an option). Official permission is needed to bring "professional" camera equipment. Foto Video and Photo Service stores sell instamatic and small digital cameras.

However, there are *no* camera stores similar to those found in North America or Europe, and 35mm SLRs, lenses, flash units, filters, etc. are unavailable. Bring spare batteries, tapes, and film, which is hard to find.

Snatch-and-grab theft of cameras is a major problem!

Photo Etiquette

Cubans love to be photographed. However, never assume an automatic right to do so. Ask permission to photograph individuals, and honor any wishing not to be photographed. Cubans often request money for being photographed, as do the mulattas in traditional costume in Habana Vieja and other Cubans who dress outrageously as a source of income. If they insist on being paid and you don't want to pay, don't take the shot. In markets, it is a courtesy to buy a small trinket from vendors you wish to photograph. *Do* send photographs to anyone you promise to send to. Few Cubans own cameras and they cherish being gifted photos.

Several foreigners have been arrested for filming "pornography," which in Cuba includes topless or nude photography.

KEY ORGANIZATIONS TO KNOW

IN THE UNITED STATES

Alamar Associates: 8305 Whitman Dr., Bethesda, MD 20817, tel. 301/520-4297, www.alamarcuba.com. Arranges Cuba-related business summits and consultation and operates the **U.S.-Cuba Trade Association,** which works to protect existing trade and promote normalization of commercial relations with Cuba.

Center for a Free Cuba: 4620 Lee Hwy., Arlington, VA 22207, tel. 703/528-7953, www.cubacenter.org. An anti-Castro organization that defines itself as "an independent, nonpartisan institution dedicated to promoting human rights and a transition to democracy on the island."

Center for Cuban Studies: 231 W. 29th St., New York, NY 10001, tel. 212/242-0559, www.cubaupdate.org. Sponsors educational forums on Cuba, organizes study tours, and has an art gallery and research library.

Cuban American Alliance Education Fund: 1010 Vermont Ave. NW, Suite 650, Washington, DC 20005, tel./fax 805/627-1959, www.cubamer.org. Sponsors an end to travel restrictions, especially those that cause hardship for Cuban-Americans, and for engagement with Cuba.

Cuban American National Foundation: 1312 SW 27th St., Miami, FL 33145, tel. 305/592-7768, www.canf.org. A conservative and highly influential lobbying group dedicated to the overthrow of Fidel Castro.

Cuba Policy Foundation: 2300 M St. NW, Washington, DC 20037, tel. 202/321-2822, www.cubafoundation.org. Comprising former senior diplomats in Republican administrations, this nonpartisan organization works to end the U.S. ban on travel to Cuba, lift the U.S. embargo against Cuba, and foster democratic change in Cuba. Currently inactive.

Fund for Reconciliation and Development: 145 Palisade St., Suite 401, Dobbs Ferry, NY 10522, tel. 914/231-6270, www.ffrd.org.

Fosters cooperation between the United States and Cuba.

IFCO/Pastors for Peace: 418 W. 145th St., New York, NY 10031, tel. 202/926-5757, www.ifconews.org. Organizes the U.S. Friendshipment Caravans to Cuba, challenging the embargo by traveling with vehicles filled with humanitarian aid. Also has study tours and organizes work brigades to assist in community projects in Cuba.

Latin America Working Group: 424 C St. NE, Washington, DC 20002, tel. 202/546-7010, www.lawg.org. A coalition of nongovernmental organizations, it works to end the Cuba embargo and travel ban and to encourage U.S. policies that promote human rights, justice, and peace.

USA*Engage: 1625 K St. NW, Washington, DC 20006, tel. 202/887-0278, www.usaengage.org. Coalition representing American business and agriculture interests; it lobbies for open trade with Cuba.

U.S.-Cuba Sister City Association: 320 Lowenhill St., Pittsburgh, PA 15216, tel. 412/563-1519, www.uscsca.org. Fosters ties between U.S. and Cuban cities.

U.S.-Cuba Trade and Economic Council: 30 Rockefeller Plaza, New York, NY 10112, tel. 212/246-1444, www.cubatrade.org. Nonpartisan business organization; currently inactive.

OUTSIDE THE UNITED STATES

The following "solidarity" organizations work to support Cuban socialism.

Australia-Cuba Friendship Society: P.O. Box 1051, Collingwood, Victoria 3066, Australia, tel. 3/9857-9249, fax 3/9857-6598.

Canadian-Cuba Friendship Association: P.O. Box 743, Station F, Toronto M4Y 2N6, Canada, tel. 416/410-8254, http://ccfatoronto.ca.

Cuba Solidarity Campaign: 218 Greenlanes, London N4 2HB, England, tel. 020/8800-0155, www.cuba-solidarity.org.uk.

BUSINESS HOURS

Banks are usually open Monday–Friday 8:30 A.M.–noon and 1:30–3 P.M., Saturday 8:30–10:30 A.M. Offices usually open Monday–Friday 8:30 A.M.–12:30 P.M. and 1:30–5:30 P.M. and every second Saturday 8:30 A.M.–noon. Pharmacies generally open daily 8 A.M.–8 P.M. (*turnos permanentes* stay open 24 hours). Post offices are usually open Monday–Saturday 8 A.M.–10 P.M., Sunday 8 A.M.–6 P.M., but vary widely. Shops are usually open Monday–Saturday 8:30 A.M.–5:30 P.M., although many remain open later, including all day Sunday. Museums vary widely, although most are closed on Monday.

Most banks, businesses, and government offices close during national holidays.

ELECTRICITY

Cuba operates on 110-volt AC (60-cycle) nationwide, although a few hotels operate on 220 volts (many have both). Most outlets use U.S. plugs: flat, parallel two-pins, and three rectangular pins. A two-prong adapter is a good idea (take one with you; they're impossible to find in Cuba). Many outlets are faulty and

dangerous. Electricity blackouts (*apagones*) are common. Take a flashlight, spare batteries, and candles plus matches or lighter.

TIME

Cuban time is equivalent to U.S. eastern standard time: five hours behind Greenwich mean time, the same as New York and Miami, and three hours ahead of the U.S. west coast. There is little seasonal variation in dawn. Cuba observes daylight saving time May–October.

TOILETS

Public toilets are few. Those that exist are disgustingly foul. Most hotels and restaurants will let you use their facilities, though most lack toilet paper, which gets stolen. An attendant usually sits outside the door, dispensing pieces of toilet paper for CUC0.50 or CUC1. *Always carry a small packet of toilet tissue with you!*

WEIGHTS AND MEASURES

Cuba operates on the metric system. Liquids are sold in liters, fruits and vegetables by the kilo. Distances are given in meters and kilometers. See the chart at the back of the book for metric conversions.

RESOURCES

Glossary

ache luck, positive vibe

aduana customs

agua mala jellyfish

alfarje Moorish-inspired ceiling layered with geometric and star patterns

aljibe well

altos upstairs unit (in street address)

americano/a citizen of the Americas (from Alaska to Tierra del Fuego); see *gringo*

animación entertainment activity involving guests (at hotels)

apagón electricity blackout

Astro national bus company

autopista freeway

azotea rooftop terrace

babalawo *santería* priest

bajos downstairs unit (in street address)

baño toilet, bathroom

bárbaro awesome, cool

batido milkshake

biblioteca library

bici-taxi bicycle taxi

bodega grocery store distributing rations; Spanish-style inn

bohío thatched rural homestead

bombo lottery for U.S. visas

bosque woodland

botella hitchhike, graft

buceo scuba dive

caballería antiquated land measurement

caballero sir, respectful address for a male

cabaret espectáculo Las Vegas-style revue

cabildo colonial-era town council

cacique Taíno chief

Cadeca foreign-exchange agency

cajita boxed meal

calle street

camarera maid or waitress

camello humped mega-bus

camión truck, crude truck-bus

campesino/a peasant, country person

campismo campsite (normally with cabins)

candela hot (as in a party scene, "promis-cuous," or "deep trouble"; literally means "flame")

cañonazo cannon-firing

carne de res beef

carnet de identidad ID card that all Cubans must carry at all times

carpeta reception

carretera road

carro automobile

cartelera cultural calendar

casa de la cultura "culture house" hosting music and other cultural events

casa de la trova same as a *casa de la cultura*

casa particular licensed room rental in a private home

casco histórico historic center of a city

cayo coral cay

CDR Comité para la Defensa de la Revolución; neighborhood watch committees

cenote flooded cave

central sugar mill

ciego blind

cigarillo cigarette

cimarrón runaway slave

circunvalación ring road around a city

claves rhythm sticks

coche horse-drawn taxi

coco-taxi three-wheeled open-air taxi

cola line, queue

colectivo collective taxi that runs along a fixed route like a bus

comemierda literally "shit-eater"; often used to refer to Communist or MININT officials

compañero/a companion, used as a Revolutionary address for another person

congrí rice with red beans

coño slang for female genitalia, equivalent to "damn" (the most utilized cuss word in Cuba)

correo post or post office

criollo Creole, used for Cuban food, or a person born in Cuba during the colonial era

cristianos y moros rice with black beans

Cuba libre "free Cuba," or rum and Coke

cuenta propista self-employed person

custodio guard (as in parking lots)

daiquiri rum cocktail served with crushed ice

diente de perro jagged limestone rock

divisa U.S. dollars

edificio building

efectivo cash

el último last person in a queue

embajada embassy

embalse reservoir

embori snitch

encomienda colonial form of slavery giving landowners usufruct rights to Indian labor

entronque crossroads

escabeche ceviche, marinated raw fish

escuela school

esquina caliente literally "hot corner," a place where baseball fans debate the sport

estación station

fábrica factory

FAR Fuerza Revolucionaria Militar, or armed forces

farmacia pharmacy

faro lighthouse

ferrocarril railway

fiesta de quince girl's 15th birthday party

filin "feeling" music, usually romantic ballads

finca farm

flota Spanish treasure fleet

FMC Federación de Mujeres Cubanas (Federation of Cuban Women)

fruta bomba papaya (see *papaya*)

fula U.S. dollars; also a messy situation

gasolinera gas station

gobernador colonial-era Spanish governor

golpe military coup

Granma yacht that carried Fidel Castro and his guerrilla army from Mexico to Cuba in 1956

gringo/a person from the United States, but can also apply to any Caucasian

guagua bus

guaguancó traditional dance with *vacunao* body movements

guajiro/a peasant or country bumpkin; also used for a type of traditional country song

guaracha satirical song

guarapo fresh-squeezed sugarcane juice

guarapería place selling *guarapo*

guayabera pleated, buttoned men's shirt

guayabita fruit native to Pinar del Río

habanero/a person from Havana

habano export-quality cigar

heladería ice-cream store

iglesia church

ingenio colonial-era sugar mill

inmigración immigration

jaba plastic bag, as at a supermarket

jefe de sector Communist *vigilante* in charge of several street blocks

jejénes minuscule sand fleas

jinetera female seeking a foreign male for pecuniary or other gain

jinetero male hustler who hassles tourists

joder slang for intercourse, but also to mess up

libreta ration book

luchar to fight; common term used to describe the difficulty of daily life

M-26-7 "26th of July Movement," Fidel Castro's underground revolutionary movement named for the date of the attack on the Moncada barracks

machetero sugarcane cutter/harvester

Mambí rebels fighting for independence from Spain; sometimes referred to as Mambises

maqueta scale model

máquina old Yankee automobile

mausoleo mausoleum

mediopunto half-moon stained-glass window

mercado market

mercado agropecuario produce market

microbrigadista brigades of unskilled volunteer labor

MININT Ministry of the Interior

mirador lookout point or tower

mogote limestone monoliths

mojito rum cocktail served with mint

moneda coins

moneda nacional Cuban pesos

Mudejar Moorish (as in architecture)

muelle pier, wharf

mulatto/a a person with both black and white heritage

negro/a black person

norteamericano/a U.S. or Canadian citizen

Oriente eastern provinces of Cuba

orisha santería deity

paladar private restaurant

palenque thatched structure

palestino derogatory term for a migrant to Havana from Oriente

papaya tropical fruit, slang term for vagina

parada bus stop

parque de diversiones amusement park

PCC Partido Comunista de Cuba

pedraplén causeway connecting offshore islands to the Cuban mainland

peninsular Spanish-born colonialist in Cuba in pre-independence days

peña social get-together for cultural enjoyment, such as a literary reading

pesos convertibles convertible pesos (tourist currency)

piropo witty or flirtatious comment

pizarra switchboard

ponchero/a puncture repair person

presa dam

prórroga visa extension

puro export-quality cigar

quinceañera girl coming of age

quinta country house of nobility

quintal Spanish colonial measure

refresco "refreshment," sugary drink

resolver to resolve or fix a problem

ropa vieja shredded beef dish

rumba a traditional Afro-Cuban dance; also a party involving such

sala room or gallery

salsa popular modern dance music

salsero/a performer of salsa

santería a syncretization of the African Yoruba and Catholic religions

santero/a adherent of santería

santiagüero/a person from Santiago de Cuba

sello postage or similar stamp

sendero walking trail

servicentro gasoline station

SIDA AIDS

son traditional music as popularized by Buena Vista Social Club

Taíno the predominant indigenous inhabitants of Cuba at the time of Spanish conquest

taquilla ticket window

taller workshop

tarjeta card, such as a credit card

telenovela soap opera

telepunto main telephone exchange

temporada alta/baja high/low season

terminal de ómnibus bus station

tienda shop

tráfico traffic cop

trago a shot of rum

trova traditional poetry-based music

UJC Unión de Jóvenes Comunistas; politically oriented youth Communist group

UNEAC Unión Nacional de Escritores y Artistas de Cuba; National Union of Cuban Writers and Artists

vaquero cowboy

vega patch of land where tobacco is grown

vigilante community-watch person, on behalf of the Revolution

verde slang for U.S. dollar

Víazul company offering scheduled tourist bus service

vitral stained-glass window

yoruba a group of peoples and a pantheistic religion from Nigeria

yuma slang for the United States

zafra sugarcane harvest

Cuban Spanish

Learning the basics of Spanish will aid your travels considerably. In key tourist destinations, however, you should be able to get along fine without it. Most larger hotels have bilingual desk staff, and English is widely spoken by the staff of car rental agencies and tour companies. Away from the tourist path, far fewer people speak English. Use that as an excuse to learn some Spanish. Cubans warm quickly to those who make an effort to speak their language.

In its literary form, Cuban Spanish is pure, classical Castilian (the Spanish of Spain). Alas, in its spoken form Cuban Spanish is the most difficult to understand in all of Latin America. Cubans speak more briskly than other Latin Americans, blurring their rapid-fire words together. The diction of Cuba is lazy and unclear. Thought Richard Henry Dana Jr. in 1859: "It strikes me that the tendency here is to enfeeble the language, and take from it the openness of the vowels and the strength of the consonants." The letter "s" is usually swallowed, especially in plurals. Thus, the typical greeting *¿Como estás?* is usually pronounced como-TAH. (The swallowed s's are apparently accumulated for use in restaurants, where they are released to get the server's attention—"S-s-s-s-s-st!" Because of this, a restaurant with bad service can sound like a pit full of snakes.) The final consonants of words are also often deleted, as are the entire last syllables of words ("If they dropped any more syllables, they would be speechless," suggests author Tom Miller).

Cubanisms to Know

Cubans are long-winded and full of flowery, passionate, rhetorical flourishes. Fidel Castro didn't inherit his penchant for long speeches from dour, taciturn Galicia—it's a purely Cuban characteristic. Cubans also spice up the language with little affectations and teasing endearments—*piropos*—given and taken among themselves without offense.

Many English (or "American") words have found their way into Cuban diction. Cubans go to *béisbol* and eat *hamburgesas*. Like the English, Cubans are clever in their use of words, imbuing their language with double entendres and their own lexicon of similes. Cubans are also great cussers. The two most common cuss words are *cojones* (balls) and *coño* (cunt), while one of the more common colloquialisms is *ojalá,* which loosely translated means "I wish" or "if only!" but which most commonly is used to mean "Some hope!"

Formal courtesies are rarely used when greeting someone. Since the Revolution, everyone is a *compañero* or *compañera* (*señor* and *señora* are considered too bourgeois), although the phrase is disdained by many Cubans as indicating approval of the Communist system. Confusingly, *¡ciao!* (used as a long-term goodbye, and spelled "chao" in Cuba) is also used as a greeting in casual passing—the equivalent of "Hi!" You will also be asked *¿Como anda?* ("How goes it?"), while younger Cubans prefer *¿Que bola?* (the Cuban equivalent of "Wassup?") rather than the traditional *¿Que pasa?* ("What's happening?").

Cubans speak to each other directly, no holds barred. Even conversations with strangers are laced with *"¡Ay, muchacha!"* ("Hey, girl!"), *"¡Mira, chica!"* ("Look, girl!"), and *"¡Hombre!"* ("Listen, man!") when one disagrees with the other. Cubans refer to one another in straightforward terms, often playing on their physical or racial characteristics: *flaco* (skinny), *gordo* (fatty), *negro* (black man), *china* (chinese woman), etc. Cubans do not refer to themselves with a single definition of "white" or "black." There are a zillion gradations of skin color and features, from *negro azul y trompudo* (blue-black and thick-lipped) and *muy negro* (very black), for example, to *leche con una gota de café* (milk with a drop of coffee). Whites, too, come in shades. *Un blanco* is a blonde- or light-haired person with blue, green, or gray eyes. *Un blanquito* is a "white" with dark hair and dark eyes.

Bárbaro is often used to attribute a positive quality to someone, as in *él es un bárbaro* ("he's a great person"). *Está en candela* ("a flame") is its equivalent, but is more commonly used to describe an alarming or complicated situation (such as "I'm broke!"), or excess (as in something that's "hot," i.e. promiscuous).

Marinovia defines a live-in girlfriend (from *marido,* for spouse, and *novia,* for girlfriend). An *asere* is one's close friend, though this street term is considered a low-class word, especially common with blacks. A *flojo* (literally, "loose guy") is a lounger who pretends to work. Cubans also have no shortage of terms referring to spies, informers, and untrustworthy souls. For example, *embori* refers to an informer in cahoots with the government. *Fronterizo* is a half-mad person. *Chispa* ("spark") is someone with vitality. To become "Cubanized" is to be *aplatanado.*

When Cubans ask home visitors if they want coffee, it is often diplomatic rather than an invitation. Replying *"gracias"* (thanks) usually signifies "thanks for the thought." *"Si, gracias* means "yes." Cubans expect you to be explicit.

Spanish Phrasebook

PRONUNCIATION GUIDE
Spanish pronunciation is much more regular than that of English, but there are still occasional variations.

Consonants
c as 'c' in "cat," before 'a,' 'o,' or 'u'; like 's' before 'e' or 'i'
d as 'd' in "dog," except between vowels, then like 'th' in "that"
g before 'e' or 'i,' like the 'ch' in Scottish loch"; elsewhere like 'g' in "get"
h always silent
j like the English 'h' in "hotel," but stronger
ll like the 'y' in "yellow"
ñ like the 'ni' in "onion"
r trilled 'r' at the beginning of words; in between vowels pronounced like the 'tt' in "butter"
rr trilled 'r'
v similar to the 'b' in "boy" (not as English 'v')
y similar to English, but with a slight 'j' sound. When standing, alone it's pronounced like the 'e' in "me."
z like 's' in "same"
b, f, k, l, m, n, p, q, s, t, w, x as in English

Vowels
a as in "father," but shorter
e as in "hen"
i as in "machine"
o as in "phone"
u usually as in "rule"; when it follows a 'q' the 'u' is silent; when it follows an 'h' or 'g,' it's pronounced like 'w,' except when it comes between 'g' and 'e' or 'i,' when it's also silent (unless it has an umlaut, when it again is pronounced as English 'w'

Stress
Spanish vowels – a, e, i, o, and u – may carry accents that determine which syllable of a word gets emphasis. The surname Chávez, for instance, is stressed on the first syllable; failure to observe this rule may mean that native speakers may not understand you.

NUMBERS
0 *cero*
1 *uno* (masculine)/*una* (feminine)
2 *dos*
3 *tres*
4 *cuatro*
5 *cinco*
6 *seis*
7 *siete*
8 *ocho*
9 *nueve*
10 *diez*
11 *once*
12 *doce*

13 *trece*
14 *catorce*
15 *quince*
16 *dieciséis*
17 *diecisiete*
18 *dieciocho*
19 *diecinueve*
20 *veinte*
21 *veintiuno*
30 *treinta*
40 *cuarenta*
50 *cincuenta*
60 *sesenta*
70 *setenta*
80 *ochenta*
90 *noventa*
100 *cien*
101 *ciento y uno*
200 *doscientos*
1,000 *mil*
10,000 *diez mil*
1,000,000 *un millón*

DAYS OF THE WEEK

Sunday *domingo*
Monday *lunes*
Tuesday *martes*
Wednesday *miércoles*
Thursday *jueves*
Friday *viernes*
Saturday *sábado*

TIME

While Latin Americans mostly use the 12-hour clock, in some instances, usually associated with plane or bus schedules, they may use the 24-hour military clock. Under the 24-hour clock, for example, *las nueve de la noche* (9 P.M.) would be *las 21 horas* (2100 hours).

What time is it? *¿Qué hora es?*
It's one o'clock *Es la una.*
It's two o'clock *Son las dos.*
At two o'clock *Á las dos.*
It's ten to three *Son tres menos diez.*
It's ten past three *Son tres y diez.*
It's three fifteen *Son las tres y cuarto.*
It's two forty-five *Son tres menos cuarto.*
It's two thirty *Son las dos y media.*

It's six A.M. *Son las seis de la mañana.*
It's six P.M. *Son las seis de la tarde.*
It's ten P.M. *Son las diez de la noche.*
today *hoy*
tomorrow *mañana*
morning *la mañana*
tomorrow morning *mañana por la mañana*
yesterday *ayer*
week *la semana*
month *mes*
year *año*
last night *anoche*
the next day *el día siguiente*

USEFUL PHRASES

Most Spanish-speaking people consider formalities important. Do not forget the appropriate salutation – good morning, good evening, etc. Standing alone, the greeting *hola* (hello) can sound brusque.

Hello. *Hola.*
Good morning. *Buenos días.*
Good afternoon. *Buenas tardes.*
Good evening. *Buenas noches.*
How are you? *¿Cómo está?*
Fine. *Muy bien.*
And you? *¿Y usted?*
So-so. *Más o menos.*
Thank you. *Gracias.*
Thank you very much. *Muchas gracias.*
You're very kind. *Muy amable.*
You're welcome. *De nada.*
yes *sí*
no *no*
I don't know. *No sé.*
It's fine; okay *Está bien.*
Good; okay. *Bueno.*
please *por favor*
Pleased to meet you. *Mucho gusto.*
Excuse me (physical) *Perdóneme.*
Excuse me (speech) *Discúlpeme.*
I'm sorry. *Lo siento.*
Goodbye. *Adios.*
See you later. *Hasta luego.*
more *más*
less *menos*
better *mejor*
much, a lot *mucho*

a little *un poco*
large *grande*
small *pequeño, chico*
quick, fast *rápido*
slowly *despacio*
bad *malo*
difficult *difícil*
easy *fácil*
He/She/It is gone. *Ya se fue.*
I don't speak Spanish well. *No hablo bien el español.*
I don't understand. *No entiendo.No entiendo.*
How do you say...in Spanish? *¿Cómo se dice...en español?*
Do you understand English? *¿Entiende el inglés?*
Is English spoken here? (Does anyone here speak English?) *¿Se habla inglés aquí?*

TERMS OF ADDRESS

When in doubt, use the formal *usted* (you) as a form of address.

I *yo*
you (formal) *usted*
you (familiar) *tú*
he/him *él*
she/her *ella*
we/us *nosotros*
you (plural) *ustedes*
they/them (all males or mixed gender) *ellos*
they/them (all females) *ellas*
Mr., sir *señor*
Mrs., madam *señora*
Miss, young lady *señorita*
wife *esposa*
husband *marido or esposo*
friend *amigo* (male), *amiga* (female)
sweetheart *novio* (male), *novia* (female)
son, daughter *hijo, hija*
brother, sister *hermano, hermana*
father, mother *padre, madre*
grandfather, grandmother *abuelo, abuela*

GETTING AROUND

Where is ... ? *¿Dónde está ... ?*
How far is it to ... ? *¿A cuánto está ... ?*
from...to ... *de...a ...*
highway *la carretera*
road *el camino*
street *la calle*
block *la cuadra*
kilometer *kilómetro*
north *norte*
south *sur*
west *oeste; poniente*
east *este; oriente*
straight ahead *al derecho; adelante*
to the right *a la derecha*
to the left *a la izquierda*

ACCOMMODATIONS

Is there a room? *¿Hay cuarto?*
May I (we) see it? *¿Puedo (podemos) verlo?*
What is the rate? *¿Cuál es el precio?*
Is that your best rate? *¿Es su mejor precio?*
Is there something cheaper? *¿Hay algo más económico?*
single room *un sencillo*
double room *un doble*
room for a couple *matrimonial*
key *llave*
with private bath *con baño*
with shared bath *con baño general; con baño compartido*
hot water *agua caliente*
cold water *agua fría*
shower *ducha*
electric shower *ducha eléctrica*
towel *toalla*
soap *jabón*
toilet paper *papel higiénico*
air-conditioning *aire acondicionado*
fan *abanico; ventilador*
blanket *frazada; manta*
sheets *sábanas*

PUBLIC TRANSPORT

bus stop *la parada*
bus terminal *terminal de buses*
airport *el aeropuerto*

launch *lancha; tiburonera*
dock *muelle*
I want a ticket to ... *Quiero un pasaje a ...*
I want to get off at ... *Quiero bajar en ...*
Here, please. *Aquí, por favor.*
Where is this bus going? *¿Adónde va este autobús?*
round-trip *ida y vuelta*
What do I owe? *¿Cuánto le debo?*

FOOD

menu *la carta, el menú*
glass *taza*
fork *tenedor*
knife *cuchillo*
spoon *cuchara*
napkin *servilleta*
soft drink *agua fresca*
coffee *café*
cream *crema*
tea *té*
sugar *azúcar*
drinking water *agua pura, agua potable*
carbonated water *agua mineral con gas*
uncarbonated water *agua sin gas*
beer *cerveza*
wine *vino*
milk *leche*
juice *jugo*
eggs *huevos*
bread *pan*
watermelon *sandía*
banana *banano, guineo*
plantain *plátano*
apple *manzana*
orange *naranja*
meat (without) *carne (sin)*
beef *carne de res*
chicken *pollo; gallina*

fish *pescado*
shellfish *mariscos*
shrimp *camarones*
fried *frito*
roasted *asado*
barbecued *a la parrilla*
breakfast *desayuno*
lunch *almuerzo*
dinner (afternoon) *comida*
dinner (evening) *cena*
the check, or bill *la cuenta*

MAKING PURCHASES

I need ... *Necesito ...*
I want ... *Deseo ... or Quiero ...*
I would like...(more polite) *Quisiera ...*
How much does it cost? *¿Cuánto cuesta?*
What's the exchange rate? *¿Cuál es el tipo de cambio?*
May I see ...? *¿Puedo ver ...?*
this one *ésta/éste*
expensive *caro*
cheap *barato*
cheaper *más barato*
too much *demasiado*

HEALTH

Help me please. *Ayúdeme por favor.*
I am ill. *Estoy enfermo.*
pain *dolor*
fever *fiebre*
stomach ache *dolor de estómago*
vomiting *vomitar*
diarrhea *diarrea*
drugstore *farmacia*
medicine *medicina*
pill, tablet *pastilla*
birth control pills *pastillas anticonceptivas*
condom *condón, preservativo*

Suggested Reading

ART AND CULTURE

Pérez, Louis A. *On Becoming Cuban: Nationality, Identity and Culture.* New York: Harper Perennial, 2001. Seminal and highly readable account of the development of Cuban culture from colonialism through communism.

BIOGRAPHY

Anderson, Jon Lee. *Che Guevara: A Revolutionary Life.* New York: Grove Press, 1997. This definitive biography reveals heretofore unknown details of Che's life and shows the dark side of this revolutionary icon.

Eire, Carlos. *Waiting for Snow in Havana.* New York: Free Press, 2004. An exquisitely told, hilarious, and heart-rending story of an exile's joyous childhood years in Havana on the eve of the Revolution, and the trauma of being put on the Peter Pan airlift, never to see his father again.

Geyer, Georgie Anne. *Guerrilla Prince: The Untold Story of Fidel Castro.* Boston: Little Brown, 1991. This sobering profile of the Cuban leader strips Castro bare, revealing his charisma and cunning, pride and paranoia, and megalomania and myth.

Gimbel, Wendy. *Havana Dreams: A Story of Cuba.* London: Virago, 1998. The moving story of Naty Revuelta's tormented love affair with Fidel Castro and the terrible consequences of a relationship as heady as the doomed romanticism of the Revolution.

Neyra, Edward J. *Cuba Lost and Found.* Cincinnati: Clerisy Press 2009. A Cuban-American's moving tale of leaving Cuba on the Peter Pan airlift and his eventual return to his roots on the island.

Ramonte, Ignacio, ed. *Fidel Castro: My Life.* London: Penguin Books, 2008. In conversation with a fawning interviewer, Fidel tells his fascinating life story and expounds on his philosophy and passions. This often amusing and eyebrow-raising autobiography reveals Castro's astounding erudition, acute grasp of history, unwavering commitment to humanistic ideals, and his delusions and pathological hatred of the United States.

Schwag, Rick. *The Literacy Brigade and Other Cuban Stories.* Lyndonville, VT: Zunzun Press, 2009. A cubaphile's exquisite humanistic recollection of his visits to Cuba and with the family of the wife he brought home.

Szulc, Tad. *Fidel: A Critical Portrait.* New York: Morrow, 1986. A riveting profile of the astonishing life of this larger-than-life figure.

CIGARS

Perelman, Richard B. *Perelman's Pocket Cyclopedia of Havana Cigars.* Perelman, Pioneer & Co, 1998. More than 160 pages with over 25 color photos, providing a complete list of cigar brands and shapes. Handy 4- by 6-inch size.

Stout, Nancy. *Habanos: The Story of the Havana Cigar.* New York: Rizzoli, 1997. Beautifully illustrated coffee-table book that tells you all you want to know about tobacco and its metamorphosis into fine cigars.

COFFEE-TABLE

Baker, Christopher P. *Cuba Classics: A Celebration of Vintage American Automobiles.* Northampton, MA: Interlink Books, 2004. This lavishly illustrated coffee-table book pays homage to Cuba's astonishing wealth of antique cars, revealing the time-worn splendor of classic American automobiles spanning eight decades. The text traces the long love affair between Cubans and the U.S. automobile and offers a paean to the owners who keep their weary *cacharros* running through resourcefulness and ingenuity.

Barclay, Juliet (photographs by Martin Charles). *Havana: Portrait of a City.* London: Cassell, 1993. A well-researched and abundantly illustrated coffee-table volume especially emphasizing the city's history.

Carley, Rachel. *Cuba: 400 Years of Architectural Legacy.* New York: Whitney Library of Design, 1997. Beautifully illustrated coffee-table book that traces the development of architectural styles, from colonial days to the Communist aesthetic hiatus and post-Soviet renaissance.

Evans, Walker. *Walker Evans: Cuba.* New York: Getty Publications, 2001. Recorded in 1933, these 60 beautiful black-and-white images capture in stark clarity the misery and hardships of life in the era.

Harvey, David Alan, and Elizabeth Newhouse. *Cuba.* Washington, D.C.: National Geographic, 2000. An acclaimed photographer and a *National Geographic* editor display their passion for Cuba in this poignant and stunningly illustrated coffee-table book.

Kenny, Jack. *Cuba.* Ann Arbor, MI: Corazon Press, 2005. Beautiful black-and-white images capture the essence of Cuba and provide an intimate portrait into its soul.

Llanes, Lillian. *Havana Then and Now.* San Diego: Thunder Bay Press, 2004. A delightful collection of images wedding centenary black-and-whites to color photos showing the same locales as they are now.

Moruzzi, Peter. *Havana Before Castro: When Cuba was a Tropical Playground.* Salt Lake City: Gibbs Smith, 2008. This superb book is stuffed with fascinating images and tidbits that recall the heyday of sin and modernism.

GENERAL

Cabrera Infante, Guillermo. *¡Mea Cuba!* New York: Farrar, Straus & Giroux, 1994. An acerbic, indignant, raw, wistful, and brilliant set of essays in which the author pours out his bile at the Castro regime.

Fuentes, Norberto. *Hemingway in Cuba.* Secaucus, NY: Lyle Stuart, 1984. The seminal, lavishly illustrated study of the Nobel Prize–winner's years in Cuba.

Henken, Ted A. *Cuba: A Global Studies Handbook.* Santa Barbara: ABC-CLIO, 2008. A thoughtful and thoroughly insightful compendium spanning everything from history and culture to "Castro as a Charismatic Hero."

Martínez-Fernández, Luis, et al. *Encyclopedia of Cuba: People, History, Culture.* Westport, CT: Greenwood Press, 2004. Comprehensive twin-volume set with chapters arranged by themes, such as history, plastic arts, and sports.

Rose, Andy, and Judy Bastyra. *Eat Cuban.* New York: Simon and Schuster, 2008. Lavishly illustrated, this coffee-table book blends recipes and cooking tips with profiles on the city landscape.

Shnookal, Deborah, and Mirta Muñiz, eds. *José Martí Reader.* New York: Ocean Press, 1999. An anthology of writings by one of the most brilliant and impassioned Latin American intellectuals of the 19th century.

HISTORY, ECONOMICS, AND POLITICS

Bardach, Ann Louise. *Cuba Confidential.* New York: Random House, 2002. A brilliant study of the failed politics of poisoned Cuban–U.S. relations, and the spiteful, self-seeking power plays and grand hypocrisies of the warring factions in Washington, Miami, and Havana.

Bardach, Ann Louise. *Without Fidel.* New York: Scribner, 2009. In this superb sequel to *Cuba Confidential,* Bardach reports on Fidel's mystery illness and twilight days, including the fall from grace of prominent Cuban politicians.

Cluster, Dick, and Rafael Hernández. *History of Havana*. New York, Palgrave-Macmillan, 2006. The co-authors imbue this historical treatise with the lively personality of the city.

Deutschmann, David, and Deborah Shnookal. *Fidel Castro Reader*. Melbourne: Ocean Press, 2007. Twenty of Castro's most important speeches are presented verbatim.

English, T. J. *Havana Nocturne: How the Mob Owned Cuba and then Lost It to the Revolution*. New York: William Morrow, 2008. A fascinating and revealing account of the heyday of Cuba's mobster connections and the sordid Batista era.

Estrada, Alfredo José. *Havana: Autobiography of a City*. New York: Palgrave Macmillan, 2009. Full of rich anecdotes, this gripping narrative brings one of the world's most romantic cities to life.

Gott, Richard. *Cuba: A New History*. New Haven, CT: Yale University Press, 2005. Erudite, entertaining, and concise, yet with all the masterful detail that commends a tour de force.

Latell, Brian. *After Fidel: The Inside Story of Castro's Regime and Cuba's Next Leader*. New York: Palgrave Macmillan, 2005. A former senior CIA analyst profiles the personalities of Fidel and Raúl Castro, providing insights into their quixotic, mutually dependent relationship and the motivations that have shaped their antagonistic relationship with the United States.

Oppenheimer, Andres. *Castro's Final Hour*. New York: Simon and Schuster, 1992. A sobering, in-depth exposé of the uglier side of both Fidel Castro and the state system, including controversial topics such as drug trading.

Smith, Wayne. *The Closest of Enemies*. New York: W. W. Norton, 1987. Essential reading, this personal account of the author's years serving as President Carter's man in Havana during the 1970s provides insights into the complexities that haunt U.S. relations with Cuba.

Sweig, Julia E. *Cuba: What Everyone Needs to Know*. Oxford: Oxford University Press, 2009. A reference to Cuba's history and politics, addressed in a clever question and answer format.

Thomas, Hugh. *Cuba: The Pursuit of Freedom, 1726–1969*. New York: Harper and Row, 1971. A seminal work—called a "magisterial conspectus of Cuban history"—tracing the evolution of conditions that eventually engendered the Revolution.

Thomas, Hugh. *The Cuban Revolution*. London: Weidenfeld and Nicolson, 1986. The definitive work on the Revolution, offering a brilliant analysis of all aspects of the country's diverse and tragic history.

Wyden, Peter. *Bay of Pigs: The Untold Story*. New York: Simon and Schuster, 1979. An in-depth and riveting exposé of the CIA's ill-conceived mission to topple Castro.

LITERATURE

Cabrera Infante, Guillermo. *Three Trapped Tigers*. New York: Avon, 1985. A poignant and comic novel that captures the essence of life in Havana before the ascendance of Castro.

García, Cristina. *Dreaming in Cuban*. New York: Ballantine Books, 1992. A poignant and sensual tale of a family divided politically and geographically by the Cuban revolution and the generational fissures that open.

Greene, Graham. *Our Man in Havana*. New York: Penguin, 1971. The story of Wormold, a British vacuum-cleaner salesman in prerevolutionary Havana. Recruited by British intelligence, Wormold finds little information to pass on, and so invents it. Full of the sensuality and tensions of Batista's last days.

Gutiérrez, Pedro Juan. *Dirty Havana Trilogy.* New York: Farrar, Straus & Giroux, 2001. A bawdy semi-biographical take on the gritty life of Havana's underclass—begging, whoring, escaping hardship through sex and *santería*—during the Special Period.

Hemingway, Ernest. *Islands in the Stream.* New York: Harper Collins, 1970. An exciting triptych set in Cuba during the war, it draws on the author's own experience hunting Nazi U-boats.

Hemingway, Ernest. *The Old Man and the Sea.* New York: Scribner's, 1952. The simple yet profound story of an unlucky Cuban angler won the Nobel Prize for Literature.

TRAVEL GUIDES

Baker, Christopher P. *Moon Spotlight Havana.* Emeryville, CA: Avalon Travel Publishing, 2010. The most thorough and up-to-date guidebook to Cuba's capital city available, with extensive maps and essential tips.

Charles, Simon. *The Cruising Guide to Cuba.* St. Petersburg, FL: Cruising Guide Publications, 1997. Invaluable reference guide for every sailor wishing to charter sailing or motorized craft.

Fernández, Anibal, and Armando Menocal. *Cuba Climbing.* Squamish, BC: Quickdraw Publications, 2009. An indispensable guide that includes photos and diagrams of scores of routes.

Lightfoot, Claudia. *Havana: A Cultural and Literary Companion.* Northampton, MA: Interlink Publishing, 2001. The author leads you through Havana past and present using literary quotations and allusions to add dimension to the sites and experiences.

Rodríguez, Eduardo Luis. *The Havana Guide: Modern Architecture 1925–65.* New York: Princeton Architectural Press, 2000. A marvelous guide to individual structures—homes, churches, theaters, government buildings—representing the best of modern architecture (1925–1965) throughout Havana.

Smith, Barbara and Walter. *Bicycling Cuba.* Woodstock, VT: Backcountry Guides, 2002. A detailed and practical guide to cycling in Cuba, with routes and maps.

TRAVEL LITERATURE

Aschkenas, Lea. *Es Cuba: Life and Love on an Illegal Island.* Emeryville, CA: Seal Press, 2006. Told with gentle compassion for a culture and country, *Es Cuba* reveals how the possibilities and hopes of the heart can surmount even the most obdurate political barriers.

Baker, Christopher P. *Mi Moto Fidel: Motorcycling through Castro's Cuba.* Washington, D.C.: National Geographic's Adventure Press, 2001. Winner of both the Lowell Thomas Award Travel Book of the Year and the North American Travel Journalist Association's Grand Prize, this erotically charged tale of the author's 7,000-mile adventure by motorcycle through Cuba offers a bittersweet look at the last Marxist "utopia."

Corbett, Ben. *This Is Cuba: An Outlaw Culture Survives.* Cambridge, MA: Westview Press, 2002. This first-person account of life in Castro's Cuba is a stinging indictment of the havoc, despair, and restraints wrought by *fidelismo.*

Miller, Tom. *Trading with the Enemy: A Yankee Travels through Castro's Cuba.* New York: Basic Books, 1996. Told by a famous author who lived in Cuba for almost a year, this travelogue is thoughtful, engaging, insightful, compassionate, and told in rich narrative.

Miller, Tom, ed. *Travelers' Tales: Cuba*. San Francisco: Travelers' Tales, 2001. Extracts from the contemporary works of 38 authors provide an at times hilarious, cautionary, and inspiring account of Cuba.

Ryan, Alan, ed. *The Reader's Companion to Cuba*. New York: Harcourt Brace and Co., 1997. A gathering of some of the best travel writing about Cuba dating from the mid-1800s, spanning an eclectic menu of authors from John Muir and Graham Greene to baseball's Tommy Lasorda.

Tattlin, Isadora. *Cuba Diaries: An American Housewife in Havana*. Chapel Hill, NC: Algonquin Books, 2002. A marvelous account of four years in Havana spent raising two children, entertaining her husband's clients (including Fidel), and contending with chronic shortages.

Suggested Viewing

Before Night Falls (2000). A poignant adaptation of Reinaldo Arenas's autobiography, in which the persecuted Cuban novelist recounts his life in Cuba and in exile in the United States. Says film critic Lucas Hilderbrand, "It's an intoxicating, intensely erotic account of sexual discovery and liberation, and a devastating record of the artist's persecution under the Castro regime."

Buena Vista Social Club (1999). An adorable documentary look at the reemergence from obscurity of veteran performers Ruben González, Omara Portuondo, Ibrahim Ferrer, Eliades Ochoa, and Compay Segundo culminating in their sellout concert at Carnegie Hall.

Death of a Bureaucrat (1966). Tomás Gutiérrez Alea's questioning portrait of the absurdities of the Cuban bureaucratic system and people's propensity to conform to absurd Kremlin-style directives that cause misery to others.

El Cuerno de Abundancia (2008). The "Horn of Plenty" is Juan Carlos Tabio's tale of how a million dollar inheritance upsets an entire town in Cuba's interior.

Fresa y Chocolate (1994). Legendary Cuban director Tomás Gutiérrez Alea's famous skit ("Strawberry and Chocolate") about the evolving friendship between a gay man and an ardent revolutionary is a classic comedic drama. David, the young Communist, is selected by Diego as a potential target for seduction. The tale that unfolds in derelict Havana is an indictment of the treatment of homosexuals in Cuba.

Guantanamera (1997). A road movie with a twist, this rueful romantic comedy by Tomás Gutiérrez Alea and Juan Carlos Tabio begins to unfold after an elderly dame dies from an excess of sexual stimulation. The farce of returning her body to Havana for proper burial provides the vehicle for a cutting yet comic parody of an overly bureaucratic contemporary Cuba.

Los Diosas Rotas (2008). An enthralling, beautifully filmed tale of pimps and prostitutes in contemporary Havana. Nominated for a 2008 Oscar as Best Foreign Film.

Memories of Underdevelopment (1968). Director Tomás Gutiérrez Alea's sensual, wide-ranging masterpiece revolves around an erotically charged, intellectual "playboy" existence in early 1960s Cuba, pinned by the tragedy of the central character's alienation from the "underdeveloped" people around him and his own inability to attain a more fulfilled state.

Miel para Ochún (2003). Humberto Solas's "Honey for Oshún" tells the tale of a Cuban-American who, aided by a taxi driver, embarks on a wild road trip through Cuba to search for the mother he thought had abandoned him as a child.

Paradise Under the Stars (1999). Set around a star-struck woman's dream of singing at the Tropicana nightclub, this buoyantly witty comedy combines exuberant musical numbers, bedroom farce, and some satiric jabs at Cuban machismo.

¡Soy Cuba! (1964). Filmed by Russian director Mikhail Kalatozov, "I Am Cuba" is a brilliant, melodramatic, agitprop black-and-white, anti-American epic to Communist kitsch that exposes the poverty, oppression, and decadence of Batista's Havana.

Suite Habana (2003). The hit of the 25th Havana Film Festival, this silent documentary by Fernando Pérez records a simple day in the life of 10 ordinary Cubans in Havana.

Internet Resources

GENERAL INFORMATION
Cuban Government
www.cubagob.cu
Official website of the Cuban government.

Cubasí
www.cubasi.cu
Generic Cuban government site with sections on travel, culture, news, etc.

CubaSource
www.cubasource.org
The Canadian Foundation for the Americas' information system.

La Empresa de Telecomunicaciones de Cuba (Etecsa)
www.etecsa.cu
The website of Cuba's telephone corporation, Etecsa, with a link to Cuba's online telephone directory.

Havana Journal
www.havanajournal.com
A news bulletin and forum on everything Cuban related.

Latin American Network Information Center
http://lanic.utexas.edu/la/cb/cuba
Portal of the Latin American Network Information Center with dozens of links relating to Cuba.

Páginas Amarillas
www.paginasamarillas.cu
Cuba has a Yellow Pages for commercial entities…this one online!

BLOGS
Along the Malecón
http://alongthemalecon.blogspot.com
Posts by Tracey Eaton, former *Dallas Morning News* Havana bureau correspondent.

Cuba & Costa Rica
www.moon.com/blogs/cuba-costa-rica
Cuba travel expert Christopher P. Baker's personal blog about Cuba.

Cuban Investments & News Digest
www.cubaninvestments.com
A daily compilation of news articles about Cuba from various news sources.

The Cuban Triangle
http://cubantriangle.blogspot.com
Politically focused posts by Phil Peters, of the Lexington Institute.

TRAVEL INFORMATION
Caribbean Tourist Organization
www.caribbeantravel.com
Official tourism website of the Caribbean.

Cuba Travel Expert
www.cubatravelexpert.com
Website of the world's foremost authority on travel and tourism to Cuba.

Cuba Web
www.cubaweb.cu
Cuban government-run tourist-focused site.

Directorio Turístico de Cuba
www.dtcuba.com
Cuban travel-related portal, with online reservation capability.

Habana Patrimonial
www.ohch.cu
Oficina del Historiador de la Ciudad Habana (Office of the City Historian). Spanish-only site relating to restoration projects, museums, hotels, and sites of interest in Habana Vieja.

Infotur
www.infotur.cu
Infotur website; information on tourist information centers in Havana.

LaHabana
www.lahabana.com
Havana supersite, dedicated to the capital city.

Ministerio de Turismo
www.cubatravel.cu
Portal of Cuba's Ministerio de Turismo (Ministry of Tourism).

United States Department of the Treasury
www.treas.gov/ofac
U.S. Treasury Department (OFAC). What you need to know about U.S. law and Cuba, direct from the horse's mouth.

Víazul
www.viazul.com
Website of Víazul, Cuba's tourist bus company, with online reservation capability.

CULTURE
Cuba Absolutely
www.cubaabsolutely.com
A superb online magazine covering travel, culture, and the arts.

Cubarte
www.cubarte.cult.cu
Cuban cultural site.

Index

List of Maps